About the Author

John J. Macionis (pronounced "ma-SHOWnis") has been in the classroom teaching sociology for almost forty years. Born and raised in Philadelphia, Pennsylvania, John earned a bachelor's degree from Cornell University, majoring in sociology, and then completed a doctorate in sociology from the University of Pennsylvania.

His publications are wide-ranging, focusing on community life in the United States, interpersonal intimacy in families, effective teaching, humor, new information technology, and the importance of global education. In addition to authoring this best-seller, Macionis has also written *Society: The Basics*, the most popular paperback text in the field, now in its twelfth edition. He collaborates on international editions of the texts: *Sociology: Canadian Edition; Society: The Basics, Canadian Edition;* and *Sociology: A Global Introduction. Sociology* is also available for high school students and in various foreign-language editions.

In addition, Macionis and Nijole V. Benokraitis have edited the best-selling anthology *Seeing Ourselves: Classic, Contemporary, and Cross-Cultural Readings in Sociology,* also available in a Canadian edition. Macionis and Vincent Parrillo have written the leading urban studies text, *Cities and Urban Life*. Macionis's most recent textbook is *Social Problems*, now in its fifth edition and the leading book in this field. The latest on all the Macionis textbooks, as well as information and dozens of Internet links of interest to students and faculty in sociology, are found at the author's personal website: www.macionis.com or www.TheSociologyPage.com. Additional information and instructor resources are found at the Pearson site: www.pearsonhighered.com

John Macionis is Professor and Distinguished Scholar of Sociology at Kenyon College in Gambier, Ohio, where he has taught for more than thirty-five years. During that time, he has chaired the Sociology Department, directed the college's multidisciplinary program in humane studies, presided over the campus senate and the college's faculty, and taught sociology to thousands of students.

In 2002, the American Sociological Association presented Macionis with the Award for Distinguished Contributions to Teaching, citing his innovative use of global material as well as the introduction of new teaching technology in his textbooks.

Professor Macionis has been active in academic programs in other countries, having traveled to some fifty nations.

He writes, "I am an ambitious traveler, eager to learn and, through the texts, to share much of what I discover with students, many of whom know little about the rest of the world. For me, traveling and writing are all dimensions of teaching. First, and foremost, I am a teacher—a passion for teaching animates everything I do."

At Kenyon, Macionis teaches a number of courses, but his favorite class is Introduction to Sociology, which he offers each academic year. He enjoys extensive contact with students and invites everyone enrolled in each of his classes to enjoy a home-cooked meal.

The Macionis family—John, Amy, and college-age children McLean and Whitney—live on a farm in rural Ohio. In his free time, Macionis enjoys tennis, swimming, hiking, and playing oldies rock-and-roll (available at his website). Macionis is as an environmental activist in the Lake George region of New York's Adirondack Mountains, where he works with a number of organizations, including the Lake George Land Conservancy, where he serves as president of the board of trustees.

Professor Macionis welcomes (and responds to) comments and suggestions about this book from faculty and students. Write to him at the Sociology Department, Ralston House, Kenyon College, Gambier, OH 43022, or send e-mail to macionis@kenyon.edu.

This book is offered to teachers of sociology in the hope that it will help our students understand their place in today's society and in tomorrow's world.

John J. Macionis

Sociology

Fifteenth Edition

John J. Macionis

KENYON COLLEGE

PEARSON

Boston   Columbus   Indianapolis   New York   San Francisco   Upper Saddle River
Amsterdam   Cape Town   Dubai   London   Madrid   Milan   Munich   Paris   Montréal   Toronto
Delhi   Mexico City   São Paulo   Sydney   Hong Kong   Seoul   Singapore   Taipei   Tokyo

Planet Friendly Publishing
✓ Made in the United States
✓ Printed on Recycled Paper
Text: 10%   Cover: 10%
Learn more: www.greenedition.org

At Pearson we're committed to producing books in an earth-friendly manner and to helping our customers make greener choices. Manufacturing books in the United States ensures compliance with strict environmental laws and eliminates the need for international freight shipping, a major contributor to global air pollution.

And printing on recycled paper helps minimize our consumption of trees, water and fossil fuels. The text of *Sociology, 15th Edition*, was printed on paper made with 10% post-consumer waste, and the cover was printed on paper made with 10% post-consumer waste. According to the Environmental Paper Network's Paper Calculator, we achieved the following environmental benefits:

Trees Saved: 105 • Air Emissions Eliminated: 10,902 pounds
Water Saved: 48,359 gallons • Solid Waste Eliminated: 3,844 pounds

For more information on our environmental practices, please visit us online at www.greenedition.org.
Courier Corporation, the manufacturer of this book, owns the Green Edition Trademark.

Editor in Chief: *Dickson Musslewhite*
Senior Acquisitions Editor: *Brita Mess*
Director of Marketing: *Brandy Dawson*
Senior Marketing Manager: *Maureen Prado Roberts*
Program Manager: *Deb Hartwell*
Development Editor: *Barbara Reilly*
Editorial Assistant: *Jessica Lombardo*
Data Researcher: *Kimberlee Klesner*
Copy Editor: *Donna Mulder*
Project Manager: *Marianne Peters-Riordan*
Manufacturing Buyer: *Diane Peirano*
Interior Designer: *Ilze Lemesis*

Cover Designer: *Bruce Kenselaar*
Creative Director: *Jayne Conte*
Cover Photo: *Joshua Paul Johnson/Pearson Education*
Digital Media Director: *Brian Hyland*
Digital Media Editor: *Alison Lorber*
Media Project Manager: *Nikhil Bramhavar*
Full-Service Project Management: *PreMediaGlobal, USA, Inc.*
Composition: *PreMediaGlobal, USA, Inc.*
Printer/Binder: *Courier Companies*
Cover Printer: *Lehigh-Phoenix Color*
Text Font: *10.5 pts MinionPro-Regular*

Credits and acknowledgments borrowed from other sources and reproduced, with permission, in this textbook appear on the appropriate page within text [or on page 769].

Microsoft® and Windows® are registered trademarks of the Microsoft Corporation in the U.S.A. and other countries. Screen shots and icons reprinted with permission from the Microsoft Corporation. This book is not sponsored or endorsed by or affiliated with the Microsoft Corporation.

Library of Congress Cataloging-in-Publication Data
Macionis, John J.
    Sociology / John J. Macionis. — Fifteenth edition.
        pages cm
    ISBN-13: 978-0-205-98560-9 (alk. paper)
    ISBN-10: 0-205-98560-2 (alk. paper)
    1. Sociology. I. Title.
    HM586.M33 2013
    301—dc23

                                                    2013028097

10 9 8 7 6 5 4 3 2

Student Version ISBN 10:   0-205-98560-2
                 ISBN 13:   978-0-205-98560-9
Books a la Carte ISBN 10:   0-13-375327-1
                 ISBN 13:   978-0-13-375327-1

Brief Contents

Contents

4 Society 98

the **Power** of **Society** to shape access to the Internet 99

5 Socialization 124

the **Power** of **Society** to shape how much television we watch 125

6   Social Interaction in Everyday Life   152

7   Groups and Organizations   178

8   Sexuality and Society   206

9   Deviance   236

the **Power** of **Society** to affect the odds of being incarcerated for using drugs   237

Part III   Social Inequality

10   Social Stratification   272

the **Power** of **Society** to affect life expectancy   273

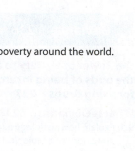

14 Race and Ethnicity   390

15 Aging and the Elderly   424

Part IV Social Institutions

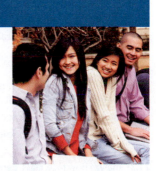

21   Health and Medicine   598

Part V   Social Change

22   Population, Urbanization, and Environment   628

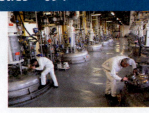

Boxes

Online Exclusive Boxes

These boxes can be found under the Student Resources tab and also in your eText in MySocLab.

Seeing Sociology in Everyday Life

Is What We Read in the Mass Media True? The Case of Extramarital Sex

Gender and Language: "You Just Don't Understand!"

Deviant Subculture: Has It Become OK to Break the Rules?

As CEOs Get Richer, the Great Mansions Return

"Happy Poverty" in India: Making Sense of a Strange Idea

Does Race Affect Intelligence?

Back to Work! Will We Ever Get to Retire?

Who's Minding the Kids?

Should Students Pray in School?

The Rumor Mill: Paul is Dead!

Tracking Change: Is Life in the United States Getting Better or Worse?

Thinking About Diversity: Race, Class, and Gender

The Importance of Gender in Research

The Development of Self among High School Students

A Third Gender: The *Muxes* of Mexico

Gender Today: Are *Men* Being Left Behind?

Women in the Mills of Lowell, Massachusetts

Gender and Eating Disorders: A Report from Fiji

Where Are the Girls? China's One-Child Policy

Controversy and Debate

Can People Lie with Statistics?

The Bell Curve Debate: Are Rich People Really Smarter?

The Market: Does the "Invisible Hand" Lift Us Up or Pick Our Pockets?

Does Science Threaten Religion?

Personal Freedom and Social Responsibility: Can We Have It Both Ways?

Thinking Globally

The Global Village: A Social Snapshot of Our World

The United States and Canada: How Do These National Cultures Differ?

Can Too Many Be Too Old? A Report from Japan

Want Equality and Freedom? Try Denmark

"Soft Authoritarianism" or Planned Prosperity? A Report from Singapore

Early to Wed: A Report from Rural India

When Health Fails: A Report from Russia

Maps

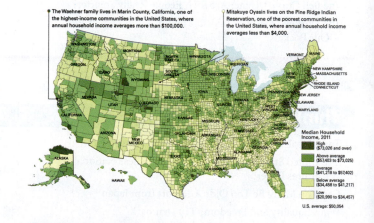

Preface

Our world challenges us like never before. Even as the economy climbs out of recession, unemployment remains high and the economic future is uncertain here in the United States and around the world. For decades, income inequality in our society has steadily increased, just as it is increasing for the world as a whole. There is a lot of anger about how our national leaders in Washington are doing—or not doing—their jobs. Technological disasters of our own making threaten the natural environment, and patterns of extreme weather only add to the mounting evidence of global warming.

Perhaps no one should be surprised to read polls that tell us most people are anxious about their economic future, unhappy with our political system, and worried about the state of the planet. Many of us simply feel overwhelmed, as if we were up against forces we can barely understand—much less control.

That's where sociology comes in. For more than 150 years, sociologists have been working to better understand how society operates. We sociologists may not have all the answers, but we have learned quite a lot that we can share with you. A beginning course in sociology is your introduction to the fascinating and very useful study of the social world. After all, we all have a stake in understanding our world and doing all we can to improve it.

Sociology, Fifteenth Edition, provides you with comprehensive understanding of how this world works. You will find this book to be informative, engaging, and even entertaining. Before you have finished the first chapter, you will discover that sociology is not only useful—it is also a great deal of fun. *Sociology is a field of study that can change the way you see the world and open the door to many new opportunities.* What could be more exciting than that?

The Text and MySocLab®: A Powerful and Interactive Learning Program

Sociology, Fifteenth Edition, places a thorough revision of the discipline's leading textbook at the center of an interactive learning program. As the fully involved author, I have been personally responsible for revising the text, as well as writing the Test Bank and all the instructor notes that are found in the Annotated Instructor's Edition and updating the Instructor's Manual. Now, convinced of the ability of Pearson's MySocLab technology to transform learning, *I have taken personal responsibility for all the content of the MySocLab that accompanies my texts.* To ensure the highest level of quality, I have written a series of interactive Social Explorer map exercises, authored all the questions that assess student learning, and personally selected all the readings and short videos that are keyed to each chapter. I have written both the book and the lab material with two goals—to set the highest standard of quality for the entire learning program and also to ensure that all parts of this program are linked seamlessly and transparently. Even if you are familiar with previous editions of this text, please do your students the favor of reviewing all that is new with *Sociology, Fifteenth Edition.*

Our outstanding learning program has been constructed with care and directed toward both high-quality content and easy and effective operation. Each major section of every chapter has a purpose, which is stated simply in the form of a **Learning Objective**. All the learning objectives are listed on the first page of each chapter; they guide students through their reading of the chapter, and they appear again as the organizing structure of the **Making the Grade** summary at the chapter's end. These learning objectives also involve a range of cognitive abilities. Some sections of the text focus on more basic cognitive skills—such as *remembering* the definitions of key concepts and *understanding* ideas to the point of being able to explain them in one's own words. In addition, questions throughout the text and especially activities in MySocLab exercises provide students with opportunities to engage in *discovery*, *analysis*, and *evaluation*. MySocLab's **Social Explorer exercises**, for example, give students the opportunity to analyze social patterns presented in colorful and interactive maps and to explore their own questions and reach their own conclusions. In addition, the MySocLab's **Sociology in Focus** blog gives readers the chance to evaluate many of the most current debates and controversies as they read frequent postings by a team of young and engaging sociologists. For each chapter of the text, I've also written a **Seeing Sociology in *Your* Everyday Life** essay, which shows the "everyday life" relevance of sociology by explaining how the material in the chapter can empower students in their personal and professional lives. Each of these essays includes learning activities designed at different intellectual levels (a "remember" exercise, an "apply" exercise, and a "create" exercise).

An exciting new element available for the first time with *Sociology, Fifteenth Edition,* is the **Core Concept Video Series**. This is a series of 126 short videos that fall into six categories.

- In *The Big Picture* videos, sociologist Jodie Lawston provides an introductory overview of the text chapter.

- *The Basics* videos presents a review of the most important concepts for each core topic in the course, using an animated, whiteboard format.

- *Sociology on the Job* videos, created by Professor Tracy Xavia Karner, connect the content of each chapter to the world of work and careers.

- *Sociology in Focus* videos feature a sociological perspective on today's popular culture.

- *Social Inequalities* videos, featuring Lester Andrist, introduce notable sociologists who highlight their own research emphasizing the importance of inequality based on race, class, and gender.

- *Thinking Like a Sociologist* videos introduce students to examples and issues using data. These friendly videos, drawing from examples in Social Explorer, help build students' quantitative analysis skills.

This entire library of videos is available to you and to your students as part of the learning program that surrounds *Sociology, Fifteenth Edition*. I have selected three videos for each chapter of the text that are identified by a "**Watch**" icon in the margin of the text at the most effective point in the chapter.

Another rich and varied resource in the learning program is the **MySocLab Library**. This is a library containing 175 articles and monographs written by notable sociologists. In the library you will find "classics" by Marx, Weber, Durkheim, and Du Bois, as well as by Jane Addams, Harriet Martineau, and Margaret Mead. Contemporary selections range from works by C. Wright Mills, Peter Berger, Bonnie Thornton Dill, Kingsley Davis, Karyn Lacy, Elijah Anderson, Karen Brodkin, Catherine Delorey, Barbara Ehrenreich, Arlie Russell Hochschild, and dozens of other sociologists. This entire sociology library is available to you and to your students as part of the *Sociology* learning program. I have selected one reading for each chapter that can be identified by the "**Read**" icon in the margin.

In addition, each chapter of the text also carries an "**Explore**" icon, which identifies a **Social Explorer®** exercise. In each of these twenty-four discovery exercises, which I have written specifically for this text, students are led on a learning journey in which they can discover important lessons for themselves. In addition, these exercises are fully interactive so that students may also engage in self-directed exploration.

To sum up, here is a list of what is available to you in the *Sociology, Fifteenth Edition*, learning program:

- **Videos**, 126 in all, with three selections placed within each chapter by John Macionis (look for the "Watch" icons in each chapter of the text, which directly link the three selected videos to chapter content). Selected videos are accompanied by assessment questions. These videos bring concepts to life and stimulate class discussion.
- **MySocLibrary** is a virtual bookshelf of classic and contemporary readings. John Macionis has selected and linked one reading to every chapter (look for the "Read" icon in each chapter, which identifies the specific reading that is part of the assessment program for that chapter).
- **Social Explorer®** activities, each written by John Macionis, provide easy access to sociological maps containing rich demographic data—largely based on the 2010 census—about the United States. An exercise, which leads students on a journey of sociological discovery, is provided for every chapter of the text (look for the "Explore" icon in each chapter).
- The **Sociology in Focus blog** can be used with each chapter of the text. Directions for accessing it are included in the list of student activities found near the end of each chapter. This blog, written by a team of young sociologists, links chapter material to the popular culture that is important to today's students.
- **Seeing Sociology in *Your* Everyday Life** essays, written by John Macionis, explain how the material found in every chapter of the text can personally and professionally benefit students in their everyday lives.
- **Writing Space** is the best way to develop and assess concept mastery and critical thinking through writing. Writing Space provides a single place within MySocLab to create, track, and grade writing assignments, access writing resources, and exchange meaningful, personalized feedback quickly and easily to improve results. For students, Writing Space provides

everything they need to keep up with writing assignments, access assignment guides and checklists, write or upload completed assignments, and receive grades and feedback—all in one convenient place. For educators, Writing Space makes assigning, receiving, and evaluating writing assignments easier. It's simple to create new assignments and upload relevant materials, see student progress, and receive alerts when students submit work. Writing Space makes student work more focused and effective with customized grading rubrics they can see, and personalized feedback. Writing Space can also check students' work for improper citation or plagiarism by comparing it against the world's most accurate text comparison database available from Turnitin.

- **Practice tests** and **flashcards**, available in MySocLab, help students prepare for quizzes and exams.
- The **Instructor's Manual**, revised for this edition by John Macionis, provides chapter outlines and supplemental lecture material and helps instructors present chapter material in greater depth.

The learning program that accompanies *Sociology, Fifteenth Edition,* offers flexibility to you as an instructor. By using the text and MySocLab, you may choose to allow students to do selected lab exercises on their own, or you can use the lab material for powerful in-class presentations. You decide the extent of integration into your course—from independent self-assessment to total course management. This learning program is also accompanied by an Instructor's Manual featuring sample syllabi, supplemental lecture material, and tips for integrating MySocLab technology into your course.

What's New in This Edition?

Here's a quick summary of the new material found throughout *Sociology, Fifteenth Edition*.

- **Learning Objectives.** Each major section of every chapter begins with a specific Learning Objective. All Learning Objectives are listed at the beginning of each chapter and they organize the summary at the end of each chapter.
- **Power of Society figures.** If you could teach your students only one thing in the introductory course, what would it be? Probably, most instructors would answer, *"To understand the power of society to shape people's lives."* Each chapter of the text now begins with a Power of Society figure that does exactly that—forcing students to give up some of their cultural common sense that points to the importance of "personal choice" in the face of evidence of how society shapes our major life decisions.
- A **new design** makes this edition of the text the cleanest and easiest ever to read.
- Much more on **social media.** More than ever before, social life revolves around computer-based technology that shapes networks and social movements. Social media are discussed throughout the text and major sections on social media are found in Chapters 6 ("Social Interaction in Everyday Life") and Chapter 7 ("Groups and Organizations").
- **New scholarship dealing with race, class, and gender**. For example, the discussion of participant observation in Chapter 2 ("Sociological Investigation") is now illustrated by Joseph Ewoodzie's recent research on homelessness among African American men and women in Jackson, Mississippi. Chapter 3 ("Culture") now has new discussion of the emergence of hip-hop music in low-income African American communities. Chapter 13 ("Gender Stratification") has new discussions of

global and multicultural feminism. Chapter 19 ("Religion") has expanded discussion of Islam.

- This revision has full coverage of the **results of the 2012 national elections** as well as important recent events such as the Newtown, Connecticut, school shootings, "Superstorm" Sandy, and the ongoing "jobless recovery."

Here is a brief summary of some of the material that is new, chapter-by-chapter:

Chapter 1: Sociology: Perspective, Theory, and Method
The new Power of Society figure shows how race, class, and age guide people's choice of partners. The revised chapter has the latest on the increasing number of states allowing same-sex marriage. There is new discussion of how the odds of going to college vary for young people from families with differing levels of income. Find updates on the number of children born to women in nations around the world; the number of high-income, middle-income, and low-income nations; and the changing share of minorities in major sports. As in every chapter, the photography program has been substantially revised and updated, with all captions written by the author.

Chapter 2: Sociological Investigation
The new Power of Society figure demonstrates how race shapes the odds of going to college or ending up in prison for young men. The revised chapter contains new data on economic inequality, extramarital relationships, and the share of the population that claims to be multiracial. The participant observation research by William Whyte has been replaced by recent research on homelessness in Jackson, Mississippi. There is a critical update on the original Hawthorne effect research. There is a new National Map showing the response rates of households to the 2010 census by county across the country.

Chapter 3: Culture
The new Power of Society figure contrasts high- and low-income nations in popular support for access to abortion. The revised chapter has updates on the income and wealth of the Asian American, Hispanic, and African American communities. There are also new data on the number of languages spoken as a measure of this country's cultural diversity, the extent of global illiteracy, patterns of immigration, the debate over official English, the number of people in the United States who speak a language other than English at home, the life goals for people entering college, the evolving texting language, and the share of all web pages written in English. There is a new Thinking About Diversity box on the origins of hip-hop music.

Chapter 4: Society
The new Power of Society figure shows the expanding use of social networking sites over time throughout the U.S. population. The revised chapter has updates on poverty in the United States as well as the latest data tracking the use of computers around the world.

Chapter 5: Socialization
The new Power of Society figure shows that class guides use of the mass media, documenting that people without a high school diploma spend much more time watching television than people with at least a college degree. The revised

chapter has the latest on the share of people who claim to be multiracial. There is also recent research on the endorsement of the presidential candidates in 2012 by major newspapers.

Chapter 6: Social Interaction in Everyday Life
The new Power of Society figure shows how age guides the extent of networking using social media. The discussion of reality building addresses how films expand people's awareness of the challenges of living with various disabilities. The discussion of nonverbal communication has been expanded to highlight its special importance to people who have some physical impairment or disability. The revised chapter has updates on the share of women in clerical or service jobs. The discussion of body language and deception has been expanded. There is a new section on social media, pointing out how computer technology has changed patterns of social networking and reality construction.

Chapter 7: Groups and Organizations
The new Power of Society figure shows that class is a powerful factor that affects the odds of being a member of a professional association. The revised chapter has updates on the size and scope of McDonalds, the extent of Internet use around the world, and the effect of race, ethnicity, and gender on having a position in management. There is a new discussion of social media and networking. Many of the chapter's images are new to this edition.

Chapter 8: Sexuality and Society
The new Power of Society figure tracks the trend toward acceptance of same-sex marriage. The revised chapter has updates on the size of the lesbian, gay, bisexual, and transgender (LGBT) community, the share of high school students who have had sexual intercourse (including new data reflecting race and ethnicity), and the share of married people who engage in extramarital sex. Included in the revision is discussion of the Supreme Court decision re the Defense of Marriage Act (DOMA) and of political changes during 2012 that have led additional states to permit same-sex marriage. The revised chapter has the latest statistics on teen pregnancy, the risk of rape, and the risks of prostitution for young women. A new discussion explores the effects of gender inequality on women's reproductive health. There is a new discussion and also a new Global Map focused on women's access to abortion around the world.

Chapter 9: Deviance
The new Power of Society figure shows that race places some categories of the U.S. population at much higher risk of being incarcerated. New discussion highlights the importance of the Sandy Hook Elementary School shootings in 2012. The updated chapter has the latest statistical information on the extent of legal gambling across the United States, the extent of legal "medical marijuana" use; the projection that, by 2015, firearms will cause more deaths than auto accidents; recent changes in capital punishment laws in the United States; recent research on the cost of incarceration; the share of white-collar criminals who end up in jail; and the number of serious crimes that are recorded in the United States for 2011. There is a complete analysis of patterns of arrest for "person crimes" and "property crimes" by age, sex, race, and ethnicity for 2011. The revised

chapter also reports the number of police in the United States and the number of people in prison, provides a statistically-based exploration of the use of the death penalty, and highlights recent legal changes to capital punishment laws.

Chapter 10: Social Stratification

The new Power of Society figure compares two communities in Florida—one affluent and one economically struggling—and finds striking effects of class on life expectancy. The revised chapter has numerous updates on social inequality in Russia, China, and South Africa, and on the extent of economic inequality in selected nations around the world. The Seeing Sociology in Everyday Life photo essay has been refreshed.

Chapter 11: Social Class in the United States

The new Power of Society figure shows how race and ethnicity set the odds that a child in the United States will live in poverty. The revised chapter has the latest data for all measures of economic inequality, including income and wealth, the economic assets of the richest families in the United States, and the educational achievement of various categories of the population. There are new data showing that the recent recession has reduced average family wealth. New data show the racial gap in home ownership, the odds of completing a four-year college degree for people at various class levels, and the extent of poverty in the United States. There is new discussion of the American dream in an age of economic recession as well as the increasing social segregation experienced by low-income families. There are 2011 data on the extent of poverty, the number of working poor, and how poverty interacts with age, sex, race, and ethnicity. There is a new estimate of the hourly wage needed to support an urban family of four above the poverty line. There are also new data on the extent of homelessness.

Chapter 12: Global Stratification

The new Power of Society figure shows how the nation into which a person is born sets the odds of surviving to the age of five. The revised chapter has updates on garment factory work in the low-income nation of Bangladesh; the number of people in the world who are poor; the distribution of income and wealth in the world; the average income for the world as a whole; the number and updated social profile of nations at high-income, middle-income, and low-income levels of development; the latest United Nations data on quality of life in various regions of the world; and the latest data on global debt. There is expanded discussion of the link between population increase and poverty. Recent data illuminate economic trends in various regions of the world and confirm the increasing economic gap between the highest- and lowest-income nations. There are updates on wealth and well-being in selected nations at each level of economic development.

Chapter 13: Gender Stratification

The new Power of Society figure shows how gender shapes people's goals and ambitions. The revised chapter has updates on life expectancy for U.S. women and men; the share of degrees earned by each sex in various fields of study; the share of U.S. women and men in the labor force and the share working full time; the share of women and men in many sex-typed occupations; the share of large corporations with women in leadership positions; the number of small businesses owned by women; and unemployment rates for women and men. The revised chapter has the latest data on income and wealth for women and men. There is discussion of new research showing that women living in states with greater access to contraception earn more over their working careers than women who live in states that provide less access. Find the most recent statistics on women in political leadership positions, including results of the 2012 national elections, which put record numbers of women in Congress. Also, the revised chapter has the latest data on women in the military, and provides updated discussions of violence against women and men. The coverage of intersection theory now reflects the most recent income data. The revised chapter has a new discussion of multicultural and global feminism.

Chapter 14: Race and Ethnicity

The new Power of Society figure shows how race and ethnicity influence voting preferences and demonstrates that Barack Obama's reelection reflected strong support among minority communities. The revised chapter has updates on the share and size of all racial and ethnic categories of the U.S. population, including the multiracial population; the share of households speaking a language other than English in the home; the share of U.S. marriages that are interracial; the number of American Indian and Alaskan Native nations and tribal groups; and the income levels and poverty rates, extent of schooling, and average age for all major racial and ethnic categories of the U.S. population. New discussion highlights important trends including the increasing share of American Indians who claim to be of mixed racial background and the increasing share of African Americans who are within the middle class.

Chapter 15: Aging and the Elderly

The new Power of Society figure shows how gender shapes the process of caregiving for older people in the United States. The revised chapter has the latest on life expectancy and the gradual "graying" of the U.S. population, and explains the effect of class and race on the way elderly people assess their health. Included are the latest figures on the income, wealth, and poverty rates of people in various age categories throughout the life course. New discussion highlights why the gender gap in income is greater among today's seniors than it is for the population as a whole; who in the family provides caregiving to older people; the extent of elder abuse; the increasing share of our population for which death takes place after reaching the age of fifty-five; and the use of Physician Orders for Life Sustaining Treatment (POLST). The latest trends on the frequency of physician-assisted suicide in states that permit this practice are included along with new data on the increasing use of hospice care. The social-conflict and feminist analysis of aging has been expanded with greater discussion of the effects of class and gender on the experience of growing old.

Chapter 16: The Economy and Work

The new Power of Society figure demonstrates how race and ethnicity guide the type of work people do. The revised chapter has updates on the increasing size of Walmart; the share of economic output in the private and public sector for the United States and for other nations; the share of the U.S. population by race and ethnicity in the labor force; the latest on the share of public and private sector workers in a union as well as the recent political conflict between several states and public service unions. There is expanded discussion of the debate concerning "right-to-work" laws and a new National Map shows which states have—and have not—enacted such laws. There are new data indicating the share of women and men who are self-employed. The discussion of unemployment now points out the emerging problem of extended unemployment and there is new discussion of the "jobless recovery."

Chapter 17: Politics and Government

The new Power of Society figure shows the effect of age on voting preferences, revealing that people under the age of thirty were critical to the outcome of the 2012 presidential election. There is updated discussion and analysis of the changing political landscape in the Middle East. The revised chapter has updates on the number of people employed in government; the cost of operating the government; voter turnout and voter preferences in the 2012 elections involving race, ethnicity, and gender; the number of lobbyists and political action committees in the country; the latest on the number of people barred from voting based on a criminal conviction; recent political trends involving college students; the latest data on the extent of terrorism and casualties resulting from such conflict; recent changes in nuclear proliferation and declining support for SDI as a peace-keeping policy; and the latest data on global and U.S. military spending as well as expanding opportunities for women in the U.S. military. There is a new National Map showing county-by-county results in the 2012 presidential election. There is new discussion of the importance of "swing states" and how the Electoral College may discourage voter turnout in most states. There is discussion of the latest nuclear disarmament negotiations.

Chapter 18: Families

The new Power of Society figure shows the effect of class on the likelihood that marriage will endure, documenting longer-term marriages among more socially privileged people and shorter-term marriages among disadvantaged people. There is expanded discussion of the importance of grandparents in the process of childrearing, the experience of loneliness and families in later life, and moving in with relatives as a strategy to cut living expenses during the current recession. There is new discussion of the "boomerang generation" made up of young people who have left home only to return when they have not found a job. A new National Map shows the divorce rate for states across the country. The revised chapter has updates on the number of U.S. households and families, the share of young women in low-income countries who marry before the age of eighteen; the cost of raising a child for parents at various class levels; the share of youngsters in the United States who are "latchkey kids"; the income gap that separates Hispanic and African American families from non-Hispanic white families; the rising average age at first marriage; the incidence of court-ordered child support and the frequency of non-payment; the rate of domestic violence against women and also children. Data for 2013 show the number of nations that permit same-sex marriage and the number of states in this country that permit same-sex marriage. There are also new data showing the increasing share of U.S. adults living alone; the child-care arrangements for working mothers with young children; and the relative frequency of various types of interracial marriage.

Chapter 19: Religion

The new Power of Society figure shows how having or lacking a religious affiliation is linked to traditional or progressive family values. The revised chapter has updates on the size of all world religions. The latest data show the extent of religious belief in the United States as well as the share of people favoring various denominations. There is new discussion of Reconstructionist Judaism in an extensively updated discussion of the Jewish religious tradition. There is expanded discussion of a trend away from religious affiliation among young people in the United States. There is expanded discussion of Islam in the United States. There is updated and expanded discussion of the secularization debate as well as more extensive application of feminist theory to religion. There is an expanded discussion of New Age spirituality, and also new discussion of celibacy among Catholic priests.

Chapter 20: Education

The new Power of Society figure shows that race and ethnicity shapes the opportunity to attend college. The revised chapter has new global data showing the relative academic performance of U.S. children, comparing them to children in Japan and other nations. There are new statistical profiles of schooling in India, Japan, and other countries. New data identify the share of U.S. adults that has completed high school and college, how income affects access to higher education, and how higher education is linked to earnings later on. There are new statistics on the number of colleges and universities in the United States as well as the financial costs of attending them. The latest data guide discussion of community colleges in the United States and the diverse student body they enroll. The revised chapter includes the latent trends in dropping out of high school, performance on the SAT, high-school grade inflation, and the spread of charter and magnet schools. A new report from the National Center for Education Statistics documents modest improvements in U.S. public schools over the last two decades.

Chapter 21: Health and Medicine

The new Power of Society figure documents a key health trend—the increasing rate of obesity among all categories of the U.S. population. The revised chapter has expanded discussion of prejudice against people based on body weight. There are updates on global patterns of health including improvements in the well-being of young children, the rate of cigarette smoking, the use of smokeless tobacco, and the frequency of illness resulting from tobacco use. The revised chapter has new discussion of how gender shapes patterns involving eating disorders, the latest on patterns of AIDS and other sexually transmitted diseases, and the ongoing debate involving euthanasia. The revised chapter reports that the government now pays for most heath care and also explains how people pay the rest of their medical bills.

Chapter 22: Population, Urbanization, and Environment

The new Power of Society figure shows that concern for environmental issues such as global warming, while typically greater in high-income nations than in low-income nations, remains low in the United States. The revised chapter has a new opening that describes recent "Superstorm" Sandy as one indication of new weather patterns that reflect changes in the natural environment and threaten people who live in flood-prone regions of the world. The revised chapter has the most recent data on the size of the U.S. population as well as rates of fertility and mortality for the United States and for various world regions. Also find new data for infant mortality and life expectancy as well as the latest global population projections. Trends involving urbanization have all been revised based on the latest research and statistics. There is a new section giving expanded coverage of social life in rural places. New discussions highlight urbanization in low-income regions of the world, increasing levels of global water consumption, and the declining size of the planet's rain forests.

Chapter 23: Collective Behavior and Social Movements

The new Power of Society figure shows in which nations people are more or less likely to engage in public demonstrations. The revised chapter illustrates important ideas with current debates such as the share of political campaign ads that are deceptive, the ongoing conflict in Syria, the controversy in the United States over the "fiscal cliff," and the deadly 2013 nightclub fire in Brazil. The revised chapter highlights the increasing importance of the Internet as a source of information about elections and other political events. Find the latest data on the share of college students who report being politically active.

Chapter 24: Social Change: Traditional, Modern, and Postmodern Societies

The new Power of Society figure identifies nations in which people look more favorably—and less favorably—on scientific advances. The revised chapter has updates on life expectancy and other demographic changes. There is new discussion of the Geechee people of Hog Hammock, where rising property values threaten to displace a historic African American community. The discussion of how life in the United States is getting better and worse has been reframed by the latest data on the well-being of the U.S. population.

Supplements for the Instructor

ANNOTATED INSTRUCTOR'S EDITION   (0-13-375300-X) The AIE is a complete student text with author-written annotations on every page. The annotations are especially useful to new instructors, but they are written to be helpful to even the most seasoned teachers. Margin notes include summaries of research findings, statistics from the United States and other nations, insightful quotations, information highlighting patterns of social diversity in the United States, and high-quality survey data from the General Social Survey conducted by the National Opinion Research Center (NORC) and from the World Values Survey conducted by the World Values Survey Association.

INSTRUCTOR'S MANUAL WITH TEST BANK   (0-205-98286-7) This learning program offers an Instructor's Manual that will be of interest even to those who have never chosen to use one before. The manual—now revised by John Macionis—goes well beyond the expected detailed chapter outlines and discussion questions to provide summaries of important current events and trends, recent articles from *Teaching Sociology* that are relevant to classroom discussions, suggestions for classroom activities, and supplemental lecture material for every

chapter of the text. In addition, this edition of the Instructor's Manual contains a great deal of information to help instructors better integrate the wide array of media assets found in MySocLab within their course content.

The Test Bank—again, written by the author—reflects the material in the text—both in content and in language—far better than the testing file available with any other introductory sociology textbook. The file contains more than 100 items per chapter—in multiple-choice, true/false, and essay formats. For all of the questions, the correct answer is provided, as well as the Bloom's level of cognitive reasoning the question requires of the student, the learning objective that the question tests, and the difficulty level.

MYTEST   (0-205-98295-6) This online, computerized software allows instructors to create their own personalized exams, to edit any or all of the existing test questions, and to add new questions. Other special features of this program include random generation of test questions, creation of alternative versions of the same test, scrambling question sequence, and test preview before printing.

POWERPOINT® LECTURE SLIDES   (0-205-98277-8) These PowerPoint slides combine graphics and text in a colorful format to help you convey sociological principles in a visual and engaging way. Each chapter of the textbook has between fifteen and twenty-five slides that effectively communicate the key concepts in that chapter. Also available are PowerPoint slides that only contain the chapter outline, for instructors who wish to build their own unique set of slides, and additionally a set of slides that only contains the art and photos within each chapter.

MYSOCLAB   (0-13-375280-1) As mentioned before, MySocLab is a learning and assessment tool that enables instructors to assess student performance and adapt course content—without investing additional time or resources. MySocLab is designed with instructor flexibility in mind—you decide the extent of integration into your course, from independent self-assessment to total course management. The lab is accompanied by an instructor's manual featuring easy-to-read media grids, activities, sample syllabi, and tips for integrating technology into your course.

Recognizing Diversity: A Word about Language

This text has a commitment to describe the social diversity of the United States and the world. This promise carries with it the responsibility to use language thoughtfully. In most cases, the text uses the terms "African American" and "person of color" rather than the word "black." Similarly, we use the terms "Latino," "Latina," and "Hispanic" to refer to people of Spanish descent. Most tables and figures refer to "Hispanics" because this is the term the Census Bureau uses when collecting statistical data about our population.

Students should realize, however, that many individuals do not describe themselves using these terms. Although the word "Hispanic" is commonly used in the eastern part of the United States and "Latino" and the feminine form "Latina" are widely heard in the West, across the United States people of Spanish descent identify with a particular ancestral nation, whether it be Argentina, Mexico, some other Latin American country, or Spain or Portugal in Europe.

The same holds for Asian Americans. Although this term is a useful shorthand in sociological analysis, most people of Asian descent think of themselves in terms of a specific country of origin, say, Japan, the Philippines, Taiwan, or Vietnam.

In this text, the term "Native American" refers to all the inhabitants of the Americas (including Alaska and the Hawaiian Islands) whose ancestors lived here prior to the arrival of Europeans. Here again, however, most people in this broad category identify with their historical society, such as Cherokee, Hopi, Seneca, or Zuni. The term "American Indian" refers to only those Native Americans who live in the continental United States, not including Native peoples living in Alaska or Hawaii.

On a global level, this text avoids the word "American"—which literally designates two continents—to refer to just the United States. For example, referring to this country, the term "the U.S. economy" is more precise than "the American economy." This convention may seem a small point, but it implies the significant recognition that we in this country represent only one society (albeit a very important one) in the Americas.

In Appreciation

The conventional practice of crediting a book to a single author hides the efforts of dozens of women and men who have helped create *Sociology, Fifteenth Edition*. I offer my deep and sincere thanks to the Pearson editorial team, including Yolanda de Rooy, division president; Craig Campanella, editorial director; Dickson Musslewhite, editor-in-chief; and Brita Mess, senior acquisitions editor in sociology, for their steady enthusiasm in the pursuit of both innovation and excellence.

Day-to-day work on the book is shared by various members of the "author team." Barbara Reilly, principal of Reilly Editorial Services, Inc., is a key member of this group. Indeed, if anyone "sweats the details" as much as I do, it is Barbara! Kimberlee Klesner works closely with me to ensure that all the data in this revision are the very latest available. Kimberlee brings enthusiasm that matches her considerable talents, and I thank her for both. I also wish to thank Joseph "Piko" Ewoodzie for permitting me to use some of his recent research. Piko will play a greater role on our team as time goes on.

I want to thank all the members of the Pearson sales staff, the men and women who have represented this text with such confidence and enthusiasm over the years. My hat goes off especially to Brandy Dawson and Maureen Prado Roberts, who share responsibility for our marketing campaign.

Thanks, also, to Anne Nieglos for managing the design, and to Melissa Sacco of PreMediaGlobal and Marianne Peters Riordan of Pearson Education for managing the production process. Copyediting of the manuscript was skillfully done by Donna Mulder.

It goes without saying that every colleague knows more about a number of topics covered in this book than the author does. For that reason, I am grateful to the hundreds of faculty and the many students who have written to me to offer comments and suggestions. Thank you, one and all, for making a difference!

Finally, I dedicate this fifteenth edition of *Sociology* to the memory of my mother, May Johnston Macionis (1917–2013). Mom, the life lessons you passed along to me, especially the importance of reaching out to other members of the community—and to people in other communities—will remain within me always. May you find peace on your journey!

With best wishes to my colleagues and with love to all,

Jan J. Macionis

1 The Sociological Perspective

((Listen to **Chapter 1** in **MySocLab**

LEARNING OBJECTIVES

1.1 Explain how the sociological perspective differs from common sense.

1.2 State several reasons that a global perspective is important in today's world.

1.3 Identify the advantages of sociological thinking for developing public policy, for encouraging personal growth, and for advancing in a career.

1.4 Link the origins of sociology to historical social changes.

1.5 Summarize sociology's major theoretical approaches.

1.6 Apply sociology's major theoretical approaches to the topic of sports.

the Power of Society

to guide our choices in marriage partners

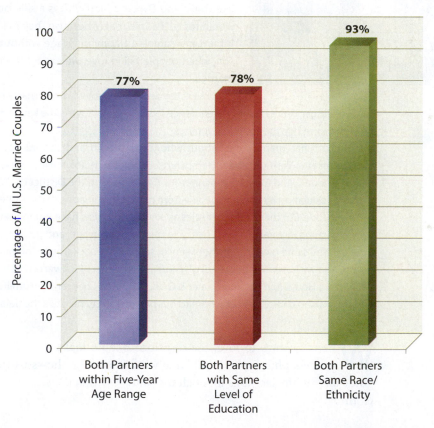

Source: U.S. Census Bureau (2012)

Do we simply "pick" our marriage partners? In 77 percent of all married couples in the United States, both partners are within five years of age of each other; in 78 percent, both partners have achieved the same level of schooling; and in 93 percent of married couples, both partners are of the same racial or ethnic category. Although we tend to think of love and marriage as very personal matters, it is clear that society guides the process of selecting a spouse.

Chapter Overview

You are about to begin a course that could change your life. Sociology is a new and exciting way of understanding the world around you. It will change what you see and how you think about the world around you, and it may well change how you think about yourself. Chapter 1 of the text introduces the discipline of sociology. The most important skill to gain from this chapter is the ability to use what we call the *sociological perspective.* This chapter also introduces *sociological theory,* which helps you build understanding from what you see using the sociological perspective.

From the moment he first saw Tonya step off the subway train, Dwayne knew she was "the one." As the two walked up the stairs to the street and entered the building where they were both taking classes, Dwayne tried to get Tonya to stop and talk. At first, she ignored him. But after class, they met again, and she agreed to join him for coffee. That was three months ago. Today, they are engaged to be married.

If you were to ask people in the United States, "Why do couples like Tonya and Dwayne marry?" it is a safe bet that almost everyone would reply, "People marry because they fall in love." Most of us find it hard to imagine a happy marriage without love; for the same reason, when people fall in love, we expect them to think about getting married.

But is the decision about whom to marry really just a matter of personal feelings? There is plenty of evidence to show that if love is the key to marriage, Cupid's arrow is carefully aimed by the society around us.

Society has many "rules" about whom we should and should not marry. In all states but Massachusetts, Vermont, New Hampshire, Connecticut, Iowa, New York, Washington, Maryland, Maine, Rhode Island, Delaware, Minnesota, California, and the District of Columbia, the law rules out half the population by banning people from marrying someone of the same sex, even if the couple is deeply in love. But there are other rules as well. Sociologists have found that people, especially when they are young, are very likely to marry someone close in age, and people of all ages typically marry others in the same racial category, of similar social class background, of much the same level of education, and with a similar degree of physical attractiveness (Schwartz & Mare, 2005; Schoen & Cheng, 2006; Feng Hou & Myles, 2008; Shafer & Qian, 2010; see Chapter 18, "Families," for details). People do end up making choices about whom to marry, but society narrows the field long before they do.

W hen it comes to love, the decisions people make do not simply result from the process philosophers call "free will." Sociology shows us the power of society to guide all our life decisions in much the same way that the seasons influence our choice of clothing.

The Sociological Perspective

(1.1) Explain how the sociological perspective differs from common sense.

S ociology is *the systematic study of human society.* At the heart of sociology is a special point of view called the *sociological perspective.*

Seeing the General in the Particular

Watch in **MySocLab**
Video: *The Basics: What Is Sociology?*

One good way to define the **sociological perspective** is *seeing the general in the particular* (Berger, 1963). This definition tells us that sociologists look for general patterns in the behavior of particular people. Although every individual is unique, a society shapes the

We can easily see the power of society over the individual by imagining how different our lives would be had we been born in place of any of these children from, respectively, Kenya, Ethiopia, Myanmar, Peru, South Korea, and India.

lives of people in patterned ways that are evident as we discover how various categories (such as children and adults, women and men, the rich and the poor) live very differently. We begin to see the world sociologically by realizing how the general categories into which we fall shape our particular life experiences.

For example, the Power of Society figure on page 3 shows how the social world guides people to select marriage partners from within their own social categories. This is why the large majority of married couples are about the same age, have similar educational backgrounds, and share the same racial and ethnic identity. What about social class? How does social class position affect what women look for in a spouse? In a classic study of women's hopes for their marriages, Lillian Rubin (1976) found that higher-income women typically expected the men they married to be sensitive to others, to talk readily, and to share feelings and experiences. Lower-income women, she found, had very different expectations and were looking for men who did not drink too much, were not violent, and held steady jobs. Obviously, what women expect in a marriage partner has a lot to do with social class position.

This text explores the power of society to guide our actions, thoughts, and feelings. We may think that marriage results simply from the personal feelings of love. Yet the sociological perspective shows us that factors such as age, schooling, race and ethnicity, sex, and social class guide our selection of a partner. It might be more accurate to think of love as a feeling we have for others who match up with what society teaches us to want in a mate.

sociology the systematic study of human society

sociological perspective sociology's special point of view that sees general patterns of society in the lives of particular people

Seeing the Strange in the Familiar

At first, using the sociological perspective may seem like *seeing the strange in the familiar.* Consider how you might react if someone were to say to you, "You fit all the right categories, which means you would make a wonderful spouse!" We are used to

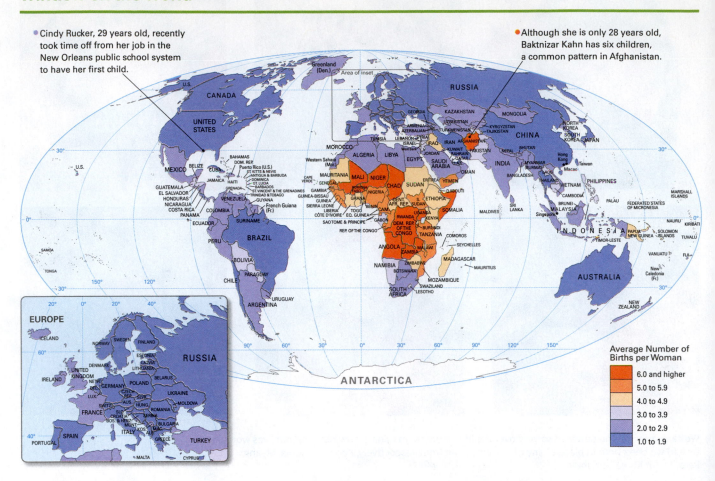

Cindy Rucker, 29 years old, recently took time off from her job in the New Orleans public school system to have her first child.

Although she is only 28 years old, Baktnizar Kahn has six children, a common pattern in Afghanistan.

Average Number of Births per Woman

- 6.0 and higher
- 5.0 to 5.9
- 4.0 to 4.9
- 3.0 to 3.9
- 2.0 to 2.9
- 1.0 to 1.9

GLOBAL MAP 1–1 Women's Childbearing in Global Perspective

Is childbearing simply a matter of personal choice? A look around the world shows that it is not. In general, women living in poor countries have many more children than women in rich nations. Can you point to some of the reasons for this global disparity? In simple terms, such differences mean that if you had been born into another society (whether you are female or male), your life might be quite different from what it is now.

Sources: Data from Population Reference Bureau (2012).

thinking that people fall in love and decide to marry based on personal feelings. But the sociological perspective reveals the initially strange idea that society shapes what we think and do.

Because we live in an individualistic society, learning to see how society affects us may take a bit of practice. If someone asked you why you "chose" to enroll at your particular college, you might offer one of the following reasons:

"I wanted to stay close to home."

"I got a basketball scholarship."

"With a journalism degree from this university, I can get a good job."

"My girlfriend goes to school here."

"I didn't get into the school I *really* wanted to attend."

Any of these responses may well be true. But do they tell the whole story?

Thinking sociologically about going to college, it's important to realize that only 7 out of every 100 people in the world have earned a college degree, with the enrollment rate much higher in high-income nations than in poor countries (Barro & Lee, 2010; OECD, 2012; World Bank, 2012). A century ago, even in the United States most people

Diversity Snapshot

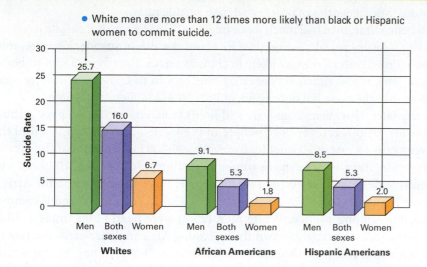

● White men are more than 12 times more likely than black or Hispanic women to commit suicide.

FIGURE 1–1 Rate of Death by Suicide, by Race and Sex, for the United States

Suicide rates are higher for white people than they are for black people and Hispanic people. Within each category, suicide rates are higher for men than for women. Rates indicate the number of deaths by suicide for every 100,000 people in each category for 2010.

Source: Centers for Disease Control and Prevention (2012).

had little or no chance to go to college. Today, enrolling in college is within the reach of far more men and women. But a look around the classroom shows that social forces still have much to do with who ends up on campus. For instance, most U.S. college students are young, generally between eighteen and about thirty. Why? Because our society links college attendance to this period of life. But more than age is involved, because just 43 percent of men and women between eighteen and twenty-four actually end up on campus.

Another factor is cost. Because higher education is so expensive, college students tend to come from families with above-average incomes. As Chapter 20 ("Education") explains, if you are lucky enough to belong to a family earning more than $115,000 a year, you are 60 percent more likely to go to college than someone whose family earns less than $27,000. Is it reasonable, in light of these facts, to ignore the power of society and say that attending college is simply a matter of personal choice?

Seeing Society in Our Everyday Lives

Another way to appreciate the power of society is to consider the number of children women have. As shown in Global Map 1–1 on page 6, the average woman in the United States has about two children during her lifetime. In Honduras, however, the average is about three; in Kenya, about four; in Yemen, five; in Afghanistan, six; and in Niger, the average woman has more than seven children (Population Reference Bureau, 2012).

What accounts for these striking differences? Because poor countries provide women with less schooling and fewer economic opportunities, women's lives are centered in the home; such women also have less access to contraception. Clearly, society has much to do with the decisions women and men make about childbearing.

Another illustration of the power of society to shape even our most private choices comes from the study of suicide. What could be a more personal choice than the decision to end your own life? But Emile Durkheim (1858–1917), one of sociology's pioneers, showed that even here, social forces are at work.

Examining official records in France, his own country, Durkheim found that some categories of people were more likely than others to take their own lives. Men, Protestants, wealthy people, and the unmarried had much higher suicide rates than women, Catholics and Jews, the poor, and married people. Durkheim explained the differences in terms of *social integration:* Categories of people with strong social ties had low suicide rates, and more individualistic categories of people had high suicide rates.

In Durkheim's time, men had much more freedom than women. But despite its advantages, freedom weakens social ties and thus increases the risk of suicide. Likewise, more individualistic Protestants were more likely to commit suicide than more tradition-bound Catholics and Jews, whose rituals encourage stronger social ties. The wealthy have much more freedom than the poor, but once again, at the cost of a higher suicide rate.

A century later, Durkheim's analysis still holds true. Figure 1–1 on page 7 shows suicide rates for various categories of people in the United States. Keep in mind that suicide is very rare—a rate of 10 suicides for every 100,000 people is about the same as 6 inches in a mile. Even so, we can see some interesting patterns. In 2010, there were 16 recorded suicides for every 100,000 white people, three times the rate for African Americans or Hispanics (5.3). For all categories of people, suicide was more common among men than among women. White men (25.7) were nearly four times as likely as white women (6.7) to take their own lives. Among African Americans, the rate for men (9.1) was about five times higher than for women (1.8). Among Hispanics, the rate for men (8.5) was more than four times higher than the rate for women (2.0) (Centers for Disease Control and Prevention, 2012). Applying Durkheim's logic, the higher suicide rate among white people and men reflects their greater wealth and freedom, just as the lower rate among women and African Americans reflects their limited social choices. As Durkheim did a century ago, we can see general patterns in the personal actions of particular individuals.

Seeing Sociologically: Marginality and Crisis

Anyone can learn to see the world using the sociological perspective. But two situations help people see clearly how society shapes individual lives: living on the margins of society and living through a social crisis.

From time to time, everyone feels like an outsider. For some categories of people, however, being an outsider—not part of the dominant group—is an everyday experience. The greater people's social marginality, the better they are able to use the sociological perspective.

For example, no African American grows up in the United States without understanding the importance of race in shaping people's lives. Songs by rapper Jay-Z express the anger he feels, not only about the poverty he experienced growing up but also about the many innocent lives lost to violence in a society with great social inequality based on race. His lyrics and those of many similar artists are spread throughout the world by the mass media as statements of how some people of color—especially African Americans living in the inner city—feel that their hopes and dreams are crushed by society. But white people, as the dominant majority, think less often about race, believing that race affects only people of color and not themselves despite the privileges provided by being white in a multiracial society. All people at the margins of social life, including not just racial minorities but also women, gay people, people with disabilities, and the very old, are aware of social patterns that others rarely think about. To become better at using the sociological perspective, we must step back from our familiar routines and look at our own lives with a new curiosity.

Periods of change or crisis make everyone feel a little off balance, encouraging us to use the sociological perspective. The sociologist C. Wright Mills (1959) illustrated this idea using the Great Depression of the 1930s. As the unemployment rate soared to 25 percent, people who were out of work could not help but see general social forces at work in their particular lives. Rather than saying, "Something must be wrong with me; I can't find a job," they took a sociological approach and realized, "The economy has collapsed; there are no jobs to be found!" Mills believed that using what he called the "sociological imagination" in this way helps people

People with the greatest privileges tend to see individuals as responsible for their own lives. Those at the margins of society, by contrast, are quick to see how race, class, and gender can create disadvantages. The rap artist Jay-Z has given voice to the frustration felt by many African Americans living in this country's inner cities.

Seeing Sociology in Everyday Life

The Sociological Imagination: Turning Personal Problems into Public Issues

As Mike opened the envelope, he felt the tightness in his chest. The letter he dreaded was in his hands—his job was finished at the end of the day. After eleven years! Years in which he had worked hard, sure that he would move up in the company. All those hopes and dreams were now suddenly gone. Mike felt like a failure. Anger at himself—for not having worked even harder, for having wasted eleven years of his life in what had turned out to be a dead-end job—swelled up inside him.

But as he returned to his workstation to pack his things, Mike soon realized that he was not alone. Almost all his colleagues in the tech support group had received the same letter. Their jobs were moving to India, where the company was able to provide telephone tech support for less than half the cost of employing workers in California.

By the end of the weekend, Mike was sitting in the living room with a dozen other ex-employees. Comparing notes and sharing ideas, they now realized that they were simply a few of the victims of a massive outsourcing of jobs that is part of what analysts call the "globalization of the economy."

In good times and bad, the power of the sociological perspective lies in making sense of our individual lives. We see that many of our particular problems (and our successes, as well) are not unique to us but are the result of larger social trends. Half a century ago, sociologist C. Wright Mills pointed to the power of what he called the sociological imagination to help us understand everyday events. As he saw it, society—not people's personal failings—is the main cause of poverty and other social problems. By turning *personal problems* into *public issues*, the sociological imagination also is the key to bringing people together to create needed change.

In this excerpt, Mills (1959:3–5) explains the need for a sociological imagination:*

> When society becomes industrialized, a peasant becomes a worker; a feudal lord is liquidated or becomes a businessman. When classes rise or fall, a man is employed or unemployed; when the rate of investment goes up or down, a man takes new heart or goes broke. When wars happen, an insurance salesman becomes a rocket launcher; a store clerk, a radar man; a wife lives alone; a child grows up without a father. Neither the life of an individual nor the history of a society can be understood without understanding both.
>
> Yet men do not usually define the troubles they endure in terms of historical change. . . . The well-being they enjoy, they do not usually impute to the big ups and downs of the society in which they live. Seldom aware of the intricate connection between the patterns of their own lives and the course of world history, ordinary men do not usually know what this connection means for the kind of men they are becoming and for the kinds of history-making in which they might take part. They do not possess the quality of mind essential to grasp the interplay of men and society, of biography and history, of self and world. . . .
>
> What they need . . . is a quality of mind that will help them [see] what is going on in the world and . . . what may be happening within themselves. It is this quality . . . [that] may be called the sociological imagination.

What Do You Think?

1. As Mills sees it, how are personal troubles different from public issues? Explain this difference in terms of what happened to Mike in the story above.

2. Living in the United States, why do we often blame ourselves for the personal problems we face?

3. How can using the sociological imagination give us the power to change the world?

*In this excerpt, Mills uses "man" and male pronouns to apply to all people. As far as gender was concerned, even this outspoken critic of society reflected the conventional writing practices of his time.

---

understand not only their society but also their own lives, because the two are closely related. The Seeing Sociology in Everyday Life box takes a closer look.

Just as social change encourages sociological thinking, sociological thinking can bring about social change. The more we learn about how "the system" operates, the more we may want to change it in some way. Becoming aware of the power of gender, for example, has caused many women and men to try to reduce gender inequality in our society.

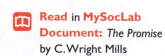 **Read** in **MySocLab Document:** *The Promise* by C. Wright Mills

The Importance of a Global Perspective

1.2 State several reasons that a global perspective is important in today's world.

As new information technology draws even the farthest reaches of the planet closer together, many academic disciplines are taking a **global perspective**, *the study of the larger world and our society's place in it.* What is the importance of a global perspective for sociology?

For a close-up look at the social shape of the world and the place of the United States within it, **Read More** in **MySocLab**, *The Global Village: A Social Snapshot of Our World*

First, global awareness is a logical extension of the sociological perspective. Sociology shows us that our place in society shapes our life experiences. It stands to reason, then, that the position of our society in the larger world system affects everyone in the United States.

The world's 195 nations can be divided into three broad categories according to their level of economic development (see Global Map 12–1 on page 335). **High-income countries** are the *nations with the highest overall standards of living.* The seventy-four countries in this category include the United States and Canada, Argentina, the nations of Western Europe, Israel, Saudi Arabia, Japan, and Australia. Taken together, these nations produce most of the world's goods and services, and the people who live there own most of the planet's wealth. Economically speaking, people in these countries are very well off, not because they are smarter or work harder than anyone else but because they were lucky enough to be born in a rich region of the world.

A second category is **middle-income countries**, *nations with a standard of living about average for the world as a whole.* People in any of these seventy-two nations—many of the countries of Eastern Europe, some of Africa, and almost all of Latin America and Asia—are as likely to live in rural villages as in cities and to walk or ride tractors, scooters, bicycles, or animals as to drive automobiles. On average, they receive eight years of schooling. Most middle-income countries also have considerable social inequality within their own borders, so that some people are extremely rich (members of the business elite in nations across North Africa, for example), but many more lack safe housing and adequate nutrition (people living in the shanty settlements that surround Lima, Peru, or Mumbai, India).

The remaining forty-nine nations of the world are **low-income countries**, *nations with a low standard of living in which most people are poor.* Most of the poorest countries in the world are in Africa, and a few are in Asia. Here again, a few people are very rich, but the majority struggle to get by with poor housing, unsafe water, too little food, and perhaps most serious of all, little chance to improve their lives.

Chapter 12 ("Global Stratification") explains the causes and consequences of global wealth and poverty. But every chapter of this text makes comparisons between the United States and other nations for five reasons:

1. **Where we live shapes the lives we lead.** As we saw in Global Map 1–1 on page 6, women living in rich and poor countries have very different lives, as suggested by the number of children they have. To understand ourselves and appreciate how others live, we must understand something about how countries differ, which is one good reason to pay attention to the global maps found throughout this text.

2. **Societies throughout the world are increasingly interconnected.** Historically, people in the United States took only passing note of the countries beyond our own borders. In recent decades, however, the United States and the rest of the world have become linked as never before. Electronic technology now transmits sounds, pictures, and written documents around the globe in seconds.

   One effect of new technology is that people the world over now share many tastes in food, clothing, and music. Rich countries such as the United States influence other nations, whose people are ever more likely to gobble up our Big Macs and Whoppers, dance to the latest hip-hop music, and speak English.

   But the larger world also has an impact on us. We all know the contributions of famous immigrants such as Arnold Schwarzenegger (who came to the United States from Austria) and Gloria Estefan (who came from Cuba). About 1.3 million immigrants enter the United States each year, bringing their skills and talents, along with their fashions and foods, greatly increasing the racial and cultural diversity of this country (Hoefer, Rytina, & Baker, 2012; U.S. Department of Homeland Security, 2012).

global perspective the study of the larger world and our society's place in it

high-income countries the nations with the highest overall standards of living

middle-income countries nations with a standard of living about average for the world as a whole

low-income countries nations with a low standard of living in which most people are poor

3. **What happens in the rest of the world affects life here in the United States.** Trade across national boundaries has created a global economy. Large corporations make and market goods worldwide. Stock traders in New York pay close attention to the financial markets in Tokyo and Hong Kong even as wheat farmers in Kansas watch the price of grain in the former Soviet republic of Georgia. Because most new jobs in the United States involve international trade, global understanding has never been more important.

    In the last several decades, the power and wealth of the United States have been challenged by what some analysts have called "the rise of the rest," meaning the increasing power and wealth of the rest of the world. As nations such as Brazil, Russia, India, and China have expanded their economic production, many of the manufacturing and office jobs that once supported a large share of the U.S. labor force have moved overseas. One consequence of this trend is that, as the country struggles to climb out of the recent recession, the unemployment rate remains high and may stay high for years to come. As many analysts see it, our current "jobless recovery" is one result of a new global economy that is reshaping societies all around the world (Zakeria, 2008).

4. **Many social problems that we face in the United States are far more serious elsewhere.** Poverty is a serious problem in the United States, but as Chapter 12 ("Global Stratification") explains, poverty in Latin America, Africa, and Asia is both more common and more serious. In the same way, although women have lower social standing than men in the United States, gender inequality is much greater in the world's poor countries.

5. **Thinking globally helps us learn more about ourselves.** We cannot walk the streets of a distant city without thinking about what it means to live in the United States. Comparing life in various settings also leads to unexpected lessons. For instance, were you to visit a squatter settlement in Chennai, India, you would likely find people thriving in the love and support of family members despite desperate poverty. Why, then, are so many poor people in our own country angry and alone? Are material things—so central to our definition of a "rich" life—the best way to measure human well-being?

In sum, in an increasingly interconnected world, we can understand ourselves only to the extent that we understand others. Sociology is an invitation to learn a new way of looking at the world around us. But is this invitation worth accepting? What are the benefits of applying the sociological perspective?

Applying the Sociological Perspective

1.3 Identify the advantages of sociological thinking for developing public policy, for encouraging personal growth, and for advancing in a career.

Applying the sociological perspective is useful in many ways. First, sociology is at work guiding many of the laws and policies that shape our lives. Second, on an individual level, making use of the sociological perspective leads to important personal growth and expanded awareness. Third, studying sociology is excellent preparation for the world of work.

Sociology and Public Policy

Sociologists have helped shape public policy—the laws and regulations that guide how people in communities live and work—in countless ways, from racial desegregation and school busing to laws regulating divorce. For example, in her study of how divorce affects people's income, the sociologist Lenore Weitzman (1985, 1996) discovered that women who leave marriages typically experience a dramatic loss of income. Recognizing this fact, many states passed laws that have increased women's claims to marital property and enforced fathers' obligations to provide support for women raising their children.

Thinking About Diversity: Race, Class, and Gender

Nickel and Dimed: On (Not) Getting By in America

All of us know people who work at low-wage jobs as waitresses at diners, clerks at drive-throughs, or sales associates at discount stores such as Walmart. We see such people just about every day. Many of us actually *are* such people. In the United States, "common sense" tells us that the jobs people have and the amount of money they make reflect their personal abilities as well as their willingness to work hard.

Barbara Ehrenreich (2001) had her doubts. To find out what the world of low-wage work is really like, the successful journalist and author decided to leave her comfortable middle-class life to live and work in the world of low-wage jobs. She began in Key West, Florida, taking a job as a waitress for $2.43 an hour plus tips. Right away, she found out that she had to work much harder than she ever imagined. By the end of a shift, she was exhausted, but after sharing tips with the kitchen staff, she averaged less than $6.00 an hour. This was barely above the minimum wage at the time and provided just enough income to pay the rent on her tiny apartment, buy food, and cover other basic expenses. She had to hope that she didn't get sick, because the job did not provide health insurance and she couldn't afford to pay for a visit to a doctor's office.

After working for more than a year at a number of other low-wage jobs, including cleaning motels in Maine and working on the floor of a Walmart in Minnesota, she had rejected quite a bit of "common sense." First, she now knew that tens of millions of people with low-wage jobs work very hard every day. If you don't think so, Ehrenreich says, try one of these jobs yourself. Second, these jobs require not just hard work (imagine thoroughly cleaning three motel rooms per hour all day long) but also special skills and real intelligence (try waiting on ten tables in a restaurant at the same time and keeping everybody happy). She found that the people she worked with were, on average, just as smart, clever, and funny as those she knew who wrote books for a living or taught at a college.

Why, then, do we think of low-wage workers as lazy or as having less ability? It surprised Ehrenreich to learn that many low-wage workers felt this way about themselves. In a society that teaches us to believe personal ability is everything, we learn to size up people by their jobs. Subject to the constant supervision, random drug tests, and other rigid rules that usually come along with low-wage jobs, Ehrenreich imagined that many people end up feeling unworthy, even to the point of not trying for anything better. Such beliefs, she concludes, help support a society of extreme inequality in which some people live very well thanks to the low wages paid to the rest.

What Do You Think?

1. Have you ever held a low-wage job? If so, would you say you worked hard? What was your pay? Were there any benefits?
2. Ehrenreich claims that most well-off people in the United States are dependent on low-wage workers. What does she mean by this?
3. How much of a chance do most people with jobs at Wendy's or Walmart have to enroll in college and to work toward a different career? Explain.

Sociology and Personal Growth

By applying the sociological perspective, we are likely to become more active and aware and to think more critically in our daily lives. Using sociology benefits us in four ways:

1. **The sociological perspective helps us assess the truth of "common sense."** We all take many things for granted, but that does not make them true. One good example is the idea that we are free individuals who are personally responsible for our own lives. If we think we decide our own fate, we may be quick to praise very successful people as superior and consider others with fewer achievements personally deficient. A sociological approach, by contrast, encourages us to ask whether such common beliefs are actually true and, to the extent that they are not, why they are so widely held. The Thinking About Diversity box takes a look at low-wage jobs and explains how the sociological perspective sometimes makes us rethink commonsense ideas about other people and their work.

2. **The sociological perspective helps us see the opportunities and constraints in our lives.** Sociological thinking leads us to see that in the game of life, society deals the cards. We have a say in how to play the hand, however, and the more we understand the game, the better players we become. Sociology helps us learn more about the world so that we can pursue our goals more effectively.

3. **The sociological perspective empowers us to be active participants in our society.** The more we understand how society works, the more active citizens we become. As C. Wright Mills (1959) explained in the box on page 9, it is the sociological perspective that turns a personal problem (such as being out of work) into a public issue (a lack of good jobs). As we come to see how society affects us, we may support society as it is, or we may set out with others to change it.

4. **The sociological perspective helps us live in a diverse world.** North Americans represent just 5 percent of the world's people, and as the remaining chapters of this book explain, many of the other 95 percent live very differently than we do. Still, like people everywhere, we tend to define our own way of life as "right," "natural," and "better." The sociological perspective encourages us to think critically about the relative strengths and weaknesses of all ways of life, including our own.

Careers: The "Sociology Advantage"

Most students at colleges and universities today are very interested in getting a good job. A background in sociology is excellent preparation for the working world. Of course, completing a bachelor's degree in sociology is the right choice for people who decide they would like to go on to graduate work and eventually become a secondary school teacher, college professor, or researcher in this field. Throughout the United States, tens of thousands of men and women teach sociology in universities, colleges, and high schools. But just as many professional sociologists work as researchers for government agencies or private foundations and businesses, gathering important information on social behavior and carrying out evaluation research. In today's cost-conscious world, agencies and companies want to be sure that the programs and policies they set in place get the job done at the lowest cost. Sociologists, especially those with advanced research skills, are in high demand for this kind of work (Deutscher, 1999).

In addition, a smaller but increasing number of professional sociologists work as clinical sociologists. These women and men work, much as clinical psychologists do, with the goal of improving the lives of troubled clients. A basic difference is that sociologists focus on difficulties not in the personality but in the individual's web of social relationships.

But sociology is not just for people who want to be sociologists. People who work in criminal justice—in police departments, probation offices, and corrections facilities—gain the "sociology advantage" by learning which categories of people are most at risk of becoming criminals as well as victims, assessing the effectiveness of various policies and programs at preventing crime, and understanding why people turn to crime in the first place. Similarly, people who work in health care—including doctors, nurses, and technicians—also gain a sociology advantage by learning about patterns of health and illness within the population, as well as how factors such as race, gender, and social class affect human well-being.

👁 **Watch** in **MySocLab**
Video: *Sociology on the Job: What Is Sociology?*

Just about every job in today's economy involves working with people. For this reason, studying sociology is good preparation for your future career. In what ways does having "people skills" help police officers perform their job?

The American Sociological Association (2002, 2011a, 2011b) reports that sociology is also excellent preparation for jobs in dozens of additional fields, including advertising, banking, business, education, government, journalism, law, public relations, and social work. In almost any type of work, success depends on understanding how various categories of people differ in beliefs, family patterns, and other ways of life. Unless you plan to have a job that never involves dealing with people, you should consider the workplace benefits of learning more about sociology.

The Origins of Sociology

1.4 Link the origins of sociology to historical social changes.

Like the "choices" made by individuals, major historical events rarely just happen. The birth of sociology was itself the result of powerful social forces.

Social Change and Sociology

Striking changes took place in Europe during the eighteenth and nineteenth centuries. Three kinds of change were especially important in the development of sociology: the rise of a factory-based industrial economy, the explosive growth of cities, and new ideas about democracy and political rights.

A New Industrial Economy

During the Middle Ages in Europe, most people plowed fields near their homes or worked in small-scale *manufacturing* (a term derived from Latin words meaning "to make by hand"). By the end of the eighteenth century, inventors used new sources of energy—the power of moving water and then steam—to operate large machines in mills and factories. Instead of laboring at home or in small groups, workers became part of a large and anonymous labor force, under the control of strangers who owned the factories. This change in the system of production took people out of their homes, weakening the traditions that had guided community life for centuries.

The Growth of Cities

Across Europe, landowners took part in what historians call the *enclosure movement*—they fenced off more and more farmland to create grazing areas for sheep, the source of wool for the thriving textile mills. Without land, countless tenant farmers had little choice but to head to the cities in search of work in the new factories.

As cities grew larger, these urban migrants faced many social problems, including pollution, crime, and homelessness. Moving through streets crowded with strangers, they faced a new and impersonal social world.

Political Change

Europeans in the Middle Ages viewed society as an expression of God's will: From the royalty to the serfs, each person up and down the social ladder played a part in the holy plan. This theological view of society is captured in lines from the old Anglican hymn "All Things Bright and Beautiful":

> The rich man in his castle,
> The poor man at his gate,
> God made them high and lowly
> And ordered their estate.

But as cities grew, tradition came under attack. In the writings of Thomas Hobbes (1588–1679), John Locke (1632–1704), and Adam Smith (1723–1790), we see a shift in focus from a moral obligation to God and king to the pursuit of self-interest. In the new political climate, philosophers spoke of *personal liberty* and *individual rights.* Echoing these sentiments, our own Declaration of Independence states that every person has "certain unalienable rights," including "life, liberty, and the pursuit of happiness."

The French Revolution, which began in 1789, was an even greater break with political and social tradition. The French social analyst Alexis de Tocqueville (1805–1859) thought the changes in society brought about by the French Revolution were so great that they amounted to "nothing short of the regeneration of the whole human race" (1955:13, orig. 1856).

A New Awareness of Society

Huge factories, exploding cities, a new spirit of individualism—these changes combined to make people more aware of their surroundings. The new discipline of sociology was born in England, France, and Germany—precisely where the changes were greatest.

Science and Sociology

And so it was that the French social thinker Auguste Comte (1798–1857) coined the term *sociology* in 1838 to describe a new way of looking at society. This makes sociology one of the youngest academic disciplines—far newer than history, physics, or economics, for example.

Of course, Comte was not the first person to think about the nature of society. Such questions fascinated many of the brilliant thinkers of ancient civilizations, including the Chinese philosopher K'ung Fu-tzu, or Confucius (551–479 B.C.E.), and the Greek philosophers Plato (c. 427–347 B.C.E.) and Aristotle (384–322 B.C.E.).[1] Over the next several centuries, the Roman emperor Marcus Aurelius (121–180), the medieval thinkers Saint Thomas Aquinas (c. 1225–1274) and Christine de Pisan (c. 1363–1431), and the English playwright William Shakespeare (1564–1616) wrote about the workings of society.

Yet these thinkers were more interested in imagining the ideal society than in studying society as it really was. Comte and other pioneers of sociology all cared about how society could be improved, but their major objective was to understand how society actually operates.

Comte (1975, orig. 1851–54) saw sociology as the product of a three-stage historical development. During the earliest, the *theological stage,* from the beginning of human history to the end of the European Middle Ages about 1350 C.E., people took a religious view that society expressed God's will.

With the dawn of the Renaissance in the fifteenth century, the theological approach gave way to a *metaphysical stage* of history in which people saw society as a natural rather than a supernatural system. Thomas Hobbes (1588–1679), for example, suggested that society reflected not the perfection of God so much as the failings of a selfish human nature.

What we see depends on our point of view. When gazing at the stars, lovers see romance, but scientists see thermal reactions. How does using the sociological perspective change what we see in the world around us?

---

[1]The abbreviation B.C.E. means "before the common era." We use this throughout the text instead of the traditional B.C. ("before Christ") to reflect the religious diversity of our society. Similarly, in place of the traditional A.D. (*anno Domini,* or "in the year of our Lord"), we use the abbreviation C.E. ("common era").

Comte's Three Stages of Society

Theological Stage
(the Church in the Middle Ages)

Metaphysical Stage
(the Enlightenment and the ideas of Hobbes, Locke, and Rousseau)

Scientific Stage
(modern physics, chemistry, sociology)

positivism a scientific approach to knowledge based on "positive" facts as opposed to mere speculation

What Comte called the *scientific stage* of history began with the work of early scientists such as the Polish astronomer Copernicus (1473–1543), the Italian astronomer and physicist Galileo (1564–1642), and the English physicist and mathematician Isaac Newton (1642–1727). Comte's contribution came in applying the scientific approach—first used to study the physical world—to the study of society.[2]

Comte's approach is called **positivism**, *a scientific approach to knowledge based on "positive" facts as opposed to mere speculation.* As a positivist, Comte believed that society operates according to its own laws, much as the physical world operates according to gravity and other laws of nature.

By the beginning of the twentieth century, sociology had spread to the United States and showed the influence of Comte's ideas. Today, most sociologists still consider science a crucial part of sociology. But as Chapter 2 ("Sociological Investigation") explains, we now realize that human behavior is far more complex than the movement of planets or even the actions of other living things. We are creatures of imagination and spontaneity, so human behavior can never be fully explained by any rigid "laws of society." In addition, early sociologists such as Karl Marx (1818–1883), whose ideas are discussed in Chapter 4 ("Society"), were troubled by the striking inequalities of industrial society. They hoped that the new discipline of sociology would not just help us understand society but also lead to change toward greater social justice.

Sociological Theory

(1.5) Summarize sociology's major theoretical approaches.

theory a statement of how and why specific facts are related

The desire to translate observations into understanding brings us to the important aspect of sociology known as *theory*. A **theory** is *a statement of how and why specific facts are related.* The job of sociological theory is to explain social behavior in the real world. For example, recall Emile Durkheim's theory that categories of people with low social integration (men, Protestants, the wealthy, and the unmarried) are at higher risk of suicide.

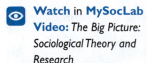

Watch in **MySocLab**
Video: *The Big Picture: Sociological Theory and Research*

As the next chapter ("Sociological Investigation") explains, sociologists test their theories by gathering evidence using various research methods. Durkheim did exactly this, finding out which categories of people were more likely to commit suicide and which were less likely and then devising a theory that best squared with all available evidence. National Map 1–1 on page 17 displays the suicide rate for each of the fifty states.

In building theory, sociologists face two basic questions: What issues should we study? And how should we connect the facts? In the process of answering these questions, sociologists look to one or more theoretical approaches as "road maps." Think of a **theoretical approach** as *a basic image of society that guides thinking and research.* Sociologists make use of three major theoretical approaches: the *structural-functional approach*, the *social-conflict approach*, and the *symbolic-interaction approach*.

theoretical approach a basic image of society that guides thinking and research

The Structural-Functional Approach

The **structural-functional approach** is *a framework for building theory that sees society as a complex system whose parts work together to promote solidarity and stability.* As its name suggests, this approach points to **social structure**, *any relatively stable pattern of social*

---

[2]Illustrating Comte's stages, the ancient Greeks and Romans viewed the planets as gods; Renaissance metaphysical thinkers saw them as astral influences (giving rise to astrology); by the time of Galileo, scientists understood planets as natural objects moving according to natural laws.

Seeing Ourselves

Explore the relationship between population density and suicide in your own community and across the United States in **MySocLab**

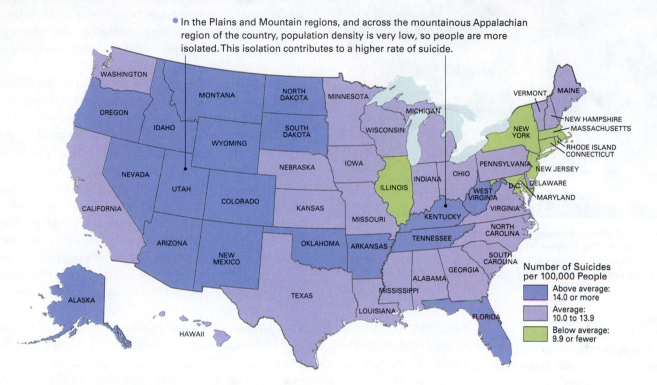

In the Plains and Mountain regions, and across the mountainous Appalachian region of the country, population density is very low, so people are more isolated. This isolation contributes to a higher rate of suicide.

Number of Suicides per 100,000 People

- Above average: 14.0 or more
- Average: 10.0 to 13.9
- Below average: 9.9 or fewer

NATIONAL MAP 1–1 Suicide Rates across the United States

This map shows which states have high, average, and low suicide rates. Look for patterns. By and large, high suicide rates occur where people live far apart from one another. More densely populated states have low suicide rates. Do these data support or contradict Durkheim's theory of suicide? Why?

Source: Centers for Disease Control and Prevention (2012).

behavior. Social structure gives our lives shape—in families, the workplace, the classroom, and the community. This approach also looks for a structure's **social functions**, *the consequences of any social pattern for the operation of society as a whole.* All social structures, from a simple handshake to complex religious rituals, function to keep society going, at least in its present form.

The structural-functional approach owes much to Auguste Comte, who pointed out the need to keep society unified at a time when many traditions were breaking down. Emile Durkheim, who helped establish the study of sociology in French universities, also based his work on this approach. A third structural-functional pioneer was the English sociologist Herbert Spencer (1820–1903). Spencer compared society to the human body. Just as the structural parts of the human body—the skeleton, muscles, and various internal organs—function interdependently to help the entire organism survive, social structures work together to preserve society. The structural-functional approach, then, leads sociologists to identify various structures of society and investigate their functions.

Robert K. Merton (1910–2003) expanded our understanding of the concept of social function by pointing out that any social structure probably has many functions, some more obvious than others. He distinguished between **manifest functions**, *the recognized and intended consequences of any social pattern,* and **latent functions**, *the unrecognized and unintended consequences of any social pattern.* For example, the manifest function of the U.S. system of higher education is to provide young people with

social structure any relatively stable pattern of social behavior

social functions the consequences of a social pattern for the operation of society as a whole

manifest functions the recognized and intended consequences of any social pattern

latent functions the unrecognized and unintended consequences of any social pattern

The Sociological Perspective   **CHAPTER 1**   **17**

The social-conflict approach points out patterns of inequality in everyday life. The TV series *Keeping Up with the Kardashians* takes a close-up look at the lives of extremely affluent women. In what ways do they depend on the work of people of lower social position?

the information and skills they need to perform jobs after graduation. Perhaps just as important, although less often acknowledged, is college's latent function as a "marriage broker," bringing together young people of similar social backgrounds. Another latent function of higher education is to limit unemployment by keeping millions of young people out of the labor market, where many of them might not easily find jobs.

But Merton also recognized that not all the effects of social structure are good. Thus a **social dysfunction** is *any social pattern that may disrupt the operation of society.* Globalization of the economy may be good for some companies, but it also can cost workers their jobs as production moves overseas. Therefore, whether any social patterns are helpful or harmful for society is a matter about which people often disagree. In addition, what is functional for one category of people (say, high profits for Wall Street bank executives) may well be dysfunctional for other categories of people (workers who lose pension funds invested in banks that fail or people who cannot pay their mortgages and end up losing their homes).

social dysfunction any social pattern that may disrupt the operation of society

EVALUATE The main idea of the structural-functional approach is its vision of society as stable and orderly. The main goal of the sociologists who use this approach, then, is to figure out "what makes society tick."

In the mid-1900s, most sociologists favored the structural-functional approach. In recent decades, however, its influence has declined. By focusing on social stability and unity, critics point out, structural-functionalism ignores inequalities of social class, race, and gender, which cause tension and conflict. In general, its focus on stability at the expense of conflict makes this approach somewhat conservative. As a critical response, sociologists developed the social-conflict approach.

CHECK YOUR LEARNING How do manifest functions differ from latent functions? Give an example of a manifest function and a latent function of automobiles in the United States.

The Social-Conflict Approach

The **social-conflict approach** is *a framework for building theory that sees society as an arena of inequality that generates conflict and change.* Unlike the structural-functional emphasis on solidarity and stability, this approach highlights inequality and change. Guided by this approach, which includes the gender-conflict and race-conflict approaches, sociologists investigate how factors such as social class, race, ethnicity, gender, sexual orientation, and age are linked to a society's unequal distribution of money, power, education, and social prestige. A conflict analysis rejects the idea that social structure promotes the operation of society as a whole, focusing instead on how social patterns benefit some people while hurting others.

Sociologists using the social-conflict approach look at ongoing conflict between dominant and disadvantaged categories of people—the rich in relation to the poor, white people in relation to people of color, and men in relation to women. Typically, people on top try to protect their privileges while the disadvantaged try to gain more for themselves.

social-conflict approach a framework for building theory that sees society as an arena of inequality that generates conflict and change

gender-conflict theory (feminist theory) the study of society that focuses on inequality and conflict between women and men

race-conflict theory the study of society that focuses on inequality and conflict between people of different racial and ethnic categories

feminism support of social equality for women and men

A conflict analysis of our educational system shows how schooling carries class inequality from one generation to the next. For example, secondary schools assign students to either college preparatory or vocational training programs. From a structural-functional point of view, such "tracking" benefits everyone by providing schooling that fits students' abilities. But conflict analysis argues that tracking often has less to do with talent than with social background, with the result that well-to-do students are placed in higher tracks while poor children end up in the lower tracks.

Thus young people from privileged families get the best schooling, which leads them to college and later to high-income careers. The children of poor families, by contrast, are not prepared for college and, like their parents before them, typically get stuck in low-paying jobs. In both cases, the social standing of one generation is passed on to the next, with schools justifying the practice in terms of individual merit (Bowles & Gintis, 1976; Oakes, 1982, 1985).

Many sociologists use the social-conflict approach not just to understand society but also to bring about societal change that would reduce inequality. Karl Marx, whose ideas are discussed at length in Chapter 4 ("Society"), championed the cause of the workers in what he saw as their battle against factory owners. In a well-known statement (inscribed on his monument in London's Highgate Cemetery), Marx asserted, "The philosophers have only interpreted the world, in various ways; the point, however, is to change it."

Feminism and Gender-Conflict Theory

One important social-conflict theory is **gender-conflict theory** (or **feminist theory**), *the study of society that focuses on inequality and conflict between women and men.* The gender-conflict approach is closely linked to **feminism**, *support of social equality for women and men.*

The importance of gender-conflict theory lies in making us aware of the many ways in which our way of life places men in positions of power over women: in the home (where men are usually considered "head of the household"), in the workplace (where men earn more income and hold most positions of power), and in the mass media (where, for instance, more men than women are hip-hop stars).

Another contribution of feminist theory is making us aware of the importance of women to the development of sociology. Harriet Martineau (1802–1876) is regarded as the first woman sociologist. Born to a wealthy English family, Martineau made her mark in 1853 by translating the writings of Auguste Comte from French into English. In her own published writings, she documented the evils of slavery and argued for laws to protect factory workers, defending workers' right to unionize. She was particularly concerned about the position of women in society and fought for changes in education policy so that women could have more options in life than marriage and raising children.

In the United States, Jane Addams (1860–1935) was a sociological pioneer whose contributions began in 1889 when she helped found Hull House, a Chicago settlement house that provided assistance to immigrant families. Although widely published—Addams wrote eleven books and hundreds of articles—she chose the life of a public activist over that of a university sociologist, speaking out on issues involving immigration and the pursuit of peace. Though her pacifism during World War I was the subject of much controversy, she was awarded the Nobel Peace Prize in 1931.

All chapters of this book consider the importance of gender and gender inequality. For an in-depth look at feminism and the social standing of women and men, see Chapter 13 ("Gender Stratification").

We can use the sociological perspective to look at sociology itself. All of the most widely recognized pioneers of the discipline were men. This is because in the nineteenth century, it was all but unheard of for women to be college professors, and few women took a central role in public life. But Jane Addams was an early sociologist in the United States, who founded Hull House, a Chicago settlement house where she spent many hours helping young people.

Race-Conflict Theory

Another important type of social-conflict theory is **race-conflict theory**, *the study of society that focuses on inequality and conflict between people of different racial and ethnic categories*. Just as men have power over women, white people have numerous social advantages over people of color, including, on average, higher incomes, more schooling, better health, and longer life expectancy.

Race-conflict theory also points out the contributions made by people of color to the development of sociology. Ida Wells Barnett (1862–1931) was born to slave parents but rose to become a teacher and then a journalist and newspaper publisher. She campaigned tirelessly for racial equality and, especially, to put an end to the lynching of black people. She wrote and lectured about racial inequality throughout her life (Lengerman & Niebrugge-Brantley, 1998).

An important contribution to understanding race in the United States was made by William Edward Burghardt Du Bois (1868–1963). Born to a poor Massachusetts family, Du Bois (pronounced doo-boyss) enrolled at Fisk University in Nashville, Tennessee, and then at Harvard University, where he earned the first doctorate awarded by that university to a person of color. Du Bois then founded the Atlanta Sociological Laboratory, which was an important center of sociological research in the early decades of the twentieth century. Like most people who follow the social-conflict approach (whether focusing on class, gender, or race), Du Bois believed that sociologists should not simply learn about society's problems but also try to solve them. He therefore studied the black communities across the United States, pointing to numerous social problems ranging from educational inequality to a political system that denied people their right to vote and the terrorist practice of lynching. Du Bois spoke out against racial inequality and participated in the founding of the National Association for the Advancement of Colored People (NAACP) (E. Wright, 2002a, 2002b). The Thinking About Diversity box on page 21 takes a closer look at the ideas of W. E. B. Du Bois.

EVALUATE The various social-conflict theories have gained a large following in recent decades, but like other approaches, they have met with criticism. Because any social-conflict theory focuses on inequality, it largely ignores how shared values and interdependence unify members of a society. In addition, say critics, to the extent that it pursues political goals, a social-conflict approach cannot claim scientific objectivity. Supporters of social-conflict theory respond that *all* theoretical approaches have political consequences.

A final criticism of both the structural-functional and the social-conflict approaches is that they paint society in broad strokes—in terms of "family," "social class," "race," and so on. A third type of theoretical analysis—the symbolic-interaction approach—views society less in general terms and more as the everyday experiences of individual people.

CHECK YOUR LEARNING Why do you think sociologists characterize the social-conflict approach as "activist"? What is it actively trying to achieve?

The Symbolic-Interaction Approach

The structural-functional and social-conflict approaches share a **macro-level orientation,** *a broad focus on social structures that shape society as a whole*. Macro-level sociology takes in the big picture, rather like observing a city from high above in a helicopter and seeing how highways help people move from place to place or how housing differs from rich to poor neighborhoods. Sociology also uses a **micro-level orientation,** *a close-up focus on social interaction in specific situations*. Exploring urban life in this way occurs at street level, where you might watch how children invent games on a school playground or how pedestrians respond to homeless people

macro-level orientation a broad focus on social structures that shape society as a whole

structural-functional approach a framework for building theory that sees society as a complex system whose parts work together to promote solidarity and stability

social-conflict approach a framework for building theory that sees society as an arena of inequality that generates conflict and change

Thinking About Diversity: Race, Class, and Gender

W. E. B. Du Bois: A Pioneer in Sociology

One of sociology's pioneers in the United States, William Edward Burghardt Du Bois saw sociology as the key to solving society's problems, especially racial inequality. Du Bois earned a Ph.D. in sociology from Harvard University and established the Atlanta Sociological Laboratory, one of the first centers of sociological research in the United States. He helped his colleagues in sociology—and people everywhere—to see the deep racial divisions in the United States. White people can simply be "Americans," Du Bois pointed out; African Americans, however, have a "double consciousness," reflecting their status as people who are never able to escape identification based on the color of their skin.

In his sociological classic *The Philadelphia Negro: A Social Study* (1899), Du Bois explored Philadelphia's African American community, identifying both the strengths and the weaknesses of people who were dealing with overwhelming social problems on a day-to-day basis. He challenged the belief—widespread at

that time—that blacks were inferior to whites, and he blamed white prejudice for creating the problems that African Americans faced. He also criticized successful people of color for being so eager to win white acceptance that they gave up all ties with the black community that needed their help.

Despite notable achievements, Du Bois gradually grew impatient with academic study, which he felt was too detached from the everyday struggles experienced by people of color. Du Bois wanted change. It was the hope of sparking public action against racial separation that led Du Bois, in 1909, to participate in the founding of the National Association for the Advancement of Colored People (NAACP), an organization that has been active in supporting racial equality for more than a century. As the editor of the organization's magazine, *Crisis*, Du Bois worked tirelessly to challenge laws and social customs that deprived African Americans of the rights and opportunities enjoyed by the white majority.

Du Bois described race as the major problem facing the United States in the twentieth century. Early in his career, he was hopeful about overcoming racial divisions. By the end of his life, however, he had grown bitter, believing that little had changed. At the age of ninety-three, Du Bois left the United States for Ghana, where he died two years later.

What Do You Think?

1. If he were alive today, what do you think Du Bois would say about racial inequality in the twenty-first century?

2. How much do you think African Americans today experience a "double consciousness"?

3. In what ways can sociology help us understand and reduce racial conflict?

Sources: Based in part on Baltzell (1967), Du Bois (1967, orig. 1899), Wright (2002a, 2002b), and personal communication with Earl Wright II.

---

they pass on the street. The **symbolic-interaction approach**, then, is *a framework for building theory that sees society as the product of the everyday interactions of individuals.*

How does "society" result from the ongoing experiences of tens of millions of people? One answer, explained in Chapter 6 ("Social Interaction in Everyday Life"), is that society is nothing more than the shared reality that people construct for themselves as they interact with one another. Human beings live in a world of symbols, attaching *meaning* to virtually everything, from the words on this page to the wink of an eye. We create "reality," therefore, as we define our surroundings, decide what we think of others, and shape our own identities.

The symbolic-interaction approach has roots in the thinking of Max Weber (1864–1920), a German sociologist who emphasized the need to understand a setting from the point of view of the people in it. Weber's approach is discussed in more detail in Chapter 4 ("Society").

Since Weber's time, sociologists have taken micro-level sociology in a number of directions. Chapter 5 ("Socialization") discusses the ideas of George Herbert Mead (1863–1931), who explored how our personalities develop as a result of social experience. Chapter 6 ("Social Interaction in Everyday Life") presents the work of Erving Goffman

micro-level orientation a close-up focus on social interaction in specific situations

symbolic-interaction approach a framework for building theory that sees society as the product of the everyday interactions of individuals

(1922–1982), whose *dramaturgical analysis* describes how we resemble actors on a stage as we play our various roles. Other contemporary sociologists, including George Homans and Peter Blau, have developed *social-exchange analysis.* In their view, social interaction is guided by what each person stands to gain or lose from the interaction. In the ritual of courtship, for example, people seek mates who offer at least as much—in terms of physical attractiveness, intelligence, and social background—as they offer in return.

EVALUATE Without denying the existence of macro-level social structures such as the family and social class, the symbolic-interaction approach reminds us that society basically amounts to *people interacting*. That is, micro-level sociology tries to show how individuals actually experience society. But on the other side of the coin, by focusing on what is unique in each social scene, this approach risks overlooking the widespread influence of culture, as well as factors such as class, gender, and race.

CHECK YOUR LEARNING How does a micro-level analysis differ from a macro-level analysis? Provide an illustration of a social pattern at both levels.

The Applying Theory table summarizes the main characteristics of sociology's major theoretical approaches: the structural-functional approach, the social-conflict approach, feminism and the gender-conflict approach, the race-conflict approach, and the symbolic-interaction approach. Each of these approaches is helpful in answering particular kinds of questions about society. However, the fullest understanding of our social world comes from using all of them, as you can see in the following analysis of sports in the United States.

Applying the Approaches: The Sociology of Sports

1.6 Apply sociology's major theoretical approaches to the topic of sports.

Who doesn't enjoy sports? Children as young as six or seven take part in organized sports, and many teens become skilled at three or more. Weekend television is filled with sporting events for viewers of all ages, and whole sections of our newspapers are devoted to teams, players, and scores. In the United States, top players such as Joe Flacco (football), Michael Phelps (swimming), LeBron James (basketball), and Serena Williams (tennis) are among our most famous celebrities. Sports in the United

Applying Theory

Major Theoretical Approaches			
	Structural-Functional Approach	**Social-Conflict, Gender-Conflict, and Race-Conflict Approaches**	**Symbolic-Interaction Approach**
What is the level of analysis?	Macro-level	Macro-level	Micro-level
What image of society does the approach have?	Society is a system of interrelated parts that is relatively stable. Each part works to keep society operating in an orderly way. Members generally agree about what is morally right and morally wrong.	Society is a system of social inequalities based on class (Marx), gender (gender-conflict theory and feminism), and race (race-conflict theory). Society operates to benefit some categories of people and harm others. Social inequality causes conflict that leads to social change.	Society is an ongoing process. People interact in countless settings using symbolic communications. The reality people experience is variable and changing.
What core questions does the approach ask?	How is society held together? What are the major parts of society? How are these parts linked? What does each part do to help society work?	How does society divide a population? How do advantaged people protect their privileges? How do disadvantaged people challenge the system seeking change?	How do people experience society? How do people shape the reality they experience? How do behavior and meaning change from person to person and from one situation to another?

States are also a multibillion-dollar industry. What can we learn by applying sociology's major theoretical approaches to this familiar part of everyday life?

The Functions of Sports

A structural-functional approach directs our attention to the ways in which sports help society operate. The manifest functions of sports include providing recreation as well as offering a means of getting in physical shape and a relatively harmless way to let off steam. Sports have important latent functions as well, which include building social relationships and also creating tens of thousands of jobs across the country. Participating in sports encourages competition and the pursuit of success, both of which are values that are central to our society's way of life.

Sports also have dysfunctional consequences. For example, colleges and universities try to field winning teams to build a school's reputation and also to raise money from alumni and corporate sponsors. In the process, however, these schools sometimes recruit students for their athletic skill rather than their academic ability. This practice not only lowers the academic standards of the college or university but also shortchanges athletes, who spend little time doing the academic work that will prepare them for later careers (Upthegrove, Roscigno, & Charles, 1999).

Sports and Conflict

A social-conflict analysis of sports points out that the games people play reflect their social standing. Some sports—including tennis, swimming, golf, sailing, and skiing—are expensive, so taking part is largely limited to the well-to-do. Football, baseball, and basketball, however, are accessible to people at almost all income levels. Thus the games people play are not simply a matter of individual choice but also a reflection of their social standing.

From a feminist point of view, we notice that, throughout history, men have dominated the world of sports. In the nineteenth century, women had little opportunity to engage in athletic competition, and those that did received little attention (Shaulis, 1999). For example, the first modern Olympic Games, held in 1896, barred women from competition. The 2012 Olympics, by contrast, included women competing in twenty-six sports, including boxing. Throughout most of the twentieth century, Little League teams barred girls based on the traditional ideas that girls and women lack the strength to play sports and risk losing their femininity if they do. Like the Olympics, Little League is now open to females as well as males. But even today, our society still encourages men to become athletes while expecting women to be attentive observers and cheerleaders. At the college level, men's athletics attracts a greater amount of attention and resources compared to women's athletics, and men greatly outnumber women as coaches, even in women's sports (Welch & Sigelman, 2007). At the professional level, women also take a back seat to men, particularly in the sports with the most earning power and social prestige.

For decades, big league sports excluded people of color, who were forced to form leagues of their own. Only in 1947 did Major League Baseball admit the first African American player when Jackie Robinson joined the Brooklyn Dodgers. More than fifty years later, professional baseball honored Robinson's amazing career by retiring his number 42 on *all* of the teams in the league. In 2011, African Americans (13 percent of the U.S. population) accounted for 9 percent of Major League Baseball players, 67 percent of National

The life of legendary baseball player Jackie Robinson, the first African American to play in Major League Baseball, is portrayed in the 2013 film *42*. Sports remain an important element of social life in countless communities across the United States. Sociology's three theoretical approaches all contribute to our understanding of the role of sports in society.

Football League (NFL) players, and 78 percent of National Basketball Association (NBA) players (Lapchick, 2012).

One reason for the high number of African Americans in some professional sports is that athletic performance—in terms of batting average or number of points scored per game—can be precisely measured and is not influenced by racial prejudice. It is also true that some people of color make a particular effort to excel in athletics, where they see greater opportunity than in other careers (Steele, 1990; Edwards, 2000; Harrison, 2000). In recent years, in fact, African American athletes have earned higher salaries, on average, than white players. *Forbes* (2012) reports that four of the five highest-earning athletes are people who are racial or ethnic minorities.

But the race-conflict approach helps us to see that racial discrimination still exists in professional sports. For one thing, race is linked to the *positions* athletes play on the field, in a pattern called "stacking." Figure 1–2 shows the results of a study of race in professional baseball. Notice that white athletes are more concentrated in the central "thinking" positions of pitcher (66 percent) and catcher (58 percent). By contrast, African Americans represent only 3 percent of pitchers and there are no black catchers at all. At the same time, 8 percent of infielders are African Americans, as are 27 percent of outfielders, positions characterized as requiring "speed and reactive ability" (Lapchick, 2012).

More broadly, African Americans have a large share of players in only five sports: baseball, basketball, football, boxing, and track. In baseball, this share has been declining, from 19 percent in 1995 to 9 percent in 2012. And across all professional sports, the vast majority of managers, head coaches, and team owners are white (Lapchick, 2012).

Who benefits most from professional sports? Although many individual players get sky-high salaries and millions of fans enjoy following their teams, the vast profits sports generate are controlled by small number of people—predominantly white men. In sum, sports in the United States are bound up with inequalities based on gender, race, and wealth.

Diversity Snapshot

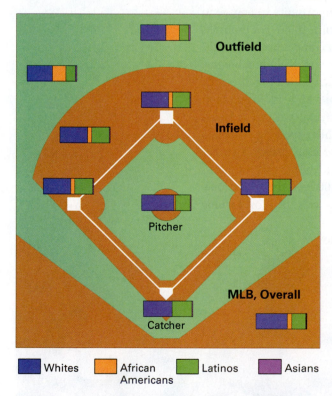

FIGURE 1–2 "Stacking" in Professional Baseball

Does race play a part in professional sports? Looking at the various positions in professional baseball, we see that white players are more likely to play the central positions in the infield, while people of color are more likely to play in the outfield. What do you make of this pattern?

Source: Lapchick (2012).

Sports as Interaction

At the micro-level, a sporting event is a complex, face-to-face interaction. In part, play is guided by the players' assigned positions and the rules of the game. But players are also spontaneous and unpredictable. Following the symbolic-interaction approach, we see sports less as a system than as an ongoing process.

From this point of view, too, we expect each player to understand the game a little differently. Some players enjoy a setting of stiff competition; for others, love of the game may be greater than the need to win.

In addition, the behavior of any single player may change over time. A rookie in professional baseball, for example, may feel self-conscious during the first few games in the big leagues but go on to develop a comfortable sense of fitting in with the team. Coming to feel at home on the field was slow and painful for Jackie Robinson, who knew that many white players, and millions of white fans, resented his presence. In time, however, his outstanding ability and his confident and cooperative manner won him the respect of the entire nation.

The major theoretical approaches—the structural-functional approach, the social-conflict approach, which includes gender-conflict/feminist theory and race-conflict theory, and the symbolic-interaction approach—provide different insights into sports, and none by itself presents the whole story. Applied to any issue, each approach generates its own interpretations. To appreciate fully the power of the sociological perspective, you should become familiar with all these approaches.

The Controversy & Debate box discusses the use of the sociological perspective and reviews many of the ideas presented in this chapter. This box raises a number of questions that will help you understand how sociological generalizations differ from the common stereotypes we encounter every day.

stereotype a simplified description applied to every person in some category

Controversy & Debate

Is Sociology Nothing More Than Stereotypes?

Jena: (*raising her eyes from her notebook*) Today in sociology class, we talked about stereotypes.

Marcia: (*trying to focus on her science lab*) OK, here's one: Roommates don't like to be disturbed when they're studying.

Jena: Seriously, my studious friend, we all have stereotypes, even professors.

Marcia: (*becoming faintly interested*) Like what?

Jena: Professor Chandler said today in class that if you're a Protestant, you're likely to kill yourself. And then Yannina—this girl from, I think, Ecuador—says something like, "You Americans are rich, you marry, and you love to divorce!"

Marcia: My brother said to me last week that "everybody knows you have to be black to play professional basketball." Now there's a stereotype!

College students, like everyone else, are quick to make generalizations about people. And as this chapter has explained, sociologists, too, love to generalize by looking for social patterns. However, beginning students of sociology may wonder if generalizations aren't really the same thing as stereotypes. For example, are the statements reported by Jena and Marcia true generalizations or false stereotypes?

Let's first be clear that a **stereotype** is *a simplified description applied to every person in some category*. Each of the statements made at the beginning of this box is a stereotype that is false for three reasons. First, rather than describing averages, each statement describes every person in some category in exactly the same way; second, even though many stereotypes often contain an element of truth, each statement ignores facts and distorts reality; and third, each statement seems to be motivated by bias, sounding more like a "put-down" than a fair-minded observation.

A sociology classroom is a good place to get at the truth behind common stereotypes.

What about sociology? If our discipline looks for social patterns and makes generalizations, does it express stereotypes? The answer is no, for three reasons. First, *sociologists do not carelessly apply any generalization to everyone in a category*. Second, *sociologists make sure that a generalization squares with the available facts*. And third, *sociologists offer generalizations fair-mindedly, with an interest in getting at the truth*.

Jena remembered her professor saying (although not in quite the same words) that the suicide rate among Protestants is higher than among Catholics or Jews. Based on information presented earlier in this chapter, that is a true statement. However, the way Jena incorrectly reported the classroom remark—"If you're a Protestant, you're likely to kill yourself"—is not good sociology. It is not a true generalization because the vast majority of Protestants do no such thing. It would be just as wrong to jump to the conclusion that a particular friend, because he is a Protestant male, is about to end his own life. (Imagine refusing to lend money to a roommate who happens to be a Baptist, explaining, "Well, given the way people like you commit suicide, I might never get paid back!")

Second, sociologists shape their generalizations to the available facts. A more factual version of the statement Yannina made in class is that on average, the U.S. population does have a high standard of living, almost everyone in our society does marry at some point in life, and although few people take pleasure in divorcing, our divorce rate is also among the world's highest.

Third, sociologists try to be fair-minded and want to get at the truth. The statement made by Marcia's brother, about African Americans and basketball, is an unfair stereotype rather than good sociology for two reasons. First, although African Americans are overly represented in professional basketball relative to their share of the population, the statement—as made above—is simply not true; second, the comment seems motivated by bias rather than truth-seeking.

The bottom line is that good sociological generalizations are *not* the same as harmful stereotypes. A college sociology course is an excellent setting for getting at the truth behind common stereotypes. The classroom encourages discussion and offers the factual information you need to decide whether a particular statement is a valid sociological generalization or a harmful or unfair stereotype.

What Do You Think?

1. Can you think of a common stereotype of sociologists? What is it? After reading this box, do you still think it is valid?

2. Do you think taking a sociology course can help correct people's stereotypes? Why or why not?

3. Can you think of a stereotype of your own that might be challenged by sociological analysis?

Seeing Sociology in Everyday Life

CHAPTER 1 The Sociological Perspective

Why do couples marry?

We asked this question at the beginning of this chapter. The commonsense answer is that people marry because they are in love. But as this chapter has explained, society guides our everyday lives, and the power of society affects everything we do, think, and feel. Look at the three photographs, each showing a couple that, we can assume, is "in love." In each case, can you provide some of the rest of the story? By looking at the categories that the people involved represent, explain how society is at work in bringing the two people together.

Beyoncé Giselle Knowles, widely known as Beyoncé, performs in New York's Madison Square Garden with her husband Jay-Z (Shawn Corey Carter). Looking at this couple, who married in 2008, what social patterns do you see?

In 2011, 85-year-old Hugh Hefner planned to marry 25-year-old Crystal Harris, only to have her call off the wedding a few days before the scheduled June event. The July issue of *Playboy* magazine featured Harris on the cover with the line "Introducing Mrs. Crystal Hefner" covered at the last minute with a sticker stating "Runaway Bride in This Issue!" What social patterns do you see in this relationship?

In 1997, during the fourth season of her hit TV show, *Ellen*, Ellen DeGeneres "came out" as a lesbian, which put her on the cover of *Time* magazine. Since then, she has been an activist on behalf of gay and lesbian issues. Following California's brief legalization of same-sex marriage in 2008, she married her longtime girlfriend, Australian actress Portia de Rossi.

HINT Society is at work on many levels. Consider (1) rules about same-sex and other-sex marriage, (2) laws defining the categories of people whom one may marry, (3) the importance of race and ethnicity, (4) the importance of social class, (5) the importance of age, and (6) the importance of social exchange (what each partner offers the other). All societies enforce various rules that state who should or should not marry whom.

Seeing Sociology in *Your* Everyday Life

1. Analyze the marriages of your parents, other family members, and friends in terms of class, race, age, and other factors. What evidence can you find that society guides the feelings that we call "love"?

2. Go to MySocLab and click on the Student Resources link to access the Sociology in Focus blog, where you can read the latest posts by a team of young sociolo-

gists who apply the sociological perspective to topics of popular culture.

3. As this chapter has explained, the time in human history when we are born and the society in which we are born, as well as our class position, race, and gender, all shape the personal experiences we have throughout our lives. Does this mean we have no power over our own destiny? No,

in fact, the more we understand how society works, the more power we have to shape our own lives. Go to the "Seeing Sociology in *Your* Everyday Life" feature in MySocLab to learn more about how the material in this chapter can help deepen your understanding of yourself and others around you so that you can more effectively pursue your life goals.

Making the Grade

The Sociological Perspective

1.1 Explain how the sociological perspective differs from common sense. (pages 4–9)

👁 **Watch** the **Video** in **MySocLab**   📖 **Read** the **Document** in **MySocLab**

The **sociological perspective** reveals the power of society to shape individual lives.

- What we commonly think of as personal choice—whether or not to go to college, how many children we will have, even the decision to end our own life—is affected by social forces.
- Peter Berger described the sociological perspective as "seeing the general in the particular."
- C. Wright Mills called this point of view the "sociological imagination," claiming it transforms personal troubles into public issues.
- The experience of being an outsider or of living through a social crisis can encourage people to use the sociological perspective.

sociology the systematic study of human society

sociological perspective sociology's special point of view that sees general patterns of society in the lives of particular people

The Importance of a Global Perspective

1.2 State several reasons that a global perspective is important in today's world. (pages 9–11)

Where we live—in a **high-income country** like the United States, a **middle-income country** such as Brazil, or a **low-income country** such as Mali—shapes the lives we lead.

Societies throughout the world are increasingly interconnected.

- New technology allows people around the world to share popular trends.
- Immigration from around the world increases the racial and ethnic diversity of the United States.
- Trade across national boundaries has created a global economy.

Many social problems that we face in the United States are far more serious in other countries.

Learning about life in other societies helps us learn more about ourselves.

global perspective the study of the larger world and our society's place in it

high-income countries nations with the highest overall standards of living

middle-income countries nations with a standard of living about average for the world as a whole

low-income countries nations with a low standard of living in which most people are poor

Applying the Sociological Perspective

1.3 Identify the advantages of sociological thinking for developing public policy, for encouraging personal growth, and for advancing in a career. (pages 11–14)

👁 **Watch** the **Video** in **MySocLab**

Research by sociologists plays an important role in shaping **public policy**.

On a **personal level**, using the sociological perspective helps us see the opportunities and limits in our lives and empowers us to be active citizens.

A background in sociology is excellent preparation for success in many different **careers**.

Origins of Sociology

1.4 Link the origins of sociology to historical social changes. (pages 14–16)

Rapid social change in the eighteenth and nineteenth centuries made people more aware of their surroundings and helped trigger the development of sociology:

- The **rise of an industrial economy** moved work from homes to factories, weakening the traditions that had guided community life for centuries.
- The **explosive growth of cities** created many social problems, such as crime and homelessness.
- **Political change** based on ideas of individual liberty and individual rights encouraged people to question the structure of society.

positivism a scientific approach to knowledge based on "positive" facts as opposed to mere speculation

Auguste Comte named sociology in 1838 to describe a new way of looking at society.
- Early philosophers had tried to describe the ideal society.
- Comte wanted to understand society as it really is by using **positivism**, a way of understanding based on science.
- Karl Marx and many later sociologists used sociology to try to make society better.

Sociological Theory

1.5 Summarize sociology's major theoretical approaches. (pages 16–22)

 Watch the **Video** in **MySocLab**   **Explore** the **Map** in **MySocLab**

A **theory** states how facts are related, weaving observations into insight and understanding. Sociologists use three major **theoretical approaches** to describe the operation of society.

 macro-level   The **structural-functional approach** explores how **social structures**—patterns of behavior, such as religious rituals or family life—work together to help society operate.

- Auguste Comte, Emile Durkheim, and Herbert Spencer helped develop the structural-functional approach.
- Thomas Merton pointed out that social structures have both **manifest functions** and **latent functions**; he also identified **social dysfunctions** as patterns that may disrupt the operation of society.

The **social-conflict approach** shows how inequality creates conflict and causes change.
- Karl Marx helped develop the social-conflict approach.
- **Gender-conflict theory**, also called **feminist theory**, focuses on ways in which society places men in positions of power over women. Harriet Martineau is regarded as the first woman sociologist.
- **Race-conflict theory** focuses on the advantages—including higher income, more schooling, and better health—that society gives to white people over people of color.
- W. E. B. Du Bois identified the "double consciousness" of African Americans.

 micro-level   The **symbolic-interaction approach** studies how people, in everyday interaction, construct reality.

- Max Weber's claim that people's beliefs and values shape society is the basis of the social-interaction approach.
- Social-exchange analysis states that social life is guided by what each person stands to gain or lose from the interaction.

theory a statement of how and why specific facts are related

theoretical approach a basic image of society that guides thinking and research

structural-functional approach a framework for building theory that sees society as a complex system whose parts work together to promote solidarity and stability

social structure any relatively stable pattern of social behavior

social functions the consequences of any social pattern for the operation of society as a whole

manifest functions the recognized and intended consequences of any social pattern

latent functions the unrecognized and unintended consequences of any social pattern

social dysfunction any social pattern that may disrupt the operation of society

social-conflict approach a framework for building theory that sees society as an arena of inequality that generates conflict and change

gender-conflict theory (feminist theory) the study of society that focuses on inequality and conflict between women and men

feminism support of social equality for women and men

race-conflict theory the study of society that focuses on inequality and conflict between people of different racial and ethnic categories

macro-level orientation a broad focus on social structures that shape society as a whole

micro-level orientation a close-up focus on social interaction in specific situations

symbolic-interaction approach a framework for building theory that sees society as the product of the everyday interactions of individuals

Applying the Approaches: The Sociology of Sports

1.6 Apply sociology's major theoretical approaches to the topic of sports. (pages 22–25)

The Functions of Sports

The structural-functional approach looks at how sports help society function smoothly.
- Manifest functions of sports include providing recreation, a means of getting in physical shape, and a relatively harmless way to let off steam.
- Latent functions of sports include building social relationships and creating thousands of jobs.

Sports and Conflict

The social-conflict approach looks at the links between sports and social inequality.
- Historically, as feminism shows us, sports have benefited men more than women.
- Some sports are accessible mainly to affluent people.
- Race-conflict theory highlights the existence of racial discrimination in professional sports.

Sports as Interaction

The social-interaction approach looks at the different meanings and understandings people have of sports.
- Within a team, players affect each other's understanding of the sport.
- The reaction of the public can affect how players perceive their sport.

stereotype a simplified description applied to every person in some category

2 Sociological Investigation

((· **Listen** to **Chapter 2** in **MySocLab**

LEARNING OBJECTIVES

2.1 Explain how scientific evidence often challenges common sense.

2.2 Describe sociology's three research orientations.

2.3 Identify the importance of gender in sociological research.

2.4 Discuss the importance of ethics to sociological research.

2.5 Explain why a researcher might choose each of sociology's research methods.

2.6 Illustrate the use of inductive and deductive logical thought.

2.7 Recall the ten important steps in carrying out sociological research.

the Power of Society
to influence our life chances

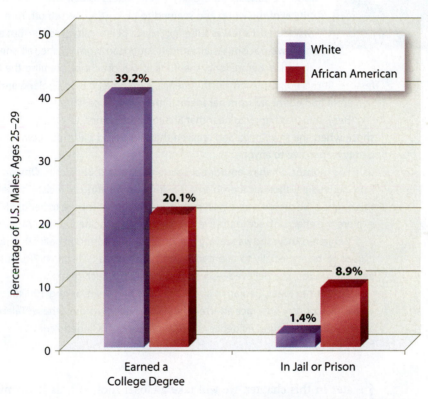

Sources: U.S. Department of Education (2012)
and U.S. Department of Justice (2012)

Do we simply "decide" our future? Among young men in their late twenties, part of the privilege of being white compared to being black is having double the odds of earning a college degree. Among African Americans, part of the disadvantage of being a person of color compared to being white is having six times the odds of being in jail or prison. While we all make choices, society sets the terrain of our life journey.

Chapter Overview

Having learned to use the sociological perspective and how to make use of sociological theory, it is time to learn how sociologists "do" research. This chapter explains the process of sociological investigation or how sociologists gather knowledge about the world. First, this chapter looks at science as a way of knowing and then discusses two limitations to scientific sociology that have given rise to two other approaches to knowing—interpretive sociology and critical sociology. Second, the chapter explains and illustrates four methods of data collection.

While on a visit to Atlanta during the winter holiday season, the sociologist Lois Benjamin (1991) called up the mother of an old college friend. Benjamin was eager to learn about Sheba; both women had dreamed about earning a graduate degree, landing a teaching job, and writing books. Now a successful university professor, Benjamin had seen her dream come true. But as she soon found out, this was not the case with Sheba.

Benjamin recalled early signs of trouble. After college, Sheba had begun graduate work at a Canadian university. But in letters to Benjamin, Sheba became more and more critical of the world and seemed to be cutting herself off from others. Some classmates wondered if she was suffering from a personality disorder. But as Sheba saw it, the problem was racism. As an African American woman, she felt she was the target of racial hostility. Before long, she flunked out of school, blaming the failure on her white professors. At this point, she left North America, earning a Ph.D. in England and then settling in Nigeria. Benjamin had not heard from her friend in the years since.

Benjamin was happy to hear that Sheba had returned to Atlanta. But her delight dissolved into shock when she saw Sheba and realized that her friend had suffered a mental breakdown and was barely responsive to anyone.

For months, Sheba's emotional collapse troubled Benjamin. Obviously, Sheba was suffering from serious psychological problems. Having felt the sting of racism herself, Benjamin wondered if this might have played a part in Sheba's story. Partly as a tribute to her old friend, Benjamin set out to explore the effects of race in the lives of bright, well-educated African Americans in the United States.

Benjamin knew she was calling into question the common belief that race is less of a barrier than it used to be, especially to talented African Americans (Wilson, 1978). But her own experiences—and Sheba's too, she believed—seemed to contradict such thinking.

To test her ideas, Benjamin spent the next two years asking 100 successful African Americans across the country how race affected their lives. In the words of these "Talented One Hundred"[1] men and women, she found evidence that even among privileged African Americans, racism remains a heavy burden.

Later in this chapter, we will take a closer look at Lois Benjamin's research. For now, notice how the sociological perspective helped her spot broad social patterns in the lives of individuals. Just as important, Benjamin's work shows us the *doing* of sociology, the process of *sociological investigation*.

Many people think that scientists work only in laboratories, carefully taking measurements using complex equipment. But as this chapter explains, although some sociologists do conduct scientific research in laboratories, most work on neighborhood streets, in homes and workplaces, in schools and hospitals, in bars and prisons—in short, wherever people can be found.

This chapter examines the methods that sociologists use to conduct research. Along the way, we shall see that research involves not just ways of gathering information but also controversies about values: Should researchers strive to be objective? Or should they point

👁 **Watch** in **MySocLab**
Video: *Sociology on the Job: Sociological Theory and Research*

---

[1]W. E. B. Du Bois used "The Talented Tenth" to refer to African American leaders.

to the need for change? Certainly Lois Benjamin did not begin her study just to show that racism exists; she wanted to bring racism out in the open as a way to challenge it. We shall tackle questions of values after presenting the basics of sociological investigation.

Basics of Sociological Investigation

2.1 Explain how scientific evidence often challenges common sense.

Sociological investigation starts with two simple requirements. The first was the focus of Chapter 1: *Apply the sociological perspective.* This point of view reveals curious patterns of behavior all around us that call for further study. It was Lois Benjamin's sociological imagination that prompted her to wonder how race affects the lives of talented African Americans.

This brings us to the second requirement: *Be curious and ask questions.* Benjamin wanted to learn more about how race affects people who are high achievers. She began by asking questions: Who are the leaders of this nation's black community? What effect does being part of a racial minority have on their view of themselves? On the way white people perceive them and their work?

Seeing the world sociologically and asking questions are basic to sociological investigation. As we look for answers, we need to realize that there are various kinds of "truth."

Science as One Type of Truth

Saying that we "know" something can mean many things. Most people in the United States, for instance, say they believe in God. Few claim to have direct contact with God, but they say they believe all the same. We call this kind of knowing "belief" or "faith."

A second kind of truth comes from recognized experts. Students with a health problem, for example, may consult a campus physician or search the Internet for articles written by experts in the field.

A third type of truth is based on simple agreement among ordinary people. Most of us in the United States would probably say we "know" that sexual intercourse among ten-year-old children is wrong. But why? Mostly because just about everyone says it is.

science a logical system that bases knowledge on direct, systematic observation

People's "truths" differ the world over, and we often encounter "facts" at odds with our own. Imagine yourself a Peace Corps volunteer just arrived in a small, traditional village in Latin America. Your job is to help local people grow more crops. On your first day in the fields, you observe a strange practice: After planting seeds, the farmers lay a dead fish on top of the soil. When you ask about this, they explain that the fish is a gift to the god of the harvest. A village elder adds sternly that the harvest was poor one year when no fish were offered.

From that society's point of view, using fish as gifts to the harvest god makes sense. The people believe in it, their experts endorse it, and everyone seems to agree that the system works. But with scientific training in agriculture, you have to shake your head and wonder. The scientific "truth" in this situation is something entirely different: The decomposing fish fertilize the ground, producing a better crop.

Science represents a fourth way of knowing. **Science** is *a logical system that bases knowledge on*

In a complex and ever-changing world, there are many different "truths." This Peace Corps volunteer on a small island in the South Pacific learned a crucial lesson—that other people often see things in a different way. There is great value in our own scientific approach to truth, but there are also important truths in the ancient traditions of people living around the world.

direct, systematic observation. Standing apart from faith, the wisdom of "experts," and general agreement, scientific knowledge rests on **empirical evidence**, that is, *information we can verify with our senses.*

Our Peace Corps example does not mean that people in traditional villages ignore what their senses tell them or that members of technologically advanced societies use only science to know things. A medical researcher using science to develop a new drug for treating cancer, for example, may still practice her religion as a matter of faith, turn to financial experts when making decisions about money, and pay attention to the political opinions of her family and friends. In short, we all hold various kinds of truths at the same time.

Common Sense versus Scientific Evidence

Like the sociological perspective, scientific evidence sometimes challenges our common sense. Here are six statements that many North Americans assume are true:

1. **"Poor people are far more likely than rich people to break the law."** Not true. If you regularly watch television shows like *COPS,* you might think that police arrest only people from "bad" neighborhoods. Chapter 9 ("Deviance") explains that poor people do stand out in the official arrest statistics. But research also shows that police and prosecutors are more likely to treat well-to-do people more leniently, as when a Hollywood celebrity is accused of shoplifting or drunk driving. Some laws are even written in a way that criminalizes poor people more and affluent people less.

2. **"The United States is a middle-class society in which most people are more or less equal."** False. Data presented in Chapter 11 ("Social Class in the United States") show that the richest 5 percent of U.S. families control 63 percent of the nation's total wealth, but almost half of all families have scarcely any wealth at all. The gap between the richest people and average people in the United States has never been greater (Wolff, 2012).

3. **"Most poor people don't want to work."** Wrong. Research described in Chapter 11 indicates that this statement is true of some but not most poor people. In fact, nearly half of poor individuals in the United States are children and elderly people who are not expected to work.

4. **"Differences in the behavior of females and males are just 'human nature.'"** Wrong again. Much of what we call "human nature" is constructed by the society in which we live, as Chapter 3 ("Culture") explains. Further, as Chapter 13 ("Gender Stratification") argues, some societies define "feminine" and "masculine" very differently from the way we do.

5. **"People change as they grow old, losing many interests as they focus on their health."** Not really. Chapter 15 ("Aging and the Elderly") reports that aging does very little to change our personalities. Problems of health increase in old age, but by and large, elderly people keep the distinctive personalities they have had throughout their adult lives.

6. **"Most people marry because they are in love."** Not always. To members of our society, few statements are so obvious. Surprisingly, however, in many societies, marriage has little to do with love. Chapter 18 ("Families") explains why.

These examples confirm the old saying that "it's not what we *don't* know that gets us into trouble as much as the things we *do* know that *just aren't so.*" While growing up we have all heard many widely accepted "truths," been bombarded by "expert" advice in the popular media, and felt pressure to accept the opinions of people around us. As adults, we need to evaluate more critically what we see, read, and hear. Sociology can help us do that.

For a closer look at why it is important to think critically about "facts" we find on the Internet and in the popular media, **Read More** in **MySocLab,** *Is What We Read in the Popular Press True? The Case of Extramarital Sex*

Three Ways to Do Sociology

2.2 Describe sociology's three research orientations.

"**D**oing" sociology means learning about the social world. There is more than one way to do this. Just as sociologists can use one or more theoretical approaches (described in Chapter 1, "The Sociological Perspective"), they may also use different research orientations. The following sections describe three ways to do research: positivist sociology, interpretive sociology, and critical sociology.

Positivist Sociology

Chapter 1 explained how early sociologists such as Auguste Comte and Emile Durkheim applied science to the study of society just as natural scientists investigate the physical world. **Positivist sociology**, then, is *the study of society based on systematic observation of social behavior.* A positivist orientation to the world assumes that an objective reality exists "out there." The job of the scientist is to discover this reality by gathering empirical evidence, facts we can verify with our senses, say, by seeing, hearing, or touching.

concept a mental construct that represents some aspect of the world in a simplified form

variable a concept whose value changes from case to case

Concepts, Variables, and Measurement

Let's take a closer look at how science works. A basic element of science is the **concept**, *a mental construct that represents some part of the world in a simplified form.* Sociologists use concepts to label aspects of social life, including "the family" and "the economy," and to categorize people in terms of their "gender" or "social class."

A **variable** is *a concept whose value changes from case to case.* The familiar variable "price," for example, has a value that changes from item to item in a supermarket. Similarly, we use the concept "social class" to describe people's social standing as "upper class," "middle class," "working class," or "lower class."

measurement a procedure for determining the value of a variable in a specific case

The use of variables depends on **measurement**, *a procedure for determining the value of a variable in a specific case.* Some variables are easy to measure, as when you step on a scale to see how much you weigh. But measuring sociological variables can be far more difficult. For example, how would you measure a person's social class? You might start by looking at the clothing people wear, listening to how they speak, or noting where they live. Or trying to be more precise, you might ask about their income, occupation, and education.

Because most variables can be measured in more than one way, sociologists often have to decide which factors to consider. For example, having a very high income might qualify a person as "upper class." But what if the income comes from selling automobiles, an occupation most people think of as "middle class"? Would having only an eighth-grade education make the person "lower class"? In a case like this, sociologists usually combine these three measures—income, occupation, and education—to determine social class, as described in Chapter 10 ("Social Stratification") and Chapter 11 ("Social Class in the United States").

Sociologists also face the problem of dealing with huge numbers of people. For example, how do you report income for thousands or even millions of U.S. families? Listing streams of numbers would carry little meaning and tells us

One principle of scientific research is that sociologists and other investigators should try to be objective in their work, so that their personal values and beliefs do not distort their findings. But such a detached attitude may discourage the connection needed for people to open up and share information. Thus sociologists have to decide how much to pursue objectivity and how much to show their own feelings.

Seeing Sociology in Everyday Life

Three Useful (and Simple) Descriptive Statistics

The admissions office at your school is preparing a new brochure, and as part of your work-study job in that office, your supervisor asks you to determine the average salary received by last year's graduating class. To keep matters simple, assume that you talk to only seven members of the class (a real study would require contacting many more) and gather the following data on their present incomes:

$30,000	$42,000	$22,000
$165,000	$22,000	$35,000
$34,000		

Sociologists use three different descriptive statistics to report averages. The simplest statistic is the *mode,* the value that occurs *most often* in a series of numbers. In this example, the mode is $22,000, since that value occurs two times and each of the others occurs only once. If all the values were to occur only once, there would be no mode; if two different values each occurred two or three times, there would be two modes. Although it is easy to identify, sociologists rarely use the mode because it reflects only some of the numbers and is therefore a crude measure of the "average."

A more common statistic, the *mean,* refers to the *arithmetic average* of a series of numbers, calculated by adding all the values together and dividing by the number of cases. The sum of the seven incomes is $350,000. Dividing by 7 yields a mean income of $50,000. But notice that the mean in this case is not a very good "average" because it is higher than six of the seven incomes and is not particularly close to any of the actual numbers. Because the mean is "pulled" up or down by an especially high or low value (in this case, the $165,000 paid to one graduate, an athlete who signed as a rookie with the Cincinnati Reds farm team), it can give a distorted picture of data that include one or more extreme scores.

The *median* is the *middle case,* the value that occurs midway in a series of numbers arranged from lowest to highest. Here the median income for the seven graduates is $34,000, because when the numbers are placed in order from lowest to highest, this value occurs exactly in the middle, with three incomes higher and three lower. (With an even number of cases, the median is halfway between the two middle cases.) Unlike the mean, the median is not affected by any extreme scores. In such cases, the median gives a better picture of what is "average" than the mean.

What Do You Think?

1. Your grade point average (GPA) is an example of an average. Is it a mode, a median, or a mean? Explain.

2. Sociologists generally use the median instead of the mean when they study people's incomes. Can you see why?

3. Do a quick calculation of the mean, median, and mode for these simple numbers: 1, 2, 5, 6, 6.

Answers: mode = 6, median = 5, mean = 4.

---

nothing about the population as a whole. To solve this problem, sociologists use *descriptive statistics* to state what is "average" for a large number of people. The Seeing Sociology in Everyday Life box above explains how.

Defining Concepts Measurement is always somewhat arbitrary because the value of any variable in part depends on how it is defined. In addition, it is easy to see that there is more than one way to measure abstract concepts such as "love," "family," or "intelligence."

Good research therefore requires that sociologists **operationalize a variable** by *specifying exactly what is to be measured before assigning a value to a variable.* Before measuring the concept of "social class," for example, you would have to decide exactly what you were going to measure—say, income level, years of schooling, or occupational prestige. Sometimes sociologists measure several of these things; in such cases, they need to specify exactly how they plan to combine these variables into one overall score. The next time you read the results of a study, notice the way the researchers operationalize each variable. How they define terms can greatly affect the results.

Even the researchers at the U.S. Census Bureau sometimes struggle with operationalizing a concept. Take the case of measuring the racial and ethnic diversity of the U.S. population. Back in 1977, researchers at the U.S. Census Bureau defined race and ethnicity by asking people to make a choice from this list: white, black, Hispanic, Asian or Pacific Islander, and American Indian or Alaska Native. One problem with this system is that someone can be both Hispanic *and* white or black; similarly, people of Arab ancestry might not identify with any of these choices. Just as important, an increasing number of people in the United States are *multiracial.* Because of the changing face of the U.S. population,

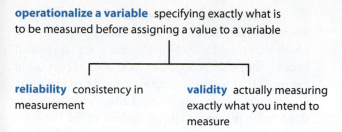

operationalize a variable specifying exactly what is to be measured before assigning a value to a variable

reliability consistency in measurement

validity actually measuring exactly what you intend to measure

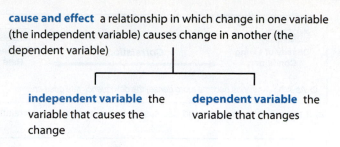

cause and effect a relationship in which change in one variable (the independent variable) causes change in another (the dependent variable)

independent variable the variable that causes the change

dependent variable the variable that changes

the 2000 census was the first one to allow people to describe their race and ethnicity by selecting more than one category from an expanded menu of choices and almost 7 million people did so. But many of these people selected both "Hispanic" and also a nationality, such as "Mexican." The result was an overcount of the number of multiracial people. In 2010, census researchers changed the process once again, providing clearer instructions and operationalizing the concept of "race" by offering five racial categories, "some other race," and fifty-seven multiracial options. In 2010, 9 million people (about 3 percent of the population) identified themselves as "multiracial."

Reliability and Validity For a measurement to be useful, it must be both reliable and valid. **Reliability** refers to *consistency in measurement*. A measurement is reliable if repeated measurements give the same result time after time. But consistency does not guarantee **validity**, which means *actually measuring exactly what you intend to measure*.

Getting a valid measurement is sometimes tricky. For instance, say you want to know just how religious the students at your college are. You might decide to ask students how often they attend religious services. But is going to a church, temple, or mosque really the same thing as being religious? People may attend religious services because of deep personal beliefs, but they may also do so out of habit or because others pressure them to go. And what about spiritual people who avoid organized religion altogether? Even when a measurement yields consistent results (making it reliable), it may not measure what we want it to (and therefore lack validity). Chapter 19 ("Religion") suggests that measuring religiosity should take account of not only participation in prayer services but also the beliefs a person holds and the degree to which a person lives by religious convictions. Good sociological research depends on careful measurement, which is always a challenge to researchers.

Relationships among Variables Once measurements are made, investigators can pursue the real payoff: seeing how variables are related. The scientific ideal is **cause and effect**, *a relationship in which change in one variable causes change in another*. Cause-and-effect relationships occur around us every day, as when studying hard for an exam results in a high grade. *The variable that causes the change* (in this case, how much you study) is called the **independent variable**. *The variable that changes* (the exam grade) is called the **dependent variable**. The value of one variable depends on the value of another. Linking variables in terms of cause and effect is important because it allows us to *predict* the outcome of future events—if we know one thing, we can accurately predict another. For example, knowing that studying hard results in a better exam grade, we can predict with confidence that a typical individual who studies hard for the next exam will receive a higher grade than if that person does not study at all.

But just because two variables change together does not mean that they are linked by a cause-and-effect relationship. For example, sociologists have long observed that juvenile delinquency is more common among young people who live in crowded housing. Say we operationalize the variable "juvenile delinquency" as the number of times a person under the age of eighteen has been arrested, and we define "crowded housing" by a home's number of square feet of living space per person. It turns out that these variables are related: Delinquency rates are high in densely populated neighborhoods. But should we conclude that crowding in the home (in this case, the independent variable) is what causes delinquency (the dependent variable)?

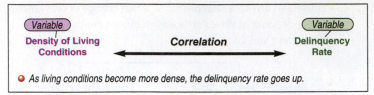

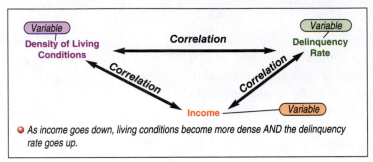

(a) If two variables increase and decrease together, they display correlation.

(b) Here we consider the effect of a third variable: income. Low income may cause *both* high-density living conditions *and* a high delinquency rate.

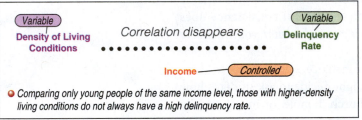

(c) When we control for income—that is, examine only young people of the same income level—we find that density of living conditions and delinquency rate no longer increase and decrease together.

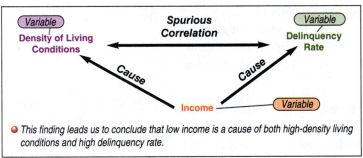

(d) Density of living conditions and delinquency rate are correlated, but their correlation is *spurious* because neither one causes the other.

FIGURE 2–1 Correlation and Cause: An Example

Correlation is not the same as cause. The four figures above explain why.

correlation a relationship in which two (or more) variables change together

spurious correlation an apparent but false relationship between two (or more) variables that is caused by some other variable

control holding constant all variables except one in order to see clearly the effect of that variable

Not necessarily. **Correlation** is *a relationship in which two (or more) variables change together*. We know that density and delinquency are correlated because they change together, as shown in part (a) of Figure 2–1. This relationship *may* mean that crowding causes more arrests, but it could also mean that some third factor is causing change in *both* of the variables under observation. To identify a third variable, think what kinds of people live in crowded housing: people with less money and few choices—the poor. Poor children are also more likely to end up with police records. In reality, crowded housing and juvenile delinquency are found together because *both* are caused by a third factor—poverty—as shown in part (b) of Figure 2–1. In short, the apparent connection between crowding and delinquency is "explained away" by a third variable—low income—that causes them both to change. So our original connection turns out to be a **spurious correlation**, *an apparent but false relationship between two (or more) variables that is caused by some other variable*.

Exposing a correlation as spurious requires a bit of detective work, assisted by a technique called **control**, *holding constant all variables except one in order to see clearly the effect of that variable*. In our example, we suspect that income level may be causing a spurious link between housing density and delinquency. To check whether the correlation between delinquency and crowding is spurious, we control for income—that is, we hold income constant by looking at only young people of one income level. If the correlation between density and delinquency remains, that is, if young people of the same income level living in more crowded housing show higher rates of arrest than young people in less crowded housing, we have more reason to think that crowding does, in fact, cause delinquency. But if the relationship disappears when we control for income, as shown in part (c) of Figure 2–1, then we know we were dealing with a spurious correlation. In fact, research shows that the correlation between crowding and delinquency just about disappears if income is controlled (Fischer, 1984). So we have now sorted out the relationship among the three variables, as illustrated in part (d) of the figure. Housing density and juvenile delinquency have a spurious correlation; evidence shows that both variables rise or fall according to income.

To sum up, correlation means only that two (or more) variables change together. To establish cause and effect, three requirements must be met: (1) a demonstrated correlation, (2) an independent (causal) variable that occurs before the dependent variable, and (3) no evidence that a third variable could be causing a spurious correlation between the two.

Natural scientists usually have an easier time than social scientists in identifying cause-and-effect relationships because most natural scientists work in laboratories, where they can control other variables. Carrying out research in a workplace or on the streets, however, makes control very difficult, so sociologists often have to settle for demonstrating only correlation. Also, human behavior is highly complex, involving dozens of causal variables at any one time, so establishing all the cause-and-effect relationships in any situation is extremely difficult.

The Ideal of Objectivity

Ten students are sitting around a dorm lounge discussing the dream vacation spot for the upcoming spring break. Do you think one place will end up being everyone's clear favorite? That hardly seems likely.

In scientific terms, each of the ten people probably operationalizes the concept "dream vacation" differently. For one, it might be a deserted, sunny beach in Mexico; for another, the choice might be New Orleans, a lively city with a very active social scene; for still another, hiking the Rocky Mountains below snow-capped peaks may be the choice. Like so many other "bests" in life, the best vacations turn out to be mostly a matter of individual taste.

Personal values are fine when it comes to choosing travel destinations, but they pose a challenge to scientific research. Remember, science assumes that reality is "out there." Scientists need to study this reality without changing it in any way, and so they strive for **objectivity**, *personal neutrality in conducting research*. Objectivity means that researchers carefully hold to scientific procedures and do not let their own attitudes and beliefs influence the results.

Scientific objectivity is an ideal rather than a reality, of course, because no one can be completely neutral. Even the topic someone chooses to study reflects a personal interest of one sort or another, as Lois Benjamin showed us in the reasons for her decision to investigate race. But the scientific ideal is to keep a professional distance or sense of detachment from the results, however they turn out. With this ideal in mind, you should do your best when conducting research to see that conscious or unconscious biases do not distort your findings. As an extra precaution, many researchers openly state their personal leanings in their research reports so that readers can interpret the conclusions with those considerations in mind.

The German sociologist Max Weber expected that people would select their research topics according to their personal beliefs and interests. Why else, after all, would one person study world hunger, another investigate the effects of racism, and still another examine how children manage in one-parent families? Knowing that people select topics that are *value-relevant*, Weber urged researchers to be *value-free* in their investigations. Only by controlling their personal feelings and opinions (as we expect any professionals to do) can researchers study the world *as it is* rather than tell us *how they think it should be*. This detachment, for Weber, is a crucial element of science that sets it apart from politics. Politicians are committed to particular outcomes; scientists try to maintain an open mind about the results of their investigations, whatever they may turn out to be.

Weber's argument still carries much weight, although most sociologists admit that we can never be completely value-free or even aware of all our biases. Keep in mind, however, that sociologists are not "average" people: Most are white, highly educated, and much more politically liberal than the population as a whole (Klein & Stern, 2004; Cardiff & Klein, 2005). Remember that sociologists, like everyone else, are influenced by their social backgrounds.

One way to limit distortion caused by personal values is **replication**, *repetition of research by other investigators*. If other researchers repeat a study using the same procedures and obtain the same results, we gain confidence that the results are accurate (both reliable and valid). The need for replication in scientific investigation probably explains why the search for knowledge is called "*re*-search" in the first place.

Keep in mind that following the logic of science does not guarantee objective, absolute truth. What science offers is an approach to knowledge that is *self-correcting* so that in the long run, researchers stand a good chance of limiting their biases. Objectivity and truth lie, then, not in any one study but in the scientific process itself as it continues over time.

Some Limitations of Scientific Sociology

Science is one important way of knowing. Yet, applied to social life, science has several important limitations.

objectivity personal neutrality in conducting research

replication repetition of research by other investigators

A basic lesson of social research is that being observed affects how people behave. Researchers can never be certain precisely how this will occur; some people resent public attention, but others become highly animated when they think they have an audience.

1. **Human behavior is too complex for sociologists to predict any individual's actions precisely.** Astronomers calculate the movement of objects in the skies with remarkable precision, but comets and planets are nonthinking objects. Humans, by contrast, have minds of their own, so no two people react to any event (whether it be a sports victory or a natural disaster) in exactly the same way. Sociologists must therefore be satisfied with showing that *categories* of people *typically* act in one way or another. This is not a failing of sociology. It simply reflects the fact that we study creative, spontaneous people.

2. **Because humans respond to their surroundings, the presence of a researcher may affect the behavior being studied.** An astronomer's gaze has no effect on a distant comet. But most people react to being observed. Try staring at someone for a few minutes and see for yourself. People being watched may become anxious, angry, or defensive; others may be especially friendly or helpful. The act of studying people can cause their behavior to change.

3. **Social patterns vary; what is true in one time or place may not hold true in another.** The same laws of physics will apply tomorrow as today, and they hold true all around the world. But human behavior is so variable that there are no universal sociological laws.

4. **Because sociologists are part of the social world they study, they can never be 100 percent value-free when conducting social research.** Barring a laboratory mishap, chemists are rarely personally affected by what goes on in their test tubes. But sociologists live in their "test tube," the society they study. Therefore, social scientists may find it difficult to control—or even to recognize—personal values that may distort their work.

Interpretive Sociology

Not all sociologists agree that science is the only way—or even the best way—to study human society. This is because, unlike planets or other elements of the natural world, humans do not simply move around as objects in ways that can be measured. Even more important, people are active creatures who attach meaning to their behavior, and meaning is not easy to observe directly.

Therefore, sociologists have developed a second research orientation, known as **interpretive sociology,** *the study of society that focuses on the meanings people attach to their social world.* Max Weber, the pioneer of this framework, argued that the proper focus of sociology is *interpretation*, or understanding the meaning that people create in their everyday lives.

The Importance of Meaning

Interpretive sociology does not reject science completely, but it does change the focus of research. Interpretive sociology differs from positivist sociology in four ways. First, positivist sociology focuses on actions—on what people do—because that is what we can observe directly. Interpretive sociology, by contrast, focuses on people's understanding of their actions and their surroundings. Second, positivist sociology claims that objective reality exists "out there," but interpretive sociology counters that reality is subjective, constructed by people in the course of their everyday lives. Third, positivist sociology tends to favor *quantitative* data—numerical measurements of people's behavior—while interpretive sociology favors *qualitative* data, or researchers' perceptions of how people understand their world. Fourth, the positivist orientation is best suited to research in a laboratory, where investigators conducting an experiment stand back and take careful measurements. On the other hand, the interpretive orientation claims that we learn more by interacting with people, focusing on subjective meaning, and learning how they make sense of their everyday lives. As the chapter will explain, this type of research often uses personal interviews or fieldwork and is best carried out in a natural or everyday setting.

Weber's Concept of *Verstehen*

Max Weber believed the key to interpretive sociology lay in *Verstehen* (pronounced "fair-SHTAY-in"), the German word for "understanding." The interpretive sociologist does not just observe *what* people do but also tries to understand *why* they do it. The thoughts and feelings of subjects, which scientists tend to dismiss because they are difficult to measure, are the focus of the interpretive sociologist's attention.

Critical Sociology

Like the interpretive orientation, critical sociology developed in reaction to what many sociologists saw as the limitations of positivist sociology. In this case, however, the problem involves the central principle of scientific research: objectivity.

Positivist sociology holds that reality is "out there" and the researcher's task is to study and document how society works. But Karl Marx, who founded the critical orientation, rejected the idea that society exists as a "natural" system with a fixed order. To assume that society is somehow "fixed," he claimed, is the same as saying that society cannot be changed. Positivist sociology, from this point of view, supports the status quo. **Critical sociology**, by contrast, is *the study of society that focuses on the need for social change.*

The Importance of Change

Rather than asking the scientific question "How does society work?" critical sociologists ask moral and political questions, such as "Should society exist in its present form?" and "Why can't our society have less inequality?" Their answers to these questions, typically, are that society should not remain as it is and that we should try to make our world more socially equal. Critical sociology does not reject science completely—Marx (like critical sociologists today) used the scientific method to learn about inequality. But critical sociology does reject the positivist claim that researchers should try to be "objective" and limit their work to studying the status quo.

One recent account of this orientation, echoing Marx, claims that the point of sociology is "not just to research the social world but to change it in the direction of democracy and social justice" (Feagin & Hernán, 2001:1). In making value judgments about how society should be improved, critical sociology rejects Weber's goal that researchers be value-free and emphasizes instead that they should be social activists in pursuit of greater social equality.

Research Orientations

positivist sociology the study of society based on systematic observation of social behavior

interpretive sociology the study of society that focuses on discovering the meanings people attach to their social world

critical sociology the study of society that focuses on the need for social change

Summing Up

Three Research Orientations in Sociology			
	Positivist Sociology	**Interpretive Sociology**	**Critical Sociology**
What is reality?	Society is an orderly system. There is an objective reality "out there."	Society is ongoing interaction. People construct reality as they attach meanings to their behavior.	Society is patterns of inequality. Reality is that some categories of people dominate others.
How do we conduct research?	Using a scientific orientation, the researcher carefully observes behavior, gathering empirical, ideally quantitative, data. Researcher tries to be a neutral observer.	Seeking to look "deeper" than outward behavior, the researcher focuses on subjective meaning. The researcher gathers qualitative data, discovering the subjective sense people make of their world. Researcher is a participant.	Seeking to go beyond positivism's focus on studying the world as it is, the researcher is guided by politics and uses research as a strategy to bring about desired social change. Researcher is an activist.
Corresponding theoretical approach	Structural-functional approach	Symbolic-interaction approach	Social-conflict approach

Sociologists using the critical orientation seek to change not just society but also the character of research itself. They often identify personally with their research subjects and encourage them to help decide what to study and how to do the work. Typically, researchers and subjects use their findings to provide a voice for less powerful people and to advance the political goal of a more equal society (Hess, 1999; Feagin & Hernán, 2001; Perrucci, 2001).

Sociology as Politics

Positivist sociologists object to taking sides in this way, charging that to the extent that critical sociology (whether feminist, Marxist, or of some other critical orientation) becomes political, it lacks objectivity and it cannot correct for its own biases. Critical sociologists reply that *all* research is political or biased—either it calls for change or it does not; sociologists thus have no choice about their work being political, but they can choose *which* positions to support.

Critical sociology is an activist orientation that ties knowledge to action and seeks not just to understand the world as it exists but also to improve it. Generally speaking, positivist sociology appeals to researchers with nonpolitical or more conservative political views; critical sociology appeals to those whose politics range from liberal to radical left.

Research Orientations and Theory

Is there a link between research orientations and sociological theory? There is no precise connection, but each of the three research orientations—positivist, interpretive, and critical—does stand closer to one of the theoretical approaches presented in Chapter 1 ("The Sociological Perspective"). The positivist orientation has an important factor in common with the structural-functional approach—both are concerned with understanding society as it is. In the same way, interpretive sociology has in common with the symbolic-interaction approach a focus on the meanings people attach to their social world. Finally, critical sociology has in common with the social-conflict approach the fact that both seek to reduce social inequality. The Summing Up table above provides a quick review of the differences among the three research orientations. Many sociologists favor one orientation over another; however, because each provides useful insights, it is a good idea to become familiar with all three (Gamson, 1999).

Gender and Research

2.3 Identify the importance of gender in sociological research.

gender the personal traits and social positions that members of a society attach to being female or male

Sociologists also know that research is affected by **gender**, *the personal traits and social positions that members of a society attach to being female or male*. Margrit Eichler (1988) identifies five ways in which gender can shape research:

1. **Androcentricity.** *Androcentricity* (literally, "focus on the male") refers to approaching an issue from a male perspective. Sometimes researchers act as if only men's activities are important, ignoring what women do. For years, researchers studying occupations focused on the paid work of men and overlooked the housework and child care traditionally performed by women. Research that seeks to understand human behavior cannot ignore half of humanity.

   Gynocentricity—seeing the world from a female perspective—can also limit good sociological investigation. However, in our male-dominated society, this problem arises less often.

2. **Overgeneralizing.** This problem occurs when researchers use data drawn from people of only one sex to support conclusions about "humanity" or "society." Gathering information by talking to only male students and then drawing conclusions about an entire campus would be an example of overgeneralizing.

3. **Gender blindness.** Failing to consider gender at all is known as gender blindness. As is evident throughout this book, the lives of men and women differ in countless ways. A study of growing old in the United States might suffer from gender blindness if it overlooked the fact that most elderly men live with their wives but elderly women typically live alone.

4. **Double standards.** Researchers must be careful not to distort what they study by judging men and women differently. For example, a family researcher who labels a couple as "man and wife" may define the man as the "head of the household" and treat him as important, paying little attention to a woman whom the researcher assumes simply plays a supporting role.

5. **Interference.** Another way gender can distort a study is if a subject reacts to the sex of the researcher, interfering with the research operation. While studying a small community in Sicily, for instance, Maureen Giovannini (1992) found that many men treated her as a woman rather than as a researcher. Some thought it was wrong for an unmarried woman to speak privately with a man. Others denied Giovannini access to places they considered off-limits to women.

There is nothing wrong with focusing research on people of one sex or the other. But all sociologists, as well as people who read their work, should be mindful of how gender can affect an investigation.

Research Ethics

(2.4) Discuss the importance of ethics to sociological research.

Like all researchers, sociologists must be aware that research can harm as well as help subjects or communities. For this reason, the American Sociological Association (ASA)—the major professional association of sociologists in North America—has established formal guidelines for conducting research (1997).

Sociologists must try to be skillful and fair-minded in their work. They must disclose all research findings without omitting significant data. They should make their results available to other sociologists who may want to conduct a similar study.

Sociologists must also make sure that the subjects taking part in a research project are not harmed, and they must stop their work right away if they suspect that any subject is at risk of harm. Researchers are also required to protect the privacy of anyone involved in a research project, even if they come under pressure from authorities, such as the police or the courts, to release confidential information. Researchers must also get the *informed consent*

If you ask only male subjects about their attitudes or actions, you may be able to support conclusions about "men" but not more generally about "people." What would a researcher have to do to ensure that research data support conclusions about all of society?

of participants, which means that the subjects must understand the responsibilities and risks that the research involves before agreeing to take part.

Another guideline concerns funding. Sociologists must reveal in their published results the sources of all financial support. They must avoid accepting money from a source if there is any question of a conflict of interest. For example, researchers must never accept funding from any organization that seeks to influence the research results for its own purposes.

The federal government also plays a part in research ethics. Colleges and universities that seek federal funding for research involving human subjects must have an *institutional review board* (IRB) to review grant applications and ensure that research will not violate ethical standards.

Thinking About Diversity: Race, Class, and Gender

Studying the Lives of Hispanics

Jorge: If you are going to include Latinos in your research, you need to learn a little about their culture.

Mark: I'm interviewing lots of different families. What's special about interviewing Latinos?

Jorge: Sit down and I'll tell you a few things you need to know….

Because U.S. society is racially, ethnically, and religiously diverse, all of us have to work with people who differ from ourselves. The same is true of sociologists. Learning, in advance, the ways of life of any category of people can ease the research process and ensure that there will be no hard feelings when the work is finished.

Gerardo Marín and Barbara Van Oss Marín (1991) have identified five areas of concern in conducting research with Hispanic people:

1. **Be careful with terms.** The Maríns point out that the term "Hispanic" is a label of convenience used by the U.S. Census Bureau. Few people of Spanish descent think of themselves as "Hispanic"; most identify with a particular country (generally, with a Latin American nation, such as Mexico or Argentina, or with Spain).

2. **Be aware of cultural differences.** By and large, the United States is individualistic and competitive. Many Hispanics, by contrast, place more value on cooperation and community. An outsider may judge the behavior of a Hispanic subject as conformist or overly trusting when in fact

the person is simply trying to be helpful. Researchers should also realize that Hispanic respondents might express agreement with a particular statement merely out of politeness.

3. **Anticipate family dynamics.** Generally speaking, Hispanic cultures have strong family loyalties. Asking subjects to reveal information about another family member may make them uncomfortable or even angry. The Maríns add that in the home, a researcher's request to speak privately with a Hispanic woman may provoke suspicion or outright disapproval from her husband or father.

4. **Take your time.** Spanish cultures, the Maríns explain, tend to place the quality of relationships above simply getting a job done. A non-Hispanic researcher who tries to hurry an interview with a Hispanic family out of a desire not to delay the family's dinner may be considered rude for not proceeding at a more sociable and relaxed pace.

5. **Think about personal space.** Finally, Hispanics typically maintain closer physical contact than many non-Hispanics. Thus researchers who seat themselves across the room from their subjects may seem standoffish. Researchers might also wrongly label Hispanics as "pushy" if they move closer than non-Hispanic people find comfortable.

Of course, Hispanics differ among themselves just as people in any category do, and these generalizations apply to some more than others. But investigators should be aware of cultural dynamics when carrying out any research, especially in the United States, where hundreds of distinctive categories of people make up our multicultural society.

What Do You Think?

1. Give a specific example of damage to a study that might take place if researchers are not sensitive to the culture of their subjects.

2. What do researchers need to do to avoid the kinds of problems noted here?

3. Discuss the research process with classmates from various cultural backgrounds. In what ways are the concerns raised by people of different cultural backgrounds similar? In what ways do they differ?

Finally, there are global dimensions to research ethics. Before beginning research in another country, an investigator must become familiar enough with that society to understand what people *there* are likely to regard as a violation of privacy or a source of personal danger. In a diverse society such as the United States, the same rule applies to studying people whose cultural background differs from your own. The Thinking About Diversity box on page 44 offers some tips on the sensitivity outsiders should apply when studying Hispanic communities.

Research Methods

(2.5) Explain why a researcher might choose each of sociology's research methods.

A **research method** is *a systematic plan for doing research*. Four commonly used methods of sociological investigation are experiments, surveys, participant observation, and the use of existing data. None is better or worse than any other. Rather, just as a carpenter selects a particular tool for a specific task, researchers select a method—or mix several methods—according to whom they want to study and what they wish to learn.

 Watch in **MySocLab**
Video: *The Basics: Sociological Theory and Research*

Testing a Hypothesis: The Experiment

The **experiment** is *a research method for investigating cause and effect under highly controlled conditions*. Experiments closely follow the logic of science, and experimental research is typically *explanatory*, asking not just what happens but also why. In most cases, researchers create an experiment to test a **hypothesis**, *a statement of a possible relationship between two (or more) variables*. A hypothesis typically takes the form of an *if-then* statement: *If* this particular thing were to happen, *then* that particular thing will result.

In an experiment, a researcher gathers the evidence needed to reject or not to reject the hypothesis in four steps: (1) State which variable is the *independent variable* (the "cause" of the change) and which is the dependent variable (the "effect," the thing that is changed). (2) Measure the initial value of the dependent variable. (3) Expose the dependent variable to the independent variable (the "cause" or "treatment"). (4) Measure the dependent variable again to see what change, if any, took place. If the expected change took place, the experiment supports the hypothesis; if not, the hypothesis must be modified.

But a change in the dependent variable could be due to something other than the supposed cause. (Think back to our discussion of spurious correlations on page 38.) To be certain that they identify the correct cause, researchers carefully control other factors that might affect the outcome of the experiment. Such control is easiest to achieve in a laboratory, a setting specially constructed to neutralize outside influences.

Another strategy to gain control is dividing subjects into an *experimental group* and a *control group*. Early in the study, the researcher measures the dependent variable for subjects in both groups but later exposes only the experimental group to the independent variable or treatment. (The control group typically gets a *placebo*, a treatment that the members of the group think is the same but really has no effect on the experiment.) Then the investigator measures the subjects in both groups again. Any factor occurring during the course of the research that influences people in the experimental group (say, a news event) would do the same to those in the control group, thus controlling or "washing out" the factor. By comparing the before and after measurements of the two groups, a researcher can learn how much of the change is due to the independent variable.

experiment a research method for investigating cause and effect under highly controlled conditions

hypothesis a statement of a possible relationship between two (or more) variables

The Hawthorne Effect

Researchers need to be aware that subjects' behavior may change simply because they are getting special attention, as one classic experiment revealed. In the late 1930s, the Western Electric Company hired researchers to investigate worker productivity in its Hawthorne factory near Chicago (Roethlisberger & Dickson, 1939). One experiment tested the hypothesis that increasing the available lighting would raise worker output. First, researchers measured worker productivity or output (the dependent variable). Then they increased the lighting (the independent variable) and measured output a second time. Productivity had gone up, a result that supported the hypothesis. But when the research team later turned the lighting back down, productivity increased again. What was going on? The researchers concluded that the employees were working harder (even if they could not see as well) simply because people were paying attention to them and measuring their output. Although this conclusion has been called into question by the results of later research, social scientists still use the term **Hawthorne effect** to refer to *a change in a subject's behavior caused simply by the awareness of being studied* (Leavitt & List, 2009).

Hawthorne effect a change in a subject's behavior caused simply by the awareness of being studied

Illustration of an Experiment: The "Stanford County Prison"

Prisons can be violent settings, but is this due simply to the "bad" people who end up there? Or as Philip Zimbardo suspected, does the prison itself somehow cause violent behavior? This question led Zimbardo to devise a fascinating experiment, which he called the "Stanford County Prison" (Zimbardo, 1972; Haney, Banks, & Zimbardo, 1973).

Zimbardo thought that once inside a prison, even emotionally healthy people are likely to engage in violence. Thus Zimbardo treated the *prison setting* as the independent variable capable of causing *violence,* the dependent variable.

To test this hypothesis, Zimbardo's research team constructed a realistic-looking "prison" in the basement of the psychology building on the campus of California's Stanford University. Then they placed an ad in the local newspaper, offering to pay young men to help with a two-week research project. To each of the seventy who responded they administered a series of physical and psychological tests and then selected the healthiest twenty-four.

The next step was to randomly assign half the men to be "prisoners" and half to be "guards." The plan called for the guards and prisoners to spend the next two weeks in the mock prison. The prisoners began their part of the experiment soon afterward when the city police "arrested" them at their homes. After searching and handcuffing the men, the police drove them to the local police station, where they were fingerprinted. Then police transported their captives to the Stanford prison, where the guards locked them up. Zimbardo started his video camera rolling and watched to see what would happen next.

The experiment turned into more than anyone had bargained for. Both guards and prisoners soon became embittered and hostile toward one another. Guards humiliated

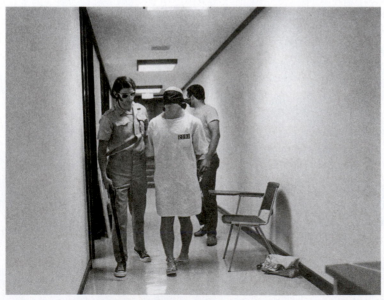

Philip Zimbardo's research helps explain why violence is a common element in our society's prisons. At the same time, his work demonstrates the dangers that sociological investigation poses for subjects and the need for investigators to observe ethical standards that protect the welfare of people who participate in research.

the prisoners by assigning them tasks such as cleaning out toilets with their bare hands. The prisoners resisted and insulted the guards. Within four days, the researchers removed five prisoners who displayed "extreme emotional depression, crying, rage and acute anxiety" (Haney, Banks, & Zimbardo, 1973:81). Before the end of the first week, the situation had become so bad that the researchers had to cancel the experiment. Zimbardo explains:

> The ugliest, most base, pathological side of human nature surfaced. We were horrified because we saw some boys (guards) treat others as if they were despicable animals, taking pleasure in cruelty, while other boys (prisoners) became servile, dehumanized robots who thought only of escape, of their own individual survival and of their mounting hatred for the guards. (Zimbardo, 1972:4)

The events that unfolded at the "Stanford County Prison" supported Zimbardo's hypothesis that prison violence is rooted in the social character of the jail setting, not in the personalities of guards and prisoners. This finding raises questions about our society's prisons, suggesting the need for basic reform. Notice, too, that this experiment shows the potential of research to threaten the physical and mental well-being of subjects. Such dangers are not always as obvious as they were in this case. Therefore, researchers must carefully consider the potential harm to subjects at all stages of their work and halt any study, as Zimbardo did, if subjects suffer harm of any kind.

EVALUATE In carrying out the "Stanford County Prison" study, the researchers chose to do an experiment because they were interested in testing a hypothesis. In this case, Zimbardo and his colleagues wanted to find out if the prison setting itself (rather than the personalities of individual guards and prisoners) is the cause of prison violence. The fact that the "prison" erupted in violence—even using guards and prisoners with "healthy" profiles—supports their hypothesis.

CHECK YOUR LEARNING What was Zimbardo's conclusion? How might Zimbardo's findings help explain the abuse of Iraqi prisoners by U.S. soldiers after the 2003 invasion?

Asking Questions: Survey Research

A **survey** is *a research method in which subjects respond to a series of statements or questions on a questionnaire or in an interview.* The most widely used of all research methods, the survey is well suited to studying what cannot be observed directly, such as political attitudes or religious beliefs. Sometimes surveys provide clues about cause and effect, but typically they yield *descriptive* findings, painting a picture of people's views on some issue.

Population and Sample

A survey targets some **population**, *the people who are the focus of research.* Lois Benjamin, in her study of racism described at the beginning of this chapter, studied a select population—talented African Americans. Other surveys, such as political polls that predict election results, treat every adult in the country as the population.

Obviously, contacting millions of people is impossible for even the best-funded and most patient researcher. Fortunately, there is an easier way that yields accurate results: Researchers collect data from a **sample**, *a part of a population that represents the whole.* Benjamin chose 100 talented African Americans as her sample. National political polls typically survey a sample of about 1,000 people.

Everyone uses the logic of sampling all the time. If you look at students sitting near you and notice five or six heads nodding off, you might conclude that the class finds the day's lecture dull. In reaching this conclusion, you are making a judgment about *all* the people in the class (the population) from observing *some* of your classmates (the sample).

But how can researchers be sure that a sample really represents the entire population? One way is through *random sampling,* in

population the people who are the focus of research

sample a part of a population that represents the whole

which researchers draw a sample from the population at random so that every person in the population has an equal chance of being selected. The mathematical laws of probability dictate that a random sample is likely to represent the population as a whole. Selecting a random sample usually involves listing everyone in the population and using a computer to make random selections to make up the sample.

Beginning researchers sometimes make the mistake of assuming that "randomly" walking up to people on the street or in a mall produces a sample that is representative of the entire city. But this technique does *not* produce a random sample because it does not give every person an equal chance to be included in the study. For one thing, on any street or in any mall whether in a rich neighborhood or near a college campus, we will find more of some kinds of people than others. The fact that the researcher may find some categories of people to be more approachable than others is another source of bias.

Although constructing a good sample is no simple task, it offers a considerable savings in time and expense. We are spared the tedious work of contacting everyone in a population, yet we can obtain essentially the same results.

Using Questionnaires

Selecting subjects is just the first step in carrying out a survey. Also needed is a plan for asking questions and recording answers. Most surveys use a questionnaire for this purpose.

A **questionnaire** is *a series of written questions a researcher presents to subjects.* One type of questionnaire provides not only the questions but also a selection of fixed responses (similar to a multiple-choice examination). This *closed-ended format* makes it fairly easy to analyze the results, but by narrowing the range of responses, it can also distort the findings. For example, Frederick Lorenz and Brent Bruton (1996) found that the number of hours per week students say they study for a college course depends on the options offered to them on the questionnaire. When the researchers presented students with options ranging from one hour or less to nine hours or more, 75 percent said that they studied four hours or less per week. But when subjects in a comparable group were given choices ranging from four hours or less to twelve hours or longer (a higher figure that suggests students should study more), they suddenly became more studious; only 34 percent reported that they studied four hours or less each week.

A second type of questionnaire, using an *open-ended format,* allows subjects to respond freely, expressing various shades of opinion. The drawback of this approach is that the researcher has to make sense out of what can be a very wide range of answers.

The researcher must also decide how to present questions to subjects. Most often, researchers use a *self-administered survey,* mailing or e-mailing questionnaires to respondents and asking them to complete the form and send it back. Since no researcher is present when subjects read the questionnaire, it must be both inviting and clearly written. *Pretesting* a self-administered questionnaire with a small number of people before sending it to the entire sample can prevent the costly problem of finding out—too late—that instructions or questions were confusing.

Using the mail or e-mail allows a researcher to contact a large number of people over a wide geographic area at minimal expense. But many people who receive such questionnaires treat them as junk mail, so typically no more than half are completed and returned (in 2010, 74 percent of people returned U.S. Census Bureau forms). Researchers must send follow-up mailings (or, as the Census Bureau does, visit people's homes) to urge reluctant subjects to respond.

Finally, keep in mind that many people are not capable of completing a questionnaire on their own. Young children obviously cannot, nor can many hospital patients or a surprising number of adults who simply lack the required reading and writing skills.

survey a research method in which subjects respond to a series of statements or questions on a questionnaire or in an interview

questionnaire a series of written questions a researcher presents to subjects

interview a series of questions a researcher asks respondents in person

Conducting Interviews

An **interview** is *a series of questions a researcher asks respondents in person.* In a closed-format design, researchers read a question or statement and then ask the subject to select a response from several that are presented. More commonly, however, interviews are open-ended so that subjects can respond as they choose and researchers can probe with follow-up questions. In either case, the researcher must guard against influencing a subject, which can be as easy as raising an eyebrow when a person begins to answer.

Although subjects are more likely to complete a survey if contacted personally by the researcher, interviews have some disadvantages: Tracking people down can be costly and takes time, especially if subjects do not live in the same area. Telephone interviews allow far greater "reach," but the impersonality of cold calls by telephone (especially when reaching answering machines) can lower the response rate.

Focus groups are a type of survey in which a small number of people representing a target population are asked for their opinions about some issue or product. Here a sociology professor asks students to evaluate textbooks for use in her introductory class.

In both questionnaires and interviews, how a question is worded greatly affects how people answer. For example, when asked during the 2008 presidential campaign if Barack Obama's race would make them less likely to vote for him, only 3 or 4 percent of people said yes. Yet if the question was changed to ask if the United States is ready to elect a black president, then almost 20 percent expressed some doubt. Similarly, if researchers asked U.S. adults if they support our military, a large majority of people said yes. Yet when researchers asked people if they supported what the military was trying to do in Iraq, most said no.

When it comes to survey questions, the exact wording will always affect responses. This is especially true if emotionally loaded language is used. Any words that trigger an emotional response in subjects will sway the results. For instance, using the expression "welfare mothers" rather than "women who receive public assistance" adds an emotional element to a question that encourages people to express a negative attitude.

Another problem is that researchers may confuse respondents by asking a double question, such as "Do you think that the government should reduce the deficit by cutting spending and raising taxes?" The issue here is that a subject could very well agree with one part of the question but not the other, so that forcing a subject to say yes or no distorts the opinion the researcher is trying to measure.

Conducting a good interview means standardizing the technique—treating all subjects in the same way. But this, too, can be problematic. Drawing people out requires establishing rapport, which in turn depends on responding naturally to the particular person being interviewed, as you would in a normal conversation. In the end, researchers have to decide where to strike the balance between uniformity and rapport (Lavin & Maynard, 2001).

Illustration of Survey Research: Studying the African American Elite

This chapter began by explaining how Lois Benjamin came to investigate the effects of racism on talented African American men and women. Benjamin suspected that personal achievement did not prevent hostility based on skin color. She believed this because of her own negative experiences after becoming the first black professor at the University of Tampa. But was she the exception or the rule? To answer this question, Benjamin set out to discover whether—and if so, how—racism affected other successful African Americans.

Benjamin chose to interview subjects rather than distribute a questionnaire because she wanted to talk with her subjects, ask follow-up questions, and pursue topics that might come up in conversation. A second reason Benjamin favored interviews over questionnaires is that racism is a sensitive topic. A supportive investigator can make it easier for subjects to respond to painful questions more freely.

Because conducting interviews takes a great deal of time, Benjamin had to limit the number of people in her study. Benjamin settled for a sample of 100 men and women. Even this small number kept Benjamin busy for more than two years as she scheduled interviews, traveled all over the country, and met with her respondents. She spent two more years analyzing the tapes of her interviews, deciding what the hours of talk told her about racism, and writing up her results.

Benjamin began by interviewing people she knew and asking them to suggest others. This strategy is called *snowball sampling* because the number of individuals included grows rapidly over time. Snowball sampling is an easy way to do research: We begin with familiar people who introduce us to their friends and colleagues. The drawback is that snowball sampling rarely produces a sample that is representative of the larger population. Benjamin's sample probably contained many like-minded individuals, and it was certainly biased toward people willing to talk openly about race. She understood these problems and tried to include in her sample people of both sexes, of different ages, and from different regions of the country. The Thinking About Diversity box presents a statistical profile of Benjamin's respondents and some tips on how to read tables.

Thinking About Diversity: Race, Class, and Gender

Lois Benjamin's African American Elite: Using Tables in Research

Say you want to present a lot of information about a diverse population. How do you do it quickly and easily? The answer is by using a *table*. A table provides a lot of information in a small amount of space, so learning to read tables can increase your reading efficiency. When you spot a table, look first at the title to see what information it contains. The title of the table presented here provides a profile of the 100 subjects participating in Lois Benjamin's research. Across the top of the table, you will see eight variables that describe these men and women. Reading down each column, note the categories within each variable; the percentages in each column add up to 100.

Starting at the top left, we see that Benjamin's sample was mostly men (63 percent, versus 37 percent women). In terms of age, most of the respondents (68 percent) were in the middle stage of life, and most grew up in a predominantly black community in the South or in the North or Midwest region of the United States.

These individuals are indeed a professional elite. Notice that half have earned either a doctorate (32 percent) or a medical or law degree (17 percent). Given their extensive education (and Benjamin's own position as a professor), we should not be surprised that the largest share (35 percent) work in academic institutions. In terms of income, these are wealthy individuals, with most (64 percent) earning more than $50,000 annually back in 1990 (a salary that only 42 percent of full-time workers make even today).

Finally, we see that these 100 individuals are generally left-of-center in their political views. In part, this reflects their extensive schooling (which encourages progressive thinking) and the tendency of academics to fall on the liberal side of the political spectrum.

What Do You Think?

1. Why are statistical data, such as those in this table, an efficient way to convey a lot of information?

2. Looking at the table, can you determine how long it took most people to become part of this elite? Explain your answer.

3. Do you see any ways in which this African American elite might differ from a comparable white elite? If so, what are the differences you see?

The Talented One Hundred: Lois Benjamin's African American Elite

Sex	Age	Childhood Racial Setting	Childhood Region	Highest Educational Degree	Job Sector	Income	Political Orientation
Male 63%	35 or younger 6%	Mostly black 71%	West 6%	Doctorate 32%	College or university 35%	More than $50,000 64%	Radical left 13%
Female 37%	36 to 54 68%	Mostly white 15%	North or Midwest 32%	Medical or law 17%	Private, for-profit 17%	$35,000 to $50,000 18%	Liberal 38%
	55 or older 26%	Racially mixed 14%	South 38%	Master's 27%	Private, non-profit 9%	$20,000 to $34,999 12%	Moderate 28%
			Northeast 12%	Bachelor's 13%	Government 22%	Less than $20,000 6%	Conservative 5%
			Other 12%	Less 11%	Self-employed 14%		Depends on issue 14%
					Retired 3%		Unknown 2%
100%	100%	100%	100%	100%	100%	100%	100%

SOURCE: Adapted from Lois Benjamin, *The Black Elite: Facing the Color Line in the Twilight of the Twentieth Century* (Chicago: Nelson-Hall, 1991), p. 276.

Benjamin based all her interviews on a series of questions with an open-ended format so that her subjects could say whatever they wished. As usually happens, the interviews took place in a wide range of settings. She met subjects in offices (hers or theirs), in hotel rooms, and in cars. So as not to be distracted by having to take notes, Benjamin tape-recorded the conversations, which lasted from two-and-one-half to three hours.

As research ethics demand, Benjamin offered full anonymity to participants. Even so, many—including notables such as Vernon E. Jordan Jr. (former president of the National Urban League) and Yvonne Walker-Taylor (first woman president of Wilberforce University)—were used to being in the public eye and allowed Benjamin to use their names.

What surprised Benjamin most about her research was how eagerly many people responded to her request for an interview. These normally busy men and women seemed to want to go out of their way to contribute to her project. Benjamin reports, too, that once the interviews were under way, many became very emotional, and about 40 of her 100 subjects cried. For them, apparently, the research provided a chance to release feelings and share experiences that they had never revealed to anyone before. How did Benjamin respond to the expression of such sentiments? She reports that she cried right along with her respondents.

Of the research orientations described earlier in the chapter, you will see that Benjamin's study fits best under interpretive sociology (she explored what race meant to her subjects) and critical sociology (she undertook the study partly to document that racial prejudice still exists). Many of her subjects reported fearing that race might someday undermine their success, and others spoke of a race-based "glass ceiling" preventing them from reaching the highest positions in our society. Benjamin concluded that despite the improving social standing of African Americans, black people in the United States still feel the sting of racial hostility.

EVALUATE Professor Benjamin chose the survey as her method because she wanted to ask a lot of questions and gather information from her subjects. Certainly, some of the information she collected could have been done using a questionnaire. But she decided to carry out interviews because she was dealing with a complex and sensitive topic. Interacting with her subjects one on one for several hours, Benjamin could put them at ease, discuss personal matters, and ask them follow-up questions.

CHECK YOUR LEARNING Do you think this research could have been carried out by a white sociologist? Why or why not?

In the Field: Participant Observation

Lois Benjamin's research demonstrates that sociological investigation takes place not only in laboratories but also "in the field," that is, where people carry on their everyday lives. The most widely used strategy for field study is **participant observation**, *a research method in which investigators systematically observe people while joining them in their routine activities.*

Read in **MySocLab** **Document:** *Strip Club: Gender, Power, and Sex Work* by Kim Price-Glynn

This method allows researchers an inside look at social life in any natural setting, from a nightclub to a religious seminary. Sociologists call their account of social life in some setting a *case study.* Cultural anthropologists use participant observation to study other societies, calling this method *fieldwork* and calling their research results an *ethnography.*

At the beginning of a field study, most investigators do not have a specific hypothesis in mind. In fact, they may not yet realize what the important questions will turn out to be. Thus most participant observation is *exploratory* and *descriptive.*

As its name suggests, participant observation has two sides. On one hand, getting an insider's look depends on becoming a participant in the setting—"hanging out" with the research subjects and trying to act, think, and even feel the way they do. Compared to experiments and survey research, participant observation has few hard-and-fast rules. But

research method a systematic plan for doing research

experiment a research method for investigating cause and effect under highly controlled conditions

survey a research method in which subjects respond to a series of statements or questions on a questionnaire or in an interview

participant observation a research method in which investigators systematically observe people while joining them in their routine activities

use of existing sources a research method in which a researcher uses data already collected by others

it is precisely this flexibility that allows investigators to explore the unfamiliar and adapt to the unexpected.

Unlike other research methods, participant observation may require that the researcher enter the setting not for a week or two but for months or even years. At the same time, however, the researcher must maintain some distance while acting as an observer, mentally stepping back to record field notes and later to interpret them. Because the investigator must both "play the participant" to win acceptance and gain access to people's lives and "play the observer" to maintain the distance needed for thoughtful analysis, there is an inherent tension in this method. Carrying out the twin roles of insider participant and outsider observer often comes down to a series of careful compromises.

Most sociologists perform participant observation alone, so they—and readers, too—must remember that the results depend on the work of a single person. Participant observation usually falls within interpretive sociology, yielding mostly qualitative data—the researcher's accounts of people's lives and what they think of themselves and the world around them—although researchers sometimes collect some quantitative (numerical) data. From a scientific point of view, participant observation is a "soft" method that relies heavily on personal judgment and lacks scientific rigor. Yet its personal approach is also a strength: Where a high-profile team of sociologists administering formal surveys might disrupt many social settings, a sensitive participant observer can often gain important insight into people's behavior.

Illustration of Participant Observation: Studying the Homeless in Jackson, Mississippi

Did you ever wonder what life was like in some new and unfamiliar place? For one young sociologist, this question has been at the center of his life. Joseph "Piko" Ewoodzie was born in Ghana, in West Africa, and moved to the United States with his family as a teenager. His father's work as a preacher required the family to move frequently, and in the process of moving, Ewoodzie had to find his way into several new communities, from midwestern Illinois to East Coast New York, and from the low-income South Bronx to the more affluent White Plains.

In 2012, Ewoodzie found himself back in the Midwest, about to embark on research for a doctoral dissertation in sociology. Already familiar with some regions of the United States, Ewoodzie had long wanted to see firsthand what life was like in the Deep South. In addition, he was curious about the lives of people whom we sometimes think of as the "poorest of the poor," those without a place to live. So he decided to study the homeless population of Jackson, Mississippi. More specifically, he set out to understand how this population, living at the margins of society, managed to get something to eat on a regular basis.

Like anyone engaged in sociological investigation, Ewoodzie considered a range of research methods. Should he develop a questionnaire and then walk around downtown Jackson asking anyone who appeared to be homeless to fill one out? Should he try to get an office on the campus of a local college and invite homeless people to come in and sit down for an interview? It was easy to see that neither of these strategies would be likely to work. Besides, Ewoodzie wanted to do more than gather information about the eating habits of homeless people. He was eager to experience their social world for himself and to discover how they lived, where they slept, and with whom they socialized. So he decided to move to Jackson and immerse himself in the homeless community. In short, he decided to become a participant observer.

Ewoodzie knew participant observation was the right method for his study, but he was still unsure of the exact steps needed to accomplish his research goal. On his first Monday morning in Jackson, he stopped by Peaches Café. He needed breakfast and this seemed as good a choice as any, and it offered the opportunity to try his hand at engaging the local people. A woman who introduced herself as Ms. Stella was single-handedly working the grill and serving the food. Ewoodzie sat down at the counter and as the bacon sizzled, tried to figure out what to do next. Should he tell her he was a graduate student in sociology? Should he mention his interest in studying food?

After a while, he mustered up the courage to engage in small talk with a couple of guys in a booth behind him. They were talking about a basketball game that, luckily, he had watched on television the night before. He chatted with them until the topic of conversation

Participant observation is a method of sociological research that allows a researcher to investigate people as they go about their everyday lives in some "natural" setting. At its best, participant observation makes you a star in your own reality show; but living in what may be a strange setting far from home for months at a time is always challenging. Here, Joseph Ewoodzie observes students from a local college helping to provide a meal to homeless people.

switched to something he knew nothing about and, feeling awkward, he disengaged. His first day on the job had already taught him how difficult starting the process of fieldwork can be.

When Ewoodzie returned to Peaches the following day, the same two gentlemen were there. He exchanged greetings with them, falling into a conversation that, this time, covered a wider range of topics. The next day, it seemed almost natural to pick up the conversation with the two men, Ms. Stella, and several other customers. Ewoodzie was well on his way to becoming a "regular." Now he was in a position to strike up conversations with others and to begin learning about life in Jackson. Researchers call this part of the research experience the process of "breaking in" to the new social scene, a step that takes patience and persistence. One thing that helped in this case was Ewoodzie's accent, which identified him as a non-Southerner. Hearing his voice, people were curious and quick to ask him where he was from. When they found out he was from Ghana, the locals—all of whom were African Americans—wanted to learn about life there.

These conversations gave Ewoodzie the opening he needed to ask about life in Jackson. But he needed to move ahead because he wanted to focus his study on homeless people. From the contacts he had made in the café, he learned about the "Opportunity Center," a nearby facility that served homeless people as a day shelter. The next step in the research was to visit the Opportunity Center.

When Ewoodzie first arrived at the Opportunity Center, affectionately known as "the OC," he met Ray and Billy, working at the reception desk. He would find out later that, at that time, they were both homeless. Within a few days, Ewoodzie was able to make friends with Ray and Billy. They were eager to help him and offered to provide information about the Opportunity Center and the people it served.

Ewoodzie soon learned that, on a typical day, the Opportunity Center served about 100 men and about a dozen women, providing a place to store personal belongings, to make phone calls, and to use bathrooms and showers. Further, the OC served as an address that clients could use to apply for a job or seek government assistance. The facility also was a social center for most of the clients, a place where they could stay informed about how others were doing and also exchange information about new opportunities for food and places to sleep.

Ray and Billy were a good source of information about Jackson's soup kitchens and shelters. They also filled Ewoodzie in on various other locations, such as parks, churches, and bus stations, where people who are homeless eat, sleep, and just hang out. With this new information in hand, Ewoodzie knew what steps were needed to complete his research. Over several months, working in the field for ten to twelve hours a day, he visited all of these facilities and locations and in the process became immersed in the lives of Jackson's homeless men.

Billie and Ray's assistance illustrates the importance of *key informants* in field research. Such people are not only a source of information but also serve to introduce a researcher to others in the community. Using a key informant allows easy access to that person's social network. Knowing people to contact in each new setting—and being able to say "I'm a friend of Billy and Ray; they said I should get in touch with you"—is obviously very helpful in gaining additional information. But using a key informant also has risks. Because any person has a particular circle of acquaintances, a key informant's guidance is certain to "spin" or bias the study in one way or another. In addition, in the eyes of others, the reputation of the key informant—whether good or bad—usually rubs off on the investigator. So although a key informant is helpful early on, a skillful participant observer will soon seek a broader range of contacts.

Over the months that followed, Ewoodzie spent most of each day joining in conversations with homeless people. He learned about their lives and about how they made it through the day. As he got to know people better, he explained more about his research project to them. Because he had taken time to build meaningful relationships with his subjects, most people not only were willing to talk to him but also offered intimate details about their lives—personal details that a researcher never would have gathered in a single meeting using a questionnaire or even an interview. Ewoodzie also credits some of this warm reception to the South's cultural tradition of hospitality.

As is typical of researchers who choose the method of participant observation, Ewoodzie jotted down notes as he engaged in conversation. Sometimes when he couldn't keep pace with the flow of information, he excused himself to go to the bathroom just so that he could have a few minutes to write down detailed notes. At times, he recorded conversations using his smart phone, but he did so only after asking and receiving the subject's permission. After each day in the field, he spent several evening hours at the apartment turning his rough notes into a detailed record of his research.

As he neared the end of his months in the field, Ewoodzie reflected about what he had learned. Some homeless people had relatives living in or near Jackson and spent some time staying with family. But most of the homeless people he had come to know were living on their own and appeared regularly at the Opportunity Center and at various soup kitchens and homeless shelters. Most of the people he studied were unemployed; some had income from paid work, and most received income assistance from the government. He was surprised to learn that they used the money they had not so much for food as for medical needs and necessities such as clothing, for entertainment, and to supply their addictions to alcohol or other drugs.

But perhaps the most surprising finding to come from Ewoodzie's (forthcoming) research was that the typical homeless person in Jackson rarely, if ever, went a day without food. Four or five soup kitchens operated in the city on any given day, and church groups and other organizations also offered food at least several days each week. Sometimes students from a nearby college would bring leftovers from the campus dining hall to feed the homeless at a nearby park. So, as long as a person stayed connected to the social network that revolved around the OC, there was no need to go hungry. At the same time, there was little choice about what to eat, and the quality of the food was uneven at best. In addition, food was not available around the clock. Breakfast and lunch were pretty much a sure thing; dinner was less certain. As a result, most homeless individuals built a "stash" from meals available earlier in the day to which they could turn later on if nothing else was available.

From his participant observation research, Ewoodzie learned much more than he intended at the outset. He saw that the greatest challenge faced by this group of homeless men was not, in fact, a lack of food. Perhaps their most immediate concern was the limited availability of safe and comfortable shelter. The homeless population of the city was greater than the number of available beds in shelters so that, especially in cold or wet weather, not everyone could find a safe space indoors. A second concern was the lack of public transportation to many places that homeless people frequented. And looking ahead, Ewoodzie concluded that the greatest long-term need among the homeless was improved literacy skills, which he saw as essential to their being able to look for, get, and hold jobs.

Research of this kind is often used by officials in government and other organizations in formulating and redefining public policy. Ewoodzie hopes that his research will result in programs that go beyond *maintaining* homeless people in their present state toward *expanding* their opportunities to become self-supporting community members.

EVALUATE To study the homeless population in Jackson, Mississippi, Joseph Ewoodzie chose participant observation as his research method. This was a good choice because he did not have a specific hypothesis to test, nor did he know at the outset exactly what the questions or issues would turn out to be. Ewoodzie was able to complete his study for very little money, although he had to spend long days for many months in the field. By moving to Jackson and then both participating in and observing the social life at the city's facilities for homeless people, Ewoodzie gradually was able to build an understanding and to prepare a detailed description of the way of life typical of the city's homeless population.

CHECK YOUR LEARNING Give an example of a topic for sociological research that would be best studied using (1) an experiment, (2) a survey, and (3) participant observation.

Using Available Data: Existing Sources

Not all research requires investigators to collect their own data. Sometimes sociologists analyze existing sources, data already collected by others.

The most widely used statistics in social science are gathered by government agencies. The U.S. Census Bureau carries out a comprehensive statistical study of the U.S. population every ten years and this agency also continuously updates a wide range of data about the U.S. population. National Map 2–1 provides a look at the share of households that filled out and returned their information forms as part of the 2010 national census.

Seeing Ourselves

Explore minority populations in your local community and in counties across the United States in **MySocLab**

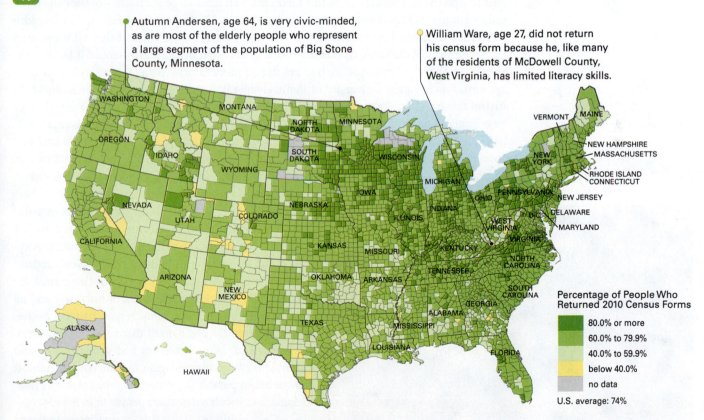

Autumn Andersen, age 64, is very civic-minded, as are most of the elderly people who represent a large segment of the population of Big Stone County, Minnesota.

William Ware, age 27, did not return his census form because he, like many of the residents of McDowell County, West Virginia, has limited literacy skills.

Percentage of People Who Returned 2010 Census Forms
- 80.0% or more
- 60.0% to 79.9%
- 40.0% to 59.9%
- below 40.0%
- no data

U.S. average: 74%

NATIONAL MAP 2-1 Census Participation Rates across the United States

Every ten years, the Census Bureau conducts a census of all U.S. households, mailing forms to each address. About 75 percent of U.S. households returned their form, as directed by law. But participation rates were higher in some places than in others. Looking at the map, what patterns do you see? What might explain lower return rates in Southwest Texas along the Mexican border and in New Mexico? What might explain the higher return rates in urban areas close to both coasts and in the Midwest?

Source: U.S. Census Bureau, 2010.

Comparable data about Canada are available from Statistics Canada, a branch of that nation's government. For international data, there are various publications of the United Nations and the World Bank. In short, data about the whole world are as close as your library or the Internet.

Using available data, whether government statistics or the findings of individual researchers, saves time and money. This approach has special appeal to sociologists with low budgets. For anyone, however, government data are generally more extensive and more accurate than what most researchers could obtain on their own.

But using existing data has problems of its own. For one thing, available data may not exist in the exact form needed. For example, you may be able to find the average salary paid to professors at your school but not separate figures for the amounts paid to women and to men. Further, there are always questions about the meaning and accuracy of work done by others. For example, in his classic study of suicide, Emile Durkheim soon discovered that there was no way to know whether a death classified as a suicide was really an accident or vice versa. In addition, various agencies use different procedures and categories in collecting data, so comparisons may be difficult. In the end, then, using existing data is a little like shopping for a used car: There are plenty of bargains out there, but you have to shop carefully.

Illustration of the Use of Existing Sources: A Tale of Two Cities

Why might one city have been home to many famous people and another have produced hardly any famous people at all? To those of us living in the present, historical data offer a key to unlocking secrets of the past. The award-winning study *Puritan Boston and Quaker Philadelphia,* by E. Digby Baltzell (1979), is a good example of how a researcher can use available data to do historical research.

This story begins when Baltzell made a chance visit to Bowdoin College in Maine. As he walked into the college library, he saw up on the wall three large portraits—of the celebrated author Nathaniel Hawthorne, the famous poet Henry Wadsworth Longfellow, and Franklin Pierce, the fourteenth president of the United States. He soon learned that all three men were members of the same class at Bowdoin, graduating in 1825. How could it be, Baltzell wondered, that this small college had graduated more famous people in a single year than his own, much bigger University of Pennsylvania had graduated in its entire history? To answer this question, Baltzell was soon paging through historical documents to see whether New England had really produced more famous people than his native Pennsylvania.

What were Baltzell's data? He turned to the *Dictionary of American Biography,* twenty volumes profiling more than 13,000 outstanding men and women in fields such as politics, law, and the arts. The dictionary told Baltzell *who* was great, and he realized that the longer the biography, the more important the person is thought to be.

By the time Baltzell had identified the seventy-five individuals with the longest biographies, he saw a striking pattern. Massachusetts had the most by far, with twenty-one of the seventy-five top achievers. The New England states, combined, claimed thirty-one of the entries. By contrast, Pennsylvania could boast of only two, and all the states in the Middle Atlantic region had just twelve. Looking more closely, Baltzell discovered that most of New England's great achievers had grown up in and around the city of Boston. Again, in stark contrast, almost no one of comparable standing came from his own Philadelphia, a city with many more people than Boston.

What could explain this remarkable pattern? Baltzell drew inspiration from the German sociologist Max Weber (1958, orig. 1904–05), who argued that a region's record of achievement was influenced by its major religious beliefs (see Chapter 4, "Society"). In the religious differences between Boston and Philadelphia, Baltzell found the answer to his puzzle.

The unexpected observation that three famous people—Nathaniel Hawthorne, Henry Wadsworth Longfellow, and Franklin Pierce—were all members of a single class at a small New England college prompted sociologist E. Digby Baltzell to analyze how different religious ethics affected patterns of achievement in New England and Pennsylvania.

Boston was originally a Puritan settlement, founded by people who highly valued the pursuit of excellence and public achievement. Philadelphia, by contrast, was settled by Quakers, who believed in equality and avoided public notice.

Both the Puritans and the Quakers were fleeing religious persecution in England, but the two religions produced quite different cultural patterns. Convinced of humanity's innate sinfulness, Boston's Puritans built a rigid society in which family, church, and school regulated people's behavior. The Puritans celebrated hard work as a means of glorifying God and viewed public success as a reassuring sign of God's blessing. In short, Puritanism fostered a disciplined life in which people both sought and respected achievement.

Philadelphia's Quakers, by contrast, built their way of life on the belief that all human beings are basically good. They saw little need for strong social institutions to "save" people from sinfulness. They believed in equality, so that even those who became rich considered themselves no better than anyone else. Thus rich and poor alike lived modestly and discouraged one another from standing out by seeking fame or running for public office.

In Baltzell's sociological imagination, Boston and Philadelphia took the form of two social "test tubes": Puritanism was poured into one, Quakerism into the other. Centuries later, we can see that different "chemical reactions" occurred in each case. The two belief systems led to different attitudes toward personal achievement, which in turn shaped the history of each region. Today, we can see that Boston's Kennedys (despite being Catholic) are only one of that city's many families who exemplify the Puritan pursuit of recognition and leadership. By contrast, there has never been even one family with such public stature in the entire history of Philadelphia.

Baltzell's study used scientific logic, but it also illustrates the interpretive orientation by showing how people understood their world. His research reminds us that sociological investigation often involves mixing research orientations to fit a particular problem.

EVALUATE The main reason Baltzell chose to use existing sources is that this is a good way to learn about history. The *Dictionary of American Biography* offers a great deal of information about people who lived long ago and obviously are not available for an interview. At the same time, existing sources were not created with the purpose of answering a modern-day sociologist's questions. For this reason, using such documents requires a critical eye and a good deal of creative thinking.

CHECK YOUR LEARNING What other questions about life in the past might you wish to answer using existing sources? What sources might you use to find the answers?

The Summing Up table provides a quick review of the four major methods of sociological investigation. We now turn to our final consideration: the link between research results and sociological theory.

Summing Up

Four Research Methods				
	Experiment	**Survey**	**Participant Observation**	**Existing Sources**
Application	For explanatory research that specifies relationships between variables Generates quantitative data	For gathering information about issues that cannot be directly observed, such as attitudes and values Useful for descriptive and explanatory research Generates quantitative or qualitative data	For exploratory and descriptive study of people in a "natural" setting Generates qualitative data	For exploratory, descriptive, or explanatory research whenever suitable data are available
Advantages	Provides the greatest opportunity to specify cause-and-effect relationships Replication of research is relatively easy.	Sampling, using questionnaires, allows surveys of large populations. Interviews provide in-depth responses.	Allows study of "natural" behavior Usually inexpensive	Saves time and expense of data collection Makes historical research possible
Limitations	Laboratory settings have an artificial quality. Unless the research environment is carefully controlled, results may be biased.	Questionnaires must be carefully prepared and may yield a low return rate. Interviews are expensive and time-consuming.	Time-consuming Replication of research is difficult. Researcher must balance roles of participant and observer.	Researcher has no control over possible biases in data. Data may only partially fit current research needs.

The Interplay of Theory and Method

2.6 Illustrate the use of inductive and deductive logical thought.

No matter how sociologists collect their data, they have to turn facts into meaning by building theory. They do this in two ways: inductive logical thought and deductive logical thought.

Inductive logical thought is *reasoning that transforms specific observations into general theory.* In this mode, a researcher's thinking runs from the specific to the general and goes something like this: "I have some interesting data here; I wonder what they mean." Baltzell's research illustrates the inductive logical model. His data showed that one region of the country (the Boston area) had produced many more high achievers than another (the Philadelphia region). He worked "upward" from ground-level observations to the high-flying theory that religious values were a key factor in shaping people's attitudes toward achievement.

A second type of logical thought moves "downward," in the opposite direction: **Deductive logical thought** is *reasoning that transforms general theory into specific hypotheses suitable for testing.* The researcher's thinking runs from the general to the specific: "I have this hunch about human behavior; let's collect some data and put it to the test." Working deductively, the researcher first states the theory in the form of a hypothesis and then selects a method by which to test it. To the extent that the data support the hypothesis, a researcher concludes that the theory is correct; on the other hand, data that refute the hypothesis suggest that the theory needs to be revised or perhaps rejected entirely.

Philip Zimbardo's "Stanford County Prison" experiment illustrates deductive logic. Zimbardo began with the general theory that a social environment can change human behavior. He then developed a specific, testable hypothesis: Placed in a prison setting, even emotionally well-balanced young men will behave violently. The violence that erupted soon after his experiment began supported Zimbardo's hypothesis. Had his experiment produced friendly behavior between prisoners and guards, his hypothesis clearly would have been wrong.

Just as researchers often employ several methods over the course of one study, they typically use *both* kinds of logical thought. Figure 2–2 illustrates both types of reasoning: inductively building theory from observations and deductively making observations to test a theory.

Finally, turning facts into meaning usually involves organizing and presenting statistical data. Precisely how sociologists arrange their numbers affects the conclusions they reach. In short, preparing their results amounts to spinning reality in one way or another.

Often we conclude that an argument must be true simply because there are statistics to back it up. However, we must look at statistics with a cautious eye. After all, researchers choose what data to present, they interpret their statistics, and they may use tables and graphs to steer readers toward particular conclusions.

inductive logical thought reasoning that transforms specific observations into general theory

deductive logical thought reasoning that transforms general theory into specific hypotheses suitable for testing

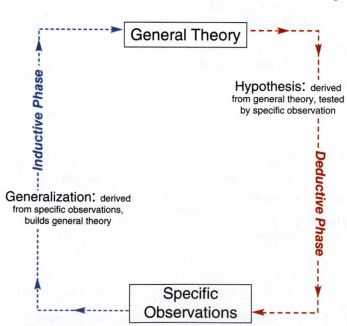

FIGURE 2–2 Deductive and Inductive Logical Thought

Sociologists link theory and method through both inductive and deductive logic.

Putting It All Together: Ten Steps in Sociological Investigation

2.7 Recall the ten important steps in carrying out sociological research.

We can summarize this chapter by outlining ten steps in the process of carrying out sociological investigation. Each step takes the form of an important question.

1. **What is your topic?** Being curious and applying the sociological perspective can generate ideas for social research at any time and in any place. Pick a topic that you find interesting and important to study.

2. **What have others already learned?** You are probably not the first person with an interest in the issue you have selected. Visit the library to see what theories and methods other researchers have applied to your topic. In reviewing the existing research, note problems that have come up to avoid repeating past mistakes.

3. **What, exactly, are your questions?** Are you seeking to explore an unfamiliar social setting? To describe some category of people? To investigate cause and effect among variables? If your study is exploratory or descriptive, identify *whom* you wish to study, *where* the research will take place, and *what* kinds of issues you want to explore. If it is explanatory, you must also formulate the hypothesis to be tested and operationalize each variable.

4. **What will you need to carry out research?** How much time and money are available to you? Is special equipment or training necessary? Will you be able to complete the work yourself? You should answer all these questions as you plan the research project.

5. **Are there ethical concerns?** Not all research raises serious ethical questions, but you must be sensitive to this possibility. Can the research cause harm or threaten anyone's privacy? How might you design the study to minimize the chances for injury? Will you promise anonymity to the subjects? If so, how will you ensure that anonymity will be maintained?

6. **What method will you use?** Consider all major research strategies, as well as combinations of methods. Keep in mind that the best method depends on the kinds of questions you are asking as well as the resources available to you.

7. **How will you record the data?** Your research method is a plan for data collection. Record all information accurately and in a way that will make sense later (it may be some time before you actually write up the results of your work). Watch out for any bias that may creep into the research.

8. **What do the data tell you?** Study the data in terms of your initial questions and decide how to interpret the data you have collected. If your study involves a specific hypothesis, you must decide whether the data you collected requires that you confirm, reject, or modify the original hypothesis. Keep in mind that there may be several ways to look at your data, depending on which theoretical approach you use, and you should consider them all.

9. **What are your conclusions?** Prepare a final report stating your conclusions. How does your work advance sociological theory? Does it suggest ways to improve research methods? Does your study have policy implications? What would the general public find interesting in your work? Finally, evaluate your own work. What problems arose during the research process? What questions were left unanswered?

10. **How can you share what you've learned?** Consider submitting your research paper to a campus newspaper or magazine or making a presentation to your class, a campus gathering, or perhaps a meeting of professional sociologists. The point is to share what you have learned with others and to let them respond to your work.

Watch in **MySocLab**
Video: *Social Inequalities: Sociological Theory and Research*

For a closer look at how statistics can be used to spin the truth, **Read More** in **MySocLab**, *Can People Lie with Statistics?*

Seeing Sociology in Everyday Life

What are friends for?

Sociological research is the key to a deeper understanding of our everyday social world and also to knowing more about ourselves. Take friendship, for example. Everyone knows that it is fun to be surrounded by friends. But did you know that friendship has real benefits for human health? What do you think these benefits might be? Take a look at the photos below and on page 61 and learn more about what research has taught us about the positive effects of having friends.

One ten-year study of older people found that those women and men who had many friends were significantly less likely to die over the course of the research than those with few or no friends. Other long-term research confirms that people with friends not only live longer but also healthier lives than those without friends. What are the variables in this study? What conclusion is drawn about the relationship between the variables?

Another study looked at 3,000 women diagnosed with breast cancer and compared the rate of survival for women with many friends with that for women with few or no friends. What do you think they concluded about the effect of friendship on surviving a serious illness?

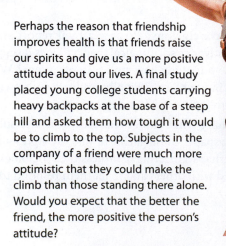

Perhaps the reason that friendship improves health is that friends raise our spirits and give us a more positive attitude about our lives. A final study placed young college students carrying heavy backpacks at the base of a steep hill and asked them how tough it would be to climb to the top. Subjects in the company of a friend were much more optimistic that they could make the climb than those standing there alone. Would you expect that the better the friend, the more positive the person's attitude?

The "friendship effect" improves the health of men, too. A study of older men found that those with many friends had lower rates of heart disease than those without friends. How could you be sure of the causal direction linking these variables? That is, how can we be sure that friendship is improving health rather than good health encouraging friendship?

HINT In the first case (*described on page 60, top right*), researchers defined having friends as the independent variable, and they defined longevity and health as the dependent variables. On average, those with friends (the experimental group) actually lived longer and were healthier than those without friends (the control group). In the second case (*on page 60, left*), researchers found that women with many friends were several times more likely to survive their illness than those without friends. In the third case (*on page 60, bottom right*), researchers found that the longer the people had been friends, the more positive the subject's attitude about making the climb turned out to be. The fourth case (above) reminds us that correlation does not demonstrate cause and effect. This study, covering over six years, looked at more than 700 men, some with many friends (the experimental group) and also other men of comparable health (the control group) and few friends. Finding those with friends had better heart health tells us that friendship is the independent or causal variable. Long live friendship!

Seeing Sociology in *Your* Everyday Life

1. The research studies discussed above demonstrate that friendship means more to people than we might think. Recall Emile Durkheim's study of suicide in Chapter 1. How did he use sociological research to uncover more about the importance of relationships? Which one of the research methods discussed in this chapter did he use in his study of suicide?

2. Go to MySocLab and click on the Student Resources link to access the Sociology in Focus blog, where you can read the latest posts by a team of young sociologists who apply the sociological perspective to topics of popular culture.

3. As this chapter has explained, sociology involves more than a distinctive perspective and theoretical approaches. The discipline is also about learning—gaining more information about the operation of society all around us. It's possible that you will go on to study more sociology and you might even end up doing sociological research. But there is value in knowing how to carry out a sound research project even if you never do it yourself. The value of such knowledge lies in this: In a society that feeds us a steady diet of information, knowing how to gather accurate information gives you the skills to assess what you read. Go to the "Seeing Sociology in *Your* Everyday Life" feature in MySocLab to learn more about how the material in this chapter enhances your critical thinking ability.

Making the Grade

Basics of Sociological Investigation

(2.1) Explain how scientific evidence often challenges common sense. (pages 33–34)

👁 **Watch** the **Video** in **MySocLab**

Two basic requirements for **sociological investigation** are

- Know how to apply the sociological perspective.
- Be curious and ready to ask questions about the world around you.

What people accept as "truth" differs around the world.

- **Science**—a logical system that bases knowledge on direct, systematic observation—is one form of truth.
- Scientific evidence gained from sociological research often challenges common sense.

science a logical system that bases knowledge on direct, systematic observation

empirical evidence information we can verify with our senses

Research Orientations: Three Ways to Do Sociology

(2.2) Describe sociology's three research orientations. (pages 35–42)

Positivist sociology studies society by systematically observing social behavior.

Positivist sociology

- requires carefully operationalizing variables and ensuring that measurement is both reliable and valid
- observes how variables are related and tries to establish cause and effect
- sees an objective reality "out there"
- favors quantitative data
- is well suited to research in a laboratory
- demands that researchers be objective and suspend their personal values and biases as they conduct research
- is loosely linked to structural-functional theory

Interpretive sociology focuses on the meanings that people attach to behavior.

Interpretive sociology

- sees reality as constructed by people in the course of their everyday lives
- favors qualitative data
- is well suited to research in a natural setting
- is linked to symbolic-interaction theory

Critical sociology uses research to bring about social change.

Critical sociology

- asks moral and political questions
- focuses on inequality
- rejects the principle of objectivity, claiming that all research is political
- is linked to social-conflict theory

positivist sociology the study of society based on systematic observation of social behavior

concept a mental construct that represents some part of the world in a simplified form

variable a concept whose value changes from case to ca

measurement a procedure for determining the value of a variable in a specific case

operationalize a variable specifying exactly what is to be measured before assigning a value to a variable

reliability consistency in measurement

validity actually measuring exactly what you intend to measure

cause and effect a relationship in which change in on variable causes change in another

independent variable the variable that causes the chang

dependent variable the variable that changes

correlation a relationship in which two (or more) variables change together

spurious correlation an apparent but false relationshi between two (or more) variables that is caused by some other variable

control holding constant all variables except one in order to see clearly the effect of that variable

objectivity personal neutrality in conducting research

replication repetition of research by other investigato

interpretive sociology the study of society that focuses on the meanings people attach to their social world

critical sociology the study of society that focuses on the need for social change

Gender and Research

(2.3) Identify the importance of gender in sociological research. (pages 42–43)

Gender, involving both researcher and subjects, can affect research in five ways:

- androcentricity
- overgeneralizing
- gender blindness
- double standards
- interference

gender the personal traits and social positions that members of a society attach to being female or male

Research Ethics

(2.4) Discuss the importance of ethics to sociological research. (pages 43–45)

Researchers must

- protect the privacy of subjects
- obtain the informed consent of subjects
- indicate all sources of funding
- submit research to an institutional review board (IRB) to ensure it doesn't violate ethical standards

Methods: Strategies for Doing Research

(2.5) Explain why a researcher might choose each of sociology's research methods. (pages 45–57)

 Watch the Video in MySocLab    Explore the Map in MySocLab

📖 Read the Document in MySocLab

The **experiment** allows researchers to study cause and effect between two or more variables in a controlled setting.

- Researchers conduct an experiment to test a **hypothesis**, a statement of a possible relationship between two (or more) variables.

Example of an experiment: Zimbardo's "Stanford County Prison"

Survey research uses questionnaires or interviews to gather subjects' responses to a series of questions.

- Surveys typically yield descriptive findings, painting a picture of people's views on some issue.

Example of a survey: Benjamin's "Talented One Hundred"

Through **participant observation**, researchers join with people in a social setting for an extended period of time.

- Participant observation, also called *fieldwork*, allows researchers an "inside look" at a social setting. Because researchers are not attempting to test a specific hypothesis, their research is exploratory and descriptive.

Example of participant observation: Ewoodzie's "Study of the Homeless in Jackson, Mississippi"

Sometimes researchers analyze **existing sources**, data collected by others.

- Using existing sources, especially the widely available data collected by government agencies, can save researchers time and money.
- Existing sources are the basis of historical research.

Example of using existing sources: Baltzell's "Puritan Boston and Quaker Philadelphia"

research method a systematic plan for doing research

experiment a research method for investigating cause and effect under highly controlled conditions

hypothesis a statement of a possible relationship between two (or more) variables

Hawthorne effect a change in a subject's behavior caused simply by the awareness of being studied

survey a research method in which subjects respond to a series of statements or questions on a questionnaire or in an interview

population the people who are the focus of research

sample a part of a population that represents the whole

questionnaire a series of written questions a researcher presents to subjects

interview a series of questions a researcher asks respondents in person

participant observation a research method in which investigators systematically observe people while joining them in their routine activities

The Interplay of Theory and Method

(2.6) Illustrate the use of inductive and deductive logical thought. (page 58)

- Using inductive logical thought, a researcher moves "upward" from the specific to the general.
- Using deductive logical thought, a researcher moves "downward" from the general to the specific.

inductive logical thought reasoning that transforms specific observations into general theory

deductive logical thought reasoning that transforms general theory into specific hypotheses suitable for testing

Putting It All Together: Ten Steps in Sociological Research

(2.7) Recall the ten important steps in carrying out sociological research. (page 59)

👁 Watch the Video in MySocLab

- The ten steps move from selecting a topic to sharing the results of research.
- Each of the steps is presented in the form of a question.

3 Culture

 Listen to Chapter 3 in MySocLab

LEARNING OBJECTIVES

3.1 Explain the development of culture as a human strategy for survival.

3.2 Identify common elements of culture.

3.3 Discuss dimensions of cultural difference and cultural change.

3.4 Apply sociology's macro-level theories to gain greater understanding of culture.

3.5 Critique culture as limiting or expanding human freedom.

the Power of Society

to guide our attitudes on social issues such as abortion

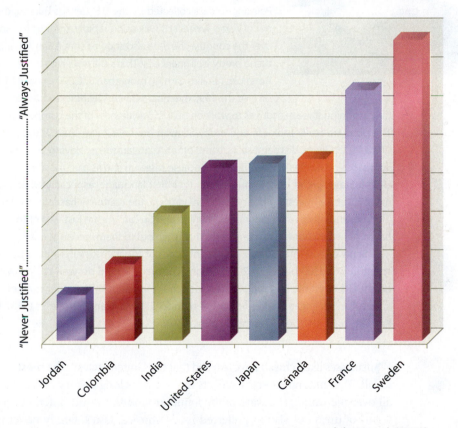

Survey Question: "Please tell me whether you think abortion can always be justified, never be justified, or something in between."

"Always Justified" ....

"Never Justified" ....

Jordan Colombia India United States Japan Canada France Sweden

Source: Inglehart et al. (2012)

Is how we feel about abortion as "personal" an opinion as we may think? If we compare the attitudes of people around the world, we see remarkable variation from country to country. People living in Sweden, for example, claim that abortion is almost always justified; people living in Jordan, by contrast, almost never support this procedure. For people living in the United States, abortion is an issue on which public opinion is fairly evenly divided. By making such global comparisons, we see that society guides people's attitudes on various issues, which is part of the way of life we call culture.

Chapter Overview

This chapter focuses on the concept of "culture," which refers to a society's entire way of life. Notice that the root of the word "culture" is the same as that of the word "cultivate," suggesting that people living together in a society actually "grow" their way of life over time.

Min-jun Lee is intently studying the computer screen when his wife, Su-bin, pulls up a chair.

"I'm trying to finish organizing our investments," Min-jun explains, speaking in Korean.

"I didn't realize that we could do that online in our own language," Su-bin says, reading the screen. "That's great. I like that a lot."

Min-jun and Su-bin are not alone in feeling this way. Back in 1990, executives of Charles Schwab & Co., a large investment brokerage corporation, gathered at the company's headquarters in San Francisco to discuss ways to expand their business. They came up with the idea that the company would profit by giving greater attention to the increasing cultural diversity of the United States. Pointing to data collected by the U.S. Census Bureau, they saw that the number of Asian Americans was rising rapidly, not just in San Francisco but also all over the country. The data also showed that Asian Americans, on average, were doing pretty well financially. That's still true, with more than half of today's Asian American families earning more than $70,000 a year (U.S. Census Bureau, 2012).

At the 1990 meeting, Schwab's leaders decided to launch a diversity initiative, assigning three executives to work on building awareness of the company among Asian Americans. The program really took off, and today Schwab employs more than 300 people who speak Korean, Chinese, Japanese, Vietnamese, or some other Asian language. Having account executives who speak languages other than English is smart because research shows that most immigrants who come to the United States prefer to communicate in their first language, especially when dealing with important matters such as investing their money. In addition, the company has launched websites using Korean, Chinese, and other Asian languages. Min-jun and Su-bin Lee are just two of the millions of people who have opened accounts with companies that reach out to them in a language other than English.

Schwab now manages a significant share of the investments made by Asian Americans, who spent about $300 billion in 2011. So any company would do well to follow the lead Schwab has taken. Other ethnic and racial categories that represent even larger markets in the United States are African Americans (spending more than $553 billion) and Hispanics ($632 billion) (Fattah, 2002; Karrfalt, 2003; U.S. Department of Labor, 2012).

Businesses like Schwab have learned that the United States is the most *multicultural* nation of all. This cultural diversity reflects the country's long history of receiving immigrants from all over the world. The ways of life found around the world differ, not only in language and forms of dress but also in preferred foods, musical tastes, family patterns, and beliefs about right and wrong. Some of the world's people have many children, while others have few; some honor the elderly, while others seem to glorify youth. Some societies are peaceful, while others are warlike; and societies around the world embrace a thousand different religious beliefs as well as particular ideas about what is polite and rude, beautiful and ugly, pleasant and repulsive. This amazing human capacity for so many different ways of life is a matter of human culture.

What Is Culture?

(3.1) Explain the development of culture as a human strategy for survival.

Culture is *the ways of thinking, the ways of acting, and the material objects that together form a people's way of life.* Culture includes what we think, how we act, and what we own. Culture is both our link to the past and our guide to the future.

Human beings around the globe create diverse ways of life. Such differences begin with outward appearance: Contrast the women shown here from Ethiopia, India, Kenya, Thailand, South Yemen, and the United States and the men from Taiwan (Republic of China), Ecuador, and Papua New Guinea. Less obvious but of even greater importance are internal differences, since culture also shapes our goals in life, our sense of justice, and even our innermost personal feelings.

To understand all that culture is, we must consider both thoughts and things. **Nonmaterial culture** is *the ideas created by members of a society*, ideas that range from art to Zen. **Material culture,** by contrast, is *the physical things created by members of a society*, everything from armchairs to zippers.

Culture shapes not only what we do but also what we think and how we feel—elements of what we commonly, but wrongly, describe as "human nature." The warlike Yąnomamö of the Brazilian rain forest think aggression is natural, but halfway around the world, the Semai of Malaysia live quite peacefully. The cultures of the United States and Japan both stress achievement and hard work, but members of our society value individualism more than the Japanese, who value collective harmony.

culture the ways of thinking, the ways of acting, and the material objects that together form a people's way of life

nonmaterial culture the ideas created by members of a society

material culture the physical things created by members of a society

Thinking Globally

Confronting the Yąnomamö: The Experience of Culture Shock

A small aluminum motorboat chugged steadily along the muddy Orinoco River, deep within South America's vast tropical rain forest. The anthropologist Napoleon Chagnon was nearing the end of a three-day journey to the home territory of the Yąnomamö, one of the most technologically simple societies on Earth.

Some 12,000 Yąnomamö live in villages scattered along the border of Venezuela and Brazil. Their way of life could not be more different from our own. The Yąnomamö wear little clothing and live without electricity, automobiles, cell phones, or other conveniences most people in the United States take for granted. Their traditional weapon, used for hunting and warfare, is the bow and arrow. Since most of the Yąnomamö knew little about the outside world, Chagnon would be as strange to them as they would be to him.

By 2:00 in the afternoon, Chagnon had almost reached his destination. The heat and humidity were becoming unbearable. He was soaked with perspiration, and his face and hands swelled from the bites of gnats swarming around him. But he hardly noticed, so excited was he that in just a few moments, he would be face to face with people unlike any he had ever known.

Chagnon's heart pounded as the boat slid onto the riverbank. He and his guide climbed from the boat and headed toward the sounds of a nearby village, pushing their way through the dense undergrowth. Chagnon describes what happened next:

> I looked up and gasped when I saw a dozen burly, naked, sweaty, hideous men staring at us down the shafts of their drawn arrows! Immense wads of green tobacco were stuck between their lower teeth and lips, making them look even more hideous, and strands of dark green slime dripped or hung from their nostrils—strands so long that they clung to their [chests] or drizzled down their chins.
>
> My next discovery was that there were a dozen or so vicious, underfed dogs snapping at my legs, circling me as if I were to be their next meal. I just stood there holding my notebook, helpless and pathetic. Then the stench of the decaying vegetation and filth hit me and I almost got sick. I was horrified. What kind of welcome was this for the person who came here to live with you and learn your way of life, to become friends with you? (1992:11–12)

Fortunately for Chagnon, the Yąnomamö villagers recognized his guide and lowered their weapons. Though reassured that he would survive the afternoon, Chagnon was still shaken by his inability to make any sense of the people surrounding him. And this was going to be his home for the next year and a half! He wondered why he had given up physics to study human culture in the first place.

What Do You Think?

1. Can you think of an experience of your own similar to the one described here? Explain what happened.

2. Do you think you ever caused culture shock in others? What did you learn from this experience?

3. Why is it difficult for people who live within different cultural systems to interact without discomfort? At the same time, are there benefits gained from doing so?

---

culture shock personal disorientation when experiencing an unfamiliar way of life

Given the extent of cultural differences in the world and people's tendency to view their own way of life as "natural," it is no wonder that travelers often find themselves feeling uneasy as they enter an unfamiliar culture. This uneasiness is **culture shock**, *personal disorientation when experiencing an unfamiliar way of life.* People can experience culture shock right here in the United States when, say, African Americans explore an Iranian neighborhood in Los Angeles, college students venture into the Amish countryside in Ohio, or New Yorkers travel through small towns in the Deep South. But culture shock is most intense when we travel abroad: The Thinking Globally box tells the story of a researcher from the United States as he makes his first visit to the home of the Yąnomamö living in the Amazon region of South America.

January 2, high in the Andes Mountains of Peru. Here in the rural highlands, people are poor and depend on one another. The culture is built on cooperation among family members and neighbors who have lived nearby for many generations. Today, we spent an hour watching a new house being constructed. A young couple had invited their families and many friends, who arrived at about 6:30 in the morning, and right away they began building. By midafternoon, most of the work was finished, and the couple then provided a large meal, drinks, and music that continued for the rest of the day.

All societies contain cultural differences that can provoke a mild case of culture shock. This woman traveling on a British subway is not sure what to make of the woman sitting next to her, who is wearing the Muslim full-face veil known as the *niqab*.

No particular way of life is "natural" to humanity, even though most people around the world view their own behavior that way. The cooperative spirit that comes naturally in small communities high in the Andes Mountains of Peru is very different from the competitive living that comes naturally to many people in, say, Chicago or New York City. Such variations come from the fact that as human beings, we join together to create our own way of life. Every other animal, from ants to zebras, behaves very much the same all around the world because behavior is guided by *instincts*, biological programming over which the species has no control. A few animals—notably chimpanzees and related primates—have the capacity for limited culture, as researchers have noted by observing them using tools and teaching simple skills to their offspring. But the creative power of humans is far greater than that of any other form of life and has resulted in countless ways of "being human." In short, *only humans rely on culture rather than instinct to create a way of life and ensure our survival* (Harris, 1987; Morell, 2008). To understand how human culture came to be, we need to look back at the history of our species.

Culture and Human Intelligence

Scientists tell us that our planet is 4.5 billion years old (see the timeline in MySocLab). Life appeared about 1 billion years later. Fast-forward another 2 to 3 billion years, and we find dinosaurs ruling Earth. It was after these giant creatures disappeared, some 65 million years ago, that our history took a crucial turn with the appearance of the animals we call primates.

The importance of primates is that they have the largest brains relative to body size of all living creatures. About 12 million years ago, primates began to evolve along two different lines, setting humans apart from the great apes, our closest relatives. Some 5 million years ago, our distant human ancestors climbed down from the trees of Central Africa to move about in the tall grasses. There, walking upright, they learned the advantages of hunting in groups and made use of fire, tools, and weapons; built simple shelters; and fashioned basic clothing. These Stone Age achievements may seem modest, but they mark the point at which our ancestors set off on a distinct evolutionary course, making culture their primary strategy for survival. By about 250,000 years ago, our own species, *Homo sapiens* (Latin for "intelligent person"), had finally emerged. Humans continued to evolve so that by about 40,000 years ago, people who looked more or less like us roamed the planet. With larger brains, these "modern" *Homo sapiens* developed culture rapidly, as the wide range of tools and cave art from this period suggests.

About 12,000 years ago, the founding of permanent settlements and the creation of specialized occupations in the Middle East (today's Iraq and Egypt) marked the "birth of civilization." About this point, the biological forces we call instincts had mostly disappeared, replaced by a more efficient survival scheme: *fashioning the natural environment for ourselves.* Ever since, humans have made and remade their world in countless ways, resulting in today's fascinating cultural diversity.

Culture, Nation, and Society

The term "culture" calls to mind other similar terms, such as "nation" and "society," although each has a slightly different meaning. *Culture* refers to a shared way of life. A *nation* is a political entity, a territory with designated borders, such as the United States, Canada, Peru, or Zimbabwe. *Society*, the topic of Chapter 4, is the organized interaction of people who typically live in a nation or some other specific territory.

The United States, then, is both a nation and a society. But many nations, including the United States, are *multicultural*; that is, their people follow various ways of life that blend (and sometimes clash).

How Many Cultures?

In the United States, how many cultures are there? One indicator of culture is language; the Census Bureau lists 382 languages spoken in this country—almost half of them (169) are native languages, with the rest brought by immigrants from nations around the world (U.S. Census Bureau, 2012).

Globally, experts document almost 7,000 languages, suggesting the existence of just as many distinct cultures. Yet with the number of languages spoken around the world declining, roughly half of those 7,000 languages now are spoken by fewer than 10,000 people. Experts expect that the coming decades may see the disappearance of hundreds of these languages, and perhaps half the world's languages may even disappear before the end of this century (Crystal, 2010). Languages on the endangered list include Gullah, Pennsylvania German, and Pawnee (all spoken in the United States), Han (spoken in northwestern Canada), Oro (spoken in the Amazon region of Brazil), Sardinian (spoken on the European island of Sardinia), Aramaic (the language of Jesus of Nazareth, still spoken in the Middle East), Nu Shu (a language spoken in southern China that is the only one known to be used exclusively by women), and Wakka Wakka as well as several other Aboriginal tongues spoken in Australia. As you might expect, when a language is becoming extinct, the last people to speak it are the oldest members of a society. What accounts for the worldwide decline in the number of spoken languages? The main reason is globalization itself, including high-technology communication, increasing international migration, and the expanding worldwide economy (UNESCO, 2001; Barovick, 2002; Hayden, 2003; Lewis, 2009).

The Elements of Culture

(3.2) Identify common elements of culture.

● **Watch** in **MySocLab**
Video: *The Basics: Culture*

Although cultures vary greatly, they all have common elements, including symbols, language, values, and norms. We begin our discussion with the one that is the basis for all the others: symbols.

Symbols

Like all creatures, humans use their senses to experience the surrounding world, but unlike others, we also try to give the world *meaning*. Humans transform elements of the world into *symbols*. A **symbol** is *anything that carries a particular meaning recognized by people who share a culture*. A word, a whistle, a wall covered with graffiti, a flashing red light, a raised fist—all serve as symbols. We can see the human capacity to create and manipulate symbols reflected in the very different meanings associated with the simple act of winking an eye, which can convey interest, understanding, or insult.

Societies create new symbols all the time. The Seeing Sociology in Everyday Life box on page 71 describes some of the "cyber-symbols" that have developed along with our increasing use of computers for communication.

We are so dependent on our culture's symbols that we take them for granted. However, we become keenly aware of the importance of a symbol when someone uses it in an

symbol anything that carries a particular meaning recognized by people who share a culture

Seeing Sociology in Everyday Life

New Symbols in the World of Instant Messaging

Molly: gr8 to c u!
Greg: u 2
Molly: jw about next time
Greg: idk, lotta work!
Molly: np, xoxoxo
Greg: thanx, bcnu

The world of symbols changes all the time. One reason that people create new symbols is that we develop new ways to communicate. Today, 88 percent of adults in the United States own cell phones and three-quarters of them—especially those who are young—use mobile text-messaging on a regular basis. Researchers report that cell phone owners between eighteen and twenty-four years of age typically send or receive more than 100 messages a day (Pew Research Center, 2011). Here are some of the most common text-messaging symbols:

b be
bff beft friends, forever
bc because
b4 before
b4n 'bye for now
bbl be back later
bcnu be seeing you
brb be right back
btw by the way
cu see you
def definitely
g2g got to go
gal get a life
gmta great minds think alike
gr8 great
hagn have a good night

h&k hugs and kisses
idc I don't care
idt I don't think
idk I don't know
imbl it must be love
irl in real life
jk just kidding
jw just wondering
j4f just for fun
kc keep cool
l8r later
lmao laugh my ass off
ltnc long time no see
myob mind your own business
np no problem
nvm never mind
omg oh my gosh
pcm please call me
plz please
prbly probably
qpsa ¿Que pasa?
rt right
sup what's up
thanx thanks
u you
uok you okay?
ur you are
w/ with
w/e whatever
w/o without
wan2 want to
wtf what the f*ck
y why
2l8 too late
? question
2 to, two
4 for, four

What Do You Think?

1. What does the creation of symbols such as those listed here suggest about culture?

2. Do you think that using such symbols is a good way to communicate? Does it lead to confusion or misunderstanding? Why or why not?

3. What other kinds of symbols can you think of that are new to your generation?

Sources: J. Rubin (2003), Berteau (2005), Bacher (2009), Lenhart (2010), Pew Research Center (2011).

unconventional way, as when a person burns a U.S. flag during a political demonstration. Entering an unfamiliar culture also reminds us of the power of symbols; culture shock is really the inability to "read" meaning in strange surroundings. Not understanding the symbols of a culture leaves a person feeling lost and isolated, unsure of how to act, and sometimes frightened.

Culture shock is a two-way process. On one hand, travelers *experience* culture shock when encountering people whose way of life is different. For example, North Americans who consider dogs beloved household pets might be put off by the Masai of eastern Africa, who ignore dogs and never feed them. The same travelers might be horrified to find that in parts of Indonesia and the People's Republic of China, people roast dogs for dinner.

On the other hand, a traveler may *inflict* culture shock on local people by acting in ways that offend them. A North American who asks for a steak in an Indian restaurant may unknowingly offend Hindus, who consider cows sacred and never to be eaten. Global travel provides almost endless opportunities for this kind of misunderstanding.

Symbolic meanings also vary within a single society. To some people in the United States, a fur coat represents a prized symbol of success, but to others it represents the inhumane treatment of animals. In the debate about flying the Confederate flag over the South Carolina statehouse a few years ago, some people saw the flag as a symbol of regional pride, but others saw it as a symbol of racial oppression.

People throughout the world communicate not just with spoken words but also with bodily gestures. Because gestures vary from culture to culture, they can occasionally be the cause of misunderstandings. For instance, the commonplace "thumbs up" gesture we use to express "Good job!" can get a person from the United States into trouble in Greece, Iran, and a number of other countries, where people take it to mean "Up yours!"

Language

An illness in infancy left Helen Keller (1880–1968) blind and deaf. Without these two senses, she was cut off from the symbolic world, and her social development was greatly limited. Only when her teacher, Anne Mansfield Sullivan, broke through Keller's isolation using sign language did Helen Keller begin to realize her human potential. This remarkable woman, who later became a famous educator herself, recalls the moment she first understood the concept of language:

We walked down the path to the well-house, attracted by the smell of honeysuckle with which it was covered. Someone was drawing water, and my teacher placed my hand under the spout. As the cool stream gushed over one hand, she spelled into the other the word *water*, first slowly, then rapidly. I stood still, my whole attention fixed upon the motions of her fingers. Suddenly I felt a misty consciousness as of something forgotten—a thrill of returning thought; and somehow the mystery of language was revealed to me. I knew then that "w-a-t-e-r" meant the wonderful cool something that was flowing over my hand. That living word awakened my soul; gave it light, hope, joy, set it free!

(Keller, 1903:24)

Language, the key to the world of culture, is *a system of symbols that allows people to communicate with one another*. Humans have created many alphabets to express the hundreds of languages we speak. Several examples are shown in Figure 3–1. Even rules for writing differ: Most people in Western societies write from left to right, but people in northern Africa and western Asia write from right to left, and people in eastern Asia write from top to bottom. Global Map 3–1 on page 73 shows where we find the three most widely spoken languages: English, Chinese, and Spanish.

Language not only allows communication but is also the key to **cultural transmission**, *the process by which one generation passes culture to the next.* Just as our bodies contain the genes of our ancestors, our culture contains countless symbols

إقرأوا	Read	독서
Arabic	English	Korean
Կարդա	διαβάζω	بخوانيد
Armenian	Greek	Farsi
អាន	קְרָא	читать
Cambodian	Hebrew	Russian
閱讀	पढ़ना	¡Ven a leer!
Chinese	Hindi	Spanish

FIGURE 3–1 Human Languages: A Variety of Symbols

Here the English word "read" is written in twelve of the thousands of languages humans use to communicate with one another.

Window on the World

GLOBAL MAP 3–1 Language in Global Perspective

Chinese
- Official language
- Widely spoken second language

Chinese (including Mandarin, Cantonese, and dozens of other dialects) is the native tongue of one-fifth of the world's people, almost all of whom live in Asia. Although all Chinese people read and write with the same characters, they use several dozen dialects. The "official" dialect, taught in schools throughout the People's Republic of China and the Republic of Taiwan, is Mandarin (the dialect of Beijing, China's capital). Cantonese, the language of Canton, is the second most common Chinese dialect; it differs in sound from Mandarin roughly the way French differs from Spanish.

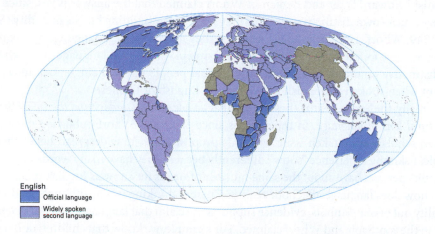

English
- Official language
- Widely spoken second language

English is the native tongue or official language in several world regions (spoken by 5 percent of humanity) and has become the preferred second language in the world.

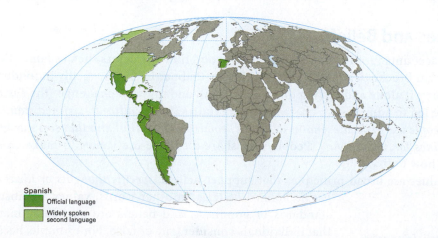

Spanish
- Official language
- Widely spoken second language

The largest concentration of Spanish speakers is in Latin America and, of course, Spain. Spanish is also the second most widely spoken language in the United States.

Sources: Lewis (2009); European Union (2012).

language a system of symbols that allows people to communicate with one another

cultural transmission the process by which one generation passes culture to the next

Sapir-Whorf thesis the idea that people see and understand the world through the cultural lens of language

of those who came before us. Language is the key that unlocks centuries of accumulated wisdom.

Throughout human history, every society has transmitted culture by using speech, a process sociologists call the "oral cultural tradition." Some 5,000 years ago, humans invented writing, although at that time only a privileged few learned to read and write. Not until the twentieth century did high-income nations boast of nearly universal literacy. Still, about 14 percent of U.S. adults (more than 30 million people) are functionally illiterate, unable to read and write in a society that increasingly demands such skills. In low-income countries of the world, at least one-third of adults are illiterate (U.S. Department of Education, 2008; World Bank, 2012).

Language skills may link us with the past, but they also spark the human imagination to connect symbols in new ways, creating an almost limitless range of future possibilities. Language sets humans apart as the only creatures who are self-conscious, aware of our limitations and ultimate mortality, yet able to dream and to hope for a future better than the present.

Does Language Shape Reality?

Does someone who thinks and speaks using Cherokee, an American Indian language, experience the world differently from other North Americans who think in, say, English or Spanish? Edward Sapir and Benjamin Whorf claimed that the answer is yes, since each language has its own distinctive symbols that serve as the building blocks of reality (Sapir, 1929, 1949; Whorf, 1956, orig. 1941). Further, they noted that each language has words or expressions not found in any other symbolic system. Finally, all languages fuse symbols with distinctive emotions so that, as multilingual people know, a single idea may "feel" different when spoken in Spanish rather than in English or Chinese.

Formally, the **Sapir-Whorf thesis** holds that *people see and understand the world through the cultural lens of language.* In the decades since Sapir and Whorf published their work, however, scholars have taken issue with this proposition. The widespread belief that, for example, Eskimos experience "snow" differently because they have many words for it is not true; Inuit speakers have about the same number of words for snow as English speakers do.

So how does language affect our reality? Current thinking is that although we do fashion reality out of our symbols, evidence supports the claim that language does not *determine* reality in the way Sapir and Whorf claimed. For example, we know that children understand the idea of "family" long before they learn that word; similarly, adults can imagine new ideas or things before devising a name for them (Kay & Kempton, 1984; Pinker, 1994).

Values and Beliefs

What accounts for the popularity of Hollywood film characters such as James Bond, Neo, Erin Brockovich, Lara Croft, and Rocky Balboa? Each is ruggedly individualistic, going it alone and relying on personal skill and savvy to challenge "the system." We are led to admire such characters by certain **values**, *culturally defined standards that people use to decide what is desirable, good, and beautiful and that serve as broad guidelines for social living.* People who share a culture use values to make choices about how to live.

Values are broad principles that support **beliefs**, *specific thoughts or ideas that people hold to be true.* In other words, values are abstract standards of goodness, and beliefs are particular matters that individuals consider true or false. For example, because most U.S. adults share the *value* of providing equal opportunities for all, they believe that a qualified woman could serve as president of the United States, as the 2008 campaign of Hillary Clinton demonstrated (NORC, 2013:403).

values culturally defined standards that people use to decide what is desirable, good, and beautiful and that serve as broad guidelines for social living

beliefs specific ideas that people hold to be true

Key Values of U.S. Culture

Because U.S. culture is a mix of ways of life from other countries all around the world, it is highly diverse. Even so, the sociologist Robin Williams Jr. (1970) identified ten values that are widespread in the United States and viewed by many people as central to our way of life:

1. **Equal opportunity.** Most people in the United States favor not *equality of condition* but *equality of opportunity.* We believe that our society should provide everyone with the chance to get ahead according to individual talents and efforts.

2. **Achievement and success.** Our way of life encourages competition so that each person's rewards should reflect personal merit. A successful person is given the respect due a "winner."

How does the popularity of the television show *American Idol* illustrate many of the key values of U.S. culture listed here?

3. **Material comfort.** Success in the United States generally means making money and enjoying what it will buy. Although we sometimes say that "money won't buy happiness," most of us pursue wealth all the same.

4. **Activity and work.** Popular U.S. heroes, from tennis champions Venus and Serena Williams to the winners of television's *American Idol,* are "doers" who get the job done. Our culture values action over reflection and taking control of events over passively accepting fate.

5. **Practicality and efficiency.** We value the practical over the theoretical, what will "get us somewhere" over what is interesting "for its own sake." Many young people hear their parents give the advice: "It's good to enjoy what you study, but major in something that will help you get a job!"

6. **Progress.** We are an optimistic people who, despite waves of nostalgia, believe that the present is better than the past. We celebrate progress, viewing the "very latest" as the "very best."

7. **Science.** We expect scientists to solve problems and improve the quality of our lives. We believe we are rational, logical people, and our focus on science probably explains our cultural tendency (especially among men) to look down on emotion and intuition as sources of knowledge.

8. **Democracy and free enterprise.** Members of our society believe that individuals have rights that governments should not take away. We believe that a just political system is based on free elections in which citizens elect government leaders and on an economy that responds to the choices of individual consumers.

9. **Freedom.** We favor individual initiative over collective conformity. While we accept the idea that everyone has at least some responsibilities to others, we believe that people should look out for themselves and be free to pursue their personal goals.

10. **Racism and group superiority.** Despite strong ideas about equal opportunity and freedom, most people in the United States still judge individuals according to gender, race, ethnicity, and social class. In general, U.S. culture values males over females, whites over people of color, rich over poor, and people with northwestern European backgrounds over those whose ancestors came from other parts of the world. Although we like to describe ourselves as a nation of equals, there is little doubt that some of us are "more equal" than others.

Values: Often in Harmony, Sometimes in Conflict

In many ways, cultural values go together. Williams's list includes examples of *value clusters* that are part of our way of life. For instance, we value activity and hard work because we expect effort to lead to achievement and success and result in greater material comfort.

Sometimes, however, one key cultural value contradicts another. Take the first and last items on Williams's list, for example: People in the United States believe in equality of opportunity, yet they may also look down on others because of their sex or race. Value conflict causes strain and often leads to awkward balancing acts in our beliefs. Sometimes we decide that one value is more important than another by, for example, supporting equal opportunity while opposing same-sex marriage. In such cases, people simply try to live with the contradictions.

Values: Change Over Time

Like all elements of culture, values change over time. People in the United States have always valued hard work. But, in recent years, more people wonder whether hard work is really enough to "get ahead." For many people, too, a single-minded focus on work is giving way to increasing importance on leisure—having time off from work to do things such as reading, travel, or community service that provide enjoyment and satisfaction. Similarly, although the importance of material comfort remains strong, more people are seeking personal growth through meditation and other spiritual activity.

Values: A Global Perspective

Values vary from culture to culture around the world. In general, the values that are important in higher-income countries differ somewhat from those common in lower-income countries.

Because lower-income nations contain populations that are vulnerable, people in these countries develop cultures that value survival. This means that people place a great deal of importance on physical safety and economic security. They worry about having enough to eat and a safe place to sleep at night. Lower-income nations also tend to be traditional, with values that celebrate the past and emphasize the importance of family and religious beliefs. These nations, in which men have most of the power, typically discourage or forbid practices such as divorce and abortion.

People in higher-income countries develop cultures that value individualism and self-expression. These countries are rich enough that most of their people take survival for granted, focusing their attention instead on which "lifestyle" they prefer and how to achieve the greatest personal happiness. In addition, these countries tend to be secular-rational, placing less emphasis on family ties and religious beliefs and more on people thinking for themselves and being tolerant of others who differ from them. In higher-income countries, too, women have social standing more equal to men and there is widespread support for practices such as divorce and abortion (World Values Survey, 2012). Figure 3–2 on page 77 shows how selected countries of the world compare in terms of their cultural values.

Norms

Most people in the United States are eager to gossip about "who's hot" and "who's not." Members of American Indian societies, however, typically condemn such behavior as rude and divisive. Both patterns illustrate the operation of **norms**, *rules and expectations by which a society guides the behavior of its members.* In everyday life, people respond to each other with *sanctions,* rewards or punishments that encourage conformity to cultural norms.

Mores and Folkways

William Graham Sumner (1959, orig. 1906), an early U.S. sociologist, recognized that some norms are more important to our lives than others. Sumner coined the term **mores** (pronounced "MORE-ayz") to refer to *norms that are widely observed and have great moral significance.* Certain mores include *taboos,* such as our society's insistence that adults not engage in sexual relations with children.

Global Snapshot

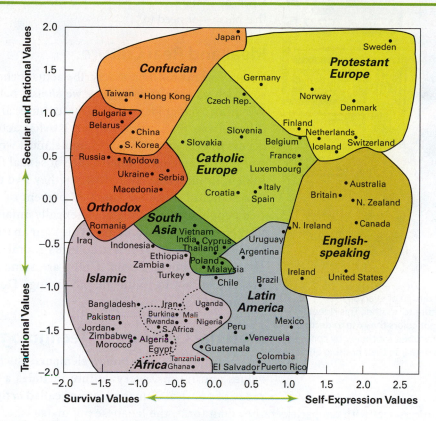

FIGURE 3–2 Cultural Values of Selected Countries

A general global pattern is that higher-income countries tend to be secular and rational and favor self-expression. By contrast, the cultures of lower-income countries tend to be more traditional and concerned with economic survival. Each region of the world has distinctive cultural patterns, including religious traditions, that affect values. Looking at the figure, what patterns can you see? How does the United States compare to Great Britain, France, and other high-income countries?

Source: Inglehart & Welzel (2010).

People pay less attention to **folkways**, *norms for routine or casual interaction*. Examples include ideas about appropriate greetings and proper dress. In short, mores distinguish between right and wrong, and folkways draw a line between right and *rude*. A man who does not wear a tie to a formal dinner party may raise eyebrows for violating folkways. If, however, he were to arrive at the party wearing *only* a tie, he would violate cultural mores and invite a more serious response.

Social Control

Mores and folkways are the basic rules of everyday life. Although we sometimes resist pressure to conform, we can see that norms make our dealings with others more orderly and predictable. Observing or breaking the rules of social life prompts a response from others in the form of either reward or punishment. Sanctions—whether an approving smile or a raised eyebrow—operate as a system of **social control**, *attempts by society to regulate people's thoughts and behavior.*

As we learn cultural norms, we gain the capacity to evaluate our own behavior. Doing wrong (say, downloading a term paper from the Internet) can cause both *shame* (the painful sense that others disapprove of our actions) and *guilt* (a negative judgment we make of ourselves). Of all living things, only cultural creatures can experience shame and

social control attempts by society to regulate people's thoughts and behavior

norms rules and expectations by which a society guides the behavior of its members

mores norms that are widely observed and have great moral significance

folkways norms for routine or casual interaction

Culture **CHAPTER 3** **77**

Standards of beauty—including the color and design of everyday surroundings—vary significantly from one culture to another. This Ndebele couple in South Africa dresses in the same bright colors they use to decorate their home. Members of North American and European societies, by contrast, make far less use of bright colors and intricate detail, so their housing and clothing appear much more subdued.

guilt. This is probably what Mark Twain had in mind when he remarked that people "are the only animals that blush—or need to."

Ideal and Real Culture

Values and norms do not describe actual behavior so much as they suggest how we *should* behave. We must remember that *ideal* culture always differs from *real* culture, which is what actually occurs in everyday life. For example, most women and men agree on the importance of sexual faithfulness in marriage, and most say they live up to that standard. Even so, about 17 percent of married people report having been sexually unfaithful to their spouses at some point in their marriage (NORC, 2013:2549). But a culture's moral standards are important even if they are sometimes broken, calling to mind the old saying "Do as I say, not as I do."

Material Culture and Technology

In addition to symbolic elements such as values and norms, every culture includes a wide range of physical human creations called *artifacts*. The Chinese eat with chopsticks rather than forks, the Japanese put mats rather than rugs on the floor, and many men and women in India prefer flowing robes to the close-fitting clothing common in the United States. The material culture of a people may seem as strange to outsiders as their language, values, and norms.

A society's artifacts partly reflect underlying cultural values. The warlike Yąnomamö carefully craft their weapons and prize the poison tips on their arrows. By contrast, our society's emphasis on individualism and independence goes a long way toward explaining our high regard for the automobile: We own more than 250 million motor vehicles—more than one for every licensed driver—and even in an age of high gasoline prices, many of these are the large sport utility vehicles we might expect rugged, individualistic people to choose.

technology knowledge that people use to make a way of life in their surroundings

In addition to reflecting values, material culture also reflects a society's **technology**, *knowledge that people use to make a way of life in their surroundings.* The more complex a society's technology is, the more its members are able (for better or worse) to shape the world for themselves. Advancements in technology have allowed us to crisscross the country with superhighways and to fill them with automobiles. At the same time, the internal-combustion engines in those cars release carbon dioxide into the atmosphere, which contributes to air pollution and global warming.

Because we attach great importance to science and praise sophisticated technology, people in our society tend to judge cultures with simpler technology as less advanced than our own. Some facts support such an assessment. For example, life expectancy for children born in the United States is more than seventy-eight years; the life span of the Yąnomamö is only about forty years.

However, we must be careful not to make self-serving judgments about other cultures. Although many Yąnomamö are eager to acquire modern technology (such as steel tools and shotguns), they are generally well fed by world standards, and most are very satisfied with their lives (Chagnon, 1992). Remember, too, that while our powerful and complex technology has produced work-reducing devices and seemingly miraculous medical treatments, it has also contributed to unhealthy levels of stress and obesity in the population and created weapons capable of destroying in a blinding flash everything that humankind has achieved.

Finally, technology is not equally distributed within our population. Although many of us cannot imagine life without a personal computer, television, and smart phone, many members of U.S. society cannot afford these luxuries. Others reject them on principle. The Amish, who live in small farming communities in Pennsylvania, Ohio, and Indiana, reject most modern conveniences on religious grounds. With their traditional black clothing and horse-drawn buggies, the Amish may seem like a curious relic of the past. Yet their communities flourish, grounded in strong families that give everyone a sense of identity and purpose. Some researchers who have studied the Amish have concluded that these communities are "islands of sanity in a culture gripped by commercialism and technology run wild" (Hostetler, 1980:4; Kraybill & Olshan, 1994).

New Information Technology and Culture

Many rich nations, including the United States, have entered a postindustrial phase based on computers and new information technology. Industrial production is centered on factories and machinery that generate material goods. By contrast, postindustrial production is based on computers and other electronic devices that create, process, store, and apply information.

In this new information economy, workers need symbolic skills in place of the mechanical skills of the industrial age. Symbolic skills include the ability to speak, write, compute, design, and create images in fields such as art, advertising, and entertainment. In today's computer-based economy, people with creative jobs are generating new cultural ideas, images, and products all the time.

Cultural Diversity: Many Ways of Life in One World

3.3 Discuss dimensions of cultural difference and cultural change.

In the United States, we are aware of our cultural diversity when we hear several different languages being spoken while eating a hot dog on the streets of New York or standing in a school yard in Los Angeles. Compared to a country like Japan, whose historic isolation makes it the most *monocultural* of all high-income nations, centuries of immigration have made the United States the most *multicultural* of all high-income countries.

Between 1820 (when the government began keeping track of immigration) and 2012, more than 80 million people came to our shores. Our cultural mix continues to increase as about 1.3 million people arrive each year. A century ago, almost all immigrants came from Europe; today, almost 80 percent arrive from Latin America or Asia (U.S. Department of Homeland Security, 2012). To understand the reality of life in the United States, we must move beyond broad cultural patterns and shared values to consider cultural diversity.

High Culture and Popular Culture

Cultural diversity involves not just immigration but also social class. In fact, in everyday talk, we usually use the term "culture" to mean art forms such as classical literature, music, dance, and painting. We describe people who regularly go to the opera or the theater as "cultured," because we think they appreciate the "finer things in life."

We speak less kindly of ordinary people, assuming that everyday culture is somehow less worthy. We are tempted to judge the music of Haydn as "more cultured" than hip-hop, couscous as better than cornbread, and polo as more polished than Ping-Pong.

These differences arise because many cultural patterns are readily available to only some members of a society. Sociologists use the term **high culture** to refer to *cultural*

Watch in **MySocLab**
Video: *Sociology in Focus: Culture*

high culture cultural patterns that distinguish a society's elite

popular culture cultural patterns that are widespread among a society's population

patterns that distinguish a society's elite and **popular culture** to designate *cultural patterns that are widespread among a society's population.*

Common sense may suggest that high culture is superior to popular culture, but sociologists are uneasy with such judgments for two reasons. First, neither elites nor ordinary people share all the same tastes and interests; people in both categories differ in many ways. Second, do we praise high culture because it is inherently better than popular culture or simply because its supporters have more money, power, and prestige? For example, there is no difference at all between a violin and a fiddle; however, we name the instrument a violin when it is used to produce classical music typically enjoyed by a person of higher position and we call it a fiddle when the musician plays country tunes appreciated by people with lower social standing.

We should also remember that our country's culture is made up of the life patterns of *all* our people. What's more, this national culture is being created all the time—not just by people whose names are familiar to all of us, but also by countless people including those living in some of the most disadvantaged neighborhoods in the country. The Thinking About Diversity box on page 81 provides a case in point.

Subculture

subculture cultural patterns that set apart some segment of a society's population

The term **subculture** refers to *cultural patterns that set apart some segment of a society's population.* People who ride "chopper" motorcycles, traditional Korean Americans, New England "Yankees," Ohio State football fans, the southern California "beach crowd," Elvis impersonators, and wilderness campers all display subcultural patterns.

It is easy but often inaccurate to place people in some subcultural category because almost everyone participates in many subcultures without necessarily having much commitment to any of them. In some cases, however, cultural differences can set people apart from one another with tragic results. Consider the former nation of Yugoslavia in southeastern Europe. The 1990s' civil war there was fueled by extreme cultural diversity. This *one* small country with a population about equal to the Los Angeles metropolitan area used *two* alphabets, embraced *three* religions, spoke *four* languages, was home to *five* major nationalities, was divided into *six* political republics, and absorbed the cultural influences of *seven* surrounding countries. The cultural conflict that plunged this nation into civil war shows that subcultures are a source not only of pleasing variety but also of tension and even violence.

Watch in **MySocLab**
Video: *Social Inequalities: Culture*

Many people view the United States as a "melting pot" where many nationalities blend into a single "American" culture (Gardyn, 2000). But given so much cultural diversity, how accurate is the "melting pot" image? For one thing, subcultures involve not just *difference* but also *hierarchy.* Too often what we view as "dominant" or "mainstream" culture are patterns favored by powerful segments of the population, and we view the lives of disadvantaged people as "subculture." But are the cultural patterns of rich skiers on the slopes of Aspen, Colorado, any less a subculture than the cultural patterns of low-income skateboarders on the streets of Los Angeles? Some sociologists therefore prefer to level the playing field of society by emphasizing multiculturalism.

Reality television is based on popular culture rather than high culture. *Here Comes Honey Boo Boo* follows seven-year-old Alana Honey Boo Boo Thompson and her parents, who live in rural Georgia. While some critics object to the show as "low-brow," others applaud the portrayal of a "real" low-income family.

Thinking About Diversity: Race, Class, & Gender

Popular Culture Born in the Inner City: The DJ Scene and Hip-Hop Music

Aaron Jerald (AJ) O'Bryant probably never thought he would help change U.S. culture. In 1960, he was born into a social world where the odds were stacked against him. His family lived in a low-income, African American neighborhood on the Lower East Side of Manhattan. Orphaned at thirteen, he moved in with his grandmother, who lived in the South Bronx, close to an intersection that was a known gathering point for local gang members.

In the 1970s, the South Bronx was brewing with social problems. As factories closed, the area lost thousands of good-paying manufacturing jobs, and unemployment and poverty were on the rise. Drug use, crime, and violence became part of everyday life.

Not surprisingly, AJ entered his teenage years thinking that violence was the way to express his frustration. He got into fights on the streets and at school, to the point of being expelled for throwing another student through a window. His grandmother enrolled him at a local school for "at-risk" young people, but he found little to like in the classroom. Within a few years, he dropped out of school and began selling drugs, which earned him fast cash as he tried to stay one step ahead of the police.

Like young people everywhere, AJ wanted to earn the respect of others. He also had a love for music. As the new "DJ" scene emerged in New York City in the mid-1970s, AJ was captivated by Afrika Bambaataa, Grandmaster Flowers, and Pete "DJ" Jones. Perhaps most of all, he idolized a young DJ named Kool Herc. AJ remembers the first time he saw Herc. "People in the Bronx were saying 'Yo, there's this dude named Herc, and this dude is *crazy*.' He was at the park on Sedgewick Avenue. So the next thing is I'm sitting there watching this dude and he's drawing a crowd." AJ was hooked on this music scene and wanted to be part of it.

AJ didn't know the first thing about DJing, but he hung out with other DJs. They became skilled at operating a turntable and playing records, figuring out *which* records to play and *what part* of records people wanted to hear, and they developed a whole set of rules and conventions that would define the new DJ scene.

In the summer of 1977, AJ did his first public performance in the local park. Although people from around New York had come to see the main act, a well-known DJ named Lovebug Star Ski, there were also many people from AJ's community who showed up to see *him*. He knew he was starting to make it as a DJ, and as his reputation spread, AJ lost interest in drug dealing. He was becoming a local hero. AJ explains, "The guys who own the stores close by the park would bring me beer or whatever I wanted for doing my music because it attracted lots of people and made money for them."

AJ's reputation continued to grow as he took part in "battles," competitions between DJs not unlike the competitions for respect in gang culture. In a battle, DJs would each play for an hour, switching back and forth. The DJ who succeeded in working the crowd into a frenzy was the winner.

AJ's big break came as the result of a challenge to battle a DJ named Flash, the star of the South Bronx DJ scene, and to do it in Flash's territory. At first, AJ refused, thinking he could never hope to sway Flash's own neighborhood crowd. But his mentor, Lovebug Star Ski, insisted, and AJ agreed.

The night of the battle, more than 500 people packed the Dixie Club in Flash's neighborhood. Even before the competition started, there were rowdy cheers for Flash. Seeing Flash haul in some new and expensive equipment further intimidated AJ as he began his set. He started with "Groove to Get Down" by T-Connection, "Catch a Groove" by Juice, and "Funky Granny" by Kool & The Gang—rhythms that were funky and new to most of the audience. As he moved from one record to the next, the crowd began to groove with him. Then AJ pulled off a wild moment when Lovebug Star Ski jumped up onto the stage to rhyme with AJ's music. The crowd lost their minds.

Flash followed with his own set and he did his usual amazing work. The crowd cheered for their local DJ, but everyone knew that *both* men had put on very impressive performances. AJ had made it in the larger South Bronx DJ scene, a feat that would lead to opportunities that no doubt saved him from the dangerous social world of drugs and gangs that surrounded him.

AJ and many other young people like him did not make headlines in the New York papers. But they created a style of musical performance—DJing—that is now popular on campuses across the United States. And the musical style that emerged from that movement—hip-hop or rap music—has become the most popular type of music among this country's young people.

What Do You Think?

1. Is the DJ scene part of popular culture or high culture? Why?
2. What does this story tell us about who creates new cultural patterns?
3. Can you think of other cultural patterns that were born among low-income people?

Source: Ewoodzie (forthcoming).

Multiculturalism

multiculturalism a perspective recognizing the cultural diversity of the United States and promoting equal standing for all cultural traditions

Eurocentrism the dominance of European (especially English) cultural patterns

Afrocentrism emphasizing and promoting African cultural patterns

Multiculturalism is *a perspective recognizing the cultural diversity of the United States and promoting equal standing for all cultural traditions.* Multiculturalism represents a sharp change from the past, when our society downplayed cultural diversity and defined itself primarily in terms of well-off European and especially English immigrants. Today there is a spirited debate about whether we should continue to focus on historical traditions or highlight contemporary diversity.

E pluribus unum, the Latin phrase that appears on all U.S. coins, means "out of many, one." This motto symbolizes not only our national political union but also the idea that immigrants from around the world have come together to form a new way of life.

But from the outset, the many cultures did not melt together as much as harden into a hierarchy. At the top were the English, who formed a majority early in U.S. history and established English as the nation's dominant language. Further down, people of other backgrounds were advised to model themselves after "their betters." In practice, then, "melting" was really a process of Anglicization—adoption of English ways. As multiculturalists see it, early in our history, this society set up the English way of life as an ideal that everyone else should imitate and by which everyone should be judged.

Ever since, historians have reported events from the point of view of the English and other people of European ancestry, paying little attention to the perspectives and accomplishments of Native Americans and people of African and Asian descent. Multiculturalists criticize this as **Eurocentrism**, *the dominance of European (especially English) cultural patterns.* Molefi Kete Asante, a supporter of multiculturalism, argues that "like the fifteenth-century Europeans who could not cease believing that the Earth was the center of the universe, many today find it difficult to cease viewing European culture as the center of the social universe" (1988:7).

One controversial issue involves language. Some people believe that English should be the official language of the United States; by 2012, legislatures in thirty-one states had enacted laws making it the official language (ProEnglish, 2012). But some 60 million men and women—one in five—speak a language other than English at home. Spanish is the second most commonly spoken language, and across the country we hear several hundred other tongues, including Italian, German, French, Filipino, Japanese, Korean, and Vietnamese, as well as many Native American languages. National Map 3–1 on page 83 shows where in the United States large numbers of people speak a language other than English at home.

Supporters of multiculturalism say it is a way of coming to terms with our country's increasing social diversity. With the Asian and Hispanic populations of this country increasing rapidly, the U.S. Census Bureau predicts that by 2043, people of African, Asian, and Hispanic ancestry will be a majority of this country's population.

Supporters also claim that multiculturalism is a good way to strengthen the academic achievement of African American children. To counter Eurocentrism, some multicultural educators call for **Afrocentrism**, *emphasizing and promoting African cultural patterns,* which they see as necessary after centuries of minimizing or ignoring the cultural achievements of African societies and African Americans.

Although multiculturalism has found favor in recent years, it has drawn its share of criticism as well. Opponents say it encourages divisiveness rather than unity because it urges people to identify with their own category rather than with the nation as a whole. In addition, critics say, multiculturalism actually harms minorities themselves. Multicultural policies (from African American studies to all-black dorms) seem to support the same racial segregation that our nation has struggled so long to overcome. Furthermore, in the early grades, an Afrocentric curriculum may deny children a wide range of important knowledge and skills by forcing them to study only certain topics from a single point of view.

Finally, the global war on terror has drawn the issue of multiculturalism into the spotlight. In 2005, British Prime Minister Tony Blair responded to a terrorist attack in London, stating, "It is important that the terrorists realize [that] our determination to defend our

Seeing Ourselves

 Explore the percentage of foreign-born people in your local community and in counties across the United States in **MySocLab**

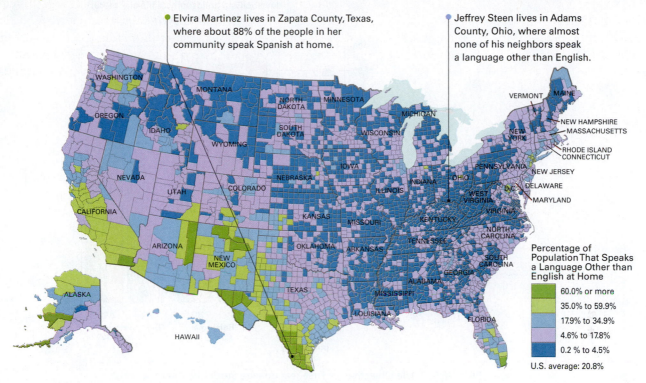

Elvira Martinez lives in Zapata County, Texas, where about 88% of the people in her community speak Spanish at home.

Jeffrey Steen lives in Adams County, Ohio, where almost none of his neighbors speak a language other than English.

Percentage of Population That Speaks a Language Other than English at Home

- 60.0% or more
- 35.0% to 59.9%
- 17.9% to 34.9%
- 4.6% to 17.8%
- 0.2 % to 4.5%

U.S. average: 20.8%

NATIONAL MAP 3–1 Language Diversity across the United States

Of more than 291 million people age five or older in the United States, the Census Bureau reports that 61 million (21 percent) speak a language other than English at home. Of these, 62 percent speak Spanish and 16 percent speak an Asian language (the Census Bureau lists a total of 37 languages and language categories, each of which is favored by more than 100,000 people). The map shows that non–English speakers are concentrated in certain regions of the country. Which ones? What do you think accounts for this pattern?

Source: U.S. Census Bureau (2012).

values and our way of life is greater than their determination to…impose their extremism on the world." He went on to warn that the British government would expel Muslim clerics who encouraged hatred and terrorism (Barone, 2005; Carle, 2008). Of course, there are also many people in other parts of the world who believe that Britain and the United States have imposed their way of life on others. In a world of cultural difference and conflict, we have much to learn about tolerance and peacemaking.

Counterculture

Cultural diversity also includes outright rejection of conventional ideas or behavior. **Counterculture** refers to *cultural patterns that strongly oppose those widely accepted within a society.*

During the 1960s, for example, a youth-oriented counterculture rejected mainstream culture as overly competitive, self-centered, and materialistic. Instead, hippies and other counterculturalists favored a cooperative lifestyle in which "being" was more important than "doing" and the capacity for personal growth—or "expanded consciousness"—was prized over material possessions like homes and cars. Such differences led some people to "drop out" of the larger society.

Countercultures are still flourishing. At the extreme, small militaristic communities (made up of people born in this country) or bands of religious militants (from other

 Read in **MySocLab Document:** *Gangstas, Thugs, and Hustlas: The Code of the Street in Rap Music* by Charis Kubrin

counterculture cultural patterns that strongly oppose those widely accepted within a society

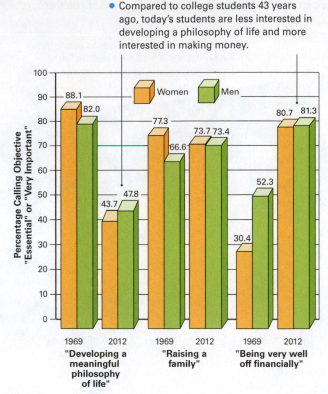

- Compared to college students 43 years ago, today's students are less interested in developing a philosophy of life and more interested in making money.

FIGURE 3–3 Life Objectives of First-Year College Students, 1969 and 2012

Researchers have surveyed first-year college students every year since 1969. While attitudes about some things such as the importance of family have stayed about the same, attitudes about other life goals have changed dramatically.

Sources: Astin et al. (2002) and Pryor et al. (2013).

countries) exist in the United States, some of them engaging in violence intended to threaten our way of life.

Cultural Change

Perhaps the most basic human truth of this world is that "all things shall pass." Even the dinosaurs, which thrived on this planet for 160 million years, exist today only as fossils. Will humanity survive for millions of years to come? All we can say with certainty is that given our reliance on culture, for as long as we survive, the human record will show continuous change.

Figure 3–3 shows changes in attitudes among first-year college students between 1969 (the height of the 1960s' counterculture) and 2012. Some attitudes have changed only slightly: Today, as a generation ago, most men and women look forward to raising a family. But today's students are less concerned with developing a philosophy of life and much more interested in making money.

Change in one dimension of a cultural system usually sparks changes in others. For example, today's college women are much more interested in making money because women are now far more likely to be in the labor force than their mothers or grandmothers were. Working for income may not change their interest in raising a family, but it does increase the age at first marriage, the age of first childbirth, and the divorce rate. Such connections illustrate the principle of **cultural integration**, *the close relationships among various elements of a cultural system.*

cultural integration the close relationships among various elements of a cultural system

Cultural Lag

Some elements of culture change faster than others. William Ogburn (1964) observed that technology moves quickly, generating new elements of material culture (things) faster than nonmaterial culture (ideas) can keep up with them. Ogburn called this inconsistency **cultural lag**, *the fact that some cultural elements change more quickly than others, disrupting a cultural system.* For example, in a world in which a woman can give birth to a child by using another woman's egg, which has been fertilized in a laboratory with the sperm of a total stranger, how are we to apply traditional ideas about motherhood and fatherhood?

cultural lag the fact that some cultural elements change more quickly than others, disrupting a cultural system

Causes of Cultural Change

Cultural changes are set in motion in three ways. The first is *invention,* the process of creating new cultural elements. Invention has given us the telephone (1876), the airplane (1903), and the computer (late 1940s); each of these elements of material culture has had a tremendous impact on our way of life. The same is true of the minimum wage (1938), school desegregation (1954), and women's shelters (1975), each an important element of nonmaterial culture. The process of invention goes on all the time, as indicated by the thousands of applications submitted every year to the U.S. Patent Office. The timeline found in MySocLab shows other inventions that have helped change our way of life.

Discovery, a second cause of cultural change, involves recognizing and understanding more fully something already in existence—perhaps a distant star or the foods of another culture or women's athletic ability. Many discoveries result from painstaking scientific research, and others happen by a stroke of luck, as in 1898, when Marie Curie left a rock on a piece of photographic paper, noticed that emissions from the rock had exposed the paper, and thus discovered radium.

The third cause of cultural change is *diffusion,* the spread of cultural traits from one society to another. Because new information technology sends information around the globe in seconds, cultural diffusion has never been greater than it is today.

Certainly our own society has contributed many significant cultural elements to the world, ranging from computers to jazz. Of course, diffusion works the other way, too, so that much of what we assume to be "American" actually comes from elsewhere. Most of the clothing we wear and the furniture we use, as well as the watch we carry and the money we spend, all had their origin in other cultures (Linton, 1937a).

It is certainly correct to talk about "American culture," especially when we are comparing our way of life to the culture of some other society. But this discussion of cultural change shows us that culture is always complex and always changing. The Thinking About Diversity box on page 86 offers a good example of the diverse and dynamic character of culture with a brief look at the history of rock-and-roll music.

Ethnocentrism and Cultural Relativism

December 10, a small village in Morocco. Watching many of our fellow travelers browsing through a tiny ceramics factory, we have little doubt that North Americans are among the world's greatest shoppers. We delight in surveying hand-woven carpets in China or India, inspecting finely crafted metals in Turkey, or collecting the beautifully colored porcelain tiles we find here in Morocco. Of course, all these items are wonderful bargains. But one major reason for the low prices is unsettling: Many products from the world's low- and middle-income countries are produced by children—some as young as five or six—who work long days for pennies per hour.

We think of childhood as a time of innocence and freedom from adult burdens like regular work. In poor countries throughout the world, however, families depend on income earned by children. So what people in one society think of as right and natural,

Thinking About Diversity: Race, Class, and Gender

Early Rock-and-Roll: Race, Class, and Cultural Change

In the 1950s, rock-and-roll emerged as a major part of U.S. popular culture. Before then, mainstream "pop" music was aimed at white adults. Songs were written by professional composers, recorded by long-established record labels, and performed by well-known artists such as Perry Como, Eddie Fisher, Doris Day, and Patti Page. Just about every big-name performer was white.

At that time, the country was rigidly segregated racially, which created differences in the cultures of white people and black people. In the subcultural world of African Americans, music had sounds and rhythms reflecting jazz, gospel singing, and rhythm and blues. These musical styles were created by African American composers and performers working with black-owned record companies broadcast on radio to an almost entirely black audience.

Class, too, divided the musical world of the 1950s, even among whites. A second musical subculture was country and western, a musical style popular among poorer whites, especially people living in the South. Like rhythm and blues, country and western music had its own composers and performers, its own record labels, and its own radio stations.

"Crossover" music was rare, meaning that very few performers or songs moved from one musical world to gain popularity in another. But this musical segregation began to break down about 1955 with the birth of rock-and-roll. Rock was a new mix of older musical patterns, blending mainstream pop with country and western and, especially, rhythm and blues.

As rock-and-roll drew together musical traditions, it soon divided society in a new way—by age. Rock was the first music clearly linked to the emergence of a youth culture—rock was all the rage among teenagers but was little appreciated by their parents. Rockers took a rebellious stand against "adult" culture, looked like what parents might have called "juvenile delinquents," and claimed to be "cool," an idea that most parents did not even understand.

Young people idolized performers sporting sideburns, turned-up collars, and black leather jackets. By 1956, the unquestioned star of rock-and-roll was a poor white southern boy from Tupelo, Mississippi, named Elvis Aron Presley. With rural roots, Elvis Presley knew country and western music, and after moving to Memphis, Tennessee, he learned black gospel and rhythm and blues.

Presley became the first superstar of rock-and-roll not just because he had talent but also because he had great crossover power. With early hits including "Hound Dog" (a rhythm and blues song originally recorded by Big Mama Thornton) and "Blue Suede Shoes" (written by country and western star Carl Perkins), Presley broke down many of the musical walls based on race and class.

By the end of the 1950s, popular music developed in many new directions, creating soft rock (Ricky Nelson, Pat Boone), rockabilly (Johnny Cash), and dozens of doo-wop groups, both black and white. In the 1960s, rock expanded further, including folk music (the Kingston Trio; Peter, Paul, and Mary; Bob Dylan), surf music (the Beach Boys, Jan and Dean), and the "British invasion" led by the Beatles.

Starting on the clean-cut, pop side of rock, the Beatles soon shared the spotlight with another British band proud of its "delinquent" clothing and street fighter looks—the Rolling Stones. By now, music was a huge business, including not just the hard rock of the Beatles and Stones but also softer "folk rock" performed by the Byrds, the Mamas and the Papas, Simon and Garfunkel, and Crosby, Stills, and Nash. In addition, "Motown" (named after the "motor city," Detroit) and "soul" music launched the careers of dozens of African American stars, including James Brown, Aretha Franklin, the Four Tops, the Temptations, and Diana Ross and the Supremes.

On the West Coast, San Francisco developed political rock music performed by Jefferson Airplane, the Grateful Dead, and Janis Joplin. West Coast spin-off styles included "acid rock," influenced by drug use, performed by the Doors and Jimi Hendrix. The jazz influence returned as "jazz rock" and was played by groups such as Chicago and Blood, Sweat, and Tears.

This brief look at the birth of rock-and-roll shows the power of race and class to shape subcultural patterns. It also shows that the production of culture became a megabusiness. Most of all, it shows us that culture does not stand still but is a living process, changing, adapting, and reinventing itself over time.

What Do You Think?

1. Our way of life shaped rock-and-roll. In what ways did the emergence of rock-and-roll change U.S. culture?

2. Throughout this period of musical change, most musical performers were men. What does this tell us about our way of life? Is today's popular music still dominated by men?

3. Carry on the story of musical change to the present. (Think of disco, heavy metal, punk rock, rap, and hip-hop.)

Source: Based on Stuessy & Lipscomb (2008).

Elvis Presley (*center*) drew together the music of rhythm and blues singers, such as Big Mama Thornton (*left*), and country and western stars, including Carl Perkins (*right*). The development of rock-and-roll illustrates the ever-changing character of U.S. culture.

people elsewhere find puzzling and even immoral. Perhaps the Chinese philosopher Confucius had it right when he noted that "all people are the same; it's only their habits that are different."

Just about every imaginable idea or behavior is commonplace somewhere in the world, and this variation from culture to culture causes travelers both excitement and, at times, distress. The Australians flip light switches down to turn them on; North Americans flip them up. The British drive on the left side of the road; North Americans drive on the right side. The Japanese give names to city blocks; North Americans name streets. Egyptians stand very close to others when engaged in conversation; North Americans are used to maintaining several feet of "personal space." Bathrooms lack toilet paper in much of rural Morocco, causing considerable discomfort for North Americans, who recoil at the thought of having to the left hand for bathroom hygiene, as the Moroccans do.

Given that a particular culture is the basis for each person's reality, it is no wonder that people everywhere exhibit **ethnocentrism**, *the practice of judging another culture by the standards of one's own culture.* Some degree of ethnocentrism is necessary for people to be emotionally attached to their way of life. But ethnocentrism also generates misunderstanding and sometimes conflict.

Members of every cultural system tend to prefer what they know and are wary about what is different. The ancient Romans took this view of difference to an extreme, using the same word for both "stranger" and "enemy." Even language is culturally biased. Centuries ago, people in Europe and North America referred to China as the "Far East." But this term, unknown to the Chinese, is an ethnocentric expression for a region that is far to the east *of us.* The Chinese name for their country translates as "Central Kingdom," suggesting that they, like us, see their own society as the center of the world.

The alternative to ethnocentrism is **cultural relativism**, *the practice of judging a culture by its own standards.* Cultural relativism can be difficult for travelers to adopt: It requires not only openness to unfamiliar values and norms but also the ability to put aside the cultural standards we have known all our lives. Even so, as people from different parts of the world come into increasing contact with one another, the importance of understanding other cultures becomes ever greater.

As the opening to this chapter explained, businesses in the United States are learning the value of marketing to a culturally diverse population. Similarly, businesses are learning that success in the global economy depends on awareness of cultural patterns around the world. IBM, for example, now provides technical support for its products using websites in thirty-three languages (IBM, 2012).

This trend is a change from the past, when many corporations used marketing strategies that lacked sensitivity to cultural diversity. When translated into Spanish, Coors's phrase "Turn It Loose" startled Spanish-speaking customers by proclaiming that the beer would cause diarrhea. Braniff Airlines translated its slogan "Fly in Leather" so carelessly into Spanish that it read "Fly Naked." Similarly, Eastern Airlines' slogan "We Earn Our Wings Every Day" became "We Fly Daily to Heaven." Even poultry giant Frank Perdue fell victim to poor marketing when his pitch "It Takes a Tough Man to Make a Tender Chicken" was transformed into the Spanish words reading "A Sexually Excited Man Will Make a Chicken Affectionate" (Helin, 1992).

But cultural relativism introduces problems of its own. If almost any kind of behavior is the norm *somewhere* in the world, does that mean everything is equally right? Does the fact that some Indian and Moroccan families benefit from having their children work long hours justify child labor? Since we

ethnocentrism the practice of judging another culture by the standards of one's own culture

cultural relativism the practice of judging a culture by its own standards

In the world's low-income countries, most children must work to provide their families with needed income. These young girls work long hours in a brick factory in the Kathmandu Valley, Nepal. Is it ethnocentric for people living in high-income nations to condemn the practice of child labor because we think youngsters belong in school? Why or why not?

are all members of a single species, surely there must be some universal standards of proper conduct. But what are they? And in trying to develop them, how can we avoid imposing our own standards on others? There are no simple answers to these questions. But when confronting an unfamiliar cultural practice, it is best to resist making judgments before grasping what people in that culture understand the issue to be. Remember also to think about your own way of life as others might see it. After all, what we gain most from studying others is better insight into ourselves.

A Global Culture?

Today more than ever, we can observe many of the same cultural practices the world over. Walking the streets of Seoul, South Korea; Kuala Lumpur, Malaysia; Chennai, India; Cairo, Egypt; or Casablanca, Morocco, we see people wearing jeans, hear familiar music, and read ads for many of the same products we use at home. Are we witnessing the birth of a single global culture?

Societies now have more contact with one another than ever before, thanks to the flow of goods, information, and people:

1. **The global economy: The flow of goods.** International trade has never been greater. The global economy has spread many of the same consumer goods—from cars and TV shows to music and fashions—throughout the world.

2. **Global communications: The flow of information.** The Internet and satellite-assisted communications enable people to experience the sights and sounds of events taking place thousands of miles away, often as they happen. Cell phone communication instantly links people all around the world, just as new technology enables text messages written in one language to be delivered in another (Simonite, 2012). In addition, although less than one-third of Internet users speak English as their first language, most of the world's Web pages are written in English. (Smartling, 2012). This fact helps explain why, as we saw in Global Map 3–1 on page 73, English is rapidly emerging as the preferred second language around the world.

3. **Global migration: The flow of people.** Knowing about the rest of the world motivates people to move to where they imagine life will be better. In addition, today's transportation technology, especially air travel, makes relocating easier than ever before. As a result, in most countries, significant numbers of people were born elsewhere, including more than 40 million people in the United States, which is 13 percent of the total population (U.S. Census Bureau, 2012).

These global links help make the cultures of the world more similar. Even so, there are three important limitations to the global culture thesis. First, the global flow of goods, information, and people is uneven in different parts of the world. Generally speaking, urban areas (centers of commerce, communication, and people) have stronger ties to one another, while many rural villages remain isolated. In addition, the greater economic and military power of North America and Western Europe means that these regions influence the rest of the world more than the rest of the world influences them.

Second, the global culture thesis assumes that people everywhere are able to *afford* various new goods and services. As Chapter 12 ("Global Stratification") explains, desperate poverty in much of the world deprives people of even the basic necessities of a safe and secure life.

Third, although many cultural practices are now found in countries throughout the world, people everywhere do not attach the same meanings to them. Do children in Tokyo draw the same lessons from reading the Harry Potter books as children in New York or

London? Similarly, we enjoy foods from around the world while knowing little about the lives of the people who created them. In short, people everywhere still see the world through their own cultural lenses.

Theories of Culture

3.4 Apply sociology's macro-level theories to gain greater understanding of culture.

Sociologists investigate how culture helps us make sense of ourselves and the surrounding world. Here we will examine several macro-level theoretical approaches to understanding culture. A micro-level approach to the personal experience of culture, which emphasizes how individuals not only conform to cultural patterns but also create new patterns in their everyday lives, is the focus of Chapter 6 ("Social Interaction in Everyday Life").

The Functions of Culture: Structural-Functional Theory

The structural-functional approach explains culture as a complex strategy for meeting human needs. Borrowing from the philosophical doctrine of *idealism,* this approach considers values the core of a culture (Parsons, 1966; Williams, 1970). In other words, cultural values direct our lives, give meaning to what we do, and bind people together. Countless other cultural traits have various functions that support the operation of society.

Thinking functionally helps us understand an unfamiliar way of life. Consider the Amish farmer plowing hundreds of acres on an Ohio farm with a team of horses. His farming methods may violate our cultural value of efficiency, but from the Amish point of view, hard work functions to develop the discipline necessary for a highly religious way of life. Long days of working together not only make the Amish self-sufficient but also strengthen family ties and unify local communities.

cultural universals traits that are part of every known culture

Of course, Amish practices have dysfunctions as well. The hard work and strict religious discipline are too demanding for some, who end up leaving the community. Then, too, strong religious beliefs sometimes prevent compromise; slight differences in religious practices have caused the Amish to divide into different communities (Kraybill, 1989; Kraybill & Olshan, 1994).

If cultures are strategies for meeting human needs, we would expect to find many common patterns around the world. **Cultural universals** are *traits that are part of every known culture.* Comparing hundreds of cultures, George Murdock (1945) identified dozens of cultural universals. One common element is the family, which functions everywhere to control sexual reproduction and to oversee the care of children. Funeral rites, too, are found everywhere, because all human communities cope with the reality of death. Jokes are another cultural universal, serving as a safe means of releasing social tensions.

All around the world, families are part of a society's way of life. From a structural-functional point of view, we might ask if this universal character reflects the fact that families carry out important tasks not easily accomplished in other ways. What tasks do families perform?

EVALUATE The strength of structural-functional theory is that it shows how culture operates to meet human needs. Yet by emphasizing a society's dominant cultural patterns, this approach largely ignores the cultural diversity that exists in many societies, including our own. Also, because this approach emphasizes cultural stability, it downplays the importance of change. In short, cultural systems are not as stable or a matter of as much agreement as structural-functional theory leads us to believe. The Applying Theory table summarizes this theoretical approach's main lessons about culture and places it alongside two other approaches that we consider next.

CHECK YOUR LEARNING In the United States, what are some of the functions of sports, July Fourth celebrations, and Black History Month?

Inequality and Culture: Social-Conflict Theory

The social-conflict approach stresses the link between culture and inequality. Any cultural trait, from this point of view, benefits some members of society at the expense of others.

Why do certain values dominate a society in the first place? Many conflict theorists, especially Marxists, argue that culture is shaped by a society's system of economic production. "It is not the consciousness of men that determines their being," Karl Marx proclaimed; "it is their social being that determines their consciousness" (Marx & Engels, 1978:4, orig. 1859). Social-conflict theory, then, is rooted in the philosophical doctrine of *materialism,* which holds that a society's system of material production (such as our own capitalist economy) has a powerful effect on the rest of a culture. This materialist approach contrasts with the idealist leanings of structural functionalism.

Social-conflict analysis ties our cultural values of competitiveness and material success to our country's capitalist economy, which serves the interests of the nation's wealthy elite. The culture of capitalism further teaches us to think that rich and powerful people work harder or longer than others and therefore deserve their wealth and privileges. It also encourages us to view capitalism as somehow "natural," discouraging us from trying to reduce economic inequality.

Eventually, however, the strains of inequality erupt into movements for social change. Two historical examples in the United States are the civil rights movement and the women's movement. A more recent example is the Occupy Wall Street movement, which has focused on our society's increasing economic inequality. All these movements seek greater equality, and all have encountered opposition from defenders of the status quo.

Gender and Culture: Feminist Theory

As Marx saw it, culture is rooted in economic production. Therefore, our society's culture largely reflects the capitalist economic system. Feminists agree with Marx's claim that culture is an arena of conflict, but they see this conflict as being rooted in gender.

Applying Theory

Culture			
	Structural-Functional Theory	**Social-Conflict and Feminist Theories**	**Sociobiology Theory**
What is the level of analysis?	Macro-level	Macro-level	Macro-level
What is culture?	Culture is a system of behavior by which members of societies cooperate to meet their needs.	Culture is a system that benefits some people and disadvantages others.	Culture is a system of behavior that is partly shaped by human biology.
What is the foundation of culture?	Cultural patterns are rooted in a society's core values and beliefs.	Marx claimed that cultural patterns are rooted in a society's system of economic production. Feminist theory says cultural conflict is rooted in gender.	Cultural patterns are rooted in humanity's biological evolution.
What core questions does the approach ask?	How does a cultural pattern help society operate? What cultural patterns are found in all societies?	How does a cultural pattern benefit some people and harm others? How does a cultural pattern support social inequality?	How does a cultural pattern help a species adapt to its environment?

Gender refers to *the personal traits and social positions that members of a society attach to being female or male*. From a feminist point of view, gender is a crucial dimension of social inequality, a topic that Chapter 10 ("Gender Stratification") examines in detail. As that chapter explains, men have greater access to the workforce than women do and so men earn more income. Men also have greater power in our national political system; for example, all forty-four of this country's presidents have been men. In addition, on the level of everyday experience, men exercise the most power in the typical household.

Feminists claim that our culture is "gendered." This means that our way of life reflects the ways in which our society defines what is male as more important than what is female. This inequality is evident in the language we use. We tend to say "man and wife," a phrase used in traditional wedding vows; we almost never hear the phrase "woman and husband." Similarly, the masculine word "king" conveys power and prestige, with a meaning that is almost entirely positive. The comparable feminine word "queen" has a range of meanings, some which are negative.

Not only does our culture define what is masculine as dominant in relation to what is feminine, but also our way of life defines this male domination as "natural." Such a system of beliefs serves to justify gender inequality by claiming it cannot be changed.

In short, cultural patterns reflect and support gender inequality. Cultural patterns also perpetuate this inequality to the extent that they carry it forward into the future.

EVALUATE Social-conflict theory suggests that cultural systems do not address human needs equally, allowing some people to dominate others. Marx focused on economic inequality and analyzed culture as an expression of capitalism. Feminists focus on gender and understand culture as a reflection of male domination. All these dimensions of inequality are "built into" our way of life. At the same time, such inequality also generates pressure toward change.

Yet by stressing the divisiveness of culture, all social-conflict analysis understates ways in which cultural patterns integrate members of a society. Thus, we should consider both social-conflict and structural-functional insights for a fuller understanding of culture.

CHECK YOUR LEARNING How might a social-conflict analysis of college fraternities and sororities differ from a structural-functional analysis?

Evolution and Culture: Sociobiology

We know that culture is a human creation, but does human biology influence how this process unfolds? A third way of thinking, standing with one leg in biology and one in sociology, is **sociobiology**, *a theoretical approach that explores ways in which human biology affects how we create culture*.

Sociobiology rests on the theory of evolution proposed by Charles Darwin in *On the Origin of Species* (1859). Darwin asserted that living organisms change over long periods of time as a result of *natural selection*, a matter of four simple principles. First, all living things live to reproduce themselves. Second, the blueprint for reproduction is in the genes, the basic units of life that carry traits of one generation into the next. Third, some random variation in genes allows a species to "try out" new life patterns in a particular environment. This variation allows some organisms to survive better than others and pass on their advantageous genes to their offspring. Fourth and finally, over thousands of generations, the genetic patterns that promote reproduction survive and become dominant. In this way, as biologists say, a species *adapts* to its environment, and dominant traits emerge as the "nature" of the organism.

Sociobiologists claim that the large number of cultural universals reflects the fact that all humans are members of a single biological species. It is our common biology that underlies, for example, the apparently universal "double standard" of sexual behavior. As the sex researcher Alfred Kinsey put it, "Among all people everywhere in the world, the

gender the personal traits and social positions that members of a society attach to being female or male

sociobiology a theoretical approach that explores ways in which human biology affects how we create culture

Using an evolutionary perspective, sociobiologists explain that different reproductive strategies give rise to a double standard: Men treat women as sexual objects more than women treat men that way. While this may be so, many sociologists counter that behavior—such as that shown here—is more correctly understood as resulting from a culture of male domination.

male is more likely than the female to desire sex with a variety of partners" (quoted in Barash, 1981:49). But why?

We all know that children result from joining a woman's egg with a man's sperm. But the biological importance of a single sperm and of a single egg is quite different. For healthy men, sperm represent a "renewable resource" produced by the testes throughout most of the life course. A man releases hundreds of millions of sperm in a single ejaculation—technically, enough to fertilize every woman in North America (Barash, 1981:47). A newborn female's ovaries, however, contain her entire lifetime supply of eggs. A woman generally releases a single egg cell from her ovaries each month. So although men are biologically capable of fathering thousands of offspring, women are able to bear only a relatively small number of children.

Given this biological difference, men reproduce their genes most efficiently by being promiscuous—readily engaging in sex with any willing partner. But women look differently at reproduction. Each of a woman's relatively few pregnancies demands that she carry the child for nine months, give birth, and provide care for years afterward. Thus efficient reproduction on the part of a woman depends on carefully selecting a mate whose qualities (beginning with the likelihood that he will simply stay around) will contribute to her child's survival and, later, successful reproduction.

The double standard certainly involves more than biology and is tangled up with the historical domination of women by men. But sociobiology suggests that this cultural pattern, like many others, has an underlying "bio-logic." Simply put, the double standard exists around the world because biological differences lead women and men everywhere to favor distinctive reproductive strategies.

EVALUATE Sociobiology has generated intriguing theories about the biological roots of some cultural patterns. The approach, however, remains controversial for two main reasons.

First, some critics fear that sociobiology may revive biological arguments, from over a century ago, that claimed the superiority of one race or sex. But defenders counter that sociobiology rejects the past pseudoscience of racial and gender superiority. In fact, they say, sociobiology unites all of humanity because all people share a single evolutionary history. Sociobiology does assert that men and women differ biologically in some ways that culture cannot easily overcome. But far from claiming that males are somehow more important than females, sociobiology emphasizes that both sexes are vital to human reproduction and survival.

Second, say the critics, sociobiologists have little evidence to support their theories. Research to date suggests that biological forces do not *determine* human behavior in any rigid sense. Rather, humans *learn* behavior within a cultural system. The contribution of sociobiology, then, lies in explaining why some cultural patterns seem easier to learn than others (Barash, 1981).

CHECK YOUR LEARNING Using the sociobiology approach, explain why a cultural pattern such as sibling rivalry (by which children in the same family often compete and even fight with one another) is widespread.

Because any analysis of culture requires a broad focus on the workings of society, the three theoretical approaches discussed in this chapter are all macro-level in scope. The symbolic-interaction approach, with its micro-level focus on behavior in everyday situations, will be explored in Chapter 6 ("Social Interaction in Everyday Life").

Culture and Human Freedom

3.5 Critique culture as limiting or expanding human freedom.

This chapter leads us to ask an important question: To what extent are human beings, as cultural creatures, free? Does culture bind us to each other and to the past? Or does culture enhance our capacity for individual thought and independent choice?

Culture as Constraint

As symbolic creatures, humans cannot live without culture. But the capacity for culture does have some drawbacks. We may be the only animal to name ourselves, but living in a symbolic world means that we are also the only creatures who experience alienation. In addition, culture is largely a matter of habit, which limits our choices and drives us to repeat troubling patterns, such as racial prejudice and sex discrimination, in each new generation.

Our society's emphasis on competitive achievement urges us toward excellence, yet this same pattern also isolates us from one another. Material things comfort us in some ways but divert us from the security and satisfaction that come from close relationships and spiritual strength.

Culture as Freedom

For better or worse, human beings are cultural creatures, just as ants and elephants are prisoners of their biology. But there is a crucial difference. Biological instincts create a ready-made world; culture forces us to make choices as we make and remake a world for ourselves. No better evidence of this freedom exists than the cultural diversity of our own society and the even greater human diversity found around the world.

Learning more about this cultural diversity is one goal shared by sociologists. Wherever we may live, the better we understand the workings of the surrounding culture, the better prepared we are to use the freedom it offers us.

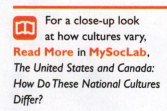

For a close-up look at how cultures vary, **Read More** in **MySocLab**, *The United States and Canada: How Do These National Cultures Differ?*

Seeing Sociology in Everyday Life

What clues do we have to a society's cultural values?

The values of any society—that is, what that society thinks is important—are reflected in various aspects of everyday life, including the things people have and the ways they behave. An interesting way to "read" our own culture's values is to look at the "superheroes" that we celebrate. Take a look at the characters in the three photos shown here and, in each case, describe what makes the character special and what each character represents in cultural terms.

In the television drama, *True Blood,* Sookie Stackhouse (Anna Paquin), a waitress with telepathic abilities and other special powers, inhabits a world in which you never know if your customer is a vampire. Heroic humans with special abilities as portrayed in the mass media rarely include women.

Superman first appeared in an *Action Comics* book in 1938, as the United States struggled to climb out of economic depression and faced the rising danger of war. Since then, Superman has been featured in a television show as well as in a string of Hollywood films. One trait of most superheroes is that they have a secret identity; in this case, Superman's everyday identity is "mild-mannered news reporter" Clark Kent.

Another longtime superhero important to our culture is Spider-Man. In the *Spider-Man* movies, Peter Parker (who transforms into Spider-Man when he confronts evil) is secretly in love with Mary Jane Watson. Again and again the male hero rescues the female from danger. But, in true superhero style, Spider-Man does not allow himself to follow his heart because with great power comes great responsibility, and that must come first.

HINT Superman (as well as all superheroes) defines our society as good; after all, Superman fights for "truth, justice, and the American way." Many superheroes have stories that draw on great people in our cultural history, including religious figures such as Moses and Jesus: They have mysterious origins (we never really know their true families), they are "tested" through great moral challenges, and they finally succeed in overcoming all obstacles. (Today's superheroes, however, are likely to win the day using force and often violence.) Having a "secret identity" means superheroes can lead ordinary lives (and means we ordinary people can imagine being superheroes). But to keep their focus on fighting evil, superheroes must place their work ahead of any romantic interests ("Work comes first!"). Sookie also illustrates the special challenge to "do it all" faced by women in our society: Besides using her special powers to fight evil, she still has to hold down a full-time job.

Seeing Sociology in *Your* Everyday Life

1. Members of every culture, as they decide how to live their lives, look to "heroes" for role models and inspiration. In modern societies, the mass media play a big part in creating heroes. What traits define popular culture heroes such as Clint Eastwood's film character "Dirty Harry," Sylvester Stallone's film characters "Rocky" as well as "Rambo," and Arnold Schwarzenegger's character "the Terminator"?

2. Go to MySocLab and click on the Student Resources link to access the Sociology in Focus blog, where you can read the latest posts by a team of young sociologists who apply the sociological perspective to topics of popular culture.

3. Do you know someone on your campus who has lived in another country or a cultural setting different from what is familiar to you? Try to engage in conversation with someone whose way of life is significantly different from your own. Try to discover something that you accept or take for granted in one way that the other person sees in a different way and try to understand why. Go to the "Seeing Sociology in *Your* Everyday Life" feature in MySocLab to learn more about cultural diversity and how we can all learn from experiencing cultural differences.

Making the Grade

What Is Culture?

3.1 Explain the development of culture as a human strategy for survival. (pages 66–70)

Culture is a **way of life**.
- Culture is shared by members of a society.
- Culture shapes how we act, think, and feel.

Culture is a **human trait**.
- Although several species display a limited capacity for culture, only human beings rely on culture for survival.

Culture is a **product of evolution**.
- As the human brain evolved, culture replaced biological instincts as our species' primary strategy for survival.

We experience **culture shock** when we enter an unfamiliar culture and are not able to "read" meaning in our new surroundings. We create culture shock for others when we act in ways they do not understand.

culture the ways of thinking, the ways of acting, and the material objects that together form a people's way of life

nonmaterial culture the ideas created by members of a society

material culture the physical things created by members of a society

culture shock personal disorientation when experiencing an unfamiliar way of life

The Elements of Culture

3.2 Identify common elements of culture. (pages 70–79)

 **Watch** the **Video** in **MySocLab**

Culture relies on **symbols** in the form of words, gestures, and actions to express meaning.
- The fact that different meanings can come to be associated with the same symbol (for example, a wink of an eye) shows the human capacity to create and manipulate symbols.
- Societies create new symbols all the time (for example, new computer technology has sparked the creation of new cyber-symbols).

Language is the symbolic system by which people in a culture communicate with one another.
- People use language—both spoken and written—to transmit culture from one generation to the next.
- Because every culture is different, each language has words or expressions not found in any other language.

Values are abstract standards of what *ought* to be (for example, equality of opportunity).
- Values can sometimes be in conflict with one another.
- Lower-income countries have cultures that value survival; higher-income countries have cultures that value individualism and self-expression.

Beliefs are specific statements that people who share a culture hold to be true (for example, "A qualified woman could be elected president").

Norms, rules that guide human behavior, are of two types:
- **mores** (for example, sexual taboos), which have great moral significance
- **folkways** (for example, greetings or dining etiquette), which are matters of everyday politeness

Technology and Culture
- A society's **artifacts**—the wide range of physical human creations that together make up a society's material culture—reflect underlying cultural values and technology.
- The more complex a society's technology, the more its members are able to shape the world as they wish.

symbol anything that carries a particular meaning recognized by people who share a culture

language a system of symbols that allows people to communicate with one another

cultural transmission the process by which one generation passes culture to the next

Sapir-Whorf thesis the idea that people see and understand the world through the cultural lens of language

values culturally defined standards that people use to decide what is desirable, good, and beautiful and that serve as broad guidelines for social living

beliefs specific ideas that people hold to be true

norms rules and expectations by which a society guides the behavior of its members

mores norms that are widely observed and have great moral significance

folkways norms for routine or casual interaction

social control attempts by society to regulate people's thoughts and behavior

technology knowledge that people use to make a way of life in their surroundings

Cultural Diversity

(3.3) Discuss dimensions of cultural difference and cultural change. (pages 79–89)

👁 **Watch** the **Video** in **MySocLab**   ✳ **Explore** the **Map** in **MySocLab**

👁 **Watch** the **Video** in **MySocLab**   📖 **Read** the **Document** in **MySocLab**

We live in a **culturally diverse society**.

- This diversity is due to our country's history of immigration.
- Diversity reflects regional differences.
- Diversity reflects differences in social class that set off **high culture** (available only to elites) from **popular culture** (available to average people).

A number of values are central to our way of life. But **cultural patterns** are not the same throughout our society.

Subculture is based on differences in interests and life experiences.

- Hip-hop fans and jocks are two examples of youth subcultures in the United States.

Multiculturalism is an effort to enhance appreciation of cultural diversity.

- Multiculturalism developed as a reaction to the earlier "melting pot" idea, which was thought to result in minorities' losing their identity as they adopted mainstream cultural patterns.

Counterculture is strongly at odds with conventional ways of life.

- Any militant group in the United States that would plot to destroy Western society would be an example of a counterculture.

Cultural change results from

- **invention** (examples include the telephone and the computer)
- **discovery** (for example, the recognition that women are capable of political leadership)
- **diffusion** (for example, the growing popularity of various ethnic foods and musical styles)

Cultural lag results when some parts of a cultural system change faster than others.

How do we understand cultural differences?

- **Ethnocentrism** links people to their society but can cause misunderstanding and conflict between societies.
- **Cultural relativism** is increasingly important as people of the world come into more contact with each other.

high culture cultural patterns that distinguish a society's elite

popular culture cultural patterns that are widespread among a society's population

subculture cultural patterns that set apart some segment of a society's population

counterculture cultural patterns that strongly oppose those widely accepted within a society

multiculturalism a perspective recognizing the cultural diversity of the United States and promoting equal standing for all cultural traditions

Eurocentrism the dominance of European (especially English) cultural patterns

Afrocentrism emphasizing and promoting African cultural patterns

cultural integration the close relationships among various elements of a cultural system

cultural lag the fact that some cultural elements change more quickly than others, disrupting a cultural system

ethnocentrism the practice of judging another culture by the standards of one's own culture

cultural relativism the practice of judging a culture by its own standards

Theories of Culture

(3.4) Apply sociology's macro-level theories to gain greater understanding of culture. (pages 89–93)

Structural–functional theory views culture as a relatively stable system built on core values. All cultural patterns play some part in the ongoing operation of society.

Social-conflict theory sees culture as a dynamic arena of inequality and conflict. Cultural patterns benefit some categories of people more than others.

Feminist theory highlights how culture is "gendered," dividing activities between the sexes in ways that give men greater power and privileges than women have.

Sociobiology explores how the long history of evolution has shaped patterns of culture in today's world.

cultural universals traits that are part of every known culture

gender the personal traits and social positions that members of a society attach to being male or female

sociobiology a theoretical approach that explores ways in which human biology affects how we create culture

Culture and Human Freedom

(3.5) Critique culture as limiting or expanding human freedom. (page 93)

- Culture can limit the choices we make.
- As cultural creatures, we have the capacity to shape and reshape our world to meet our needs and pursue our dreams.

4 Society

((• Listen to Chapter 4 in MySocLab

LEARNING OBJECTIVES

4.1 Describe how technological development has shaped the history of human societies.

4.2 Analyze the importance of class conflict to the historical development of human societies.

4.3 Demonstrate the importance of ideas to the development of human societies.

4.4 Contrast the social bonds typical of traditional and modern societies.

4.5 Summarize the contributions of Lenski, Marx, Weber, and Durkheim to our understanding of social change.

the Power of Society

to shape access to the Internet

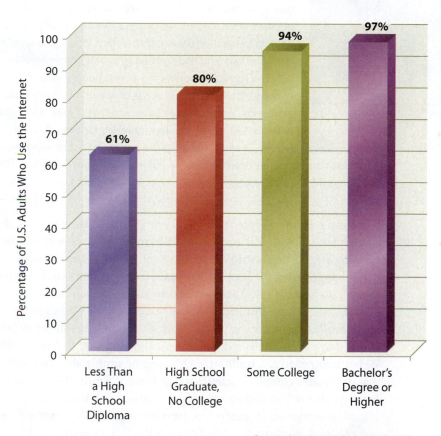

Percentage of U.S. Adults Who Use the Internet

Less Than a High School Diploma	61%
High School Graduate, No College	80%
Some College	94%
Bachelor's Degree or Higher	97%

Source: Pew Research Center (2012)

Does everyone have the same opportunity to use new computer technology such as the Internet? While for some people, the Internet is as close as their smartphone, others know little about this technology. In general, people with more education have more resources—including greater access to computer technology—than people who are more disadvantaged.

Chapter Overview

We all live within a social world. This chapter explores how societies are organized and also explains how societies have changed over the centuries. The story of human societies over time is guided by the work of one of today's leading sociologists, Gerhard Lenski, and three of sociology's founders, Karl Marx, Max Weber, and Emile Durkheim.

Sididi Ag Inaka has never sent a text message. He has never spoken on a cell phone. And he has never logged on to the Internet. Does such a person really exist in today's high-technology world? Well, how about this: Neither Inaka nor anyone in his family has ever been to a movie, watched television, or even read a newspaper.

Are these people visitors from another planet? Prisoners on some remote island? Not at all. They are Tuareg nomads who wander over the vast Sahara in the western African nations of Mali and Niger. Known as the "blue men of the desert" for the flowing blue robes worn by both men and women, the Tuareg herd camels, goats, and sheep and live in camps where the sand blows and the daytime temperature often reaches 120 degrees Fahrenheit. Life is hard, but most Tuareg try to hold on to traditional ways. With a stern look, Inaka says, "My father was a nomad. His father was a nomad. I am a nomad. My children will be nomads."

The Tuareg are among the world's poorest people. When the rains fail to come, they and their animals are at risk of losing their lives. Perhaps someday the Tuareg people can gain some of the wealth that comes from mining uranium below the desert across which they have traveled for centuries. But whatever their economic fate, Inaka and his people are a society set apart, with little knowledge of the larger world and none of its advanced technology. But Inaka does not complain: "This is the life of my ancestors. This is the life that we know" (Buckley, 1996; Matloff, 1997; Lovgren, 1998; McConnell, 2007).

Society refers to *people who interact in a defined territory and share a culture.* In this chapter, you will learn more about human societies with the help of four important sociologists. We begin with the approach of **Gerhard Lenski**, who describes how societies have changed over the past 10,000 years. Lenski points to the importance of *technology* in shaping any society. Then we turn to three of sociology's founders. **Karl Marx**, like Lenski, took a long historical view of societies. But Marx's story of society is all about *social conflict* that arises as people work within an economic system to produce material goods. **Max Weber** tells a different tale, showing that the power of *ideas* shapes society. Weber contrasted the traditional thinking of simple societies with the rational thought that dominates complex societies today. Finally, **Emile Durkheim** helps us see the different ways that traditional and modern societies hang together.

All four visions of society answer a number of important questions: What makes the way of life of people such as the Tuareg of the Sahara so different from your life as a college student in the United States? How and why do all societies change over time? What forces divide a society? What forces hold a society together? This chapter will provide answers to all of these questions as we look at the work of important sociologists.

Gerhard Lenski: Society and Technology

4.1 Describe how technological development has shaped the history of human societies.

Members of our society, who take things like television and texting for granted, must wonder at the nomads of the Sahara, who live the same simple life their ancestors did centuries ago. The work of Gerhard Lenski (Nolan & Lenski, 2010) helps us understand the great differences among societies that have existed throughout human history.

Lenski uses the term **sociocultural evolution** to mean *changes that occur as a society gains new technology*. With only simple technology, societies such as the Tuareg have little control over nature, so they can support just a small number of people. Societies with complex technology such as cars and cell phones, while not necessarily "better," are certainly more productive so that they can support hundreds of millions of people with far more material affluence.

Inventing or adopting new technology sends ripples of change throughout a society. When our ancestors first discovered how to make a sail so that the power of the wind could move a boat, they created a new form of transportation that eventually would take them to new lands, greatly expand their economy, and increase their military power. In addition, the more technology a society has, the faster it changes. Technologically simple societies change very slowly; Sididi Ag Inaka says he lives "the life of my ancestors." How many people in U.S. society can say that they live the way their grandparents or great-grandparents did? Because modern, high-technology societies such as our own change so fast, people usually experience major social changes during a single lifetime. Imagine how surprised your great-grandmother would be to hear about "Googling" and text-messaging, replacement hearts and test-tube babies, or 4G phones and iPads.

Drawing on Lenski's work, we will examine five types of societies defined by their technology: hunting and gathering societies, horticultural and pastoral societies, agrarian societies, industrial societies, and postindustrial societies. Characteristics of each of these types of society are reviewed in the Summing Up table on page 103.

After a nearby forest was burned, these Aboriginal women in Australia spent the day collecting roots, which they will use to make dye for their clothing. Members of such societies live closely linked to nature.

Hunting and Gathering Societies

In the simplest of all societies, people live by **hunting and gathering**, *making use of simple tools to hunt animals and gather vegetation for food*. From the time that our species appeared 3 million years ago until about 12,000 years ago, *all* humans were hunters and gatherers. Even in 1800, many hunting and gathering societies could be found around the world. But today just a few remain, including the Aka and Pygmies of Central Africa, the Bushmen of southwestern Africa, the Aborigines of Australia, the Kaska Indians of northwestern Canada, the Batek and Semai of Malaysia, and isolated native people living in the Amazon rain forest.

With little ability to control their environment, hunters and gatherers spend most of their time looking for game and collecting plants to eat. Only in lush areas with lots of food do hunters and gatherers have much chance for leisure. Because it takes a large amount of land to support even a few people, hunting and gathering societies have just a few dozen members. They must also be nomadic, moving on to find new sources of vegetation or to follow migrating animals. Although they may return to favored sites, they rarely form permanent settlements.

society people who interact in a defined territory and share a culture

Gerhard Lenski (society is defined by level of technology)

Karl Marx (society is defined by type of social conflict)

Max Weber (society is defined by ideas/mode of thinking)

Emile Durkheim (society is defined by type of solidarity)

Hunting and gathering societies depend on the family to do many things. The family must get and distribute food, protect its members, and teach their way of life to the children. Everyone's life is much the same; people spend most of their time getting their next meal. Age and gender have some effect on what individuals do. Healthy adults do most of the work, leaving the very young and the very old to help out as they can. Women gather vegetation—which provides most of the food—while men take on the less certain job of hunting. Although men and women perform different tasks, most hunters and gatherers probably see the sexes as having about the same social importance (Leacock, 1978).

Hunting and gathering societies usually have a *shaman,* or spiritual leader, who enjoys high prestige but has to work to find food like everyone else. In short, people in hunting and gathering societies come close to being socially equal.

Hunters and gatherers use simple weapons—the spear, bow and arrow, and stone knife—but rarely do they use them to wage war. Their real enemy is the forces of nature: Severe storms and droughts can kill off their food supply in a short span of time, and there is little they can do for someone who has a serious accident or illness. Being constantly at risk in this way encourages people to cooperate and share, a strategy that raises everyone's chances of survival. But the truth is that many die in childhood, and no more than half reach the age of twenty.

During the past century, societies with more powerful technology have closed in on the few remaining hunters and gatherers, reducing their food supply. As a result, hunting and gathering societies are disappearing. Fortunately, study of this way of life has given us valuable information about human history and our basic ties to the natural world.

Horticultural and Pastoral Societies

Some 10,000 to 12,000 years ago, as the timeline found in MySocLab shows, a new technology began to change the lives of human beings. People developed **horticulture**, *the use of hand tools to raise crops.* Using a hoe to work the soil and a digging stick to punch holes in the ground to plant seeds may not seem like something that would change the world, but these inventions allowed people to give up gathering in favor of growing food for themselves. The first humans to plant gardens lived in fertile regions of the Middle East. Cultural diffusion spread this knowledge to America and Asia and eventually all over the world.

Not all societies were quick to give up hunting and gathering for horticulture. Hunters and gatherers living where food was plentiful probably saw little reason to change their ways. People living in dry regions (such as the deserts of Africa or the Middle East) or mountainous areas found little use for horticulture because they could not grow much anyway. Such people (including the Tuareg) were more likely to adopt **pastoralism**, *the domestication of animals.* Today, societies that mix horticulture and pastoralism can be found throughout South America, Africa, and Asia.

Growing plants and raising animals greatly increased food production, so populations expanded from dozens to hundreds of people. Pastoralists remained nomadic, leading their herds to fresh grazing lands. But horticulturalists formed settlements, moving only when the soil gave out. Joined by trade, these settlements formed extended societies with populations reaching into the thousands.

Once a society is capable of producing a *material surplus*—more resources than are needed to feed the population—not everyone has to work at providing food. Greater specialization results: Some make crafts, while others engage in trade, cut hair, apply tattoos, or serve as priests. Compared to hunting and gathering societies, horticultural and pastoral societies are more socially diverse.

But being more productive does not make a society "better" in every sense. As some families

What would it be like to live in a society with simple technology? That's the premise of the television show *Survivor.* What advantages do societies with simple technology afford their members? What disadvantages do you see?

produce more than others, they become richer and more powerful. Horticultural and pastoral societies have greater inequality, with elites using government power—and military force—to serve their own interests. But leaders do not have the ability to travel or to communicate over large distances, so they can control only a small number of people rather than rule over vast empires.

Religion also differs among types of societies. Hunters and gatherers believe that many spirits inhabit the world. Horticulturalists, however, are more likely to think of one God as the creator of the world. Pastoral societies carry this belief further, seeing God as directly involved in the well-being of the entire world. The pastoral roots of Judaism and Christianity are evident in the term "pastor" and the common view of God as a shepherd ("The Lord is my shepherd," says Psalm 23) who stands watch over us all.

Agrarian Societies

About 5,000 years ago, another revolution in technology was taking place in the Middle East, one that would end up changing life on Earth. This was the emergence of **agriculture**, *large-scale cultivation using plows harnessed to animals or more powerful energy sources.* So important was the invention of the animal-drawn plow, along with other breakthroughs of the period—including irrigation, the wheel, writing, numbers, and the use of various metals—that this moment in history is often called the "dawn of civilization."

Summing Up

Sociocultural Evolution

Type of Society	Historical Period	Productive Technology	Population Size	Settlement Pattern	Social Organization	Examples
Hunting and Gathering Societies	Only type of society until about 12,000 years ago; still common several centuries ago; the few examples remaining today are threatened with extinction	Primitive weapons	25–40 people	Nomadic	Family-centered; specialization limited to age and sex; little social inequality	Pygmies of Central Africa, Bushmen of southwestern Africa, Aborigines of Australia, Semai of Malaysia, Kaska Indians of Canada
Horticultural and Pastoral Societies	From about 12,000 years ago, with decreasing numbers after about 3000 B.C.E.	Horticultural societies use hand tools for cultivating plants; pastoral societies are based on the domestication of animals.	Settlements of several hundred people, connected through trading ties to form societies of several thousand people	Horticulturalists form small permanent settlements; pastoralists are nomadic.	Family-centered; religious system begins to develop; moderate specialization; increased social inequality	Middle Eastern societies about 5000 B.C.E., various societies today in New Guinea and other Pacific islands, Yąnomamö today in South America
Agrarian Societies	From about 5,000 years ago, with large but decreasing numbers today	Animal-drawn plow	Millions of people	Cities become common, but they generally contain only a small proportion of the population.	Family loses significance as distinct religious, political, and economic systems emerge; extensive specialization; increased social inequality	Egypt during construction of the Great Pyramids, medieval Europe, numerous predominantly agrarian societies of the world today
Industrial Societies	From about 1750 to the present	Advanced sources of energy; mechanized production	Millions of people	Cities contain most of the population.	Distinct religious, political, economic, educational, and family systems; highly specialized; marked social inequality persists, lessening somewhat over time	Most societies today in Europe, North America, Australia, and Japan, which generate most of the world's industrial production
Postindustrial Societies	Emerging in recent decades	Computers that support an information-based economy	Millions of people	Population remains concentrated in cities but begins to decentralize.	Similar to industrial societies, with information processing and other service work gradually replacing industrial production	Industrial societies are now entering the postindustrial stage.

Using animal-drawn plows, farmers could cultivate fields far bigger than the garden-sized plots planted by horticulturalists. Plows have the added advantage of turning and aerating the soil, making it more fertile. As a result, farmers could work the same land for generations, encouraging the development of permanent settlements. With the ability to grow a surplus of food and to transport goods using animal-powered wagons, agrarian societies greatly expanded in size and population. About 100 c.e., for example, the agrarian Roman Empire contained some 70 million people spread over 2 million square miles (Nolan & Lenski, 2010).

Greater production meant even more specialization. Now there were dozens of distinct occupations, from farmers to builders to metalworkers. With so many people producing so many different things, people invented money as a common standard of exchange, and the old barter system—in which people traded one thing for another—was abandoned.

Agrarian societies have extreme social inequality, typically even more than modern societies such as our own. In most cases, a large number of the people are peasants or slaves, who do most of the work. Elites therefore have time for more "refined" activities, including the study of philosophy, art, and literature. This explains the historical link between "high culture" and social privilege noted in Chapter 3 ("Culture").

Among hunters and gatherers and also among horticulturalists, women provide most of the food, which gives them social importance. Agriculture, however, raises men to a position of social dominance. Using heavy metal plows pulled by large animals, agrarian societies put men in charge of food production. Women are left with the support tasks, such as weeding and carrying water to the fields (Boulding, 1976; Fisher, 1979).

In agrarian societies, religion reinforces the power of elites by defining both loyalty and hard work as moral obligations. Many of the "Wonders of the Ancient World," such as the Great Wall of China and the Great Pyramids of Egypt, were possible only because emperors and pharaohs had almost absolute power and could order their people to work for a lifetime without pay.

Of the societies described so far, agrarian societies have the most social inequality. Agrarian technology also gives people a greater range of life choices, which is the reason that agrarian societies differ more from one another than horticultural and pastoral societies do.

Industrial Societies

Industrialism, which first took hold in the rich nations of today's world, is *the production of goods using advanced sources of energy to drive large machinery*. Until the industrial era began, the major source of energy had been the muscles of humans and the animals they tended. Around the year 1750, people turned to water power and then steam boilers to operate mills and factories filled with larger and larger machines.

Industrial technology gave people such power to alter their environment that change took place faster than ever before. It is probably fair to say that the new industrial societies changed more in one century than the earlier agrarian societies had changed over the course of the previous thousand years. As explained in Chapter 1 ("The Sociological Perspective"), change was so rapid that it sparked the birth of sociology itself. By 1900, railroads crossed the land, steamships traveled the seas, and steel-framed skyscrapers reached far higher than any of the old cathedrals that symbolized the agrarian age.

But that was only the beginning. Soon automobiles allowed people to move quickly almost anywhere, and electricity powered homes full of modern "conveniences" such as refrigerators, washing machines, air conditioners, and entertainment centers. Electronic communication, beginning with the telegraph and the telephone and followed by radio, television, and computers, gave people the ability to reach others instantly, all over the world.

Work also changed. In agrarian communities, most men and women worked in the home or in the fields nearby. Industrialization drew people away from home to factories situated near energy sources (such as coalfields) that powered their machinery. The result was a weakening of close working relationships, strong family ties, and many of the traditional values, beliefs, and customs that guide agrarian life.

Explore the difference industrialization makes in your local community and in counties across the United States in **MySocLab**

December 28, Moray, in the Andes highlands of Peru. We are high in the mountains in a small community of several dozen families, miles from the nearest electric line or paved road. At about 12,000 feet, breathing is hard for people not used to the thin air, so we walk slowly. But hard work seems to be no problem for the man and his son out on a field near their home tilling the soil with a horse and plow. Too poor to buy a tractor, these people till the land in the same way that their ancestors did 500 years ago.

With industrialization, occupational specialization became greater than ever. Today, the kind of work you do has a lot to do with your standard of living, so people now often size up one another in terms of their jobs rather than according to their family ties, as agrarian people do. Rapid change and people's tendency to move from place to place also make social life more anonymous, increase cultural diversity, and promote subcultures and countercultures, as described in Chapter 3 ("Culture").

Industrial technology changes the family, too, reducing its traditional importance as the center of social life. No longer does the family serve as the main setting for work, learning, and religious worship. As Chapter 18 ("Families") explains, technological change also plays a part in making families more diverse, with a greater share of single people, divorced people, single-parent families, and stepfamilies.

Perhaps the greatest effect of industrialization has been to raise living standards, which increased fivefold in the United States over the past century. Although at first new technology only benefits the elite few, industrial technology is so productive that over time just about everyone's income rises so that people live longer and more comfortable lives. Even social inequality decreases slightly, as explained in Chapter 10 ("Social Stratification"), because industrial societies provide extended schooling and greater political rights for everyone. Around the world, industrialization has had the effect of increasing the demand for a greater political voice, a pattern evident in South Korea, Taiwan, the People's Republic of China, the nations of Eastern Europe and the former Soviet Union, and in 2011, in Egypt and other nations of the Middle East.

Postindustrial Societies

Many industrial societies, including the United States, have now entered a new phase of technological development, and we can extend Lenski's analysis to take account of recent trends. A generation ago, the sociologist Daniel Bell (1973) coined the term **postindustrialism** to refer to *the production of information using computer technology.* Production in industrial societies centers on factories and machinery generating material goods; postindustrial production relies on computers and other electronic devices that create, process, store, and apply information. Just as people in industrial societies learn mechanical skills, people in postindustrial societies such as ours develop information-based skills and carry out their work using computers and other forms of high-technology communication.

As Chapter 16 ("The Economy and Work") explains, a postindustrial society uses less and less of its labor force for industrial production, and the work can be performed almost anywhere. At the same time, more jobs become available for clerical workers, teachers, writers, sales managers, and marketing representatives, all of whom have in common jobs that involve processing information.

sociocultural evolution changes that occur as a society gains new technology

hunting and gathering the use of simple tools to hunt animals and gather vegetation for food

horticulture the use of hand tools to raise crops
pastoralism the domestication of animals

agriculture large-scale cultivation using plows harnessed to animals or more powerful energy sources

industrialism the production of goods using advanced sources of energy to drive large machinery

postindustrialism the production of information using computer technology

Does advancing technology make society better? In some ways, perhaps. However, many films and TV shows—as far back as *Frankenstein* (*left*) in 1931 and as recently as the 2013 film *Iron Man 3* (*right*)—have expressed the concern that new technology not only solves old problems but also creates new ones. All the sociological theorists discussed in this chapter shared this ambivalent view of the modern world.

The Information Revolution, which is at the heart of postindustrial society, is most evident in rich nations, yet new information technology affects people in all countries around the world. As discussed in Chapter 3 ("Culture"), a worldwide flow of products, people, and information now links societies and has advanced a global culture. In this sense, the postindustrial society is at the heart of globalization.

The Limits of Technology

More complex technology has made life better by raising productivity, reducing infectious disease, and sometimes just relieving boredom. But technology provides no quick fix for social problems. Poverty, for example, remains a reality for some 46.3 million women and men in the United States (see Chapter 11, "Social Class in the United States") and 1.3 billion people worldwide (Chen & Ravaillon, 2012; U.S. Census Bureau, 2012; see Chapter 12, "Global Stratification").

Technology also creates new problems that our ancestors (and people like Sididi Ag Inaka today) could hardly imagine. Industrial and postindustrial societies give us more personal freedom, but they often lack the sense of community that was part of preindustrial life. Most seriously, an increasing number of the world's nations have used nuclear technology to build weapons that could send the entire world back to the Stone Age—if humanity survives at all.

Advancing technology has also threatened the physical environment. Each stage in sociocultural evolution has introduced more powerful sources of energy and increased our appetite for Earth's resources. Ask yourself whether we can continue to pursue material prosperity without permanently damaging our planet by consuming its limited resources or poisoning it with pollution (see Chapter 22, "Population, Urbanization, and Environment").

Technological advances have improved life and brought the world's people closer. But establishing peace, ensuring justice, and protecting the environment are problems that technology alone cannot solve.

Karl Marx: Society and Conflict

4.2 Analyze the importance of class conflict to the historical development of human societies.

The first of our classic visions of society comes from Karl Marx (1818–1883), an early giant in the field of sociology whose influence continues today. Keenly aware of how the Industrial Revolution had changed Europe, Marx spent most of his adult life in

London, the capital of what was then the vast British Empire. He was awed by the size and productive power of the new factories going up all over Britain. Along with other industrial nations, Britain was producing more goods than ever before, drawing raw materials from around the world and churning out finished products at a dizzying rate.

👁 **Watch** in **MySocLab**
Video: *Social Inequalities: Social Stratification*

What astounded Marx even more was that the riches produced by this new technology ended up in the hands of only a few people. As he walked around the city of London, he could see for himself that a handful of aristocrats and industrialists enjoyed lives of luxury and privilege, living in fabulous mansions staffed by many servants. At the same time, most people lived in slums and labored long hours for low wages. Some even slept in the streets, where they were likely to die young from diseases brought on by cold and poor nutrition.

social conflict the struggle between segments of society over valued resources

capitalists people who own and operate factories and other businesses in pursuit of profits

proletarians people who sell their labor for wages

Marx saw his society in terms of a basic contradiction: In a country so rich, how could so many people be so poor? Just as important, he asked, how can this situation be changed? Many people think Marx set out to tear societies apart. But he was motivated by compassion and wanted to help a badly divided society create a new and more just social order.

At the heart of Marx's thinking is the idea of **social conflict**, *the struggle between segments of society over valued resources.* Social conflict can, of course, take many forms: Individuals quarrel, colleges have long-standing sports rivalries, and nations sometimes go to war. For Marx, however, the most important type of social conflict was *class conflict* arising from the way a society produces material goods.

social institutions the major spheres of social life, or societal subsystems, organized to meet human needs

Society and Production

Living in the nineteenth century, Marx observed the early decades of industrial capitalism in Europe. This economic system, Marx explained, turned a small part of the population into **capitalists**, *people who own and operate factories and other businesses in pursuit of profits.* A capitalist tries to make a profit by selling a product for more than it costs to produce. Capitalism turns most of the population into industrial workers, whom Marx called **proletarians**, *people who sell their labor for wages.* To Marx, a system of capitalist production always ends up creating conflict between capitalists and workers. To keep profits high, capitalists keep wages low. But workers want higher wages. Since profits and wages come from the same pool of funds, the result is conflict. As Marx saw it, this conflict could end only with the end of capitalism itself.

All societies are composed of **social institutions**, *the major spheres of social life, or societal subsystems, organized to meet human needs.* Examples of social institutions include the economy, the political system, the family, religion, and education. In his analysis of society, Marx argued that one institution—the economy—dominates all the others and defines the character of the entire society. Drawing on the philosophical approach called *materialism,* which says that how humans produce material goods shapes their experiences, Marx believed that the other social institutions all operate in a way that supports a society's economy. Lenski focused on how technology molds a society but, for Marx, it is the economy that forms a society's "real foundation" (1959:43, orig. 1859).

Marx viewed the economic system as society's *infrastructure* (*infra* is Latin, meaning "below"). Other social institutions, including the family, the political system, and religion, are built on this foundation; they form society's *superstructure* and support the economy. Marx's theory is illustrated in Figure 4–1. For example, under capitalism, the legal system protects capitalists' wealth, and the family allows capitalists to pass their property from one generation to the next.

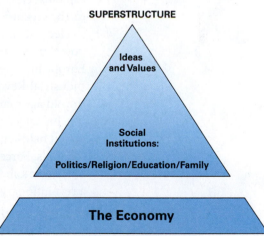

SUPERSTRUCTURE

Ideas and Values

Social Institutions:

Politics/Religion/Education/Family

The Economy

INFRASTRUCTURE

FIGURE 4–1 Karl Marx's Model of Society

This diagram illustrates Marx's materialist view that the system of economic production shapes the entire society. Economic production involves both technology (industry, in the case of capitalism) and social relationships (for capitalism, the relationship between the capitalists, who own the factories and businesses, and the workers). On this infrastructure, or foundation, rests society's superstructure, including its major social institutions as well as core cultural values and ideas. Marx maintained that every part of a society supports the economic system.

false consciousness Marx's term for explanations of social problems as the short-comings of individuals rather than as the flaws of society

Marx was well aware that most people living in an industrial capitalist system do not recognize how capitalism shapes the operation of their entire society. Most people, in fact, regard the right to own private property or pass it on to their children as "natural." In the same way, many of us tend to see rich people as having "earned" their money through long years of schooling and hard work; we see the poor, on the other hand, as lacking skills and the personal drive to make more of themselves. Marx rejected this type of thinking, calling it **false consciousness**, *explaining social problems as the shortcomings of individuals rather than as the flaws of society.* Marx was saying, in effect, that it is not "people" who make society so unequal but rather the system of capitalist production. False consciousness, he believed, hurts people by hiding the real cause of their problems.

Conflict and History

For Marx, conflict is the engine that drives social change. Sometimes societies change at a slow, *evolutionary* rate. But they may erupt in rapid, *revolutionary* change.

To Marx, early hunters and gatherers formed primitive communist societies. *Communism* is a system in which people commonly own and equally share food and other things they produce. People in hunting and gathering societies do not have much, but they share what they have. In addition, because everyone does the same kind of work, there are no class differences and thus little chance of social conflict.

With technological advance comes social inequality. Among horticultural, pastoral, and early agrarian societies—which Marx lumped together as the "ancient world"—warfare was frequent, and the victors turned their captives into slaves.

Agriculture brings still more wealth to a society's elite but does little for most other people, who labor as serfs and are barely better off than slaves. As Marx saw it, the state supported the feudal system (in which the elite or nobility had all the power), assisted by the church, which claimed that this arrangement reflected the will of God. This is why Marx thought that feudalism was simply "exploitation, veiled by religious and political illusions" (Marx & Engels, 1972:337, orig. 1848).

Gradually, new productive forces started to break down the feudal order. As trade steadily increased, cities grew, and merchants and skilled craftsworkers formed the new capitalist class or *bourgeoisie* (a French word meaning "people of the town"). After 1800, the bourgeoisie also controlled factories, becoming richer and richer so that they soon rivaled the ancient landowning nobility. For their part, the nobles looked down their noses at this upstart "commercial" class, but in time, these capitalists took control of European societies. To Marx's way of thinking, then, new technology was only part of the Industrial Revolution; it also served as a class revolution in which capitalists overthrew the old agrarian elite.

Industrialization also led to the formation of the proletariat. English landowners converted fields once plowed by serfs into grazing land for sheep to produce wool for the textile mills. Forced from the land, millions of people migrated to cities and had little choice but to work in factories. Marx envisioned these workers one day joining together to form a revolutionary class that would overthrow the capitalist system.

Capitalism and Class Conflict

"The history of all hitherto existing society is the history of class struggles." With these words, Marx and his collaborator, Friedrich Engels, began their best-known statement, the *Manifesto of the Communist Party* (1972:335, orig. 1848). Industrial capitalism, like earlier types of society, contains two major social classes: the ruling class, whose members (capitalists or bourgeoisie) own productive property, and the oppressed (proletarians), who sell their labor, reflecting the two basic positions in the productive system. Like masters and slaves in the ancient world and like nobles and serfs in feudal systems, capitalists and proletarians are engaged in class conflict today. Currently, as in the past, one class controls the other as productive property. Marx used the term **class conflict** (and sometimes *class struggle*) to refer to *conflict between entire classes over the distribution of a society's wealth and power.*

Class conflict is nothing new. What distinguishes the conflict in capitalist society, Marx pointed out, is how out in the open it is. Agrarian nobles and serfs, for all their differences, were bound together by traditions and mutual obligations. Industrial capitalism dissolved those ties so that loyalty and honor were replaced by "naked self-interest." Because the proletarians had no personal ties to the capitalists, Marx saw no reason for them to put up with their oppression.

Marx knew that revolution would not come easily. First, workers must *become aware* of their oppression and see capitalism as its true cause. Second, they must *organize and act* to address their problems. This means that false consciousness must be replaced with **class consciousness**, *workers' recognition of themselves as a class unified in opposition to capitalists and ultimately to capitalism itself.* Because the inhumanity of early capitalism was plain for him to see, Marx concluded that industrial workers would soon rise up to destroy this economic system.

How would the capitalists react? Their wealth made them strong. But Marx saw a weakness in the capitalist armor. Motivated by a desire for personal gain, capitalists feared competition with other capitalists. Marx predicted, therefore, that capitalists would be slow to band together despite their common interests. In addition, he reasoned, capitalists kept employees' wages low in order to maximize profits, which made the workers' misery ever greater. In the long run, Marx believed, capitalists would bring about their own undoing.

class conflict conflict between entire classes over the distribution of a society's wealth and power

class consciousness workers' recognition of themselves as a class unified in opposition to capitalists and ultimately to capitalism itself

Read in **MySocLab Document:** *Manifesto of the Communist Party* by Karl Marx and Friedrich Engels

Capitalism and Alienation

Marx also condemned capitalist society for producing **alienation**, *the experience of isolation and misery resulting from powerlessness.* To the capitalists, workers are nothing more than a source of labor, to be hired and fired at will. Dehumanized by their jobs (repetitive factory work in the past and processing orders on a computer today), workers find little satisfaction and feel unable to improve their situation. Here we see another contradiction of capitalist society: As people develop technology to gain power over the world, the capitalist economy gains more control over people.

alienation the experience of isolation and misery resulting from powerlessness

Marx noted four ways in which capitalism alienates workers:

1. **Alienation from the act of working.** Ideally, people work to meet their needs and to develop their personal potential. Capitalism, however, denies workers a say in what they make or how they make it. Further, much of the work is a repetition of routine tasks. The fact that today we replace workers with machines whenever possible would not have surprised Marx. As far as he was concerned, capitalism had turned human beings into machines long ago.

2. **Alienation from the products of work.** The product of work belongs not to workers but to capitalists, who sell it for profit. Thus, Marx reasoned, the more of themselves workers invest in their work, the more they lose.

3. **Alienation from other workers.** Through work, Marx claimed, people build bonds of community. Industrial capitalism, however, makes work competitive rather than cooperative, setting each person apart from everyone else and offering little chance for companionship.

A common fear among thinkers in the early industrial era was that people, now slaves to the new machines, would be stripped of their humanity. No one captured this idea better than the comic actor Charlie Chaplin, who wrote and starred in the 1936 film *Modern Times*.

4. **Alienation from human potential.** Industrial capitalism alienates workers from their human potential. Marx argued that a worker "does not fulfill himself in his work but denies himself, has a feeling of misery rather than well-being, does not freely develop his physical and mental energies, but is physically exhausted and mentally debased. The worker, therefore, feels himself to be at home only during his leisure time, whereas at work he feels homeless" (1964:124–25, orig. 1848). In short, industrial capitalism turns an activity that should express the best qualities in human beings into a dull and dehumanizing experience.

Marx viewed alienation, in its various forms, as a barrier to social change. But he hoped that industrial workers would overcome their alienation by uniting into a true social class, aware of the cause of their problems and ready to change society.

Revolution

The only way out of the trap of capitalism, Marx argued, is to remake society. He imagined a system of production that could provide for the social needs of all. He called this system *socialism*. Although Marx knew that such a dramatic change would not come easily, he must have been disappointed that he did not live to see workers in England rise up. Still, convinced that capitalism was a social evil, he believed that in time the working majority would realize they held the key to a better future. This change would certainly be revolutionary and perhaps even violent. Marx believed that a socialist society would bring class conflict to an end.

Chapter 10 ("Social Stratification") explains more about changes in industrial-capitalist societies since Marx's time and why the revolution he envisioned never took place. In addition, as Chapter 17 ("Politics and Government") explains, Marx failed to foresee that the revolution he imagined could take the form of repressive regimes, such as Stalin's government in the Soviet Union, that would end up killing tens of millions of people (R. F. Hamilton, 2001). But in his own time, Marx looked toward the future with hope: "The proletarians have nothing to lose but their chains. They have a world to win" (Marx & Engels, 1972:362, orig. 1848).

Max Weber: The Rationalization of Society

4.3 Demonstrate the importance of ideas to the development of human societies.

With a wide-ranging knowledge of law, economics, religion, and history, Max Weber (1864–1920) produced what many experts regard as the greatest individual contribution ever made to sociology. This scholar, born to a prosperous family in Germany, had much to say about how modern society differs from earlier types of social organization.

Weber understood the power of technology, and he shared many of Marx's ideas about social conflict. But he disagreed with Marx's philosophy of materialism. Weber's philosophical approach, called *idealism*, emphasized how human ideas—especially beliefs and values—shape society. He argued that the most important difference among societies is not how people produce things but how people think about the world. In Weber's view, modern society was the product of a new way of thinking.

Weber compared societies in different times and places. To make the comparisons, he relied on the **ideal type**, *an abstract statement of the essential characteristics of any social phenomenon*. Following Weber's approach, for example, we might speak of "preindustrial" and "industrial" societies as ideal types. The use of the word "ideal" does not mean that one or the other is "good" or "best." Nor does an ideal type refer to any actual society. Rather, think of an ideal type as a way of defining a type of society in its pure form. We have already used ideal types in comparing "hunting and gathering societies" with "industrial societies" and "capitalism" with "socialism."

Watch in MySocLab
Video: *The Big Picture: What Is Sociology?*

ideal type an abstract statement of the essential characteristics of any social phenomenon

Two Worldviews: Tradition and Rationality

Rather than categorizing societies according to their technology or productive systems, Weber focused on ways that people think about their world. Members of preindustrial societies, Weber explained, are bound by *tradition,* and people in industrial-capitalist societies are guided by *rationality.*

By **tradition**, Weber meant *values and beliefs passed from generation to generation.* In other words, traditional people are guided by the past, and they feel a strong attachment to long-established ways of life. They consider particular actions right and proper mostly because they have been accepted for so long.

People in modern societies, however, favor **rationality**, *a way of thinking that emphasizes deliberate, matter-of-fact calculation of the most efficient way to accomplish a particular task.* Sentimental ties to the past have no place in a rational worldview, and tradition becomes simply one type of information. Typically, modern people think and act on the basis of what they see as the present and future consequences of their choices. They evaluate jobs, schooling, and even relationships in terms of what they put into them and what they expect to receive in return.

Weber viewed both the Industrial Revolution and the development of capitalism as evidence of modern rationality. Such changes are all part of the **rationalization of society**, *the historical change from tradition to rationality as the main type of human thought.* Weber went on to describe modern society as "disenchanted" because scientific thinking has swept away most of people's sentimental ties to the past.

The willingness to adopt the latest technology is one strong indicator of how rationalized a society is. To illustrate the global pattern of rationalization, Global Map 4–1 on page 112 shows where in the world personal computers are found. In general, members of high-income societies in North America and Europe use personal computers the most, but these devices are rare in low-income nations.

Why are some societies more eager than others to adopt new technology? Those with a more rational worldview might consider new computer or medical technology a breakthrough, but those with a very traditional culture might reject such devices as a threat to their way of life. The Tuareg nomads of northern Mali, described at the beginning of this chapter, shrug off the idea of using telephones: Why would anyone herding animals in the desert need a cell phone? Similarly, in the United States, the Amish refuse to have telephones in their homes because it is not part of their traditional way of life.

In Weber's view, the amount of technological innovation depends on how a society's people understand their world. Many people throughout history have had the opportunity to adopt new technology, but only in the rational cultural climate of Western Europe did people exploit scientific discoveries to spark the Industrial Revolution (Weber, 1958, orig. 1904–05).

To the outside observer, the trading floor of a stock exchange may look like complete craziness. But in such activity Weber saw the essence of modern rationality.

rationalization of society the historical change from tradition to rationality as the main type of human thought

tradition values and beliefs passed from generation to generation

rationality a way of thinking that emphasizes deliberate, matter-of-fact calculation of the most efficient way to accomplish a particular task

Is Capitalism Rational?

Is industrial capitalism a rational economic system? Here again, Weber and Marx ended up on different sides. Weber considered industrial capitalism highly rational because capitalists

Window on the World

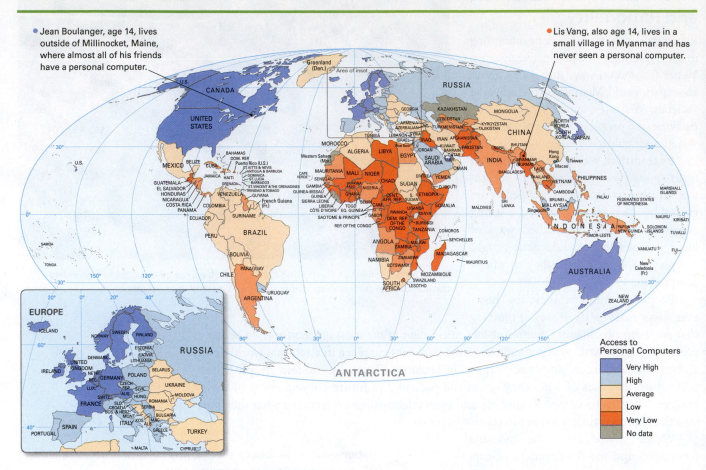

● Jean Boulanger, age 14, lives outside of Millinocket, Maine, where almost all of his friends have a personal computer.

● Lis Vang, also age 14, lives in a small village in Myanmar and has never seen a personal computer.

Access to Personal Computers

- Very High
- High
- Average
- Low
- Very Low
- No data

GLOBAL MAP 4–1 High Technology in Global Perspective

Countries with traditional cultures cannot afford, choose to ignore, or even intentionally resist new technology that nations with highly rationalized ways of life quickly embrace. Personal computers, central to today's high technology, are commonplace in high-income countries such as the United States. In low-income nations, by contrast, they are unknown to most people.

Source: United Nations (2010) and International Telecommunication Union (2012).

try to make money in any way they can. Marx, however, thought capitalism irrational because it fails to meet the basic needs of most of the people (Gerth & Mills, 1946:49).

Weber's Great Thesis: Protestantism and Capitalism

Weber spent many years considering how and why industrial capitalism developed in the first place. Why did it emerge in parts of Western Europe during the eighteenth and nineteenth centuries?

Weber claimed that the key to the birth of industrial capitalism lay in the Protestant Reformation. Specifically, he saw industrial capitalism as the major outcome of Calvinism, a Christian religious movement founded by John Calvin (1509–1564). Calvinists approached life in a formal and rational way that Weber characterized as *inner-worldly asceticism*. This mind-set leads people to deny themselves worldly pleasures in favor of a highly disciplined focus on economic pursuits. In practice, Calvinism encouraged people to put their time and energy into their work; in modern terms, we might say that such people become good businesspeople or entrepreneurs (Berger, 2009).

Another of Calvin's most important ideas was *predestination,* the belief that an all-knowing and all-powerful God had predestined some people for salvation and others for damnation. Believing that everyone's fate was set before birth, early Calvinists thought that people could only guess at what their destiny was and that, in any case, they could do nothing to change it. So Calvinists swung between hopeful visions of spiritual salvation and anxious fears of eternal damnation.

Frustrated at not knowing their fate, Calvinists gradually came to a resolution of sorts. Wouldn't those chosen for glory in the next world, they reasoned, see signs of divine favor in *this* world? In this way, Calvinists came to see worldly prosperity as a sign of God's grace. Eager to gain this reassurance, Calvinists threw themselves into a quest for business success, applying rationality, discipline, and hard work to their tasks. They were certainly pursuing wealth, but they were not doing this for the sake of money, at least not to spend on themselves because any self-indulgence would be sinful. Neither were Calvinists likely to use their wealth for charity. To share their wealth with the poor seemed to go against God's will because they viewed poverty as a sign of God's rejection. Calvinists' duty was pressing forward in what they saw as their personal *calling* from God, reinvesting the money they made for still greater success. It is easy to see how such activity—saving money, using wealth to create more wealth, and adopting new technology—became the foundation of capitalism.

Other world religions did not encourage the rational pursuit of wealth the way Calvinism did. Catholicism, the traditional religion in most of Europe, taught a passive, "otherworldly" view: Good deeds performed humbly on Earth would bring rewards in heaven. For Catholics, making money had none of the spiritual significance it had for Calvinists. Weber concluded that this was the reason that industrial capitalism developed primarily in areas of Europe where Calvinism was strong.

Weber's study of Calvinism provides striking evidence of the power of ideas to shape society. Not one to accept simple explanations, Weber knew that industrial capitalism had many causes. But by stressing the importance of ideas, Weber tried to counter Marx's strictly economic explanation of modern society.

As the decades passed, later generations of Calvinists lost much of their early religious enthusiasm. But their drive for success and personal discipline remained, and what started out as a *religious* ethic was gradually transformed into a *work* ethic. In this sense, Weber considered industrial capitalism to be a "disenchanted" religion, with wealth no longer valued as a sign of salvation but for its own sake. This transformation is seen in the fact that the practice of "accounting," which to early Calvinists meant keeping a daily record of their moral deeds, before long came to mean simply keeping track of money.

Rational Social Organization

According to Weber, rationality is the basis of modern society, giving rise to both the Industrial Revolution and capitalism. He went on to identify seven characteristics of rational social organization:

1. **Distinctive social institutions.** In hunting and gathering societies, the family is the center of all activity. Gradually, however, religious, political, and economic systems develop as separate social institutions. In modern societies, new institutions—including education and health care—also appear. Specialized social institutions are a rational strategy to meet human needs efficiently.

2. **Large-scale organizations.** Modern rationality can be seen in the spread of large-scale organizations. As early as the horticultural era, small groups of political officials made decisions concerning religious observances, public works, and warfare. By the time Europe had developed agrarian societies, the Catholic church had grown into a much larger organization with thousands of officials. In today's modern, rational society, almost everyone works for large formal organizations, and federal and state governments employ tens of millions of workers.

3. **Specialized tasks.** Unlike members of traditional societies, people in modern societies are likely to have very specialized jobs. The Yellow Pages of any city's telephone directory suggest just how many thousands of different occupations there are today.

4. **Personal discipline.** Modern societies put a premium on self-discipline. Most business and government organizations expect their workers to be disciplined, and discipline is also encouraged by our cultural values of achievement and success.

5. **Awareness of time.** In traditional societies, people measure time according to the rhythm of sun and seasons. Modern people, by contrast, schedule events precisely by the hour and even the minute. Clocks began appearing in European cities some 500 years ago, about the same time commerce began to expand. Soon people began to think (to borrow Benjamin Franklin's phrase) that "time is money."

6. **Technical competence.** Members of traditional societies size up one another on the basis of *who* they are—their family ties. Modern rationality leads us to judge people according to *what* they are, with an eye toward their education, skills, and abilities. Most workers have to keep up with the latest skills and knowledge in their field in order to be successful.

7. **Impersonality.** In a rational society, technical competence is the basis for hiring, so the world becomes impersonal. People interact as specialists concerned with particular tasks rather than as individuals concerned with one another as people. Because showing your feelings can threaten personal discipline, modern people tend to devalue emotion.

All these characteristics can be found in one important expression of modern rationality: bureaucracy.

Rationality, Bureaucracy, and Science

Weber considered the growth of large, rational organizations one of the defining traits of modern societies. Another term for this type of organization is *bureaucracy*. Weber believed that bureaucracy has much in common with capitalism—another key factor in modern social life:

> Today, it is primarily the capitalist market economy which demands that the official business of public administration be discharged precisely, unambiguously, continuously, and with as much speed as possible. Normally, the very large capitalist enterprises are themselves unequaled models of strict bureaucratic organization. (1978:974, orig. 1921)

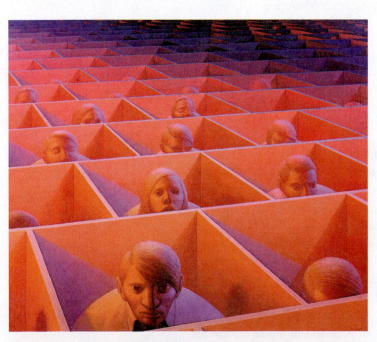

Max Weber agreed with Karl Marx that modern society is alienating to the individual, but they identified different causes of this problem. For Marx, economic inequality is the reason; for Weber, the problem is isolating and dehumanizing bureaucracy. George Tooker's painting *Landscape with Figures* echoes Weber's sentiments.
George Tooker, *Landscape with Figures*, 1963, egg tempera on gesso panel, 26 × 30 in. Private collection. Reproduction courtesy D. C. Moore Gallery, New York.

As Chapter 7 ("Groups and Organizations") explains, we find aspects of bureaucracy in today's businesses, government agencies, labor unions, and universities. Weber considered bureaucracy highly rational because its elements—offices, duties, and policies—help achieve specific goals as efficiently as possible. To Weber, capitalism, bureaucracy, and also science—the highly disciplined pursuit of knowledge—are all expressions of the same underlying factor that defines modern society: rationality.

Rationality and Alienation

Weber agreed with Marx that industrial capitalism was highly productive. Weber also agreed with Marx that modern society generates widespread alienation, although Weber pointed to different reasons. Marx thought alienation was caused by economic inequality. Weber blamed alienation on bureaucracy's countless rules and regulations. Bureaucracies, Weber warned, treat a human being as a "number" or a "case" rather than as a unique individual. In addition, working for large organizations demands highly specialized and often tedious routines. In the end, Weber saw modern society as a vast and growing system of rules trying to regulate everything, and he feared that modern society would end up crushing the human spirit.

Like Marx, Weber found it ironic that modern society, meant to serve humanity, turns on its creators and enslaves them. Just as Marx described the dehumanizing effects of industrial capitalism, Weber portrayed the modern individual as "only a small cog in a ceaselessly moving mechanism that prescribes to him an endlessly fixed routine of march" (1978:988, orig. 1921). Although Weber could see the advantages of modern society, he was deeply pessimistic about the future. He feared that in the end, the rationalization of society would reduce human beings to robots.

Emile Durkheim: Society and Function

(4.4) Contrast the social bonds typical of traditional and modern societies.

"To love society is to love something beyond us and something in ourselves." These are the words (1974:55, orig. 1924) of the French sociologist Emile Durkheim (1858–1917), another of the discipline's founders. In Durkeim's ideas we find another important vision of human society.

Structure: Society beyond Ourselves

Emile Durkheim's great insight was recognizing that society exists beyond ourselves. Society is more than the individuals who compose it. Society was here long before we were born, it shapes us while we live, and it will remain long after we are gone. Patterns of human behavior—cultural norms, values, and beliefs—exist as established structures, or *social facts,* that have an objective reality beyond the lives of individuals.

Because society is bigger than any one of us, it has the power to guide our thoughts and actions. This is why studying individuals alone (as psychologists or biologists do) can never capture the heart of the social experience. A classroom of college students taking a math exam, a family gathered around a table sharing a meal, people quietly waiting their turn in a doctor's office—all are examples of the countless situations that have a familiar organization apart from any particular individual who has ever been part of them.

Once created by people, Durkheim claimed, society takes on a life of its own and demands a measure of obedience from its creators. We experience the power of society when we see lives falling into common patterns or when we feel the tug of morality during a moment of temptation.

Function: Society as System

Having established that society has structure, Durkheim turned to the concept of *function.* The significance of any social fact, he explained, is more than what individuals see in their immediate lives; social facts help along the operation of society as a whole.

Consider crime. As victims of crime, individuals experience pain and loss. But taking a broader view, Durkheim saw that crime is vital to the ongoing life of society itself. As Chapter 9 ("Deviance") explains, only by defining acts as wrong do people construct and defend morality, which gives direction and meaning to our collective life. For this reason, Durkheim rejected the common view of crime as abnormal. On the contrary, he concluded, crime is "normal" for the most basic of reasons: A society could not exist without it (1964a, orig. 1893; 1964b, orig. 1895).

Personality: Society in Ourselves

Durkheim said that society is not only "beyond ourselves" but also "in ourselves," helping to form our personalities. How we act, think, and feel is drawn from the society that nurtures us. Society shapes us in another way as well—by providing the moral discipline that guides our behavior and controls our desires. Durkheim believed that human beings need the restraint of society because as creatures who can want more and more, we are in constant danger of being overpowered by our own desires. As he put it, "The more one

Durkheim's observation that people with weak social bonds are prone to self-destructive behavior stands as stark evidence of the power of society to shape individual lives. When rock-and-roll singers become famous, they are wrenched out of familiar life patterns and existing relationships, sometimes with deadly results. The history of rock-and-roll contains many tragic stories of this kind, including (*from left*) Janis Joplin's and Jimi Hendrix's deaths by drug overdose (both 1970), Kurt Cobain's suicide (1994), the drugs-induced death of Michael Jackson (2009), and the death of Amy Winehouse by alcohol poisoning (2011).

Watch in **MySocLab**
Video: *Sociology in Focus: What Is Sociology?*

has, the more one wants, since satisfactions received only stimulate instead of filling needs" (1966:248, orig. 1897).

Nowhere is the need for societal regulation better illustrated than in Durkheim's study of suicide (1966, orig. 1897), which was described in Chapter 1 ("The Sociological Perspective"). Why is it that rock stars—from Del Shannon, Elvis Presley, Janis Joplin, and Jim Morrison to Jimi Hendrix, Keith Moon, Kurt Cobain, Michael Jackson, and Amy Winehouse—seem so prone to self-destruction? Durkheim had the answer long before the invention of the electric guitar: Now as back then, the *highest* suicide rates are found among categories of people with the *lowest* level of societal integration. In short, the enormous freedom of the young, rich, and famous carries a high price in terms of the risk of suicide.

Modernity and Anomie

Compared to traditional societies, modern societies impose fewer restrictions on everyone. Durkheim acknowledged the advantages of modern-day freedom, but he warned of increased **anomie**, *a condition in which society provides little moral guidance to individuals*. The pattern by which many celebrities are "destroyed by fame" well illustrates the destructive effects of anomie. Sudden fame tears people from their families and familiar routines, disrupts established values and norms, and breaks down society's support and regulation of the individual—sometimes with fatal results. Therefore, Durkheim explained, an individual's desires must be balanced by the claims and guidance of society—a balance that is sometimes difficult to achieve in the modern world. Durkheim would not have been surprised to see a rising suicide rate in modern societies such as the United States.

anomie Durkheim's term for a condition in which society provides little moral guidance to individuals

Evolving Societies: The Division of Labor

Like Marx and Weber, Durkheim lived through the rapid social change that swept across Europe during the nineteenth century as the Industrial Revolution unfolded. But Durkheim offered his own understanding of this change.

In preindustrial societies, he explained, tradition operates as the social cement that binds people together. In fact, what he termed the *collective conscience* is so strong that the community moves quickly to punish anyone who dares to challenge conventional ways of life. Durkheim used the term **mechanical solidarity** to refer to *social bonds, based on common sentiments and shared moral values, that are strong among members of preindustrial societies*. In practice, mechanical solidarity is based on *similarity*. Durkheim called these bonds "mechanical" because people are linked together in lockstep, with a more or less automatic sense of belonging together and acting alike.

mechanical solidarity social bonds, based on common sentiments and shared moral values, that are strong among members of preindustrial societies

organic solidarity social bonds, based on specialization and interdependence, that are stong among members of industrial societies

division of labor specialized economic activity

With industrialization, Durkheim continued, mechanical solidarity becomes weaker and weaker, and people are much less bound by tradition. But this does not mean that society dissolves. Modern life creates a new type of solidarity. Durkheim called this new social integration **organic solidarity**, defined as *social bonds, based on specialization and interdependence, that are strong among members of industrial societies*. The solidarity that was once rooted in likeness is now based on *differences* among people who find that their specialized work—as plumbers, college students, midwives, or sociology instructors—makes them rely on other people for most of their daily needs.

For Durkheim, then, the key to change in a society is an expanding **division of labor**, or *specialized economic activity*. Weber said that modern societies specialize in order to become more efficient, and Durkheim filled out the picture by showing that members of modern societies count on tens of thousands of others—most of them strangers—for the goods and services needed every day. As members of modern societies, we depend more and more on people we trust less and less. Why do we look to people we hardly know and whose beliefs may well differ from our own? Durkheim's answer was "because we can't live without them."

So modern society rests far less on *moral consensus* and far more on *functional interdependence*. Herein lies what we might call "Durkheim's dilemma": The technological power and greater personal freedom of modern society come at the cost of declining morality and the rising risk of anomie.

Like Marx and Weber, Durkheim worried about the direction society was taking. But of the three, Durkheim was the most optimistic. He saw that large, anonymous societies gave people more freedom and privacy than small towns. Anomie remains a danger, but Durkheim hoped we would be able to create laws and other norms to regulate our behavior.

In traditional societies, people dress the same and everyone does much the same work. These societies are held together by strong moral beliefs. Modern societies, illustrated by urban areas in this country, are held together by a system of production in which people perform specialized work and rely on one another for all the things they cannot do for themselves.

Seeing Sociology in Everyday Life

Today's Information Revolution: What Would Durkheim, Weber, and Marx Have Thought?

Colleen: Didn't Marx predict there'd be a class revolution?
Masako: Well, yes, but in the information age, what are the classes that are supposed to be in conflict?

New technology is changing our society at a dizzying pace. Were they alive today, the founding sociologists discussed in this chapter would be eager observers of the current scene. Imagine for a moment the kinds of questions Emile Durkheim, Max Weber, and Karl Marx might ask about the effects of computer technology on our everyday lives.

Durkheim, who emphasized the increasing division of labor in modern society, would probably wonder if new information technology is pushing work specialization even further. There is good reason to think that it is. Because electronic communication (say, a website) gives anyone a vast market (currently about 2.3 billion people access the Internet), people can specialize far more than if they were trying to make a living in a small geographic area. For example, while most small-town lawyers have a general practice, an information age attorney, living anywhere, can provide specialized guidance on, say, prenuptial agreements or electronic copyright law. As we move into the electronic age, the number of highly specialized small businesses (some of which end up becoming very large) in all fields is increasing rapidly.

Durkheim might also point out that the Internet threatens to increase our experience of anomie. Using computers has a tendency to isolate people from personal relationships with others. Perhaps, as one analyst puts it, as we expect more from our machines, we expect less from each other (Turkle, 2011). An additional problem is that, although the Internet offers a flood of information, it provides little in the way of moral guidance about what is wise or good or worth knowing.

Weber believed that modern societies are distinctive because their members share a rational worldview, and nothing illustrates this worldview better than bureaucracy. But will bureaucracy be as important during the twenty-first century? Here is one reason to think it may not: Although organizations will probably continue to regulate workers performing the kinds of routine tasks that were common in the industrial era, much work in the postindustrial era involves imagination. Consider such "new age" work as designing homes, composing music, and writing software. This kind of creative work cannot be regulated in the same way as putting together automobiles as they move down an assembly line. Perhaps this is the reason many high-technology companies have done away with worker dress codes and having employees punch in and out on a time clock.

Finally, what might Marx make of the Information Revolution? Since Marx considered the earlier Industrial Revolution a *class* revolution that allowed the owners of industry to dominate society, he would probably be concerned about the emergence of a new symbolic elite. Some analysts point out that film and television writers, producers, and performers now enjoy vast wealth, international prestige, and enormous power. Just as people without industrial skills stayed at the bottom of the class system in past decades, so people without symbolic skills may well become the "underclass" of the twenty-first century. Globally, there is a "digital divide" by which most people in rich countries, but few people in poor countries, are part of the Information Revolution (ITU, 2012).

Durkheim, Weber, and Marx greatly improved our understanding of industrial societies. As we continue into the postindustrial age, there is plenty of room for new generations of sociologists to carry on.

What Do You Think?

1. As we try to understand the Information Revolution that defines our postindustrial society, which of the founding sociologists considered in this chapter—Marx, Weber, or Durkheim—do you find most useful? Why?

2. In what ways do you think the development of computer technology has made our lives better? Try to be specific about what has improved.

3. In what ways do you think computer technology has harmed our society or made life more challenging? Again, be specific about the problems you see.

How can we apply Durkheim's views to the Information Revolution? The Seeing Sociology in Everyday Life box suggests that Durkheim, as well as two of the other theorists whose ideas we have considered in this chapter, would have had much to say about today's new computer technology.

Critical Review: Four Visions of Society

4.5 Summarize the contributions of Lenski, Marx, Weber, and Durkheim to our understanding of social change.

This chapter opened with several important questions about society. We will conclude by summarizing how each of the four visions of society answers these questions.

What Holds Societies Together?

How is something as complex as society possible? Lenski claims that members of a society are united by a shared culture, although cultural patterns become more diverse as a society gains more complex technology. He also points out that as technology becomes more complex, inequality divides a society more and more, although industrialization reduces inequality somewhat.

Marx saw in society not unity but social division based on class position. From his point of view, elites may force an uneasy peace, but true social unity can occur only if production becomes a cooperative process. To Weber, the members of a society share a worldview. Just as tradition joined people together in the past, so modern societies have created rational, large-scale organizations that connect people's lives. Finally, Durkheim made solidarity the focus of his work. He contrasted the mechanical solidarity of preindustrial societies, which is based on shared morality, with modern society's organic solidarity, which is based on specialization.

How Have Societies Changed?

According to Lenski's model of sociocultural evolution, societies differ mostly in terms of changing technology. Modern society stands out from past societies in terms of its enormous productive power. Marx, too, noted historical differences in productivity yet pointed to continuing social conflict (except perhaps among simple hunters and gatherers). For Marx, modern society is distinctive mostly because it brings that conflict out into the open. Weber considered the question of change from the perspective of how people look at the world. Members of preindustrial societies have a traditional outlook; modern people take a rational worldview. Finally, for Durkheim, traditional societies are characterized by mechanical solidarity based on moral likeness. In modern industrial societies, mechanical solidarity gives way to organic solidarity based on productive specialization.

Why Do Societies Change?

As Lenski sees it, social change comes about through technological innovation that over time transforms an entire society. Marx's materialist approach highlights the struggle between classes as the engine of change, pushing societies toward revolution. Weber, by contrast, pointed out that ideas contribute to social change. He demonstrated how a particular worldview—Calvinism—set in motion the Industrial Revolution, which ended up reshaping all of society. Finally, Durkheim pointed to an expanding division of labor as the key dimension of social change.

The fact that these four approaches are so different does not mean that any one of them is right or wrong in an absolute sense. Society is exceedingly complex, and our understanding of society benefits from applying all four visions.

How do we understand something as complex as human society? Each of the thinkers profiled in this chapter offers insights about the meaning and importance of modern society. Each has a somewhat different view and provides a partial answer to a very complex issue.

Seeing Sociology in Everyday Life

Does having advanced technology make a society better?

The four thinkers discussed in this chapter all had their doubts. Here's a chance for you to do some thinking about the pros and cons of computer technology in terms of its effect on our everyday lives. For each of the three photos shown here and on page 121, answer these questions: What do you see as the advantages of this technology for our everyday lives? What are the disadvantages?

Mark has recently started a new job and he decided to carry a laptop equipped so that he can access the Internet and receive email even out on the lake. What advantages and disadvantages do you think this technology provides to Mark?

Andy's parents have learned that letting him play video games on a computer tablet ensures that they'll be able to enjoy a distraction-free restaurant meal. Assess the use of computer technology as a form of recreation.

Whether we're college students or famous actresses, most of us have become accustomed to staying in touch with friends as we ride in a car, wait for our dinner in a restaurant, go for a daily walk, or pass the time during a break in a sporting event. What advantages and disadvantages do you see in cell phone technology?

HINT In the first case, being linked to the Internet allows us to stay in touch with the office, and this may help our careers. At the same time, being "connected" in this way blurs the line between work and play, just as it may allow work to come into our lives at home. In addition, employers may expect us to be on call 24-7.

In the second case, computer gaming can certainly be fun and it may develop various sensory-motor skills. At the same time, the rise of computer gaming discourages physical play and plays a part in the alarming increase of obesity, which now affects more than one in five children. Also, personal computer technology has the effect of isolating individuals, not only from the natural world but also from other people.

In the third case, cell phones allow us to talk with others and to send and receive text messages. Of course, we all know that cell phones and cars don't add up to safe driving. In addition, doesn't talking on cell phones in public end up reducing our privacy? And what about the other people around us? How do you feel about having to listen to the personal conversations of people sitting nearby?

Seeing Sociology in *Your* Everyday Life

1. The defining trait of a postindustrial society is computer technology. Spend a few minutes walking around your apartment, dorm room, or home trying to identify every device that has a computer chip in it. How many did you find? Were you surprised by the number?

2. Go to MySocLab and click on the Student Resources link to access the Sociology in Focus blog, where you can read the latest posts by a team of young sociologists who apply the sociological perspective to topics of popular culture.

3. Is modern society good for us? This chapter makes clear that the founders of sociology were aware that modern societies provide many benefits, but all of them were also critical of modern society. Based on what you have read in this chapter, list three ways in which you would argue modern society is better than traditional societies. Also point to three ways in which you think traditional societies are better than modern societies. Go to the "Seeing Sociology in *Your* Everyday Life" feature in MySocLab to learn more about the experience of living in modern society and how we can learn to face up to the challenges of modern life.

Making the Grade

Gerhard Lenski: Society and Technology

4.1 Describe how technological development has shaped the history of human societies. (pages 100–106)

 Explore the **Map** in **MySocLab**

Gerhard Lenski points to the importance of **technology** in shaping any society.

Hunting and gathering societies

- have only a few dozen members, are built around the family, and are nomadic
- consider men and women roughly equal in social importance; men use simple tools to hunt animals and women gather vegetation

Horticultural and pastoral societies

- raise animals for food and use hand tools to raise crops
- show greater specialization of work
- show increasing levels of social inequality

Agrarian societies

- use plows harnessed to animals or more powerful energy sources to enable large-scale cultivation
- show even greater specialization, with dozens of distinct occupations
- have extreme social inequality, and reduce the importance of women

Industrialization

- uses advanced sources of energy to drive large machinery
- moves work from home to factory, and reduces the traditional importance of the family
- reduces the traditional importance of the family
- raises living standards

Postindustrialization

- shifts production from heavy machinery making material things to computers processing information
- requires a population with information-based skills
- is the driving force behind the Information Revolution, a worldwide flow of information that now links societies with an emerging global culture

society people who interact in a defined territory and share a culture

sociocultural evolution Lenski's term for the changes that occur as a society gains new technology

hunting and gathering making use of simple tools to hunt animals and gather vegetation for food

horticulture the use of hand tools to raise crops

pastoralism the domestication of animals

agriculture large-scale cultivation using plows harnessed to animals or more powerful energy sources

industrialism the production of goods using advanced sources of energy to drive large machinery

postindustrialism the production of information using computer technology

Karl Marx: Society and Conflict

4.2 Analyze the importance of class conflict to the historical development of human societies. (pages 106–10)

 Watch the **Video** in **MySocLab**    **Read** the **Document** in **MySocLab**

Karl Marx's **materialist approach** claims that societies are defined by their economic systems: How humans produce material goods shapes their experiences.

Conflict and History

Marx traced conflict between social classes in societies as the source of social change throughout history:

- In "ancient" societies, masters dominated slaves.
- In agrarian societies, nobles dominated serfs.
- In industrial-capitalist societies, capitalists dominate proletarians.

Capitalism

Marx focused on the role of **capitalism** in creating inequality and class conflict in modern societies.

social conflict the struggle between segments of society over valued resources

capitalists people who own and operate factories and other businesses in pursuit of profits

proletarians people who sell their labor for wages

social institutions the major spheres of social life, or societal subsystems, organized to meet human needs

false consciousness Marx's term for explanations of social problems as the short-comings of individuals rather than as the flaws of society

- The ruling class (capitalists) oppresses the working class (proletarians).
- Capitalism alienates workers from the act of working, from the products of work, from other workers, and from their own potential.
- Marx predicted that a workers' revolution would overthrow capitalism and replace it with socialism, a system of production that would provide for the social needs of all.

class conflict conflict between entire classes over the distribution of a society's wealth and power

class consciousness Marx's term for workers' recognition of themselves as a class unified in opposition to capitalists and ultimately to capitalism itself

alienation the experience of isolation and misery resulting from powerlessness

Max Weber: The Rationalization of Society

4.3 Demonstrate the importance of ideas to the development of human societies. (pages 110–15)

👁 Watch the Video in MySocLab

Max Weber's **idealist approach** emphasizes the power of ideas to shape society.

Ideas and History

Weber traced the ideas—especially beliefs and values—that have shaped societies throughout history.
- Members of preindustrial societies are bound by **tradition**.
- Members of industrial-capitalist societies are guided by **rationality**.

The Rise of Rationality

Weber focused on the growth of large, rational organizations as the defining characteristic of modern societies.
- Increasing rationality gave rise to both the Industrial Revolution and capitalism.
- Protestantism (specifically, Calvinism) encouraged the rational pursuit of wealth, laying the groundwork for the rise of industrial-capitalism.
- Weber feared that excessive rationality, while promoting efficiency, would stifle human creativity.

ideal type an abstract statement of the essential characteristics of any social phenomenon

tradition values and beliefs passed from generation to generation

rationality a way of thinking that emphasizes deliberate, matter-of-fact calculation of the most efficient way to accomplish a particular task

rationalization of society Weber's term for the historical change from tradition to rationality as the main type of human thought

Emile Durkheim: Society and Function

4.4 Contrast the social bonds typical of traditional and modern societies. (pages 115–18)

👁 Watch the Video in MySocLab

Emile Durkheim claimed that society has an existence apart from its individual members.

Structure and Function

Durkheim believed that because society is bigger than any one of us, it dictates how we are expected to act in any given social situation.
- Social elements (such as crime) have functions that help society operate.
- Society also shapes our personalities and provides the moral discipline that guides our behavior and controls our desires.

Evolving Societies

Durkheim traced the evolution of social change by describing the different ways societies throughout history have guided the lives of their members.
- In preindustrial societies, **mechanical solidarity** guides the social life of individuals.
- Industrialization and the **division of labor** weaken traditional bonds, so that social life in modern societies is characterized by **organic solidarity**.
- Durkheim warned of increased **anomie** in modern societies, as society provides little moral guidance to individuals.

anomie Durkheim's term for a condition in which society provides little moral guidance to individuals

mechanical solidarity Durkheim's term for social bonds, based on common sentiments and shared moral values, that are strong among members of preindustrial societies

organic solidarity Durkheim's term for social bonds, based on specialization and interdependence, that are strong among members of industrial societies

division of labor specialized economic activity

Critical Review: Four Visions of Society

4.5 Summarize the contributions of Lenski, Marx, Weber, and Durkheim to our understanding of social change. (page 119)

- All four see modern societies as distinct from societies of the past.
- Each thinker highlights a difference dimension of change: For Lenski, it is technology; for Marx it is social conflict; for Weber it is ideas; for Durkheim it is the increasing degree of specialization.

5 Socialization

((• Listen to Chapter 5 in MySocLab

LEARNING OBJECTIVES

5.1 Describe how social interaction is the foundation of personality.

5.2 Explain six major theories of socialization.

5.3 Analyze how the family, school, peer groups, and the mass media guide the socialization process.

5.4 Discuss how our society organizes human experience into distinctive stages of life.

5.5 Characterize the operation of total institutions.

the Power of Society

to shape how much television we watch

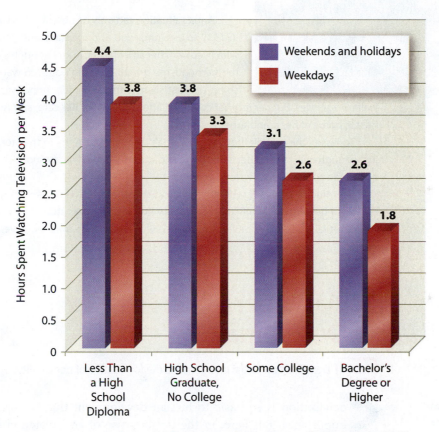

Hours Spent Watching Television per Week

- Weekends and holidays
- Weekdays

	Weekends and holidays	Weekdays
Less Than a High School Diploma	4.4	3.8
High School Graduate, No College	3.8	3.3
Some College	3.1	2.6
Bachelor's Degree or Higher	2.6	1.8

Source: U.S. Department of Labor, Bureau of Labor Statistics (2012)

How conscious is our decision to spend time in front of the television? People with less than a high school diploma watch considerably more television—spending roughly twice as much time per week in front of the screen—than people who have earned a college degree. Although we tend to think we make choices about television watching (as well as our use of other mass media), society guides our behavior in this respect as it does in so many others.

Chapter Overview

Having completed two macro-level chapters, Chapters 3 ("Culture") and 4 ("Society"), exploring our social world, we turn now to a micro-level look at how individuals become members of society through the process of socialization.

On a cold winter day in 1938, a social worker walked quickly to the door of a rural Pennsylvania farmhouse. Investigating a case of possible child abuse, the social worker entered the home and soon discovered a five-year-old girl hidden in a second-floor storage room. The child, whose name was Anna, was wedged into an old chair with her arms tied above her head so that she couldn't move. She was wearing filthy clothes, and her arms and legs were as thin as matchsticks (Davis, 1940).

Anna's situation can only be described as tragic. She had been born in 1932 to an unmarried and mentally impaired woman of twenty-six who lived with her strict father. Angry about his daughter's "illegitimate" motherhood, the grandfather did not even want the child in his house, so for the first six months of her life, Anna was passed among several welfare agencies. But her mother could not afford to pay for her care, and Anna was returned to the hostile home of her grandfather.

To lessen the grandfather's anger, Anna's mother kept Anna in the storage room and gave her just enough milk to keep her alive. There she stayed—day after day, month after month, with almost no human contact—for five long years.

Learning of Anna's rescue, the sociologist Kingsley Davis immediately went to see the child. He found her with local officials at a county home. Davis was stunned by the emaciated girl, who could not laugh, speak, or even smile. Anna was completely unresponsive, as if alone in an empty world.

Social Experience: The Key to Our Humanity

(**5.1**) Describe how social interaction is the foundation of personality.

Watch in **MySocLab**
Video: *The Big Picture: Socialization*

Socialization is so basic to human development that we sometimes overlook its importance. But here, in the terrible case of an isolated child, we can see what humans would be like without social contact. Although physically alive, Anna hardly seems to have been human. We can see that without social experience, a child is not able to act or communicate in a meaningful way and seems to be as much an object as a person.

Sociologists use the term **socialization** to refer to *the lifelong social experience by which people develop their human potential and learn culture.* Unlike other living species, whose behavior is mostly or entirely set by biology, humans need social experience to learn their culture and to survive. Social experience is also the foundation of **personality**, *a person's fairly consistent patterns of acting, thinking, and feeling.* We build a personality by internalizing—taking in—our surroundings. But without social experience, as Anna's case shows, personality hardly develops at all.

socialization the lifelong social experience by which people develop their human potential and learn culture

personality a person's fairly consistent patterns of acting, thinking, and feeling

Human Development: Nature and Nurture

Anna's case makes clear that humans depend on others to provide the care and nurture needed not only for physical growth but also for personality to develop. A century ago, however, people mistakenly believed that humans were born with instincts that determined their personality and behavior.

 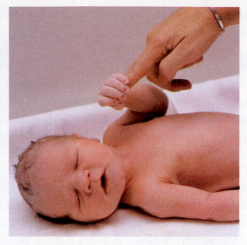 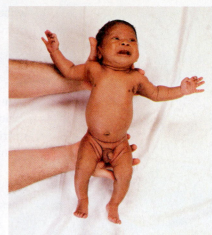

Human infants display various *reflexes*—biologically based behavior patterns that enhance survival. The sucking reflex, which actually begins before birth, enables the infant to obtain nourishment. The grasping reflex, triggered by placing a finger on the infant's palm, causing the hand to close, helps the infant to maintain contact with a parent and, later on, to grasp objects. The Moro reflex, activated by startling the infant, has the infant swinging both arms outward and then bringing them together across the chest. This action, which disappears after several months of life, probably developed among our evolutionary ancestors so that a falling infant could grasp the body hair of a parent.

The Biological Sciences: The Role of Nature

Charles Darwin's groundbreaking 1859 study of evolution, described in Chapter 3 ("Culture"), led people to think that human behavior was instinctive, simply our "nature." Such ideas led to claims that the U.S. economic system reflects "instinctive human competitiveness," that some people are "born criminals," or that women are "naturally" emotional while men are "naturally" rational.

People trying to understand cultural diversity also misunderstood Darwin's thinking. Centuries of world exploration had taught Western Europeans that people behaved quite differently from one society to another. But Europeans linked these differences to biology rather than culture. It was an easy, although incorrect and very damaging, step to claim that members of technologically simple societies were biologically less evolved and therefore "less human." This ethnocentric view helped justify colonialism: Why not take advantage of others if they seem not to be human in the same sense that you are?

The Social Sciences: The Role of Nurture

In the twentieth century, biological explanations of human behavior came under fire. The psychologist John B. Watson (1878–1958) developed a theory called *behaviorism,* which holds that behavior is not instinctive but learned. Thus people everywhere are equally human, differing only in their cultural patterns. In short, Watson rooted human behavior not in nature but in *nurture.*

Today, social scientists are cautious about describing *any* human behavior as instinctive. This does not mean that biology plays no part in human behavior. Human life, after all, depends on the functioning of the body. We also know that children often share biological traits (like height and hair color) with their parents and that heredity plays a part in intelligence, musical and artistic talent, and personality (such as how you react to frustration). However, whether you develop your inherited potential depends on how you are raised. For example, unless children use their brain early in life, the brain does not fully develop (Goldsmith, 1983; Begley, 1995).

Without denying the importance of nature, then, we can correctly say that nurture matters more in shaping human behavior. More precisely, *nurture is our nature.*

Social Isolation

As the story of Anna shows, being cut off from the social world is very harmful to human beings. For ethical reasons, researchers can never place people in total isolation to study what happens. But in the past, they have studied the effects of social isolation on non-human primates.

Research with Monkeys

In a classic study, the psychologists Harry and Margaret Harlow (1962) placed rhesus monkeys—whose behavior is in some ways surprisingly similar to that of humans—in various conditions of social isolation. They found that complete isolation (with adequate nutrition) for even six months seriously disturbed the monkeys' development. When returned to their group, these monkeys were passive, anxious, and fearful.

The Harlows then placed infant rhesus monkeys in cages with an artificial "mother" made of wire mesh with a wooden head and the nipple of a feeding tube where the breast would be. These monkeys also survived but were unable to interact with others when placed in a group.

But monkeys in a third category, isolated with an artificial wire mesh "mother" covered with soft terry cloth, did better. Each of these monkeys would cling to its mother closely. Because these monkeys showed less developmental damage than earlier groups, the Harlows concluded that the monkeys benefited from this closeness. The experiment confirmed how important it is that adults cradle infants affectionately.

Finally, the Harlows discovered that infant monkeys could recover from about three months of isolation. But by about six months, isolation caused irreversible emotional and behavioral damage.

Studies of Isolated Children

Tragic cases of children isolated by abusive family members show the damage caused by depriving human beings of social experience. We will review three such cases.

Anna: The Rest of the Story The rest of Anna's story squares with the Harlows' findings. After her discovery, Anna received extensive medical attention and soon showed improvement. When Kingsley Davis visited her after ten days, he found her more alert and even smiling (perhaps for the first time in her life). Over the next year, Anna made slow but steady progress, showing more interest in other people and gradually learning to walk. After a year and a half, she could feed herself and play with toys.

But as the Harlows might have predicted, five long years of social isolation had caused permanent damage. At age eight, her mental development was less than that of a two-year-old. Not until she was almost ten did she begin to use words. Because Anna's mother was mentally retarded, perhaps Anna was also. The riddle was never solved, however, because Anna died at age ten of a blood disorder, possibly related to the years of abuse she suffered (Davis, 1940, 1947).

The personalities we develop depend largely on the environment in which we live. When a child's world is shredded by violence, the damage (including losing the ability to trust) can be profound and lasting. This drawing was made by a child living through the daily violence of the civil war in Syria. What are the likely effects of such experiences on a young person's self-confidence and capacity to form trusting ties?

Another Case: Isabelle A second case involves another girl found at about the same time as Anna and under similar circumstances. After more than six years of virtual isolation, this girl, named Isabelle, displayed the same lack of responsiveness as Anna. But Isabelle had the benefit of an intensive learning program directed by psychologists. Within a week, Isabelle was trying to speak, and a year and a half later, she knew some 2,000 words. The psychologists concluded that intensive effort had pushed Isabelle through six years of normal development in only two years. By the time she was fourteen, Isabelle was attending sixth-grade classes, damaged by her early ordeal but on her way to a relatively normal life (Davis, 1947).

A Third Case: Genie A more recent case of childhood isolation involves a California girl abused by her parents (Curtiss, 1977; Rymer, 1994). From the time she

Read in **MySocLab**
Document: *Final Note on an Extreme Case of Isolation* by Kingsley Davis

was two, Genie was tied to a potty chair in a dark garage. In 1970, when she was rescued at age thirteen, Genie weighed only fifty-nine pounds and had the mental development of a one-year-old. With intensive treatment, she became physically healthy, but her language ability remains that of a young child. Today, Genie lives in a home for developmentally disabled adults.

EVALUATE All evidence points to the crucial importance of social experience in personality development. Human beings can recover from abuse and short-term isolation. But there is a point—precisely when is unclear from the small number of cases studied—at which isolation in childhood causes permanent developmental damage.

CHECK YOUR LEARNING What do studies of isolated children teach us about the importance of social experience?

Understanding Socialization

5.2 Explain six major theories of socialization.

Socialization is a complex, lifelong process. The following discussions highlight the work of six researchers—Sigmund Freud, Jean Piaget, Lawrence Kohlberg, Carol Gilligan, George Herbert Mead, and Erik H. Erikson—who have made lasting contributions to our understanding of human development.

Sigmund Freud's Elements of Personality

Sigmund Freud (1856–1939) lived in Vienna at a time when most Europeans considered human behavior to be biologically fixed. Trained as a physician, Freud gradually turned to the study of personality and mental disorders and eventually developed the celebrated theory of psychoanalysis.

Basic Human Needs

Freud claimed that biology plays a major part in human development, although not in terms of specific instincts, as is the case in other species. Rather, he theorized that humans have two basic needs or drives that are present at birth. First is a need for sexual and emotional bonding, which he called the "life instinct," or *eros* (named after the Greek god of love). Second, we share an aggressive drive he called the "death instinct," or *thanatos* (the Greek word for "death"). These opposing forces, operating at an unconscious level, create deep inner tension.

Freud's Model of Personality

Freud combined basic needs and the influence of society into a model of personality with three parts: id, ego, and superego. The **id** (Latin for "it") represents *the human being's basic drives,* which are unconscious and demand immediate satisfaction. Rooted in biology, the id is present at birth, making a newborn a bundle of demands for attention, touching, and food. But society opposes the self-centered id, which is why one of the first words a child typically learns is "no."

To avoid frustration, a child must learn to approach the world realistically. This is done through the **ego** (Latin for "I"), which is *a person's conscious efforts to balance innate pleasure-seeking drives with the demands of society.* The ego arises as we become aware of our distinct existence and face the fact that we cannot have everything we want.

In the human personality, the **superego** (Latin for "above or beyond the ego") is

Freud's Model of Personality

id the human being's basic drives

ego a person's conscious efforts to balance innate pleasure-seeking drives with the demands of society

superego the cultural values and norms internalized by an individual

the cultural values and norms internalized by an individual. The superego operates as our conscience, telling us *why* we cannot have everything we want. The superego begins to form as a child becomes aware of parental demands and matures as the child comes to understand that everyone's behavior should take account of cultural norms.

Personality Development

To the id-centered child, the world is a bewildering assortment of physical sensations that bring either pleasure or pain. As the superego develops, however, the child learns the moral concepts of right and wrong. Initially, in other words, children can feel good only in a physical way (such as by being held and cuddled), but after three or four years, they feel good or bad according to how they judge their behavior against cultural norms (doing "the right thing").

The id and superego remain in conflict, but in a well-adjusted person, the ego manages these two opposing forces. If conflicts are not resolved during childhood, Freud claimed, they may surface as personality disorders later on.

Culture, in the form of the superego, *represses* selfish demands, forcing people to look beyond their own desires. Often the competing demands of self and society result in a compromise that Freud called *sublimation.* Sublimation redirects selfish drives into socially acceptable behavior. For example, marriage makes the satisfaction of sexual urges socially acceptable, and competitive sports are an outlet for aggression.

EVALUATE In Freud's time, few people were ready to accept sex as a basic human drive. More recent critics have charged that Freud's work presents humans in male terms and devalues women (Donovan & Littenberg, 1982). Freud's theories are also difficult to test scientifically. But Freud influenced everyone who later studied human personality. Of special importance to sociology are his ideas that we internalize social norms and that childhood experiences have a lasting impact on personality.

CHECK YOUR LEARNING What are the three elements in Freud's model of personality? Explain how each one operates.

Jean Piaget's Theory of Cognitive Development

The Swiss psychologist Jean Piaget (1896–1980) studied human *cognition,* how people think and understand. As Piaget watched his own three children grow, he wondered not just what they knew but also how they made sense of the world. Piaget went on to identify four stages of cognitive development.

The Sensorimotor Stage

Stage one is the **sensorimotor stage**, *the level of human development at which individuals experience the world only through their senses.* For about the first two years of life, the infant knows the world only through the five senses: touching, tasting, smelling, looking, and listening. "Knowing" to young children amounts to what their senses tell them.

Piaget's Stages of Development

sensorimotor stage the level of human development at which individuals experience the world only through their senses

preoperational stage the level of human development at which individuals first use language and other symbols

concrete operational stage the level of human development at which individuals first see causal connections in their surroundings

formal operational stage the level of human development at which individuals think abstractly and critically

The Preoperational Stage

About age two, children enter the **preoperational stage**, *the level of human development at which individuals first use language and other symbols.* Now children begin to think about the world mentally and use imagination. But "pre-op" children between about two and six still attach meaning only to specific experiences and objects. They can identify a toy as their "favorite" but cannot explain what *types* of toys they like.

Lacking abstract concepts, a child also cannot judge size, weight, or volume. In one of his best-known experiments, Piaget placed two identical glasses containing equal amounts of water on a table. He asked several children aged five and six if the amount in each glass was the same. They nodded that it was. The children then watched Piaget take one of the glasses and pour its contents into a taller, narrower glass so that the level of the water in the glass was higher. He asked again if each glass held the same amount. The typical five- or six-year-old now insisted that the taller glass held more water. By about age seven, children are able to think abstractly and realize that the amount of water stays the same.

The Concrete Operational Stage

Next comes the **concrete operational stage**, *the level of human development at which individuals first see causal connections in their surroundings.* Between the ages of seven and eleven, children focus on how and why things happen. In addition, children now attach more than one symbol to a particular event or object. If, for example, you say to a child of five, "Today is Wednesday," she might respond, "No, it's my birthday!"—indicating that she can use just one symbol at a time. But a ten-year-old at the concrete operational stage would be able to respond, "Yes, and it's also my birthday."

The Formal Operational Stage

The last stage in Piaget's model is the **formal operational stage**, *the level of human development at which individuals think abstractly and critically.* At about age twelve, young people begin to reason abstractly rather than thinking only of concrete situations. If, for example, you were to ask a seven-year-old, "What would you like to be when you grow up?" you might receive a concrete response such as "a teacher." But most teenagers can think more abstractly and might reply, "I would like a job that helps others." As they gain the capacity for abstract thought, young people also learn to understand metaphors. Hearing the phrase "A penny for your thoughts" might lead a child to ask for a coin, but a teenager will recognize a gentle invitation to intimacy.

EVALUATE Freud saw human beings torn by opposing forces of biology and culture. Piaget saw the mind as active and creative. He saw an ability to engage the world unfolding in stages as the result of both biological maturation and social experience.

But do people in all societies pass through all four of Piaget's stages? Living in a traditional society that changes slowly probably limits a person's capacity for abstract and critical thought. Even in the United States, perhaps 30 percent of people never reach the formal operational stage (Kohlberg & Gilligan, 1971).

CHECK YOUR LEARNING What are Piaget's four stages of cognitive development? What does his theory teach us about socialization?

Lawrence Kohlberg's Theory of Moral Development

Lawrence Kohlberg (1981) built on Piaget's work to study *moral reasoning,* or how individuals judge situations as right or wrong. Here again, development occurs in stages.

Young children who experience the world in terms of pain and pleasure (Piaget's sensorimotor stage) are at the *preconventional* level of moral development. At this early stage, in other words, "rightness" amounts to "what feels good to me." For example, a young child may simply reach for something on a table that looks shiny, which is the reason parents of young children have to "childproof" their homes.

The *conventional* level, Kohlberg's second stage, appears by the teen years (corresponding to Piaget's final, formal operational stage). At this point, young people lose some of their selfishness as they learn to define right and wrong in terms of what pleases parents and conforms to cultural norms. Individuals at this stage also begin to assess intention in reaching moral judgments instead of simply looking at what people do. For example, they understand that stealing food to feed one's hungry children is not the same as stealing an iPod to sell for pocket change.

In Kohlberg's final stage of moral development, the *postconventional* level, people move beyond their society's norms to consider abstract ethical principles. Now they think about liberty, freedom, or justice, perhaps arguing that what is legal still may not be right. When the African American activist Rosa Parks refused to give up her seat on a bus in Montgomery, Alabama, in 1955, she violated that city's segregation laws in order to call attention to the racial injustice of the law.

EVALUATE Like the work of Piaget, Kohlberg's model explains moral development in terms of distinct stages. But whether this model applies to people in all societies remains unclear. Further, many people in the United States apparently never reach the postconventional level of moral reasoning, although exactly why is still an open question.

Another problem with Kohlberg's research is that his subjects were all boys. He committed a common research error, described in Chapter 2 ("Sociological Investigation"), by generalizing the results of male subjects to all people. This problem led a colleague, Carol Gilligan, to investigate how gender affects moral reasoning.

CHECK YOUR LEARNING What are Kohlberg's three stages of moral development? What does his theory teach us about socialization?

Carol Gilligan's Theory of Gender and Moral Development

For a closer look at Carol Gilligan's study, **Read More** in **MySocLab**, *The Importance of Gender in Research*

Carol Gilligan compared the moral development of girls and boys and concluded that the two sexes use different standards of rightness.

Boys, Gilligan (1982, 1990) claims, have a *justice perspective,* relying on formal rules to define right and wrong. Girls, by contrast, have a *care and responsibility perspective,* judging a situation with an eye toward personal relationships and loyalties. For example, as boys see it, stealing is wrong because it breaks the law. Girls are more likely to wonder why someone would steal and to be sympathetic toward a person who steals, say, to feed her family.

Kohlberg treats rule-based male reasoning as superior to the person-based female approach. Gilligan notes that impersonal rules dominate men's lives in the workplace, but personal relationships are more relevant to women's lives as mothers and caregivers. Why, then, Gilligan asks, should we set up male standards as the norms by which to judge everyone?

EVALUATE Gilligan's work sharpens our understanding of both human development and gender issues in research. Yet the question remains, does nature or nurture account for the differences between females and males? In Gilligan's view, cultural conditioning is at work, a view that finds support in other research. Nancy Chodorow (1994) claims that children grow up in homes in which, typically, mothers do much more nurturing than fathers. As girls identify with mothers, they become more concerned with care and responsibility to others. By contrast, boys become more like fathers, who are often detached from the home, and develop the same formal and detached personalities. Perhaps the moral reasoning of females and males will become more similar as more women organize their lives around the workplace.

CHECK YOUR LEARNING According to Gilligan, how do boys and girls differ in their approach to understanding right and wrong?

George Herbert Mead's Theory of the Social Self

George Herbert Mead (1863–1931) developed the theory of *social behaviorism* to explain how social experience develops an individual's personality (1962, orig. 1934).

The Self

Mead's central concept is the **self**, *the part of an individual's personality composed of self-awareness and self-image.* Mead's genius was in seeing the self as the product of social experience.

First, said Mead, *the self is not there at birth; it develops.* The self is not part of the body, and it does not exist at birth. Mead rejected the idea that personality is guided by biological drives (as Freud asserted) or biological maturation (as Piaget claimed).

Second, *the self develops only with social experience,* as the individual interacts with others. Without interaction, as we see from cases of isolated children, the body grows, but no self emerges.

Third, Mead continued, *social experience is the exchange of symbols.* Only people use words, a wave of the hand, or a smile to create meaning. We can train a dog using reward and punishment, but the dog attaches no meaning to its actions. Human beings, by contrast, find meaning in almost every action.

Fourth, Mead stated that *seeking meaning leads people to imagine other people's intentions.* In short, we draw conclusions from people's actions, imagining their underlying intentions. A dog responds to *what you do;* a human responds to *what you have in mind* as you do it. You can train a dog to go to the hallway and bring back an umbrella, which is handy on a rainy day. But because the dog doesn't understand intention, if the dog cannot find the umbrella, it is incapable of the *human* response: to look for a raincoat instead.

Fifth, Mead explained that *understanding intention requires imagining the situation from the other's point of view.* Using symbols, we imagine ourselves "in another person's shoes" and see ourselves as that person does. We can therefore anticipate how others will respond to us even before we act. A simple toss of a ball requires stepping outside ourselves to imagine how another will catch our throw. All social interaction involves seeing ourselves as others see us—a process that Mead termed *taking the role of the other.*

The Looking-Glass Self

As we interact with others, the people around us become a mirror (an object that people used to call a "looking glass") in which we can see ourselves. What we think of ourselves, then, depends on how we think others see us. For example, if we think others see us as clever, we will think of ourselves in the same way. But if we feel they think of us as clumsy, then that is how we will see ourselves. Charles Horton Cooley (1864–1929) used the phrase **looking-glass self** to mean *a self-image based on how we think others see us* (1964, orig. 1902).

The I and the Me

Mead's sixth point is that *by taking the role of the other, we become self-aware.* Another way of saying this is that the self has two parts. One part of the self operates as the subject, being active and spontaneous. Mead called the active side of the self the "I" (the subjective form of the personal pronoun). The other part of the self works as an object, that is, the way we imagine others see us. Mead called the objective side of the self the "me" (the objective form of the personal pronoun). All social experience has both components: We initiate an action (the I-phase, or subject side, of self), and then we continue the action based on how others respond to us (the me-phase, or object side, of self).

Childhood is a time to learn principles of right and wrong. According to Carol Gilligan, however, boys and girls define what is "right" in different ways. After reading about Gilligan's theory, can you suggest what these two children might be arguing about?

self George Herbert Mead's term for the part of an individual's personality composed of self-awareness and self-image

looking-glass self Cooley's term for a self-image based on how we think others see us

Watch in **MySocLab** Video: *The Basics: Socialization*

George Herbert Mead wrote, "No hard-and-fast line can be drawn between our own selves and the selves of others." This statement helps to explain the immense importance of "significant others" in our lives. How does this father affect the self emerging in his son?

significant others people, such as parents, who have special importance for socialization

generalized other George Herbert Mead's term for widespread cultural norms and values we use as references in evaluating ourselves

Development of the Self

According to Mead, the key to developing the self is learning to take the role of the other. Because of their limited social experience, infants can do this only through *imitation*. They mimic behavior without understanding underlying intentions, and so at this point, they have no self.

As children learn to use language and other symbols, the self emerges in the form of *play*. Play involves assuming roles modeled on **significant others**, *people, such as parents, who have special importance for socialization*. Playing "mommy and daddy" is an important activity that helps young children imagine the world from a parent's point of view.

Gradually, children learn to take the roles of several others at once. This skill lets them move from simple play (say, playing catch) with one other to complex *games* (such as baseball) involving many others. By about age seven, most children have the social experience needed to engage in team sports.

Figure 5–1 on page 135 charts the progression from imitation to play to games. But there is a final stage in the development of the self. A game involves taking the role of specific people in just one situation. Everyday life demands that we see ourselves in terms of cultural norms as *any* member of our society might. Mead used the term **generalized other** to refer to *widespread cultural norms and values we use as references in evaluating ourselves*.

As life goes on, the self continues to change along with our social experiences. But no matter how much the world shapes us, we always remain creative beings, able to react to the world around us. Thus, Mead concluded, we play a key role in our own socialization.

EVALUATE Mead's work explores the character of social experience itself. In the symbolic interaction of human beings, he believed he had found the root of both self and society.

Mead's view is completely social, allowing no biological element at all. This is a problem for critics who stand with Freud (who said our general drives are rooted in the body) and Piaget (whose stages of development are tied to biological maturity).

Be careful not to confuse Mead's concepts of the I and the me with Freud's id and superego. For Freud, the id originates in our biology, but Mead rejected any biological element of the self (although he never clearly spelled out the origin of the I). In addition, the id and the superego are locked in continual combat, but the I and the me work cooperatively together (Meltzer, 1978).

CHECK YOUR LEARNING Explain the meaning and importance of Mead's concepts of the I and the me. What did Mead mean by "taking the role of the other"? Why is this process so important to socialization?

Erik H. Erikson's Eight Stages of Development

Although some analysts (including Freud) point to childhood as the crucial time when personality takes shape, Erik H. Erikson (1902–1994) took a broader view of socialization. He explained that we face challenges throughout the life course (1963, orig. 1950).

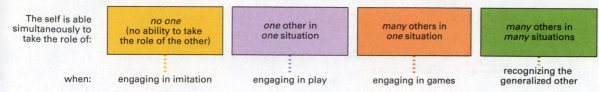

The self is able simultaneously to take the role of:	*no one* (no ability to take the role of the other)	*one* other in *one* situation	*many* others in *one* situation	*many* others in *many* situations
when:	engaging in imitation	engaging in play	engaging in games	recognizing the generalized other

FIGURE 5–1 Building on Social Experience

George Herbert Mead described the development of the self as a process of gaining social experience. That is, the self develops as we expand our capacity to take the role of the other.

Stage 1: Infancy—the challenge of trust (versus mistrust). Between birth and about eighteen months, infants face the first of life's challenges: to establish a sense of trust that their world is a safe place. Family members play a key part in how any infant meets this challenge.

Stage 2: Toddlerhood—the challenge of autonomy (versus doubt and shame). The next challenge, up to age three, is to learn skills to cope with the world in a confident way. Failing to gain self-control leads children to doubt their abilities.

Stage 3: Preschool—the challenge of initiative (versus guilt). Four- and five-year-olds must learn to engage their surroundings—including people outside the family—or experience guilt at failing to meet the expectations of parents and others.

Stage 4: Preadolescence—the challenge of industriousness (versus inferiority). Between ages six and thirteen, children enter school, make friends, and strike out on their own more and more. They either feel proud of their accomplishments or fear that they do not measure up.

Stage 5: Adolescence—the challenge of gaining identity (versus confusion). During the teen years, young people struggle to establish their own identity. In part, teenagers identify with others, but they also want to be unique. Almost all teens experience some confusion as they struggle to establish an identity.

Stage 6: Young adulthood—the challenge of intimacy (versus isolation). The challenge for young adults is to form and maintain intimate relationships with others. Making close friends (and especially falling in love) involves balancing the need to bond with the need to have a separate identity.

Stage 7: Middle adulthood—the challenge of making a difference (versus self-absorption). The challenge of middle age is contributing to the lives of others in the family, at work, and in the larger world. Failing at this, people become self-centered, caught up in their own limited concerns.

Stage 8: Old age—the challenge of integrity (versus despair). As the end of life approaches, people hope to look back on what they have accomplished with a sense of integrity and satisfaction. For those who have been self-absorbed, old age brings only a sense of despair over missed opportunities.

EVALUATE Erikson's theory views personality formation as a lifelong process, with success at one stage (say, as an infant gaining trust) preparing us to meet the next challenge. However, not everyone faces these challenges in the exact order presented by Erikson. Nor is it clear that failure to meet the challenge of one stage of life means that a person is doomed to fail later on. A broader question, raised earlier in our discussion of Piaget's ideas, is whether people in other cultures and in other times in history would define a successful life in Erikson's terms.

In sum, Erikson's model points out that many factors, including the family and school, shape our personalities. In the next section, we take a close look at these important agents of socialization.

CHECK YOUR LEARNING In what ways does Erikson take a broader view of socialization than other thinkers presented in this chapter?

Agents of Socialization

5.3 Analyze how the family, school, peer groups, and the mass media guide the socialization process.

Every social experience we have affects us in at least a small way. However, several familiar settings have special importance in the socialization process. These include the family, school, peer group, and the mass media.

The Family

The family affects socialization in many ways. For most people, in fact, the family may be the most important socialization agent of all.

Nurture in Early Childhood

Infants are totally dependent on others for care. The responsibility for providing a safe and caring environment typically falls on parents and other family members. For several years—at least until children begin school—the family also has the job of teaching children skills, values, and beliefs. Overall, research suggests, nothing is more likely to produce a happy, well-adjusted child than a loving family (Gibbs, 2001).

Not all family learning results from intentional teaching by parents. Children also learn from the type of environment adults create for them. Whether children learn to see themselves as strong or weak, smart or stupid, loved or simply tolerated—and as Erik Erikson suggests, whether they see the world as trustworthy or dangerous—depends largely on the quality of the surroundings provided by parents and other caregivers.

Race and Class

Through the family, parents give a social identity to children. In part, social identity involves race. Racial identity can be complex because, as Chapter 14 ("Race and Ethnicity") explains, societies define race in various ways. The U.S. Census Bureau reports that, in 2011, 8.7 million people or 2.8 percent of the nation's population considered themselves to be of two or more racial categories. This share is twice the figure of 1.4 percent that was reported back in 2000. The share is certain to keep going up because about 6 percent of all births in the United States are now recorded as interracial (U.S. Census Bureau, 2012). National Map 5–1 on page 137 shows where people who describe themselves as racially mixed live.

Social class, like race, plays a large part in shaping a child's personality. Whether born into families of high or low social position, children gradually come to realize that their family's social standing affects how others see them and, in time, how they come to see themselves.

In addition, research shows that class position affects not just how much money parents have to spend on their children but also what parents expect of them (Ellison, Bartkowski, & Segal, 1996). Parents of all social class backgrounds want their children to be successful and to make a difference in the world. But when asked to pick from a list of traits that are desirable in a child, lower-class parents are far more likely than upper-class parents to point to "obedience" as a key trait in a child. By contrast, well-to-do parents are more likely than low-income parents to praise children who can "think for themselves" (NORC, 2013).

What accounts for the difference? Melvin Kohn (1977) explains that people of lower social standing usually have limited education and perform routine jobs under close

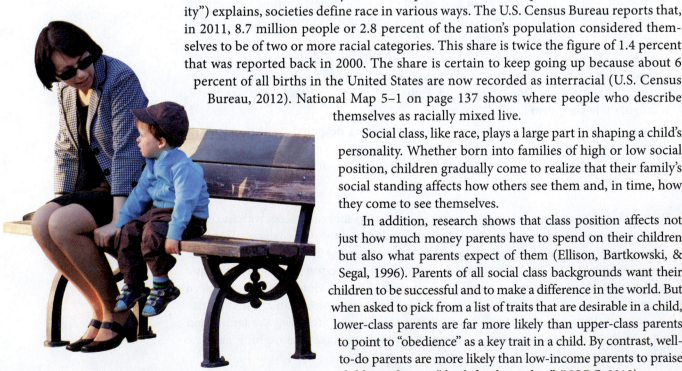

Wealthy parents give their children advantages that go beyond money. Research shows that they talk more to their children, enhancing their intellectual development. All parents can help their children simply by engaging them in conversation.

Seeing Ourselves

Explore the percentage of racially mixed people in your local community and in counties across the United States in **MySocLab**

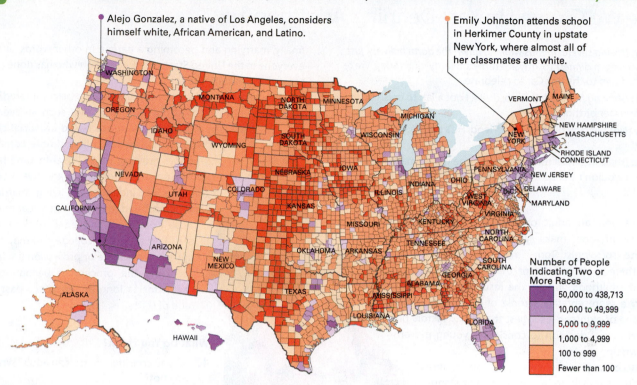

Alejo Gonzalez, a native of Los Angeles, considers himself white, African American, and Latino.

Emily Johnston attends school in Herkimer County in upstate New York, where almost all of her classmates are white.

Number of People Indicating Two or More Races
- 50,000 to 438,713
- 10,000 to 49,999
- 5,000 to 9,999
- 1,000 to 4,999
- 100 to 999
- Fewer than 100

NATIONAL MAP 5–1 Racially Mixed People across the United States

This map shows, for 2011, the county-by-county distribution of people who described themselves as racially mixed. How do you think growing up in an area with a high level of racially mixed people (such as Los Angeles or Miami) would be different from growing up in an area with few such people (for example, in upstate New York or the Plains States in the middle of the country)?

Source: U.S. Census Bureau (2012).

supervision. Expecting that their children will hold similar positions, they encourage obedience and may even use physical punishment like spanking to get it. Because well-off parents have had more schooling, they usually have jobs that demand independence, imagination, and creativity, so they try to inspire the same qualities in their children. Consciously or not, all parents act in ways that encourage their children to follow in their footsteps.

Wealthier parents are more likely to push their children to achieve, and they also typically provide their daughters and sons with an extensive program of leisure activities, including sports, travel, and music lessons. These enrichment activities—far less available to children growing up in low-income families—build *cultural capital*, which advances learning and creates a sense of confidence in these children that they will succeed later in life (Lareau, 2002; NORC, 2013).

Social class also affects how long the process of growing up takes, as the Seeing Sociology in Everyday Life box on page 138 explains.

The School

Schooling enlarges children's social world to include people with backgrounds different from their own. It is only as they encounter people who differ from themselves that children come to understand the importance of factors such as race and social position. As they do, they are likely to cluster in playgroups made up of one class, race, and gender.

Seeing Sociology in Everyday Life

Are We Grown Up Yet? Defining Adulthood

Solly: *(seeing several friends walking down the dorm hallway, just returned from dinner)* Yo, guys! Jeremy's twenty-one today. We're going down to the Box Car to celebrate.

Matt: *(shaking his head)* Dunno, dude. I got a lab to finish up. It's just another birthday.

Solly: Not just any birthday, my friend. He's twenty-one—an *adult*!

Matt: *(sarcastically)* If turning twenty-one would make me an adult, I wouldn't still be clueless about what I want to do with my life!

Are you an adult or still an adolescent? Does turning twenty-one make you a "grown-up"? According to the sociologist Tom Smith (2003), in our society, there is no one factor that announces the onset of adulthood. In fact, the results of his survey—using a representative sample of 1,398 people over the age of eighteen—suggest that many factors play a part in our decision to consider a young person "grown up."

According to the survey, the single most important transition in claiming adult standing in the United States today is the completion of schooling. But other factors are also important: Smith's respondents linked adult standing to taking on a full-time job, gaining the ability to support a family financially, no longer living with parents, and

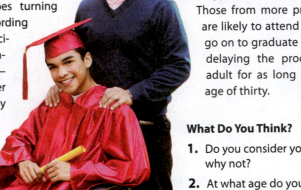

What significance does graduating from college have in the process of becoming an adult?

finally, marrying and becoming a parent. In other words, almost everyone in the United States thinks a person who has done *all* of these things is fully "grown up."

At what age are these transitions likely to be completed? On average, the answer is about twenty-six. But such an average masks an important difference based on social class. People who do not attend college (more common among people growing up in lower-income families) typically finish school before age twenty, and a full-time job, independent living, marriage, and parenthood may follow in a year or two. Those from more privileged backgrounds are likely to attend college and may even go on to graduate or professional school, delaying the process of becoming an adult for as long as ten years, past the age of thirty.

What Do You Think?

1. Do you consider yourself an adult? Why or why not?

2. At what age do you think adulthood begins? Why? Do patterns of growing up differ for females and males? Explain.

3. What importance do you think social class has in the process of becoming an adult?

Gender

Schools join with families in socializing children into gender roles. Studies show that at school, boys engage in more physical activities and spend more time outdoors, and girls are more likely to help teachers with various housekeeping chores. Boys also engage in more aggressive behavior in the classroom, while girls are typically quieter and better behaved (Best, 1983; Jordan & Cowan, 1995).

What Children Learn

Schooling is not the same for children living in rich and poor communities. As Chapter 20 ("Education") explains, children from well-off families typically have a far better experience in school than those whose families are poor.

What children learn in school goes beyond the formally planned lessons. Schools also informally teach many things, which together might be called the *hidden curriculum*. Activities such as spelling bees teach children not only how to spell words but also how society divides the population into "winners" and "losers." Organized sports help students develop their strength and skills and also teach children important life lessons in cooperation and competition.

For most children, school is also the first experience with bureaucracy. The school day is based on impersonal rules and a strict time schedule. Not surprisingly, these are also the traits of the large organizations that will employ young people later in life.

The Peer Group

By the time they enter school, children have discovered the **peer group**, *a social group whose members have interests, social position, and age in common*. Unlike the family and the school, the peer group lets children escape the direct supervision of adults. Among their peers, children learn how to form relationships on their own. Peer groups also offer the chance to discuss interests that adults may not share with their children (such as clothing and popular music) or permit (such as drugs and sex).

It is not surprising, then, that parents often express concern about who their children's friends are. In a rapidly changing society, peer groups have great influence, and the attitudes of young and old may differ because of a "generation gap." The importance of peer groups typically peaks during adolescence, when young people begin to break away from their families and think of themselves as adults.

Even during adolescence, however, parental influence on children remains strong. Peers may affect short-term interests such as music or films, but parents have greater influence on long-term goals, such as going to college (Davies & Kandel, 1981).

Finally, any neighborhood or school is made up of many peer groups. As Chapter 7 ("Groups and Organizations") explains, individuals tend to view their own group in positive terms and put down other groups. In addition, people are influenced by peer groups they would like to join, a process sociologists call **anticipatory socialization**, *learning that helps a person achieve a desired position*. In school, for example, young people may copy the styles and slang of a group they hope will accept them. Later in life, a young lawyer who hopes to become a partner in the law firm may conform to the attitudes and behavior of the firm's partners in order to be accepted.

peer group a social group whose members have interests, social position, and age in common

anticipatory socialization learning that helps a person achieve a desired position

The Mass Media

August 30, Isle of Coll, off the west coast of Scotland. The last time we visited this remote island, there was no electricity and most of the people spoke the ancient Gaelic language. Now that a power cable comes from the mainland, homes have electric lights, modern appliances, television, and computers that access the Internet. Today, most of the islanders have cell phones and routinely text others all over Britain and around the world. Technology and the new social media have pushed this remote place into a vastly larger, more connected world. It is no surprise that traces of the island's own culture have all but disappeared, with only rare performances of its traditional dancing or music. Today, most of the population consists of mainlanders who ferry over with their cars to spend time in their vacation homes. And everyone now speaks English.

The **mass media** are *the means for delivering impersonal communications to a vast audience*. The term *media* (plural of *medium*) comes from the Latin word for "middle," suggesting that the media connect people. *Mass* media resulted as communications technology (first newspapers and then radio, television, films, and the Internet) spread information on a massive scale. The mass media are important not only because they are so powerful but also because their influence is likely to differ from that of the family, the local school, and the peer group. In short, the mass media introduce people to ideas and images that reflect the larger society and the entire world.

In the United States today, the mass media have an enormous influence on our attitudes and behavior. Today, 76 percent of U.S. households have a personal computer, and 72 percent of households are connected to the Internet. Television, introduced in the 1930s, became the dominant medium after World War II, and 97 percent of U.S. households now have at least one set (the same share of households that have a telephone). Nine out of ten of the households with television also have cable or satellite connections. As Figure 5–2 on page 140 shows, the United States has one of the highest rates of

mass media the means for delivering impersonal communications to a vast audience

Global Snapshot

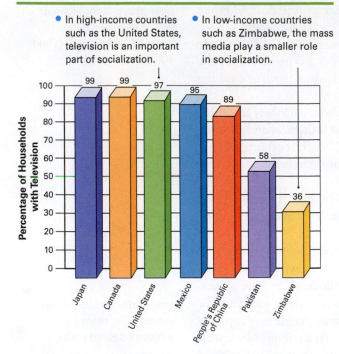

- In high-income countries such as the United States, television is an important part of socialization.
- In low-income countries such as Zimbabwe, the mass media play a smaller role in socialization.

FIGURE 5–2 Television Ownership in Global Perspective

Television is popular in high and middle-income countries, where almost every household owns at least one TV set.

Sources: International Telecommunication Union (2012); TVB (2012).

Watch in **MySocLab**
Video: *Sociology in Focus: Socialization*

television ownership in the world. Almost everyone in our country spends some time watching television but, as the Power of Society figure at the beginning of this chapter points out, it is people with less education (who are also those with lower incomes) who spend the most time watching TV, a pattern that also holds for playing video games (TVB, 2012; U.S. Census Bureau, 2012; U.S. Department of Labor, 2012).

The Extent of Mass Media Exposure

Just how "glued to the tube" are we? Survey data show that the average household has at least one television set turned on for eight hours each day and that people spend more than half their free time watching television. One study, by the Kaiser Family Foundation, found that compared to adults, who average about five hours a day, school-age youngsters typically spend even more time—about seven and a half hours each day—watching television or playing video games. African American children spend slightly more time watching television than Hispanic children and both categories spend considerably more time watching TV than white children do.

About two-thirds of U.S. children report that the television is typically on during meals, and more than 70 percent claim that parents do not limit the amount of time they spend in front of the screen. Younger children favor watching television and playing video games; as children get older, music videos and web surfing become a bigger part of the mix. At all ages, boys favor video games and girls lean toward music videos (Rideout, Foehr, & Roberts, 2010; Nielsen Media Research, 2012; TVB, 2012; U.S. Census Bureau, 2012).

In today's society, years before children learn to read, television watching is a part of their daily routine. As they grow, children spend as many hours in front of a television as they do in school or interacting with their parents. This extensive television viewing shows no signs of change despite the fact that, according to research, the more children watch television the slower their cognitive development, the more passive they become, the less they use their imagination, and the higher their risk of obesity. It is not that television is directly harmful to children; rather, extensive television takes time away from interaction with parents and peers, as well as exercise and other activities that are more likely to promote development and good health (American Psychological Association, 1993; Fellman, 1995; Shute, 2010).

Television and Politics

The comedian Fred Allen once quipped that we call television a "medium" because it is "rarely well done." For a number of reasons, television (as well as other mass media) provokes plenty of criticism. Some liberal critics argue that for most of television's history, racial and ethnic minorities have not been visible or have been included only in stereotypical roles (such as African Americans playing butlers and maids, Asian Americans playing gardeners, or Hispanics playing new immigrants). In recent years, however, minorities have moved closer to center stage on television. There are ten times as many Hispanic actors on prime-time television as there were in the 1970s, and they play a far larger range of characters (Lichter & Amundson, 1997; Fetto, 2003b).

From another perspective, conservative critics charge that the television and film industries are dominated by a liberal "cultural elite." In recent years, they claim, "politically correct" media have advanced liberal causes, including feminism and gay rights (Rothman, Powers, & Rothman, 1993; Goldberg, 2002). But not everyone agrees, and some counter that the popularity of Fox News, home to Sean Hannity, Bill O'Reilly, and other conservative commentators, suggests that television programming offers "spin" from both sides of the political spectrum (Rothman, Powers, & Rothman, 1993; B. Goldberg, 2002; Pew Center for People and the Press, 2012).

One study of the 2008 presidential election found that the Democratic candidate Barack Obama was endorsed by almost three times as many U.S. newspapers as Republican candidate John McCain ("Ongoing Tally," 2008). In 2012, of the 100 U.S. newspapers with the largest circulation, Barack Obama was endorsed by forty-one newspapers; Republican Mitt Romney was endorsed by thirty-five newspapers, while the remaining twenty-four did not make a clear endorsement of one or the other candidate (Peters & Woolley, 2012). So there appears to be some basis for the claim that, overall, the print media lean in a liberal direction. But research also suggests that a wide range of political opinion is available in all of today's mass media. In addition, while most people claim to want the news presented "without a point of view," a majority of people focus on those media sources, whether more liberal or more conservative, that provide news and analysis that are closer to their own personal opinions (Pew Research Center, 2012).

Television and Violence

In 1996, the American Medical Association (AMA) issued the startling statement that violence in television and films had reached such a high level that it posed a hazard to our health. Surveys confirm that three-fourths of U.S. adults say they have either walked out of a movie or turned off television because of too much violence. Almost two-thirds of television programs contain violence, and in most such scenes, characters engaging in violence show no remorse and are not punished (Rideout, 2007).

Public concern about violence in the mass media is especially high when it comes to children. About two-thirds of parents say that they are "very concerned" that their children are exposed to too much media violence. Research has found a correlation between the amount of time school children spend watching television and using video games and aggressive behavior such as fighting, the early use of alcohol and other illegal drugs, and even trouble sleeping. In 2011, the American Academy of Pediatrics issued a recommendation that children's television time be limited to two hours a day, and that parents not permit children under the age of two to watch television at all (Robinson et al., 2001; Centers for Disease Control and Prevention, 2011; Garrison, et al, 2011).

Back in 1997, the television industry adopted a rating system for programming. In addition, televisions manufactured after 2000 have a "V-chip" that allows parents to block programming that they do not wish their children to watch. But we are left to wonder whether watching sexual or violent programming is itself the cause of harm to young people or whether, for example, children who receive little attention from parents or who suffer from other risk factors end up watching more television. In any case, we might well ask why the mass media contain so much sex and violence in the first place.

Television and the other mass media enrich our lives with entertaining and educational programming. The media also increase our exposure to diverse cultures and provoke discussion of current issues. At the same time, the power of the media—especially television—to shape how we think remains highly controversial.

Concern with violence and the mass media extends to the world of video games, especially those popular with young boys. Among the most controversial games, which include high levels of violence, is *The Sopranos: Road to Respect*. Do you think the current rating codes are sufficient to guide parents and children who buy video games, or would you support greater restrictions on game content?

EVALUATE This section shows that socialization is complex, with many different factors shaping our personalities as we grow. In addition, these factors do not always work together. For instance, children learn certain things from peer groups and the mass media that may conflict with what they learn at home.

Beyond family, school, peer group, and the media, other spheres of life also play a part in social learning. For most people in the United States, these include the workplace, religious organizations, the military, and social clubs. In the end, socialization proves to be not just a simple matter of learning but a complex balancing act as we absorb information from a variety of sources. In the process of sorting and weighing all the information we receive, we form our own distinctive personalities.

CHECK YOUR LEARNING Identify all the major agents of socialization discussed in this section of the chapter. What are some of the unique ways that each of these helps us develop our individual personalities?

Socialization and the Life Course

5.4 Discuss how our society organizes human experience into distinctive stages of life.

Although childhood has special importance in the socialization process, learning continues throughout our lives. An overview of the life course reveals that our society organizes human experience according to age— namely, the stages of life we know as childhood, adolescence, adulthood, and old age.

In recent decades, some people have become concerned that U.S. society is shortening childhood, pushing children to grow up faster and faster. The television show *Toddlers and Tiaras* shows young girls performing and acting much like older women might do. Do television programs such as this one contribute to a "hurried child syndrome"? Do you see this as a problem or not? Why?

Childhood

The next time you go shopping for athletic shoes, check where the shoes on display are made. Most brands are manufactured in countries such as Taiwan and Indonesia where wages are far lower than they are in the United States. What is not stated anywhere on the shoes is that many are made by children who spend their days working in factories instead of going to school. About 215 million of the world's children work, with 60 percent of working children doing farming. Half of the world's working children are in Asia, while another one-fourth are in Africa. About half of them labor full time, and one-half of these boys and girls do work that is dangerous to their physical and mental health. For their efforts, they earn very little—typically, about 50 cents an hour (Human Rights Watch, 2006; Thrupkaew, 2010; International Labour Organization, 2011; U.S. Department of Labor, 2012). Global Map 5–1 on page 143 shows that child labor is most common in Africa and Asia.

The idea of children working long days in factories may be disturbing to people who live in high-income nations because we think of *childhood*—roughly the first twelve years of life—as a carefree time of learning and play. Yet as the historian Philippe Ariès (1965) explains, the whole idea of "childhood" is fairly new. During the Middle Ages, children of four or five were treated like adults and expected to fend for themselves.

We defend our idea of childhood because children are biologically immature. But a look back in time and around the world shows that the concept of childhood is grounded not in biology but in culture (LaRossa & Reitzes, 2001). In rich countries, not

Window on the World

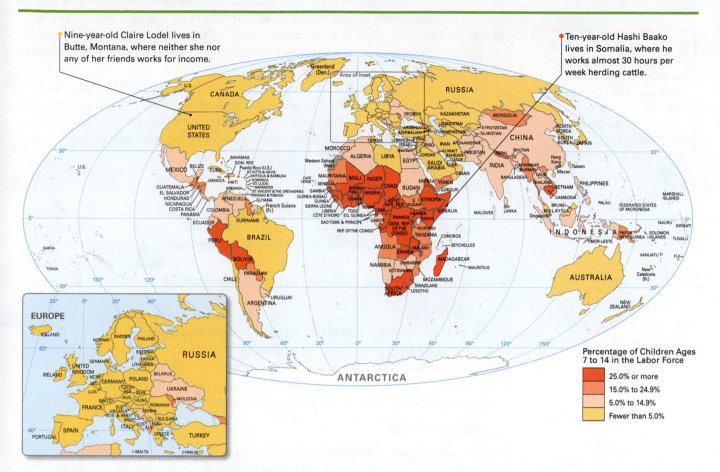

Nine-year-old Claire Lodel lives in Butte, Montana, where neither she nor any of her friends works for income.

Ten-year-old Hashi Baako lives in Somalia, where he works almost 30 hours per week herding cattle.

Percentage of Children Ages 7 to 14 in the Labor Force
- 25.0% or more
- 15.0% to 24.9%
- 5.0% to 14.9%
- Fewer than 5.0%

GLOBAL MAP 5–1 Child Labor in Global Perspective

Because industrialization extends childhood and discourages children from working and other activities considered suitable only for adults, child labor is uncommon in the United States and other high-income countries. In less economically developed nations of the world, however, children are a vital economic asset, and they typically begin working as soon as they are able. How would childhood in, say, the African nation of Chad or Ghana differ from that in the United States or Canada?

Sources: UNICEF (2012).

everyone has to work, so childhood can be extended to allow time for young people to learn the skills they will need in a high-technology workplace.

Because childhood in the United States lasts such a long time, some people worry when children seem to be growing up too fast. In part, this "hurried child" syndrome results from changes in the family—including high divorce rates and both parents in the labor force—that leave children with less supervision. In addition, "adult" programming on television (not to mention in films and on the Internet) carries grown-up concerns such as sex, drugs, and violence into young people's lives. Today's ten- to twelve-year-olds, says one executive of a children's television channel, have about the same interests and experiences typical of twelve- to fourteen-year-olds a generation ago. Perhaps this is why today's children, compared to kids fifty years ago, have higher levels of stress and anxiety (Hymowitz, 1998; Gorman, 2000; Hoffman, 2010).

Adolescence

At the same time that industrialization created childhood as a distinct stage of life, adolescence emerged as a buffer between childhood and adulthood. We generally link *adolescence*, or the teenage years, with emotional and social turmoil as young people struggle to develop their own identities. Again, we are tempted to attribute teenage

For a close-up look at how race and ethnicity can shape the academic performance of high school students, **Read More** in **MySocLab**, *The Development of Self among High School Students*

rebelliousness and confusion to the biological changes of puberty. But it is in fact the result of cultural inconsistency. For example, the mass media glorify sex and schools hand out condoms, even as parents urge restraint. Consider, too, that an eighteen-year-old may face the adult duty of going to war but lacks the adult right to drink a beer. In short, adolescence is a time of social contradictions, when people are no longer children but not yet adults.

As is true of all stages of life, adolescence varies according to social background. Most young people from working-class families move directly from high school into the adult world of work and parenting. Wealthier teens, however, have the resources to attend college and perhaps graduate school, stretching their adolescent years into the late twenties and even the thirties (Smith, 2003).

Adulthood

If stages of the life course were based on biological changes, it would be easy to define *adulthood*. Regardless of exactly when it begins, adulthood is the time when most of life's accomplishments take place, including pursuing a career and raising a family. Personalities are largely formed by then, although marked changes in a person's environment—such as unemployment, divorce, or serious illness—may cause significant changes to the self.

Early Adulthood

During early adulthood—until about age forty—young adults learn to manage day-to-day affairs for themselves, often juggling conflicting priorities: schooling, job, partner, children, and parents. During this stage of life, many women try to "do it all," a pattern that reflects the fact that our culture gives them the major responsibility for child rearing and housework even if they have demanding jobs outside the home.

Middle Adulthood

In middle adulthood—roughly ages forty to sixty-five—people sense that their life circumstances are pretty well set. They also become more aware of the fragility of health, which the young typically take for granted. Women who have spent many years raising a family find middle adulthood emotionally trying. Children grow up and require less attention, and husbands become absorbed in their careers, leaving some women with spaces in their lives that are difficult to fill. Many women who divorce also face serious financial problems (Weitzman, 1985, 1996). For all these reasons, an increasing number of women in middle adulthood return to school and seek new careers.

For everyone, growing older means experiencing physical decline, a prospect our culture makes especially challenging for women. Because good looks are considered more important for women, the appearance of wrinkles and graying hair can be traumatic. Men have their own particular difficulties as they get older. Some must admit that they are never going to reach earlier career goals. Others realize that the price of career success has been neglect of family or personal health.

Old Age

Old age—the later years of adulthood and the final stage of life itself—begins around the mid-sixties. In the United States, about one in eight people is at least age sixty-five, and the elderly now outnumber teenagers (U.S. Census Bureau, 2012).

Once again, societies attach different meanings to this stage of life. As explained in Chapter 15 ("Aging and the Elderly"), it is older members of traditional societies who typically control most of the land and other wealth. Also, since traditional societies change slowly, older people possess useful wisdom gained over their lifetime, which earns them much respect.

In industrial societies, however, most younger people work and live apart from their parents, becoming independent of their elders. Rapid change also gives our society a "youth orientation" that defines the young as more "hip" and "with it," and what is old as unimportant or even obsolete. To younger people, the elderly may seem out of touch with new trends and fashions, and their knowledge and experience may seem of little value.

Perhaps this anti-elderly bias will decline as the share of older people in the United States steadily increases. The percentage of the U.S. population over age sixty-five has more than tripled in the past hundred years. With life expectancy still increasing, most men and women in their mid-sixties today (the "young elderly") can look forward to living decades longer. Analysts predict that by 2050, the number of seniors will double to more than 83 million, and the "average" person in the United States will be older than forty (U.S. Census Bureau, 2012).

Old age differs in an important way from earlier stages in the life course. Growing up typically means entering new roles and taking on new responsibilities, but growing old is the opposite experience—leaving roles that provided both satisfaction and social identity. For some people, retirement is a period of restful activity, but for others, it can mean losing valued routines and even outright boredom. Like any life transition, retirement demands learning new patterns while at the same time letting go of habits from the past.

Death and Dying

Throughout most of human history, low living standards and limited medical technology meant that death from accident or disease could come at any stage of life. Today, however, 86 percent of people in the United States die after age fifty-five (Hoyert & Xu, 2012).

After observing many people as they were dying, the psychiatrist Elisabeth Kübler-Ross (1969) described death as an orderly transition involving five distinct stages. Typically, a person first faces death with *denial*, perhaps out of fear and perhaps because our culture tends to ignore the reality of death. The second phase is *anger*, when a person facing death sees it as a gross injustice. Third, anger gives way to *negotiation* as the person imagines the possibility of avoiding death by striking a bargain with God. The fourth response, *resignation*, is often accompanied by psychological depression. Finally, a complete adjustment to death requires *acceptance*. At this point, no longer paralyzed by fear and anxiety, the person whose life is ending sets out to find peace and makes the most of whatever time remains.

More recent research has shown that Kübler-Ross simplified the process of dying—not everyone passes through these stages or does so in the order in which she presents them (Konigsberg, 2011). At the same time, this research has helped draw attention to death and dying. As the share of women and men in old age increases, we can expect our culture to become more comfortable with the idea of death. In recent years, people in the United States have started talking about death more openly, and the trend is toward viewing dying as preferable to prolonged suffering. More married couples now prepare for death with legal and financial planning. This openness may ease somewhat the pain of the surviving spouse, a consideration for women, who, more often than not, outlive their husbands.

The Life Course: Patterns and Variations

This brief look at the life course points to two major conclusions. First, although each stage of life is linked to the biological process of aging, the life course is largely a social construction. For this reason, people in other societies may experience a stage of life quite differently or, for that matter, not at all. Second, in any society, the stages of the life course present certain problems and transitions that involve learning something new and, in many cases, unlearning familiar routines.

A cohort is a category of similar-age people who share common life experiences. Just as audiences at Rolling Stones concerts in the 1960s were mainly young people, so many of the group's fans today are the same people, now over age sixty. Mick Jagger (*left*) recently turned seventy.

Societies organize the life course according to age, but other forces, such as class, race, ethnicity, and gender, also shape people's lives. This means that the general patterns described in this chapter apply somewhat differently to various categories of people.

cohort a category of people with something in common, usually their age

People's life experiences also vary, depending on when, in the history of the society, they were born. A **cohort** is *a category of people with something in common, usually their age*. Because members of a particular age cohort are generally influenced by the same economic and cultural trends, they tend to have similar attitudes and values. Women and men born in the 1940s and 1950s, for example, grew up during a time of economic expansion that gave them a sense of optimism. Today's college students, who have grown up in an age of economic uncertainty, are less confident about the future.

Resocialization: Total Institutions

5.5 Characterize the operation of total institutions.

A final type of socialization, experienced by more than 3 million people in the United States, involves being confined—usually against their will—in prisons or mental hospitals (CDC, 2012; U.S. Department of Justice, 2012). This is the world of the **total institution**, *a setting in which people are isolated from the rest of society and manipulated by an administrative staff.*

total institution a setting in which people are isolated from the rest of society and manipulated by an administrative staff

According to Erving Goffman (1961), total institutions have three important characteristics. First, staff members supervise all aspects of daily life, including when and where residents (often called "inmates") eat, sleep, and work. Second, life in a total institution is controlled and standardized, with the same food, uniforms, and activities for everyone. Third, formal rules dictate when, where, and how inmates perform their daily routines.

resocialization radically changing an inmate's personality by carefully controlling the environment

The purpose of such rigid routines is **resocialization**, *radically changing an inmate's personality by carefully controlling the environment*. Prisons and mental hospitals physically isolate inmates behind fences, barred windows, and locked doors and limit their access to the telephone, mail, and visitors. The institution becomes their entire world, making it easier for the staff to bring about personality change—or at least obedience—in the inmate.

Resocialization is a two-part process. First, the staff breaks down the new inmate's existing identity. For example, an inmate must give up personal possessions, including clothing and grooming articles used to maintain a distinctive appearance. Instead, the staff provides standard-issue clothes so that everyone looks alike. The staff subjects new inmates to "mortifications of self," which can include searches, head shaving, medical examinations, fingerprinting, and assignment of a serial number. Once inside the walls, individuals also give up their privacy as guards routinely inspect their living quarters.

In the second part of the resocialization process, the staff tries to build a new self in the inmate through a system of rewards and punishments. Having a book to read, watching television, or making a telephone call may seem like minor pleasures to the outsider, but in the rigid environment of the total institution, gaining such simple privileges as these can be a powerful motivation to conform. The length of confinement typically depends on how well the inmate cooperates with the staff.

Prisons are one example of a total institution in which inmates dress alike and carry out daily routines under the direct supervision and control of institutional staff. What do we expect prison to do to young people convicted of crimes? How well do you think prisons do what people expect them to?

Total institutions affect people in different ways. Some inmates may end up "rehabilitated" or "recovered," but others may change little, and still others may become hostile and bitter. Over a long period of time, living in a rigidly controlled environment can leave some people *institutionalized*, without the capacity for independent living.

But what about the rest of us? Does socialization crush our individuality or empower us to reach our creative potential? The Controversy & Debate box takes a closer look at this question.

Controversy & Debate

Are We Free within Society?

Mike: Sociology is a really interesting course. Since my professor started telling us how to look at the world with a sociological eye, I'm realizing that a lot of who I am and where I am is because of society.

Kim: (*teasingly*) Oh, so *society* is responsible for you turning out so smart and witty and good-looking?

Mike: No, that's all me. But I'm seeing that being at college and playing football is maybe not all me. I mean, it's at least also about social class and gender. What people are and the society around them can never be completely separated.

This chapter stresses one key theme: Society shapes how we think, feel, and act. If this is so, then in what sense are we free? To answer this important question, consider the Muppets, puppet stars of television and film that many of us remember from childhood. Watching the antics of Kermit the Frog, Miss Piggy, and the rest of the troupe, we almost believe they are real rather than objects controlled from backstage or below. As the sociological perspective points out, human beings are like puppets in that we, too, respond to backstage forces. Society, after all, gives us

Does understanding more about how society shapes our lives give us greater power to "cut the strings" and choose for ourselves how to live?

a culture and also shapes our lives according to class, race, and gender. If this is so, can we really claim to be free?

Sociologists answer this question with many voices. The politically liberal response is that individuals are *not* free of society—in fact, as social creatures, we never could be. But if we have to live in a society with power over us, then it is important to do what we can to make our world more socially just. We can do this by trying to lessen inequality, working to reduce class differences and to eliminate barriers to opportunity that hold back minorities, including women. A more conservative response is that, yes, society does shape our lives but we should also realize that we can remain free all the same because, first, to the extent that we believe in our way of life, society does not seem oppressive. Second, even when we run up against social barriers that we do not accept, we remain free because society can never dictate our dreams. Our history as a nation, right from the revolutionary acts that led to its founding, is one story after another of people pursuing personal goals despite great odds.

All of these arguments can be found in George Herbert Mead's analysis of socialization. Mead knew that society makes demands on us, sometimes limiting our options. But he also saw that human beings are spontaneous and creative, capable of continually acting on society both with acceptance and with efforts to bring about change. Mead noted the power of society while still affirming the human capacity to evaluate, criticize, and ultimately choose and change.

In the end, then, we may seem like puppets, but this impression is correct only on the surface. A crucial difference is that we have the ability to stop, look up at the "strings" that make us move, decide what we think about them, and even yank on the strings defiantly (Berger, 1963:176). If our pull is strong enough, we can accomplish more than we might think. As Margaret Mead once remarked, "Never doubt that a small group of thoughtful, committed citizens can change the world. Indeed, it is the only thing that ever has."

What Do You Think?

1. Do you think that our society gives more freedom to males than to females? Why or why not?

2. Do you think that most people in our society feel that they have some control over their lives or not? Why?

3. Has learning about socialization increased or decreased your feeling of freedom? Why?

Seeing Sociology in Everyday Life

On the San Carlos Reservation in Arizona, young Apache girls perform the Sunrise Dance to mark their transition to adulthood. Carefully painted by an elder according to Apache tradition, each girl holds a special staff, which symbolizes her hope for a long and healthy life and spiritual happiness. Many of the world's societies time these coming-of-age rituals to correspond to a girl's first menstrual cycle. Why do you think this is so?

When do we grow up and become adults?

As this chapter explains, many factors come into play in the process of moving from one stage of the life course to another. In global perspective, what makes our society unusual is that there is no one event that clearly tells everyone (and us, too) that the milestone of adulthood has been reached. We have important events that say, for example, when someone completes high school (graduation ceremony) or becomes married (wedding ceremony). Look at the photos shown here and on page 149. In each case, what do we learn about how the society defines the transition from one stage of life to another?

Among the Hamer people in the Omo Valley of Ethiopia, young boys must undergo a test to mark their transition to manhood. Usually the event is triggered by the boy's expressing a desire to marry. In this ritual, witnessed by everyone in his society, the boy must jump over a line of bulls selected by the girl's family. If he succeeds in doing this three times, he is declared a man and the wedding can take place (marking the girl's transition to womanhood). Does our society have any ceremony or event similar to this to mark the transition to adulthood?

These young men and women in Seoul, South Korea, are participating in a Confucian ceremony to mark their becoming adults. This ritual, which takes place on the twentieth birthday, defines young people as full members of the community and also reminds them of all the responsibilities they are now expected to fulfill. If we had such a ritual in the United States, at what age would it take place? Would a person's social class affect the timing of this ritual?

HINT Societies differ in how they structure the life course, including which stages of life are defined as important, which years of life various stages correspond to, and how clearly movement from one stage to another is marked. Given our cultural emphasis on individual choice and freedom, many people tend to say "You're only as old as you feel" and let people decide these things for themselves. When it comes to reaching adulthood, our society is not very clear—the box on page 138 points out many factors that figure into becoming an adult. So there is no widespread "adult ritual" as we see in these photos. Keep in mind that, for us, class matters a lot in this process, with young people from more affluent families staying in school and delaying full adulthood until well into their twenties or even their thirties. Finally, in these tough economic times, the share of young people in their twenties living with parents goes way up, which can delay adulthood for an entire cohort.

Seeing Sociology in *Your* Everyday Life

1. Across the United States, many families plan elaborate parties to celebrate a young person's graduation from high school. In what respects is this event a ritual that symbolizes a person reaching adulthood? How does social class affect whether or not people define high school graduation as an achievement that marks the beginning of adulthood?

2. Go to MySocLab and click on the Student Resources link to access the Sociology in Focus blog, where you can read the latest posts by a team of young sociologists who apply the sociological perspective to topics of popular culture.

3. In what sense are human beings free? After reading through this chapter, develop a personal statement of the extent to which you think you are able to guide your own life. Notice that some of the thinkers discussed in this chapter (such as Sigmund Freud) argued that there are sharp limits on our ability to act freely; by contrast, others (especially George Herbert Mead) claimed that human beings have significant ability to be creative. What is your personal statement about the extent of human freedom? Go to the "Seeing Sociology in *Your* Everyday Life" feature in MySocLab to learn more about the extent of personal freedom in society as well as suggestions about ways of making the most of the freedom we have.

Making the Grade

Social Experience: The Key to Our Humanity

5.1 Describe how social interaction is the foundation of personality. (pages 126–29)

 Watch the **Video** in **MySocLab**   **Read** the **Document** in **MySocLab**

Socialization is a **lifelong process**.

- Socialization develops our humanity as well as our particular personalities.
- The importance of socialization is seen in the fact that extended periods of social isolation result in permanent damage (cases of Anna, Isabelle, and Genie).

Socialization is a matter of **nurture** rather than **nature**.

- A century ago, most people thought human behavior resulted from biological instinct.
- For us as human beings, it is our nature to nurture.

socialization the lifelong social experience by which people develop their human potential and learn culture

personality a person's fairly consistent patterns of acting, thinking, and feeling

Understanding Socialization

5.2 Explain six major theories of socialization. (pages 129–35)

 Watch the **Video** in **MySocLab**

Sigmund Freud's model of the human personality has three parts:

- **id:** innate, pleasure-seeking human drives
- **superego:** the demands of society in the form of internalized values and norms
- **ego:** our efforts to balance innate, pleasure-seeking drives and the demands of society

Jean Piaget believed that human development involves both biological maturation and gaining social experience. He identified four stages of cognitive development:

- The **sensorimotor stage** involves knowing the world only through the senses.
- The **preoperational stage** involves starting to use language and other symbols.
- The **concrete operational stage** allows individuals to understand causal connections.
- The **formal operational stage** involves abstract and critical thought.

Lawrence Kohlberg applied Piaget's approach to stages of moral development:

- We first judge rightness in **preconventional** terms, according to our individual needs.
- Next, **conventional** moral reasoning takes account of parental attitudes and cultural norms.
- Finally, **postconventional** reasoning allows us to criticize society itself.

Carol Gilligan found that gender plays an important part in moral development, with males relying more on abstract standards of rightness and females relying more on the effects of actions on relationships.

To **George Herbert Mead:**

- The **self** is part of our personality and includes self-awareness and self-image.
- The self develops only as a result of social experience.
- Social experience involves the exchange of symbols.
- Social interaction depends on understanding the intention of another, which requires taking the role of the other.
- Human action is partly spontaneous (the I) and partly in response to others (the me).
- We gain social experience through imitation, play, games, and understanding the **generalized other**.

id Freud's term for the human being's basic drives

ego Freud's term for a person's conscious efforts to balance innate pleasure-seeking drives with the demands of society

superego Freud's term for the cultural values and norms internalized by an individual

sensorimotor stage Piaget's term for the level of human development at which individuals experience the world only through their senses

preoperational stage Piaget's term for the level of human development at which individuals first use language and other symbols

concrete operational stage Piaget's term for the level of human development at which individuals first see causal connections in their surroundings

formal operational stage Piaget's term for the level of human development at which individuals think abstractly and critically

self George Herbert Mead's term for the part of an individual's personality composed of self-awareness and self-image

looking-glass self Cooley's term for a self-image based on how we think others see us

Charles Horton Cooley used the term **looking-glass self** to explain that we see ourselves as we imagine others see us.

Erik H. Erikson identified challenges that individuals face at each stage of life from infancy to old age.

significant others people, such as parents, who have special importance for socialization

generalized other George Herbert Mead's term for widespread cultural norms and values we use as references in evaluating ourselves

Agents of Socialization

5.3 Analyze how the family, school, peer groups, and the mass media guide the socialization process. (pages 136–42)

 Explore the **Map** in **MySocLab**   **Watch** the **Video** in **MySocLab**

The **family** is usually the first setting of socialization.
- Family has the greatest impact on attitudes and behavior.
- A family's social position, including race and social class, shapes a child's personality.
- Ideas about gender are learned first in the family.

Schools give most children their first experience with bureaucracy and impersonal evaluation.
- Schools teach knowledge and skills needed for later life.
- Schools expose children to greater social diversity.
- Schools reinforce ideas about gender.

The **peer group** helps shape attitudes and behavior.
- The peer group takes on great importance during adolescence.
- The peer group frees young people from adult supervision.

The **mass media** have a huge impact on socialization in modern, high-income societies.
- The average U.S. child spends as much time watching television and videos as attending school and interacting with parents.
- The mass media often reinforce stereotypes about gender and race.
- The mass media expose people to a great deal of violence.

peer group a social group whose members have interests, social position, and age in common

anticipatory socialization learning that helps a person achieve a desired position

mass media the means for delivering impersonal communications to a vast audience

Socialization and the Life Course

5.4 Discuss how our society organizes human experience into distinctive stages of life. (pages 142–46)

The concept of **childhood** is grounded not in biology but in culture. In high-income countries, childhood is extended.

The emotional and social turmoil of **adolescence** results from cultural inconsistency in defining people who are not children but not yet adults. Adolescence varies by social class.

Adulthood is the stage of life when most accomplishments take place. Although personality is now formed, it continues to change with new life experiences.

Old age is defined as much by culture as biology.
- Traditional societies give power and respect to elders.
- Industrial societies define elders as unimportant and out of touch.

Acceptance of **death and dying** is part of socialization for the elderly. This process typically involves five stages: denial, anger, negotiation, resignation, and acceptance.

cohort a category of people with something in common, usually their age

Resocialization: Total Institutions

5.5 Characterize the operation of total institutions. (pages 146–47)

Total institutions include prisons, mental hospitals, and monasteries.
- Staff members supervise all aspects of life.
- Life is standardized, with all inmates following set rules and routines.

Resocialization is a two-part process:
- breaking down inmates' existing identity
- building a new self through a system of rewards and punishments

total institution a setting in which people are isolated from the rest of society and manipulated by an administrative staff

resocialization radically changing an inmate's personality by carefully controlling the environment

6 Social Interaction in Everyday Life

((• **Listen** to **Chapter 6** in **MySocLab**

LEARNING OBJECTIVES

6.1 Explain how social structure helps us to make sense of everyday situations.

6.2 State the importance of status to social organization.

6.3 State the importance of role to social organization.

6.4 Describe how we socially construct reality.

6.5 Apply Goffman's analysis to several familiar situations.

6.6 Construct a sociological analysis of three aspects of everyday life: emotions, language, and humor.

the Power of Society
to guide the way we do social networking

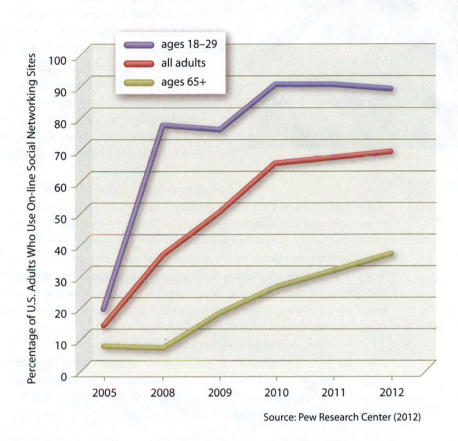

Percentage of U.S. Adults Who Use On-line Social Networking Sites

ages 18–29
all adults
ages 65+

Source: Pew Research Center (2012)

Is our use of social networking sites as much of a personal choice as we may think? In 2005, just 10 percent of U.S. adults were making use of social networking sites such as Facebook; today, almost two out of three adults are. But age is a powerful predictor of who uses social media: While just 34 percent of people over the age of sixty-five use social networking sites, 86 percent of people between the ages of eighteen and twenty-nine do so.

Chapter Overview

This chapter takes a "micro-level" look at society, examining patterns of everyday social interaction. First, the chapter identifies important social structures, including status and role, which guide our behavior in the presence of others. Then it explains how we construct reality in social interaction. Finally, the chapter applies the lessons learned to three everyday experiences: emotions, language, and humor.

Harold and Sybil are on their way to another couple's home in an unfamiliar area near Fort Lauderdale, Florida. For the last twenty minutes, as Sybil sees it, they have been driving in circles, searching in vain for Coconut Palm Road.

"Look, Harold," says Sybil. "There are some people up ahead. Let's ask for directions." Harold, gripping the wheel ever more tightly, begins muttering under his breath. "I know where I am. I don't want to waste time talking to strangers. Just let me get us there."

"I'm sure you know where you are, Harold," Sybil responds, looking straight ahead. "But I don't think you know where you're going."

Harold and Sybil are lost in more ways than one: Not only can't they find where their friends live, but they also cannot understand why they are growing angrier with each other with each passing minute.

What's going on? Like most men, Harold cannot stand getting lost. The longer he drives around, the more incompetent he feels. Sybil can't understand why Harold doesn't pull over to ask someone the way to Coconut Palm Road. If she were driving, she thinks to herself, they would already be comfortably settled in with their friends.

Why don't men like to ask for directions? Because men are so eager to claim competence and independence, they are uncomfortable asking for any type of help and are reluctant to accept it. In addition, to ask another person for assistance is the same as saying, "You know something I don't know." If it takes Harold a few more minutes to find Coconut Palm Road on his own—and to keep his sense of being in control—he thinks that's the way to go.

Women are more in tune with others and strive for connectedness. From Sybil's point of view, asking for help is right because sharing information builds social bonds and at the same time gets the job done. Asking for directions seems as natural to Sybil as searching on his own is to Harold. Obviously, getting lost is sure to create conflict for Harold and Sybil as long as neither one understands the other's point of view.

S uch everyday social patterns are the focus of this chapter. The central concept is **social interaction**, *the process by which people act and react in relation to others.* We begin by presenting the rules and building blocks of everyday experience and then explore the almost magical way in which face-to-face interaction creates the reality in which we live.

social interaction the process by which people act and react in relation to others

Social Structure: A Guide to Everyday Living

(**6.1**) Explain how social structure helps us to make sense of everyday situations.

◉ **Watch** in **MySocLab** **Video:** *The Basics: Social Interaction*

October 21, Ho Chi Minh City, Vietnam. This morning we leave the ship and make our way along the docks toward the center of Ho Chi Minh City, known to an earlier generation as Saigon. The government security officers wave us through the heavy metal gates. Pressed against the fence are dozens of men who operate *cyclos* (bicycles with small carriages attached to the front), the Vietnamese version of taxicabs. We wave them off and spend the next twenty minutes shaking our heads at several drivers who pedal alongside, pleading for our business. The pressure is uncomfortable. We decide to cross the street but realize suddenly that there are no stop signs or signal lights—and the street is an unbroken stream of bicycles, cyclos, motorbikes, and small trucks. The locals don't bat an eye; they just walk at a steady pace across the street, parting waves of vehicles that immediately close in again behind them. Walk right into traffic? With our small children on our backs? Yup, we did it; that's the way it works in Vietnam.

Members of every society rely on social structure to make sense of everyday situations. As our family's introduction to the busy streets of Vietnam suggests, the world can be confusing, even frightening, when society's rules are unclear. Let's take a closer look at the ways in which societies organize everyday life.

Status

6.2 State the importance of status to social organization.

In every society, people build their everyday lives using the idea of **status**, *a social position that a person holds*. In everyday use, the word *status* generally means "prestige," as when we say that a college president has more "status" than a newly hired assistant professor. But sociologically speaking, both "president" and "professor" are statuses, or positions, within the collegiate organization.

Status is part of our social identity and helps define our relationship to others. As Georg Simmel (1950:307, orig. 1902), one of the founders of sociology, once pointed out, before we can deal with anyone, we need to know who the person is.

Status Set

Each of us holds many statuses at once. The term **status set** refers to *all the statuses a person holds at a given time*. A teenage girl may be a daughter to her parents, a sister to her brother, a student at her school, and a goalie on her soccer team.

Status sets change over the life course. A child grows up to become a parent, a student graduates to become a lawyer, and a single person marries to become a husband or wife, sometimes becoming single again as a result

Members of our society celebrate the achievements of super-stars such as Jennifer Lopez (J.Lo) not only because of her success as a musician and actress as well as a fashion designer, but also because she grew up in a poor neighborhood of the Bronx, New York, and had to "make it" mostly on her own.

status a social position that a person holds

ascribed status a social position a person receives at birth or takes on involuntarily later in life

achieved status a social position a person takes on voluntarily that reflects personal ability and effort

of death or divorce. Joining an organization or finding a job enlarges our status set; withdrawing from activities makes it smaller. Over a lifetime, people gain and lose dozens of statuses.

Ascribed and Achieved Status

Sociologists classify statuses in terms of how people attain them. An **ascribed status** is *a social position a person receives at birth or takes on involuntarily later in life*. Examples of ascribed statuses include being a daughter, a Cuban, a teenager, or a widower. Ascribed statuses are matters about which we have little or no choice.

By contrast, an **achieved status** refers to *a social position a person takes on voluntarily that reflects personal ability and effort*. Achieved statuses in the United States include honors student, Olympic athlete, nurse, software writer, and thief.

In the real world, of course, most statuses involve a combination of ascription and achievement. That is, people's ascribed statuses influence the statuses they achieve.

Thinking About Diversity: Race, Class, and Gender

Physical Disability as a Master Status

Physical disability works in much the same ways as class, gender, or race in defining people in the eyes of others. In the following interviews, two women explain how a physical disability can become a master status—a trait that overshadows everything else about them. The first voice is that of twenty-nine-year-old Donna Finch, who lives with her husband and son in Muskogee, Oklahoma, and holds a master's degree in social work. She is also blind.

> Most people don't expect handicapped people to grow up; they are always supposed to be children…. You aren't supposed to date, you aren't supposed to have a job, somehow

you're just supposed to disappear. I'm not saying this is true of anyone else, but in my own case I think I was more intellectually mature than most children, and more emotionally immature. I'd say that not until the last four or five years have I felt really whole.

Rose Helman is an elderly woman who has retired from her job and lives near New York City. She suffers from spinal meningitis and is also blind.

> You ask me if people are really different today than in the '20s and '30s. Not too much. They are still fearful of the handicapped. I don't know if *fearful* is the right word, but uncomfortable at least. But I can understand it somewhat; it happened to me. I once asked a man to tell me which staircase to use to get from the subway out to the street. He started giving me directions that were confusing, and I said, "Do you mind taking me?" He said, "Not at all." He grabbed me on the side with my dog on it, so I asked him to take my other arm. And he said, "I'm sorry, I have no other arm." And I said, "That's all right, I'll hold onto the jacket." It felt funny hanging onto the sleeve without the arm in it.

Modern technology means that most soldiers who lose limbs in war now survive. How do you think the loss of an arm or a leg affects a person's social identity and sense of self?

What Do You Think?

1. Have you ever had a disease or disability that became a master status? If so, how did others react?

2. How might such a master status affect someone's personality?

3. Can being very fat or very thin serve as a master status? Why or why not?

Source: Based on Orlansky & Heward (1981).

People who achieve the status of lawyer, for example, are likely to share the ascribed benefit of being born into relatively well-off families. By the same token, many less desirable statuses, such as criminal, drug addict, or unemployed worker, are more easily achieved by people born into poverty.

Master Status

Some statuses matter more than others. A **master status** is *a status that has special importance for social identity, often shaping a person's entire life*. For most people, a job is a master status because it reveals a great deal about a person's social background, education, and income. In a few cases, name is a master status; being in the Bush or Kennedy family attracts attention and creates opportunities.

A master status can be negative as well as positive. Take, for example, serious illness. Sometimes people, even longtime friends, avoid cancer patients or people with AIDS because of their illnesses. As another example, the fact that all societies limit the opportunities of women makes gender a master status.

Sometimes a physical disability serves as a master status to the point where we dehumanize people by seeing them only in terms of their disability. The Thinking About Diversity box on page 156 shows how.

status set all the statuses a person holds at a given time

master status a status that has special importance for social identity, often shaping a person's entire life

Role

6.3 State the importance of role to social organization.

A second important social structure is **role**, *behavior expected of someone who holds a particular status*. A person *holds* a status and *performs* a role (Linton, 1937b). For example, holding the status of student leads you to perform the role of attending classes and completing assignments.

Both statuses and roles vary by culture. In the United States, the status of "uncle" refers to the brother of a mother or a father. In Vietnam, the word for "uncle" is different on the mother's and father's sides of the family, and the two men have different responsibilities. In every society, actual role performance varies with an individual's unique personality, and some societies permit more individual expression of a role than others.

role behavior expected of someone who holds a particular status

role set a number of roles attached to a single status

Role Set

Because we hold many statuses at once—a status set—everyday life is a mix of many roles. Robert Merton (1968) introduced the term **role set** to identify *a number of roles attached to a single status*.

Figure 6-1 shows four statuses of one person, each status linked to a different role set. First, as a professor, this woman interacts with students (the teacher role) and with other academics (the colleague role). Second, in her work as a researcher, she gathers and analyzes data (the fieldwork role) that she uses in her publications (the author role). Third, the woman occupies the status of "wife," with a marital role (such as confidante and sexual partner) toward her husband, with whom she shares household duties (domestic role). Fourth, she holds the status of "mother," with routine responsibilities for her children (the maternal role), as well as toward their school and other organizations in her community (the civic role).

A global perspective shows that the roles people use to define their lives differ from society to society. In low-income countries,

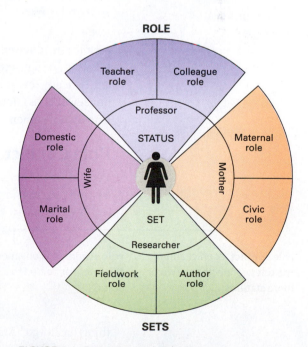

FIGURE 6-1 Status Set and Role Sets

A status set includes all the statuses a person holds at a given time. The status set defines *who we are* in society. The many roles linked to each status define *what we do*.

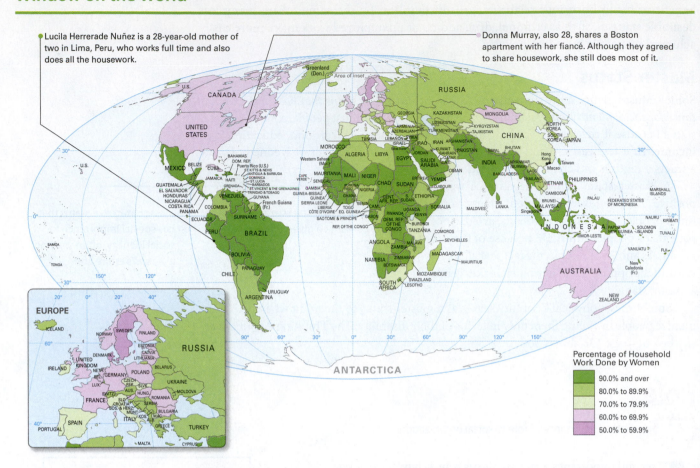

Lucila Herrerade Nuñez is a 28-year-old mother of two in Lima, Peru, who works full time and also does all the housework.

Donna Murray, also 28, shares a Boston apartment with her fiancé. Although they agreed to share housework, she still does most of it.

Percentage of Household Work Done by Women

- 90.0% and over
- 80.0% to 89.9%
- 70.0% to 79.9%
- 60.0% to 69.9%
- 50.0% to 59.9%

GLOBAL MAP 6-1 Housework in Global Perspective

Throughout the world, housework is a major part of women's routines and identities. This is especially true in poor nations of Latin America, Africa, and Asia, where the social position of women is far below that of men. But our society also defines housework and child care as "feminine" activities, even though women and men have the same legal rights and most women work outside the home.

Source: United Nations (2010).

people spend fewer years as students, and family roles are often very important to social identity. In high-income nations, people spend more years as students, and family roles are typically less important to social identity. Another dimension of difference involves housework. As Global Map 6-1 above shows, especially in poor countries, housework falls heavily on women.

Role Conflict and Role Strain

People in modern, high-income nations juggle many responsibilities demanded by their various statuses and roles. As most mothers (and more and more fathers) can testify, the combination of parenting and working outside the home is physically and emotionally draining. Sociologists thus recognize **role conflict** as *conflict among the roles connected to two or more statuses.*

We experience role conflict when we find ourselves pulled in various directions as we try to respond to the many statuses we hold. One response to role conflict is deciding that "something has to go." More than one politician, for example, has decided not to run for office because of the conflicting demands of a hectic campaign schedule and family life. In other cases, people put off having children in order to stay on the "fast track" for career success.

Even roles linked to a single status may make competing demands on us. **Role strain** refers to *tension among the roles connected to a single status.* A college professor

role conflict conflict among the roles connected to two or more statuses

role strain tension among the roles connected to a single status

may enjoy being friendly with students. At the same time, however, the professor must maintain the personal distance needed to evaluate students fairly. In short, performing the various roles attached to even one status can be something of a balancing act.

One strategy for minimizing role conflict is separating parts of our lives so that we perform roles for one status at one time and place and carry out roles connected to another status in a completely different setting. A familiar example of this idea is deciding to "leave the job at work" before heading home to the family.

Role Exit

After she left the life of a Catholic nun to become a university sociologist, Helen Rose Fuchs Ebaugh began to study her own experience of *role exit,* the process by which people disengage from important social roles. Studying a range of "exes," including ex-nuns, ex-doctors, ex-husbands, and ex-alcoholics, Ebaugh identified elements common to the process of becoming an "ex."

According to Ebaugh (1988), the process begins as people come to doubt their ability to continue in a certain role. As they imagine alternative roles, they ultimately reach a tipping point when they decide to pursue a new life. Even as they are moving on, however, a past role can continue to influence their lives. Exes carry with them a self-image shaped by an earlier role, which can interfere with building a new sense of self. For example, an ex-nun may hesitate to wear stylish clothing and makeup.

Exes must also rebuild relationships with people who knew them in their earlier life. Learning new social skills is another challenge. For example, Ebaugh reports, ex-nuns who enter the dating scene after decades in the church are often surprised to learn that sexual norms are very different from those they knew when they were teenagers.

The Social Construction of Reality

(6.4) Describe how we socially construct reality.

In 1917, the Italian playwright Luigi Pirandello wrote a play called *The Pleasure of Honesty* about a character named Angelo Baldovino, a brilliant man with a checkered past. Baldovino enters the fashionable home of the Renni family and introduces himself in a peculiar way:

> Inevitably we construct ourselves. Let me explain. I enter this house and immediately I become what I have to become, what I can become: I construct myself. That is, I present myself to you in a form suitable to the relationship I wish to achieve with you. And, of course, you do the same with me. (1962:157–58)

Baldovino suggests that although behavior is guided by status and role, we have the ability to shape who we are and to guide what happens from moment to moment. In other words, "reality" is not as fixed as we may think.

The **social construction of reality** is *the process by which people creatively shape reality through social interaction.* This idea is the foundation of the symbolic-interaction approach, described in Chapter 1 ("The Sociological Perspective"). As Baldovino's remark suggests, quite a bit of "reality" remains unclear in everyone's mind, especially in unfamiliar situations. So we present ourselves in terms that suit the setting and our purposes, we try to guide what happens next, and as others do the same, reality takes shape. Social interaction, then, is a complex negotiation that builds reality. Most everyday situations involve at least some agreement about what's going on. But how people see events depends on their different backgrounds, interests, and intentions.

Explore how education shapes reality construction in your local community and in counties across the United States in **MySocLab**

social construction of reality the process by which people creatively shape reality through social interaction

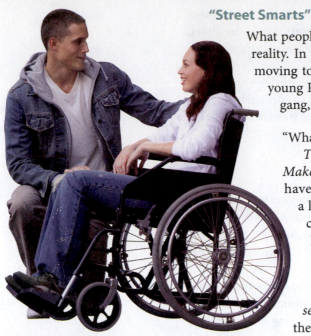

Flirting is an everyday experience in reality construction. Each person offers information to the other and hints at romantic interest. Yet the interaction proceeds with a tentative and often humorous air so that either individual can withdraw at any time without further obligation.

"Street Smarts"

What people commonly call "street smarts" is actually a form of constructing reality. In his autobiography *Down These Mean Streets,* Piri Thomas recalls moving to an apartment in Spanish Harlem. Returning home one evening, young Piri found himself cut off by Waneko, the leader of the local street gang, who was flanked by a dozen others.

"Whatta ya say, Mr. Johnny Gringo," drawled Waneko.

Think man, I told myself, *think your way out of a stomping. Make it good.* "I hear you 104th Street coolies are supposed to have heart," I said. "I don't know this for sure. You know there's a lot of streets where a whole 'click' is made out of punks who can't fight one guy unless they all jump him for the stomp." I hoped this would push Waneko into giving me a fair one. His expression didn't change.

"Maybe we don't look at it that way."

Crazy, man, I cheer inwardly, *the* cabron *is falling into my setup….* . "I wasn't talking to you," I said. "Where I come from, the pres is president 'cause he got heart when it comes to dealing."

Waneko was starting to look uneasy. He had bit on my worm and felt like a sucker fish. His boys were now light on me. They were no longer so much interested in stomping me as seeing the outcome between Waneko and me. "Yeah," was his reply…. .

I knew I'd won. Sure, I'd have to fight; but one guy, not ten or fifteen. If I lost, I might still get stomped, and if I won I might get stomped. I took care of this with my next sentence. "I don't know you or your boys," I said, "but they look cool to me. They don't feature as punks."

I had left him out purposely when I said "they." Now his boys were in a separate class. I had cut him off. He would have to fight me on his own, to prove his heart to himself, to his boys, and most important, to his turf. He got away from the stoop and asked, "Fair one, Gringo?" (1967:56–57)

This situation reveals the drama—sometimes subtle, sometimes savage—by which human beings creatively build reality. But, of course, not everyone enters a situation with equal standing. If a police officer had happened to drive by when Piri and Waneko were fighting, both young men might have ended up in jail.

The Thomas Theorem

By displaying his wits and fighting with Waneko until they both tired, Piri Thomas won acceptance by the gang. What took place that evening in Spanish Harlem is an example of the **Thomas theorem**, named after W. I. Thomas and Dorothy Thomas (1928; Thomas, 1966:301, orig. 1931): *Situations that are defined as real are real in their consequences.*

Applied to social interaction, the Thomas theorem means that although reality is initially "soft" as it is being shaped, it can become "hard" in its effects. In the case just described, local gang members saw Piri Thomas act in a worthy way, so in their eyes, he *became* worthy.

Ethnomethodology

Most of the time, we take social reality for granted. To become more aware of the world we help create, Harold Garfinkel (1967) devised **ethnomethodology**, *the study of the way people make sense of their everyday surroundings.* This approach begins by pointing out that everyday behavior rests on a number of assumptions. When you ask someone the simple question "How are you?" you usually want to know how the person is doing in

Watch in **MySocLab** **Video:** *Sociology on the Job: Social Interaction*

Thomas theorem
W. I. Thomas's claim that situations defined as real are real in their consequences

ethnomethodology Harold Garfinkel's term for the study of the way people make sense of their everyday surroundings

general, but you might really be wondering how the person is dealing with a specific physical, mental, spiritual, or financial challenge. However, the person being asked probably assumes that you are not really interested in details about any of these things, that you are just "being polite."

One good way to try to uncover the assumptions we make about reality is to break the rules. For example, the next time someone greets you by saying, "How are you?" offer details from your last physical examination or explain all the good and bad things that have happened since you woke up that morning and see how the person reacts.

The results are predictable, because we all have some idea of the "rules" of everyday interaction. The person will most likely become confused or irritated by your unexpected behavior—a reaction that helps us see not only what the rules are but also how important they are to everyday reality.

Reality Building: Class and Culture

People do not build everyday experience out of thin air. In part, how we act or what we see in our surroundings depends on our interests. Gazing at the sky on a starry night, for example, lovers discover romance, and scientists see hydrogen atoms fusing into helium. Social background also affects what we see, which is why residents of Spanish Harlem experience a different world than people living on Manhattan's pricey Upper East Side.

In global perspective, reality construction varies even more. Consider these everyday situations: People waiting for their luggage in a Swedish airport stand behind a yellow line about ten feet from the conveyor belt that carries the bags and then step forward only when they see their bags passing by; in the United States, people in the luggage claim area of an airport typically push right up to the conveyor system and lean forward looking for their own bags to appear. In Saudi Arabia, the law forbids women to drive cars, a ban unthinkable in the United States. In this country, people assume that "a short walk" means a few blocks or a few minutes; in the Andes Mountains of Peru, this same phrase means traveling a few miles.

The point is that people build reality from the surrounding culture. Chapter 3 "Culture") explains how people the world over find different meanings in specific gestures, so inexperienced travelers can find themselves building an unexpected and unwelcome reality. Similarly, in a study of popular culture, JoEllen Shively (1992) screened western films to men of European descent and to Native American men. The men in both categories claimed to enjoy the films, but for very different reasons. White men interpreted the films as praising rugged people striking out for the West and conquering the forces of nature. Native American men saw in the same films a celebration of land and nature. Given their different cultures, it is as if people in the two categories saw two different films.

Films also have an effect on the reality we all experience. In 2012, the New York Disabilities Film Festival screened films dealing with autism, blindness, cerebral palsy, and mental illness. These films, which were also screened in ten other urban areas, raised awareness of the lives of people and their families as they cope with these serious personal challenges.

People build reality from their surrounding culture. Yet because cultural systems are marked by diversity and even outright conflict, reality construction always involves tensions and choices. Turkey is a nation with a mostly Muslim population, but it has also embraced Western culture. Here women confront starkly different definitions of what is "feminine."

Staton R. Winter, *The New York Times*.

In 2012, the Chinese government decided to require all students to take "patriotism" classes supporting the Chinese Communist Party. In an age of social media, the reaction was immediate as millions of students, linked by smart phone technology, mobilized against a plan they denounced as "brainwashing." Have you ever used social networking sites to engage in political action?

The Increasing Importance of Social Media

The social construction of reality has always involved face-to-face social interaction. In recent years, however, this process has also been aided by computer technology. The concept of **social media** refers to *technology that links people in social activity*. Although newspapers and other print media are older examples of social media, more recent computer technology is much more powerful because it connects a far larger number of people. In addition, computer-based technology is interactive, allowing individuals not only to receive messages but also to send information to others.

In the past, when people came together to form communities based on a common interest, they gathered in a single location. Even a generation ago, few people imagined the dramatic changes that computer technology would bring to the landscape of social interaction. Today, of course, most people in the United States and nations around the world participate in various online communities with countless others who share some interest. Participants may be anywhere in physical space, and they are people whom we may or may not ever meet in person.

The expansion of social media can be seen in the explosive increase in the public's use of social networking sites. Facebook, which began formal operation in 2004, now has some 1 billion members worldwide. Similarly, Twitter was launched in 2006 as a social networking and micro-blogging system that allows users to send and receive short text messages called "tweets." It now boasts some 175 million registered users.

Some sociologists have argued that the rise of social media has connected people in new ways but weakened social ties among people who share physical space. Take the case of two college roommates, each of whom might be interacting with thousands of other people while sitting just a few feet apart in the same dorm room, barely paying attention to each other. Much the same argument was made about the spread of telephone technology more than a century ago.

Like every major change in society, the rise of social media will spark controversy and debate. But there is little doubt that this trend is reshaping all aspects of everyday life from the way people engage in social movements to the way they look for romance (Farrell, 2011; Turkle, 2012).

social media technology that links people in social activity

Dramaturgical Analysis: The "Presentation of Self"

Read in **MySocLab Document:** *The Presentation of Self in Everyday Life* by Erving Goffman

6.5 Apply Goffman's analysis to several familiar situations.

dramaturgical analysis Erving Goffman's term for the study of social interaction in terms of theatrical performance

Erving Goffman (1922–1982) was another sociologist who analyzed social interaction, explaining that people live their lives much like actors performing on a stage. If we imagine ourselves as directors observing what goes on in the theater of everyday life, we are doing what Goffman called **dramaturgical analysis**, *the study of social interaction in terms of theatrical performance.*

Dramaturgical analysis offers a fresh look at the concepts of status and role. A status is like a part in a play, and a role serves as a script, supplying dialogue and action for the characters. Goffman described each individual's "performance" as the **presentation of self**, *a person's efforts to create specific impressions in the minds of others.* This process, sometimes called *impression management,* begins with the idea of personal performance (Goffman, 1959, 1967).

Performances

As we present ourselves in everyday situations, we reveal information to others both consciously and unconsciously. Our performance includes how we dress (in theatrical terms, our costume), the objects we carry (props), and our tone of voice and gestures (our demeanor). In addition, we vary our performance according to where we are (the set). We may joke loudly in a restaurant, for example, but lower our voice when entering a church or a temple. People design settings, such as homes or offices, to bring about desired reactions in others.

An Application: The Doctor's Office

Consider how physicians set up their offices to convey particular information to an audience of patients. The fact that medical doctors enjoy high prestige and power in the United States is clear upon entering a doctor's office. First, the doctor is nowhere to be seen. Instead, in what Goffman describes as the "front region" of the setting, the patient encounters a receptionist, or gatekeeper, who decides whether and when the patient can meet the doctor. A simple glance around the doctor's waiting room, with patients (often impatiently) waiting to be invited into the inner sanctum, leaves little doubt that the doctor and the staff are in charge.

The "back region" is composed of the examination room plus the doctor's private office. Once inside the office, the patient can see a wide range of props, such as medical books and framed degrees, that give the impression that the doctor has the specialized knowledge necessary to call the shots. The doctor is usually seated behind a desk—the larger the desk, the greater the statement of power—and the patient is given only a chair.

The doctor's appearance and manner offer still more information. The white lab coat (costume) may have the practical function of keeping clothes from becoming dirty, but its social function is to let others know at a glance the physician's status. A stethoscope around the neck and a medical chart in hand (more props) have the same purpose. A doctor uses highly technical language that is often mystifying to the patient, again emphasizing that the doctor is in charge. Finally, patients use the title "doctor," but they, in turn, are often addressed by their first names, which further shows the doctor's dominant position. The overall message of a doctor's performance is clear: "I will help you, but you must allow me to take charge."

Nonverbal Communication

The novelist William Sansom describes a fictional Mr. Preedy, an English vacationer on a beach in Spain:

> He took care to avoid catching anyone's eye. First, he had to make it clear to those potential companions of his holiday that they were of no concern to him whatsoever. He stared through them, round them, over them—eyes lost in space.

presentation of self
Erving Goffman's term for a person's efforts to create specific impressions in the minds of others

The beach might have been empty. If by chance a ball was thrown his way, he looked surprised; then let a smile of amusement light his face (Kindly Preedy), looked around dazed to see that there were people on the beach, tossed it back with a smile to himself and not a smile *at* the people... .

[He] then gathered together his beach-wrap and bag into a neat sand-resistant pile (Methodical and Sensible Preedy), rose slowly to stretch his huge frame (Big-Cat Preedy), and tossed aside his sandals (Carefree Preedy, after all). (1956:230–31)

nonverbal communication
communication using body movements, gestures, and facial expressions rather than speech

Without saying a single word, Mr. Preedy offers a great deal of information about himself to anyone watching him. This is the process of **nonverbal communication**, *communication using body movements, gestures, and facial expressions rather than speech.*

People use many parts of the body to convey information through *body language*. Facial expressions are the most important type of body language. Smiling, for instance, shows pleasure, although we distinguish among the deliberate smile of Kindly Preedy on the beach, a spontaneous smile of joy at seeing a friend, a pained smile of embarrassment after spilling a cup of coffee, and the full, unrestrained smile of self-satisfaction that we often associate with winning some important contest.

Eye contact is another key element of nonverbal communication. Generally, we use eye contact to invite social interaction. Someone across the room "catches our eye," sparking a conversation. Avoiding another's eyes, by contrast, discourages communication. Hands, too, speak for us. Common hand gestures in our society convey, among other things, an insult, a request for a ride, an invitation for someone to join us, or a demand that others stop in their tracks. Gestures also supplement spoken words. For example, pointing at someone in a threatening way gives greater emphasis to a word of warning, just as shrugging the shoulders adds an air of indifference to the phrase "I don't know" and rapidly waving the arms adds urgency to the single word "Hurry!"

In everyday interaction, body language is an important way in which we transmit information to an audience as well as "read" information in the behavior of others. To people who have limited skills in the spoken language used by those around them, body language takes on special importance. Similarly, to people who have a physical impairment—perhaps older people who have lost some of their ability to hear—"reading" body language can enhance understanding (Stepanikova et al., 2011).

Body Language and Deception

As any actor knows, it is very difficult to pull off a perfect performance in front of others. In everyday interaction, unintended body language can contradict our planned meaning: A teenage boy offers an explanation for getting home late, for example, but his mother

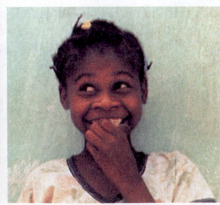

Hand gestures vary widely from one culture to another. Yet people everywhere chuckle, grin, or smirk to indicate that they don't take another person's performance seriously. Therefore, the world over, people who cannot restrain their mirth tactfully cover their faces.

begins to doubt his words because he avoids looking her in the eye. The teenage celebrity on a television talk show claims that her recent musical flop is "no big deal," but the nervous swing of her leg suggests otherwise. Because nonverbal communication is hard to control, it offers clues to deception in much the same way that changes in breathing, pulse rate, perspiration, and blood pressure recorded on a lie detector indicate that a person is lying.

Detecting dishonest performances is difficult because no single bodily gesture tells us for sure that someone is lying. But nervous movement of the hands or feet can be a sign of deception. Similarly, moving the head back or stepping away from someone—ways of adding to the distance between people—may be signs of deception. More generally, because any performance involves so much body language, few people can engage in deception (especially when they feel a strong emotion) without some slip-up or "leaking" information that raises the suspicions of a careful observer. The key to detecting lies is to view the whole performance with an eye for inconsistencies.

Gender and Performances

Because women are socialized to respond to others, they tend to be more sensitive than men to nonverbal communication. Research suggests that women "read" men better than men "read" women (Farris et al., 2008). Gender is also one of the key elements in the presentation of self, as the following sections explain.

Watch in **MySocLab** Video: *The Big Picture: Social Interaction*

Demeanor

Demeanor—the way we act and carry ourselves—is a clue to social power. Simply put, powerful people enjoy more freedom in how they act. At the office, off-color remarks, swearing, or putting your feet on the desk may be acceptable for the boss but rarely, if ever, for employees. Similarly, powerful people can interrupt others; less powerful people are expected to show respect through silence (Smith-Lovin & Brody, 1989; Henley, Hamilton, & Thorne, 1992; Johnson, 1994).

Because women generally occupy positions of lesser power, demeanor is a gender issue as well. As Chapter 13 ("Gender Stratification") explains, 38 percent of all working women in the United States hold clerical or service jobs under the control of supervisors, typically men (U.S. Department of Labor, 2012). Women, then, learn to craft their personal performances more carefully than men and to defer to men more often in everyday interaction.

Use of Space

How much space does a personal performance require? Power plays a key role here; the more power you have, the more space you use. Men typically command more space than women, whether pacing back and forth before an audience or casually sitting on a bench. Why? Our culture has traditionally measured femininity by how *little* space women occupy—the standard of "daintiness"—and masculinity by how *much* territory a man controls—the standard of "turf" (Henley, Hamilton, & Thorne, 1992).

For both sexes, the concept of **personal space** refers to *the surrounding area over which a person makes some claim to privacy*. In the United States, people typically position themselves several feet apart when speaking; throughout the Middle East, by contrast, people stand much closer. Just about everywhere, men (with their greater social power) often intrude into women's personal space. If a woman moves into a man's personal space, however, he is likely to take it as a sign of sexual interest.

personal space
the surrounding area over which a person makes some claim to privacy

Staring, Smiling, and Touching

Eye contact encourages interaction. In conversations, women hold eye contact more than men. But men have their own brand of eye contact: staring. When men stare at women, they are claiming social dominance and defining women as sexual objects.

Although it often shows pleasure, smiling can also be a sign of trying to please someone or submission. In a male-dominated world, it is not surprising that women smile more than men (Henley, Hamilton, & Thorne, 1992).

Finally, mutual touching suggests intimacy and caring. Apart from close relationships, touching is generally something men do to women (but less often, in our culture, to other men). A male physician touches the shoulder of his female nurse as they examine a report, a young man touches the back of his woman friend as he guides her across the street, or a male tennis instructor touches young women as he teaches them to hit a serve. In such examples, the intent of touching may be harmless and may bring little response, but it amounts to a subtle ritual by which men claim dominance over women.

Idealization

People behave the way they do for many, often complex reasons. Even so, Goffman suggests, we construct performances to *idealize* our intentions. That is, we try to convince others (and perhaps ourselves) that what we do reflects ideal cultural standards rather than selfish motives.

Idealization is easily illustrated by returning to the world of doctors and patients. In a hospital, doctors engage in a performance commonly described as "making rounds." Entering the room of a patient, the doctor often stops at the foot of the bed and silently reads the patient's chart. Afterward, doctor and patient talk briefly. In ideal terms, this routine involves a doctor making a personal visit to check on a patient's condition.

In reality, the picture is not so perfect. A doctor may see several dozen patients a day and remember little about many of them. Reading the chart is a chance to recall the patient's name and medical problems, but revealing the impersonality of medical care would undermine the cultural ideal of the doctor as deeply concerned about the welfare of others.

Doctors, college professors, and other professionals typically idealize their motives for entering their chosen careers. They describe their work as "making a contribution to science," "helping others," "serving the community," and even "answering a calling from God." Rarely do they admit the more common, less honorable, motives: the income, power, prestige, and leisure time that these occupations provide.

We all use idealization to some degree. When was the last time you smiled and spoke politely to someone you do not like? Have you acted interested in a class that was really boring? Such little lies in our performances help us get through everyday life. Even when we suspect that others are putting on an act, we are unlikely to challenge their performances for reasons that we shall examine next.

Embarrassment and Tact

The famous speaker giving a campus lecture keeps mispronouncing the college's name; the head coach rises to speak at the team's end-of-season banquet unaware of the napkin still tucked in her dress; the student enters the lecture hall late and soaking wet, attracting the gaze of hundreds of classmates. As carefully as individuals may try to craft their performances, slip-ups of all kinds occur. The result is *embarrassment*, discomfort following a spoiled performance. Goffman describes embarrassment as "losing face."

Embarrassment is an ever-present danger because idealized performances usually contain some deception. In addition, most performances involve juggling so many elements that one thoughtless moment can shatter the intended impression.

A curious fact is that an audience often overlooks flaws in a performance, allowing the actor to avoid embarrassment. If we do point out a misstep ("Excuse me, but your fly is open"), we do it quietly and only to help someone avoid even greater loss of face. In Hans Christian Andersen's classic fable "The Emperor's New Clothes," the child who blurts out the truth, that the emperor is parading about naked, is scolded for being rude.

Often members of an audience actually help the performer recover from a flawed performance. *Tact* is helping someone "save face." After hearing a supposed expert make an embarrassingly inaccurate remark, for example, tactful people may ignore the comment, as if it had never been spoken, or react with mild laughter treating what was said as a joke. Or they may simply respond, "I'm sure you didn't mean that," an indication that someone heard the statement but will not allow it to destroy the actor's performance. With such efforts in mind, we can understand Abraham Lincoln's comment that "tact is the ability to describe others the way they see themselves."

Why is tact so common? Because embarrassment creates discomfort not just for the actor but for everyone else as well. Just as a theater audience feels uneasy when an actor forgets a line, people who observe awkward behavior are reminded of how fragile their own performances often are. Socially constructed reality thus functions like a dam holding back a sea of chaos. When one person's performance springs a leak, others tactfully help make repairs. Everyone lends a hand in building reality, and no one wants it suddenly swept away.

In sum, Goffman's research shows that although behavior is spontaneous in some respects, it is more patterned than we like to think. Four centuries ago, William Shakespeare captured this idea in lines that still ring true:

All the world's a stage,
And all the men and women merely players:
They have their exits and their entrances;
And one man in his time plays many parts.
                    (*As You Like It*, act 2, scene 7)

Interaction in Everyday Life: Three Applications

6.6 Construct a sociological analysis of three aspects of everyday life: emotions, language, and humor.

The final sections of this chapter illustrate the major elements of social interaction by focusing on three dimensions of everyday life: emotions, language, and humor.

Emotions: The Social Construction of Feeling

Emotions, more commonly called *feelings,* are an important element of human social life. In truth, what we *do* often matters less than how we *feel* about it. Emotions seem very personal because they are "inside." Even so, just as society guides our behavior, it guides our emotional life.

The Biological Side of Emotions

Studying people all over the world, Paul Ekman (1980a, 1980b, 1998, 2003) reports that people everywhere express six basic emotions: happiness, sadness, anger, fear, disgust, and surprise. In addition, Ekman found that people in every society use much the same facial

To most people in the United States, these expressions convey anger, fear, disgust, happiness, surprise, and sadness. But do people elsewhere in the world define them in the same way? Research suggests that all human beings experience the same basic emotions and display them to others in the same basic ways. But culture plays a part by specifying the situations that trigger one emotion or another.

expressions to show these emotions. Ekman believes that some emotional responses are "wired" into human beings; that is, they are biologically programmed in our facial features, muscles, and central nervous system.

Why might this be so? Over centuries of evolution, emotions developed in the human species because they serve a social purpose: supporting group life. Emotions are powerful forces that allow us to overcome our self-centeredness and build connections with others. Thus the capacity for emotion arose in our ancestors along with the capacity for culture (Turner, 2000).

The Cultural Side of Emotions

But culture does play an important role in guiding human emotions. First, Ekman explains, culture defines *what triggers* an emotion. Whether people define the departure of an old friend as joyous (causing happiness), insulting (arousing anger), a loss (producing sadness), or mystical (provoking surprise and awe) has a lot to do with culture. Second, culture provides rules for the *display* of emotions. For example, most people in the United States express emotions more freely with family members than with colleagues in the workplace. Similarly, we expect children to express emotions freely to parents, but parents tend to hide their emotions from their children. Third, culture guides how we *value* emotions. Some societies encourage the expression of emotion; others expect members to control their feelings and maintain a "stiff upper lip." Gender also plays a part; traditionally, at least, many cultures expect women to show emotions, but they discourage emotional expression by men as a sign of weakness. In some cultures, of course, this pattern is less pronounced or even reversed.

Emotions on the Job

In the United States, most people are freer to express their feelings at home than on the job. The reason, as sociologist Arlie Russell Hochschild (1979, 1983) explains, is that the typical company tries to regulate not only the behavior of its employees but also their emotions. Take the case of the busy airline flight attendant who offers each passenger a drink, a bag of pretzels, and a smile. Do you think that this smile may convey real pleasure at serving the customer? It may. But Hochschild's study points to a different conclusion: The smile is an emotional script demanded by the airline management as the right way

Many of us think that emotions are simply part of our biological makeup. While there is a biological foundation to human emotion, sociologists have learned that what triggers an emotion—as well as when, where, and to whom the emotion is displayed—is shaped by culture. Similarly, every society has situations or settings in which some people are forbidden to display any emotion at all. Look at each of these photos and explain why members of the palace guard, courtside assistants at professional tennis matches, and soldiers facing those of higher rank typically must "keep a straight face."

Controversy & Debate

Managing Feelings: Women's Abortion Experiences

Liz: I just *can't* be pregnant! I'm going to see my doctor tomorrow about an abortion. There's no way I can deal with a baby at this point in my life!

Jen: I can't believe you'd do that, Liz! How are you going to feel a few years from now when you think about what that *child* would be doing if you'd let it live?

Few issues today generate as much emotion as abortion. In a study of women's abortion experiences, the sociologist Jennifer Keys (2002) discovered emotional scripts or "feeling rules" that guided how women feel about ending a pregnancy.

Keys explains that emotional scripts arise from the political controversy surrounding abortion. The antiabortion movement defines abortion as a personal tragedy, the "killing of an unborn child." Given this definition, women who terminate a pregnancy through abortion are doing something morally wrong and can expect to feel grief, guilt, and regret. So intense are these feelings, according to supporters of this position, that such women often suffer from "postabortion syndrome."

Those who take the pro-choice position have an opposing view of abortion. From this point of view, the woman's problem is the *unwanted pregnancy*; abortion is an acceptable medical solution. Therefore, the emotion common to women who terminate a pregnancy should be not guilt but relief.

In her research, Keys conducted in-depth interviews with forty women who had recently had abortions and found that all of them used such scripts to "frame" their situation in an antiabortion or pro-choice manner. In part, this construction of reality reflected the women's own attitudes about abortion. In addition, however, the women's partners and friends typically encouraged specific feelings about the event. Ivy, one young woman in the study, had a close friend who was also pregnant. "Congratulations!" she exclaimed when she learned of Ivy's condition. "We're going to be having babies together!" Such a statement established one "feeling rule"—having a baby is *good*—which sent the message to Ivy that her planned abortion should trigger guilt. Working in the other direction, Jo's partner was horrified by the news that she was pregnant. Doubting his own ability to be a father, he blurted out, "I would rather put a gun to my head than have this baby!" His panic not only defined having the child as a mistake but alarmed Jo as well. Clearly, her partner's reaction made the decision to end the pregnancy a matter of relief from a terrible problem.

Medical personnel also play a part in this process of reality construction by using specific terms. Nurses and doctors who talk about "the baby" encourage the antiabortion framing of abortion and provoke grief and guilt. On the other hand, those who use language such as "pregnancy tissue," "fetus," or "the contents of the uterus" encourage the pro-choice framing of abortion as a fairly routine medical procedure leading to relief. Olivia began using the phrase "products of conception," which she picked up from her doctor. Denise spoke of her procedure as "taking the extra cells out of my body. Yeah, I did feel some guilt when I thought that this was the beginning of life, but my body is full of life—you have lots of cells in you."

After undergoing the procedure, most women reported actively trying to manage their feelings. Explained Ivy, "I never used the word 'baby.' I kept saying to myself that it was not formed yet. There was nothing there yet. I kept that in my mind." On the other hand, Keys found that all of the women in her study who leaned toward the antiabortion position did use the term "baby." Gina explained, "I do think of it as a baby. The truth is that I ended my baby's life.... Thinking that makes me feel guilty. But—considering what I did—maybe I *should* feel guilty." Believing that what she had done was wrong, in other words, Gina actively called out the feeling of guilt—in part, Keys concluded, to punish herself.

The words that doctors and nurses use guide whether a woman having an abortion defines the experience in positive or negative terms.

What Do You Think?

1. In your own words, what are "emotional scripts" or "feeling rules"?

2. Can you apply the idea of "feeling rules" to the experience of getting married?

3. In light of this discussion, how accurate is it to say that our feelings are not quite as personal as we may think they are?

to perform the job. Therefore, from Hochschild's research we see an added dimension of the "presentation of self" described by Erving Goffman. Not only do our everyday life presentations to others involve surface acting but they also involve the "deep acting" of emotions.

With these patterns in mind, it is easy to see that we socially construct our emotions as part of our everyday reality, a process sociologists call *emotion management*. The Controversy & Debate box on page 169 links the emotions displayed by women who decide to have an abortion to their political views and to their personal view of terminating a pregnancy.

Language: The Social Construction of Gender

As Chapter 3 ("Culture") explains, language is the thread that weaves members of a society into the symbolic web we call culture. Language communicates not only a surface reality but also deeper levels of meaning. One such level involves gender. Language defines men and women differently in terms of both power and value (Henley, Hamilton, & Thorne, 1992; Thorne, Kramarae, & Henley, 1983).

Language and Power

A young man proudly rides his new motorcycle up his friend's driveway and boasts, "Isn't she a beauty?" On the surface, the question has little to do with gender. Yet why does he use the pronoun *she* instead of *he* or *it* to refer to his prized possession?

The answer is that men often use language to establish control over their surroundings. A man attaches a female pronoun to a motorcycle (or car, boat, or other object) because it reflects the power of *ownership*. Perhaps this is also why, in the United States and elsewhere, a woman who marries traditionally takes the last name of her husband. Because many of today's married women value their independence, some (at least 10 percent) now keep their own name or combine the two family names (Gooding & Kreider, 2010).

Language and Value

Typically, the English language treats as masculine whatever has greater value, force, or significance. For instance, the word *virtuous,* meaning "morally worthy" or "excellent," comes from the Latin word *vir,* meaning "man." On the other hand, the adjective *hysterical,* meaning "emotionally out of control," comes from the Greek word *hystera,* meaning "uterus."

In many familiar ways, language also confers different value on the two sexes. Traditional masculine terms such as *king* and *lord* have a positive meaning, while comparable feminine terms, such as *queen, madam,* and *dame,* can have negative meanings. Similarly, use of the suffixes *-ette* and *-ess* to denote femininity usually devalues the words to which they are added. For example, a *major* has higher standing than a *majorette,* as does a *host* in relation to a *hostess* or a *master* in relation to a *mistress.* Language both mirrors social attitudes and helps perpetuate them.

Given the importance of gender in everyday life, perhaps we should not be surprised that women and men sometimes have trouble communicating with each other. In fact, some people comment,

For a closer look at how women and men use language differently, **Read More** in **MySocLab**, *Gender and Language: "You Just Don't Understand!"*

Most of us have had the unpleasant experience of being "chewed out" at work for doing something that displeased the boss. Do you think women and men in positions of power can show anger with the same response from an audience? In other words, do we tolerate more of this type of emotional expression from managers of one sex than the other?

with more than a little seriousness, that the two sexes often seem to be speaking different languages.

Reality Play: The Social Construction of Humor

Humor plays an important part in everyday life. Everyone laughs at a joke, but few people stop to think about what makes something funny. We can apply many of the ideas developed in this chapter to explain how, by using humor, we "play with reality" (Macionis, 1987).

The Foundation of Humor

Humor is produced by the social construction of reality; it arises as people create and contrast two different realities. Generally, one reality is *conventional*, that is, what culture leads people to expect in a specific situation. The other reality is *unconventional*, an unexpected violation of cultural patterns. Humor arises from the contradictions, ambiguities, and double meanings found in differing definitions of the same situation.

There are countless ways to mix realities and generate humor. Reality play can be found in single statements that contradict themselves, such as "Nostalgia is not what it used to be"; statements that repeat themselves, such as Yogi Berra's line "It's *déjà vu* all over again"; or statements that mix up words, such as Oscar Wilde's line "Work is the curse of the drinking class." Even switching around syllables does the trick, as in the case of the country song "I'd Rather Have a Bottle in Front of Me than a Frontal Lobotomy."

You can also build a joke the other way around, leading the audience to expect an unconventional answer and then delivering a very ordinary one. When a reporter asked the famous gangster Willy Sutton why he continued to rob banks, for example, he replied dryly, "Because that's where the money is." Regardless of how a joke is constructed, the greater the opposition or difference that is created between the two definitions of reality, the greater is the humor that results.

When telling jokes, the comedian uses various strategies to strengthen this opposition and make the joke funnier. One common technique is to present the first, or conventional, remark in conversation with another actor and then to turn toward the audience (or the camera) to deliver the second, unexpected line. In a Marx Brothers movie, Groucho remarks, "Outside of a dog, a book is a man's best friend." Then, raising his voice and turning to the camera, he adds, "And *inside* of a dog, it's too dark to read!" Such "changing channels" emphasizes the difference between the two realities. Following the same logic, stand-up comedians may "reset" the audience to conventional expectations by interjecting the phrase, "But seriously, folks, …" between jokes. Monty Python comedian John Cleese did this with his trademark line, "And now for something completely different."

Comedians pay careful attention to their performances—the precise words they use and the timing of their delivery. A joke is well told if the comedian creates the sharpest possible opposition between the realities; in a careless performance, the joke falls flat. Because the key to humor lies in the collision of realities, we can see why the climax of a joke is termed the "*punch* line."

The Dynamics of Humor: "Getting It"

After hearing a joke, did you ever say, "I don't get it"? To "get" humor, members of the audience must understand both the conventional and the unconventional realities well enough to appreciate their difference. A comedian may make getting a joke harder by leaving out some important information. In such cases, listeners must pay attention to the stated elements of the joke and then fill in the missing pieces on their own. A simple example is the comment of the movie producer Hal Roach on his one hundredth birthday: "If I had known I would live to be one hundred, I would have taken better care of myself!" Here, getting the joke depends on realizing that Roach must have taken pretty good care of himself because he did make it to one hundred. Or as my own father, who lived to the age of ninety-five, used to say, "At my age, I don't even buy green bananas anymore!" "Sure, who knows how long he's going to live!", we would think to ourselves to "finish" the joke.

Here is an even more complex joke: What do you get if you cross an insomniac, an agnostic, and a dyslexic? Answer: A person who stays up all night wondering if there is a dog. To get this one, you need a good bit of information: you must know that insomnia is an inability to sleep, that an agnostic doubts the existence of God, and dyslexia causes a person to reverse the letters in words.

Why would a comedian want the audience to make this sort of effort to understand a joke? Our enjoyment of a joke is increased by the pleasure of figuring out for ourselves all the pieces needed to "get it." In addition, getting the joke makes you an "insider" compared to those who don't get it. We have all experienced the frustration of *not* getting a joke: fear of being judged stupid, along with a sense of being excluded from a pleasure shared by others. Sometimes someone may tactfully explain the joke so that the other person doesn't feel left out. But as the old saying goes, if a joke has to be explained, it isn't very funny.

The Topics of Humor

All over the world, people smile and laugh, making humor a universal element of human culture. But because the world's people live in different cultures, humor rarely travels well.

October 1, Kobe, Japan. Is it possible share a joke with people who live halfway around the world? At dinner, I ask two Japanese college women to tell me a joke. "You know 'crayon'?" Asako asks. I nod. "How do you ask for a crayon in Japanese?" I respond that I have no idea. She laughs out loud as she says what sounds like "crayon crayon." Her companion Mayumi laughs too. My wife and I sit awkwardly, with a quizzical look on our faces. Asako relieves some of our embarrassment by explaining that the Japanese word for "give me" is *kureyo*, which sounds like "crayon." I force a smile.

What is humorous to the Japanese may be lost on the Chinese, South Africans, or people in the United States. Even the social diversity of our own country means that different types of people will find humor in different situations. New Englanders, southerners, and westerners have their own brands of humor, as do Latinos and Anglos, fifteen- and fifty-year-olds, construction workers and rodeo riders.

But for everyone, topics that lend themselves to double meanings or controversy generate humor. In the United States, the first jokes many of us learned as children concerned bodily functions kids are not supposed to talk about. The mere mention of "unmentionable acts" or even certain parts of the body can dissolve young faces in laughter.

Are there jokes that do break through the culture barrier? Yes, but they must touch on universal human experiences such as, say, turning on a friend:

I think of a number of jokes, but none seems likely to work. Understanding jokes about the United States is difficult for people who know little of our culture. Is there something more universal? Inspiration: "Two fellows are walking in the woods and come upon a huge bear. One guy leans over and tightens up the laces on his running shoes. 'Jake,' says the other, 'what are you doing? You can't outrun this bear!' 'I don't have to outrun the bear,' responds Jake. 'All I have to do is outrun you!'" Smiles all around.

Because humor involves challenging established conventions, most U.S. comedians—including Aziz Ansari—have been social "outsiders," members of racial or ethnic minorities.

Humor often walks a fine line between what is funny and what is "sick" or offensive. During the Middle Ages, people used the word *humors* (derived from the Latin *humidus*, meaning "moist") to refer to the various bodily fluids believed to regulate a person's health. Researchers today document the power of humor to reduce stress and improve health. One recent study of cancer patients, for example, found that the greater people's sense of humor, the greater their odds of surviving the disease. Such findings confirm the old saying that "laughter is the best medicine" (Bakalar, 2005; Svebak, cited in M. Elias, 2007). At the extreme, however, people who always take conventional reality lightly risk being defined as deviant or even mentally ill (a common stereotype shows insane people laughing uncontrollably, and for a long time mental hospitals were known as "funny farms").

Then, too, every social group considers certain topics too sensitive for humorous treatment, and joking about them risks criticism for having a "sick" sense of humor (and being labeled "sick" yourself). People's religious beliefs, tragic accidents, or appalling crimes are some of the topics of sick jokes or no jokes at all. Even years later, there have been no jokes about the victims of the September 11, 2001, terrorist attacks.

The Functions of Humor

Humor is found everywhere because it works as a safety valve for potentially disruptive sentiments. Put another way, humor provides an acceptable way to discuss a sensitive topic without appearing to be serious or offending anyone. Having said something controversial, people can use humor to defuse the situation by simply stating, "I didn't mean anything by what I said—it was just a joke!"

People also use humor to relieve tension in uncomfortable situations. One study of medical examinations found that most patients try to joke with doctors to ease their own nervousness (Baker et al., 1997).

Humor and Conflict

Humor may be a source of pleasure, but it can also be used to put down other people. Men who tell jokes about women, for example, are typically expressing some measure of hostility toward them (Powell & Paton, 1988; Benokraitis & Feagin, 1995). Similarly, jokes about gay people reveal tensions about sexual orientation. Real conflict can be masked by humor in situations where one or both parties choose not to bring the conflict out into the open (Primeggia & Varacalli, 1990).

"Put-down" jokes make one category of people feel good at the expense of another. After collecting and analyzing jokes from many societies, Christie Davies (1990) confirmed that ethnic conflict is one driving force behind humor in most of the world. The typical ethnic joke makes fun of some disadvantaged category of people, at the same time making the joke teller feel superior. Given the Anglo-Saxon traditions of U.S. society, Poles and other ethnic and racial minorities have long been the butt of jokes in the United States, as have Newfoundlanders in eastern Canada, the Irish in Scotland, Sikhs in India, Turks in Germany, Hausas in Nigeria, Tasmanians in Australia, and Kurds in Iraq.

Disadvantaged people also make fun of the powerful, although usually with some concern about who might be listening. Women in the United States joke about men, just as African Americans find humor in white people's ways and poor people poke fun at the rich. Throughout the world, people target their leaders with humor, and officials in some countries take such jokes seriously enough to arrest those who do not show proper respect (Speier, 1998).

In sum, humor is much more important than we may think. It is a means of mental escape from a conventional world that is never entirely to our liking (Flaherty, 1984, 1990; Yoels & Clair, 1995). This fact helps explain why so many of our nation's comedians are from the ranks of historically marginalized peoples, including Jews and African Americans. As long as we maintain a sense of humor, we assert our freedom and are not prisoners of reality. By putting a smile on our faces, we can change ourselves and the world just a little and for the better.

Seeing Sociology in Everyday Life

How do we construct the reality we experience?

This chapter suggests that Shakespeare may have had it right when he said, "All the world's a stage." And if so, then the Internet may be the latest and greatest stage so far. When we use social media websites, as Goffman explains, we present ourselves as we want others to see us. Everything we write about ourselves as well as how we arrange our page creates an impression in the mind of anyone interested in "checking us out." Take a look at the website page below, paying careful attention to all the details. What is the young man explicitly saying about himself? What can you read "between the lines"? That is, what information can you identify that he may be trying to conceal, or at least purposely not be mentioning? How honest do you think his "presentation of self" is? Why? Do a similar analysis of the young woman's profile shown on the next page.

HINT Just about every element of a presentation conveys information about us to others, so all the information found on a website like this one is significant. Some information is intentional—for example, what people write about themselves and the photos they choose to post. Other information may be unintentional but is nevertheless picked up by the careful viewer who may be noting such things as these:

- The length and tone of the person's profile. Is it a long-winded list of talents and accomplishments or humorous and modest?
- The language used. Poor grammar may be a clue to educational level.
- What hour of the day or night the person wrote the material. A person creating his profile at 11 P.M. on a Saturday night may not be quite the party person he describes himself to be.

Seeing Sociology in *Your* Everyday Life

1. Identify five important ways in which you "present yourself" to others including, for example, the way you decorate your dorm room, apartment, or house; the way you dress; and the way you behave in the classroom. In each case, think about what you are trying to say about yourself. Do you present a different self to various others, such as friends, professors, and parents? If so, how do you account for the differences?

2. Go to MySocLab and click on the Student Resources link to access the Sociology in Focus blog, where you can read the latest posts by a team of young sociologists who apply the sociological perspective to topics of popular culture.

3. This chapter has explained that we all engage in a process called the social construction of reality. What that means is that each of us plays a part in shaping the reality we experience. Let's apply this idea to the issue of personal freedom. To what extent does the material presented in this chapter support a claim that humans are free to shape their own lives? Go to the "Seeing Sociology in *Your* Everyday Life" feature in MySocLab to learn more about the social construction of reality as well as suggestions for ways you can help construct a more positive social world.

Making the Grade

Social Structure: A Guide to Everyday Living

6.1 Explain how social structure helps us to make sense of everyday situations. (pages 154–55)

👁 **Watch** the **Video** in **MySocLab**

Social structure refers to social patterns that guide our behavior in everyday life. The building blocks of social structure are status and role.

social interaction the process by which people act and react in relation to others

Status

6.2 State the importance of status to social organization. (pages 155–57)

Status is a social position that is part of our social identity and that defines our relationships to others.

A status can be either an

- **ascribed status**, which is involuntary (for example, being a teenager, an orphan, or a Mexican American), or an
- **achieved status**, which is earned (for example, being an honors student, a pilot, or a thief).

A **master status**, which can be either ascribed or achieved, has special importance for a person's identity (for example, being blind, a doctor, or a Kennedy).

status a social position that a person holds
status set all the statuses a person holds at a given time
ascribed status a social position a person receives at birth or takes on involuntarily later in life
achieved status a social position a person takes on voluntarily that reflects personal ability and effort
master status a status that has special importance for social identity, often shaping a person's entire life

Role

6.3 State the importance of role to social organization. (pages 157–59)

Role is behavior expected of someone who holds a particular status.

Role conflict results from tension among roles linked to two or more statuses (for example, a woman who juggles her responsibilities as a mother and a corporate CEO).

Role strain results from tension among roles linked to a single status (for example, the college professor who enjoys personal interaction with students but at the same time knows that social distance is necessary in order to evaluate students fairly).

role behavior expected of someone who holds a particular status
role set a number of roles attached to a single status
role conflict conflict among the roles connected to two or more statuses
role strain tension among the roles connected to a single status

The Social Construction of Reality

6.4 Describe how we socially construct reality. (pages 159–62)

✳ **Explore** the **Map** in **MySocLab**   👁 **Watch** the **Video** in **MySocLab**

Through **social interaction**, we construct the reality we experience.
- For example, two people interacting both try to shape the reality of their situation.

The **Thomas theorem** says that the reality people construct in their interaction has real consequences for the future.
- For example, a teacher who believes a certain student to be intellectually gifted may well encourage exceptional academic performance.

social construction of reality the process by which people creatively shape reality through social interaction
Thomas theorem W. I. Thomas's claim that situations defined as real are real in their consequences

Ethnomethodology is a strategy to reveal the assumptions people have about their social world.

- We can expose these assumptions by intentionally breaking the "rules" of social interaction and observing the reactions of other people.

Both **culture** and **social class** shape the reality people construct.

- For example, a "short walk" for a New Yorker is a few city blocks, but for a peasant in Latin America, it could be a few miles.

The expansion of **social media** has dramatically changed how people interact.

- The social construction of reality no longer requires people to have face-to-face interaction.

> **ethnomethodology** Harold Garfinkel's term for the study of the way people make sense of their everyday surroundings
>
> **social media** technology that links people in social activity

Dramaturgical Analysis: The "Presentation of Self"

6.5 Apply Goffman's analysis to several familiar situations. (pages 162–67)

 **Read** the **Document** in **MySocLab**   **Watch** the **Video** in **MySocLab**

Dramaturgical analysis explores social interaction in terms of theatrical performance: A status operates as a part in a play, and a role is a script.

Performances are the way we present ourselves to others.

- Performances are both conscious (intentional action) and unconscious (nonverbal communication).
- Performances include costume (the way we dress), props (objects we carry), and demeanor (tone of voice and the way we carry ourselves).

Gender affects performances because men typically have greater social power than women. Gender differences involve *demeanor*, *use of space*, and *smiling*, *staring*, and *touching*.

- **Demeanor**—With greater social power, men have more freedom in how they act.
- **Use of space**—Men typically command more space than women.
- **Staring** and **touching** are generally done by men to women.
- **Smiling**, as a way to please another, is more commonly done by women.

Idealization of performances means we try to convince others that our actions reflect ideal culture rather than selfish motives.

Embarrassment is the "loss of face" in a performance. People use **tact** to help others "save face."

> **dramaturgical analysis** Erving Goffman's term for the study of social interaction in terms of theatrical performance
>
> **presentation of self** Erving Goffman's term for a person's efforts to create specific impressions in the minds of others
>
> **nonverbal communication** communication using body movements, gestures, and facial expressions rather than speech
>
> **personal space** the surrounding area over which a person makes some claim to privacy

Interaction in Everyday Life: Three Applications

6.6 Construct a sociological analysis of three aspects of everyday life: emotions, language, and humor. (pages 167–73)

Emotions: The Social Construction of **Feeling**

The same basic emotions are biologically programmed into all human beings, but culture guides what triggers emotions, how people display emotions, and how people value emotions. In everyday life, the presentation of self involves managing emotions as well as behavior.

Language: The Social Construction of **Gender**

Gender is an important element of everyday interaction. Language defines women and men as different types of people, reflecting the fact that society attaches greater power and value to what is viewed as masculine.

Reality Play: The Social Construction of **Humor**

Humor results from the difference between conventional and unconventional definitions of a situation. Because humor is a part of culture, people around the world find different situations funny.

7 Groups and Organizations

((Listen to **Chapter 7** in **MySocLab**

LEARNING OBJECTIVES

7.1 Explain the importance of various types of groups to social life.

7.2 Describe the operation of large, formal organizations.

7.3 Summarize the changes to formal organizations over the course of the last century.

7.4 Assess the consequences of modern social organization for social life.

the Power of Society

to link people into groups

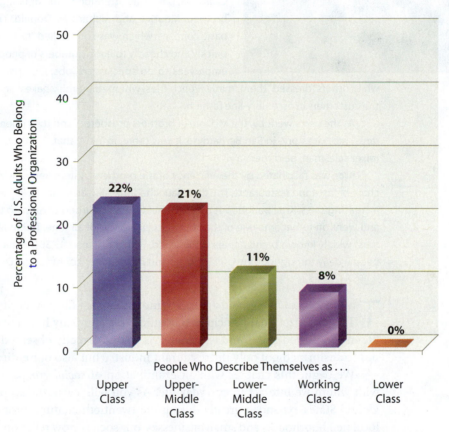

Percentage of U.S. Adults Who Belong to a Professional Organization

22% — Upper Class
21% — Upper-Middle Class
11% — Lower-Middle Class
8% — Working Class
0% — Lower Class

People Who Describe Themselves as . . .

Source: Inglehart et al. (2012)

Does your social class influence which groups and organizations you join? Professional organizations attract people who work as physicians, nurses, lawyers, and college teachers. Look at how social class affects membership in such organizations—people who identified themselves as being "upper class" or "upper-middle class" were three times more likely to be members of professional organizations than people who said they were "working class." And no one who claimed to be "lower class" reported being in such an organization. Membership in groups and organizations is not simply a matter of choice; it is also a reflection of the way society is organized.

Chapter Overview

We spend much of our lives within the collectivities that sociologists call social groups and formal organizations. This chapter begins by analyzing social groups, both small and large, highlighting the differences between them. Then the focus shifts to formal organizations that carry out various tasks in our modern society.

With the workday over, Juan and Jorge pushed through the doors of the local McDonald's restaurant. "Man, am I hungry," announced Juan, heading right into line. "Look at all the meat I'm gonna eat." But Jorge, a recent immigrant from a small village in Guatemala, is surveying the room with a sociological eye. "There is much more than food to see here. This place is all about America!"

And so it is, as we shall see. Back in 1948, people in Pasadena, California, paid little attention to the opening of a new restaurant by brothers Maurice and Richard McDonald. The McDonald brothers' basic concept, which was soon called "fast food," was to serve meals quickly and cheaply to large numbers of people. The brothers trained employees to do specialized jobs: One person grilled hamburgers while others "dressed" them, made French fries, whipped up milkshakes, and presented the food to the customers in assembly-line fashion.

As the years went by, the McDonald brothers prospered, and they opened several more restaurants, including one in San Bernardino. It was there, in 1954, that Ray Kroc, a traveling blender and mixer salesman, paid them a visit.

Kroc was fascinated by the efficiency of the brothers' system and saw the potential for a whole chain of fast-food restaurants. The three launched the plan as partners. In 1961, in the face of rapidly increasing sales, Kroc bought out the McDonalds (who returned to running their original restaurant) and went on to become one of the great success stories of all time. Today, McDonald's is one of the most widely known brand names in the world, with more than 33,500 restaurants serving 69 million people daily throughout the United States and in 118 other countries (McDonald's, 2012).

The success of McDonald's points to more than just the popularity of burgers and fries. The organizational principles that guide this company have come to dominate social life in the United States and elsewhere. As Jorge correctly observed, this one small business transformed not only the restaurant industry but also our entire way of life.

We begin this chapter with an examination of *social groups,* the clusters of people with whom we interact in everyday life. As you will learn, the scope of group life in the United States expanded greatly during the twentieth century. From a world of families, local neighborhoods, and small businesses, our society now relies on the operation of huge corporations and other bureaucracies that sociologists describe as *formal organizations.* Understanding this expanding scale of social life and appreciating what it means for us as individuals are the main objectives of this chapter.

Social Groups

7.1 Explain the importance of various types of groups to social life.

Almost everyone wants a sense of belonging, which is the essence of group life. A **social group** is *two or more people who identify with and interact with one another.* Human beings come together in couples, families, circles of friends, churches, clubs, businesses, neighborhoods, and large organizations. Whatever the form, a group is made up of people with shared experiences, loyalties, and interests. In short, while keeping their individuality, members of social groups also think of themselves as a special "we."

Not every collection of individuals forms a group. People all over the country with a status in common, such as women, homeowners, soldiers, millionaires, college graduates, and Roman Catholics, are not a group but a *category*. Though they know that others hold the same status, most are strangers to one another. Similarly, students sitting in a large stadium interact to a very limited extent. Such a loosely formed collection of people in one place is a *crowd* rather than a group.

However, the right circumstances can quickly turn a crowd into a group. Unexpected events, from power failures to terrorist attacks, can make people bond quickly with strangers.

social group two or more people who identify with and interact with one another

primary group a small social group whose members share personal and lasting relationships

secondary group a large and impersonal social group whose members pursue a specific goal or activity

Primary and Secondary Groups

Friends often greet one another with a smile and the simple phrase "Hi! How are you?" The response is usually "Fine, thanks. How about you?" This answer is often more scripted than sincere. Explaining how you are *really* doing might make people feel so awkward that they would beat a hasty retreat.

Social groups are of two types, depending on their members' degree of personal concern for one another. According to Charles Horton Cooley (1864–1929), a **primary group** is *a small social group whose members share personal and lasting relationships*. Joined by *primary relationships,* people spend a great deal of time together, engage in a wide range of activities, and feel that they know one another pretty well. In short, they show real concern for one another. The family is every society's most important primary group.

Cooley called personal and tightly integrated groups "primary" because they are among the first groups we experience in life. In addition, family and friends have primary importance in the socialization process, shaping our attitudes, behavior, and social identity.

Members of primary groups help one another in many ways, but they generally think of the group as an end in itself rather than as a means to some goal. In other words, we prefer to think that family and friendship link people who "belong together." Members of a primary group also tend to view each other as unique and irreplaceable. Especially in the family, we are bound to others by emotion and loyalty. Brothers and sisters may not always get along, but they always remain "family."

In contrast to the primary group, the **secondary group** is *a large and impersonal social group whose members pursue a specific goal or activity*. In most respects, secondary groups have characteristics opposite to those of primary groups. *Secondary relationships* involve weak emotional ties and little personal knowledge of one another. Many secondary groups exist for only a short time, beginning and ending without particular significance. Students enrolled in the same course at a large university—who may or may not see one another again after the semester ends—are one example of a secondary group.

Secondary groups include many more people than primary groups. For example, dozens or even hundreds of people may work together in the same company, yet most of them pay only passing attention to one another. In some cases, time may transform a group from secondary to primary, as with co-workers who share an office for many years and develop closer relationships. But generally, members of a secondary group do not think of themselves as "we." Secondary ties need not be hostile or cold, of course.

Watch in **MySocLab**
Video: *The Basics: Societies, Groups, and Organizations*

As human beings, we live our lives as members of groups. Such groups may be large or small, temporary or long-lasting, and can be based on kinship, cultural heritage, or some shared interest.

Interactions among students, co-workers, and business associates are often quite pleasant even if they are impersonal.

Unlike members of primary groups, who display a *personal orientation*, people in secondary groups have a *goal orientation*. Primary group members define each other according to *who* they are in terms of family ties or personal qualities, but people in secondary groups look to one another for *what* they are, that is, what they can do for each other. In secondary groups, we tend to "keep score," aware of what we give others and what we receive in return. This goal orientation means that secondary group members usually remain formal and polite. In a secondary relationship, therefore, we ask the question "How are you?" without expecting a truthful answer.

The Summing Up table reviews the characteristics of primary and secondary groups. Keep in mind that these traits define two types of groups in ideal terms; most real groups contain elements of both. For example, a women's group on a university campus may be quite large (and therefore secondary), but its members may identify strongly with one another and provide lots of mutual support (making it seem primary).

Many people think that small towns and rural areas have mostly primary relationships and that large cities are characterized by more secondary ties. This generalization is partly true, but some urban neighborhoods—especially those populated by people of a single ethnic or religious category—are very tightly knit.

Group Leadership

How do groups operate? One important element of group dynamics is leadership. Though a small circle of friends may have no leader at all, most large secondary groups place leaders in a formal chain of command.

Two Leadership Roles

instrumental leadership group leadership that focuses on the completion of tasks

expressive leadership group leadership that focuses on the group's well-being

Groups typically benefit from two kinds of leadership. **Instrumental leadership** refers to *group leadership that focuses on the completion of tasks*. Members look to instrumental leaders to make plans, give orders, and get things done. **Expressive leadership**, by contrast, is *group leadership that focuses on the group's well-being*. Expressive leaders take less interest in achieving goals than in raising group morale and minimizing tension and conflict among members.

Because they concentrate on performance, instrumental leaders usually have formal secondary relationships with other members. These leaders give orders and reward or punish members according to how much the members contribute to the group's efforts. Expressive leaders build more personal primary ties. They offer sympathy to a member going through tough times, keep the group united, and lighten serious moments with humor. Typically, successful instrumental leaders enjoy more *respect* from members, and expressive leaders generally receive more personal *affection*.

Three Leadership Styles

Sociologists also describe leadership in terms of decision-making style. *Authoritarian leadership* focuses on instrumental concerns, takes personal charge of decision making,

Summing Up

Primary Groups and Secondary Groups		
	Primary Group	**Secondary Group**
Quality of relationships	Personal orientation	Goal orientation
Duration of relationships	Usually long-term	Variable; often short-term
Breadth of relationships	Broad; usually involving many activities	Narrow; usually involving few activities
Perception of relationships	Ends in themselves	Means to an end
Examples	Families, circles of friends	Co-workers, political organizations

and demands that group members obey orders. Although this leadership style may win little affection from the group, a fast-acting authoritarian leader is appreciated in a crisis.

Democratic leadership is more expressive and makes a point of including everyone in the decision-making process. Although less successful in a crisis situation, democratic leaders generally draw on the ideas of all members to develop creative solutions to problems.

Laissez-faire leadership allows the group to function more or less on its own (*laissez-faire* in French means "leave it alone"). This style is typically the least effective in promoting group goals (White & Lippitt, 1953; Ridgeway, 1983).

Group Conformity

Groups influence the behavior of their members by promoting conformity. "Fitting in" provides a secure feeling of belonging, but at the extreme, group pressure can be unpleasant and even dangerous. As experiments by Solomon Asch and Stanley Milgram showed, even strangers can encourage conformity.

Asch's Research

Solomon Asch (1952) recruited students for what he told them was a study of visual perception. Before the experiment began, he explained to all but one member in a small group that their real purpose was to put pressure on the remaining person. Arranging six to eight students around a table, Asch showed them a "standard" line, as drawn on Card 1 in Figure 7–1, and asked them to match it to one of three lines on Card 2.

Anyone with normal vision could easily see that the line marked "A" on Card 2 is the correct choice. At the beginning of the experiment, everyone made the matches correctly. But then Asch's secret accomplices began answering incorrectly, leaving the uninformed student (seated at the table so as to answer next to last) bewildered and uncomfortable.

What happened? Asch found that one-third of all subjects chose to conform by answering incorrectly. Apparently, many of us are willing to compromise our own judgment to avoid the discomfort of being seen as different, even by people we do not know.

Milgram's Research

Stanley Milgram, a former student of Solomon Asch's, conducted conformity experiments of his own. In Milgram's controversial study (1963, 1965; Miller, 1986), a researcher explained to male recruits that they would be taking part in a study of how punishment affects learning. One by one, he assigned the subjects to the role of teacher and placed another person—actually an accomplice of Milgram's—in a connecting room to pose as a learner.

The teacher watched as the learner was seated in what looked like an electric chair. The researcher applied electrode paste to one of the learner's wrists, explaining that this would "prevent blisters and burns." The researcher then attached an electrode to the wrist and secured the leather straps, explaining that these would "prevent excessive movement while the learner was being shocked." The researcher assured the teacher that although the shocks would be painful, they would cause "no permanent tissue damage."

The researcher then led the teacher back to the next room, explaining that the "electric chair" was connected to a "shock generator," actually a phony but realistic-looking piece of equipment with a label that read "Shock Generator, Type ZLB, Dyson Instrument Company, Waltham, Mass." On the front was a dial that appeared to regulate electric shock from 15 volts (labeled "Slight Shock") to 300 volts (marked "Intense Shock") to 450 volts (marked "Danger: Severe Shock").

Seated in front of the "shock generator," the teacher was told to read aloud pairs of words. Then the teacher was to repeat the first word of each pair and wait for the learner to recall the second word. Whenever the learner failed to answer correctly, the teacher was told to apply an electric shock.

The researcher directed the teacher to begin at the lowest level (15 volts) and to increase the shock by another 15 volts every time the learner made a mistake. And so the teacher did. At 75, 90, and 105 volts, the

Card 1 Card 2

FIGURE 7–1 Cards Used in Asch's Experiment in Group Conformity

In Asch's experiment, subjects were asked to match the line on Card 1 to one of the lines on Card 2. Many subjects agreed with the wrong answers given by others in their group.

Source: Asch (1952).

teacher heard moans from the learner; at 120 volts, shouts of pain; at 270 volts, screams; at 315 volts, pounding on the wall; after that, dead silence. None of forty subjects assigned to the role of teacher during the initial research even questioned the procedure before reaching 300 volts, and twenty-six of the subjects—almost two-thirds—went all the way to 450 volts. Even Milgram was surprised at how readily people obeyed authority figures.

Milgram (1964) then modified his research to see if groups of ordinary people—not authority figures—could pressure people to administer electrical shocks, as Asch's groups had pressured individuals to match lines incorrectly.

This time, Milgram formed a group of three teachers, two of whom were his accomplices. Each of the three teachers was to suggest a shock level when the learner made an error; the rule was that the group would then administer the *lowest* of the three suggested levels. This arrangement gave the person not "in" on the experiment the power to deliver a lesser shock regardless of what the others said.

The accomplices suggested increasing the shock level with each error, putting pressure on the third member to do the same. The subjects in these groups applied voltages three to four times higher than the levels applied by subjects acting alone. In this way, Milgram showed that people are likely to follow the lead of not only legitimate authority figures but also groups of ordinary individuals, even when it means harming another person.

Janis's "Groupthink"

Experts also cave in to group pressure, says Irving L. Janis (1972, 1989). Janis argues that a number of U.S. foreign policy errors, including the failure to foresee Japan's attack on Pearl Harbor during World War II and our ill-fated involvement in the Vietnam War, resulted from group conformity among our highest-ranking political leaders.

Common sense tells us that group discussion improves decision making. Janis counters that group members often seek agreement that closes off other points of view. Janis called this process **groupthink**, *the tendency of group members to conform, resulting in a narrow view of some issue.*

A classic example of groupthink led to the failed invasion of Cuba at the Bay of Pigs in 1961. Looking back, Arthur Schlesinger Jr., an adviser to President John F. Kennedy, confessed to feeling guilty for "having kept so quiet during those crucial discussions in the Cabinet Room," adding that the group discouraged anyone from challenging what, in hindsight, Schlesinger considered "nonsense" (quoted in Janis, 1972:30, 40). Groupthink may also have been a factor in the U.S. invasion of Iraq in 2003 when U.S. leaders were led to believe—erroneously—that Iraq had stockpiles of weapons of mass destruction. Closer to home, one professor suggests that college faculties are subject to groupthink because they share political attitudes that are overwhelmingly liberal (Klein, 2010).

groupthink the tendency of group members to conform, resulting in a narrow view of some issue

Reference Groups

How do we assess our own attitudes and behavior? Frequently, we use a **reference group**, *a social group that serves as a point of reference in making evaluations and decisions.*

A young man who imagines his family's response to a woman he is dating is using his family as a reference group. A supervisor who tries to predict her employees' reaction to a new vacation policy is using them in the same way. As these examples suggest, reference groups can be primary or secondary. In either case, our need to conform shows how others' attitudes affect us.

We also use groups that we do *not* belong to for reference. Being well prepared for a job interview means showing up dressed the way people in that company dress for work. Conforming to groups we do not belong to is a strategy to win acceptance by others and illustrates the process of *anticipatory socialization*, described in Chapter 5 ("Socialization").

reference group a social group that serves as a point of reference in making evaluations and decisions

Stouffer's Research

Samuel Stouffer and his colleagues (1949) conducted a classic study of reference group dynamics during World War II. Researchers asked soldiers to rate their own or any competent soldier's chances of promotion in their army unit. You might guess that soldiers serving in outfits with a high promotion rate would be optimistic about advancement. Yet Stouffer's research pointed to the opposite conclusion: Soldiers in army units with low promotion rates were actually more positive about their chances to move ahead.

The key to understanding Stouffer's results lies in the groups against which soldiers measured themselves. Those assigned to units with lower promotion rates looked around them and saw people making no more headway than they were. That is, although they had not been promoted, neither had many others, so they did not feel slighted. However, soldiers in units with a higher promotion rate could easily think of people who had been promoted sooner or more often than they had. With such people in mind, even soldiers who had been promoted were likely to feel shortchanged.

The point is that we do not make judgments about ourselves in isolation, nor do we compare ourselves with just anyone. Regardless of our situation in *absolute* terms, we form a subjective sense of our well-being by looking at ourselves *relative* to specific reference groups.

⊙ **Watch** in **MySocLab**
Video: *Social Inequalities: Societies, Groups, and Organizations*

In-Groups and Out-Groups

Each of us favors some groups over others, based on political outlook, social prestige, or even just manner of dress. On the college campus, for example, left-leaning student activists may look down on fraternity members, whom they consider too conservative; fraternity members, in turn, may snub the "nerds," who they feel work too hard. People in every social setting make positive and negative evaluations of members of other groups.

Such judgments illustrate another important element of group dynamics: the opposition of in-groups and out-groups. An **in-group** is *a social group toward which a member feels respect and loyalty.* An in-group exists in relation to an **out-group**, *a social group toward which a person feels a sense of competition or opposition.* In-groups and out-groups are based on the idea that "we" have valued traits that "they" lack.

Tensions between groups sharpen the groups' boundaries and give people a clearer social identity. However, members of in-groups generally hold overly positive views of themselves and unfairly negative views of various out-groups.

Power also plays a part in intergroup relations. A powerful in-group can define others as a lower-status out-group. Historically, in countless U.S. towns and cities, many white people viewed people of color as an out-group and subordinated them socially, politically, and economically. Minorities who internalize these negative attitudes often struggle to overcome negative self-images. In this way, in-groups and out-groups foster loyalty but also generate conflict (Tajfel, 1982; Bobo & Hutchings, 1996).

in-group a social group toward which a member feels respect and loyalty

out-group a social group toward which a person feels a sense of competition or opposition

Group Size

The next time you go to a small party or gathering, try to arrive first. If you do, you will be able to watch some fascinating group dynamics. Until about six people enter the room, every person who arrives shares a single conversation. As more people arrive, the group divides into two clusters, and it divides again and again as the party grows. Size plays an important role in how group members interact.

To understand why, note the mathematical number of relationships among two to seven people. As shown in Figure 7–2, two people form a single relationship; adding a third person results in three relationships; adding a fourth person yields six. Increasing the number of people one at a time, then, expands the number of relationships much more rapidly since every new individual can interact with everyone already there. Thus by the time seven people join one conversation, twenty-one "channels"

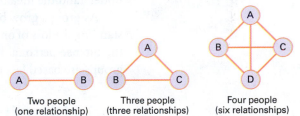

Two people (one relationship)   Three people (three relationships)   Four people (six relationships)

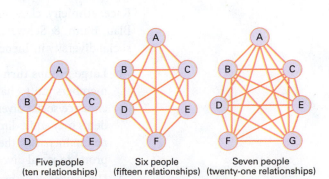

Five people (ten relationships)   Six people (fifteen relationships)   Seven people (twenty-one relationships)

FIGURE 7–2 Group Size and Relationships

As the number of people in a group increases, the number of relationships that link them increases much faster. By the time six or seven people share a conversation, the group usually divides into two. Why are relationships in smaller groups typically more intense?

Source: Created by the author.

A triad is a group made up of three people. A triad is more stable than a dyad because conflict between any two persons can be mediated by the third member. Even so, should the relationship between any two become more intense in a positive sense, those two are likely to exclude the third.

connect them. With so many open channels, at this point the group usually divides into smaller conversation groups.

The Dyad

The German sociologist Georg Simmel (1858–1918) studied social dynamics in the smallest groups. Simmel (1950, orig. 1902) used the term **dyad** (Greek for "pair") to designate *a social group with two members.* Simmel explained that social interaction in a dyad is usually more intense than in larger groups because neither member shares the other's attention with anyone else. In the United States, love affairs, marriages, and the closest friendships are typically dyadic.

But like a stool with only two legs, dyads are unstable. Both members of a dyad must work to keep the relationship going; if either withdraws, the group collapses. Because the stability of marriages is important to society, the marital dyad is supported by legal, economic, and often religious ties.

The Triad

dyad a social group with two members

triad a social group with three members

Simmel also studied the **triad**, *a social group with three members,* which contains three relationships, each uniting two of the three people. A triad is more stable than a dyad because one member can act as a mediator should the relationship between the other two become strained. Such group dynamics help explain why members of a dyad (say, a married couple) often seek out a third person (such as a counselor) to discuss tensions between them.

On the other hand, two of the three can pair up at times to press their views on the third, or two may intensify their relationship, leaving the other feeling left out. For example, when two of the three develop a romantic interest in each other, they will come to understand the meaning of the old saying, "Two's company, three's a crowd."

As groups grow beyond three people, they become more stable and capable of withstanding the loss of one or more members. At the same time, increases in group size reduce the intense personal interaction possible only in the smallest groups. This is why larger groups are based less on personal attachment and more on formal rules and regulations.

Social Diversity: Race, Class, and Gender

Race, ethnicity, class, and gender each play a part in group dynamics. Peter Blau (1977; Blau, Blum, & Schwartz, 1982; South & Messner, 1986) points out three ways in which social diversity influences intergroup contact:

1. **Large groups turn inward.** Blau explains that the larger a group is, the more likely its members are to have relationships just among themselves. Say a college is trying to enhance social diversity by increasing the number of international students. These students may add a dimension of difference, but as the number of students from a particular nation increases, they become more likely to form their own social group. Thus efforts to promote social diversity may have the unintended effect of promoting separatism.

2. **Heterogeneous groups turn outward.** The more internally diverse a group is, the more likely its members are to interact with outsiders. Members of campus groups that recruit people of both sexes and various social backgrounds typically have more intergroup contact than those with members of one social category.

3. **Physical boundaries create social boundaries.** To the extent that a social group is physically segregated from others (by having its own dorm or dining area, for example), its members are less likely to interact with other people.

Networks

A **network** is *a web of weak social ties.* Think of a network as a "fuzzy" group containing people who come into occasional contact but who lack a sense of boundaries and belonging. If you think of a *group* as a "circle of friends," think of a network as a "social web" expanding outward, often reaching great distances and including large numbers of people.

The largest network of all is the World Wide Web of the Internet. But the Internet has expanded much more in some global regions than in others. Global Map 7–1 shows that Internet use is high in rich countries such as the United States and the countries of Western Europe and far less common in poor nations in Africa and Southeast Asia.

Closer to home, some networks come close to being groups, as is the case with college classmates who stay in touch after graduation through class newsletters and annual reunions. More commonly, however, a network includes people we know of or who know of us but with whom we interact only rarely, if at all. As one woman known as a community organizer explains, "I get calls at home, [and] someone says, 'Are you Roseann Navarro? Somebody told me to call you. I have this problem…'" (quoted in Kaminer, 1984:94).

Network ties often give us the sense that we live in a "small world." In a classic experiment, Stanley Milgram (1967; Watts, 1999) gave letters to subjects in Kansas and Nebraska intended for a few specific people in Boston who were unknown to the original subjects. No addresses were supplied, and the subjects in the study were told to send the letters

network a web of weak social ties

Window on the World

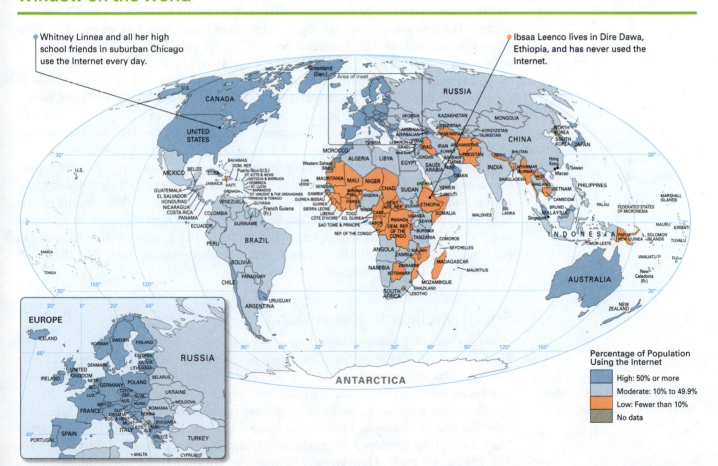

GLOBAL MAP 7–1 Internet Users in Global Perspective

This map shows how the Information Revolution has affected countries around the world. In most high-income nations, at least one-half of the population uses the Internet. By contrast, only a small share of people in low-income nations does so. What effect does this pattern have on people's access to information? What does this mean for the future in terms of global inequality?

Source: International Telecommunications Union (2012).

The 2010 film *The Social Network* depicts the birth of Facebook, now one of the largest social networking sites in the world. In what ways have Internet-based social networks changed social life in the United States?

to others they knew personally who might know the target people. Milgram found that the target people received the letters with, on average, six subjects passing them on. This result led Milgram to conclude that just about everyone is connected to everyone else by "six degrees of separation." Later research, however, has cast doubt on Milgram's conclusions. Examining Milgram's original data, Judith Kleinfeld points out that most of Milgram's letters (240 out of 300) never arrived at their destinations (Wildavsky, 2002). Those that did were typically given to people who were wealthy, a fact that led Kleinfeld to conclude that rich people are far better connected across the country than ordinary men and women. Illustrating this assertion, convicted swindler Bernard Madoff was able to recruit more than 5,000 clients entirely through his extensive business networks, with one new client encouraging others to sign up. In the end, these people and organizations lost some $50 billion in the largest Ponzi pyramid scheme of all time (Lewis, 2010).

Network ties may be weak, but they can be a powerful resource. For immigrants who are trying to become established in a new community, businesspeople seeking to expand their operations, or new college graduates looking for a job, *who* you know is often as important as *what* you know (Hagan, 1998; Petersen, Saporta, & Seidel, 2000).

Networks are based on people's colleges, clubs, neighborhoods, political parties, and personal interests. Obviously, some networks contain people with considerably more wealth, power, and prestige than others; that explains the importance of being "well connected." The networks of more privileged categories of people—such as the members of an expensive country club—are a valuable form of "social capital," which can lead to benefits such as higher-paying jobs (Green, Tigges, & Diaz, 1999; Lin, Cook, & Burt, 2001).

Some people also have denser networks than others; that is, they are connected to more people. Typically, the largest social networks include people who are affluent, young, well educated, and living in large cities. Networks are also dynamic. Typically, about half of the individuals in a person's social network change over a period of about seven years (Fernandez & Weinberg, 1997; Podolny & Baron, 1997; Mollenhorst, 2009).

Gender shapes networks. Although the networks of men and women are typically the same size, women include more relatives (and more women) in their networks, and men include more co-workers (and more men). Research suggests that women's ties do not carry quite the same clout as the "old-boy" networks that men often rely on for career and social advancement. Even so, research suggests that as gender equality increases in the United States, the networks of women and men are becoming more alike (Reskin & McBrier, 2000; Torres & Huffman, 2002).

Social Media and Networking

Networks have long operated as webs of weak social ties involving dozens, hundreds, and for the very "well connected," even thousands of people. In recent decades, networks have become far larger along with the development of social media based on computer technology. **Social media** refers to *technology that links people in social activity*.

social media technology that links people in social activity

Computer-based social media have exploded in popularity over the past decade. Consider the case of Facebook, which began when a Harvard University sophomore named Mark Zuckerberg developed a simple interactive website for part of his campus in 2003. This site quickly evolved into an early form of what we know today and, within a month, half the campus was using it. Facebook expanded to other campuses, invited high school students to join, and by 2006 was open to anyone over age thirteen with computer access and an email account. By 2011, 600 million people were involved in Facebook networks—double the population of the United States—and by the end of 2012, the number had passed 1 billion. Today, Facebook, Twitter, and other social networking sites connect people all over the world.

Formal Organizations

7.2 Describe the operation of large, formal organizations.

A century ago, most people lived in small groups of family, friends, and neighbors. Today, our lives revolve more and more around **formal organizations**, *large secondary groups organized to achieve their goals efficiently.* Formal organizations, such as business corporations and government agencies, differ from families and neighborhoods in their impersonality and their formally planned atmosphere.

When you think about it, organizing more than 300 million people in this country into a single society is truly remarkable, whether it involves paving roads, collecting taxes, schooling children, or delivering the mail. To carry out most of these tasks, we rely on different types of large formal organizations.

Types of Formal Organizations

Amitai Etzioni (1975) identified three types of formal organizations, distinguished by the reasons people participate in them: utilitarian organizations, normative organizations, and coercive organizations.

Utilitarian Organizations

Just about everyone who works for income belongs to a *utilitarian organization,* one that pays people for their efforts. Large businesses, for example, generate profits for their owners and income for their employees. Becoming part of a utilitarian organization such as a business or government agency is usually a matter of individual choice, although most people must join one or another such organization to make a living.

Normative Organizations

People join *normative organizations* not for income but to pursue some goal they think is morally worthwhile. Sometimes called *voluntary associations,* these include community service groups (such as the PTA, the Lions Club, the League of Women Voters, and the Red Cross), as well as political parties and religious organizations. In global perspective, people living in the United States and other high-income nations with relatively democratic political systems are likely to join voluntary associations. A recent study found that 74 percent of first-year college students in the United States claimed to have participated in some volunteer activity within the past year (Pryor et al., 2013).

Coercive Organizations

Membership in *coercive organizations* is involuntary. People are forced to join these organizations as a form of punishment (prisons) or treatment (some psychiatric hospitals). Coercive organizations have special physical features, such as locked doors and barred windows, and are supervised by security personnel. They isolate people, whom they label "inmates" or "patients," for a period of time in order to radically change their attitudes and behavior. Recall from Chapter 5 ("Socialization") the power of a total institution to change a person's sense of self.

It is possible for a single organization to fall into *all* three categories from the point of view of different individuals. For example, a mental hospital serves as a coercive organization for a patient, a utilitarian organization for a psychiatrist, and a normative organization for a hospital volunteer.

Origins of Formal Organizations

Formal organizations date back thousands of years. Elites who controlled early empires relied on government officials to collect taxes, undertake military campaigns, and build monumental structures, from the Great Wall of China to the pyramids of Egypt.

formal organization a large secondary group organized to achieve its goals efficiently

 Explore membership in one of our country's largest formal organizations—the military—in your local community and in counties across the United States in **MySocLab**

rationalization of society the historical change from tradition to rationality as the main type of human thought

tradition behavior, values, and beliefs passed from generation to generation

rationality a way of thinking that emphasizes deliberate, matter-of-fact calculation of the most efficient way to accomplish a particular task

However, early organizations had two limitations. First, they lacked the technology to let people travel over large distances, to communicate quickly, and to gather and store information. Second, the preindustrial societies they were trying to rule had traditional cultures. **Tradition**, according to German sociologist Max Weber, consists of *behavior, values, and beliefs passed from generation to generation*. Tradition makes a society conservative, Weber explained, because it limits an organization's productive efficiency and ability to change.

By contrast, Weber described the modern worldview as based on **rationality**, *a way of thinking that emphasizes deliberate, matter-of-fact calculation of the most efficient way to accomplish a particular task*. A rational worldview pays little attention to the past and encourages productive efficiency because it is open to any changes that might get the job done better or more quickly.

The rise of the modern world rests on what Weber called the **rationalization of society**, *the historical change from tradition to rationality as the main type of human thought*. Modern society, he claimed, becomes "disenchanted" as sentimental ties give way to a rational focus on science, complex technology, and the organizational structure called "bureaucracy."

Characteristics of Bureaucracy

bureaucracy an organizational model rationally designed to perform tasks efficiently

Bureaucracy is *an organizational model rationally designed to perform tasks efficiently*. Bureaucratic officials regularly create and revise policy to increase efficiency. To appreciate the power and scope of bureaucratic organization, consider that any one of more than 400 million telephones in the United States can connect you within seconds to any other phone in a home, business, automobile, or even a hiker's backpack on a remote trail in the Rocky Mountains. Such instant communication was beyond the imagination of people who lived in the ancient world.

Our telephone system depends on technology such as electricity, fiber optics, and computers. But the system could not exist without the bureaucracy that keeps track of every telephone call—noting which phone calls which other phone, when, and for how long—and then presents the relevant information to some 300 million telephone users in the form of a monthly bill (FCC, 2010; CTIA, 2012).

What specific traits promote organizational efficiency? Max Weber (1978, orig. 1921) identified six key elements of the ideal bureaucratic organization:

1. **Specialization.** Our ancestors spent most of their time performing the general task of looking for food and shelter. Bureaucracy, by contrast, assigns people highly specialized jobs.

2. **Hierarchy of positions.** Bureaucracies arrange workers in a vertical ranking. Each person is supervised by someone "higher up" in the organization while in turn supervising others in lower positions. Usually, with few people at the top and many at the bottom, bureaucratic organizations take the form of a pyramid.

3. **Rules and regulations.** Cultural tradition counts for little in a bureaucracy. Instead, rationally enacted rules and regulations guide a bureaucracy's operation. Ideally, a bureaucracy operates in a completely predictable way.

4. **Technical competence.** Bureaucratic officials have the technical competence to carry out their duties. Bureaucracies typically hire new members according to set standards and then monitor their performance. Such impersonal evaluation contrasts with the ancient custom of favoring relatives, whatever their talents, over strangers.

Weber described the operation of the ideal bureaucracy as rational and highly efficient. In real life, however, organizations often operate very differently than Weber's model, as can be seen in the television show *The Mindy Project*.

Summing Up

Small Groups and Formal Organizations		
	Small Groups	**Formal Organizations**
Activities	Much the same for all members	Distinct and highly specialized
Hierarchy	Often informal or nonexistent	Clearly defined according to position
Norms	General norms, informally applied	Clearly defined rules and regulations
Membership criteria	Variable; often based on personal affection or kinship	Technical competence to carry out assigned tasks
Relationships	Variable and typically primary	Typically secondary, with selective primary ties
Communications	Typically casual and face-to-face	Typically formal and in writing
Focus	Person-oriented	Task-oriented

5. **Impersonality.** Bureaucracy puts rules ahead of personal whim so that both clients and workers are treated in the same way. From this impersonal approach comes the image of the "faceless bureaucrat."

6. **Formal, written communications.** It is said that the heart of bureaucracy is not people but paperwork. Instead of the casual, face-to-face talk that characterizes interaction within small groups, bureaucracy relies on formal, written memos and reports, which accumulate in vast files.

Bureaucratic organization promotes efficiency by carefully hiring workers and limiting the unpredictable effects of personal taste and opinion. The Summing Up table reviews the differences between small social groups and large bureaucratic organizations.

Organizational Environment

No organization operates in a vacuum. The performance of any organization depends not only on its own goals and policies but also on the **organizational environment**, *factors outside an organization that affect its operation*. These factors include technology, economic and political trends, current events, the available workforce, and other organizations.

Modern organizations are shaped by *technology*, including copiers, fax machines, telephones, and computers. This technology gives employees access to more information and more people than ever before. At the same time, modern technology allows managers to monitor worker activities much more closely than in the past (Markoff, 1991).

Economic and political trends affect organizations. All organizations are helped or hurt by periodic economic growth or recession. Most industries also face competition from abroad as well as changes in laws—such as new environmental standards—at home.

Population patterns also affect organizations. The average age, typical level of education, social diversity, and size of a local community determine the available workforce and sometimes the market for an organization's products or services.

Current events can have significant effects on organizations that are far removed from the location of the events themselves. Events such as the sweeping political revolutions in the Middle East in 2011 and the reelection of President Obama in the 2012 presidential election affect the operation of both government agencies and business organizations.

Other organizations also contribute to the organizational environment. To be competitive, a hospital must be responsive to the insurance industry and to organizations representing doctors, nurses, and other health care workers. It must also be aware of the equipment and procedures available at nearby facilities, as well as their prices.

organizational environment factors outside an organization that affect its operation

The Informal Side of Bureaucracy

Weber's ideal bureaucracy deliberately regulates every activity. In actual organizations, however, human beings are creative (and stubborn) enough to resist bureaucratic regulation. Informality may amount to simply cutting corners on your job, but it can also provide the flexibility needed to adapt and prosper.

In part, informality comes from the personalities of organizational leaders. Studies of U.S. corporations document that the qualities and quirks of individuals—including personal charisma, interpersonal skills, and the willingness to recognize problems—can have a great effect on organizational outcomes (Halberstam, 1986; Baron, Hannan, & Burton, 1999).

Authoritarian, democratic, and laissez-faire types of leadership (described earlier in this chapter) reflect individual personality as much as any organizational plan. In the "real world" of organizations, leaders sometimes seek to benefit personally by abusing organizational power. Many of the corporate leaders of banks and insurance companies that collapsed during the financial meltdown of 2008 walked off with huge "golden parachutes." Throughout the business world, leaders take credit for the efforts of the people who work for them, at least when things go well. In addition, the importance of many secretaries to how well a boss performs is often much greater than most people think (and greater than a secretary's official job title and salary suggest).

Communication offers another example of organizational informality. Memos and other written communications are the formal way to spread information throughout an organization. Typically, however, individuals also create informal networks, or "grapevines," that spread information quickly, if not always accurately. Grapevines, using both word of mouth and e-mail, are particularly important to rank-and-file workers because higher-ups often try to keep important information from them.

The spread of e-mail has "flattened" organizations somewhat, allowing even the lowest-ranking employee to bypass immediate superiors and communicate directly with the organization's leader or with all fellow employees at once. Some organizations object to such "open-channel" communication and limit the use of e-mail. Microsoft Corporation (whose founder, Bill Gates, has an unlisted e-mail address that helps him limit his mail to a few hundred messages a day) pioneered the development of screens that filter out messages from everyone except certain approved people (Gwynne & Dickerson, 1997).

Using new information technology as well as age-old human ingenuity, members of organizations often try to break free of rigid rules in order to personalize procedures and surroundings. Such efforts suggest that we should take a closer look at some of the problems of bureaucracy.

Problems of Bureaucracy

We rely on bureaucracy to manage everyday life efficiently, but many people are uneasy about large organizations. Bureaucracy can dehumanize and manipulate us, and some say it poses a threat to political democracy. These dangers are discussed in the following sections.

Bureaucratic Alienation

Max Weber held up bureaucracy as a model of productivity. However, Weber was keenly aware of bureaucracy's ability to *dehumanize* the people it is supposed to serve. The same impersonality that fosters efficiency also keeps officials and clients from responding to one another's unique personal needs. Typically, officials at large government and corporate agencies must treat each client impersonally as a standard "case." In 2008, for example, the U.S. Army accidently sent letters to family members of soldiers killed in Iraq and Afghanistan, addressing the recipients as "John Doe" ("Army Apologizes," 2009).

Formal organizations breed *alienation,* according to Weber, by reducing the human being to "a small cog in a ceaselessly moving mechanism" (1978:988, orig. 1921). Although formal organizations are designed to benefit people, Weber feared that people might well end up serving formal organizations.

Bureaucratic Inefficiency and Ritualism

On Labor Day 2005, as people in New Orleans and other coastal areas were battling to survive in the wake of Hurricane Katrina, 600 firefighters from around the country assembled in a hotel meeting room in Atlanta awaiting deployment. Officials of the Federal Emergency

Management Agency (FEMA) explained to the crowd that they were first going to be given a lecture on "equal opportunity, sexual harassment, and customer service." Then, the official continued, they would each be given a stack of FEMA pamphlets with the agency's phone number to distribute to people in the devastated areas. A firefighter stood up and shouted, "This is ridiculous! Our fire departments and mayors sent us down here to save lives, and you've got us doing *this*?" The FEMA official thundered back, "You are now employees of FEMA, and you will follow orders and do what you are told!" ("Places," 2005:39).

People sometimes describe this inefficiency as too much "red tape," a reference to the ribbon used by slow-working eighteenth-century English administrators to wrap official parcels and records (Shipley, 1985).

To Robert Merton (1968), red tape amounts to a new twist on the already familiar concept of group conformity. He coined the term **bureaucratic ritualism** to describe *a focus on rules and regulations to the point of undermining an organization's goals.* In short, rules and regulations should be a means to an end, not an end in themselves that takes the focus away from the organization's stated goals. After the terrorist attacks of September 11, 2001, for example, the U.S. Postal Service continued to help deliver mail addressed to Osama bin Laden at a post office in Afghanistan, despite the objections of the FBI. It took an act of Congress to change the policy (Bedard, 2002).

George Tooker's painting *Government Bureau* is a powerful statement about the human costs of bureaucracy. The artist paints members of the public in a drab sameness—reduced from human beings to mere "cases" to be disposed of as quickly as possible. Set apart from others by their positions, officials are "faceless bureaucrats" concerned more with numbers than with providing genuine assistance (notice that the artist places the fingers of the officials on calculators).

George Tooker, *Government Bureau*, 1956. Egg tempera on gesso panel, 19 × 29 inches. The Metropolitan Museum of Art, George A. Hearn Fund, 1956 (56.78). Photograph © 1984 The Metropolitan Museum of Art/Image source: Art Resource, NY.

bureaucratic ritualism a focus on rules and regulations to the point of undermining an organization's goals

Bureaucratic Inertia

If bureaucrats sometimes have little reason to work very hard, they have every reason to protect their jobs. Officials typically work to keep an organization going even after its original goal has been realized. As Weber put it, "Once fully established, bureaucracy is among the social structures which are hardest to destroy" (1978:987, orig. 1921).

Bureaucratic inertia refers to *the tendency of bureaucratic organizations to perpetuate themselves.* Formal organizations tend to take on a life of their own beyond their formal objectives. For example, the U.S. Department of Agriculture has offices in nearly every county in all fifty states, even though only one county in seven has any working farms. Usually, an organization stays in business by redefining its goals. For example, the Agriculture Department now performs a broad range of work not directly related to farming, including nutritional and environmental research.

bureaucratic inertia the tendency of bureaucratic organizations to perpetuate themselves

Oligarchy

Early in the twentieth century, Robert Michels (1876–1936) pointed out the link between bureaucracy and political **oligarchy**, *the rule of the many by the few* (1949, orig. 1911). According to what Michels called the "iron law of oligarchy," the pyramid shape of bureaucracy places a few leaders in charge of the resources of the entire organization.

Weber believed that a strict hierarchy of responsibility resulted in high organizational efficiency. But Michels countered that this hierarchical structure also concentrates power and thus threatens democracy because officials can and often do use their access to information, resources, and the media to promote their own personal interests.

Furthermore, bureaucracy helps distance officials from the public, as in the case of the corporate president or public official who is "unavailable for comment" to the local

oligarchy the rule of the many by the few

press or the U.S. president who withholds documents from Congress claiming "executive privilege." Oligarchy, then, thrives in the hierarchical structure of bureaucracy and reduces leaders' accountability to the people.

Political competition, term limits, and a legal system that includes various checks and balances prevent the U.S. government from becoming an out-and-out oligarchy. Even so, incumbents, who generally have more visibility, power, and money than their challengers, enjoy a significant advantage in U.S. politics. In recent congressional elections, 90 percent of congressional officeholders on the ballot were able to win reelection.

The Evolution of Formal Organizations

7.3 Summarize the changes to formal organizations over the course of the last century.

The problems of bureaucracy—especially the alienation it produces and its tendency toward oligarchy—stem from two organizational traits: hierarchy and rigidity. To Weber, bureaucracy was a top-down system: Rules and regulations made at the top guide every facet of people's lives down the chain of command. A century ago in the United States, Weber's ideas took hold in an organizational model called *scientific management*. We take a look at this model and then examine three challenges over the course of the twentieth century that gradually led to a new model: the *flexible organization*.

Scientific Management

Frederick Winslow Taylor (1911) had a simple message: Most businesses in the United States were sadly inefficient. Managers had little idea of how to increase their business's output, and workers relied on the same tired skills of earlier generations. To increase efficiency, Taylor explained, business should apply the principles of science. **Scientific management** is thus *the application of scientific principles to the operation of a business or other large organization.*

Scientific management involves three steps. First, managers carefully observe the task performed by each worker, identifying all the operations involved and measuring the time needed for each. Second, managers analyze their data, trying to discover ways for workers to perform each job more efficiently. For example, managers might decide to give the worker different tools or to reposition various work operations within the factory. Third, management provides guidance and incentives for workers to do their jobs more quickly. If a factory worker moves 20 tons of pig iron in one day, for example, management shows the worker how to do the job more efficiently and then provides higher wages as the worker's productivity rises. Taylor concluded that if scientific principles were applied in this way, companies would become more profitable, workers would earn higher wages, and consumers would benefit by paying lower prices.

A century ago, auto pioneer Henry Ford put it this way: "Save ten steps a day for each of 12,000 employees, and you will have saved fifty miles of wasted motion and misspent energy" (Allen & Hyman, 1999:209). In the early 1900s, the Ford Motor Company and many other businesses followed Taylor's lead and made improvements in efficiency. Today, corporations carefully review every aspect of their operation in a never-ending effort to increase efficiency.

The principles of scientific management suggested that workplace power should reside with owners and executives, who have historically paid little attention to the ideas of their workers. Formal organizations have also faced important challenges, involving race and gender, rising competition from abroad, and the changing nature of work. We now take a brief look at each of these challenges.

The First Challenge: Race and Gender

In the 1960s, critics charged that big businesses and other organizations engaged in unfair hiring practices. Rather than hiring on the basis of competence as Weber had proposed, organizations excluded women and other minorities, especially from positions of power.

scientific management
Frederick Taylor's term for the application of scientific principles to the operation of a business or other large organization

Hiring on the basis of competence is only partly a matter of fairness; it is also a matter of enlarging the talent pool to promote efficiency.

Patterns of Privilege and Exclusion

Even in the early twenty-first century, as shown in Figure 7–3, non-Hispanic white men in the United States—32 percent of the working-age population—still held 64 percent of management jobs. Non-Hispanic white women made up 32 percent of the population but held just 25 percent of managerial positions (U.S. Equal Employment Opportunity Commission, 2012). The members of other minorities lagged further behind.

Rosabeth Moss Kanter (1977; Kanter & Stein, 1979) claims that excluding women and minorities from the workplace ignores the talents of half the population. Furthermore, underrepresented people in an organization often feel like socially isolated out-groups—uncomfortably visible, taken less seriously, and given fewer chances for promotion. Sometimes what passes for "merit" or good work in an organization is simply being of the right social category (Castilla, 2008).

Opening up an organization so that change and advancement happen more often, Kanter claims, improves everyone's on-the-job performance by motivating employees to become "fast-trackers" who work harder and are more committed to the company. By contrast, an organization with many dead-end jobs turns workers into less productive "zombies" who are never asked for their opinion on anything. An open organization encourages leaders to seek out the input of all employees, which usually improves decision making.

The "Female Advantage"

Some organizational researchers argue that women bring special management skills that strengthen an organization. According to Deborah Tannen (1994), women have a greater "information focus" and more readily ask questions in order to understand an issue.

Diversity Snapshot

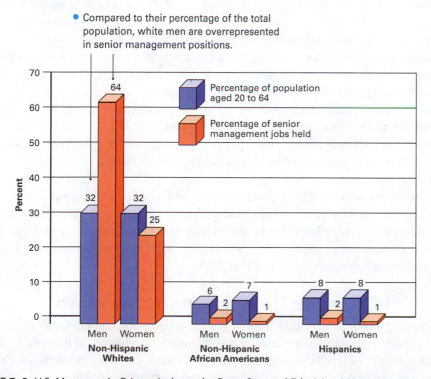

• Compared to their percentage of the total population, white men are overrepresented in senior management positions.

Percentage of population aged 20 to 64

Percentage of senior management jobs held

FIGURE 7–3 U.S. Managers in Private Industry by Race, Sex, and Ethnicity, 2011

White men are more likely than their population size suggests to be managers in private industry. The opposite is true for white women and other minorities. What factors do you think may account for this pattern?

Sources: U.S. Census Bureau (2012) and U.S. Equal Employment Opportunity Commission (2012).

Men, by contrast, have an "image focus" that makes them wonder how asking questions in a particular situation will affect their reputation.

In another study of women executives, Sally Helgesen (1990) found three other gender-linked patterns. First, women place greater value on communication skills than men and share information more than men do. Second, women are more flexible leaders who typically give their employees greater freedom. Third, compared to men, women tend to emphasize the interconnectedness of all organizational operations. These patterns, which Helgesen dubbed the *female advantage*, help make companies more flexible and democratic.

In sum, one challenge to conventional bureaucracy is to become more open and flexible in order to take advantage of the experience, ideas, and creativity of everyone, regardless of race or gender. The result goes right to the bottom line: greater profits.

The Second Challenge: The Japanese Work Organization

In 1980, the U.S. corporate world was shaken to discover that the most popular automobile model sold in this country was not a Chevrolet, Ford, or Plymouth but the Honda Accord, made in Japan. Recently, the Japanese corporation Toyota passed General Motors to become the largest carmaker in the world (Meier, 2012). This is quite a change. As late as the 1950s, U.S. automakers dominated car production, and the label "Made in Japan" was generally found on products that were cheap and poorly made. The success of the Japanese auto industry, as well as companies making cameras and other products, drew attention to the "Japanese work organization." How was so small a country able to challenge the world's economic powerhouse?

Japanese organizations reflect that nation's strong collective spirit. In contrast to the U.S. emphasis on rugged individualism, the Japanese value cooperation. In effect, formal organizations in Japan are more like large primary groups. A generation ago, William Ouchi (1981) highlighted five differences between formal organizations in Japan and those in the United States. First, Japanese companies hired new workers in groups, giving everyone the same salary and responsibilities. Second, many Japanese companies hired workers for life, fostering a strong sense of loyalty. Third, with the idea that employees would spend their entire careers there, many Japanese companies trained workers in all phases of their operations. Fourth, although Japanese corporate leaders took final responsibility for their organization's performance, they involved workers in "quality circles" to discuss decisions that affected them. Fifth, Japanese companies played a large role in the lives of workers, providing home mortgages, sponsoring recreational activities, and scheduling social events. Together, such policies encourage much more loyalty among members of Japanese organizations than is typically the case in their U.S. counterparts.

Not everything has worked well for Japan's corporations. About 1990, the Japanese economy entered a recession that has lasted for two decades. During this downturn, many Japanese companies have changed their policies, no longer offering workers jobs for life or many of the other benefits noted by Ouchi. But the long-term outlook for Japan's business organizations remains bright.

In recent years, the widely admired Toyota corporation has also seen challenges. After expanding its operations to become the world's largest carmaker, Toyota was forced to recall millions of automobiles due to mechanical problems, suggesting that one consequence of the company's rapid growth was losing focus on what had been the key to its success all along—quality (Saporito, 2010).

The Third Challenge: The Changing Nature of Work

Beyond rising global competition and the need to provide equal opportunity for all, pressure to modify conventional organizations is coming from changes in the nature of work itself. Chapter 4 ("Society") described the shift from industrial to postindustrial production. Rather than working in factories using heavy machinery to make *things*, more and more people are using computers and other electronic technology to create or process *information*. The postindustrial society, then, is characterized by information-based organizations.

Frederick Taylor developed his concept of scientific management at a time when jobs involved tasks that, though often backbreaking, were routine and repetitive. Workers shoveled coal, poured liquid iron into molds, welded body panels to automobiles on an assembly line, or shot hot rivets into steel girders to build skyscrapers. In addition, many of the industrial workers in Taylor's day were immigrants, most of whom had little schooling and many of whom knew little English. The routine nature of industrial jobs, coupled with the limited skills of the labor force, led Taylor to treat work as a series of fixed tasks, set down by management and followed by employees.

Many of today's information age jobs are very different: The work of designers, artists, writers, composers, programmers, business owners, and others now demands individual creativity and imagination. Here are several ways in which today's organizations differ from those of a century ago:

1. **Creative freedom.** As one Hewlett-Packard executive put it, "From their first day of work here, people are given important responsibilities and are encouraged to grow" (cited in Brooks, 2000:128). Today's organizations now treat employees with information age skills as a vital resource. Executives can set production goals but cannot dictate how a worker is to accomplish tasks that require imagination and discovery. This gives highly skilled workers *creative freedom,* which means less day-to-day supervision as long as they generate good results in the long run.

2. **Competitive work teams.** Organizations typically give several groups of employees the freedom to work on a problem, offering the greatest rewards to those who come up with the best solution. Competitive work teams, a strategy first used by Japanese organizations, draw out the creative contributions of everyone and at the same time reduce the alienation often found in conventional organizations (Maddox, 1994; Yeatts, 1994).

3. **A flatter organization.** By spreading responsibility for creative problem solving throughout the workforce, organizations take on a flatter shape. That is, the pyramid shape of conventional bureaucracy is replaced by an organizational form with fewer levels in the chain of command, as shown in Figure 7-4.

4. **Greater flexibility.** The typical industrial age organization was a rigid structure guided from the top. Such organizations may accomplish a large amount of work, but they are not especially creative or able to respond quickly to changes in the larger environment. The ideal model in the information age is a more open, *flexible* organization that both generates new ideas and adapts quickly to the rapidly changing global marketplace.

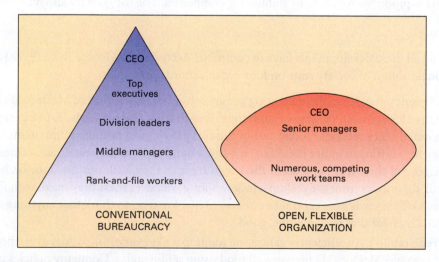

FIGURE 7-4 Two Organizational Models

The conventional model of bureaucratic organizations has a pyramid shape, with a clear chain of command. Orders flow from the top down, and reports of performance flow from the bottom up. Such organizations have extensive rules and regulations, and their workers have highly specialized jobs. More open and flexible organizations have a flatter shape, more like a football. With fewer levels in the hierarchy, responsibility for generating ideas and making decisions is shared throughout the organization. Many workers do their jobs in teams and have a broad knowledge of the entire organization's operation.

Source: Created by the author.

What does all this mean for formal organizations? As David Brooks puts it, "The machine is no longer held up as the standard that healthy organizations should emulate. Now it's the ecosystem" (2000:128). Today's "smart" companies seek out intelligent, creative people (AOL's main building is called "Creative Center 1") and nurture the growth of their talents.

Keep in mind, however, that many of today's jobs do not involve creative work at all. More correctly, the postindustrial economy has created two very different types of work: high-skill creative work and low-skill service work. Work in the fast-food industry, for example, is routine and highly supervised and thus has much more in common with the factory work of a century ago than with the creative teamwork typical of today's information organizations. Therefore, at the same time that some organizations have taken on a flexible, flatter form, others continue to use the rigid chain of command.

The "McDonaldization" of Society

As noted in the opening to this chapter, McDonald's has enjoyed enormous success, now operating more than 33,500 restaurants in the United States and around the world. Japan has more than 3,300 Golden Arches; Europe has 7,100 restaurants, and McDonald's prepared for the 2012 Olympics in London by building a giant restaurant that employed 500 people and seated 1,500 customers.

McDonald's is far more than a restaurant chain; it is a symbol of U.S. culture. Not only do people around the world associate McDonald's with the United States, but also here at home, one poll found that 98 percent of schoolchildren could identify Ronald McDonald, making him as well known as Santa Claus.

Even more important, the organizational principles that underlie McDonald's are coming to dominate our entire society. Our culture is becoming "McDonaldized," an awkward way of saying that we model many aspects of life on this restaurant chain: Parents buy toys at worldwide chain stores all carrying identical merchandise; we drop in for a ten-minute oil change while running errands; face-to-face communication is being replaced more and more by e-mail, voice mail, and texting; more vacations take the form of resorts and tour packages; television packages the news in the form of ten-second sound bites; college admissions officers size up students they have never met by glancing at their GPA and SAT scores; and professors assign ghost-written textbooks[1] and evaluate students with tests mass-produced for them by publishing companies. The list goes on and on.

Four Principles

What do all these developments have in common? According to George Ritzer (1993), the McDonaldization of society rests on four organizational principles:

1. **Efficiency.** Ray Kroc, the marketing genius behind the expansion of McDonald's back in the 1950s, set out to serve a hamburger, French fries, and a milkshake to a customer in exactly fifty seconds. Today, one of the company's most popular menu items is the Egg McMuffin, an entire breakfast in a single sandwich. In the restaurant, customers dispose of their trash and stack their own trays as they walk out the door or, better still, drive away from the pickup window taking whatever mess they make with them. Such efficiency is now central to our way of life. We tend to think that anything done quickly is, for that reason alone, good.

2. **Predictability.** An efficient organization wants to make everything it does as predictable as possible. McDonald's prepares all food using set formulas. Company policies guide the performance of every job.

3. **Uniformity.** The first McDonald's operating manual set the weight of a regular raw hamburger at 1.6 ounces, its size at 3.875 inches across, and its fat content at

---

[1] A number of popular sociology books were not written by the person whose name appears on the cover. This book is not one of them. Even the test bank and the material in MySocLab that accompanies this text were written by the author.

The best of today's information age jobs—including working at Google, the popular search engine website—allow people lots of personal freedom as long as they produce good ideas. At the same time, many other jobs, such as working the counter at McDonald's, involve the same routines and strict supervision found in factories a century ago.

19 percent. A slice of cheese weighs exactly half an ounce. Fries are cut precisely 9/32 of an inch thick.

Think about how many objects around your home, the workplace, and the campus are designed and mass-produced according to a standard plan. Not just our environment but also our life experiences—from traveling the nation's interstates to sitting at home viewing television—are more standardized than ever before.

Almost anywhere in the world, a person can walk into a McDonald's restaurant and purchase the same sandwiches, drinks, and desserts prepared in precisely the same way.[2] Uniformity results from a highly rational system that specifies every action and leaves nothing to chance.

4. **Control.** The most unreliable element in the McDonald's system is the human beings who work there. After all, people have good and bad days, sometimes let their minds wander, or simply decide to try something a different way. To minimize the unpredictable human element, McDonald's has automated its equipment to cook food at a fixed temperature for a set length of time. Even the cash register at McDonald's is keyed to pictures of the items so that ringing up a customer's order is as simple as possible.

Similarly, automatic teller machines are replacing bank tellers, highly automated bakeries now produce bread while people stand back and watch, and chickens and eggs (or is it eggs and chickens?) emerge from automated hatcheries. In supermarkets, laser scanners at self-checkouts are phasing out human checkers. We do most of our shopping in malls, where everything from temperature and humidity to the kinds of stores and products sold are subject to continuous control and supervision (Ide & Cordell, 1994).

Can Rationality Be Irrational?

There is no doubt about the popularity or efficiency of McDonald's. But there is another side to the story.

Max Weber was alarmed at the increasing rationalization of the world, fearing that formal organizations would cage our imaginations and crush the human spirit. As Weber

---

[2]As McDonald's has "gone global," a few products have been added or changed according to local tastes. For example, in Uruguay, customers enjoy the McHuevo (hamburger with poached egg on top); Norwegians can buy McLaks (grilled salmon sandwiches); the Dutch favor the Groenteburger (vegetable burger); in Thailand, McDonald's serves Samurai pork burgers (pork burgers with teriyaki sauce); the Japanese can purchase a Chicken Tatsuta Sandwich (chicken seasoned with soy and ginger); Filipinos eat McSpaghetti (spaghetti with tomato sauce and bits of hot dog); and in India, where Hindus eat no beef, McDonald's sells a vegetarian Maharaja Mac (Sullivan, 1995).

Controversy & Debate

Computer Technology, Large Organizations, and the Assault on Privacy

Jake completes a page on Facebook, which includes his name and college, e-mail address, photo, biography, and current personal interests. It can be accessed by billions of people around the world.

Late for a meeting with a new client, Sarah drives her car through a yellow light as it turns red at a main intersection. A computer linked to a pair of cameras notes the violation and takes one picture of her license plate and another of her sitting in the driver's seat. In seven days, she receives a summons to appear in traffic court.

Julio looks through his mail and finds a letter from a data services company telling him that he is one of about 145,000 people whose name, address, Social Security number, and credit file have recently been sold to criminals posing as businesspeople. With this information, other people can obtain credit cards or take out loans in his name.

These cases show that today's organizations—which know more about us than ever before and more than most of us realize—pose a growing threat to personal privacy. Large organizations are necessary for today's society to operate. In some cases, organizations using or selling information about us may actually be helpful. But cases of identity theft are on the rise, and personal privacy is on the decline.

In the past, small-town life gave people little privacy. But at least if people knew something about you, you were just as likely to know something about them. Today, unknown people "out there" can access information about each of us all the time without our learning about it.

In part, the loss of privacy is a result of more and more complex computer technology. Are you aware that every e-mail you send and every website you visit leaves a record in one or more computers? These records can be retrieved by people you don't know as well as by employers and other public officials.

Another part of today's loss of privacy reflects the number and size of formal organizations. As explained in this chapter, large organizations tend to treat people impersonally, and they have a huge appetite for information. Mix large organizations with ever more complex computer technology, and it is no wonder that many people are concerned about who knows what about them and what other people are doing with this information.

For decades, the level of personal privacy in the United States has been declining. Early in the twentieth century, when state agencies began issuing driver's licenses, they generated files for every licensed driver. Today, officials can send this information at the touch of a button to the police and to all sorts of other organizations. The Internal Revenue Service and the Social Security Administration, as well as government agencies that benefit veterans, students, the unemployed, and the poor, all collect mountains of personal information.

Business organizations now do much the same thing. Most of us use credit—the U.S. population now has more than 1 billion credit cards, an average of five per adult—but the companies that do "credit checks" collect and distribute information about us to almost anyone who asks.

Then there are the small cameras found not only at traffic intersections but also in stores, public buildings, and parking garages and across college campuses. So-called security cameras may increase public safety—say, by discouraging a mugger or even a terrorist—at the cost of the little privacy we have left. In the United Kingdom, the typical resident of London appears on closed-circuit television about 300 times every day, and all this "tracking" is stored in computer files. Here in the United States, New York City already has 4,000 surveillance cameras in the streets and subway system, which city officials claim might well have prevented an attack such as the 2013 Boston Marathon bombing (Rossen and Connor, 2013).

Government monitoring of the population has been expanding steadily in recent years. After the September 11, 2001, terrorist attacks, the federal government took steps (including passage of the USA PATRIOT Act) to strengthen national security. Today, government officials closely monitor not only people entering the country but also the activities of all of us. It is possible that these efforts increase national security, but it is certain that they erode personal privacy.

Some legal protections remain. Every state has laws that give citizens the right to examine some records about themselves kept by employers, banks, and credit bureaus. The federal Privacy Act of 1974 also limits the exchange of personal information among government agencies and permits citizens to examine and correct most government files. In response to rising levels of identity theft, Congress is likely to pass more laws to regulate the sale of credit information. But the danger to privacy and individual rights is rising. One recent analysis concluded that within a few years governments will have access to the technology needed to completely monitor and record virtually everything people say or do within a country. Many organizations—private as well as public—already have information about us and experts estimate that 90 percent of U.S. households are profiled in databases somewhere. Can current laws ensure that privacy will remain part of our way of life?

What Do You Think?

1. Do you think that the use of surveillance cameras in public places enhances or reduces personal security? Explain.

2. What about automatic toll payment technology (such as E-ZPass) that allows you to move more quickly through highway toll gates but also collects information on where you go and when you get there?

3. Do you think laws will ensure that some privacy remains, or are we on a road to the elimination of personal privacy?

Sources: "Online Privacy" (2000), Heymann (2002), O'Harrow (2005), Tingwall (2008), Werth (2008), Hui (2010), and Stein (2011).

saw it, rational systems were efficient but dehumanizing. McDonaldization bears him out. Each of the four principles just discussed limits human creativity, choice, and freedom. Echoing Weber, Ritzer states that "the ultimate irrationality of McDonaldization is that people could lose control over the system and it would come to control us" (1993:145). Perhaps even McDonald's understands this—the company has now expanded its more upscale offerings to include premium roasted coffee and salad selections that are more sophisticated, fresh, and healthful (Philadelphia, 2002).

The Future of Organizations: Opposing Trends

7.4 Assess the consequences of modern social organization for social life.

Early in the twentieth century, ever-larger organizations arose in the United States, most taking on the bureaucratic form described by Max Weber. In many respects, these organizations resembled armies led by powerful generals who issued orders to their captains and lieutenants. Foot soldiers, working in the factories, did what they were told.

With the emergence of a postindustrial economy around 1950, as well as rising competition from abroad, many organizations evolved toward a flatter, more flexible model that prizes communication and creativity. Such "intelligent organizations" (Pinchot & Pinchot, 1993; Brooks, 2000) have become more productive than ever. Just as important, for highly skilled people who now enjoy creative freedom, these organizations cause less of the alienation that so worried Weber.

But this is only half the story. Although the postindustrial economy has created many highly skilled jobs over the past half-century, it has created even more routine service jobs. Fast-food companies now represent the largest pool of low-wage labor, aside from migrant workers, in the United States (Schlosser, 2002). Work of this kind, which Ritzer terms "McJobs," offers few of the benefits that today's highly skilled workers enjoy. On the contrary, the automated routines that define work in the fast-food industry, telemarketing, and similar fields are very much the same as those that Frederick Taylor described a century ago.

Today, organizational flexibility gives better-off workers more freedom but often means the threat of "downsizing" and job loss for many rank-and-file employees. Organizations facing global competition seek out creative employees, but they are also eager to cut costs by eliminating as many routine jobs as possible. The net result is that some people are better off than ever, while others worry about holding their jobs and struggle to make ends meet—a trend that Chapter 11 ("Social Class in the United States") explores in detail.

U.S. organizations are the envy of the world for their productive efficiency. For example, there are few places on Earth where the mail arrives as quickly and dependably as it does in this country. But we should remember that the future is far brighter for some workers than for others. In addition, as the Controversy & Debate box on page 200 explains, organizations pose an increasing threat to our privacy—something to keep in mind as we envision our organizational future.

This new data center for the National Security Administration (NSA) in Utah will have the capacity to store a hundred times more data than humanity has created in the entire history of the computer. The NSA's pattern of monitoring telephone calls and emails caused national alarm in 2013, sparking criticism that this practice represents a large loss of personal privacy. How much are you willing to allow government officials to oversee your personal communications with the goal of keeping terrorism at bay?

Seeing Sociology in Everyday Life

What have we learned about the way modern society is organized?

This chapter explains that since the opening of the first McDonald's restaurant in 1948, the principles that underlie the fast-food industry—efficiency, predictability, uniformity, and control—have spread to many aspects of our everyday lives. Here is a chance to identify aspects of McDonaldization in several familiar routines. In each of the two photos on page 203, can you identify specific elements of McDonaldization? That is, in what ways does the organizational pattern or the technology involved increase efficiency, predictability, uniformity, and control? In the photo below, what elements do you see that are clearly not McDonaldization? Why?

Small, neighborhood businesses like this one were once the rule in the United States. But the number of "mom and pop" businesses is declining as "big box" discount stores and fast-food chains expand. Why are small stores disappearing? What social qualities of these stores are we losing in the process?

Automated teller machines became common in the United States in the early 1970s. A customer with an electronic identification card can complete certain banking operations (such as withdrawing cash) without having to deal with a human bank teller. What makes the ATM one example of McDonaldization? Do you like using ATMs? Why or why not?

At checkout counters in many supermarkets, customers lift each product through a laser scanner linked to a computer in order to identify what the product is and what it costs. The customer then inserts a credit or debit card to pay for the purchases.

HINT This process, which is described as the "McDonaldization of society," has made our lives easier in some ways, but it has also made our society ever more impersonal, gradually diminishing our range of human contact. Also, although this organizational pattern is intended to serve human needs, it may end up doing the opposite by forcing people to live according to the demands of machines. Max Weber feared that our future would be an overly rational world in which we all might lose much of our humanity.

Seeing Sociology in *Your* Everyday Life

1. Have colleges and universities been affected by the process called McDonaldization? Do large, anonymous lecture courses qualify as an example? Why? What other examples of McDonaldization can you identify on the college campus?

2. Go to MySocLab and click on the Student Resources link to access the Sociology in Focus blog, where you can read the latest posts by a team of young sociologists who apply the sociological perspective to topics of popular culture.

3. What experiences do you have that are similar to using an ATM or a self-checkout at a discount store? Identify several examples and explain ways that you benefit from using them. In what ways might you be harmed by using these devices? Go to the "Seeing Sociology in *Your* Everyday Life" feature in MySocLab to learn more about the advantages and disadvantages of living in a highly rational society as well as suggestions about ways of making choices that enhance the quality of your own life.

Making the Grade

What Are Social Groups?

7.1 Explain the importance of various types of groups to social life. (pages 180–88)

 Watch the Video in MySocLab   Watch the Video in MySocLab

Social groups are two or more people who identify with and interact with one another.

- A **primary group** is small, personal, and lasting (examples include family and close friends).
- A **secondary group** is large, impersonal and goal-oriented, and often of shorter duration (examples include a college class or a corporation).

Elements of Group Dynamics

Group leadership

- **Instrumental leadership** focuses on completing tasks.
- **Expressive leadership** focuses on a group's well-being.
- *Authoritarian leadership* is a "take charge" style that demands obedience; *democratic leadership* includes everyone in decision making; *laissez-faire leadership* lets the group function mostly on its own.

Group conformity

- The Asch, Milgram, and Janis research shows that group members often seek agreement and may pressure one another toward conformity.
- Individuals use **reference groups**—including both **in-groups** and **out-groups**—to form attitudes and make evaluations.

Group size and diversity

- Georg Simmel described the **dyad** as intense but unstable; the **triad**, he said, is more stable but can dissolve into a dyad by excluding one member.
- Peter Blau claimed that larger groups turn inward, socially diverse groups turn outward, and physically segregated groups turn inward.

Networks are relational webs that link people with little common identity and limited interaction. Being "well connected" in networks is a valuable type of social capital.

- **Social media** based on computer technology have involved people in more and more social networks that now extend around the world

social group two or more people who identify with and interact with one another

primary group a small social group whose members share personal and lasting relationships

secondary group a large and impersonal social group whose members pursue a specific goal or activity

instrumental leadership group leadership that focuses on the completion of tasks

expressive leadership group leadership that focuses on the group's well-being

groupthink the tendency of group members to conform, resulting in a narrow view of some issue

reference group a social group that serves as a point of reference in making evaluations and decisions

in-group a social group toward which a member feels respect and loyalty

out-group a social group toward which a person feels a sense of competition or opposition

dyad a social group with two members

triad a social group with three members

network a web of weak social ties

social media technology that links people in social activity

What Are Formal Organizations?

7.2 Describe the operation of large, formal organizations. (pages 189–94)

 Explore the Map in MySocLab

Formal organizations are large secondary groups organized to achieve their goals efficiently.

- **Utilitarian organizations** pay people for their efforts (examples include a business or government agency).
- **Normative organizations** have goals people consider worthwhile (examples include voluntary associations such as the PTA).
- **Coercive organizations** are organizations people are forced to join (examples include prisons and mental hospitals).

formal organization a large secondary group organized to achieve its goals efficiently

tradition behavior, values, and beliefs passed from generation to generation

rationality a way of thinking that emphasizes deliberate, matter-of-fact calculation of the most efficient way to accomplish a particular task

rationalization of society the historical change from tradition to rationality as the main type of human thought

All formal organizations operate in an **organizational environment**, which is influenced by

- technology
- political and economic trends
- current events
- population patterns
- other organizations

Modern Formal Organizations: Bureaucracy

Bureaucracy, which Max Weber saw as the dominant type of organization in modern societies, is based on

- specialization
- hierarchy of positions
- rules and regulations
- technical competence
- impersonality
- formal, written communications

Problems of bureaucracy include

- bureaucratic alienation
- bureaucratic inefficiency and ritualism
- bureaucratic inertia
- oligarchy

organizational environment factors outside an organization that affect its operation
bureaucracy an organizational model rationally designed to perform tasks efficiently
bureaucratic ritualism a focus on rules and regulations to the point of undermining an organization's goals
bureaucratic inertia the tendency of bureaucratic organizations to perpetuate themselves
oligarchy the rule of the many by the few

The Evolution of Formal Organizations

 7.3 Summarize the changes to formal organizations over the course of the last century. (pages 194–201)

 Read the **Document** in **MySocLab**   👁 **Watch** the **Video** in **MySocLab**

scientific management Frederick Taylor's term for the application of scientific principles to the operation of a business or other large organization

Conventional Bureaucracy

- In the early 1900s, Frederick Taylor's **scientific management** applied scientific principles to increase productivity.

More Open, Flexible Organizations

- In the 1960s, Rosabeth Moss Kanter proposed that opening up organizations for all employees, especially women and other minorities, increased organizational efficiency.
- In the 1980s, global competition drew attention to the Japanese work organization's collective orientation.

The Changing Nature of Work

Recently, the rise of a postindustrial economy has created two very different types of work:

- highly skilled and creative work (examples include designers, consultants, programmers, and executives)
- low-skilled service work associated with the "McDonaldization" of society, based on efficiency, uniformity, and control (examples include jobs in fast-food restaurants and telemarketing)

The Future of Organizations: Opposing Trends

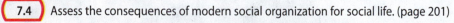 **7.4** Assess the consequences of modern social organization for social life. (page 201)

- In our postindustrial society, many organizations are evolving toward a "flatter," more flexible model that encourages worker creativity.
- At the same time, other organizations that provide services require more workers to perform "McJobs," which describes low-wage, routine work.

8 Sexuality and Society

((• Listen to Chapter 8 in MySocLab

LEARNING OBJECTIVES

8.1 Describe how sexuality is both a biological and a cultural issue.

8.2 Explain changes in sexual attitudes in the United States.

8.3 Analyze factors that shape sexual orientation.

8.4 Discuss several current controversies involving sexuality.

8.5 Apply sociology's major theories to the topic of sexuality.

the Power of Society

to shape our attitudes on social issues involving sexuality

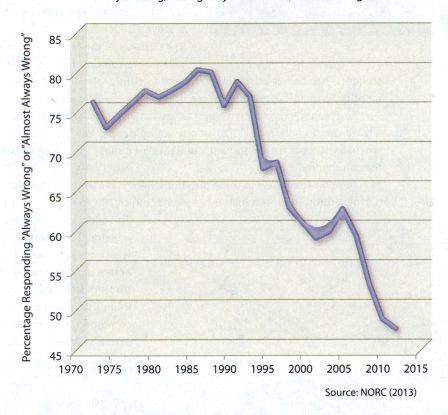

Survey Question: "What about sexual relations between two adults of the same sex—do you think it is always wrong, almost always wrong, wrong only sometimes, or not wrong at all?"

Percentage Responding "Always Wrong" or "Almost Always Wrong"

Source: NORC (2013)

Does society shape our opinions on issues involving sexuality? Back in 1973, more than three-fourths of U.S. adults expressed the opinion that sexual relations between two people of the same sex was wrong. By about 1990, however, this attitude began to change, and by 2012, such disapproval was expressed by less than half of the population. This change in public opinion about same-sex relations is a key reason for the expansion of same-sex marriage, which now has the support of most U.S. adults. Although we tend to think of our attitudes as personal choices, larger social trends are also at work.

Chapter Overview

Sex. No one can doubt that it is an important dimension of our lives. But, as this chapter explains, sex is not simply a biological process linked to reproduction. It is society, including culture and patterns of inequality, that shapes patterns of sexual behavior and gives meaning to sexuality in our everyday lives.

Pam Goodman walks along the hallway with her friends Jen Delosier and Cindy Thomas. The three young women are sophomores at Jefferson High School, in Jefferson City, a small town in the Midwest.

"What's happening after school?" Pam asks.

"Dunno," replies Jennifer. "Maybe Todd is coming over."

"Got the picture," adds Cindy. "We're so gone."

"Shut up!" Pam stammers, smiling. "I hardly know Todd."

"OK, but …" The three girls break into laughter.

It is no surprise that young people spend a lot of time thinking and talking about sex. And as the sociologist Peter Bearman discovered, sex involves more than just talk. Bearman and two colleagues (Bearman, Moody, & Stovel, 2004) conducted confidential interviews with 832 students at the high school in a midwestern town he called Jefferson City, learning that 573 (69 percent of the students) had had at least one "sexual and romantic relationship" during the previous eighteen months. So most, but not all, of these students are sexually active.

Bearman wanted to learn about sexual activity in order to understand the problem of sexually transmitted diseases (STDs) among young people. Why are the rates of STDs so high? And what can account for the sudden "outbreaks" of disease that involve dozens of young people in the community?

To find the answers to these questions, Bearman asked the students to identify their sexual partners (promising, as a matter of research ethics, not to reveal any confidential information). This allowed him to trace connections between individual students in terms of sexual activity, which revealed a surprising pattern: Sexually active students were linked to each other through networks of common partners much more than anyone might have expected. In all, common partners linked half of the sexually active students, as shown in the diagram at the left.

- Men
- Women

Other relationships
(If a pattern was observed more than once, numeral indicates frequency.)

2   2   9   12   63

Source: Bearman, Moody, & Stovel (2004).

Awareness of the connections among people can help us understand how STDs spread from one infected person to many others in a short period of time. Bearman's study also shows that research can teach us a great deal about human sexuality, which is an important dimension of social life. You will also see that sexual attitudes and behavior have changed dramatically over the past century in the United States.

Understanding Sexuality

8.1 Describe how sexuality is both a biological and a cultural issue.

How much of your thoughts and actions every day involve sexuality? If you are like most people, your answer would have to be "quite a lot," because sexuality is about much more than having sex. Sexuality is a theme found almost everywhere—in sports, on campus, in the workplace, and especially in the mass media. There is also a sex industry that includes pornography and prostitution, both of which are multibillion-dollar businesses in this country. The bottom line is that sexuality is an important part of how we think about ourselves as well as how others think about us. For this reason, there are few areas of everyday life in which sexuality does not play some part.

Although sex is a big part of everyday life, U.S. culture has long treated sex as taboo; even today, many people avoid talking about it. As a result, although sex can produce much pleasure, it also causes confusion, anxiety, and sometimes outright fear. Even scientists long considered sex off limits as a topic of research. Not until the middle of the twentieth century did researchers turn their attention to this vital dimension of social life. Since then, as this chapter explains, we have discovered a great deal about human sexuality.

Sex: A Biological Issue

Sex refers to *the biological distinction between females and males*. From a biological point of view, sex is the way the human species reproduces. A female ovum and a male sperm, each containing twenty-three matching chromosomes (biological codes that guide physical development), combine to form an embryo. To one of these pairs of chromosomes—the

sex the biological distinction between females and males

We claim that beauty is in the eye of the beholder, which suggests the importance of culture in setting standards of attractiveness. All of the people pictured here—from Kenya, Arizona, Saudi Arabia, Thailand, Ethiopia, and Ecuador—are considered beautiful by members of their own society. At the same time, sociobiologists point out that in every society on Earth, people are attracted to youthfulness. The reason, as sociobiologists see it, is that attractiveness underlies our choices about reproduction, which is most readily accomplished in early adulthood.

primary sex characteristics the genitals, organs used for reproduction

secondary sex characteristics bodily development, apart from the genitals, that distinguishes biologically mature females and males

pair that determines the child's sex—the mother contributes an X chromosome and the father contributes either an X or a Y. Should the father contribute an X chromosome, a female (XX) embryo results; a Y from the father produces a male (XY) embryo. A child's sex is thereby determined biologically at the moment of conception.

The sex of an embryo guides its development. If the embryo is male, the growth of testicular tissue starts to produce large amounts of testosterone, a hormone that triggers the development of male genitals (sex organs). If little testosterone is present, the embryo develops female genitals.

Sex and the Body

Some differences in the body set males and females apart. Right from birth, the two sexes have different **primary sex characteristics**, namely, *the genitals, organs used for reproduction*. At puberty, as people reach sexual maturity, additional sex differentiation takes place. At this point, people develop **secondary sex characteristics**, *bodily development, apart from the genitals, that distinguishes biologically mature females and males*. Mature females have wider hips for giving birth, milk-producing breasts for nurturing infants, and deposits of soft, fatty tissue that provide a reserve supply of nutrition during pregnancy and breast feeding. Mature males typically develop more muscle in the upper body, more extensive body hair, and deeper voices. Of course, these are general differences; some males are smaller and have less body hair and higher voices than some females.

Keep in mind that sex is not the same thing as gender. *Gender* is an element of culture and refers to the personal traits and patterns of behavior (including responsibilities, opportunities, and privileges) that a culture attaches to being female or male. Chapter 13 ("Gender Stratification") explains that gender is an important dimension of social inequality.

intersexual people people whose bodies (including genitals) have both female and male characteristics

transsexuals people who feel they are one sex even though biologically they are the other

Intersexual People

Sex is not always as clear-cut as has just been described. The term **intersexual people** refers to *people whose bodies (including genitals) have both female and male characteristics*. Intersexuality is both natural and very rare, involving well below 1 percent of a society's population. An older term for intersexual people is *hermaphrodites* (derived from Hermaphroditus, the child of the mythological Greek gods Hermes and Aphrodite, who embodied both sexes). A true hermaphrodite has both a female ovary and a male testis.

However, our culture demands that sex be clear-cut, a fact evident in the requirement that parents record the sex of their new child at birth as either female or male. In the United States, some people respond to intersexual individuals with confusion or even disgust. But attitudes in other societies can be quite different: The Pokot of eastern Africa, for example, pay little attention to what they consider a rare biological error, and the Navajo look on intersexual people with awe, seeing in them the full potential of both the female and the male (Geertz, 1975).

We are used to thinking of sex as a clear-cut issue of being female or male. But transsexual people do not fit such simple categories. In 2008, Thomas Beatie, age 34, became pregnant and gave birth to a healthy baby girl; since then, he has given birth to two additional children. Beatie, who was born a woman, had surgery to remove his breasts and legally changed his sex from female to male, but nonetheless chose to bear children. What is your response to cases such as this?

Transsexuals

Transsexuals are *people who feel they are one sex even though biologically they are the other*. Estimates suggest that one or two out of every 1,000 people who are born experience the feeling of being trapped in a body of the wrong sex and have a desire to be the other sex.

Some people in this situation respond to this feeling by undergoing *gender reassignment*, surgical alteration of their genitals and breasts, usually accompanied by hormone treatments. This medical process is complex and takes months or even years, but it helps many people gain a joyful sense of finally becoming on the outside the person that they feel they are on the inside (Gagné, Tewksbury, & McGaughey, 1997; Olyslager & Conway, 2007).

Sex: A Cultural Issue

Sexuality has a biological foundation. But like all aspects of human behavior, sexuality is also very much a cultural issue. Biology may explain some animals' mating rituals, but humans have no similar biological program. Although there is a biological "sex drive" in the sense that people find sex pleasurable and may want to engage in sexual activity, our biology does not dictate any specific ways of being sexual any more than our desire to eat dictates any particular foods or table manners.

Cultural Variation

Almost every sexual practice shows considerable variation from one society to another. In his pioneering research study of sexuality in the United States, Alfred Kinsey and his colleagues (1948) found that most heterosexual couples reported having intercourse in a single position—face to face, with the woman on the bottom and the man on top. Halfway around the world, however, on islands in the South Seas, most couples *never* have sex in this way. In fact, when the people of the South Seas learned of this practice from Western missionaries, they poked fun at it as the strange "missionary position."

Even the simple practice of showing affection varies from society to society. Most people in the United States kiss in public, but the Chinese kiss only in private. The French kiss publicly, often twice (once on each cheek), and the Belgians kiss three times (starting on either cheek). The Maoris of New Zealand rub noses, and most people in Nigeria don't kiss at all.

Modesty, too, is culturally variable. If a woman stepping into a bath is disturbed by someone entering the room, what body parts do you think she would cover? Helen Colton (1983) reports that an Islamic woman covers her face, a Laotian woman covers her breasts, a Samoan woman covers her navel, a Sumatran woman covers her knees, and a European woman covers her breasts with one hand and her genital area with the other.

Around the world, some societies restrict sexuality, and others are more permissive. In China, for example, norms closely regulate sexuality so that few people have sexual intercourse before their wedding day. In the United States, at least over the last few decades, intercourse prior to marriage has become the norm, and some people choose to have sex even without strong commitment.

The Incest Taboo

When it comes to sex, do all societies agree on anything? The answer is yes. One cultural universal—an element that is found in every society the world over—is the **incest taboo**, *a norm forbidding sexual relations or marriage between certain relatives*. In the United States, both law and cultural mores prohibit close relatives (including brothers and sisters, parents and children) from having sex or marrying. But in another example of cultural variation, exactly which family members are included in a society's incest taboo varies from state to state. National Map 8–1 on page 212 shows that half the states outlaw marriage between first cousins and half do not; a few states permit this practice but with restrictions (National Conference of State Legislatures, 2012).

Some societies (such as the North American Navajo) apply incest taboos only to the mother and others on her side of the family. Throughout history, in a number of countries members of the nobility intermarried with relatives. There are even societies on record (including ancient Peru and Egypt) in which noble families formed brother-sister marriages. This pattern was a strategy to keep power within a single family (Murdock, 1965, orig. 1949).

Why does at least some form of incest taboo exist in every society around the world? Part of the reason is rooted in biology: Reproduction between close relatives of any species

incest taboo a norm forbidding sexual relations or marriage between certain relatives

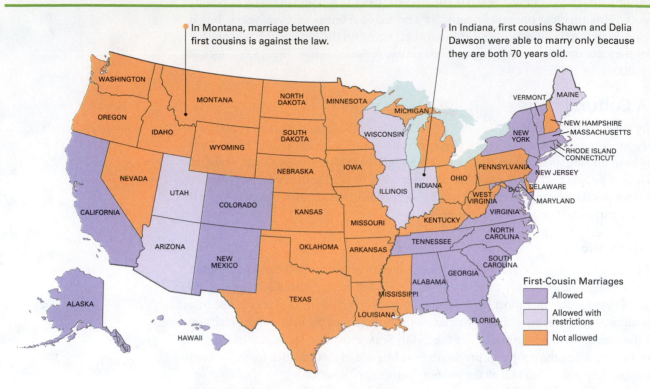

In Montana, marriage between first cousins is against the law.

In Indiana, first cousins Shawn and Delia Dawson were able to marry only because they are both 70 years old.

First-Cousin Marriages
- Allowed
- Allowed with restrictions
- Not allowed

NATIONAL MAP 8–1 First-Cousin Marriage Laws across the United States

There is no single view on first-cousin marriages in the United States: Twenty-five states forbid such unions, nineteen allow them, and six allow them with restrictions.* In general, states that permit first-cousin marriages are found in New England, the Southeast, and the Southwest.

*Of the six states that allow first-cousin marriages with restrictions, five states permit such marriages when couples are past childbearing age.

Source: National Conference of State Legislatures (2012).

raises the odds of producing offspring with mental or physical problems. But why, of all living species, do only humans observe an incest taboo? This fact suggests that controlling sexuality among close relatives is a necessary element of *social* organization. For one thing, the incest taboo limits sexual competition in families by restricting sex to spouses (ruling out, for example, a sexual relationship between parent and child). Second, because family ties define people's rights and obligations toward one another, reproduction between close relatives would hopelessly confuse kinship lines: If a mother and son had a daughter, would the child consider the male a father or a brother? Third, by requiring people to marry outside their immediate families, the incest taboo serves to integrate the larger society as people look beyond their close kin when seeking to form new families.

The incest taboo has long been a sexual norm in the United States and throughout the world. But many other sexual norms have changed over time. In the twentieth century, as the next section explains, our society experienced both a sexual revolution and a sexual counterrevolution.

Sexual Attitudes in the United States

8.2 Explain changes in sexual attitudes in the United States.

Watch in **MySocLab**
Video: *The Big Picture: Sex and Sexuality*

What do people in the United States think about sex? Our cultural attitudes about sexuality have always been somewhat contradictory. Most European immigrants arrived with rigid ideas about "correct" sexuality, typically limiting sex to reproduction within marriage. The early Puritan settlers of New England demanded strict conformity in attitudes and behavior, and they imposed severe penalties for any sexual misconduct, even if it took place in the privacy of the home. Some regulation of sexuality has continued ever since. As late as the 1960s, several states prohibited the sale of condoms in stores. Until 2003, when the Supreme Court struck them down, laws in thirteen states banned sexual acts between partners of the same sex. Even today, "fornication" laws, which forbid intercourse by unmarried couples, are still on the books in eight states.

But this is just one side of the story. As Chapter 3 ("Culture") explains, because U.S. culture is individualistic, many of us believe that people should be free to do pretty much as they wish as long as they cause no direct harm to others. The idea that what people do in the privacy of their own home is no one else's business makes sex a matter of individual freedom and personal choice.

When it comes to sexuality, is the United States restrictive or permissive? The answer is both. On one hand, many people in the United States still view holding oneself back sexually to be an important indicator of personal morality (for women even more than for men). On the other hand, sex is more and more a part of the mass media that people encounter every day. One recent study concluded that young people feel that most of the television shows they watch and the music they listen to has sexual themes. Furthermore, researchers claim that the number of scenes in television shows with sexual content has been increasing over time (Kunkel et al., 2005; DeAngellis, 2011). Within this complex framework, we now turn to changes in sexual attitudes and behavior that have taken place in the United States over the past century.

The Sexual Revolution

Over the past century, the United States witnessed profound changes in sexual attitudes and practices. The first indications of this change came with industrialization in the 1920s, as millions of women and men migrated from farms and small towns to rapidly growing cities. There, living apart from their families and meeting new people in the workplace, young people enjoyed considerable sexual freedom, one reason that decade became known as the "Roaring Twenties."

In the 1930s and 1940s, the Great Depression and World War II slowed the rate of change. But in the postwar period, after 1945, a researcher named Alfred Kinsey set the stage for what later came to be known as the *sexual revolution*. In 1948, Kinsey and his colleagues published their first study of sexuality in the United States, and it raised eyebrows everywhere. The national uproar resulted not so much from what he said as from the fact that scientists were actually studying sex, a topic many people were uneasy talking about even in the privacy of their homes.

Over the course of the past century, social attitudes in the United States have become more accepting of most aspects of human sexuality. What do you see as some of the benefits of this greater openness? What are some of the negative consequences?

Kinsey also had some interesting things to say. His two books (Kinsey, Pomeroy, & Martin, 1948; Kinsey et al., 1953) became best sellers partly because they revealed that people in the United States, on average, were far less conventional in sexual matters than most had thought. These books encouraged a new openness toward sexuality, which helped set the sexual revolution in motion.

In the late 1960s, the revolution truly came of age. Youth culture dominated public life, and expressions like "sex, drugs, and rock-and-roll" and "if it feels good, do it" summed up a new, freer attitude toward sex. The baby boom generation, born between 1946 and 1964, became the first cohort in U.S. history to grow up with the idea that sex was part of people's lives, whether they were married or not.

New technology also played a part in the sexual revolution. The birth control pill, introduced in 1960, not only prevented pregnancy but also made "protected" sex more convenient. Unlike a condom or a diaphragm, which must be applied at the time of intercourse, the pill could be taken like a daily vitamin supplement. Now women as well as men could engage in sex spontaneously without any special preparation.

Because women were historically subject to greater sexual regulation than men, the sexual revolution had special significance for them. Society's "double standard" allows (and even encourages) men to be sexually active but expects women to be virgins until marriage and faithful to their husbands afterward. The survey data in Figure 8–1 show the narrowing of the double standard as a result of the sexual revolution. Among people born between 1933 and 1942 (that is, people who are in their seventies and early eighties today), 56 percent of men but just 16 percent of women report having had two or more sexual partners by the time they reached age twenty. Compare this wide gap to the pattern among the baby boomers born between 1953 and 1962 (people now in their fifties and early sixties), who came of age after the sexual revolution. In this category, 62 percent of men and 48 percent of women say they had two or more sexual partners by age twenty (Laumann et al., 1994:198). The sexual revolution increased sexual activity overall, but it changed women's behavior more than men's.

Greater openness about sexuality develops as societies become richer and the opportunities for women increase. With these facts in mind, look for a pattern in the global use of birth control shown in Global Map 8–1 on page 215.

The Sexual Counterrevolution

The sexual revolution made sex a topic of everyday discussion and sexual activity more a matter of individual choice. However, by 1980, the climate of sexual freedom that had marked the late 1960s and 1970s was criticized by some people as evidence of our country's moral decline, and the *sexual counterrevolution* began.

Politically speaking, the sexual counterrevolution was a conservative call for a return to "family values" and a change from sexual freedom back toward what critics saw as the sexual responsibility valued by earlier generations. Critics of the sexual revolution objected not just to the idea of "free love" but also to trends such as cohabitation (heterosexual couples living together without being married) and unmarried couples having children.

Looking back, the sexual counterrevolution did not greatly change the idea that people should decide for themselves when and with whom to have a sexual relationship. But whether for moral reasons or concerns about sexually transmitted diseases, more people began limiting their number of sexual partners or choosing not to have sex at all.

Is the sexual revolution over? It is true that many people are making more careful decisions about sexuality. But as the rest of

Diversity Snapshot

- Nancy Houck, now 76 years old, has lived most of her life in a social world where men have had much more sexual freedom than women.
- Sarah Roholt, 55, is a baby boomer who feels that she and her women friends have pretty much the same sexual freedom as men.

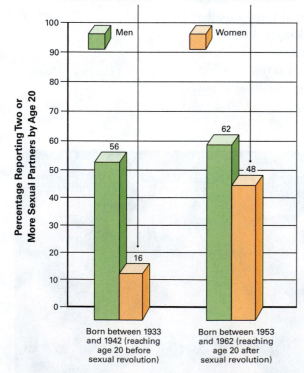

FIGURE 8–1 The Sexual Revolution: Closing the Double Standard

Although a larger share of men than women reports having had two or more sexual partners by age twenty, the sexual revolution greatly reduced this gender difference.

Source: Laumann et al. (1994:198)

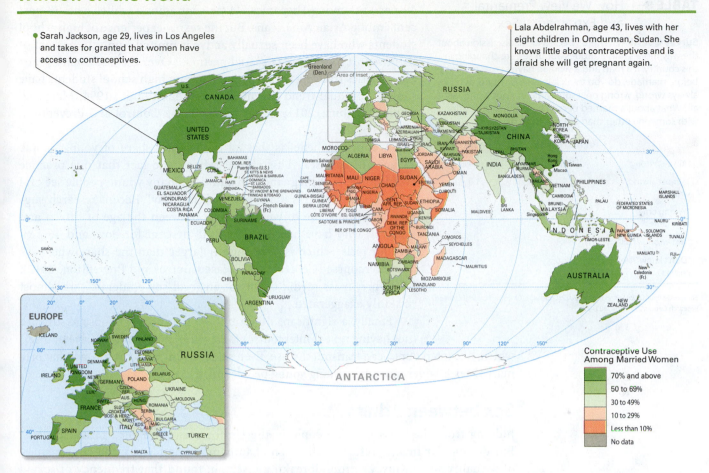

Sarah Jackson, age 29, lives in Los Angeles and takes for granted that women have access to contraceptives.

Lala Abdelrahman, age 43, lives with her eight children in Omdurman, Sudan. She knows little about contraceptives and is afraid she will get pregnant again.

Contraceptive Use Among Married Women

- 70% and above
- 50 to 69%
- 30 to 49%
- 10 to 29%
- Less than 10%
- No data

GLOBAL MAP 8–1 Contraceptive Use in Global Perspective

The map shows the percentage of married women using modern contraceptive methods (such as barrier methods, contraceptive pill, implants, injectables, intrauterine devices, or sterilization). In general, how do high-income nations differ from low-income nations? Can you explain this difference?

Sources: Data from United Nations (2008) and Population Reference Bureau (2012).

this chapter explains, the ongoing sexual revolution is evident in the fact that there is now greater acceptance of premarital sex as well as increasing tolerance for various sexual orientations.

Premarital Sex

In light of the sexual revolution and the sexual counterrevolution, how much has sexual behavior in the United States really changed? One interesting trend involves premarital sex—sexual intercourse before marriage—among young people.

Consider, first, what U.S. adults *say* about premarital intercourse. Table 8–1 on page 216 shows that about 27 percent characterize sexual relations before marriage as "always wrong" or "almost always wrong." Another 16 percent consider premarital sex "wrong only sometimes," and about 54 percent say premarital sex is "not wrong at all" (NORC, 2013:421). Public opinion is much more accepting of premarital sex today than a generation ago, but even so, our society remains divided on this issue.

Now let's look at what young people actually *do*. For women, there has been a marked change over time. The Kinsey studies reported that among people born in the early 1900s, about 50 percent of men but just 6 percent of women had had premarital sexual intercourse before age nineteen. Studies of baby boomers, born after World War II, show a slight increase in premarital intercourse among men and a large increase—to about one-third—among women. The most recent studies show that 47 percent of high school students have had premarital sexual intercourse. Broken down by race and

TABLE 8–1 How We View Premarital and Extramarital Sex

Survey Question: "There's been a lot of discussion about the way morals and attitudes about sex are changing in this country. If a man and a woman have sexual relations before marriage, do you think it is always wrong, almost always wrong, wrong only sometimes, or not wrong at all? What about a married person having sexual relations with someone other than the marriage partner?"

	Premarital Sex	Extramarital Sex
"Always wrong"	21.0%	78.4%
"Almost always wrong"	5.5	11.9
"Wrong only sometimes"	15.8	6.7
"Not wrong at all"	54.1	1.2
"Don't know"/No answer	3.6	1.8

Source: *General Social Surveys, 1972–2012: Codebook* (Chicago: National Opinion Research Center, 2013), pp. 421–22.

ethnicity, this share is 60 percent among African American students, 49 percent among Hispanics, 44 percent among whites, and 30 percent among Asian Americans. But the sexual experience of high school students who have been sexually active is limited—only 15 percent of them report four or more sexual partners. Over the last twenty years, the statistics tracking sexual activity among high school students have shown a gradual trend downward (Laumann et al., 1994; Martinez, Copen, & Abma, 2011; Centers for Disease Control and Prevention, 2012).

A common belief is that an even larger share of young people engages in oral sex. This choice reflects the fact that this practice avoids the risk of pregnancy; in addition, many young people see oral sex as something less than "going all the way." Recent research suggests that the share of young people between the age of fifteen and nineteen who have had oral sex is 48 percent for boys and 46 percent for girls, which is only slightly larger than the share who have had intercourse (Centers for Disease Control and Prevention, 2012). Therefore, mass media claims of an "oral sex epidemic" are almost certainly exaggerated.

Finally, a significant minority of young people choose abstinence (not having sexual intercourse). Many also choose not to have oral sex, which, like intercourse, can transmit disease. Even so, research confirms the fact that premarital sex is widely accepted among young people today.

Sex between Adults

Judging from the mass media, people in the United States are very active sexually. But do popular images reflect reality? The Laumann study (1994), the largest study of sexuality since Kinsey's groundbreaking research, found that frequency of sexual activity varies widely in the U.S. population. One-third of adults report having sex with a partner a few times a year or not at all, another one-third have sex once or several times a month, and the remaining one-third have sex with a partner two or more times a week. In short, no single stereotype accurately describes sexual activity in the United States.

Despite the widespread image of "swinging singles" promoted on television shows such as *Sex and the City,* it is married people who have sex with partners the most. Married people also report the highest level of satisfaction—both emotional and physical—with their partners (Laumann et al., 1994).

Extramarital Sex

What about married people having sex outside of marriage? This practice, commonly called "adultery" (sociologists prefer the more neutral term *extramarital sex*), is widely condemned. Table 8–1 shows that about 90 percent of U.S. adults consider a married person having sex with someone other than the marital partner "always wrong" or "almost always wrong." The norm of sexual fidelity within marriage has been and remains a strong element of U.S. culture.

But, of course, actual behavior does not always live up to the cultural ideal. Research suggests that about 17 percent of married people report having been sexually unfaithful to a spouse. Researchers also report that this share is higher among men (about 19 percent) than among women (about 12 percent). Stating this the other way around, 81 percent of men and 88 percent of women remain sexually faithful to their partners throughout their married lives. Research indicates that the incidence of extramarital sex is higher among the young than the old, higher among people of low social position than among those who are well off, higher among those who report no religious affiliation and, as we might expect, also higher among those who report a low level of happiness in their marriage (Laumann et al., 1994:214; Smith, 2006; NORC, 2013:2549).

Sex over the Life Course

Patterns of sexual activity change with age. In the United States, most young men and women become sexually active by the age of seventeen. By the time they reach their mid-twenties, about 90 percent of both women and men report being sexually active with a partner at least once during the past year (Reece et al., 2010; Chandra et al., 2011; Centers for Disease Control and Prevention, 2012).

Overall, adults report having sexual intercourse about sixty-two times a year, which is slightly more often than once a week. Young adults report the highest frequency of sexual intercourse at eighty-four times per year. This number falls to sixty-four times for adults in their forties and declines further to about ten times per year for adults in their seventies.

From another angle, by about age sixty, less than half of adults (54 percent of men and 42 percent of women) say they have had sexual intercourse one or more times during the past year. By age seventy, just 43 percent of men and 22 percent of women report the same behavior (Smith, 2006; Reece et al., 2010).

Sexual Orientation

8.3 Analyze factors that shape sexual orientation.

Watch in **MySocLab**
Video: *Social Inequalities: Sex and Sexuality*

Sexual orientation is *a person's romantic and emotional attraction to another person.* The norm in all human societies is **heterosexuality** (*hetero* is Greek for "the other of two"), meaning *sexual attraction to someone of the other sex.* Yet in every society, a significant share of people experience **homosexuality** (*homo* is Greek for "the same"), *sexual attraction to someone of the same sex.* Keep in mind that people do not necessarily fall into just one of these categories; they may have varying degrees of attraction to both sexes.

The idea that sexual orientation is not always clear-cut is confirmed by the existence of **bisexuality**, *sexual attraction to people of both sexes.* Some bisexual people are equally attracted to males and females; many others are more attracted to one sex than the other. Finally, **asexuality** refers to *a lack of sexual attraction to people of either sex.* Figure 8–2 shows each of these sexual orientations in relation to the others.

It is important to remember that sexual *attraction* is not the same thing as sexual *behavior.* Many people, perhaps even most people, have experienced attraction to someone of the same sex, but far fewer ever engage in same-sex behavior. This is in large part because our culture discourages such actions.

In the United States and around the world, heterosexuality emerged as the norm because, biologically speaking, heterosexual relations permit human reproduction. Even so, most societies tolerate homosexuality, and some have even celebrated it. Among the ancient Greeks, for example, upper-class men considered homosexuality the highest form of relationship, partly because they looked down on women as intellectually inferior. As men saw it, heterosexuality was necessary only so they could have children, and "real" men preferred homosexual relations (Kluckhohn, 1948; Ford & Beach, 1951; Greenberg, 1988).

What Gives Us a Sexual Orientation?

The question of how people come to have a particular sexual orientation is strongly debated. The arguments cluster into two general positions: sexual orientation as a product of society and sexual orientation as a product of biology.

Diversity Snapshot

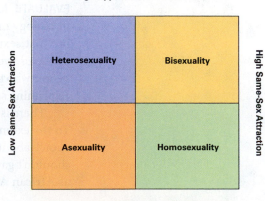

FIGURE 8–2 Four Sexual Orientations

A person's levels of same-sex attraction and opposite-sex attraction are two distinct dimensions that combine in various ways to produce four major sexual orientations.

Source: Adapted from Storms (1980).

Sexual Orientation: A Product of Society

This approach argues that people in any society attach meanings to sexual activity, and these meanings differ from place to place and over time. As Michel Foucault (1990, orig. 1978) points out, for example, there was no distinct category of people called "homosexuals" until just over a century ago, when scientists and eventually the public as a whole began defining people that way. Throughout history, many people no doubt had what we would call "homosexual experiences," but neither they nor others saw in this behavior the basis for any special identity.

Anthropological studies show that patterns of homosexuality differ from one society to another. In Siberia, for example, the Chukchee Eskimo have a practice in which one man dresses as a female and does a woman's work. The Sambia, who dwell in the Eastern Highlands of New Guinea, have a ritual in which young boys perform oral sex on older men in the belief that eating semen will make them more masculine. In southeastern Mexico, a region in which ancient religions recognize gods who are both female and male, the local culture defines people not only as female and male but also as *muxes* (MOO-shays), a third sexual category. *Muxes* are men who dress and act as women, some only on ritual occasions, some all the time. Such diversity around the world shows that sexual expression is not fixed by human biology but is socially constructed (Murray & Roscoe, 1998; Blackwood & Wieringa, 1999; Rosenberg, 2008).

Sexual Orientation: A Product of Biology

A growing body of evidence suggests that sexual orientation is innate, or rooted in human biology, in much the same way that people are born right-handed or left-handed. Arguing this position, Simon LeVay (1993) links sexual orientation to the structure of a person's brain. LeVay studied the brains of both homosexual and heterosexual men and found a small but important difference in the size of the hypothalamus, a part of the brain that regulates hormones. Such an anatomical difference, he claims, plays a part in shaping a person's sexual orientation.

Genetics may also influence sexual orientation. One study of forty-four pairs of brothers, all homosexual, found that thirty-three pairs had a distinctive genetic pattern involving the X chromosome. The gay brothers also had an unusually high number of gay male relatives—but only on their mother's side. Such evidence leads some researchers to think there may be a "gay gene" located on the X chromosome (Hamer & Copeland, 1994).

One factor that has advanced the social acceptance of homosexuality is the inclusion of openly gay characters in the mass media, especially films and television shows. In the popular musical-drama series *Glee*, Chris Colfer plays Kurt Hummel, who came out as being gay during the first season of the show. How would you assess the portrayal of homosexuality in the mass media?

EVALUATE Mounting evidence supports the conclusion that sexual orientation is rooted in biology or "nature," although it is also likely that nurture plays some part. Remember that sexual orientation is not a matter of neat categories. Most people who think of themselves as homosexual have had some heterosexual experiences, just as many people who think of themselves as heterosexual have had some homosexual experiences. Explaining sexual orientation, then, is not easy.

There is also a political issue here with great importance for gay men and lesbians. To the extent that sexual orientation is based in biology, homosexuals have no more choice about their sexual orientation than they do about their skin color. If this is so, shouldn't gay men and lesbians expect the same legal protection from discrimination as African Americans?

sexual orientation a person's romantic and emotional attraction to another person

heterosexuality sexual attraction to someone of the other sex

homosexuality sexual attraction to someone of the same sex

bisexuality sexual attraction to people of both sexes

asexuality a lack of sexual attraction to people of either sex

What evidence supports the position that sexual behavior is constructed by society? What evidence supports the position that sexual orientation is rooted in biology?

For a closer look at the acceptance of sexual identity in central Mexico, **Read More** in **MySocLab**, *A Third Gender: The Muxes of Mexico*

How Many Gay People Are There?

What share of our population is gay? This is a difficult question to answer because, as noted earlier, sexual orientation is not a matter of neat categories. In addition, not all people are willing to reveal their sexuality to strangers or even to family members. Kinsey estimated that about 4 percent of males and 2 percent of females have an exclusively same-sex orientation, although he pointed out that most people experience same-sex attraction at some point in their lives.

The results of research surveys show that how homosexuality is defined makes a big difference in the size of the homosexual population. Some social scientists put the gay share of the population at 10 percent. This is about the share of U.S. adults who say that they have *ever* felt any sexual attraction to a person of the same sex. But feeling some sexual attraction and acting on it are two different issues. As Figure 8–3 shows, 5.6 percent of U.S. men and 12.7 percent of U.S. women between the ages of fifteen and forty-four reported engaging in homosexual activity *at some time in their lives*. Then there is the issue of sexual identity. When asked how they define themselves in terms of sexual orientation, just 1.7 percent of men and 1.1 percent of women said that they defined themselves as "partly" or "entirely" homosexual.

In recent surveys, 1.1 percent of men and 3.5 percent of women described themselves as bisexual. But bisexual experiences appear to be fairly common (at least for a time) among younger people, especially on college and university campuses (Laumann et al., 1994; Leland, 1995; Reece et al., 2010; Chandra et al., 2011). Many bisexuals do not think of themselves as either gay or straight, and their behavior reflects aspects of both gay and straight living.

The Gay Rights Movement

In recent decades, public opinion about sexual orientation has shown a remarkable change. In the United States and in much of the world, public attitudes toward homosexuality have been moving toward greater acceptance. Back in 1973, as shown in the Power of Society figure at the beginning of this chapter, about three-fourths of adults in the United States claimed that homosexual relations were "always wrong" or "almost always wrong." Although that percentage changed little during the 1970s and 1980s, by 2012 it had dropped to 46 percent (NORC, 2013:422; Pew Research Center, 2012). Among college students, who are typically more tolerant of homosexuality than the general population, we see a similar trend toward acceptance. In 1980, as Figure 8–4 on page 220 shows, about half of college students supported laws prohibiting homosexual relationships; in the following decades, that share declined dramatically. The most recent surveys on this issue asked students whether they supported same-sex couples having the legal right to marry; by 2012, as the figure shows, three-quarters of college students claimed to support legal same-sex marriage (Astin et al., 2002; Pryor et al., 2013).

In large measure, this change was brought about by the gay rights movement, which began in the middle of the twentieth century. Up to that time, most people in this country did not discuss homosexuality, and it was common for employers (including the federal government and the armed forces) to fire anyone who was gay or lesbian (or was even *accused* of being gay). Mental health professionals, too, took a hard line, describing homosexual people as "sick" and sometimes placing them in mental hospitals where, it was hoped, they might be "cured."

Diversity Snapshot

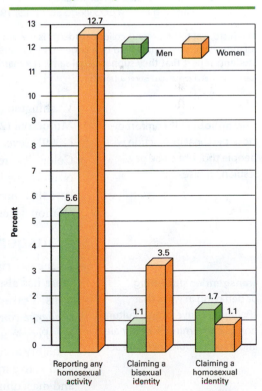

FIGURE 8–3 Share of the Population That Is Bisexual or Homosexual

Although more women than men report having had a homosexual experience, more men than women claim to have a homosexual identity.

Source: Adapted from Chandra et al. (2011).

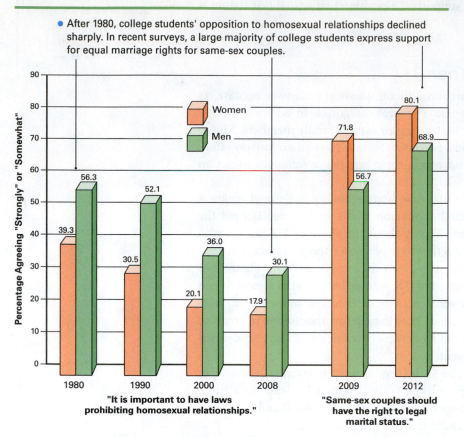

- After 1980, college students' opposition to homosexual relationships declined sharply. In recent surveys, a large majority of college students express support for equal marriage rights for same-sex couples.

FIGURE 8–4 Attitudes about Homosexual Relationships and Same-Sex Marriage among First-Year College Students, 1980–2012

The historical trend among college students is toward greater tolerance of homosexual relationships, a view now held by a large majority. Three-quarters of first-year college students report that they support legal same-sex marriage.

Sources: Astin et al. (2002) and Pryor et al. (2013).

homophobia discomfort over close personal interaction with people thought to be gay, lesbian, or bisexual

transgender appearing or behaving in ways that challenge conventional cultural norms concerning how females and males should look and act

Facing such prejudice, it is no surprise that most lesbians and gay men remained "in the closet," closely guarding the secret of their sexual orientation. But the gay rights movement gained strength during the 1960s. One early milestone occurred in 1973, when the American Psychiatric Association (APA) declared that it would no longer define homosexuality as an illness; the organization stated that it was nothing more than "a form of sexual behavior." In 2009, the APA went a step further and condemned the use of psychological therapy in an effort to make gay people straight (Cracy, 2009).

The gay rights movement also began using the term **homophobia** to describe *discomfort over close personal interaction with people thought to be gay, lesbian, or bisexual* (Weinberg, 1973). The concept of homophobia turns the tables on society: Instead of asking "What's wrong with gay people?" the question becomes "What's wrong with people who can't accept a different sexual orientation?"

In 2004, a number of cities and towns in the United States began to allow gay couples to marry, although these unions were later declared illegal. But gay marriage became legal in Massachusetts in 2004 and now it is also legal in Connecticut (2008), Vermont (2009), Iowa (2009), New Hampshire (2009), New York (2011), Washington (2012), Maryland (2012), Maine (2012), Delaware (2013), Rhode Island (2013), Minnesota (2013), California (briefly in 2008, then in 2013), and the District of Columbia (2009). Several other states—New Jersey, Oregon, Nevada, Wisconsin, Illinois, Hawaii, and Colorado—recognize either "domestic partnerships" or "civil unions," which provide most or all of the benefits of marriage. At the same time, a majority of the states have enacted laws that forbid gay marriage and prohibit recognizing gay marriages performed elsewhere (National Conference of State Legislatures, 2013).

Transgender

As the gay rights movement has gained acceptance for gay, lesbian, and bisexual people, there has also been greater tolerance of people who challenge conventional gender patterns. **Transgender** is a broad concept that refers to *appearing or behaving in ways that challenge conventional cultural norms concerning how females and males should look and act*. People in the transgender community do not think of themselves or express their sexuality according to conventional standards. In other words, transgender people disregard conventional ideas about femininity or masculinity in favor of combining feminine and masculine traits or perhaps embodying something entirely different.

Transgender is not a sexual orientation. Transgender people may think of themselves as gay or lesbian, heterosexual, bisexual, asexual, as some combination of these categories, or in entirely different terms.

Researchers estimate that about three in every 1,000 adults in the United States have a transgender identity. This amounts to about 700,000 people (Gates, 2011). It is becoming common to speak about the lesbian, gay, bisexual, and transgender (LGBT) population. Because someone may identify with more than one of these categories, no exact number can be placed on the size of the LGBT population. But estimates suggest that almost 4 percent of the U.S. adult population—or about 9 million people—are within the LGBT community (Gates, 2011).

Sexual Issues and Controversies

(8.4) Discuss several current controversies involving sexuality.

Sexuality lies at the heart of a number of controversies in the United States today. Here we take a look at four key issues: teen pregnancy, pornography, prostitution, and sexual violence.

Teen Pregnancy

Because being sexually active carries the risk of pregnancy, this behavior demands a high level of personal responsibility. Teenagers may be biologically mature enough to conceive, but many are not emotionally mature enough to appreciate the consequences of their actions. Surveys lead researchers to estimate that there are some 768,000 teen pregnancies in the United States each year, most of them unplanned. This country's rate of births to teens is higher than that of most other high-income countries and is twice the rate in Canada (Alan Guttmacher Institute, 2012; Ventura et al., 2012).

Among people in all racial and ethnic categories, low levels of parental education and income sharply increase the likelihood that a young woman will become sexually active and have an unplanned child. In addition, compared to young women who live with both biological parents, those who live with a mother and a stepfather or in some other family arrangement have triple the odds of having a child by age nineteen. To add to the challenge, having unplanned children raises the risk that young women (as well as young fathers-to-be) will not complete high school and will end up living in poverty (Martinez, Copen, & Abma, 2011).

Did the sexual revolution raise the level of teenage pregnancy? Perhaps surprisingly, the answer is no. The rate of pregnancy among U.S. teens in 1950 was higher than it is today, partly because people back then married at a younger age. Because abortion was against the law, many pregnancies led to quick marriages. As a result, many teens became pregnant, but almost 90 percent of these women were already married or married soon after. In recent years, the teenage pregnancy rate has fallen to its lowest level in decades. However, although this rate is lower, about 80 percent of these women are unmarried. In a slight majority (58 percent) of such cases, the women keep their babies; in the remainder, they have abortions (26 percent) or miscarriages (17 percent) (Ventura et al., 2012). National Map 8–2 on page 222 shows the pregnancy rates for women between the ages of fifteen and nineteen throughout the United States.

pornography sexually explicit material intended to cause sexual arousal

Pornography

Pornography is *sexually explicit material intended to cause sexual arousal*. But what is or is not pornographic has long been a matter of debate. Recognizing that different people view portrayals of sexuality differently, the U.S. Supreme Court gives local communities the power to decide for themselves what violates "community standards" of decency and lacks "redeeming social value."

Definitions aside, pornography is very popular in the United States: sexually

Pregnancy among unmarried teenage women, once a social taboo, has become part of the mass media with shows like MTV's *Teen Mom* and *16 and Pregnant*. Such shows clearly convey the many challenges that face young mothers-to-be. Would you expect these shows to have any effect on the country's teen pregnancy rate? Explain.

Explore the percentage of fifteen- to seventeen-year-olds who are married in your local community and in counties across the United States in **MySocLab**

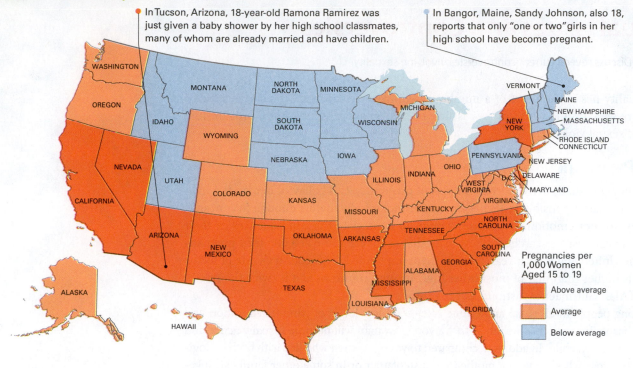

In Tucson, Arizona, 18-year-old Ramona Ramirez was just given a baby shower by her high school classmates, many of whom are already married and have children.

In Bangor, Maine, Sandy Johnson, also 18, reports that only "one or two" girls in her high school have become pregnant.

Pregnancies per 1,000 Women Aged 15 to 19

- Above average
- Average
- Below average

NATIONAL MAP 8–2 Teenage Pregnancy Rates across the United States

The map shows pregnancy rates for women aged fifteen to nineteen in 2010. In what regions of the country are rates high? Where are they low? What explanation can you offer for these patterns?

Source: Alan Guttmacher Institute (2010).

explicit videos, movies, and magazines, telephone "sex lines," and thousands of Internet websites make up a thriving industry that takes in approximately $10 billion each year. Most pornography in the United States is created in California, and the vast majority of consumers of pornography are men (Steinhauer, 2008).

Traditionally, people have criticized pornography on *moral* grounds. As national surveys confirm, 60 percent of U.S. adults are concerned that "sexual materials lead to a breakdown of morals" (NORC, 2013:423). Today, however, pornography is also seen as a *power* issue because most of it degrades women, portraying them as the sexual playthings of men.

Some critics also claim that pornography is a cause of violence against women. Although it is difficult to prove a scientific cause-and-effect relationship between what people view and how they act, the public shares a concern about pornography and violence, with almost half of adults holding the opinion that pornography encourages people to commit rape (NORC, 2013:424).

Although people everywhere object to sexual material they find offensive, many also value the principle of free speech and the protection of artistic expression. Nevertheless, pressure to restrict pornography is building from an unlikely coalition of conservatives (who oppose pornography on moral grounds) and liberals (who condemn it for political reasons).

Prostitution

prostitution the selling of sexual services

Prostitution is *the selling of sexual services*. Often called "the world's oldest profession," prostitution has been widespread throughout recorded history. In the United States today, about one in eleven adult men reports having paid for sex at some time (NORC, 2013). Because most people think of sex as an expression of intimacy between two people, they find the idea of sex for money disturbing. As a result, prostitution is against the law everywhere in the United States except for parts of rural Nevada.

Around the world, prostitution is most common in poor countries, where patriarchy is strong and traditional cultural norms limit women's ability to earn a living.

Types of Prostitution

Most prostitutes (many prefer the morally neutral term "sex workers") are women, and they fall into different categories. *Call girls* are elite prostitutes, typically young, attractive, and well-educated women who arrange their own "dates" with clients by texting or telephone. The classified pages of any large city newspaper contain numerous ads for "escort services," by which women (and sometimes men) offer both companionship and sex for a fee.

In the middle category are prostitutes who are employed in "massage parlors" or brothels under the control of managers. These sex workers have less choice about their clients, receive less money for their services, and get to keep no more than half of the money they earn.

At the bottom of the hierarchy are *streetwalkers,* women and men who "work the streets" of large cities around the country. Some female streetwalkers are under the control of male pimps who take most of their earnings. Many others are people with a substance addiction who sell sex in order to buy drugs. Both types of people are at high risk of becoming the victims of violence (Davidson, 1998; Estes, 2001).

The lives of sex workers, then, are diverse, with some earning more than others and some at greater risk of violence. But studies point to one thing that most of these women have in common: They consider their work degrading. As one researcher suggested, one minute the sex worker is adored as "the most beautiful woman," while the next she is condemned as a "slut" (Barton, 2006).

Most prostitutes offer heterosexual services. However, gay male prostitutes also trade sex for money. Researchers report that many gay prostitutes end up selling sex after having suffered rejection by family and friends because of their sexual orientation (Weisberg, 1985; Boyer, 1989; Kruks, 1991).

Read in **MySocLab**
Document: *Human Rights, Sex Trafficking, and Prostitution* by Alice Leuchtag

A Victimless Crime?

Prostitution is against the law almost everywhere in the United States, but many people consider it a *victimless crime* (defined in Chapter 9, "Deviance," as a crime in which there is no obvious victim). As a result, instead of enforcing prostitution laws all the time, police stage only occasional crackdowns. This policy reflects a desire to control prostitution while also recognizing that it is impossible to eliminate it entirely.

Many people take a "live and let live" attitude about prostitution and say that adults ought to be able to do as they please so long as no one is harmed or forced to do anything. But is prostitution really victimless? The sex trade subjects many women to kidnapping, emotional abuse, and outright violence and also plays a part in spreading sexually transmitted diseases, including AIDS. In addition, many poor women—especially in low-income nations—become trapped in a life of selling sex. Thailand, in Southeast Asia, has as many as 2 million prostitutes, representing about 10 percent of all women in the labor force. The younger the person is who begins to work in prostitution, the greater the risks of harm. About half of the women working as prostitutes in Thailand are teenagers—many begin working before they even reach their teens—and these women typically suffer physical and emotional abuse and run a high risk of becoming infected with HIV (Wonders & Michalowski, 2001; Kapstein, 2006; UNAIDS, 2010; Silverman, 2011).

In the past, the focus of attention has been on the women who earn money as sex workers. But prostitution would not exist at all if it were not for demand on the part of men. For this reason, law enforcement is now more likely to target "Johns" when they attempt to buy sex.

Sexual Violence: Rape and Date Rape

Ideally, sexual activity occurs within a loving relationship between consenting adults. In reality, however, sex can be twisted by hate and violence. Here we consider two types of sexual violence: rape and date rape.

Watch in **MySocLab**
Video: *Sociology on the Job: Sex and Sexuality*

Experts agree that one factor that contributes to the problem of sexual violence on the college campus is the widespread use of alcoholic beverages. What policies are in force on your campus to discourage the kind of drinking that leads to one person imposing sex on another?

Rape

Although some people think rape is motivated only by a desire for sex, it is actually an expression of power—a violent act that uses sex to hurt, humiliate, or control another person. According to the U.S. Department of Justice (2012), more than 80,000 women each year report to the police that they have been raped. This reflects only the reported cases; the actual number of rapes is almost certainly several times higher.

The official government definition of rape is "the carnal knowledge of a female forcibly and against her will." Thus official rape statistics include only victims who are women. But men, too, are raped—in perhaps 15 percent of all cases. Most men who rape men are not homosexual; they are heterosexuals who are motivated by a desire not for sex but to dominate another person.

Date Rape

A common myth is that rape involves strangers. In reality, however, only about 30 percent of rapes fit this pattern. About 70 percent of known cases of rape involve people who know one another—more often than not, pretty well—and these crimes usually take place in familiar surroundings, especially the home and the campus. For this reason, the term "date rape" or "acquaintance rape" is used to refer to forcible sexual violence against women by men they know (Laumann et al., 1994; U.S. Department of Justice, 2012).

A second myth, often linked to date rape, is that the woman must have done something to encourage the man and made him think she wanted to have sex. Perhaps the victim agreed to go out with the offender. Maybe she even invited him into her room. But, of course, acting in this way no more justifies rape than it would any other type of physical assault.

Although rape is a physical attack, it often leaves emotional and psychological scars. Beyond the brutality of being physically violated, rape by an acquaintance also undermines a victim's sense of trust. Psychological scars are especially serious among the two-thirds of rape victims who are under eighteen and even more so among the one-third who are under the age of twelve. The home is no refuge from rape: One-third of all victims under the age of eighteen are attacked by their own fathers or stepfathers (Snyder, 2000).

How common is date rape? One study found that about 9 percent of a sample of high school students in the United States reported being the victim of sexual or physical violence inflicted by boys they were dating. About 12 percent of high school girls and 5 percent of high school boys reported being forced into having sexual intercourse against their will. The risk of abuse is especially high among girls who become sexually active before reaching the age of fifteen (Dickinson, 2001; Centers for Disease Control and Prevention, 2012).

Nowhere has the issue of date rape been more widely discussed in recent years than on college campuses, where the danger of date rape is high. The collegiate environment promotes easy friendships and encourages trust among young people who still have much to learn about relationships and about themselves. As the Seeing Sociology in Everyday Life box on page 225 explains, the same college environment that encourages communication provides few social norms to help guide young people's sexual experiences. To counter the problem, many schools now actively address myths about rape through on-campus workshops. In addition, greater attention is now focused on the abuse of alcohol, which increases the likelihood of sexual violence.

Seeing Sociology in Everyday Life

When Sex Is Only Sex: The Campus Culture of "Hooking Up"

Brynne: My mom told me once that she didn't have sex with my dad until after they were engaged.

Katy: I guess times have really changed!

Have you ever been in a sexual situation and not been sure of the right thing to do? Most colleges and universities highlight two important rules. First, sexual activity must take place only when both participants have given clear statements of consent. The consent principle is what makes "having sex" different from date rape. Second, no one should knowingly expose another person to a sexually transmitted disease, especially when the partner is unaware of the danger.

These rules are very important, but they say little about the larger issue of what sex *means*. For example, when is it "right" to have a sexual relationship? How well do you have to know the other person? If you do have sex, are you obligated to see the person again?

Two generations ago, there were informal rules for campus sex. Dating was considered part of the courtship process. That is, "going out" was the way in which women and men evaluated each other as possible marriage partners while they sharpened their own sense of what they wanted in a mate. Because, on average, marriage took place in the early twenties, many college students became engaged and married while they were still in school. In this cultural climate, sex was viewed by college students as part

of a relationship that carried a commitment—a serious interest in the other person as a possible marriage partner.

Today, the sexual culture of the campus is very different. Partly because people now marry much later, the culture of courtship has declined dramatically. About three-fourths of women in a national survey point to a relatively new campus pattern, the culture of "hooking up." What exactly is "hooking up"? Most describe it in words like these: "When a girl and a guy get together for a physical encounter—anything from kissing to having sex—and don't necessarily expect anything further."

Student responses to the survey suggest that hookups have three characteristics. First, most couples who hook up know little about each other. Second, a typical hookup involves people who have been drinking alcohol, usually at a campus party. Third, most women are critical of the culture of hooking up and express little satisfaction with these encounters. Certainly, some women (and men) who hook up simply walk away, happy to have enjoyed a sexual experience free of further obligation. But given the powerful emotions that sex can unleash, hooking up often leaves someone wondering what to expect next: "Will you call me tomorrow?" "Will I see you again?"

The survey asked women who had experienced a recent hookup to report how they felt about the experience a day later. A majority of respondents said they felt "awkward," about half felt "disappointed" and "confused," and one in four felt "exploited." Clearly, for many people, sex is more than a physical encounter. In addition, because today's campus climate is very sensitive to charges of sexual exploitation, there is a need for clearer standards of fair play.

What Do You Think?

1. How extensive is the pattern of hooking up on your campus?

2. What do you see as the advantages of sex without commitment? What are the disadvantages of this kind of relationship?

3. Do you think men and women are likely to answer the preceding questions differently? Explain.

Source: Based in part on Marquardt & Glenn (2001).

Theories of Sexuality

8.5 Apply sociology's major theories to the topic of sexuality.

Applying sociology's various theoretical approaches gives us a better understanding of human sexuality. The following sections discuss the three major approaches, and the Applying Theory table on page 226 highlights the key insights of each approach.

Sexuality			
	Structural-Functional Theory	**Symbolic-Interaction Theory**	**Social-Conflict and Feminist Theories**
What is the level of analysis?	Macro-level	Micro-level	Macro-level
What is the importance of sexuality for society?	Society depends on sexuality for reproduction. Society uses the incest taboo and other norms to control sexuality in order to maintain social order.	Sexual practices vary among the many cultures of the world. Some societies allow individuals more freedom than others in matters of sexual behavior.	Sexuality is linked to social inequality. U.S. society regulates women's sexuality more than men's, which is part of the larger pattern of men dominating women.
Has sexuality changed over time? How?	Yes. As advances in birth control technology separate sex from reproduction, societies relax some controls on sexuality.	Yes. The meanings people attach to virginity and other sexual matters are all socially constructed and subject to change.	Yes and no. Some sexual standards have relaxed, but society still defines women in sexual terms, just as homosexual people are harmed by society's heterosexual bias.

Structural-Functional Theory

The structural-functional approach highlights the contribution of any social pattern to the overall operation of society. Because sexuality can have such important consequences, society regulates this type of behavior.

The Need to Regulate Sexuality

From a biological point of view, sex allows our species to reproduce. But culture and social institutions regulate *with whom* people reproduce. For example, most societies condemn a married person for having sex with someone other than his or her spouse. To allow sexual passion to go unchecked would threaten family life, especially the raising of children.

The fact that the incest taboo exists everywhere shows that no society permits completely free choice in sexual partners. Reproduction by family members other than married partners would break down the system of kinship and hopelessly confuse human relationships.

Historically, the social control of sexuality was strong, mostly because sex often led to childbirth. We see these controls at work in the traditional distinction between "legitimate" reproduction (within marriage) and "illegitimate" reproduction (outside marriage). But once a society develops the technology to control births, its sexual norms become more permissive. In the United States, over the course of the twentieth century, sex moved beyond its basic reproductive function and became accepted as a form of intimacy and even recreation (Giddens, 1992).

Latent Functions: The Case of Prostitution

It is easy to see that prostitution is harmful because it spreads disease and exploits women. But are there latent functions that help explain why prostitution is so widespread? According to Kingsley Davis (1971), prostitution performs several useful functions. It is one way to meet the sexual needs of a large number of people who may not have ready access to sex, including soldiers, travelers, people who are not physically attractive, or people too poor to attract a marriage partner. Some people favor prostitution because they want sex without the "hassle" of a relationship. As a number of analysts have pointed out, "Men don't pay for *sex*; they pay so they can *leave*" (Miracle, Miracle, & Baumeister, 2003:421).

The control of women's sexuality is a common theme in human history. During the Middle Ages, Europeans devised the "chastity belt"—a metal device locked about a woman's groin that prevented sexual intercourse (and probably interfered with other bodily functions as well). While such devices are all but unknown today, the social control of sexuality continues. Can you point to examples?

EVALUATE The structural-functional approach helps us see the important part sexuality plays in the organization of society. The incest taboo and other cultural norms also suggest that society has always paid attention to who has sex with whom and, especially, who reproduces with whom.

Functionalist analysis sometimes ignores gender; when Kingsley Davis wrote of the benefits of prostitution for society, he was really talking about the benefits *to men*. In addition, the fact that sexual patterns change over time, just as they differ in remarkable ways around the world, is ignored by this perspective. To appreciate the varied and changeable character of sexuality, we now turn to the symbolic-interaction approach.

CHECK YOUR LEARNING Compared to traditional societies, why do modern societies give people more choice about matters involving sexuality?

Symbolic-Interaction Theory

The symbolic-interaction approach highlights how, as people interact, they construct everyday reality. As Chapter 6 ("Social Interaction in Everyday Life") explains, people sometimes construct very different realities, so the views of one group or society may well differ from those of another. In the same way, our understanding of sexuality can and does change over time, just as it differs from one society to another.

The Social Construction of Sexuality

Almost all social patterns involving sexuality saw considerable change over the course of the twentieth century. One good illustration is the changing importance of virginity. A century ago, our society's norm—for women, at least—was virginity before marriage. This norm was strong because there was no effective means of birth control, and virginity was the only guarantee a man had that his bride-to-be was not carrying another man's child.

Today, in a society that uses birth control to separate sex from reproduction, people define sexual activity differently. Attitudes toward sex become more permissive and, as a result, the virginity norm has weakened considerably. In the United States, among people born between 1963 and 1974, just 16.3 percent of men and 20.1 percent of women reported being virgins at first marriage (Laumann et al., 1994:503). Of course, among some categories of the population, the virginity norm is defined as more important; in others, it is less so.

In the same way, the rule that priests in the Catholic Church should be celibate is officially defended as a means to ensure that, by giving up marriage and children, a priest will have greater commitment to the work of the Church. Yet, the Catholic Church did not enact this rule until the twelfth century—more than a thousand years after Christ. Clearly, whether members of the clergy should be celibate is a matter of disagreement from one religious organization to another (Shipley, 2009).

A final example of our society's construction of sexuality involves young people. A century ago, childhood was a time of innocence in sexual matters. In recent decades, however, thinking has changed. Although few people encourage sexual activity between children, most people believe that children should be educated about sex by the time they are teenagers so that they can make intelligent choices about their behavior as they grow older.

Global Comparisons

Around the world, different societies attach different meanings to sexuality. For example, the anthropologist Ruth Benedict (1938), who spent years learning the ways of life of the Melanesian people of southeastern New Guinea, reported that adults paid little attention when young children engaged in sexual experimentation with one another. Parents in Melanesia shrugged off such activity because, before puberty, sex cannot lead to reproduction. Is it likely that most parents in the United States would respond the same way?

Sexual practices also vary from culture to culture. Male circumcision of infant boys (the practice of removing all or part of the foreskin of the penis) is common in the United States but rare in most other parts of the world. A practice sometimes referred to incorrectly as female circumcision (removal of the clitoris) is rare in the United States and much of the world but common in parts of Africa and the Middle East (Crossette, 1995; Huffman, 2000). (For more about this practice, more accurately called "female genital mutilation," see the Thinking About Diversity box on page 375.)

EVALUATE The strength of the symbolic-interaction approach lies in revealing the constructed character of familiar social patterns. Understanding that people "construct" sexuality, we can better appreciate the variety of sexual attitudes and practices found over the course of history and around the world.

One limitation of this approach, however, is that not all sexual practices are so variable. Men everywhere have always been more likely to see women in sexual terms than the other way around. Some broader social structure must be at work in a pattern that is this widespread, as we shall see in the following section, on the social-conflict approach.

CHECK YOUR LEARNING What evidence can you provide that human sexuality is socially constructed?

Social-Conflict and Feminist Theories

As you have seen in earlier chapters, the social-conflict approach (particularly the gender-conflict or feminist approach) highlights dimensions of inequality. This approach shows how sexuality both reflects patterns of social inequality and helps perpetuate them. Feminism, a social-conflict approach focusing on gender inequality, links sexuality to the domination of women by men.

Sexuality: Reflecting Social Inequality

Recall our discussion of prostitution, a practice outlawed almost everywhere in the United States. Enforcement of prostitution laws is uneven at best, especially when it comes to who

is and is not likely to be arrested. Gender bias is evident here: Although two people are involved, the record shows that police are far more likely to arrest (less powerful) female prostitutes than (more powerful) male clients. Similarly, of all women engaged in prostitution, it is streetwalkers—women with the least income and most likely to be minorities—who face the highest risk of arrest (Saint James & Alexander, 2004). We might also wonder whether so many women would be involved in prostitution in the first place if they had the economic opportunities equal to those of men.

More generally, which categories of people in U.S. society are most likely to be defined in terms of their sexuality? The answer, once again, is those with less power: women compared to men, people of color compared to whites, and gays and lesbians compared to heterosexuals. In this way, sexuality, a natural part of human life, is used by society to define some categories of people as less worthy.

Sexuality: Creating Social Inequality

Social-conflict theorists, especially feminists, point to sexuality as the root of inequality between women and men. Defining women in sexual terms amounts to devaluing them from full human beings into objects of men's interest and attention. Is it any wonder that the word *pornography* comes from the Greek word *porne*, meaning "harlot" or "prostitute"?

If men define women in sexual terms, it is easy to see pornography—almost all of which is consumed by males—as a power issue. Because pornography typically shows women focused on pleasing men, it supports the idea that men have power over women.

From a social-conflict point of view, sexuality is not so much a "natural" part of our humanity as it is a socially constructed pattern of behavior. Sexuality plays an important part in social inequality: By defining women in sexual terms, men devalue them as objects. Would you consider the behavior shown here to be "natural" or socially directed? Why?

Men have power over women in the world of reproductive health care as well. During 2012, more than 400 laws were introduced in state legislatures across the country to limit the right of a woman and her doctor to make decisions about abortion. In recent years, many state legislatures—made up mostly of men—have mandated that women must endure waiting periods, look at ultrasound images of a fetus, and undergo various medically unnecessary physical procedures before a woman and her doctor can make a decision to terminate a pregnancy. As former Michigan governor Jennifer Granholm suggests, men can better appreciate this gender-based power imbalance by imagining a legislature in which 80 percent of members were women requiring that men, before they can obtain a prescription for Viagra, present a letter from a sexual partner testifying to their inability to have an erection, or requiring men to watch an ultrasound of their testicles while listening to a doctor point to millions of "pre-human lives" that are about to end (Granholm, 2012).

Reformers such as Granholm would like to end legislation that limits women's choices. But some radical critics doubt that the element of power can ever be removed from heterosexual relations (Dworkin, 1987). Most social-conflict theorists do not object to heterosexuality, but they do agree that sexuality can and does degrade women. Our culture often describes sexuality in terms of sport (men "scoring" with women) and violence ("slamming," "banging," and "hitting on," for example, are verbs used for both fighting and sex).

Another recent development by African American feminists and people in other minority communities centers on the concept of *reproductive justice*. While many women and men have debated whether or not women should be able to obtain abortions or otherwise control their own bodies, the reproductive justice movement points out that many women are disadvantaged to the point that they really are not able to make choices about their own lives. Only when women and girls have social, economic, and political equality in the United States, in other words, will there be reproductive justice. From another angle, it is important to understand the social conditions that contribute, for example, to an abortion rate among African American women that is more than three times higher than among white women (Pickert, 2013; Ross, 2013).

Queer Theory

Finally, social-conflict theory has taken aim not only at men dominating women but also at heterosexuals dominating homosexuals. In recent years, as lesbians and gay men have sought public acceptance, a gay voice has arisen in sociology. The term **queer theory** refers to *a body of research findings that challenges the heterosexual bias in U.S. society.*

Queer theory begins with the claim that our society is characterized by **heterosexism**, *a view that labels anyone who is not heterosexual as "queer."* Our heterosexual culture victimizes a wide range of people, including gay men, lesbians, bisexuals, intersexuals, transsexuals, and even asexual people. Although most people agree that bias against women (sexism) and people of color (racism) is wrong, heterosexism is widely tolerated and sometimes well within the law. For example, U.S. military forces cannot legally discharge a female soldier simply for "acting like a woman" because this would be a clear case of gender discrimination. But, until the law changed at the end of 2010, the military forces could and did discharge women and men for homosexuality if they were sexually active.

Heterosexism is also part of everyday culture (Kitzinger, 2005). When we describe something as "sexy," for example, don't we really mean attractive to *heterosexuals*?

queer theory a body of research findings that challenges the heterosexual bias in U.S. society

heterosexism a view that labels anyone who is not heterosexual as "queer"

Watch in **MySocLab**
Video: *Social Inequalities: Sex and Sexuality*

EVALUATE The social-conflict approach shows that sexuality is both a cause and an effect of inequality. In particular, it helps us understand men's power over women and heterosexual people's domination of homosexual people.

At the same time, this approach overlooks the fact that many people do not see sexuality as a power issue. On the contrary, many couples enjoy a vital sexual relationship that deepens their commitment to one another. In addition, the social-conflict approach pays little attention to steps U.S. society has taken toward reducing inequality. Today's men are less likely to describe women as sex objects than they were a few decades ago. One of the most important issues in the workplace today is ensuring that all employees remain free from sexual harassment. Rising public

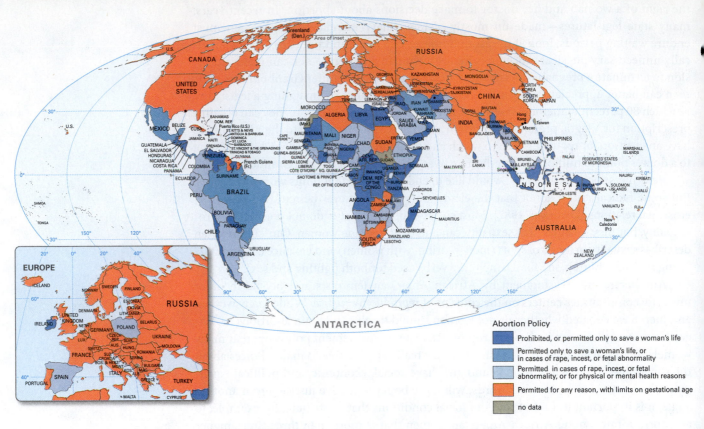

GLOBAL MAP 8–2 Women's Access to Abortion in Global Perspective

In global perspective, just sixty-eight nations permit a woman to obtain an abortion for a wide variety of reasons. Generally, these are high-income nations, including many countries in Europe and North America. What pattern do you see involving countries that place the greatest restriction on abortion?
Source: Population Reference Bureau (2012).

Abortion Policy
- Prohibited, or permitted only to save a woman's life
- Permitted only to save a woman's life, or in cases of rape, incest, or fetal abnormality
- Permitted in cases of rape, incest, or fetal abnormality, or for physical or mental health reasons
- Permitted for any reason, with limits on gestational age
- no data

concern (see Chapter 13, "Gender Stratification") has reduced the abuse of sexuality in the workplace. Likewise, there is ample evidence that the gay rights movement has secured greater opportunities and social acceptance for gay people.

CHECK YOUR LEARNING How does sexuality play a part in creating social inequality?

abortion the deliberate termination of a pregnancy

This chapter closes with a look at what is perhaps the most divisive issue involving sexuality: **abortion**, *the deliberate termination of a pregnancy*. According to global research carried out in 2008, about one in five of all pregnancies ended in abortion. In addition, researchers concluded that half of all abortions performed during that year were "unsafe." For any nation, the level of economic development is closely linked to the abortion rate. Around the world, 86 percent of all abortions took place in less economically developed countries, as did 98 percent of the "unsafe" abortions (Alan Guttmacher Institute, 2012; Sedgh et al., 2012). A major reason for the high rate of unsafe procedures is that, as Global Map 8–2 shows, most nations either prohibit or place substantial restrictions on a woman's ability to have an abortion.

In the United States, the U.S. Supreme Court has supported a woman's legal access to abortion since 1973. But the debate over this procedure—which some see as a moral issue and others see as the foundation of social equality between the sexes—goes on. There seems to be no middle ground in the debate over this controversial issue. The Controversy & Debate box on page 231 helps explain why.

Controversy & Debate

The Abortion Controversy

Frank: The abortion people are marching again across campus.

Marvin: For or against?

Frank: Both. I'm not sure which came first, but somebody said there have already been some fights…

A black van pulls up in front of the storefront in a busy section of the city. Two women get out of the front seat and cautiously look up and down the street. After a moment, one nods to the other, and they open the rear door to let a third woman out of the van. Standing to the right and left of the woman, the two quickly escort her inside the building.

This scene might describe two federal marshals taking a convict to a police station, but it is actually an account of two clinic workers helping a woman who has decided to have an abortion. Why are they so cautious? Anyone who has read the papers in recent years knows about the angry confrontations at abortion clinics across North America. Some opponents have even targeted and killed doctors who carried out abortions, some 1.2 million of which are performed in the United States each year (Ventura et al., 2012). It is one of the most hotly debated issues of our day.

Abortion has not always been so controversial. In colonial times, midwives and other healers performed abortions with little community opposition and with full approval of the law. But controversy arose about 1850, when early medical doctors wanted to eliminate the competition they faced from midwives and other traditional health providers, whose income came largely from ending pregnancies. By 1900, medical doctors had succeeded in getting every state to pass a law banning abortion.

Such laws greatly reduced the number of abortions. Those that did occur were performed "underground," as secretly as possible. Many women who wanted abortions—especially those who were poor—had little choice but to seek help from unlicensed "back alley" abortionists, sometimes with tragic results due to unsanitary conditions and the use of medically dangerous techniques.

By the 1960s, opposition to antiabortion laws was rising. In 1973, the U.S. Supreme Court made a landmark decision (in the cases of *Roe* v. *Wade* and *Doe* v. *Bolton*), striking down all state laws banning abortion. In effect, this action established a woman's legal access to abortion nationwide.

Even so, the abortion controversy continues and about 40 percent of people in the United States claim that abortion is "very important" in making a choice of political candidates (Pew Research Center, 2012). On one side of the issue are people who describe themselves as "pro-choice," supporting a woman's right to choose abortion. On the other side are those who call themselves "pro-life," opposing abortion as morally wrong; these people would like to see the Supreme Court reverse its 1973 decision.

How strong is the support for each side of the abortion controversy? A recent national survey asked a sample of adults the question "Should it be possible for a pregnant woman to obtain a

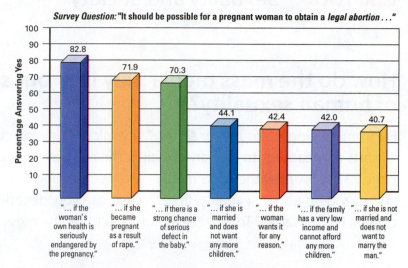

Survey Question: "It should be possible for a pregnant woman to obtain a *legal abortion* . . ."

- 82.8 — "… if the woman's own health is seriously endangered by the pregnancy."
- 71.9 — "… if she became pregnant as a result of rape."
- 70.3 — "… if there is a strong chance of serious defect in the baby."
- 44.1 — "… if she is married and does not want any more children."
- 42.4 — "… if the woman wants it for any reason."
- 42.0 — "… if the family has a very low income and cannot afford any more children."
- 40.7 — "… if she is not married and does not want to marry the man."

When Should the Law Allow a Woman to Choose Abortion?
The extent of public support for legal abortion depends on how the issue is presented.
Source: NORC (2013:407–9).

legal abortion if the woman wants it for any reason?" In response, 42 percent said yes (placing them in the pro-choice camp) and 53 percent said no (expressing the pro-life position); the remaining 5 percent offered no opinion (NORC, 2013:409).

A closer look shows that circumstances make a big difference in how people see this issue. The figure shows that large majorities of U.S. adults favor legal abortion if a pregnancy seriously threatens a woman's health, if the pregnancy is a result of rape, or if a fetus is likely to have a serious defect. The bottom line is that about 42 percent support access to abortion under *any* circumstances, but about 83 percent support access to abortion under *some* circumstances (NORC, 2013:407-9).

Many of those who take the pro-life position feel strongly that abortion amounts to killing unborn children—nearly 50 million since *Roe* v. *Wade* was passed in 1973. To them, people never have the right to end innocent life in this way. But pro-choice advocates are no less committed to the position that women must have control over their own bodies. If pregnancy decides the course of women's lives, women will never be able to compete with men on equal terms, whether it is on campus or in the workplace. Therefore, access to legal, safe abortion is a necessary condition to women's full participation in society (Alan Guttmacher Institute, 2011).

What Do You Think?

1. The more conservative, pro-life position sees abortion as a moral issue, and the more liberal, pro-choice position views abortion as a power issue. Compare these positions to how conservatives and liberals view the issue of pornography.

2. Surveys show that men and women have almost the same opinions about abortion. Does this surprise you? Why or why not?

3. Why do you think the abortion controversy is often so bitter? Do you think our nation can find a middle ground on this issue?

Seeing Sociology in Everyday Life

How do the mass media play into our society's views of human sexuality?

Far from it being a "natural" or simply "biological" concept, cultures around the world attach all sorts of meanings to human sexuality. The magazine covers presented here and on page 233 show how the mass media—in this case, popular magazines—reflect our own culture's ideas about sexuality. In each case, can you "decode" the magazine cover and explain its messages? To what extent do you think the messages are true?

Magazines like this one are found at the checkout lines of just about every supermarket and discount store in the United States. Looking just at the cover, what can you conclude about women's sexuality in our society?

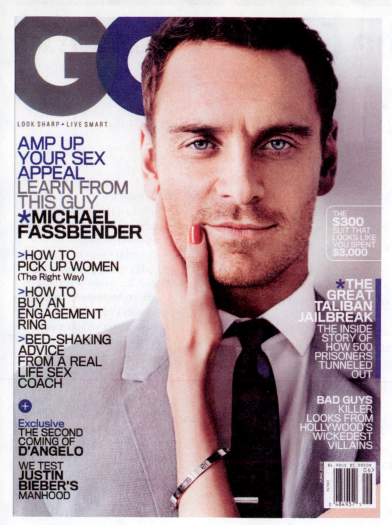

Messages about sexuality are directed to men as well as to women. Here is a recent issue of *GQ*. What messages about masculinity can you find? Do you see any evidence of heterosexual bias?

HINT The messages we get from mass media sources like these not only tell us about sexuality but also tell us what sort of people we ought to be. There is a lot of importance attached to sexuality for women, placing pressure on women to look good to men and to define life success in terms of attracting men with their sexuality. Similarly, being masculine means being successful, sophisticated, in charge, and able to attract desirable women. When the mass media endorse sexuality, it is almost always according to the norm of heterosexuality.

Seeing Sociology in *Your* Everyday Life

1. Looking at the *Cosmopolitan* cover, what evidence of heterosexual bias do you see? Explain.

2. Go to MySocLab and click on the Student Resources link to access the Sociology in Focus blog, where you can read the latest posts by a team of young sociologists who apply the sociological perspective to topics of popular culture.

3. Based on what you have read in this chapter, what evidence supports the argument that sexuality is constructed by society? For more on how sexuality is a societal issue, go to the "Seeing Sociology in *Your* Everyday Life" feature in MySocLab, where you will also find suggestions about the benefits of seeing sexuality using the sociological perspective.

Making the Grade

What Is Sexuality?

8.1 Describe how sexuality is both a biological and a cultural issue. (pages 209–12)

Sex is biological, referring to bodily differences between females and males.

Gender is cultural, referring to behavior, power, and privileges a society attaches to being female or male.

Sexuality is a **biological issue**.

- Sex is determined at conception as a male sperm joins a female ovum.
- Males and females have different genitals (*primary sex characteristics*) and bodily development (*secondary sex characteristics*).
- *Intersexual people (hermaphrodites)* have some combination of male and female genitalia.
- *Transsexual people* feel they are one sex although biologically they are the other.

Sexuality is a **cultural issue**.

- For humans, sex is a matter of cultural meaning and personal choice rather than biological programming.
- Sexual practices vary considerably from one society to another (examples include kissing, ideas about modesty, and standards of beauty).
- The *incest taboo* exists in all societies because regulating sexuality, especially reproduction, is a necessary element of social organization. Specific taboos vary from one society to another.

sex the biological distinction between females and males
primary sex characteristics the genitals, organs used for reproduction
secondary sex characteristics bodily development, apart from the genitals, that distinguishes biologically mature females and males
intersexual people people whose bodies (including genitals) have both female and male characteristics
transsexuals people who feel they are one sex even though biologically they are the other
incest taboo a norm forbidding sexual relations or marriage between certain relatives

Sexual Attitudes in the United States

8.2 Explain changes in sexual attitudes in the United States. (pages 212–17)

 Watch the Video in MySocLab

The **sexual revolution**, which peaked in the 1960s and 1970s, drew sexuality out into the open. Baby boomers were the first generation to grow up with the idea that sex was a normal part of social life.

The **sexual counterrevolution**, which began around 1980, aimed criticism at "permissiveness" and urged a return to more traditional "family values."

Beginning with the work of Alfred Kinsey, researchers have studied sexual behavior in the United States and reached many interesting conclusions:

- Premarital sexual intercourse became more common during the twentieth century.
- About 47%t of high school students in the United States have had sexual intercourse; only 15% report having had four or more sexual partners.
- Among all U.S. adults, sexual activity varies: One-third report having sex with a partner a few times a year or not at all; another one-third have sex once to several times a month; the remaining one-third have sex two or more times a week.
- Extramarital sex is widely viewed as wrong, and just 17% of married people (19% of married men and 12% of married women) report being sexually unfaithful to their spouses at some time.
- By their mid-twenties, about 90% of men and women report becoming sexually active with at least one partner; by age seventy, 43% of men and 22% of women report having had sexual intercourse during the previous year.

Sexual Orientation

8.3 Analyze factors that shape sexual orientation. (pages 217–21)

 Watch the Video in MySocLab

Sexual orientation is a person's romantic and emotional attraction to another person.
Four sexual orientations are

- heterosexuality
- homosexuality

sexual orientation a person's romantic and emotional attraction to another person
heterosexuality sexual attraction to someone of the other sex
homosexuality sexual attraction to someone of the same sex

- bisexuality
- asexuality

Most research supports the claim that sexual orientation is rooted in biology in much the same way as being right-handed or left-handed.

Sexual orientation is not a matter of neat categories because many people who think of themselves as heterosexual have homosexual experiences; the reverse is also true.

- The share of the U.S. population that is homosexual depends on how you define "homosexuality."
- About 6% of adult men and 13% of adult women report engaging in homosexual activity at some point in their lives; 1.7% of men and 1.1% of women define themselves as homosexual; 1.1% of men and 3.5% of women claim a bisexual identity.

The gay rights movement helped change public attitudes toward greater acceptance of homosexuality. Still, a substantial share (46%) of U.S. adults say homosexuality is wrong.

Transgender refers not to a sexual orientation, but to appearing or behaving in ways that challenge conventional cultural norms about how females and males should look and act.

bisexuality sexual attraction to people of both sexes
asexuality a lack of sexual attraction to people of either sex
homophobia discomfort over close personal interaction with people thought to be gay, lesbian, or bisexual
transgender appearing or behaving in ways that challenge conventional cultural norms concerning how females and males should look and act

Sexual Issues and Controversies

8.4 Discuss several current controversies involving sexuality. (pages 221–24)

 Explore the **Map** in **MySocLab**   **Read** the **Document** in **MySocLab**

 Watch the **Video** in **MySocLab**

Teen Pregnancy About 768,000 U.S. teenagers become pregnant each year. The rate of teenage pregnancy has dropped since 1950, when many teens married and had children. Today, most pregnant teens are not married and are at high risk of dropping out of school and being poor.

Pornography The law allows local communities to set standards of decency. Conservatives condemn pornography on moral grounds; liberals view pornography as a power issue, condemning it as demeaning to women.

Prostitution The selling of sexual services is illegal almost everywhere in the United States. Many people view prostitution as a victimless crime, but it victimizes women and spreads sexually transmitted diseases.

Sexual Violence More than 80,000 rapes are reported each year in the United States, but the actual number is probably several times higher. About 15% of rape cases involve men as victims. Rape is a violent crime in which victim and offender typically know one another.

Abortion Laws banned abortion in all states by 1900. Opposition to these laws rose during the 1960s, and in 1973, the U.S. Supreme Court declared these laws unconstitutional. Today, some 1.2 million abortions are performed each year. People who describe themselves as "pro-choice" support a woman's right to choose abortion; people who call themselves "pro-life" oppose abortion on moral grounds.

pornography sexually explicit material intended to cause sexual arousal
prostitution the selling of sexual services
abortion the deliberate termination of a pregnancy

Theories of Sexuality

8.5 Apply sociology's major theories to the topic of sexuality. (pages 225–30)

Structural-functional theory highlights society's need to regulate sexual activity and especially reproduction. One universal norm is the incest taboo, which keeps family relations clear.

Symbolic-interaction theory emphasizes the various meanings people attach to sexuality. The social construction of sexuality can be seen in sexual differences between societies and in changing sexual patterns over time.

Social-conflict theory links sexuality to social inequality. **Feminist theory** claims that men dominate women by devaluing them to the level of sexual objects. **Queer theory** claims our society has a heterosexual bias, defining anything different as "queer."

queer theory a body of research findings that challenges the heterosexual bias in U.S. society
heterosexism a view that labels anyone who is not heterosexual as "queer"

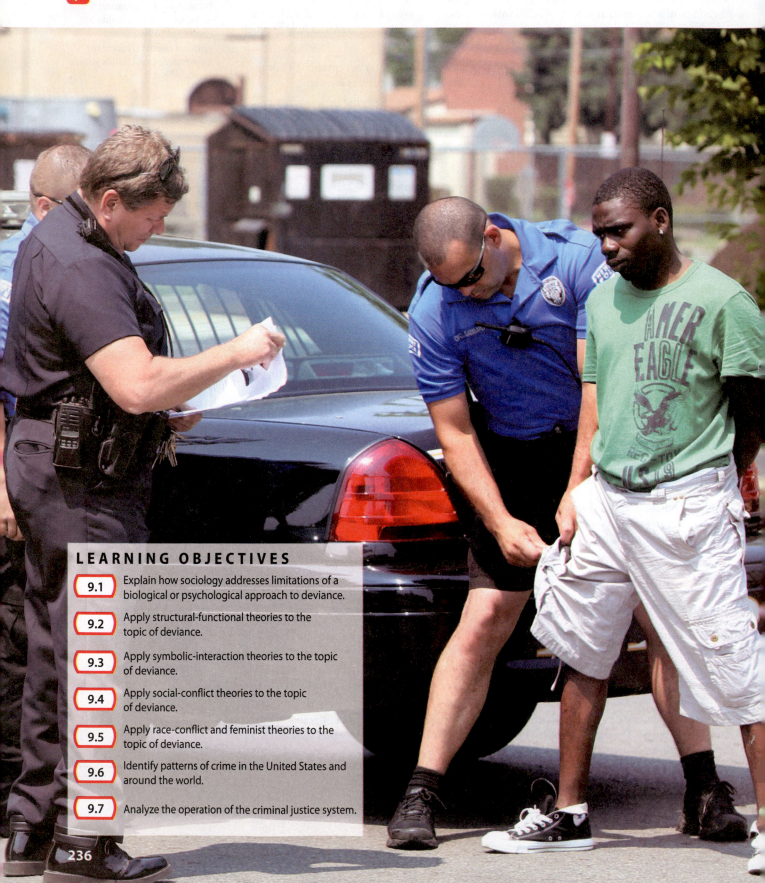

LEARNING OBJECTIVES

9.1 Explain how sociology addresses limitations of a biological or psychological approach to deviance.

9.2 Apply structural-functional theories to the topic of deviance.

9.3 Apply symbolic-interaction theories to the topic of deviance.

9.4 Apply social-conflict theories to the topic of deviance.

9.5 Apply race-conflict and feminist theories to the topic of deviance.

9.6 Identify patterns of crime in the United States and around the world.

9.7 Analyze the operation of the criminal justice system.

the Power of Society

to affect the odds of being incarcerated for using drugs

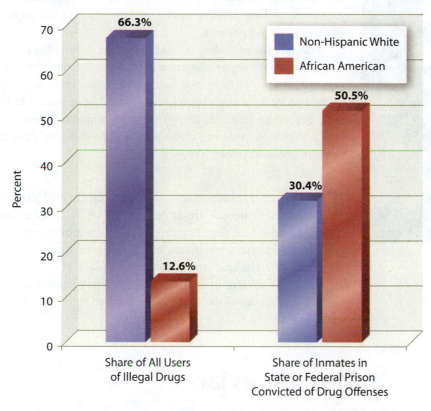

66.3%

70

60

50.5%

50

Percent

40

30.4%

30

20

12.6%

10

0

Non-Hispanic White

African American

Share of All Users
of Illegal Drugs

Share of Inmates in
State or Federal Prison
Convicted of Drug Offenses

Sources: U.S. Department of Justice (2011) and U.S.
Department of Health and Human Services (2012)

Does everyone—regardless of race—run the same risk of being sent to prison if they engage in illegal drug use? Non-Hispanic whites account for 66.3 percent of all people over the age of fifteen who report using any illegal drug. By contrast, African Americans account for 12.6 percent of all people using any illegal drug. Yet, African Americans represent just over half of all inmates in federal and state prisons locked up for drug offenses, which is four times what we might expect based on their share of the population using drugs. Non-Hispanic whites account for 30.4 percent of drug-offense inmates, which is half the expected percentage based on population share. The types of illegal drugs people use and the way our society views both drug use and race combine to place African Americans at much higher risk of being incarcerated for these offenses.

Chapter Overview

Common sense may suggest that some things are simply "right" and some things are simply "wrong." We also tend to think—or hope—that most of us, at least most of the time, know the difference. But the line between "good" and "bad" is constructed by society in a way that is far from simple. This chapter investigates how and why society encourages both conformity and deviance. This chapter also introduces the concept of crime and surveys the operation of the criminal justice system.

"I was like the guy lost in another dimension, a stranger in town, not knowing which way to go." With these words, Bruce Glover recalls the day he returned to his hometown of Detroit, Michigan, after being away for twenty-six years—a long stretch in a state prison. Glover was a young man of thirty when he was arrested for running a call girl ring. Found guilty at trial, he was given a stiff jail sentence.

Now fifty-six, he shakes his head as he says, "My mother passed while I was gone. I lost everything." On the day he walked out of prison, he had nowhere to go and no way to get there. He had no driver's license or other valid identification, which our society requires of people who are looking for a job and a place to live. Glover had no money to buy the clothes he needed to go out and begin his life all over again. He turned to a prison official and asked for help. Only with the assistance of a state agency was he finally able to get some money and locate temporary housing (Jones, 2007).

This chapter explores issues involving crime and criminals, asking why some categories of people are at higher risk of being offenders—and victims—than others. In addition, the chapter explains how our criminal justice system handles offenders and also how it tackles the broader question of why societies develop standards of right and wrong in the first place. As you will see, law is simply one part of a complex system of social control: Society teaches us all to conform to countless rules, at least most of the time. We begin our investigation by defining several basic concepts.

What Is Deviance?

9.1 Explain how sociology addresses limitations of a biological or psychological approach to deviance.

Watch in **MySocLab**
Video: *The Big Picture: Deviance*

Deviance is *the recognized violation of cultural norms.* Norms guide almost all human activities, so the concept of deviance is quite broad. One category of deviance is **crime**, *the violation of a society's formally enacted criminal law.* Even criminal deviance spans a wide range, from minor traffic violations to prostitution, sexual assault, and murder.

Most familiar examples of nonconformity are negative instances of rule breaking, such as stealing from a campus bookstore, assaulting a fellow student, or driving a car while intoxicated. But we also define especially righteous people—students who speak up too much in class or people who are overly enthusiastic about new computer technology—as deviant, even if we give them a measure of respect. What deviant actions or attitudes, whether negative or positive, have in common is some element of *difference* that causes us to think of another person as an "outsider" (Becker, 1966).

Not all deviance involves action or even choice. The very *existence* of some categories of people can be troublesome to others. To the young, elderly people may seem hopelessly "out of it," and to some whites, the mere presence of people of color may cause discomfort. Able-bodied

---

deviance the recognized violation of cultural norms

crime the violation of a society's formally enacted criminal law

people often view people with disabilities as an out-group, just as rich people may shun the poor for falling short of their high-class standards.

social control attempts by society to regulate people's thoughts and behavior

criminal justice system the organizations—police, courts, and prison officials—that respond to alleged violations of the law

Social Control

All of us are subject to **social control**, *attempts by society to regulate people's thoughts and behavior.* Often this process is informal, as when parents praise or scold their children or when friends make fun of our choice of music or style of dress. Cases of serious deviance, however, may involve the **criminal justice system**, *the organizations—police, courts, and prison officials—that respond to alleged violations of the law.*

How a society defines deviance, who is branded as deviant, and what people decide to do about deviance all have to do with the way society is organized. Only gradually, however, have people recognized that the roots of deviance are deep in society, as the chapter now explains.

The Biological Context

Chapter 5 ("Socialization") explained that a century ago, most people assumed—incorrectly, as it turns out—that human behavior was the result of biological instincts. Early interest in criminality therefore focused on biological causes. In 1876, Cesare Lombroso (1835–1909), an Italian physician who worked in prisons, theorized that criminals stand out physically, with low foreheads, prominent jaws and cheekbones, hairiness, and unusually long arms. In other words, Lombroso claimed that criminals look like our apelike ancestors.

Had Lombroso looked more carefully, he would have found the physical features he linked to criminality throughout the entire population. We now know that no physical traits distinguish criminals from noncriminals.

In the middle of the twentieth century, William Sheldon took a different approach, suggesting that general body structure might predict criminality (Sheldon, Hartl, & McDermott, 1949). He cross-checked hundreds of young men for body type and criminal history and concluded that criminality was most likely among boys with muscular, athletic builds. Sheldon Glueck and Eleanor Glueck (1950) confirmed Sheldon's conclusion but cautioned that a powerful build does not necessarily *cause* or even *predict* criminality. Parents, they suggested, tend to be somewhat distant from powerfully built sons, who in turn grow up to show less sensitivity toward others. Moreover, in a self-fulfilling prophecy, people who expect muscular boys to be bullies may act in ways that bring about the aggressive behavior they expect.

Today, researchers in the field of genetics are cautiously investigating possible links between biology and crime. Some research already suggests that such a link may exist. In 2003, scientists at the University of Wisconsin reported results of a twenty-five-year study of crime among 400 boys. The researchers collected DNA samples from each boy and noted any history of trouble with the law. The researchers concluded that genetic factors (especially defective genes that, say, make too much of an enzyme) together with environmental factors (especially abuse early in life) were strong predictors of adult crime and violence. They noted, too, that these factors together were a better predictor of crime than either one alone (Lemonick, 2003; Pinker, 2003; Cohen, 2011; Shanks, 2011).

Deviance is always a matter of difference. Deviance emerges in everyday life as we encounter people whose appearance or behavior differs from what we consider "normal." Who is the "deviant" in this photograph? From whose point of view?

EVALUATE Biological theories offer a limited explanation of crime. The best guess at present is that biological traits in combination with environmental factors explain some serious crime. Or, put another way, learning more about human genetics may help social researchers better direct their attention to specific aspects of the social environment that may encourage or discourage criminal behavior. But the biggest problem with a purely biological approach to understanding crime is that most of the actions we define as deviant are carried out by people who are biologically quite normal.

In addition, because a biological approach looks at the individual, it offers no insight into how some kinds of behaviors come to be defined as deviant in the first place. Therefore, although there is much to be learned about how human biology may affect behavior, research currently puts far greater emphasis on social influences.

CHECK YOUR LEARNING What does biological research add to our understanding of crime? What are the limitations of this approach?

Personality Factors

Like biological theories, psychological explanations of deviance focus on abnormality in the individual personality. Some personality traits are inherited, but most psychologists think that personality is shaped primarily by social experience. Deviance, then, is viewed as the result of "unsuccessful" socialization.

Classic research by Walter Reckless and Simon Dinitz (1967) illustrates the psychological approach. Reckless and Dinitz began by asking a number of teachers to categorize twelve-year-old male students as either likely or unlikely to get into trouble with the law. They then interviewed both the boys and their mothers to assess each boy's self-concept and how he related to others. Analyzing their results, Reckless and Dinitz found that the "good boys" displayed a strong conscience (what Freud called superego), could handle frustration, and identified with conventional cultural norms and values. The "bad boys," by contrast, had a weaker conscience, displayed little tolerance of frustration, and felt out of step with conventional culture.

As we might expect, the "good boys" went on to have fewer run-ins with the police than the "bad boys." Because all the boys lived in an area where delinquency was widespread, the investigators attributed staying out of trouble to a personality that controlled deviant impulses. Based on this conclusion, Reckless and Dinitz called their analysis *containment theory.*

In a more recent study, researchers followed 500 nonidentical twin boys from birth until they reached the age of thirty-two. Twins were used so that researchers could compare each of the twins to his brother controlling for social class and family environment. Observing the boys when they were young, parents, teachers, and the researchers assessed their level of self-control, ability to withstand frustration, and ability to delay gratification. Echoing the earlier conclusions of Reckless and Dinitz, the researchers found that the brother who had lower scores on these measures in childhood almost always went on to get into more trouble, including criminal activity (Moffitt et al., 2011).

EVALUATE Psychologists have shown that personality patterns have some connection to deviance. Some serious criminals are psychopaths who do not feel guilt or shame, have no fear of punishment, and have little or no sympathy for the people they harm (Herpertz & Sass, 2000). More generally, the capacity for self-control and the ability to withstand frustration do seem to be skills that promote conformity. However, as noted in the case of the biological approach, most serious crimes are committed by people whose psychological profiles are normal.

Both the biological and psychological approaches view deviance as a trait of individuals. The reason that these approaches have had limited value in explaining deviance is that wrongdoing has more to do with the organization of society. We now turn to a sociological approach, which explores where ideas of right and wrong come from, why people define some rule breakers but not others as deviant, and what role power plays in this process.

CHECK YOUR LEARNING Why do biological and psychological analyses fail to explain deviance very well?

The Social Foundations of Deviance

Although we tend to view deviance as the free choice or personal failings of individuals, all behavior—deviance as well as conformity—is shaped by society. Three social foundations of deviance identified here will be detailed later in this chapter:

1. **Deviance varies according to cultural norms.** No thought or action is inherently deviant; it becomes deviant only in relation to particular norms. Because norms vary from place to place, deviance also varies. State law permits prostitution in rural areas of Nevada, although the practice is outlawed in the rest of the United States. Medical use of marijuana is legal in eighteen states plus Washington, D.C., and illegal in other states. Just two states—Colorado and Washington—allow adults to engage in recreational use of marijuana, a practice that is illegal in other states. Drivers on a new highway in western Texas can legally travel at 85 miles per hour, a speed that will draw quick attention from police everywhere else in the country. Just two states (Utah and Hawaii) do not have any form of legal gambling; forty-eight states do. Thirty-nine states have gambling casinos, including twenty-nine that permit casinos on Indian reservations, and fourteen that permit casinos at racetracks. Text messaging while driving is legal in eleven states but against the law in thirty-six others (three other states forbid the practice for young drivers). Would you think that everyone could at least agree that fresh milk is good for you? Not so fast: Selling raw milk is legal in ten states and banned or heavily regulated in all the others (American Gaming Association, 2012; Ozersky, 2010; National Conference of State Legislatures, 2012).

   Further, most cities and towns have at least one unique law. For example, Fort Lee, New Jersey, bans texting while walking; Mobile, Alabama, outlaws the wearing of stiletto-heeled shoes; Pine Lawn, Missouri, bans saggy, "low-rider" pants; in Juneau, Alaska, it is illegal to bring a flamingo into a barbershop; South Padre Island, Texas, bans the wearing of neckties; Mount Prospect, Illinois, has a law against keeping pigeons or bees; Topeka, Kansas, bans snowball fights; Hoover, South Dakota, does not allow fishing by the light of a kerosene lantern; and Beverly Hills, California, regulates the number of tennis balls allowed on the court at one time (Steele, 2000; Wittenauer, 2007; Belofsky, 2010; Newcomb, 2012).

   Around the world, deviance is even more diverse. Albania outlaws any public display of religious faith, such as the Catholic practice of "crossing" oneself; Cuba regulates private ownership of personal computers and limits access to the Internet; Vietnam can prosecute citizens for meeting with foreigners; Malaysia does not allow women to wear tight-fitting jeans; Saudi Arabia bans the sale of red flowers on Valentine's Day; and Iran bans wearing makeup by women and forbids anyone from playing rap music (Chopra, 2008).

2. **People become deviant as others define them that way.** Everyone violates cultural norms at one time or

Why is it that street-corner gambling like this is usually against the law but playing the same games in a fancy casino is not?

another. Have you ever walked around talking to yourself or "borrowed" a pen from your workplace? Whether such behavior defines us as mentally ill or criminal depends on how others perceive, define, and respond to it.

3. **How societies set norms and how they define rule breaking both involve social power.** The law, declared Karl Marx, is the means by which powerful people protect their interests. A homeless person who stands on a street corner speaking out against the government risks arrest for disturbing the peace; a mayoral candidate during an election campaign who does exactly the same thing gets police protection. In short, norms and how we apply them reflect social inequality.

The Functions of Deviance: Structural-Functional Theories

(9.2) Apply structural-functional theories to the topic of deviance.

The key insight of the structural-functional approach is that deviance is a necessary part of social organization. This point was made a century ago by Emile Durkheim.

Durkheim's Basic Insight

In his pioneering study of deviance, Emile Durkheim (1964a, orig. 1893; 1964b, orig. 1895) made the surprising claim that there is nothing abnormal about deviance. In fact, it performs four essential functions:

1. **Deviance affirms cultural values and norms.** As moral creatures, people must prefer some attitudes and behaviors to others. But any definition of virtue rests on an opposing idea of vice: There can be no good without evil and no justice without crime. Deviance is needed to define and support morality.

⊙ **Watch** in **MySocLab** **Video:** *Social Inequalities: Deviance*

2. **Responding to deviance clarifies moral boundaries.** By defining some individuals as deviant, people draw a boundary between right and wrong. For example, a college marks the line between academic honesty and cheating by disciplining students who cheat on exams.

3. **Responding to deviance brings people together.** People typically react to serious deviance with shared outrage. In doing so, Durkheim explained, they reaffirm the moral ties that bind them. For example, after the December 2012 shooting rampage at the Sandy Hook Elementary School in Newtown, Connecticut, that killed twenty elementary school children and six adults, people across the United States were joined by a common desire to control this type of senseless violence.

4. **Deviance encourages social change.** Deviant people push a society's moral boundaries, suggesting alternatives to the status quo and encouraging change. Today's deviance, declared Durkheim, can become tomorrow's morality (1964b:71, orig. 1895). For example, rock-and-roll, condemned as immoral in the 1950s, became a

Durkheim claimed that deviance is a necessary element of social organization, serving several important functions. After a twenty-year-old man gunned down twenty children and six adults in a mass murder at the Sandy Hook Elementary School in Newtown, Connecticut, people across the country came together to affirm their community ties as they sought to understand how such an action could occur. Has any event on your campus caused a similar community reaction?

multibillion-dollar industry just a few years later (see the Thinking About Diversity box on page 86). In recent years, hip-hop music has followed the same path toward respectability.

An Illustration: The Puritans of Massachusetts Bay

Kai Erikson's classic study of the Puritans of Massachusetts Bay brings Durkheim's theory to life. Erikson (2005b, orig. 1966) shows that even the Puritans, a disciplined and highly religious group, created deviance to clarify their moral boundaries. In fact, Durkheim might well have had the Puritans in mind when he wrote this:

> Imagine a society of saints, a perfect cloister of exemplary individuals. Crimes, properly so called, will there be unknown; but faults which appear [insignificant] to the layman will create there the same scandal that the ordinary offense does in ordinary consciousness.... For the same reason, the perfect and upright man judges his smallest failings with a severity that the majority reserve for acts more truly in the nature of an offense. (1964b:68–69, orig. 1895)

Deviance is thus not a matter of a few "bad apples" but a necessary condition of "good" social living.

Deviance may be found in every society, but the *kind* of deviance people generate depends on the moral issues they seek to clarify. The Puritans, for example, experienced a number of "crime waves," including the well-known outbreak of witchcraft in 1692. With each response, the Puritans answered questions about the range of proper beliefs by celebrating some of their members and condemning others as deviant.

Erikson discovered that even though the offenses changed, the proportion of people the Puritans defined as deviant remained steady over time. This stability, he concluded, confirms Durkheim's claim that society creates deviants to mark its changing moral boundaries. In other words, by constantly defining a small number of people as deviant, the Puritans maintained the moral shape of their society.

Merton's Strain Theory

Some deviance may be necessary for a society to function, but Robert Merton (1938, 1968) argued that society can be set up in a way that encourages too much deviance. Specifically, the extent and type of deviance people engage in depend on whether a society provides the *means* (such as schooling and job opportunities) to achieve cultural *goals* (such as financial success). Merton's strain theory is illustrated in Figure 9–1.

Conformity lies in pursuing cultural goals through approved means. Therefore, the U.S. "success story" is someone who gains wealth and prestige through talent, schooling, and hard work. But not everyone who wants conventional success has the opportunity to attain it. For example, people raised in poverty may have little hope of becoming successful if they play by the rules. According to Merton, the strain between our culture's emphasis on wealth and the lack of opportunities to get rich may encourage some people, especially the poor, to engage in stealing, drug dealing, or other forms of street crime. Merton called this type of deviance *innovation*—using unconventional means (street crime) rather than conventional means (hard work at a "straight" job) to achieve a culturally approved goal (wealth).

The inability to reach a cultural goal may also prompt another type of deviance that Merton calls *ritualism*. For example, many people may not care much about becoming rich but rigidly stick to the rules (the conventional means) anyway in order to at least feel "respectable."

A third response to the inability to succeed is *retreatism*: rejecting both cultural goals and conventional means so that a person in effect

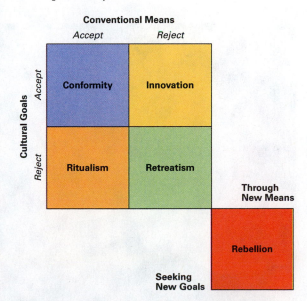

FIGURE 9–1 Merton's Strain Theory of Deviance

Combining a person's view of cultural goals and the conventional means to obtain them allowed Robert Merton to identify various types of deviance.

Source: Merton (1968).

"drops out." Some alcoholics, drug addicts, and street people can be described as retreatists. The deviance of retreatists lies in their unconventional lifestyle and also in what seems to be their willingness to live this way.

The fourth response to failure is *rebellion.* Like retreatists, rebels such as radical "survivalists" reject both the cultural definition of success and the conventional means of achieving it, but they go one step further by forming a counterculture supporting alternatives to the existing social order.

Deviant Subcultures

Richard Cloward and Lloyd Ohlin (1966) extended Merton's theory, proposing that crime results not simply from limited legitimate (legal) opportunity but also from readily accessible illegitimate (illegal) opportunity. In short, deviance or conformity arises from the *relative opportunity structure* that frames a person's life.

The life of Al Capone, a notorious gangster, illustrates Cloward and Ohlin's theory. As the son of poor immigrants, Capone faced barriers of poverty and ethnic prejudice, which lowered his odds of achieving success in conventional terms. Yet as a young man during Prohibition (when alcoholic beverages were banned in the United States between 1920 and 1933), Capone found in his neighborhood people who could teach him how to sell alcohol illegally—a source of illegitimate opportunity. Where the structure of opportunity favors criminal activity, Cloward and Ohlin predict the development of *criminal subcultures,* such as Capone's criminal organization or today's inner-city street gangs.

But what happens when people are unable to find *any* opportunity, legal or illegal? Then deviance may take one of two forms. One is *conflict subcultures,* such as armed street gangs that engage in violence out of frustration and a desire for respect. Another possible outcome is the development of *retreatist subcultures,* in which deviants drop out and abuse alcohol or other drugs.

Albert Cohen (1971, orig. 1955) suggests that delinquency is most common among lower-class youths because they have the least opportunity to achieve conventional success. Neglected by society, they seek self-respect by creating a delinquent subculture that defines as worthy the traits these youths do have. Being feared on the street may not win many points with society as a whole, but it may satisfy a young person's desire to "be somebody" in the local neighborhood.

Walter Miller (1970, orig. 1958) adds that delinquent subcultures are characterized by (1) *trouble,* arising from frequent conflict with teachers and police; (2) *toughness,* the value placed on physical size and strength, especially among males; (3) *smartness,* the ability to succeed on the streets, to outsmart or "con" others, and to avoid being similarly taken advantage of; (4) a *need for excitement,* the search for thrills or danger; (5) a *belief in fate,* a sense that people lack control over their own lives; and (6) a *desire for freedom,* often expressed as anger toward authority figures.

Finally, Elijah Anderson (1994, 2002; Kubrin, 2005) explains that in poor urban neighborhoods, most people manage to conform to conventional or "decent" values. Yet faced with neighborhood crime and violence, indifference or even hostility from police, and sometimes neglect by their own parents, some young men decide to live by the "street code." To show that they can survive on the street, a young man displays "nerve," a willingness to stand up to any threat. Following this street code, which is

Young people cut off from legitimate opportunity often form subcultures that many people view as deviant. Gang subcultures are one way young people gain the sense of belonging and respect denied to them by the larger culture.

also evident in much recent rap music, the young man believes that a violent death is better than being "dissed" (disrespected) by others. Some manage to escape the dangers, but the risk of ending up in jail—or worse—is very high for these young men, who have been pushed to the margins of our society.

EVALUATE Durkheim made an important contribution by pointing out the functions of deviance. However, there is evidence that a community does not always come together in reaction to crime; sometimes fear of crime causes people to withdraw from public life (Liska & Warner, 1991; Warr & Ellison, 2000).

Merton's strain theory has been criticized for explaining some kinds of deviance (stealing, for example) better than others (such as crimes of passion or mental illness). Also, not everyone seeks success in the conventional terms of wealth, as strain theory suggests.

The general argument of Cloward and Ohlin, Cohen, Miller, and Anderson—that deviance reflects the opportunity structure of society—has been confirmed by subsequent research (Allan & Steffensmeier, 1989; Uggen, 1999). However, these theories fall short by assuming that everyone shares the same cultural standards for judging right and wrong. In addition, if we define crime to include not only burglary and auto theft but also fraud and other crimes carried out by corporate executives and Wall Street tycoons, then more high-income people will be counted as criminals.

Finally, all structural-functional theories suggest that everyone who breaks important rules will be labeled deviant. However, becoming deviant is actually a highly complex process, as the next section explains.

CHECK YOUR LEARNING Why do you think many of the theories just discussed seem to say that crime is more common among people with lower social standing?

Defining Deviance: Symbolic-Interaction Theories

(9.3) Apply symbolic-interaction theories to the topic of deviance.

The symbolic-interaction approach explains how people define deviance in everyday situations. From this point of view, definitions of deviance and conformity are surprisingly flexible.

Labeling Theory

The main contribution of symbolic-interaction analysis is **labeling theory**, *the idea that deviance and conformity result not so much from what people do as from how others respond to those actions.* Labeling theory stresses the relativity of deviance, meaning that people may define the same behavior in any number of ways.

Consider these situations: A college student takes a sweater off the back of a roommate's chair and packs it for a weekend trip, a married woman at a convention in a distant city has sex with an old boyfriend, and a city mayor gives a big contract to a major campaign contributor. We might define the first situation as carelessness, borrowing, or theft. The consequences of the second case depend largely on whether the woman's behavior becomes known back home. In the third situation, is the official choosing the best contractor or paying off a political debt? The social construction of reality is a highly variable process of detection, definition, and response.

Primary and Secondary Deviance

Edwin Lemert (1951, 1972) observed that some norm violations—say, skipping school or underage drinking—provoke slight reaction from others and have little effect on a person's self-concept. Lemert calls such passing episodes *primary deviance.*

For a closer look at how people of all social backgrounds are becoming more casual about wrongdoing, **Read More** in **MySocLab**, *Deviant Subcultures: Has It Become OK to Break the Rules?*

But what happens if people take notice of someone's deviance and really make something of it? After an audience has defined some action as primary deviance, the individual may begin to change, taking on a deviant identity by talking, acting, or dressing in a different way, rejecting the people who are critical, and repeatedly breaking the rules. Lemert (1951:77) calls this change of self-concept *secondary deviance*. He explains that "when a person begins to employ ... deviant behavior as a means of defense, attack, or adjustment to the ... problems created by societal reaction," deviance becomes secondary. For example, say that people have begun describing a young man as an "alcohol abuser," which establishes primary deviance. These people may then exclude him from their friendship network. His response may be to become bitter toward them, start drinking even more, and seek the company of others who approve of his drinking. These actions mark the beginning of secondary deviance, a deeper deviant identity.

Stigma

👁 **Watch** in **MySocLab**
Video: *Sociology in Focus: Deviance*

Secondary deviance marks the start of what Erving Goffman (1963) calls a *deviant career*. As people develop a stronger commitment to deviant behavior, they typically acquire a **stigma**, *a powerfully negative label that greatly changes a person's self-concept and social identity*.

A stigma operates as a master status(see Chapter 6, "Social Interaction in Everyday Life"), overpowering other aspects of social identity so that a person is discredited in the minds of others and becomes socially isolated. Often a person gains a stigma informally as others begin to see the individual in deviant terms. Sometimes, however, an entire community formally stigmatizes an individual through what Harold Garfinkel (1956) calls a *degradation ceremony*. A criminal trial is one example, operating much like a high school graduation ceremony in reverse: A person stands before the community and is labeled in negative rather than positive terms.

Retrospective and Projective Labeling

Once people stigmatize an individual, they may engage in *retrospective labeling,* interpreting someone's past in light of some present deviance (Scheff, 1984). For example, after discovering

that a priest has sexually molested a child, others rethink his past, perhaps musing, "He always did want to be around young children." Retrospective labeling, which distorts a person's biography by being highly selective, typically deepens a deviant identity.

Similarly, people may engage in *projective labeling* of a stigmatized person, using the person's deviant identity to predict future actions. Regarding the priest, people might say, "He's going to keep at it until he gets caught." The more people in someone's social world think such things, the more these definitions affect the individual's self-concept, increasing the chance that they will come true.

Labeling Difference as Deviance

Is a homeless man who refuses to allow police to take him to a city shelter on a cold night simply trying to live independently, or is he "crazy"? People have a tendency to treat behavior that irritates or threatens them not simply as different but as deviance or even mental illness.

The psychiatrist Thomas Szasz (1961, 1970, 2003, 2004) charges that people are too quick to apply the label of mental illness to conditions that simply amount to a difference we don't like. The only way to avoid this troubling practice, Szasz continues, is to abandon the idea of mental illness entirely. The world is full of people who think or act differently in ways that may irritate us, but such differences are not grounds for defining someone as mentally ill. Such labeling, Szasz claims, simply enforces conformity to the standards of people powerful enough to impose their will on others.

Most mental health care professionals reject the idea that mental illness does not exist. But they agree that it is important to think critically about

James Egan Holmes is currently facing charges after allegedly entering a movie theater in Aurora, Colorado, in 2012 and fatally shooting twelve people and injuring fifty-eight others. Does simply committing such a horrific crime lead us to wonder about a suspect's sanity? Should society respond differently to someone considered "insane" rather than "guilty" of the crime? Explain.

how we define "difference." First, people who are mentally ill are no more to blame for their condition than people who suffer from cancer or some other physical problem. Therefore, having a mental or physical illness is no grounds for a person being labeled "deviant." Second, ordinary people without the medical knowledge to diagnose mental illness should avoid using such labels just to make people conform to their own standards of behavior.

labeling theory the idea that deviance and conformity result not so much from what people do as from how others respond to those actions

stigma a powerfully negative label that greatly changes a person's self-concept and social identity

medicalization of deviance the transformation of moral and legal deviance into a medical condition

The Medicalization of Deviance

Labeling theory, particularly the ideas of Szasz and Goffman, helps explain an important shift in the way our society understands deviance. Over the past fifty or sixty years, the growing influence of psychiatry and medicine in the United States has led to the **medicalization of deviance**, *the transformation of moral and legal deviance into a medical condition.*

Medicalization amounts to swapping one set of labels for another. In moral terms, we evaluate people or their behavior as "bad" or "good." However, the scientific objectivity of medicine passes no moral judgment, instead using clinical diagnoses such as "sick" or "well."

To illustrate, until the mid-twentieth century, people generally viewed alcoholics as morally weak people easily tempted by the pleasure of drink. Gradually, however, medical specialists redefined alcoholism so that most people now consider it a disease, rendering people "sick" rather than "bad." In the same way, obesity, drug addiction, child abuse, sexual promiscuity, and other behaviors that used to be strictly moral matters are widely defined today as illnesses for which people need help rather than punishment.

Similarly, behaviors that used to be defined as criminal—such as smoking marijuana—are more likely today to be seen as a form of treatment. By the beginning of 2013, eighteen states had enacted medical marijuana laws (National Conference of State Legislatures, 2012).

The Difference Labels Make

Whether we define deviance as a moral or a medical issue has three consequences. First, it affects *who responds* to deviance. An offense against common morality usually brings about a reaction from members of the community or the police. A medical label, however, places the situation under the control of clinical specialists, including counselors, psychiatrists, and physicians.

A second issue is *how people respond* to deviance. A moral approach defines deviants as offenders subject to punishment. Medically, however, they are patients who need treatment. Punishment is designed to fit the crime, but treatment programs are tailored to the patient and may involve virtually any therapy that a specialist thinks might prevent future deviance.

Third, and most important, the two labels differ on the *personal competence of the deviant person.* From a moral standpoint, whether we are right or wrong, at least we take responsibility for our own behavior. Once we are defined as sick, however, we are seen as unable to control (or if "mentally ill," even to understand) our actions. People who are labeled incompetent are in turn subjected to treatment, often against their will. For this reason alone, attempts to define deviance in medical terms should be made with extreme caution.

Sutherland's Differential Association Theory

Learning any behavioral pattern, whether conventional or deviant, is a process that takes place in groups. According to Edwin Sutherland (1940), a person's tendency toward conformity or deviance depends on the amount of contact with others who encourage or reject conventional behavior. This is Sutherland's theory of *differential association.*

A number of research studies confirm the idea that young people are more likely to engage in delinquency if they believe members of their peer groups encourage such

All social groups teach their members skills and attitudes that encourage certain behavior. In recent years, discussion on college campuses has focused on the dangers of binge drinking, which results in several dozen deaths each year among young people in the United States. How much of a problem is binge drinking on your campus?

activity (Akers et al., 1979; Miller & Mathews, 2001). One investigation focused on sexual activity among eighth-grade students. Two strong predictors of such behavior for young girls was having a boyfriend who encouraged sexual relations and having girlfriends they believed would approve of such activity. Similarly, boys were encouraged to become sexually active by friends who rewarded them with high status in their peer group (Little & Rankin, 2001).

Hirschi's Control Theory

The sociologist Travis Hirschi (1969; Gottfredson & Hirschi, 1995) developed *control theory*, which states that social control depends on people anticipating the consequences of their behavior. Hirschi assumes that everyone finds at least some deviance tempting. But the thought of a ruined career keeps most people from breaking the rules; for some, just imagining the reactions of family and friends is enough. On the other hand, individuals who feel they have little to lose by deviance are likely to become rule breakers.

Specifically, Hirschi links conformity to four different types of social control:

1. **Attachment.** Strong social attachments encourage conformity. Weak family, peer, and school relationships leave people freer to engage in deviance.

2. **Opportunity.** The greater a person's access to legitimate opportunity, the greater the advantages of conformity. By contrast, someone with little confidence in future success is more likely to drift toward deviance.

3. **Involvement.** Extensive involvement in legitimate activities—such as holding a job, going to school, or playing sports—inhibits deviance (Langbein & Bess, 2002). By contrast, people who simply "hang out" waiting for something to happen have time and energy to engage in deviant activity.

4. **Belief.** Strong belief in conventional morality and respect for authority figures restrain tendencies toward deviance. People who have a weak conscience (and who are left unsupervised) are more open to temptation (Stack, Wasserman, & Kern, 2004).

Hirschi's analysis combines a number of earlier ideas about the causes of deviant behavior. Note that a person's relative social privilege as well as family and community environment is likely to affect the risk of deviant behavior (Hope, Grasmick, & Pointon, 2003).

EVALUATE The various symbolic-interaction theories all see deviance as a reality that may emerge within the process of interaction. Labeling theory links deviance not to the action but to the *reaction* of others. Thus some people are defined as deviant but others who think or behave in the same way are not. The concepts of secondary deviance, deviant career, and stigma show how being labeled deviant can become a lasting self-concept.

Yet labeling theory has several limitations. First, because it takes a highly relative view of deviance, labeling theory ignores the fact that some kinds of behavior—such as murder—are condemned just about everywhere. Therefore, labeling theory is most usefully applied to less serious issues, such as sexual promiscuity or mental illness. Second, research on the consequences of deviant labeling does not clearly show whether deviant labeling produces further deviance or discourages it (Smith & Gartin, 1989; Sherman & Smith, 1992). Third, not everyone resists being labeled deviant; some people actively seek it out (Vold & Bernard, 1986). For example, people take part in civil disobedience and willingly subject themselves to arrest in order to call attention to social injustice.

Sociologists consider Sutherland's differential association theory and Hirschi's control theory important contributions to our understanding of deviance. But why do society's norms and laws define certain kinds of activities as deviant in the first place? This question is addressed by social-conflict analysis, the focus of the next section.

CHECK YOUR LEARNING Clearly define primary deviance, secondary deviance, deviant career, and stigma.

Deviance and Inequality: Social-Conflict Theories

9.4 Apply social-conflict theories to the topic of deviance.

The social-conflict approach, as summarized in the Applying Theory table, links deviance to social inequality. That is, who or what is labeled deviant depends on which categories of people hold power in a society.

Deviance and Power

Alexander Liazos (1972) points out that the people we tend to define as deviants—the ones we dismiss as "nuts" and "sluts"—are typically not as bad or harmful as they are *powerless*. Bag ladies and unemployed men on street corners, not corporate polluters or international arms dealers, carry the stigma of deviance.

Social-conflict theory explains this pattern in three ways. First, all norms—especially the laws of any society—generally reflect the interests of the rich and powerful. People who threaten the wealthy are likely to be labeled deviant, either for taking people's property ("common thieves") or for advocating a more egalitarian society ("political radicals"). As noted in Chapter 4 ("Society"), Karl Marx argued that the law and all other social institutions support the interests of the rich. Or as Richard Quinney puts it, "Capitalist justice is by the capitalist class, for the capitalist class, and against the working class" (1977:3).

Second, even if their behavior is called into question, the powerful have the resources to resist deviant labels. The majority of the executives involved in recent corporate scandals have yet to be arrested; only a few have gone to jail.

Third, the widespread belief that norms and laws are natural and good masks their political character. For this reason, although we may condemn the unequal application of the law, we give little thought to whether the laws themselves are really fair or not.

Applying Theory

Deviance				
	Structural-Functional Theory	**Symbolic-Interaction Theory**	**Social-Conflict Theory**	**Race-Conflict and Feminist Theories**
What is the level of analysis?	Macro-level	Micro-level	Macro-level	Macro-level
What is deviance? **What part does it play in society?**	Deviance is a basic part of social organization. By defining deviance, society sets its moral boundaries.	Deviance is part of socially constructed reality that emerges in interaction. Deviance comes into being as individuals label something deviant.	Deviance results from social inequality. Norms, including laws, reflect the interests of powerful members of society.	Deviance reflects racial and gender inequality. Deviant labels are more readily applied to women and other minorities.
What is important about deviance?	Deviance is universal: It exists in all societies.	Deviance is variable: Any act or person may or may not be labeled deviant.	Deviance is political: People with little power are at high risk of being labeled deviant.	Deviance is a means of control: Dominant categories of people discredit others as a means to dominate them.

Deviance and Capitalism

In the Marxist tradition, Steven Spitzer (1980) argues that deviant labels are applied to people who interfere with the operation of capitalism. First, because capitalism is based on private control of wealth, people who threaten the property of others—especially the poor who steal from the rich—are prime candidates for being labeled deviant. On the other hand, the rich who take advantage of the poor are less likely to be labeled deviant. For example, landlords who charge poor tenants high rents and evict anyone who cannot pay are not considered criminals; they are simply "doing business."

Second, because capitalism depends on productive labor, people who cannot or will not work risk being labeled deviant. Many members of our society think people who are out of work, even through no fault of their own, are somehow deviant.

Third, capitalism depends on respect for authority figures, causing people who resist authority to be labeled deviant. Examples are children who skip school or talk back to parents and teachers and adults who do not cooperate with employers or police.

The television show *Arrested Development* tells the story of the Bluth family, whose success in business has not come without trouble with the law. George Bluth is an untrustworthy character who has been the target of a police investigation for securities fraud and looting company coffers for his own purposes, and he has spent some time in jail. Do you think that white-collar criminals are treated fairly by our criminal justice system? Why or why not?

Fourth, anyone who directly challenges the capitalist status quo is likely to be defined as deviant. Such has been the case with labor organizers, radical environmentalists, and antiwar activists.

On the other side of the coin, society positively labels whatever supports the operation of capitalism. For example, winning athletes enjoy celebrity status because they express the values of individual achievement and competition, both vital to capitalism. Also, Spitzer notes, we condemn using drugs of escape (marijuana, psychedelics, heroin, and crack) as deviant but encourage drugs (such as alcohol and caffeine) that promote adjustment to the status quo.

The capitalist system also tries to control people who are not economically productive. The elderly, people with mental or physical disabilities, and Robert Merton's retreatists (people addicted to alcohol or other drugs) are a "costly yet relatively harmless burden" on society. Such people, claims Spitzer, are subject to control by social welfare agencies. But people who openly challenge the capitalist system, including the inner-city underclass and revolutionaries—Merton's innovators and rebels—are controlled by the criminal justice system and, in times of crisis, military forces such as the National Guard.

Note that both the social welfare and criminal justice systems blame individuals, not the system, for social problems. Welfare recipients are considered unworthy freeloaders, poor people who express rage at their plight are labeled rioters, anyone who challenges the government is branded a radical or a communist, and those who try to gain illegally what they will never get legally are rounded up as common criminals.

White-Collar Crime

In a sign of things to come, a Wall Street stockbroker named Michael Milken made headlines back in 1987 when he was jailed for business fraud. Milken attracted attention because not since the days of Al Capone had anyone made so much money in one year: $550 million—about $1.5 million a day (Swartz, 1989).

Milken engaged in **white-collar crime**, defined by Edwin Sutherland (1940) as *crime committed by people of high social position in the course of their occupations*. White-collar crimes do not involve violence and rarely attract police to the scene with guns drawn. Rather, white-collar criminals use their powerful offices to illegally enrich themselves and others, often causing significant public harm in the process. For this reason, sociologists sometimes call white-collar offenses that occur in government offices and corporate boardrooms "crime in the suites" as opposed to "crime in the streets."

The most common white-collar crimes are bank embezzlement, business fraud, bribery, and antitrust violations. Sutherland (1940) explains that such white-collar offenses typically end up in a civil hearing rather than a criminal courtroom. *Civil law* regulates business dealings between private parties, and *criminal law* defines the individual's moral responsibilities to society. In practice, then, someone who loses a civil case pays for damage or injury but is not labeled a criminal. Corporate officials are also protected by the fact that most charges of white-collar crime target the organization rather than individuals.

When white-collar criminals are charged and convicted, they usually escape punishment. A government study found that those convicted of fraud and punished with a fine ended up paying less than 10 percent of what they owed; most managed to hide or transfer their assets to avoid paying up. Among white-collar criminals convicted of the more serious crime of embezzlement, only about half ever served a day in jail. One accounting found that just 53 percent of the embezzlers convicted in the U.S. federal courts served prison sentences; the rest were put on probation or issued a fine (U.S. Department of Justice, Bureau of Justice Statistics, 2012). As some analysts see it, until courts impose more prison terms, we should expect white-collar crime to remain widespread (Shover & Hochstetler, 2006).

Corporate Crime

Sometimes whole companies, not just individuals, break the law. **Corporate crime** is *the illegal actions of a corporation or people acting on its behalf.*

Corporate crime ranges from knowingly selling faulty or dangerous products to deliberately polluting the environment (Derber, 2004). The collapse of a number of major U.S. corporations in recent years cost tens of thousands of people their jobs and their pensions. Even more seriously, 151 people died in underground coal mines between 2007 and 2012; hundreds more died from "black lung" disease caused by years of inhaling coal dust. The annual death toll for all job-related hazards in the United States runs into the thousands, and each year more than a million people are injured on the job seriously enough to require time away from work (Frank, 2007; Jafari, 2008; U.S. Department of Labor, Mine Safety and Health Administration, 2012; U.S. Department of Labor, 2012).

Organized Crime

Organized crime is *a business supplying illegal goods or services.* Sometimes criminal organizations force people to do business with them, as when a gang extorts money from shopkeepers for "protection." In most cases, however, organized crime involves the sale of illegal goods and services—often sex, drugs, and gambling—to willing buyers.

Organized crime has flourished in the United States for more than a century. The scope of its operations expanded among immigrants, who found that this society was not willing to share its opportunities with them. Some ambitious

The television series *Boardwalk Empire* offers an inside look at the lives of gangsters in this country's history. How accurately do you think the mass media portray organized crime? Explain.

individuals (such as Al Capone, mentioned earlier) made their own success, especially during Prohibition, when the government banned the production and sale of alcohol.

The Italian Mafia is a well-known example of organized crime. But other criminal organizations involve African Americans, Chinese, Colombians, Cubans, Haitians, Nigerians, and Russians, as well as others of almost every racial and ethnic category. Today, organized crime involves a wide range of activities, from selling illegal drugs to prostitution to credit card fraud to selling false identification papers to illegal immigrants (Valdez, 1997; U.S. Department of Justice, Federal Bureau of Investigation, 2011).

EVALUATE According to social-conflict theory, a capitalist society's inequality in wealth and power shapes its laws and how they are applied. The criminal justice and social welfare systems thus act as political agents, controlling categories of people who are a threat to the capitalist system.

Like other approaches to deviance, social-conflict theory has its critics. First, this approach implies that laws and other cultural norms are created directly by the rich and powerful. At the very least, this is an oversimplification, as laws also protect workers, consumers, and the environment, sometimes opposing the interests of corporations and the rich.

Second, social-conflict analysis argues that criminality springs up only to the extent that a society treats its members unequally. However, as Durkheim noted, deviance exists in all societies, whatever their economic system and their degree of inequality.

CHECK YOUR LEARNING Define white-collar crime, corporate crime, and organized crime.

Deviance, Race, and Gender: Race-Conflict and Feminist Theories

9.5 Apply race-conflict and feminist theories to the topic of deviance.

What people consider deviant reflects the relative power and privilege of different categories of people. The following sections offer two examples: how racial and ethnic hostility motivates hate crimes and how gender is linked to deviance.

Race-Conflict Theory: Hate Crimes

A **hate crime** is *a criminal act against a person or a person's property by an offender motivated by racial or other bias.* A hate crime may express hostility toward someone's race, religion, ethnicity or ancestry and, since 2009, sexual orientation, or physical disability. The federal government recorded 6,222 hate crimes in 2011 (U.S. Department of Justice, Federal Bureau of Investigation, 2012).

In 1998, people across the country were stunned by the brutal killing of Matthew Shepard, a gay student at the University of Wyoming, by two men filled with hatred toward homosexuals. The National Coalition of Anti-Violence Programs (2012) reported that 30 murders and 2,092 hate crimes against gay and lesbian people occurred in 2011. People who contend with multiple stigmas, such as gay men of color, are especially likely to be victims. Yet it can happen to anyone: In 2011, 17 percent of hate crimes based on race targeted white people (U.S. Department of Justice, Federal Bureau of Investigation, 2012).

By 2012, forty-five states and the federal government had enacted legislation that increased penalties for crimes motivated by hatred (Anti-Defamation League, 2012). Supporters are gratified, but opponents charge that such laws, which increase penalties based on the attitudes of the offender, punish "politically incorrect" thoughts. The Thinking About Diversity box on page 253 takes a closer look at the issue of hate crime laws.

hate crime a criminal act against a person or a person's property by an offender motivated by racial or other bias

Thinking About Diversity: Race, Class, and Gender

Hate Crime Laws: Should We Punish Attitudes as Well as Actions?

On a cool October evening, nineteen-year-old Todd Mitchell, an African American, was standing with some friends in front of their apartment complex in Kenosha, Wisconsin. They had just seen the film *Mississippi Burning* and were fuming over a scene that showed a white man beating a young black boy while he knelt in prayer.

"Do you feel hyped up to move on some white people?" asked Mitchell. Minutes later, they saw a young white boy walking toward them on the other side of the street. Mitchell commanded, "There goes a white boy; go get him!" The group swarmed around the youngster, beating him bloody and leaving him on the ground in a coma. The attackers took the boy's tennis shoes as a trophy.

Police soon arrested the teenagers and charged them with the beating. Mitchell went to trial as the ringleader, and the jury found him guilty of aggravated battery *motivated by racial hatred*. Instead of the usual two-year sentence, Mitchell went to jail for four years.

As this case illustrates, hate crime laws punish a crime more severely if the offender is motivated by bias against some category of people. Supporters make three arguments in favor of hate crime legislation. First, as noted in the text discussion of crime, the offender's intentions are always important in weighing criminal responsibility, so considering hatred an intention is nothing new. Second, victims of hate crimes typically suffer greater injury than victims of crimes with other motives. Third, a crime motivated by racial or other bias is more harmful because it inflames the public mood more than a crime carried out, say, for money.

Critics counter that while some hate crime cases involve hardcore racism, most are impulsive acts by young people. Even more important, critics maintain, hate crime laws are a threat to First Amendment guarantees of free speech. Hate crime laws allow courts to sentence offenders not just for their actions but also for their attitudes. As the Harvard University law professor Alan Dershowitz cautions, "As much as I hate bigotry, I fear much more the Court attempting to control the minds of its citizens." In short, according to critics, hate crime statutes open the door to punishing beliefs rather than behavior.

In 1993, the U.S. Supreme Court upheld the sentence handed down to Todd Mitchell. In a unanimous decision, the justices stated that the government should not punish an individual's beliefs. But, they reasoned, a belief is no longer protected when it becomes the motive for a crime.

Do you think this example of vandalism should be prosecuted as a hate crime? In other words, should the punishment be more severe than if the spray painting were just "normal" graffiti? Why or why not?

What Do You Think?

1. Do you think crimes motivated by hate are more harmful than those motivated by greed? Why or why not?

2. Do you think minorities such as African Americans should be subject to the same hate crime laws as white people? Why or why not?

3. Do you favor or oppose hate crime laws? Why?

Sources: Terry (1993), Sullivan (2002), and Hartocollis (2007).

Feminist Theory: Deviance and Gender

In 2009, several women in Sudan were convicted of "dressing indecently." The punishment was imprisonment and, in several cases, ten lashes. The crime was wearing trousers (BBC, 2009).

This is an exceptional case, but the fact is that virtually every society in the world places stricter controls on women than on men. Historically, our own society has centered the lives of women on the home. In the United States even today, women's opportunities in the workplace, in politics, in athletics, and in the military are more limited than men's.

Elsewhere in the world, as the preceding example suggests, the constraints on women are greater still. In Saudi Arabia, women cannot vote or legally operate motor vehicles; in Iran, women who dare to expose their hair or wear makeup in public can be whipped; and not long ago, a Nigerian court convicted a divorced woman of bearing a child out of wedlock and sentenced her to death by stoning; her life was later spared out of concern for her child (Eboh, 2002; Jefferson, 2009).

Gender also figures in the theories of deviance you read about earlier in the chapter. Robert Merton's strain theory, for example, defines cultural goals in terms of financial success. Traditionally, at least, this goal has had more to do with the lives of men because women have been taught to define success in terms of relationships, particularly marriage and motherhood (Leonard, 1982). A more woman-focused theory might recognize the "strain" that results from the cultural ideal of equality clashing with the reality of gender-based inequality.

According to labeling theory, gender influences how we define deviance because people commonly use different standards to judge the behavior of females and males. Further, because society puts men in positions of power over women, men often escape direct responsibility for actions that victimize women. In the past, at least, men who sexually harassed or assaulted women were labeled only mildly deviant and sometimes escaped punishment entirely.

By contrast, women who are victimized may have to convince others—even members of a jury—that they were not to blame for their own sexual harassment or assault. Research confirms an important truth: Whether people define a situation as deviance—and, if so, who the deviant is—depends on the sex of both the audience and the actors (King & Clayson, 1988).

Finally, despite its focus on social inequality, much social-conflict analysis does not address the issue of gender. If economic disadvantage is a primary cause of crime, as conflict theory suggests, why do women (whose economic position is much worse than men's) commit far *fewer* crimes than men?

Crime

9.6 Identify patterns of crime in the United States and around the world.

Crime is the violation of criminal laws enacted by a locality, a state, or the federal government. All crimes are composed of two elements: the *act* itself (or in some cases, the failure to do what the law requires) and *criminal intent* (in legal terminology, *mens rea*, or "guilty mind"). Intent is a matter of degree, ranging from willful conduct to negligence. Someone who is negligent does not deliberately set out to hurt anyone but acts (or fails to act) in a way that results in harm. Prosecutors weigh the degree of intent in deciding whether, for example, to charge someone with first-degree murder, second-degree murder, or negligent manslaughter. Alternatively, they may consider a killing justifiable, as in self-defense.

Types of Crime

In the United States, the Federal Bureau of Investigation (FBI) gathers information on criminal offenses and regularly reports the results in a publication called *Crime in the United States.* Two major types of crime make up the FBI "crime index."

Crimes against the person, also called *violent crimes*, are *crimes that direct violence or the threat of violence against others.* Violent crimes include murder and manslaughter (legally defined as "the willful killing of one human being by another"), aggravated assault ("an unlawful attack by one person upon another for the purpose of inflicting severe or aggravated bodily injury"), forcible rape ("the carnal knowledge

Seeing Ourselves

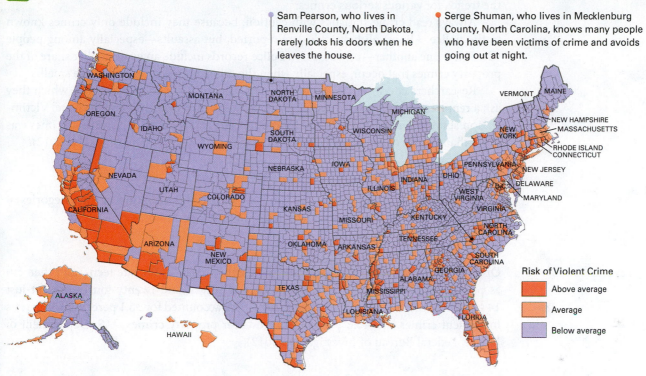

Explore the share of the population in prison in your local community and in counties across the United States in **MySocLab**

Sam Pearson, who lives in Renville County, North Dakota, rarely locks his doors when he leaves the house.

Serge Shuman, who lives in Mecklenburg County, North Carolina, knows many people who have been victims of crime and avoids going out at night.

Risk of Violent Crime

- Above average
- Average
- Below average

NATIONAL MAP 9–1 The Risk of Violent Crime across the United States

This map shows the risk of becoming a victim of violent crime. In general, the risk is highest in low-income, rural counties that have a large population of men between the ages of fifteen and twenty-four. After reading this section of the text, see whether you can explain this pattern.

Source: CAP Index (2009).

of a female forcibly and against her will"), and robbery ("taking or attempting to take anything of value from the care, custody, or control of a person or persons by force or threat of force or violence and/or putting the victim in fear"). National Map 9–1 shows a person's risk of becoming a victim of violent crime in counties all across the United States.

Crimes against property, also called *property crimes*, are *crimes that involve theft of property belonging to others*. Property crimes include burglary ("the unlawful entry of a structure to commit a [serious crime] or a theft"), larceny-theft ("the unlawful taking, carrying, leading, or riding away of property from the possession of another"), auto theft ("the theft or attempted theft of a motor vehicle"), and arson ("any willful or malicious burning or attempt to burn the personal property of another").

A third category of offenses, not included in major crime indexes, is **victimless crimes**, *violations of law in which there are no obvious victims*. Also called *crimes without complaint*, they include illegal drug use, prostitution, and gambling. The term "victimless crime" is misleading, however. How victimless is a crime when young people steal to support a drug habit? What about a young pregnant woman who, by smoking crack, permanently harms her baby? Perhaps it is more correct to say that people who commit such crimes are both offenders and victims.

Because public views of victimless crimes vary greatly, laws differ from place to place. In the United States, although gambling and prostitution are legal in only limited areas, both activities are common across the country.

crimes against the person (violent crimes) crimes that direct violence or the threat of violence against others

crimes against property (property crimes) crimes that involve theft of money or property belonging to others

victimless crimes violations of law in which there are no obvious victims

Criminal Statistics

Statistics gathered by the FBI show crime rates rising from 1960 to 1990 and then declining. Even so, police count more than 10 million serious crimes each year. Figure 9–2 shows the trends for various serious crimes.

Always read crime statistics with caution, because they include only crimes known to the police. Almost all homicides are reported, but assaults—especially among people who know one another—often are not. Police records include an even smaller share of the property crimes that occur, especially when the crime involves losses that are small.

Researchers check official crime statistics using *victimization surveys,* in which they ask a representative sample of people if they have had any experience with crime. Victimization surveys carried out in 2011 showed that the actual number of serious crimes was more than twice as high as police reports indicate (U.S. Department of Justice, 2012).

The Street Criminal: A Profile

Using government crime reports, we can gain a general description of the categories of people most likely to be arrested for violent and property crimes.

Age

Official crime rates rise sharply during adolescence, peak in the late teens, and then fall as people get older. People between the ages of fifteen and twenty-four represent just 14 percent of the U.S. population, but in 2011, they accounted for 38.1 percent of all arrests for violent crimes and 45.6 percent of arrests for property crimes (U.S. Department of Justice, Federal Bureau of Investigation, 2012).

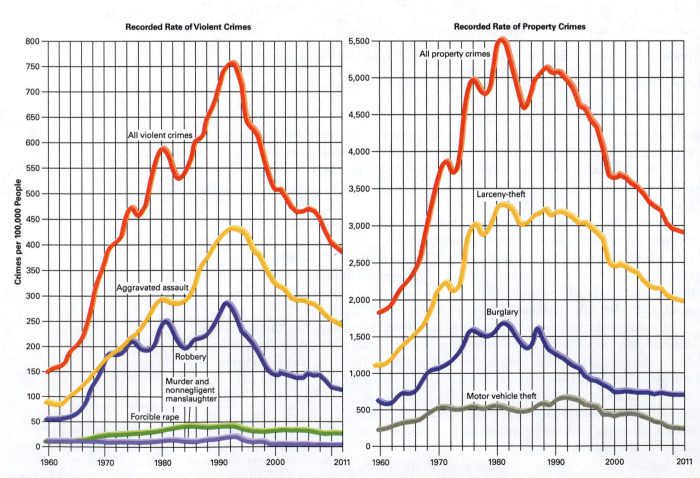

FIGURE 9–2 Crime Rates in the United States, 1960–2011

The graphs show the rates for various violent crimes and property crimes during recent decades. Since about 1990, the trend in crime rates has been downward.

Source: U.S. Department of Justice, Federal Bureau of Investigation (2012).

Gender

Although each sex makes up roughly half the country's population, police collared males in 62.9 percent of all property crime arrests in 2011; the other 37.1 percent of arrests involved women. In other words, men are arrested almost twice as often as women for property crimes. In the case of violent crimes, the difference is even greater, with 80.4 percent of arrests by police involving males and just 19.6 percent of the arrests involving females (more than a four-to-one ratio).

How do we account for the dramatic difference? It may be that some law enforcement officials are reluctant to define women as criminals. In fact, all over the world, the greatest gender differences in crime rates occur in societies that most severely limit the opportunities of women. In the United States, however, the difference in arrest rates for women and men is narrowing, which probably indicates increasing sexual equality in our society. Between 2002 and 2011, there was an 5.8 percent *increase* in arrests of women and an 11.0 percent *decrease* in arrests of men (U.S. Department of Justice, Federal Bureau of Investigation, 2012).

What actions a society allows or outlaws sometimes seem curious. For example, almost everywhere, our society forbids consenting adults from buying or selling sex. Yet, it's perfectly legal for film producers to pay people to have sex in front of a camera. Why do you think this might be the case?

Social Class

The FBI does not assess the social class of arrested persons, so no statistical data of the kind given for age and gender are available. But research has long indicated that street crime is more widespread among people of lower social position (Thornberry & Farnsworth, 1982; Wolfgang, Thornberry, & Figlio, 1987).

Yet the link between class and crime is more complicated than it appears on the surface. For one thing, many people look on the poor as less worthy than the rich, whose wealth and power confer "respectability" (Tittle, Villemez, & Smith, 1978; Elias, 1986). And although crime—especially violent crime—is a serious problem in the poorest inner-city communities, most of these crimes are committed by a few repeat offenders. The majority of the people who live in poor communities have no criminal record at all (Wolfgang, Figlio, & Sellin, 1972; Elliott & Ageton, 1980; Harries, 1990).

The connection between social standing and criminality also depends on the type of crime. If we expand our definition of crime beyond street offenses to include white-collar crime and corporate crime, the "common criminal" suddenly looks much more affluent and may live in a $100 million home.

Race and Ethnicity

Both race and ethnicity are strongly linked to crime rates, although the reasons are many and complex. Official statistics show that 69.2 percent of arrests for FBI index crimes in 2011 involved white people. However, the African American arrest rate was higher than the rate for whites in proportion to their representation in the general population. African Americans make up 13.1 percent of the population but account for 29.5 percent of arrests for property crimes (versus 68.1 percent for whites) and 38.3 percent of arrests for violent crimes (versus 59.4 percent for whites) (U.S. Department of Justice, Federal Bureau of Investigation, 2012).

There are several reasons for the disproportionate number of arrests among African Americans. First, race in the United States closely relates to social standing, which, as already explained, affects the likelihood of engaging in street crimes. Many poor people living in the midst of wealth come to perceive society as unjust and are therefore more likely to turn to crime to get their share (Blau & Blau, 1982; Anderson, 1994; Martinez, 1996).

Second, black and white family patterns differ: 72.5 percent of non-Hispanic black children (compared to 53.4 percent of Hispanic children and 29.0 percent of non-Hispanic

"You look like this sketch of someone who's thinking about committing a crime."

white children) are born to single mothers. Single parenting carries two risks: Children receive less supervision and are at greater risk of living in poverty. With more than one-third of African American children growing up poor (compared to one in eight white children), no one should be surprised at the proportionately higher crime rates for African Americans (Hamilton et al., 2012; U.S. Census Bureau, 2012).

Third, prejudice prompts white police to arrest black people more readily and leads citizens to report African Americans more willingly, so people of color are overly criminalized (Chiricos, McEntire, & Gertz, 2001; Quillian & Pager, 2001; Demuth & Steffensmeier, 2004).

Fourth, remember that the official crime index does not include arrests for offenses ranging from drunk driving to white-collar violations. This omission contributes to the view of the typical criminal as a person of color. If we broaden our definition of crime to include drunk driving, business fraud, embezzlement, stock swindles, and cheating on income tax returns, the proportion of white criminals rises dramatically.

Keep in mind, too, that categories of people with high arrest rates are also at higher risk of being victims of crime. In the United States, for example, African Americans are six times as likely as white people to die as a result of homicide (Rogers et al., 2001; Kochanek et al., 2011).

Finally, some categories of the population have unusually low rates of arrest. People of Asian descent, who account for about 5 percent of the population, figure in less the 1 percent of all arrests. As Chapter 14 ("Race and Ethnicity") explains, Asian Americans enjoy higher than average educational achievement and income. Also, Asian American culture emphasizes family solidarity and discipline, both of which keep criminality down.

Crime in Global Perspective

By world standards, the crime rate in the United States is high. Although recent crime trends are downward, there were 14,612 murders in the United States in 2011, which amounts to one every thirty-six minutes around the clock. In large cities such as New York, rarely does a day go by without someone being killed as a result of criminal violence.

The rates of violent crime and also property crime in the United States are several times higher than in Europe. The contrast is even greater between our country and the nations of Asia, especially Japan, where rates of violent and property crime are among the lowest in the world.

Elliott Currie (1985) suggests that crime stems from our culture's emphasis on individual economic success, frequently at the expense of strong families and neighborhoods. The United States also has extraordinary cultural diversity—a result of centuries of immigration—that can lead to conflict. In addition, economic inequality is higher in this country than in most other high-income nations. Thus our society's relatively weak social fabric, combined with considerable frustration among the poor, increases the level of criminal behavior.

Another factor contributing to violence in the United States is extensive private ownership of guns. About two-thirds of murder victims in the United States die from shootings. The U.S. rate of handgun homicides is almost seven times higher than the rate in Canada, a country that strictly limits handgun ownership. By 2015, deaths from firearms (which have been rising) are expected to surpass deaths from auto accidents (which have been falling) for the first time in U.S. history (Statistics Canada, 2011; Goodwin, 2012).

Across all regions of the United States, the trend in gun ownership is down. In the 1970s, half of U.S. households had at least one gun. This share fell to about 40 percent by the mid-1990s. Surveys conducted in 2012 suggest that one or more guns are found in just about one-third of all U.S. households. But even at that level, there are more guns (about 285 million) than adults in this country, and 40 percent of these weapons are handguns, the weapons commonly used in violent crimes. In large part, gun ownership reflects people's fear of crime, yet the easy availability of guns in this country also makes crime more deadly (NORC, 2013:438; Brady Campaign, 2012).

Supporters of gun control claim that restricting gun ownership would reduce the number of murders in the United States. For example, the number of murders each year in the nation of Canada (598), where the law prevents most people from owning guns, is lower than the number of killings in just the New York metropolitan area (852). But as critics of gun control point out, laws regulating gun ownership do not keep guns out of the hands of criminals, who almost always obtain guns illegally. They also claim that gun control is no magic bullet in the war on crime: The number of people in the United States killed each year by knives alone is almost three times the number of Canadians killed by weapons of all kinds (J. D. Wright, 1995; Munroe, 2007; U.S. Department of Justice, Federal Bureau of Investigation, 2012; Statistics Canada, 2012).

The U.S. population remains evenly divided over the issue of gun control, with 46 percent of people saying it is more important to protect the personal right to own a gun and 47 percent saying it is more important to control gun ownership. But the momentum in this debate may be shifting in the wake of the fatal shooting of twenty children and six adults at the Sandy Hook Elementary School in Connecticut in 2012. This tragic mass killing stunned the nation and rallied the forces seeking greater gun control (Pew Research Center, 2012).

Crime rates are high in some of the largest cities of the world, including Lima, Peru; São Paulo, Brazil; and Manila, Philippines—all of which have rapid population growth and millions of desperately poor people. Outside of big cities, however, the traditional character of low-income societies and their strong families allow local communities to control crime informally.

Some types of crime have always been multinational, such as terrorism, espionage, and arms dealing (Martin & Romano, 1992). But today, the globalization we are experiencing on many fronts also extends to crime. A recent case in point is the illegal drug trade. In part, the problem of illegal drugs in the United States is a *demand* issue. That is, the demand for cocaine and other drugs in this country is high, and many people risk arrest or even a violent death for a chance to get rich in the drug trade. But the *supply* side of the issue is just as important. The South American nation of Colombia has long looked to cocaine production as a significant part of its national economy. Similarly, about 90 percent of cocaine that enters the United States comes through Mexico, enriching at least some of that nation's people (and causing violence that affects many more). Clearly, drug dealing and many other crimes are closely related to social and economic conditions both in the United States and elsewhere.

Different countries have different strategies for dealing with crime. The use of capital punishment (the death penalty) is one example. According to Amnesty International (2012), China executes more people than the rest of the world combined—probably in the thousands—but does not divulge its numbers. Of the 680 documented executions in 2011, 87 percent were in Iran, Saudi Arabia, Iraq, Yemen, and the United States. Global Map 9–1 shows which countries currently use capital punishment. The global trend is toward abolishing the death penalty: Amnesty International (2012) reports that since 1985, sixty-seven nations have ended this practice.

When economic activity such as selling illegal drugs takes place outside of the law, people turn to violence rather than courts to settle disagreements. In Central America, drug violence has pushed the homicide rate to the highest level in the world.

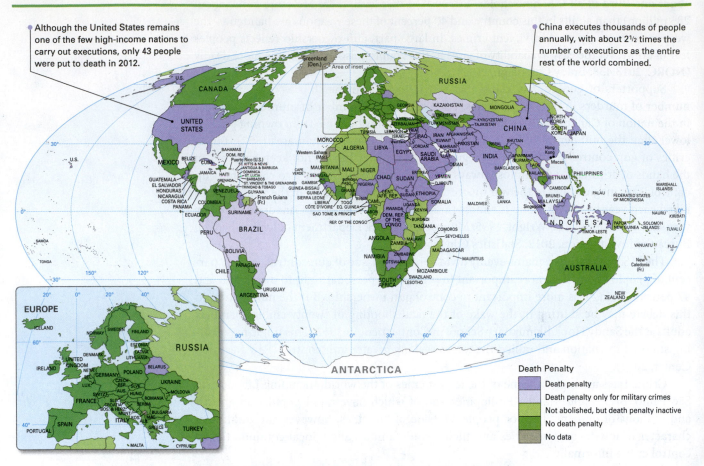

Although the United States remains one of the few high-income nations to carry out executions, only 43 people were put to death in 2012.

China executes thousands of people annually, with about 2½ times the number of executions as the entire rest of the world combined.

Death Penalty

- Death penalty
- Death penalty only for military crimes
- Not abolished, but death penalty inactive
- No death penalty
- No data

GLOBAL MAP 9–1 Capital Punishment in Global Perspective

The map identifies fifty-eight countries in which the law allows the death penalty for ordinary crimes; in eight more, the death penalty is reserved for exceptional crimes under military law or during times of war. The death penalty does not exist in ninety-seven countries; in thirty-five more, although the death penalty remains in law, no execution has taken place in more than ten years. Compare rich and poor nations: What general pattern do you see? In what way are the United States and Japan exceptions to this pattern?

Source: Amnesty International (2012).

The U.S. Criminal Justice System

9.7 Analyze the operation of the criminal justice system.

The criminal justice system is a society's formal system of social control. We shall briefly examine the key elements of the U.S. criminal justice system: police, courts, and the system of punishment and corrections. First, however, we must understand an important principle that underlies the entire system, the idea of due process.

Due Process

Due process is a simple but very important idea: The criminal justice system must operate according to law. This principle is grounded in the first ten amendments to the U.S. Constitution—known as the Bill of Rights—adopted by Congress in 1791. The Constitution offers various protections to any person charged with a crime. Among these are the right to counsel, the right to refuse to testify against oneself, the right to confront all accusers, freedom from being tried twice for the same crime, and freedom from being "deprived of life, liberty, or property without due process of law." Furthermore, the Constitution gives all people the right to a speedy and public trial by jury and freedom from excessive bail and from "cruel and unusual" punishment.

In general terms, the concept of due process means that anyone charged with a crime must receive (1) fair notice of legal proceedings, (2) the opportunity to present a defense during a hearing on the charges, which must be conducted according to law, and (3) a judge or jury that weighs evidence impartially (Inciardi, 2000).

Due process limits the power of government, with an eye toward this nation's cultural support of individual rights and freedoms. Deciding exactly how far government can go is an ongoing process that makes up much of the work of the judicial system, especially the U.S. Supreme Court.

Police must be allowed discretion if they are to handle effectively the many different situations they face every day. At the same time, it is important for police to treat people fairly. Here we see police deciding to make an arrest at an Occupy Wall Street rally in New York City in 2012. What factors do you think enter into this decision?

Police

The police generally serve as the primary point of contact between a society's population and the criminal justice system. In principle, the police maintain public order by enforcing the law. Of course, there is only so much that the 698,460 full-time police officers in the United States can do to monitor the activities of 311 million people. As a result, the police use a great deal of personal judgment in deciding which situations warrant their attention and how to handle them.

How do police officers carry out their duties? In a study of police behavior in five cities, Douglas Smith and Christy Visher (1981; Smith, 1987) concluded that because they must act swiftly, police officers quickly size up situations in terms of six factors. First, the more serious they think the situation is, the more likely they are to make an arrest. Second, officers take account of the victim's wishes in deciding whether or not to make an arrest. Third, the odds of arrest go up the more uncooperative a suspect is. Fourth, officers are more likely to take into custody someone they have arrested before, presumably because this suggests guilt. Fifth, the presence of observers increases the chances of arrest. According to Smith and Visher, the presence of observers prompts police to take stronger control of a situation, if only to move the encounter from the street (the suspect's turf) to the police department (where law officers have the edge). Sixth, all else being equal, police officers are more likely to arrest people of color than whites, perceiving suspects of African or Latino descent as either more dangerous or more likely to be guilty.

Courts

After arrest, a court determines a suspect's guilt or innocence. In principle, U.S. courts rely on an adversarial process involving attorneys—one representing the defendant and another the state—in the presence of a judge, who monitors legal procedures.

In practice, however, 97 percent of criminal convictions result from the process of **plea bargaining**, *a legal negotiation in which a prosecutor reduces a charge in exchange for a defendant's guilty plea.* Without ever going to trial, for example, the state may offer a defendant charged with burglary a lesser charge, perhaps possession of burglary tools, in exchange for a guilty plea (U.S. Department of Justice, 2012).

Plea bargaining is widespread because it spares the system the time and expense of trials. A trial is usually unnecessary if there is little disagreement over the facts of the case. In addition, because the number of cases entering the system annually has doubled over the past decade, prosecutors could not bring every case to trial even if they wanted to. By quickly resolving most of their work, the courts channel their resources into the most important cases.

plea bargaining a legal negotiation in which a prosecutor reduces a charge in exchange for a defendant's guilty plea

Television shows like *Suits* suggest that the criminal justice system carefully weighs the guilt and innocence of defendants. But as explained here, only 3 percent of criminal cases are actually resolved through a formal trial.

Read in **MySocLab**
Document: *Trend to Lighten Harsh Sentences Catches On in Conservative States* by Charlie Savage

But a system of plea bargaining pressures defendants (who are presumed innocent) to plead guilty. A person can exercise the right to a trial, but only at the risk of receiving a more severe sentence if found guilty at trial. Furthermore, low-income defendants enter the process with the guidance of a public defender—typically an overworked and underpaid attorney who may devote little time to even the most serious cases. In a 2012 decision, the U.S. Supreme Court recognized that although plea bargaining may be efficient, it can compromise due process by undercutting both the adversarial process and the rights of defendants to effective legal representation.

Punishment

In 2011, on a sunny Saturday morning in Tucson, Arizona, Congressional Representative Gabrielle Giffords sat down behind a folding table positioned in front of a supermarket. At two minutes before 10 o'clock, she tweeted "My 1ˢᵗ Congress on Your Corner starts now. Please stop by to let me know what's on your mind." Shortly after that, a taxi pulled to the curb nearby and dropped off a single passenger, a troubled young man who had violence on his mind. He paid the cab fare with a $20 bill, and then he walked toward Ms. Giffords and pulled out a Glock 19 pistol loaded with thirty-one cartridges. Gunshots rang out for fifteen deadly seconds. The human toll: twenty people shot, including six who died (von Drehle, 2011).

Such cases force us to wonder about the reasons for acts of violence and also to ask how a society should respond to such acts. In the case of the Tucson shootings, the offender appears to have been suffering from serious mental illness, so there is some question about the extent to which he is responsible for his actions (Cloud, 2011). But typically, of course, the question of responsibility is resolved when a suspect is apprehended and put on trial. If found to be responsible for the actions, the next step is punishment.

What does a society gain through the punishment of wrongdoers? Scholars answer with four basic reasons: retribution, deterrence, rehabilitation, and societal protection.

Retribution

The oldest justification for punishment is to satisfy people's need for **retribution**, *an act of moral vengeance by which society makes the offender suffer as much as the suffering caused by the crime.* Retribution rests on a view of society as a moral balance. When criminality upsets this balance, punishment in equal measure restores the moral order, as suggested in the ancient code calling for "an eye for an eye, a tooth for a tooth."

In the Middle Ages, most Europeans viewed crime as sin—an offense against God as well as society that required a harsh response. Today, although critics point out that retribution does little to reform the offender, many people consider vengeance reason enough for punishment.

Deterrence

A second justification for punishment is **deterrence**, *the attempt to discourage criminality through the use of punishment.* Deterrence is based on the eighteenth-century Enlightenment idea that humans, as calculating and rational creatures, will not break the law if they think that the pain of punishment will outweigh the pleasure of the crime.

Deterrence emerged as a reform measure in response to the harsh punishments based on retribution. Why put someone to death for stealing if theft can be discouraged with a prison sentence? As the concept of deterrence gained acceptance in industrial nations, the execution and physical mutilation of criminals in most high-income societies were replaced by milder forms of punishment such as imprisonment.

Punishment can deter crime in two ways. *Specific deterrence* is used to convince an individual offender that crime does not pay. Through *general deterrence,* the punishment of one person serves as an example to others.

Rehabilitation

The third justification for punishment is **rehabilitation**, *a program for reforming the offender to prevent later offenses.* Rehabilitation arose along with the social sciences in the nineteenth century. Since then, sociologists have claimed that crime and other deviance spring from a social environment marked by poverty or a lack of parental supervision. Logically, then, if offenders learn to be deviant, they can also learn to obey the rules; the key is controlling their environment. *Reformatories* or *houses of correction* provided controlled settings where people could learn proper behavior (recall the description of total institutions in Chapter 5, "Socialization").

Like deterrence, rehabilitation motivates the offender to conform. In contrast to deterrence and retribution, which simply make the offender suffer, rehabilitation encourages constructive improvement. Unlike retribution, which demands that the punishment fit the crime, rehabilitation tailors treatment to each offender. Thus identical crimes would prompt similar acts of retribution but different rehabilitation programs.

Societal Protection

A final justification for punishment is **societal protection**, *rendering an offender incapable of further offenses temporarily through imprisonment or permanently by execution.* Like deterrence, societal protection is a rational approach to punishment intended to protect society from crime.

Currently, about 2.3 million people are jailed in the United States. Although the crime rate has gone down in recent years, the number of offenders locked up across the country has gone up, more than quadrupling since 1980. This rise in the prison population reflects tougher public attitudes toward crime and punishing offenders and stiffer sentences handed down by courts. The trend also reflects an increasing number of drug-related arrests—half of all federal inmates are serving time for drug offenses. As a result, the United States now incarcerates about one of every one hundred adults—a larger share of its population than any other country in the world—a fact that leads some critics to label this country the "incarceration nation." Although the "get-tough" policies enacted decades ago were initially praised for reducing street crime, now analysts claim that sending so many people to prison actually may be pushing up poverty rates (Pew Center on the States, 2010; U.S. Department of Justice, 2011; International Centre for Prison Studies, 2012; Zakaria, 2012; Tierney, 2013).

EVALUATE The Summing Up table on page 264 reviews the four justifications for punishment. However, an accurate assessment of the consequences of punishment is no simple task.

The value of retribution lies in Durkheim's claim that punishing the deviant person increases society's moral awareness. For this reason, punishment was traditionally a public event. Although the last public execution in the United States took place in Kentucky more than seventy years ago, today's mass media ensure public awareness of executions carried out inside prison walls (Kittrie, 1971).

Four Justifications for Punishment

retribution an act of moral vengeance by which society makes the offender suffer as much as the suffering caused by the crime

deterrence the attempt to discourage criminality through the use of punishment

rehabilitation a program for reforming the offender to prevent later offenses

societal protection rendering an offender incapable of further offenses temporarily through imprisonment or permanently by execution

Summing Up

Four Justifications for Punishment	
Retribution	The oldest justification for punishment.
	Punishment is society's revenge for a moral wrong.
	In principle, punishment should be equal in severity to the crime itself.
Deterrence	An early modern approach.
	Crime is considered social disruption, which society acts to control.
	People are viewed as rational and self-interested; deterrence works because the pain of punishment outweighs the pleasure of crime.
Rehabilitation	A modern strategy linked to the development of social sciences.
	Crime and other deviance are viewed as the result of social problems (such as poverty) or personal problems (such as mental illness).
	Social conditions are improved; treatment is tailored to the offender's condition.
Societal protection	A modern approach easier to carry out than rehabilitation.
	Even if society is unable or unwilling to rehabilitate offenders or reform social conditions, people are protected by the imprisonment or execution of the offender.

criminal recidivism later offenses by people previously convicted of crimes

Does punishment deter crime? Despite our extensive use of punishment, our society has a high rate of **criminal recidivism**, *later offenses by people previously convicted of crimes*. About three-fourths of prisoners in state penitentiaries have been jailed before, and about two-thirds of people released from prison are arrested again within three years (DeFina & Arvanites, 2002; U.S. Department of Justice, 2008). So does punishment really deter crime? According to researchers, just 49 percent of all violent crimes and 37 percent of all property crimes are known to police, and of what is known, only about one in five crimes results in an arrest. Most crimes, therefore, go unpunished, so the old saying that "crime doesn't pay" rings hollow.

Prisons provide short-term societal protection by keeping offenders off the streets, but they do little to reshape attitudes or behavior in the long term (Carlson, 1976; R. A. Wright, 1994). Perhaps rehabilitation is an unrealistic expectation, because according to Sutherland's theory of differential association, locking up criminals together for years probably strengthens criminal attitudes and skills. Imprisonment also stigmatizes prisoners, making it harder for them to find legitimate employment later on (Pager, 2003). Finally, prison breaks the social ties inmates may have in the outside world, which, following Hirschi's control theory, makes inmates more likely to commit new crimes upon release.

CHECK YOUR LEARNING What are society's four justifications for punishment? Does sending offenders to prison accomplish each of them? Why?

The Death Penalty

Perhaps the most controversial issue involving punishment is the death penalty. Between 1977 and 2013, more than 7,500 people were sentenced to death in U.S. courts; 1,320 executions were carried out.

In thirty-three states, the law allows the state to execute offenders convicted of very serious crimes such as first-degree murder. But although a majority of states do permit capital punishment, only a few states are likely to carry out executions. Across the United States, half of the 3,170 people on death row in April 2012 were in just four states: California, Texas, Florida, and Pennsylvania (U.S. Department of Justice, Bureau of Justice Statistics, 2011; Death Penalty Information Center, 2012).

Opponents of capital punishment point to research suggesting that the death penalty has limited value as a crime deterrent. Countries such as Canada, where the death penalty has been abolished, have not seen a rise in the number of murders. Critics also point out that the United States is the only Western, high-income nation that routinely executes offenders. As public concern about the death penalty has increased, the use of capital punishment has declined, falling from 85 executions in 2000 to 43 in 2012.

Public opinion surveys reveal that the share of U.S. adults who claim to support the death penalty as a punishment for murder remains high (60 percent) and has been fairly stable over time (NORC, 2013:253). College students hold about the same attitudes as everyone else, with about two-thirds of first-year students expressing support for the death penalty (Pryor et al., 2013).

But judges, criminal prosecutors, and members of trial juries are less and less likely to call for the death penalty. One reason is that because the crime rate has come down in recent years, the public now has less fear of crime and is less interested in applying the most severe punishment.

To increase the power of punishment to deter crime, capital punishment was long carried out in public. Here is a photograph from the last public execution in the United States, with twenty-two-year-old Rainey Bethea standing on the scaffold moments from death in Owensboro, Kentucky, on August 16, 1937. Children as well as adults were in the crowd. Now that the mass media report the story of executions across the country, states carry out capital punishment behind closed doors.

A second reason is public concern that the death penalty may be applied unjustly. The analysis of DNA evidence—a recent advance—from old crime scenes has shown that many people were wrongly convicted of a crime. Across the country, between 1973 and 2013, 141 people who had been sentenced to death were released from death row, including 18 in which new DNA evidence demonstrated their innocence. Such findings were one reason that in 2011, the governor of Oregon declared a moratorium on executions, claiming that he could no longer support what he characterized as a "compromised and inequitable system" (State of Oregon, 2011).

A third reason for the decline in the use of the death penalty is that more states now permit judges and juries to sentence serious offenders to life in prison without the possibility of parole. Such punishment offers to protect society from dangerous criminals who can be "put away" forever without requiring an execution.

Fourth and finally, many states now shy away from capital punishment because of the high cost of prosecuting capital cases. Death penalty cases require more legal work and demand superior defense lawyers, often at public expense. In addition, such cases commonly include testimony by various paid "experts," including physicians and psychiatrists, which also runs up the costs of trial. Then there is the cost of many appeals that almost always follow a conviction leading to the sentence of death. When all these factors are put together, the cost of a death penalty case typically exceeds the cost of sending an offender to prison for life. So it is easy to see why states often choose not to seek the death penalty (Dwyer, 2011).

Organizations opposed to the death penalty are challenging this punishment in court. In 2008, for example, the U.S. Supreme Court upheld the use of lethal injection against the charge that this procedure amounts to cruel and unusual punishment, which would be unconstitutional (Greenhouse, 2008). In 2012, the people of California voted in a state referendum to uphold the use of the death penalty, although that state has executed just thirteen offenders in the last thirty-five years. Overall, there is no indication at present that the United States will end the use of the death penalty. But the trend is away from this type of punishment.

Community-Based Corrections

Prisons certainly keep convicted criminals off the streets, but the evidence suggests that they do little to rehabilitate most offenders. Furthermore, prisons are expensive to operate. One study put the average cost of supporting one prison inmate for a year at $31,286. This amount is in addition to the initial cost of building the detention facilities (Vera Institute of Justice, 2012).

One alternative to the traditional prison that has been adopted by cities and states across the country is **community-based corrections**, *correctional programs operating within society at large rather than behind prison walls*. Community-based corrections have three main advantages: They reduce costs, reduce overcrowding in prisons, and allow for supervision of convicts while eliminating the hardships of prison life and the stigma that accompanies going to jail. In general, the idea of community-based corrections is not so much to punish as to reform; such programs are therefore usually offered to individuals who have committed less serious offenses and appear to be good prospects for avoiding future criminal violations. In principle, community-based corrections promise to lower the cost of the criminal justice system. At the same time, limited implementation of this approach has not resulted in any significant decrease in the country's prison population (Vera Institute of Justice, 2012).

community-based corrections correctional programs operating within society at large rather than behind prison walls

Probation

One form of community-based corrections is *probation,* a policy permitting a convicted offender to remain in the community under conditions imposed by a court, including regular supervision. Courts may require that a probationer receive counseling, attend a drug treatment program, hold a job, avoid associating with "known criminals," or anything else a judge thinks is appropriate. Typically, a probationer must check in with an officer of the court (the probation officer) on a regular schedule to make sure the guidelines are being followed. Should the probationer fail to live up to the conditions set by the court or commit a new offense, the court may revoke probation and send the offender to jail.

Shock Probation

A related strategy is *shock probation,* a policy by which a judge orders a convicted offender to prison for a short time but then suspends the remainder of the sentence in favor of probation. Shock probation is thus a mix of prison and probation, used to impress on the offender the seriousness of the situation without resorting to full-scale imprisonment. In some cases, shock probation takes place in a special "boot camp" facility where offenders might spend one to three months in a military-style setting intended to teach discipline and respect for authority (Cole & Smith, 2002).

Parole

Parole is a policy of releasing inmates from prison to serve the remainder of their sentences in the local community under the supervision of a parole officer. Although some sentences specifically deny the possibility of parole, most inmates become eligible for parole after serving a certain portion of their sentences behind bars. At that time, a parole board evaluates the risks and benefits of the inmate's early release from prison. If parole is granted, the parole board monitors the offender's conduct until the sentence is completed. Should the offender not comply with the conditions of parole or be arrested for another crime, the board can revoke parole and return the offender to prison to complete the sentence.

EVALUATE Researchers have carefully studied both probation and parole to see how well these programs work. Evaluations of both these policies are mixed. There is little question that probation and parole programs are much less expensive than conventional imprisonment; they also free up room in prisons for people who commit more serious crimes. Yet research suggests that although probation and shock probation do seem to work for some people, they do not significantly reduce recidivism. Parole is also useful to prison officials as a means to encourage good behavior among inmates. But levels of crime among those released on parole are so high that a number of states as well as the federal government have terminated their parole programs entirely.

Such evaluations point to a sobering truth: The criminal justice system—operating on its own—cannot eliminate crime. As the Controversy & Debate box explains, although police, courts, and prisons do have an effect on crime rates, crime and other forms of deviance are not just the acts of "bad people" but reflect the operation of society itself.

Controversy & Debate

Violent Crime Is Down—But Why?

Duane: I'm a criminal justice major, and I want to be a police officer. Crime is a huge problem in America, and police are what keep the crime rate low.

Sandy: I'm a sociology major. As for the crime rate, I'm not sure it's quite that simple… .

During the 1980s, crime rates shot upward. Just about everyone lived in fear of violent crime, and in many large cities, the numbers killed and wounded made whole neighborhoods seem like war zones. There seemed to be no solution to the problem.

Yet in the 1990s, serious crime rates began to fall, until by 2000, they were at levels not seen in more than a generation. Why? Researchers point to several reasons:

1. **A reduction in the youth population.** It was noted earlier that young people (particularly males) are responsible for much violent crime. During the 1990s, the population aged fifteen to twenty-four dropped by 5 percent (in part because of the legalization of abortion in 1973).

2. **Changes in policing.** Much of the drop in crime (as well as the earlier rise in crime) took place in large cities. In New York City, the number of murders fell from 2,245 in 1990 to just 515 in 2011. Part of the reason for the decline is that the city has adopted a policy of *community policing,* which means that police are concerned not just with making arrests but also with preventing crime before it happens. Officers get to know the areas they patrol and stop young

men for jaywalking or other minor infractions so they can check them for concealed weapons (the word has gotten around that you can be arrested for carrying a gun). There are also *more* police at work in large cities. Los Angeles added more than 2,000 police officers in the 1990s, which contributed to its drop in violent crime during that period.

3. **More prisoners.** Between 1985 and 2011, the number of inmates in jails and prisons soared from 750,000 to more than 2.3 million. The main reason for this increase is tough laws that demand prison time for certain crimes, such as drug offenses. Mass incarceration has consequences. As one analyst put it, "When you lock up an extra million people, it's got to have some effect on the crime rate" (Franklin Zimring, quoted in Witkin, 1998:31).

4. **A better economy.** The U.S. economy boomed during the 1990s. Unemployment was down, reducing the likelihood that some people would turn to crime out of economic desperation. The logic here is simple: More jobs equal fewer crimes. But although we may see crime rates rise as the recent economic downturn continues, government data show that, through the end of 2011, crime rates have continued to fall.

5. **The declining drug trade.** Many analysts agree that the most important factor in reducing rates of violent crime was the decline of crack cocaine. Crack came on the scene about 1985, and violence spread as young people—especially in the inner cities and increasingly armed with guns—became part of a booming drug trade. By the early 1990s, however, the popularity of crack began to fall as people saw the damage it was causing to entire communities. This realization, coupled with steady economic improvement and stiffer sentences for drug offenses, helped bring about the turnaround in violent crime.

The current picture looks better relative to what it was a decade or two ago. But one researcher cautions, "It looks better… only because the early 1990s were so bad. So let's not fool ourselves into thinking everything is resolved. It's not."

What Do You Think?

1. Do you support the policy of community policing? Why or why not?

2. What are the pros and cons of building more prisons?

3. Which of the factors mentioned here do you think is the most important in crime control? Which is least important? Why?

Sources: Winship & Berrien (1999), Donahue & Leavitt (2000), Rosenfeld (2002), Liptak (2008), Mitchell (2008), Antlfinger (2009), and U.S. Department of Justice, Federal Bureau of Investigation (2012).

One reason that crime has gone down is that there are more than 2 million people incarcerated in this country. This has caused severe overcrowding of facilities such as this Chino, California, prison.

Seeing Sociology in Everyday Life

Heroes and villains: Helping us (at least most of the time) obey the rules

As this chapter has explained, every society is a system of social control that encourages conformity to certain norms and discourages deviance or norm breaking. One way society does this is through the construction of heroes and villains. Heroes, of course, are people we are supposed to "look up to" and use as role models. Villains are people whom we "look down on" and reject their example, allowing them to become "anti-heroes" who point us in the opposite direction. Organizations of all types create heroes and villains that serve as guides to everyday behavior. In each case that follows, who is being made into a hero? Why? What are the values or behaviors that we are encouraged to copy in our own lives?

Colleges and universities create heroes in various ways. Here we see the president of Washington College (Maryland) awarding the Sophie Kerr Prize at a recent graduation ceremony. This prize, which included a check for more than $50,000, recognized English major Claire Tompkins's ability to write outstanding short stories. What is heroic in this case? What does graduating with honors or a Latin praise (*cum laude* and so on) define as heroic? What about villains—how do colleges and universities create them, too?

Religious organizations, too, use heroes to encourage certain behavior and beliefs. The Roman Catholic Church has defined the Virgin Mary and more than 10,000 other men and women as "saints." For what reasons might someone be honored in this way? What do saints do for the rest of us?

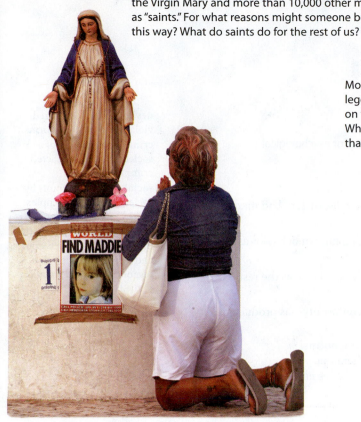

Most sports have a "hall of fame." A larger-than-life-size statue of the legendary slugger Babe Ruth attracts these New York City children on their visit to the Baseball Hall of Fame in Cooperstown, New York. What are the qualities that make an athlete "legendary"? Isn't it more than just how far someone hits a ball?

HINT A society without heroes and villains would be one in which no one cared what people thought or how they acted. Societies create heroes as role models that should inspire us to be more like them. Societies create heroes by emphasizing one aspect of someone's life and ignoring lots of other things. For example, Babe Ruth was a great ball player, but his private life was sometimes less than inspiring. Perhaps this is why the Catholic church never considers anyone a candidate for sainthood until after—usually long after—the person has died.

Seeing Sociology in *Your* Everyday Life

1. Do athletic teams, fraternities and sororities, and even people in a college classroom create heroes and villains? Explain how and why.

2. Go to MySocLab and click on the Student Resources link to access the Sociology in Focus blog, where you can read the latest posts by a team of young sociologists who apply the sociological perspective to topics of popular culture.

3. Based on the material presented in this chapter, we might say that "Deviance is a difference that makes a difference." That is, deviance is constructed as part of social life because, as Emile Durkheim argued, it is a necessary part of society. Make a (private) list of ten negative traits that have been directed at you (or that you have directed at yourself). Then look at your list and try to determine what it says about the society we live in. Why, in other words, do these differences make a difference to members of our society? Go to the "Seeing Sociology in *Your* Everyday Life" feature in MySocLab to learn more about how sociological thinking can give you a deeper understanding of right and wrong and find suggestions for how to respond to difference.

Making the Grade

Chapter 9
Deviance

What Is Deviance?

 9.1 Explain how sociology addresses limitations of a biological or psychological approach to deviance. (pages 238–42)

👁 **Watch** the **Video** in **MySocLab**

Deviance refers to norm violations ranging from minor infractions, such as bad manners, to major infractions, such as serious violence.

Biological theories focus on individual abnormality and explain human behavior as the result of biological instincts.

Psychological theories focus on individual abnormality and see deviance as the result of "unsuccessful socialization."

Sociological theories view all behavior—deviance as well as conformity—as products of society. Sociologists point out that

- what is deviant varies from place to place according to cultural norms
- behavior and individuals become deviant as others define them that way
- what and who a society defines as deviant reflect who has and does not have social power

deviance the recognized violation of cultural norms
crime the violation of a society's formally enacted criminal law
social control attempts by society to regulate people's thoughts and behavior
criminal justice system the organizations—police, courts, and prison officials—that respond to alleged violations of the law

The Functions of Deviance: Structural-Functional Theories

 9.2 Apply structural-functional theories to the topic of deviance. (pages 242–45)

👁 **Watch** the **Video** in **MySocLab**

Durkheim claimed that deviance is a normal element of society that affirms cultural norms and values, clarifies moral boundaries, brings people together, and encourages social change.

Merton's **strain theory** explains deviance in terms of a society's cultural goals and the means available to achieve them.

Deviant subcultures are discussed by Cloward and Ohlin, Cohen, Miller, and Anderson.

Defining Deviance: Symbolic-Interaction Theories

 9.3 Apply symbolic-interaction theories to the topic of deviance. (pages 245–49)

👁 **Watch** the **Video** in **MySocLab**

Labeling theory claims that deviance depends less on what someone does than on how others react to that behavior. If people respond to primary deviance by stigmatizing a person, secondary deviance and a deviant career may result.

The **medicalization of deviance** is the transformation of moral and legal deviance into a medical condition. In practice, this means a change in labels, replacing "good" and "bad" with "sick" and "well."

Sutherland's **differential association theory** links deviance to how much others encourage or discourage such behavior.

Hirschi's **control theory** states that imagining the possible consequences of deviance often discourages such behavior. People who are well integrated into society are less likely to engage in deviant behavior.

labeling theory the idea that deviance and conformity result not so much from what people do as from how others respond to those actions
stigma a powerfully negative label that greatly changes a person's self-concept and social identity
medicalization of deviance the transformation of moral and legal deviance into a medical condition

270 CHAPTER 9 Deviance

Deviance and Inequality: Social-Conflict Theories

9.4 Apply social-conflict theories to the topic of deviance. (pages 249–52)

Based on Karl Marx's ideas, social-conflict theory holds that laws and other norms operate to protect the interests of powerful members of any society. In a capitalist society, law operates to support the capitalist economy.

- **White-collar offenses** are committed by people of high social position as part of their jobs. Sutherland claimed that such offenses are rarely prosecuted and are most likely to end up in civil rather than criminal court.
- **Corporate crime** refers to illegal actions by a corporation or people acting on its behalf. Although corporate crimes cause considerable public harm, most cases of corporate crime go unpunished.
- **Organized crime** has a long history in the United States, especially among categories of people with few legitimate opportunities.

white-collar crime crime committed by people of high social position in the course of their occupations
corporate crime the illegal actions of a corporation or people acting on its behalf
organized crime a business supplying illegal goods or services

Deviance, Race, and Gender: Race-Conflict and Feminist Theories

9.5 Apply race-conflict and feminist theories to the topic of deviance. (pages 252–54)

- Race-conflict theory and feminist theory explain that what people consider deviant reflects the relative power and privilege of different categories of people.
- **Hate crimes** are crimes motivated by racial or other bias; they target people who are already disadvantaged based on race, gender, or sexual orientation.
- In the United States and elsewhere, societies control the behavior of women more closely than that of men.

hate crime a criminal act against a person or a person's property by an offender motivated by racial or other bias

Crime

9.6 Identify patterns of crime in the United States and around the world. (pages 254–60)

 Explore the **Map** in **MySocLab**

Crimes against the person (violent crime) include murder, aggravated assault, and forcible rape. **Crimes against property** (property crime) include burglary, larceny-theft, and arson.

- 63% of people arrested for property crimes and 80% of people arrested for violent crimes are male.
- Street crime is more common among people of lower social position. Including white-collar and corporate crime makes class differences in criminality smaller.
- More whites than African Americans are arrested for street crimes. However, African Americans are arrested more often than whites in relation to their population size. Asian Americans have a lower-than-average rate of arrest.

crimes against the person crimes that direct violence or the threat of violence against others; also known as *violent crimes*
crimes against property crimes that involve theft of property belonging to others; also known as *property crimes*
victimless crimes violations of law in which there are no obvious victims

The U.S. Criminal Justice System

9.7 Analyze the operation of the criminal justice system. (pages 260–67)

 Read the **Document** in **MySocLab**

The **police** maintain public order by enforcing the law.

- Police use personal discretion in deciding whether and how to handle a situation.
- Research suggests that police are more likely to make an arrest if the offense is serious, if bystanders are present, or if the suspect is African American or Latino.

Courts rely on an adversarial process in which attorneys—one representing the defendant and one representing the state—present their cases in the presence of a judge who monitors legal procedures.

- In practice, U.S. courts resolve most cases through plea bargaining. Though efficient, this method puts less powerful people at a disadvantage.

There are four justifications for **punishment**: retribution, deterrence, rehabilitation, and societal protection.

- The **death penalty** remains controversial in the United States, the only high-income Western nation that routinely executes serious offenders. The trend is toward fewer executions.
- **Community-based corrections** include probation and parole. These programs lower the cost of supervising people convicted of crimes and reduce prison overcrowding but have not been shown to reduce recidivism.

plea bargaining a legal negotiation in which a prosecutor reduces a charge in exchange for a defendant's guilty plea
retribution an act of moral vengeance by which society makes the offender suffer as much as the suffering caused by the crime
deterrence the attempt to discourage criminality through the use of punishment
rehabilitation a program for reforming the offender to prevent later offenses
societal protection rendering an offender incapable of further offenses temporarily through imprisonment or permanently by execution
criminal recidivism later offenses by people previously convicted of crimes
community-based corrections correctional programs operating within society at large rather than behind prison walls

10 Social Stratification

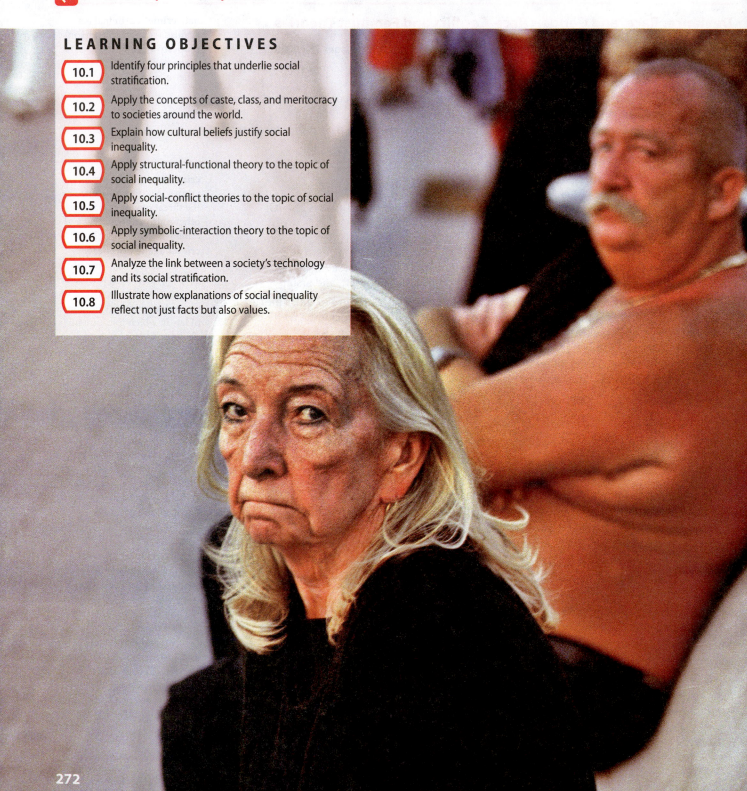

((• Listen to Chapter 10 in MySocLab

LEARNING OBJECTIVES

10.1 Identify four principles that underlie social stratification.

10.2 Apply the concepts of caste, class, and meritocracy to societies around the world.

10.3 Explain how cultural beliefs justify social inequality.

10.4 Apply structural-functional theory to the topic of social inequality.

10.5 Apply social-conflict theories to the topic of social inequality.

10.6 Apply symbolic-interaction theory to the topic of social inequality.

10.7 Analyze the link between a society's technology and its social stratification.

10.8 Illustrate how explanations of social inequality reflect not just facts but also values.

the Power of Society
to affect life expectancy

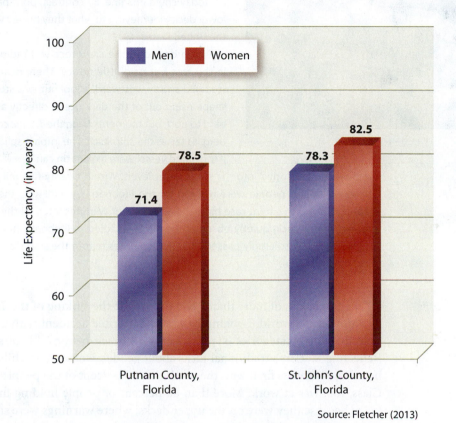

Source: Fletcher (2013)

How does where we reside affect our chances to live to a ripe old age? In the state of Florida, two northern counties near Jacksonville that are situated side by side provide an answer to this question. Putnam County has relatively low average income, while oceanfront St. John's County has higher average income and home values that are twice as high. In 2010, men in Putnam County had a life expectancy of 71.4 years; in St. John's County, the figure was 78.3 years. Among women, life expectancy was 78.5 years in Putnam County compared to 82.5 years in St. John's County. In these differences we see the power of society—in this case, the importance of social class—to affect not only people's quality of life but also how long they live.

Chapter Overview

This chapter introduces the central concept of social stratification, the focus of the next six chapters of the text. Social stratification is very important because our social standing affects almost everything about our lives.

On April 10, 1912, the ocean liner *Titanic* slipped away from the docks of Southampton, England, on its maiden voyage across the North Atlantic to New York. A proud symbol of the new industrial age, the towering ship carried 2,300 men, women, and children. Some of the passengers were enjoying more luxury than most travelers today could imagine. By contrast, poor passengers crowded the lower decks, journeying to what they hoped would be a better life in the United States.

Two days out, the crew received radio warnings of icebergs in the area but paid little notice. Then, near midnight, as the ship steamed swiftly westward, a lookout was stunned to see a massive shape rising out of the dark ocean directly ahead. The ship steered hard to port, but moments later, the *Titanic* collided with a huge iceberg, as tall as the ship itself. The impact split open the ship's side as if the grand vessel were a giant tin can.

Seawater exploded into the ship's lower levels. Within twenty-five minutes of impact, alarms had sounded and people were rushing for the lifeboats. By 2:00 A.M., the bow was completely submerged, and the stern rose high above the water. Minutes later, all the ship's lights went out. Clinging to the deck, quietly observed by those huddled in lifeboats, hundreds of helpless passengers and crew solemnly passed their final minutes before the ship disappeared into the frigid Atlantic (Lord, 1976).

The tragic loss of more than 1,600 lives made the sinking of the *Titanic* headline news around the world. Looking back at this terrible accident with a sociological eye, we note that some categories of passengers had much better odds of survival than others. Reflecting that era's traditional ideas about gender, women and children were allowed to board the lifeboats first, with the result that 80 percent of the people who died were men. Class, too, was at work. More than 60 percent of people holding first-class tickets were saved because they were on the upper decks, where warnings were sounded first and lifeboats were accessible. Only 36 percent of the second-class passengers survived, and of the third-class passengers on the lower decks, only 24 percent escaped drowning. On board the *Titanic,* class turned out to mean much more than the quality of accommodations—it was a matter of life or death.

The fate of the passengers on the *Titanic* dramatically illustrates how social inequality affects the way people live and sometimes whether they live at all. This chapter explains the meaning of social stratification and explores how patterns of inequality differ around the world and throughout human history. Chapter 11 continues the story by examining social inequality in the United States, and Chapter 12 takes a broader look at how our country fits into a global system of wealth and poverty.

What Is Social Stratification?

10.1 Identify four principles that underlie social stratification.

For tens of thousands of years, humans lived in small hunting and gathering societies. Although members of these bands might single out one person as swifter, stronger, or more skillful in collecting food, everyone had roughly the same social standing. As societies became more complex—a process detailed in Chapter 4 ("Society")—a major change came about. Societies began to elevate specific categories of people above others, giving some parts of the population more wealth, power, and prestige than others.

Social stratification, *a system by which a society ranks categories of people in a hierarchy,* is based on four important principles:

1. **Social stratification is a trait of society, not simply a reflection of individual differences.** Many of us think of social standing in terms of personal talent and effort, and as a result, we often exaggerate the extent to which we control our own fate. Did a higher percentage of the first-class passengers on the *Titanic* survive because they were better swimmers than second- and third-class passengers? No. They did better because of their privileged position on the ship, which gave them first access to the lifeboats. Similarly, children born into wealthy families are more likely than children born into poverty to enjoy good health, do well in school, succeed in a career, and live a long life. Neither the rich nor the poor created social stratification, yet this system shapes the lives of us all.

2. **Social stratification carries over from generation to generation.** We have only to look at how parents pass their social position on to their children to see that stratification is a trait of societies rather than individuals. Some people, especially in high-income societies, do experience **social mobility,** *a change in position within the social hierarchy.* Social mobility may be upward or downward. We celebrate the achievements of rare individuals such as Gisele Bundchen (from Brazil) and rapper Jay-Z (United States), neither of whom ever finished high school but both of whom nevertheless managed to rise to fame and fortune. Some people move downward in the social hierarchy because of business failures, illness, divorce, or economic recession and rising unemployment. More often people move *horizontally*; they switch from one job to another at about the same social level. The social standing of most people remains much the same over their lifetime.

3. **Social stratification is universal but variable.** Social stratification is found everywhere. Yet *what* is unequal and *how* unequal it is varies from one society to another. In some societies, inequality is mostly a matter of prestige; in others, wealth or power is the key element of difference. In addition, some societies contain more inequality than others.

4. **Social stratification involves not just inequality but beliefs as well.** Any system of inequality not only gives some people more than others but also defines these arrangements as fair. Just as the details of inequality vary, the explanations of *why* people should be unequal differ from society to society.

The personal experience of poverty is clear in this photograph of mealtime in a homeless shelter. The main sociological insight is that although we feel the effects of social stratification personally, our social standing is largely the result of the way society (or a world of societies) structures opportunity and reward. To the core of our being, we are all products of social stratification.

Watch in **MySocLab** **Video:** *Sociology in Focus: Social Stratification*

social stratification a system by which a society ranks categories of people in a hierarchy

social mobility a change in position within the social hierarchy

Caste and Class Systems

10.2 Apply the concepts of caste, class, and meritocracy to societies around the world.

Sociologists distinguish between *closed systems,* which allow for little change in social position, and *open systems,* which permit much more social mobility. Closed systems are called *caste systems*, and more open systems are called *class systems*.

Watch in **MySocLab** **Video:** *The Basics: Social Stratification*

The Caste System

A **caste system** is *social stratification based on ascription, or birth.* A pure caste system is closed because birth alone determines a person's entire future, allowing little or no social mobility based on individual effort. People live out their lives in the rigid categories assigned to them, without the possibility of change for the better or worse.

An Illustration: India

Many of the world's societies, most of them agrarian, are caste systems. In India, much of the population still lives in traditional villages where the caste system continues to be part of everyday life. The traditional Indian system identifies four major castes (or *varnas,* from a Sanskrit word that means "color"): Brahman, Kshatriya, Vaishya, and Sudra. On the local level, each of these is composed of hundreds of subcaste groups (*jatis*).

From birth, a caste system determines the direction of a person's life. First, with the exception of farming, which is open to everyone, families in each caste perform one type of work, as priests, soldiers, barbers, leather workers, street sweepers, and so on.

Second, a caste system demands that people marry others of the same ranking. If people were to enter into "mixed" marriages with members of other castes, what rank would their children hold? Sociologists call this pattern of marrying within a social category *endogamous* marriage (*endo-* stems from the Greek word for "within"). According to tradition—this practice is now rare and is found only in remote rural areas—Indian parents select their children's future marriage partners, often before the children reach their teens.

Third, caste guides everyday life by keeping people in the company of "their own kind." Norms reinforce this practice by teaching, for example, that a "purer" person of a higher caste is "polluted" by contact with someone of lower standing.

Fourth, caste systems rest on powerful cultural beliefs. Indian culture is built on the Hindu tradition that doing the caste's life work and accepting an arranged marriage are moral duties.

Caste and Class Systems

caste system social stratification based on ascription, or birth

class system social stratification based on both birth and individual achievement

meritocracy social stratification based on personal merit

Caste and Agrarian Life

Caste systems are typical of agrarian societies because agriculture demands a lifelong routine of hard work. By teaching a sense of moral duty, a caste system ensures that people are disciplined for a lifetime of work and are willing to perform the same jobs as their parents. Thus the caste system has hung on in rural areas of India some seventy years after being

In rural India, the traditional caste system still shapes people's lives. This girl is a member of the "untouchables," a category below the four basic castes. She and her family are clothes washers, people who clean material "polluted" by blood or human waste. Such work is defined as unclean for people of higher caste position. In the cities, by contrast, caste has given way to a class system where achievement plays a greater part in social ranking and income and consumption are keys to social standing.

formally outlawed. People living in the industrial cities of India have many more choices about work and marriage partners than people in rural areas.

Another country long dominated by caste is South Africa, although the system of *apartheid*, or separation of the races, is no longer legal and is now in decline. The Thinking Globally box takes a closer look.

Thinking Globally

Race as Caste: A Report from South Africa

Jerome: Wow. I've been reading about racial caste in South Africa. I'm glad that's history.

Reggie: But racial inequality is far from over....

At the southern tip of the African continent lies South Africa, a country about the size of Alaska with a population of about 51 million. For 300 years, the native Africans who lived there were ruled by white people, first by the Dutch traders and farmers who settled there in the mid-seventeenth century and then by the British, who colonized the area early in the nineteenth century. By the early 1900s, the British had taken over the entire country, naming it the Union of South Africa.

In 1961, the nation declared its independence from Britain, calling itself the Republic of South Africa, but freedom for the black majority was still decades away. To ensure their political control over the black population, whites instituted the policy of *apartheid*, or racial separation. Apartheid, written into law in 1948, denied blacks national citizenship, ownership of land, and any voice in the nation's government. As a lower caste, blacks received little schooling and performed menial, low-paying jobs. White people with even average wealth had at least one black household servant.

The members of the white minority claimed that apartheid protected their cultural traditions from the influence of people they considered inferior. When blacks resisted apartheid, whites used brutal military repression to maintain their power. Even so, steady resistance—especially from younger blacks, who demanded a political voice and economic opportunity—gradually forced the country to change. Criticism from other industrial nations added to the pressure. By the mid-1980s, the tide began to turn as the South African government granted limited political rights to people of mixed race and Asian ancestry. Next came the right of all people to form labor unions, to enter occupations once limited to whites, and to own property. Officials also repealed apartheid laws that separated the races in public places.

The pace of change increased in 1990 with the release from prison of Nelson Mandela, who led the fight against apartheid. In 1994, the first national election open to all races made Mandela president, ending centuries of white minority rule.

Despite this dramatic political change—and strong economic growth during the last decade—social stratification in South Africa is still based on race. Even with the right to own property, one-fourth of black South Africans have no work, and one-fourth of the population lives below the poverty line. The worst off are some 7 million *ukuhleleleka,* which means "marginal people" in the Xhosa language. Soweto-by-the-Sea may sound like a summer getaway, but it is a shantytown, home to thousands of people who live crammed into shacks made of packing crates, corrugated metal, cardboard, and other discarded materials. Recent years have seen increasing signs of prosperity, some shopping centers have been built, and most streets are now paved. But the poverty rate stands at about 25 percent, and some families still live without electricity for lights or refrigeration. Some also lack plumbing, forcing people to use buckets to haul sewage. In some communities, women line up to take a turn at a single water tap that serves as many as 1,000 people. Jobs are hard to come by, with an unemployment rate of about 25 percent. For those who do find work, most feel lucky to earn $250 a month.

South Africa's current president, Jacob Zuma, who was elected in 2009, leads a nation still crippled by its history of racial caste. Tourism is up and holds the promise of an economic boom in years to come, but the economy is still dominated by the white minority. The country can break from the past only by providing real opportunity to all its people.

What Do You Think?

1. How has race been a form of caste in South Africa?

2. Although apartheid is no longer law, why does racial inequality continue to shape South African society?

3. Does race operate as an element of caste in the United States? Explain your answer.

Sources: Mabry & Masland (1999), Murphy (2002), Perry (2009), McGroarty & Maylie (2012), and World Bank (2012).

The Class System

Because a modern economy must attract people to work in many occupations other than farming, it depends on developing people's talents in diverse fields. This gives rise to a **class system**, *social stratification based on both birth and individual achievement*.

Class systems are more open than caste systems, so people who gain schooling and skills may experience social mobility. As a result, class distinctions become blurred, and even blood relatives may have different social standings. Categorizing people according to their color, sex, or social background comes to be seen as wrong in modern societies as all people gain political rights and, in principle, equal standing before the law. In addition, work is no longer fixed at birth but involves some personal choice. Greater individuality also translates into more freedom in selecting a marriage partner.

Meritocracy

The concept of **meritocracy** refers to *social stratification based on personal merit*. Because industrial societies need to develop a broad range of abilities beyond farming, stratification is based not just on the accident of birth but also on *merit* (from a Latin word meaning "earned"), which includes a person's knowledge, abilities, and effort. A rough measure of merit is the importance of a person's job and how well it is done. To increase the extent of meritocracy, industrial societies expand equality of opportunity and teach people to expect unequal rewards based on individual performance.

A pure meritocracy has never existed, but in such a system social position would depend entirely on a person's ability and effort. Such a system would have ongoing social mobility, blurring social categories as individuals continuously move up or down in the system, depending on their latest performance.

Caste societies define merit in different terms, emphasizing loyalty to the system—that is, dutifully performing whatever job comes with the social position a person has from birth. Because they assign jobs before anyone can know anything about a person's talents or interests, caste systems waste human potential. On the other hand, because caste systems clearly assign everyone a "place" in society and a general type of work, they are very stable and orderly. A need for some amount of order is one reason industrial and postindustrial societies keep some elements of caste—such as letting wealth pass from generation to generation—rather than becoming complete meritocracies. A pure meritocracy would have individuals moving up and down the social ranking all the time. Such extreme social mobility would pull apart families and other social groupings. After all, economic performance is not everything: Would we want to evaluate our family members solely on how successful they are in their jobs outside the home? Probably not. Class systems in industrial societies develop some meritocracy to promote productivity and efficiency, but they keep caste elements, such as family, to maintain order and social unity.

Status Consistency

status consistency the degree of uniformity in a person's social standing across various dimensions of social inequality

Status consistency is *the degree of uniformity in a person's social standing across various dimensions of social inequality*. A caste system has limited social mobility and high status consistency, so the typical person has the same relative ranking with regard to wealth, power, and prestige. The greater mobility of class systems produces less status consistency, so people are ranked higher on some dimensions of social standing and lower on others. In the United States, for example, most college professors with advanced academic degrees enjoy high social prestige but earn only modest incomes. Low status consistency means that it is harder to define people's social position. Therefore, the lines between *classes* are much harder to define than the lines that separate *castes*.

Caste and Class: The United Kingdom

The mix of caste and meritocracy in class systems is well illustrated by the United Kingdom (Great Britain—consisting of England, Wales, and Scotland—and Northern Ireland), an industrial nation with a long agrarian history.

Aristocratic England

In the Middle Ages, England had an aristocratic society that resembled a caste system. At the top, the aristocrats included the leading members of the church, who were thought to speak with the authority of God. Some clergy were local priests who were not aristocrats and who lived simple lives. But the highest church officials lived in palaces and presided over an organization that owned much land, which was the major source of wealth. Church leaders, typically referred to as the *first estate* in France and other European countries, also had a great deal of power to shape the political events of the day.

The rest of the aristocracy, which in France and other European countries was known as the *second estate*, was a hereditary nobility that made up barely 5 percent of the population. The royal family—the king and queen at the top of the power structure—as well as lesser nobles (including several hundred families headed by men titled as dukes, earls, and barons) together owned most of the nation's land. Most of the men and women within the aristocracy were wealthy due to their ownership of land, and they had many servants for their homes as well as ordinary farmers to work their fields. With all their work done for them by others, members of the aristocracy had no occupation and came to believe that engaging in a trade or any other work for income was beneath them. Aristocrats used their leisure time to develop skills in horseback riding and warfare and to cultivate refined tastes in art, music, and literature.

To prevent their vast landholdings from being divided by heirs after they died, aristocrats devised the law of *primogeniture* (from the Latin meaning "firstborn"), which required that all property pass to the oldest son or other male relation. Younger sons had to find other means of support. Some of these men became leaders in the church—where they would live as well as they were used to—and helped tie together the church and the state by having members of the same families running both. Other younger sons within the aristocracy became military officers or judges or took up other professions considered honorable for gentlemen. In an age when no woman could inherit her father's property and few women had the opportunity to earn a living on their own, a noble daughter depended for her security on marrying well.

Below the high clergy and the rest of the aristocracy, the vast majority of men and women were simply called *commoners* or, in France and other European countries, the *third estate*. Most commoners were serfs working land owned by nobles or the church. Unlike members of the aristocracy, most commoners had little schooling and were illiterate.

As the Industrial Revolution expanded England's economy, some commoners living in cities made enough money to challenge the nobility. More emphasis on meritocracy, the increasing importance of money, and the expansion of schooling and legal rights eventually blurred the difference between aristocrats and commoners and gave rise to a class system.

Perhaps it is a sign of the times that these days, traditional titles are put up for sale by aristocrats who need money. In 1996, for example, Earl Spencer—the brother of the late Princess Diana—sold one of his titles, Lord of Wimbledon, to raise the $300,000 he needed to redo the plumbing in one of his large homes (McKee, 1996).

The United Kingdom Today

The United Kingdom has a class system, but caste elements from England's aristocratic past still play a part in social standing. A small number of British families continue to hold considerable inherited wealth and enjoy high prestige, receive schooling at excellent universities,

In 2011, Prince William, second in line to the British throne, married commoner Catherine Middleton, who then took the title, "Her Royal Highness the Duchess of Cambridge." They now take their place as part of a royal family that traces its ancestry back more than a thousand years—an element of caste that remains in the British class system.

and are members of social networks in which people have substantial political influence. A traditional monarch, Queen Elizabeth II, is the United Kingdom's head of state, and Parliament's House of Lords is composed of "peers," about half of whom are aristocrats of noble birth. However, control of government has passed to the House of Commons, where the prime minister and other leaders reach their positions by achievement—winning an election—rather than by birth.

Lower in the class hierarchy, roughly one-fourth of the British people form the middle class. Many earn comfortable incomes from professions and business and are likely to have investments in the form of stocks and bonds. Below the middle class, perhaps half of all Britons consider themselves "working-class," earning modest incomes through manual labor. The remaining one-fourth of the British people make up the lower class, the poor who lack steady work or who work full time but are paid too little to live comfortably. Most lower-class Britons live in the nation's northern and western regions, which have been further impoverished by the closings of mines and factories.

The British mix of caste elements and meritocracy has produced a highly stratified society with some opportunity to move upward or downward, much the same as exists in the United States (Long & Ferrie, 2007). Historically, British society has been somewhat more castelike than the United States, a fact reflected in the importance attached to linguistic accent. Distinctive patterns of speech develop in any society when people are set off from one another over several generations. People in the United States treat accent as a clue to where a person lives or grew up (we can easily identify a midwestern "twang" or a southern "drawl"). In the United Kingdom, however, accent is a mark of social class, with upper-class people speaking "the King's English" but most people speaking "like commoners." So different are these two accents that the British seem to be, as the saying goes, "a single people divided by a common language."

Another Example: Japan

Social stratification in Japan also mixes caste and meritocracy. Japan is both the world's oldest continuously operating monarchy and a modern society where wealth follows individual achievement.

Aristocratic Japan

By the fifth century C.E., Japan was an agrarian society with a rigid caste system, ruled by an imperial family, containing both aristocrats and commoners. The emperor ruled by divine right (meaning that he claimed that God intended him to rule), and his military leader (*shogun*) enforced the emperor's rule with the help of regional nobles or warlords.

Below the nobility were the *samurai,* a warrior caste whose name means "to serve." This second rank of Japanese society was made up of soldiers who learned martial arts and who lived by a code of honor based on absolute loyalty to their leaders.

As in Great Britain, most people in Japan at this time in history were commoners who worked very hard to live from day to day. Unlike their European counterparts, however, Japanese commoners were not lowest in rank. At the bottom were the *burakumin,* or "outcasts," looked down on by both lord and commoner. Like the lowest-caste groups in India, these outcasts lived apart from others, performed the most distasteful work, and could not change their social standing.

Modern Japan

By the 1860s (the time of the Civil War in the United States), the nobles realized that Japan's traditional caste system would prevent the country from entering the modern industrial era. Besides, as in Britain, some nobles were happy to have their children marry wealthy commoners who had more money than they did. As Japan opened up to the larger world, the traditional caste system weakened. In 1871, the Japanese legally banned the social category of *burakumin,* although some people still looked down on those whose ancestors held this rank. After Japan's defeat in World War II, the nobles lost their privileges and, although the emperor remains as a symbol of Japan's traditions, he has little real power.

Social stratification in Japan is very different from the rigid caste system of centuries ago. Today, Japanese society consists of "upper," "upper-middle," "lower-middle," and "lower" classes. The exact lines between these classes are unclear to most Japanese, and many people do move between classes over time. But because Japanese culture tends to respect tradition, family background is never far from the surface when sizing up someone's social standing. Officially, everyone is equal before the law, but in reality, many people still look at one another through the centuries-old lens of caste.

Finally, traditional ideas about gender continue to shape Japanese society. Legally, the two sexes are equal, but men dominate women in many ways. Because Japanese parents are more likely to send sons than daughters to college, there is a significant gender gap in education. With the recent economic downturn in Japan, many more women have entered the labor force. But most working women fill lower-level support positions in the corporate world. In Japan, only about 10 percent of corporate and political leaders are women. In short, individual achievement in Japan's modern class system operates in the shadow of centuries of traditional male privilege (Norbeck, 1983; Brinton, 1988; French, 2002; OECD, 2009).

Classless Societies? The Former Soviet Union

Nowhere in the world do we find a society without some degree of social inequality. Yet some nations have claimed to be classless.

The Second Russian Revolution

The Union of Soviet Socialist Republics (USSR), which rivaled the United States as a military superpower in the mid- to late twentieth century, was born out of a revolution in Russia in 1917. The Russian Revolution ended the feudal aristocracy in which a nobility ruled the country and transferred farms, factories, and other productive property from private ownership to state control.

The Russian Revolution was guided by the ideas of Karl Marx, who believed that private ownership of productive property was the basis of social classes (see Chapter 4, "Society"). When the state took control of the economy, Soviet officials boasted that they had created the first modern classless society.

Critics, however, pointed out that based on their jobs, the Soviet people were actually stratified into four unequal categories. At the top were high government officials, known as *apparatchiks*. Next came the Soviet intelligentsia, including lower government officials, college professors, scientists, physicians, and engineers. Below them were manual workers and, at the lowest level, the rural peasantry.

In reality, the Soviet Union was not classless at all. But putting factories, farms, colleges, and hospitals under state control did create more economic equality (although with sharp differences in power) than in capitalist societies such as the United States.

The Modern Russian Federation

In 1985, Mikhail Gorbachev came to power in the Soviet Union with a new economic program known as *perestroika* ("restructuring"). Gorbachev saw that although the Soviet system had reduced economic inequality, living standards lagged far behind those of other industrial nations. Gorbachev tried to generate economic growth by reducing the inefficient centralized control of the economy, which had proved to be inefficient.

One of the major events of the twentieth century was the socialist revolution in Russia, which led to the creation of the Soviet Union. Following the ideas of Karl Marx, the popular uprising overthrew a feudal aristocracy, as depicted in the 1920 painting *Bolshevik* by Boris Mikhailovich Kustodiev.

Gorbachev's economic reforms turned into one of the most dramatic social movements in history. People in the Soviet Union and in other socialist countries of Eastern Europe blamed their poverty and their lack of basic freedoms on the repressive ruling class of Communist party officials. Beginning in 1989, people throughout Eastern Europe toppled their socialist governments, and at the end of 1991, the Soviet Union itself collapsed, with its largest republic remaking itself as the Russian Federation.

The Soviet Union's story shows that social inequality involves more than economic resources. Soviet society did not have the extremes of wealth and poverty found in the United Kingdom, Japan, and the United States. But an elite class existed all the same, based on political power rather than wealth.

What about social mobility in so-called classless societies? During the twentieth century, there was as much upward social mobility in the Soviet Union as in the United States. Rapidly expanding industry and government drew many poor rural peasants into factories and offices. This trend illustrates what sociologists call **structural social mobility**, *a shift in the social position of large numbers of people due more to changes in society itself than to individual efforts.*

structural social mobility a shift in the social position of large numbers of people due more to changes in society itself than to individual efforts

November 24, Odessa, Ukraine. The first snow of our voyage flies over the decks as our ship docks at Odessa, the former Soviet Union's southernmost port on the Black Sea. We gaze up the Potemkin Steps, the steep stairway up to the city, where bloody violence that eventually led to the Russian Revolution took place. It has been several years since our last visit, and much has changed; in fact, the Soviet Union itself has collapsed. Has life improved? For some people, certainly: There are now chic boutiques where well-dressed shoppers buy fine wines, designer clothes, and imported perfumes. But for most people, life seems much worse. Flea markets line the curbs as families sell their home furnishings. When meat costs $4 a pound and the average person earns about $30 a month, people become desperate. Even the city has to save money by turning off streetlights after 8:00 P.M. The spirits of most people seem as dim as Odessa's streets.

During the 1990s, the forces of structural social mobility in the new Russian Federation turned downward. One indicator is that the average life span for Russian men dropped by five years and for women by two years. Many factors are involved in this decline, including Russia's poor health care system, but the Russian people clearly have suffered in the turbulent period of economic change that began in 1991 (Gerber & Hout, 1998; Mason, 2004; World Bank, 2012).

The hope was that in the long run, closing inefficient state industries would improve the nation's economic performance. The economy has expanded and, compared to many struggling nations in Western Europe, Russia is doing pretty well economically. Today, fewer people are in poverty than at any time in the last two decades. But many Russians continue to face hard times. In addition, there is widespread concern both inside and outside of Russia that President Putin's increasing control over the country is eroding political freedoms (Zuckerman, 2006; Wendle, 2009; World Bank, 2012).

China: Emerging Social Classes

Sweeping political and economic change has affected not just the former Soviet Union but also the People's Republic of China. After the Communist revolution in 1949, the state took control of all farms, factories, and other productive property. Communist party leader Mao Zedong declared all types of work to be equally important, so officially, social classes no longer existed.

The new program greatly reduced economic inequality. But as in the Soviet Union, social differences remained. The country was ruled by a political elite with enormous power and considerable privilege; below them were managers of large factories as well as skilled professionals; next came industrial workers; at the bottom were rural peasants, who were not even allowed to leave their villages and migrate to cities.

Further economic change came in 1978 when Mao died and Deng Xiaoping became China's leader. The state gradually loosened its hold on the economy, allowing a new class of business owners to emerge. In 2012, Xi Jinping became the leader of the Chinese Communist Party, which continues to control the country. In recent years, many political leaders have prospered and they have joined the ranks of the small but wealthy elite who control new privately run industries. China's economy has experienced years of rapid growth and only recently shows signs of slowing. One sign of this prosperity is the fact that the nation is now included among the middle-income countries. Much of this recent economic growth has been concentrated in cities, especially in coastal areas, where living standards have soared far above those in China's rural interior. A sign of the times is that the luxury automobile producer Bentley now sells more of its cars in China than in its home nation, Great Britain (Richburg, 2011; United Nations, 2011).

China has the fastest-growing economy of all the major nations and currently manufactures more products than even the United States. With more and more money to spend, the Chinese are now a major consumer of automobiles—a fact that probably saved the Buick brand from extinction.

Since the late 1990s, the booming cities along China's coast have become home to many thousands of people made rich by the expanding economy. In addition, these cities have attracted more than 100 million young migrants from rural areas in search of better jobs and a better life. Many more have wanted to move to the booming cities, but the government still restricts movement, which has the effect of slowing upward social mobility. For those who have been able to move, the jobs that are available are generally better than the work that people knew before. But many of these new jobs are dangerous, and most pay wages that barely meet the higher costs of living in the city, so that the majority of the migrants remain poor.

In general, however, China's population has experienced structural upward mobility as the economy has expanded by about 10 percent annually over the past three decades. China now has the world's second largest economy (after that of the United States). This rise reflects in part how much of the world's manufacturing takes place in China (Wu & Treiman, 2007; Chang, 2008; Powell, 2008; World Bank, 2011).

One new category in China's social hierarchy consists of the *hai gui*, a term derived from words meaning "returned from overseas" or "sea turtles." The ranks of the "sea turtles" are increasing by tens of thousands each year as young women and men return from education in other countries, in many cases from college and university campuses in the United States. These young people, most from privileged families to begin with, typically return to China to find many opportunities and soon become very influential (Liu & Hewitt, 2008).

The young members of rich and politically well-connected families have emerged as a new economic and political aristocracy. To illustrate, Xi Jinping, the new Communist Party leader and since 2013 the nation's president, is himself the son of an early leader in the Chinese Communist Party. Sometimes called "princelings," these powerful people (who are mostly men) may feud among themselves as they seek to gain influence. But most observers of the current scene in China agree that they represent another force to be reckoned with (Beech, 2012; Johnson, 2012).

In China, a new class system is emerging, with the nation's elite now a mix of the old Party officials, new business leaders, and a new "aristocratic" class of well-connected people. Economic inequality in China has increased as many members of this new business and political elite have become millionaires and even billionaires.

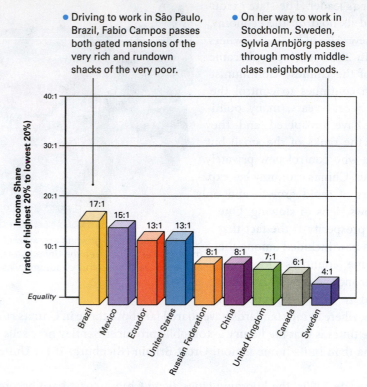

- Driving to work in São Paulo, Brazil, Fabio Campos passes both gated mansions of the very rich and rundown shacks of the very poor.

- On her way to work in Stockholm, Sweden, Sylvia Arnbjörg passes through mostly middle-class neighborhoods.

FIGURE 10–1 Economic Inequality in Selected Countries, 2012

Many low- and middle-income countries have greater economic inequality than the United States. But the United States has more economic inequality than most high-income nations.

Sources: U.S. Census Bureau (2012) and World Bank (2012).

As Figure 10–1 shows, economic inequality in China is now slightly greater than it is in the United Kingdom. With so much change under way in China, that country's social stratification is likely to remain dynamic for some time to come (Bian, 2002; Johnson, 2012).

Ideology: Supporting Stratification

10.3 Explain how cultural beliefs justify social inequality.

How do societies persist without sharing resources more equally? The highly stratified British aristocracy and the caste system in Japan each survived for centuries, and for 2,000 years, people in India accepted the idea that they should be privileged or poor based on the accident of birth.

A major reason that social hierarchies endure is **ideology**, *cultural beliefs that justify particular social arrangements, including patterns of inequality.* A belief—for example, the idea that rich people are smart and poor people are lazy—is ideological to the extent that it supports inequality by defining it as fair.

Plato and Marx on Ideology

According to the ancient Greek philosopher Plato (427–347 B.C.E.), every culture considers some type of inequality just. Although Karl Marx understood this, he was far more critical of inequality than Plato. Marx criticized capitalist societies for defending wealth and power in the hands of a few as "a law of the marketplace." Capitalist law, he continued, defines the right to own property and ensures that money stays within the same families

ideology cultural beliefs that justify particular social arrangements, including patterns of inequality

from one generation to the next. In short, Marx concluded, culture and institutions combine to support a society's elite, which is why established hierarchies last such a long time.

Historical Patterns of Ideology

Ideology changes along with a society's economy and technology. Because agrarian societies depend on most people's lifelong labor, they develop caste systems that make carrying out the duties of a person's social position or "station" a moral responsibility. With the rise of industrial capitalism, an ideology of meritocracy emerges, defining wealth and power as prizes to be won by the individuals who perform the best. This change means that the poor—often given charity under feudalism—come to be looked down on as personally undeserving. This harsh view is found in the ideas of the early sociologist Herbert Spencer, as explained in the Thinking About Diversity box.

History shows how difficult it is to change social stratification. However, challenges to the status quo always arise. The traditional idea that "a woman's place is in the home," for example, has given way to increased economic opportunities for women in many societies today. The continuing progress toward racial equality in South Africa is another case of the widespread rejection of the ideology of apartheid. The popular uprisings against political dictatorships across the Middle East that began in 2011 show us that this process of challenging entrenched social stratification continues.

Thinking About Diversity: Race, Class, and Gender

The Meaning of Class: Is Getting Rich "the Survival of the Fittest"?

Jake: "My dad is amazing. He's really smart!"

Frank: "You mean he's rich. He owns I don't know how many businesses."

Jake: "Do you think people get rich without being smart?"

It's a question we all wonder about. How much is our social position a matter of intelligence? What about hard work? Being born to the "right family"? Even "dumb luck"?

More than in most societies, in the United States we link social standing to personal abilities including intelligence. In 2010, *Time* magazine put Mark Zuckerberg on the cover and announced that he was "Person of the Year" for inventing Facebook. For this achievement, and amassing a fortune estimated at about $7 billion, it is easy to imagine that this Harvard dropout is a pretty smart guy (Grossman, 2010).

But the idea that social standing is linked to intelligence goes back a long time. We have all heard the words "the survival of the fittest," which describe our society as a competitive jungle in which the "best" survive and the rest fall behind. The phrase was coined by one of sociology's pioneers, Herbert Spencer (1820–1903), whose ideas about social inequality are still widespread today.

Spencer, who lived in England, eagerly followed the work of the natural scientist Charles Darwin (1809–1882). Darwin's theory of biological evolution held that a species changes physically over many generations as it adapts to the natural environment. Spencer incorrectly applied Darwin's theory to the operation of society, which does not operate according to biological principles. In Spencer's distorted view, society became the "jungle," with the "fittest" people rising to wealth and the "failures" sinking into miserable poverty.

It is no surprise that Spencer's views, wrong as they were, were popular among the rising U.S. industrialists of the day. John D. Rockefeller (1839–1937), who made a vast fortune building the oil industry, recited Spencer's "social gospel" to young children in Sunday school. As Rockefeller saw it, the growth of giant corporations—and the astounding wealth of their owners—was merely the result of the survival of the fittest, a basic fact of nature. Neither Spencer nor Rockefeller had much sympathy for the poor, seeing poverty as evidence of individuals' failing to measure up in a competitive world. Spencer opposed social welfare programs because he thought they penalized society's "best" people (through taxes) and rewarded its "worst" members (through welfare benefits). By incorrectly using Darwin's theory, the rich could turn their backs on everyone else, assuming that inequality was inevitable and somehow "natural."

Today, sociologists point out that our society is far from a meritocracy, as Spencer claimed. And it is not the case that companies or individuals who generate lots of money necessarily benefit society. The people who made hundreds of millions of dollars selling subprime mortgages in recent years certainly ended up hurting just about everyone. But Spencer's view that the "fittest" rise to the top remains widespread in our very unequal and individualistic culture.

What Do You Think?

1. How much do you think inequality in our society can correctly be described as "the survival of the fittest"? Why?

2. Why do you think Spencer's ideas are still popular in the United States today?

3. Is how much you earn a good measure of your importance to society? Why or why not?

Explaining Stratification: Structural-Functional Theory

10.4 Apply structural-functional theory to the topic of social inequality.

Why does social stratification exist at all? One answer, consistent with the structural-functional approach, is that social inequality plays a vital part in the smooth operation of society. This argument was set forth more than sixty years ago by Kingsley Davis and Wilbert Moore (1945).

The Davis-Moore Thesis

The **Davis-Moore thesis** states that *social stratification has beneficial consequences for the operation of society.* How else, ask Davis and Moore can we explain the fact that some form of social stratification has been found in every society?

Davis and Moore note that modern societies have hundreds of occupational positions of varying importance. Certain jobs—say, washing windows or answering a telephone—are fairly easy and can be performed by almost anyone. Other jobs—such as designing new generations of computers or transplanting human organs—are difficult and demand the scarce talents of people with extensive and expensive training.

Therefore, Davis and Moore explain, the greater the functional importance of a position, the more rewards a society attaches to it. This strategy promotes productivity and efficiency because rewarding important work with income, prestige, power, and leisure encourages people to do these jobs and to work better, longer, and harder. In short, unequal rewards (the foundation of social stratification) benefit society as a whole.

Davis and Moore claim that any society could be egalitarian, but only to the extent that people are willing to let *anyone* perform *any* job. Equality would also demand that someone who carries out a job poorly be rewarded the same as someone who performs it well. Such a system would offer little incentive for people to try their best, thereby reducing the society's productive efficiency.

The Davis-Moore thesis suggests the reason stratification exists; it does not state what rewards a society should give to any occupational position or how unequal the rewards should be. It merely points out that positions a society considers more important must offer enough rewards to draw talented people away from less important work.

Oprah Winfrey reported income of $165 million in 2011. Guided by the Davis-Moore thesis, why would societies reward some people with so much more fame and fortune than others? How would Karl Marx answer this question?

Read in **MySocLab** **Document:** *Some Principles of Stratification* by Kingsley Davis and Wilbert E. Moore, and the response by Melvin Tumin

Davis-Moore thesis the functional analysis claiming that social stratification has beneficial consequences for the operation of society

EVALUATE Although the Davis-Moore thesis is an important contribution to understanding social stratification, it has provoked criticism. Melvin Tumin (1953) wondered, first, how we assess the importance of a particular occupation. Perhaps the high rewards our society gives to physicians result partly from deliberate efforts by the medical profession to limit the supply of physicians and thereby increase the demand for their services.

Furthermore, do rewards actually reflect the contribution someone makes to society? With income of about $85 million per year, boxer Floyd Mayweather, the world's highest-paid athlete in 2011, earned more in four days than President Obama earned all year. Would anyone argue that boxing is more important than leading a country? What about members of the U.S. military serving in Iraq or Afghanistan? Facing the risks of combat, a private first-class in the U.S. Army earned only $22,000 in 2012 (Pomerantz & Rose, 2010; Defense Finance and Accounting Service, 2012). And we might also wonder about the heads of the big Wall Street financial firms that collapsed in 2008. It seems reasonable to conclude that these corporate leaders made some bad and harmful decisions, yet their salaries were astronomical. Even after finishing its worst year ever, with losses of $27 billion, Merrill Lynch paid bonuses of more than $1 million to each of more than

700 employees. Lloyd Blankfein, CEO of Goldman Sachs, paid himself a stock bonus worth $12.6 million (an amount that it would take an army private 600 years to earn), despite his company's falling profits during 2010, a year in which salaries and benefits in the financial industry hit an all-time high. Increased government regulation and lackluster performance led most Wall Street companies to trim salaries and bonuses in 2011 and 2012. Even so, as one analyst put it, "while payouts may be disappointing, they are still far higher than what most people will ever see" (Moore, 2012; see also *New York Times,* 2011; Roth, 2011; Badenhausen, 2012).

Even top executives who perform badly and lose their jobs do surprisingly well. During the recent financial industry meltdown, Chuck Prince was forced to resign as head at Citigroup, but not before receiving a "severance package" worth more than $30 million. When insurance giant AIG failed, corporate leader Martin Sullivan left the company, receiving $47 million on the way out (Beck & Simon, 2008; Scherer, 2008). Do corporate executives deserve such megasalaries for their contributions to society?

Second, Tumin claimed that Davis and Moore ignore how caste elements of social stratification can prevent the development of individual talent. Born to privilege, rich children have opportunities to develop their abilities that many gifted poor children never have.

Third, living in a society that places so much emphasis on money, we tend to overestimate the importance of high-paying work; what do stockbrokers or people who trade international currencies really contribute to society? For the same reason, it is difficult for us to see the value of work that is not oriented toward making money, such as parenting, creative writing, playing music in a symphony, or just being a good friend to someone in need (Packard, 2002).

Finally, the Davis-Moore thesis ignores how social inequality may promote conflict and even outright revolution. This criticism leads us to the social-conflict approach, which provides a very different explanation for social inequality.

CHECK YOUR LEARNING State the Davis-Moore thesis in your own words. What are Tumin's criticisms of this thesis?

Explaining Stratification: Social-Conflict Theories

10.5 Apply social-conflict theories to the topic of social inequality.

Social-conflict analysis argues that rather than benefiting society as a whole, social stratification benefits some people and disadvantages others. This analysis draws heavily on the ideas of Karl Marx, with contributions from Max Weber.

Karl Marx: Class Conflict

Karl Marx, whose ideas are discussed at length in Chapter 4 ("Society"), explained that most people have one of two basic relationships to the means of production: They either own productive property or labor for others. Different productive roles arise from different social classes. In medieval Europe, aristocratic families, including high church officials and titled nobles, owned the land on which peasants labored as farmers. In industrial class systems, the capitalists (or the bourgeoisie) own the factories, which use the labor of workers (the proletarians).

Watch in **MySocLab**
Video: *Sociology in Focus: Economy and Work*

Back in the Great Depression of the 1930s, "tent cities" that were home to desperately poor people could be found in much of the United States. The depression came to an end, but poverty persisted. The recent recession sparked a resurgence of tent cities, including this one in Fresno, California. How would structural-functional analysis explain such poverty? What about the social-conflict approach?

Marx lived during the nineteenth century, a time when a small number of industrialists in the United States were amassing great fortunes. The business tycoons who led the country's move into the industrial age included Andrew Carnegie (steel), J. P. Morgan (finance and steel), John D. Rockefeller (oil), and John Jacob Astor (real estate; Astor was the richest passenger on the *Titanic* and one of the few very rich passengers to drown when the ship sank). All of them lived in fabulous mansions staffed by dozens of servants. Even by today's standards, their incomes were staggering. For example, Carnegie earned about $20 million a year in 1900 (more than $550 million in today's dollars), when the average worker earned roughly $500 a year (Baltzell, 1964; Williamson, 2012).

Marx explained that capitalist society *reproduces the class structure* in each new generation. This happens as families gain wealth and pass it down from generation to generation. But, he predicted, oppression and misery would eventually drive the working majority to come together to overthrow capitalism in favor of a socialist system that would put an end to class differences.

EVALUATE Marx has had enormous influence on sociological thinking. But his revolutionary ideas, calling for the overthrow of capitalist society, also make his work highly controversial.

One of the strongest criticisms of Marxism is that it denies a central idea of the Davis-Moore thesis: that a system of unequal rewards is necessary to place talented people in the right jobs and to motivate them to work hard. Marx separated reward from performance; his egalitarian ideal was based on the principle "from each according to his ability; to each according to his needs" (Marx & Engels, 1972:388, orig. 1848). However, failure to reward individual performance may be precisely what caused the low productivity of the former Soviet Union and other socialist economies around the world. Defenders of Marxism respond to such criticism by asking why people assume that humanity is inherently selfish rather than social, and they note that individual rewards are not the only way to motivate people to perform their social roles (Clark, 1991).

A second problem is that the revolutionary change Marx predicted has failed to happen, at least in advanced capitalist societies. The next section explains why.

CHECK YOUR LEARNING How does Marx's view of social stratification differ from the Davis-Moore thesis?

Why No Marxist Revolution?

Despite Marx's prediction, capitalism is still thriving. Why have industrial workers not overthrown capitalism? Ralf Dahrendorf (1959) suggested four reasons:

1. **Fragmentation of the capitalist class.** Today, millions of stockholders, rather than single families, own most large companies. Day-to-day corporate operations are in the hands of a large class of managers, who may or may not be major stockholders. With stock widely held—about half of households in the United States own stocks—more

and more people have a direct stake in the capitalist system (Federal Reserve Board, 2012).

2. **A higher standard of living.** As Chapter 16 ("The Economy and Work") explains, a century ago, most workers were in factories or on farms employed in **blue-collar occupations**, *lower-prestige jobs that involve mostly manual labor.* Today, most workers are engaged in **white-collar occupations**, *higher-prestige jobs that involve mostly mental activity.* These jobs are in sales, customer support, management, and other service fields. Most of today's white-collar workers do not think of themselves as an "industrial proletariat." Just as important, the average income in the United States rose almost tenfold over the course of the twentieth century, even allowing for inflation, and the number of hours in the workweek decreased. For that reason, even in tough economic times, most of today's workers are better off than workers were a century ago, an example of structural social mobility. One result of this rising standard of living is that more people are content with the status quo and less likely to press for change.

3. **More worker organizations.** Workers today have the right to form labor unions, to make demands of management, and to back up their demands with threats of work slowdowns and strikes. As a result, labor disputes are settled without threatening the capitalist system.

4. **Greater legal protections.** Over the past century, the government passed laws to make workplaces safer. In addition, unemployment insurance, disability protection, and Social Security now provide workers with greater financial security.

A Counterpoint

These developments suggest that U.S. society has smoothed many of capitalism's rough edges. Yet some observers claim that Marx's analysis of capitalism is still largely valid (Domhoff, 1983; Hout, Brooks, & Manza, 1993; Foroohar, 2011). First, wealth remains highly concentrated, with 35 percent of all privately owned property in the hands of just 1 percent of the U.S. population (Wolff, 2012). Second, many of today's white-collar jobs offer no more income, security, or satisfaction than factory work did a century ago. Third, many, if not most, of today's workers feel squeezed by high unemployment, company downsizing, jobs moving overseas, and job benefits being cut to balance budgets. Fourth, the income and benefits that today's workers do enjoy came about through exactly the class conflict Marx described. In addition, as the conflict between public worker labor unions and state government in Wisconsin, Ohio, and other states in 2011 shows, workers still struggle to hold on to what they have. Fifth, although workers have gained some legal protections, ordinary people still face disadvantages that the law cannot overcome. Therefore, social-conflict theorists conclude, even without a socialist revolution in the United States, Marx was still mostly right about capitalism.

Max Weber: Class, Status, and Power

Max Weber, whose approach to social analysis is described in Chapter 4 ("Society"), agreed with Karl Marx that social stratification causes social conflict, but he viewed Marx's economics-based model as simplistic. Instead, he claimed that social stratification involves three distinct dimensions of inequality.

The first dimension is economic inequality—the issue so important to Marx—which Weber termed *class position.* Weber did not think of classes as well-defined categories but as a continuum ranging from high to low. Weber's second dimension is *status,* or social prestige, and the third is *power.*

Weber's Socioeconomic Status Hierarchy

Marx viewed social prestige and power as simple reflections of economic position and did not treat them as distinct dimensions of inequality. But Weber noted that status

blue-collar occupations
lower-prestige jobs that involve mostly manual labor

white-collar occupations
higher-prestige jobs that involve mostly mental activity

Explore dimensions of inequality in your local community and in counties across the United States in **MySocLab**

The extent of social inequality in agrarian systems is greater than that found in industrial societies. One indication of the unchallenged power of rulers is the monumental structures built over years with the unpaid labor of common people. Although the Taj Mahal in India is among the world's most beautiful buildings, it was built as a tomb for a single individual.

socioeconomic status (SES)

a composite ranking based on various dimensions of social inequality

consistency in modern societies is often quite low: For instance, a local official might exercise great power yet have little wealth or social prestige.

Weber, then, portrays social stratification in industrial societies as a multidimensional ranking rather than a hierarchy of clearly defined classes. In line with Weber's thinking, sociologists use the term **socioeconomic status (SES)** to refer to *a composite ranking based on various dimensions of social inequality.*

Inequality in History

Weber claimed that each of his three dimensions of social inequality stands out at different points in the evolution of human societies. Status or social prestige is the main difference in agrarian societies, taking the form of honor. Members of these societies (whether nobles or servants) gain status by conforming to cultural norms that apply to their particular rank.

Industrialization and the development of capitalism eliminate traditional rankings based on birth but create striking financial inequality. Thus in an industrial society, the crucial difference between people is the economic dimension of class.

Over time, industrial societies witness the growth of a bureaucratic state. Bigger government and the spread of all sorts of other organizations make power more important in the stratification system. Especially in socialist societies, where government regulates many aspects of life, high-ranking officials become the new ruling elite.

This historical analysis points to a final difference between Weber and Marx. Marx thought societies could eliminate social stratification by abolishing the private ownership of productive property that is the basis of capitalism. Weber doubted that overthrowing capitalism would significantly lessen social stratification. It might reduce economic differences, he reasoned, but socialism would increase inequality by expanding government and concentrating power in the hands of a political elite. Popular uprisings against socialist bureaucracies in Eastern Europe and the former Soviet Union show that discontent can be generated by socialist political elites, a fact that supports Weber's position.

EVALUATE Max Weber's multidimensional view of social stratification has greatly influenced sociological thinking. But critics (particularly those who favor Marx's ideas) argue that although social class boundaries may have blurred, industrial and postindustrial societies still show striking patterns of social inequality.

As you will see in Chapter 11 ("Social Class in the United States"), income inequality has been increasing in the United States. Although some people still favor Weber's multidimensional hierarchy, in light of this trend, others think that Marx's view of the rich versus the poor is closer to the truth.

Explaining Stratification: Symbolic-Interaction Theory

(10.6) Apply symbolic-interaction theory to the topic of social inequality.

Because social stratification has to do with the way an entire society is organized, sociologists (Marx and Weber included) typically treat it as a macro-level issue. But a micro-level analysis of social stratification is also important because people's social standing affects their everyday interactions. The Applying Theory table summarizes the contributions of the three approaches to an understanding of social stratification.

In most communities, people interact primarily with others of about the same social standing. To some extent, this is because people tend to live with others like themselves. In larger public spaces, such as a shopping mall, we see couples or groups made up of individuals whose appearance and shopping habits are similar. People with very different social standing commonly keep their distance from one another. Well-dressed people walking down the street on their way to an expensive restaurant, for example, might move across the sidewalk or even cross the street to avoid getting close to others they think are homeless people. The Seeing Sociology in Everyday Life box on page 292 gives another example of how differences in social class position can affect interaction.

Finally, just about everyone realizes that the way we dress, the car we drive (or the bus we ride), and even the food and drink we order at the campus snack bar say something about our budget and personal tastes. Sociologists use the term **conspicuous consumption** to refer to *buying and using products because of the "statement" they make about social position*. Ignoring the water fountain in favor of paying for bottled water tells people you have extra money to spend. And no one needs a $100,000 automobile to get around, of course, but driving up in such a vehicle says "I have arrived" in more ways than one.

conspicuous consumption buying and using products because of the "statement" they make about social position

Applying Theory

Social Stratification			
	Structural-Functional Theory	Social-Conflict Theory	Symbolic-Interaction Theory
What is the level of analysis?	Macro-level	Macro-level	Micro-level
What is social stratification?	Stratification is a system of unequal rewards that benefits society as a whole.	Stratification is a division of a society's resources that benefits some people and harms others.	Stratification is a factor that guides people's interactions in everyday life.
What is the reason for our social position?	Social position reflects personal talents and abilities in a competitive economy.	Social position reflects the way society divides resources.	The products we consume all say something about social position.
Are unequal rewards fair?	Yes. Unequal rewards boost economic production by encouraging people to work harder and try new ideas. Linking greater rewards to more important work is widely accepted.	No. Unequal rewards only serve to divide society, creating "haves" and "have-nots." There is widespread opposition to social inequality.	Maybe. People may or may not define inequality as fair. People may view their social position as a measure of self-worth, justifying inequality in terms of personal differences.

Seeing Sociology in Everyday Life

When Class Gets Personal: Picking (with) Your Friends

The sound of banjo music drifted across the field late one summer afternoon. I lay down my brush, climbed over the fence I had been painting, and walked toward the sound of the music to see what was going on. That's how I met my neighbor Max, a retired factory worker who lived just up the road. Max was a pretty good "picker," and within an hour, I was back on his porch with my guitar. I called Howard, a friend who teaches at the college, and he showed up a little while later, six-string in hand. The three of us jammed for a couple of hours, smiling all the while.

The next morning, I was mowing the grass in front of the house when Max came walking down the road. I turned off the mower as he got closer. "Hi, Max," I said. "Thanks for having us over last night. I really had fun."

"Don't mention it," Max responded with a wave. Then he stopped and shook his head a little and added, "Ya know, I was thinkin' after you guys left. I mean, it was really somethin' how you guys were having a great time. With somebody like *me!*"

"Well, yeah," I replied, a bit awkwardly, not sure exactly what he meant. "You sure played better than we did."

Max looked down at the ground, embarrassed by the compliment. Then he added, "What I mean is that you guys were having a good time with somebody like *me*. You're both professors, right? *Doctors,* even…"

What Do You Think?

1. Why did Max assume that two college teachers would not enjoy spending time with him?

2. How does his reaction suggest that people take social position personally?

3. Can you think of a similar experience you have had with someone of a different social position (higher or lower) than you have?

Social Stratification and Technology: A Global Perspective

10.7 Analyze the link between a society's technology and its social stratification.

We can weave together a number of observations made in this chapter to show that a society's technology affects its type of social stratification. This analyis draws on Gerhard Lenski's model of sociocultural evolution, detailed in Chapter 4 ("Society").

Hunting and Gathering Societies

With simple technology, members of hunting and gathering societies produce only what is necessary for day-to-day living. Some people may produce more than others, but the group's survival depends on all sharing what they have. Thus no categories of people are better off than others.

Horticultural, Pastoral, and Agrarian Societies

As technological advances create a surplus, social inequality increases. In horticultural and pastoral societies, a small elite controls most of the surplus. Large-scale agriculture is

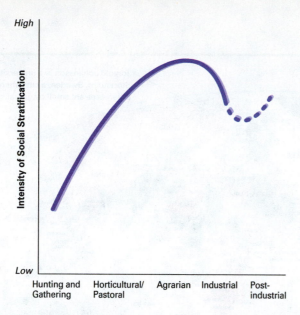

FIGURE 10–2 Social Stratification and Technological Development: The Kuznets Curve

The Kuznets curve shows that greater technological sophistication is generally accompanied by more pronounced social stratification. The trend reverses itself as industrial societies relax rigid, castelike distinctions in favor of greater opportunity and equality under the law. Political rights are more widely extended, and there is even some leveling of economic differences. However, the emergence of postindustrial society has brought an upturn in economic inequality, as indicated by the broken line added by the author.

Sources: Based on Kuznets (1955) and Lenski (1966).

more productive still, and striking inequality—as great as at any time in history—places the nobility in an almost godlike position over the masses.

Industrial Societies

Industrialization turns the tide, pushing inequality downward. Prompted by the need to develop individual talents, meritocracy takes hold and weakens the power of traditional aristocracy. Industrial productivity also raises the living standards of the historically poor majority. Specialized work demands schooling for all, sharply reducing illiteracy. A literate population, in turn, presses for a greater voice in political decision making, reducing social inequality and lessening men's domination of women.

Over time, even wealth becomes somewhat less concentrated (contradicting Marx's prediction). In the 1920s, the richest 1 percent of the U.S. population owned about 40 percent of all wealth in the country, a figure that fell to 30 percent by the 1980s as taxes—which have higher rates for people with higher incomes—paid for new government programs benefiting the poor (Williamson & Lindert, 1980; Beeghley, 1989; U.S. House of Representatives, 1991). Such trends help explain why Marxist revolutions occurred in *agrarian* societies—such as Russia (1917), Cuba (1959), and Nicaragua (1979)—where social inequality is most pronounced, rather than in industrial societies as Marx had predicted. However, wealth inequality in the United States turned upward again after 1990, and it is once again at about the same level that it was in the 1920s (Wolff, 2012). With the goal of reducing this trend of increasing economic inequality, the Obama administration in 2013 won the support of Congress to modestly increase federal income tax rates on high-income individuals.

The Kuznets Curve

In human history, then, technological advances first increase but then moderate the extent of social stratification. Greater inequality is functional for agrarian societies, but industrial societies benefit from a more equal system. This historical trend, recognized by the Nobel

Window on the World

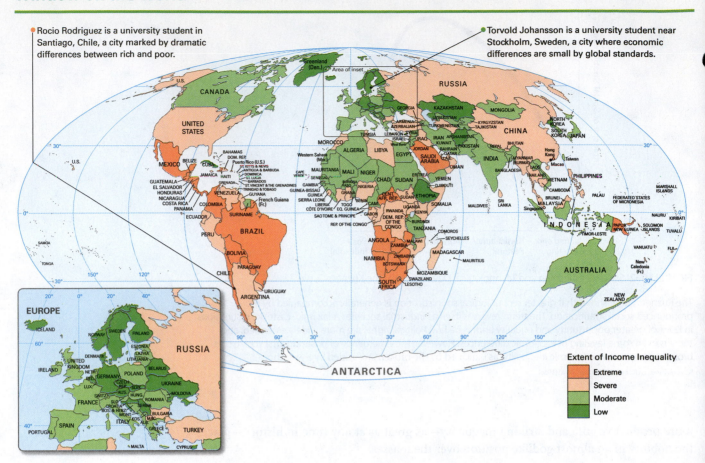

● Rocio Rodriguez is a university student in Santiago, Chile, a city marked by dramatic differences between rich and poor.

● Torvold Johansson is a university student near Stockholm, Sweden, a city where economic differences are small by global standards.

Extent of Income Inequality
- Extreme
- Severe
- Moderate
- Low

GLOBAL MAP 10–1 Income Inequality in Global Perspective

Societies throughout the world differ in the rigidity and extent of their social stratification and their overall standard of living. This map highlights income inequality. Generally speaking, the United States stands out among high-income nations, such as Great Britain, Sweden, Japan, and Australia, as having greater income inequality. The less economically developed countries of Latin America and Africa, including Colombia, Brazil, and the Central African Republic, as well as much of the Arab world, exhibit the most pronounced inequality of income. Is this pattern consistent with the Kuznets curve?

Source: Based on Gini coefficients obtained from Central Intelligence Agency (2012) and World Bank (2012).

Prize–winning economist Simon Kuznets (1955, 1966), is illustrated by the Kuznets curve, shown in Figure 10–2 on page 293.

Social inequality around the world generally supports the Kuznets curve. Global Map 10–1 shows that high-income nations that have passed through the industrial era (including the United States, Canada, and the nations of Western Europe) have somewhat less income inequality than nations in which a larger share of the labor force remains in farming (as is common in Latin America and Africa). At the same time, it is important to remember that income inequality reflects not just technological development but also the political and economic priorities of a country. Income disparity in the United States may have declined during much of the last century, but this country still has more economic inequality than Canada, European nations, and Japan (although less than some other high-income nations, including Chile and Singapore).

Another criticism of the Kuznets curve is that it was developed by comparing societies at different levels of economic development (what sociologists call "cross-sectional data"). Such data do not let us predict the future of any one society. In the United States, recent trends showing increases in economic inequality suggest that the Kuznets curve may require serious revision—represented by the broken line in Figure 10–2. The fact that

U.S. society is experiencing greater economic inequality as the Information Revolution moves forward (see Chapter 11) suggests that the long-term trend may differ from what Kuznets projected half a century ago.

Social Stratification: Facts and Values

10.8   Illustrate how explanations of social inequality reflect not just facts but also values.

The year was 2081 and everybody was finally equal. They weren't only equal before God and the law. They were equal every which way. Nobody was smarter than anybody else. Nobody was better looking than anybody else. Nobody was stronger or quicker than anybody else. All this equality was due to the 211th, 212th, and 213th Amendments to the Constitution and the unceasing vigilance of agents of the Handicapper General.

With these words, the novelist Kurt Vonnegut Jr. (1968:7) begins the story of Harrison Bergeron, an imaginary account of a future United States in which all social inequality has been abolished. Vonnegut warns that although attractive in principle, equality can be a dangerous concept in practice. His story describes a nightmare of social engineering in which every individual talent that makes one person different from another is systematically neutralized by the government.

To eliminate differences that make one person "better" than another, Vonnegut's state requires that physically attractive people wear masks that make them average-looking, that intelligent people wear earphones that generate distracting noise, and that the best athletes and dancers be fitted with weights to make them as clumsy as everyone else. In short, although we may imagine that social equality would liberate people to make the most of their talents, Vonnegut concludes that an egalitarian society could exist only if everyone is reduced to the lowest common denominator. In Vonnegut's view, this would amount not to liberation but to oppression.

Like Vonnegut's story, all of this chapter's explanations of social stratification involve value judgments. The Davis-Moore thesis states not only that social stratification is universal but also that it is necessary to make society highly productive. Class differences in U.S. society, from this point of view, reflect both variation in human abilities and the relatively unequal importance of different jobs. Taken together, these facts lead us to see complete equality as undesirable because it could be achieved only in a rigid and inefficient society that cared little for developing individual talent and rewarding excellence.

Social-conflict analysis, advocated by Karl Marx, takes a much more positive view of equality. Marx thought that inequality is harmful because it causes both human suffering and conflict between haves and have-nots. As he saw it, social stratification springs from injustice and greed. As a result, Marx wanted people to share resources equally.

The connection between intelligence and social class is one of the most troublesome issues in social science. For one thing, defining and measuring "intelligence" is difficult. Also, the idea that elites are somehow "better" than others challenges our democratic culture.

The next chapter ("Social Class in the United States") examines inequality in our own nation, highlighting recent economic polarization. Then Chapter 12 ("Global Stratification") surveys social inequality throughout the world, explaining why some nations have so much more wealth than others. As you will learn, at all levels, the study of social stratification involves a mix of facts and values about the shape of a just society.

For a closer look at the issue of how intelligence may be linked to social class, **Read More** in **MySocLab**, *The Bell Curve Debate: Are Rich People Really Smarter?*

Seeing Sociology in Everyday Life

Can you identify elements of caste and meritocracy in U.S. society?

This chapter explains that modern societies are class systems that combine elements of caste and meritocracy. Using the sociological perspective, you can see both caste and meritocracy in operation in many everyday situations. Here are three examples to get you started. Look at the photos below and on page 297, and then start your own list.

One of the most demanding jobs you can ever have is being a parent. And traditionally at least, most parenting is performed by women, with gender operating as a caste element. Why do you think our society does not pay parents for their work? What difference in meaning can you see between the phrases "fathering a child" and "mothering a child"?

Justin Bieber is a Canadian singer who was born to a single teen mother who raised her son in low-income housing. After his first record went platinum in the United States, he became one of the highest-paid entertainers—an example of a "rags to riches" move upward in social standing.

In 2009, Judge Sonia Sotomayor became the first Hispanic woman to join the U.S. Supreme Court. Her record of achievement began at Cardinal Spellman High School in the Bronx (New York), where she was valedictorian. Of more than 100 justices who have served on the Supreme Court, how many do you think have been Hispanic? How many have been women?

HINT The fact that parenting is not paid work means that people should raise children not for money but out of moral duty. "Fathering a child" may suggest only biological paternity; "mothering a child" implies deep involvement in a child's life, indicating how gender has long been a caste element linking women to nurturing. Careers that emphasize merit are typically those jobs that are regarded as especially important and that require rare talents; even so, most successful musical performers have been male. Judge Sotomayor is the first Hispanic and just the third woman (along with Sandra Day O'Connor and Ruth Bader Ginsburg) to serve on the U.S. Supreme Court. There have been just two African American justices (Thurgood Marshall and Clarence Thomas).

Seeing Sociology in *Your* Everyday Life

1. The "seven deadly sins," the human failings recognized by the Roman Catholic Church during the Middle Ages, were pride, greed, envy, anger, lust, gluttony, and sloth. Why are these traits likely to be viewed as dangerous by people who live in an agrarian caste system with a strong traditional culture? Are these traits a threat to today's capitalist class system? In what ways might most of them (perhaps all but sloth) actually be *necessary* to our way of life?

2. Go to MySocLab and click on the Student Resources link to access the Sociology in Focus blog, where you can read the latest posts by a team of young sociologists who apply the sociological perspective to topics of popular culture.

3. Identify three ways in which social stratification is evident in the everyday lives of students on your campus. In each case, explain exactly what is unequal and what difference it makes. Do you think individual talent or family background is more important in creating these social differences? Go to the "Seeing Sociology in *Your* Everyday Life" feature in MySocLab to learn more about the interplay of caste and class and why members of our society tend to see social class standing as simply the result of personal abilities and effort.

Making the Grade

What Is Social Stratification?

(10.1) Identify four principles that underlie social stratification. (pages 274–75)

 **Watch** the **Video** in **MySocLab**

Social stratification

- is a trait of society, not simply a reflection of individual differences
- is found in all societies but varies according to *what* is unequal and *how* unequal it is
- carries over from one generation to the next
- is supported by a system of cultural beliefs that defines certain kinds of inequality as just
- takes two general forms: caste systems and class systems

social stratification a system by which a society ranks categories of people in a hierarchy

social mobility a change in position within the social hierarchy

Caste and Class Systems

(10.2) Apply the concepts of caste, class, and meritocracy to societies around the world. (pages 275–84)

Watch the **Video** in **MySocLab**

Caste Systems

- are based on birth (ascription) and permit little or no social mobility
- shape a person's entire life, including occupation and marriage
- are common in traditional, agrarian societies

An Illustration: India

Although the caste system is formally outlawed in India, it is still observed in rural areas, where agriculture demands a lifetime of hard work and discipline.

- In traditional villages, caste determines the work people perform and whom they may marry.
- Powerful cultural beliefs make observing caste rules a moral duty.

Class Systems

- are based on both birth (ascription) and **meritocracy** (individual achievement)
- permit some social mobility based on individual achievement
- are common in modern industrial and postindustrial societies
- **Status consistency** in class systems is low due to increased social mobility.

Caste and Class: The United Kingdom

- In the Middle Ages, England had a castelike aristocracy, including the leading clergy and a hereditary nobility. The vast majority of people were commoners.
- Today's British class system mixes caste and meritocracy, producing a highly stratified society with some social mobility.

Caste and Class: Japan

- In the Middle Ages, Japan had a rigid caste system in which an imperial family ruled over nobles and commoners.
- Today's Japanese class system still places great importance on family background and traditional gender roles.

Classless Societies? The Former Soviet Union

- Although the Russian Revolution in 1917 attempted to abolish social classes, the new Soviet Union was still stratified based on unequal job categories and the concentration of power in the new political elite. Economic development created new types of jobs, which resulted in **structural social mobility**.
- Since the collapse of the Soviet Union in the early 1990s, the forces of structural social mobility have turned downward and the gap between rich and poor has increased.

caste system social stratification based on ascription, or birth

class system social stratification based on both birth and individual achievement

meritocracy social stratification based on personal merit

status consistency the degree of uniformity in a person's social standing across various dimensions of social inequality

structural social mobility a shift in the social position of large numbers of people due more to changes in society itself than to individual efforts

China: Emerging Social Classes

- Economic reforms introduced after the Communist revolution in 1949—including state control of factories and productive property—greatly reduced economic inequality, although social differences remained.
- In the last thirty years, China's government has loosened control of the economy, causing the emergence of a new class of business owners and an increase in economic inequality.

Ideology: Supporting Stratification

(10.3) Explain how cultural beliefs justify social inequality. (pages 284–85)

- Cultural beliefs justify patterns of social inequality.
- Ideology reflects both a society's economic system and its level of technology.

ideology cultural beliefs that justify particular social arrangements, including patterns of inequality

Explaining Stratification: Structural-Functional Theory

(10.4) Apply structural-functional theory to the topic of social inequality. (pages 286–87)

📖 Read the Document in MySocLab

Structural-functional theory points to ways social stratification helps society operate.

- The Davis-Moore thesis states that social stratification is universal because of its functional consequences.
- In caste systems, people are rewarded for performing the duties of their position at birth.
- In class systems, unequal rewards attract the ablest people to the most important jobs and encourage effort.

Davis-Moore thesis the functional analysis claiming that social stratification has beneficial consequences for the operation of society

Explaining Stratification: Social-Conflict Theories

(10.5) Apply social-conflict theories to the topic of social inequality. (pages 287–91)

👁 Watch the Video in MySocLab   ✴ Explore the Map in MySocLab

Social-conflict theory claims that stratification divides societies in classes, benefiting some categories of people at the expense of others and causing social conflict.

- Karl Marx claimed that capitalism places economic production under the ownership of capitalists, who exploit the proletarians who sell their labor for wages.
- Max Weber identified three distinct dimensions of social stratification: economic class, social status or prestige, and power. Conflict exists between people at various positions on a multidimensional hierarchy of **socioeconomic status (SES)**.

blue-collar occupations lower-prestige jobs that involve mostly manual labor
white-collar occupations higher-prestige jobs that involve mostly mental activity
socioeconomic status (SES) a composite ranking based on various dimensions of social inequality

Explaining Stratification: Symbolic-Interaction Theory

(10.6) Apply symbolic-interaction theory to the topic of social inequality. (pages 291–92)

- **Symbolic-interaction theory**, a micro-level analysis, explains that we size up people by looking for clues to their social standing.
- **Conspicuous consumption** refers to buying and displaying products that make a "statement" about social class.

conspicuous consumption buying and using products because of the "statement" they make about social position

Stratification and Technology: A Global Perspective

(10.7) Analyze the link between a society's technology and its social stratification. (pages 292–94)

Hunting and Gathering → Horticultural and Pastoral → Agrarian → Industrial → Postindustrial

- Gerhard Lenski explains that advancing technology initially increases social stratification, which is most intense in agrarian societies.
- Industrialization reverses the trend, reducing social stratification.
- In postindustrial societies, social stratification again increases.

Social Stratification: Facts and Values

(10.8) Illustrate how explanations of social inequality reflect not just facts but also values (page 295).

People's beliefs about social inequality reflect not just facts but also politics and values concerning how a society should be organized.

11 Social Class in the United States

(((**Listen** to **Chapter 11** in **MySocLab**

LEARNING OBJECTIVES

11.1 Describe the distribution of income and wealth in the United States.

11.2 Explain how someone's position at birth affects social standing later in life.

11.3 Describe the various social class positions in U.S. society.

11.4 Analyze how social class position affects health, values, politics, and family life.

11.5 Assess the extent of social mobility in the United States.

11.6 Discuss patterns and explanations of poverty in the U.S. population.

11.7 Assess the trend toward increasing economic inequality in the United States.

the Power of Society

to shape our chances of living in poverty

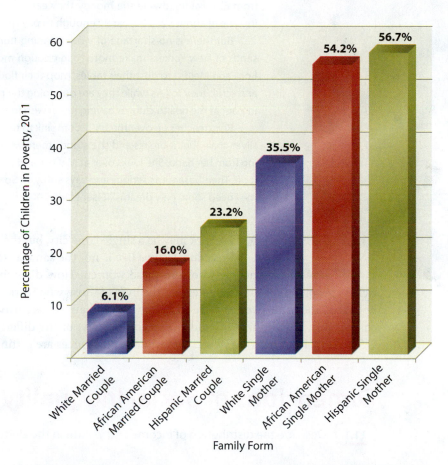

Percentage of Children in Poverty, 2011

- White Married Couple: 6.1%
- African American Married Couple: 16.0%
- Hispanic Married Couple: 23.2%
- White Single Mother: 35.5%
- African American Single Mother: 54.2%
- Hispanic Single Mother: 56.7%

Family Form

Source: U.S. Census Bureau (2012)

What are a person's odds of being born into poverty? Our social position reflects factors such as our race and ethnicity as well as the marital status of our parents. Of all white children born to a U.S. married couple, 6.1 percent (about six out of every 100 children) are poor. By contrast, the share in poverty is almost three times higher for comparable African American children, and almost four times higher for comparable Hispanic children. The same pattern holds for children born to single mothers, except that the odds of being poor jump even more dramatically for African American and Hispanic children.

Chapter Overview

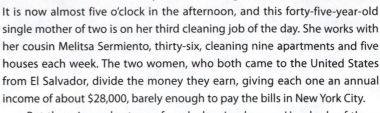

How much social inequality is there in the United States? This chapter will help you to understand the extent of social class differences in this country. The chapter begins with a close-up look at important measures of social stratification. You will discover that there are numerous dimensions of inequality in our society, and that the amount of social inequality is increasing.

Rosa Urias leans forward, pushing and pulling the vacuum cleaner across the thick carpet, a motion she has repeated thousands of times to the point that her right wrist and elbow are sore.

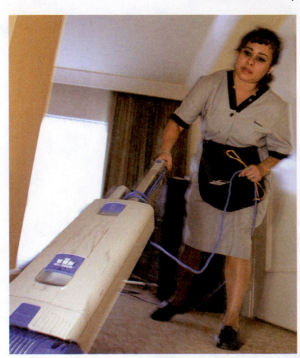

It is now almost five o'clock in the afternoon, and this forty-five-year-old single mother of two is on her third cleaning job of the day. She works with her cousin Melitsa Sermiento, thirty-six, cleaning nine apartments and five houses each week. The two women, who both came to the United States from El Salvador, divide the money they earn, giving each one an annual income of about $28,000, barely enough to pay the bills in New York City.

But there is no shortage of work cleaning homes. Hundreds of thousands of New Yorkers make more than enough money to hire people like Rosa and Melitsa to dust their tables, mop their floors, and clean their sinks and scrub their toilets while they are out doing their high-paying jobs, working out at the health club, or having lunch with friends.

Rosa reaches up over the bathroom sink to turn on a light. She pulls the silver chain, but it breaks and she stands there with part of the chain hanging from her hand. She looks over at Melitsa, and both do their best to laugh it off. Then Rosa turns serious and says softly, in Spanish, "My daughter tells me I need some new dreams" (Eisenstadt, 2004).

New York may be a single large city, but the social world in which Rosa and Melitsa live is not the same as the social world of the people who hire these women. How different are the lives of the richest people in the United States and the lives of those who work hard all day just to get by? What about the lives of those who do not even have the security of steady work? This chapter answers all these questions, explaining some of the different "worlds" found in U.S. society, how different we are, and why the differences are getting bigger.

Dimensions of Social Inequality

(11.1) Describe the distribution of income and wealth in the United States.

The United States differs from most European nations and Japan in never having had a titled nobility. With the significant exception of our racial history, we have never known a caste system that rigidly ranks categories of people.

Even so, U.S. society is highly stratified. Not only do the rich have most of the money, but they also receive the most schooling, enjoy the best health, and consume the most goods and services. Such privilege contrasts sharply with the poverty of millions of women and men who worry about money for next month's rent or to pay a doctor's bill when a child becomes ill. Many people think of the United States as a middle-class society, but is this really the case?

Income

One important dimension of inequality is **income,** *earnings from work or investments.* The Census Bureau reports that the median U.S. family income in 2011 was $60,974. The pie chart in the middle of Figure 11–1 on page 303 illustrates the distribution of income

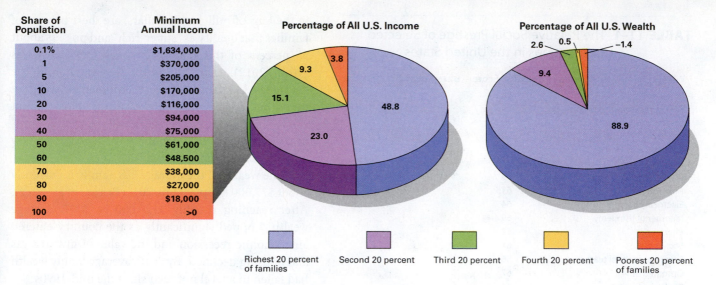

Share of Population	Minimum Annual Income
0.1%	$1,634,000
1	$370,000
5	$205,000
10	$170,000
20	$116,000
30	$94,000
40	$75,000
50	$61,000
60	$48,500
70	$38,000
80	$27,000
90	$18,000
100	>0

Percentage of All U.S. Income

48.8
23.0
15.1
9.3
3.8

Percentage of All U.S. Wealth

88.9
9.4
2.6
0.5
−1.4

Richest 20 percent of families   Second 20 percent   Third 20 percent   Fourth 20 percent   Poorest 20 percent of families

FIGURE 11–1 Distribution of Income and Wealth in the United States, 2011

Income, and especially wealth, are divided unequally in U.S. society.

Sources: Income data from U.S. Census Bureau (2012); wealth data based on Wolff (2012) and author estimates.

among all U.S. families.[1] The richest 20 percent of families (earning at least $116,000 annually, with a mean of about $198,000) received 48.8 percent of all income, while the bottom 20 percent (earning less than $27,000, with a mean of about $15,000) received only 3.8 percent (U.S. Census Bureau, 2012).

The table at the left in Figure 11–1 provides a closer look at income distribution. In 2011, the highest-paid 5 percent of U.S. families earned at least $205,000 (averaging $345,000), or 21.3 percent of all income, more than the total earnings of the lowest-paid 40 percent. At the very top of the income pyramid, the richest one-tenth of 1 percent earned at least $1.6 million.

During recent decades, income inequality has increased. One part of this trend is that the very richest people now receive a much larger share of all income. For example, in 1978, the highest-paid 0.1 percent of all earners received 2.7 percent of all income. By 2010, this elite category (people making $1.6 million or more a year) took home a share that is more than three times larger, equaling 9 percent of all income (Fox, 2009; Internal Revenue Service, 2012).

Watch in **MySocLab**
Video: *The Big Picture: Social Class in the United States*

Wealth

Income is only a part of a person's or family's **wealth**, *the total value of money and other assets, minus outstanding debts.* Wealth—including stocks, bonds, and real estate—is distributed more unequally than income. The reductions in taxes on income earned by individuals and on wealth passed from one generation to the next that were enacted by Congress a decade ago have made this inequality even greater (Wahl, 2003; Keister & Southgate, 2012).

The pie chart on the right in Figure 11–1 shows the distribution of wealth. The richest 20 percent of U.S. families own roughly 89 percent of the country's wealth. High up in this privileged category are the wealthiest 5 percent of families—the "very rich," who own 63 percent of all private property. Richer still, with wealth

income earnings from work or investments

wealth the total value of money and other assets, minus outstanding debts

[1] The Census Bureau reports both mean and median incomes for families ("two or more persons related by blood, marriage, or adoption") and households ("two or more persons sharing a living unit"). In 2011, mean family income was $81,007, higher than the median ($60,974) because high-income families pull up the mean but not the median. For households, these figures are somewhat lower—a mean of $69,677 and a median of $50,054—largely because families average 3.13 people and households average 2.55.

TABLE 11–1 The Relative Social Prestige of Selected Occupations in the United States

White-Collar Occupations	Prestige Score	Blue-Collar Occupations
Physician	86	
College/university professor	74	
Lawyer	75	
Dentist	72	
Physicist, astronomer	73	
Architect	73	
Psychologist	69	
Airplane pilot	61	
Electrical engineer	64	
Member of the clergy	69	
Pharmacist	68	
Sociologist	61	
Secondary school teacher	66	
Optometrist	67	
Registered nurse	66	
Dental hygienist	52	
	60	Police officer
Elementary school teacher	66	
Veterinarian	62	
Actor	58	
Accountant	65	
Economist	63	
	51	Electrician
Painter, sculptor	52	
Librarian	54	
	53	Aircraft mechanic
	53	Firefighter
Social worker	52	
Athlete	65	
Computer programmer	61	
Editor, reporter	60	
Radio or TV announcer	55	
	49	
Real estate agent	49	
Bookkeeper	47	
	47	Machinist
Musician, composer	47	
	46	Secretary
	47	Mail carrier
Photographer	45	
Bank teller	43	
	42	Tailor
	40	Farmer
	39	Carpenter
	31	Auto body repairer
	36	Bricklayer, stonemason
	35	Baker
	34	Bulldozer operator
	36	Hairdresser
	30	Truck driver
Cashier	29	
Retail apparel salesperson	30	
	28	Waiter, waitress
	25	Bartender
	36	Child care worker
	23	Household laborer
	22	Door-to-door salesperson
	22	Janitor
	28	Taxi driver
	28	Garbage collector
	27	Bellhop
	9	Shoe shiner

Source: Adapted from General Social Surveys, 1972–2012: Cumulative Codebook (Chicago: National Opinion Research Center, 2013:2993–3000).

in the tens of millions of dollars, are the 1 percent of families that qualify as "super-rich" and possess about 35 percent of this nation's privately held resources (Wolff, 2012). At the top of the wealth pyramid, the ten richest U.S. families have a combined net worth of more than $347 billion (*Forbes*, 2012). This amount equals the total property of 4.5 million average families, including enough people to fill the cities of New York, Houston, and Los Angeles.

The wealth of the average U.S. family is currently about $77,000 (Applebaum, 2012; Bricker et al., 2012). After reaching roughly $120,000 in 2007, average wealth dropped significantly as the country entered an economic recession and the value of investments and housing declined. By 2010, average family wealth had fallen to a level not seen since the mid-1990s.

Family wealth reflects the value of homes, cars, investments, insurance policies, retirement pensions, furniture, clothing, and all other personal property, minus a home mortgage and other debts. The wealth of average people is not only less than that of the rich, however, but also different in kind. Most people's wealth centers on a home and a car—that is, property that generates no income—but the wealth of the rich is mostly in the form of stocks and other income-producing investments.

When financial assets are balanced against debts, the lowest-ranking 40 percent of U.S. families have little or no wealth at all. The negative percentage that is shown in Figure 11–1 on page 303 for the poorest 20 percent of the population means that these families actually live in debt.

Power

In the United States, wealth is an important source of power. The small proportion of families that controls most of the nation's wealth also shapes the agenda of the entire society. As explained in Chapter 17 ("Politics and Government"), some sociologists argue that such concentrated wealth weakens democracy because the political system serves the interests of the super-rich.

Occupational Prestige

In addition to generating income, work is also an important source of social prestige. We commonly evaluate each other according to the kind of work we do, giving greater respect to those who do what we consider important work and less respect to others with more modest jobs. Sociologists measure the relative prestige of various occupations (NORC, 2011). Table 11–1 shows that people give high prestige to occupations such as physician, lawyer, and engineer that require extensive training and generate high income. By contrast, less prestigious work—as a waitress or janitor, for example—pays less and requires less schooling. Occupational prestige rankings are much the same in all high-income nations (Lin & Xie, 1988).

In any society, high-prestige occupations go to privileged categories of people. In Table 11–1, for example, the highest-ranking occupations are dominated by men. We have to go more than a dozen jobs down the list to find "secondary school teacher" and "registered nurse," careers chosen mostly by women. Similarly, many of the lowest-prestige jobs are commonly performed by people of color.

Schooling

Industrial societies have expanded opportunities for schooling, but some people still receive much more education than others. About 88 percent of women and men aged twenty-five and older have completed high school. But just 31 percent of men and 30 percent of women have completed a four-year college degree.

Schooling affects both occupation and income, since most (but not all) of the better-paying white-collar jobs shown in Table 11–1 require a college degree or other advanced study. Most blue-collar jobs, which bring lower income and social prestige, require less schooling.

U.S. Stratification: Merit and Caste

(11.2) Explain how someone's position at birth affects social standing later in life.

As we discussed in Chapter 10 ("Social Stratification"), the U.S. class system is partly a meritocracy in that social position reflects individual talent and effort. But it also has caste elements, because birth—which socially locates each person in a particular family, as well as assigning traits such as race, ethnicity, and gender—plays a part in what we become later in life.

Ancestry

Nothing affects social standing in the United States as much as being born into a particular family, which has a strong bearing on schooling, occupation, and income. Research suggests that more than one-third of our country's richest individuals—those with hundreds of millions of dollars in wealth—acquired some of their fortunes from inheritance (Miller & Newcomb, 2005; Harford, 2007). Inherited poverty shapes the future of tens of millions of others.

Race and Ethnicity

Race is closely linked to social position in the United States. On average, whites have a higher occupational position than African Americans and also receive more schooling. The median African American family's income was $40,495 in 2011, just 58 percent of the $69,829 earned by non-Hispanic white families. This inequality in income makes a real difference in people's lives. For example, the share of non-Hispanic white families (74 percent) who own their homes is significantly larger than the comparable share of black families (44 percent) (U.S. Census Bureau, 2012).

Families that include married couples earn more than families with a single parent. With this fact in mind, some of the racial difference in income results from the larger share of single-parent families among African Americans. Comparing only families headed by married couples, African Americans earned 83 percent as much as non-Hispanic white families.

Over time, the income difference builds into a huge wealth gap. A recent survey of families by the Federal Reserve found that median wealth for minority families, including African Americans, Hispanics, and Asian Americans ($20,400), is just 16 percent of the median ($130,600) for non-Hispanic white families (Bricker et al., 2012).

Social ranking involves ethnicity as well. People of English ancestry have always enjoyed the most wealth and the greatest power in U.S. society. The Latino population—the largest U.S. racial or ethnic minority—has long been disadvantaged. In 2011, the median income among Hispanic families was $40,061, which is 57 percent of the median income for non-Hispanic white families. A detailed examination of how race and ethnicity affect social standing is presented in Chapter 14 ("Race and Ethnicity").

Gender

Of course, both men and women are found in families at every class level. Yet on average, women have less income, wealth, and occupational prestige than men. Among single-parent families, those headed by a woman are more than twice as likely to be poor than those headed by a man. Chapter 13 ("Gender Stratification") examines the link between gender and social stratification.

Social Classes in the United States

11.3 Describe the various social class positions in U.S. society.

As Chapter 10 ("Social Stratification") explained, rankings in a caste system are rigid and obvious to all. Defining social categories in a more fluid class system such as ours, however, is not so easy.

There is an old joke about two friends who order a pizza, asking that it be cut into six slices because they aren't hungry enough to eat eight. Sociologists do the same thing with social class: Some slice the population into more classes than others. At one extreme, people find as many as six or even seven social classes; at the other, some follow Karl Marx and see two major classes: capitalists and proletarians. Still others side with Max Weber, claiming that stratification creates not clear-cut classes but a multidimensional status hierarchy.

Defining classes in U.S. society is difficult because of our relatively low level of status consistency. Especially toward the middle of the hierarchy, people's standing in one dimension may not be the same as their standing in another. For example, a government official may have the power to administer a multimillion-dollar budget yet may earn only a modest personal income. Similarly, many members of the clergy enjoy ample prestige but only moderate power and low pay. Or consider a "card shark," a skillful gambler who hustles other people, winning little public respect but lots of money.

Finally, the social mobility characteristic of class systems—again, most pronounced around the middle—means that social position may change during a person's lifetime, further blurring class boundaries. With these issues in mind, we will examine four general rankings: the upper class, the middle class, the working class, and the lower class.

The Upper Class

Families in the upper class—5 percent of the U.S. population—earn at least $205,000 a year, and some earn ten times that much or more. Along with high income comes significant wealth. The core of the upper class is a much smaller share of the population, including people whose wealth can only be described as vast. In 2012, *Forbes* magazine profiled the richest 400 people in the country, who were worth at least $1 billion (and as much as $66 billion).

Karl Marx described these men and women as "capitalists"—the owners of the means of production along with most of the nation's private wealth. Many upper-class people are business owners, executives in large corporations, or senior government officials. Historically, the upper class has been composed mostly of white Anglo-Saxon Protestants, but this is less true today (Pyle & Koch, 2001).

These women have appeared on the television program *Real Housewives of New Jersey*. Using the categories discussed in the pages that follow, within which social class category do you think they fall? Why?

Upper-Uppers

The *upper-upper class,* sometimes called "blue bloods" or simply "society," includes less than 1 percent of the U.S. population (Coleman & Neugarten, 1971; Baltzell, 1995). Membership is almost always the result of birth, as suggested by the joke that the easiest way to become an upper-upper is to be born one. Most but not all of these families possess enormous wealth, which is primarily inherited. As a general rule, the more a family's income comes from inherited wealth in the form of stocks and bonds, real estate, and other investments, the stronger a family's claim to being a member of the upper-upper class. For this reason, members of the upper-upper class are said to have "old money."

Set apart by their wealth, upper-uppers live in old, exclusive neighborhoods, such as Beacon Hill in Boston, Rittenhouse Square in Philadelphia, the Gold Coast of Chicago, and Nob Hill in San Francisco. Their children typically attend private schools with others of similar background and complete their schooling at high-prestige colleges and universities. In the tradition of European aristocrats, they study liberal arts rather than vocational skills.

Women of the upper-upper class do volunteer work for charitable organizations. Such activities serve a dual purpose: They help the larger community, and they build networks that broaden this elite's power (Ostrander, 1980, 1984).

Watch in **MySocLab** **Video:** *Sociology in Focus: Social Class in the United States*

Lower-Uppers

Most upper-class people actually fall into the *lower-upper class.* The queen of England has a fortune of $500 million—more than enough to be included in the upper class—but her membership in the upper-upper class reflects not only money but her family tree. J. K. Rowling, author of the Harry Potter books, is probably worth twice as much—more than $1 billion—but this self-made woman (who was once on welfare) stands at the top of the lower-upper class. The major difference, in other words, is that members of the lower-upper class are the "working rich" who get their money mostly by earning it rather than from inheritance. These well-to-do families—who make up 3 or 4 percent of the U.S. population—generally live in large homes in expensive neighborhoods, own vacation homes near the water or in the mountains, and send their children to private schools and good colleges. Yet most of the "new rich" do not gain entry into the most exclusive clubs and associations of "old money" families.

In the United States, what we often call the American dream has been to earn enough to join the ranks of the lower-upper class. The athlete who signs a multimillion-dollar contract, the actress who lands a starring role in a Hollywood film, the computer whiz who creates the latest Internet site to capture the public's attention, and even the person who hits it big by winning a huge lottery jackpot are the talented achievers and lucky people who reach the lower-upper class.

People often distinguish between the "new rich" and families with "old money." Men and women who suddenly begin to earn high incomes tend to spend their money on status symbols because they enjoy the new thrill of high-roller living and they want others to know of their success. Those who grow up surrounded by wealth, by contrast, are used to a privileged way of life and are more quiet about it. Thus the conspicuous consumption of the lower-upper class (*left*) can differ dramatically from the more private pursuits and understatement of the upper-upper class (*right*).

The Middle Class

Made up of 40 to 45 percent of the U.S. population, the large middle class has a tremendous influence on our culture. Television programs and movies usually show middle-class people, and most commercial advertising is directed at these average consumers. The middle class contains far more racial and ethnic diversity than the upper class.

Upper-Middles

People in the top half of this category are called the *upper-middle class,* based on above-average income in the range of $116,000 to $205,000 a year. Such income allows upper-middle-class families to live in comfortable homes in fairly expensive areas, own several automobiles, and build investments. Two-thirds of upper-middle-class children graduate from college, and postgraduate degrees are common. Many go on to high-prestige careers as physicians, engineers, lawyers, accountants, and business executives. Lacking the power of the richest people to influence national or international events, upper-middles often play an important role in local political affairs.

Average-Middles

The rest of the middle class falls close to the center of the U.S. class structure. *Average-middles* typically work at less prestigious white-collar jobs as bank branch managers, high school teachers, and government office workers or in highly skilled blue-collar jobs such as electrical work and carpentry. Family income is between $48,500 and $116,000 a year, which is roughly the national average.[2]

Middle-class people typically build up a small amount of wealth over the course of their working lives, mostly in the form of a house and a retirement investment account. Middle-class men and women are likely to be high school graduates, but the odds are less than fifty-fifty that they will complete a four-year college degree, and those who do will typically attend a less expensive, state-supported college or university.

What would you say about the social class standing of the Harrison family and their friend Chumlee, who star in the popular reality television show *Pawn Stars*? What about the work of running a family business? What about their dress and interests? What about the fact that they have recently made a lot of money from their television show? Doesn't their situation show that social class position is often complex and contradictory?

The Working Class

About one-third of the population falls within the working class (sometimes called the *lower-middle class*). In Marxist terms, the working class forms the core of the industrial proletariat. The blue-collar jobs held by members of the working class yield a family income of between $27,000 and $48,500 a year, somewhat below the national average. Working-class families have little or no wealth and are vulnerable to financial problems caused by unemployment or illness.

Many working-class jobs provide little personal satisfacion—because the work requires discipline but rarely imagination—and jobs subject workers to continual supervision. These jobs also offer fewer benefits, such as medical insurance and pension plans. More than half of working-class families own their own homes, which are usually located in lower-cost neighborhoods. Earning a four-year college degree becomes a reality for only about one-quarter of working-class children.

---

[2]In some parts of the United States where the cost of living is very high (say, New York City or San Francisco), a family might need $150,000 or more in annual income to reach the middle class.

The Lower Class

The remaining 20 percent of our population make up the lower class. Low income makes their lives insecure and difficult. In 2011, the federal government classified 46.3 million people (15 percent of the population) as poor. Millions more—called the "working poor"—are slightly better off, holding low-wage jobs that provide little satisfaction and minimal income. Seventy percent of lower-class children manage to complete high school, but only about 15 percent ever complete a four-year college degree.

Society segregates the lower class, especially when the poor are racial or ethnic minorities. About 43 percent of lower-class families own their own homes, typically in the least desirable neighborhoods. Although poor neighborhoods are usually found in our inner cities, lower-class families also live in rural communities, especially in the South.

The recent recession has increased the size of the lower class all over the United States. Yuma, Arizona, recently recorded the highest official unemployment rate for all U.S. cities (about 30 percent) and average income for residents has fallen to about $18,000 a year. Many cities in the West (including El Centro, California), the South (such as Macon, Georgia), and the Midwest (including Zanesville, Ohio) struggle with high unemployment and have reported per-person income of barely $20,000 a year, well below the national average (U.S. Census Bureau, 2012; U.S. Department of Labor, 2012). National Map 11–1 shows an important measure of social class—median household income—for all the counties in the United States.

Seeing Ourselves

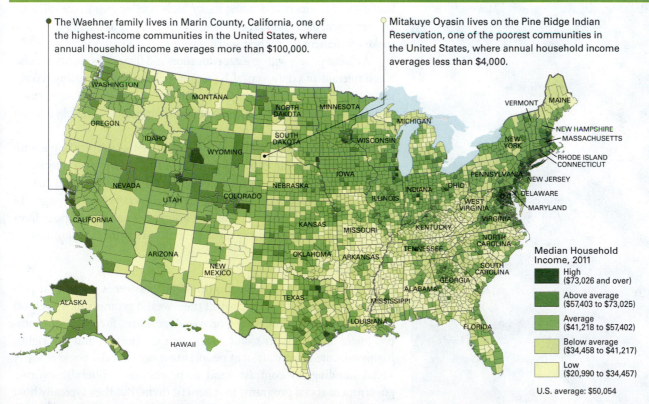

• The Waehner family lives in Marin County, California, one of the highest-income communities in the United States, where annual household income averages more than $100,000.

○ Mitakuye Oyasin lives on the Pine Ridge Indian Reservation, one of the poorest communities in the United States, where annual household income averages less than $4,000.

Median Household Income, 2011

High ($73,026 and over)
Above average ($57,403 to $73,025)
Average ($41,218 to $57,402)
Below average ($34,458 to $41,217)
Low ($20,990 to $34,457)

U.S. average: $50,054

NATIONAL MAP 11–1 Household Income across the United States, 2011

This map shows the median household income (that is, how much money, on average, a household earned) in the more than 3,000 counties that make up the United States for the year 2011. The richest counties, shown in the darker shades of green, are not spread randomly across the country. Nor are the poorest U.S. counties, which are shown in the lightest colors. Looking at the map, what patterns do you see in the distribution of wealth and poverty across the United States? What can you say about wealth and poverty in urban and rural areas?

Source: U.S. Census Bureau (2012).

The Difference Class Makes

(11.4) Analyze how social class position affects health, values, politics, and family life.

Social stratification affects nearly every dimension of our lives. We will briefly examine some of the ways social standing is linked to our health, values and attitudes, politics, and family life.

Health

Health is closely related to social standing. Children born into poor families are twice as likely to die from disease, neglect, accidents, or violence during their first years of life as children born into privileged families. Among adults, people with above-average incomes are almost twice as likely as low-income people to describe their health as excellent.

Government researchers have found that income level has a lot to do with whether or not people get the medical care they need. When compared with people in the highest-income category, people in the lowest-income category were thirteen times more likely to go without needed medical attention. The long-term consequence of not getting medical attention, typically coupled to a lower level of nutrition and living in a more stressful environment, is easy to guess: Average life expectancy for low-income people is five years less than for affluent people (Singh, 2010; Adams, Kirzinger, & Martinez, 2012).

Watch in **MySocLab**
Video: *The Basics: Social Class in the United States*

Values and Attitudes

Some cultural values vary from class to class. The "old rich" have an unusually strong sense of family history because their social position is based on wealth passed down from generation to generation. Secure in their birthright privileges, upper-uppers also favor understated manners and tastes; many "new rich" engage in conspicuous consumption, using homes, cars, and even airplanes as status symbols to make a statement about their social position.

Affluent people with greater education and financial security are also more tolerant of controversial behavior such as homosexuality. Working-class people, who grow up in an atmosphere of greater supervision and discipline and are less likely to attend college, tend to be less tolerant (Lareau, 2002; NORC, 2011).

Social class has a great deal to do with self-concept. People with higher social standing experience more confidence in everyday interaction for the simple reason that others tend to view them as having greater importance. The Thinking About Diversity box on page 311 describes the challenges faced by one young woman from a poor family attending a college where most students are from elite families.

Politics

Do political attitudes follow class lines? The answer is yes, but the pattern is complex. A desire to protect their wealth prompts most well-off people to be more conservative on *economic* issues, favoring, for example, lower taxes. But on *social* issues such as abortion and gay rights, highly educated, more affluent people are more liberal. People of lower social standing, by contrast, tend to be economic liberals, favoring government social programs that benefit them. But they typically hold more conservative views on social issues (NORC, 2011).

A more clear-cut pattern emerges when it comes to political involvement. Higher-income people, who are better served by the system, are more likely to vote and to join political organizations than people with low incomes. In the 2012 presidential elections, 78 percent of adults with family incomes of $100,000 voted, compared to 54 percent of those with family incomes of less than $40,000 (U.S. Census Bureau, 2013).

Compared to high-income people, low-income people are only half as likely to report good health and, on average, live about five fewer years. The toll of low income—played out in inadequate nutrition, little medical care, and high stress—is easy to see on the faces of the poor, who look old before their time.

Thinking About Diversity: Race, Class, and Gender

The Power of Class: A Low-Income Student Asks, "Am I as Good as You?"

Marcella grew up without the privileges that most other students on the campus of this private, liberal arts college take for granted. During her senior year, she and I talked at length about her college experiences and why social class presented a huge challenge to her. Marcella is not her real name; she wishes to remain anonymous. I have summarized what she has said about her college life in the story that follows.

When I came here, I entered a new world. I found myself in a place that seemed strange and sometimes dangerous. All around me were people with habits and ideas I did not understand. A thousand times, I thought to myself, I hope all of you will realize that there are other worlds out there and that I am from one of them. Will you accept me?

I am a child of poverty, a young woman raised in a world of want and violence. I am now on the campus of an elite college. I may have a new identity as a college student. But my old life is still going on in my head. I have not been able to change how I think of myself.

Do you want to find out more about me? Learn more about the power of social class to shape how we feel about ourselves? Here is what I want to say to you.

When I was growing up, I envied most of you. You lived in a middle-class bubble, a world that held you, protected you, and comforted you. Not me. While your parents were discussing current events, planning family trips, and looking out for you, my father and mother were screaming at each other. I will never be able to forget summer nights when I lay in my bed, sticky with sweat, biting my fingernails as a telephone crashed against the wall that separated my room from theirs. My father was drunk and out of control; my mother ducked just in time.

Your fathers and mothers work in office buildings. They have good jobs, as doctors, lawyers, and architects; they are corporate managers; they run small businesses. Your mothers and fathers are people who matter. My mom takes the bus to a hospital where she works for $10 an hour cleaning up after people. She spends her shift doing what she is told. My dad?

Who knows. He was a deadbeat, a drunk, a drug addict. I don't know if he still is or not. I haven't heard from him in eight years.

You grew up in a nice neighborhood and probably lived for many years in one house. My family lived in low-cost rental housing. We moved a lot. When there was no money for rent, we packed up our stuff and moved to a new place. It seemed like we were always running away from something.

You grew up with books, with trips to the library, with parents who read to you. You learned how to speak well and have an impressive vocabulary. I never heard a bedtime story, and I had maybe one inspiring teacher. Most of what I know I had to learn on my own. Maybe that's why I always feel like I am trying to catch up to you.

You know how to use forks, knives, and spoons the right way. You know how to eat Chinese food and what to order at a Thai restaurant. You have favorite Italian dishes. You know how to order wine. You know about German beers, Danish cheeses, and French sauces. Me? I grew up having Thanksgiving dinner on paper plates, eating turkey served by social service volunteers. When you ask me to go with you to some special restaurant, I make some excuse and stay home. I can't afford it. More than that, I am afraid you will find out how little I know about things you take for granted.

How did I ever get to this college? I remember one of my teachers telling me "You have promise." The college admissions office accepted me. But I am not sure why. I was given a scholarship that covers most of my tuition. That solved one big problem, and now I am here. But sometimes I am not sure I will stay. I have to study more than many of you to learn things you already know. I have to work two part-time jobs to make the money I needed to buy a used computer, clothes, and the occasional pizza at the corner place where many of you spend so much time.

It's amazing to me that I am here. I realize how lucky I am. But now that I am here, I realize that the road is so much longer than I thought it would be. Getting to this college was only part of the journey. The scholarship was only part of the answer. The biggest challenge for me is what goes on every day—the thousands of ways in which you live a life that I still don't really understand, the thousands of things that I won't know or that I will do wrong that will blow my cover, and show me up for the fraud I am.

What Do You Think?

1. How does this story show that social class involves much more than how much money a person has?

2. Why does Marcella worry that other people will think she is a "fraud"? If you could speak to her about this fear, what would you say?

3. Have you ever had similar feelings about being less important than—or better than—someone else based on social class position? Explain.

Family and Gender

Social class also shapes family life. Generally, lower-class families are somewhat larger than middle-class families because of earlier marriage and less use of birth control. Another family pattern is that working-class parents encourage children to conform to conventional norms and to respect authority figures. Parents of higher social standing pass on different "cultural capital" to their children, teaching them to express their individuality and to use their imagination more freely. In both cases, parents are looking to the future: The odds are that less privileged children will have jobs that require them to follow rules and that more privileged children will have careers that require more creativity (Kohn, 1977; McLeod, 1995; Lareau, 2002).

The more money a family has, the more resources parents have to develop their children's talents and abilities. Researchers estimate that affluent families with earnings greater than $102,870 a year will spend $490,830 raising a child born in 2011 to the age of eighteen. Middle-class people, with an annual income between $59,410 and $102,870, will spend $295,560, and a lower-income family, earning less than $59,410, will spend $212,370 (Lino, 2012). Privilege leads to privilege as family life reproduces the class structure in each generation.

Class also shapes our world of relationships. In a classic study of married life, Elizabeth Bott (1971, orig. 1957) found that most lower-income couples divide their responsibilities according to gender roles, so that men and women live rather different lives. More affluent couples, by contrast, are more egalitarian, sharing more activities and expressing greater intimacy. More recently, Karen Walker (1995) discovered that friendships among less well-off people typically serve as sources of material assistance; among those with higher incomes, friendships are likely to involve shared interests and leisure pursuits.

Social Mobility

(11.5) Assess the extent of social mobility in the United States.

Ours is a dynamic society marked by quite a bit of social movement. Earning a college degree, landing a higher-paying job, or marrying someone who earns a good income contributes to *upward social mobility;* dropping out of school, losing a job, or becoming divorced (especially for women) may result in *downward social mobility.*

Over the long term, social mobility is not so much a matter of changes in individuals as changes in society itself. In the first half of the twentieth century, for example, industrialization expanded the U.S. economy, pushing up living standards. Even people who were not good swimmers rode the rising tide of prosperity. In recent decades, the closing of U.S. factories has pushed *structural social mobility* in a downward direction, dealing economic setbacks to many people. The economic downturn that hit hard at the end of 2007 and continues several years later reduced the income and economic opportunities of millions of people.

Sociologists distinguish between shorter- and longer-term changes in social position. **Intragenerational social mobility** is *a change in social position occurring during a person's lifetime* (*intra* is Latin for "within"). **Intergenerational social mobility**, *upward or downward social mobility of children in relation to their parents,* is important because it usually reveals long-term changes in society, such as industrialization, that affect everyone (*inter* is Latin for "between").

Research on Mobility

In few societies do people think about "getting ahead" as much as in the United States. Lady Gaga claims her parents both grew up in lower-class families; last year, she earned more than $60 million. Johnny Depp was born in Kentucky to a father who was an engineer and a mother who was a waitress; last year, he earned $100 million. Moving up—if not always to the point of becoming a superstar—is the American dream. But does everyone move up, even a little? Is there as much social mobility as we like to think?

intragenerational social mobility a change in social position occurring during a person's lifetime

intergenerational social mobility upward or downward social mobility of children in relation to their parents

One recent study of intergenerational mobility shows that about 32 percent of U.S. men have the same type of work as their fathers, 37 percent have been upwardly mobile (for example, a son born to a father with a blue-collar job now does white-collar work), and 32 percent have been downwardly mobile (for example, the father has a white-collar job and the son does blue-collar work). Among women, 27 percent showed no change in relation to their fathers, 46 percent were upwardly mobile, and 28 percent were downwardly mobile (Beller & Hout, 2006). The Thinking About Diversity box provides the results of another study of long-term social mobility.

Thinking About Diversity: Race, Class, and Gender

Is Social Mobility the Exception or the Rule?

How likely is it to move up in U.S. society? What about the odds of moving down? What share of people, as adults, ends up staying right where they started as children? To answer these questions, Lisa A. Keister used data from the National Longitudinal Survey of Youth (NLSY), a long-term study of 9,500 men and women. These people were first studied in 1979 during their youth—when they were between fourteen and twenty-two years old and living at home with one or both parents. The same people were studied again as adults in 2000, when they ranged in age from thirty-five to forty-three years old. About 80 percent of the subjects were married and all had households of their own.

What Keister wanted to know was how the economic standing of the subjects may have changed over their lifetimes, which she measured by estimating (from NLSY data) their amount of wealth at two different times. In 1979, because the subjects were young and living at home, she measured the family wealth of the subjects' parents. Keister placed each subject's family in one of five wealth quintiles—from the richest 20 percent down to the poorest 20 percent—and these quintiles are shown in the vertical axis of the accompanying table. In 2000, she measured the wealth of the same people, who were now living in households of their own. Wealth rankings in 2000 are shown in the horizontal axis of the table.

So what did Keister learn? How much social mobility, in terms of household wealth, took place over the course of twenty-one years? Looking at the table, we can learn a great deal. The cell in the upper left corner shows us that, of the richest 20 percent of subjects in 1979, 55 percent of these young people went on to remain in the top wealth category in 2000. Obviously, because these people were starting out in the top category, there could be no upward movement (although some of the subjects were richer as adults than they were when they were young). Twenty-five percent of the richest subjects in 1979 had dropped one level to the second quintile. That means that 80 percent of the richest

people in 1979 were still quite well off in 2000; only 20 percent of the richest people were downwardly mobile across two or more categories (9 percent who fell two levels, 6 percent who fell three levels, and 5 percent who fell to the lowest wealth level).

A similar pattern is seen as we begin with the poorest subjects—those who were in the lowest wealth quintile in 1979. Obviously, again, because these people started out in the lowest category, they had nowhere to go but up. But 45 percent of these men and women remained in the lowest wealth category as adults (the bottom-right box), and 27 percent moved up one quintile. Another 28 percent of the poorest people moved up two or more quintiles as adults (11 percent who rose two levels, 9 percent who rose three levels, and 8 percent who rose to the richest level).

For subjects in the middle ranges, the data show that mobility was somewhat more pronounced. For those who started in the second richest quintile, just 33 percent ended up in the same place. The remaining 67 percent moved up or down at least one level, although the most common move was rising or falling one level. Of those in the third (or middle) quintile, 35 percent ended up in the same rank as adults, and 65 percent moved up or down at least one level. Again, most of those who moved shifted just one level. Similarly, of those who started out in the fourth quintile, 35 percent ended up in the same ranking as adults, and 65 percent moved in most cases one level up or down.

So what can we conclude about patterns of wealth mobility over a generation between 1979 and 2000? The first conclusion is that a majority of people did experience some mobility, moving up or down one or more levels. So mobility was the rule rather than the exception. Second, movement downward was about as common as movement upward. Third, movement was somewhat more common among people closer to the middle of the wealth hierarchy—the largest share of people who "stayed put" (55 percent among those who started out at the top and 45 percent of those who started out at the bottom) were at one or the other extreme.

What Do You Think?

1. What about the results presented here surprises you? Explain.

2. Overall, how well do the results presented here square with what you imagine most people in this country think about mobility?

3. How do you think the recent economic recession has affected patterns of social mobility?

Childhood Standing, 1979	Adult Standing, 2000				
	Richest 20%	Second 20%	Third 20%	Fourth 20%	Poorest 20%
Richest 20% →	55	25	9	6	5
Second 20% →	25	33	23	11	8
Third 20% →	13	21	35	20	11
Fourth 20% →	7	14	20	35	24
Poorest 20% →	8	9	11	27	45

Horizontal social mobility—changing jobs at the same class level—is even more common; overall, about 80 percent of children show at least some type of change in occupational work in relation to their fathers (Hout, 1998; Beller & Hout, 2006).

Research points to five general conclusions about social mobility in the United States:

1. **Social mobility over the past century has been fairly high.** A high level of mobility is what we would expect in an industrial class system. Most men and women show some mobility in relation to their parents.

2. **Within a single generation, social mobility is usually small.** Most young families increase their income over time as they gain education and skills—some social mobility occurs as people move through the life course. For example, a typical family headed by a thirty-year-old earned about $56,000 in 2011; a typical family headed by a fifty-year-old earned $80,000 (U.S. Census Bureau, 2012). Yet only a few people move "from rags to riches" (the way author J. K. Rowling did) or lose a lot of money (a number of rock stars who made it big had little money a few years later). Most social mobility involves limited movement within one class level rather than striking moves between classes.

3. **The long-term trend in social mobility has been upward.** Industrialization, which greatly expanded the U.S. economy, and the growth of white-collar work over the course of the twentieth century have raised living standards. In recent decades, however, mobility has been downward about as often as it has been upward (Keister, 2005).

4. **Since the 1970s, social mobility has been uneven.** Real income (adjusted for inflation) rose steadily during the twentieth century until the 1970s. Since then, as shown in Figure 11–2, real income has risen and fallen with overall smaller gains than was the case before 1970.

5. **The short-term trend in social mobility has been downward.** Especially since the beginning of the recent recession in 2007, the middle class has become smaller as income and wealth have declined. As a result, 85 percent of people who identify themselves as

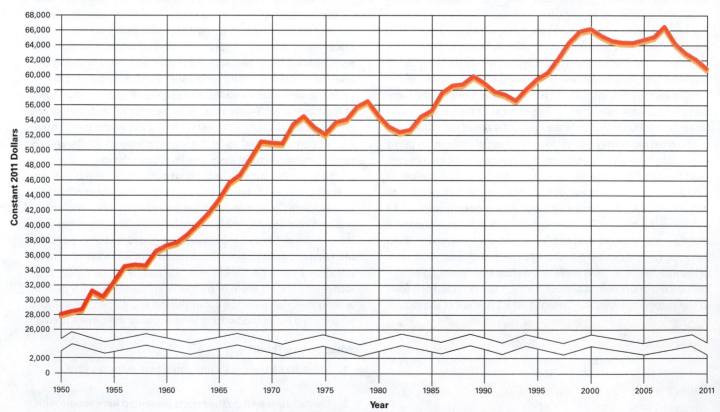

FIGURE 11–2 Median Annual Income, U.S. Families, 1950–2011

Average family income in the United States grew rapidly between 1950 and 1970. In the decades since then, however, income increased at a lower and less even rate. After 2007, the economic recession pushed median income downward.

Source: U.S. Census Bureau (2012).

"middle class" say that keeping the same standard of living has become more difficult (Pew Research Center, 2012).

Mobility by Income Level

The experience of social mobility depends on where in the social class system you happen to be. Figure 11–3 shows how U.S. families at different income levels made out between 1980 and 2011. Well-to-do families (the highest 20 percent at each point in time, but not all the same families over the entire period) saw their incomes jump 55 percent, from an average of $127,983 in 1980 to $197,932 in 2011. People in the middle of the population also had gains, but more modest ones. The lowest-income 20 percent saw an 8.3 percent decrease in earnings.

For the families at the top of the income scale (the highest 5 percent), recent decades have brought a windfall. Families in this category, with average income of more than $182,000 in 1980, were making $345,000 in 2011—almost twice as much as in 1980 (U.S. Census Bureau, 2012).

Mobility: Race, Ethnicity, and Gender

White people in the United States have always been in a more privileged position than people of African or Hispanic descent. Through the economic expansion of the 1980s and 1990s, many more African Americans entered the ranks of the wealthy. But overall, the real income of African Americans has changed little in three decades. African American family income as a percentage of white family income has fallen slightly to 58 percent in 2011 from 61 percent in 1975. Compared with white families, Latino families in the United States lost more ground, earning 66 percent as much as white families in 1975 and just 57 percent as much in 2011 (U.S. Census Bureau, 2012).

Feminists point out that historically women in U.S. society have had limited opportunity for upward mobility because the clerical jobs (such as secretary) and service positions (such as food server) widely held by women offer few opportunities for advancement.

Over time, however, the earnings gap between women and men has been narrowing. Women working full time in 1980 earned 60 percent as much as men working full time; by 2011, women were earning 77 percent as much (U.S. Census Bureau, 2012).

Mobility and Marriage

Research points to the conclusion that marriage has an important effect on social standing. In a study of women and men in their forties, Jay Zagorsky (2006) found that people who marry and stay married accumulate about twice as much wealth as people who remain single or who divorce. Reasons for this difference include the fact that couples who live together typically enjoy double incomes and also pay roughly half the bills they would have if they were single and living in separate households.

It is also likely that compared to single people, married men and women work harder in their jobs and save more money. Why? The main reason is that they are working not just for themselves but also to support others who are counting on them.

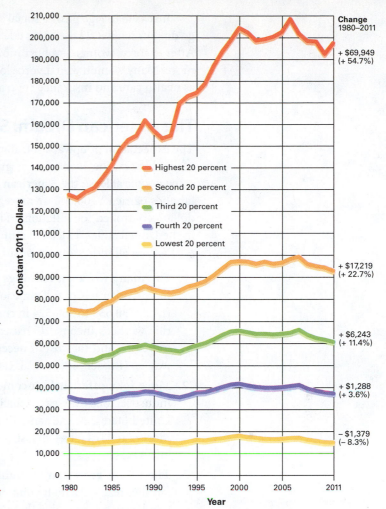

FIGURE 11–3 Mean Annual Income, U.S. Families, 1980–2011 (in 2011 dollars, adjusted for inflation)

The gap between high-income and low-income families is wider today than it was in 1980.

Source: U.S. Census Bureau (2012).

Just as marriage pushes social standing upward, divorce usually makes social position go down. Couples who divorce take on the financial burden of supporting two households. After divorce, women are hurt more than men because it is typically the man who earns more. Many women who divorce lose not only most of their income but also benefits such as health care and insurance coverage (Weitzman, 1996).

The American Dream: Still a Reality?

The expectation of upward social mobility is deeply rooted in U.S. culture. Through most of our history, the economy has grown steadily, raising living standards. Even today, for some people at least, the American dream is alive and well. In 2011, about one in four U.S. families earned $100,000 or more, compared with just one in thirteen back in 1967 (in dollars controlled for inflation). There are now almost 8 million millionaire households in the United States, twice the number in 1995 (U.S. Census Bureau, 2012; Wolff, 2012).

Yet not all indicators are positive. Note these disturbing trends:

1. **For many workers, earnings have stalled.** The annual income of a fifty-year-old male worker with a full-time job climbed by about 65 percent between 1958 and 1974 (from $30,653 to $50,524 in constant 2011 dollars). Between 1974 and 2011, however, this worker's income *decreased* by 9 percent, even as the number of hours worked increased and the cost of necessities like housing, education, and medical care went way up (Russell, 1995a; U.S. Census Bureau, 2012).

2. **More jobs offer little income.** The expanding global economy has moved many industrial jobs overseas, reducing the number of high-paying factory jobs here in the United States. At the same time, the expansion of our service economy means that more of today's jobs—in fast-food restaurants or large discount stores—offer relatively low wages.

3. **The recent recession brought economic decline.** The median net worth for U.S. families reached a high point of about $120,000 in 2007. With the economic recession that began by the end of that year, this figure had fallen to $77,000 by 2010. This drop reflected both a drop in housing values throughout most of the United States and also a decline in the value of other investments.

4. **Young people are remaining at home.** Currently, more than half of young people aged eighteen to twenty-four (61 percent of men and 52 percent of women) are living with their parents. Since 1975, the average age at marriage has moved upward five years (to 26.6 years for women and 28.6 years for men).

Over the past generation, more people have become rich. In the last few years, however, the number of people worth more than $5 million has actually gone down, as the recession has eroded the value of investments and homes. In this sense, some of the rich have "shared the pain," although they are not suffering like most "ordinary" people. But at the top of the class system, the very rich continue to claim an increasing share of all wealth (Wolff, 2012). Over the past several decades, the highest-paid corporate executives have enjoyed a runaway rise in their earnings.

The picture is different at the middle of the class structure and below that. The increasing share of low-paying jobs has brought downward mobility for millions of families, feeding the fear that the chance to enjoy a middle-class lifestyle is slipping away. Two generations ago, most people defined being "middle class" in terms of having a college education, a professional job, and a house in the suburbs. Today, according to one recent survey, more than 80 percent said being "middle class" meant having a secure job. Surveys also confirm that fewer and fewer people think of themselves as "middle class" and that the share of people who say they are in the "lower-middle class" or the "lower class" is on the rise. Some sobering numbers underlie these trends. As a glance back at Figure 11–2 on page 314 shows, although median family income doubled in the generation between 1950 and 1973, it grew by only 12 percent over almost two generations. In the last few years, median income has actually fallen (CNBC, 2012; Pew Research Center, 2012; U.S. Census Bureau, 2012).

For a closer look at how the very rich have prospered in recent years, **Read More** in **MySocLab**, *As CEOs Get Richer, the Great Mansions Return*

The Global Economy and the U.S. Class Structure

Underlying the shifts in U.S. class structure is global economic change. Much of the industrial production that gave U.S. workers high-paying jobs a generation ago has moved overseas. With less industry at home, the United States now serves as a vast market for industrial goods such as cars and popular items like stereos, cameras, and computers made in China, Japan, South Korea, and elsewhere.

High-paying jobs in manufacturing, held by 28 percent of the U.S. labor force in 1960, support only 9 percent of workers today (U.S. Department of Labor, 2012). In their place, the economy now offers service work, which often pays far less. A traditionally high-paying corporation like USX (formerly United States Steel) now employs fewer people than the expanding McDonald's chain, and fast-food clerks make only a fraction of what steelworkers earn.

The global reorganization of work has not been bad news for everyone. On the contrary, the global economy is driving upward social mobility for educated people who specialize in law, finance, marketing, and computer technology. Even allowing for the economic downturn that began in 2008, the global economic expansion helped push up the stock market more than thirteen-fold between 1980 and 2013, increasing the wealth of families with money to invest over this period.

But the same trend has hurt many average workers, who have lost their factory jobs and now perform low-wage service work. In addition, many companies (General Motors and Ford are recent examples) have downsized, cutting the ranks of their workforce in their efforts to stay competitive in world markets. As a result, even though 52 percent of all families contain two or more workers—more than twice the share in 1950—many families are working harder simply to hold on to what they have (U.S. Census Bureau, 2012).

Poverty in the United States

(11.6) Discuss patterns and explanations of poverty in the U.S. population.

Social stratification creates both "haves" and "have-nots." All systems of social inequality create poverty, or at least **relative poverty**, *the lack of resources of some people in relation to those who have more*. A more serious but preventable problem is **absolute poverty**, *a lack of resources that is life-threatening*.

As Chapter 12 ("Global Stratification") explains, about 1.3 billion human beings—one person in five—are at risk of absolute poverty. Even in the affluent United States, families go hungry, live in inadequate housing, and suffer poor health because of a serious lack of resources.

The Extent of Poverty

In 2011, the government classified 46 million men, women, and children—15 percent of the population—as poor. This count of relative poverty refers to families with incomes below an official poverty line, which for a family of four in that year was set at $23,021. The poverty line is about three times what the government estimates people must spend for food. But the income of the average poor family was just 59 percent of this amount. This means that the typical poor family had to get by on an income of about $13,500 (U.S. Census Bureau, 2012). Figure 11–4 shows that the official poverty rate fell during the 1960s, and then rose and fell within a narrow range in the decades since, rising with the recent recession.

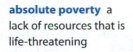

absolute poverty a lack of resources that is life-threatening

relative poverty the lack of resources of some people in relation to those who have more

FIGURE 11–4 The Poverty Rate in the United States, 1960–2011

The share of our population in poverty fell dramatically between 1960 and 1970. Since then, the poverty rate has remained between 10 and 15 percent of the population.

Source: U.S. Census Bureau (2012).

Who Are the Poor?

Although no single description fits all poor people, poverty is pronounced among certain categories of our population. Where these categories overlap, the problem is especially serious.

Age

A generation ago, the elderly were at greatest risk for poverty. But thanks to better retirement programs offered today by private employers and the government, the poverty rate for people over age sixty-five fell from 30 percent in 1967 to 8.7 percent—well below the national average—in 2011. Looking at it from another angle, about 7.8 percent (3.6 million) of the poor are elderly (U.S. Census Bureau, 2012).

Today the burden of poverty falls more heavily on children. In 2011, 21.9 percent of people under age eighteen (16.1 million children) and 20.6 percent of people age eighteen to twenty-four (6.2 million young adults) were poor. Put another way, 48 percent of the U.S. poor are young people no older than twenty-four.

Race and Ethnicity

Two-thirds of all poor people are white (including those who also say they are Hispanic); 24 percent are African Americans. But in relation to their overall numbers, African Americans are almost three times as likely as non-Hispanic whites to be poor. In 2011, 27.6 percent of African Americans (10.9 million people) lived in poverty, compared to 25.3 percent of Hispanics (13.2 million), 12.3 percent of Asians and Pacific Islanders (2 million), and 9.8 percent of non-Hispanic whites (19.2 million). The poverty gap between whites and minorities has changed little since 1975.

People of color have especially high rates of child poverty. Among African American children, 38.8 percent are poor; the comparable figures are 34.1 percent among Hispanic children and 12.5 percent among non-Hispanic white children (U.S. Census Bureau, 2012).

Gender and Family Patterns

feminization of poverty the trend of women making up an increasing proportion of the poor

Of all poor people age eighteen or older, 59 percent are women and 41 percent are men. This difference reflects the fact that women who head households are at high risk of poverty. Of all poor families, 52 percent are headed by women with no husband present; just 10 percent of poor families are headed by single men.

The United States has thus experienced a **feminization of poverty**, *the trend of women making up an increasing proportion of the poor*. In 1960, only 25 percent of all poor households were headed by women; the majority of poor families had both wives and husbands in the home. By 2011, however, the share of poor households headed by a single woman had more than doubled to 52 percent.

The feminization of poverty is one result of a larger trend: the rapidly increasing number of households at all class levels headed by single women. This trend, coupled with the fact that households headed by women are at high risk of poverty, helps explain why women and their children make up an increasing share of the U.S. poor.

Urban and Rural Poverty

In the United States, the greatest concentration of poverty is found in central cities, where the 2011 poverty rate stood at

Henry Ossawa Tanner captured the humility and humanity of impoverished people in his painting *The Thankful Poor*. This insight is important in a society that tends to define poor people as morally unworthy and deserving of their bitter plight.

Source: Henry Ossawa Tanner (1859–1937), *The Thankful Poor*. Private collection. Art Resource, New York.

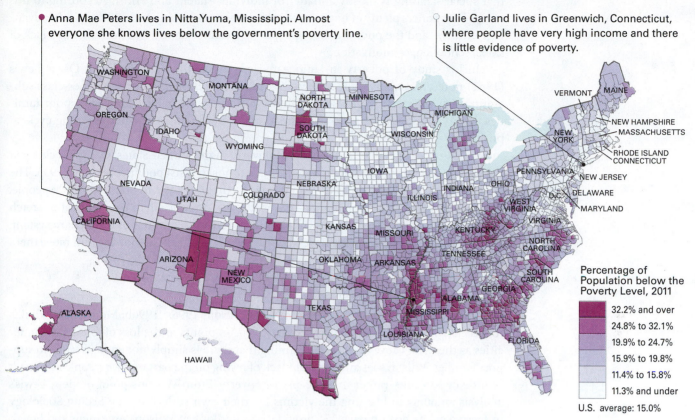

● Anna Mae Peters lives in Nitta Yuma, Mississippi. Almost everyone she knows lives below the government's poverty line.

○ Julie Garland lives in Greenwich, Connecticut, where people have very high income and there is little evidence of poverty.

Percentage of Population below the Poverty Level, 2011

	32.2% and over
	24.8% to 32.1%
	19.9% to 24.7%
	15.9% to 19.8%
	11.4% to 15.8%
	11.3% and under

U.S. average: 15.0%

NATIONAL MAP 11–2 Poverty across the United States, 2011

This map shows that the poorest counties in the United States—where the poverty rate is more than twice the national average—are in Appalachia, across the Deep South, along the border with Mexico, near the Four Corners region of the Southwest, and in the Dakotas. Can you suggest some reasons for this pattern?
Source: U.S. Census Bureau (2012).

20 percent. The poverty rate in suburbs is 11.3 percent. Thus the poverty rate for urban areas as a whole is 14.6 percent—somewhat lower than the 17 percent found in rural areas. National Map 11–2 shows that most of the counties with the highest poverty rate in the United States are rural.

Wherever poor families may live, they are becoming more socially segregated. That is, as income inequality increases, the odds that poor families live in communities in which most people are poor are also increasing. A majority of low-income families still live in communities in which most people are not poor. But almost 30 percent of the poor now live in mostly poor communities, a sharp increase from about 20 percent in 1980 (Pew Research Center, 2012; Taylor, 2012).

Explaining Poverty

The richest nation on Earth contains tens of millions of poor people, a fact that raises serious questions. It is true, as some analysts remind us, that most poor people in the United States are far better off than the poor in other countries: 32 percent of U.S. poor families own a home, at least 64 percent own a car, and about 82 percent say they usually have enough food (U.S. Census Bureau, 2012; U.S. Department of Agriculture, 2012). But there is little doubt that poverty harms the overall well-being of millions of people in this country.

Why is there poverty in the first place? We will examine two opposing explanations for poverty that lead to a lively and important political debate.

One View: Blame the Poor

One approach holds that *the poor are mostly responsible for their own poverty*. Throughout this nation's history, people have placed a high cultural value on self-reliance, convinced that social standing is mostly a matter of individual talent and effort. According to this view, society offers plenty of opportunities to anyone who is able and willing to take advantage of them, and the poor are those people who cannot or will not work due to a lack of skills, schooling, or motivation.

In his study of poverty in Latin American cities, the anthropologist Oscar Lewis (1961) noted that many poor become trapped in a *culture of poverty*, a lower-class subculture that can destroy people's ambition to improve their lives. Raised in poor families, children become resigned to their situation, producing a self-perpetuating cycle of poverty.

In 1996, hoping to break the cycle of poverty in the United States, Congress changed the welfare system, which had provided federal funds to assist poor people since 1935. The federal government continues to send money to the states to distribute to needy people, but benefits carry strict time limits—in most cases, no more than two years at a stretch and a lifetime total of five years as an individual moves in and out of the welfare system. The stated purpose of this reform was to force people to be self-supporting and move them away from dependency on government.

Another View: Blame Society

A different position, argued by William Julius Wilson (1996a, 1996b; Mouw, 2000), holds that *society is mostly responsible for poverty*. Wilson points to the loss of jobs in the inner cities as the main cause of poverty, claiming that there is simply not enough work to support families. Wilson sees any apparent lack of trying on the part of poor people as a result of little opportunity rather than a cause of poverty. From Wilson's point of view, Lewis's analysis amounts to blaming the victims for their own suffering. The Seeing Sociology in Everyday Life box on page 321 provides a closer look at Wilson's argument and how it would shape public policy.

EVALUATE The U.S. public is evenly divided over whether the government or people themselves should take responsibility for reducing poverty (NORC, 2013:508). And here's what we know about poverty and work: Government statistics show that 56 percent of the heads of poor households did not work at all during 2011, and an additional 30 percent worked only part time (U.S. Census Bureau, 2012). Such facts seem to support the "blame the poor" side of the argument, because one major cause of poverty is not holding a job.

But the *reasons* that people do not work seem more in step with the "blame society" position. Middle-class women may be able to combine working and child rearing, but this is much harder for poor women who cannot afford child care, and few employers provide child care programs. As Wilson explains, many people are idle not because they are avoiding work but because there are not enough jobs to go around. In short, the most effective way to reduce poverty is to ensure a greater supply of jobs as well as child care for parents who work (Wilson, 1996a; Bainbridge, Meyers, & Waldfogel, 2003).

CHECK YOUR LEARNING Explain the view that the poor should take responsibility for poverty and the view that society is responsible for poverty. Which is closer to your own view?

The Working Poor

Not all poor people are jobless. The *working poor* command the sympathy and support of people on both sides of the poverty debate. In 2011, some 15 percent of heads of poor families (1.4 million women and men) worked at least fifty weeks

Seeing Sociology in Everyday Life

When Work Disappears, the Result Is Poverty

The U.S. economy has created tens of millions of new jobs in recent decades. Yet African Americans who live in inner cities have faced a catastrophic loss of work. Unemployment rates were sky high even before the recent recession, which has only made the problem worse. William Julius Wilson points out that although people continue to talk about welfare reform, few Democratic or Republican leaders have said anything about the lack of work in central cities.

With the loss of inner-city jobs, Wilson continues, for the first time in U.S. history a large majority of the adults in our inner cities are not working. Studying the Washington Park area of Chicago, Wilson found a troubling trend. Back in 1950, most adults in this African American community had jobs, but by the mid-1990s, two-thirds did not. As one elderly woman who moved to the neighborhood in 1953 explained:

> When I moved in, the neighborhood was intact. It was intact with homes, beautiful homes, mini-mansions, with stores, laundromats, with Chinese cleaners. We had drugstores. We had hotels. We had doctors over on 39th Street. We had doctors' offices in the neighborhood. We had the middle class and the upper-middle class. It has gone from affluent to where it is today. (Wilson, 1996b:28)

Why has this neighborhood declined? Wilson's eight years of research point to one answer: There are barely any jobs. It is the loss of work that has pushed people into desperate poverty,

weakened families, and made people turn to welfare. In nearby Woodlawn, Wilson identified more than 800 businesses that had operated in 1950; today, just 100 remain. In addition, a number of major employers in the past—including Western Electric and International Harvester—closed their plant doors in the late 1960s. The inner cities have fallen victim to economic change, including downsizing and the loss of industrial jobs that have moved overseas.

Wilson paints a grim picture. But he also believes we have the power to create new jobs. Wilson proposes attacking the problem in stages. First, the government could hire people to do all kinds of work, from clearing slums to putting up new housing. Such a program, modeled on the Works Progress Administration (WPA) created in 1935 during the Great Depression, would move people from welfare to work and in the process create much-needed hope. In addition, federal and state governments must improve schools by enacting performance standards and providing more funding. Of special importance is teaching children language skills and computer skills to prepare them for the jobs being created by the Information Revolution. Improved regional public transportation would connect cities (where people need work) and suburbs (where most jobs now are). In addition, more affordable child care would help single mothers and fathers balance the responsibilities of employment and parenting.

Wilson claims that his proposals are well grounded in research. But he knows that politics revolves around other considerations as well. For one thing, if the public *thinks* there are jobs available, it is hard to change the perception that the poor are simply avoiding work. He also concedes that his proposals, at least in the short term, are more expensive than continuing to funnel welfare assistance to jobless communities.

But what are the long-term costs of allowing our cities to decay while suburbs prosper? On the other hand, what would be the benefits of giving everyone the hope and satisfaction that are supposed to define our way of life?

What Do You Think?

1. If Wilson were running for public office, do you think he would be elected? Why or why not?

2. In your opinion, why are people so reluctant to see inner-city poverty as a problem?

3. Where do you agree with Wilson's analysis of poverty? Where do you disagree?

William Julius Wilson spent years studying neighborhoods like this one in Chicago. He now teaches at Harvard University in Cambridge, Massachusetts.

of the year and yet could not escape poverty. Another 30 percent of these heads of families (2.8 million people) remained poor despite part-time employment. Put differently, 3.5 percent of full-time workers earn so little that they remain poor (U.S. Census Bureau, 2012). Congress set the minimum wage at $6.55 per hour in 2008, raising it to $7.25 per hour in July 2009. But even this increase cannot end working poverty—even at $8.00 an hour, a full-time worker still cannot lift an urban family of four above the poverty line. Currently, it would take an hourly wage of about $11.07 to do that.

Individual ability and personal effort do play a part in shaping social position. So do decisions like dropping out of school and deciding to have a child without enough family income to support everyone. However, the weight of sociological evidence points to society, not individual character traits, as the primary cause of poverty because more and more of the jobs that are available offer only low wages. In addition, the poor are *categories* of people—female heads of families, people of color, people isolated from the larger society in inner-city areas—who face special barriers and limited opportunities.

The Controversy & Debate box on page 323 takes a closer look at current welfare policy. Understanding this important social issue can help us decide how our society should respond to the problem of poverty, as well as the problem of homelessness, discussed next.

Homelessness

In 2011, the government's Department of Housing and Urban Development (HUD) conducted a national survey of cities and towns to find out how many people in the United States were homeless on a single night in January. The answer was about 636,000, including people living in shelters, in transitional housing, and on the street. As with earlier estimates of the homeless population, critics claimed that the HUD survey undercounted the homeless, who may well number several million people. In addition, they add, evidence suggests that the number of homeless people in the United States is increasing (Kaufman, 2004; U.S. Department of Housing and Urban Development, 2011).

The familiar stereotypes of homeless people—men sleeping in doorways and women carrying everything they own in a shopping bag—have been replaced by the "new homeless": people thrown out of work because of plant closings, women who take their children and leave home to escape domestic violence, women and men forced out of apartments by rent increases, and others unable to meet mortgage or rent payments because of low wages or no work at all. Today, no stereotype paints a complete picture of the homeless.

The large majority of homeless people report that they do not work, although about 15 percent have at least a part-time job (U.S. Conference of Mayors, 2011). Working or not, all homeless people have one thing in common: *poverty*. For that reason, the explanations of poverty just presented also apply to homelessness. Some (more conservative) people blame the *personal traits* of the homeless themselves. One-third of homeless people are

Is society responsible for poverty or are individuals themselves to blame? When it comes to homeless families, most people think society should do more.

Controversy & Debate

The Welfare Dilemma

Marco: (rushing in the door) Sorry I'm late. I stopped at the store and got stuck behind some welfare mother in the checkout line.

Sergi: (looking back with a confused grin) Exactly what does a person on welfare look like?

What is *your* image of a "welfare recipient"? If you are like many people in the United States, you might think of a middle-aged African American woman. But you would be wrong. In truth, the typical person receiving welfare in this country is a child who is white.

There is a lot of confusion about welfare. There is also disagreement about whether this type of assistance is a good or bad idea. In 1996, Congress debated the issue and enacted new law that ended the federal government's role in providing income assistance to poor households. In place of this federal program, new state-run programs now offer limited help to the poor, but they require people who receive aid to get job training or find work—or have their benefits cut off.

To understand how we got to where we are, let's begin by explaining what, exactly, welfare is. The term "welfare" refers to an assortment of policies and programs designed to improve the well-being of some low-income people. Until the welfare reform of 1996, most people used the term to refer to just one part of the overall system, Aid for Families with Dependent Children (AFDC), a federal program of monthly financial support for parents (mostly single women) to care for themselves and their children. In 1996, about 5 million households received AFDC for some part of the year.

Conservatives opposed AFDC, claiming that rather than reducing child poverty, AFDC made the problem worse, in two ways. First, they claimed that AFDC weakened families, because for years after the program began, it paid benefits to poor mothers only if no husband lived in the home. As a result, the government was providing an economic incentive to women to have children outside of marriage, and critics blame this policy for the rapid rise of out-of-wedlock births among poor people. To conservatives, marriage is key to reducing poverty: Only one in sixteen married-couple families is poor; more than nine in ten AFDC families were headed by an unmarried woman.

Second, conservatives believe that welfare encourages poor people to become dependent on government handouts, the main reason that eight out of ten poor heads of households did not have full-time jobs. Furthermore, only 5 percent of single mothers receiving AFDC worked full time, compared to more than half of nonpoor single mothers. Conservatives say that welfare gradually moved well beyond its original purpose of short-term help to nonworking women with children (say, after divorce or death of a husband) and gradually became a way of life. Once trapped in dependency, poor women would raise children who were themselves likely to be poor as adults.

Liberals have a different view. Why, they ask, do people object to government money going to poor mothers and children when most "welfare" actually goes to richer people? The cost of AFDC was as high as $25 billion annually—no small sum, to be sure, but much less than the $596 billion in annual Social Security benefits

Uncle Sam provides to 44.8 million senior citizens, most of whom are not poor. And it is just a small fraction of the more than $1 trillion "bailout money" Congress voted in 2008 and 2009 to assist the struggling financial industry.

Liberals insist that most poor families who turn to public assistance are truly needy. Most of the people who are helped in this way are children. And they don't get very much. The typical household receives only about $391 per month in assistance, hardly enough to attract people to a life of welfare dependency. Even with some additional money in the form of food stamps, households assisted by welfare still struggle well below the poverty line everywhere in the country. Therefore, liberals see public assistance as a "Band-Aid approach" to the serious social problems of too few jobs and too much income inequality in the United States. As for the charge that public assistance weakens families, liberals agree that the share of families with one parent has gone up, but they see single parenting as a broad trend found at all class levels in many countries.

Back in 1996, the conservative arguments carried the day, ending the AFDC program. Our society's individualistic culture has always encouraged us to blame people themselves (rather than society) for poverty, which becomes a sign not of need but of laziness and personal failure. This view of the poor is probably the biggest reason that led Congress to replace the federal AFDC program with state-run programs called Temporary Assistance for Needy Families (TANF), requiring poor adults to get job training and limiting income assistance to two consecutive years with a lifetime limit of five years.

By 2008, the new TANF policy had reduced the number of households receiving income assistance by about 60 percent. This means that many single parents who were once on welfare have taken jobs or are receiving job training. In addition, the rate of out-of-wedlock births has fallen. With these facts in mind, conservatives who supported welfare reform see the new program as a huge success. The welfare rolls have been cut by more than half, and more people have moved from receiving a check to working in order to support themselves. But liberals claim that the reform is far from successful. They point out that many of the people who are now working earn so little pay that they are hardly better off than before. In addition, half of these workers have no health insurance. In other words, the reform has greatly reduced the number of people receiving welfare but has done little to reduce the extent of poverty.

What Do You Think?

1. How does our cultural emphasis on self-reliance help explain the controversy surrounding public assistance? Why do people not criticize benefits (such as home mortgage interest deductions) for people who are better off?

2. Do you approve of the time limits on benefits built into the TANF program? Why or why not?

3. Do you think the Obama administration will reduce poverty? Explain your answer.

Sources: Lichter & Crowley (2002), Lichter & Jayakody (2002), Von Drehle (2008); U.S. Census Bureau (2012); U.S. Department of Health and Human Services (2012).

substance abusers, and one-fourth are mentally ill. More broadly, a fraction of 1 percent of our population, for one reason or another, seems unable to cope with our complex and highly competitive society (U.S. Conference of Mayors, 2011; U.S. Department of Housing and Urban Development, 2011).

Other (more liberal) people see homelessness as resulting from *societal factors*, including low wages and a lack of low-income housing (Kozol, 1988; Bohannan, 1991; Kaufman, 2004). Supporters of this position note that 37 percent of the homeless consists of entire families, and they point to children as the fastest-growing category of the homeless.

No one disputes that a large proportion of homeless people are personally impaired to some degree, but untangling what is cause and what is effect is not so easy. Long-term, structural changes in the U.S. economy, cutbacks in social service budgets, and the recent economic downturn have all contributed to the problem of homelessness.

Increasing Inequality, Increasing Controversy

11.7 Assess the trend toward increasing economic inequality in the United States.

This chapter has explained that there is a rising level of debate about income inequality in the United States. Economic inequality has reached levels not seen in this country since 1929, just before the Great Depression. As shown in Figure 11–5, the 1920s was a decade that saw steady gains in income for the highest-earning 1 percent of the population who, just before the stock market crash, were receiving almost 25 percent of all income.

For several decades following the Depression, the trend was toward greater income equality. By the 1970s, as the figure shows, the richest 1 percent received less than 10 percent of all income. During the last thirty years, however, the trend has reversed direction. Today, the highest-paid 1 percent of the population enjoys about the same share of all income that the top earners received in 1929.

The United States has always been a nation in which most people expect some degree of economic inequality. This country's core values of competitive individualism and personal responsibility support the idea that people should receive rewards in proportion to their talents, abilities, and efforts.

Even so, people are now losing confidence that this is, in fact, the case. In a recent survey, U.S. adults were presented with the statement, "Differences in income in America are too large." In response, 63 percent agreed and only 16 percent disagreed (the remainder said that they neither agreed nor disagreed or that they did not know) (NORC, 2013:2225). Other surveys find that a large majority of people agree with the statement, "This is a country in which the rich get richer and the poor get poorer" (Kohut, 2011).

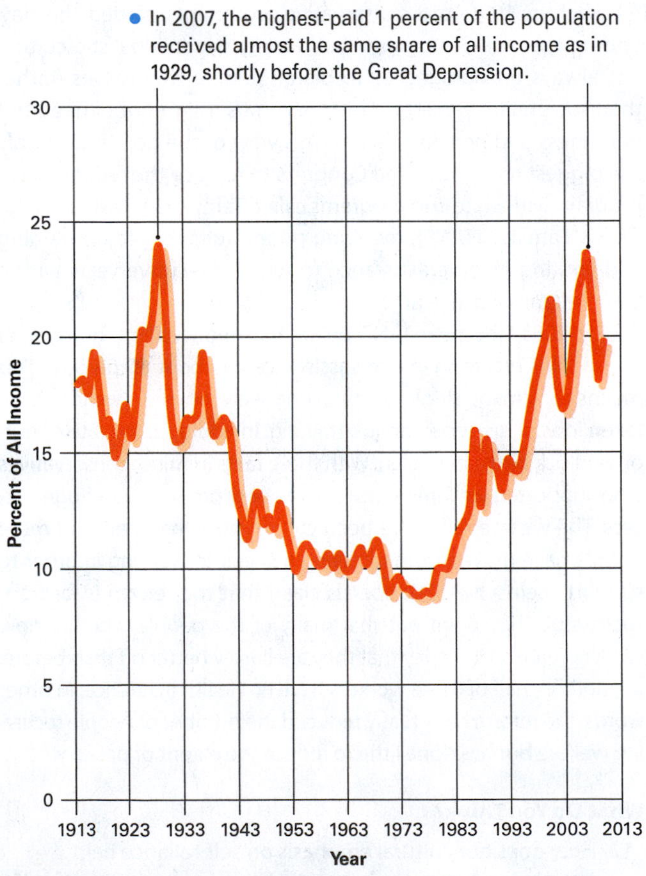

• In 2007, the highest-paid 1 percent of the population received almost the same share of all income as in 1929, shortly before the Great Depression.

FIGURE 11–5 The Share of All Income Earned by the Richest 1 Percent, 1913–2010

In 1929, the richest 1 percent of the U.S. population earned almost one-fourth of all income. This share declined in the decades that followed, dipping below 10 percent by the mid-1970s. In recent decades, however, the trend has been toward greater income inequality. By 2007, the top 1 percent was earning almost one-fourth of all income once again, although this share fell with the onset of the economic recession.

Sources: Internal Revenue Service (2011); Saez & Piketty (2012).

Are the Very Rich Worth the Money?

Such widespread concern about economic inequality suggests serious problems. First, in a society in which most think there is too much income inequality, people doubt that the highest-paid individuals are really worth the money they are paid. Certainly, there are some very smart, very talented, and very hardworking women and men in our country who are rewarded with high incomes. People in the entertainment industry, like television personalities Mariska Hargitay (who is paid about $10 million a year), Conan O'Brien ($14 million), and Jay Leno ($30 million), earn more money than most of us may ever see. Even bigger stars like Johnny Depp and Beyoncé bring home far more (each earns close to $100 million a year). Such rewards are what we have come to expect very popular media stars to receive, and we may justify such pay because of the power these celebrities have to attract viewers and advertising money.

But we should be careful not to assume that income is directly related to talent, ability, and effort. In 2011, Alex Rodriguez of the New York Yankees took home the biggest paycheck among major league ballplayers, at $32 million. This amount almost equals the money paid that season to the entire Kansas City Royals team, whose players surely offer more talent, ability, and effort than even the single best player on the Yankees. Another Yankee—Babe Ruth—who was arguably the greatest ballplayer of all time earned only $80,000 (or $1.2 million in today's dollars) in his highest-paid seasons (1930 and 1931) with the Yankees.

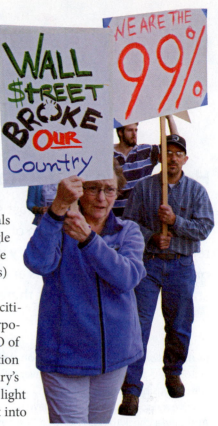

The Occupy Wall Street movement gained support across the nation and inspired citizen action around the world for criticizing the very high pay that a small share of corporate leaders receives. In 2011, according to *Forbes* magazine, John Hammergren, CEO of McKesson Pharmaceuticals, was the highest-earning CEO, receiving total compensation of $131 million in salary, bonus, stock options, and other perks. That year, the country's ten highest-paid CEOs averaged just over $60 million each in earnings. Noteworthy, in light of the movement's focus on Wall Street, is the fact that no Wall Street CEOs made it into the top ten (although Wall Street's top hedge-fund managers made much more). Surveying U.S. corporations, CEOs are earning more than ever. Back in 1970, the compensation of top CEOs was about 40 times what the average company employee earned. In 2011, top CEOs earned more than 400 times the company average and took home pay increases of about 25 percent, so the upward trend shows no sign of ending (Corporate Library, 2012; Helman, 2011; Roth, 2011; U.S. Census Bureau, 2012; U.S. Department of Commerce, Bureau of Economic Analysis, 2012).

In 2011, with economic inequality increasing, the Occupy Wall Street movement emerged. This groundswell of anger and activism put much of the blame for the recent recession on the very rich.

Defenders of such high pay claim that companies pay whatever it takes to attract the most talented people to top leadership, which helps companies perform better. Critics counter that company performance is not clearly linked to CEO rewards—half of the companies paying top salaries to CEOs actually lost money in their most recent year (Helman, 2011; NORC, 2011).

Can the Rest of Us Get Ahead?

A second problem accompanying increasing inequality is rising doubt that people who are willing to work hard can get ahead. The idea that those willing to make the effort can enjoy economic security and expect to improve social standing over time is at the heart of the American dream. But, in recent decades, while people at the top of the income hierarchy have been generously rewarded, average people who work hard have been struggling to hang on to what they have. With good-paying jobs harder to find, it is not surprising that the share of people who say that they believe their family can achieve the American dream has declined—from 76 percent in 2001 to 50 percent in 2011 (IBOPE Inteligência, 2012).

Today, some analysts are claiming that the United States is no longer the "land of opportunity" (Stiglitz, 2012). In addition, the public's awareness of economic inequality is as high as it has been since the Great Depression of the 1930s. Should the trend toward greater economic inequality persist, and should the loss of confidence in our system of social inequality continue, the demands for basic change to our society are sure to intensify.

Finally, as we debate the shape of inequality here at home, we must remember that the drama of social stratification extends far beyond the borders of the United States. The most striking social inequality is found not by looking inside one country but by comparing living standards in various parts of the world. In Chapter 12, we broaden our focus by investigating global stratification.

Seeing Sociology in Everyday Life

How do we understand inequality in the United States?

This chapter sketches the class structure of the United States and how people end up in their position in our system of social inequality. How accurately do you think the mass media reflect the reality of inequality in our society? Look at the three photos of television shows, one from back in the 1950s and the other two from today. What messages about social standing, and how we get there, does each show convey?

In *The Millionaire,* a popular television show that ran from 1955 until 1960, a very rich man (who was never fully shown on camera) had the curious hobby of giving away $1 million to other people he had never even met. Each week, he gave his personal assistant, Michael Anthony, a check to pass along to "the next millionaire." Anthony tracked down the person and handed over the money, and the story went on to reveal how such great wealth from out of nowhere changed someone's life for better (or sometimes for worse). What does this story line seem to suggest about social class position?

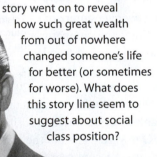

In the TV show *The Bachelor,* first aired in 2002, a young bachelor works his way through a collection of twenty-five attractive young women, beginning with group dates, moving on to overnight visits with three "finalists," and (in most cases) proposing to his "final selection." Much of the interaction takes place in a lavish, 7,500-square-foot home somewhere in southern California. What does this show suggest is the key to social position? What message does this show promote about the importance of marriage for women?

Project Runway, which began in 2004, places twelve or more fashion designers in competition, gradually eliminating them until only one "winner" remains. What messages about social position and achieving success does this show present to young people?

HINT In general, the mass media present social standing as a reflection of an individual's personal traits and sometimes sheer luck. In *The Millionaire,* wealth was visited on some people for no apparent reason at all. In *The Bachelor,* women try to gain the approval of a man. In *Project Runway,* the key to success is fashion sense and ingenuity. But social structure is also involved in ways that we easily overlook. Is becoming a millionaire really a matter of luck? Is there any significance to the fact that (as of 2011) all the bachelors on that show have been white? Does everyone with a lot of creativity have an equal chance to achieve success? Does social standing result from personal competition as much as television shows suggest?

Seeing Sociology in *Your* Everyday Life

1. During an evening of television viewing, assess the social class level of the characters you see on various shows. In each case, explain why you assign someone a particular social position. Do you find many clearly upper-class people? Middle-class people? Working-class people? Poor people? Describe the patterns you find.

2. Go to MySocLab and click on the Student Resources link to access the Sociology in Focus blog, where you can read the latest posts by a team of young sociologists who apply the sociological perspective to topics of popular culture.

3. Social stratification involves how a society distributes resources. It also has a relational dimension—social inequality guides *with whom* we do and do not interact and also *how* we interact with people. Can you give examples of how social class differences guide social interaction in your everyday life? Go to the "Seeing Sociology in *Your* Everyday Life" feature in MySocLab for additional discussion of the relational aspects of social stratification, including suggestions for how to relate to people whose social backgrounds differ from your own.

Making the Grade

Dimensions of Social Inequality

(11.1) Describe the distribution of income and wealth in the United States. (pages 302–5)

📖 **Read** the **Document** in **MySocLab**   👁 **Watch** the **Video** in **MySocLab**

income earnings from work or investments
wealth the total value of money and other assets, minus outstanding debts

Social stratification involves many dimensions:

- *Income*—Earnings from work and investments are unequal, with the richest 20% of families earning thirteen times as much as the poorest 20% of families.
- *Wealth*—The total value of all assets minus debts, wealth is distributed more unequally than income, with the richest 20% of families holding 89% of all wealth.
- *Power*—Income and wealth are important sources of power.
- *Occupational prestige*—Work generates not only income but also prestige. White-collar jobs generally offer more income and prestige than blue-collar jobs. Many lower-prestige jobs are performed by women and people of color.
- *Schooling*—Schooling affects both occupation and income. Some categories of people have greater opportunities for schooling than others.

U.S. Stratification: Merit and Caste

(11.2) Explain how someone's position at birth affects social standing later in life. (pages 305–6)

Although the United States is a meritocracy, social position in this country involves some caste elements:

- **Ancestry**—Being born into a particular family affects a person's opportunities for schooling, occupation, and income.
- **Race and Ethnicity**—Non-Hispanic white families enjoy high social standing based on income and wealth. By contrast, African American and Hispanic families remain disadvantaged.
- **Gender**—On average, women have less income, wealth, and occupational prestige than men.

Social Classes in the United States

(11.3) Describe the various social class positions in U.S. society. (pages 306–9)

👁 **Watch** the **Video** in **MySocLab**

Defining **social classes** in the United States is difficult because of low status consistency and relatively high social mobility. But we can describe four general rankings:

- the upper class
- the middle class
- the working class
- the lower class

$205,000

upper class—5% of the population. Most members of the *upper-upper class*, or "old rich," inherited their wealth; members of the *lower-upper class*, or "new rich," work at high-paying jobs.

$205,000
$48,500

middle class—40% to 45% of the population. People in the *upper-middle class* have significant wealth; *average-middles* have less prestige, do white-collar work, and most attend college.

$48,500
$27,000

working class—30% to 35% of the population. People in the *lower-middle class* do blue-collar work; only about one-third of children attend college.

$27,000

lower class—20% of the population. Most people in the lower class lack financial security due to low income; many live below the poverty line; just 70% of children complete high school.

The Difference Class Makes

 11.4 Analyze how social class position affects health, values, politics, and family life. (pages 310–12)

 Watch the **Video** in **MySocLab**

Health

- Rich people, on average, live longer and receive better health care than poor people.

Values and Attitudes

- Affluent people, with greater education and financial security, display greater tolerance than working-class people.

Politics

- Affluent people tend to be more conservative on economic issues and more liberal on social issues than poor people.
- Affluent people, who are better served by the political system, are more likely to vote than poor people.

Family and Gender

- Affluent families pass on advantages in the form of "cultural capital" to their children.
- Class also shapes the division of family responsibilities, with lower-class people maintaining more traditional gender roles.

Social Mobility

11.5 Assess the extent of social mobility in the United States. (pages 312–17)

- Social mobility is common in the United States, as it is in other high-income countries, but typically only small changes occur from one generation to the next.
- Between 1980 and 2011, the richest 20% of U.S. families enjoyed a 54.7% jump in annual income, while the 20% of families with the lowest income experienced an 8.3% decrease.
- Historically, African Americans, Hispanic Americans, and women have had less opportunity for upward mobility in U.S. society than white men.
- The American dream—the expectation of upward social mobility—is deeply rooted in our culture. Although high-income families are earning more and more, many average families are struggling to hold on to what they have.
- Marriage encourages upward social mobility. Divorce lowers social standing.
- The global reorganization of work has created upward social mobility for educated people in the United States but has hurt average workers, whose factory jobs have moved overseas and who are forced to take low-wage service work.

intragenerational social mobility a change in social position occurring during a person's lifetime

intergenerational social mobility upward or downward social mobility of children in relation to their parents

Poverty in the United States

11.6 Discuss patterns and explanations of poverty in the U.S. population. (pages 317–24)

 Explore the **Map** in **MySocLab**

Poverty Profile

- The government classifies 46.25 million people, 15% of the population, as poor.
- About 48% of the poor are under age twenty-five.
- Sixty-seven percent of the poor are white (both Hispanic and non-Hispanic), but in relation to their population size, African Americans are more likely to be poor.
- The **feminization of poverty** refers to the trend by which more poor families are headed by women.
- About 44% of the heads of poor families are among the "working poor" who work at least part time but do not earn enough to lift a family of four above the poverty line.
- An estimated 1.6 million people are homeless for some time during the course of a year.

Explanations of Poverty

- Blame individuals: The *culture of poverty* thesis states that poverty is caused by shortcomings in the poor themselves (Oscar Lewis).
- Blame society: Poverty is caused by society's unequal distribution of wealth and lack of good jobs (William Julius Wilson).

relative poverty the lack of resources of some people in relation to those who have more

absolute poverty a lack of resources that is life-threatening

feminization of poverty the trend of women making up an increasing proportion of the poor

Increasing Social Inequality

11.7 Assess the trend toward increasing economic inequality in the United States. (pages 324–25)

- In recent decades, inequality of income and wealth has increased.
- Surveys show that most people think that income differences in the United States are too large.
- Many people are concerned that hard work may not be enough to get ahead.

12 Global Stratification

((¢ **Listen** to **Chapter 12** in **MySocLab**

LEARNING OBJECTIVES

12.1 Describe the division of the world into high-, middle-, and low-income countries.

12.2 Discuss patterns and explanations of poverty around the world.

12.3 Apply sociological theories to the topic of global inequality.

12.4 Evaluate trends in global inequality.

the Power of Society

to determine a child's chance of survival to age five

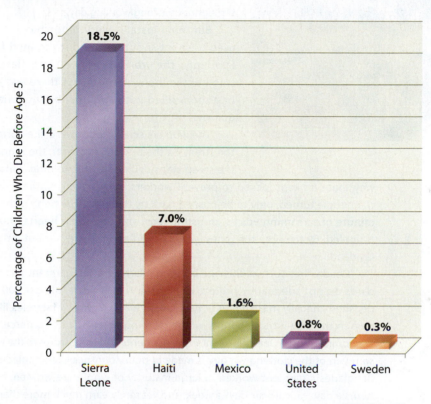

Source: UNICEF (2012)

In a world of unequal economic development, how does a child's country of birth affect the chances of survival? Of all children born in Sierra Leone, a low-income nation on Africa's western coast, 18.5 percent die before reaching the age of five. In Haiti, another low-income nation, 7 percent of children suffer this fate. In high-income nations, the share is much lower. In the United States, less than 1 percent of children will die so early in life. And in nations with more extensive social welfare systems, such as Sweden, the share is even lower.

Chapter Overview

Social stratification involves not just people within a single country; it is also a worldwide pattern with some nations far more economically productive than others. This chapter shifts the focus from inequality within the United States to inequality found in the world as a whole. The chapter begins by describing global inequality and then provides two theoretical models that explain global stratification.

More than 1,000 workers were busily sewing together polo shirts on the fourth floor of the garment factory in Narsingdi, a small town about 30 miles northeast of Bangladesh's capital city of Dhaka. The thumping of hundreds of sewing machines produced a steady roar throughout the long working day.

But in an instant everything changed when an electric gun used to shoot spot remover onto stained fabric gave off a spark. Suddenly, the worktable burst into flames. People rushed to smother the fire with shirts, but there was no stopping the blaze: In a room filled with combustible materials, the flames spread quickly.

The workers scrambled toward the narrow staircase that led to the street. At the bottom, however, the human wave pouring down the steep steps collided with a folding metal gate across the doorway that was kept locked to prevent workers from leaving during working hours. Panicked, the people turned, only to be pushed back by the hundreds behind them. In a single terrifying minute of screaming voices, thrusting legs, and pounding hearts, dozens were crushed and trampled. By the time the gates were opened and the fire put out, fifty-two garment workers lay dead.

Deadly fires such as this one occur regularly in Asian garment factories, where safety standards do not adequately protect workers. In recent years, almost 100 garment workers have perished annually in such fires in Bangladesh alone. Garment factories like this one are big business in this low-income nation, where clothing accounts for 78 percent of Bangladesh's total economic exports. One-quarter of these garments end up in stores in the United States. The reason so much of the clothing we buy is made in poor countries like Bangladesh is simple economics: Bangladeshi garment workers, a large majority of whom are women, labor for close to twelve hours a day, typically six days a week, and yet rarely earn much more than that nation's minimum wage of $443 a month, which is less than $2 an hour and a small share of what garment workers earn in the United States.

Tanveer Chowdhury manages the garment factory owned by his family. Speaking to reporters, he complained bitterly about the tragedy. "This fire has cost me $586,373, and that does not include $70,000 for machinery and $20,000 for furniture. I made commitments to meet deadlines, and I still have the deadlines. I am now paying for air freight at $10 a dozen when I should be shipping by sea at 87 cents a dozen."

There was one other cost Chowdhury did not mention. To compensate families for the loss of their loved ones in the fire, he eventually agreed to pay $1,952 per person. In Bangladesh, life—like labor—is cheap (based on Bearak, 2001; Hossain, 2011; Bangladesh Garment Manufacturers & Exporters Association, 2012; World Bank, 2012).

Garment workers in Bangladesh are among the roughly 1.3 billion of the world's people who work hard every day and yet remain poor (Chen & Ravallion, 2012). As this chapter explains, although poverty is a reality in the United States and other nations, the greatest social inequality is not *within* nations but *between* them (Goesling, 2001). We can understand the full dimensions of poverty only by exploring **global stratification**, *patterns of social inequality in the world as a whole.*

Global Stratification: An Overview

12.1 Describe the division of the world into high-, middle-, and low-income countries.

Chapter 11 ("Social Class in the United States") described social inequality in the United States. In global perspective, however, social stratification is far greater. The pie chart at the left in Figure 12–1 divides the world's total income by fifths of the population. Recall from Chapter 11 that the richest 20 percent of the U.S. population earn about 49 percent of the national income (see Figure 11–1 on page 303). The richest 20 percent of global population, however, receive about 77 percent of world income. At the other extreme, the poorest 20 percent of the U.S. population earn slightly less than 4 percent of our national income; the poorest fifth of the world's people struggles to survive on just 2 percent of global income.

In terms of wealth, as the pie chart at the right in Figure 12–1 shows, global inequality is even greater. A rough estimate is that the richest 20 percent of the world's adults own about 94 percent of the planet's wealth. About half of all wealth is owned by about 1 percent of the world's adult population. On the other extreme, the poorest half of the world's adults own less than 1 percent of all global wealth. In terms of dollars, about half the world's families have less than $3,710 in total wealth, far less than the $77,000 in wealth for the typical family in the United States (Bricker et al., 2012; Davies, Lluberas, & Shorrocks, 2012).

Because the United States is among the world's richest countries, even people in the United States with income well below the government's poverty line live far better than the majority of people on the planet (Milanovic, 2011). The average person living in a rich nation such as the United States is extremely well off by world standards. Any one of the world's richest people (in 2011, the world's three richest *people*—Carlos Slim Helú in Mexico, Bill Gates and Warren Buffett in the United States—were *each* worth more than $44 billion) has personal wealth that exceeds the total economic output of more than 100 of the world's *countries* (*Forbes*, 2012; World Bank, 2012).

Watch in **MySocLab**
Video: *The Big Picture: Social Stratification*

A Word about Terminology

Classifying the 195 independent nations on Earth into categories ignores many striking differences. These nations have rich and varied histories, speak different languages, and take pride in distinctive cultures. However, various models have been developed that help distinguish countries on the basis of global stratification.

One global model, developed after World War II, labeled the rich, industrial countries the "First World"; the less industrialized, socialist countries the "Second World"; and the nonindustrialized, poor countries the "Third World." But the "three worlds" model is less useful today. For one thing, it was a product of Cold War politics by which the capitalist West (the First World) faced off against the socialist East (the Second World) while other nations (the Third World) remained more or less on the sidelines. But the sweeping changes in Eastern Europe and the

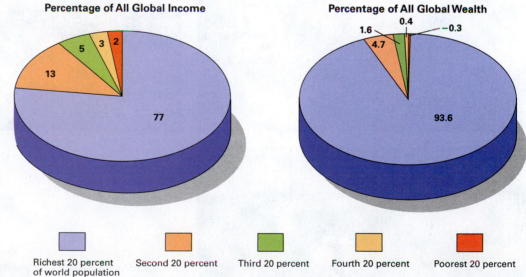

FIGURE 12–1 Distribution of Global Income and Wealth

Global income is very unequal, with the richest 20 percent of the world's people earning almost forty times as much as the poorest 20 percent. Global wealth is even more unequally divided, with the richest 20 percent owning 94 percent of private wealth and the poorest half of the world's people having barely anything at all.

Sources: Based on Milanovic (2009, 2011) and Davies, Lluberas, & Shorrocks (2012).

global stratification patterns of social inequality in the world as a whole

high-income countries the nations with the highest overall standards of living

middle-income countries nations with a standard of living about average for the world as a whole

low-income countries nations with a low standard of living in which most people are poor

collapse of the former Soviet Union in the early 1990s mean that a distinctive Second World no longer exists.

Another problem is that the "three worlds" model lumped together more than 100 countries as the Third World. In reality, some relatively better-off nations of the Third World (such as Chile in South America) have fifteen times the per-person productivity of the poorest countries of the world (such as Ethiopia in East Africa).

These facts call for a modestly revised system of classification. The seventy-four **high-income countries** are defined as *the nations with the highest overall standards of living*. These nations have a per capita gross national income (GNI) greater than $12,500. The world's seventy-two **middle-income countries** are not as rich; they are *nations with a standard of living about average for the world as a whole*. Their per capita GNI is less than $12,500 but greater than $2,500. The remaining forty-nine **low-income countries** are *nations with a low standard of living in which most people are poor*. In these nations, per capita GNI is less than $2,500 (United Nations Development Programme, 2012; World Bank, 2012).

This model has two advantages over the older "three worlds" system. First, it focuses on economic development rather than political structure (capitalist or socialist). Second, it gives a better picture of the relative economic development of various countries because it does not lump together all less developed nations into a single "Third World."

When envisioning global stratification, keep in mind that there is social stratification within every nation. In Bangladesh, for example, members of the Chowdhury family, who own the garment factory described in the chapter-opening story, earn as much as $1 million per year, which is several thousand times more than their workers earn. The full

The United States is among the world's high-income countries, in which industrial technology and economic expansion have produced material prosperity. The presence of market forces is evident in this view of New York City (*above, left*). India has recently become one of the world's middle-income countries (*above, right*). An increasing number of motor vehicles fill city streets. Afghanistan (*left*) is among the world's low-income countries. As the photograph suggests, these nations have limited economic development and rapidly increasing populations. The result is widespread poverty.

extent of global inequality is even greater, because the wealthiest people in rich countries such as the United States live worlds apart from the poorest people in low-income nations such as Bangladesh, Haiti, and Sudan.

High-Income Countries

In nations where the Industrial Revolution first took place more than two centuries ago, productivity increased more than one hundredfold. To understand the power of industrial and computer technology, consider that South Korea—a small Asian nation about the size of the state of Oregon—is as economically productive as the whole continent of Africa south of the Sahara, which has a land area more than twice the size of the United States.

Global Map 12–1 shows that the high-income nations of the world include the United States, Canada, Mexico, Argentina, Chile, the nations of Western Europe, Israel, Saudi

Window on the World

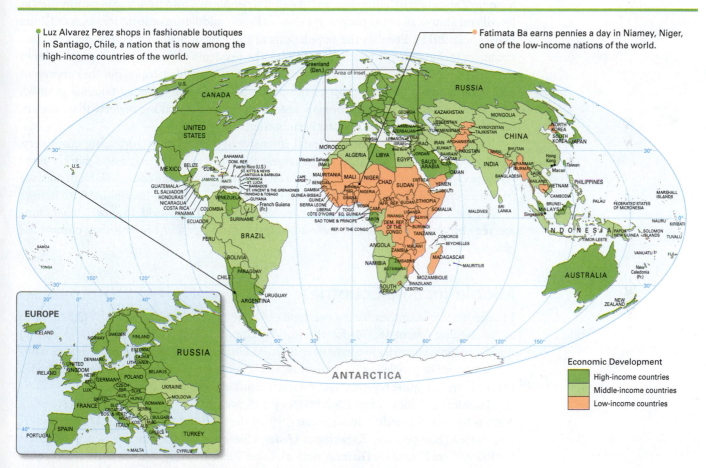

Luz Alvarez Perez shops in fashionable boutiques in Santiago, Chile, a nation that is now among the high-income countries of the world.

Fatimata Ba earns pennies a day in Niamey, Niger, one of the low-income nations of the world.

Economic Development
- High-income countries
- Middle-income countries
- Low-income countries

GLOBAL MAP 12–1 Economic Development in Global Perspective

In high-income countries—including the United States, Canada, Mexico, Chile, Argentina, the nations of Western Europe, Israel, Saudi Arabia, Singapore, Hong Kong, South Korea, Malaysia, Australia, the Russian Federation, Japan, and New Zealand—a highly productive economy provides people, on average, with material plenty. Middle-income countries—including most of Latin America and Asia—are less economically productive, with a standard of living about average for the world as a whole but far below that of the United States. These nations also have a significant share of poor people who are barely able to feed and house themselves. In the low-income countries of the world, poverty is severe and widespread. Although small numbers of elites live very well in the poorest nations, most people struggle to survive on a small fraction of the income common in the United States.

Note: Data for this map are provided by the United Nations and the World Bank. Each country's economic productivity is measured in terms of its gross national income (GNI), which is the total value of all the goods and services produced by a country's economy within its borders in a given year, plus net compensation and property income from abroad. Dividing each country's GNI by the country's population gives us the per capita (per-person) GNI and allows us to compare the economic performance of countries of different population sizes. High-income countries have a per capita GNI of more than $12,500. Many are far richer than this, however; the figure for the United States exceeds $48,000. Middle-income countries have a per capita GNI ranging from $2,500 to $12,500. Low-income countries have a per capita GNI of less than $2,500. Figures used here reflect the World Bank's "purchasing power parities" system, which is an estimate of what people can buy using their income in the local economy.

Source: Data from United Nations Development Programme (2012) and the World Bank (2012).

Arabia, Singapore, Hong Kong (part of the People's Republic of China), Japan, South Korea, the Russian Federation, Malaysia, Australia, and New Zealand.

These countries cover roughly 47 percent of Earth's land area, including parts of five continents, and they lie mostly in the Northern Hemisphere. In 2011, the total population of these nations was about 1.6 billion, or about 23 percent of the world's people. About three-fourths of the people in high-income countries live in or near cities (Population Reference Bureau, 2012; World Bank, 2012).

Significant cultural differences exist among high-income countries; for example, the nations of Europe recognize more than thirty official languages. But these societies all produce enough economic goods and services to enable their people to lead comfortable lives. Per capita income (that is, average income per person per year) ranges from about $13,000 annually (in Venezuela, Bulgaria, and Lebanon) to more than $45,000 annually (in the United States, Norway, and Singapore). In fact, people in high-income countries enjoy 64 percent of the world's total income.

In a high-income nation such as the United States, even the poor have a higher economic standard of living than about half the people in a middle-income nation such as Brazil and almost all of the people in a (less well-off) middle-income nation such as China (Milanovic, 2011). Even so, the populations of the United States and other high-income countries include many low-income people. The residents of the poorest communities in the United States may be better off than about half the world's people, but they represent a striking contrast to what most of the people living in this country take for granted. The Thinking About Diversity box on page 337 profiles the striking poverty that exists in *las colonias* along our country's southern border.

Production in rich nations is capital-intensive; it is based on factories, big machinery, and advanced technology. Most of the largest corporations that design and market computers, as well as most computer users, are located in high-income countries. High-income countries control the world's financial markets, so daily events in the financial exchanges of New York, London, and Tokyo affect people throughout the world. In short, rich nations are very productive because of their advanced technology and because they control the global economy.

Middle-Income Countries

Middle-income countries have a per capita income of between $2,500 and $12,500, close to the median (about $8,350) for the world's nations. About 52 percent of the people in middle-income countries live in or near cities, and industrial jobs are common. The remaining 48 percent of people live in rural areas, where most are poor and lack access to schools, medical care, adequate housing, and even safe drinking water.

Looking at Global Map 12–1 on page 335, we see that seventy-two of the world's nations fall into the middle-income category. At the high end are Costa Rica (Latin America), Serbia (Europe), and Kazakhstan (Asia), where annual income is about $11,000. At the low end are Nicaragua (Latin America), Cape Verde (Africa), and Vietnam (Asia), with roughly $3,000 annually in per capita income.

One cluster of middle-income countries used to be part of the Second World. These countries, found in Eastern Europe and Western Asia, had mostly socialist economies until popular revolts between 1989 and 1991 swept their governments aside. Since then, these nations have introduced more free-market systems. These middle-income countries include Ukraine, Uzbekistan, Georgia, and Turkmenistan.

Watch in **MySocLab**
Video: *Sociology on the Job: Social Stratification*

Other middle-income nations include Peru and Brazil in South America and Namibia and South Africa in Africa. Both India and the People's Republic of China have entered the middle-income category, which now includes most of Asia.

Taken together, middle-income countries span roughly 35 percent of Earth's land area and are home to about 4.2 billion people, or about 60 percent of humanity. Some very large countries (such as China) are far less crowded than other smaller nations (such as El Salvador), but compared to high-income countries, these societies are densely populated.

Thinking About Diversity: Race, Class, and Gender

Las Colonias: "America's Third World"

"We wanted to have something for ourselves," explains Olga Ruiz, who has lived in the border community of College Park, Texas, for eleven years. There is no college in College Park, nor does this dusty stretch of rural land have sewer lines or even running water. Yet this town is one of some 2,300 settlements that have sprouted up in southern Texas along the 1,200-mile border with Mexico that runs from El Paso to Brownsville. Together, they are home to roughly 500,000 people.

Many people speak of *las colonias* (Spanish for "the colonies") as "America's Third World" because these desperately poor communities look much like their counterparts in Mexico or many other middle- or low-income nations. But this is the United States, and almost all of the people living in the *colonias* are Mexican Americans, 85 percent of them legal residents and more than half U.S. citizens.

Anastacia Ledsema, now seventy-two years old, moved to a *colonia* called Sparks more than forty years ago. Born in Mexico, Ledsema married a Texas man, and together they paid $200 for

a quarter-acre lot in a new border community. For months, they camped out on their land. Step by step, they invested their labor and their money to build a modest house. Not until 1995 did their small community get running water—a service that had been promised by developers years before. When the water line finally did arrive, however, things changed more than they expected. "When we got water," recalls Ledsema, "that's when so many people came in." The population of Sparks quickly doubled to about 3,000, overwhelming the water supply so that sometimes the faucet does not run at all.

The residents of all the *colonias* know that they are poor, and with annual per capita income of about $6,000, they are. The Census Bureau has declared the county surrounding one border community to be the poorest in the United States. Concerned over the lack of basic services in so many of these communities, Texas officials have banned new settlements. But most of the people who move here—even those who start off sleeping in their cars or trucks—see these communities as the first step on the path to the American dream. Oscar Solis, a neighborhood leader in Panorama Village, a community with a population of about 150, is proud to show visitors around the small but growing town. "All of this work we have done ourselves," he says with a smile, "to make our dream come true."

What Do You Think?

1. Are you surprised that such intense poverty exists in a rich country like the United States? Why or why not?

2. Have you ever had experiences with poverty such as that described here in other parts of the United States? If so, where?

3. What do you think the future holds for the families living in *las colonias*? Explain your prediction.

Source: Based on Schaffer (2002) and *The Economist* (2011).

Low-Income Countries

Low-income countries, where most people are very poor, are mostly agrarian societies with some industry. Forty-nine low-income countries, identified in Global Map 12–1 on page 335, are spread across Central and East Africa and Asia. Low-income countries cover 17 percent of the planet's land area and are home to about 1.2 billion people, or 17 percent of humanity. Population density is generally high, although it is greater in Asian countries (such as Bangladesh) than in Central African nations (such as Chad and the Democratic Republic of the Congo).

In poor countries, 35 percent of the people live in cities; most inhabit villages and farms as their ancestors have done for centuries. In fact, half the world's people are farmers, most of whom follow cultural traditions. With limited industrial technology, they cannot be very productive, one reason that many suffer severe poverty. Hunger, disease, and unsafe housing shape the lives of the world's poorest people.

Those of us who live in rich nations such as the United States find it hard to understand the scope of human need that exists in much of the world. From time to time, televised

In general, when natural disasters strike high-income nations, property damage may be great, but loss of life is low. Hurricane Sandy, which was characterized as a "superstorm," (*left*) struck the East Coast of the United States in 2012, resulting in more than $60 billion in damage and seventy-two deaths. The earthquake that hit Haiti (*right*) in 2010, by contrast, resulted in more than 300,000 deaths.

pictures of famine in very poor countries such as Ethiopia and Bangladesh give us shocking glimpses of the poverty that makes every day a life-and-death struggle for many people in low-income nations. Behind these images lie cultural, historical, and economic forces that we shall explore in the remainder of this chapter.

Global Wealth and Poverty

12.2 Discuss patterns and explanations of poverty around the world.

October 14, Manila, Philippines. What caught my eye was how clean she was— a girl no more than seven or eight years old. She was wearing a freshly laundered dress, and her hair was carefully combed. She stopped to watch us, following us with her eyes: Camera-toting Americans stand out here, one of the poorest neighborhoods in the entire world.

Fed by methane from decomposing garbage, the fires never go out on Smokey Mountain, the vast garbage dump on the north side of Manila. Smoke covers the hills of refuse like a thick fog. But Smokey Mountain is more than a dump; it is a neighborhood that is home to thousands of people. It is hard to imagine a setting more hostile to human life. Amid the smoke and the squalor, men and women do what they can to survive. They pick plastic bags from the garbage and wash them in the river, and they collect cardboard boxes or anything else they can sell. What chance do their children have, coming from families that earn only a few hundred dollars a year, with hardly any opportunity for schooling, year after year breathing this foul air? Against this backdrop of human tragedy, one lovely little girl has put on a fresh dress and gone out to play.

Now our taxi driver threads his way through heavy traffic as we head for the other side of Manila. The change is amazing: The smoke and smell of the dump give way to neighborhoods that could be in Miami or Los Angeles. A cluster of yachts floats on the bay in the distance. No more rutted streets; now we glide quietly along wide boulevards lined with trees and filled with expensive Japanese cars. We pass shopping plazas, upscale hotels, and high-rise office buildings. Every block or so we see the gated entrance to yet another exclusive residential community with security guards standing watch. Here, in large, air-conditioned homes, the rich of Manila live—and many of the poor work.

Low-income nations are home to some rich and many poor people. The fact that most people live on incomes of just a few hundred dollars a year means that the burden of poverty is far greater there than among the poor of the United States. This is not to suggest that U.S. poverty is a minor problem. In so rich a country, too little food, substandard housing, and no medical care for tens of millions of people—almost half of them children—amount to a national tragedy.

The Severity of Poverty

Poverty in poor countries is more severe than it is in rich countries. A key reason that the quality of life differs so much around the world is that economic productivity is lowest in precisely the regions where population growth is highest. Figure 12–2 shows the proportion of world population and global income for countries at each level of economic development. High-income countries are by far the most advantaged, with 64 percent of global income supporting just 23 percent of humanity. In middle-income nations, 60 percent of the world's people earn 33 percent of global income. This leaves 17 percent of the planet's population with just 3 percent of global income. In short, for every dollar received by individuals in a low-income country, someone in a high-income country takes home $14.

Table 12–1 on page 340 shows the extent of wealth and well-being in specific countries around the world. The first column of figures gives gross national income (GNI) for a number of high-, middle-, and low-income countries.[1] The United States, a large and highly productive nation, had a 2011 GNI of more than $15 trillion; Japan's GNI was $4.5 trillion. A comparison of GNI figures shows that the world's richest nations are thousands of times more productive than the poorest countries.

The second column of figures in Table 12–1 divides GNI by the entire population size to give an estimate of what people can buy with their income in the local economy. The per capita GNI for rich countries like the United States, Sweden, and Canada is very high, exceeding $39,000. For middle-income countries, the figures range from about $3,600 in India to almost $12,000 in Costa Rica. In the world's low-income countries, per capita GNI is just one or two thousand dollars. In Niger or in Ethiopia, for example, a typical person labors all year to make what the average worker in the United States earns in a week.

The last column of Table 12–1 is a measure of the quality of life in the various nations. This index, calculated by the United Nations (2011), is based on income, education (extent of adult literacy and average years of schooling), and longevity (how long people typically live). Index values are decimals that fall between extremes of 1 (highest) and 0 (lowest). By this calculation, Norwegians enjoy the highest quality of life (.943), with residents of the United States close behind (.910). At the other extreme, people in the Democratic Republic of the Congo in Africa have the lowest quality of life (.286).

Relative versus Absolute Poverty

The distinction between relative and absolute poverty, made in Chapter 11 ("Social Class in the United States"), has an important application to global inequality. People living in rich countries generally focus on *relative poverty*, meaning that some people lack resources that are taken for granted by others. By definition, relative poverty exists in every society, rich or poor.

More important in global perspective, however, is *absolute poverty*, a lack of resources that is life-threatening. Human beings in absolute poverty lack the nutrition necessary for health and long-term survival. To be sure, some absolute poverty exists in the United States. But such immediately life-threatening poverty strikes only a very small proportion of the

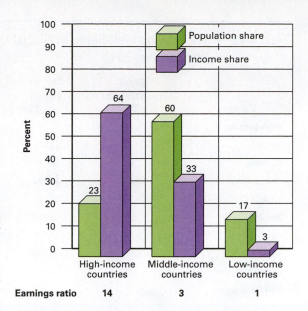

FIGURE 12–2 The Relative Share of Income and Population by Level of Economic Development

For every dollar earned by people in low-income countries, people in high-income countries earn $14

Source: Based on Population Reference Bureau (2012) and World Bank (2012).

 Read in **MySocLab Document:** *More or Less* by Branko Milanovic

---

[1]Gross national income is the value of all the goods and services produced by a country's economy within its borders in a given year, plus all the income earned abroad by its people and companies.

TABLE 12–1 Wealth and Well-Being in Global Perspective, 2011

Country	Gross National Income ($ billions)	GNI per Capita (PPP US$)*	Quality of Life Index
High-Income			
Norway	311	62,970	.943
Australia	812	34,431	.929
United States	15,232	48,890	.910
Canada	1,370	39,730	.908
Sweden	399	42,200	.904
Japan	4,541	35,530	.901
South Korea	1,510	30,340	.897
United Kingdom	2,251	35,940	.863
Middle-Income			
Eastern Europe			
Serbia	85	11,640	.766
Albania	29	8,900	.739
Ukraine	324	7,080	.729
Latin America			
Costa Rica	57	11,950	.744
Ecuador	122	8,310	.720
Brazil	2,261	11,500	.718
Asia			
People's Republic of China	11,361	8,450	.687
Thailand	583	8,390	.682
India	4,491	3,620	.547
Middle East			
Iran	833	10,164	.707
Syria	104	4,243	.632
Africa			
Algeria	301	8,370	.698
Namibia	15	6,600	.625
Low-Income			
Latin America			
Haiti	12	1,190	.454
Asia			
Laos	16	2,600	.524
Cambodia	32	2,260	.523
Bangladesh	291	1,940	.500
Africa			
Kenya	72	1,720	.509
Guinea	11	1,050	.344
Ethiopia	94	1,110	.363
Mali	17	1,050	.359
Democratic Republic of the Congo	23	350	.286

*These data are purchasing power parity (PPP) calculations, which avoid currency rate distortion by showing the local purchasing power of each domestic currency.

Source: United Nations Development Programme (2012), World Bank (2012).

U.S. population. In low-income countries, by contrast, almost one-half of the people live on about $1.25 a day and are in desperate need.

Because absolute poverty is deadly, people in low-income nations face an elevated risk of dying young. Global Map 12–2 on page 341 lets us explore this pattern by presenting the odds of living to the age of sixty-five that are typical for the nations of the world. In many rich societies, more than 85 percent of people reach this age; the figure for the United States is 83 percent. In the world's poorest countries, however, the odds of living to age sixty-five are less than one in three and two in ten children do not survive to the age of five (United Nations, 2011, 2012).

The Extent of Poverty

Poverty in poor countries is more widespread than it is in rich nations such as the United States. Chapter 11 ("Social Class in the United States") noted that the U.S. government officially classifies 15 percent of the population as poor. In low-income countries, however, most people live no better than the poor in the United States, and many are far worse off. As Global Map 12–2 shows, the low odds of living to the age of sixty-five in the countries of sub-Saharan Africa indicate that absolute poverty is greatest there, where more than one-fourth of the population is malnourished. In the world as a whole, at any given time, 12.5 percent of the people—about 868 million—suffer from chronic hunger, which leaves them less able to work and puts them at high risk of disease (United Nations Food and Agriculture Organization, 2012).

The typical adult in a rich nation such as the United States consumes about 3,750 calories a day, an excess that contributes to widespread obesity and related health problems. The typical adult in a low-income country not only consumes just 2,350 calories a day but also does more physical labor. Together, these factors result in undernourishment: too little food or not enough of the right kinds of food (United Nations Food and Agriculture Organization, 2012).

In the ten minutes it takes to read this section of the chapter, about 100 people in the world who are sick and weakened from hunger will die. This number amounts to about 25,000 people a day, or 9 million people each year. Clearly, easing world hunger is one of the most serious responsibilities facing humanity today (United Nations World Food Programme, 2008).

Poverty and Children

Death comes early in poor societies, where families lack adequate food, safe water, secure housing, and access to medical care. In the world's low-income nations, one-quarter of all children do not receive enough nutrition to be healthy (World Bank, 2012).

Poor children live in poor families, and many share in the struggle to get through each day. Organizations fighting

Window on the World

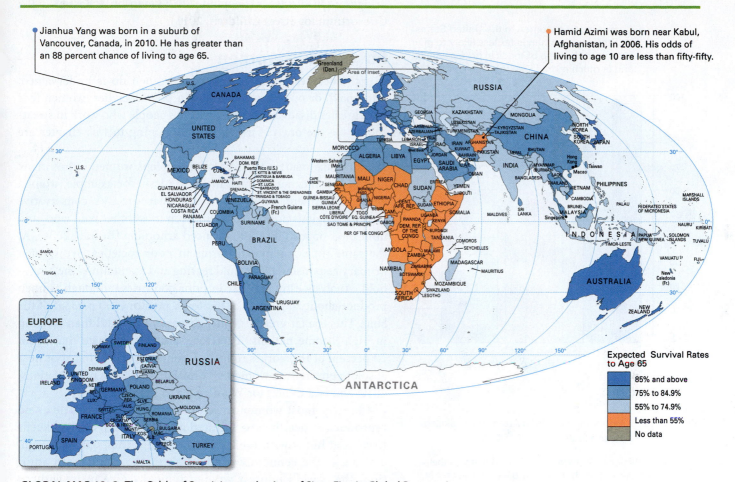

Jianhua Yang was born in a suburb of Vancouver, Canada, in 2010. He has greater than an 88 percent chance of living to age 65.

Hamid Azimi was born near Kabul, Afghanistan, in 2006. His odds of living to age 10 are less than fifty-fifty.

Expected Survival Rates to Age 65

- 85% and above
- 75% to 84.9%
- 55% to 74.9%
- Less than 55%
- No data

GLOBAL MAP 12–2 The Odds of Surviving to the Age of Sixty-Five in Global Perspective

This map identifies expected survival rates to the age of sixty-five for nations around the world. In thirty-nine of the world's nations, including most high-income countries, more than 85 percent of people live to this age. In the United States, due to lower survival rates among the poor, the share is 83 percent. But in low-income nations, death often comes early, with just one-third of people reaching the age of sixty-five.

Source: United Nations (2011).

child poverty estimate that as many as 100 million children living in cities in poor countries beg, steal, sell sex, or work for drug gangs to provide income for their families. Such a life almost always means dropping out of school and puts children at high risk of disease and violence. Many girls, with little or no access to medical assistance, become pregnant—a case of children who cannot support themselves having children of their own.

Analysts estimate that tens of millions of the world's children are orphaned or have left their families altogether, sleeping and living on the streets as best they can or perhaps trying to migrate to the United States. Roughly half of all street children are found in Latin American cities such as Mexico City and Rio de Janeiro, where half of all children grow up in poverty. Many people in the United States know these cities as exotic travel destinations, but they are also home

Tens of millions of children fend for themselves every day on the streets of poor cities where many fall victim to disease, drug abuse, and violence. What do you think should be done to ensure that children like these in Bangalore, India, receive adequate nutrition and a quality education?

Global Stratification **CHAPTER 12** **341**

Global Snapshot

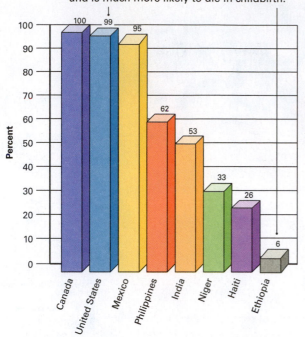

- Compared to a woman in the United States, an Ethiopian woman is far less likely to give birth with the help of medical professionals and is much more likely to die in childbirth.

FIGURE 12–3 Percentage of Births Attended by Skilled Health Staff

In the United States, most women give birth with the help of medical professionals, but this is usually not the case in low-income nations.

Source: World Bank (2012).

to thousands of street children living in makeshift huts, under bridges, or in alleyways (Leopold, 2007; Levinson & Bassett, 2007; Consortium for Street Children, 2011).

Poverty and Women

In rich societies, much of the work women do is undervalued, underpaid, or overlooked entirely. In poor societies, women face even greater disadvantages. Most of the people who work in sweatshops like the one described in the opening to this chapter are women.

To make matters worse, tradition keeps women out of many jobs in low-income nations. In Bangladesh, for example, women work in garment factories because that society's conservative Muslim religious norms bar them from most other paid work and limit their opportunity for advanced schooling (Bearak, 2001). At the same time, traditional norms in poor societies give women primary responsibility for child rearing and maintaining the household. Analysts estimate that in poor countries, although women produce about 70 percent of the food, men own 90 percent of the land. This is a far greater gender disparity in wealth than is found in high-income nations. Therefore, analysts estimate that about 70 percent of the world's roughly 1 billion people living at or near absolute poverty are women (World Bank, 2008; United Nations, 2010; Landsea Center for Women's Land Rights, 2011).

Finally, most women in poor countries receive little or no reproductive health care. Limited access to birth control keeps women at home with their children, keeps the birth rate high, and limits the economic production of the country. In addition, the world's poorest women typically give birth without help from trained health care personnel. Figure 12–3 illustrates a stark difference between low- and high-income countries in this regard.

Slavery

Poor societies have many problems in addition to hunger, including illiteracy, warfare, and even slavery. The British Empire banned slavery in 1833, followed by the United States in 1865. But slavery is a reality for at least 20 million men, women, and children (International Labour Organization, 2012).

Anti-Slavery International describes five types of slavery. The first is *chattel slavery,* in which one person owns another. In spite of the fact that this practice is against the law almost everywhere in the world, several million people fall into this category. The buying and selling of slaves—generally people of one ethnic or caste group enslaving members of another—still takes place in many countries throughout Asia, the Middle East, and especially Africa. The Thinking Globally box on page 343 describes the reality of one slave's life in the African nation of Mauritania.

A second type of bondage is *slavery imposed by the state.* In this case, a government imposes forced labor on people convicted of criminal violations or on others simply because the government needs their labor. In China, for example, people who engage in prostitution or other crimes or who are addicted to drugs or engage in political dissent are subject to forced labor. In North Korea, the government can force people to work for almost any reason at all.

A third and common form of bondage is *child slavery,* in which desperately poor families send their children out into the streets to beg or steal or do whatever they can to survive. Probably tens of millions of children—many in the poorest countries of Latin

Thinking Globally

"God Made Me to Be a Slave"

Fatma Mint Mamadou is a young woman living in North Africa's Islamic Republic of Mauritania. Asked her age, she pauses, smiles, and shakes her head. She has no idea when she was born. Nor can she read or write. What she knows is tending camels, herding sheep, hauling bags of water, sweeping, and serving tea to her owners. This young woman is one of perhaps 500,000 slaves in Mauritania, which represents about 18 percent of that nation's population.

In the central region of this nation, having dark brown skin almost always means being a slave to an Arab owner. Fatma accepts her situation; she has known nothing else. She explains in a matter-of-fact voice that she is a slave like her mother before her and her grandmother before that. "Just as God created a camel to be a camel," she shrugs, "he created me to be a slave."

Fatma, her mother, and her brothers and sisters live in a squatter settlement on the edge of Nouakchott, Mauritania's

Human slavery continues to exist in the twenty-first century.

capital city. Their home is a 9-by-12-foot hut that they built from wood scraps and other materials found at construction sites. The roof is nothing more than a piece of cloth; there is no plumbing or furniture. The nearest water comes from a well a mile down the road.

In this region, slavery began more than 500 years ago, about the time Columbus sailed west toward the Americas. As Arab and Berber tribes raided local villages, they made slaves of the people, and so it has been for dozens of generations ever since. In 1905, the French colonial rulers of Mauritania banned slavery. After the nation gained independence in 1961, the new government reaffirmed the ban. However, slavery was not officially abolished until 1981, and even then, it was not made a crime. In 2007, the nation passed legislation making the practice of slavery an offense punishable by up to ten years in prison, and the government now provides monetary compensation to victims of slavery. But the new laws have done little to change strong traditions. The sad truth is that people like Fatma still have no conception of "freedom to choose."

The next question is more personal: "Are you and other girls ever raped?" Again, Fatma hesitates. With no hint of emotion, she responds, "Of course, in the night the men come to breed us. Is that what you mean by rape?"

What Do You Think?

1. How does tradition play a part in keeping people in slavery?

2. What might explain the fact that the world still tolerates slavery?

3. Explain the connection between slavery and poverty.

Source: Based on Burkett (1997), Fisher (2011); Anti-Slavery International (2012).

America and Africa—fall into this category. In addition, an estimated 10 million children are forced to labor daily in the production of tobacco, sugar cane, cotton, and coffee in more than seventy nations.

Fourth, *debt bondage* is the practice by which an employer pays wages to workers that are less than what the employer charges the workers for company-provided food and housing. Under such an arrangement, workers can never pay their debts so, for practical purposes, workers are enslaved. Many sweatshop workers in low-income nations fall into this category.

Fifth, *servile forms of marriage* may also amount to slavery. In India, Thailand, and some African nations, families marry off women against their will. Many end up as slaves working for their husband's family; some are forced into prostitution.

An additional form of slavery is *human trafficking*, the moving of men, women, and children from one place to another for the purpose of performing forced labor. Women or men are brought to a new country with the promise of a job and then forced to become prostitutes or farm laborers, or "parents" adopt children from another country and then force them to work in sweatshops. Such activity is big business: Next to trading in guns and drugs, trading in people brings the greatest profit to organized crime around the world (Orhant, 2002; Anti-Slavery International, 2012; International Labor Organization, 2012; U.S. Department of Labor, 2012).

In 1948, the United Nations issued its Universal Declaration of Human Rights, which states, "No one shall be held in slavery or servitude; slavery and the slave trade shall be prohibited in all their forms." Unfortunately, more than six decades later, this social evil still exists.

Explanations of Global Poverty

What accounts for severe and extensive poverty in so much of the world? The rest of this chapter provides answers using the following facts about poor societies:

1. **Technology.** About one-quarter of people in low-income countries farm the land using human muscle or animal power. With limited energy sources, economic production is modest.

2. **Population growth.** As Chapter 22 ("Population, Urbanization, and Environment") explains, theThe poorest countries have the world's highest birth rates. Despite the death toll from poverty, the populations of poor countries in Africa double every twenty-five years. In sub-Saharan Africa, 43 percent of the people are under the age of fifteen. With so many people entering their childbearing years, the wave of population increase will roll into the future. The result is more poverty. Why? The population of Uganda, for example, has swelled by about 5 percent annually in recent years; even with some economic development, living standards there have fallen. This is far from an isolated case. Globally, just about all future population increase will be in lower-income countries (Population Reference Bureau, 2012).

3. **Cultural patterns.** Poor societies are usually traditional. Holding on to long-established ways of life means resisting change—even change that promises a richer material life.

4. **Social stratification.** Low-income societies distribute their wealth very unequally. Chapter 10 ("Social Stratification") explained that social inequality is greater in agrarian societies than in industrial societies. In Brazil, for example, 75 percent of all farmland is owned by just 4 percent of the people (Galano, 1998; IBGE, 2006; Frayssinet, 2009).

5. **Gender inequality.** Gender inequality in poor societies keeps women from holding jobs, which typically means they have many children. An expanding population, in turn, slows economic development. Many analysts conclude that raising living standards in much of the world depends on improving the social standing of women.

6. **Global power relationships.** A final cause of global poverty lies in the relationships between the nations of the world. Historically, wealth flowed from poor societies to rich nations through **colonialism**, *the process by which some nations enrich themselves through political and economic control of other nations.* The countries of Western Europe colonized much of Latin America beginning just over five centuries ago. Such global exploitation allowed some nations to develop economically at the expense of other nations.

Although 130 former colonies gained their independence over the course of the twentieth century, exploitation continues today through **neocolonialism** (*neo* is Greek for "new"), *a new form of global power relationships that involves not direct political control but economic exploitation by multinational corporations.* A **multinational corporation** is *a large business that operates in many countries.* Corporate leaders often impose their will on countries in which they do business to create favorable economic conditions for the operation of their corporations, just as colonizers did in the past (Bonanno, Constance, & Lorenz, 2000).

For a close-up look at why traditional people may respond to their poverty differently than poor people in the United States, **Read More** in **MySocLab**, *"Happy Poverty" in India: Making Sense of a Strange Idea*

Theories of Global Stratification

(12.3) Apply sociological theories to the topic of global inequality.

There are two major explanations for the unequal distribution of the world's wealth and power: *modernization theory* and *dependency theory*. Each theory suggests a different solution to the suffering of hungry people in much of the world.

Modernization Theory

Modernization theory is *a model of economic and social development that explains global inequality in terms of technological and cultural differences between nations.* Modernization theory, which follows the structural-functional approach, emerged in the 1950s, a time when U.S. society was fascinated by new developments in technology. To showcase the power of productive technology and also to counter the growing influence of the Soviet Union, U.S. policymakers drafted a market-based foreign policy that has been with us ever since (Rostow, 1960, 1978; Bauer, 1981; Berger, 1986; Firebaugh, 1996; Firebaugh & Sandhu, 1998).

Historical Perspective

Until a few centuries ago, the entire world was poor. Because poverty is the norm throughout human history, modernization theory claims that it is *affluence* that demands an explanation.

Affluence came within reach of a growing share of people in Western Europe during the late Middle Ages as world exploration and trade expanded. Soon after, the Industrial Revolution transformed first Western Europe and then North America. Industrial technology and the spirit of capitalism created new wealth as never before. At first, this wealth benefited only a few individuals. But industrial technology was so productive that gradually the living standards of even the poorest people began to improve. Absolute poverty, which had plagued humanity throughout history, was finally in decline.

In high-income countries, where the Industrial Revolution began in the late 1700s or early 1800s, the standard of living jumped at least fourfold during the twentieth century. As middle-income nations in Asia and Latin America have industrialized, they too have become richer. But with limited industrial technology, low-income countries have changed much less.

The Importance of Culture

Why didn't the Industrial Revolution sweep away poverty throughout the world? Modernization theory points out that not every society wants to adopt new technology. Doing so requires a cultural environment that emphasizes the benefits of material wealth and new ideas.

Modernization theory identifies *tradition* as the greatest barrier to economic development. In some societies, strong family systems and a reverence for the past discourage people from adopting new technologies that would raise their living standards. Even today, many traditional people—from the Amish in North America to Islamic people in the Middle East to the Semai of Malaysia—oppose new technology as a threat to their families, customs, and religious beliefs. Max Weber (1958, orig. 1904–05) found that at the end of the Middle Ages, Western Europe's cultural environment favored change. As discussed in Chapter 4 ("Society"), the Protestant Reformation reshaped traditional Christian beliefs to generate a progress-oriented way of life. Wealth—looked on with suspicion by the Catholic church—became a sign of personal virtue, and the growing importance of individualism steadily replaced the traditional emphasis on family and community. Taken together, these new cultural patterns nurtured the Industrial Revolution.

Rostow's Stages of Modernization

Modernization theory holds that the door to affluence is open to all. As technological advances spread around the world, all societies should gradually industrialize. According to Walt Rostow (1960, 1978), modernization occurs in four stages:

1. **Traditional stage.** Socialized to honor the past, people in traditional societies cannot easily imagine that life could or should be any different. They therefore build their lives around families and local communities, following well-worn paths that allow little individual freedom or change. Life is often spiritually rich but lacking in material goods.

   A century ago, much of the world was in this initial stage of economic development. Nations such as Bangladesh, Niger, and Somalia are still at the traditional stage and remain poor. Even in countries, such as India, that have recently joined the ranks of middle-income nations, certain elements of the population have remained highly traditional.

2. **Take-off stage.** As a society shakes off the grip of tradition, people start to use their talents and imagination, sparking economic growth. A market emerges as people produce goods not just for their own use but also to trade with others for profit. Greater individualism, a willingness to take risks, and a desire for material goods also take hold, often at the expense of family ties and time-honored norms and values.

   Great Britain reached take-off by about 1800, the United States by 1820. Thailand, a middle-income country in eastern Asia, is now in this stage. Such development is typically speeded by help from rich nations, including foreign aid, the availability of advanced technology and investment capital, and opportunities for schooling abroad.

3. **Drive to technological maturity.** As this stage begins, "growth" is a widely accepted idea that fuels a society's pursuit of higher living standards. A diversified economy drives a population eager to enjoy the benefits of industrial technology. At the same time, however, people begin to realize (and sometimes regret) that industrialization is eroding traditional family and local community life. Great Britain reached this point by about 1840, the United States by 1860. Today, Mexico, the U.S. territory of Puerto Rico, and Poland are among the nations driving to technological maturity.

   At this stage of development, absolute poverty is greatly reduced. Cities swell with people who leave rural villages in search of economic opportunity. Specialization creates the wide range of jobs that we find in our economy today. An increasing focus on work makes relationships less personal. Growing individualism generates social movements demanding greater political rights. Societies approaching technological maturity also provide basic schooling for all their people and advanced training for some. The newly educated consider tradition "backward" and push for further change. The social position of women steadily approaches that of men.

In rich nations such as the United States, most parents expect their children to enjoy years of childhood, largely free from the responsibilities of adult life. This is not the case in poor nations across Latin America, Africa, and Asia. Poor families depend on whatever income their children can earn, and many children as young as six or seven work full days weaving or performing other kinds of manual labor. Child labor lies behind the low prices of many products imported for sale in this country.

4. **High mass consumption.** Economic development steadily raises living standards as mass production stimulates mass consumption. Simply put, people soon learn to "need" the expanding array of goods that their society produces. The United States, Japan, and other rich nations moved into this stage by 1900. Now entering this level of economic development are two former British colonies that are prosperous small societies of eastern Asia: Hong Kong (part of the People's Republic of China since 1997) and Singapore (independent since 1965).

The Role of Rich Nations

Modernization theory claims that high-income countries play four important roles in global economic development:

1. **Controlling population.** Because population growth is greatest in the poorest societies, rising population can overtake economic advances. Rich nations can help limit population growth by exporting birth control technology and promoting its use. Once economic development is under way, birth rates should decline, as they have in industrialized nations, because children are no longer an economic asset.

2. **Increasing food production.** Rich nations can export high-tech farming methods to poor nations to increase agricultural yields. Such techniques, collectively referred to as the Green Revolution, include new hybrid seeds, modern irrigation methods, chemical fertilizers, and pesticides for insect control.

3. **Introducing industrial technology.** Rich nations can encourage economic growth in poor societies by introducing machinery and information technology, which raise productivity. Industrialization also shifts the labor force from farming to skilled industrial and service jobs.

4. **Providing foreign aid.** Investment capital from rich nations can boost the prospects of poor societies trying to reach Rostow's take-off stage. Foreign aid can raise farm output by helping poor countries buy more fertilizer and build irrigation projects. In the same way, financial and technical assistance can help build power plants and factories to improve industrial output. Each year, the United States provides more than $35 billion in foreign aid to developing countries (U.S. Agency for International Development, 2012).

EVALUATE Modernization theory has many influential supporters among social scientists (Parsons, 1966; Moore, 1977, 1979; Bauer, 1981; Berger, 1986; Firebaugh & Beck, 1994; Firebaugh, 1996, 1999; Firebaugh & Sandu, 1998). For decades, it has shaped the foreign policy of the United States and other rich nations. Supporters point to rapid economic development in Asia—especially in South Korea, Taiwan, Singapore, and Hong Kong—as proof that the affluence achieved in Western Europe and North America is within the reach of all countries.

But modernization theory comes under fire from socialist countries (and left-leaning analysts in the West) as little more than a defense of capitalism. Its most serious flaw, according to critics, is that modernization simply has not occurred in many poor countries. Economic indicators reported by the United Nations show that living standards in a number of nations, including Haiti and Nicaragua in Latin America and Sudan, Ghana, and Rwanda in Africa, are little changed—and are in some cases worse—than in 1960 (United Nations Development Programme, 2008).

A second criticism of modernization theory is that it fails to recognize how rich nations, which benefit from the status quo, often block the path to development for poor countries. Centuries ago, critics charge, rich countries industrialized from a position of global strength. Can we expect poor countries today to do so from a position of global weakness?

Third, modernization theory treats rich and poor societies as separate worlds, ignoring the ways in which international relations have affected all nations. Many countries in Latin America and Asia are still struggling to overcome the harm caused by colonialism, which boosted the fortunes of Europe.

Explore which areas of the United States have attracted large numbers of immigrants seeking the high standard of living available in a country at this stage of modernization in **MySocLab**

Watch in **MySocLab** Video: *The Big Picture: Population, Urbanization, and Environment*

Fourth, modernization theory holds up the world's most developed countries as the standard for judging the rest of humanity, revealing an ethnocentric bias. We should remember that our Western idea of "progress" has caused us to rush headlong into a competitive, materialistic way of life, which uses up the world's scarce resources and pollutes the natural environment.

Fifth and finally, modernization theory suggests that the causes of global poverty lie almost entirely in the poor societies themselves. Critics see this analysis as little more than blaming the victims for their own problems. Instead, they argue, an analysis of global inequality should focus just as much on the behavior of rich nations as it does on the behavior of poor ones and also on the global economic system. Concerns such as these reflect a second major approach to understanding global inequality, dependency theory.

CHECK YOUR LEARNING State the important ideas of modernization theory, including Rostow's four stages of economic development. Point to several strengths and weaknesses of this theory.

Dependency Theory

Dependency theory is *a model of economic and social development that explains global inequality in terms of the historical exploitation of poor nations by rich ones.* This analysis, which follows the social-conflict approach, puts the main responsibility for global poverty on rich nations, which for centuries have systematically impoverished low-income countries and made them dependent on the rich ones—a destructive process that continues today.

Historical Perspective

Everyone agrees that before the Industrial Revolution, there was little affluence in the world. Dependency theory asserts, however, that people living in poor countries were actually better off economically in the past than their descendants are now. André Gunder Frank (1975), a noted supporter of this theory, argues that the colonial process that helped develop rich nations also *underdeveloped* poor societies.

Dependency theory is based on the idea that the economic positions of rich and poor nations of the world are linked and cannot be understood apart from each other. Poor nations are not simply lagging behind rich ones on the "path of progress"; rather, the prosperity of the most developed countries came largely at the expense of less developed ones. In short, some nations became rich only because others became poor. Both are products of the global commerce that began five centuries ago.

The Importance of Colonialism

Late in the fifteenth century, Europeans began exploring the Americas to the west, Africa to the south, and Asia to the east in order to establish colonies. They were so successful that a century ago, Great Britain controlled about one-fourth of the world's land, boasting that "the sun never sets on the British Empire." The United States, itself originally a collection of small British colonies on the eastern seaboard of North America, soon pushed across the continent, purchased Alaska, and gained control of Haiti, Puerto Rico, Guam, the Philippines, the Hawaiian Islands, part of Panama, and Guantanamo Bay in Cuba.

Modernization theory claims that corporations that build factories in low-income nations help people by providing them with jobs and higher wages than they had before; dependency theory views these factories as "sweatshops" that exploit workers. In response to the Olympic Games selling sports clothing produced by sweatshops, these women staged a protest in Athens, Greece; they are wearing white masks to symbolize the "faceless" workers who make much of what we wear. Is any of the clothing you wear made in sweatshop factories?

As colonialism spread, there emerged a brutal form of human exploitation—the international slave trade—beginning about 1500 and continuing until 1850. Even as the world was turning away from slavery, Europeans took control of most of the African continent, as Figure 12–4 shows, and dominated most of the continent until the early 1960s.

Formal colonialism has almost disappeared from the world. However, according to dependency theory, political liberation has not translated into economic independence. Far from it—the economic relationship between poor and rich nations continues the colonial pattern of domination. This neocolonialism is the heart of the capitalist world economy.

Wallerstein's Capitalist World Economy

Immanuel Wallerstein (1974, 1979, 1983, 1984) explains global stratification using a model of the "capitalist world economy." Wallerstein's term *world economy* suggests that the prosperity of some nations and the poverty and dependency of other countries result from a global economic system. He traces the roots of the global economy to the beginning of colonization more than 500 years ago, when Europeans began gathering wealth from the rest of the world. Because the world economy is based in the high-income countries, it is capitalist in character.[2]

Wallerstein calls the rich nations the *core* of the world economy. Colonialism enriched this core by funneling raw materials from around the world to Western Europe, where they fueled the Industrial Revolution. Today, multinational corporations operate profitably worldwide, channeling wealth to North America, Western Europe, Australia, and Japan.

Low-income countries represent the *periphery* of the world economy. Drawn into the world economy by colonial exploitation, poor nations continue to support rich ones by providing inexpensive labor and a vast market for industrial products. The remaining countries are considered the *semiperiphery* of the world economy. They include middle-income countries like India and Brazil that have closer ties to the global economic core.

According to Wallerstein, the world economy benefits rich societies (by generating profits) and harms the rest of the world (by causing poverty). The world economy thus makes poor nations dependent on rich ones. This dependency involves three factors:

1. **Narrow, export-oriented economies.** Poor nations produce only a few crops for export to rich countries. Examples include coffee and fruit from Latin American nations, oil from Nigeria, hardwoods from the Philippines, and palm oil from Malaysia. Today's multinational corporations purchase raw materials

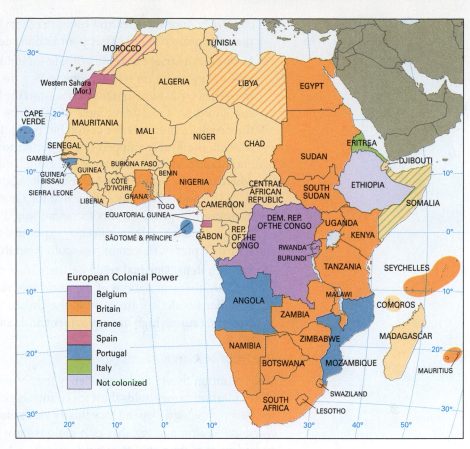

FIGURE 12–4 Africa's Colonial History

For more than a century, most of Africa was colonized by European nations, with France dominating in the northwestern region of the continent and Great Britain dominating in the east and south.

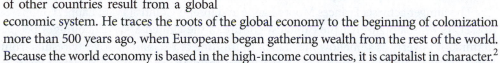

modernization theory
a model of economic and social development that explains global inequality in terms of technological and cultural differences between nations

dependency theory
a model of economic and social development that explains global inequality in terms of the historical exploitation of poor nations by rich ones

---

[2]This discussion also draws on A. G. Frank (1980, 1981), Delacroix & Ragin (1981), Bergesen (1983), Dixon & Boswell (1996), and Kentor (1998).

cheaply in poor societies and transport them to core nations, where factories process them for profitable sale. Thus poor nations develop few industries of their own.

2. **Lack of industrial capacity.** Without an industrial base, poor societies face a double bind: They count on rich nations to buy their inexpensive raw materials, and they must then try to buy from the rich nations the few expensive manufactured goods they can afford. In a classic example of this dependency, British colonialists encouraged the people of India to raise cotton but prevented them from weaving their own cloth. Instead, the British shipped Indian cotton to their own textile mills in Birmingham and Manchester, manufactured the cloth, and shipped finished goods back to India, where the very people who harvested the cotton bought the garments.

Dependency theorists claim that the Green Revolution—widely praised by modernization theorists—works the same way. Poor countries sell cheap raw materials to rich nations and then must buy expensive fertilizers, pesticides, and machinery in return. Typically, rich countries profit from this exchange far more than poor nations.

3. **Foreign debt.** Unequal trade patterns have plunged poor countries into debt. Collectively, the poor nations of the world owe rich countries some $4 trillion; hundreds of billions of dollars are owed to the United States. Such staggering debt paralyzes a country, causing high unemployment and rampant inflation (World Bank, 2012).

The Role of Rich Nations

Modernization theory and dependency theory assign very different roles to rich nations. Modernization theory holds that rich countries *produce wealth* through capital investment and new technology. Dependency theory views global inequality in terms of how countries *distribute wealth,* arguing that rich nations have *overdeveloped* themselves as they have *underdeveloped* the rest of the world.

Dependency theorists dismiss the idea that programs developed by rich countries to control population and boost agricultural and industrial output raise living standards in poor countries. Instead, they claim, such programs actually benefit rich nations and the ruling elites, not the poor majority, in low-income countries (Kentor, 2001).

The hunger activists Frances Moore Lappé and Joseph Collins (1986; Lappé, Collins, & Rosset, 1998) maintain that the capitalist culture of the United States encourages people to think of poverty as somehow inevitable. In this line of reasoning, poverty results from "natural" processes, including having too many children, and natural disasters such as droughts. But global poverty is far from inevitable; in their view, it results from deliberate policies. Lappé and Collins point out that the world already produces enough food to allow every person on the planet to become quite fat. Moreover, India and most of Africa actually *export* food, even though many people in African nations go hungry.

According to Lappé and Collins, the contradiction of poverty amid plenty stems from the rich-nation policy of producing food for profit, not people. That is, corporations in rich nations cooperate with elites in poor countries to grow and export profitable crops such as coffee, which means using land that could otherwise produce basics such as beans and corn for local families. Governments of poor countries support the practice of growing for export because they need food profits to repay foreign debt. According to Lappé and Collins, the capitalist corporate structure of the global economy is at the core of this vicious cycle.

EVALUATE The main idea of dependency theory is that no nation becomes rich or poor in isolation, because a single global economy shapes the destiny of all nations. Pointing to continuing poverty in Latin America, Africa, and Asia, dependency theorists claim that development simply cannot proceed under the constraints now imposed by rich countries. Rather, they call for radical reform of the entire world economy so that it operates in the interests of the majority of people.

Critics charge that dependency theory wrongly treats wealth as if no one gets richer without someone else getting poorer. Corporations, small business owners, and farmers can and do create new wealth through hard work and imaginative use of new technology. After all, they point out, the entire world's wealth has increased tenfold since 1950.

Second, dependency theory is wrong in blaming rich nations for global poverty because many of the world's poorest countries (such as Ethiopia) have had little contact with rich nations. On the contrary, a long history of trade with rich countries has dramatically improved the economies of many nations, including Sri Lanka, Singapore, and Hong Kong (all former British colonies), as well as South Korea and Japan. In short, say the critics, most evidence shows that foreign investment by rich nations encourages economic growth, as modernization theory claims, and not economic decline, as dependency theory holds (Vogel, 1991; Firebaugh, 1992).

Third, critics call dependency theory simplistic for pointing the finger at a single factor—the capitalist market system—as the cause of global inequality (Worsley, 1990). Dependency theory views poor societies as passive victims and ignores factors inside these countries that contribute to their economic problems. Sociologists have long recognized the vital role of culture in shaping people's willingness to embrace or resist change. Under the rule of the ultratraditional Muslim Taliban, for example, Afghanistan became economically isolated, and its living standards sank to among the lowest in the world. Is it reasonable to blame capitalist nations for that country's stagnation?

Although the world continues to grow richer, billions of people are being left behind. This shantytown of Cité Soleil, Haiti, is typical of many cities in low-income countries. What can you say about the quality of life in such a place?

Nor can rich societies be held responsible for the reckless behavior of foreign leaders whose corruption and militarism impoverish their countries. Examples include the regimes of Ferdinand Marcos in the Philippines, François Duvalier in Haiti, Manuel Noriega in Panama, Mobutu Sese Seko in Zaire (today's Democratic Republic of the Congo), Robert Mugabe in Zimbabwe, Saddam Hussein in Iraq, Hosni Mubarak in Egypt, and Muammar el-Qaddafi in Libya. Some leaders even use food supplies as weapons in internal political struggles, leaving the masses starving, as in the African nations of Ethiopia, Sudan, and Somalia. Likewise, many countries throughout the world have done little to improve the status of women or control population growth.

Fourth, critics say that dependency theory is wrong to claim that global trade always makes rich nations richer and poor nations poorer. For example, in 2011, the United States had a trade deficit of $738 billion, meaning that this nation imports nearly three-quarters of a trillion dollars' more goods than it sells abroad. The single greatest debt ($296 billion) was owed to China, whose profitable trade has now pushed that country into the ranks of the world's middle-income nations (U.S. Census Bureau, 2012).

Fifth, critics fault dependency theory for offering only vague solutions to global poverty. Most dependency theorists urge poor nations to end all contact with rich countries, and some call for nationalizing foreign-owned industries. In other words, dependency theory is really an argument for some type of world socialism. In light of the difficulties that socialist societies (even better-off socialist countries such as Russia) have had in meeting the needs of their own people, critics ask, should we really expect such a system to rescue the entire world from poverty?

CHECK YOUR LEARNING State the main ideas of dependency theory. What are several of its strengths and weaknesses?

The Applying Theory table on page 352 summarizes the main arguments of modernization theory and dependency theory.

Global Poverty	Modernization Theory	Dependency Theory
Which theoretical approach is applied?	Structural-functional approach	Social-conflict approach
How did global poverty come about?	The whole world was poor until some countries developed industrial technology, which allowed mass production and created affluence.	Colonialism moved wealth from some countries to others, making some nations poor as it made other nations rich.
What are the main causes of global poverty today?	Traditional culture and a lack of productive technology.	Neocolonialism—the operation of multinational corporations in the global, capitalist economy.
Are rich countries part of the problem or part of the solution?	Rich countries are part of the solution, contributing new technology, advanced schooling, and foreign aid.	Rich countries are part of the problem, making poor countries economically dependent and in debt.

The Future of Global Stratification

12.4 Evaluate trends in global inequality.

Among the most important trends in recent decades is the development of a global economy. In the United States, rising production and sales abroad bring profits to many corporations and their stockholders, especially those who already have substantial wealth. At the same time, the global economy has moved manufacturing jobs abroad, closing factories in this country and hurting many average workers. The net result: greater economic inequality in the United States.

People who support the global economy claim that the expansion of trade results in benefits for all countries involved. For this reason, they endorse policies like the North American Free Trade Agreement (NAFTA) signed by the United States, Canada, and Mexico. Critics of expanding globalization make other claims: Manufacturing jobs are being lost in the United States, and more manufacturing now takes place abroad in factories where workers are paid little and few laws ensure workplace safety. In addition, other critics of expanding globalization point to the ever-greater stresses that our economy places on the natural environment.

But perhaps the greatest concern is the vast economic inequality that exists between the world's countries. The concentration of wealth in high-income countries, coupled with the grinding poverty in low-income nations, may well be the biggest problem facing humanity in the twenty-first century.

Both modernization theory and dependency theory offer some understanding of this urgent problem. In evaluating these theories, we must consider empirical evidence. Over the course of the twentieth century, living standards rose in most of the world. Even the economic output of the poorest 25 percent of the world's people almost tripled during those 100 years. As a result, the share of the world's population living on less than $1.25 a day fell from about 52 percent in 1981 to about 43 percent in 1990 and to about 22 percent in 2008 (Chen & Ravallion, 2012).

So far, the greatest reduction in poverty has taken place in Asia, a region generally regarded as an economic success story. Back in 1981, about 77 percent of the population of East Asia was living on less than $1.25 per day. By 2008, however, that share had declined dramatically to about 14 percent. Signaling this trend toward greater prosperity, in 2005, two very large Asian countries—India and China—joined the ranks of the middle-income nations (Sala-i-Martin, 2002; Bussolo et al., 2007; Davies et al., 2008; Chen & Ravallion, 2012).

During the 1970s, Latin America enjoyed significant economic growth, which pushed the share of its population living in $1.25-per-day poverty down to 12 percent by 1981.

During the 1980s and 1990s, however, this number changed very little, with additional small gains after about 2005. By 2008, the share of people living in poverty was about 7 percent (Chen & Ravallion, 2012).

Sub-Saharan Africa represents the greatest challenge in humanity's efforts to reduce poverty. By 2008, for the first time, less than half the people (47 percent) of this global region were living at $1.25-per-day poverty or less. This poverty rate is still well above that of other world regions. Yet analysts are optimistic about Africa's future, pointing out that this region has enjoyed average economic growth of more than 5 percent a year over the past decade. In addition, six of the ten fastest developing countries in the world are now in southern Africa (Sala-i-Martin, 2002; Chen & Ravillion, 2012; Perry, 2012).

Looking at the world as a whole, the good news is that, in *absolute* terms, living standards are rising. Over the course of the last century, economic output has increased for both rich and poor nations. But the troubling trend is that living standards in rich and poor countries are not rising at the same rate. As a result, the *relative* gap between the rich and the poor in the world is increasing and, in 2011, this divide was more than five times larger than it was back in 1900. Figure 12–5 shows that the lower-income people in the world are being left behind.

Recent trends suggest the need to look critically at both modernization and dependency theories. The fact that governments have played a large role in the economic growth that has occurred in Asia and elsewhere challenges modernization theory and its free-market approach to development. On the other hand, since the upheavals in the former Soviet Union and Eastern Europe, a global reevaluation of socialism has been taking place. Because socialist nations have a record of decades of poor economic performance and political repression, many low-income nations are unwilling to follow the advice of dependency theory and place economic development entirely under government control.

Although the world's future is uncertain, we have learned a great deal about global stratification. One insight offered by modernization theory is that poverty is partly a *problem of technology.* A higher standard of living for a surging world population depends on the ability of poor nations to raise their agricultural and industrial productivity. A second insight, derived from dependency theory, is that global inequality is also a *political issue.* Even with higher productivity, the human community must address crucial questions concerning how resources are distributed, both within societies and around the globe.

Although economic development raises living standards, it also places greater strains on the natural environment. As nations such as India and China—with a combined population of 2.6 billion—become more affluent, their people will consume more energy and other resources (China has recently passed Japan to become the second-largest consumer of oil, behind the United States, which is one reason that oil prices and supplies have been under pressure). Richer nations also produce more solid waste and create more pollution.

Finally, the vast gulf that separates the world's richest and poorest people puts everyone at greater risk of war and terrorism as the poorest people challenge the social arrangements that threaten their existence (Lindauer & Weerapana, 2002). In the long run, we can achieve peace on this planet only by ensuring that all people enjoy a significant measure of dignity and security.

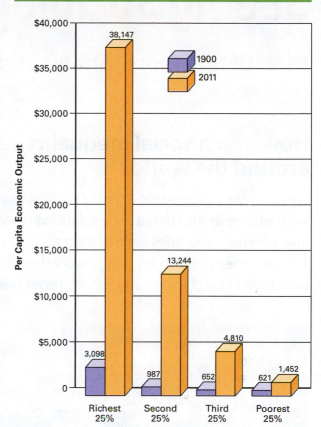

FIGURE 12–5 The World's Increasing Economic Inequality

The gap between the richest and poorest people in the world in 2011 was more than five times bigger than it was in 1900.
Source: World Bank (2012).

Seeing Sociology in Everyday Life

How much social inequality can we find if we look around the world?

This chapter explains that a global perspective reveals even more social stratification than we find here in the United States. Around the world, an increasing number of people in lower-income countries are traveling to higher-income nations in search of jobs. As "guest workers," they perform low-wage work that the country's own more well-off citizens do not wish to do. In such cases, the rich and poor truly live "worlds apart."

Many guest workers come to Dubai from India to take jobs building this country's new high-rise hotels and business towers. With very little income, they often sleep six to a small room. How do you think living in a strange country, with few legal rights, affects these workers' ability to improve their working conditions?

Guest workers in Dubai labor about twelve hours a day but earn only between $50 and $175 a month. Do you think the chance to take a job like this in a foreign country is an opportunity (income is typically twice what people can earn at home), or is it a form of exploitation?

Oil wealth has made some of the people of Dubai, in the United Arab Emirates, among the richest in the world. Dubai's wealthiest people can afford to ski on snow—in one of the hottest regions of the world—on enormous indoor ski slopes like this one. Is there anything about this picture that makes you uncomfortable? Explain your reaction.

HINT Dubai's recent building boom has been accomplished using the labor of about 1 million guest workers, who actually make up about 85 percent of the population of the United Arab Emirates. Recent years have seen a rising level of social unrest, including labor strikes, which has led to some improvements in working and living conditions and better health care. But guest workers have no legal rights to form labor unions, nor do they have any chance to gain citizenship.

Seeing Sociology in *Your* Everyday Life

1. What comparisons can you make between the pattern of guest workers coming to places like Dubai in the Middle East and workers coming to the United States from Mexico and other countries in Latin America?

2. Go to MySocLab and click on the Student Resources link to access the Sociology in Focus blog, where you can read the latest posts by a team of young sociologists who apply the sociological perspective to topics of popular culture.

3. Have you ever traveled in a low-income nation? Do you think people from a high-income nation such as the United States should feel guilty when seeing the daily struggles of the world's poorest people? Why or why not? Go to the "Seeing Sociology in *Your* Everyday Life" feature in MySocLab to learn more about global stratification and also to read some suggestions for travelers who have the chance to interact with people in low-income nations.

Making the Grade

Global Stratification: An Overview

12.1 Describe the division of the world into high-, middle-, and low-income countries. (pages 333–38)

 Watch the **Video** in **MySocLab**   **Watch** the **Video** in **MySocLab**

High-Income Countries

- contain 23% of the world's people
- receive 64% of global income
- have a high standard of living based on advanced technology
- produce enough economic goods to enable their people to lead comfortable lives
- include 74 nations, among them the United States, Canada, Mexico, Argentina, Chile, the nations of Western Europe, Israel, Saudi Arabia, the Russian Federation, Japan, South Korea, Malaysia, and Australia

Middle-Income Countries

- contain 60% of the world's people
- receive 33% of global income
- have a standard of living about average for the world as a whole
- include 72 nations, among them the nations of Eastern Europe, Peru, Brazil, Namibia, Egypt, Indonesia, India, and the People's Republic of China

Low-Income Countries

- contain 17% of the world's people
- receive 3% of global income
- have a low standard of living due to limited industrial technology
- include 49 nations, generally in Central and East Africa and Asia, among them Chad, the Democratic Republic of the Congo, Ethiopia, and Bangladesh.

global stratification patterns of social inequality in the world as a whole

high-income countries the nations with the highest overall standards of living

middle-income countries nations with a standard of living about average for the world as a whole

low-income countries nations with a low standard of living in which most people are poor

Global Wealth and Poverty

12.2 Discuss patterns and explanations of poverty around the world. (pages 338–44)

Read the **Document** in **MySocLab**

All societies contain **relative poverty**, but low-income nations face widespread **absolute poverty** that is life-threatening.

- Worldwide, about 868 million people are at risk due to poor nutrition.
- About 9 million people each year die each year from diseases caused by poverty.
- Throughout the world, women are more likely than men to be poor. Gender bias is strongest in poor societies.
- At least 20 million men, women, and children live in conditions that can be described as slavery.

Factors Causing Poverty

- Lack of technology limits production.
- High birth rates produce rapid population increase.
- Traditional cultural patterns make people resist change.
- Extreme social inequality distributes wealth very unequally.
- Extreme gender inequality limits the opportunities of women.
- Colonialism allowed some nations to exploit other nations; neocolonialism continues today.

colonialism the process by which some nations enrich themselves through political and economic control of other nations

neocolonialism a new form of global power relationships that involves not direct political control but economic exploitation by multinational corporations

multinational corporation a large business that operates in many countries

Theories of Global Stratification

(12.3) Apply sociological theories to the topic of global inequality. (pages 345–52)

✳ **Explore** the **Map** in **MySocLab**   👁 **Watch** the **Video** in **MySocLab**

Modernization theory maintains that nations achieve affluence by developing advanced technology. This process depends on a culture that encourages innovation and change.

Walt Rostow identified four stages of development:

- *Traditional stage*—People's lives are built around families and local communities. (Example: Democratic Republic of the Congo)
- *Take-off stage*—A market emerges as people produce goods not just for their own use but also to trade with others for profit. (Example: Thailand)
- *Drive to technological maturity*—Economic growth and higher living standards are goals; schooling is widely available; women's social standing improves. (Example: Mexico)
- *High mass consumption*—Advanced technology fuels mass production and mass consumption as people now "need" countless goods. (Example: the United States)

Modernization theory claims …

- Rich nations can help poor nations by providing technology to control population size, increase food production, and expand industrial and information economy output and by providing foreign aid to pay for new economic development.
- Rapid economic development in Asia shows that affluence is within reach of other nations.

Critics claim …

- Rich nations do little to help poor countries and benefit from the status quo. Low living standards in much of Africa and South America result from the policies of rich nations.
- Because rich nations, including the United States, control the global economy, many poor nations struggle to support their people and cannot follow the path to development taken by rich countries centuries ago.

Dependency theory maintains that global wealth and poverty were created by the colonial process beginning 500 years ago that developed rich nations and underdeveloped poor nations. This capitalist process continues today in the form of neocolonialism—economic exploitation of poor nations by multinational corporations.

Immanuel Wallerstein's identified three categories of nations in a capitalist world economy:

- *Core*—the world's high-income countries, which are home to multinational corporations
- *Semiperiphery*—the world's middle-income countries, with ties to core nations
- *Periphery*—the world's low-income countries, which provide low-cost labor and a vast market for industrial products

Dependency theory claims …

- Three key factors—export-oriented economies, a lack of industrial capacity, and foreign debt—make poor countries dependent on rich nations and prevent their economic development.
- Radical reform of the entire world economy is needed so that it operates in the interests of the majority of people.

Critics claim …

- Dependency theory overlooks the tenfold increase in global wealth since 1950 and the fact that the world's poorest countries have had weak, not strong, ties to rich countries.
- Rich nations are not responsible for cultural patterns and political corruption that block economic development in many poor nations.

modernization theory
a model of economic and social development that explains global inequality in terms of technological and cultural differences between nations

dependency theory
a model of economic and social development that explains global inequality in terms of the historical exploitation of poor nations by rich ones

The Future of Global Stratification

(12.4) Evaluate trends in global inequality. (pages 352-53)

- Global stratification is partly a matter of national differences in productive technology and partly a political matter involving how economic resources are distributed among nations and within nations.
- Although all regions of the world have made economic gains in absolute terms, the gap between rich and poor nations is more than five times larger than it was a century ago.

13 Gender Stratification

LEARNING OBJECTIVES

13.1 Describe research that points to how society creates gender stratification.

13.2 Explain the importance of gender to socialization.

13.3 Analyze the extent of gender inequality in various social institutions.

13.4 Apply sociology's major theories to gender stratification.

13.5 Contrast liberal, radical, and socialist feminism.

the Power of Society

to guide our life choices

Survey Question: "If you were free to do either, would you prefer to have a job outside the home, or would you prefer to stay at home and take care of the house and family?"

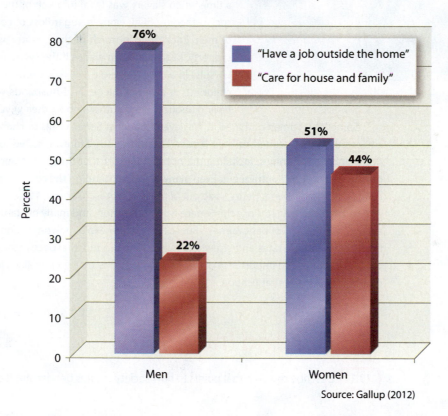

Source: Gallup (2012)

A recent survey asked U.S. adults this question, and men and women gave different answers. Among men it was no contest, with a large majority choosing the job outside the home. Among women, however, it was much closer, with only a very slight majority choosing the job. Or, from another angle, women were twice as likely as men to choose taking care of home and family. The difference in female and male responses shows the power of gender to shape our lives down to the very personal choices we make about how to live.

Chapter Overview

We live in a world organized around not only the differences of social class but also around the concepts of feminine and masculine, which sociologists call "gender." This chapter examines gender, explores the meaning societies attach to being female or male, and explains why gender is an important dimension of social stratification.

At first we traveled quite alone … but before we had gone many miles, we came on other wagonloads of women, bound in the same direction. As we reached different cross-roads, we saw wagons coming from every part of the country and, long before we reached Seneca Falls, we were a procession.

So wrote Charlotte Woodward in her journal as she made her way in a horse-drawn wagon along the rutted dirt roads leading to Seneca Falls, a small town in upstate New York. The year was 1848, a time when slavery was legal in much of the United States and the social standing of all women, regardless of color, was far below that of men. Back then, in much of the country, women could not own property, keep their own wages if they were married, draft a will, file lawsuits in a court (including lawsuits seeking custody of their own children), or attend college, and husbands were widely viewed as having unquestioned authority over their wives and children.

Some 300 women gathered at Wesleyan Chapel in Seneca Falls to challenge this second-class citizenship. They listened as their leader, Elizabeth Cady Stanton, called for expanding women's rights and opportunities, including the right to vote. At that time, most people considered such a proposal absurd and outrageous. Even many of those attending the conference were shocked by the idea: Stanton's husband, Henry, rode out of town in protest (Gurnett, 1998).

Much has changed since the Seneca Falls convention, and many of Stanton's proposals are now accepted as matters of basic fairness. But as this chapter explains, women and men still lead different lives in the United States and elsewhere in the world; in most respects, men are still in charge. This chapter explores the importance of gender and explains that gender, like class position, is a major dimension of social stratification.

Gender and Inequality

(**13.1**) Describe research that points to how society creates gender stratification.

Chapter 8 ("Sexuality and Society") explained that biological differences divide the human population into categories of female and male. **Gender** refers to *the personal traits and social positions that members of a society attach to being female or male.* Gender, then, is a dimension of social organization, shaping how we interact with others and even how we think about ourselves. More important, gender also involves *hierarchy,* placing men and women in different positions in terms of power, wealth, and other resources. This is why sociologists speak of **gender stratification**, *the unequal distribution of wealth, power, and privilege between men and women.* In short, gender affects the opportunities and constraints we face throughout our lives.

Male-Female Differences

Many people think there is something "natural" about gender distinctions because the two sexes do have some biological differences. But we must be careful not to think of social differences in biological terms. In 1848, for example, women were denied the vote because many people assumed that women did not have enough intelligence or any interest in politics. Such attitudes had nothing to do with biology; they reflected the *cultural* patterns of that time and place.

Another example is athletic performance. In 1925, most people—both women and men—believed that the best women runners could never compete with men in a marathon. Today, as Figure 13–1 shows, the gender gap has greatly narrowed, and the best women runners routinely post better times than the fastest men of decades past. Here again, most of the differences between men and women turn out to be socially created.

Differences in physical ability between the sexes do exist. On average, males are 10 percent taller than females, 20 percent heavier, and 30 percent stronger, especially in the upper body. On the other hand, women outperform men in the ultimate game of life itself: Life expectancy for men is 76.3 years, and women can expect to live 81.1 years (Ehrenreich, 1999; Fryar, Gu, & Ogden, 2012; Hoyert & Xu, 2012).

In adolescence, males do a bit better on the mathematics and reading parts of the SAT, while females show stronger writing skills, and researchers claim that these differences reflect both biology and socialization (Lewin, 2008; College Board, 2012). However, research does not point to any overall differences in intelligence between males and females.

Biologically, then, men and women differ in limited ways, with neither one naturally superior. But culture can define the two sexes differently, as the global study of gender described in the next section shows.

Gender in Global Perspective

The best way to see how gender is based in culture is by comparing one society to another. Three important studies highlight just how different "masculine" and "feminine" can be.

The Israeli Kibbutz

In Israel, collective settlements are called *kibbutzim*. The *kibbutz* (the singular form of the word) has been an important setting for gender research because gender equality is one of its stated goals; men and women share in both work and decision making.

In recent decades, kibbutzim have become less collective and thus less distinctive organizations. But for much of their history, both sexes shared most everyday jobs. Many men joined women in taking care of children, and women joined men in repairing buildings and providing armed security. Both sexes made everyday decisions for the group. Girls and boys were raised in the same way; in many cases, young children were raised together in dormitories away from parents. Women and men in the kibbutzim achieved remarkable (although not complete) social equality, evidence that cultures define what is feminine and what is masculine.

Margaret Mead's Research

The anthropologist Margaret Mead carried out groundbreaking research on gender. If gender is based in the biological differences between men and women, she reasoned, people everywhere should define "feminine" and "masculine" in the same way; if gender is cultural, these concepts should vary.

Mead (1963, orig. 1935) studied three societies in New Guinea. In the mountainous home of the Arapesh, Mead observed men and women with remarkably similar attitudes and behavior. Both sexes, she reported, were cooperative and sensitive to others—in short, what our culture would label "feminine."

Diversity Snapshot

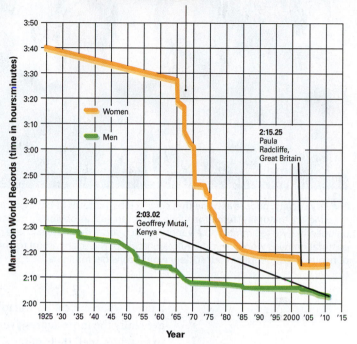

• The women's movement of the 1960s encouraged women to show their true abilities.

FIGURE 13–1 Men's and Women's Athletic Performance

Do men naturally outperform women in athletic competition? The answer is not obvious. Early in the twentieth century, men outpaced women by more than an hour in marathon races. But as opportunities for women in athletics have increased, women have been closing the performance gap. Only twelve minutes separate the current world marathon records for women (set in 2003) and for men (set in 2011).

Source: Marathonguide.com (2012).

gender the personal traits and social positions that members of a society attach to being female or male

gender stratification the unequal distribution of wealth, power, and privilege between men and women

Gender Stratification **CHAPTER 13** **361**

In every society, people assume that certain jobs, patterns of behavior, and ways of dressing are "naturally" feminine while others are just as obviously masculine. But in global perspective, we see remarkable variety in such social definitions. These men, Wodaabe pastoral nomads who live in the African nation of Niger, are proud to engage in a display of beauty most people in our society would consider feminine.

Moving south, Mead then studied the Mundugumor, whose headhunting and cannibalism stood in striking contrast to the gentle ways of the Arapesh. In this culture, both sexes were typically selfish and aggressive, traits we define as "masculine."

Finally, traveling west to the Tchambuli, Mead discovered a culture that, like our own, defined females and males differently. But, Mead reported, the Tchambuli *reversed* many of our ideas of gender: Females were dominant and rational, and males were submissive, emotional, and nurturing toward children. Based on her observations, Mead concluded that culture is the key to gender distinctions, because what one society defines as masculine another may see as feminine.

Some critics view Mead's findings as "too neat," as if she saw in these societies just the patterns she was looking for. Deborah Gewertz (1981) challenged what she called Mead's "reversal hypothesis," pointing out that Tchambuli males are really the more aggressive sex. Gewertz explains that Mead visited the Tchambuli (who themselves spell their name Chambri) during the 1930s, after they had lost much of their property in tribal wars, and observed men rebuilding their homes, a temporary role for Chambri men.

George Murdock's Research

In a broader study of more than 200 preindustrial societies, George Murdock (1937) found some global agreement on which tasks are feminine and which masculine. Hunting and warfare, Murdock observed, generally fall to men, and home-centered tasks such as cooking and child care tend to be women's work. With their simple technology, preindustrial societies apparently assign roles reflecting men's and women's physical characteristics. With their greater size and strength, men hunt game and protect the group; because women bear children, they do most of the work in the home.

Beyond this general pattern, Murdock found much variety. Consider agriculture: Women did the farming in about the same number of societies as men; in most societies, the two sexes divided this work. When it came to many other tasks, from building shelters to tattooing the body, Murdock found that preindustrial societies of the world were as likely to turn to one sex as the other.

EVALUATE Global comparisons show that, overall, societies do not consistently define tasks as feminine or masculine. With industrialization, the importance of muscle power declines, further reducing gender differences (Nolan & Lenski, 2010). In sum, gender is too variable to be a simple expression of biology; what it means to be female and male is mostly a creation of society.

CHECK YOUR LEARNING By comparing many cultures, what do we learn about the origin of gender differences?

Patriarchy and Sexism

Conceptions of gender vary, and there is evidence of societies in which women have greater power than men. One example is the Musuo, a very small society in southwestern China's Yunnan province, in which women control most property, select their sexual partners, and make most decisions about everyday life. The Musuo appear to be a case of **matriarchy** ("rule by mothers"), *a form of social organization in which females dominate males*, which has only rarely been documented in human history.

The pattern found almost everywhere in the world is **patriarchy** ("rule by fathers"), *a form of social organization in which males dominate females*. Global Map 13–1 shows the great variation in the relative power and privilege of women that exists from country to country. According to the United Nations's Gender Inequality Index, the Netherlands, Sweden, Denmark, and Switzerland give women the highest social standing; by contrast, women in Saudi Arabia, Niger, Afghanistan, and Yemen have the lowest social standing compared with men. Of the world's 195 nations, the United States was ranked 42nd in terms of gender equality (United Nations Development Programme, 2013).

The justification for patriarchy is **sexism**, *the belief that one sex is innately superior to the other*. Sexism is not just a matter of individual attitudes; it is also built into the institutions of society. *Institutional sexism* is found throughout the economy, with women highly concentrated in low-paying jobs. Similarly, the legal system has long excused violence against women, especially on the part of boyfriends, husbands, and fathers.

matriarchy a form of social organization in which females dominate males

patriarchy a form of social organization in which males dominate females

sexism the belief that one sex is innately superior to the other

Window on the World

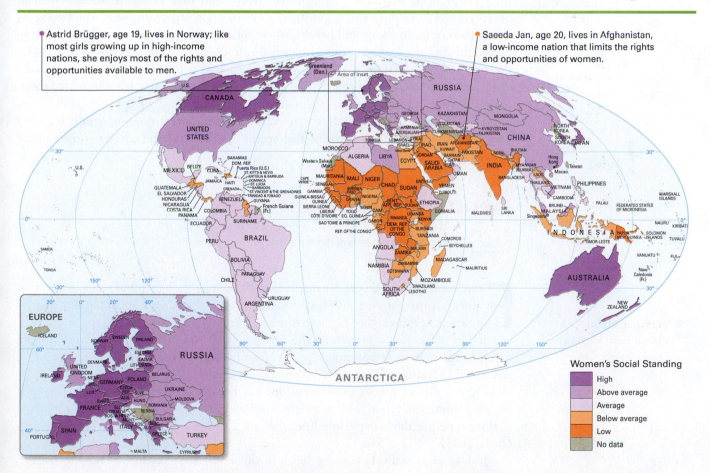

Astrid Brügger, age 19, lives in Norway; like most girls growing up in high-income nations, she enjoys most of the rights and opportunities available to men.

Saeeda Jan, age 20, lives in Afghanistan, a low-income nation that limits the rights and opportunities of women.

Women's Social Standing
- High
- Above average
- Average
- Below average
- Low
- No data

GLOBAL MAP 13–1 Women's Power in Global Perspective

Women's social standing in relation to men's varies around the world. In general, women live better in rich countries than in poor countries. Even so, some nations stand out: In the Netherlands, Sweden, Denmark, and Switzerland women come closest to social equality with men.

Source: Data from United Nations Development Programme (2013).

The Costs of Sexism

Sexism limits the talents and the ambitions of the half of the human population, who are women. Although men benefit in some respects from sexism, their privilege comes at a high price. Masculinity in our culture encourages men to engage in many high-risk behaviors: using tobacco and alcohol, playing dangerous sports, and even driving recklessly. As Marilyn French (1985) argues, patriarchy drives men to relentlessly seek control, not only of women but also of themselves and their world. Thus masculinity is linked not only to accidents but also to suicide, violence, and stress-related diseases. The *Type A personality*—marked by chronic impatience, driving ambition, competitiveness, and free-floating hostility—is one cause of heart disease and an almost perfect match with the behavior our culture considers masculine (Ehrenreich, 1983).

Finally, as men seek control over others, they lose opportunities for intimacy and trust. As one analyst put it, competition is supposed to "separate the men from the boys." In practice, however, it separates men from men and from everyone else (Raphael, 1988).

Must Patriarchy Go On?

In preindustrial societies, women have little control over pregnancy and childbirth, which limits the scope of their lives. In those same societies, men's greater height and physical strength are valued resources that give them power. But industrialization, including birth control technology, increases people's choices about how to live. In societies like our own, biological differences offer little justification for patriarchy.

But males are socially dominant in the United States and elsewhere. Does this mean that patriarchy is inevitable? Some researchers claim that biological factors such as differences in hormones and slight differences in brain structure "wire" the two sexes with different motivations and behaviors—especially aggressiveness in males—making patriarchy difficult or perhaps even impossible to change (Goldberg, 1974; Rossi, 1985; Popenoe, 1993b; Udry, 2000). However, most sociologists believe that gender is socially constructed and *can* be changed. The fact that no society has completely eliminated patriarchy does not mean that we must remain prisoners of the past.

To understand why patriarchy continues today, we must examine how gender is rooted and reproduced in society, a process that begins in childhood and continues throughout our lives.

Gender and Socialization

13.2 Explain the importance of gender to socialization.

From birth until death, gender shapes human feelings, thoughts, and actions. Children quickly learn that their society considers females and males different kinds of people; by about age three, they begin to think of themselves in these terms.

In the past, many people in the United States traditionally described women using terms such as "emotional," "passive," and "cooperative." By contrast, men were described as "rational," "active," and "competitive." It is curious that we were taught for so long to think of gender in terms of one sex being opposite to the other, especially because women and men have so much in common and also because research suggests that most people develop personalities that are a mix of feminine and masculine traits (Bem, 1993).

Just as gender affects how we think of ourselves, so it teaches us how to behave. **Gender roles** (also known as **sex roles**) are *attitudes and activities that a society links to each sex.* A culture that defines males as ambitious and competitive encourages them to seek out positions of leadership and play team sports. To the extent that females are defined as deferential and emotional, they are expected to be supportive helpers and quick to show their feelings.

Watch in **MySocLab**
Video: *Social Inequalities: Gender*

gender roles (also known as **sex roles**) attitudes and activities that a society links to each sex

Gender and the Family

The first question people usually ask about a newborn—"Is it a boy or a girl?"—has great importance because the answer involves not just sex but the likely direction of the child's life. In fact, gender is at work even before a child is born, especially in lower-income nations, because parents hope their firstborn will be a boy rather than a girl (Pappas, 2011).

Soon after birth, family members welcome infants into the "pink world" of girls or the "blue world" of boys (Bernard, 1981). People even send gender messages in the way they handle infants. One researcher at an English university presented an infant dressed as either a boy or a girl to a number of women; her subjects handled the "female" child tenderly, with frequent hugs and caresses, while treating the "male" child more aggressively, often lifting him up high in the air or bouncing him on a knee (Bonner, 1984; Tavris & Wade, 2001). The lesson is clear: The female world revolves around cooperation and emotion, and the male world puts a premium on independence and action.

Gender and the Peer Group

About the time they enter school, children begin to move outside the family and make friends with others of the same age. Considerable research points to the fact that young children tend to form single-sex play groups (Martin & Fabes, 2001).

Peer groups teach additional lessons about gender. After spending a year watching children at play, Janet Lever (1978) concluded that boys favor team sports with complex rules and clear objectives such as scoring runs or making touchdowns. Such games nearly always have winners and losers, reinforcing masculine traits of aggression and control.

Girls, too, play team sports. But, Lever explains, girls also play hopscotch, jump rope, or simply talk, sing, or dance. These activities have few rules, and rarely is victory the ultimate goal. Instead of teaching girls to be competitive, Lever explains, female peer groups promote the interpersonal skills of communication and cooperation, presumably the basis for girls' future roles as wives and mothers.

The games we play offer important lessons for our later lives. Lever's observations recall Carol Gilligan's gender-based theory of moral reasoning, discussed in Chapter 5 ("Socialization"). Boys, Gilligan (1982) claims, reason according to abstract principles. For them, "rightness" amounts to "playing by the rules." By contrast, girls consider morality a matter of responsibility to others.

Sex is a biological distinction that develops prior to birth. Gender is the meaning that a society attaches to being female or male. Gender differences are a matter of power, because what is defined as masculine typically has more importance than what is defined as feminine. Infants begin to learn the importance of gender by the way parents treat them. Do you think this child is a girl or a boy? Why?

Gender and Schooling

Gender shapes our interests and beliefs about our own abilities, guiding areas of study and, eventually, career choices (Correll, 2001). The types of courses people take in high school still reflect traditional gender patterns. For example, more girls than boys learn secretarial skills and take vocational classes such as cosmetology and food services. On the other hand, classes in woodworking and auto mechanics attract mostly young men.

Because women represent 57 percent of people on the campus and earn 59 percent of all associate's and bachelor's degrees, it is no surprise that they are now well represented in many fields of study that once excluded them, including mathematics, chemistry, and biology. But men still predominate in many fields, including engineering (earning 82 percent of all bachelor's degrees), computer science (82 percent), and the physical sciences (59 percent). Women tend to cluster in library science (87 percent of all bachelor's degrees), education (80 percent), and psychology (77 percent). In sociology, for 2010, women earned 70 percent of bachelor's degrees, 67 percent of master's degrees, and 61 percent of doctorates (U.S. Department of Education, National Center for Education Statistics, 2012; American Sociological Association, 2013).

Gender and the Mass Media

Since television captured the public imagination in the early 1950s, white males have held center stage; racial and ethnic minorities were all but absent from television until the early 1970s. Even when both sexes appeared on camera, men generally played the

Seeing Sociology in Everyday Life

The Beauty Myth

Beth: I can't eat lunch. I need to be sure I can get into that black dress for tonight.

Sarah: Maybe eating is more important than looking good for Tom.

Beth: That's easy for you to say. You're a size 2, and Jake adores you!

The Duchess of Windsor once remarked, "A woman cannot be too rich or too thin." The first half of her observation might apply to men as well, but certainly not the second. After all, the vast majority of ads placed by the $11-billion-a-year U.S. cosmetics industry and the $60-billion diet industry target women.

According to Naomi Wolf (1990), certain cultural patterns add up to a "beauty myth" that is damaging to women. First, the foundation of the beauty myth is the notion, taught from an early

One way our culture supports the beauty myth is through beauty pageants for women; over the years, contestants have become thinner and thinner.

age, that women should measure their worth in terms of physical appearance or, more specifically, how physically attractive they are *to men*. Of course, the standards of beauty embodied by the *Playboy* centerfold or the 100-pound New York fashion model are out of reach for most women.

Second, our society teaches women to prize relationships with men, whom they presumably attract with their beauty. Striving for beauty not only drives women to be extremely disciplined but also forces them to be highly attentive to and responsive to men. In short, beauty-minded women try to please men and avoid challenging male power.

Belief in the beauty myth is one reason that so many young women are focused on body image, particularly being as thin as possible, often to the point of endangering their health. During the past several decades, the share of young women who develop an eating disorder such as anorexia nervosa (dieting to the point of starvation) or bulimia (binge eating followed by vomiting) has risen dramatically.

The beauty myth, then, is the idea that striving to be physically attractive to men is the key to women's happiness. As Wolf sees it, however, such efforts are more likely to end up standing between women and their power and worthwhile accomplishments.

The beauty myth affects males as well: Men are told repeatedly that they should want to possess beautiful women. Such ideas about beauty reduce women to objects and motivate thinking about women as if they were dolls rather than human beings.

There can be little doubt that the idea of beauty is important in everyday life. According to Wolf, the question is whether beauty is about how we look or how we act.

What Do You Think?

1. Is there a "money myth" that states that people's income is a simple reflection of their talent? Does it apply more to one sex than to the other?

2. Can you see a connection between the beauty myth and the rise of eating disorders among young women in the United States?

3. Among people with physical disabilities, do you think that issues of "looking different" are more serious for women or for men? Why?

---

brilliant detectives, fearless explorers, and skilled surgeons. Women played the less capable characters, often unnecessary except for the sexual interest they added to the story. In recent years, more women have taken starring roles, but female stars earn less than their male counterparts. Before he left the show *Two and a Half Men*, for example, Charlie Sheen was the highest-paid male television actor, earning $875,000 an episode. Mariska Hargitay has been the highest-paid female actor, earning $400,000 an episode for *Law & Order: SVU*.

Historically, advertisements have shown women in the home, cheerfully using cleaning products, serving food, trying out appliances, and modeling clothes. Men predominate in ads for cars, travel, banking services, industrial companies, and alcoholic beverages.

The authoritative voiceover—the voice that describes a product on television and radio—is almost always male (Davis, 1993; Coltrane & Messineo, 2000; Messineo, 2008).

A careful study of gender in advertising reveals that men usually appear taller than women, implying male superiority. Women, by contrast, are more frequently presented lying down (on sofas and beds) or, like children, seated on the floor. Men's facial expressions and behavior give off an air of competence and imply dominance; women often appear childlike, submissive, and sexual. Men focus on the products being advertised, and women often focus on the men (Goffman, 1979; Cortese, 1999).

Advertising also perpetuates what Naomi Wolf (1990) calls the "beauty myth." The Seeing Sociology in Everyday Life box on page 366 takes a closer look at how this myth affects both women and men.

In our society, the mass media have enormous influence on our attitudes and behavior, and what we see shapes our view of gender. In the 2012 film *Hunger Games*, we see Jennifer Lawrence playing Katniss Everdeen, a take-charge, female lead character. Such a portrayal is an exception to the conventional pattern by which active males play against more passive females. In your opinion, how much can the mass media change conventional ideas about gender? Why?

Gender and Social Stratification

13.3 Analyze the extent of gender inequality in various social institutions.

Gender involves more than how people think and act. It is also about how society is organized, how our lives are affected by social hierarchy. The reality of gender stratification can be seen in just about every aspect of our everyday lives. We look, first, to the world of working women and men.

Working Women and Men

In 1900, just 20 percent of women but 80 percent of men were in the U.S. labor force. Today, the share of women has tripled, to almost 60 percent, while the share of men has fallen to 71 percent. As the Power of Society figure at the beginning of this chapter points out, our society continues to encourage men more than women to work for income.

Among people in the labor force, 70 percent of women and 85 percent of men work full time. From another angle, 47 percent of all U.S. jobs are held by women, and 53 percent are held by men (U.S. Department of Labor, 2012). Men may still dominate the labor force, but the once common view that earning income is a man's role no longer holds true.

Factors that have contributed to change in the U.S. labor force include the decline of farming, the growth of cities, shrinking family size, and a rising divorce rate. In the United States, along with most other nations of the world, women in the labor force working for income is now the rule rather than the exception. Women make up almost half the U.S. paid labor force, and 52 percent of U.S. married couples depend on two incomes.

In the past, many younger women in the labor force were childless. But today, 59 percent of married women with children under age six are in the labor force, as are 71 percent of married women with children between six and seventeen years of age. For families maintained by a woman (including single, widowed, divorced, or separated women with children), the comparable figures are 59 percent of women with younger children and 71 percent of women with older children (U.S. Department of Labor, 2012).

Gender and Occupations

Although women are closing the gap with men as far as working for income is concerned, the work done by the two sexes remains very different. The U.S. Department of Labor (2012) reports a high concentration of women in two types of jobs. Administrative support work

TABLE 13–1 Jobs with the Highest Concentrations of Women, 2011

Occupation	Number of Women Employed	Percentage in Occupation Who Are Women
1. Dental assistant	301,000	97.9%
2. Preschool or kindergarten teacher	691,000	97.7
3. Dental hygienist	144,000	97.5
4. Secretary or administrative assistant	2,753,000	95.9
5. Speech-language pathologist	120,000	95.6
6. Medical transcriptionist	70,596	95.4
7. Child care worker	1,163,000	94.5
8. Medical assistant	369,000	93.4
9. Hairdresser or cosmetologist	705,000	93.0
10. Teacher assistant	876,000	92.2

Source: U.S. Department of Labor (2012)

draws 22 percent of working women, most of whom are secretaries or other office workers. These are called "pink-collar jobs" because 73 percent are filled by women. Another 16 percent of employed women perform service work. Most of these jobs are in the food service industries, child care, and health care.

Table 13–1 shows the ten occupations with the highest concentrations of women. These jobs tend to be at the low end of the pay scale, with limited opportunities for advancement and with men as supervisors (U.S. Department of Labor, 2012).

Men dominate most other job categories, including the building trades, where 99 percent of brickmasons, stonemasons, and heavy-equipment mechanics are men. Likewise, men make up 86 percent of architects and engineers, 88 percent of police officers, 68 percent of lawyers, 66 percent of physicians and surgeons, and 57 percent of corporate managers. According to a recent survey, just nineteen of the Fortune 500 companies in the United States have a woman as their chief executive officer, and just 16 percent of the seats on corporate boards of directors are held by women. Of the 500 highest-paid corporate chief executive officers (CEOs), just seventeen are women. Such a gender imbalance leads many people to support increasing the leadership role of women in the business world. This claim is made not only as a matter of fairness but also because research into the earnings of this country's largest corporations shows that the companies with more women in leadership positions are more profitable (Graybow, 2007; Catalyst, 2012; *Forbes*, 2012; U.S. Department of Labor, 2012).

Gender stratification in everyday life is easy to see: Female nurses assist male physicians, female secretaries serve male executives, and female flight attendants are under the command of male airline pilots. In any field, the greater a job's income and prestige, the more likely it is to be held by a man. For example, women represent 98 percent of kindergarten teachers, 82 percent of elementary and middle school teachers, 58 percent of secondary school educators, 46 percent of professors in colleges and universities, and 26 percent of college and university presidents (*Chronicle of Higher Education*, 2012; U.S. Department of Labor, 2012).

How are women kept out of certain jobs? By defining some kinds of work as "men's work," society defines women as less competent than men. In a study of coal mining in southern West Virginia, Suzanne Tallichet (2000) found that most men considered it "unnatural" for women to work in the mines. Women who did so were defined as deviant and subject to labeling as "sexually loose" or as lesbians. Such labeling made these women outcasts, presented a challenge to holding the job, and made advancement all but impossible.

In the corporate world, too, the higher in the company we look, the fewer women we find. You hardly ever hear anyone say out loud that women don't belong at the top levels of a company. But many people seem to feel this way, which can prevent women from being promoted. Sociologists describe this barrier as a *glass ceiling* that is not easy to see but blocks women's careers all the same.

One challenge to male domination in the workplace comes from women who are entrepreneurs. There are now more than 8 million woman-owned businesses in the United States, double the number of a decade ago; they employ 7.6 million people and generate $1.2 trillion in sales. By starting their own businesses, women have shown that they can make opportunities for themselves apart from large, male-dominated companies (U.S. Census Bureau, 2010).

 **Watch** in **MySocLab** Video: *Sociology on the Job: Gender*

Gender and Unemployment

The unemployment rates for women and men typically rise and fall together, with men having a slightly higher level of joblessness. By the end of 2012, the unemployment rate for adult women stood at 6.7 percent, just below the figure of 6.8 percent for adult men (U.S. Department of Labor, 2012).

High unemployment among men reflects the fact that men's work is heavily in manufacturing, and many factory jobs have moved abroad. But the recent recession also brought job losses in the administrative support and service work that is performed mostly by women. During the last two years, as the nation has struggled to climb out of recession, the unemployment rate for men has fallen faster than the rate among women (Kochlar, 2011; U.S. Department of Labor, 2012).

Gender, Income, and Wealth

In 2011, the median earnings for women working full time were $37,118, and men working full time earned $48,202. This means that for every dollar earned by men, women earned about 77 cents. These earnings differences are greatest among older workers because older working women typically have less education and seniority than older working men. Earning differences are smaller among younger workers because younger men and women tend to have similar schooling and work experience.

The gender gap also varies according to occupation. Among pharmacists, for example, the gender gap is relatively small, with women earing 95 percent as much as men. Among corporate CEOs, however, the gap is much greater, with women earning just 69 percent as much as men (Goudreau, 2012).

Among all full-time workers regardless of age, 23 percent of women earned less than $25,000 in 2011, compared with 15 percent of comparable men. At the upper end of the income scale, men were twice as likely as women (25 percent versus 12.5 percent) to earn more than $75,000 (U.S. Census Bureau, 2012).

The main reason women earn less is the *type* of work they do: largely clerical and service jobs. In effect, jobs and gender interact. People still perceive jobs with less clout as "women's work," just as people devalue certain work simply because it is performed by women (England, Hermsen, & Cotter, 2000; Cohen & Huffman, 2003).

In recent decades, supporters of gender equality have proposed a policy of "comparable worth," paying people not according to the historical double standard but according to the level of skill and responsibility involved in the work. As an example of the problem, consider the case of floral designers, the people who make attractive displays of flowers. These workers—most of whom are women—earn about $12 an hour. At the same time, the people who drive the vans and other small trucks to deliver these flower arrangements—most of whom are men—earn about $16 an hour (U.S. Department of Labor, 2012). It is hard to see why floral arrangers would earn just 77 percent as much as van drivers. Is there a difference in the level of skill or training required? Or does the disparity reflect gender stratification?

In response to such patterns, several nations, including Great Britain and Australia, have adopted comparable worth policies, but these policies have found limited acceptance in the United States. As a result, women in this country lose as much as $1 billion in income annually.

A second cause of gender-based income disparity has to do with society's view of the family. Both men and women have children, of course, but our culture gives more of the responsibility of parenting to women. Pregnancy and raising small children keep many younger women out of the labor force at a time when their male peers are making significant career advancements. When women workers return to the labor force, they have less job experience and seniority than their male counterparts. These facts help explain a pattern documented by researchers: Women who live in states with greater access to oral contraceptives earn more over their careers than women who live in states that provide less access to contraception (Stier, 1996; Waldfogel, 1997; Grandoni, 2012).

In addition, women who choose to have children may be unable or unwilling to take on fast-paced jobs that tie up their evenings and weekends. To avoid role strain, they may take jobs that offer shorter commuting distances, more flexible hours, and employer-provided child care services. Women pursuing both a career and a family are torn between their dual responsibilities in ways that men are not. One study found that almost half of women in competitive jobs took time off to have children, compared to about 12 percent of men. Similarly, later in life, women are more likely than men to take time off from work to care for aging parents (Hewlett, 2005; Hewlett & Luce, 2010). Role conflict is also experienced by women on campus: Several studies confirm that young female professors with at least one child are less likely to have tenure than comparable men in the same field (Shea, 2002; Ceci & Williams, 2011).

The two factors noted so far—type of work and family responsibilities—account for about two-thirds of the earnings difference between women and men. A third factor—discrimination against women—accounts for most of the remainder (Fuller & Schoenberger, 1991). Because overt discrimination is illegal, it is practiced in subtle ways. Women on their way up the corporate ladder often run into the glass ceiling described earlier; company officials may deny its existence, but it effectively prevents many women from rising above middle management.

For all these reasons, women earn less than men in all major occupational categories. Even so, many people think that women own most of the country's wealth, perhaps because women typically outlive men. Government statistics tell a different story: Fifty-four percent of people with $2 million or more in assets are men, although widows are highly represented in this elite club (Johnson & Raub, 2006; Internal Revenue Service, 2012). Just 11 percent of the people identified by *Forbes* magazine as the richest people in the United States in 2012 were women (*Forbes*, 2012).

Housework: Women's "Second Shift"

In the United States, housework has always presented a cultural contradiction: We claim that keeping a home is essential for family life, but people get little reward for doing it (Bernard, 1981). Here, as around the world, taking care of the home and children has been considered "women's work"(see Global Map 6–1 on page 158). As women have entered the labor force, the amount of housework women do has gone down, but the *share* done by women has stayed the same. Figure 13–2 shows that overall women average 15.7 hours a week of housework, compared to 9.0 hours for men. As the figure shows, women in all categories do significantly more housework than men (U.S. Bureau of Labor Statistics, 2012).

Men do support the idea of women entering the paid labor force, and most count on the money women earn. But many men resist taking on an equal share of household duties (Heath & Bourne, 1995; Harpster & Monk-Turner, 1998; Stratton, 2001).

Gender and Education

A century ago, college was considered appropriate only for (well-to-do) men. By 1980, however, women earned a majority of all associate and bachelor's degrees. In 2010, women were a majority (57 percent) of the students on college and university campuses across the United States, earning 59 percent of all associate's and bachelor's degrees (U.S. Department of Education, National Center for Education Statistics, 2012).

According to recent research, women have a more positive view of the value of a college degree compared to men. This is a gender-linked difference that holds among all major racial and ethnic categories. As a result, among U.S. adults between the ages of twenty-five and twenty-nine, 36 percent of women have completed a four-year college degree, compared to just 28 percent of men (Wang & Parker, 2011).

As college doors have opened wider to women in recent decades, differences in men's and women's majors have become smaller. In 1970, for example, women accounted for just 17 percent of bachelor's degrees in the natural sciences, computer science, and engineering; by 2010, the proportion had more than doubled to 36 percent.

In 1992, for the first time, women earned a majority of postgraduate degrees, which are often a springboard to high-prestige jobs. In all areas of study in 2010, women earned 60 percent of all

Diversity Snapshot

- On average, women spend considerably more time doing housework than men.

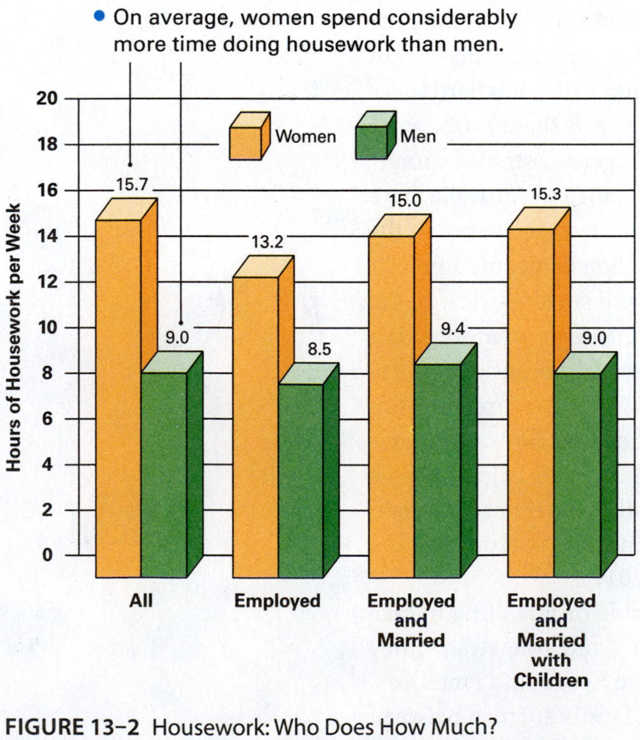

FIGURE 13–2 Housework: Who Does How Much?

Regardless of employment or family status, women do more housework than men. What effect do you think the added burden of housework has on women's ability to advance in the workplace?

Source: U.S. Bureau of Labor Statistics (2012).

master's degrees and 52 percent of all doctorates (including 61 percent of all Ph.D. degrees in sociology). Women have also broken into many graduate fields that used to be almost all male. For example, in 1970, only a few hundred women received a master's of business administration (M.B.A.) degree, compared to more than 80,000 women in 2010 (46 percent of all such degrees) (U.S. Department of Education, National Center for Education Statistics, 2012).

Despite this progress, men still predominate in some professional fields. In 2010, men received 53 percent of law degrees (LL.B. and J.D.), 52 percent of medical degrees (M.D.), and 54 percent of dental degrees (D.D.S. and D.M.D.) (U.S. Department of Education, National Center for Education Statistics, 2012). Many people in our society may still define high-paying professions (and the drive and competitiveness needed to succeed in them) as masculine. But the share of women in all these professions has risen and is now close to half. When will statistical parity be reached? Probably not for at least a few more years. For example, the American Bar Association (2012) reports that in 2012, men still accounted for 53 percent of law school students across the United States.

Based on the educational gains women have made, some analysts suggest that education is the one social institution where women rather than men predominate. More broadly, women's relative advantages in school performance have prompted a national debate about whether men are in danger of being left behind.

Gender and Politics

A century ago, almost no women held elected office in the United States. In fact, women were legally barred from voting in national elections until the passage of the Nineteenth Amendment to the Constitution in 1920. However, a few women were candidates for political office even before they could vote. The Equal Rights party supported Victoria Woodhull for the U.S. presidency in 1872; perhaps it was a sign of the times that she spent Election Day in a New York City jail. Table 13–2 identifies milestones in women's gradual movement into U.S. political life.

For a closer look at the position of men in society today, **Read More** in **MySocLab**, *Gender Today: Are Men Being Left Behind?*

TABLE 13–2 Significant Firsts for Women in U.S. Politics

1869	Law allows women to vote in Wyoming Territory.
1872	First woman to run for the presidency (Victoria Woodhull) represents the Equal Rights party.
1917	First woman elected to the House of Representatives (Jeannette Rankin of Montana).
1924	First women elected state governors (Nellie Taylor Ross of Wyoming and Miriam "Ma" Ferguson of Texas); both followed their husbands into office. First woman to have her name placed in nomination for the vice-presidency at the convention of a major political party (Lena Jones Springs, a Democrat).
1931	First woman to serve in the Senate (Hattie Caraway of Arkansas); completed the term of her husband upon his death and won reelection in 1932.
1932	First woman appointed to the presidential cabinet (Frances Perkins, secretary of labor in the cabinet of President Franklin D. Roosevelt).
1964	First woman to have her name placed in nomination for the presidency at the convention of a major political party (Margaret Chase Smith, a Republican).
1972	First African American woman to have her name placed in nomination for the presidency at the convention of a major political party (Shirley Chisholm, a Democrat).
1981	First woman appointed to the U.S. Supreme Court (Sandra Day O'Connor).
1984	First woman to be successfully nominated for the vice-presidency (Geraldine Ferraro, a Democrat).
1988	First woman chief executive to be elected to a consecutive third term (Madeleine Kunin, governor of Vermont).
1992	Political "Year of the Woman" yields record number of women in the Senate (six) and the House (forty-eight), as well as first African American woman to win election to U.S. Senate (Carol Moseley-Braun of Illinois), first state (California) to be served by two women senators (Barbara Boxer and Dianne Feinstein), and first woman of Puerto Rican descent elected to the House (Nydia Velazquez of New York).
1996	First woman appointed secretary of state (Madeleine Albright).
2000	First former First Lady to win elected political office (Hillary Rodham Clinton, senator from New York).
2001	First woman to serve as national security adviser (Condoleezza Rice); first Asian American woman to serve in a presidential cabinet (Elaine Chao).
2005	First African American woman appointed secretary of state (Condoleezza Rice).
2007	First woman elected as Speaker of the House (Nancy Pelosi).
2008	For the first time, women make up a majority of a state legislature (New Hampshire).
2013	Record number of women in the Senate (twenty) and the House (seventy-eight). Also, New Hampshire becomes the first state to have all-women leadership as the governor and all U.S. senators and members of Congress are women.

Explore the percentage of women in management, business, and finance in your local community and in counties across the United States in **MySocLab**

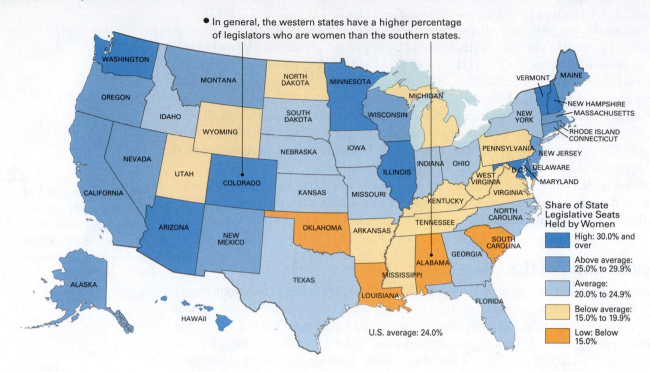

• In general, the western states have a higher percentage of legislators who are women than the southern states.

Share of State Legislative Seats Held by Women

- High: 30.0% and over
- Above average: 25.0% to 29.9%
- Average: 20.0% to 24.9%
- Below average: 15.0% to 19.9%
- Low: Below 15.0%

U.S. average: 24.0%

NATIONAL MAP 13–1 Women in State Government across the United States

Although women make up half of U.S. adults, in 2013 just 24 percent of the seats in state legislatures are held by women. Look at the state-by-state variations in the map. In which regions of the country have women gained the greatest political power? What do you think accounts for this pattern?

Source: Center for American Women and Politics (2012).

Today, thousands of women serve as mayors of cities and towns across the United States, and tens of thousands hold responsible administrative jobs in the federal government. At the state level, 24 percent of state legislators in 2013 were women (up from just 5 percent in 1971). National Map 13–1 shows where in the United States women have made the greatest political gains.

Change is also coming to the highest levels of power. The 113th Congress, which was sworn in in 2013, included 77 women (18 percent of 435 members) in the House of Representatives) and 20 women (20 percent of 100 members) in the Senate. These percentages are the highest ever in the history of the United States. In addition, 5 of the 50 state governors (10 percent) were women (Center for American Women and Politics, 2012; Litvan, 2012).

Women make up half of Earth's population, but they hold just 20 percent of seats in the world's 190 parliamentary governments. This number is considerably higher than the 3 percent of seats women held fifty years ago. In part, this rise reflects the fact that almost 100 countries have adopted some form of gender quota (either constitutional, enacted into legislation, or a voluntary goal of political parties) that ensures women a greater political voice. Even so, only in twenty-four countries, among them Sweden and Norway, do women represent at least one-third of the members of parliament (Paxton, Hughes, & Green, 2006; Inter-Parliamentary Union, 2012).

Finally, gender is linked to politics in another way—by shaping political attitudes. In general, women are somewhat more likely than men to favor liberal positions, such as expanding social programs that provide a "safety net" for people who are in need. On the other hand, men are somewhat more likely than women to favor conservative positions, such as building a stronger military. This difference in political attitudes is sometimes called the *gender gap*. In the 2012 presidential election, 55 percent of women, but just 45 percent of men, voted to reelect the Democratic presidential candidate, Barack Obama.

Gender and the Military

Since colonial times, women have served in the U.S. armed forces. Yet in 1940, at the outset of World War II, just 2 percent of armed forces personnel were women. In the fall of 2012, women represented 15 percent of all deployed U.S. troops as well as people serving in all capacities in the armed forces.

Clearly, women make up a growing share of the U.S. military, and virtually all military assignments are now open to both women and men. In 2013, Defense Secretary Leon Panetta announced that women would be allowed to serve in ground-combat operations, where gaining leadership experience is widely viewed as crucial for career advancement. For years, of course, women have been engaged in combat operations, because in today's high-tech military, the line between troop support and outright combat is not easy to draw, as women serving in Iraq have learned. In fact, between May 2003 and January 2013, the wars in Iraq and Afghanistan claimed the lives of 152 female soldiers (U.S. Department of Defense, 2012; Domi, 2013).

The debate on women's role in the military has been going on for centuries. Some people object to opening doors in this way, claiming that women lack the physical strength of men. Others point out that military women are better educated and score higher on intelligence tests than military men. But the heart of the issue is our society's deeply held view of women as *nurturers*—people who give life and help others—which clashes with the image of women trained to kill.

Whatever our views of women and men, the reality is that military women are in harm's way. In part, this fact reflects the strains of a military short of personnel. In addition, the type of insurgency that surrounds our troops in Iraq and Afghanistan can bring violent combat to any soldier at any time. Finally, our modern warfare technology blurs the distinction between combat and noncombat personnel. A combat pilot can fire missiles at a target miles away; by contrast, non-fighting medical evacuation teams must travel directly into the line of fire (Segal & Hansen, 1992; Kaminer, 1997; McGirk, 2006).

Read in **MySocLab**
Document: *Women in the U.S. Military: Growing Share, Distinctive Profile* by Eileen Patten and Kim Parker

Are Women a Minority?

A **minority** is *any category of people distinguished by physical or cultural difference that a society sets apart and subordinates.* Given the clear economic disadvantage of being a woman in our society, it seems reasonable to say that women are a minority in the United States even though they outnumber men.[1]

Even so, most white women do not think of themselves in this way. This is partly because, unlike racial minorities (including African Americans) and ethnic minorities (say, Hispanics), white women are well represented at all levels of the class structure, including the very top.

Bear in mind, however, that at every class level, women typically have less income, wealth, education, and power than men. Patriarchy makes women dependent on men—first their fathers and later their husbands—for their social standing (Bernard, 1981).

minority any category of people distinguished by physical or cultural difference that a society sets apart and subordinates

Violence against Women

In the nineteenth century, men claimed the right to rule their households, even to the point of using physical discipline against their wives, and a great deal of "manly" violence is still directed against women. A government report estimates that 452,232 aggravated assaults against women occur annually. To this number can be added 208,987 rapes or sexual assaults and 1.7 million simple assaults (U.S. Department of Justice, 2012).

Gender violence is also an issue on college and university campuses. According to research carried out by the U.S. Department of Justice, in a given academic year, about 3 percent of female college students become victims of rape (either attempted or completed). Over a typical college career, estimates suggest that between 10 and 20 percent of

**Watch** in **MySocLab**
Video: *The Basics: Gender*

---

[1] Sociologists use the term "minority" instead of "minority group" because, as explained in Chapter 7 ("Groups and Organizations"), women make up a *category*, not a group. People in a category share a status or identity but generally do not know one another or interact.

Window on the World

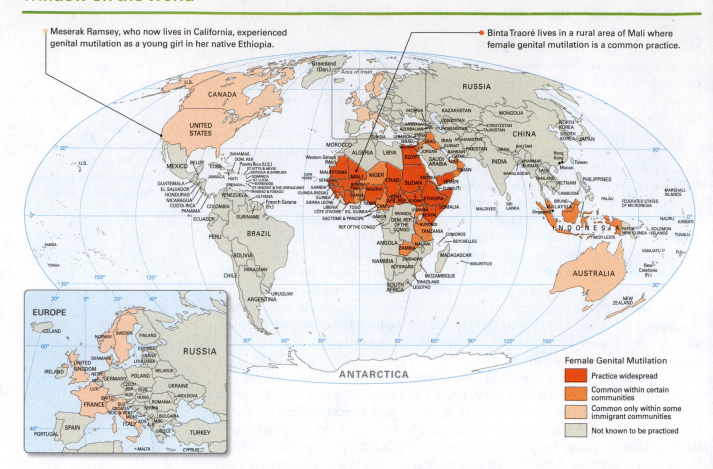

Meserak Ramsey, who now lives in California, experienced genital mutilation as a young girl in her native Ethiopia.

Binta Traoré lives in a rural area of Mali where female genital mutilation is a common practice.

Female Genital Mutilation

- ■ Practice widespread
- ■ Common within certain communities
- ■ Common only within some immigrant communities
- ■ Not known to be practiced

GLOBAL MAP 13–2 Female Genital Mutilation in Global Perspective

Female genital mutilation is known to be performed in at least twenty-nine countries around the world. Across Africa, the practice is common and affects a majority of girls in the eastern African nations of Sudan, Ethiopia, and Somalia. In several Asian nations, the practice is limited to a few ethnic minorities. In the United States, Canada, several European nations, and Australia, there are reports of the practice among some immigrants.

Sources: Population Reference Bureau (2010), World Health Organization (2006, 2011), and United Nations (2012).

college women experience rape or attempted rape. In 90 percent of all cases, the victim knew the offender, and most of the assaults took place in the woman's living quarters (U.S. Department of Justice, 2012).

Off campus as well, most gender-linked violence occurs where men and women interact most: in the home. Richard Gelles (cited in Roesch, 1984) argues that with the exception of the police and the military, the family is the most violent organization in the United States, and it is women who suffer most of the injuries. The risk of violence is especially great for low-income women living in families that face a great deal of stress; low-income women also have fewer options to get out of a dangerous home (Smolowe, 1994; Frias & Angel, 2007).

Violence toward women also occurs in casual relationships. As noted in Chapter 9 ("Deviance"), most rapes involve men known, and often trusted, by their victims. Dianne Herman (2001) claims that abuse of women is built into our way of life. All forms of violence against women—from the catcalls that intimidate women on city streets to a pinch in a crowded subway to physical assaults that occur at home—express what she calls a "rape culture" of men trying to dominate women. Feminists explain that sexual violence is fundamentally about *power*, not sex, and therefore should be understood as a dimension of gender stratification.

In global perspective, violence against women is built into other cultures in many different ways. One case in point is the practice of female genital mutilation, a painful and often dangerous surgical procedure that is performed in more than two dozen countries and is also known to occur in the United States, as shown in Global Map 13–2 . The

Thinking About Diversity: Race, Class, and Gender

Female Genital Mutilation: Violence in the Name of Morality

Meserak Ramsey, a woman born in Ethiopia and now working as a nurse in California, paid a visit to an old friend's home. Soon after arriving, she noticed her friend's eighteen-month-old daughter huddled in the corner of a room in obvious distress. "What's wrong with her?" she asked.

Ramsey was shocked when the woman said her daughter had recently had a clitoridectomy, the surgical removal of the clitoris. This type of female genital mutilation—performed by a midwife, a tribal practitioner, or a doctor and typically without anesthesia—is common in Nigeria, Sierra Leone, Senegal, Sudan, Ethiopia, Somalia, and Egypt, and is known to be practiced in certain cultural groups in other nations around the world. It is illegal in the United States.

Among members of highly patriarchal societies, husbands demand that their wives be virgins at marriage and remain sexually faithful thereafter. The point of female genital mutilation is to eliminate sexual feeling, which, people assume, makes women less likely to violate sexual norms and thus be more desirable to men who seek to control them. In about one-fifth of all cases an even more severe procedure, called infibulation, is performed, in which the entire external genital area is removed and the surfaces are stitched together, leaving only a small hole for urination and menstruation. Before marriage, a husband retains the right to open the wound and ensure himself of his bride's virginity.

How many women have undergone female genital mutilation? Worldwide, estimates suggest that at least 3 million girls (most live in Africa) undergo this procedure annually. Although the annual number is declining, globally, the number of women who have been cut in this way is at least 75 million and probably exceeds 100 million (Kristof & Wu Dunn, 2010; World Health Organization, 2012). In the United States, hundreds or even thousands of such procedures are performed every year. In most cases, immigrant mothers and grandmothers who have themselves been mutilated insist that young girls in their family follow their example. Indeed, many immigrant women demand the procedure *because* their daughters now live in the United States, where sexual mores are more lax. "I don't have to worry about her now," the girl's mother explained to Meserak Ramsey. "She'll be a good girl."

Medically, the consequences of genital mutilation include more than the loss of sexual pleasure. Pain is intense and can persist for years. There is also danger of infection, infertility, and even death. Ramsey knows the anguish all too well: She herself underwent genital mutilation as a young girl. She is one of the lucky ones who has had few medical problems since. But the extent of her suffering is suggested by this story: She invited a young U.S. couple to stay at her home. Late at night, she heard the woman's cries and burst into their room to investigate, only to learn that the couple was making love and the woman had just had an orgasm. "I didn't understand," Ramsey recalls. "I thought that there must be something wrong with American girls. But now I know that there is something wrong with me." Or with a system that inflicts such injury in the name of traditional morality.

What Do You Think?

1. Is female genital mutilation a medical procedure or a means of social control? Explain your answer.

2. Can you think of other examples of physical mutilation imposed on women? What are they?

3. What do you think should be done about female genital mutilation in places where it is widespread? Do you think respect for human rights should override respect for cultural differences in this case?

Sources: Crossette (1995), Boyle, Songora, & Foss (2001), and Sabatini (2011).

These young women have just undergone female genital mutilation. What do you think should be done about this practice?

Thinking About Diversity box describes an instance of female genital mutilation that took place in California and asks whether this practice, which some people defend as promoting "morality," amounts to a case of violence against women.

Violence against Men

If our way of life encourages violence against women, it may encourage even more violence against men. As noted in Chapter 9 ("Deviance"), in more than 80 percent of cases in which police make an arrest for a violent crime, including murder, robbery, and assault, the offender is a male. In addition, 78 percent of murder victims (and 55 percent of the victims of all of violent crime) are men (U.S. Department of Justice, Federal Bureau of Investigation, 2012; U.S. Bureau of Justice Statistics, 2012).

Our culture tends to define masculinity in terms of aggression and violence. "Real men" work and play hard, speed on the highways, and let nothing stand in their way. A higher crime rate is one result. But even when no laws are broken, men's lives involve more stress and isolation than women's lives, which is one reason that the suicide rate for men is four times higher than for women (Centers for Disease Control and Prevention, 2012). In addition, as noted earlier, men live, on average, about five fewer years than women.

Violence is not simply a matter of choices made by individuals. It is cultural—that is, built into our very way of life, with resulting harm to both men and women. In short, the way any society constructs gender plays an important part in how violent or peaceful that society will be.

Sexual Harassment

sexual harassment comments, gestures, or physical contacts of a sexual nature that are deliberate, repeated, and unwelcome

Sexual harassment refers to *comments, gestures, or physical contacts of a sexual nature that are deliberate, repeated, and unwelcome.* During the 1990s, sexual harassment became an issue of national importance that rewrote the rules for workplace interaction between women and men.

Most (but not all) victims of sexual harassment are women. The reason is that, first, our culture encourages men to be sexually assertive and to see women in sexual terms. As a result, social interaction between men and women in the workplace, on campus, and elsewhere can easily take on sexual overtones. Second, most people in positions of power—including business executives, doctors, bureau chiefs, assembly line supervisors, professors, and military officers—are men who oversee the work of women. Surveys carried out in widely different work settings show that about 3 percent of women claim that they have been harassed on the job in the last year and about half of women say they receive unwanted sexual attention (NORC, 2013:1486).

Sexual harassment is sometimes obvious and direct: A supervisor may ask for sexual favors from an employee and make threats if the advances are refused. Courts have declared that such *quid pro quo* sexual harassment (the Latin phrase means "one thing in return for another") is a violation of civil rights.

More often, however, the problem of unwelcome sexual attention is a matter of subtle behavior—sexual teasing, off-color jokes, comments about someone's looks—that may or may not be intended to harass anyone. But based on the *effect* standard favored by many feminists, such actions add up to creating a *hostile environment* for women in the workplace. Incidents of this kind are far more complex because they involve different perceptions of the same behavior. For example, a man may think that repeatedly complimenting a co-worker on her appearance is simply being friendly. The co-worker, on the other hand, may believe that the man is thinking of her in sexual terms and is not taking her work seriously, an attitude that could harm her job performance and prospects for advancement.

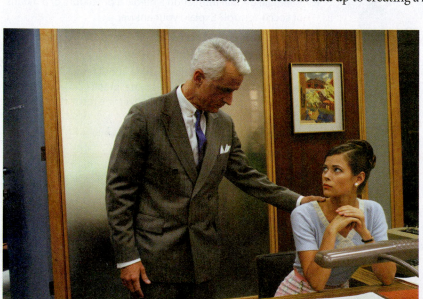

In recent decades, our society has recognized sexual harassment as an important problem. At least officially, unwelcome sexual attention is no longer tolerated in the workplace. The television show *Mad Men*, which gives us a window back to the early 1960s, shows us our society before the more recent wave of feminism began.

Pornography

Chapter 8 ("Sexuality and Society") defined *pornography* as sexually explicit material that causes sexual arousal. However, people take different views of exactly what is and what is not pornographic; the law gives local communities the power to define whether sexually explicit material violates "community standards of decency" and lacks "any redeeming social value."

Traditionally, people have raised concerns about pornography as a *moral* issue. But pornography also plays a part in gender stratification. From this point of view, pornography is really a *power* issue because most pornography dehumanizes women, depicting them as the playthings of men.

In addition, there is widespread concern that pornography encourages violence against women by portraying them as weak and undeserving of respect. Men show contempt for women defined in this way by striking out against them. Surveys show that about half of U.S. adults think that pornography encourages people to commit rape (NORC, 2013:424).

Like sexual harassment, pornography raises complex and sometimes conflicting concerns. Despite the fact that some material may offend just about everyone, many people defend the rights of free speech and artistic expression. Nevertheless, pressure to restrict pornography has increased in recent decades, reflecting both the long-standing concern that pornography weakens morality and the more recent concerns that it is demeaning and threatening to women.

Theories of Gender

13.4 Apply sociology's major theories to gender stratification.

Why does gender exist in all known societies? Sociology's macro-level approaches—the structural-functional and social-conflict approaches—address the central place of gender in social organization. In addition, the symbolic-interaction approach helps us see the importance of gender in everyday life. The Applying Theory table summarizes the important insights offered by each of these approaches.

Structural-Functional Theory

The structural-functional approach views society as a complex system of many separate but integrated parts. From this point of view, gender serves as a means to organize social life.

As Chapter 3 ("Culture") explained, the earliest hunting and gathering societies had little power over biology. Lacking effective birth control, women could do little to prevent pregnancy, and the responsibilities of child care kept them close to home. At the same time, men's greater strength made them better suited for warfare and hunting. Over the

Applying Theory

Gender			
	Structural-Functional Theory	**Symbolic-Interaction Theory**	**Social-Conflict and Intersection Theories**
What is the level of analysis?	Macro-level	Micro-level	Macro-level
What does gender mean?	Parsons described gender in terms of two complementary patterns of behavior: masculine and feminine.	Numerous sociologists have shown that gender is part of the reality that guides social interaction in everyday situations.	Engels described gender in terms of the power of one sex over the other. Gender interacts with class, race, and ethnicity to create various levels of disadvantage.
Is gender helpful or harmful?	Helpful. Gender gives men and women distinctive roles and responsibilities that help society operate smoothly. Gender builds social unity as men and women come together to form families.	Hard to say; gender is both helpful and harmful. In everyday life, gender is one of the factors that help us relate to one another. At the same time, gender shapes human behavior, placing men in control of social situations. Men tend to initiate most interactions, while women typically act in a more deferential manner.	Harmful. Gender limits people's personal development. Gender divides society by giving power to men to control the lives of women. Intersection theory explains that minority women face multiple disadvantages.

In the 1950s, Talcott Parsons proposed that sociologists interpret gender as a matter of *differences*. As he saw it, masculine men and feminine women formed strong families and made for an orderly society. In recent decades, however, social-conflict theory has reinterpreted gender as a matter of *inequality*. From this point of view, U.S. society places men in a position of dominance over women.

centuries, this sex-based division of labor became institutionalized and largely taken for granted (Lengermann & Wallace, 1985; Freedman, 2002).

Industrial technology opens up a much greater range of cultural possibilities. With human muscle power no longer the main energy source, the physical strength of men becomes less important. In addition, the ability to control reproduction gives women greater choices about how to live. Modern societies relax traditional gender roles as the societies become more meritocratic because rigid roles waste an enormous amount of human talent. Yet change comes slowly because gender is deeply rooted in culture.

Gender and Social Integration

As Talcott Parsons (1942, 1951, 1954) observed, gender helps integrate society, at least in its traditional form. Gender forms a *complementary* set of roles that links women and men into family units and gives each sex responsibility for carrying out important tasks. Women take the lead in managing the day-to-day life of the household and raising children. Men connect the family to the larger world as they participate in the labor force.

Thus gender plays an important part in socialization. Society teaches boys—presumably destined for the labor force—to be rational, self-assured, and competitive. Parsons called this complex of traits *instrumental* qualities. To prepare girls for child rearing, socialization stresses *expressive* qualities, such as emotional responsiveness and sensitivity to others.

Society encourages gender conformity by instilling in men and women a fear that straying too far from accepted standards of masculinity or femininity will cause rejection by the opposite sex. In simple terms, women learn to reject nonmasculine men as sexually unattractive, and men learn to reject unfeminine women. In sum, gender integrates society both structurally (in terms of what we do) and morally (in terms of what we believe).

EVALUATE Influential in the 1950s, this approach has lost much of its standing today. First, structural-functionalism assumes a singular vision of society that is not shared by everyone. For example, historically, many women have worked outside the home because of economic necessity, a fact not reflected in Parsons's conventional, middle-class view of social life. Second, Parsons's analysis ignores the personal strains and social costs of rigid gender roles. Third, in the eyes of those seeking sexual equality, Parsons's gender "complementarity" amounts to little more than women submitting to male domination.

CHECK YOUR LEARNING In Parsons's analysis, what functions does gender perform for society?

Symbolic-Interaction Theory

The symbolic-interaction approach takes a micro-level view of society, focusing on face-to-face interaction in everyday life. As suggested in Chapter 6 ("Social Interaction in Everyday Life"), gender affects everyday interaction in a number of ways.

Gender and Everyday Life

If you watch women and men interacting, you will probably notice that women typically engage in more eye contact than men do. Why? Holding eye contact is a way of encouraging the conversation to continue; in addition, looking directly at someone clearly shows the other person that you are paying attention.

This pattern is an example of sex roles, defined earlier as the way a society defines how women and men should think and behave. To understand such patterns, consider the fact that people with more power tend to take charge of social encounters. When men and women engage one another, as they do in families and in the workplace, it is men who typically initiate the interaction. That is, men speak first, set the topics of discussion, and control the outcomes. With less power, women are expected to be more *deferential,* meaning that they show respect for others of higher social position. In many cases, this means that women (just like children or others with less power) spend more time being silent and also encouraging men (or others with more power) not just with eye contact but by smiling or nodding in agreement. As a technique to control a conversation, men often interrupt others, just as they typically feel less need to ask the opinions of other people, especially those with less power (Tannen, 1990, 1994; Henley, Hamilton, & Thorne, 1992; Ridgeway & Smith-Lovin, 1999).

Gender and Reality Construction

If a woman is planning to marry a man, should she take his last name or keep her own? This decision is about more than how she will sign a check: It also affects how employers will see her and even her future pay.

In the United States today, about 8 percent of women who marry men keep their own name. This is a decline from the 1990s, when the share peaked at about 23 percent. Research shows that women who marry in their thirties (after they have started a career) are much more likely to keep their own name than women who marry in their early twenties. Research also shows that subjects asked to assess women's personal traits typically perceive those who take their husband's last name as more caring, dependent, and emotional (traditional feminine qualities). By contrast, they assess women who keep their maiden names as more ambitious, talented, and capable (more competitive against others, including men). Data on salaries reveal a significant difference in pay: Married women who keep their own name end up earning about 40 percent more than those who adopt their husband's name (Shellenbarger, 2011).

Such patterns demonstrate how gender shapes the reality we experience in everyday life. They also suggest that women who face a decision about surnames when they marry may consider the choice they make will carry particular meaning to others and have important consequences.

EVALUATE The strength of the symbolic-interaction approach is helping us see how gender plays a part in shaping almost all our everyday experiences. Our society defines men (and everything we consider to be masculine) as having more value than women (and what is defined as feminine). For this reason, just about every familiar social encounter is "gendered" so that men and women interact in distinctive and unequal ways.

The symbolic-interaction approach suggests that individuals socially construct the reality they experience as they interact every day, using gender-linked traits such as clothing and demeanor (and, for women, also last name) as elements of their personal "performances" that shape ongoing reality.

Gender plays a part in the reality we experience. Yet, as a structural dimension of society, gender is at least largely beyond the immediate control of any of us as individuals as it gives some people power over others. In other words, patterns of everyday social interaction reflect our society's gender stratification. Everyday interaction also helps reinforce this inequality. For example, to the extent that fathers take the lead in dinner table discussions, the entire family learns to expect men to "display leadership" and "show their wisdom." As mothers do the laundry, children learn that women are expected to do household chores.

A limitation of the symbolic-interaction approach is that by focusing on situational social experience, it says little about the broad patterns of inequality that set the rules for our everyday lives. To understand the roots of gender stratification, we have to "kick it up a level" to see more closely how society makes men and women unequal. We will do this using the social-conflict approach.

CHECK YOUR LEARNING Point to several ways that gender shapes the everyday face-to-face interactions of individuals.

Social-Conflict Theory

From a social-conflict point of view, gender involves much more than differences in behavior—gender is a structural system of *power* that provides privilege to some and disadvantage to others. Consider the striking similarity between the way traditional ideas about gender benefit men and harm women and the way ideas about race benefit men and disadvantage racial and ethnic minorities. Conventional ideas about gender do not make society operate smoothly, as a structural-functional analysis suggests. On the contrary, gender is a societal structure that creates division and tension, with men seeking to protect their privileges as women challenge the status quo.

As earlier chapters noted, the social-conflict approach draws heavily on the ideas of Karl Marx. Yet as far as gender is concerned, Marx was a product of his times, and his writings focused almost entirely on men. However, his friend and collaborator Friedrich Engels did develop a theory of gender stratification.

Gender and Class Inequality

Looking back through history, Engels saw that in hunting and gathering societies, the activities of women and men, though different, had equal importance. A successful hunt brought men great prestige, but the vegetation gathered by women provided most of a group's food supply. As technological advances led to a productive surplus, social equality and communal sharing gave way to private property and ultimately a class hierarchy, and men gained significant power over women. With surplus wealth to pass on to heirs, upper-class men needed to be sure that their sons were their own, which led them to control the sexuality of women. The desire to control both women's sexuality and private property brought about monogamous marriage and the family. Women were taught to remain virgins until marriage, to remain faithful to their husbands thereafter, and to build their lives around bearing and raising one man's children. Family law ensures that property is transmitted within families from one generation to the next, keeping the class system intact.

According to Engels (1902, orig. 1884), the rise of capitalism makes male domination even stronger. First, capitalism uses trade and industrial production to create more wealth, which gives greater power to men as income earners and owners of property. Second, an expanding capitalist economy depends on turning people, especially women, into consumers who seek personal fulfillment by buying and using products. Third, society assigns women the task of maintaining the home to free men to work in factories. The double exploitation of capitalism, as Engels saw it, lies in paying low wages for male labor and paying women no wages at all.

EVALUATE Social-conflict analysis is strongly critical of conventional ideas about gender, claiming that society would be better off if we minimized or even did away with this dimension of social structure. That is, this approach regards conventional families, which traditionalists consider personally and socially positive, as a social evil. A problem with social-conflict analysis, then, is that it minimizes the extent to which women and men live together cooperatively and often happily in families. A second problem lies in the assertion that capitalism is the basis of gender stratification. In fact, agrarian societies are typically more patriarchal than industrial-capitalist societies. In addition, although socialist nations, including the People's Republic of China and the former Soviet Union, did move women into the labor force, by and large they provided women with very low pay in sex-segregated jobs (Rosendahl, 1997; Haney, 2002).

CHECK YOUR LEARNING According to Engels, how does gender support social inequality in a capitalist class system?

Intersection Theory

In recent years, an additional social-conflict approach has gained great importance in sociology: intersection theory. The key insight of intersection theory is that there are multiple systems of stratification based on race, class, and gender, and these systems do not operate independently of one another. On the contrary, these dimensions of inequality intersect and interact. Formally, then, **intersection theory** is *analysis of the interplay of race, class, and gender, which often results in multiple dimensions of disadvantage.* Research shows that disadvantages linked to race and gender often combine to produce especially low social standing for some people (Ovadia, 2001).

Income data confirm the basic claim of intersection theory. Looking first at race and ethnicity, the median income in 2011 for African American women working full time was $33,727, which is 83 percent as much as the $40,554 earned by non-Hispanic white women; Hispanic women earned $29,537—just 73 percent as much as their white counterparts. Looking at gender, African American women earned 86 percent as much as African American men, and Hispanic women earned 92 percent as much as Hispanic men.

To explore the "intersection" of these dimensions of inequality, we find that some categories of women experience greater disadvantages. African American women earned only 64 percent as much as non-Hispanic white men, and Hispanic women earned just 56 percent as much (U.S. Census Bureau, 2012). These income differences reflect minority women's lower positions in the occupational and educational hierarchies.

Intersection theory helps us to see that although gender has a powerful effect on our lives, it does not operate alone. Class position, race and ethnicity, gender, and sexual orientation form a multilayered system that provides disadvantages for some and privileges for others (Saint Jean & Feagin, 1998).

The basic insight of intersection theory is that various dimensions of social stratification—including race and gender—can add up to great disadvantages for some categories of people. Just as African Americans earn less than whites, women earn less than men. Thus African American women confront a "double disadvantage," earning just 64 cents for every dollar earned by non-Hispanic white men. How would you explain the fact that some categories of people are much more likely to end up in low-paying jobs like this one?

EVALUATE If it is true that women are disadvantaged, it is also the case that some women are disadvantaged more than others. This insight is the first contribution of intersection theory. In addition, this approach helps us understand that, although the lives of all women are shaped by gender, there is no single "woman's experience." Rather, white women, Hispanic women, women of color (and also older women, women with disabilities, and lesbians) all have particular social standing and experiences that must be understood on their own terms.

A remaining issue that must be addressed is what people should *do* about gender stratification. This concern leads to another expression of social-conflict theory—feminism.

CHECK YOUR LEARNING State the basic idea of intersection theory. How does this theory help us understand the complexity of social stratification?

intersection theory analysis of the interplay of race, class, and gender, which often results in multiple dimensions of disadvantage

Feminism

(**13.5**) Contrast liberal, radical, and socialist feminism.

Feminism is *support of social equality for women and men, in opposition to patriarchy and sexism.* The first wave of feminism in the United States began in the 1840s as women opposed to slavery, including Elizabeth Cady Stanton and

feminism support of social equality for women and men, in opposition to patriarchy and sexism

In her recent book, Sheryl Sandberg, an executive at *Facebook*, describes the workplace barriers—including discrimination and sexual harassment—faced by women in our society. Sandberg also claims that to overcome these barriers, women must reject societal definitions of women as second-class citizens and "lean in" toward the goal of greater leadership positions. Critics suggest that the barriers to success faced by average women are far greater than those overcome by privileged women such as Sandberg.

Lucretia Mott, drew parallels between the oppression of African Americans and the oppression of women. Their main objective was obtaining the right to vote, which was finally achieved in 1920. But other disadvantages persisted, causing a second wave of feminism to arise in the 1960s that continues today.

Basic Feminist Ideas

Feminism views the everyday lives of women and men through the lens of gender. How we think of ourselves (gender identity), how we act (gender roles), and our social standing as women or men (gender stratification) are all rooted in the operation of society.

Although feminists disagree about many things, most support five general principles:

1. **Taking action to increase equality.** Feminist thinking is political; it links ideas to action. Feminism is critical of the status quo, pushing for change toward social equality for women and men. Many feminists are also guided by intersection theory to seek equality based on race and class as well as gender.

2. **Expanding human choice.** Feminists argue that cultural ideas about gender divide the full range of human qualities into two opposing and limiting spheres: the female world of emotion and cooperation and the male world of rationality and competition. As an alternative, feminists propose a "reintegration of humanity" by which all individuals develop all human traits (French, 1985).

3. **Eliminating gender stratification throughout society.** Feminism opposes laws and cultural norms that limit the education, income, and job opportunities of women. For this reason, feminists have long supported passage of the Equal Rights Amendment (ERA) to the U.S. Constitution, which states, in its entirety, "Equality of rights under the law shall not be denied or abridged by the United States or any State on account of sex." The ERA was first proposed in Congress in 1923. Although it has widespread support, it has yet to become law.

4. **Ending sexual violence.** Today's women's movement seeks to eliminate sexual violence. Feminists argue that patriarchy distorts the relationships between women and men, encouraging violence against women in the form of rape, domestic abuse, sexual harassment, and pornography (Dworkin, 1987; Freedman, 2002).

5. **Promoting sexual freedom.** Finally, feminism advocates women having control over their sexuality and reproduction. Feminists support the free availability of birth control information. As Figure 13–3 on page 383 shows, about three-quarters of married women of childbearing age in the United States use contraception; the use of contraceptives is far less common in many lower-income nations. Most feminists also support a woman's right to choose whether to have children or to end a pregnancy, rather than allowing men—as husbands, physicians, and legislators—to control their reproduction. Many feminists also support gay people's efforts to end prejudice and discrimination in a largely heterosexual culture (Ferree & Hess, 1995; Armstrong, 2002).

Types of Feminism

Although feminists agree on the importance of gender equality, they disagree on how to achieve it: through liberal feminism, socialist feminism, or radical feminism (Stacey, 1983; Vogel, 1983; Ferree & Hess, 1995; Armstrong, 2002; Freedman, 2002). The Applying Theory table highlights the key arguments made by each type of feminist thinking.

Liberal Feminism

Liberal feminism is rooted in classic liberal thinking that individuals should be free to develop their own talents and pursue their own interests. Liberal feminists accept the basic organization of our society but seek to expand the rights and opportunities of women. As they see it, gender should not operate as a form of caste, to the disadvantage of women. As an important step to achieving this goal, they support the passage of the Equal Rights Amendment. Liberal feminists also support reproductive freedom for all women. They respect the family as a social institution but seek changes in society, including more widely available maternity and paternity leave and child care for parents who work.

Given their beliefs in the rights of individuals, liberal feminists think that women should advance according to their individual efforts and merit, rather than by working collectively for change. Both women and men, through personal achievement, are capable of improving their lives, as long as society removes legal and cultural barriers.

Socialist Feminism

Socialist feminism evolved from the ideas of Karl Marx and Friedrich Engels. From this point of view, capitalism increases patriarchy by concentrating wealth and power in the hands of a small number of men. Socialist feminists do not think the reforms supported by liberal feminists go far enough. They believe that the family form fostered by capitalism must change in order to replace "domestic slavery" with some collective means of carrying out housework and child care. Replacing the traditional family can come about only through a socialist revolution that creates a state-centered economy to meet the needs of all.

Radical Feminism

Like socialist feminism, *radical feminism* finds liberal feminism inadequate. Radical feminists believe that patriarchy is so firmly entrenched that even a socialist revolution would not end it. Instead, reaching the goal of gender equality means that society must eliminate gender itself.

One possible way to achieve this goal is to use new reproductive technology that has been developed by scientists in recent decades (see Chapter 18, "Families"). This technology has the ability to separate women's bodies from the process of childbearing. With an end to motherhood, radical feminists reason, society could leave behind the entire family system,

Global Snapshot

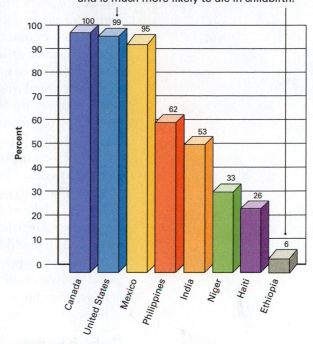

● Compared to a woman in the United States, an Ethiopian woman is far less likely to give birth with the help of medical professionals and is much more likely to die in childbirth.

FIGURE 13–3 Use of Contraception by Married Women of Childbearing Age

In the United States, most married women of childbearing age use contraception. In many lower-income countries, however, most women do not have the opportunity to make this choice.

Source: Population Reference Bureau (2012).

Applying Theory

Feminism			
	Liberal Feminism	**Socialist Feminism**	**Radical Feminism**
Does it accept the basic order of society?	Yes. Liberal feminism seeks change only to ensure equality of opportunity.	No. Socialist feminism supports an end to social classes and to family gender roles that encourage "domestic slavery."	No. Radical feminism supports an end to the family system.
How do women improve their social standing?	Individually, according to personal ability and effort.	Collectively, through socialist revolution.	Collectively, by working to eliminate gender itself.

liberating women, men, and children from the oppression of family, gender, and sex itself (Dworkin, 1987). Radical feminism seeks an egalitarian and gender-free society, a revolution much more sweeping than that sought by Marx.

Multicultural and Global Feminism

The three types of feminism considered so far are strategies for change. They also tend to portray women as a single category of humanity, defined by their sex and subordinated by their society. In recent decades, however, new feminist perspectives have highlighted not only the common situation faced by all women but also their social and cultural differences (Collins, 2000; hooks, 2000; Tong, 2009).

Multicultural feminism draws on the insights provided by intersection theory. That is, while all women have a common position of oppression in relation to men, the life experiences of women differ according to their race, ethnicity, and class position. To put this differently, gender stratification cannot be completely understood without also taking account of racial oppression and class differences. In other words, systems of hierarchy are multidimensional with various types of oppression that combine in their effects.

In the same way, global feminism attempts to recognize the common oppression in the lives of all the world's women, while also paying attention to their different positions within a world of nations set apart from one another by the system of global stratification. This simply means that the life experiences of women living in high-income nations are shaped by both oppression linked to gender and privilege linked to living in the core of the global capitalist economy. Similarly, the life experiences of women living in low-income nations reflect both gender stratification and their social location in an exploited region of the world.

Public Support for Feminism

Because all of the various types of feminism call for significant change, feminism has always been controversial. Today, about 18 percent of U.S. adults support the idea that "women should return to their traditional roles in society" (Pew Research Center, 2012). It is also true that only about 20 percent of U.S. adults claim that they are willing to identify themselves as feminists ("The Barrier That Didn't Fall," 2008).

But, over time, the share of the population seeking opportunity and equality for women has steadily increased. The most dramatic changes took place in the early 1970s; later changes have been far smaller. A larger share of women than men express support for feminism.

Most men and women who express criticism of feminism hold conventional ideas about gender. Some men oppose gender equality for the same reason that many white people have historically opposed social equality for people of color: They do not want to give up their privileges. Other men and women, including those who are neither rich nor powerful, distrust a social movement (especially its radical expressions) that attacks the traditional family and rejects social patterns that have guided male-female relations for centuries.

Men who have been socialized to value strength and dominance may feel uneasy about feminist ideals of men as gentle and warm (Doyle, 1983). Similarly, some women whose lives center on their husbands and children may think that feminism does not value the social roles that give meaning to their lives. In general, opposition to feminism is greatest among women who have the least education and those who do not work outside the home (Marshall, 1985; Ferree & Hess, 1995; CBS News, 2005).

Race and ethnicity play some part in shaping people's attitudes toward feminism. In general, African Americans (especially African American women) express the greatest support of feminist goals, followed by whites, with Hispanic Americans holding somewhat more traditional attitudes when it comes to gender (Kane, 2000).

Support for feminism is strong and widely evident in academic circles. But this does not mean that feminism is accepted uncritically. Some sociologists charge that feminism ignores a growing body of evidence that men and women think and act in somewhat different ways, and these differences may make complete gender equality impossible. Furthermore, say critics, with its drive to increase women's presence in the workplace, feminism undervalues the crucial and unique contribution women make to the development of children, especially in the first years of life (Baydar & Brooks-Gunn, 1991; Popenoe, 1993b; Gibbs, 2001).

Finally, there is the question of *how* women should go about improving their social standing. A large majority of adults in the United States think that women should have equal rights, but 70 percent also say that women should advance individually, according to their training and abilities; only 10 percent favor women's rights groups or collective action (NORC, 2013:585).

For these reasons, most opposition to feminism is directed toward its socialist and radical forms, while support for liberal feminism is widespread. In addition, we are seeing an unmistakable trend toward greater gender equality. In 1977, 65 percent of all adults endorsed the statement "It is much better for everyone involved if the man is the achiever outside the home and the woman takes care of the home and family." By 2012, the share supporting this statement had dropped sharply, to 31 percent (NORC, 2013: 449).

Gender: Looking Ahead

Predictions about the future are no more than educated guesses. Just as economists disagree about the likely inflation rate a year from now, sociologists can offer only general observations about the likely future of gender and society.

Looking back, change has been remarkable. A century ago, women were second-class citizens, without access to many jobs, barred from public office, and with no right to vote. Although women remain socially disadvantaged, the movement toward equality has surged ahead. Two-thirds of people entering the workforce in the 1990s were women, and by 2000, for the first time, a majority of families had both husband and wife in the paid labor force. Today's economy depends a great deal on the earnings of women. In addition, more than one in five married men in the United States have wives who earn more than they do (Fry & Cohn, 2010). As the share of women in higher education continues to rise, women's participation in the labor force has gone up along with the range of work that they perform.

Many factors have contributed to this long-term transformation. Perhaps most important, industrialization and advances in computer technology have shifted the nature of work from physically demanding tasks that favored male strength to jobs that require thought and imagination. This change puts women and men on an even footing. Also, because birth control technology has given us greater control over reproduction, women's lives are less constrained by unwanted pregnancies.

Many women and men have deliberately pursued social equality. For example, sexual harassment complaints in the workplace are taken much more seriously today than they were a generation ago. Another important trend is the increasing share of college degrees that are earned by women. This trend, in turn, is likely to reduce the earnings gap in the years to come as more women assume positions of power in the corporate and political worlds (Foroohar, 2011). As these trends unfold, social change involving gender in the twenty-first century may turn out to be as great as those that have already taken place.

How much do you think conceptions of gender will change over your lifetime? Will there be more change in the lives of women or men? Why?

Seeing Sociology in Everyday Life

Can you spot "gender messages" in the world around you?

As this chapter makes clear, gender is one of the basic organizing principles of everyday life. Most of the places we go and most of the activities we engage in as part of our daily routines are "gendered," meaning that they are defined as either more masculine or more feminine. Understanding this fact, corporations keep gender in mind when they market products to the public. Take a look at the ads shown on this page and on page 387. In each case, can you explain how companies use gender to sell these products?

There are a lot of gender dynamics going on in this ad. What do you see?

Generally, our society defines cosmetics as feminine because most cosmetics are marketed toward women. How and why is this ad different?

What gender messages do you see in this ad?

HINT Looking for "gender messages" in ads is a process that involves several levels of analysis. Start on the surface by noting everything obvious in the ad, including the setting, the background, and especially the people. Then notice how the people are shown—what they are doing, how they are situated, their facial expressions, how they are dressed, and how they appear to relate to each other. Finally, state what you think is the message of the ad, based on both the ad itself and also what you know about the surrounding society.

Seeing Sociology in *Your* Everyday Life

1. Look through some recent magazines and select three advertisements that involve gender. In each case, provide analysis of how gender is used in the ad.

2. Go to MySocLab and click on the Student Resources link to access the Sociology in Focus blog, where you can read the latest posts by a team of young sociologists who apply the sociological perspective to topics of popular culture.

3. Do some research on the history of women's issues in your state. When was the first woman sent to Congress? What laws once existed that restricted the work women could do? Do any such laws exist today? Go to the "Seeing Sociology in *Your* Everyday Life" feature in MySocLab to read more about how gender can be changed and learn some of the personal benefits that come from recognizing this fact.

Making the Grade

Gender and Inequality

(13.1) Describe research that points to how society creates gender stratification. (pages 360–64)

Gender refers to the meaning a culture attaches to being female or male.

- Evidence that gender is rooted in culture includes global comparisons by Margaret Mead and others showing how societies define what is feminine and masculine in various ways.
- Gender is not only about difference: Because societies give more power and other resources to men than to women, gender is an important dimension of social stratification. **Sexism** is built into the operation of social institutions.
- Although some degree of **patriarchy** is found almost everywhere, it varies throughout history and from society to society.

gender the personal traits and social positions that members of a society attach to being female or male

gender stratification the unequal distribution of wealth, power, and privilege between men and women

matriarchy a form of social organization in which females dominate males

patriarchy a form of social organization in which males dominate females

sexism the belief that one sex is innately superior to the other

Gender and Socialization

(13.2) Explain the importance of gender to socialization. (pages 364–67)

👁 **Watch** the **Video** in **MySocLab**

Through the socialization process, gender becomes part of our personalities (**gender identity**) and our actions (**gender roles**). All the major agents of socialization—family, peer groups, schools, and the mass media—reinforce cultural definitions of what is feminine and masculine.

gender roles (also known as sex roles) attitudes and activities that a society links to each sex

Gender and Social Stratification

(13.3) Analyze the extent of gender inequality in various social institutions. (pages 367–77)

👁 **Watch** the **Video** in **MySocLab**   ✳ **Explore** the **Map** in **MySocLab**

📖 **Read** the **Document** in **MySocLab**   👁 **Watch** the **Video** in **MySocLab**

Gender stratification shapes **the workplace**:
- A majority of women are now in the paid labor force, but 38% hold clerical or service jobs.
- Comparing full-time U.S. workers, women earn 77% as much as men.

Gender stratification shapes **family life**:
- Most unpaid housework is performed by women, whether or not they hold jobs outside the home.
- Pregnancy and raising small children keep many women out of the labor force at a time when their male peers are making important career gains.

Gender stratification shapes **education**:
- Women now earn 59% of all associate and bachelor's degrees.
- Women make up 47% of law school students and are an increasing share of graduates in professions traditionally dominated by men, including medicine and business administration.

Gender stratification shapes **politics**:
- Although the number of women in politics has increased significantly, the vast majority of elected officials, especially at the national level, are men.
- Women make up only about 15% of U.S. military personnel.

Violence against women and men is a widespread problem linked to how a society defines gender.
- **Sexual harassment** mostly victimizes women because our culture encourages men to be assertive and to see women in sexual terms.
- **Pornography** portrays women as sexual objects. Many see pornography as a moral issue; because pornography dehumanizes women, it is also a power issue.

minority any category of people distinguished by physical or cultural difference that a society sets apart and subordinates

sexual harassment comments, gestures, or physical contacts of a sexual nature that are deliberate, repeated, and unwelcome

Theories of Gender

13.4 Apply sociology's major theories to gender stratification. (pages 377–81)

Structural-functional theory suggests that

- in preindustrial societies, distinctive roles for males and females reflect biological differences between the sexes.
- in industrial societies, marked gender inequality becomes dysfunctional and gradually decreases.

Talcott Parsons described gender differences in terms of complementary roles that promote the social integration of families and society as a whole.

Symbolic-interaction theory suggests that

- individuals use gender as one element of their personal performances as they socially construct reality through everyday interactions.
- gender plays a part in shaping almost all our everyday experiences.

Because our society defines men as having more value than women, the sex roles that define how women and men should behave place men in control of social situations; women play a more deferential role.

Social-conflict theory suggests that

- gender is an important dimension of social inequality and social conflict.
- gender inequality benefits men and disadvantages women.

Friedrich Engels tied gender stratification to the rise of private property and a class hierarchy. Marriage and the family are strategies by which men control their property through control of the sexuality of women. Capitalism exploits everyone by paying men low wages and assigning women the task of maintaining the home.

Intersection theory suggests that

- particular dimensions of difference in women's lives combine in a multi-layered system, creating unique disadvantage for various categories of women.
- women of color encounter greater social disadvantages than white women and earn much less than white men.

intersection theory analysis of the interplay of race, class, and gender, which often results in multiple dimensions of disadvantage

Feminism

13.5 Contrast liberal, radical, and socialist feminism. (pages 381–85)

Feminism

- endorses the social equality of women and men and opposes patriarchy and sexism.
- seeks to eliminate violence against women.
- advocates giving women control over their reproduction.

There are three types of feminism:

- Liberal feminism seeks equal opportunity for both sexes within the existing society.
- Socialist feminism claims that gender equality will come about by replacing capitalism with socialism.
- Radical feminism seeks to eliminate the concept of gender itself and to create an egalitarian and gender-free society.

Multicultural feminism expands the focus on gender stratification to take into account the intersection of gender with race and ethnicity; global feminism points out that gender inequality also involves the varying positions of women around the world in the system of global stratification.

Today, support for social equality for women and men is widespread. Just 18% of U.S. adults say that women should return to their traditional roles in society. Support for liberal feminism is widespread, with greater opposition directed toward socialist and radical feminism.

feminism support of social equality for women and men, in opposition to patriarchy and sexism

14 Race and Ethnicity

(((Listen to **Chapter 14** in **MySocLab**

LEARNING OBJECTIVES

14.1 Explain the social construction of race and ethnicity.

14.2 Describe the extent and causes of prejudice.

14.3 Distinguish discrimination from prejudice.

14.4 Identify examples of pluralism, assimilation, segregation, and genocide.

14.5 Assess the social standing of racial and ethnic categories of U.S. society.

the Power of Society

to shape political attitudes

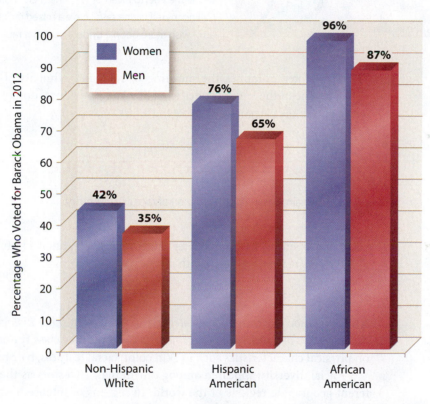

Percentage Who Voted for Barack Obama in 2012

- Women
- Men

Non-Hispanic White		Hispanic American		African American	
42%	35%	76%	65%	96%	87%

Source: Center for American Women and Politics (2012)

Is our choice to cast a vote for a particular candidate a purely "personal" decision? In the 2012 presidential election, just 42 percent of non-Hispanic white women and 35 percent of non-Hispanic white men voted for Barack Obama. But Hispanic Americans and especially African Americans supported him overwhelmingly, ensuring his victory. The political choices people make when they vote in elections are not simply personal but also reflect race, ethnicity, and other societal factors.

Chapter Overview

This chapter explains how race and ethnicity are created by society. The United States is a nation as racially and ethnically diverse as any in the world. Here and elsewhere, both race and ethnicity are not only matters of difference but also dimensions of social inequality.

On a cool November morning in New York City, the instructor of a sociology class at Bronx Community College is leading a small-group discussion of race and ethnicity. He explains that the meaning of both concepts is far less clear than most people think. Then he asks, "How do you describe yourself?"

Eva Rodriguez leans forward in her chair and is quick to respond. "Who am I? Or should I say *what* am I? This is hard for me to answer. Most people think of race as black and white. But it's not. I have both black and white ancestry in me, but you know what? I don't think of myself in that way. I don't think of myself in terms of race at all. It would be better to call me Puerto Rican or Hispanic. Personally, I prefer the term 'Latina.' Calling myself Latina says I have a mixed racial heritage, and that's what I am. I wish more people understood that race is not clear-cut."

This chapter examines the meaning of race and ethnicity. There are now millions of people in the United States who, like Eva Rodriguez, do not think of themselves in terms of a single category but as having a mix of ancestry.

The Social Meaning of Race and Ethnicity

14.1 Explain the social construction of race and ethnicity.

As the opening to this chapter suggests, people often confuse race and ethnicity. For this reason, we begin with some basic definitions.

Race

A **race** is *a socially constructed category of people who share biologically transmitted traits that members of a society consider important.* People may classify one another racially based on physical characteristics such as skin color, facial features, hair texture, and body shape.

Racial diversity appeared among our human ancestors as the result of living in different geographic regions of the world. In regions of intense heat, for example, humans developed darker skin (from the natural pigment melanin) as protection from the sun; in regions with moderate climates, people have lighter skin. Such differences are literally only skin deep because human beings the world over are members of a single biological species.

The striking variety of physical traits found today is also the product of migration; genetic characteristics once common to a single place (such as light skin or curly hair) are now found in many lands. Especially pronounced is the racial mix in the Middle East (that is, western Asia), historically a crossroads of migration. Greater physical uniformity characterizes more isolated people, such as the island-dwelling Japanese. But every population has some genetic mixture, and increasing contact among the world's people ensures even more blending of physical characteristics in the future.

Although we think of race in terms of biological elements, race is a socially constructed concept. It is true that human beings differ in any number of ways involving physical traits, but a "race" comes into being only when the members of a society decide that some physical trait (such as skin color or eye shape) actually *matters*.

race a socially constructed category of people who share biologically transmitted traits that members of a society consider important

ethnicity a shared cultural heritage

The range of biological variation in human beings is far greater than any system of racial classification allows. This fact is made obvious by trying to place all of the people pictured here into simple racial categories.

Because race involves social definitions, it is a highly variable concept. For example, the members of U.S. society consider racial differences more important than people of many other countries. We also tend to "see" three racial categories—typically, black, white, and Asian—while people in other societies identify many more categories. People in Brazil, for example, distinguish between *branca* (white), *parda* (brown), *morena* (brunette), *mulata* (mulatto), *preta* (black), and *amarela* (yellow) (Inciardi, Surratt, & Telles, 2000).

In addition, race may be defined differently by various categories of people within a society. In the United States, for example, research shows that white people "see" black people as having darker skin than black people do (Hill, 2002).

The meanings and importance of race not only differ from place to place but also change over time. Back in 1900, for example, it was common in the United States to consider people of Irish, Italian, or Jewish ancestry as "nonwhite." By 1950, however, this was no longer the case, and such people today are considered part of the "white" category (Loveman, 1999; Brodkin, 2007).

Today, the Census Bureau allows people to describe themselves using more than one racial category (offering six single-race options and fifty-seven multiracial options). Our society officially recognizes a wide range of multiracial people (U.S. Census Bureau, 2012).

Racial Types

Scientists invented the concept of race more than a century ago as they tried to organize the world's physical diversity into three racial types. They called people with lighter skin and fine hair *Caucasoid,* people with darker skin and coarse hair *Negroid,* and people with yellow or brown skin and distinctive folds on the eyelids *Mongoloid.*

Sociologists consider such terms misleading at best and harmful at worst. For one thing, no society contains biologically "pure" people. The skin color of people we might call "Caucasoid" (or "Indo-European," "Caucasian," or more commonly "white") ranges from very light (typical in Scandinavia) to very dark (in southern India). The same variation exists among so-called "Negroids" ("Africans" or more commonly "black" people) and "Mongoloids" ("Asians"). In fact, many "white" people (say, in southern India) actually have darker skin than many "black" people (the Aborigines of Australia). Overall, the three racial categories differ in just 6 percent of their genes, and there is actually more genetic variation *within* each category than *between* categories. This means that two people in the

Read in MySocLab Document: *The Souls of Black Folk* by W.E.B. Du Bois

European nation of Sweden, randomly selected, are likely to have at least as much genetic difference as a Swede and a person in the African nation of Senegal (Harris & Sim, 2002; American Sociological Association, 2003; California Newsreel, 2003).

So how important is race? From a biological point of view, the only significance of knowing people's racial category is assessing the risk factors for a few diseases. Why, then, do societies make so much of race? Such categories allow societies to rank people in a hierarchy, giving some people more money, power, and prestige than others and allowing some people to feel that they are inherently "better" than others. Because race may matter so much, societies may construct racial categories in extreme ways. Throughout much of the twentieth century, for example, many southern states labeled as "colored" anyone with as little as one thirty-second African ancestry (that is, one African American great-great-great-grandparent). Today, the law allows parents to declare the race of a child (or not) as they wish. Even so, most members of U.S. society are still very sensitive to people's racial backgrounds.

A Trend toward Mixture

Over many generations and throughout the Americas, the genetic traits from around the world have become mixed. Many "black" people have a significant Caucasoid ancestry, just as many "white" people have some Negroid genes. Whatever people may think, race is not a black-and-white issue.

Today, people are more willing to define themselves as multiracial. On the most recent U.S. Census survey for 2011, 8.7 million people described themselves by checking two or more racial categories. In 2011, 6 percent of children under the age of five were multiracial compared to less than 1 percent of people age 65 and older.

Ethnicity

Ethnicity is *a shared cultural heritage*. People define themselves—or others—as members of an *ethnic category* based on common ancestry, language, or religion that gives them a distinctive social identity. The United States is a multiethnic society. Even though we favor the English language, more than 60 million people (21 percent of the U.S. population) speak Spanish, Italian, German, French, Chinese, or some other language in their homes. In California, about 44 percent of the population does so (U.S. Census Bureau, 2012).

With regard to religion, the United States is a predominantly Protestant nation, but most people of Spanish, Italian, and Polish descent are Roman Catholic, and many of Greek, Ukrainian, and Russian descent belong to the Eastern Orthodox Church. More than 5.2 million Jewish Americans have ancestral ties to various nations around the world.

TABLE 14–1 Racial and Ethnic Categories in the United States, 2011

Racial or Ethnic Classification*	Approximate U.S. Population	Share of Total Population
Hispanic descent	**52,045,277**	**16.7%**
Mexican	33,557,922	10.8%
Puerto Rican	4,885,294	1.6%
Cuban	1,891,014	0.6%
Other Hispanic	11,605,686	3.7%
African descent	**40,750,746**	**13.1%**
Nigerian	275,174	0.1%
Ethiopian	192,045	0.1%
Somalian	131,894	<
Other African	40,151,633	12.9%
Native American descent	**2,547,006**	**0.8%**
American Indian	2,064,928	0.7%
Alaska Native Tribes	121,883	<
Other Native American	360,195	0.1%
Asian or Pacific Island descent	**16,270,474**	**5.2%**
Chinese	3,520,150	1.1%
Asian Indian	2,908,204	0.9%
Filipino	2,538,325	0.8%
Vietnamese	1,669,447	0.5%
Korean	1,449,876	0.5%
Japanese	756,898	0.2%
Cambodian	253,830	0.1%
Other Asian or Pacific Islander	3,173,744	1.0%
West Indian descent	**2,768,024**	**0.9%**
Arab descent	**1,822,447**	**0.6%**
Non-Hispanic European descent	**197,510,927**	**63.4%**
German	47,392,523	15.2%
Irish	34,520,787	11.1%
English	25,696,424	8.2%
Italian	17,460,857	5.6%
Polish	9,447,939	3.0%
French	8,596,126	2.8%
Scottish	5,412,820	1.7%
Dutch	4,441,071	1.4%
Norwegian	4,398,767	1.4%
Other non-Hispanic European	42,483,926	13.6%
Two or more races	**8,721,818**	**2.8%**

*People of Hispanic descent may be of any race. Many people also identify with more than one ethnic category. Therefore, figures total more than 100 percent.

Source: U.S. Census Bureau (2012).

The population of Muslim men and women is generally estimated at between 2 and 3 million and is rapidly increasing due to both immigration and a high birthrate (Pew Research Center, 2011; ARDA, 2012).

Like race, the concept of "ethnicity" is socially constructed, becoming important only because society defines it that way. For example, U.S. society defines people of Spanish descent as "Latin," even though Italy has a more "Latin" culture than Spain. People of Italian descent are not viewed as Latin but as "European" and therefore less different from the point of view of the European majority (Camara, 2000; Brodkin, 2007). Like racial differences, the importance of ethnic differences can change over time. A century ago, Catholics and Jews were considered "different" in the mostly Protestant United States. This is much less true today.

Keep in mind that race is constructed from *biological* traits and ethnicity is constructed from *cultural* traits. However, the two often go hand in hand. For example, Japanese Americans have distinctive physical traits and, for those who hold to a traditional way of life, a distinctive culture as well. Table 14–1 on page 394 presents the most recent data on the racial and ethnic diversity of the United States.

minority any category of people distinguished by physical or cultural difference that a society sets apart and subordinates

On an individual level, people play up or play down cultural traits, depending on whether they want to fit in or stand apart from the surrounding society. Immigrants may drop their cultural traditions or, like many people of Native American descent in recent years, try to revive their heritage. For most people, ethnicity is more complex than race because they identify with several ethnic backgrounds. Rock-and-roll legend Jimi Hendrix was African American, white, and Cherokee; news anchor Soledad O'Brian considers herself both white and black, both Australian and Irish, and both Anglo and Hispanic.

Minorities

March 3, Dallas, Texas. *The lobby of just about any hotel in a major U.S. city presents a lesson in contrasts: The majority of the guests checking in are white; the majority of hotel employees who carry luggage, serve food, and clean the rooms are racial or ethnic minorities.*

As defined in Chapter 13 ("Gender Stratification"), a **minority** is *any category of people distinguished by physical or cultural difference that a society sets apart and subordinates.* Minority standing can be based on race, ethnicity, or both. As shown in Table 14–1, non-Hispanic white people (63 percent of the total) are still a majority of the U.S. population. But the share of minorities is increasing. Today, minorities are a majority in four states (California, New Mexico, Texas, and Hawaii) and in more than half of the country's 100 largest cities. By 2011, a majority of the births in the United States were racial and ethnic minorities. This fact—coupled to the effects

Diversity Snapshot

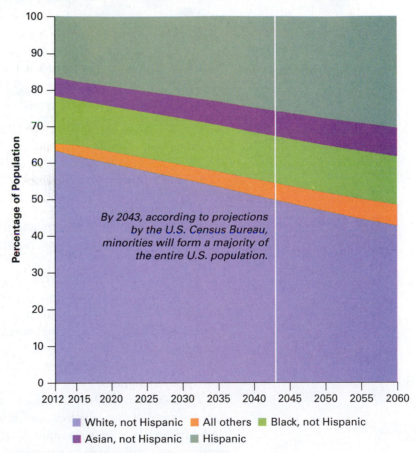

By 2043, according to projections by the U.S. Census Bureau, minorities will form a majority of the entire U.S. population.

■ White, not Hispanic   ■ All others   ■ Black, not Hispanic
■ Asian, not Hispanic   ■ Hispanic

FIGURE 14–1 The Coming Minority Majority

According to projections from the Census Bureau, the United States will have a minority majority in the year 2043, less than thirty years from now. By that time, as the figure shows, the white, non-Hispanic population will actually decline, as the number of Asian Americans, African Americans, and especially Hispanic Americans increases. What changes do you expect this trend will bring to the United States?

Source: U.S. Census Bureau (2012).

Seeing Ourselves

 Explore the percentage of minority people in your local community and in counties across the United States in **MySocLab**

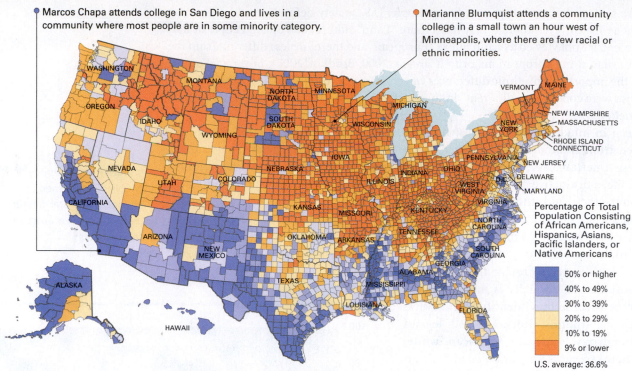

● Marcos Chapa attends college in San Diego and lives in a community where most people are in some minority category.

● Marianne Blumquist attends a community college in a small town an hour west of Minneapolis, where there are few racial or ethnic minorities.

Percentage of Total Population Consisting of African Americans, Hispanics, Asians, Pacific Islanders, or Native Americans

- 50% or higher
- 40% to 49%
- 30% to 39%
- 20% to 29%
- 10% to 19%
- 9% or lower

U.S. average: 36.6%

NATIONAL MAP 14–1 Where the Minority Majority Already Exists

Racial and ethnic minorities are now a majority of the population in four states—Hawaii, California, New Mexico, and Texas—as well as in the District of Columbia. At the other extreme, Vermont and Maine have the smallest share (about 6 percent) of minorities. Why do you think states with high minority populations are located in the South and Southwest?

Source: U.S. Census Bureau (2012).

of immigration—means that the minority share of the population will steadily increase. By 2043, according the U.S. Census Bureau (2012), minorities are likely to form a majority of the entire U.S. population. Figure 14–1 on page 395 shows how this trend is projected to unfold over time. National Map 14–1 shows where a minority majority already exists.

Minorities have two important characteristics. First, they share a *distinctive identity*, which may be based on physical or cultural traits. Second, minorities experience *subordination*. As the rest of this chapter shows, U.S. minorities typically have lower income, lower occupational prestige, and limited schooling. These facts mean that class, race, and ethnicity, as well as gender, are overlapping and reinforcing dimensions of social stratification. The Thinking About Diversity box on page 397 profiles the struggles of recent Latin American immigrants.

Of course, not all members of any minority category are disadvantaged. Some Latinos are quite wealthy, certain Chinese Americans are celebrated business leaders, and African Americans are among our nation's political leaders. But even job success rarely allows individuals to escape their minority standing. As described in Chapter 6 ("Social Interaction in Everyday Life"), race or ethnicity often serves as a *master status* that overshadows personal accomplishments.

Minorities usually make up a small proportion of a society's population, but this is not always the case. Black South Africans are disadvantaged even though they are a numerical majority in their country. In the United States, women represent slightly more than half the population but are still struggling for all the opportunities and privileges enjoyed by men.

Watch in **MySocLab**
Video: *Sociology on the Job: Race and Ethnicity*

Thinking About Diversity: Race, Class, and Gender

Hard Work: The Immigrant Life in the United States

Early in the morning, it is already hot on the streets of Houston as a line of pickup trucks snakes slowly into a dusty yard, where 200 laborers have been gathering since dawn, each hoping for a day's work. The driver of the first truck opens his window and tells the foreman that he is looking for a crew to spread boiling tar on a roof. Abdonel Cespedes, the foreman, turns to the crowd, and after a few minutes, three workers step forward and climb into the back of the truck. The next driver is looking for two experienced housepainters. The scene is repeated over and over as men and a few women leave to dig ditches, spread cement, hang drywall, open clogged septic tanks, or crawl under houses to poison rats.

As each driver pulls into the yard, the foreman asks, "How much?" Most offer $5 an hour. Cespedes automatically responds, "$7.25; the going rate is $7.25 for an hour's hard work." Sometimes he convinces them to pay that much, but usually not. The workers, who come from Mexico, El Salvador, and Guatemala, know that dozens of them will end up with no work at all this day. Most accept $5 or $6 an hour because they know that when the day is over, $50 is better than nothing.

Labor markets like this one are common in large cities, especially across the southwestern United States. The surge in immigration in recent years has brought millions of people to this country in search of work, and most have little schooling and speak little English.

Manuel Barrera has taken a day's work moving the entire contents of a store to a storage site. He arrives at the boarded-up building and gazes at the mountains of heavy furniture that he must carry out to a moving van, drive across town, and then carry again. He sighs when he thinks about how hot it is outside and realizes that it is even hotter inside the building. He will have no break for lunch. No one says anything about toilets. Barrera shakes his head: "I will do this kind of work because it puts food on the table. But I did not foresee it would turn out like this."

The hard truth is that immigrants to the United States do the jobs that no one else wants. At the bottom level of the national economy, they perform low-skill jobs in restaurants and hotels and on construction crews, and they work in private homes cooking, cleaning, and caring for children. Across the United States, about half of all housekeepers, household cooks, tailors, and restaurant waiters are men or women born abroad. Few immigrants make much more than the official minimum wage ($7.25 in 2012), and rarely do immigrant workers receive any health or pension benefits. Many well-off families take the labor of immigrants as much for granted as their air-conditioned cars and comfortable homes.

What Do You Think?

1. In what ways do you or members of your family depend on the low-paid labor of immigrants?

2. Do you favor allowing the 11.5 million people who entered this country illegally to earn citizenship? What should be done?

3. Should the U.S. government act to reduce the number of immigrants entering this country in the future? Why or why not?

Sources: Booth (1998), Tumulty (2006), U.S. Department of Homeland Security (2012), and U.S. Department of Labor (2012).

These immigrants gather on a New York City street corner every morning hoping to be hired for construction work that pays about $60 a day with no benefits.

Prejudice and Stereotypes

14.2 Describe the extent and causes of prejudice.

November 19, Jerusalem, Israel. We are driving along the outskirts of this historical city—a holy place to Jews, Christians, and Muslims—when Razi, our taxi driver, spots a small group of Falasha—Ethiopian Jews—on a street corner. "Those people over there," he points as he speaks, "they are different. They don't drive cars. They don't want to improve themselves. Even when our country offers them schooling, they don't take it." He shakes his head at the Ethiopians and drives on.

Prejudice is *a rigid and unfair generalization about an entire category of people*. Prejudice is unfair because *all* people in some category are described as the same, based on little or no direct evidence. Prejudice may target people of a particular social class, sex, sexual orientation, age, political affiliation, physical disability, race, or ethnicity.

Prejudices are *prejudgments* that can be either positive or negative. Our positive prejudices tend to exaggerate the virtues of people like ourselves, and our negative prejudices condemn those who differ from us. Negative prejudice can be expressed as anything from mild dislike to outright hostility. Because such attitudes are rooted in culture, everyone has at least some prejudice.

Prejudice often takes the form of a **stereotype** (*stereo* is derived from a Greek word meaning "solid"), *a simplified description applied to every person in some category*. Many white people hold stereotypical views of minorities. Stereotyping is especially harmful to minorities in the workplace. If company officials see workers only in terms of a stereotype, they will make assumptions about their abilities, steering them toward certain jobs and limiting their access to better opportunities (Kaufman, 2002).

Minorities, too, stereotype whites and other minorities (T. W. Smith, 1996; Cummings & Lambert, 1997). Surveys show, for example, that African Americans are more likely than whites to express the belief that Asians engage in unfair business practices and Asians are more likely than whites to criticize Hispanics for having too many children (Perlmutter, 2002).

Measuring Prejudice: The Social Distance Scale

One measure of prejudice is *social distance,* how closely people are willing to interact with members of some category. In the 1920s, Emory Bogardus developed the *social distance scale* shown in Figure 14–2 on page 398. Bogardus (1925) asked students at U.S. colleges and universities to look at this scale and indicate how closely they were willing to interact with people in thirty racial and ethnic categories. People express the greatest social distance (most negative prejudice) by declaring that a particular category of people should be barred from the country entirely (point 7); at the other extreme, people express the least social distance (most social acceptance) by saying they would accept members of a particular category into their family through marriage (point 1).

Bogardus (1925, 1967; Owen, Elsner, & McFaul, 1977) found that people felt much more social distance from some categories than from others. In general, students in his surveys expressed the most social distance from Hispanics, African Americans, Asians, and Turks, indicating that they would be willing to tolerate such people as co-workers but not as neighbors, friends, or family members. Students expressed the least social distance from those from northern and western Europe, including English and Scottish people, and also Canadians, indicating that they were willing to include them in their families by marriage.

What patterns of social distance do we find among college students today? A recent study using the same social distance scale reported three major findings (Parrillo & Donoghue, 2005):[1]

1. **Student opinion shows a trend toward greater social acceptance.** Today's students express less social distance from all minorities than students did several decades ago. Figure 14–2 shows that the mean (average) score on the social distance scale declined from 2.14 in 1925 to 1.93 in 1977 and 1.44 in 2001. Respondents (81 percent of whom were white) showed notably greater acceptance of African Americans, a category that moved up from near the bottom in 1925 to the top one-third in 2001.

---

[1]Parrillo and Donoghue dropped seven of the categories used by Bogardus (Armenians, Czechs, Finns, Norwegians, Scots, Swedes, and Turks), claiming they were no longer visible minorities. They added nine new categories (Africans, Arabs, Cubans, Dominicans, Haitians, Jamaicans, Muslims, Puerto Ricans, and Vietnamese), claiming that these are visible minorities today. This change probably encouraged higher social distance scores, making the trend toward decreasing social distance all the more significant.

Student Snapshot

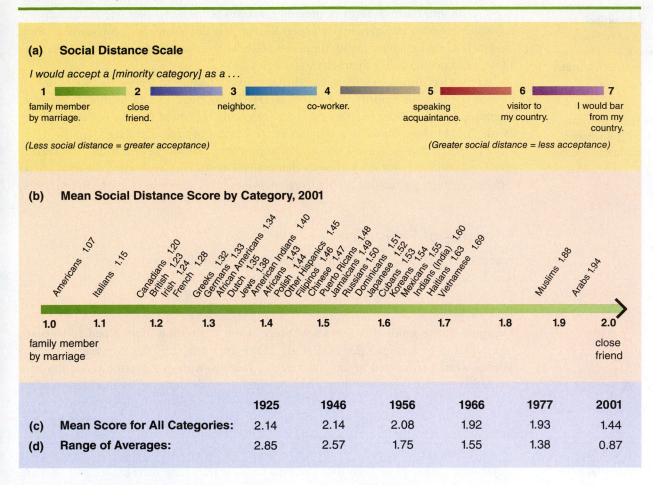

(a) Social Distance Scale

I would accept a [minority category] as a . . .

1	2	3	4	5	6	7
family member by marriage.	close friend.	neighbor.	co-worker.	speaking acquaintance.	visitor to my country.	I would bar from my country.

(Less social distance = greater acceptance)   *(Greater social distance = less acceptance)*

(b) Mean Social Distance Score by Category, 2001

Americans 1.07, Italians 1.15, Canadians 1.20, British 1.23, Irish 1.24, French 1.28, Greeks 1.32, Germans 1.33, African Americans 1.34, Dutch 1.35, Jews 1.38, American Indians 1.40, Africans 1.43, Polish 1.44, Other Hispanics 1.45, Filipinos 1.46, Chinese 1.47, Puerto Ricans 1.48, Jamaicans 1.49, Russians 1.50, Dominicans 1.51, Japanese 1.52, Cubans 1.53, Koreans 1.54, Mexicans 1.55, Indians (India) 1.60, Haitians 1.63, Vietnamese 1.69, Muslims 1.88, Arabs 1.94

1.0 1.1 1.2 1.3 1.4 1.5 1.6 1.7 1.8 1.9 2.0

family member by marriage   close friend

		1925	1946	1956	1966	1977	2001
(c)	Mean Score for All Categories:	2.14	2.14	2.08	1.92	1.93	1.44
(d)	Range of Averages:	2.85	2.57	1.75	1.55	1.38	0.87

FIGURE 14–2 Bogardus Social Distance Research

The social distance scale is a good way to measure prejudice. Part (a) illustrates the complete social distance scale, from least social distance at the far left to greatest social distance at the far right. Part (b) shows the mean (average) social distance score received by each category of people in 2001. Part (c) presents the overall mean score in specific years (the average of the scores received by all racial and ethnic categories). These scores have fallen from 2.14 in 1925 to 1.44 in 2001, showing that students express less social distance toward minorities today than they did in the past. Part (d) shows the range of averages, the difference between the highest and lowest scores in given years (in 2001, for instance, it was 0.87, the difference between the high score of 1.94 for Arabs and the low score of 1.07 for Americans). This figure has also become smaller since 1925, indicating that today's students tend to see fewer differences between various categories of people.

Source: Parrillo and Donoghue (2005).

2. **People see less difference between various minorities.** The earliest studies found the difference between the highest- and lowest-ranked minorities (the range of averages) equal to almost three points on the scale. As the figure shows, the most recent research produced a range of averages of less than one point, indicating that today's students see fewer differences between various categories of people.

3. **The terrorist attacks of September 11, 2001, may have reduced social acceptance of Arabs and Muslims.** The most recent study was conducted just a few weeks after September 11, 2001. Perhaps the fact that the nineteen men who attacked the World Trade Center and the Pentagon were Arabs and Muslims is part of the reason that students ranked these categories last on the social distance scale. However, not a single student gave Arabs or Muslims a 7, indicating that they should be barred from the country. On the contrary, the 2001 mean scores (1.94 for Arabs and 1.88 for Muslims) show higher social acceptance than students in 1977 expressed toward eighteen of the thirty categories of people studied.

For a closer look at studies of race and intelligence, **Read More** in **MySocLab**, *Does Race Affect Intelligence?*

racism the belief that one racial category is innately superior or inferior to another

Racism

A powerful and harmful form of prejudice, **racism** is *the belief that one racial category is innately superior or inferior to another*. Racism has existed throughout world history. Despite their many achievements, the ancient Greeks, the peoples of India, and the Chinese all regarded people unlike themselves as inferior.

Racism has also been widespread throughout the history of the United States, where ideas about racial inferiority supported slavery. Today, overt racism in this country has decreased because more people believe in evaluating others, in Martin Luther King Jr.'s words, "not by the color of their skin but by the content of their character."

Even so, racism remains a serious social problem, as some people think that certain racial and ethnic categories are smarter than others. As studies have shown, however, racial differences in mental abilities result from environment rather than biology (Sowell, 1994, 1995).

Theories of Prejudice

Where does prejudice come from? Social scientists provide several answers to this question, focusing on frustration, personality, culture, and social conflict.

Scapegoat Theory

Scapegoat theory holds that prejudice springs from frustration among people who are themselves disadvantaged (Dollard et al., 1939). For instance, take the case of a white woman who is frustrated by the low pay she receives from her assembly-line job in a textile factory. Directing hostility at the powerful factory owners carries the obvious risk of being fired; therefore, she may blame her low pay on the presence of minority co-workers. Her prejudice does not improve her situation, but it is a relatively safe way to express anger, and it may give her the comforting feeling that at least she is superior to someone.

A **scapegoat**, then, is *a person or category of people, typically with little power, whom people unfairly blame for their own troubles*. Because they have little power and thus are usually "safe targets," minorities often are used as scapegoats.

scapegoat a person or category of people, typically with little power, whom people unfairly blame for their own troubles

Authoritarian Personality Theory

Theodor Adorno and colleagues (1950) considered extreme prejudice a personality trait of certain individuals. This conclusion is supported by research showing that people who show strong prejudice toward one minority are usually intolerant of all minorities. These *authoritarian personalities* rigidly conform to conventional cultural values and see moral issues as clear-cut matters of right and wrong. People with authoritarian personalities also view society as naturally competitive and hierarchical, with "better" people (like themselves) inevitably dominating those who are weaker (all minorities).

Adorno and his colleagues also found the opposite pattern to be true: People who express tolerance toward one minority are likely to be accepting of all. They tend to be more flexible in their moral judgments and treat all people as equals.

Adorno thought that people with little schooling and those raised by cold and demanding parents tend to develop authoritarian personalities. Filled with anger and anxiety as children, they grow into hostile, aggressive adults who seek out scapegoats.

Culture Theory

A third theory claims that although extreme prejudice may be found in some people, some prejudice is found in everyone. Why? Because prejudice is part of the culture in which we all live and learn. The Bogardus social distance studies help prove the point. Bogardus found that students across the country had much the same attitudes toward specific racial and ethnic categories, feeling closer to some and more distant from others.

More evidence that prejudice is rooted in culture is the fact that minorities express the same attitudes as white people toward categories other than their own. Such patterns suggest that individuals hold prejudices because we live in a "culture of prejudice" that has taught us all to view certain categories of people as "better" or "worse" than others.

discrimination unequal treatment of various categories of people

institutional prejudice and discrimination bias built into the operation of society's institutions

Conflict Theory

A fourth explanation proposes that prejudice is used as a tool by powerful people to oppress others. Anglos who look down on Latino immigrants in the Southwest, for example, can get away with paying the immigrants low wages for long hours of hard work. Similarly, all elites benefit when prejudice divides the labor force along racial and ethnic lines and discourages them from working together to advance their common interests (Geschwender, 1978; Olzak, 1989; Rothenberg, 2008).

According to another conflict-based argument, made by Shelby Steele (1990), minorities themselves encourage *race consciousness* to win greater power and privileges. Because of their historical disadvantage, minorities claim that they are victims entitled to special consideration based on their race. This strategy may bring short-term gains, but Steele cautions that such thinking often sparks a backlash from whites or others who oppose "special treatment" on the basis of race or ethnicity.

Discrimination

14.3 Distinguish discrimination from prejudice.

Closely related to prejudice is **discrimination**, *unequal treatment of various categories of people. Prejudice* refers to *attitudes,* but *discrimination* is a matter of *action.* Like prejudice, discrimination can be either positive (providing special advantages) or negative (creating obstacles) and ranges from subtle to extreme.

Institutional Prejudice and Discrimination

We typically think of prejudice and discrimination as the hateful ideas or actions of specific people. But Stokely Carmichael and Charles Hamilton (1967) pointed out that far greater harm results from **institutional prejudice and discrimination,** *bias built into the operation of society's institutions,* including schools, hospitals, the police, and the workplace. For example, researchers have found that banks reject home mortgage applications from minorities at a higher rate than those from white people, even when income and quality of neighborhood are held constant (Gotham, 1998; Blanton, 2007).

According to Carmichael and Hamilton, people are slow to condemn or even recognize institutional prejudice and discrimination because it often involves respected public officials and long-established traditions. A case in point is *Brown* v. *Board of Education of Topeka,* the 1954 Supreme Court decision that ended the legal segregation of schools. The principle of "separate but equal" schooling had been the law of the land, supporting racial inequality by allowing school segregation. Despite this change in the law, half a century later, most U.S. students still attend schools in which one race overwhelmingly predominates (KewalRamani et al., 2007). In 1991, the courts pointed out that

Watch in **MySocLab**
Video: *The Basics: Race and Ethnicity*

In 2012, seventeen-year old Trayvon Martin was shot and killed by twenty-eight-year old George Zimmerman, who was the coordinator of his Florida community's neighborhood watch program. From the outset, questions arose about whether racial bias played a part in the shooting. Eventually, Zimmerman was charged with murder, and in 2013 a jury found him not guilty. The high level of national concern over this event—especially within the African American community—suggests that many believe race continues to shape the operation of the U.S. criminal justice system.

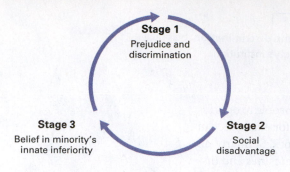

Stage 1
Prejudice and discrimination

Stage 3
Belief in minority's innate inferiority

Stage 2
Social disadvantage

Stage 1: Prejudice and discrimination begin, often as an expression of ethnocentrism or an attempt to justify economic exploitation.

Stage 2: As a result of prejudice and discrimination, a minority is socially disadvantaged, occupying a low position in the system of social stratification.

Stage 3: This social disadvantage is then interpreted not as the result of earlier prejudice and discrimination but as evidence that the minority is innately inferior, unleashing renewed prejudice and discrimination by which the cycle repeats itself.

FIGURE 14–3 Prejudice and Discrimination: The Vicious Circle

Prejudice and discrimination can form a vicious circle, thereby perpetuating themselves.

neighborhood schools will never provide equal education as long as our population is segregated, with most African Americans living in central cities and most white people and Asian Americans living in suburbs.

Prejudice and Discrimination: The Vicious Circle

Prejudice and discrimination reinforce each other. The Thomas theorem, discussed in Chapter 6 ("Social Interaction in Everyday Life"), offers a simple explanation of this fact: *Situations that are defined as real become real in their consequences* (Thomas & Thomas, 1928; Thomas, 1966:301, orig. 1931).

Applying the Thomas theorem, we understand how stereotypes can become real to people who believe them and sometimes even to those who are victimized by them. Prejudice on the part of white people toward people of color does not produce *innate* inferiority, but it can produce *social* inferiority, pushing minorities into low-paying jobs, inferior schools, and racially segregated housing. Then, as white people interpret that social disadvantage as evidence that minorities do not measure up, they unleash a new round of prejudice and discrimination, giving rise to a vicious circle in which each perpetuates the other, as shown in Figure 14–3.

Majority and Minority: Patterns of Interaction

14.4 Identify examples of pluralism, assimilation, segregation, and genocide.

Sociologists describe patterns of interaction among racial and ethnic categories in a society in terms of four models: pluralism, assimilation, segregation, and genocide.

Pluralism

Pluralism is *a state in which people of all races and ethnicities are distinct but have equal social standing*. In other words, people who differ in appearance or social heritage all share resources roughly equally.

The United States is pluralistic to the extent that all people have equal standing under the law. Also, many large cities contain "ethnic villages," where people proudly display the traditions of their immigrant ancestors. These include New York's Spanish Harlem, Little Italy, and Chinatown; Philadelphia's Italian "South Philly"; Chicago's Little Saigon; and Latino East Los Angeles. New York City alone has more than 300 magazines, newspapers, and radio stations that publish in more than ninety languages (Logan, Alba, & Zhang, 2002; Center for Community and Ethnic Media, CUNY, 2013).

But the United States is not truly pluralistic, for three reasons. First, although most people value their cultural heritage, few want to live exclusively with others exactly like themselves (NORC, 2013:671–673). Second, our tolerance of social diversity goes only so far. One reaction to the rising number of U.S. minorities is a social movement to make English the nation's official language. Third, as you will see later in this chapter, people of various colors and cultures do *not* have equal social standing.

Assimilation

Many people think of the United States as a "melting pot" in which different nationalities blend together. But rather than everyone "melting" into some new cultural pattern, most minorities have adopted the dominant culture established by our earliest settlers. Why? Because doing so is both the path to upward social mobility and a way to escape the prejudice and discrimination directed at more visible foreigners. Sociologists use the term **assimilation** to describe *the process by which minorities gradually adopt patterns of the dominant culture.* Assimilation can involve changing modes of dress, values, religion, language, and friends.

The amount of assimilation varies by category. For example, Canadians have "melted" more than Cubans, the Dutch more than Dominicans, Germans more than the Japanese. Multiculturalists oppose making assimilation a goal because it suggests that minorities are a problem and the ones who need to do all the changing.

Note that assimilation involves changes in ethnicity but not in race. For example, many descendants of Japanese immigrants discard their ethnic traditions but retain their racial identity. For racial traits to diminish over generations, **miscegenation**, or *biological reproduction by partners of different racial categories*, must occur. Although interracial marriage is becoming more common, it still amounts to only 8 percent of all U.S. marriages (U.S. Census Bureau, 2012).

Should we expect people who come to the United States to change their language and other cultural patterns in order to "fit in," or should we expect them to hold onto their own traditions? Why?

Segregation

Segregation is *the physical and social separation of categories of people.* Some minorities, especially religious orders like the Amish, voluntarily segregate themselves. However, majorities usually segregate minorities by excluding them. Residential neighborhoods, schools, occupations, hospitals, and even cemeteries may be segregated. Pluralism encourages distinctiveness without disadvantage, but segregation enforces separation that harms a minority.

Racial segregation has a long history in the United States, beginning with slavery and evolving into racially separated housing, schools, buses, and trains. Court decisions such as the 1954 *Brown* case have reduced *de jure* (Latin, "by law") discrimination in this country. However, *de facto* ("in actual fact") segregation continues in the form of countless neighborhoods that are home to people of a single race.

Despite some recent decline, segregation persists in the United States. For example, Livonia, Michigan, is 89 percent white, and neighboring Detroit is 82 percent African American. Kurt Metzger (2001) explains, "Livonia was pretty much created by white flight [from Detroit]." Further, research shows that across the country, many whites (especially those with young children) avoid neighborhoods where African Americans live (Emerson, Yancey, & Chai, 2001; Krysan, 2002). At the extreme, Douglas Massey and Nancy Denton (1989) document the *hypersegregation* of poor African Americans in some inner cities. Hypersegregation means having little contact of any kind with people outside the local community.

miscegenation biological reproduction by partners of different racial categories

Patterns of Majority and Minority Interaction

pluralism a state in which people of all races and ethnicities are distinct but have equal social standing

assimilation the process by which minorities gradually adopt patterns of the dominant culture

segregation the physical and social separation of categories of people

genocide the systematic killing of one category of people by another

Hypersegregation is the daily experience of about 20 percent of poor African Americans and is a pattern found in about twenty-five large U.S. cities (Wilkes & Iceland, 2004; Iceland et al., 2010).

Genocide

Genocide is *the systematic killing of one category of people by another*. This deadly form of racism and ethnocentrism violates nearly every recognized moral standard, yet it has occurred time and again in human history.

Genocide was common in the history of contact between Europeans and the original inhabitants of the Americas. From the sixteenth century on, the Spanish, Portuguese, English, French, and Dutch forcibly colonized vast empires. Although most native people died from diseases brought by Europeans, against which they had no natural defenses, many who opposed the colonizers were killed deliberately (Matthiessen, 1984; Sale, 1990).

Genocide also occurred during the twentieth century. During World War I, at least 1 million Armenians in Eastern Europe perished under the rule of the Ottoman Empire. Soon after that, European Jews experienced a reign of terror known as the Holocaust during Adolf Hitler's rule in Germany. From about 1935 to 1945, the Nazis murdered more than 6 million Jewish men, women, and children, and another 5 million people including gay people, Gypsies, and people with handicaps. During the same period, the Soviet dictator Josef Stalin murdered on an even greater scale, killing perhaps 30 million real and imagined enemies during decades of violent rule. Between 1975 and 1980, Pol Pot's Communist regime in Cambodia butchered all "capitalists," a category that included anyone able to speak a Western language. In all, some 2 million people (one-fourth of the population) perished in the Cambodian "killing fields."

Tragically, genocide continues in the modern world. Recent examples include Hutus killing Tutsis in the African nation of Rwanda, Serbs killing Bosnians in the Balkans of Eastern Europe, and the killing of hundreds of thousands of people in the Darfur region of Sudan in Africa.

These four patterns of minority-majority interaction have all been played out in the United States. Although many people proudly point to patterns of pluralism and assimilation, it is also important to recognize the degree to which U.S. society has been built on segregation (of African Americans) and genocide (of Native Americans). The remainder of this chapter examines how these four patterns have shaped the history and present social standing of major racial and ethnic categories in the United States.

Race and Ethnicity in the United States

14.5 Assess the social standing of racial and ethnic categories of U.S. society.

> Give me your tired, your poor,
> Your huddled masses yearning to breathe free,
> The wretched refuse of your teeming shore,
> Send these, the homeless, tempest-tossed to me:
> I lift my lamp beside the golden door.

These words by Emma Lazarus, inscribed on the Statue of Liberty, express cultural ideals of human dignity, personal freedom, and economic opportunity. The United States has provided more of the "good life" to more immigrants than any other nation. About 1.3 million immigrants come to this country every year, and their many ways of life create a social mosaic that is especially evident in large cities with many distinctive racial and ethnic neighborhoods.

However, as a survey of this country's racial and ethnic minorities will show, our country's golden door has opened more widely for some than for others. We turn next to the history and current social standing of the major categories of the U.S. population.

Native Americans

The term "Native Americans" refers to the hundreds of societies—including the Aztec, Inca, Aleuts, Cherokee, Zuni, Sioux, and Mohawk—that first settled the Western Hemisphere. Some 15,000 years before Christopher Columbus landed in the Americas in 1492, migrating peoples crossed a land bridge from Asia to North America where the Bering Strait (off the coast of Alaska) lies today. Gradually, they spread throughout North and South America.

When the first Europeans arrived late in the fifteenth century, Native Americans numbered in the millions. But by 1900, after centuries of conflict and even acts of genocide, the "vanishing Americans" numbered just 250,000 (Dobyns, 1966; Tyler, 1973). The land they controlled also shrank dramatically, as National Map 14–2 shows.

Columbus first referred to Native Americans that he encountered as "Indians" because he mistakenly thought he had reached the coast of India. Columbus found the native people passive and peaceful, in stark contrast to the materialistic and competitive Europeans. Yet Europeans justified the seizure of Native American land by calling their victims thieves and murderers (Josephy, 1982; Matthiessen, 1984; Sale, 1990).

After the Revolutionary War, the new U.S. government took a pluralistic approach to Native American societies, seeking to gain more land through treaties. Payment for the land was far from fair, however, and when Native Americans resisted the surrender of their homelands, the U.S. government simply used its superior military power to evict them. By the early 1800s, few Native Americans remained east of the Mississippi River.

Seeing Ourselves

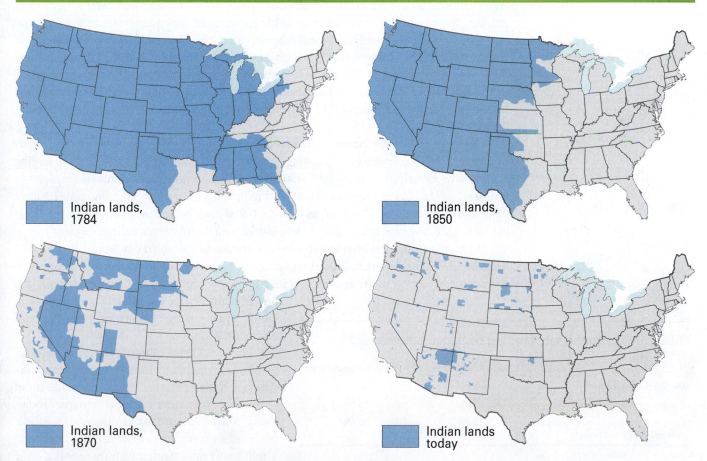

Indian lands, 1784

Indian lands, 1850

Indian lands, 1870

Indian lands today

NATIONAL MAP 14–2 Land Controlled by Native Americans, 1784 to Today

In 1784, Native Americans controlled three-fourths of the land (blue-shaded areas) that eventually became the United States. Today, Native Americans control 436 reservations, scattered across the United States, that account for just 5.3 percent of the country's land area. How would you characterize these locations?

Source: Waldman (2000) and U.S. Census Bureau (2011).

In an effort to force assimilation, the U.S. Bureau of Indian Affairs took American Indian children from their families and placed them in boarding schools like this one, the U.S. Indian School in Carlisle, Pennsylvania. There they were taught to speak English by non-Indian teachers with the goal of making them into "Americans."

In 1871, the United States declared Native Americans wards of the government and adopted a strategy of forced assimilation. Relocated to specific territories designated as "reservations," Native Americans continued to lose their land and were well on their way to losing their culture as well. Reservation life encouraged dependency, replacing ancestral languages with English and traditional religion with Christianity. Officials of the Bureau of Indian Affairs took children from their parents and put them in boarding schools, where they were resocialized as "Americans." Authorities gave local control of reservation life to the few Native Americans who supported government policies, and they distributed reservation land, traditionally held collectively, as private property to individual families (Tyler, 1973).

Not until 1924 were Native Americans entitled to U.S. citizenship. After that, many migrated from reservations, adopting mainstream cultural patterns and marrying non–Native Americans. Today, half of Native Americans consider themselves biracial or multiracial (U.S. Census Bureau, 2011), and many large cities now contain sizable Native American populations. However, as Table 14–2 shows, Native American income is far below the U.S. average, and relatively few Native Americans earn a college degree.[2]

From in-depth interviews with Native Americans in a western city, Joan Albon (1971) linked low Native American social standing to a range of cultural factors, including a noncompetitive view of life and a reluctance to pursue higher education. In addition, she noted, many Native Americans have dark skin, which makes them targets of prejudice and discrimination.

The U.S. Census Bureau (2012) recognizes forty-one American Indian nations and six Alaskan Native nations, which are made up of more than 600 smaller tribal groups. Today, many Native Americans are displaying ethnic pride as they reclaim their cultural heritage. Traditional cultural organizations report a surge

TABLE 14–2 The Social Standing of Native Americans, 2011

	Native Americans	Entire U.S. Population
Median family income	$40,962	$60,974
Percentage in poverty	29.5%	15.0%
Completion of four or more years of college (age 25 and over)	13.3%	30.9%

Source: U.S. Census Bureau (2012).

[2]In making comparisons of education and especially income, keep in mind that various categories of the U.S. population have different median ages. In 2011, the median age for all U.S. people was 37.3 years; for Native Americans, the figure was 31.3 years. Because people's schooling and income increase over time, this age difference accounts for some of the disparities seen in Table 14–2.

in new membership applications, and many children can speak native languages better than their parents. The legal right of Native Americans to govern their reservations has enabled some tribes to build profitable gaming casinos. But the wealth produced from gambling has enriched relatively few Native peoples, and most profits go to non-Indian investors (Bartlett & Steele, 2002). While some prosper, most Native Americans remain severely disadvantaged and share a profound sense of the injustice they have suffered at the hands of white people.

White Anglo-Saxon Protestants

White Anglo-Saxon Protestants (WASPs) were not the first people to inhabit the United States, but they soon dominated after European settlement began. Most WASPs are of English ancestry, but the category also includes people from Scotland and Wales. With some 33 million people claiming English, Scottish, or Welsh ancestry, 9.2 percent of our society has some WASP background, and WASPs are found at all class levels (U.S. Census Bureau, 2012).

Many people associate WASPs with elite communities along the East and West Coasts. But the highest concentrations of WASPs are in Utah (because of migrations of Mormons with English ancestry), Appalachia, and northern New England (also due to historical patterns of immigration).

Looking back in time, WASP immigrants were highly skilled and motivated to achieve by what we now call the Protestant work ethic. Because of their high social standing, WASPs were not subject to the prejudice and discrimination experienced by other categories of immigrants. In fact, the historical dominance of WASPs has led others to want to become more like them (Jones, 2001).

WASPs were never one single group; especially in colonial times, considerable hostility separated English Anglicans and Scottish Presbyterians (Parrillo, 1994). But in the nineteenth century, most WASPs joined together to oppose the arrival of "undesirables" such as Germans in the 1840s and Italians in the 1880s. Those who could afford it sheltered themselves in exclusive suburbs and restrictive clubs. Thus the 1880s—the decade when the Statue of Liberty first welcomed immigrants to the United States—also saw the founding of the first country club with exclusively WASP members (Baltzell, 1964).

By about 1950, however, WASP wealth and power had peaked, as indicated by the 1960 election of John Fitzgerald Kennedy, the first Irish Catholic president. Yet the WASP cultural legacy remains. English is this country's dominant language and Protestantism its majority religion. Our legal system also reflects our English origins. But the historical dominance of WASPs is most evident in the widespread assumption that the terms "race" and "ethnicity" apply to everyone but them.

African Americans

Africans accompanied European explorers to the New World in the fifteenth century. But most accounts date the beginning of black history in the United States to 1619, when a Dutch trading ship brought twenty Africans to Jamestown, Virginia. Many more ships filled with African laborers followed. Whether these people arrived as slaves or as indentured servants (who paid for their passage by agreeing to work for a period of time), being of African descent on these shores soon became virtually synonymous with being a slave. In 1661, Virginia enacted the first law in the new colonies recognizing slavery (Sowell, 1981).

Slavery was the foundation of the southern colonies' plantation system. White people ran plantations using slave labor, and until 1808, some were also slave traders. Traders—Europeans, Africans, and North Americans—forcibly transported some 10 million Africans to various countries in the Americas, including 400,000 to the United States. On small sailing ships, hundreds of slaves were chained together for the several weeks it took to cross the Atlantic Ocean. Filth and disease killed many and drove others to suicide. Overall, perhaps half died en route (Franklin, 1967; Sowell, 1981).

The reward for surviving the miserable journey was a lifetime of servitude. Although some slaves worked in cities at various trades, most labored in the fields, often from

The efforts of these four women greatly advanced the social standing of African Americans in the United States. Pictured from left to right: Sojourner Truth (1797–1883), born a slave, became an influential preacher and outspoken abolitionist who was honored by President Lincoln at the White House. Harriet Tubman (1820–1913), after escaping from slavery herself, masterminded the flight from bondage of hundreds of African American men and women via the "Underground Railroad." Ida Wells-Barnett (1862–1931), born to slave parents, became a partner in a Memphis newspaper and served as a tireless crusader against the terror of lynching. Marian Anderson (1902–1993), an exceptional singer whose early career was restrained by racial prejudice, broke symbolic "color lines" by singing in the White House in 1936 and on the steps of the Lincoln Memorial to a crowd of almost 100,000 people in 1939.

daybreak until sunset and even longer during the harvest. The law allowed owners to use whatever disciplinary measures they deemed necessary to ensure that slaves were obedient and hardworking. Even killing a slave rarely prompted legal action. Owners also divided slave families at public auctions, where human beings were bought and sold as property. Unschooled and dependent on their owners for all their basic needs, slaves had little control over their lives (Franklin, 1967; Sowell, 1981).

Some free persons of color lived in both the North and the South, laboring as small-scale farmers, skilled workers, and small business owners. But the lives of most African Americans stood in glaring contradiction to the principles of equality and freedom on which the United States was founded. The Declaration of Independence states:

> We hold these Truths to be self-evident, that all Men are created equal, that they are endowed by their Creator with certain unalienable Rights, that among these are Life, Liberty, and the Pursuit of Happiness.

However, most white people did not apply these ideals to black people, and certainly not to slaves. In the *Dred Scott* case of 1857, the U.S. Supreme Court addressed the question "Are slaves citizens?" by writing, "We think they are not, and that they are not included, and were not intended to be included, under the word 'citizens' in the Constitution, and can therefore claim none of the rights and privileges which that instrument provides for and secures for citizens of the United States" (quoted in Blaustein & Zangrando, 1968:160). Thus arose what the Swedish sociologist Gunnar Myrdal (1944) called the "American dilemma": a democratic society's denial of basic rights and freedoms to one category of people. People would speak of equality, in other words, but do little to make all categories of people equal. Many white people resolved this dilemma by defining black people as naturally inferior and undeserving of equality (Leach, 2002).

In 1865, the Thirteenth Amendment to the Constitution outlawed slavery. Three years later, the Fourteenth Amendment reversed the *Dred Scott* ruling, giving citizenship to all people born in the United States. The Fifteenth Amendment, ratified in 1870, stated that neither race nor previous condition of servitude could deprive anyone of the right to vote. However, so-called *Jim Crow laws*—classic cases of institutional discrimination—segregated U.S. society into two racial castes. Especially in the South, white people beat and lynched black people (and some white people) who challenged the racial hierarchy.

The twentieth century brought dramatic changes for African Americans. After World War I, tens of thousands of men, women, and children left the rural South for jobs in northern factories. Although most did find economic opportunities, few escaped racial prejudice and discrimination, which placed them lower in the social hierarchy than white immigrants arriving from Europe.

In the 1950s and 1960s, a national civil rights movement led to landmark judicial decisions outlawing segregated schools and overt discrimination in employment and public accommodations. The Black Power movement gave African Americans a renewed sense of pride and purpose.

TABLE 14–3 The Social Standing of African Americans, 2011

	African Americans	Entire U.S. Population
Median family income	$40,495	$60,974
Percentage in poverty	27.6%	15.0%
Completion of four or more years of college (age 25 and over)	21.2%	30.9%

Source: U.S. Census Bureau (2012).

Despite these gains, people of African descent continue to occupy a lower social position in the United States, as shown in Table 14–3. The median income of African American families in 2011 ($40,495) was only 58 percent of non-Hispanic white family income ($69,829), a ratio that has changed little in thirty years.[3] Black families remain almost three times as likely as white families to be poor.

The number of African Americans securely in the middle class rose by more than half between 1980 and 2012; 43 percent earn $48,500 or more. This means that the African American community is now economically diverse. Even so, a majority of African Americans are still working class or poor. In recent years, many have seen earnings slip as urban factory jobs, vital to residents of central cities, have been lost to other countries where labor costs are lower. This is one reason that black unemployment (13.8 percent in 2012) is almost twice as high as white unemployment (7.2 percent); among African American teenagers, the figure exceeds 38 percent (R. A. Smith, 2002; Pattillo, 2007; U.S. Department of Labor, 2013).

Since 1980, African Americans have made remarkable educational progress. The share of adults completing high school rose from half to 85 percent in 2011, nearly closing the gap between whites and blacks. Between 1980 and 2011, the share of African American adults with at least a college degree rose from 8 to 21 percent. But as Table 14–3 shows, African Americans are still well below the national standard when it comes to completing four years of college.

The Congressional Black Caucus represents the increasing political power of African Americans in the United States. Even so, in 2012, African Americans accounted for just forty-two members of the House of Representatives, one state governor, and no members of the U.S. Senate.

---

[3]Here again, a median age difference (non-Hispanic whites, 42.3; blacks, 32.7) accounts for some of the income and educational disparities. More important is a higher proportion of one-parent families among blacks than whites. If we compare only married-couple families, African Americans (median income $64,626 in 2011) earned 83 percent as much as non-Hispanic whites ($78,311).

The political clout of African Americans has also increased. As a result of black migration to the cities and white flight to the suburbs, African Americans have gained greater political power in urban places, and many of this country's largest cities have elected African American mayors. At the national level, the election of Barack Obama as this country's forty-fourth president—the first African American to hold this office—is a historic and hugely important event. It demonstrates that our society has moved beyond the assumption that race is a barrier to the highest office in the land (West, 2008). Yet in 2012, African Americans accounted for just forty-two members of the House of Representatives (10 percent of 435), no members of the Senate (out of 100), and only one of fifty state governors (National Governors Association, 2012).

In sum, for nearly 400 years, people of African ancestry in the United States have struggled for social equality. As a nation, we have come far in this pursuit. Overt discrimination is now illegal, and research documents a long-term decline in prejudice against African Americans (Firebaugh & Davis, 1988; Wilson, 1992).

Fifty years after the abolition of slavery, W. E. B. Du Bois (1913) pointed to the extent of black achievement but cautioned that racial caste remained strong in the United States. Almost a century later, this racial hierarchy persists.

Watch in **MySocLab**
Video: *Social Inequalities: Race and Ethnicity*

Asian Americans

Although Asian Americans share some racial traits, enormous cultural diversity characterizes this category of people with ancestors from dozens of nations. In 2011, the total number of Asian Americans exceeded 16 million, or about 5.2 percent of the U.S. population. Asian Americans represent the largest number and share of immigrants to the United States (430,000 immigrants in 2010 or 36 percent of the total), even compared to Hispanics (370,000 immigrants or 31 percent) (Pew Research Center, 2011). National Map 14–3 on page 411 shows the distribution of the Asian American, as well as the Hispanic American, African American, and Arab American populations across the United States.

The largest category of Asian Americans is people of Chinese ancestry (3.5 million), followed by those of Asian Indian (2.9 million), Filipino (2.5 million), Vietnamese (1.7 million), Korean (1.5 million), and Japanese (757,000) descent. Almost one-third of Asian Americans live in California.

Young Asian Americans command attention and respect as high achievers and are disproportionately represented at our country's best colleges and universities. Many of their elders, too, have made economic and social gains; most Asian Americans now live in middle-class suburbs, and an increasing number of Asian Americans live in some of the highest-income neighborhoods in the country. Yet despite (and sometimes because of) this achievement, Asian Americans often find that others are aloof or outright hostile toward them (O'Hare, Frey, & Fost, 1994; Chua-Eoan, 2000; Lee & Marlay, 2007).

The achievement of some Asian Americans has given rise to a "model minority" stereotype that is misleading because it hides the sharp differences in class standing found among their ranks. We will focus first on the history and current standing of Chinese Americans and Japanese Americans—the longest-established Asian American minorities—and conclude with a brief look at the more recent arrivals.

On average, Asian Americans have income above the national median. At the same time, however, the poverty rate in many Asian American communities—including San Francisco's Chinatown—is well above average.

Chinese Americans

Chinese immigration to the United States began in 1849 as a result of the economic boom of California's Gold Rush. New towns and businesses sprang up overnight, and the demand for cheap labor attracted some 100,000 Chinese immigrants. Most Chinese workers were young men who were willing to take difficult, low-status jobs that whites did not want. But the economy soured in the 1870s, and desperate whites began to compete with the

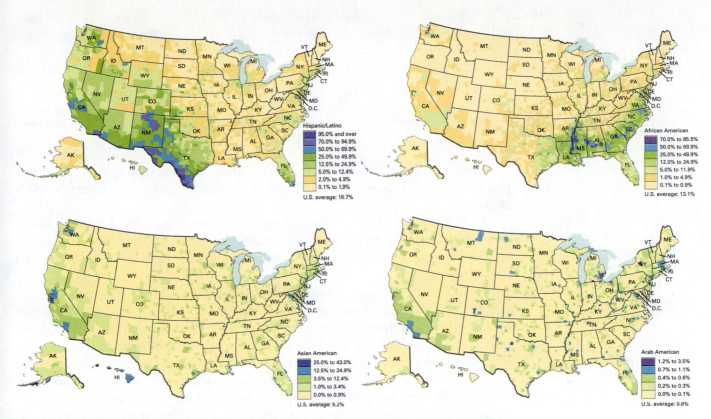

NATIONAL MAP 14–3 The Concentration of Hispanics or Latinos, African Americans, Asian Americans, and Arab Americans, by County

In 2011, people of Asian descent represented 5.2 percent of the U.S. population, compared with 16.7 percent Hispanic Americans, 13.1 percent African Americans, and 0.6 percent Arab Americans. These maps show the geographic distribution of these categories of people in 2011 (data for Arab Americans is 2010). Comparing them we see that the southern half of the United States is home to far more minorities than the northern half. But do they all concentrate in the same areas? What patterns do the maps reveal?

Source: U.S. Census Bureau (2011, 2012).

Chinese for whatever work could be found. Suddenly, the hardworking Chinese were seen as a threat. Economic hard times led to prejudice and discrimination (Ling, 1971; Boswell, 1986). Soon laws were passed barring Chinese people from many occupations, and public opinion turned strongly against the "Yellow Peril."

In 1882, the U.S. government passed the first of several laws limiting Chinese immigration. This action caused domestic hardship in the United States, because Chinese men in effect were then living in a "bachelor society" where they outnumbered Chinese women by twenty to one. This sex imbalance drove the Chinese population down to only 60,000 by 1920. Because Chinese women already in the United States were in high demand, they soon lost much of their traditional submissiveness to men (Hsu, 1971; Lai, 1980; Sowell, 1981).

Responding to racial hostility, some Chinese moved east; many more sought the relative safety of urban Chinatowns. There Chinese traditions flourished, and kinship networks, called *clans,* provided financial assistance to individuals and represented the interests of all. At the same time, however, living in an all-Chinese community discouraged residents from learning English, which limited their job opportunities (Wong, 1971).

A renewed need for labor during World War II prompted President Franklin Roosevelt to end the ban on Chinese immigration in 1943 and to extend the rights of citizenship to Chinese Americans born abroad. Many responded by moving out

TABLE 14–4 The Social Standing of Asian Americans, 2011

	All Asian Americans	Chinese Americans	Japanese Americans	Asian Indian Americans	Filipino Americans	Korean Americans	Entire U.S. Population
Median family income	$72,996	$77,209	$90,550	$102,894	$85,222	$61,452	$60,974
Percentage in poverty	12.3%	15.1%	7.8%	8.1%	6.4%	15.6%	15.0%
Completion of four or more years of college (age 25 and over)	51.0%	52.3%	48.3%	71.1%	47.6%	52.6%	30.9%

Source: U.S. Census Bureau (2012).

of Chinatowns and pursuing cultural assimilation. In Honolulu in 1900, for example, 70 percent of Chinese people lived in Chinatown; today, the figure is below 20 percent.

By 1950, many Chinese Americans had experienced upward social mobility. Today, people of Chinese ancestry are no longer limited to self-employment in laundries and restaurants; many hold high-prestige positions, especially in fields related to science and technology.

As shown in Table 14–4, the median family income of Chinese Americans in 2011 was $77,209, which is above the national average of $60,974. However, the higher income of all Asian Americans reflects a larger number of family members in the labor force.[4] Chinese Americans also have a record of educational achievement, with the share of college graduates (52.3 percent) well above the national average (30.9 percent).

Despite their successes, many Chinese Americans still deal with subtle (and sometimes blatant) prejudice and discrimination. Such hostility is one reason that poverty remains a problem for many Chinese Americans. The problem of poverty is most common among people who remain in the socially isolated Chinatowns working in restaurants or other low-paying jobs, which raises the question of whether racial and ethnic enclaves help their residents or exploit them (Portes & Jensen, 1989; Kinkead, 1992; Gilbertson & Gurak, 1993).

Japanese Americans

Japanese immigration to the United States began slowly in the 1860s, reaching only 3,000 by 1890. Most were men who came to the Hawaiian Islands (annexed by the United States in 1898 and made a state in 1959) as a source of cheap labor. After 1900, however, as the number of Japanese immigrants to California rose (reaching 140,000 by 1915), white hostility increased (Takaki, 1998). In 1907, the United States signed an agreement with Japan curbing the entry of men—the chief economic threat—while allowing women to enter this country to ease the Japanese sex ratio imbalance. In the 1920s, state laws in California and elsewhere segregated the Japanese and banned interracial marriage, just about ending further Japanese immigration. Not until 1952 did the United States extend citizenship to foreign-born Japanese.

Immigrants from Japan and China differed in three important ways. First, there were fewer Japanese immigrants, so they escaped some of the hostility directed toward the more numerous Chinese. Second, the Japanese knew more about the United States than the Chinese did, which helped them assimilate (Sowell, 1981). Third, Japanese immigrants preferred rural farming to clustering in cities, which made them less visible. But many white people objected to Japanese ownership of farmland, so in 1913, California barred further purchases. Many foreign-born Japanese (called *Issei*) responded by placing farmland in the names of their U.S.-born children (*Nisei*), who were constitutionally entitled to citizenship.

---

[4]Median age for all Asian Americans in 2011 was 35.9 years, somewhat below the national median of 37.3 and the non-Hispanic white median of 42.3. But specific categories vary widely in median age: Japanese, 48.6; Filipino, 39.5; Chinese, 38.1; Korean, 37.0; Asian Indian, 32.5; Cambodian, 29.3; Hmong, 21.8 (U.S. Census Bureau, 2012).

Japanese Americans faced their greatest crisis after Japan bombed the U.S. naval fleet at Hawaii's Pearl Harbor on December 7, 1941. Rage was directed at the Japanese living in the United States. Some people feared that Japanese Americans would spy for Japan or commit acts of sabotage. Within a year, President Franklin Roosevelt signed Executive Order 9066, an unprecedented action designed to ensure national security by detaining people of Japanese ancestry in military camps. Authorities soon relocated 120,000 people of Japanese descent (90 percent of all U.S. Japanese) to remote inland reservations (Sun, 1998; Ewers, 2008).

Concern about national security always rises in times of war, but Japanese internment was sharply criticized. First, it targeted an entire category of people, not a single one of whom was known to have committed a disloyal act. Second, most of those imprisoned were *Nisei,* U.S. citizens by birth. Third, the United States was also at war with Germany and Italy, but no comparable action was taken against people of German or Italian ancestry.

Relocation meant selling homes, furnishings, and businesses on short notice for pennies on the dollar. As a result, almost the entire Japanese American population was economically devastated. In military prisons—surrounded by barbed wire and guarded by armed soldiers—families crowded into single rooms, often in buildings that had previously sheltered livestock. The internment ended in 1944 when the U.S. Supreme Court declared it unconstitutional, although the last camp did not close until 1946 (after the war had ended). In 1988, Congress awarded $20,000 to each of the victims as token compensation for the hardships they endured.

After World War II, Japanese Americans staged a dramatic recovery. Having lost their traditional businesses, many entered new occupations; driven by cultural values stressing the importance of education and hard work, Japanese Americans have enjoyed remarkable success. In 2011, the median income of Japanese American families was more than 48 percent higher than the national average, and the rate of poverty among Japanese Americans (7.8 percent) was well below the national figure (15.0 percent).

Upward social mobility has encouraged cultural assimilation and intermarriage. Younger generations of Japanese Americans rarely live in residential enclaves, as many Chinese Americans do, and most marry non-Japanese partners. In the process, some have abandoned their traditions, including the Japanese language. A high proportion of Japanese Americans, however, belong to ethnic associations as a way of maintaining their ethnic identity. Still, some appear to be caught between two worlds: no longer culturally Japanese yet, because of racial differences, not completely accepted in the larger society.

Recent Asian Immigrants

More recent immigrants from Asia include Filipinos, Indians, Koreans, Vietnamese, Guamanians, and Samoans. The Asian American population more than doubled between 1990 and 2011 and currently accounts for more than forty percent of all immigration to the United States (U.S. Department of Homeland Security, 2012).

The entrepreneurial spirit is strong among Asian immigrants. In part this reflects cultural patterns that stress achievement and self-reliance, but having one's own small business is also a strategy for dealing with societal prejudice and discrimination. Small business success is one reason that Asian American family income is above the national average, but it is also true that in many of these businesses, a number of family members work long hours.

Another factor that raises the family income of Asian Americans is a high level of schooling. As shown in Table 14–4, for all categories of Asian Americans, the share of adults with a four-year college degree is well above the national average. Among Asian Indian Americans, who have the highest evducational achievement of all Asian Americans, more than seventy percent of all men and women over the age of twenty-five have completed college, a proportion that is more than twice the national average. This remarkable educational achievement is one reason that Asian Indian Americans had a

TABLE 14–5 The Social Standing of Hispanic Americans, 2011

	All Hispanics	Mexican Americans	Puerto Ricans	Cuban Americans	Entire U.S. Population
Median family income	$40,061	$39,528	$41,168	$46,026	$60,974
Percentage in poverty	25.3%	27.5%	27.4%	19.3%	15.0%
Completion of four or more years of college (age 25 and over)	14.5%	9.6%	16.1%	24.2%	30.9%

Source: U.S. Census Bureau (2012).

median family income of $102,894 in 2011, about 69 percent higher than the national average.

In sum, a survey of Asian Americans presents a complex picture. The Japanese come closest to having achieved social acceptance. But some surveys reveal greater prejudice against Asian Americans than against African Americans (Parrillo & Donoghue, 2005). Median income data suggest that many Asian Americans have prospered. But these numbers reflect the fact that many Asian Americans live in Hawaii, California, or New York, where incomes are high but so are living costs. Then, too, many Asian Americans remain poor. One thing is clear—their high immigration rate and their increasing political clout mean that people of Asian ancestry will play a central role in U.S. society in the decades to come (Takaki, 1998; Barbassa, 2009).

Hispanic Americans/Latinos

In 2011, the number of people of Hispanic descent in the United States topped 52 million (16.7 percent of the population), surpassing the number of Asian Americans (16.3 million, or 5.2 percent of the U.S. population) and even African Americans (40.8 million, or 13.1 percent) and making Hispanics the largest racial or ethnic minority.

However, keep in mind that most people who fall into this category do not describe themselves primarily as "Hispanic" or "Latino." Like Asian Americans, Hispanics are really a cluster of distinct populations, each of which identifies with a particular ancestral nation. In one recent survey, 69 percent of U.S. Hispanics said that Latinos have many cultures and just 24 percent claimed to identify with one "Hispanic community" (Marín & Marín, 1991; Jiménez, 2007; Taylor et al., 2012). About two out of three Hispanics (some 33.6 million) are Mexican Americans, or "Chicanos." Puerto Ricans are next in population size (4.9 million), followed by Cuban Americans (1.9 million). Many other nations of Latin America are represented by smaller numbers.

Although the Hispanic population is increasing all over the country, most Hispanic Americans still live in the Southwest. Almost 40 percent of Californians are Latino (in greater Los Angeles, half the people are).

Median family income for all Hispanics—$40,061 in 2011, as shown in Table 14–5—is well below the national average.[5] As the following sections explain, however, some categories of Hispanics have fared better than others.

Mexican Americans

Some Mexican Americans are descendants of people who lived in a part of Mexico annexed by the United States after the Mexican American War (1846–48). Most, however, are more recent immigrants. Currently, more immigrants come to the United States from Mexico (13.5 percent of the total) than from any other country.

Like many other immigrants, many Mexican Americans have worked as low-wage laborers on farms and in factories. As shown in Table 14–5, the 2011 median family income for Mexican Americans was $39,528, which is two-thirds of the national average.

---

[5]The 2011 median age of the U.S. Hispanic population was 27.5 years, far below the non-Hispanic white median of 42.3 years. This difference accounts for some of the disparity in income and education.

More than one-fourth of Chicano families are poor—a rate that is above the national average. Finally, despite gains since 1980, Mexican Americans still have a high dropout rate and receive much less schooling, on average, than the U.S. population as a whole.

Puerto Ricans

The island of Puerto Rico, like the Philippines, became a U.S. possession when the Spanish-American War ended in 1898. In 1917, Congress passed the Jones Act, which made Puerto Ricans (but not Filipinos) U.S. citizens and made Puerto Rico a territory of the United States. In a 2012 referendum, 61 percent of Puerto Rican voters expressed the wish that Puerto Rico become the fifty-first state, although there is no indication that this might happen any time soon (Patterson, 2012).

Many Hispanic Americans, the largest racial or ethnic minority in the United States, form multigenerational homes. As the country moves toward a minority majority, housing construction is likely to shift in response to the attitudes and desires of the evolving population. What other changes in everyday life might you expect to see as the share of Hispanics and other minorities continues to rise?

New York City is home to more than 750,000 Puerto Ricans. However, about one-third of this community is severely disadvantaged, with 37 percent of families with children living below the poverty line. Adjusting to cultural patterns on the mainland—including, for many, learning English—is one major challenge; also, Puerto Ricans with dark skin encounter prejudice and discrimination. As a result, more people return to Puerto Rico each year than arrive. Between 1990 and 2011, the Puerto Rican population of New York actually fell by about 135,000 (Navarro, 2000; Marzán, Torres, & Luecke, 2008; U.S. Census Bureau, 2012).

This "revolving door" pattern limits assimilation. Sixty-three percent of Puerto Rican families in the United States speak Spanish at home. Speaking Spanish keeps ethnic identity strong but limits economic opportunity. Puerto Ricans also have a higher incidence of female-headed households (39 percent) than most other Hispanics (27 percent) and double the national average (20 percent), a pattern that puts families at greater risk of poverty (U.S. Census Bureau, 2012).

As Table 14–5 shows, the 2011 median family income for Puerto Ricans was $41,168, or about 68 percent of the national average. Although long-term mainland residents have made economic gains, more recent immigrants from Puerto Rico continue to struggle to find work. Overall, Puerto Ricans remain the most socially disadvantaged Hispanic minority.

Cuban Americans

Within a decade after the 1959 Marxist revolution led by Fidel Castro, 400,000 Cubans had fled to the United States. Most settled with other Cuban Americans in Miami, Florida. Many were highly educated business and professional people who wasted little time becoming as successful in the United States as they had been in their homeland.

As Table 14–5 shows, the 2011 median family income for Cuban Americans was $46,026, above that of other Hispanics but still well below the national average of $60,974. The 1.9 million Cuban Americans living in the United States today have managed a delicate balancing act, achieving in the larger society while holding on to much of their traditional culture. Of all Hispanics, Cubans are the most likely to speak Spanish in their homes: Eight out of ten Cuban families do so. However, cultural distinctiveness and highly visible communities, such as Miami's Little Havana, provoke hostility from some people.

Arab Americans

Arab Americans are another U.S. minority that is increasing in size. Like Hispanic Americans, these are people whose ancestors lived in a variety of countries. What is sometimes called "the Arab world" includes twenty-two nations and stretches across northern Africa, from Mauritania and Morocco on Africa's west coast to Egypt and Sudan on Africa's east coast, and extends into the Middle East (western Asia), including Iraq and Saudi Arabia. Not all the people who live in these nations are Arabs, however; for example, the Berber people in Morocco and the Kurds of Iraq are not Arabs.

Arab cultures differ from society to society, but they share widespread use of the Arabic alphabet and language and have Islam as their dominant religion. But keep in mind that "Arab" (an ethnic category) is not the same as "Muslim" (a follower of Islam). A majority of the people living in most Arab countries are Muslims, but some Arabs are Christians or followers of other religions. In addition, most of the world's Muslims do not live in Africa or the Middle East and are not Arabs.

Because many of the world's nations have large Arab populations, immigration to the United States has created a culturally diverse population of Arab Americans. Some Arab Americans are Muslims, and some are not; some speak Arabic, and some do not; some maintain the traditions of their homeland, and some do not. As is the case with Hispanic Americans and Asian Americans, some are recent immigrants, and some have lived in this country for decades or even for generations.

As noted in Table 14–1 on page 394, the government gives the official number of Arab Americans as 1.8 million, but because people may not wish to declare their ethnic background, the actual number may be twice as high.[6] The largest populations of Arab Americans have ancestral ties to Lebanon (27 percent of all Arab Americans), Egypt (12 percent), and Syria (8 percent). Most Arab Americans (65 percent) report ancestral ties to one nation, but 35 percent report both Arab and non-Arab ancestry (U.S. Census Bureau, 2012). A look at National Map 14–3 on page 411 shows the Arab American population is distributed throughout the United States.

Included in the Arab American population are people of all social classes. Some are highly educated professionals who work as physicians, engineers, and professors; others are working-class people who perform various skilled jobs in factories or on construction sites; still others do service work in restaurants, hospitals, or other settings or work in small family businesses. As shown in Table 14–6, median family income for Arab Americans is about the same as the national average ($60,854 compared to the national median of $60,974 in 2011), but Arab Americans have a much higher than average poverty rate (22.8 percent versus 15.0 percent for the population as a whole) (U.S. Census Bureau, 2012).

There are large, visible Arab American communities in a number of U.S. cities, including New York, Chicago, Los Angeles, Houston, and Dearborn (Michigan). Even so, Arab Americans may choose to downplay

Arab American communities can be found in many large cities on the East and West Coasts of the United States, but the heaviest concentrations are found across the upper Midwest. This mosque rises above the cornfields in a rural area near Toledo, Ohio.

TABLE 14–6 The Social Standing of Arab Americans, 2011

	Arab Americans	Entire U.S. Population
Median family income	$60,854	$60,974
Percentage in poverty	22.8%	15.0%
Completion of four or more years of college (age 25 and over)	45.5%	30.9%

Source: U.S. Census Bureau (2012).

[6]The 2011 median age for Arab Americans was 29.9 years, below the national median of 37.3 years.

White ethnic communities persist in many U.S. cities, especially in the Northeast region of the country. These communities are primarily home to working-class men and women whose ancestors came here as immigrants. To many more people, areas such as Philadelphia's Italian Market are a source of attractive cultural diversity.

their ethnicity as a way to avoid prejudice and discrimination. The fact that many terrorist attacks against the United States and other nations have been carried out by Arabs has fueled a stereotype that links being Arab (or Muslim) with being a terrorist. This stereotype is unfair because it blames an entire category of people for actions by a few individuals. But it is probably the reason that the social distance research discussed earlier in this chapter shows students expressing more negative attitudes toward Arabs than toward any other racial or ethnic category. It also helps explain why Arab Americans have been targets of an increasing number of hate crimes and why many Arab Americans feel that they are subject to "ethnic profiling" that threatens their privacy and freedom (Ali & Juarez, 2003; Ali, Lipper, & Mack, 2004; Hagopian, 2004).

White Ethnic Americans

The term "white ethnics" recognizes the ethnic heritage and social disadvantages of many white people. White ethnics are non-WASPs whose ancestors lived in Ireland, Poland, Germany, Italy, or other European countries. More than half (53 percent in 2011) of the U.S. population falls into one or more white ethnic categories.

High rates of emigration from Europe during the nineteenth century first brought Germans and Irish and then Italians and Jews to our shores. Despite cultural differences, all shared the hope that the United States would offer greater political freedom and economic opportunity than their homelands. Most did live better in this country, but the belief that "the streets of America were paved with gold" turned out to be a far cry from reality. Most immigrants found only hard labor for low wages.

White ethnics also endured their share of prejudice and discrimination. Many employers shut their doors to immigrants, posting signs that warned, "None need apply but Americans" (Handlin, 1941:67). In 1921, Congress enacted a quota system that greatly limited immigration, especially by southern and eastern Europeans, who were likely to have darker skin and different cultural backgrounds than the dominant WASPs. This quota system continued until 1968.

Controversy & Debate

Affirmative Action: Solution or Problem?

Gina: I think Gruttner get a raw deal. She should've gotten in.
Ed: Maybe. But diversity is important. I believe in affirmative action.
Natalie: I guess some people do get into college more easily. But that includes guys like me whose father went here.

Barbara Gruttner, who is white, charged that the University of Michigan Law School had unfairly denied her application for admission while admitting many less qualified African American applicants. She claimed that Michigan, a state university, accepted just 9 percent of white students with her grade point average and law school aptitude test scores while admitting 100 percent of African American applicants with comparable scores.

In 2003, in a 6-3 decision, the U.S. Supreme Court ruled against Gruttner, claiming that the University of Michigan Law School could use a policy of affirmative action that takes account of the race of applicants in the interest of creating a socially diverse student body. At the same time, however, the Court struck down the university's undergraduate admissions policy, which awarded points not only for grades and college board scores but also for being a member of an underrepresented minority. A point system of this kind, the Court ruled, is too close to the rigid quota systems rejected by the Court in the past.

With this ruling, the Supreme Court opposed quotalike systems while affirming the importance of racial diversity on campus. Thus colleges and universities can take account of race in order to increase the number of traditionally underrepresented students as long as race is treated as just one variable in a process that evaluates each applicant as an individual (Stout, 2003).

How did the controversial policy of affirmative action begin? At the end of World War II, the U.S. government funded higher education for veterans of all races. The so-called G.I. Bill held special promise for African Americans, most of whom needed financial assistance to enroll in college. By 1960, government funding helped 350,000 black men and women attend college.

However, these individuals were not finding the kinds of jobs for which they were qualified. So the Kennedy administration devised "affirmative action" to broaden opportunities for qualified minorities. Employers were required to monitor hiring, promotion, and admissions policies to eliminate discrimination against minorities, even if unintended.

Defenders of affirmative action see it, first, as a sensible response to our nation's racial and ethnic history, especially for African Americans, who suffered through two centuries of slavery and a century of segregation under Jim Crow laws. Throughout our history, they claim, being white gave people a big advantage. They see minority preference today as a step toward fair compensation for unfair majority preference in the past.

Second, many analysts doubt that we will ever become a color-blind society. They claim that because prejudice and discrimination are rooted deep in U.S. culture, simply saying that we are color-blind does not mean that everyone will be treated fairly.

Third, supporters ask, where would minorities be if the government had not enacted this policy in the 1960s? Major employers, such as fire and police departments in large cities, began hiring minorities, including women, only because of affirmative action. This program expanded the black middle class and increased racial diversity on campuses and in the workplace.

Only about 15 percent of white people say they support racial preferences for African Americans. Even among African Americans themselves, just 43 percent support this policy (NORC, 2013). Critics point out, first of all, that affirmative action began as a temporary remedy to ensure fair competition but soon became a system of "group preferences" and quotas—in short, a form of "reverse discrimination," favoring people not because of performance but because of race, ethnicity, or sex.

Second, critics say, if racial preferences were wrong in the past, they are wrong now. Why should whites today, many of whom are far from privileged, be penalized for past discrimination that was in no way their fault? Giving entire categories of people special treatment compromises standards of excellence.

A third argument against affirmative action is that any policy that lowers standards for a category of people may set them up for disappointment later on. Researchers have found that students who benefit from "group preferences" (whether based on race or having alumni parents) are more likely to struggle academically and may select less challenging majors.

A final argument against affirmative action is that it benefits those who need it least. Favoring minority-owned corporations or holding places in law school for minority applicants helps people who are already relatively privileged. Affirmative action does little for the African American underclass.

There are good arguments for and against affirmative action, and people who want our society to have more racial or ethnic equality fall on both sides of the debate. The disagreement is not whether people of all colors should have equal opportunity but whether the current policy of affirmative action is part of the solution or part of the problem.

What Do You Think?

1. What are the benefits of affirmative action?
2. What drawbacks or problems do you see with this policy?
3. On balance, do you support this policy? Why or why not?

Sources: Bowen and Bok (1999), Kantrowitz and Wingert (2003), Flynn (2008), Sander and Taylor, Jr. (2012), and NORC (2013).

In response to prejudice and discrimination, many white ethnics formed supportive residential enclaves. Some also established footholds in certain businesses and trades: Italian Americans entered the construction industry; the Irish worked in construction and in civil service jobs; Jews predominated in the garment industry; many Greeks (like the Chinese) worked in the retail food business (Newman, 1973).

Many working-class people still live in traditional neighborhoods, although those who prospered have gradually assimilated. Most descendants of immigrants who labored in sweatshops and lived in crowded tenements now lead more comfortable lives. As a result, their ethnic heritage has become a source of pride.

Race and Ethnicity: Looking Ahead

The United States has been and will remain a land of immigrants. Immigration has brought striking cultural diversity and tales of hope, struggle, and success told in hundreds of languages.

Millions of immigrants arrived in a great wave that peaked about 1910. The next two generations saw gradual economic gains and at least some assimilation into the larger society. The government also extended citizenship to Native Americans (1924), foreign-born Filipinos (1942), Chinese Americans (1943), and Japanese Americans (1952).

Another wave of immigration began after World War II and swelled as the government relaxed immigration laws in the 1960s. Today, about 1.25 million people come to the United States each year—about 1.0 million legally and another 250,000 illegally. Today's immigrants come not from Europe but from Latin America and Asia, with Mexicans, Chinese, Indians, and Filipinos arriving in the largest numbers.

As the Power of Society figure that opened this chapter suggests, the growing minority population of the United States will bring changes to this country. In 2012, the political support of African Americans and Hispanics was key to President Obama's reelection. The eyes of both major political parties are now on the country's Hispanic population. Not only is the Hispanic community now the largest minority category, but the size of the Hispanic electorate is projected to double by 2030 as well (Taylor et al., 2012b).

Many of the immigrants who will arrive in the decades to come will face the same type of prejudice and discrimination experienced by those who came before them. In fact, recent years have witnessed rising hostility toward foreigners (an expression of *xenophobia*, from Greek roots meaning "fear of what is strange"). In 1994, California voters passed Proposition 187, which stated that illegal immigrants should be denied health care, social services, and public education; it was later overturned in federal court. More recently, voters there mandated that all children learn English in school. Some landowners in the Southwest have taken up arms to discourage the large number of illegal immigrants crossing the border from Mexico, and our nation is increasing border security as we also wonder how to best deal with the 11.5 million illegal immigrants already here.

Even minorities who have been in the United States for generations feel the sting of prejudice and discrimination. Affirmative action, a policy meant to provide opportunities for members of racial and ethnic minorities, continues to be hotly debated in this country. The Controversy & Debate box on page 418 describes this issue in greater detail.

Like other minorities, today's immigrants hope to gain acceptance and to blend into U.S. society without completely giving up their traditional culture. Some still build racial and ethnic enclaves so that in many cities across the country, the Little Havanas and Koreatowns of today stand alongside the Little Italys and Chinatowns of the past. In addition, new arrivals still carry the traditional hope that their racial and ethnic identities can be a source of pride rather than a badge of inferiority.

Does race still matter in people's social standing?

This chapter explores the importance of race and ethnicity to social standing in the United States. You already know, for example, that the rate of poverty is almost three times higher for African Americans than for whites, and you have also learned that the typical black family earns just 58 percent as much as the typical (non-Hispanic) white family. But rich people—here, we'll define "rich" as a family earning more than $75,000 a year—come in all colors. Here's a chance to test your sociological thinking by answering several questions about how race affects being rich. Look at each of the statements below: Does the statement reflect reality or is it a myth?

Q

1. In the United States, all rich people are white. *Reality or myth?*
2. Rich white families are actually richer than rich African American families. *Reality or myth?*
3. People in rich black families don't work as hard as members of rich white families. *Reality or myth?*
4. When you are rich, color doesn't matter. *Reality or myth?*

1. *Of course, this is a myth.* But when it comes to being rich, race does matter: About 24 percent of African American families are affluent (for Hispanic families, 22 percent), compared to about 46 percent of non-Hispanic white families.

2. *Reality.* Rich white, non-Hispanic families have a mean (average) income more than $214,000 per year. Rich African American families average about $140,000 per year.

3. *Myth.* On average, rich black families are more likely to rely on multiple incomes (that is, they have more people working) than their white counterparts. In addition, rich white families receive more unearned income—income from investments—than rich African American families.

4. *Myth.* Rich African Americans still face social barriers based on their race, just as rich whites benefit from the privileges linked to their color.

Seeing Sociology in *Your* Everyday Life

1. Give several of your friends or family members a quick quiz, asking them what share of the U.S. population is white, Hispanic, African American, and Asian (see Table 14–1 on page 394). Why do you think most white people exaggerate the minority population of this country? (Gallagher, 2003)

2. Go to MySocLab and click on the Student Resources link to access the Sociology in Focus blog, where you can read the latest posts by a team of young sociologists who apply the sociological perspective to topics of popular culture.

3. Do you think people tend to see race in terms of biological traits or as categories constructed by society? What about you? Go to the "Seeing Sociology in *Your* Everyday Life" feature in MySocLab to read more about how society constructs the meaning of race and also for some suggestions about how you might think about the meaning of race.

Making the Grade

Chapter 14
Race and
Ethnicity

The Social Meaning of Race and Ethnicity

14.1 Explain the social construction of race and ethnicity. (pages 392–97)

📖 **Read** the **Document** in **MySocLab**   ✴ **Explore** the **Map** in **MySocLab**

👁 **Watch** the **Video** in **MySocLab**

Race refers to socially constructed categories based on biological traits a society defines as important.
- The meaning and importance of race vary from place to place and over time.
- Societies use racial categories to rank people in a hierarchy, giving some people more money, power, and prestige than others.
- In the past, scientists created three broad categories—Caucasoids, Mongoloids, and Negroids—but there are no biologically pure races.

Ethnicity refers to socially constructed categories based on cultural traits a society defines as important.
- Ethnicity reflects common ancestors, language, and religion.
- The importance of ethnicity varies from place to place and over time.
- People choose to play up or play down their ethnicity.
- Societies may or may not set categories of people apart based on differences in ethnicity.

race a socially constructed category of people who share biologically transmitted traits that members of a society consider important
ethnicity a shared cultural heritage
minority any category of people distinguished by physical or cultural difference that a society sets apart and subordinates

Prejudice and Stereotypes

14.2 Describe the extent and causes of prejudice. (pages 397–401)

Prejudice is a rigid and unfair generalization about a category of people.
- The social distance scale is one measure of prejudice.
- One type of prejudice is the **stereotype**, an exaggerated description applied to every person in some category.
- **Racism**, a very destructive type of prejudice, asserts that one race is innately superior or inferior to another.

There are four **theories of prejudice**:
- **Scapegoat theory** claims that prejudice results from frustration among people who are disadvantaged.
- **Authoritarian personality theory** (Adorno) claims that prejudice is a personality trait of certain individuals, especially those with little education and those raised by cold and demanding parents.
- **Culture theory** (Bogardus) claims that prejudice is rooted in culture; we learn to feel greater social distance from some categories of people.
- **Conflict theory** claims that prejudice is a tool used by powerful people to divide and control the population.

prejudice a rigid and unfair generalization about an entire category of people
stereotype a simplified description applied to every person in some category
racism the belief that one racial category is innately superior or inferior to another
scapegoat a person or category of people, typically with little power, whom people unfairly blame for their own troubles

Discrimination

14.3 Distinguish discrimination from prejudice. (pages 401–2)

👁 **Watch** the **Video** in **MySocLab**

Discrimination refers to actions by which a person treats various categories of people unequally.
- Prejudice refers to *attitudes*; discrimination involves *actions*.
- **Institutional prejudice and discrimination** are biases built into the operation of society's institutions, including schools, hospitals, the police, and the workplace.
- Prejudice and discrimination perpetuate themselves in a vicious circle, resulting in social disadvantage that fuels additional prejudice and discrimination.

discrimination unequal treatment of various categories of people
institutional prejudice and discrimination bias built into the operation of society's institutions

Majority and Minority: Patterns of Interaction

14.4 Identify examples of pluralism, assimilation, segregation, and genocide. (pages 402–4)

Pluralism means that racial and ethnic categories, although distinct, have roughly equal social standing.

- U.S. society is pluralistic in that all people in the United States, regardless of race or ethnicity, have equal standing under the law.
- U.S. society is not pluralistic in that all racial and ethnic categories do not have equal social standing.

Assimilation is a process by which minorities gradually adopt the patterns of the dominant culture.

- Assimilation involves changes in dress, language, religion, values, and friends.
- Assimilation is a strategy to escape prejudice and discrimination and to achieve upward social mobility.
- Some categories of people have assimilated more than others.

Segregation is the physical and social separation of categories of people.

- Although some segregation is voluntary (as by the Amish), majorities usually segregate minorities by excluding them from neighborhoods, schools, and occupations.
- *De jure* segregation is segregation by law; *de facto* segregation describes settings that contain only people of one category.
- Hypersegregation means having little social contact with people beyond the local community.

Genocide is the systematic killing of one category of people by another.

- Historical examples of genocide include the extermination of Jews by the Nazis and the killing of Western-leaning people in Cambodia by Pol Pot.
- Recent examples of genocide include Hutus killing Tutsis in the African nation of Rwanda, Serbs killing Bosnians in the Balkans of Eastern Europe, and systematic killing in the Darfur region of Sudan.

pluralism a state in which people of all races and ethnicities are distinct but have equal social standing

assimilation the process by which minorities gradually adopt patterns of the dominant culture

miscegenation biological reproduction by partners of different racial categories

segregation the physical and social separation of categories of people

genocide the systematic killing of one category of people by another

Race and Ethnicity in the United States

14.5 Assess the social standing of racial and ethnic categories of U.S. society. (pages 404–19)

 Watch the **Video** in **MySocLab**

Native Americans, the earliest human inhabitants of the Americas, have endured genocide, segregation, and forced assimilation. Today, the social standing of Native Americans is well below the national average.

White Anglo-Saxon Protestants (WASPs) were most of the original European settlers of the United States, and many continue to enjoy high social position today.

African Americans experienced more than two centuries of slavery. Emancipation in 1865 gave way to segregation by law (the so-called Jim Crow laws). In the 1950s and 1960s, a national civil rights movement resulted in legislation that outlawed segregated schools and overt discrimination in employment and public accommodations. Today, despite legal equality, African Americans are still disadvantaged.

Asian Americans have suffered both racial and ethnic hostility. Although some prejudice and discrimination continue, both Chinese and Japanese Americans now have above-average income and schooling. Asian immigrants—especially Koreans, Indians, and Filipinos—now account for more than 40% of all immigration to the United States.

Hispanic Americans/Latinos, the largest U.S. minority, include many ethnicities sharing a Spanish heritage. Mexican Americans, the largest Hispanic minority, are concentrated in the southwestern region of the country and are the poorest Hispanic category. Cubans, concentrated in Miami, are the most affluent Hispanic category.

Arab Americans are a growing U.S. minority. Because they come to the United States from so many different nations, Arab Americans are a culturally diverse population, and they are represented in all social classes. They have been a target of prejudice and hate crimes in recent years as a result of a stereotype that links all Arab Americans with terrorism.

White ethnic Americans are non-WASPs whose ancestors emigrated from Europe in the nineteenth and twentieth centuries. In response to prejudice and discrimination, many white ethnics formed supportive residential enclaves.

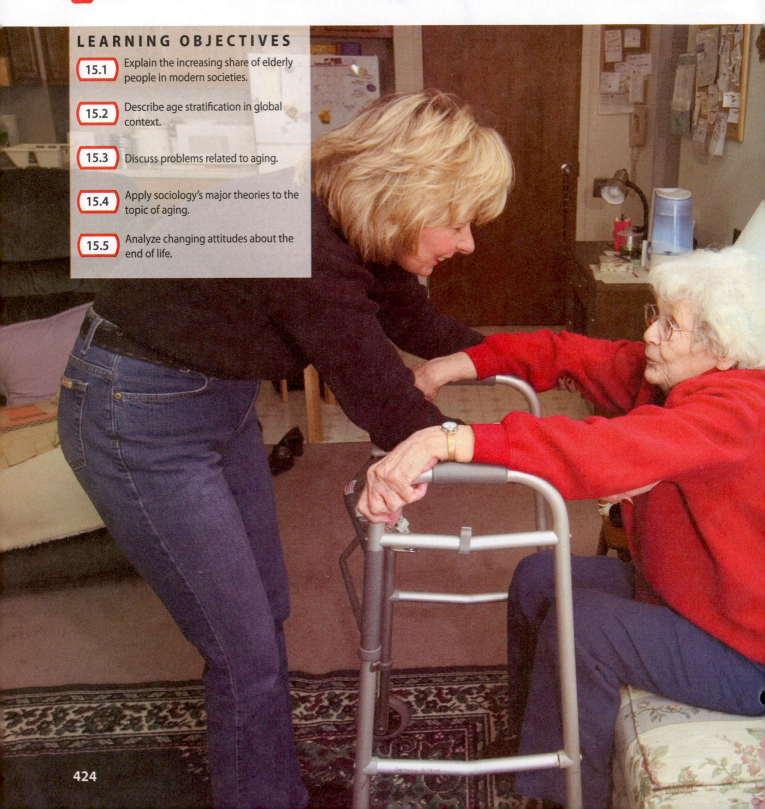

15 Aging and the Elderly

((•)) **Listen** to **Chapter 15** in **MySocLab**

LEARNING OBJECTIVES

15.1 Explain the increasing share of elderly people in modern societies.

15.2 Describe age stratification in global context.

15.3 Discuss problems related to aging.

15.4 Apply sociology's major theories to the topic of aging.

15.5 Analyze changing attitudes about the end of life.

the Power of Society

to shape caregiving for older people

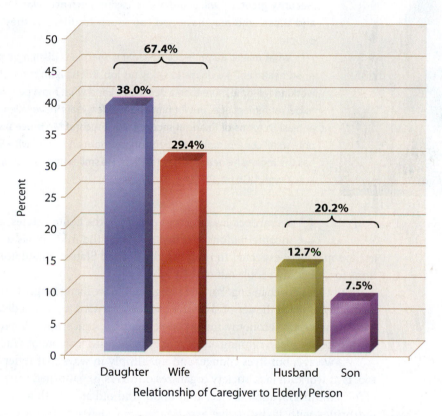

Percent

Relationship of Caregiver to Elderly Person

Source: U.S. Department of Health and Human Services (2012)

What is the likelihood that each of us will serve as a caregiver to an elderly parent or spouse? The answer is "pretty high," and the reason is that as people in our lives move into old age, the odds increase that they will need assistance with some of life's tasks and responsibilities. In the United States, most caregiving comes from members of the aging person's family. But some family members are far more likely to assist than others. Men provide only about 20 percent of caregiving, while women provide more than three times as much. This pattern shows the power of society to define caregiving as a feminine task.

Chapter Overview

For all of us, life is a process of growing older. This chapter explores the consequences of growing old and explains why aging is a dimension of social stratification. The importance of understanding aging is increasing along with the elderly share of our population.

Ralph Bruce smiles at a young couple as they approach the casino entrance. "How are you folks, today?" The pair hold out their ID cards, which Mr. Bruce scans with an electronic reader to be sure both people are over the age of twenty-one. The computer flashes its approval and he waves them through with a cheerful, "Good luck to you!"

It is a normal Friday afternoon at the *Lucky Lady*, a popular gambling casino located in Caruthersville, Missouri, on the Mississippi River. Ralph Bruce is working the "swing shift" from 3 P.M. until 11 P.M. For eight hours, he and two dozen other "security greeters" will stand at the casino entrance, watching for underage people and those who may have had too much to drink, as they welcome hundreds of people.

What makes Ralph Bruce unusual is that he is pushing eighty. He is glad to be in good health and he claims to enjoy his job. But he admits that he never expected to be working full-time more than a decade beyond what most people in our society consider to be "retirement age." But for him, the "golden years" have fallen short of their promise—at least in terms of financial security. For much of Mr. Bruce's working life, he received only small contributions to a pension program and, even with Social Security, he barely has the money he needs to pay the bills. He smiles and says simply, "I guess I'll work until I can't work" (Carrns, 2012).

Several decades ago, most people in the United States, and also in other high-income nations, defined reaching the mid-sixties as "getting old." At that age, people were expected to retire. In the United States, "mandatory retirement" regulations forced many people out of their jobs.

But times are changing. For one thing, people are living longer than ever before. Men and women who reach the age of sixty-five can look forward to several decades more of life. And with the uncertain economy, many people share the concerns of Ralph Bruce that leaving the workforce will mean running out of money before they run out of time.

As we age, our lives change, and not simply in ways that reflect our biology. Society, too, is at work. In fact, society organizes our lives in patterned ways that we call the *stages of life*: childhood, adolescence, adulthood, and old age. As this chapter explains, growing old brings with it distinctive experiences and also significant disadvantages, including lower income and sometimes the experience of prejudice and discrimination, both in and beyond the workplace. For this reason, like class, gender, and race, growing old is a dimension of social stratification. The importance of learning about old age is increasing all the time because the number of older people in the U.S. population is greater than ever and rising rapidly.

The Graying of the United States

(15.1) Explain the increasing share of elderly people in modern societies.

A quiet but powerful revolution is reshaping the United States. As shown in Figure 15–1 on page 427, in 1900, the United States was a nation of young people, with half the population under age twenty-three; just 4 percent had reached sixty-five. But the number of elderly people—women and men aged sixty-five or older—increased tenfold during the

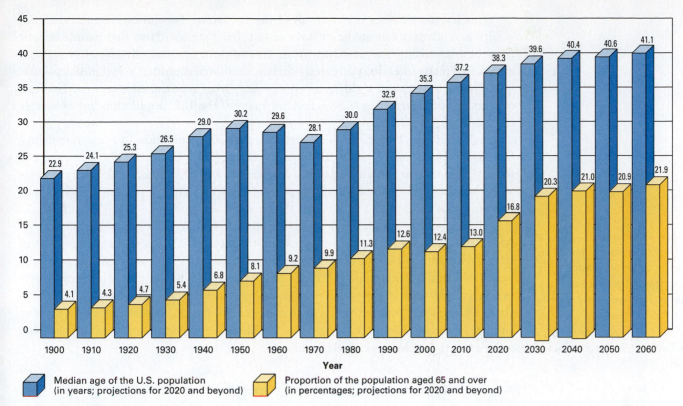

FIGURE 15–1 The Graying of U.S. Society

The proportion of the U.S. population over the age of sixty-five tripled during the last century. The median age of the U.S. population has now passed thirty-seven years and will continue to rise.

Source: U.S. Census Bureau (2012).

last century. By 2011, the number of seniors exceeded 41 million and half the population was over thirty-seven. Seniors now easily outnumber teenagers, and they account for 13 percent of the entire population. By 2050, the number of seniors will double again to more than 83 million, and half the country's people will be over forty (U.S. Census Bureau, 2012).

In nearly all high-income nations, the share of elderly people is increasing rapidly. There are two reasons for this increase: low birth rates (people are having fewer children) and increasing longevity (people are living longer).

In the United States, the ranks of the elderly will swell even more rapidly, as the first of the baby boomers—some 76 million strong—reached age sixty-five in 2011. As recent political debate shows, there are serious questions about the ability of the current Social Security system to meet the needs of so many older people.

Birth Rate: Going Down

The U.S. birth rate has been falling for more than a century. This is the usual trend as societies industrialize. Why? Because in industrial societies, children are more likely to survive into adulthood, and so couples have fewer children. In addition, although to farming families children are an economic asset, to families in industrial societies children are an economic liability. In other words, children no longer add to their family's financial income but instead are a major expense.

Finally, as more and more women work outside the home, they choose to have fewer children. This trend reflects both the rising standing of women and advances in birth control technology over the past century.

Life Expectancy: Going Up

Life expectancy in the United States is going up. In 1900, a typical female born here could expect to live just 48 years, and a male, 46 years. By contrast, females born in 2011 can look forward to living 81.1 years, and males can expect to live 76.3 years (Hoyert & Xu, 2012).

This longer life span is one result of the Industrial Revolution. Greater material wealth and advances in medicine have raised living standards so that people benefit from better housing and more nutrition. In addition, medical advances have almost eliminated many infectious diseases—such as smallpox, diphtheria, and measles—that killed many infants and children a century ago. Other medical advances help us fend off cancer and heart disease, which claim most of the U.S. population but now later in life.

As life becomes longer, the oldest segment of the U.S. population—people over eighty-five—is increasing rapidly and is already forty times greater than in 1900. These men and women now number 5.8 million (almost 2 percent of the total population). Their numbers will grow to about 18 million (about 4.3 percent of the total) by the year 2060 (U.S. Census Bureau, 2012).

This major increase in the elderly population will change our society in many ways. As the number of older people retiring from the labor force goes up, the proportion of nonworking adults—already about ten times greater than in 1900—will demand ever more health care and other resources. The ratio of working-age adults to nonworking elderly people, called the *old-age dependency ratio,* will fall from the current level of four to one to about 2.5 to one by the year 2050 (U.S. Social Security Administration, 2012). With fewer and fewer workers to support tomorrow's swelling elderly population, what security can today's young people expect in their old age?

An Aging Society: Cultural Change

As the average age of the population rises and the share over age sixty-five climbs ever higher, cultural patterns are likely to change. Through much of the twentieth century, the young rarely mixed with the old, so most people learned little about old age. But as this country's elderly population steadily increases, age segregation will decline. Younger people will see more seniors on the highways, at shopping malls, and at sporting events. In addition, the design of buildings—including homes, stores, stadiums, and college classrooms—is likely to change in order to ease access for older shoppers, sports fans, and students.

Colleges are also opening their doors to more older people, and seniors are becoming a familiar sight on many campuses. As baby boomers (people born between 1946 and 1964) enter old age, many are deciding to put off retirement and complete degrees or train for new careers. Community colleges, which offer extensive programs that prepare people for new types of work, are now offering a wide range of "second career" programs that attract older people (Olson, 2006).

Of course, the extent of contact with older people depends a great deal on where in the country you live. The elderly represent a far larger share of the population in some regions, especially in the midsection, from North Dakota and Minnesota down to Texas, as shown in National Map 15–1 on page 429.

When thinking about how an aging population will change our ways of life, keep in mind that seniors are socially diverse. Being "elderly" is a category open to everyone, if we are lucky enough to live that long. Elders in the United States are women and men of all classes, races, and ethnic backgrounds.

The "Young Old" and the "Old Old"

Analysts sometimes distinguish two cohorts of the elderly, roughly equal in size. The younger elderly, who are between sixty-five and seventy-five, typically live independently with good health and financial security; they are likely to be living as couples. The older elderly, those past age seventy-five, are more likely to have health and money problems and to be dependent on others. Because of their greater longevity, women outnumber men in the elderly population, an imbalance that grows greater with advancing age. Among the "oldest old," those over age eighty-five, 67 percent are women.

For a close-up look at a country where the graying of the population is taking place even faster than in the United States, **Read More** in **MySocLab**, *Can Too Many Be Too Old? A Report from Japan*

Explore the elderly population in your local community and in counties across the United States in **MySocLab**

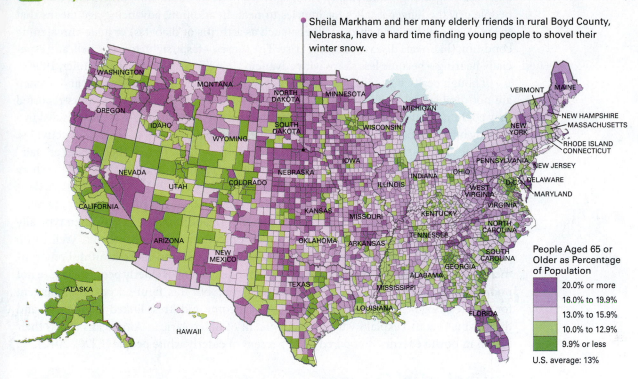

Sheila Markham and her many elderly friends in rural Boyd County, Nebraska, have a hard time finding young people to shovel their winter snow.

People Aged 65 or Older as Percentage of Population

- 20.0% or more
- 16.0% to 19.9%
- 13.0% to 15.9%
- 10.0% to 12.9%
- 9.9% or less

U.S. average: 13%

NATIONAL MAP 15–1 The Elderly Population across the United States

Common sense suggests that elderly people live in the Sunbelt, enjoying the warmer climate of the South and Southwest. Although it is true that Florida has a disproportionate share of people over age sixty-five, it turns out that most counties with high percentages of older people are in the Midwest. What do you think accounts for this pattern? Hint: Which regions of the United States do younger people leave in search of jobs?

Source: U.S. Census Bureau (2012).

Growing Old: Biology and Culture

15.2 Describe age stratification in global context.

Studying the graying of a society's population is the focus of **gerontology** (derived from the Greek word *geron*, meaning "old person"), *the study of aging and the elderly*. Gerontologists—who work in many disciplines, including medicine, psychology, and sociology—investigate not only how people change as they grow old but also the different ways in which societies around the world define old age.

gerontology the study of aging and the elderly

Biological Changes

Aging consists of gradual, ongoing changes in the body. But how we experience life's transitions—whether we welcome our maturity or complain about physical decline—depends largely on how our cultural system defines the various stages of life. In general, U.S. culture takes a positive view of biological changes that occur early in life. Through childhood and adolescence, people look forward to expanding opportunities and responsibilities.

But today's youth-oriented culture takes a dimmer view of the biological changes that happen later on. Few people receive congratulations for getting old, at least not until they reach eighty-five or ninety. Rather, we offer sympathy to friends as they turn forty, fifty, and sixty and make jokes to avoid facing up to the fact that advancing age will put us all on a slippery slope of physical and mental decline. In short, we assume that by age fifty or sixty, people stop growing *up* and begin growing *down*.

Growing old brings on predictable changes: gray hair, wrinkles, height and weight loss, and declining strength and vitality. After age fifty, bones become more brittle, and the older people get, the longer it takes for injuries to heal. In addition, advancing age means that the odds of developing a chronic illness (such as arthritis or diabetes) or a life-threatening condition (like heart disease or cancer) rise. The senses—taste, sight, touch, smell, and especially hearing—become less sharp with advancing age (Treas, 1995; Metz & Miner, 1998).

Though health becomes more fragile as people get older, most elderly men and women are not disabled by their physical condition. In 2010, only 16 percent of seniors reported they could not walk a quarter-mile by themselves, and fewer than one in twenty resided in a nursing home. About 12 percent needed help with shopping, chores, or other daily activities. Overall, only 26 percent of people over age seventy-five characterized their health as "fair" or "poor"; 74 percent consider their overall condition "good" or "excellent." In fact, the share of seniors reporting good or excellent health is going up (CDC, 2012; Schiller et al., 2012).

Of course, some elders have better health than others. Health problems become more common after people reach the age of seventy-five. In addition, because women typically live longer than men, they suffer more from chronic disabilities like arthritis. Well-to-do people also fare better because they live and work in safer and more healthful environments and can afford better medical care. Eighty-one percent of elderly people who are not poor assess their own health as "excellent" or "good," but that figure drops to 57 percent for people living below the poverty level. Lower income and stress linked to prejudice and discrimination also explain why only 62 percent of older African Americans assess their health in positive terms, compared to 78 percent of elderly white people (CDC, 2012).

Psychological Changes

Just as we tend to overstate the physical problems of old age, we sometimes exaggerate the psychological changes that accompany growing old. The common view about intelligence over the life course can be summed up as "What goes up must come down."

If we measure skills such as sensorimotor coordination—the ability to arrange objects to match a drawing—we do find a steady decline after midlife. The ability to learn new material and to think quickly also declines, although not until around age seventy. Even then, only about 7 percent of adults over age seventy suffer symptoms ranging from mild memory loss to more serious mental conditions. For most, the ability to apply familiar ideas holds steady with advancing age, and the capacity for thoughtful reflection and spiritual growth actually increases (Baltes & Schaie, 1974; Metz & Miner, 1998; Cortez, 2008).

We all wonder if we will think or feel differently as we get older. Gerontologists report that for better or worse, the answer is usually no. The most common personality changes with advancing age are becoming less materialistic, more mellow in attitudes, and more thoughtful. Generally, two elderly people who had been childhood friends would recognize in each other the same personality traits that brought them together as youngsters (Neugarten, 1977; Wolfe, 1994).

Aging and Culture

November 1, Kandy, Sri Lanka. Our little van struggles up the steep mountain incline. Breaks in the lush vegetation offer spectacular views that interrupt our conversation about growing old. "Then there are no old-age homes in your country?" I ask. "In Colombo and other cities, I am sure," our driver responds, "but not many. We are not like you Americans." "And how is that?" I counter, stiffening a bit. His eyes remain fixed on the road: "We would not leave our fathers and mothers to live alone."

When do people grow old? How do younger people regard society's oldest members? How do elderly people view themselves? The answers people give to these questions vary from society to society, showing that although aging is a biological process, it is also a matter of culture.

The reality of growing old is as much a matter of culture as it is of biology. In the United States, being elderly often means being inactive; yet in many other countries of the world elders often continue many familiar and productive routines.

How long and how well people live depend, first, on a society's technology and standard of living. Through most of human history, as the English philosopher Thomas Hobbes (1588–1679) famously put it, people's lives were "nasty, brutish, and short" (although Hobbes himself made it to the ripe old age of ninety-one). In his day, most people married and had children as teenagers, became middle-aged in their twenties, and died from various illnesses in their thirties and forties. Many of history's great men and women never reached what we would call old age at all: The English poet Keats died at age twenty-six; Mozart, the Austrian composer, at thirty-five. Among famous writers, none of the three Brontë sisters lived to the end of her thirties; Edgar Allan Poe died at forty, Henry David Thoreau at forty-five, Oscar Wilde at forty-six, and William Shakespeare at fifty-two.

By about 1900, however, rising living standards and advancing medical technology in the United States and Western Europe combined to extend longevity to about age fifty. As Global Map 15–1 on page 432 shows, this is still the figure in many low-income countries today. In high-income nations, however, increasing affluence has added almost thirty years to the average life span.

Just as important as longevity is the value societies attach to their senior members. As Chapter 10 ("Social Stratification") explains, all societies distribute basic resources unequally. We now turn to the importance of age in this process.

Age Stratification: A Global Survey

Like race, ethnicity, and gender, age is a basis for social ranking. **Age stratification** is *the unequal distribution of wealth, power, and privilege among people at different stages of the life course.* Age stratification varies according to a society's level of technological development.

Hunting and Gathering Societies

As Chapter 4 ("Society") explains, without the technology to produce a surplus of food, hunters and gatherers must be nomadic. This means that survival depends on physical strength and stamina. As members of these societies grow old (in this case, about age thirty), they become less active and may even be considered an economic burden and, when food is in short supply, abandoned (Sheehan, 1976).

Pastoral, Horticultural, and Agrarian Societies

Once societies develop the technology to raise their own crops and animals, they produce a surplus. In such societies, some individuals build up considerable wealth over a lifetime. Of all age categories, the most privileged are typically the elderly, a pattern called

age stratification the unequal distribution of wealth, power, and privilege among people at different stages of the life course

gerontocracy a form of social organization in which the elderly have the most wealth, power, and prestige

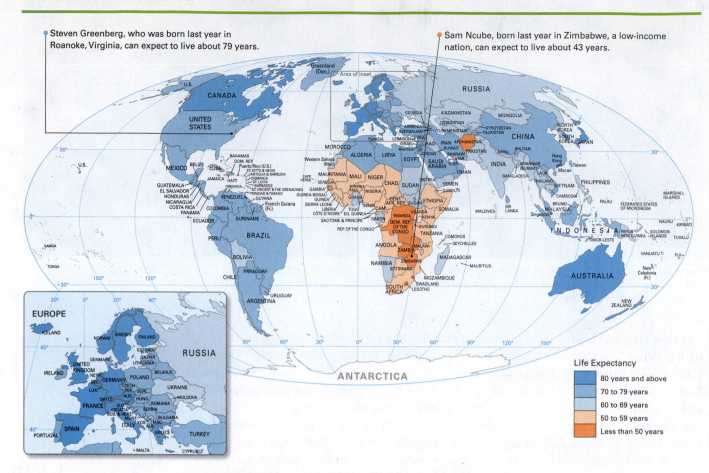

Steven Greenberg, who was born last year in Roanoke, Virginia, can expect to live about 79 years.

Sam Ncube, born last year in Zimbabwe, a low-income nation, can expect to live about 43 years.

Life Expectancy

	80 years and above
	70 to 79 years
	60 to 69 years
	50 to 59 years
	Less than 50 years

GLOBAL MAP 15–1 Life Expectancy in Global Perspective

Life expectancy shot up during the twentieth century in high-income countries, including Canada, the United States, Western Europe, Japan, and Australia. A newborn in the United States can now expect to live about seventy-nine years, and our life expectancy would be greater still were it not for the high risk of death among infants born into poverty. Because poverty is the rule in much of the world, lives are correspondingly shorter, especially in parts of Africa, where life expectancy may be less than fifty years.

Source: Population Reference Bureau (2012).

gerontocracy, *a form of social organization in which the elderly have the most wealth, power, and prestige.* Old people, particularly men, are honored and sometimes feared by their families, and they remain active leaders of society until they die. This respect for the elderly also explains the widespread practice of ancestor worship in agrarian societies.

Industrial and Postindustrial Societies

Industrialization pushes living standards upward and advances medical technology, both of which increase human life expectancy. But although industrialization adds to the *quantity* of life, it can harm the *quality* of life for older people. Contrary to the practice in traditional societies, industrial societies give little power and prestige to the elderly. The reason is that with industrialization, the prime source of wealth shifts from land (typically controlled by the oldest members of society) to businesses and other goods (usually owned and managed by younger people). For all low-income nations, 37 percent of men and 14 percent of women over the age of sixty-five remain in the labor force. Across high-income countries, even with greater life expectancy, these percentages are far smaller: 15 percent of men and 8 percent of women over the age of sixty-five are still working for income. The fact that many older people move out of the paid labor force in the United States is one reason that average income declines after the age of seventy (U.S. Census Bureau, 2012; International Labour Organization, 2012).

In high-income countries, younger people move away from their parents to pursue careers, depending less on their parents and more on their own earning power. In addition, because industrial, urban societies change rapidly, the skills, traditions, and life experiences that served the old may seem unimportant to the young. Finally, the tremendous productivity of industrial nations means that not all members of a society need to work, so most of the very old and the very young play nonproductive roles.

The long-term effect of all these factors transforms *elders* (a word with positive connotations) into *the elderly* (a term that carries far less prestige). In postindustrial societies such as the United States and Canada, economic and political leaders are usually people between the ages of forty and sixty who combine experience with up-to-date skills. Even as the U.S. population, on average, is getting older, the country's corporate executives are getting younger, declining from an average age of fifty-nine in 1980 to fifty-two today (U.S. Department of Labor, 2012).

In rapidly changing sectors of the economy, especially the high-tech fields, many key executives are younger still, sometimes barely out of college. Industrial societies often give older people only marginal participation in the economy because they lack the knowledge and training demanded in a fast-changing marketplace.

Some occupations are dominated by older people. The average farmer is fifty-five, well above the age of the typical U.S. worker, which is only forty-two. One-fourth of today's farmers are over the age of sixty-five. Older people also predominate in other traditional occupations, working as barbers, tailors, and shop clerks, and in jobs that involve minimal physical activity, such as night security guards (Yudelman & Kealy, 2000; U.S. Department of Agriculture, 2009; U.S. Department of Labor, Bureau of Labor Statistics, 2012).

Japan: An Exceptional Case

Throughout the last century, Japan stood out as an exception to the rule that industrialization lowers the social standing of older people. Not only is the share of seniors in Japan increasing as fast as anywhere in the world, but Japan's more traditional culture gives older people great importance. Most elders in Japan live with an adult daughter or son, and they play a significant role in family life. Elderly men in Japan are also more likely than their U.S. counterparts to stay in the labor force, and in many Japanese corporations, the oldest employees enjoy the greatest respect. But Japan is becoming more like other industrial nations, where growing old means giving up some measure of social importance. In addition, a long economic downturn has left Japanese families less able to care for their older members, which may further weaken the traditional importance of elders (Ogawa & Retherford, 1997; Onishi, 2006; Lah, 2008).

Transitions and Challenges of Aging

15.3 Discuss problems related to aging.

We confront change at each stage of life. Old age has its rewards, but of all stages of the life course, it presents the greatest challenges.

Physical decline in old age is less serious than most younger people think. But even so, older people endure pain, limit their activities, increase their dependency on others, lose dear friends and relatives, and face up to their own mortality. Because our culture places such a high value on youthfulness, aging in the United States often means added fear and self-doubt. As one retired psychologist quipped about old age, "Don't let the current hype about the joys of retirement fool you. They are not the best of times. It's just that the alternative is even worse" (Rubenstein, 1991).

Finding Meaning

Chapter 5 ("Socialization") presented Erik Erikson's theory that elderly people must resolve a tension of "integrity versus despair." No matter how much they still may be learning and achieving, older people recognize that their lives are nearing an end. Thus elderly people spend

Although finding meaning can be challenging for people at all stages of the life course, this process can be especially difficult for older people nearing or in old age, who tend to see their lives in terms of what they have lost or what they can no longer do. The television show *Hot in Cleveland* follows the lives of three past-their-prime actresses who leave southern California for a less youth-obsessed culture in Cleveland, Ohio, where they share a home and contend with an older caretaker (Betty White), who shows them that older people can still have plenty of attitude.

more time reflecting on their past, remembering disappointments as well as accomplishments. Integrity, to Erikson (1963, orig. 1950; 1980), means assessing your life realistically. Without such honesty, this stage of life may turn into a time of despair—a dead end with little positive meaning.

In a classic study of people in their seventies, Bernice Neugarten (1971) found that some people cope with growing older better than others. Worst off are those who fail to come to terms with aging; they develop *disintegrated and disorganized personalities* marked by despair. Many of these people end up as passive residents of hospitals or nursing homes.

Slightly better off are people with *passive-dependent personalities*. They have little confidence in their abilities to cope with daily events, sometimes seeking help even if they do not really need it. Always in danger of social withdrawal, their life satisfaction level is relatively low.

A third category develops *defended personalities,* living independently but fearful of aging. They try to shield themselves from the reality of old age by fighting to stay youthful and physically fit. Although it is good to be concerned about health, setting unrealistic standards breeds stress and disappointment.

Most of Neugarten's subjects, however, displayed what she termed *integrated personalities,* coping well with the challenges of growing old. As Neugarten sees it, the key to successful aging lies in keeping personal dignity and self-confidence while accepting growing old.

Social Isolation

Being alone can cause anxiety at any age, but isolation is most common among elderly people. Retirement closes off one source of social interaction, physical problems may limit mobility, and negative stereotypes of the elderly as "over the hill" may discourage younger people from close social contact with them.

But the greatest cause of social isolation is the death of significant others, especially the death of a spouse. One study found that almost three-fourths of widows and widowers cited loneliness as their most serious problem (Lund, 1989).

But loneliness is not the same as being alone. On the contrary, one recent study found that more than half of the older people who said they felt lonely were married. The problem of loneliness can result from being alone, but it also results from physical or emotional issues that isolate people from those around them. In other cases, social isolation results from living in fear. An older person who is afraid of falling, for example, is much more likely to avoid social activities that require walking, resulting in social isolation. Whatever its cause, the more social isolation people experience, the greater the chances they will experience dementia or other types of mental and physical decline (Cornwell & Waite, 2009; Holwerda et al., 2012).

Gender plays a part in patterns of social isolation. The problem of social isolation falls more heavily on women because they typically outlive their husbands. Table 15–1 shows that 72 percent of men aged sixty-five and over live with spouses, but only 42 percent of elderly women do. In

TABLE 15–1 Living Arrangements of the Elderly, 2012

	Men	Women
Living alone	19%	37%
Living with spouse	72	42
Living with other relatives or nonrelatives	9	21

Note: In 2012, some 3.5 percent of elderly people lived in nursing homes. This number includes people from all of these categories.

Source: U.S. Census Bureau (2012), Federal Interagency Forum on Aging-Related Statistics (2012).

addition, 37 percent of older women (especially the "older elderly") live alone, compared to 19 percent of older men (Federal Interagency Forum, 2012).

For most older people, family members are the major source of social support. The majority of U.S. seniors have at least one adult child living no more than 10 miles away. About half of these nearby children visit their parents at least once a week, although research confirms that daughters are more likely than sons to visit regularly (Lin & Rogerson, 1994; Rimer, 1998).

Retirement

Beyond earnings, work provides us with an important part of our personal identity. Therefore, retirement means not only a reduction in income but also less social prestige and perhaps some loss of purpose in life.

Some organizations help ease this transition. Colleges and universities, for example, confer the title "professor emeritus" (*emeritus* in Latin means "fully earned") on retired faculty members, many of whom are permitted to keep library privileges, a parking space, and an e-mail account. These highly experienced faculty members can be a valuable resource not only to students but to younger professors as well (Parini, 2001).

Because seniors are socially diverse, there is no single formula for successful retirement. Part-time work occupies many people entering old age and provides some extra cash as well. Grandparenting is an enormous source of pleasure for many older people. Volunteer work is another path to rewarding activity, especially for those who have saved enough so that they do not have to work—one reason that volunteerism is increasing more among seniors than in any other age category (Gardyn, 2000; Savishinsky, 2000; Shapiro, 2001).

Although retirement is a familiar idea, the concept developed only within the past century or so in high-income countries. High-income societies are so productive that not everyone needs to work; in addition, advanced technology places a premium on up-to-date skills. Therefore, retirement emerged in these societies as a strategy to permit younger workers—presumably those with the most current knowledge and training—to have a larger presence in the labor force. Fifty years ago, most companies in the United States even had a mandatory retirement age, typically between sixty-five and seventy, although in the 1970s, Congress enacted laws phasing out such policies so that they apply to only a few occupations today. For example, air traffic controllers hired after 1972 must retire at age fifty-six, commercial airline pilots must retire at age sixty, and most police officers and firefighters must retire between fifty-five and sixty (Gokhale, 2004). In most high-income societies, then, retirement is a personal choice made possible by private and government pension programs. In low-income nations, most people do not have the opportunity to retire from paid work.

Even in high-income nations, of course, people can choose to retire only if they can afford to do so. Generally speaking, when economic times are good, people save more and retire earlier in life. This was generally the case in the United States during the second half of the twentieth century. By 2010, the median net worth of senior households had swelled to about $210,000. Greater wealth permitted more people to retire earlier, and so the median retirement age fell from sixty-eight in 1950 to sixty-three by 2005.

However, for a large share of seniors, the economic downturn that began in 2007 has had the opposite effect. The recession has forced many older people to confront the harsh reality that their retirement "nest egg" has been cracked by the sinking stock market, disappearing pensions, and declining home values. With so much wealth suddenly gone, many had little choice but to continue working. In 1998, for example, 11.9 percent of people age sixty-five and older were still in the labor force. By 2011, this share had increased to 16.1 percent. Many other high-income nations, faced with rapidly rising costs of pension programs, are considering legislation to encourage or even mandate later retirement (Toossi, 2009; Brandon, 2010; U.S. Department of Labor, Bureau of Labor Statistics, 2012).

For a closer look at how the recent recession has affected people's retirement plans, **Read More** in **MySocLab**, *Back to Work! Will We Ever Get to Retire?*

A recent policy to deal with hard times is "staged retirement," in which people continue working well past the age of sixty-five, reducing their hours at work in stages as they build greater financial security (Kadlec, 2002; McCartney, 2005; Koskela, 2008; Trumbull, 2011).

Some retired people, including many whose investments have declined in value or who now face expenses that they cannot afford, are being forced to go back to paid work. Some are taking courses at community colleges to gain the skills they need to find a good job (Leland, 2009). But, even with schooling and the determination to succeed, the road back to a paycheck is not always easy.

Aging and Poverty

By the time they reach sixty-five, most people have paid off their home mortgages and their children's college expenses. But the costs of medical care, household help, and home utilities (like heat) typically go up. At the same time, retirement often means a significant decline in income. The good news is that over recent decades, seniors have built up more wealth than ever before (as noted, a median net worth of about $210,000 in 2010). However, most of this wealth is tied up in the value of their homes, so it is not readily available to help pay expenses. The economic downturn has also hurt many seniors, as employers have cut back retirement pensions and benefits at the same time that investment income has declined. Today's reality, then, is that for about 60 percent of people over the age of sixty-five, the largest source of income is from the government in the form of Social Security. Even so, the poverty rate of 8.7 percent for people over the age of sixty-five (and even the 10.4 percent rate for people over the age of seventy-five) is well below the national average of 15.0 percent, as shown in Figure 15–2.

Diversity Snapshot

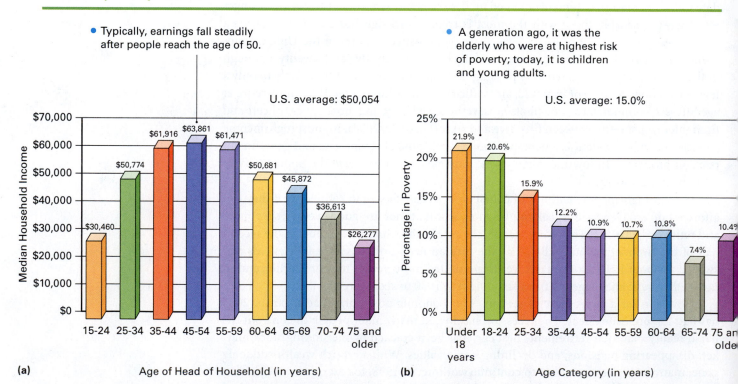

FIGURE 15–2 U.S. Poverty Rates, by Age, 2011

In a dramatic shift from several generations ago, the highest poverty rate in the United States is not for the elderly but for young people under the age of twenty-five. Although millions of seniors are poor, the poverty rate for older people is well below the national average.

Source: U.S. Census Bureau (2012).

Looking back in time, we see a dramatic change: The poverty rate among the elderly fell from about 35 percent in 1960 to 8.7 percent in 2011, or just about half the poverty rate for the entire U.S. population. The long-term trend since about 1980 shows that seniors have posted a 45 percent increase in average income (in constant dollars), which is vastly bigger than the one percent increase in income among people between the ages of twenty-five and thirty-four (U.S. Census Bureau, 2012).

Several factors have boosted the financial strength of seniors. Better health now allows people who wish to work to stay in the labor force, and more of today's older couples earn two incomes. Government policy, too, has helped older people, because programs that benefit the elderly—including Social Security—now amount to almost half of all government spending, even as spending on children has remained flat. Of course, the recent economic downturn has canceled out some of these advantages as people have lost a share of the pension income they were counting on; as more companies reduce or cancel retirement benefits, workers and retirees are receiving less to fund their future. As a result, about 40 percent of adults in the United States claim to lack confidence that they will have enough money in retirement—a share that is higher than it was when the recession hit hard in 2009 (Morin & Fry, 2012).

In the United States, it is common for businesses to offer a "senior discount" to people over sixty-five (sometimes even fifty-five). What is the reason for this practice? Would you prefer a policy of offering discounts to single parents with children, a category of people at much higher risk of poverty?

As we have seen in earlier chapters, some categories of people face particular challenges. Disadvantages that are linked to race and ethnicity throughout the life course persist in old age. In 2011, the poverty rate among elderly Hispanics (18.7 percent) and African Americans (17.3 percent) was two to three times higher than the rate for elderly non-Hispanic whites (6.7 percent) (U.S. Census Bureau, 2012).

Gender also shapes the lives of people as they age. Among full-time workers, women over sixty-five had median earnings of $36,282 in 2011, compared to $50,342 for men over sixty-five. A quick calculation shows that these older full-time working women earned 72 percent as much as comparable men. Recall from Chapter 13 ("Gender Stratification") that all working women earn 77 percent as much as *all* working men. Thus the income gap linked to gender among people of all ages is even greater among people in old age.

But because most elderly people have retired from the labor force, a more realistic financial picture must take account of all seniors. When we include both those who are working and those who are not, median individual income is far lower: $19,260 for women, which is 62 percent of the $30,841 earned by men (U.S. Census Bureau, 2012). In light of these low averages, it is easy to see why seniors—and especially women, who are less likely to have pensions or income other than Social Security—are concerned about rising expenses such as the costs of health care and prescription drugs (Fetto, 2003a; Institute for Women's Policy Research, 2007; AARP Public Policy Institute, 2012).

In the United States, today as in decades past, growing old (especially for women and other minorities) increases the risk of poverty. One government study found that elderly households typically spend about 80 percent of their income on housing, food, health care, and other basic necessities. This fact points to the conclusion that most seniors are just getting by (Federal Interagency Forum, 2012).

Finally, poverty among the elderly is often hidden from view. Because of personal pride and a desire to remain independent, many elderly people hide financial problems, even from their own families. People who have supported their children for years find it difficult to admit that they can no longer provide for themselves.

Caregiving

In an aging society, the need for caregiving is bound to increase. **Caregiving** refers to *informal and unpaid care provided to a dependent person by family members, other relatives, or friends.* Although parents provide caregiving to children, the term is more often applied to the needs of elderly men and women. Indeed, today's middle-aged adults are called the "sandwich generation" because many will spend as much time caring for their aging parents as for their own children.[1]

Who Are the Caregivers?

Surveys show that more than 80 percent of caregiving to elders is provided by family members, in most cases by one person, and without financial compensation. Most caregivers live close to the older person; many live in the same house. In addition, as shown in the Power of Society figure at the beginning of the chapter, about 80 percent of all caregiving is provided by women, most often daughters or wives.

About three-quarters of caregivers are married, and almost one-third are also responsible for young children. When we add the fact that more than one-quarter of all caregivers also have a part- or full-time job, it is clear that caregiving is a responsibility over and above what most people already consider a full day's work. Eighty-six percent of all primary caregivers spend more than twenty hours per week providing elder care (U.S. Administration on Aging, 2012).

Elder Abuse

Abuse of older people takes many forms, from passive neglect to active torment; it includes verbal, emotional, financial, and physical harm. At least 1 million elderly people (3 percent of the total) suffer serious maltreatment each year, and three times as many (about 10 percent) suffer abuse at some point. Like other forms of family violence, abuse of the elderly often goes unreported because the victims are reluctant to talk about their plight (Holmstrom, 1994; Thompson, 1997, 1998; National Center on Elder Abuse, 2005, 2010).

Many caregivers experience fatigue, emotional distress, and guilt over not being able to do more. Abuse is most likely to occur if the caregiver (1) works full time, (2) cares for young children, (3) is poor, (4) feels little affection for the older person, (5) finds the elderly person very difficult, and (6) gets no support or help from others.

But the relatively small share of cases involving abuse should not overshadow the positive side of caregiving. Helping another person is a selfless act of human kindness that affirms the best in us and provides a source of personal enrichment and satisfaction (Lund, 1993).

Ageism

Earlier chapters explained how ideology—including racism and sexism—serves to justify the social disadvantages of minorities. In the same way, sociologists use the term **ageism** for *prejudice and discrimination against older people.* Elderly people are the primary targets of ageism, although middle-aged people can suffer as well. Examples of ageism include passing over qualified older job applicants in favor of younger workers or firing older workers first.

Like racism and sexism, ageism can be blatant (as when a company decides not to hire a sixty-year-old applicant because of her age) or subtle (as when a nurse speaks to elderly patients in a condescending tone, as if they were children). Also like racism and sexism, ageism builds physical traits into stereotypes. In the case of the elderly, some people consider gray hair, wrinkled skin, and stooped posture signs of personal incompetence. Negative stereotypes portray the aged as helpless, confused, unable to deal with change, and generally unhappy. Even "positive" images of sweet little old ladies and eccentric old gentlemen are stereotypes that gloss over individuality and ignore years of experience and accomplishment (Butler, 1975; Cohen, 2001).

---

[1]This discussion of caregiving reflects Lund (1993) and personal communication from Dale Lund.

Sometimes ageism reflects a bit of truth. Statistically speaking, older people are more likely than younger people to be mentally and physically impaired. But we slip into ageism when we make unfair generalizations about an entire category of people.

Betty Friedan (1993), a pioneer of the modern feminist movement, believes that ageism is deeply rooted in our culture. She points out that few elderly people appear in the mass media; only a small percentage of television shows, for example, feature main characters over age sixty. More generally, when most of us think about older people, it is often in negative terms: This older man *lacks* a job, that older woman has *lost* her vitality, and seniors *look back* to their youth. In short, says Friedan, we often treat being old as if it were a disease, marked by decline and deterioration, for which there is no cure.

Even so, Friedan believes that older women and men in the United States are discovering that they have more to contribute than others give them credit for. Advising small business owners, designing housing for the poor, teaching children to read—there are countless ways in which older people can help others and at the same time enhance their own lives.

The Elderly: A Minority?

Elderly people in the United States face social disadvantages. Does that mean that the elderly are a minority in the same way as, say, African Americans or women?

The elderly appear to meet the definition of a minority because they have a clear social identity based on their age and they are subject to prejudice and discrimination. But Gordon Streib (1968) counters that we should not think of elderly people as a minority. First, minority status is usually both permanent and exclusive. That is, a person is an African American or a woman *for life* and cannot become part of the dominant category of whites or men. But being elderly is an *open* status because people are elderly for only part of their lives, and everyone who has the good fortune to live long enough grows old.

Second, the seniors at highest risk of being poor or otherwise disadvantaged fall into categories of people—women, African Americans, Hispanics—who are at highest risk of being poor throughout the life course. As Streib sees it, it is not so much that the old grow poor as that the poor grow old.

If so, old people are not a minority in the same sense as other categories. It might be better to say that the elderly are a part of our population that faces special challenges as they age.

Theories of Aging

15.4 Apply sociology's major theories to the topic of aging.

Let us now apply sociology's theoretical approaches to gain insight into how society shapes the lives of the elderly. We will consider the structural-functional, symbolic-interaction, and social-conflict approaches in turn.

Structural-Functional Theory: Aging and Disengagement

Drawing on the ideas of Talcott Parsons—an architect of the structural-functional approach—Elaine Cumming and William Henry (1961) explain that the physical decline and death that accompany aging can disrupt society. In response, society *disengages* the elderly, gradually transferring statuses and roles from the old to the young so that tasks are performed with minimal interruption. **Disengagement theory** is *the idea that society functions in an orderly way by removing people from positions of responsibility as they reach old age.*

Disengagement ensures the orderly operation of society by removing aging people from productive roles before they are no longer able to perform them. Another benefit of disengagement in a rapidly changing society is that it makes room for young workers, who

Watch in **MySocLab**
Video: *Sociology in Focus: Aging and the Elderly*

Watch in **MySocLab**
Video: *The Basics: Aging and the Elderly*

typically have the most up-to-date skills and training. Disengagement provides benefits to aging people as well. Although most sixty-year-olds in the United States wish to keep working, most begin to think about retirement and perhaps cut back a bit on their workload. Exactly when people begin to disengage from their careers, of course, depends on their health, enjoyment of the job, and financial situation.

Retiring does not mean being inactive. Some people start a new career and others pursue hobbies or engage in volunteer work. In general, people in their sixties start to think less about what they *have been doing* and begin to think more about what they *want to do* with the rest of their lives (Palmore, 1979; Schultz & Heckhausen, 1996).

EVALUATE Disengagement theory explains why rapidly changing high-income societies tend to define their oldest members as socially marginal. But there are several limitations to this approach.

First, especially in recent years, many workers have found that they cannot disengage from paid work because they need the income. Second, some elderly people, rich or poor, do not want to disengage from work they enjoy. Disengagement may also mean losing friends and social prestige. Third, it is not clear that the societal benefits of disengagement outweigh its social costs, which include the loss of human resources and the need to take care of people who might otherwise be able to support themselves. As the number of elderly people swells, finding ways to help seniors remain independent is a high priority. Fourth, any rigid system of disengagement does not take account of the widely differing abilities of the elderly. This concern leads us to the symbolic-interaction approach.

CHECK YOUR LEARNING State clearly the basic idea behind disengagement theory. How does disengagement benefit the aging individual? How does it benefit society?

disengagement theory the idea that society functions in an orderly way by removing people from positions of responsibility as they reach old age

activity theory the idea that a high level of activity increases personal satisfaction in old age

Symbolic-Interaction Theory: Aging and Activity

Drawing on the symbolic-interaction approach, **activity theory** is *the idea that a high level of activity increases personal satisfaction in old age*. Because everyone bases social identity on many roles, disengagement is bound to reduce satisfaction and meaning in the lives of older people. What seniors need is not to be pushed out of roles but to have many productive or recreational options. The importance of having choices is especially great for today's sixty-five-year-old, who can look forward to about twenty more years of life (Smart, 2001; Walsh, 2001).

Activity theory does not reject the idea of job disengagement; it simply says that people need to find new roles to replace those they leave behind. Research confirms that elderly people who maintain a high activity level find the most satisfaction in their lives.

Activity theory also recognizes that the elderly are diverse with a variety of interests, needs, and physical abilities. For this reason, the activities that people choose and the pace at which they pursue them are always an individual matter (Neugarten, 1977; Moen, Dempster-McClain, & Williams, 1992).

Disengagement theory suggests that society gradually removes responsibilities from people as they grow old. Activity theory counters that like people at any stage of life, elders find life worthwhile to the extent that they stay active. As a result, many older men and women seek out new jobs, hobbies, and social activities.

EVALUATE Activity theory shifts the focus of analysis from the needs of society (as stated in disengagement theory) to the needs of the elderly themselves. It emphasizes the social diversity of elderly people and highlights the importance of choice in any government policy.

A limitation of this approach is that it assumes that elders are both healthy and competent, which may or may not be the case. Another problem with this approach is that it ignores the fact that many of the problems older people face—such as poverty—have more to do with society than with themselves. We turn now to that point of view: social-conflict theory.

CHECK YOUR LEARNING Explain what activity theory says about aging. How does this approach challenge disengagement theory?

Social-Conflict and Feminist Theories: Aging and Inequality

A social-conflict analysis of aging is based on the idea that opportunities and social resources are unequally distributed among people in different age categories. For this reason, age is a dimension of social stratification. Feminist theory adds to our understanding by pointing out that gender operates along with age to create multidimensional social inequality.

In the United States, middle-aged people enjoy the greatest power and the most opportunities and privileges, and the elderly and people under the age of twenty-five have a higher risk of poverty. Employers who replace senior workers with younger men and women in order to keep wages low may not intend to discriminate against older people. However, according to recent court rulings, if such policies have the effect of causing special harm to older people, they amount to discrimination.

The social-conflict approach claims that our industrial-capitalist economy creates an age-based hierarchy. In line with Marxist thought, Steven Spitzer (1980) points out that a profit-oriented society devalues any category of people that is less economically productive. To the extent that older people do not work for income, a capitalist society labels them as mildly deviant.

Social-conflict analysis also draws attention to additional dimensions of social inequality within the elderly population. Differences of class, gender, and race and ethnicity divide older people as they do everyone else. More affluent people entering old age are generally well-prepared financially for the rising costs of health care; these people have enjoyed decades of good salaries and favorable investment outcomes. At the same time, many working-class people entering old age have experienced decades of falling wages and economic cutbacks. Their financial prospects in old age are far less favorable (Brooks & Collins, 2012). Keep in mind, too, that women—an increasing majority of the population as people age—suffer the social and economic disadvantages of both sexism and ageism; the income gap between older working women and older working men is even greater than it is between the sexes in the younger working population. Finally, elderly white people typically enjoy advantages and opportunities denied to older people of color and those in other minority categories.

In general, then, growing old is a process shaped by the complex forces of social inequality that affect people at every stage of the life course. In old age, some seniors have far greater economic security, access to better medical care, and more options for personal satisfaction than others.

EVALUATE The social-conflict approach adds to our understanding of the aging process by highlighting age-based inequality and pointing out that capitalism devalues elderly people who are less productive. But critics claim that the real culprit is *industrialization*. As evidence they point to the fact that the elderly are not better off under a socialist system, as Marxist theory implies. Furthermore, the idea that either industrialization or capitalism necessarily causes the elderly to suffer is challenged by the long-term rise in income and well-being experienced by seniors in the United States. Even though, as feminist theory points out, older women are relatively disadvantaged in relation to older

Aging and the Elderly			
	Structural-Functional Theory	**Symbolic-Interaction Theory**	**Social-Conflict and Feminist Theories**
What is the level of analysis?	Macro-level	Micro-level	Macro-level
How do we understand growing old?	The fact that people grow old and eventually die can disrupt the operation of society. Therefore, societies disengage the elderly from important tasks and other responsibilities as they reach old age.	For elders, like everyone else, being active encourages both health and happiness. Therefore, elders strive to maintain a high activity level, replacing roles they leave with new roles.	Aging is one dimension of social stratification. Generally, middle-aged people have the most wealth and power. Poor people, women, and other minorities face the greatest disadvantages as they grow old.

men, the U.S. population over the age of sixty is doing pretty well, as reflected in their much lower rate of poverty. The Applying Theory table summarizes what we learn from each of the theoretical approaches.

CHECK YOUR LEARNING What does Marxist theory teach us about aging in a capitalist society? What insights does feminist theory offer?

Death and Dying

15.5 Analyze changing attitudes about the end of life.

To every thing there is a season,
And a time for every matter under heaven:
A time to be born and a time to die…

These lines from the biblical book of Ecclesiastes state two basic truths about human existence: the fact of birth and the inevitability of death. Just as life varies throughout history and around the world, death has many faces. We conclude this chapter with a brief look at the changing character of death, the final stage in the process of growing old.

Historical Patterns of Death

In the past, death was a familiar part of life. Many children died soon after birth, a fact that led many parents to delay naming children until they were one or two years old. For those fortunate enough to survive infancy, illness, accidents, and natural catastrophes made life uncertain at best.

Sometimes food shortages forced societies to protect the majority by sacrificing the least productive members. *Infanticide* is the killing of newborn infants, and *geronticide* is the killing of the elderly.

Because death was commonplace, it was readily accepted. Medieval Christianity assured believers that death fit into the divine plan for human existence. Here is how the historian Philippe Ariès describes Sir Lancelot, one of King Arthur's knights of the Round Table, preparing for death when he thinks he is mortally wounded:

His gestures were fixed by old customs, ritual gestures which must be carried out when one is about to die. He removed his weapons and lay quietly upon the ground…. He spread his arms out, his body forming a cross… in such a way that his head faced east toward Jerusalem. (1974:7–8)

As societies gradually learned more about health and medicine, death became less of an everyday experience. Fewer children died at birth, and accidents and disease took a smaller toll among adults. As a result, most people living in high-income societies today view dying as extraordinary, something that happens to the very old or to younger people in rare and tragic cases. Back in 1900, about one-third of all deaths in the United States occurred before the age of five and fully two-thirds before the age of fifty-five. Today, by contrast, 91 percent of people in the United States die *after* reaching the age of fifty-five (Arias, 2012). Death and old age are closely linked in our culture.

The Modern Separation of Life and Death

Now removed from everyday experience, death seems somehow unnatural. Social conditions prepared our ancestors to accept death, but modern society's youth culture and aggressive medical technology foster a desire for eternal youth and immortality. Death has become separated from life.

Death is also *physically* removed from everyday activities. The clearest evidence of this is that many of us have never seen a person actually die. Our ancestors typically died at home in the presence of family and friends, but most deaths today occur in impersonal settings such as hospitals and nursing homes. Even in hospitals, dying patients occupy a special part of the building, and hospital morgues are located well out of sight of patients and visitors alike (Ariès, 1974; Lee, 2002).

Ethical Issues: Confronting Death

In a society in which technology gives us the power to prolong life, moral questions about when and how people should die are more pressing than ever. For example, the national debate in 2005 surrounding the death of Terri Schiavo, who was kept alive by mechanical means for fifteen years, was not just about the fate of one woman; many people feel we need a better understanding of what the "right to die" rules should be.

When Does Death Occur?

Perhaps the most basic question is the most difficult: Exactly how do we define death? Common sense suggests that life ceases when breathing and heartbeat stop. But the ability of medical personnel to resuscitate someone after a heart attack and artificially sustain breathing makes such definitions of death obsolete. Medical and legal experts in the United States continue to debate the meaning of death, but many now consider death an *irreversible* state involving no response to stimulation, no movement or breathing, no reflexes, and no indication of brain activity (Wall, 1980; Jones, 1998).

The Right-to-Die Debate

Terri Schiavo remained alive without evidence of being conscious or responsive to her surroundings for fifteen years following a heart attack that cut off blood to her brain. Debate surrounding this case, which ended with her death after her feeding tube was removed, shows that many people are less afraid of death than of the prospect of being kept alive at all costs. In other words, medical technology that can sustain life also threatens personal freedom by letting doctors or others rather than the dying person decide when life is to end. In response, people who support a "right to die" seek control over their own deaths just as they seek control over their lives (Ogden, 2001).

After thoughtful discussion, patients, families, and physicians may decide not to take "heroic measures" to keep a person alive. *Living wills*—documents stating which medical procedures an individual wants and does not want under specific conditions—are now widely used. An increasing number of states also have enacted laws creating Physician Orders for Life Sustaining Treatment (POLST), which is a document created to ensure that a patient's wishes about treatment are clear and followed by hospital staff and other medical personnel. Ideally, when completing such a form, a physician, physician assistant, or a nurse practitioner meets with the patient, family members, and those with legal authorization to speak for a patient to determine whether a person with an advanced illness wishes to have aggressive life-sustaining treatment, more limited medical intervention, or simply palliative care that will make the end-of-life as comfortable as possible.

Cases in which a patient does not wish aggressive treatment may lead to physicians and family members agreeing to issue a "do not resuscitate" order. This medical directive will

Watch in **MySocLab**
Video: *Sociology on the Job: Aging and the Elderly*

euthanasia assisting in the death of a person suffering from an incurable disease; also known as *mercy killing*

allow a patient who stops breathing to die. A more difficult issue involves **euthanasia** (also known as "mercy killing")—*assisting in the death of a person suffering from an incurable disease.* Euthanasia (from the Greek, meaning "a good death") poses an ethical dilemma because it involves not just refusing treatment but also actively taking steps to end a life. Some people see euthanasia as an act of kindness, while others consider it a form of murder.

People with incurable diseases can choose not to have treatment that might prolong their lives. But whether such people can ask a doctor to help bring about death is a matter of debate. Should there be a right to die? In 1997, voters in Oregon passed a right-to-die initiative (the Death with Dignity Act). Although this law has been challenged repeatedly ever since, Oregon physicians can legally assist in ending the lives of patients; since 1997, Oregon physicians have legally assisted in the deaths of about 596 patients (Oregon Public Health Division, 2012). However, in 1997, the U.S. Supreme Court, in *Vacco* v. *Quill,* declared that the U.S. Constitution recognizes no right to die. This decision discouraged other states from considering laws similar to the one in Oregon; only in neighboring Washington in 2008 did voters pass a ballot initiative permitting physician-assisted suicide. In a third state, Montana, a Supreme Court decision concluded that Montana law did not prohibit assisted suicide, although the legislature has yet to enact law to regulate this practice. And in 2013, Vermont became the first state to enact legislation legalizing physician-assisted suicide.

Supporters of the right-to-die movement hold up as a model the Netherlands, which has the most permissive euthanasia law in the world. How does the Dutch system operate? The Thinking Globally box on page 445 takes a closer look.

Should the United States hold the line on euthanasia or follow the lead of the Dutch? Right-to-die advocates maintain that a person facing extreme suffering should be able to choose to live or die. And if death is the choice, medical assistance can help people toward a "good death." Surveys show that two-thirds of U.S. adults support giving people the option of dying with a doctor's help (NORC, 2013:427).

On the other side of the debate, opponents fear that laws allowing physician-assisted suicide invite abuse. Pointing to the Netherlands, critics cite surveys indicating that in most cases the five conditions for physician-assisted suicide are not met. In particular, most physicians do not consult with another doctor or even report the euthanasia to authorities. Of greater concern is the fact that in about one-fifth of all physician-assisted suicides, the patient never explicitly asks to die. This is so even though half of these patients are conscious and capable of making decisions themselves (Gillon, 1999). This fact—and the steadily rising number of physician-assisted suicides in the Netherlands—leads opponents to argue that legalizing physician-assisted suicide puts a nation on a slippery slope toward more and more euthanasia. In 2012, in Belgium, two deaf brothers were euthanized by their doctor at their request after learning that they were losing their eyesight. The doctor claimed that ending their lives in this way avoided "suffering," although neither man had any other disease (Goldman, 2013). In light of such cases, how can we be sure, critics ask, that ill people won't be pushed into accepting death by doctors who consider suicide the right choice for the terminally ill or even the not-terminally ill? What about pressure to undergo euthanasia from family members who are weary of providing care or want to avoid the expenses of medical treatment?

Evidence drawn from the United States does not confirm such fears. In Oregon, the number of annual cases of physician-assisted suicide has remained low—around seventy each a year. No matter how the right-to-die debate eventually turns out, we have entered a new era when it comes to dying. Today, individuals, family members, and medical personnel must face death not as a medical fact but as a negotiated outcome.

Bereavement

Elisabeth Kübler-Ross (1969) found that most people confront their own death in stages (see Chapter 5, "Socialization"). Initially, individuals react with *denial,* followed by *anger;* then they try *negotiation,* hoping for divine intervention. Gradually, they fall into *resignation* and finally reach *acceptance.*

According to some researchers, bereavement follows the same pattern of stages. The people closest to a dying person may initially deny the reality of impending death and then gradually reach a point of acceptance. Other researchers, however, question any linear "stage

Thinking Globally

Death on Demand: Euthanasia in the Netherlands

Marcus Erich picked up the telephone and called his brother Arjen. In a quiet voice, thirty-two-year-old Marcus announced, "Friday at five o'clock." When the time came, Arjen was there, having driven to his brother's farmhouse south of Amsterdam. They said their final good-byes. Soon afterward, Marcus's physician arrived. Marcus and the doctor spoke for a few moments, and then the doctor prepared a "cocktail" of barbiturates and other drugs. As Marcus drank the mixture, he made a face, joking, "Can't you make this sweeter?"

As the minutes passed, Marcus lay back and his eyes closed. But after half an hour, he was still breathing. At that point, according to their earlier agreement, the physician administered a lethal injection. Minutes later, Marcus's life came to an end.

Events like this take us to the heart of the belief that people have a "right to die." Marcus Erich was dying of AIDS. For five years, his body had been wasting away, and he was suffering greatly with no hope of recovery. He wanted his doctor to end his life.

The Netherlands, a small nation in northwestern Europe, has gone further than any other in the world in allowing mercy killing, or euthanasia. A 1981 Dutch law allows a physician to assist in a suicide if the following five conditions are met:

1. The patient must make a voluntary, well-considered, and repeated request to a doctor for help in dying.

2. The patient's suffering must be unbearable and without hope of improvement.

3. The doctor and the patient must discuss alternatives.

4. The doctor must consult with at least one colleague who has access to the patient and the patient's medical records.

5. The assisted suicide must be performed in accordance with sound medical practice.

Official records indicate that doctors end about 2,000 lives a year in the Netherlands, and the number has been rising slowly but steadily. But because many cases are never reported, the actual number may be two or three times as high. Critics point to the fact that in recent years, Dutch doctors have brought about the death of people who, due to their illness, were not able to clearly state their desire to die. The Dutch policy of euthanasia enjoys widespread popular support in the Netherlands, and similar policies have been enacted in Belgium (2002), Switzerland (2005), and Luxembourg (2010). But this policy remains hotly debated in much of the world.

What Do You Think?

1. What advantages and benefits do you see in the Dutch law permitting physician-assisted suicide?

2. What are the disadvantages or dangers of such a law?

3. What about cases in which a person is very ill and cannot state the desire to die or not to die? Should euthanasia be permitted in such cases? If so, when and why?

Sources: Della Cava (1997), Mauro (1997), and Barr (2004).

---

theory," arguing that bereavement is a very personal and unpredictable process and that the stages identified by Kübler-Ross often do not apply at all (Lund, Caserta, & Dimond, 1986; Lund, 1989; Cutcliffe, 1998; Konigsberg, 2011). What experts do agree on, however, is the fact that how family and friends view an impending death has an effect on the person who is dying. By accepting an approaching death, others can help the dying person do the same; denying the death isolates the dying person, who is not able to share feelings and experiences with others.

Many dying people find support in the *hospice movement.* Of all deaths in the United States in 2011, 40 percent involved hospice care. Unlike a hospital, which is designed to cure disease, a hospice helps people have a good death. Hospices try to minimize pain and suffering—either at a center or at home—and encourage family members to stay close by. Most hospices also provide social support for family members experiencing bereavement (Foliart & Clausen, 2001).

Under the best of circumstances, bereavement often involves profound grief. Research documents that bereavement is less intense for someone who accepts the death of a loved

Unlike a hospital, which tries to save and extend life, the hospice movement tries to give dying people greater comfort, including the companionship and support of family members.

one and has brought satisfactory closure to the relationship. Such closure also allows family and friends to comfort one another more effectively after a death occurs.

Reaching closure is not possible when a death is unexpected, and survivors' social disorientation may last for years. One study of middle-aged women who had recently experienced the death of their husbands found that many felt they had lost not only a spouse but also their reason for living. Therefore, dealing successfully with bereavement requires the time and social support necessary to form a new sense of self and recognize new life options (Atchley, 1983; Danforth & Glass, 2001). With the number of older people in the United States increasing so fast, understanding death and dying is taking on greater importance.

Aging: Looking Ahead

This chapter has explored the graying of the United States and other high-income nations. By 2035, the number of elderly people in this country will exceed the entire country's population in 1900. In addition, one in four of today's seniors are over the age of eighty. In decades to come, then, society's oldest members will gain a far greater voice in everyday life. Younger people will find that careers relating to gerontology—the study of the elderly—are sure to gain in importance.

With more elderly people living longer, will our society have the support services to sustain them? Remember that as the needs of the elderly increase, a smaller share of younger people will be there to respond and pay the bills with their taxes. What about the spiraling medical costs of an aging society? As the baby boomers enter old age, some analysts paint a doomsday picture of the United States, with desperate and dying elderly people everywhere (Longino, 1994). This is one reason that addressing the need for health care—for old and young alike—has been a major priority of the Obama administration, leading to Congress passing the Affordable Care for America Act in 2010. Even so, the country is a long way from solving the problem of how to pay for this care.

But there is also good news. For one thing, the health of tomorrow's elderly people— today's middle-aged adults—will be better than ever: Smoking is way down, and more people are eating more healthfully. Such trends suggest that the elderly may well become more vigorous and independent. Tomorrow's seniors will also enjoy the benefits of steadily advancing medical technology, although, as the Controversy & Debate box on page 447 explains, how much of the country's medical resources older people can claim is already being hotly debated.

Another positive sign over the past several decades is the growing financial strength of the elderly. The economic downturn after 2000, which intensified in 2008, has been stressful, and many elderly people have lost income, retirement benefits, and equity in their homes. But it is likely that the long-term trend will remain fairly bright for most seniors, and it may turn out that tomorrow's elderly—the baby boomers—will be more affluent than ever. Why? One important fact is that the baby boomers are the first generation of the U.S. population whose women have been in the labor force most of their lives. For this reason, the boomers are likely to have substantial savings and pension income.

At the same time, younger adults will face a mounting responsibility to care for aging parents in years to come. A falling birth rate coupled with a growing elderly population

Controversy & Debate

Setting Limits: Must We "Pull the Plug" on Old Age?

Simone: I'm almost sixty now. When I'm eighty-five, I want the best medical care I can find. Why shouldn't I get it?

Juan: I'll tell you why—because our society can't spend more and more money on extending the lives of old people when so many children are at risk.

Sergio: I guess the answer depends on whether you're young or old.

As the U.S. elderly population soars, as new technology gives us more power to prolong life, and as medical care gets increasingly expensive, many people now wonder just how much old age we can afford. Currently, about half the average person's lifetime spending for medical care occurs during the final years of life, and the share is rising. Against the spiraling costs of prolonging life, we well may ask if what is medically *possible* is morally *desirable*. In the decades to come, warns the gerontologist Daniel Callahan (1987), an elderly population ready and eager to extend their lives will eventually force us either to "pull the plug" on old age or to shortchange everyone else.

Just raising this issue, Callahan admits, seems cold and heartless. But consider that the bill for Medicare, the program that pays for the elderly's healthcare topped $549 billion in 2011—five times what it cost in 1990. This dramatic increase reflects the current policy of directing more and more medical resources to studying and treating the diseases and disabilities of old age.

So Callahan makes the case for limits. First, the more we spend on behalf of the elderly, the less we can provide for others. With poverty a growing problem among children, can we afford to spend more and more on the oldest members of our society?

Second, a *longer* life does not necessarily mean a *better* life. Cost aside, does heart surgery that prolongs the life of an eighty-four-year-old woman a year or two necessarily improve the quality of her life? Might such a procedure only end up prolonging her decline? Cost considered, would those resources yield more "quality of life" if used, say, to give a ten-year-old child a kidney transplant or to provide basic care and comfort to hundreds of low-income seniors?

Third, we need to reconsider our view of death as an enemy to be conquered at all costs. Rather, he suggests, a more realistic position for an aging society is to treat death as a natural end to the life course. If we cannot make peace with death for our own well-being, then in a society with limited resources, we must do it for the benefit of others.

Not everyone agrees. Shouldn't people who have worked all their lives and made our society what it is enjoy our generosity in their final years? Would it be right to deny medical care to aging people who are able and willing to pay for it?

Today, we face questions that few people would have imagined even fifty years ago: Is peak longevity good for everyone? Is it even *possible* for everyone?

The share of our population over the age of sixty-five is going up. In addition, older people are very likely to vote. What do these facts lead you to predict about government policy dealing with health care for the elderly?

What Do You Think?

1. Do you think that a goal of doctors and other medical personnel should be to extend life at all costs? Explain your view.

2. How should society balance the needs of high-income seniors with the needs of those with little or no money to pay for medical care as they age?

3. Do you think people should decide for themselves what care they need, consistent with their income? Or should government regulate how care is distributed to everyone? Why?

Sources: Callahan (1987, 2009) and Centers for Medicare and Medicaid Services (2012).

---

will demand that middle-aged people perform an increasing share of caregiving for the very old.

Most of us need to learn more about caring for aging parents, which includes far more than meeting their physical needs. More important lessons involve communicating with them, expressing love, and facing up to eventual death. In caring for our parents, we will also teach important lessons to our children, including the skills they will need, one day, to care for us.

Seeing Sociology in Everyday Life

How are older adults changing today's society?

A lot has been said about the baby boomers—the women and men born between 1945 and 1964—who were the driving force behind many of the changes that took place in the 1960s and 1970s. Civil rights, women's rights, and gay rights reflect just some of the social movements they initiated or carried on. Now, as this cohort begins to enter old age, they are rewriting the rules once again, this time about what it means to be old.

Mick Jagger and Keith Richard launched the Rolling Stones almost fifty years ago and continue to perform as they both turn seventy in 2013. What do these stars of popular culture say about older men?

A much younger Paul McCartney wrote the lyrics to "When I'm Sixty-Four," probably never imagining that he would still be writing music and performing today—he reached age seventy-one in 2013. In what ways is he a role model for elders?

Judy Collins turned seventy in 2009 and continues a busy career as a folk singer and political activist. As they enter old age, how have the baby boomers reshaped U.S. politics?

Joan Baez has also been a folk singer and political activist for more than half a century. Both she and Judy Collins have supported numerous social movements, ranging from opposition to the use of land mines to the antiwar movement. In what ways do you expect your generation to reshape U.S. society as you reach old age?

HINT The baby boomers have been a cohort responsible for major societal change, and as they have aged they have redefined every stage of life. As elders, they appear determined to maintain active lives well beyond the traditional time of retirement. The celebrities pictured here also suggest that older people can be sexy—and the generation that brought sex out into the open for young people is defining sex as a part of growing old. The social justice values that defined the boomers as young people seem to still drive them as seniors. Most of all, they appear determined that their political voice will be heard.

Seeing Sociology in *Your* Everyday Life

1. Look through an issue of a popular magazine, such as *Time* or *People,* and study the pictures of men and women in news stories and advertising. What share of the pictures show elderly people? In what types of advertising are they featured?

2. Go to MySocLab and click on the Student Resources link to access the Sociology in Focus blog, where you can read the latest posts by a team of young sociologists who apply the sociological perspective to topics of popular culture.

3. Based on what you have read in this chapter, how is old age (like all stages of the life course) linked to biological changes but mainly a creation of society? Go to the "Seeing Sociology in *Your* Everyday Life" feature in MySocLab to learn more about how society constructs the stages of life and also to understand some of the benefits of seeing old age sociologically.

Making the Grade

The Graying of the United States

15.1 Explain the increasing share of elderly people in modern societies. (pages 426–29)

Explore the **Map** in **MySocLab**

The "graying of the United States" means that the average age of the U.S. population is steadily going up.

- In 1900, the median age was 23, and elderly people were 4% of the population.
- By 2050, the median age will be more than 40, and elderly people will represent 21% of the U.S. population.

In high-income countries like the United States, the share of elderly people has been increasing for two reasons:

- Birth rates have been falling as families choose to have fewer children.
- Life expectancy has been rising as living standards improve and medical advances reduce deaths from infectious diseases.

Growing Old: Biology and Culture

15.2 Describe age stratification in global context. (pages 429–33)

Biological and psychological changes are associated with aging.

- Although people's health becomes more fragile with advancing age, affluent elderly people experience fewer health problems than poor people, who cannot afford quality medical care.
- Psychological research confirms that growing old does not result in overall loss of intelligence or major changes in personality.

Although aging is a biological process, how elderly people are regarded by society is a matter of **culture**.

The age at which people are defined as old varies:

- Until several centuries ago, old age began as early as 30.
- In poor societies today, where life expectancy is low, people become old at 50 or even 40.

Age Stratification: A Global Survey

- In *hunting and gathering societies*, where survival depends on physical stamina, both the very young and the very old contribute less to society.
- In *agrarian societies*, elders are typically the most privileged and respected members of society, a pattern known as **gerontocracy**.
- In *industrial* and *postindustrial societies*, the social standing of the elderly is low because the fast pace of social change is dominated by the young.

age stratification the unequal distribution of wealth, power, and privilege among people at different stages of the life course

gerontocracy a form of social organization in which the elderly have the most wealth, power, and prestige

gerontology the study of aging and the elderly

Transitions and Challenges of Aging

15.3 Discuss problems related to aging. (pages 433–39)

Read the **Document** in **MySocLab**   **Watch** the **Video** in **MySocLab**

Personal challenges that elderly people face include

- the realization that one's life is nearing an end
- social isolation caused by the death of friends or a spouse, physical disability, or retirement from one's job
- reduced social prestige and a loss of purpose in life due to retirement

caregiving informal and unpaid care provided to a dependent person by family members, other relatives, or friends

ageism prejudice and discrimination against older people

A person's risk of **poverty** rises after midlife, although since 1960, the poverty rate for the elderly has fallen and is now below the poverty rate for the population as a whole.

- The aged poor include categories of people—such as single women and people of color—who are at high risk of poverty at any age.
- Some retired people have had to return to work in order to make ends meet, a result of the recent economic downturn.

The need for **caregiving** is increasing in our aging society.

- Most caregiving for the elderly is performed by family members, typically women.
- At least 1 million elderly people are victims of **elder abuse** each year.

Ageism—prejudice and discrimination against older people—is used to justify age stratification.

- Like racism and sexism, ageism builds physical traits into stereotypes that make unfair generalizations about all elderly people.

Theories of Aging

15.4 Apply sociology's major theories to the topic of aging. (pages 439–42)

 Watch the **Video** in **MySocLab**

Structural-functional theory points to the role that aging plays in the orderly operation of society.

- **Disengagement theory** suggests that society helps the elderly disengage from positions of social responsibility before the onset of disability or death.
- The process of disengagement provides for the orderly transfer of statuses and roles from the older to the younger generation.

Symbolic-interaction theory focuses on the meanings that people attach to growing old.

- **Activity theory** claims that a high level of activity increases people's personal satisfaction in old age.
- People must find new roles in old age to replace the ones they left behind.

Social-conflict theory and **feminist theory** highlight the inequalities in opportunities and social resources available to people in different age and gender categories.

- A capitalist society's emphasis on economic efficiency leads to the devaluation of those who are less productive, including the elderly.
- Some categories of elderly people—namely, women and other minorities—have less economic security, less access to quality medical care, and fewer options for personal satisfaction in old age than others.

disengagement theory the idea that society functions in an orderly way by removing people from positions of responsibility as they reach old age

activity theory the idea that a high level of activity increases personal satisfaction in old age

Death and Dying

15.5 Analyze changing attitudes about the end of life. (pages 442–46)

 Watch the **Video** in **MySocLab**

Historical Perspective

- In the past, death was a familiar part of everyday life and was accepted as a natural event that might occur at any age.
- Modern society has set death physically apart from everyday activities, and advances in medical technology have resulted in people's inability or unwillingness to accept death.
- This avoidance of death also reflects the fact that most people in high-income societies die in old age.

Ethical Issues: Confronting Death

- Our society's power to prolong life has sparked a debate as to the circumstances under which a dying person should be kept alive by medical means.
- People who support a person's right to die seek control over the process of their own dying.
- **Euthanasia** poses an ethical dilemma because it involves not just refusing treatment but also actively taking steps to end a person's life.

Bereavement

- Some researchers believe that the process of bereavement follows the same pattern of stages as a dying person coming to accept approaching death: denial, anger, negotiation, resignation, and acceptance.
- The **hospice movement** offers support to dying people and their families.

euthanasia assisting in the death of a person suffering from an incurable disease; also known as *mercy killing*

16 The Economy and Work

((• Listen to Chapter 16 in MySocLab

LEARNING OBJECTIVES

16.1 Summarize historical changes to the economy.

16.2 Assess the operation of capitalist and socialist economies.

16.3 Analyze patterns of employment and unemployment in the United States.

16.4 Discuss the importance of corporations to the U.S. economy.

the Power of Society

to shape our choices in jobs

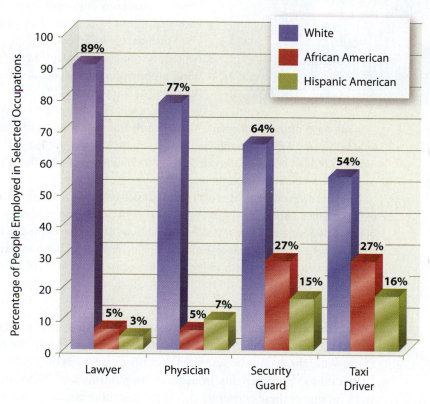

Percentage of People Employed in Selected Occupations

- White
- African American
- Hispanic American

Lawyer: 89%, 5%, 3%
Physician: 77%, 5%, 7%
Security Guard: 64%, 27%, 15%
Taxi Driver: 54%, 27%, 16%

Source: U.S. Department of Labor (2012)

Will the jobs you take throughout your life reflect choices you make based on your personal abilities and interests? To some extent, yes. But the work we have has a lot to do with our position in a society that distributes opportunity unequally. Look at the "high-prestige" jobs such as lawyer and physician—notice how these jobs are overwhelmingly filled by people born with the relative advantages that go with being white. By contrast, "low-prestige" jobs are far more likely to be filled by people born into a disadvantaged racial or ethnic category. Society has a lot to say about the type of work we all do.

Chapter Overview

This chapter begins a survey of the major social institutions. We begin with the economy, which is the institution widely regarded as having the greatest impact on society as a whole. The chapter explores the operation of the economy and also explains how revolutionary changes in economic production have reshaped society.

Here's a quick quiz about the U.S. economy. (Hint: All six questions have the same correct answer.)

- Which U.S. business do more than 200 million people around the world visit each week?
- Which business sells products made by more than 100,000 companies?
- Which U.S. company, on average, opens three new stores somewhere in the world every day?
- Which U.S. company buys more than $25 billion worth of goods each year from China, making it a larger trading partner for China than the United Kingdom?
- Which U.S. company employs 2.2 million people around the world, including approximately 1.4 million in the United States?
- Which single company actually grew in size during the recent economic downturn?

You have probably guessed that the correct answer is Walmart, the global discount chain founded by Sam Walton, who opened his first store in Arkansas in 1962. In 2012, Walmart announced revenues of $444 billion from more than 4,600 stores in the United States and 5,964 stores in other countries from Brazil to China.

But not everyone is pleased with the expansion of Walmart. Across the United States, many people have joined a social movement to keep Walmart out of their local communities, fearing the loss of local businesses and, in some cases, local culture. Critics also claim that the merchandising giant pays low wages, keeps out labor unions, and sells many products made in sweatshops abroad. Since 2010, Walmart also has defended itself in the courts against claims of sex discrimination (Saporito, 2003; Walsh, 2007; Walmart, 2012).

This chapter examines the economy, widely considered the most influential of all social institutions. As the story of Walmart's expansion suggests, the economy of the United States—and the economic system of the entire world—is dominated by a number of giant corporations. Who benefits from these megabusinesses? Who loses? What is it like to work for one of these corporations? To answer these questions, sociologists study how the economy operates as well as the nature of work and what jobs mean to each of us.

The Economy: Historical Overview

(16.1) Summarize historical changes to the economy.

economy the social institution that organizes a society's production, distribution, and consumption of goods and services

The **economy** is *the social institution that organizes a society's production, distribution, and consumption of goods and services.* As an institution, the economy operates, for better or worse, in a generally predictable manner. *Goods* are commodities ranging from necessities (food, clothing, shelter) to luxury items (cars, swimming pools, yachts). *Services* are activities that benefit others (for example, the work of priests, physicians, teachers, and computer software specialists).

We value goods and services because they ensure survival or because they make life easier or more interesting. Also, what people produce as workers and what they buy as consumers are important parts of social identity, as when we say, "He's a steelworker," or "She drives a Mercedes." How goods and services are distributed, too, shapes the lives

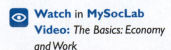

Watch in **MySocLab**
Video: *The Basics: Economy and Work*

of everyone by giving more resources to some and fewer to others.

The economies of modern high-income nations are the result of centuries of social change. We turn now to three technological revolutions that reorganized production and, in the process, transformed social life.

The Agricultural Revolution

The earliest human societies were made up of hunters and gatherers living off the land. In these technologically simple societies, there was no distinct economy. Rather, producing and consuming were part of family life.

As Chapter 4 ("Society") explained, when people harnessed animals to plows, beginning some 5,000 years ago, a new agricultural economy was created that was fifty times more productive than hunting and gathering. The resulting surplus meant that not everyone had to produce food, so many took on specialized work: making tools, raising animals, or building dwellings. Soon towns sprang up, linked by networks of traders dealing in food, animals, and other goods. These four factors—agricultural technology, job specialization, permanent settlements, and trade—made the economy a distinct social institution.

As societies industrialize, a smaller share of the labor force works in agriculture. In the United States, much of the agricultural work that remains is performed by immigrants from lower-income nations. These farm workers from Mexico travel throughout Florida during the tomato harvest.

The Industrial Revolution

By the mid-eighteenth century, a second technological revolution was under way, first in England and then in North America. The development of industry was even more powerful than the rise of agriculture in bringing change to the economy. Industrialization changed the economy in five fundamental ways:

1. **New sources of energy.** Throughout history, "energy" had meant the muscle power of people or animals. But in 1765, the English inventor James Watt introduced the steam engine. One hundred times more powerful than animal muscles, early steam engines soon drove heavy machinery.

2. **Centralization of work in factories** Steam-powered machines soon moved work from homes to factories, the centralized and impersonal workplaces that housed the machines.

3. **Manufacturing and mass production.** Before the Industrial Revolution, most people grew or gathered raw materials such as grain, wood, or wool. In an industrial economy, the focus shifts so that most people work to turn raw materials into a wide range of finished products such as processed foods, furniture, and clothing.

4. **Specialization.** Centuries ago, people worked at home, making products from start to finish. In the factory, a worker repeats a single task over and over, making only a small contribution to the finished product.

5. **Wage labor.** Instead of working for themselves, factory workers became wage laborers working for strangers, who often cared less for them than for the machines they operated.

The Industrial Revolution gradually raised the standard of living as countless new products and services fueled an expanding marketplace. Yet the benefits of industrial technology were shared very unequally, especially at the beginning. Some factory owners made vast fortunes, while the majority of industrial workers lived close to poverty. Children, too, worked in factories or in coal mines for pennies a day. Women working

For a close-up look at the special problems endured by women workers in textile factories, **Read More in MySocLab**, *Women in the Mills of Lowell, Massachusetts*

in factories were among the lowest paid, and their rigid supervision left them with little personal freedom.

The Information Revolution and Postindustrial Society

postindustrial economy
a productive system based on service work and high technology

By about 1950, the nature of production was changing once again. The United States was creating a **postindustrial economy**, *a productive system based on service work and high technology*. Automated machinery (and later, robotics) reduced the role of human labor in factory production and expanded the ranks of clerical workers and managers. The postindustrial era is marked by a shift from industrial work to service work.

Driving this change is a third technological breakthrough: the computer. Just as the Industrial Revolution did two-and-a-half centuries ago, the Information Revolution has introduced new kinds of products and new forms of communication and has altered the character of work. In general, there have been three significant changes:

1. **From tangible products to ideas.** The industrial era was defined by the production of goods; in the postindustrial era, people work with symbols. Computer programmers, writers, financial analysts, advertising executives, architects, editors, and all sorts of consultants make up more of the labor force in the information age.

2. **From mechanical skills to literacy skills.** The Industrial Revolution required that workers have mechanical skills, but the Information Revolution requires literacy skills: speaking and writing well and, of course, knowing how to use a computer. People able to communicate effectively are likely to do well; people without these skills face fewer opportunities in the job market.

3. **From factories to almost anywhere.** Industrial technology drew workers into factories located near power sources, but computer technology allows people to work almost anywhere. Laptop and wireless computers and cell phones now turn the home, a car, or even an airplane into a "virtual office." What this means for everyday life is that new information technology blurs the line between our lives at work and at home.

Global Snapshot

- In high-income nations such as the United States, three out of four jobs are in the tertiary or service sector of the economy.

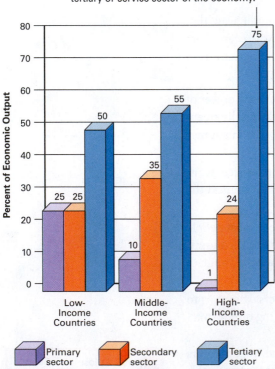

FIGURE 16–1 The Size of Economic Sectors, by Income Level of Country

As countries become richer, the primary sector becomes a smaller part of the economy and the tertiary or service sector becomes larger.

Source: Estimates based on World Bank (2012).

Sectors of the Economy

The three revolutions just described reflect a shifting balance among the three sectors of a society's economy. The **primary sector** is *the part of the economy that draws raw materials from the natural environment*. The primary sector—agriculture, raising animals, fishing, forestry, and mining—is largest in low-income nations. Figure 16–1 shows that 25 percent of the economic output of low-income countries is from the primary sector, compared with 10 percent of economic activity in middle-income nations and just 1 percent in high-income countries such as the United States.

The **secondary sector** is *the part of the economy that transforms raw materials into manufactured goods*. This sector grows quickly as societies industrialize. It includes operations such as refining petroleum into gasoline and turning metals into tools and automobiles. The globalization of industry means that just about all the world's countries have a significant share of their workers in the secondary sector. Figure 16–1 shows that the secondary sector now accounts for about the same share of economic output in low-income nations as it does in high-income countries.

The **tertiary sector** is *the part of the economy that involves services rather than goods*. The tertiary sector grows with industrialization, accounting for 50 percent of economic output in low-income countries, 55 percent in middle-income countries, and 75 percent in high-income nations. About 85 percent of the U.S. labor force is in service work, including secretarial and clerical work and positions in food

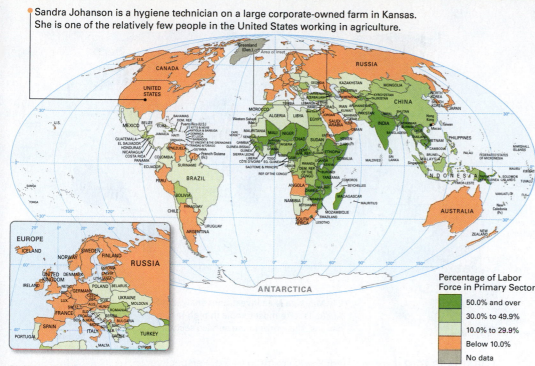

Sandra Johanson is a hygiene technician on a large corporate-owned farm in Kansas. She is one of the relatively few people in the United States working in agriculture.

Percentage of Labor Force in Primary Sector

- 50.0% and over
- 30.0% to 49.9%
- 10.0% to 29.9%
- Below 10.0%
- No data

GLOBAL MAP 16–1 Agricultural Employment in Global Perspective

The primary sector of the economy is largest in the nations that are least developed. Thus in the poor countries of Africa and Asia, up to half of all workers are farmers. This picture is altogether different in the world's most economically developed countries—including the United States, Canada, Great Britain, and Australia—which have only about 1 percent of their labor force in agriculture.

Source: Data from International Labour Organization (2012).

service, sales, law, health care, law enforcement, advertising, and teaching (U.S. Department of Labor, 2012; World Bank, 2012).

The Global Economy

New information technology is drawing people around the world closer together and creating a **global economy**, *economic activity that crosses national borders*. The development of a global economy has five major consequences.

First, we see a global division of labor: Different regions of the world specialize in one sector of economic activity. As Global Map 16–1 shows, agriculture represents about half the total economic output of the world's poorest countries. Global Map 16–2 on page 458 indicates that most of the economic output of high-income countries, including the United States, is in the service sector. In short, the world's poorest nations specialize in producing raw materials, and the richest nations specialize in the production of services.

Second, an increasing number of products pass through more than one nation. Look no further than your morning coffee: The beans may have been grown in Colombia and transported to New Orleans on a freighter registered in Liberia, made in a shipyard in Japan using steel from Korea, and fueled by oil from Venezuela.

global economy economic activity that crosses national borders

Sectors of the Economy

primary sector the part of the economy that draws raw materials from the natural environment

secondary sector the part of the economy that transforms raw materials into manufactured goods

tertiary sector the part of the economy that involves services rather than goods

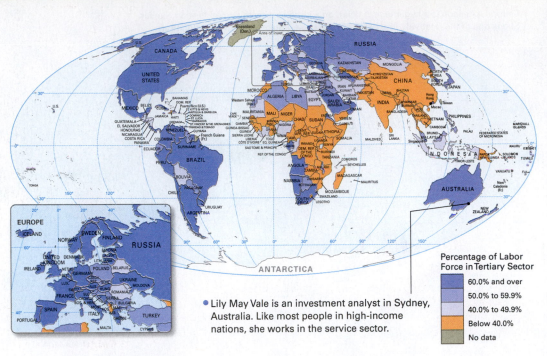

- Lily May Vale is an investment analyst in Sydney, Australia. Like most people in high-income nations, she works in the service sector.

Percentage of Labor Force in Tertiary Sector

- 60.0% and over
- 50.0% to 59.9%
- 40.0% to 49.9%
- Below 40.0%
- No data

GLOBAL MAP 16–2 Service-Sector Employment in Global Perspective

The tertiary sector of the economy becomes ever larger as a nation's income level rises. In the United States, Canada, the countries of Western Europe, much of South America, Australia, and Japan, about two-thirds of the labor force performs service work.

Source: Data from International Labour Organization (2012).

Third, national governments no longer control the economic activity that takes place within their borders. In fact, governments cannot even regulate the value of their national currencies because dollars, euros, pounds sterling, and yen are traded around the clock in the financial markets of New York, London, and Tokyo.

A fourth consequence of the global economy is that a small number of businesses, operating internationally, now control a vast share of the world's economic activity. Based on the latest available data, the 1,500 largest multinational companies (with sales of about $35 trillion) account for half of the economic output of the entire world (DeCarlo, 2012; World Bank, 2012).

Fifth and finally, the globalization of the economy raises concerns about the rights and opportunities of workers. Critics of this trend claim that the United States is losing jobs—especially factory jobs—to low-income nations. This means that workers here face lower wages and higher unemployment; many workers abroad are paid extremely low wages. As a result, say critics, the global expansion of capitalism threatens the well-being of workers throughout the world.

The world is still divided into 195 politically distinct nations. But increasing international economic activity makes nationhood less significant than it was even a decade ago.

Economic Systems: Paths to Justice

16.2 Assess the operation of capitalist and socialist economies.

Every society's economic system makes a statement about *justice* by determining who is entitled to what. Two general economic models are capitalism and socialism. No nation anywhere in the world has an economy that is completely one or the other; capitalism and socialism represent two ends of a continuum along which all real-world economies can be located. We will look at each of these two models in turn.

Watch in **MySocLab**
Video: *The Big Picture: Economy and Work*

Capitalism

Capitalism is *an economic system in which natural resources and the means of producing goods and services are privately owned.* An ideal capitalist economy has three distinctive features:

1. **Private ownership of property.** In a capitalist economy, individuals can own almost anything. The more capitalist an economy is, the more private ownership there is of wealth-producing property, such as factories, real estate, and natural resources.

2. **Pursuit of personal profit.** A capitalist society seeks to create profit and wealth. The profit motive is the reason people take new jobs, open new businesses, or try to improve products. Making money is considered the natural way of economic life. Just as important, the Scottish philosopher Adam Smith (1723–1790) claimed that as individuals pursue their self-interest, the entire society prospers (1937, orig. 1776).

3. **Competition and consumer choice.** A purely capitalist economy is a free-market system with no government interference (sometimes called a *laissez-faire economy,* from the French words meaning "leave it alone"). Adam Smith stated that a freely competitive economy regulates itself by the "invisible hand" of the law of supply and demand.

   Consumers regulate a free-market economy, Smith explained, by selecting the goods and services offering the greatest value. As producers compete for the customer's business, they provide the highest-quality goods at the lowest possible prices. In Smith's time-honored phrase, from narrow self-interest comes the "greatest good for the greatest number of people." Government control of an economy, on the other hand, distorts market forces by reducing the quantity and quality of goods, shortchanging consumers in the process.

Justice in a capitalist system amounts to freedom of the marketplace, where a person can produce, invest, and buy according to individual self-interest. The increasing popularity of Walmart, described in the opening to this chapter, reflects the fact that people think they get a lot for their money when shopping there.

The United States is considered a capitalist nation because most businesses are privately owned. However, it is not purely capitalist because government plays a large role in the economy. The government owns and operates a number of businesses, including almost all of this country's schools, roads, parks and museums, the U.S. Postal Service, the Amtrak railroad system, and the entire U.S. military. The U.S. government also had a major hand in building the Internet. In addition, governments use taxation and other forms of regulation to influence what companies produce, control the quality and cost of merchandise, and motivate consumers to conserve natural resources.

The U.S. government also sets minimum wage levels, enforces workplace safety standards, regulates corporate mergers, provides farm price supports, and supplements the income of a majority of its people in the form of Social Security, public assistance, student loans, and veterans' benefits. Local, state, and federal governments combined are the country's biggest employer, with 17 percent of the nonfarm labor force on their payrolls (U.S. Department of Labor, 2012).

Socialism

Socialism is *an economic system in which natural resources and the means of producing goods and services are collectively owned.* In its ideal form, a socialist economy rejects each of the three characteristics of capitalism just described in favor of three opposite features:

1. **Collective ownership of property.** A socialist economy limits rights to private property, especially property used to generate income. Government controls such property and makes housing and other goods available to all, not just to the people with the most money.

Capitalism still thrives in Hong Kong (*left*), evident in streets choked with advertising and shoppers. Socialism is more the rule in China's capital, Beijing (*right*), a city dominated by government buildings rather than a downtown business district.

2. **Pursuit of collective goals.** The individualistic pursuit of profit goes against the collective orientation of socialism. What capitalism celebrates as the "entrepreneurial spirit," socialism condemns as greed; individuals are expected to work for the common good of all.

3. **Government control of the economy.** Socialism rejects capitalism's laissez-faire approach in favor of a *centrally controlled* or *command economy* operated by the government. Commercial advertising thus plays little role in socialist economies.

Justice in a socialist context means not competing to gain wealth but meeting everyone's basic needs in a roughly equal manner. From a socialist point of view, the common capitalist practice of giving workers as little in pay and benefits as possible to boost company earnings is unjust because it puts profits before people.

Venezuela, Cuba, North Korea, the People's Republic of China, and more than two dozen other nations in Asia, Africa, and Latin America model their economies on socialism, placing almost all wealth-generating property under state control (Miller, Holmes, & Feulner, 2012). The extent of world socialism declined during the 1990s as most of the countries in Eastern Europe and the former Soviet Union have geared their economies toward a market system. More recently, however, voters in Bolivia, Venezuela, Ecuador, and other nations in South America have elected leaders who have moved the national economies in a socialist direction.

Socialism and Communism

Many people think of *socialism* and *communism* as the same thing, but they are not. **Communism** is *a hypothetical economic and political system in which all members of a society are socially equal.* Karl Marx viewed socialism as one important step on the path toward the ideal of a communist society that abolishes all class divisions. In many socialist societies today, the dominant political party describes itself as communist, but the communist goal has not been achieved in any country.

Why? For one thing, social stratification involves differences in power as well as wealth. Socialist societies have reduced economic differences by regulating people's range of choices. In the process, government did not "wither away," as Marx imagined it would.

capitalism an economic system in which natural resources and the means of producing goods and services are privately owned

socialism an economic system in which natural resources and the means of producing goods and services are collectively owned

communism a hypothetical economic and political system in which all members of a society are socially equal

Rather, government has grown, giving socialist political elites enormous power and privilege.

Marx might have agreed that a communist society is a *utopia* (from Greek words meaning "no place"). Yet Marx considered communism a worthy goal and might well have objected to so-called Marxist societies such as North Korea, the People's Republic of China, and Cuba for falling short of the promise of communism.

welfare capitalism an economic and political system that combines a mostly market-based economy with extensive social welfare programs

state capitalism an economic and political system in which companies are privately owned but cooperate closely with the government

Welfare Capitalism and State Capitalism

Some nations of Western Europe, including Sweden and Italy, have market-based economies but also offer broad social welfare programs. Analysts call this type of economic system **welfare capitalism**, *an economic and political system that combines a mostly market-based economy with extensive social welfare programs.*

Under welfare capitalism, the government owns some of the largest industries and services, such as transportation, the mass media, and health care. In Greece, France, and Sweden, almost half of economic production is "nationalized," or state-controlled. Most industry is left in private hands, although it is subject to extensive government regulation. High taxation (aimed especially at the rich) funds a wide range of social welfare programs, including universal health care and child care. In Sweden, for example, government-provided social services represent 28 percent of all economic output, much higher than the 19 percent share in the United States (OECD, 2012).

Another blend of capitalism and socialism is **state capitalism**, *an economic and political system in which companies are privately owned but cooperate closely with the government.* State capitalism is the rule among the nations along the Pacific Rim. Japan, South Korea, and Singapore are all capitalist countries, but their governments work in partnership with large companies, supplying financial assistance and controlling foreign imports to help their businesses compete in world markets (Gerlach, 1992).

Relative Advantages of Capitalism and Socialism

Which economic system works best? Comparing economic models is difficult because all countries mix capitalism and socialism to varying degrees. In addition, nations differ in cultural attitudes toward work, access to natural resources, levels of technological development, and patterns of trade. Despite such complicating factors, some crude comparisons are revealing.

Economic Productivity

One key dimension of economic performance is productivity. A commonly used measure of economic output is gross domestic product (GDP), the total value of all goods and services produced annually. Per capita (per-person) GDP allows us to compare the economic performance of nations of different population sizes.

The output of mostly capitalist countries at the end of the 1980s—before the fall of the socialist systems in the Soviet Union and Eastern Europe—varied somewhat but averaged about $13,500 per person. The comparable figure for the mostly socialist former Soviet Union and nations of Eastern Europe was about $5,000. This means that the capitalist countries outproduced the socialist nations by a ratio of 2.7 to 1 (United Nations Development Programme, 1990). A recent comparison of socialist North Korea (per capita GDP of $1,800) and capitalist South Korea ($22,424) provides an even sharper contrast (Central Intelligence Agency, 2012; World Bank, 2012).

Economic Equality

The distribution of resources within a population is another important measure of how well an economic system works. A comparative study of Europe in the mid-1970s, when that region was split between mostly capitalist and mostly socialist countries, compared the earnings of

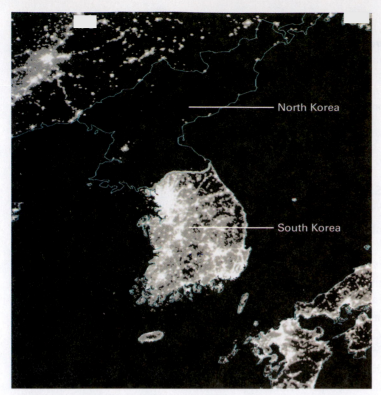

the richest 5 percent of the population and the poorest 5 percent (Wiles, 1977). Societies with capitalist economies had an income ratio of about 10 to 1; the ratio for socialist countries was about 5 to 1. In other words, capitalist economies support a higher overall standard of living, but with greater income inequality; socialist economies create more economic equality but with a lower overall living standard.

Personal Freedom

One additional consideration in evaluating capitalism and socialism is the personal freedom each gives its people. Capitalism emphasizes the *freedom to pursue self-interest* and depends on the ability of producers and consumers to interact with little interference by the state. Socialism, by contrast, emphasizes *freedom from basic want*. The goal of equality requires the state to regulate the economy, which in turn limits personal choices and opportunities for citizens.

Can a single society offer both political freedom and economic equality? In the capitalist United States, our political system offers many personal freedoms, but the economy generates a lot of inequality, and freedom is not worth as much to a poor person as to a rich one. By contrast, North Korea or Cuba has considerable economic equality, but people cannot speak out or travel freely within or outside of the country.

Directly comparing the economic performance of capitalism and socialism is difficult because nations differ in many ways. But a satellite image of socialist North Korea and capitalist South Korea at night shows the dramatically different electrical output of the two nations, one indication of economic activity.

For a close-up look at welfare capitalism in Denmark, **Read More** in **MySocLab**, *Want Equality and Freedom? Try Denmark*

Perhaps the closest any country has come to "having it all" is Denmark, where welfare capitalism combines a market economy with broad government programs that provide for the welfare of all citizens.

Changes in Socialist and Capitalist Countries

In 1989 and 1990, the nations of Eastern Europe, which had been seized by the Soviet Union at the end of World War II, overthrew their socialist regimes. These nations—including the former German Democratic Republic (reunited with Germany), the Czech Republic, Slovakia, Hungary, Romania, and Bulgaria—have been moving toward capitalist market systems after decades of state-controlled economies. In 1991, the Soviet Union itself formally dissolved, and many of its former republics introduced some free-market principles. Within a decade, three-fourths of former Soviet government enterprises were partly or entirely in private hands (Montaigne, 2001).

There were many reasons for these sweeping changes. First, the capitalist economies far outproduced their socialist counterparts. The socialist economies were successful in achieving economic equality, but living standards were low compared to those of Western Europe. Second, Soviet socialism was heavy-handed, rigidly controlling the media and restricting individual freedoms. In short, socialism did away with *economic* elites, as Karl Marx predicted, but as Max Weber foresaw, socialism increased the power of *political* elites.

So far, the market reforms in Eastern Europe have proceeded unevenly. Some nations, such as Kazakhstan, Uzbekistan, and Turkmenistan, all with extensive reserves of oil and natural gas, did well even during the recent global recession. Other nations, including Lithuania, Latvia, and Azerbaijan, have seen their economies shrink and have faced rising unemployment. In just about every formerly socialist nation, the introduction of a market economy has brought with it an increase in economic inequality (Ignatius, 2007; Pew Research Center, 2011; World Bank, 2012).

A number of other countries have recently begun moving toward more socialist economies. In 2005, the people of Bolivia elected Evo Morales, a former farmer, union leader, and activist, as their new president. This election placed Bolivia in a group of nations—including Ecuador, Venezuela, Brazil, Chile, and Uruguay—that are moving toward more socialist economies. The reasons for this shift vary from country to country, but the common element is economic inequality. In Bolivia, for example, economic production has increased in recent decades, but most of the benefits have gone to a wealthy business elite. By contrast, more than half of the country's people remain very poor (Howden, 2005).

Work in the Postindustrial U.S. Economy

16.3 Analyze patterns of employment and unemployment in the United States.

Economic change is occurring not just in the socialist world but in the United States as well. In 2012, a total of 144 million people in the United States—59 percent of those aged sixteen and over—were working for income. A larger share of men (65 percent) than women (54 percent) had jobs, a gap that has been holding steady over time. Among men, 59 percent of African Americans were employed, compared with 69 percent of whites and 74 percent of Hispanics. Among women, 55 percent of African Americans were employed, compared to 55 percent of whites, and 53 percent of Hispanics. For both sexes, 60 percent of Asian Americans were employed (U.S. Department of Labor, 2012).

The Decline of Agricultural Work

In 1900, roughly 40 percent of U.S. workers were farmers. In 2011, just 1.6 percent were in agriculture. Although recent years have seen a small resurgence of family farms—reflecting the growing popularity of organic and locally grown foods—the larger trend is that the family farm of a century ago has been replaced by *corporate agribusinesses*. Farmland is now more productive, but this change in output has caused painful adjustments across the country as a traditional way of life is lost (Dudley, 2000; Carlson, 2008). Figure 16–2 illustrates the shrinking role of the primary sector in the U.S. economy over the last century.

From Factory Work to Service Work

A century ago, industrialization swelled the ranks of blue-collar workers. By 1950, however, a white-collar revolution had moved a majority of workers into service occupations. By 2011, more than 80 percent of the labor force worked in the service sector, and almost all of this country's new jobs were being created in this sector (U.S. Department of Labor, 2012).

As Chapter 11 ("Social Class in the United States") explained, the expansion of service work is one reason many people call the United States a middle-class society. But much service work—including sales and clerical positions and jobs in hospitals and restaurants—pays much less than former factory jobs. This means that many of the jobs in today's postindustrial society provide only a modest standard of living. Women and other minorities, as well as many young people just starting their working careers, are the most likely to have jobs doing low-paying service work (Kalleberg, Reskin, & Hudson, 2000; Greenhouse, 2006).

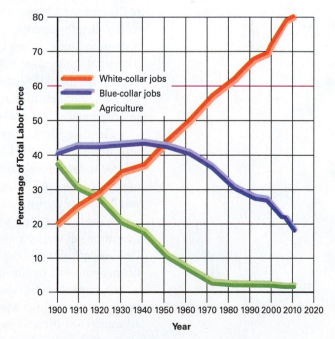

FIGURE 16–2 The Changing Pattern of Work in the United States, 1900–2011

Compared to a century ago, when the economy involved a larger share of factory and farm work, making a living in the United States now involves mostly white-collar service jobs.

Source: Estimates based on U.S. Department of Labor (2012).

The Dual Labor Market

Sociologists see the jobs in today's economy falling into two categories. The **primary labor market** offers *jobs that provide extensive benefits to workers*. This segment of the labor market includes the traditional white-collar professions such as medicine and law, as well as upper-management positions. These are jobs that people think of as *careers,* interesting work that provides high income, job security, and opportunity for advancement.

Few of these advantages apply to work in the **secondary labor market**, *jobs that provide minimal benefits to workers*. This segment of the labor force is employed in low-skilled, blue-collar assembly-line operations and low-level service-sector jobs, including clerical positions. Workers in the secondary labor market receive lower income, have less job security and fewer benefits, and find less satisfaction in their work. Women and other minorities are overly represented in the secondary labor market workforce (Nelson, 1994; Kalleberg, Reskin, & Hudson, 2000).

Labor Unions

labor unions organizations of workers that seek to improve wages and working conditions through various strategies, including negotiations and strikes

The changing U.S. economy has seen a decline in **labor unions**, *organizations of workers that seek to improve wages and working conditions through various strategies, including negotiations and strikes*. During the Great Depression of the 1930s, union membership increased rapidly; by 1950, it had reached more than one-third of nonfarm workers. Union rolls peaked at almost 25 million around 1970. Since then, membership has declined to about 12 percent of nonfarm workers, or some 15 million men and women. Looking more closely, 37 percent of government workers are members of unions, compared to just 7 percent of private-sector (nongovernment) workers. In terms of absolute numbers, by 2010, government workers had become a majority of all union members (Clawson & Clawson, 1999; Riley, 2011; U.S. Department of Labor, 2012).

The pattern of union decline holds in other high-income countries, yet unions elsewhere claim a higher share of workers than they do in the United States. Union membership is around 19 percent in Japan, between 15 and 40 percent in much of Europe, 29 percent in Canada, and reaches a high of 70 percent in Finland (OECD, 2012).

The widespread decline in union memberships reflects the shrinking industrial sector of the economy. Newer service jobs—such as sales jobs at retailers like Walmart, described in the chapter opening—generally have not become unionized. Citing low wages and numerous worker complaints, unions are trying to organize Walmart employees, so far without winning over a single store. In the end, long-term gains in membership probably depend on the ability of unions to adapt to the new global economy. Union members in the United States, used to seeing foreign workers as "the enemy," will have to build new international alliances (Rousseau, 2002; Dalmia, 2008; Allen, 2009).

The strength of unions in the economy depends in large part on the laws that regulate how unions are formed. Over the course of this country's history, even when employees wanted to form a labor union, a company did not have to recognize the union as representing the workers. A common strategy used by unions to gain the right to represent workers was "majority sign-up," which means that if a majority of workers at a particular company sign a card saying they wish to form a union then the company would have to recognize the union, all workers would pay union dues, and the union would represent all workers. Unions defend this policy as both democratic and preventing some workers from enjoying the benefits won by the union without paying their share of the union's support.

Opponents of this strategy support a different policy, generally called a "right-to-work" law. Such a law allows a union to represent workers, but it prevents a union from requiring all workers to join and pay dues as a condition of working at the company. In other words, all people have a "right to work," whether or not they wish to join a union.

National Map 16–1 on page 465 shows which states across the country have and have not enacted "right-to-work" laws.

In 2011, the nation's attention was drawn to efforts by several states to limit the power of

primary labor market jobs that provide extensive benefits to workers

secondary labor market jobs that provide minimal benefits to workers

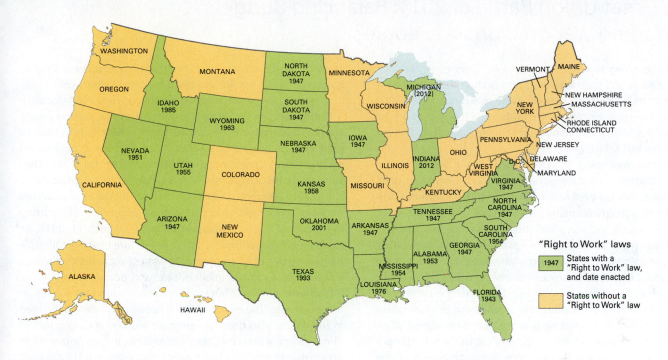

Explore self-employment in your local community and in counties across the United States in **MySocLab**

NATIONAL MAP 16–1 Right-to-Work Laws across the United States

Unions oppose "right-to-work" laws because these laws limit the power of unions to organize workers. In general, right-to-work laws have been enacted in the South and in many of the Plains States and western states. By contrast, states in the Northeast, in much of the Midwest, and on the West Coast have not enacted right-to-work laws. How do you think the two categories of states typically voted in the 2012 presidential election?

Source: National Conference of State Legislatures (2012).

government employee unions. On one side of the debate were people who claim that high wages and generous benefits for public employees threaten to bankrupt state treasuries. On the other side of the debate were people claiming that such benefits are deserved by people who do important and often dangerous work for modest pay. In addition, critics charge that some political leaders are trying to destroy the union movement. The Controversy & Debate box on page 466 provides details.

Professions

Many types of jobs today are called *professional*—we hear of professional tennis players, professional housecleaners, even professional exterminators. As distinct from *amateur* (from the Latin for "lover," meaning someone who does something just for the love of doing it), a professional performs some task to make a living. But does this term mean something more? What exactly is a profession?

A **profession** is *a prestigious white-collar occupation that requires extensive formal education*. People performing this kind of work make a *profession*, or public declaration, of their willingness to work according to certain ethical principles. Professions include the ministry, medicine, law, academia, architecture, accountancy, and social work. An occupation is considered a profession to the extent that it demonstrates the following four basic characteristics (Goode, 1960; Ritzer & Walczak, 1990):

profession a prestigious white-collar occupation that requires extensive formal education

1. **Theoretical knowledge.** Professionals have a theoretical understanding of their field rather than mere technical training. Anyone can master first-aid skills, for example, but physicians have a theoretical understanding of human health. This means that tennis players, housecleaners, and exterminators do not really qualify as professionals.

Controversy & Debate

The Great Union Battle of 2011: Balancing Budgets or Waging War on Working People?

"We're going to reform government," Ohio governor John Kasich told state legislators on March 8, 2011, as he gave his first "state of the state" speech. As he spoke, more than 1,000 firefighters—state employees—crowded the lobby outside the doors of the legislative chamber and chanted in unison, "Kill the bill! Kill the bill! Kill the bill!"

So what was going on? Ohio was facing a desperate economic situation—the state government was $8 billion in debt. Governor Kasich believed one major cause of that enormous deficit was past agreements made between state officials and public employee unions, including firefighters, police, and teachers.

As Kasich saw it, the problem was a system that gives public employee unions too much power and threatens to bankrupt the state. Under that system, unions effectively require every public employee to be a union member and to pay hefty dues through payroll deductions. These dues give unions huge political power to elect Democratic leaders who, in the past, have signed off on labor contracts that not only exceed what workers in the private sector earn but also that the state simply cannot afford. The reforms Kasich and the Republican-controlled state government enacted in 2011 would have continued collective bargaining by public employee unions for salary but no longer allowed it as the means to set benefits. In addition, pay was to be linked to a performance-based merit system rather than seniority, and public employee unions would not have been allowed to strike.

Harold Schaltberger, representing the International Association of Fire Fighters, saw the "reforms" as nothing less than a war on unions. The proposed measures, he claimed, "move us back decades to when there were no true workers' rights." As a result, unions organized a massive effort to overturn the new Ohio law. In the fall of 2011, they succeeded when a majority of voters supported the union position.

In 2010, Wisconsin voters elected Scott Walker as governor on a platform of reducing that state's budget deficit by cutting the power of public employee unions. On March 11, 2011, he signed a bill passed by the state's legislature limiting collective bargaining by public employees to wages (not benefits), limiting wage increases to the inflation rate, and decreasing the share the government contributes toward their health care and retirement pensions. The new law, which has already been challenged in the courts, also gives government workers the right to join or not to join a union. As they did in Ohio, unions organized in opposition to this new law by seeking to remove Scott Walker from office. But, in this case, the outcome was a defeat for the unions: Walker survived a recall election in 2012.

Because many states—as well as the federal government—are facing large budget deficits, the conflicts seen in Ohio and Wisconsin are likely to be repeated across the country in the future.

What Do You Think?

1. Do you think all workers—including government employees—should have the right to form unions? Explain.

2. Should public service employees receive roughly the same pay and benefits earned by comparable workers in the private sector? What about firefighters and police who face danger in their daily work?

3. Do you support the position taken by Governors Kasich and Walker to reduce union power? Or do you side with these unions and want to see them remain strong? Explain.

Sources: Gray (2011), Murphy (2011), Rasmussen (2011), Ripley (2011), Sulzberger (2011), and Kelleher (2012).

---

2. **Self-regulating practice.** The typical professional is self-employed, "in private practice," rather than working for a company. Professionals oversee their own work guided by a code of ethics.

3. **Authority over clients.** Because of their expertise, professionals are sought out by clients, who value their advice and follow their directions.

4. **Community orientation rather than self-interest.** The traditional professing of duty states an intention to serve others rather than merely to seek income.

In almost all cases, professional work requires not just a college degree but also a graduate degree. Not surprisingly, therefore, professions are well represented among the occupations beginning college students say they hope to enter after graduation, as shown in Figure 16–3 on page 467.

Many occupations that do not qualify as true professions nonetheless may seek to *professionalize* their services. Claiming professional standing often begins by renaming the work to suggest special, theoretical knowledge, moving the field away from its original, lesser reputation. Stockroom workers become "inventory supply managers," and exterminators are reborn as "insect control specialists."

Interested parties may also form a professional association that certifies their skills and ethical conduct. This organization then licenses its members, writes a code of ethics, and emphasizes the work's importance in the community. To win public acceptance, a professional association may also establish schools or other training facilities and publish a professional journal. Not all occupations try to claim professional status. Some *paraprofessionals,* including paralegals and medical technicians, possess specialized skills but lack the extensive theoretical education required of full professionals.

Self-Employment

Self-employment—earning a living without being on the payroll of a large organization—was once common in the United States. About 80 percent of the labor force was self-employed in 1800, compared to just 7 percent of workers today (8 percent of men and 6 percent of women) (U.S. Department of Labor, 2012).

Lawyers, physicians, and other professionals are well represented among the ranks of the self-employed. But most self-employed workers are small business owners, plumbers, carpenters, freelance writers, editors, artists, and long-distance truck drivers. In all, the self-employed are more likely to have blue-collar than white-collar jobs.

Women own 30 percent of this country's businesses, and the share is rising. The 7.8 million firms owned by U.S. women employ 6.4 percent of the labor force and generate $1.2 trillion in annual sales (U.S. Census Bureau, 2012).

Unemployment and Underemployment

Every society has some unemployment. Few young people entering the labor force find a job right away; workers may leave their jobs to seek new work or stay at home raising children; others may be on strike or suffer from long-term illnesses; still others lack the skills to perform useful work.

But unemployment is not just an individual problem; it is also caused by the economy. Jobs disappear as occupations become obsolete and companies change the way they operate. Since 1980, the 500 largest U.S. businesses eliminated more than 5 million jobs while creating an even larger number of new ones.

Generally, companies downsize to become more competitive, or firms close in the face of foreign competition or economic recession. During the recent recession in the United States, several million jobs were lost with unemployment rising in just about every part of the economy. Not only blue-collar workers but also white-collar workers who had typically weathered downturns in the past have lost jobs during this recession.

In 2008, just as the economy was falling into recession, 7 million people over the age of sixteen were unemployed, about 4.6 percent of the civilian labor force. But by the end of 2012, 12.2 million were officially counted as unemployed pushing up the annual unemployment rate to 8.1 (8.2 percent for men and 7.9 percent for women). This figure was below the high of 10.6 percent at the start of 2010. Even with this drop in the unemployment rate, however, the number of unemployed people had increased by more than 70 percent since 2008, and the length of time people had been out of work had also increased—in 2012, 40 percent of unemployed people had been out of work for more than half a year (U.S. Department of Labor, 2012). The unemployment rate is not the same everywhere in the country,

- In a society such as ours, with so many different types of work, no one career attracts the interest of more than a small share of today's students.

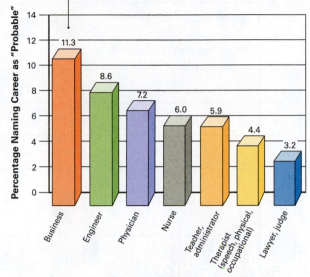

FIGURE 16–3 The Careers Most Commonly Named as "Probable" by First-Year College Students, 2012

Today's college students expect to enter careers that pay well and carry high prestige.

Source: Pryor et al. (2013).

 Read in **MySocLab Document:** *A Sociology of Bubbles* by Bruce G. Carruthers, about the factors that played a role in the recent economic crisis

Diversity Snapshot

- The best strategy to reduce your risk of being without a job is to complete a college education.

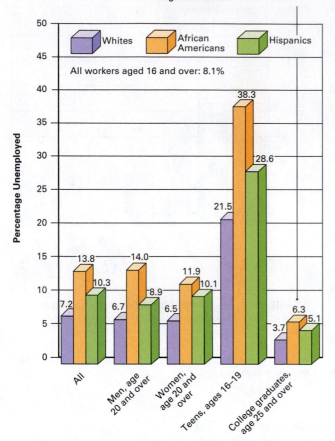

FIGURE 16–4 Official Unemployment Rates for Various Categories of the U.S. Population, 2012

Although college graduates have a low risk of unemployment, race is related to unemployment for all categories of people.

Source: U.S. Department of Labor (2013).

of course. For example, the western states have been particularly hard hit while the Plains States in the middle of the country have fared better. In addition, counting the people without jobs who have given up looking for work (and, therefore, are not counted in the official unemployment statistics), the number of jobless people almost certainly exceeds 20 million making the actual unemployment rate about 13 percent.

Figure 16–4 shows that in 2012, unemployment among African Americans (13.8 percent) was almost twice the rate among white people (7.2 percent). Regardless of sex or age, unemployment is lower among whites than among African Americans; the gap between white and black teenagers was especially large. For all categories of people, one of the best ways to avoid unemployment is to earn a college degree: As the figure shows, the unemployment rate for college graduates is about half the national average (U.S. Department of Labor, 2013).

For those who experience unemployment, finding another job is more difficult than ever. The median length of unemployment has increased to 18.1 weeks, meaning that half of all unemployed people are out of work longer than this. But the mean length of unemployment is more than twice this long—37 weeks—because many workers are out of work for a year or more. In short, our society now faces a problem of *extended unemployment,* with unemployment not only more widespread but also longer lasting than it has been in the recent past (U.S. Department of Labor, 2012).

Underemployment is also a problem for millions of workers. In an era of corporate bankruptcy, the failure of large banks, and downsizing by companies throughout the U.S. economy, millions of workers—the lucky ones who still have their jobs—have been left with lower salaries, fewer benefits such as health insurance, and disappearing pensions. Rising global competition, weaker worker organizations, and economic recession have combined to allow many people to keep their jobs only by agreeing to cutbacks in pay or to the loss of other benefits (Clark, 2002; Gutierrez, 2007; McGeehan, 2009).

In addition, the government reports that more than 27 million people work part time, defined as less than thirty-five hours a week. Although most say they are satisfied with this arrangement, 30 percent of part-timers claim that they want more work but cannot find it (U.S. Department of Labor, 2012). In all, as the country struggles to climb out of the recent recession, it is likely that one in five workers is working fewer hours than desired, is out of work and looking for a job, or is a "discouraged worker" who has given up entirely.

The "Jobless Recovery"

The economy operates in cycles, with periods of prosperity followed by periods of recession—what we commonly call "boom and bust." In the past, periods of high job loss during economic recession have typically been followed by a rapid increase in jobs as good times returned, bringing down the unemployment rate within a few years.

This time around, the recovery in jobs has not been as quick. Corporate profits have returned to their pre-recession levels, but U.S. corporations are operating with about 7 million fewer workers. This means that the nation's unemployment remains stubbornly high. One reason for this pattern—sometimes described as the "jobless recovery"—is that, even before the economy went into recession, companies were finding ways to operate with a smaller workforce. Computer technology allows fewer people to do more work; in many cases, too, a smaller number of workers have simply been given more to do. In addition, companies are making more use of temporary workers.

Second, more companies have opened factories and office hubs abroad—often in China, India, or Brazil, where wages and benefits will cost far less. In China, for example, workers earn about 10 percent as much as they do in the United States. For this reason, many global corporations are making record profits while adding almost no jobs here in the United States.

A third issue is that the U.S. economy is simply not growing fast enough—and hasn't been for many years—to absorb all the people looking for jobs. That is why, according to government reports, for every new job that is available, there are almost five people looking for work.

Fourth and finally, in global terms, U.S. workers are simply too expensive and do not have the high level of skills needed to fare well in today's economy. Perhaps, as some analysts suggest, large investments will have to be made in education and job training in order to get the unemployment rate here in the United States back to pre-recession levels (Faroohar, 2011; Wessel, 2011; Zakaria, 2011).

The Underground Economy

The U.S. government requires individuals and businesses to report their economic activity, especially earnings. Unreported income makes a transaction part of the **underground economy**, *economic activity involving income not reported to the government as required by law*.

Most of us participate in the underground economy in small ways from time to time: A family makes extra money by holding a garage sale, or teenagers baby-sit for neighbors without reporting the income. Much more of the underground economy is due to criminal activity, such as prostitution, bribery, theft, illegal gambling, loan-sharking, and the sale of illegal drugs.

But the largest segment of contributors to the underground economy is people who fail to report some or all of their legally earned income when it comes time to file income tax returns. Self-employed persons such as carpenters, physicians, and small business owners may understate their income on tax forms; food servers and other service workers may not report their earnings from tips. Individually, the amounts people do not report may be small, but taken together, U.S. taxpayers fail to pay as much as $450 billion annually in federal taxes (Internal Revenue Service, 2012).

Although the economy has been getting stronger, employment has not returned to pre-recession levels. The television show *Girls* follows the everyday lives of recent college graduates trying to make it in New York City working low-wage jobs while they chase their dreams..

underground economy economic activity involving income not reported to the government as required by law

Workplace Diversity: Race and Gender

In the past, white men have been the mainstay of the U.S. labor force. However, the nation's proportion of minorities is rising rapidly. The African American population is increasing faster than the population of non-Hispanic white people. The rate of increase in the Asian American and Hispanic populations is even greater.

Such dramatic changes are likely to affect U.S. society in countless ways. Not only will more and more workers be women and other minorities, but also the workplace will have to develop programs and policies that meet the needs of a socially diverse workforce while encouraging everyone to work together effectively and respectfully. The Thinking About Diversity box on page 470 takes a closer look at some of the issues involved in our changing workplace.

New Information Technology and Work

July 2, Ticonderoga, New York. *The manager of the local hardware store scans the bar codes of a bagful of items. "The computer doesn't just total the costs," she explains. "It also keeps track of inventory, placing orders from the warehouse and deciding which products to continue to sell and which to drop." "Sounds like what you used to do, Maureen," I respond with a smile. "Yep," she nods, with no smile at all.*

Thinking about Diversity: Race, Class, and Gender

Diversity 2020: Changes Coming to the Workplace

An upward trend in the U.S. minority population is changing the workplace. As the figure shows, the number of non-Hispanic white men in the U.S. labor force actually will decline by 2 percent by 2020. During the same period, the number of African American men will increase by 9 percent, the number of Hispanic men will rise by 25 percent, and the number of Asian American men will go up by 21 percent.

Among non-Hispanic white women, the projected change by 2020 is a slight decline of 1 percent; among African American women, an increase of 7 percent; and among Asian women, an increase of 25 percent. Hispanic women will show the greatest gains, estimated at 28 percent.

By 2020, non-Hispanic white men will represent just 33 percent of all workers, a figure that will continue to drop. As a result, companies that welcome social diversity will tap the largest pool of talent and enjoy a competitive advantage leading to higher profits (Graybow, 2007; Harford, 2008; U.S. Department of Labor, 2012).

Welcoming social diversity means, first, recruiting talented workers of both sexes and all racial and cultural backgrounds. But developing the potential of all employees requires meeting the needs of women and other minorities, which may not be the same as those of white men. For example, child care at the workplace is a big issue for working mothers with small children.

Second, businesses must develop effective ways to deal with tensions that arise from social differences. They will have to work harder to ensure that workers are treated equally and respectfully, which means having zero tolerance for racial or sexual harassment.

Third, companies will have to rethink current promotion practices. The latest research shows that 75 percent of the directors of Fortune 100 companies are white men; 25 percent are women or other minorities. Of these 100 large companies, 96 percent of the chairs of the boards of directors are white men (Alliance for Board Diversity, 2011). In a survey of U.S. companies, the U.S. Equal Employment Opportunity Commission (2012) confirmed that non-Hispanic white men, who make up 32 percent of adults aged twenty to sixty-four, hold 52 percent of management jobs; the comparable figures are 33 and 29 percent, respectively, for non-Hispanic white women, 13 and 6 percent for non-Hispanic African Americans, and 16 and 6 percent for Hispanics.

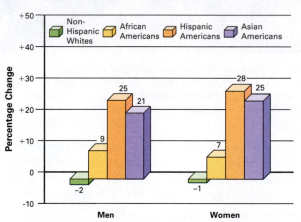

Projected Increase in the Number of People in the U.S. Labor Force, 2012–2020
Looking ahead, the share of minorities in the U.S. labor force will increase while the share of non-Hispanic whites will decline.

Source: U.S. Department of Labor (2012).

What Do You Think?

1. What underlying factors are increasing the diversity of the U.S. workplace?

2. In what specific ways do you think businesses should support minority workers?

3. In what other settings (such as schools) is social diversity becoming more important?

Watch in **MySocLab**
Video: *Sociology on the Job: Economy and Work*

Another workplace issue is the increasing role of computers and other information technology. The Information Revolution is changing what people do in a number of ways (Rule & Brantley, 1992; Vallas & Beck, 1996):

1. **Computers are deskilling labor.** Just as industrial machinery replaced the master craftsworkers of an earlier era, computers now threaten the skills of managers. More business operations are based not on executive decisions but on computer modeling. In other words, a machine decides whether to place an order, stock a dress in a certain size and color, or approve a loan application.

2. **Computers are making work more abstract.** Most industrial workers have a hands-on relationship with their product. Postindustrial workers use symbols to perform abstract tasks, such as making a company more profitable, making software more user-friendly, or hiding risky assets inside financial "derivatives."

3. **Computers limit workplace interaction.** As workers spend more time at computer terminals, they become increasingly isolated from one another.

4. **Computers increase employers' control of workers.** Computers allow supervisors to monitor employees' output continuously, whether they work at computer terminals or on assembly lines.

5. **Computers allow companies to relocate work.** Because computer technology allows information to flow almost anywhere instantly, the symbolic work in today's economy may not take place where we might think. We have all had the experience of calling a business (say, a hotel or bookstore) located in our own town only to find that we are talking to a person at a computer workstation thousands of miles away. Computer technology provides the means to outsource many jobs—especially service work—to other places where wages may be lower.

In today's corporate world, computers are changing the nature of work just as factories did more than a century ago. In what ways is computer-based work different from factory work? In what ways do you think it is very much the same?

Perhaps, in the wake of widespread failures on Wall Street, there will be a trend away from allowing computers to manage risk, putting responsibility for business decisions back in the hands of people (Kivant, 2008). Or perhaps both computers and people have flaws that will always prevent us from living in a perfect world. But the rapidly increasing reliance on computers in business reminds us that new technology is never socially neutral. It changes the relationships between people in the workplace, shapes the way we work, and often alters the balance of power between employers and employees. Understandably, then, people welcome some aspects of the Information Revolution and oppose others.

Corporations

16.4 Discuss the importance of corporations to the U.S. economy.

At the core of today's capitalist economy lies the **corporation**, *an organization with a legal existence, including rights and liabilities, separate from that of its members*. Incorporating makes an organization a legal entity, able to enter into contracts and own property. Of the 32 million businesses in the United States, 5.8 million are incorporated (Internal Revenue Service, 2012). Incorporating protects the wealth of owners from lawsuits that result from business debts or harm to consumers; it can also mean a lower tax rate on the company's profits.

Economic Concentration

Most U.S. corporations are small, with assets of less than $500,000, so it is the largest corporations that dominate our nation's economy. In 2009, the government listed 2,604 corporations with assets exceeding $2.5 billion, representing 81 percent of all corporate assets (Internal Revenue Service, 2012).

The largest U.S. corporation in terms of sales is Walmart. Its annual sales ($444 billion in 2012) equal the combined tax revenues of forty-four of the fifty states.

Conglomerates and Corporate Linkages

Economic concentration has created the **conglomerate**, *a giant corporation composed of many smaller corporations*. Conglomerates form as corporations enter new markets, spin off new companies, or merge with other companies. For example, PepsiCo is a

corporation an organization with a legal existence, including rights and liabilities, separate from that of its members

conglomerate a giant corporation composed of many smaller corporations

conglomerate that includes Pepsi-Cola, Frito-Lay, Gatorade, Tropicana, and Quaker.

Many conglomerates are linked because they own each other's stock, the result being worldwide corporate alliances of staggering size. In 2012, for example, General Motors owned Opel (Germany), Vauxhall (Great Britain), Holden (Australia), and a share of Daewoo (South Korea) and had partnerships with Suzuki and Toyota (Japan) and several new brands in China.

Corporations are also linked through *interlocking directorates,* networks of people who serve as directors of many corporations (Weidenbaum, 1995; Kono et al., 1998). These boardroom connections give corporations access to valuable information about other companies' products and marketing strategies. While perfectly legal, such linkages may encourage illegal activity, such as price fixing, as the companies share information about their pricing policies.

Corporations: Are They Competitive?

According to the capitalist model, businesses operate independently in a competitive market. But in light of the extensive linkages that exist between them, it is obvious that large corporations do not operate independently. Also, a few large corporations dominate many markets, so they are not truly competitive.

Federal law forbids any company from establishing a **monopoly**, *the domination of a market by a single producer,* because with no competition, such a company could simply charge whatever it wanted for its products. But **oligopoly**, *the domination of a market by a few producers*, is both legal and common. Oligopoly arises because the huge investment needed to enter a major market, such as the auto industry, is beyond the reach of all but the biggest companies. In addition, competition means risk, which big business tries to avoid. Even so, we have recently seen that even the largest corporations are not immune to economic crisis, as shown by the 2009 bankruptcy of General Motors. They can also face rising competition, as the U.S. auto industry has seen from companies such as Kia and Hyundai.

The federal government seeks to regulate corporations in order to protect the public interest. Yet as recent corporate scandals have shown—most recently involving the housing mortgage business and the collapse of so many banks—regulation is often too little too late, resulting in companies harming millions of people. The U.S. government is the corporate world's single biggest customer, and in 2008 and 2009 it stepped in to support many struggling corporations with multibillion-dollar bailout programs. Especially during tough economic times, the public tends to support a greater role for the government in the economy (Sachs, 2009).

Corporations and the Global Economy

Corporations have grown so large that they now account for most of the world's economic output. The biggest corporations are based in the United States, Japan, and Western Europe, but their marketplace is the entire world. In fact, many large U.S. companies such as McDonald's and the chipmaker Intel earn most of their money outside the United States. In 2011, General Motors sold almost three-fourths of its cars outside of the United States, especially in the "emerging markets" of Brazil, Russia, India, and China (General Motors, 2012).

Global corporations know that lower-income countries contain most of the world's people and natural resources. In addition, labor costs are attractively low: A manufacturing worker in Mexico earns about $6.23 an

monopoly the domination of a market by a single producer

oligopoly the domination of a market by a few producers

hour and labors for a week to earn what a worker in Japan (who averages about $32 an hour) or the United States ($35 per hour) earns in a single day. (U.S. Department of Labor, 2012).

As Chapter 12 ("Global Stratification") explained, the impact of multinational corporations on poor countries is controversial. Modernization theorists claim that by unleashing the great productive power of capitalism, multinational corporations help to raise living standards in poor nations, offering them tax revenues, new jobs, and advanced technology that together accelerate economic growth (Berger, 1986; Firebaugh & Beck, 1994; Firebaugh & Sandu, 1998).

Dependency theorists respond that multinationals make global inequality worse by blocking the development of local industries and pushing poor countries to make goods for export rather than food and other products for local people. From this standpoint, multinationals make poor nations increasingly dependent on rich nations (Wallerstein, 1979; Dixon & Boswell, 1996; Kentor, 1998).

In short, modernization theory praises the market as the key to progress and affluence for all the world's people, and dependency theory calls for replacing market systems with government-based economic policies.

For a closer look at the issue of market versus government economies, **Read More** in **MySocLab**, *The Market: Does the "Invisible Hand" Lift Us Up or Pick Our Pockets?*

The Economy: Looking Ahead

Social institutions are a society's way of meeting people's needs. But as we have seen, the U.S. economy only partly succeeds in accomplishing this goal. Over the years, our national economy experiences periods of expansion and periods of recession. In addition, in both good times and bad, our economy provides for some people much better than for others.

One important trend that underlies change in the economy is the shift from industrial work to jobs created by the Information Revolution. First, the share of the U.S. labor force in industrial manufacturing is just one-third of what it was in 1960; service work, especially computer-related jobs, makes up the difference. For industrial workers, the postindustrial economy has brought rising unemployment and declining wages. Our society must face up to the challenge of providing millions of men and women with the language and computer skills they need to succeed in the new economy.

A second transformation of recent years is the expansion of the global economy. Two centuries ago, the ups and downs people experienced reflected events and trends in their own town. One century ago, communities were economically linked so that one town's prosperity depended on producing goods demanded by people elsewhere in the country. Today, we have to look beyond the national economy because, for example, the historical rise in the cost of gasoline in our local communities has much to do with increasing demand for oil around the world, especially in China and India. As both producers and consumers, we are now responding to factors and forces that are both distant and unseen.

Finally, analysts around the world are rethinking conventional economic models. The global economy shows that socialism is less productive than capitalism, which is one important reason behind the collapse of the socialist regimes in Eastern Europe and the Soviet Union. But capitalism has its own problems, including high levels of inequality and a steady stream of corporate scandal—two important reasons that the economy now operates with significant government regulation.

What will be the long-term effects of all these changes? Two conclusions seem certain. First, the economic future of the United States and other nations will be played out in a global arena. The new postindustrial economy in the United States has emerged as more industrial production has moved to other nations. Second, it is imperative that we address the related issues of global inequality and population increase. Whether the world reduces or enlarges the gap between rich and poor societies may well steer our planet toward peace or war.

Seeing Sociology in Everyday Life

CHAPTER 16   The Economy and Work

What are the challenges of today's economy?

This chapter explains that the economy is the social institution that organizes the production, distribution, and consumption of goods and services. It's no secret that we are living in tough economic times. Unemployment has been high, earning a living wage is harder than it used to be, and public confidence in a secure future has taken a hit. As C. Wright Mills might have said, the problems we face as individuals are issues that are deeply rooted in the economy. Look at the three photos and ask yourself: What changes in today's economy create challenges for today's labor force?

Walk around a big-box store and examine products to see where they are made. It will not take long to see a pattern: What is it? As the share of manufactured goods made abroad rises, what happens to manufacturing jobs here in the United States?

Have you ever called an 800 support line and wondered where the person on the other end of the line was located? It is not only manufacturing jobs that have moved overseas. Lower wages have led corporations to relocate many service jobs—including many skilled office jobs—to places such as India, where service employment is skyrocketing. In short, is anyone safe from the trend we call "outsourcing"?

Advancing technology makes our economy more productive, right? Generally, yes. But adopting new technology can make organizations more productive with fewer employees. Have you ever taken a "distance learning" class in which the professor was not in the classroom with you? How can computer technology enable colleges to teach more students using fewer faculty?

HINT Industrial production has been moving from the United States to countries where wages are lower. In China, for example, industrial workers earn roughly 10 percent of what a worker is paid in this country. Lower labor cost is the key reason that China produces 70 percent of all products sold in Walmart stores around the world. China's economy is still less than half as large as that of the United States, despite having a labor force five times larger. But since 2000, China's industrial production has increased, on average, about 10 percent a year. U.S. industrial production has actually declined in five years of the new century, and averages less than a 1 percent annual increase. Economic activity is also expanding in India, a country that has seen striking growth in service jobs, such as those shown in the photo at the bottom of page 474 of a call-center in the city of Kolkata. Back home in the United States, even highly skilled people such as college professors are facing challenges in today's economy. Computer technology is being used to allow professors to teach larger classes and also to allow a single faculty member to teach students in multiple classrooms in various places at the same time. In short, even when a corporation or organization becomes more productive, it does not always end up employing more people, which helps us to understand why some analysts have been talking about a "jobless recovery."

Seeing Sociology in *Your* Everyday Life

1. Visit a discount store such as Walmart or Kmart and do a little "fieldwork" in an area of the store that interests you. Pick ten products, and see where each is made. Do the results support the existence of a global economy?

2. Go to MySocLab and click on the Student Resources link to access the Sociology in Focus blog, where you can read the latest posts by a team of young sociologists who apply the sociological perspective to topics of popular culture.

3. Based on what you have read in this chapter, make three predictions about the nature of work and jobs twenty years from now. That is, what trends have you noted that seem likely to continue? To read more about how information in this chapter can assist you in your own career, go to the "Seeing Sociology in *Your* Everyday Life" feature in MySocLab, where you will find some facts of interest.

Making the Grade

The Economy: Historical Overview

(**16.1**) Summarize historical changes to the economy. (pages 454–58)

 Watch the **Video** in **MySocLab**

In technologically simple societies, economic activity is simply part of family life.

The **agricultural revolution** (5,000 years ago) made the economy a distinct social institution based on

- agricultural technology
- specialized work
- permanent settlements
- trade

The **Industrial Revolution** (beginning around 1750) expanded the economy based on

- new sources of energy
- centralization of work in factories
- specialization and mass production
- wage labor

The **postindustrial economy**, propelled by the **Information Revolution**, which began around 1950, is based on

- a shift from industrial work to service work
- computer technology

The **primary sector** of the economy

- draws raw materials from the natural environment
- is of greatest importance (25% of the economy) in low-income nations

Examples: agriculture, fishing, mining

The **secondary sector** of the economy

- transforms raw materials into manufactured goods
- is a significant share (24%–35%) of the economy in low-, middle-, and high-income nations

Examples: automobile and clothing manufacturing

The **tertiary sector** of the economy

- produces services rather than goods
- is the largest sector (50%–74%) in low-, middle-, and high-income countries

Examples: secretarial work, sales, teaching

economy the social institution that organizes a society's production, distribution, and consumption of goods and services

postindustrial economy a productive system based on service work and high technology

primary sector the part of the economy that draws raw materials from the natural environment

secondary sector the part of the economy that transforms raw materials into manufactured goods

tertiary sector the part of the economy that involves services rather than goods

global economy economic activity that crosses national borders

Economic Systems: Paths to Justice

(**16.2**) Assess the operation of capitalist and socialist economies. (pages 458–63)

 Watch the **Video** in **MySocLab**

Capitalism is based on private ownership of property and the pursuit of profit in a competitive marketplace. Capitalism results in

- greater productivity ⟷
- higher overall standard of living ⟷
- greater income inequality ⟷
- freedom to act according to self-interest ⟷

Socialism is grounded in collective ownership of productive property through government control of the economy. Socialism results in

- less productivity
- lower overall standard of living
- less income inequality
- freedom from basic want

Example: The United States has a mostly capitalist economy.

Examples: The People's Republic of China and Venezuela have mostly socialist economies.

capitalism an economic system in which natural resources and the means of producing goods and services are privately owned

socialism an economic system in which natural resources and the means of producing goods and services are collectively owned

communism a hypothetical economic and political system in which all members of a society are socially equal

welfare capitalism an economic and political system that combines a mostly market-based economy with extensive social welfare programs

Under **welfare capitalism,**

- government may own some large industries such as transportation and the mass media
- most industry is privately owned but highly regulated by government
- high taxation of the rich helps pay for extensive government services for all

Examples: Sweden and Italy have welfare capitalist economies.

Under **state capitalism**, government works in partnership with large companies by

- supplying financial assistance
- controlling foreign imports

Examples: Japan and Singapore have state capitalist economies.

state capitalism an economic and political system in which companies are privately owned but cooperate closely with the government

---

Work in the Postindustrial U.S. Economy

16.3 Analyze patterns of employment and unemployment in the United States. (pages 463–71)

 Explore the **Map** in **MySocLab**   **Read** the **Document** in **MySocLab**

 Watch the **Video** in **MySocLab**

- Agricultural work represents only 1.6% of jobs.
- Blue-collar, industrial work has declined to 17% of jobs.
- White-collar, service work has increased to 81% of jobs.

- Jobs in the **primary labor market** involve interesting work that provides high income, benefits, and job security.
- Jobs in the **secondary labor market** have lower pay, less job security, and fewer benefits and provide less personal satisfaction.

- 6.8% of U.S. workers are **self-employed**.
- Many professionals fall into this category, but most self-employed people have blue-collar jobs.

- **Unemployment** has many causes, including the operation of the economy itself.
- In 2012, 8.1% of the country's labor force was unemployed.
- At highest risk for unemployment are young people and African Americans.

Information technology is changing the workplace and how people work. Computers are

- deskilling labor
- making work more abstract
- limiting interaction among workers
- increasing employers' control over workers
- allowing companies to relocate work

primary labor market jobs that provide extensive benefits to workers

secondary labor market jobs that provide minimal benefits to workers

labor unions organizations of workers that seek to improve wages and working conditions through various strategies, including negotiations and strikes

profession a prestigious white-collar occupation that requires extensive formal education

underground economy economic activity involving income not reported to the government as required by law

---

Corporations

16.4 Discuss the importance of corporations to the U.S. economy. (pages 471–73)

Corporations form the core of the U.S. economy. Incorporation

- makes an organization a legal entity
- shields owners' wealth from lawsuits brought against the company
- can result in a lower tax rate on the company's profits

The largest corporations, which are **conglomerates**, account for most corporate assets and profits (examples: PepsiCo, General Motors).

- Corporations are linked through interlocking directorates.
- Recognizing that corporate linkages and the domination of certain markets by large corporations reduce competition, federal laws forbid **monopoly** and price fixing.

Many large corporations operate as **multinationals**, producing and distributing products in nations around the world.

- Modernization theorists claim that multinationals raise living standards in poor countries by offering them more jobs and advanced technology.
- Dependency theorists claim that multinationals make global inequality worse by pushing poor countries to produce goods for export and making them more dependent on rich nations.

corporation an organization with a legal existence, including rights and liabilities, separate from that of its members

conglomerate a giant corporation composed of many smaller corporations

monopoly the domination of a market by a single producer

oligopoly the domination of a market by a few producers

17 Politics and Government

((• Listen to Chapter 17 in MySocLab

LEARNING OBJECTIVES

17.1 Distinguish traditional, rational-legal, and charismatic authority.

17.2 Compare monarchy and democracy as well as authoritarian and totalitarian political systems.

17.3 Analyze economic and social issues using the political spectrum.

17.4 Apply the pluralist, power-elite, and Marxist models to the U.S. political system.

17.5 Describe causes of both revolution and terrorism.

17.6 Identify factors encouraging war or peace.

the Power of Society

to shape voting patterns

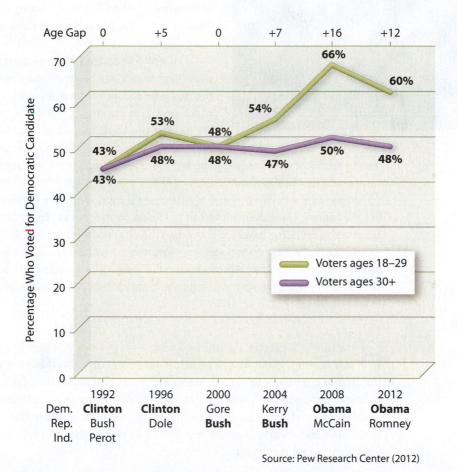

| Age Gap | 0 | +5 | 0 | +7 | +16 | +12 |

Percentage Who Voted for Democratic Candidate

- 66%
- 60%
- 54%
- 53%
- 48%
- 43%
- 43%
- 48%
- 48%
- 47%
- 50%
- 48%

Voters ages 18–29
Voters ages 30+

	1992	1996	2000	2004	2008	2012
Dem.	**Clinton**	**Clinton**	Gore	Kerry	**Obama**	**Obama**
Rep.	Bush	Dole	**Bush**	**Bush**	McCain	Romney
Ind.	Perot					

Source: Pew Research Center (2012)

Does a person's age affect political leanings? If the only voters in the 2012 presidential election had been people over the age of thirty, Republican Mitt Romney would have won. The support of young people was key to Democrat Barack Obama's reelection. Young people have not always voted differently than their elders: In 1992 and 2000, there was no overall difference between people above and below age thirty; in 1996, there was a small difference. But in 2004, 2008, and 2012, young people moved dramatically toward greater support for the Democratic candidate. If this trend holds, young people will continue to play a major role in our nation's elections.

Chapter Overview

Politics is the social institution through which a society distributes power, sets goals, and makes decisions. This chapter explores politics and explains the operation of government. In addition, the chapter analyzes the character and causes of war and terrorism.

The sun has barely come up and already several thousand people have gathered at a major intersection in Manama, the capital city of Bahrain. Some have come from their homes, some have come from nearby college campuses, some have been sleeping there all night. Many people hold cell phones, checking the latest news on what is planned for the day. And over the whole scene drifts the sound of music—rap music—written by a young Tunisian known as "El Général." "Mister President," the song goes, "your people are dying...I see injustice everywhere."

In the Middle East, we will remember the year 2011 as a time when rage mixed with rap to produce revolution. And added to this mix is one more key element—young people. The majority of the people in the streets of Bahrain, as elsewhere across the Middle East, are under thirty. Equipped with the handheld computer technology that has defined their generation, these young people are full of ambition and hope and tired of unemployment, hunger, and having little or no voice in their political systems.

It started in Tunisia at the end of 2010 when a popular uprising forced that nation's dictator to flee the country. The movement spread to Algeria, Jordan, Yemen, Egypt (forcing out that country's longtime leader), Libya (resulting in the death of a dictator there), as well as Syria (where yet another dictator has so far held on to power only by using the military against his own people). We cannot predict the full outcome of this movement, but the goal of young people across the Middle East is clear—they have been trying to change the world (Ghosh, 2011; Zakaria, 2011; Yom & Gause, 2012; Al Arabiya, 2013).

How power is exercised within a society—who has it and how it is used—is the focus of this chapter. What we call **politics**—or more formally, the "polity"—is *the social institution that distributes power, sets a society's goals, and makes decisions.* We will examine the political system in the United States and, from various points of view, assess the extent to which our society can claim to be democratic. Then we will turn our attention to the world as a whole, including a focus on revolution, as well as the international use of power in the form of war and terrorism.

Power and Authority

(17.1) Distinguish traditional, rational-legal, and charismatic authority.

The sociologist Max Weber (1978, orig. 1921) claimed that every society is based on **power**, which he defined as *the ability to achieve desired ends despite resistance from others.* The use of power is the business of **government**, *a formal organization that directs the political life of a society.* Governments demand compliance on the part of a population; yet Weber noted that most governments do not openly threaten their people. Most of the time, people respect, or at least accept, their society's political system.

No government, Weber explained, is likely to keep its power for long if compliance comes *only* from the threat of brute force. Even the most brutal dictator must wonder if

Watch in **MySocLab**
Video: *The Basics: Politics and Government*

politics the social institution that distributes power, sets a society's goals, and makes decisions

government a formal organization that directs the political life of a society

power the ability to achieve desired ends despite resistance from others

authority power that people perceive as legitimate rather than coercive

there can ever be enough police to watch everyone—and who would watch the police? Every government, therefore, tries to make itself seem legitimate in the eyes of the people. This fact brings us to Weber's concept of **authority**, *power that people perceive as legitimate rather than coercive.* How do governments transform raw power into more stable authority? Weber pointed to three ways: traditional authority, rational-legal authority, and charismatic authority.

Traditional Authority

Preindustrial societies, said Weber, rely on **traditional authority**, *power legitimized by respect for long-established cultural patterns.* Woven into a population's collective memory, traditional authority means that people accept a system, usually one of hereditary leadership, simply because it has always been that way. Chinese emperors in centuries past were legitimized by tradition, as were aristocratic rulers in medieval Europe. The power of tradition can be so strong that, for better or worse, people typically come to view traditional rulers as almost godlike.

Traditional authority declines as societies industrialize. Hannah Arendt (1963) pointed out that traditional authority remains strong only as long as everyone shares the same beliefs and way of life. Modern scientific thinking, the specialization demanded by industrial production, and the social changes and cultural diversity resulting from immigration all combine to weaken tradition. Therefore, a U.S. president would never claim to rule "by the grace of God," as many rulers in the ancient world did. Even so, some upper-class families with names like Bush, Kennedy, Roosevelt, and Rockefeller are so well established in our country's political life that their members may enter the political arena with some measure of traditional authority (Baltzell, 1964). Around the world, there are still hereditary rulers who claim a traditional right to rule. But this claim is increasingly out of step with modern society. Some traditional rulers persist by relinquishing most of their power (as in the United Kingdom) or at the other extreme by keeping their people cut off from the world and in a state of total subjugation (as in North Korea).

Traditional authority is also a source of strength for *patriarchy,* the domination of women by men. This traditional form of power is still widespread, although it is increasingly challenged. Less controversial is the traditional authority parents have over their children. As children, most of us can remember challenging a parent's demand by asking "Why?" only to hear the response "Because I said so!" Answering this way, the parent makes clear that the demand is not open to debate; to respond otherwise would ignore the parent's traditional authority over the child and put the two on an equal footing.

Rational-Legal Authority

Weber defined **rational-legal authority** (sometimes called *bureaucratic authority*) as *power legitimized by legally enacted rules and regulations.* Rational-legal authority is power legitimized in the operation of lawful government.

As Chapter 7 ("Groups and Organizations") explains, Weber viewed bureaucracy as the type of organization that dominates in rational-thinking, modern societies. The same rational worldview that promotes bureaucracy also erodes traditional customs and practices. Instead of looking to the past, members of today's high-income societies seek justice through the operation of a political system that follows formally enacted rules of law.

Rationally enacted rules also guide the use of power in everyday life. The authority of deans and classroom teachers, for example, rests on the offices they hold in bureaucratic colleges and universities. The police, too, depend on rational-legal authority. In contrast to

traditional authority power legitimized by respect for long-established cultural patterns

rational-legal authority power legitimized by legally enacted rules and regulations (also known as *bureaucratic authority*)

charismatic authority power legitimized by extraordinary personal abilities that inspire devotion and obedience

traditional authority, rational-legal authority comes not from family background but from a position in government organization. A traditional monarch rules for life, but a modern president or prime minister first accepts and later on gives up power according to law, which shows that the authority resides not in the person but in the office.

Charismatic Authority

Finally, Weber claimed that power can turn into authority through charisma. **Charismatic authority** is *power legitimized by extraordinary personal abilities that inspire devotion and obedience.* Unlike traditional and rational-legal authority, charismatic authority depends less on a person's ancestry or office and more on personality.

Charismatic leaders have surfaced throughout history, using their personal skills to turn an audience into followers. Often they make their own rules and challenge the status quo. Examples of charismatic leaders can be as different as Jesus of Nazareth and Adolf Hitler. The fact that they and others, such as India's liberator, Mahatma Gandhi, and the U.S. civil rights leader Martin Luther King Jr., succeeded in transforming the society around them certainly shows the power of charisma. And it probably explains why charismatics are highly controversial and why few of them die of old age.

routinization of charisma
the transformation of charismatic authority into some combination of traditional and bureaucratic authority

Because charismatic authority flows from a single individual, the leader's death creates a crisis. Survival of a charismatic movement, Weber explained, requires the **routinization of charisma**, *the transformation of charismatic authority into some combination of traditional and bureaucratic authority.* After the death of Jesus, for example, followers institutionalized his teachings in a church, built on tradition and bureaucracy. Routinized in this way, the Roman Catholic Church has lasted for 2,000 years.

Politics in Global Perspective

17.2 Compare monarchy and democracy as well as authoritarian and totalitarian political systems.

Political systems have changed over the course of history. Technologically simple hunting and gathering societies, once found all over the planet, operated like large families without formal governments. Leadership generally fell to a man with unusual strength, hunting skill, or personal charisma. But with few resources, such leaders might control their own people but could never rule a large area (Nolan & Lenski, 2010).

Agrarian societies are larger with specialized jobs and material surpluses. In these societies, a small elite gains control of most of the wealth and power, so that politics is not just a matter of powerful individuals but a more complex social institution in its own right. This is the point in history when power passed from generation to generation within a single family and leaders start to claim a divine right to rule, gaining some measure of Weber's traditional authority. Leaders may also benefit from rational-legal authority to the extent that their rule is supported by law.

As societies grow bigger, politics takes the form of a national government, or *political state*. But the effectiveness of a political state depends on the available technology. Centuries ago, armies moved slowly on foot, and communication over even short distances was uncertain. For this reason, the early political empires—such as Mesopotamia in the Middle East about 5,000 years ago—took the form of many small *city-states*.

More complex technology brings about the larger-scale system of *nation-states*. Currently, the world has 195 independent nation-states, each with a somewhat distinctive political system. Generally, however, these political systems fall into four categories: monarchy, democracy, authoritarianism, and totalitarianism.

Monarchy

Monarchy (with Latin and Greek roots meaning "one ruler") is *a political system in which a single family rules from generation to generation.* Monarchy is commonly found in the ancient agrarian societies; the Bible, for example, tells of great kings such as David and Solomon. In the world today, twenty-six nations have royal families;[1] some trace their ancestry back for centuries. In Weber's terms, then, monarchy is legitimized by tradition.

During the Middle Ages, *absolute monarchs* in much of the world claimed a monopoly of power based on divine right. Today, claims of divine right are rare, although monarchs in a

Monarchy is typically found in societies that have yet to industrialize. The recent political unrest throughout the Middle East indicates growing resistance to this form of political system in today's world. Even so, King Abdullah and members of his royal family strengthen their control of Saudi Arabia through their support of Arabic heritage and culture.

number of nations—including Saudi Arabia and Oman—still exercise almost absolute control over their people, although not necessarily with divine support. Worth noting is that the leaders who managed to survive the recent uprisings in the Middle East were all monarchs rather than nontraditional leaders (Yom & Gause, 2012).

With industrialization, however, the general trend is for monarchs to gradually pass from the scene in favor of elected officials. All the European nations with royal families today are *constitutional monarchies,* meaning that their monarchs are little more than symbolic heads of state; actual governing is the responsibility of elected officials, led by a prime minister and guided by a constitution. In these nations, nobility formally *reigns*, but elected officials actually *rule*.

Democracy

The historical trend in the modern world has been toward **democracy**, *a political system that gives power to the people as a whole.* More accurately, because it would be impossible for *all* citizens to act as leaders, we have devised a system of *representative democracy* that puts authority in the hands of leaders chosen by the people in elections.

In most high-income countries of the world, including those that still have royal families, political leaders claim their system is democratic. Industrialization and democratic government go together because both require a literate populace. Also, with industrialization, the legitimization of power in a tradition-based monarchy gives way to rational-legal authority. Thus, democracy and rational-legal authority go together, just like monarchy and traditional authority.

Of course, some high-income nations, such as Saudi Arabia, do not give the population much political voice. More broadly, even high-income countries such as the United States are not truly democratic, for two reasons. First, there is the problem of bureaucracy. The U.S. federal government has 2.8 million regular employees and several million more government workers paid for by special funding. Add to these workers 1.6 million uniformed military personnel and 64,000 legislative and judicial branch personnel, which add up to 4.4 million federal government

monarchy a political system in which a single family rules from generation to generation

democracy a political system that gives power to the people as a whole

[1]In Europe: Sweden, Norway, Denmark, Great Britain, the Netherlands, Liechtenstein, Luxembourg, Belgium, Spain, and Monaco; in the Middle East: Jordan, Saudi Arabia, Oman, Qatar, Bahrain, and Kuwait; in Africa: Lesotho, Swaziland, and Morocco; in Asia: Brunei, Tonga, Thailand, Malaysia, Cambodia, Bhutan, and Japan (U.S. Department of State, 2012).

workers in all. Another 19.4 million people work in almost 90,700 local governments across the country. Most people who run the government are never elected by anyone and do not have to answer directly to the people.

The second problem with our nation's claim to being democratic involves economic inequality, since rich people have far more political power than poor people. Many of the most politically influential people—from President Obama (who has made millions on book sales) and Bill Clinton (who has earned lots of money since leaving the presidency) to Mitt Romney (who made a fortune on Wall Street) and former vice-presidential candidate Sarah Palin (now a high-paid media celebrity)—are among the country's richest people. Of course, in the game of politics, "money talks." Given the even greater resources of billion-dollar corporations and their super-rich CEOs, how well does our "democratic" system hear the voices of "average people"?

Still, democratic nations do provide many rights and freedoms. Global Map 17–1 shows one assessment of the extent of political freedom around the world. According to Freedom House, an organization that tracks political trends, ninety of the world's nations (with 43 percent of the global population) were "free," respecting many civil liberties, in 2013. This represents a gain for freedom: Just seventy-five nations were considered free two decades earlier (Freedom House, 2013).

Window on the World

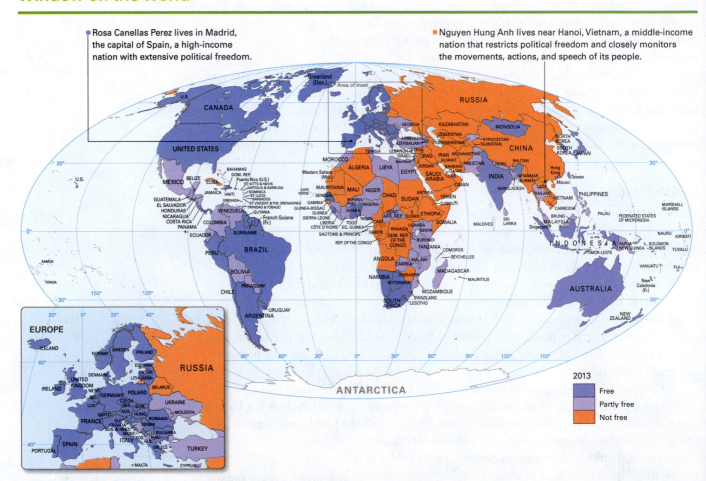

GLOBAL MAP 17–1 Political Freedom in Global Perspective

In 2013, a total of 90 of the world's 195 nations, containing 43 percent of all people, were politically "free"; that is, they offered their citizens extensive political rights and civil liberties. Another 58 countries, which included 23 percent of the world's people, were "partly free," with more limited rights and liberties. The remaining 47 nations, home to 34 percent of humanity, fall into the category of "not free." In these countries, government sharply restricts individual initiative. Between 1980 and 2013, democracy made significant gains, largely in Latin America.

Source: Freedom House (2013).

Democracy and Freedom: Capitalist and Socialist Approaches

Despite the problems just described, rich capitalist nations such as the United States claim to operate as democracies. Of course, socialist countries such as Cuba and the People's Republic of China make the same claim. This curious fact suggests that perhaps we need to look more closely at *political economy,* the interplay of politics and economics.

The political life of the United States, Canada, and the nations of Europe is largely shaped by the economic principles of capitalism, described in Chapter 16 ("The Economy and Work"). The pursuit of profit in a market system requires that "freedom" be defined in terms of people's right to act in their own self-interest. Thus the capitalist approach to political freedom translates into personal liberty, the freedom to act in whatever ways maximize profit or other personal advantage. From this point of view, political "democracy" means that individuals have the right to select their leaders from among those running for office.

However, capitalist societies are marked by a striking inequality of income and wealth. If everyone acts according to self-interest, the inevitable result is that some people have much more power to get their way than others. In practice, a market system creates unequal wealth and transforms wealth into power. Critics of capitalism claim that a wealthy elite dominates the economic and political life of the society.

By contrast, socialist systems claim they are democratic because their economies meet everyone's basic needs for housing, schooling, work, and medical care. Despite being a much poorer country than the United States, for example, Cuba provides basic medical care to all its people regardless of their ability to pay.

But critics of socialism counter that the extensive government regulation of social life in these countries is oppressive. The socialist governments of China and Cuba, for example, do not allow their people to move freely across or even within their borders and tolerate no organized political opposition.

These contrasting approaches to democracy and freedom raise an important question: Can economic equality and political liberty go together? To foster economic equality, socialism limits the choices of individuals. Capitalism, on the other hand, provides broad political liberties, which in practice mean much more to the rich than to the poor.

Authoritarianism

Some nations prevent their people from having any voice at all in politics. **Authoritarianism** is *a political system that denies the people participation in government.* An authoritarian government is indifferent to people's needs, offers them no voice in selecting leaders, and uses force in response to dissent or opposition. The absolute monarchies in Saudi Arabia and Oman are authoritarian, as is the military junta in Ethiopia. Sometimes, as the recent political movements in the Middle East illustrate, people stand up and oppose heavy-handed government. But not always. A largely peaceful system of "soft authoritarianism" thrives in the small Asian nation of Singapore, where political freedom is limited but people are secure and prosperous.

> For a closer look at how authoritarianism works in Singapore, **Read More** in **MySocLab**, *"Soft Authoritarianism" or Planned Prosperity? A Report from Singapore*

Totalitarianism

October 30, Beijing, China. Several U.S. students are sitting around a computer in the lounge of a Chinese university dormitory. They are taking turns running Google searches on keywords such as "democracy" and "Amnesty International." They soon realize that China's government monitors the Internet, filtering the results of online searches so that only officially approved sites appear. One Chinese student who is watching points out that things could be worse—in North Korea, she explains, the typical person has no access to computers at all.

The most intensely controlled political form is **totalitarianism**, *a highly centralized political system that extensively regulates people's lives.* Totalitarianism emerged in the twentieth century as technological advances gave governments the ability to rigidly control their populations. The Vietnamese government closely monitors the activities of not just visitors but also all its citizens. Similarly, the government of North Korea, perhaps the most

In totalitarian nations, government controls all aspects of people's lives. During the funeral of Kim Jong-il, absolute ruler of North Korea, people were told to line the route used for his public funeral and display appropriate anguish at his death. After the event, government officials examined photographs of the crowds and prosecuted those whose sorrow did not measure up to their demands.

totalitarian in the world, keeps its people in poverty and uses not only police to control people but also surveillance equipment and powerful computers to collect and store information about them.

Although some totalitarian governments claim to represent the will of the people, most seek to bend people to the will of the government. As the term itself implies, such governments have a *total* concentration of power, allowing no organized opposition. Denying the people the right to assemble and controlling access to information, these governments create an atmosphere of personal isolation and fear. In the final decades of the Soviet Union, for example, ordinary citizens had no access to telephone directories, copiers, fax machines, or even accurate city maps. Only in recent years has the Cuban government allowed ordinary citizens to own personal computers and cell phones.

Socialization in totalitarian societies is intensely political with the goal of obedience and commitment to the system. In North Korea, people are denied access to social media but they see pictures of leaders and political messages everywhere, reminding them that they owe total allegiance to the state. Government-controlled schools and mass media present only official versions of events. When that nation's leader, Kim Jong-il, died in 2011, the official government news agency reported the nation's people were in "utter despair" at the loss of the "Glorious Leader Who Descended from Heaven" but would find comfort in the "absolute surety that the leadership of [his son] Comrade Kim Jong-un will lead the great task of revolutionary enterprise." Since 1948, three generations of the same family have tightly controlled this impoverished nation (Chance & Kim, 2011; Rogers, 2011).

Totalitarian governments span the political spectrum from fascist (as in Nazi Germany) to communist (as in North Korea). In all cases, however, one party claims total control of the society and permits no opposition.

authoritarianism a political system that denies the people participation in government

totalitarianism a highly centralized political system that extensively regulates people's lives

A Global Political System?

Chapter 16 ("The Economy and Work") described the emergence of a global economy in which large corporations operate with little regard to national boundaries. Is globalization changing politics in the same way? On one level, the answer is no. Although most of the world's economic activity is international, the planet remains divided into nation-states, just as it has been for centuries. The United Nations (founded in 1945) was a small step in the direction of global government, but to date its political role in the world has been limited.

On another level, however, politics has become a global process. For some analysts, multinational corporations have created a new political order because of their enormous power to shape events throughout the world. In other words, politics is dissolving into business as corporations grow larger than governments.

Also, the Information Revolution has moved national politics onto the world stage. Social media, including e-mail, text messaging, and Twitter networks, mean that few countries can conduct their political affairs in complete privacy. The recent "WikiLeaks" controversy shows that just about anyone can easily transmit information—even that guarded by governments—so that it can become available to anyone and everyone (Gellman, 2011).

At the same time, social media based on computer technology add a global dimension to even local politics. Most of the young people who participated in the political opposition that swept the Middle East in 2011 and 2012 were motivated by an awareness of the greater political voice available to most people elsewhere in the world. Using cell phone networks, they rapidly spread information and quickly organized political events. No wonder, as the Middle East drama unfolded, China clamped down on Internet use, creating what some analysts called the "Great Firewall of China" (Xia, 2011; Zakaria, 2011).

Finally, as part of the global political process, several thousand *nongovernmental organizations* (NGOs) seek to advance issues such as human rights (Amnesty International) or an ecologically sustainable world (Greenpeace). NGOs will continue to play a key part in expanding the global political culture.

To sum up, just as individual nations can no longer control much of their own economies, governments cannot fully manage the political events occurring within their borders.

Politics in the United States

(17.3) Analyze economic and social issues using the political spectrum.

After fighting a war against Britain to gain political independence, the United States replaced the British monarchy with a representative democracy. Our nation's political development reflects a cultural history as well as its capitalist economy.

U.S. Culture and the Rise of the Welfare State

The political culture of the United States can be summed up in one word: individualism. This emphasis is found in the Bill of Rights of the U.S. Constitution, which guarantees freedom from undue government interference. It was this individualism that the nineteenth-century poet and essayist Ralph Waldo Emerson had in mind when he said, "The government that governs best is the government that governs least."

But most people stop short of Emerson's position, believing that government is necessary to defend the country, operate highway systems and schools, maintain law and order, and help people in need. To accomplish these things, the U.S. government has grown into a vast and complex **welfare state**, *a system of government agencies and programs that provides benefits to the population*. Government benefits begin even before birth (through prenatal nutrition programs), include adult benefits (such as medical care), and continue during old age (through Social Security and Medicare). Some programs are especially important to the poor, who are not well served by our capitalist economic system. But students, farmers, homeowners, small business operators, veterans, performing artists, and even executives of giant corporations all get various subsidies and supports. In fact, a majority of U.S. adults look to government for at least part of their income.

Today's welfare state is the result of a gradual increase in the size and scope of government. In 1789, the presence of the federal government amounted to little more than a flag in most communities, and the entire federal budget was a mere $4.5 million ($1.50 for each person in the nation). Since then, it has risen steadily, reaching $3.8 trillion in 2013 ($12,118 per person) (U.S. Office of Management and Budget, 2012).

Similarly, when our nation was founded, one government employee served every 1,800 citizens. Today, about one in six workers in the United States is a government employee, which is a larger share of our workforce than is engaged in manufacturing (U.S. Census Bureau, 2012; U.S. Department of Labor, 2013).

Despite this growth, the U.S. welfare state is still smaller than those of many other high-income nations. As Figure 17–1 on page 488 shows, government is larger in most of Europe, especially in France and the Scandinavian countries such as Denmark and Sweden.

welfare state a system of government agencies and programs that provides benefits to the population

The Political Spectrum

Who supports a bigger welfare state? Who wants to cut it back? Answers to these questions reveal attitudes that form the *political spectrum*, beliefs that range from extremely liberal to extremely conservative. In a 2013 survey of U.S. adults, 27 percent said they were "liberal" (the political "left"), 32 percent described themselves as "conservative" (the political "right"), and 36 percent claimed to be political "moderates" (the political "middle") (NORC, 2013:218).

Watch in **MySocLab**
Video: *The Big Picture: Politics and Government*

Global Snapshot

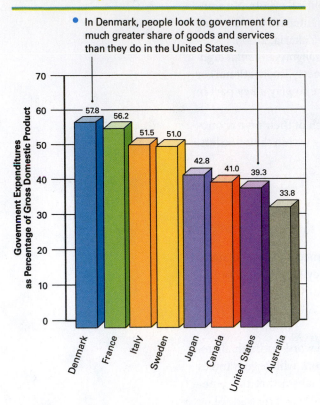

- In Denmark, people look to government for a much greater share of goods and services than they do in the United States.

FIGURE 17–1 The Size of Government, 2013

Government activity accounts for a smaller share of economic output in the United States than in most other high-income countries.

Source: OECD (2013).

The political spectrum helps us understand two types of issues: *Economic issues* focus on economic inequality; *social issues* involve moral questions about how people ought to live.

Economic Issues

Economic liberals support both extensive government regulation of the economy and a larger welfare state in order to reduce income inequality. The government can reduce inequality by taxing the rich more heavily and providing more benefits to the poor. Economic conservatives want to limit the hand of government in the economy and allow market forces more freedom, claiming that this produces more jobs and makes the economy more productive.

Social Issues

Social issues are moral questions about how people ought to live, ranging from abortion and the death penalty to gay rights and the treatment of minorities. Social liberals support equal rights and opportunities for all categories of people, view abortion as a matter of individual choice, and oppose the death penalty because it has been unfairly applied to minorities. The "family values" agenda of social conservatives supports traditional gender roles and opposes gay marriage, affirmative action, and other "special programs" for minorities. At the same time, social conservatives condemn abortion as morally wrong and support the death penalty.

Of the two major political parties in the United States, the Republican party is more conservative on both economic and social issues, and the Democratic party is more liberal. But both political parties favor big government when it advances their particular aims. During the 2012 presidential campaign, for example, Republican Mitt Romney supported bigger government in the form of a stronger military; Democrat Barack Obama favored enlarging government to expand the social "safety net" that would provide benefits to much of the population, including "investments" in education, transportation infrastructure, and new forms of energy. The fact that both political parties look to government to advance their goals is certainly one reason that, no matter which party controls the White House, government has increased in size along with the national debt.

Class, Race, Gender, and Age

Most people hold a mix of conservative and liberal attitudes. Surveys taken during the 2012 election showed, for example, that a majority of people favored smaller government (a conservative position) but also supported legal abortion and a pathway to citizenship for immigrants who entered the country illegally (both liberal positions).

Class position helps explain political attitudes. With wealth to protect, well-to-do people tend to be conservative on economic issues, but their extensive schooling and secure social standing lead most to be social liberals. Low-income people display the opposite pattern with most being liberal on economic issues but leaning in a more conservative direction on social issues (Ohlemacher, 2008; Kohut, 2012).

African Americans, whether they are rich or poor, tend to be more liberal than whites, especially when it comes to economic issues. For half a century African Americans have voted overwhelmingly Democratic and, in 2012, 93 percent of African American voters cast ballots for the Democratic candidate, Barack Obama. Historically, Latinos, Asian Americans, and Jews have also supported the Democratic party. If none of these racial or ethnic categories of the population had voted in the 2012 presidential election, Republican Mitt Romney easily would have become president. Because the minority population of the country is increasing, minorities represent an ever more important force in U.S. politics (Pew Research Center, 2012).

Gender matters, too, because women tend to be somewhat more liberal than men. Among U.S. adults, more women lean toward the Democrats, and more men vote for Republican candidates. In 2012, for example, 55 percent of women but just 45 percent of men voted for Barack Obama.

Finally, as indicated by the Power of Society figure at the beginning of this chapter, younger voters have been moving in a liberal direction. Figure 17–2 on page 490 shows the voting pattern over time among college students. During the 1970s, student attitudes moved to the right and then, by the mid-1990s, student attitudes shifted to the left. During this entire period, however, college women remained consistently more liberal than college men (Astin et al., 2002; Sax et al., 2003; Pryor et al., 2013).

Party Identification

Surveys conducted in late 2012 show that about 46 percent favor or lean toward the Democratic party, 36 percent favor or lean toward the Republican party, and about 18 percent say they are "independent" or favor some other party (Pew Research Center, 2012). But because many people hold mixed political attitudes, with liberal views on some issues and conservative stands on others, party identification in this country is not very strong. Relatively weak party identification is one reason that each of the two major parties gains or loses power from election to election. Democrats held the White House in 1996 and gained ground in Congress in 1996, 1998, and 2000. In 2002 and 2004, the tide turned as Republicans made gains in Congress and kept control of the White House. In 2006, the tide turned again, with Democrats gaining control of Congress and winning the White House in 2008. By the 2010 elections, however, Republicans had picked up seats in Congress, gaining a majority in the House of Representatives. Then, in the 2012 elections, Democrats held the presidency and gained ground in Congress (Schouten, 2012).

There is also an urban-rural divide in U.S. politics: People in urban areas typically vote Democratic and those in rural areas generally vote Republican. The Seeing Sociology in Everyday Life box on page 491 takes a closer look at the national political scene, and National Map 17–1 on page 491 shows the county-by-county results for the 2012 presidential election.

Special-Interest Groups and Campaign Spending

Especially since the 2012 shooting at the Sandy Hook Elementary School in Newtown, Connecticut, there has been a raging debate across the United States about the private ownership of firearms. Organizations such as the Brady Campaign to Prevent Gun

Lower-income people have more pressing financial needs, and so they tend to focus on economic issues, such as job wages and benefits. Higher-income people, by contrast, provide support for many social issues, such as animal rights.

FIGURE 17–2 Left-Right Political Identification of College Students, 1970–2012

Student attitudes moved to the right after 1970 and shifted left in the late 1990s. College women tend to be more liberal than college men.

Sources: Astin et al. (2002), Sax et al. (2003), and Pryor et al. (2013).

 Read in **MySocLab Document:** *Campaign Finance (Super PACs)* by Adam Liptak

special-interest group people organized to address some economic or social issue

political action committee (PAC) an organization formed by a special-interest group, independent of political parties, to raise and spend money in support of political goals

Violence support stricter gun laws; other organizations, including the National Rifle Association, strongly oppose such measures. Each of these organizations is an example of a **special-interest group**, *people organized to address some economic or social issue*. Special-interest groups, which include associations of older adults, fireworks producers, environmentalists, and even sociologists, are strong in nations where political parties are relatively weak. Special-interest groups employ *lobbyists* to work on their behalf, trying to get members of Congress to support their goals. Washington, D.C., is home to about 12,000 lobbyists (Center for Responsive Politics, 2012).

A **political action committee (PAC)** is *an organization formed by a special-interest group, independent of political parties, to raise and spend money in support of political goals*. Political action committees channel most of their funds directly to candidates likely to support their interests. Since they were created in the 1970s, the number of PACs has grown rapidly to more than 5,200 (Federal Election Commission, 2012).

Because of the rising costs of political campaigns, most candidates eagerly accept support from PACs. In 2012, members of the House of Representatives seeking reelection spent an average of $1.5 million on their campaigns, with most of the money coming from outside organizations, including PACs. Senators seeking reelection spent an average of $11 million on their races.

In presidential elections, contributions run much higher. In 2012, Barack Obama and Mitt Romney together received and spent $2.6 billion on their presidential campaigns, including more than $500 million from PACs and other organizations (Center for Responsive Politics, 2012). Supporters of this pattern of large contributions and great spending defend PACs, claiming that they represent the interests of a vast assortment of businesses, unions, and church groups, thereby increasing political participation. Critics counter that organizations supplying cash to politicians expect to be treated favorably in return, so in effect, PACs are attempting to buy political influence ("Abramoff Effect," 2006; Federal Election Commission, 2012).

Does raising the most money matter? The answer is yes—in the 2012 elections, in 94 percent of the House races and 79 percent of the Senate races, the candidate who spent the most money ended up winning the election. Concerns about the power of money have led to much discussion of campaign financing. In 2002, Congress passed a modest campaign finance reform, limiting the amount of unregulated money that candidates are allowed to collect. Despite this change, all presidential races since then have set new records for campaign spending. In addition, in 2010 "super PACs" emerged as political action committees that raise money—without limits—to engage in political activity for or against any candidate for public office. It seems unlikely that this pattern will change any time soon. The courts seem to agree. In 2010, the Supreme Court rejected limits on the election spending of corporations, unions, and other large organizations (Liptak, 2010; Gorenstrin, 2011; Center for Responsive Politics, 2012).

Voter Apathy

A disturbing fact of U.S. political life is that many people in this country do not vote. In fact, U.S. citizens are less likely to vote today than they were a century ago. In the 2000 presidential election, which was decided by a few hundred votes, only half the people eligible to vote went to the polls. In 2008, participation rose to 63 percent, which was the highest turnout since 1960 but still lower than in almost all other high-income countries.

Seeing Sociology in Everyday Life

Election 2012: The Rural-Urban Divide

Jorge: Just about everyone I know in L.A. voted Democratic. I mean, *nobody* voted for Romney!

Harry: If you lived in my county in rural Ohio, you'd see the exact opposite. Obama did not do well there at all.

As this conversation suggests, the reality of everyday politics in the United States depends on where you live. Political attitudes and voting patterns in rural and urban places are quite different. Sociologists have long debated why these differences exist.

Take a look at National Map 17–1, which shows the county-by-county results for the 2012 presidential election. The first thing that stands out is that the Republican candidate, Mitt Romney, won 78 percent of U.S. counties—2,259 out of 2,908 ("Romney" counties appear in red on the map). Democrat Barack Obama won in 649 counties ("Obama" counties appear in blue).

How did Obama win the election when Romney won so many more counties? Obama won 51 percent of the popular vote, doing well in counties with large populations. Democrats do very well in large cities, for example, where Obama won 70 percent of the popular vote in 2008 and 69 percent in 2012. Rural counties, with relatively small populations, tend to lean Republican. John McCain received 53 percent of the rural vote in 2008 and Mitt Romney received 59 percent in 2012. In many states, it is easy to see the rural-urban divide. In Ohio, for example, Obama won enough votes in and around Cleveland, Columbus, and Cincinnati to carry the entire state even though most of the state's counties went for Romney.

The national pattern has led many political analysts to distinguish urban "blue states" that vote Democratic and rural "red states" that vote Republican. Looking more closely, at the county level, there appears to be a political divide between "liberal, urban America" and "conservative, rural America."

What accounts for this difference? Typically, rural counties are home to people who have lived in one place for a long time, are more traditional and family-oriented in their values, and are more likely to be religious. Such people tend to vote Republican. By contrast, urban areas are home to more minorities, young and single people, college students, and lower-income people, all of whom are more likely to vote Democratic.

What Do You Think?

1. Can you find your county on the map? Which way did most people vote? Can you explain why?

2. In most elections, more Republicans than Democrats claim they are concerned about "moral values"; more Democrats than Republicans say they care about "the economy and jobs." Can you explain why?

3. How might Democratic candidates do better in rural areas? How might Republican candidates do better in urban areas?

Seeing Ourselves

Explore patterns of voting in presidential elections in your local community and in counties across the United States in **MySocLab**

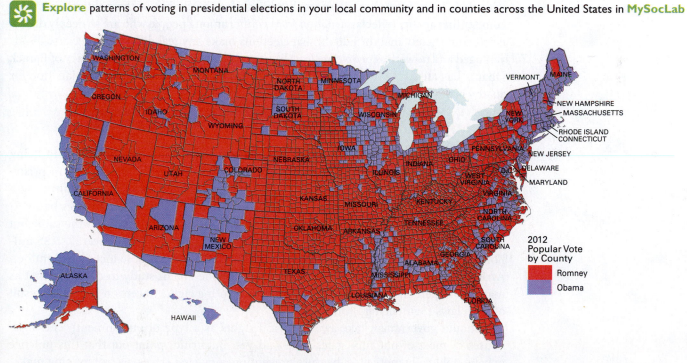

NATIONAL MAP 17–1 The Presidential Election, 2012: Popular Vote by County

Barack Obama won the 2012 presidential election with 51 percent of the total popular vote, but he received a majority of the vote in only about one-fourth of the nation's counties. Obama and other Democrats did well in more densely populated urban areas, while Mitt Romney and other Republicans did well in less populated rural areas. Can you explain why urban areas are mostly Democratic and rural areas are mostly Republican? What other social characteristics do you think distinguish the people who vote Democratic from those who vote Republican?

Source: The Guardian (2012).

In the 2012 presidential election, partly due to Hurricane Sandy hitting shortly before the election, turnout fell to 57.5 percent of eligible voters (Bipartisan Policy Center, 2012).

Who is and is not likely to vote? Research shows that women are slightly more likely than men to cast a ballot. People over sixty-five are much more likely to vote than college-age adults (almost half of whom have not even registered). Non-Hispanic white people are just slightly more likely to vote (66 percent voted in 2008 and 2012) than African Americans (65 percent in 2008 and 2012), and Hispanics (50 percent, also in both 2008 and 2012) are the least likely of all to vote (Bipartisan Policy Center, 2012; Pew Research Center, 2012).

Generally speaking, people with a bigger stake in U.S. society—homeowners, parents with young children, people with more schooling and good jobs—are more likely to vote. Income matters, too: People earning more than $100,000 are much more likely to vote (78 percent in 2012) than people earning less than $20,000 (47 percent) (U.S. Census Bureau, 2013).

Of course, we should expect some nonvoting because, at any given time, millions of people are sick or away from home or have recently moved to a new neighborhood and have forgotten to reregister. In addition, registering and voting depend on the ability to read and write, which discourages tens of millions of U.S. adults with limited literacy skills. Finally, people with physical disabilities that limit mobility have a lower turnout than the general population (Schur & Kruse, 2000; Brians & Grofman, 2001).

But the political system itself may cause voter apathy. Under our nation's Electoral College system, in forty-eight states (all but Nebraska and Maine) the presidential candidate who wins a majority of votes takes all the state's electoral votes. Most of these states vote predictably Democratic or Republican, so that people who favor either party may reasonably conclude that their individual votes will not matter. By contrast, in a small number of "swing states" or "battleground states," candidates spend much of their money on saturation media advertising and voter mobilization in an effort to win a majority of the state's votes. In these states, voter turnout was about 63 percent, compared to 55 percent in the rest of the states (Bipartisan Policy Center, 2012).

There is also a political debate over the cause of voter apathy. Conservatives suggest that apathy is really *indifference to politics* among people who are, by and large, content with their lives. Liberals and especially radicals on the far left of the political spectrum counter that apathy reflects *alienation from politics* among people who are so deeply dissatisfied with society that they doubt that elections make any real difference. Because disadvantaged and powerless people are least likely to vote, and because the candidacy of Barack Obama has raised the level of participation among minorities, the liberal explanation for apathy is probably closer to the truth.

Should Convicted Criminals Vote?

Although the right to vote is at the very foundation of our country's claim to being democratic, all states except Vermont and Maine have laws that bar people in prison from voting. Thirty-one states do not allow people on probation after committing a felony to vote; thirty-five states do the same for people on parole. Four states ban voting even after people have completed their sentences, and eight others do the same but offer people a process to appeal for restoration of their voting rights. Overall, 5.85 million people in the United States do not have the right to vote. These include 2.2 million African Americans, a fact that led researchers in one recent study to conclude that as many as 40 percent of black men may lose their voting rights in certain states as a result of such laws (Sentencing Project, 2012).

Should government take away political rights as a type of punishment? The legislatures of most of our fifty states have said yes. But critics point out that this practice may be politically motivated, because preventing convicted criminals from voting makes a difference in the way elections in this country turn out. Convicted felons (who tend to be lower-income people) show better than a two-to-one preference for Democratic over Republican candidates. If these laws had not been in effect back in 2000, Democrat Al Gore would have defeated George W. Bush for the presidency (Uggen & Manza, 2002). In 2011, such political considerations led Democrats in Congress to propose legislation called the Democracy Restoration Act, which would establish a process to restore voting rights for convicted criminals who have completed their sentences.

Theories of Power in Society

17.4 Apply the pluralist, power-elite, and Marxist models to the U.S. political system.

Sociologists have long debated how power is spread throughout the U.S. population. Power is a very difficult topic to study because decision making is complex and often takes place behind closed doors. Despite this difficulty, researchers have developed three competing models of power in the United States. The Applying Theory table provides a summary of each.

The Pluralist Model: The People Rule

The **pluralist model**, closely linked to structural-functional theory, is *an analysis of politics that sees power as spread among many competing interest groups.* Pluralists claim, first, that politics is an arena of negotiation. With limited resources, no organization can expect to achieve all its goals. Organizations therefore operate as *veto groups,* realizing some success but mostly keeping opponents from achieving all their ends. The political process relies heavily on creating alliances and compromises among numerous interest groups so that policies gain wide support. In short, pluralists see power as spread widely throughout society, with all people having at least some voice in the political system (Dahl, 1961, 1982; Rothman & Black, 1998).

The Power-Elite Model: A Few People Rule

The **power-elite model**, based on social-conflict theory, is *an analysis of politics that sees power as concentrated among the rich.* The term *power elite* was coined by C. Wright Mills (1956), who argued that a small upper class holds most of society's wealth, prestige, and power.

Mills claimed that members of the power elite head up the three major sectors of U.S. society: the economy, the government, and the military. The power elite is made up of the "super-rich" (corporate executives and major stockholders); top officials in Washington, D.C., and state capitals around the country; and the highest-ranking officers in the U.S. military.

Further, Mills explained, these elites move from one sector to another, building power as they go. Former Vice President Dick Cheney, for example, has moved back and forth between powerful positions in the corporate world and the federal government. Colin Powell moved

One of the most significant political forces to develop in recent years is the Tea Party movement. Supporters claim that government has grown too big, too expensive, and now threatens the freedom of ordinary people. Do you see government as a "problem" the way many people on the right side of the political spectrum do? Or do you see it as the "solution" the way many people on the left side of the political spectrum do? Why?

Applying Theory

Politics			
	Pluralist Model	Power-Elite Model	Marxist Political-Economy Model
Which theoretical approach is applied?	Structural-functional approach	Social-conflict approach	Social-conflict approach
How is power spread throughout society?	Power is spread widely so that all groups have some voice.	Power is concentrated in the hands of top business, political, and military leaders.	Power is directed by the operation of the capitalist economy.
Is the United States a democracy?	Yes. Power is spread widely enough to make the country a democracy.	No. Power is too concentrated for the country to be a democracy.	No. The capitalist economy sets political decision making, so the country is not a democracy.

from a top position in the U.S. military to become secretary of state. More broadly, when presidents pick cabinet officials, most of these powerful public officials are millionaires. This was true in the Bush administration as it is in the Obama administration. Power-elite theorists say that the United States is not a democracy because the influence of a few people with great wealth and power is so strong that the average person's voice cannot be heard. They reject the pluralist idea that various centers of power serve as checks and balances on one another. According to the power-elite model, those at the top are so powerful that they face no real opposition (Bartlett & Steele, 2000; Moore et al., 2002).

The Marxist Model: The System Is Biased

A third approach to understanding U.S. politics is the **Marxist political-economy model**, *an analysis that explains politics in terms of the operation of a society's economic system*. Like the power-elite model, the Marxist model rejects the idea that the United States operates as a political democracy. But whereas the power-elite model focuses on just the enormous wealth and power of certain individuals, the Marxist model goes further and sees bias rooted in the nation's institutions,

pluralist model an analysis of politics that sees power as spread among many competing interest groups

power-elite model an analysis of politics that sees power as concentrated among the rich

Marxist political-economy model an analysis that explains politics in terms of the operation of a society's economic system

especially its economy. As noted in Chapter 4 ("Society"), Karl Marx claimed that a society's economic system (capitalist or socialist) shapes its political system. Therefore, the power elites do not simply appear out of nowhere; they are creations of the capitalist economy.

From this point of view, reforming the political system—say, by limiting the amount of money that rich people can contribute to political candidates—is unlikely to bring about true democracy. The problem does not lie in the people who exercise great power or the people who do not vote; the problem is rooted in the system itself, or what Marxists call the "political economy of capitalism." In other words, as long as the United States has a mostly capitalist economy, the majority of people will be shut out of politics, just as they are exploited in the workplace.

EVALUATE Which one of the three models is most accurate? Over the years, research has shown support for each one. In the end, how you think our political system ought to work is as much a matter of political values as of scientific fact.

Classic research by Nelson Polsby (1959) supports the pluralist model. Polsby studied the political scene in New Haven, Connecticut, and concluded that key decisions on various issues—including education, urban renewal, and the electoral nominating process—were made by different groups. Polsby concluded that in New Haven, no one group—not even the upper class—ruled all the others.

Robert Lynd and Helen Lynd (1937) studied Muncie, Indiana (which they called "Middletown," to suggest that it was a typical city), and documented the fortune amassed by a single family, the Balls, from their business manufacturing glass canning jars. Their findings support the power-elite position. The Lynds showed how the Ball family dominated the city's life, pointing to that family's name on a local bank, a university, a hospital, and a department store. In Muncie, according to the Lynds, the power elite boiled down, more or less, to a single family.

From the Marxist perspective, the point is not to look at which individuals make decisions. Rather, as Alexander Liazos (1982:13) explains in his analysis of the United States, "The basic tenets of capitalist society shape everyone's life: the inequalities of social classes and the importance of profits over people." As long as the basic institutions of society are organized to meet the needs of the few rather than the many, Liazos concludes, a democratic society is impossible.

Clearly, the U.S. political system gives almost everyone the right to participate in the political process through elections. But the power-elite and Marxist models point out that, at the very least, the U.S. political system is far less democratic than most people think. Most citizens may have the right to vote, but the major political parties and their candidates typically support only positions that are acceptable to the most powerful segments of society and consistent with the operation of our capitalist economy.

Whatever the reasons, unhappiness with government in the United States is not limited to a small number of people in the Tea Party (a movement that seeks a smaller government). Less than half of U.S. adults report having "some" or "a great deal" of confidence that members of Congress and other government officials will do what is best for the country (NORC, 2013:343–46).

CHECK YOUR LEARNING What is the main argument of the pluralist model of power? What about the power-elite model? The Marxist political-economy model?

Power beyond the Rules

17.5 Describe causes of both revolution and terrorism.

In politics, there is always disagreement over a society's goals and the best means to achieve them. A political system tries to resolve these controversies within a system of rules. But political activity sometimes breaks the rules or tries to do away with the entire system.

Revolution

Political revolution is *the overthrow of one political system in order to establish another.* Reform involves change *within* a system, either through modification of the law or, in the extreme case, through a *coup d'état* (in French, literally, "blow to the state"), in which one leader topples another. Revolution involves change in the type of system itself.

> **political revolution** the overthrow of one political system in order to establish another

No political system is immune to revolution, nor does revolution produce any one kind of government. Our country's Revolutionary War (1775–1783) replaced colonial rule by the British monarchy with a representative democracy. French revolutionaries in 1789 also overthrew a monarch, only to set the stage for the return of monarchy in the person of Napoleon. In 1917, the Russian Revolution replaced monarchy with a socialist government built on the ideas of Karl Marx. In 1979, an uprising in Iran overthrew an unpopular dictator but led to the rule of unpopular religious clerics. In 1991, a second Russian revolution dismantled the socialist Soviet Union, and the nation was reborn as fifteen independent republics, the largest of which—known as the Russian Federation—initially moved closer to a market system and a government offering greater political rights but has more recently become more tightly controlled by a central government. As a final example, the 2011 political uprising in Egypt forced that country's leader from office and led to a government dominated by the Muslim Brotherhood, an Islamic movement; in 2013, that nation's military forced the new president from office.

Despite their striking variety, revolutions share a number of traits (Tocqueville, 1955, orig. 1856; Skocpol, 1979; Tilly, 1986):

1. **Rising expectations.** Common sense suggests that revolution would be more likely when people are severely deprived, but history shows that most revolutions occur when people's lives are improving. Rising expectations, rather than bitterness and despair, make revolution more likely. Driving the recent uprisings across the Middle East are people who may be living better than their families did generations ago but not as well as they see people living in other parts of the world.

2. **Unresponsive government.** Revolutions become more likely when a government is unwilling to reform itself, especially when demands for reform

In 2011, as part of the popular movement that swept across northern Africa and the Middle East, Egyptians forced President Hosni Mubarak from office. In 2013, Mohamed Morsi was elected president. A year later, however, he too was forced from office by popular opposition, although many of his supporters continue to demand his return to power. Do you think the recent political changes in Egypt have been *revolutionary* or are they examples of *reform*? Why?

by powerful segments of society are ignored. In Egypt, for example, the government led by Hosni Mubarak had done little to benefit the people or reform its own corruption over many decades.

3. **Radical leadership by intellectuals.** The English philosopher Thomas Hobbes (1588–1679) claimed that intellectuals provide the justification for revolution, and universities are often the center of political change. Students played a critical role in China's prodemocracy movement in the 1990s, the uprisings in Eastern Europe, and the recent uprisings across the Middle East.

4. **Establishing a new legitimacy.** Overthrowing a political system is not easy, but ensuring a revolution's long-term success is harder still. Some revolutionary movements are held together mostly by hatred of the past regime and fall apart once new leaders are installed. This fact is one reason that it is difficult to predict the long-term outcome of recent political changes in the Middle East. Revolutionaries must also guard against counterrevolutionary drives led by overthrown leaders. This explains the speed and ruthlessness with which victorious revolutionaries typically dispose of former leaders.

Scientific analysis cannot declare that a revolution is good or bad. The full consequences of such an upheaval depend on the personal values of the observer and, in any case, typically become evident only after many years. For example, nearly two decades after the revolutions that toppled their governments in the early 1990s, the future of many of the former Soviet states remains uncertain.

Similarly, it is far from clear that the "prodemocracy" movement that has transformed parts of the Middle East will result in a long-term trend toward democracy. For one thing, polls show that just 60 percent of Egyptians, for example, claim that democracy is the best form of government. In addition, in the vacuum created by deposing an authoritarian ruler, many organizations—some more democratic than others—quickly compete for power (Bell, 2011).

Terrorism

The terrorist attacks on the United States on September 11, 2001, involving four commercial airliners, killed nearly 3,000 innocent people, injured many thousands more, completely destroyed the twin towers of the World Trade Center in New York City, and seriously damaged the Pentagon in Washington, D.C. Not since the attack on Pearl Harbor at the outbreak of World War II had the United States suffered such a blow. Indeed, this event was the most serious terrorist act ever recorded.

Terrorism refers to *acts of violence or the threat of violence used as a political strategy by an individual or a group.* Like revolution, terrorism is a political act beyond the rules of established political systems. According to Paul Johnson (1981), terrorism has four distinguishing characteristics.

First, terrorists try to paint violence as a legitimate political tactic, even though such acts are condemned by virtually every nation. Terrorists also bypass (or are excluded from) established channels of political negotiation. Therefore, terrorism is a strategy used by a weaker organization against a stronger enemy. Terrorism can also be carried out by a single individual in support of some larger cause or movement as illustrated by the 2009 killing of thirteen people at the Fort Hood army base in Texas by a U.S. Army major (Gibbs, 2009).

In recent decades, terrorism has become commonplace in international politics. In 2012, there were almost 7,000 acts of terrorism worldwide, which claimed 11,098 lives and injured nearly 22,000 people. More than half of the dead were civilians and hundreds of victims were children. Almost two-thirds of all attacks in 2012 took place in just three nations: Afghanistan, Pakistan, and Iraq U.S. Department of State, 2013).

Terrorism is a complex political process typically involving parties with differing levels of global power. The television series *Homeland* illustrates that terrorism is also a matter of defining some parties as "good" and others as "evil" and sometimes never being sure which is which. How accurately do you think the mass media in the United States portray the global conflicts we call "terrorism"?

Second, terrorism is used not just by groups but also by governments against their own people. *State terrorism* is the use of violence, generally without support of law, by government officials as a way to control the population. State terrorism is lawful in some authoritarian and totalitarian states, which survive by creating widespread fear and intimidation among the population. The dictator Saddam Hussein, for example, relied on secret police and state terror to protect his power in Iraq. More recently, Syrian president Bashar al-Assad has attempted to remain in power by using that country's military against a popular uprising that has turned into a bloody civil war.

Third, democratic societies reject terrorism in principle, but they are especially vulnerable to terrorists because they give broad civil liberties to people and have less extensive police networks. In contrast, totalitarian regimes make widespread use of state terrorism, but their extensive police power gives individuals few opportunities to commit acts of terror against the government.

Fourth and finally, terrorism is always a matter of definition. Governments claim the right to maintain order, even by force, and may label opposition groups that use violence as "terrorists." Political differences may explain why one person's "terrorist" is another's "freedom fighter" (Jenkins, 2003).

Although hostage taking and outright killing provoke popular anger, taking action against terrorists is difficult. Because most terrorist groups are shadowy organizations with no formal connection to any established state, identifying the parties responsible may be difficult. In addition, a military response may risk confrontation with other governments—recall the heightened tensions with Pakistan in 2011 after U.S. soldiers entered the country in a mission to kill Osama bin Laden. Yet as the terrorism expert Brian Jenkins warns, the failure to respond "encourages other terrorist groups, who begin to realize that this can be a pretty cheap way to wage war" (quoted in Whitaker, 1985:29).

War and Peace

17.6 Identify factors encouraging war or peace.

Perhaps the most critical political issue is **war**, *organized, armed conflict among the people of two or more nations, directed by their governments.* War is as old as humanity, but understanding it is crucial today because humanity now has weapons that can destroy the entire planet.

At almost any moment during the twentieth century, nations somewhere in the world were engaged in violent conflict. In its short history, the United States has participated in eleven large-scale wars. From the Revolutionary War to the Iraq War, more than 1.3 million U.S. men and women have been killed in armed conflicts, as shown in Figure 17–3, and many times that number have been injured. Thousands more died in "undeclared wars" and limited military actions in the Dominican Republic, Nicaragua, Lebanon, Grenada, Panama, Haiti, Bosnia, Afghanistan, and elsewhere.

The Causes of War

Wars occur so often that we might think that there is something natural about armed confrontation. But there is no evidence that human beings must wage war under any particular circumstances. On the contrary, governments around the world usually have to force their people to go to war.

Like all forms of social behavior, warfare is a product of *society* that is more common in some places than in others. The Semai of Malaysia, among the most peace-loving of the world's peoples,

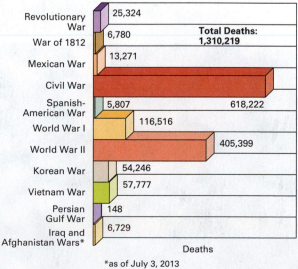

War	Deaths
Revolutionary War	25,324
War of 1812	6,780
Mexican War	13,271
Civil War	618,222
Spanish-American War	5,807
World War I	116,516
World War II	405,399
Korean War	54,246
Vietnam War	57,777
Persian Gulf War	148
Iraq and Afghanistan Wars*	6,729

Total Deaths: 1,310,219

*as of July 3, 2013

FIGURE 17–3 Deaths of Americans in Eleven U.S. Wars

Almost half of all U.S. deaths in war occurred during the Civil War (1861–65).

Sources: Compiled from various sources by Maris A. Vinovskis (1989) and the author.

terrorism refers to acts of violence or the threat of violence used as a political strategy by an individual or a group

war organized, armed conflict among the people of two or more nations, directed by their governments

rarely resort to violence. In contrast, the Yąnomamö of South America (see the box on page 68) are quick to wage war.

If society holds the key to war or peace, under what circumstances do humans go to battle? Quincy Wright (1987) cites five factors that promote war:

1. **Perceived threats.** Nations mobilize in response to a perceived threat to their people, territory, or culture. Leaders justified the U.S.-led military campaign to disarm Iraq, for example, by stressing the threat that Saddam Hussein posed to the United States.

2. **Social problems.** When internal problems generate widespread frustration at home, a nation's leaders may divert public attention by attacking an external "enemy" as a form of scapegoating. Although U.S. leaders claimed that the war in Iraq was a matter of national security, there is little doubt that the onset of the war diverted attention from the struggling national economy and boosted the popularity of President George W. Bush.

3. **Political objectives.** Poor nations, such as Vietnam, have used wars to end foreign domination. Powerful countries, such as the United States, may benefit from a periodic show of force (recall the deployments of troops in Somalia, Haiti, Bosnia, and Afghanistan) to increase global political standing.

4. **Moral objectives.** Nations rarely claim that they are going to war to gain wealth and power. Instead, their leaders infuse military campaigns with moral urgency. By calling the 2003 invasion of Iraq "Operation Iraqi Freedom," U.S. leaders portrayed the mission as a morally justified war of liberation from an evil tyrant.

5. **The absence of alternatives.** A fifth factor promoting war is the absence of alternatives. Although the goal of the United Nations is to maintain international peace by finding alternatives to war, the UN has had limited success in preventing conflict between nations.

Social Class, Gender, and the Military

In World War II, three-fourths of the men in the United States in their late teens and twenties served in the military, either voluntarily or by being *drafted*—called to service. Only those who had some physical or mental impairment were freed from the obligation to serve. Today, by contrast, there is no draft, and fighting is done by a volunteer military. But not every member of our society is equally likely to volunteer.

One study revealed that the military has few young people who are rich and also few who are very poor. Rather, it is primarily working-class people who look to the military for a job, to earn some money to go to college, or simply to get out of the small town they grew up in. In

In 2013, the U.S. armed forces announced plans to integrate women into military combat operations by 2016. Do you see this as a step forward for women? Why or why not?

addition, the largest number of young enlistees comes from the South, where local culture is more supportive of the military and where most military bases are located. As two analysts put it, "America's military seems to resemble the makeup of a two-year commuter or trade school outside Birmingham or Biloxi far more than that of a ghetto or barrio or four-year university in Boston" (Halbfinger & Holmes, 2003:1). The Controversy and Debate box on page 499 asks whether this nation's dependence on a volunteer army is creating a "warrior caste."

Throughout our nation's history, women have been a part of the U.S. military. In recent decades, women have taken on greater importance in the armed forces. For one thing, the share of women is on the rise, now standing at 14.6 percent of all military personnel. Just as important, although regulations continue to keep many military women out of harm's way, more women are now engaging in

Controversy & Debate

The Volunteer Army: Have We Created a Warrior Caste?

In 2008, having completed three combat tours in Iraq, Marine Sergeant Alex Lemons returned to the United States. But his arrival did not feel like a homecoming. "I felt as alien here as I felt in Iraq," Lemons remarked, sitting on the front deck of his house in Utah. After getting back, Lemons explained, he saw no signs that this country was engaged in a war. Most people didn't want to think about the war in Iraq. And perhaps that's the problem—the vast majority of our population is no longer linked to the military.

It was not always that way. During World War II, about 9 percent of the U.S. population served in the military. Almost everyone else was involved in the war effort by working in a defense plant, participating in programs that rationed vital materials, or buying bonds to finance the war effort. Today, by contrast, less than half of 1 percent of our nation's population is in the military, and most families have no member who has worn a military uniform. Over more than a decade since the September 2001 attacks, just 1 percent of the population over the age of eighteen has served in the military. That leaves 99 percent of adults with no direct involvement in military service.

There are many reasons that military service now involves a small slice of the U.S. population. The most important factor is

that, in 1973 as the Vietnam War was winding down, Congress ended the draft, which created today's all-volunteer military. A second factor is gender, because 86 percent of today's military personnel are males. Third, the military is overwhelmingly from certain regions of the country with the South most heavily represented. In fact, more than 40 percent of new recruits are from the South and half of all active-duty military personnel are stationed in just five states: Virginia, North Carolina, Georgia, Texas, and California. Surprisingly, perhaps, most adults in the United States would be ineligible to enlist in the military even if they wanted to, due to having criminal records or being overweight.

When all things are considered, today's military personnel are physically fit men from rural areas and small towns in more traditional regions of the country, where military values such as honor, discipline, and patriotism are more pronounced. These people are not poor but generally are from working-class families. Typically, they see in military service a way to gain economic security and work experience.

The fact that the burden of military service falls on a thin slice of U.S. society is also evident in the country's leadership. In the years immediately after the Vietnam War, almost 80 percent of members of Congress were veterans; today, that share has fallen to 20 percent. Beyond the world of politics, almost no one who works in the mass media—including newspapers, television, and films—has engaged in military service. With that fact in mind, it is easy to understand the frustration of one military wife, who lives in Washington State and has a husband fighting in Afghanistan. The Taliban, she recounts, blew up "a bus last week and killed 17 people, and I didn't know anything about it because it wasn't on the news. It makes me think nobody cares. They're putting on things like Kardashians getting divorced—it's on the news constantly—but we have soldiers over there dying, and you just don't hear about it."

What Do You Think?

1. Should the responsibility for military service be shouldered by just 1 percent of the adult population?

2. Would you support restoring the draft as a means of spreading this responsibility throughout the class structure?

3. Do veterans deserve more than they now receive from our society? Explain.

Sources: Thompson (2011), U.S. Department of Defense (2012), U.S. House Committee on Veterans Affairs (2013).

combat. Battle experience is significant because it is widely regarded as necessary for soldiers to reach the highest levels of leadership (Military Diversity Leadership Commission, 2011; U.S. Department of Defense, 2012).

Is Terrorism a New Kind of War?

In recent years, we have heard government officials speak of terrorism as a new kind of war. War has historically followed certain patterns: It is played out according to basic rules, the warring parties are known to each other, and the objectives of the warring parties—which generally involve control of territory—are clearly stated.

Terrorism breaks from these patterns. The identity of terrorist individuals and organizations may not be known, those involved may deny their responsibility, and their goals may be unclear. The 2001 terrorist attacks against the United States were not attempts to defeat the nation militarily or to secure territory. Carried out by people representing not a country but a cause, the terrorist acts were not well understood in the United States. In short, these attacks were expressions of anger and hate, an effort to destabilize the country and create widespread fear.

Conventional warfare is symmetrical with two nations sending their armies into battle. By contrast, terrorism is an unconventional form of warfare, an asymmetrical conflict in which a small number of attackers uses terror and their own willingness to die to level the playing field against a much more powerful enemy. Although the terrorists may be ruthless, the nation under attack must exercise restraint in its response to terrorism because little may be known about the identity and location of the parties responsible.

The Costs and Causes of Militarism

The cost of armed conflict extends far beyond battlefield casualties. Together, the world's nations spend more than $1.7 trillion annually for military purposes (Stockholm International Peace Research Institute, 2012). Spending this much diverts resources from the desperate struggle for survival by hundreds of millions of poor people.

After Social Security, defense is the U.S. government's single largest expenditure, accounting for 19 percent of all federal spending and amounting to more than $700 billion in the 2013 budget. In recent years, the United States has emerged as the world's only superpower, accounting for about 41 percent of the world's military spending. Put another way, the United States spends nearly as much on the military as the rest of the world's nations combined (Stockholm International Peace Research Institute, 2012; U.S. Office of Management and Budget, 2012).

For decades, military spending went up as a result of the *arms race* between the United States and the Soviet Union, which ended with the collapse of the USSR in 1991. But some analysts (those who support power-elite theory) link high military spending to the domination of U.S. society by a **military-industrial complex**, *the close association of the federal government, the military, and defense industries.* The roots of militarism, then, lie not just in external threats to our security but also in the institutional structures here at home (Marullo, 1987; Barnes, 2002b).

A final reason for continuing militarism is regional conflict. During the 1990s, for example, localized wars broke out in Bosnia, Chechnya, and Zambia, and tensions today run high between Israel and Palestine and between India and Pakistan. Even limited wars have the potential to grow and draw in other countries, including the United States. India and Pakistan—both nuclear powers—moved to the brink of war in 2002 and then pulled back. In 2003, the announcement by North Korea that it, too, had nuclear weapons raised tensions in Asia. Iran continues to develop nuclear technology, raising fears that this nation may soon have an atomic bomb.

military-industrial complex
the close association of the federal government, the military, and defense industries

Nuclear Weapons

Despite the easing of superpower tensions, the world still contains approximately 4,000 operational nuclear warheads, representing a destructive power of several tons of TNT for every person on the planet. If even a small fraction of this stockpile is used in war, life as we know it would end. Albert Einstein, whose

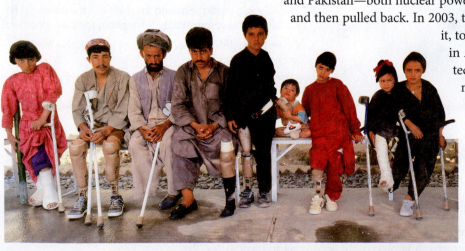
One reason to pursue peace is the rising toll of death and mutilation caused by millions of land mines placed in the ground during wartime and left there afterward. Civilians—many of them children—maimed by land mines receive treatment in this clinic in Kabul, Afghanistan.

genius contributed to the development of nuclear weapons, reflected, "The unleashed power of the atom has changed everything *save our modes of thinking,* and we thus drift toward unparalleled catastrophe." In short, nuclear weapons make unrestrained war unthinkable in a world not yet capable of peace.

The United States, the Russian Federation, Great Britain, France, the People's Republic of China, Israel, India, Pakistan, and probably North Korea all have nuclear weapons. The danger of catastrophic war increases with **nuclear proliferation**, *the acquisition of nuclear weapons technology by more and more nations.* A few nations stopped the development of nuclear weapons—Argentina and Brazil halted work in 1990, and South Africa dismantled its arsenal in 1991. But by 2015, there could be several additional nations in the "nuclear club" and some analysts predict that there could be as many as fifty nuclear nations by 2025 (Grier, 2006). Such a trend makes even the smallest regional conflict very dangerous to the entire planet.

nuclear proliferation
the acquisition of nuclear weapons technology by more and more nations

Mass Media and War

The Iraq War (2003–2010) was the first war in which television crews traveled with U.S. troops, reporting to the world as the campaign unfolded. The mass media provided ongoing and detailed reports of events; cable television made available live coverage of the war twenty-four hours a day, seven days a week.

Media outlets critical of the war—especially the Arab news channel Al-Jazeera—tended to report the slow pace of the conflict, the casualties to the U.S. and allied forces, and the deaths and injuries suffered by Iraqi civilians, information that would increase pressure to end the war. Media outlets supportive of the war—including most news organizations in the United States—tended to report the rapid pace of the war and the casualties to Saddam Hussein's forces and to downplay harm to Iraqi civilians as minimal and unintended. In short, the power of the mass media to provide selective information to a worldwide audience means that television and other media are almost as important to the outcome of a conflict as the military forces that are doing the actual fighting.

Pursuing Peace

How can the world reduce the dangers of war? Here are the most recent approaches to peace:

Deterrence

The logic of the arms race linked security to a "balance of terror" between the superpowers. The principle of *mutual assured destruction* (MAD) means that the side launching a first-strike nuclear attack against the other will face greater retaliation. This deterrence policy kept the peace during more than fifty years of the Cold War between the United States and the Soviet Union. But this strategy fueled an enormously expensive arms race and had little effect on nuclear proliferation, which represents a growing threat to peace. Deterrence also does little to stop terrorism, the internal military conflict that recently divided Libya, or to prevent war started by a powerful nation (such as the United States) against a weaker foe (such as the Taliban regime in Afghanistan or Saddam Hussein's Iraq).

High-Technology Defense

If technology created the weapons, perhaps it can also protect us from them. Such is the claim made by supporters of the *strategic defense initiative* (SDI). Under SDI, which emerged in the 1980s under the Reagan administration, satellites and ground installations would destroy enemy missiles soon after they were launched (Thompson & Waller, 2001).

In a survey shortly after the 2001 terrorist attacks, two-thirds of U.S. adults supported SDI (Thompson & Waller, 2001; "Female Opinion," 2002). However, critics claim that the system, which they refer to as "Star Wars," would be, at best, a leaky umbrella. Others worry that building such a system will spark another massive arms race. In recent years, the Obama administration has turned away from further development of SDI in favor of more focused defense against short-range missiles that might be launched from Iran.

Diplomacy and Disarmament

Some analysts believe that the best path to peace is diplomacy rather than technology (Dedrick & Yinger, 1990). Teams of diplomats working together can increase security by reducing, rather than building, weapons stockpiles.

But disarmament has limitations. No nation wants to be weakened by letting down its defenses. Successful diplomacy depends on everyone involved making efforts to resolve a common problem (Fisher & Ury, 1988). The United States and Russia continue to negotiate arms reduction agreements. In 2010, the New Start treaty required each country to reduce nuclear stockpiles to 1,550 warheads within seven years; it also provided for a new system of monitoring compliance with this limitation. Even so, each nation will still have more than enough weapons to destroy the entire planet. In addition, the world now faces increasing threats from other nations including North Korea and Iran.

Resolving Underlying Conflict

In the end, reducing the dangers of war may depend on resolving underlying conflicts by promoting a more just world. Poverty, hunger, and illiteracy are all root causes of war. Perhaps the world needs to reconsider the wisdom of spending thousands of times as much money on militarism as we do on efforts to find peaceful solutions (Sivard, 1988; Kaplan & Schaffer, 2001).

Politics: Looking Ahead

Change in political systems is ongoing. Several problems and trends are likely to be important in the decades to come.

One troublesome problem in the United States is the inconsistency between our democratic ideals and our low turnout at the polls. Perhaps, as conservative pluralist theorists say, many people do not bother to vote because they are content with their lives. On the other hand, liberal power-elite theorists may be right in their view that people withdraw from a system that concentrates wealth and power in the hands of so few people. Or perhaps, as radical Marxist critics claim, people find that our political system gives little real choice, limiting options and policies to those that support our capitalist economy. In any case, the current high level of apathy certainly undermines our nation's claim that our political system operates according to the will of all the people.

A second issue is the global rethinking of political models. The Cold War between the United States and the Soviet Union encouraged people to think of politics in terms of the two opposing models, capitalism and socialism. Today, however, people are more likely to consider a broader range of political systems that links government to the economy in various ways. "Welfare capitalism," as found in Sweden, and "state capitalism," as found in Japan and South Korea, are just two possibilities. In all cases, promoting the broadest democratic participation is an important goal. The Thinking Globally box on page 503 helps us understand the current political transformation in the Middle East by looking at the recent political history of the world's Islamic countries.

Third, we still face the danger of war in many parts of the world. Even as the United States and the Russian Federation dismantle some warheads, vast stockpiles of nuclear weapons remain, and nuclear technology continues to spread around the world. In addition, new superpowers are likely to arise (the People's Republic of China and India are likely candidates), regional conflicts are likely to continue, and there is no end in sight to global terrorism. We can only hope for—*and vote for*—leaders who will find nonviolent solutions to the age-old problems that provoke war and put us on the road to world peace.

Thinking Globally

Uprisings Across the Middle East: An End to the Islamic "Democracy Gap"?

The wave of popular political protest that swept across the Middle East in 2011 is the largest global political movement in the two decades since change swept through the former Soviet Union and the nations of Eastern Europe. What's going on? Why are so many nations in this part of the world erupting with political opposition?

Is there a "democracy gap" in the Middle East? Is there a lack of democracy in Islamic nations? Making any assessment of global democracy is more difficult than it may appear. For one thing, in a world marked by striking cultural diversity, can we assume that democracy and the related ideas about political freedoms are the same everywhere? The answer cannot be a simple "yes," because with their various political histories, concepts such as "democracy" and "freedom" mean different things in different cultural settings.

What have researchers found? Freedom House is an organization that monitors political freedom by tracking people's right to vote, to express ideas, and to move about without undue interference from government in nations around the world. Freedom House classifies nations in one of three categories: "not free," "partly fee," and "free."

Freedom House reports that many of the nations that are classified as "not free" have populations that are largely Islamic. Around the world, 46 of 195 nations had an Islamic majority population in 2012. Just 10 (22 percent) of these 46 countries had democratic governments, and Freedom House rated only three (6.6 percent)—Indonesia, Senegal, and Sierra Leone—as "free." Of the remainder, 18 (39.1 percent) were considered to be "partly free" and 25 (54.3 percent) were classified as "not free." Of the 149 nations without a majority Islamic population, 108 (73 percent) had democratic governments, and 87 (58.4 percent) were rated as "free." When you put these facts together, countries without Islamic majorities were three times more likely than countries with Islamic majorities to have democratic governments. Based on this finding, Freedom House concluded that countries with an Islamic majority display a "democracy gap."

This relative lack of democracy was found not just in the Middle East but also in all world regions that contain Islamic-majority nations, including Africa, central Europe, and Asia. But the pattern was especially strong among the sixteen Islamic-majority states in the Middle East and North Africa that are ethnically Arabic—as of early 2013, only two, Libya and Tunisia, are electoral democracies.

What explains this "democracy gap"? Freedom House points to four factors. First, countries with Islamic-majority populations are typically less developed economically with limited schooling for their people and widespread poverty. Second, these countries have cultural traditions that rigidly control the lives of women, limiting their economic, educational, and political opportunities. Third, although most other countries restrict the power of religious elites in government, and some (including the United States) even recognize a "separation of church and state," Islamic-majority nations support a political role for Islamic leaders. In just two recent cases—Iran and Afghanistan under the Taliban—Islamic leaders have actually taken formal control of the government; more commonly, religious leaders do not hold office but exert considerable influence on political outcomes.

Fourth and finally, the enormous wealth that comes from Middle Eastern oil also plays a part in preventing democratic government. In Iraq, Saudi Arabia, Kuwait, Qatar, and other nations, this natural resource has provided astounding riches to a small number of families, money that they can use to shore up their political control. In addition, oil wealth permits elites to build airports and other modern facilities without encouraging broader economic development that raises the living standards of the majority.

For all these reasons, Freedom House concludes that the road to democracy for Islamic-majority nations is likely to be long. But it is worthwhile remembering that, looking back to 1950, very few Catholic-majority countries (mostly in Europe and Latin America) had democratic governments. Today, however, most of these nations are democratic.

What is the future for democracy in Islamic-majority nations? Keep in mind that 43 percent of the world's Muslims live in Nigeria, Turkey, Bangladesh, India, Indonesia, Germany, France, and the United States, where they already live under democratic governments. But perhaps the best indicator that change is under way is the widespread demands for a political voice now rising from people throughout the Middle East. The pace of political change is increasing.

What Do You Think?

1. How do you think the political conflict in the Middle East will turn out? Will the cause of democracy be advanced? Explain your view.

2. Over the coming decades, do you think the Islamic "democracy gap" just described will disappear? Why or why not?

3. What role should the United States play in this process? Do you think the United States is a force that advances democracy? Why or why not?

Sources: Karatnycky (2002), Pew Research Center, Forum on Religion and Public Life (2012), and Freedom House (2013).

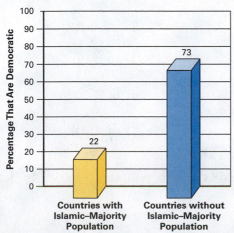

Democracy and Islam
Today, democratic government is much less common in countries with Islamic-majority populations. Fifty years ago, the same was true of countries with Catholic-majority populations.

Seeing Sociology in Everyday Life

How important are you to the political process?

Historically, as this chapter explains, younger people have been less likely than older people to take part in politics. But, as the results of the 2008 and 2012 elections suggest, that trend may be changing as evidence builds that young people intend to have their voices heard.

Thousands of young people volunteered to assist the 2012 presidential candidates in their campaigns. In what ways can young people help their candidates simply by using the telephone?

You don't need to be a campaign worker to make a difference. What is the easiest—and in the end, the most important—way to be a part of the political process?

In 2011, Stephanie Joanne Angelina Germanotta, better known as Lady Gaga, participated in the National Equality March in Washington, D.C., in support of changing the law to permit openly gay and lesbian people to serve in this country's armed forces. Can you identify other celebrities who have tried to shape public opinion?

HINT In the 2012 presidential campaign, thousands of young people served as volunteers for the candidates of both major political parties, telephoning voters or walking door-to-door in an effort to increase public interest, raise money, and get people to the polls on Election Day. Many celebrities—including musicians and members of the Hollywood entertainment scene—also spoke out in favor of a candidate and, as has been the case in recent years, most of them favored the Democratic party. But voting is most important of all, and your vote counts as much as that of any celebrity. Are you registered to vote? Will you turn out next Election Day?

Seeing Sociology in *Your* Everyday Life

1. Analysis of recent election results, including how gender, race, income, religion, and other variables shaped people's choices, can be found at http://www.cnn.com/ELECTION/2012/. Visit this site and develop a profile of the typical Democratic voter and the typical Republican voter. Which variables best predict differences in voting preference?

2. Go to MySocLab and click on the Student Resources link to access the Sociology in Focus blog, where you can read the latest posts by a team of young sociologists who apply the sociological perspective to topics of popular culture.

3. What do you think a more democratic United States would look like?

What about a more democratic world? For more about political democracy, go to the "Seeing Sociology in *Your* Everyday Life" feature in MySocLab, where you will also find suggestions about ways that you can advance the cause of democracy.

Making the Grade

Politics: Power and Authority

 17.1 Distinguish traditional, rational-legal, and charismatic authority. (pages 480–82)

👁 **Watch** the **Video** in **MySocLab**

Politics is the major social institution by which a society distributes power and organizes decision making. Max Weber claimed that raw power is transformed into *legitimate authority* in three ways:

- Preindustrial societies rely on tradition to transform power into authority. **Traditional authority** is closely linked to kinship.
- As societies industrialize, tradition gives way to rationality. **Rational-legal authority** underlies the operation of bureaucratic offices as well as the law.
- At any time, however, some individuals transform power into authority through charisma. **Charismatic authority** is based on extraordinary personal qualities (as found in Jesus of Nazareth, Adolf Hitler, and Mahatma Gandhi).

politics the social institution that distributes power, sets a society's goals, and makes decisions

power the ability to achieve desired ends despite resistance from others

government a formal organization that directs the political life of a society

authority power that people perceive as legitimate rather than coercive

traditional authority power legitimized by respect for long-established cultural patterns

rational-legal authority power legitimized by legally enacted rules and regulations; also known as *bureaucratic authority*

charismatic authority power legitimized by extraordinary personal abilities that inspire devotion and obedience

routinization of charisma the transformation of charismatic authority into some combination of traditional and bureaucratic authority

Politics in Global Perspective

17.2 Compare monarchy and democracy as well as authoritarian and totalitarian political systems. (pages 482–87)

Monarchy is common in agrarian societies.

- Leadership is based on kinship.
- During the Middle Ages, absolute monarchs claimed to rule by divine right.

Democracy is common in modern societies.

- Leadership is linked to elective office.
- Bureaucracy and economic inequality limit true democracy in high-income countries today.

Authoritarianism is any political system that denies the people participation in government.

- Absolute monarchies and military juntas are examples of authoritarian regimes.

Totalitarianism concentrates all political power in one centralized leadership.

- Totalitarian governments allow no organized opposition, and they rule by fear.

- The world is divided into 195 independent nation-states, 90 of which were politically "free" in 2012. Another 58 countries were "partly free," and the remaining 47 countries were "not free."
- Multinational corporations have created a new political order because their enormous wealth gives them power to shape world events.
- In an age of computers and other new information technology, governments can no longer control the flow of information across their borders.

monarchy a political system in which a single family rules from generation to generation

democracy political system that gives power to the people as a whole

authoritarianism a political system that denies the people participation in government

totalitarianism a highly centralized political system that extensively regulates people's lives

Politics in the United States

17.3 Analyze economic and social issues using the political spectrum. (pages 487–93)

👁 **Watch** the **Video** in **MySocLab**   📖 **Read** the **Document** in **MySocLab**

✳ **Explore** the **Map** in **MySocLab**

welfare state a system of government agencies and programs that provides benefits to the population

special-interest group people organized to address some economic or social issue

- U.S. government has expanded over the past two centuries, although the **welfare state** in the United States is smaller than in most other high-income nations.

- The **political spectrum**, from the liberal left to the conservative right, involves attitudes on both economic issues and social issues.
- Affluent people tend to be conservative on economic issues and liberal on social issues.
- Party identification in the United States is weak.

- **Special-interest groups** advance the political aims of specific segments of the population.
- **Political action committees** play a powerful role in electoral politics.
- Spending in the 2012 presidential campaigns totaled some $2.6 billion.

- **Voter apathy** runs high in the United States.
- Only 57.5% of eligible voters went to the polls in the 2012 presidential election.

political action committee (PAC) an organization formed by a special-interest group, independent of political parties, to raise and spend money in support of political goals

Theories of Power in Society

17.4 Apply the pluralist, power-elite, and Marxist models to the U.S. political system. (pages 493–95)

 Watch the **Video** in **MySocLab**

- The **pluralist model** claims that political power is spread widely in the United States. It is linked to structural-functional theory
- The **power-elite model** claims that power is concentrated in a small, wealthy segment of the population. It is based on the ideas of C. Wright Mills and is linked to social-conflict theory.
- The **Marxist political-economy model** claims that our political agenda is determined by a capitalist economy, so true democracy is impossible. It is based on the ideas of Karl Marx and is linked to social-conflict theory.

pluralist model an analysis of politics that sees power as spread among many competing interest groups
power-elite model an analysis of politics that sees power as concentrated among the rich
Marxist political-economy model an analysis that explains politics in terms of the operation of a society's economic system

Power beyond the Rules

17.5 Describe causes of both revolution and terrorism. (pages 495–97)

- **Revolution** radically transforms a political system. Revolutions occur during periods of rising expectations and when governments are unwilling to reform themselves. They are usually led by intellectuals.
- **Terrorism** is an unconventional form of warfare that employs violence in the pursuit of political goals and is used by a group against a much more powerful enemy. Who or what is defined as terrorist depends on one's political perspective.
- **State terrorism** is the use of violence by government officials as a way to control the population.

political revolution the overthrow of one political system in order to establish another
terrorism acts of violence or the threat of violence used as a political strategy by an individual or a group

War and Peace

17.6 Identify factors encouraging war or peace. (pages 497–502)

Like all forms of social behavior, **war** is a product of society. Societies go to war when
- people perceive a threat to their way of life
- governments want to divert public attention from social problems at home
- governments want to achieve a specific political or moral objective
- governments can find no alternatives to resolving conflicts

- The U.S. military is composed mainly of members of the working class.
- Military spending rose dramatically in the second half of the twentieth century because of the *arms race* between the United States and the former Soviet Union.
- Some analysts point to the domination of U.S. society by a **military-industrial complex**.
- The development and spread of nuclear weapons have increased the threat of global catastrophe.

- The most recent approaches to peace include deterrence; high-technology defense; diplomacy and disarmament; resolution of underlying conflict.
- In the end, pursuing peace means ending poverty, hunger, and illiteracy and promoting social justice for all people.

war organized, armed conflict among the people of two or more nations, directed by their governments
military-industrial complex the close association of the federal government, the military, and defense industries
nuclear proliferation the acquisition of nuclear weapons technology by more and more nations

18 Families

((· **Listen** to **Chapter 18** in **MySocLab**

LEARNING OBJECTIVES

18.1 Describe families and how they differ around the world.

18.2 Apply sociology's major theories to family life.

18.3 Analyze changes in the family over the life course.

18.4 Explain how class, race, and gender shape family life.

18.5 Analyze the effects of divorce, remarriage, and violence on family life.

18.6 Describe the diversity of family life in the United States.

the **Power** of **Society**

to affect the odds that a marriage will end in divorce

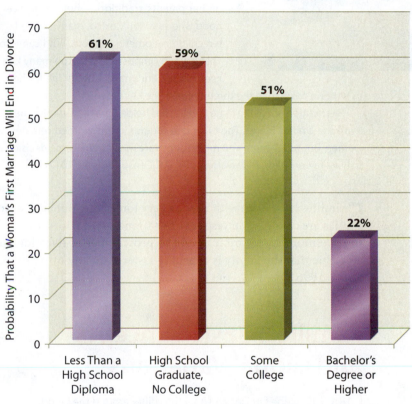

Probability That a Woman's First Marriage Will End in Divorce

- Less Than a High School Diploma: **61%**
- High School Graduate, No College: **59%**
- Some College: **51%**
- Bachelor's Degree or Higher: **22%**

Source: Copen et al. (2012)

Why do some marriages last longer than others? At some point in their lives, about 95 percent of people in the United States marry. But not all marriages have the same odds of lasting. In general, more socially privileged people who tie the knot have the best chances of staying married. For women who have at least a bachelor's degree, just 22 percent of first marriages end in divorce. By contrast, for women who have less than a high school diploma, divorce is almost three times more likely, with 61 percent of first marriages ending in divorce. Just as society guides people in their selection of a marriage partner, it also shapes the chances that the marriage will last.

Chapter Overview

This chapter explores the family, a major social institution. Families are important for many reasons, which helps explain why they are found in every society. The chapter identifies various forms of family life and tracks changes in families over time. We begin by introducing a number of important concepts that sociologists use to describe and analyze families.

Rosa Yniguez is one of seven children who grew up together in Jalisco, Mexico, in a world in which families worked hard, went to church regularly, and were proud of having many children. Rosa remembers visiting the home of friends of her parents who had a clock in their living room with a picture of each of their twelve children where the numbers on the clock face would be.

Now thirty-five years old, Rosa is living in San Francisco and working as a cashier in a department store. In some respects, she has carried on her parents' traditions—but not in every way. Recalling her childhood, she says, "In Mexico, many of the families I knew had six, eight, ten children. Sometimes more. But I came to this country to get ahead. That is simply impossible with too many kids." As a result of her desire to keep her job and make a better life for her family, Yniguez has decided to have no more than the three children she has now.

A tradition of having large families has helped make Hispanics the largest racial or ethnic minority in the United States. The birth rate for immigrant women remains higher than for native-born women. But today more and more Latinas are making the same decision as Rosa Yniguez and opting to have fewer children (Navarro, 2004; U.S. Census Bureau, 2012).

Families have been with us for a very long time. But as this story indicates, U.S. families are changing in response to a number of factors, including the desire of women to have more career options and to provide better lives for their children. It is probably true that the family is changing faster than any other social institution (Bianchi & Spain, 1996).

Families: Basic Concepts and Global Variations

(18.1) Describe families and how they differ around the world.

kinship a social bond based on common ancestry, marriage, or adoption

family a social institution found in all societies that unites people in cooperative groups to care for one another, including any children

extended family a family composed of parents and children as well as other kin; also known as a *consanguine family*

nuclear family a family composed of one or two parents and their children; also known as a *conjugal family*

The **family** is *a social institution found in all societies that unites people in cooperative groups to care for one another, including any children.* Family ties are also called **kinship**, *a social bond based on common ancestry, marriage, or adoption.* All societies contain families, but exactly who people call their kin has varied through history and varies today from one culture to another. From the point of view of any individual, families change as we grow up, leaving the family into which we were born to form a family of our own.

Here as in other countries, families form around **marriage**, *a legal relationship, usually involving economic cooperation, sexual activity, and childbearing.* The traditional belief in the United States is that people should marry before having children; this expectation is found in the word *matrimony*, which in Latin means "the condition of motherhood." Today, 59 percent of children are born

marriage a legal relationship, usually involving economic cooperation, sexual activity, and childbearing

endogamy marriage between people of the same social category

exogamy marriage between people of different social categories

monogamy marriage that unites two partners

polygamy marriage that unites a person with two or more spouses

polygyny marriage that unites one man and two or more women

polyandry marriage that unites one woman and two or more men

to married couples, but 41 percent are born to single women who may or may not live with a partner.

Families, then, have become more diverse. Which relationships are and are not considered a family can have important consequences because employers typically extend benefits such as health care only to family members. The U.S. Census Bureau, which collects data used by sociologists, counts as families only people living together who are linked by "birth, marriage, or adoption."[1] All Census Bureau data on families in this chapter are based on that definition. However, the trend in the United States is toward a broader definition of families to include both homosexual and heterosexual partners and unmarried as well as married couples who live together. These *families of affinity* are made up of people who think of themselves as a family and wish others to see them that way.

How closely related do people have to be to consider themselves a "family"? In preindustrial societies, people commonly recognize the **extended family**, *a family consisting of parents and children as well as other kin.* This group is sometimes called the *consanguine family* because it includes everyone with "shared blood." With industrialization, however, increased social mobility and geographic migration give rise to the **nuclear family**, *a family composed of one or two parents and their children.* The nuclear family is also called the *conjugal family* (*conjugal* means "based on marriage"). Although many people in our society think of kinship in terms of extended families, most people carry out their everyday routines within a nuclear family.

The family is changing most quickly in nations that have a large welfare state (see Chapter 17, "Politics and Government"). In the Thinking Globally box on page 512, the sociologist David Popenoe takes a look at Sweden, which, he claims, is home to the weakest families in the world.

Watch in **MySocLab**
Video: *The Basics: Families*

Marriage Patterns

Cultural norms, and often laws, identify people as suitable or unsuitable marriage partners. Some marital norms promote **endogamy**, *marriage between people of the same social category.* Endogamy limits potential partners to people of the same age, race, religion, or social class. By

What does the modern family look like? If we look to the mass media, this is a difficult question to answer. In the television series *Modern Family*, Jay Pritchett's family includes his much younger wife, his stepson Manny, his daughter Claire (who is married with three children), and his son Mitchell (who, with his gay partner, has an adopted Vietnamese daughter). How would you define "the family"?

[1] According to the U.S. Census Bureau, there were 121.1 million U.S. households in 2012. Of these, 80.5 million (67 percent) met the bureau's definition of "family." The remaining living units contained single people or unrelated individuals living together. In 1950, fully 90 percent of all households were families.

Thinking Globally

The Weakest Families on Earth? A Report from Sweden

Inge: In Sweden, we have a government that takes care of every person!

Sam: In the United States, we have families to do that….

We in the United States can envy the Swedes for avoiding many of our worst social problems, including violent crime, drug abuse, and savage poverty. Instead, this Scandinavian nation seems to fulfill the promise of the modern welfare state with a large and professional government bureaucracy that sees to virtually every human need.

But according to David Popenoe (1991), one drawback of such a large welfare state is that big government weakens families. In simple terms, this is because people look to the government, not spouses or other family members, for economic assistance. For the same reason, Sweden also has a high share of adults living alone (40 percent, compared to 27 percent in the United States). In addition, a large proportion of couples live together outside marriage (11 percent, versus 6 percent in the United States), and 54 percent of all Swedish children (compared to 41 percent in the United States) are born to unmarried parents. Average household size in Sweden is almost the smallest in the world (2.1 persons, versus 2.6 in the United States). So families appear to play a less central role in Swedish society than they do in the United States.

Popenoe claims that, back in the 1960s, a growing culture of individualism and self-fulfillment, along with the declining influence of religion, began eroding Swedish families. The movement of women into the labor force also played a part. Today, Sweden has the lowest proportion of women who are homemakers (10 percent, versus 22 percent in the United States) and the highest percentage of women in the labor force (72 percent, versus 58 percent in the United States).

But most important, according to Popenoe, is the expansion of the welfare state. The Swedish government offers its citizens a lifetime of services. Swedes can count on the government to deliver and school their children, provide comprehensive health care, support them when they are out of work, and pay for their funerals.

Many Swedes supported this welfare state, thinking it would strengthen families. But as Popenoe sees it, government is really *replacing* families. Take the case of child care: The Swedish government operates child care centers that are staffed by professionals and available regardless of parents' income. However, the government gives nothing to parents who wish to care for their children in their own home. In effect, government benefits encourage people to let the state do what family members used to do for themselves.

But if Sweden's system has solved so many social problems, why should anyone care about the family getting weaker? For two reasons, says Popenoe. First, it is very expensive for government to provide many "family" services; this is the main reason that Sweden has one of the highest rates of taxation in the world. Second, at any price, Popenoe says that government employees in large child care centers cannot provide children with the same love and emotional security given by two parents living as a family. When it comes to taking care of people—especially young children—small, intimate groups do the job better than large, impersonal organizations.

What Do You Think?

1. Do you agree with Popenoe's concern that we should not get on the path to government replacing families? Explain your answer.

2. In the United States, we have a much smaller welfare state than Sweden has. Should our government do more for its people? Why or why not?

3. With regard to children, list two specific things that you think government can do better than parents and two things that parents do better than government. Explain your list.

Sources: Martin et al. (2012); European Union Statistical Division (2012); OECD (2012); United Nations Economic Commission for Europe (2012); U.S. Bureau of Labor Statistics (2012); and U.S. Census Bureau (2012).

contrast, **exogamy** is *marriage between people of different social categories.* In rural areas of India, for example, people are expected to marry someone of the same caste (endogamy) but from a different village (exogamy). The reason for endogamy is that people of similar position pass along their standing to their offspring, maintaining the traditional social hierarchy. Exogamy, on the other hand, links communities and encourages the spread of culture.

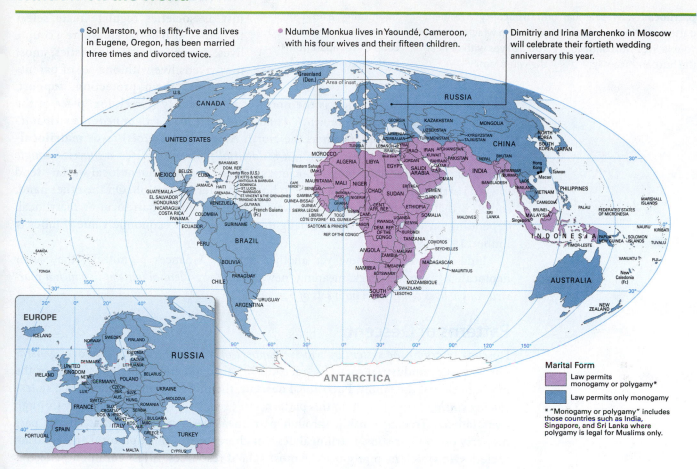

Sol Marston, who is fifty-five and lives in Eugene, Oregon, has been married three times and divorced twice.

Ndumbe Monkua lives in Yaoundé, Cameroon, with his four wives and their fifteen children.

Dimitriy and Irina Marchenko in Moscow will celebrate their fortieth wedding anniversary this year.

Marital Form

Law permits monogamy or polygamy*

Law permits only monogamy

* "Monogamy or polygamy" includes those countries such as India, Singapore, and Sri Lanka where polygamy is legal for Muslims only.

GLOBAL MAP 18–1 Marital Form in Global Perspective

Monogamy is the only legal form of marriage throughout the Western Hemisphere and in much of the rest of the world. In most African nations and in southern Asia, however, polygamy is permitted by law. In many cases, this practice reflects the influence of Islam, a religion that allows a man to have up to four wives. Even so, most marriages in these countries are monogamous, primarily for financial reasons.

Source: *Peters Atlas of the World* (1990) with updates by the author.

In high-income nations, laws permit only **monogamy** (from the Greek, meaning "one union"), *marriage that unites two partners.* As Global Map 18–1 shows, monogamy is the rule throughout North and South America as well as Europe, although many countries in Africa and southern Asia permit **polygamy** (from the Greek, meaning "many unions"), *marriage that unites a person with two or more spouses.* Polygamy has two forms. By far the more common form is **polygyny** (from the Greek, meaning "many women"), *marriage that unites one man and two or more women.* For example, Islamic nations in the Middle East and Africa permit men up to four wives. Even so, most Islamic families are monogamous because few men can afford to support several wives and even more children.

Polyandry (from the Greek, meaning "many men" or "many husbands") is *marriage that unites one woman and two or more men.* This extremely rare pattern exists in Tibet, a mountainous land where agriculture is difficult. There, polyandry discourages the division of land into parcels too small to support a family and divides the hard work of farming among many men.

Most of the world's societies have at some time permitted more than one marital pattern. Even so, most marriages have been monogamous (Murdock, 1965, orig. 1949). This historical preference for monogamy reflects two facts of life: Supporting several spouses is very expensive, and the number of men and women in most societies is roughly equal.

patrilocality a residential pattern in which a married couple lives with or near the husband's family

matrilocality a residential pattern in which a married couple lives with or near the wife's family

neolocality a residential pattern in which a married couple lives apart from both sets of parents

Residential Patterns

Just as societies regulate mate selection, they also designate where a couple lives. In preindustrial societies, most newlyweds live with one set of parents who offer them protection, support, and assistance. Most common is the norm of **patrilocality** (Greek for "place of the father"), *a residential pattern in which a married couple lives with or near the husband's family.* But some societies (such as the North American Iroquois) favor **matrilocality** (meaning "place of the mother"), *a residential pattern in which a married couple lives with or near the wife's family.* Societies that engage in frequent local warfare tend toward patrilocality, so sons are close to home to offer protection. On the other hand, societies that engage only in distant warfare may be either patrilocal or matrilocal, depending on whether its sons or daughters have greater economic value (Ember & Ember, 1971, 1991).

Industrial societies show yet another pattern. Finances permitting, they favor **neolocality** (from the Greek, meaning "new place"), *a residential pattern in which a married couple lives apart from both sets of parents.*

Patterns of Descent

Descent refers to *the system by which members of a society trace kinship over generations.* Most preindustrial societies trace kinship through either the father's side or the mother's side of the family. **Patrilineal descent**, the more common pattern, is *a system tracing kinship through men.* In this pattern, children are related to others only through their fathers. Tracing kinship through patrilineal descent ensures that fathers pass property on to their sons. Patrilineal descent characterizes most pastoral and agrarian societies, in which men produce the most valued resources. A less common pattern is **matrilineal descent**, a system tracing kinship through women. Matrilineal descent, in which mothers pass property to their daughters, is found more frequently in horticultural societies, where women are the main food producers.

Industrial societies with greater gender equality recognize **bilateral descent** ("two-sided descent"), *a system tracing kinship through both men and women.* In this pattern, children include people on both the father's side and the mother's side among their relatives.

descent the system by which members of a society trace kinship over generations

patrilineal descent a system tracing kinship through men

matrilineal descent a system tracing kinship through women

bilateral descent a system tracing kinship through both men and women

Patterns of Authority

Worldwide, polygyny, patrilocality, and patrilineal descent are dominant and reflect the common global pattern of patriarchy. In industrial societies like the United States, men are still typically heads of households, and most U.S. parents give children their father's last name. However, more egalitarian family patterns are evolving, especially as the share of women in the labor force goes up.

Theories of the Family

18.2 Apply sociology's major theories to family life.

A
s in earlier chapters, applying sociology's major theoretical approaches offers a range of insights about the family. The Applying Theory table on page 515 summarizes what we can learn from each approach.

Family

	Structural-Functional Theory	Social-Conflict and Feminist Theories	Symbolic-Interaction and Social-Exchange Theories
What is the level of analysis?	Macro-level	Macro-level	Micro-level
What is the importance of family for society?	The family performs vital tasks, including socializing the young and providing emotional and financial support for members.	The family perpetuates social inequality by handing down wealth from one generation to the next.	Symbolic-interaction theory explains that the reality of family life is constructed by members in their interaction.
	The family helps regulate sexual activity.	The family supports patriarchy as well as racial and ethnic inequality.	Social-exchange theory shows that courtship typically brings together people who offer the same level of advantages.

Functions of the Family: Structural-Functional Theory

According to the structural-functional approach, the family performs many vital tasks. For this reason, the family is often called the "backbone of society."

1. **Socialization.** As explained in Chapter 5 ("Socialization"), the family is the first and most important setting for child rearing. Ideally, parents help children become well-integrated, contributing members of society. Of course, family socialization continues throughout the life cycle. Adults change within marriage and, as any parent knows, mothers and fathers learn as much from their children as their children learn from them.

2. **Regulation of sexual activity.** Every culture regulates sexual activity in the interest of maintaining kinship organization and property rights. The **incest taboo** is *a norm forbidding sexual relations or marriage between certain relatives.* Although the incest taboo exists in every society, exactly which relatives cannot marry varies from one culture to another. The matrilineal Navajo, for example, forbid marrying any relative of one's mother. Our bilateral society applies the incest taboo to both sides of the family but limits it to close relatives, including parents, grandparents, siblings, aunts, and uncles (National Map 8–1 on page 212 shows which states allow or forbid first-cousin marriages). But even brother-sister (but not parent-child) marriages were accepted among the ancient Egyptian, Incan, and Hawaiian nobility (Murdock, 1965, orig. 1949).

incest taboo a norm forbidding sexual relations or marriage between certain relatives

Why does some form of the incest taboo exist in every society? Part of the reason is rooted in biology: Reproduction between close relatives of any species raises the odds of producing offspring with mental or physical damage. But why of all living species do just human beings observe an incest taboo? The answer is that controlling reproduction among close relatives is necessary for social organization. For one thing, the incest taboo limits sexual competition in families by restricting sex to spouses. Second, because kinship defines people's rights and obligations toward one another, reproduction among close relatives would hopelessly confuse kinship ties and threaten social

Often, we experience modern society as cold and impersonal. In this context, the family can be a haven in a heartless world. Not every family lives up to this promise, of course, but people in families do live happier and longer than those who live alone.

order. Third, by requiring people to marry beyond their immediate families, the incest taboo serves to tie together the larger society as various kinship groups are linked in marriage.

3. **Social placement.** Families are not needed for people to reproduce, but they do help maintain social organization. Parents pass on their own social identity—in terms of race, ethnicity, religion, and social class—to their children at birth.

4. **Material and emotional security.** Many people view the family as a "haven in a heartless world," offering physical protection, emotional support, and financial assistance. Perhaps this is why people living in families tend to be happier, healthier, and wealthier than people living alone (Goldstein & Kenney, 2001; U.S. Census Bureau, 2012).

EVALUATE Structural-functional theory explains why society, at least as we know it, is built on families. But this approach glosses over the diversity of U.S. family life and ignores how other social institutions (such as government) could meet some of the same human needs. Finally, structural-functionalism overlooks negative aspects of family life, including patriarchy and family violence.

CHECK YOUR LEARNING What four important functions does the family provide for the operation of society?

Inequality and the Family: Social-Conflict and Feminist Theories

Read in **MySocLab**
Document: *How History and Sociology Can Help Today's Families* by Stephanie Coontz

Like the structural-functional approach, the social-conflict approach, including feminist theory, considers the family central to our way of life. But rather than focusing on ways that kinship benefits society, this approach points out how the family perpetuates social inequality.

1. **Property and inheritance.** Friedrich Engels (1902, orig. 1884) traced the origin of the family to men's need (especially in the higher classes) to identify heirs so that they could hand down property to their sons. Families thus concentrate wealth and reproduce the class structure in each new generation.

2. **Patriarchy.** Feminists link the family to patriarchy. To know their heirs, men must control the sexuality of women. Families therefore transform women into the sexual and economic property of men. A century ago in the United States, most wives' earnings belonged to their husbands. Today, women still bear most of the responsibility for child rearing and housework (England, 2001; U.S. Department of Labor, 2012).

3. **Race and ethnicity.** Racial and ethnic categories persist over generations because most people marry others like themselves. Endogamous marriage supports racial and ethnic inequality.

EVALUATE Social-conflict and feminist theories show another side of family life: its role in social stratification. Engels criticized the family as part and parcel of capitalism. But noncapitalist societies also have families (and family problems). The family may be linked to social inequality, as Engels argued, and to gender inequality, as feminist theory claims. But it carries out societal functions not easily accomplished by other means.

CHECK YOUR LEARNING Point to three ways in which families support social inequality.

Constructing Family Life: Micro-Level Theories

Both the structural-functional and social-conflict approaches view the family as a structural system. By contrast, micro-level analysis explores how individuals shape and experience family life.

Symbolic-Interaction Theory

Ideally, family living offers an opportunity for *intimacy*, a word with Latin roots meaning "sharing fear." As family members share many activities over time, they identify with each other and build emotional bonds. Of course, the fact that parents act as authority figures often limits their closeness with younger children. But as children approach adulthood, kinship ties typically open up to include sharing confidences with greater intimacy (Macionis, 1978).

Social-Exchange Theory

Social-exchange theory, another micro-level approach, describes courtship and marriage as forms of negotiation (Blau, 1964). Dating allows each person to assess the advantages and disadvantages of a potential spouse. In essence, exchange theory suggests, people "shop around" for partners to make the best "deal" they can.

In patriarchal societies, gender roles dictate the elements of exchange: Traditionally, men bring wealth and power to the marriage marketplace, and women bring beauty. The importance of beauty explains women's historical concern with their appearance and sensitivity about revealing their age. But as women have joined the labor force, they are less dependent on men to support them, and so the terms of exchange are converging for men and women.

EVALUATE Micro-level analysis provides a counterpart to structural-functional and social-conflict visions of the family as an institutional system. Both symbolic-interaction and social-exchange theories focus on the individual experience of family life. However useful micro-level analysis may be, it misses the bigger picture: The experience of family life is similar for people in the same social and economic categories.

CHECK YOUR LEARNING How does a micro-level approach to understanding family differ from a macro-level approach? State the main ideas of symbolic-interaction theory and social-exchange theory.

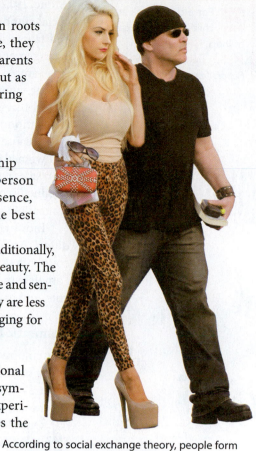

According to social exchange theory, people form relationships based on what each offers to the other. Generally partners see the exchange as fair or "about even." What do you think is the exchange involved in this marriage between actor Doug Hutchinson (who was 51 at the time of their marriage) and aspiring actress Courtney Stodden (who was 16)?

Stages of Family Life

(18.3) Analyze changes in the family over the life course.

The family is a dynamic institution. Not only does the family itself change over time, but the way any of us *experiences* family changes as well as we move through the life course. A new family begins with the couple engaged in courtship and evolves as the new partners settle into the realities of married life. Next, for most couples at least, come the years spent developing careers and raising children, leading to the later years of marriage, after the children have left home to form families of their own. We will look briefly at each of these four stages.

Courtship

November 2, Kandy, Sri Lanka. Winding through the rain forest of this beautiful island, our van driver, Harry, recounts how he met his wife. Actually, he explains, it was more of an arrangement: The two families were both Buddhist and of the same caste. "We got along well, right from the start," recalls Harry. "We had the same background. I suppose she or I could have said no. But 'love marriages' happen in the city, not in the village where I grew up."

In rural Sri Lanka, as in rural areas of low- and middle-income countries throughout the world, most people consider courtship too important to be left to the young

For a closer look at child marriage in parts of India, **Read More** in **MySocLab**, *Early to Wed: A Report from Rural India*

(Stone, 1977). *Arranged marriages* are alliances between two extended families of similar social standing and usually involve an exchange not just of children but also of wealth and favors. Romantic love has little to do with marriage, and parents may make such arrangements when their children are very young. A century ago in Sri Lanka and India, for example, half of all girls married before they reached age fifteen. Today, perhaps one in nine young women in low-income nations is married before the age of fifteen; about one in three is married before the age of eighteen (Mayo, 1927; Mace & Mace, 1960; Population Reference Bureau, 2013).

Because traditional societies are more culturally homogeneous, almost all young men and women have been well socialized to be good spouses. Therefore, parents can arrange marriages without having to worry about whether or not the two individuals involved are *personally* compatible because they know that the partners are being raised to be *culturally* compatible.

Industrialization both erodes the importance of extended families and weakens tradition. As young people begin the process of choosing their own mate, dating sharpens courtship skills and allows sexual experimentation. Marriage is delayed until young people complete their schooling, build the financial security needed to live apart from their parents, and gain the experience needed to select a suitable partner.

Romantic Love

Our culture celebrates *romantic love*—affection and sexual passion for another person—as the basis for marriage. We find it hard to imagine marriage without love, and popular culture—from fairy tales like "Cinderella" to today's television sitcoms and dramas—portrays love as the key to a successful marriage.

Our society's emphasis on romance motivates young people to "leave the nest" to form new families of their own, and sexual passion can help a new couple through the often difficult adjustments of living together (Goode, 1959). On the other hand, because feelings change over time, romantic love is a less stable foundation for marriage than social and economic considerations, which is one reason that the divorce rate is much higher in the United States than it is in nations in which culture is a stronger guide in the choice of a marriage partner.

But even in our country, sociologists point out, society aims Cupid's arrow more than we like to think. Most people fall in love with others of the same race, of comparable age, and of similar social class. Our society "arranges" marriages by encouraging **homogamy** (literally, "like marrying like"), *marriage between people with the same social characteristics.* The extent of homogamy is greater for some categories of our population (such as older people and immigrants from traditional societies) than for others (younger people and those who live with less concern for cultural traditions).

homogamy marriage between people with the same social characteristics

Settling In: Ideal and Real Marriage

Our culture gives the young an idealized, "happily ever after" picture of marriage. Such optimism can lead to disappointment, especially for women, who are taught to view marriage as the key to personal happiness. Also, romantic love involves a good deal of fantasy: We fall in love with others not always as they are but as we want them to be.

Sexuality, too, can be a source of disappointment. In the romantic haze of falling in love, people may see marriage as an endless sexual honeymoon, only to face the sobering realization that sex becomes a less-than-all-consuming passion. Although the frequency of marital sex does decline over time, about two in three married people report that they are satisfied with the sexual dimension of their relationship. In general, couples with the best sexual relationships experience the most satisfaction in their marriages. Sex may not be the key to marital bliss, but more often than not, good sex and good relationships go together (Laumann et al., 1994; Smith, 2006).

Infidelity—*sexual activity outside one's marriage*—is another area where the reality of marriage does not match our cultural ideal. In a recent survey, 78 percent of adults in the United States said sex outside of marriage is "always wrong" or "almost always wrong."

infidelity sexual activity outside one's marriage

Even so, 19 percent of married men and 12 percent of married women indicated (in a private, written questionnaire) that they had been sexually unfaithful to their spouses at least once (NORC, 2013).

Child Rearing

Despite the demands children make on us, adults in this country overwhelmingly identify raising children as one of life's greatest joys (Wang & Taylor, 2011; NORC, 2013:2262). Today, about half of U.S. adults say that two children is the ideal number, and few people say they want more than three (NORC, 2013:405). This is a change from two centuries ago, when eight children was the average.

Big families pay off in preindustrial societies because children supply needed labor. People therefore regard having children as a wife's duty, and without effective methods of birth control, childbearing is a regular event. Of course, a high death rate in preindustrial societies prevents many children from reaching adulthood; as late as 1900, one-third of all children born in the United States died by age ten.

Economically speaking, industrialization transforms children from an asset to a liability. It now costs low-income parents about $200,000 to raise one child, including college tuition; middle-class parents commonly spend about $300,000; and high-income families spend $500,000 and more (Lino, 2012). No wonder the average size of the U.S. family dropped steadily during the twentieth century to one child per family![2]

"Son, you're all grown up now. You owe me two hundred and fourteen thousand dollars."

The trend toward smaller families is most evident in high-income nations. The picture differs in low-income countries in Latin America, Asia, and especially Africa, where many women have few alternatives to bearing children. In such societies, as a glance back at Global Map 1–1 on page 6 shows, four or five children is still the norm.

Parenting is a very expensive, lifelong commitment. As our society has given people greater choices about family life, more U.S. adults have decided to delay childbirth or to remain childless. In 1960, almost 90 percent of women between twenty-five and twenty-nine who had ever married had at least one child; today, this proportion has declined to just 70 percent (U.S. Census Bureau, 2012).

About half of parents in the United States claim that they would like to devote more time to child rearing (Cohn, 2007). But unless we accept a lower standard of living, economic realities demand that most parents pursue careers outside the home, even if that means devoting less time to their children. For many families, including the Yniguez family described in the opening to this chapter, having fewer children is an important step toward resolving the tension between work and parenting (Gilbert, 2005).

Children of working parents spend most of the day at school. But after school, some 4.6 million children (12 percent of five- to fourteen-year-olds) are latchkey kids who are left to fend for themselves (U.S. Census Bureau, 2011). Traditionalists in the "family values" debate charge that many mothers work at the expense of their children, who receive less parenting. Progressives counter that such criticism targets women for wanting the same opportunities men have long enjoyed.

Congress took a step toward easing the conflict between family and job responsibilities by passing the Family and Medical Leave Act in 1993. This law allows up to ninety days of unpaid leave from work to care for a new child or to deal with a serious family emergency. Still, most adults in this country have to juggle parental and job responsibilities.

For a close-up look at who cares for the kids when parents work, **Read More** in **MySocLab**, *Who's Minding the Kids?*

---

[2]According to the U.S. Census Bureau, the median number of children per family was 0.90 in 2011. Among all families, the means were 0.75 for whites, 1.15 for African Americans, and 1.37 for Hispanics.

The Family in Later Life

Increasing life expectancy in the United States means that couples who remain married will stay together for a long time. By about age sixty, most have finished the task of raising children. At this point, marriage brings a return to living with only a spouse.

Like the birth of children, their departure—creating an "empty nest"—requires adjustments, although a marriage often becomes closer and more satisfying. Years of living together may have lessened a couple's sexual passion, but understanding and commitment often increase.

Personal contact with children usually continues because most older adults live a short distance from at least one of their children. One-third of all U.S. adults (about 60 million) are grandparents. A majority of grandparents provide at least some grandchild care. One-third of working mothers with young children rely on the child's grandparents for child care during working hours. About 7 million of our nation's grandparents have grandchildren under the age of eighteen living at home with them. For some categories of the population, grandparents play an especially large role in child rearing. Among African Americans, who have a high rate of single parenting, grandmothers have a central position in family life (AARP Foundation, 2007; Luo et al., 2012).

The other side of the coin is that more adults in midlife now care for aging parents. The empty nest may not be filled by a parent coming to live in the home, but many adults find that caring for parents, who now live to eighty, ninety, and beyond, can be as taxing as raising young children. About 27 percent of U.S. women and 19 percent of U.S. men between the ages of forty-five and fifty-four reported being elder care providers in 2011. The oldest of the baby boomers—now reaching sixty-five—are called the "sandwich generation" because many (especially women) will spend as many years caring for their aging parents as they did caring for their children (Lund, 1993; U.S. Bureau of Labor Statistics, 2012).

The final and surely the most difficult transition in married life comes with the death of a spouse. Wives typically outlive their husbands because of their greater life expectancy and the fact that women usually marry men several years older than themselves. Wives can thus expect to spend some years as widows. The challenge of living alone following the death of a spouse is especially great for men, who usually have fewer friends than widows and may lack housekeeping skills.

Keep in mind that loneliness is not the same as being alone. One recent study of loneliness among older people found that more than half of those who said they felt lonely were married. Loneliness can result from being alone, but it also results from physical or emotional issues that isolate people from those around them (Cornwell & Waite, 2009; Holwerda et al., 2012).

The experience of family life changes as we move through the life course. One important responsibility for many people as they move through middle age is caring for aging parents. In what ways does the process of aging change the relationship between parents and their sons and daughters?

U.S. Families: Class, Race, and Gender

18.4   Explain how class, race, and gender shape family life.

Watch in **MySocLab**
Video: *Sociology on the Job: Families*

Dimensions of inequality—social class, ethnicity and race, and gender—are powerful forces that shape marriage and family life. This discussion addresses each factor in turn, but bear in mind that they overlap in our lives.

Social Class

Social class determines both a family's financial security and its range of opportunities. Interviewing working-class women, Lillian Rubin (1976) found that wives thought a good husband was one who held a steady job, did not drink too much, and was not violent. Rubin's middle-class respondents, by contrast, never mentioned such things; these women simply *assumed* that a husband would provide a safe and secure home. Their ideal husband was someone they could talk to easily, sharing feelings and experiences.

Clearly, what women (and men) think they can hope for in marriage—and what they end up with—is linked to their social class. Much the same holds for children; those lucky enough to be born into affluent families enjoy better mental and physical health, develop more self-confidence, and go on to greater achievement than children born to poor parents (McLeod & Shanahan, 1993; Duncan et al., 1998).

When economic bad times bring economic challenges to the United States, we can expect to see changes in family patterns. In the wake of the Great Recession that began in 2007, one notable trend was a rise in the number of people moving in with relatives. Just before the recession began in 2007, 46 million adults were living in households with a parent, adult child, or adult sibling. By 2009, this number was almost 52 million. By sharing household expenses, relatives who live together boost their standard of living and cut their risk of poverty. Among unemployed adults, for example, the poverty rate for people who had moved in with relatives was about 18 percent—well below the level of 30 percent for those who had not done so (Pew Research Center, 2011).

Ethnicity and Race

As Chapter 14 ("Race and Ethnicity") discusses, ethnicity and race are powerful social forces that can affect family life. Keep in mind, however, that American Indian, Latino, and African American families (like all families) are diverse and do not fit any single generalization or stereotype (Allen, 1995).

American Indian Families

American Indians display a wide variety of family types. Some patterns emerge, however, among people who migrate from tribal reservations to cities. Women and men who arrive in cities often seek out others—especially kin and members of the same tribe—for help getting settled. One study, for example, tells the story of two women migrants to the San Francisco area who met at a meeting of an Indian organization and realized that they were of the same tribe. The women and their children decided to share an apartment, and soon after, the children began to refer to one another as brothers, sisters, and cousins. As the months passed, the two mothers came to think of themselves as sisters (Lobo, 2002).

Migration also creates many "fluid households" with changing membership. In another case from the same research, a large apartment in San Francisco was rented by a woman, her aunt, and their children. Over the course of the next month, however, they welcomed into their home more than thirty other urban migrants, who stayed for a short time until they found housing of their own. Such patterns of mutual assistance, often involving real and fictional kinship, are common among all low-income people.

American Indians who leave tribal reservations for the cities are typically better off than those who stay behind. Because people on reservations have a hard time finding

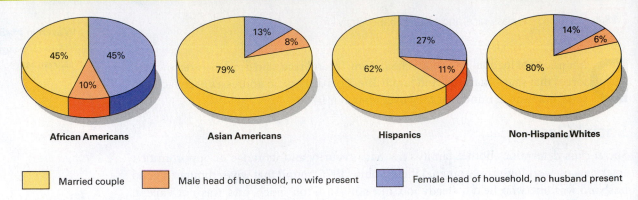

African Americans · **Asian Americans** · **Hispanics** · **Non-Hispanic Whites**

Married couple · Male head of household, no wife present · Female head of household, no husband present

FIGURE 18–1 Family Form in the United States, 2012

All racial and ethnic categories show variations in family form.

Source: U.S. Census Bureau (2012).

work, they cannot easily form stable marriages, and problems such as alcoholism and drug abuse can shatter the ties between parent and child.

Latino Families

Many Latinos enjoy the loyalty and support of extended families. Traditionally, too, Latino parents exercise considerable control over children's courtship, considering marriage an alliance of families, not just a union based on romantic love. Some Latino families also follow conventional gender roles, encouraging *machismo*—strength, daring, and sexual conquest—among men and treating women with respect but also subjecting them to close supervision.

However, assimilation into the larger society is changing these traditional patterns. As the story opening this chapter explained, many women who come to California from Mexico favor smaller families. Similarly, many Puerto Ricans who migrate to New York do not maintain the strong extended family ties they knew in Puerto Rico. Traditional male authority over women has also lessened, especially among affluent Latino families, whose number has more than tripled in the past twenty-five years (Raley, Durden, & Wildsmith, 2004; U.S. Census Bureau, 2012).

Overall, however, the typical Hispanic family had an income of $40,061 in 2011, or 66 percent of the national average (U.S. Census Bureau, 2012). Many Hispanic families suffer the stress of unemployment and other poverty-related problems.

African American Families

African American families face economic disadvantages: The typical African American family earned $40,495 in 2011, which was 66 percent of the national average. People of African ancestry are almost three times as likely as non-Hispanic whites to be poor, and poverty means that both parents and children are likely to experience unemployment, substandard housing, and poor health.

Under these circumstances, maintaining a stable marriage is difficult. Consider that 34 percent of African American women in their forties have never married, compared to about 10 percent of white women of the same age. This means that African American women—often with children—are more likely to be single heads of households. Figure 18–1 shows that women headed 45 percent of all African American families in 2012, compared to 27 percent of Hispanic families, 14 percent of non-Hispanic white families, and 13 percent of Asian or Pacific Islander families (U.S. Census Bureau, 2012).

Regardless of race, single-mother families are always at high risk of poverty. Thirty-three percent of single families with children headed by non-Hispanic white women are poor. Higher yet, the poverty rate among families with children headed by African

American women (47 percent) and Hispanic women (49 percent) is strong evidence of how the intersection of class, race, and gender can put women at a disadvantage. African American families with both wife and husband in the home, which represent 45 percent of the total, are much stronger economically, earning 83 percent as much as comparable non-Hispanic white families. But 73 percent of African American children are born to single women, and 39 percent of African American boys and girls are growing up poor today, meaning that these families carry much of the burden of child poverty in the United States (Martin et al., 2012; U.S. Census Bureau, 2012).

Ethnically and Racially Mixed Marriages

Marriage involves homogamy: Most spouses have similar social backgrounds with regard to factors such as class and race. But over the course of the twentieth century, when it came to choosing a marriage partner, ethnicity came to matter less and less. Even fifty years ago, for example, a woman of German and French ancestry might readily marry a man of Irish and English background without inviting any particular reaction from their families or from society in general.

Race has been a more powerful factor in mate selection. Before a 1967 Supreme Court decision (*Loving* v. *Virginia*), interracial marriage was actually illegal in sixteen states. Today, African, Asian, and Native Americans represent 19.5 percent of the U.S. population; if people ignored race in choosing spouses, we would expect about the same share of marriages to be mixed. The actual proportion of racially mixed marriages is 4.4 percent, showing that race remains important in social relations.

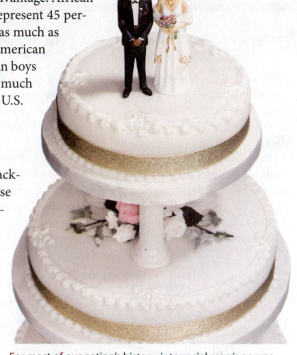

For most of our nation's history, interracial marriage was illegal. The last of these laws was struck down forty-six years ago. Although race and ethnicity continue to guide the process of courtship and marriage, interracial relationships are becoming more and more common.

But this pattern, too, is changing. For one thing, the age at first marriage has been rising to an average of 28.6 for men and 26.6 for women. Young people who marry when they are older are likely to make choices about partners with less input from parents. One consequence of this increasing freedom of choice is that the share of ethnically and racially mixed marriages is increasing (Rosenfeld & Kim, 2005; Kent, 2011; U.S. Census Bureau, 2012).

The most common type of interracial married couple is a white husband and an Asian wife, accounting for about 24 percent of all interracial married couples. When ethnicity is considered, the most common type of "mixed" couple, representing 43 percent of all cases, includes one partner who is Hispanic (the largest racial or ethnic minority category) and one who is not.

But today's couples include just about every imaginable combination. In about 47 percent of all "mixed" marriages, one or both partners claim to have a multiracial or multiethnic identity. "Mixed" marriage couples are likely to live in the West; in seven states—Hawaii, Oklahoma, Alaska, Nevada, California, New Mexico, and Washington, plus the District of Columbia—more than 10 percent of all married couples are interracial (Passel, Wang, & Taylor, 2010; U.S. Census Bureau, 2012). The Thinking About Diversity box on page 524 demonstrates how acceptance of "mixed" relationships varies according to age.

Gender

The sociologist Jessie Bernard (1982) claimed that every marriage is actually two different relationships: the woman's marriage and the man's marriage. The reason is that few marriages have two equal partners. Although patriarchy has weakened, most people still expect husbands to be older and taller than their wives and to have more important, better-paid jobs.

Why, then, do many people think that marriage benefits women more than men? The positive stereotype of the carefree bachelor contrasts sharply with the negative image of the lonely spinster, suggesting that women are fulfilled only through being wives and mothers.

Thinking About Diversity: Race, Class, and Gender

Dating and Marriage: The Declining Importance of Race

In 1961, a young anthropology student from Kansas named Ann Dunham married a foreign student from Kenya named Barack Obama. This marriage was quite unusual at that time for the simple reason that Dunham was white and Obama was black.

Fifty years ago, barely two of every one hundred marriages involved partners of different racial categories. There were strong cultural forces opposing such unions. Survey data from the 1960s show that 42 percent of adults living in the northern United States said they wanted the law to ban marriage between people of different racial classifications. In the South, almost three-fourths of

adults held the same opinion. And, in fact, until 1967 when the Supreme Court declared such laws to be unconstitutional, sixteen states actually did outlaw interracial marriage.

Today, their son, Barack Obama, Jr. has been elected to his second term as president. Today, as well, interracial romantic relationships have become much more common. As the figure shows, almost all young people between the ages of eighteen and twenty-nine claim that they accept interracial dating. Most young people also accept interracial marriage. Among people who are older, however, a more traditional norm of racial homogamy is still in play and they show somewhat lower support for interracial dating. But, since 2000, majorities of people in all age categories support this practice.

Even among people who say that they accept interracial marriage, however, most actual marriages still join people of the same racial category. Considering both race and ethnicity, 85 percent of U.S. marriages join people of the same category. Asians are the mostly likely to "marry out," and about 28 percent do. Hispanics are next, with about 26 percent marrying non-Hispanics. About 17 percent of African Americans marry non–African Americans. Finally, about 9 percent of non-Hispanic whites marry people of other categories.

Even in the "Age of Obama," race and ethnicity continue to guide the selection of a marriage partner, but not as much as they once did. And, in terms of marriage, racial homogamy is certainly no longer the law.

What Do You Think?

1. What are your views on interracial dating and marriage? What are your personal experiences?

2. What patterns involving dating and race do you see on your campus?

3. Do you think you will live to see the day when race no longer guides people's choices of marriage partners? Why or why not?

Sources: Based on Kent (2010), Pew Research Center (2012); U.S. Census Bureau (2012); and Wang (2012).

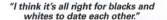
"I think it's all right for blacks and whites to date each other."

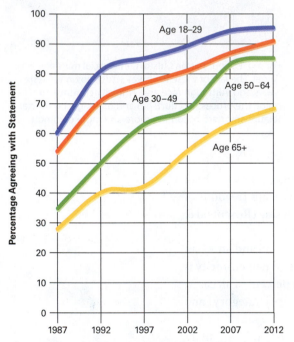

Share of People Who Support Interracial Dating, by Age

Source: Pew Research Center (2012)

However, Bernard claimed, married women actually have poorer mental health, less happiness, and more passive attitudes toward life than single women. Married men, on the other hand, generally live longer, are mentally better off, and report being happier overall than single men (Fustos, 2010). These differences suggest why, after divorce, men are more eager than women to find a new partner.

Bernard concluded that there is no better assurance of long life, health, and happiness for a man than a woman well socialized to devote her life to taking care of him and providing the security of a well-ordered home. She is quick to add that marriage *could* be healthful for women if husbands did not dominate wives and expect them to do almost all the housework. Survey responses confirm that couples rank "sharing household chores" as among the most important factors that contribute to a successful marriage (Pew Research Center, 2007a).

Transitions and Problems in Family Life

18.5 Analyze the effects of divorce, remarriage, and violence on family life.

The newspaper columnist Ann Landers once remarked that one marriage in twenty is wonderful, five in twenty are good, ten in twenty are tolerable, and the remaining four are "pure hell." Families can be a source of joy, but for some, the reality falls far short of the ideal.

Divorce

U.S. society strongly supports marriage, and 90 percent of people who have reached the age of forty have at some point "tied the knot." But many of today's marriages unravel. Figure 18–2 shows that the U.S. divorce rate has more than tripled over the past century. Today, about 20 percent of marriages end in separation or divorce within five years, and about half eventually do so (for African Americans, the share is above 60 percent). From another angle, of all people over the age of fifteen, 21 percent of men and 22 percent of women have been divorced at some point. Our divorce rate is the fourth highest in the world—almost twice as high as in Canada and Japan and more than four times higher than in Italy and Ireland (Fustos, 2010; European Union, 2012; United Nations, 2012). National Map 18–1 on page 526 shows where in the United States divorce rates are especially high and low.

The high U.S. divorce rate has many causes (Furstenberg & Cherlin, 1991; Etzioni, 1993; Popenoe, 1999; Greenspan, 2001):

1. **Individualism is on the rise.** Today's family members spend less time together. We have become more individualistic and more concerned about personal happiness and earning income than about the well-being of our partners and children.

2. **Romantic love fades.** Because our culture bases marriage on romantic love, relationships may fail as sexual passion fades. Many people end a marriage in favor of a new relationship that promises renewed excitement and romance.

3. **Women are less dependent on men.** Women's increasing participation in the labor force has reduced wives' financial dependence on husbands. Therefore, women find it easier to leave unhappy marriages.

4. **Many of today's marriages are stressful.** With both partners working outside the home in most cases, jobs leave less time and energy for family life. This makes raising children harder than ever. Children do stabilize some marriages, but divorce is most common during the early years of marriage, when many couples have young children.

5. **Divorce has become socially acceptable.** Divorce no longer carries the powerful stigma it did several generations ago. Family and friends are now less likely to discourage couples in conflict from divorcing.

6. **Legally, a divorce is easier to get.** In the past, courts required divorcing couples to show that one or both were guilty of behavior such as adultery or physical abuse. Today, all states allow divorce if a couple simply declares that the marriage has failed. Concern about easy divorces, shared by more than one-third of U.S. adults, has led a few states to consider rewriting their marriage laws (Phillips, 2001; NORC, 2013:418).

Who Divorces?

At greatest risk of divorce are young spouses—especially those who marry after a brief courtship—who lack money and emotional maturity.

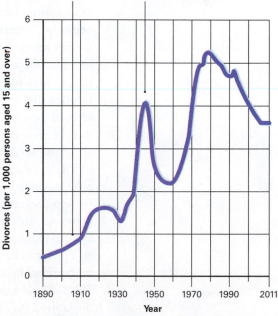

● A century ago, many people regarded divorce as a mark of personal failure.

● The divorce rate rose during World War II, when many couples were separated for long periods of time.

FIGURE 18–2 Divorce Rate for the United States, 1890–2011

Over the long term, the U.S. divorce rate has gone up. Since about 1980, however, the trend has been downward.

Sources: CDC (2013) and U.S. Census Bureau (2012).

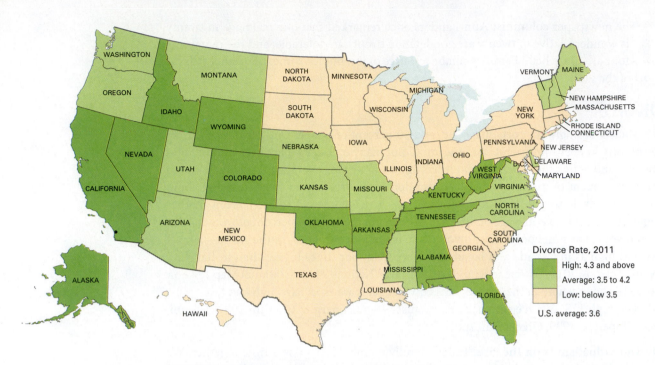

NATIONAL MAP 18–1 Divorce across the United States

The divorce rate (the number of divorces for every 1,000 people regardless of age) is higher in some states than it is in others. In general, divorce rates are higher in the West (and especially in Nevada, a state with very liberal divorce laws), less common in the East, and much less common in the middle of the country. Research points out some patterns: Divorce is more likely among people who are younger, have weaker religious ties, and who move away from their parents' hometown. Can you apply these facts to make sense of this map?

Source: CDC (2012).

The chance of divorce also rises if the couple marries after an unexpected pregnancy or if one or both partners have substance abuse problems. Research also shows that people who are not religious are more likely to divorce than those who have strong religious beliefs. In addition, people whose parents divorced also have a higher divorce rate themselves. Researchers suggest that a role-modeling effect is at work: Children who see parents go through divorce are more likely to consider divorce themselves. People who live in rural areas of the country are less likely to divorce than people who live in large cities, although this difference is smaller than it used to be (Amato, 2001; Pew Research Center, 2008; Tavernise & Gebeloff, 2011; Copen et al., 2012).

Rates of divorce (and marriage) have remained about the same among people with a college education and those with high-paying jobs. At the same time, as suggested by the Power of Society figure at the beginning of this chapter, divorce rates are much higher (and marriage rates are lower) among those who do not attend college and among people with low-paying work. Some researchers suggest that more disadvantaged members of our society appear to be turning away from marriage, not so much because they do not wish to be married but because they lack the economic security needed for a stable family life (Kent, 2011). This trend shows how the recent recession and increasing economic inequality in the United States are affecting marriage and family life.

Finally, men and women who have already divorced once are more likely to divorce than people who have married for the first time. Government data show that, among U.S. women between the ages of fifteen and forty-four, 32 percent of first marriages ended in divorce within ten years; for second marriages, the share rose to 46 percent (CDC, National Center for Health Statistics, 2012). Why? For many people the factors raising the odds of divorce follow them from one marriage to the next. Perhaps, too, having decided once to leave a marriage makes people more likely to reach the same conclusion again. This fact helps to explain why the divorce rate has been increasing among older people (Glenn & Shelton, 1985; Moeller, 2012).

Divorce and Children

Because mothers usually gain custody of children but fathers typically earn more income, the well-being of children often depends on fathers making court-ordered child support payments. As Figure 18–3 indicates, courts award child support in 51 percent of all divorces involving children. Yet in any given year, more than half the children legally entitled to support receive only partial payments or no payments at all. Some 3.5 million "deadbeat dads" fail to support their youngsters. In response, federal legislation now mandates that employers withhold money from the earnings of fathers or mothers who fail to pay up; it is a serious crime to refuse to make child support payments or to move to another state to avoid making them (U.S. Census Bureau, 2011).

The effects of divorce on children go beyond financial support. Divorce can tear young people from familiar surroundings, entangle them in bitter feuding, and distance them from a parent they love. Most serious of all, many children blame themselves for their parents' breakup. Divorce changes the course of many children's lives, causing emotional and behavioral problems and raising the risk of dropping out of school and getting into trouble with the law. Many experts counter that divorce is better for children than staying in a family torn by tension and violence. In any case, parents should remember that if they consider divorce, more than their own well-being is at stake (Wallerstein & Blakeslee, 1989; Amato & Sobolewski, 2001).

Divorce may be a solution for a couple in an unhappy marriage, but it can be a problem for children who experience the withdrawal of a parent from their social world. In what ways can divorce be harmful to children? Is there a positive side to divorce? How might separating parents better prepare their children for the transition of parental divorce?

family violence emotional, physical, or sexual abuse of one family member by another

Remarriage and Blended Families

More than half of all people who divorce remarry, most within four years. Nationwide, more than one-quarter of all new marriages are now remarriages for at least one partner. Men, who benefit more from wedlock, are more likely than women to remarry (Kreider & Ellis, 2011).

Remarriage often creates *blended families,* composed of children and some combination of biological parents and stepparents. With brothers, sisters, half-siblings, a stepparent—not to mention a biological parent who may live elsewhere and be married to someone else with other children—young people in blended families face the challenge of defining many new relationships and deciding just who is part of the nuclear family. Parents often have trouble defining responsibilities for household work among people unsure of their relationships to each other. When the custody of children is an issue, ex-spouses can be an unwelcome presence for people in a new marriage. Although blended families require that members adjust to their new circumstances, they offer both young and old the chance to relax rigid family roles (Furstenberg & Cherlin, 2001; McLanahan, 2002).

Family Violence

The ideal family is a source of pleasure and support. However, the disturbing reality of many homes is **family violence**, *emotional, physical, or sexual abuse of one family member by another.* With the exception of the

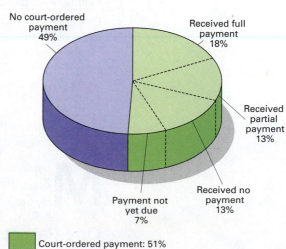

FIGURE 18–3 Payment of Child Support after Divorce

In almost half of all cases of court-ordered child support, the full payment is never received.

Source: U.S. Census Bureau (2011).

police and the military, says the sociologist Richard J. Gelles, the family is "the most violent group in society" (quoted in Roesch, 1984:75).

Violence against Women

Family brutality often goes unreported to police. Even so, the U.S. Department of Justice (2012) estimates that about 500,000 adults are victims of domestic violence each year. Family violence harms both sexes but not equally—women are three times more likely than men to be victims. Government statistics show us that 37 percent of female victims of homicide—but just 3 percent of male victims—are killed by spouses, partners, or ex-partners. Nationwide, the death toll from family violence is about 1,150 women each year. Overall, women are more likely to be injured by a family member than to be mugged or raped by a stranger or hurt in an automobile accident (Shupe, Stacey, & Hazlewood, 1987; Blankenhorn, 1995; U.S. Department of Justice, 2012).

Historically, the law defined wives as the property of their husbands, so no man could be charged with raping his wife. Today, however, all states have enacted *marital rape laws*. The law no longer regards domestic violence as a private family matter; it gives victims more options. Now, even without a formal separation or divorce, a woman can obtain court protection from an abusive spouse, and all states have "stalking laws" that forbid one ex-partner from following or otherwise threatening the other. Communities across the United States have established shelters to provide counseling and temporary housing for women and children driven from their homes by domestic violence.

Finally, the harm caused by domestic violence goes beyond the physical injuries. Victims often lose their ability to trust others. One study found that women who had been physically or sexually abused were much less likely than nonvictims to form stable relationships later on (Cherlin et al., 2004).

Violence against Children

Family violence also victimizes children. In 2011, there were more than 3 million reports of alleged child abuse or neglect. Of these, 677,000 were confirmed to be victims and 1,545 children died from abuse or neglect. Child abuse entails more than physical injury; abusive adults misuse power and trust to damage a child's emotional well-being in ways that may last a lifetime. Child abuse and neglect are most common among the youngest and most vulnerable children (Besharov & Laumann, 1996; U.S. Department of Health and Human Services, 2012).

Although child abusers conform to no simple stereotype, they are slightly more likely to be women (54 percent) than men (46 percent). But almost all abusers share one trait—having been abused themselves as children. Research shows that violent behavior in close relationships is learned; in families, violence begets violence (Levine, 2001; U.S. Department of Health and Human Services, 2012).

Alternative Family Forms

(18.6) Describe the diversity of family life in the United States.

Most families in the United States are composed of married couples that raise children. But in recent decades, our society has displayed increasing diversity in family life.

One-Parent Families

Watch in **MySocLab**
Video: *The Big Picture: Families*

Thirty-two percent of U.S. families with children under eighteen have only one parent in the household, a proportion that more than doubled during the last generation. Put another way, 32 percent of U.S. children now live with only one parent or no natural parent, and almost half will do so before reaching eighteen. One-parent families, 84 percent of which are headed by a single mother, result from divorce, death, or an unmarried woman's decision to have a child (U.S. Census Bureau, 2012).

Single parenthood increases a woman's risk of poverty because it limits her ability to work and to further her education. The opposite is also true: Poverty raises the odds that a young woman will become a single mother. But single parenthood goes well beyond the poor: There are about 1.6 million births to unmarried women each year, which represents more than 40 percent of all births in this country. In recent decades, the rate of childbirth to younger single women has declined; at the same time, the rate of childbirth to unmarried women over the age of forty is on the rise (Pew Research Center, 2007a; Martin et al., 2012).

Looking back at Figure 18–1 on page 522, note that 55 percent of African American families are headed by a single parent. Single parenting is less common among Hispanics (38 percent), Asian Americans (21 percent), and non-Hispanic whites (20 percent). In many single-parent families, mothers turn to their own mothers for support. In the United States, then, the rise in single parenting is tied to a declining role for fathers and the growing importance of grandparenting (Luo at al., 2012).

Research shows that growing up in a one-parent family usually puts children at a disadvantage. Some studies claim that because a father and a mother each make distinctive contributions to a child's social development, one parent has a hard time doing as good a job alone. But the most serious problem for one-parent families, especially if that parent is a woman, is poverty. On average, children growing up in a single-parent family start out poorer, get less schooling, and end up with lower incomes as adults. In addition, 32 percent of adults whose parents never married are single parents themselves compared to 5 percent of adults in the general population (Blankenhorn, 1995; Kantrowitz & Wingert, 2001; McLanahan, 2002; U.S. Census Bureau, 2012).

Cohabitation

Cohabitation is *the sharing of a household by an unmarried couple.* As a long-term form of family life, with or without children, cohabitation is especially common in the Scandinavian countries and is gaining popularity in other European nations. In the United States, the number of cohabiting couples increased from about 500,000 in 1970 to more than 6.7 million today (6.1 million heterosexual couples and 606,000 homosexual couples), or about 6 percent of all households. About half of all people (52 percent of women and 49 percent of men) between fifteen and forty-four years of age have cohabited at some point (CDC, National Center for Health Statistics, 2012; U.S. Census Bureau, 2012).

Cohabiting tends to appeal to more independent-minded individuals as well as those who favor gender equality. At the same time, cohabiting is also somewhat more common among people with less education (Brines & Joyner, 1999; Copen at al., 2012). Most couples cohabit for no more than a few years. After three years, three in ten couples continue to cohabit, four in ten have decided to marry, and three in ten have split up. Mounting evidence suggests that living together may actually discourage marriage because partners become used to low-commitment relationships. For this reason, cohabiting couples who have children—currently representing about one in eight births in the United States—may not always be long-term active parents. Figure 18–4 shows that just 5 percent of children born to cohabiting couples will live until age eighteen with both biological parents if the parents remain unmarried. The share rises to 36 percent among children whose parents marry at some point, but even this is half of the 70 percent figure among children whose parents married before they were born. When cohabiting couples with children separate, their parental involvement, including financial support, is highly uncertain (Popenoe & Whitehead, 1999; Booth & Crouter, 2002; Fustos, 2010; CDC, National Center for Health Statistics, 2012; U.S. Census Bureau, 2012).

cohabitation the sharing of a household by an unmarried couple

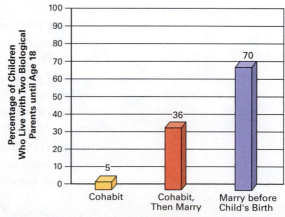

FIGURE 18–4 Parental Involvement in Children's Lives: Cohabiting and Married Parents

Marriage increases the odds that children will remain in the same household with both biological parents as they grow up.

Source: Phillips (2001).

Gay and Lesbian Couples

In 1989, Denmark became the first country to permit registered partnerships with the benefits of marriage for same-sex couples. This change extended social legitimacy to gay and lesbian couples and equalized advantages in inheritance, taxation, and joint property ownership. Since then, more than twenty countries including Norway (1993), Sweden (1994), Iceland (1996), Finland (2001), the United Kingdom (2004), Australia (2008), and Ireland (2011) have followed suit. However, only fifteen countries have extended marriage—in name as well as practice—to same-sex couples: the Netherlands (2001), Belgium (2003), Canada (2005), Spain (2005), South Africa (2006), Norway (2008), Sweden (2009), Portugal (2010), Iceland (2010), Argentina (2010), Denmark (2012), France (2013), Uruguay (2013), New Zealand (2013), and Great Britain (2013).

In 2013, the Supreme Court struck down a provision of the federal Defense of Marriage Act, a decision that gave legally-wed same-sex couples marital status under federal law. Soon after, supporters of same-sex marriage celebrated in New York City's Gay Pride parade. Do you expect same-sex marriage to become the law across the United States? If so, when?

In the United States, Massachusetts became the first state to legalize same-sex marriage in 2004. As of 2013, Iowa, Connecticut, Vermont, New Hampshire, New York, Maine, Maryland, Washington, Delaware, Rhode Island, Minnesota, California, and the District of Columbia have also changed their laws to allow same-sex marriage. New Jersey, Illinois, Colorado, Oregon, Nevada, Wisconsin, and Hawaii permit same-sex unions with all the rights of marriage (National Conference of State Legislatures, 2013).

Back in 1996, Congress passed the Defense of Marriage Act (DOMA), defining marriage as joining one man and one woman. Since then, thirty-five states have amended their constitutions to permit marriage only between one man and one woman. In February 2011, the Obama administration announced that the Department of Justice would no longer defend the DOMA in court. Soon afterward, Congress began debating whether or not to overturn the DOMA but that debate ended in 2013, when the Supreme Court struck down this law. Such changes reflect a steady upward trend in public acceptance of same-sex marriage. Currently, about half of U.S. adults say they support gay marriage—more than the 40 percent of adults who say they oppose it. (Newport, 2005; NORC, 2011:2313; Pew Research Center, 2011, 2012).

Most gay couples with children in the United States are raising the offspring of previous heterosexual unions; others have adopted children. But many gay parents are quiet about their sexual orientation, not wishing to draw unwelcome attention to their children or to themselves. In several widely publicized cases, courts have removed children from the custody of homosexual couples, citing a concern for the "best interests" of the children.

Same-sex couples raising children challenges many traditional ideas. But it also shows that many same-sex people value family life as highly as heterosexuals do.

Singlehood

Because nine out of ten people in the United States marry, we tend to view singlehood as a temporary stage of life. However, increasing numbers of people are choosing to live alone. In 1950, only one household in ten contained a single person. By 2012, this share had risen to 27 percent, a total of 33.2 million single adults (U.S. Census Bureau, 2012).

Most striking is the rising number of single young women. In 1960, 28 percent of U.S. women aged twenty to twenty-four were single; by 2012, the proportion had soared to 81 percent. Underlying this trend is the increasing number of women going to college, which has pushed back the age at first marriage.

Women who complete college do marry later in life, but they are actually more likely to marry than women who do not attend college. The reason is simply that the more education people have, the more they will earn and the more attractive they are as marriage partners (Kent, 2011).

By midlife, many unmarried women sense a lack of available men. Because we expect a woman to marry a man older than she is, and because women tend to be healthier and live longer than men do, the older a woman becomes the more difficulty she has finding a suitable husband.

Extended Family Households

A popular idea in U.S. culture is that individual family members should try to establish their own residence. In large part, this idea has gained public favor because living on one's own is a symbol of financial independence.

But, of course, many people—especially people facing economic challenges—have always recognized the economic advantages of sharing a household. Countless immigrants have come to the United States and lived with extended family members, if only until they have been able to "make it on their own." Similarly, American Indians moving from reservations to large cities often join together with kin (or tribal members they come to define as kin) as a way of caring for one another and also as a strategy to save money. More recently, an increasing share of young people who have completed college but who have not yet found a job have returned "home" to live with parents, a pattern that has earned them the label of "boomerang kids." In addition, more young people who might have expected to strike out on their own have remained at home. Overall, researchers report, almost half of young people between the ages of eighteen and thirty have lived at home with parents for at least some period of time (Parker, 2012).

For people of all ages, as noted earlier in this chapter, the recent recession has sparked an increase in extended family households as people move in with relatives and in-laws. More than 50 million people in the United States live in a household with a parent, adult child, or adult sibling. Sharing a household with other family members carries both joys and challenges. But research shows that it is an effective strategy to save money and cut the odds of falling below the poverty line (Pew Research Center, 2011; Green, 2012).

New Reproductive Technologies and Families

Medical advances involving reproductive technologies are also changing families. In 1978, England's Louise Brown became the world's first "test-tube baby"; since then, tens of thousands of children have been conceived outside the womb.

Test-tube babies are the product of *in vitro fertilization,* in which doctors unite a woman's egg and a man's sperm "in glass" (usually not a test tube but a shallow dish) rather than in a woman's body. Doctors then either implant the resulting embryo in the womb of the woman who is to bear the child or freeze it for implantation at a later time.

New reproductive technology has special importance to same-sex couples who wish to raise children. The television show *The New Normal* features two gay men in a committed relationship who have a child using a surrogate mother.

Modern reproductive technologies allow some couples who cannot conceive by conventional means to have children. These techniques may also eventually help reduce the incidence of birth defects. Genetic screening of sperm and eggs allows medical specialists to increase the odds of having a healthy baby. But new reproductive technologies also raise difficult and troubling questions: When one woman carries an embryo developed from the egg of another, who is the mother? When a couple divorces, which spouse is entitled to use, or destroy, their frozen embryos? Should parents use genetic screening to select the traits of their child such as sex or hair color? Such questions remind us that technology changes faster than our ability to understand all the consequences of its use.

Families: Looking Ahead

Family life in the United States will continue to change in the years ahead, and with change comes controversy. Advocates of "traditional family values" line up against those who support greater personal choice; the Controversy & Debate box on page 533 outlines some of the issues. Sociologists cannot predict the outcome of this debate, but we can suggest five likely future trends.

First, the divorce rate is likely to remain high, even in the face of evidence that marital breakups harm children. In truth, today's marriages are about as durable as they were a century ago, when many were cut short by death. The difference is that now more couples *choose* to end marriages that fail to live up to their expectations. So even though the divorce rate has declined since 1980, it is unlikely to return to the low rates that marked the early decades of the twentieth century.

Second, family life in the twenty-first century will be more diverse. Cohabiting couples, one-parent families, gay and lesbian families, blended families, and multigenerational households are all on the rise. Most families still include people who are married, and most married couples still have children. But the diversity of family forms reflects a trend toward more personal choice as well as people responding to economic challenges.

Third, men continue to play a limited role in child rearing. In the 1950s, a decade that many people view as the "golden age" of families, men began to withdraw from active parenting (Snell, 1990; Stacey, 1990). In recent years, a countertrend has become evident with some older, highly educated men staying at home with young children, many using computer technology to continue their work. But the stay-at-home dad represents no more than 1 percent of fathers with young children (U.S. Census Bureau, 2012). The bigger picture is that the high U.S. divorce rate and the increase in single motherhood are weakening children's ties to fathers and increasing children's risk of poverty.

Fourth, families will continue to feel the effects of economic changes. In many homes today, both household partners work, reducing marriage and family life to the interaction of weary men and women who must try to fit a little "quality time" with their children into an already full schedule. The long-term effects of the two-career couple on families as we have known them are likely to be mixed.

Fifth and finally, the importance of new reproductive technologies will increase. Ethical concerns about whether what *can* be done *should* be done will slow these developments, but new approaches to reproduction will continue to alter the traditional experience of parenthood.

Despite the changes and controversies that have shaken the family in the United States, most people still report being happy as partners and parents (NORC, 2013:2296). Marriage and family life are likely to remain foundations of our society for generations to come.

Controversy & Debate

Should We Save the Traditional Family?

What are "traditional families"? Are they vital to our way of life or a barrier to progress? People use the term *traditional family* to mean a married man and woman who at some point in their lives raise children. Statistically speaking, traditional families are less common than they used to be. In 1950, 90 percent of U.S. households were families—using the Census Bureau's definition of two or more persons related by birth, marriage, or adoption. By 2012, just 67 percent of households were families, due to rising levels of divorce, cohabitation, and singlehood.

"Traditional family" is more than just a handy expression; it is also a moral statement. Belief in the traditional family implies giving high value to becoming and staying married, putting children ahead of careers, and favoring two-parent families over various alternatives.

"Traditional Families Are the Solution"

On one side of the debate, David Popenoe (1993a) has warned of a serious erosion of the traditional family since 1960. At that time, married couples with young children accounted for almost half of all households; today, the figure is 20 percent. Singlehood is up, from 10 percent of households in 1960 to 27 percent today. And the divorce rate has risen by 59 percent since 1960, so that almost half of today's marriages end in permanent separation. Because of both divorce and the increasing number of children born to single women, the share of youngsters who live with just one parent has almost tripled since 1960 to 28 percent. Put another way, just one in four of today's children will grow up with two parents in the home and go on to maintain a stable marriage as an adult (U.S. Census Bureau, 2012).

In light of such data, Popenoe suggests that it may not be an exaggeration to say that the family is falling apart. He sees a fundamental shift from a "culture of marriage" to a culture of divorce," where traditional vows of marital commitment—"till death do us part"—now amount to little more than "as long as I am happy." Negative consequences of this cultural trend are obvious: As we pay less and less attention to children, the crime rate among young people goes up, along with other problem behaviors including underage smoking and drinking, premarital sex, and teen suicide.

As Popenoe sees it, we must work hard and act quickly to reverse current trends. Government cannot be the solution and may even be part of the problem: Since 1960, as families have weakened, government spending on social programs has soared. To save the traditional family, says Popenoe, we need a cultural turnaround similar to what happened with regard to cigarette smoking. In this case, we must replace our "me first" attitudes with commitment to our spouse and children and publicly endorse the two-parent family as best for the well-being of children.

"Traditional Families Are the Problem"

Judith Stacey (1993) provides an opposing, feminist viewpoint, saying "good riddance" to the traditional family. In her view, the traditional family is more problem than solution: "The family is not here to stay. Nor should we wish it were. On the contrary, I believe that all democratic people, whatever their kinship preferences, should work to hasten its demise" (Stacey, 1990:269).

The main reason for rejecting the traditional family, Stacey explains, is that it perpetuates social inequality. Families play a key role in maintaining the class hierarchy by transferring wealth as well as "cultural capital" from one generation to another. Feminists criticize the traditional family's patriarchal form, which subjects women to their husbands' authority and gives them most of the responsibility for housework and child care. From a gay rights perspective, she adds, a society that values traditional families also denies homosexual men and women equal participation in social life.

Stacey thus applauds the breakdown of the family as social progress. She does not view the family as a necessary social institution but as a political construction that elevates one category of people—affluent white males—above others, including women, homosexuals, and poor people.

Stacey also claims that the concept of the "traditional family" is increasingly irrelevant in a diverse society in which both men and women work for income. What our society needs, Stacey concludes, is not a return to some golden age of the family but political and economic change, including income parity for women, universal health care and child care, programs to reduce unemployment, and expanded sex education in the schools. Such measures ensure that people in diverse family forms receive the respect and dignity they deserve.

What Do You Think?

1. To strengthen families, David Popenoe suggests that parents put children ahead of their own careers by limiting their joint workweek to sixty hours. Do you agree? Why or why not?

2. Judith Stacey thinks that marriage is weaker today because women are rejecting patriarchal relationships. What do you think about this argument?

3. Do we need to change family patterns for the well-being of our children? What specific changes are called for?

Whether the traditional family is a positive force in U.S. society or a negative one depends on your point of view.

Seeing Sociology in Everyday Life

CHAPTER 18   Families

How do the mass media portray the family?

Many are familiar with the traditional families portrayed in popular television shows of the 1950s such as *The Adventures of Ozzie and Harriet* and *Leave It to Beaver*. Both of these shows had a working father, homemaker mother, and two (wonderful) sons. But, as the images below and on page 535 suggest, today's television shows present a far wider range of family types.

While television shows fifty years ago presented the family as a cultural ideal, today's shows are far more likely to present the reality of family life. This means not only a variety of family types but, as shown in the popular television show *Breaking Bad*, the struggles and conflicts within families.

In the sitcom *New Girl*, Jess Day is a twenty-something teacher who needs a place to live after ending a relationship. Responding to an ad seeking a roommate, she moves in with three young men. In what ways does this group resemble a family?

The recent television show *Shameless* follows the dysfunctional family life of Frank Gallagher, a single father suffering from alcoholism, and his six children who try their best to cope without much parenting.

HINT The general pattern found in the mass media today is certainly different from that common in the 1950s, the so-called "golden age of families." Today's television shows portray careers that leave little time for families, provide fewer examples of stable marriages, and show the many ways in which people create family-like groups. Some people might say that Hollywood has an anti-family bias. Perhaps, but scriptwriters find that nonconventional family forms make for more interesting stories. To what extent do you agree with the view that most people today are capable of finding satisfying relationships, whether or not these relationships correspond to a traditional family form?

Seeing Sociology in *Your* Everyday Life

1. After reading through the photo essay, list your own favorite television shows and, in each case, evaluate the importance of family life in the show. Is family life included in the show? If so, what family forms are presented? Are families a source of happiness for people or not?

2. Go to MySocLab and click on the Student Resources link to access the Sociology in Focus blog, where you can read the latest posts by a team of young sociologists who apply the sociological perspective to topics of popular culture.

3. This chapter explains that family life in today's society is more and more about making choices. What are the underlying reasons that family life is more varied today than it was, say, a century ago? For suggestions about how you can make better choices about relationships and family life in today's world, go to the "Seeing Sociology in *Your* Everyday Life" feature in MySocLab and read more about how what you have learned in this chapter can benefit you.

Making the Grade

Chapter 18
Families

Families: Basic Concepts and Global Variations

 18.1 Describe families and how they differ around the world. (pages 510–14)

 Watch the **Video** in **MySocLab**

All societies are built on *kinship*. The **family** varies across cultures and over time:

- In industrialized societies, such as the United States, *marriage* is monogamous.
- Preindustrial societies recognize the *extended family*; industrialization gives rise to the *nuclear family*.
- Many preindustrial societies permit *polygamy*, of which there are two types: *polygyny* and *polyandry*.
- In global perspective, *patrilocality* is most common, but industrial societies favor *neolocality* and a few societies have *matrilocal residence*.
- Industrial societies use *bilateral descent*; preindustrial societies are either *patrilineal* or *matrilineal*.
- *Monogamy* is the most common global pattern. In most of Africa and in much of South Asia, the law also permits polygamy.

family a social institution found in all societies that unites people in cooperative groups to care for one another, including any children

kinship a social bond based on common ancestry, marriage, or adoption

marriage a legal relationship, usually involving economic cooperation, sexual activity, and childbearing

extended family a family consisting of parents and children as well as other kin; also known as a *consanguine family*

nuclear family a family composed of one or two parents and their children; also known as a *conjugal family*

endogamy marriage between people of the same social category

exogamy marriage between people of different social categories

monogamy marriage that unites two partners

polygamy marriage that unites a person with two or more spouses

polygyny marriage that unites one man and two or more women

polyandry marriage that unites one woman and two or more men

patrilocality a residential pattern in which a married couple lives with or near the husband's family

matrilocality a residential pattern in which a married couple lives with or near the wife's family

neolocality a residential pattern in which a married couple lives apart from both sets of parents

descent the system by which members of a society trace kinship over generations

patrilineal descent a system tracing kinship through men

matrilineal descent a system tracing kinship through women

bilateral descent a system tracing kinship through both men and women

Theories of the Family

 18.2 Apply sociology's major theories to family life. (pages 514–17)

📖 **Read** the **Document** in **MySocLab**

incest taboo a norm forbidding sexual relations or marriage between certain relatives

Structural-functional theory identifies major family functions that help society operate smoothly:

- socialization of children to help them become well-integrated members of society
- regulation of sexual activity to maintain kinship organization and property rights
- giving children a social identity in terms of race, ethnicity, religion, and social class
- providing material and emotional support to family members

Social-conflict theory and **feminist theory** point to ways in which families perpetuate social inequality.

- Families ensure the continuation of the class structure by passing on wealth to their children.
- Families perpetuate gender roles by establishing men as the heads of the household and by assigning the responsibility for child rearing and housework to women.
- The tendency of people to marry others like themselves supports racial and ethnic hierarchies.

Symbolic-interaction theory explores how family members build emotional bonds in the course of everyday family life.

Social-exchange theory sees courtship and marriage as a process of negotiation in which each person weighs the advantages and disadvantages of a potential partner.

Stages of Family Life

18.3 Analyze changes in the family over the life course. (pages 517–20)

- Arranged marriages are common in preindustrial societies; courtship based on romantic love is central to mate selection in the United States.

homogamy marriage between people with the same social characteristics

536 CHAPTER 18 Families

- Large families are necessary in preindustrial societies because children are a source of needed labor.
- Family size has decreased over time as industrialization increases the costs of raising children.
- As more women choose to go to school or join the labor force, fewer children are born.
- The "family values" debate revolves around who cares for children when both parents work outside the home.
- The departure of children, known as the "empty nest," requires adjustments to family life.
- Many middle-aged couples care for aging parents.
- The final transition in marriage begins with the death of a spouse.

infidelity sexual activity outside one's marriage

U.S. Families: Class, Race, and Gender

(18.4) Explain how class, race, and gender shape family life. (pages 521–24) 👁 **Watch** the **Video** in **MySocLab**

- **Social class** determines a family's financial security and opportunities available to family members.
- Children born into rich families typically have better mental and physical health and go on to achieve more in life than children born into poor families.
- Economic challenges linked to the recent recession have resulted in more people joining households with other relatives.
- **Ethnicity** and **race** can affect a person's experience of family life, although no single generalization fits all families within a particular category.
- Migration of American Indians from reservations to cities creates "fluid households" with changing membership.
- The traditional pattern of extended Latino families is changing as Latinos assimilate into the larger U.S. society.
- African American families face severe economic disadvantages; more than one-third of African American children are growing up poor.
- **Gender** affects family dynamics because husbands dominate in most marriages.
- Research suggests that marriage provides more benefits for men than for women.
- After divorce, men are more likely than women to remarry.

Transitions and Problems in Family Life

(18.5) Analyze the effects of divorce, remarriage, and violence on family life. (pages 525–28)

✳ **Explore** the **Map** in **MySocLab**

family violence emotional, physical, or sexual abuse of one family member by another

- The **divorce** rate is more than three times what it was a century ago; almost half of today's marriages will end in divorce. Researchers point to six causes: Individualism is on the rise; romantic love fades; women are less dependent on men; many of today's marriages are stressful; divorce is socially acceptable; legally, a divorce is easier to get.
- More than half of all people who divorce eventually remarry; **remarriage** creates blended families that include children from previous marriages.
- **Family violence**, which victimizes mostly women and children, is far more common than official records indicate; most adults who abuse family members were themselves abused as children.

Alternative Family Forms

(18.6) Describe the diversity of family life in the United States. (pages 528-31)

👁 **Watch** the **Video** in **MySocLab**

cohabitation the sharing of a household by an unmarried couple

- The proportion of one-parent families—now 32% of all U.S. families—more than doubled during the last generation; single parenthood increases a woman's risk of poverty, which puts children at a disadvantage.
- About half of all people 25 to 44 years of age have cohabited at some point; research shows that children born to cohabiting couples are less likely to live with both biological parents until age 18 than children born to married parents.
- Although only Massachusetts, Connecticut, Vermont, New Hampshire, Iowa, New York, Maine, Maryland, Washington, Delaware, Rhode Island, Minnesota, California, and the District of Columbia allow same-sex marriage, many gay men and lesbians form long-lasting relationships and, increasingly, are becoming parents.
- 27% of households today—up from one in ten in 1950—contain a single person. The number of young women who are single is rising dramatically, a result of women's greater participation in the workforce and lessened dependence on men for material support.
- Almost 50 million people live in extended family households; almost half of young adults under age thirty have lived at home with parents for some period of time, typically because they have not been able to find a job that allows them to live on their own.

19 Religion

 **Listen** to **Chapter 19** in **MySocLab**

LEARNING OBJECTIVES

19.1 Apply sociology's major theories to religion.

19.2 Analyze how religion encourages social change.

19.3 Distinguish among church, sect, and cult.

19.4 Contrast religious patterns in preindustrial and industrial societies.

19.5 Contrast six major world religions.

19.6 Analyze patterns of religiosity in the United States.

19.7 Discuss recent trends in religious life.

the Power of Society

to shape our values and beliefs

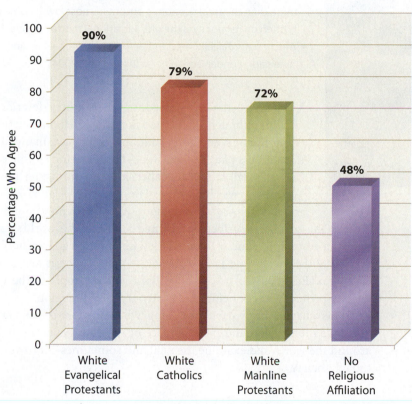

Survey Statement: "I have old-fashioned values about family and marriage."

Percentage Who Agree

- White Evangelical Protestants: 90%
- White Catholics: 79%
- White Mainline Protestants: 72%
- No Religious Affiliation: 48%

Source: Pew Research Center for the People & the Press (2012)

Can a person's religious affiliation (or lack of it) give us any clues about that person's attitudes on family life? In a recent survey of U.S adults (a survey that was limited to white people, to control for race), 90 percent of those who described themselves as evangelical Protestants also said they had "old-fashioned" values about family and marriage. The share of self-described Catholics or mainline Protestants who said the same was lower. And less than half of those who claimed to have no religious affiliation shared these traditional values. Clearly, people's values—whether "old-fashioned" or progressive—are not just a matter of personal choice; they also reflect people's social background, including their religious affiliation.

Chapter Overview

This chapter explores the meaning and importance of religion, a major social institution. Although religion varies around the world, it is always based on the concept of the sacred.

With its many churches, synagogues, temples, and mosques (a recent study put the figure at one house of worship for every 900 people), one country stands out as among the most religious nations on Earth.

- For its entire history, its leaders have proclaimed that God is responsible for its prosperity and liberty.
- Today, four out of five of this nation's people say they "never doubt the existence of God."
- Together, its people give almost $100 billion each year to religious organizations—more than the total economic output of most low-income countries.
- Written on its money is the official national motto, "In God We Trust."
- And in schools, children stand before the national flag and pledge their allegiance to "one nation under God" (Sheler, 2002; Aprill, 2004).

You have already guessed that the country described is the United States. But although the United States is a religious nation, it is also a country of immigrants, and as a result, its people have many different images of God. In countless places of worship—from soaring Gothic cathedrals in New York City to small storefront tabernacles in sprawling Los Angeles—Christians, Muslims, Jews, Buddhists, Hindus, Sikhs, Jains, Zoroastrians, and followers of dozens of other religions can be found (Yang & Ebaugh, 2001; Sheler, 2002). One scholar described the United States as the world's most religiously diverse nation, a country in which Hindu and Jewish children go to school together and Muslims and Buddhists, Sikhs and Jains work in the same factories and offices as Protestants and Catholics (Eck, 2001). And as you will see, many people in the United States today are deeply spiritual without being part of any organized religion.

This chapter begins by explaining what religion is from a sociological point of view. We then explore the changing face of religious belief throughout history as well as around the world and examine the vital and sometimes controversial place of religion in today's society.

Religion: Concepts and Theories

(19.1)   Apply sociology's major theories to religion.

The French sociologist Emile Durkheim stated that religion involves "things that surpass the limits of our knowledge" (1965:62, orig. 1915). We define most objects, events, or experiences as **profane** (from Latin, meaning "outside the temple"), *included as an ordinary element of everyday life*. But we also consider some things **sacred**, *set apart as extraordinary, inspiring awe and reverence*. Setting the sacred apart from the profane is the essence of all religious belief. **Religion**, then, is *a social institution involving beliefs and practices based on recognizing the sacred*.

There is great diversity in matters of faith, and nothing is sacred to everyone on Earth. Although people regard most books as profane, Jews believe that the Torah (the first five books of the Hebrew Bible or Old Testament) is sacred, in the same way that Christians revere the Old and New Testaments of the Bible and Muslims exalt the Qur'an (Koran).

religion a social institution involving beliefs and practices based on recognizing the sacred

Watch in **MySocLab**
Video: *Sociology in Focus: Religion*

But no matter how a community of believers draws religious lines, Durkheim explained, people understand profane things in terms of their everyday usefulness: We log on to the Internet with our laptop or turn a key to start our car. What is sacred we reverently set apart from daily life, giving it a "forbidden" or "holy" aura. Marking the boundary between the sacred and the profane, for example, Muslims remove their shoes before entering a mosque to avoid defiling a sacred place with soles that have touched the profane ground outside.

The sacred is embodied in **ritual**, or *formal, ceremonial behavior.* Holy Communion is the central ritual of Christianity; to the Christian faithful, the wafer and wine consumed during Communion are never treated in a profane way as food but as the sacred symbols of the body and blood of Jesus Christ.

Although rituals take countless forms, all religion deals with what surpasses ordinary or everyday understanding. In Venezuela, these "devil dancers" take part in the annual Corpus Christi Day celebration.

Religion and Sociology

Because religion deals with ideas that transcend everyday experience, neither common sense nor sociology can prove or disprove religious doctrine. Religion is a matter of **faith**, *belief based on personal conviction rather than on scientific evidence.* The New Testament of the Bible defines faith as "the conviction of things not seen" (Hebrews 11:1) and urges Christians to "walk by faith, not by sight" (2 Corinthians 5:7).

Some people with strong faith may be disturbed by the thought of sociologists turning a scientific eye on what they hold sacred. However, a sociological study of religion is no threat to anyone's faith. Sociologists study religion just as they study the family, to understand religious experiences around the world and how religion is tied to other social institutions. They make no judgments that a specific religion is right or wrong in terms of ultimate truth. Rather, scientific sociology takes a more worldly approach, asking why religions take a particular form in one society or another and how religious activity affects society as a whole.

Sociologists apply the major theoretical approaches to the study of religion just as they do to any other topic. Each approach provides distinctive insights into the way religion shapes social life.

faith belief based on personal conviction rather than on

Functions of Religion: Structural-Functional Theory

According to Durkheim (1965, orig. 1915), society has a life and power of its own beyond the life of any individual. In other words, society itself is godlike, shaping the lives of its members and living on beyond them. Practicing religion, people celebrate the awesome power of their society.

No wonder people around the world transform certain everyday objects into sacred symbols of their collective life. Members of technologically simple societies do this with a **totem**, *an object in the natural world collectively defined as sacred.* The totem—perhaps an animal or an elaborate work of art—becomes the centerpiece of ritual, symbolizing the power of society over the individual. In our society, the flag is treated with respect and is not used in a profane way (say, as clothing) or allowed to touch the ground.

Similarly, putting the words "In God We Trust" on U.S. currency (a practice started in the 1860s at the time of the Civil War) or adding the words "under God" to the Pledge of Allegiance (in 1954) symbolizes some widespread beliefs that tie society together. Across the United States, local communities also gain a sense of unity by linking totems to sports teams, from the New England Patriots to the Iowa State

Watch in **MySocLab**
Video: *The Basics: Religion*

totem an object in the natural world collectively defined as sacred

profane included as an ordinary element of everyday life

sacred set apart as extraordinary, inspiring awe and reverence

University Cyclones to the San Francisco 49ers. Durkheim identified three major functions of religion that contribute to the operation of society:

1. **Establishing social cohesion.** Religion unites people through shared symbolism, values, and norms. Religious thought and ritual establish rules of fair play, organizing our social life.

2. **Promoting social control.** Every society uses religious ideas to promote conformity. By defining God as a "judge," many religions encourage people to obey cultural norms. Religion can also be used to back up the power of political systems. In medieval Europe, for example, monarchs claimed to rule by "divine right," so that obedience was seen as doing God's will. Even today, our leaders ask for God's blessing, implying that their efforts are right and just.

3. **Providing meaning and purpose.** Religious belief offers the comforting sense that our brief lives serve some greater purpose. Strengthened by such beliefs, people are less likely to despair in the face of change or even tragedy. For this reason, we mark major life course transitions—including birth, marriage, and death—with religious observances.

EVALUATE In Durkheim's structural-functional analysis, religion represents the collective life of society. The major weakness of this approach is that it downplays religion's dysfunctions, especially the fact that strongly held beliefs can generate social conflict. Terrorists have claimed that God supports their actions, and many nations march to war under the banner of their God. A study of conflict in the world would probably show that religious beliefs have provoked more violence than differences of social class.

CHECK YOUR LEARNING What are Durkheim's three functions of religion for society?

Constructing the Sacred: Symbolic-Interaction Theory

From a symbolic-interaction point of view, religion (like all of society) is socially constructed (although perhaps with divine inspiration). Through various rituals—from daily prayers to annual religious observances such as Easter, Passover, or Ramadan—people sharpen the distinction between the sacred and the profane. Peter Berger (1967:35–36) claims that placing our small, brief lives within some "cosmic frame of reference" gives us the appearance of "ultimate security and permanence."

Marriage is a good example. If two people look on marriage as merely a contract, they can agree to split up whenever they want. Their bond makes far stronger claims on them when it is defined as holy matrimony, which is surely one reason that the divorce rate is lower among people with strong religious beliefs. More generally, whenever human beings face uncertainty or life-threatening situations—such as illness, natural disaster, terrorist attack, or war—we turn to our sacred symbols.

Religion is founded on the concept of the sacred—aspects of our existence that are set apart as extraordinary and demand our submission. Bowing, kneeling, or prostrating oneself are all ways of symbolically surrendering to a higher power. These Filipino Christians seek atonement for their sins in an annual Lenten ritual.

EVALUATE Using the symbolic-interaction approach, we see how people turn to religion to give everyday life sacred meaning. Berger notes that the sacred's ability to give special meaning to society requires that we ignore the fact that it is socially constructed. After all, how much strength could we gain from beliefs if we saw them merely as strategies for coping with tragedy? Also, this micro-level view ignores religion's link to social inequality, to which we turn next.

Inequality and Religion: Social-Conflict Theory

The social-conflict approach highlights religion's support of social inequality. Religion, proclaimed Karl Marx, serves ruling elites by legitimizing the status quo and diverting people's attention from social inequities.

Today, the British monarch is the formal head of the Church of England, illustrating the close ties between religious and political elites. In practical terms, linking the church and the state means that opposing the government amounts to opposing the church and, by implication, opposing God as well. Religion also encourages people to accept the social problems of this world while they look hopefully to a "better world to come." In a well-known statement, Marx dismissed religion as preventing revolutionary change; religion is, in his words, "the sigh of the oppressed creature, the sentiment of a heartless world, and the soul of soulless conditions. It is the opium of the people" (1964:27, orig. 1848).

Gender and Religion: Feminist Theory

Feminist theory explains that religion and social inequality are also linked through gender because virtually all the world's major religions are patriarchal. For example, the Qur'an (Koran), the sacred text of Islam, gives men social dominance over women by defining gender roles: "Men are in charge of women.... Hence good women are obedient.... As for those whose rebelliousness you fear, admonish them, banish them from your bed, and scourge them" (Qur'an 4:34, quoted in Kaufman, 1976:163).

Christianity, the major religion of the Western world, also supports patriarchy. Many Christians revere Mary, the mother of Jesus, but the New Testament also includes the following passages:

A man... is the image and glory of God; but woman is the glory of man. For man was not made from woman, but woman from man. Neither was man created for woman, but woman for man. (1 Corinthians 11:7–9)

As in all the churches of the saints, the women should keep silence in the churches. For they are not permitted to speak, but should be subordinate, as even the law says. If there is anything they desire to know, let them ask their husbands at home. For it is shameful for a woman to speak in church. (1 Corinthians 14:33–35)

Wives, be subject to your husbands, as to the Lord. For the husband is the head of the wife as Christ is the head of the church.... As the church is subject to Christ, so let wives also be subject in everything to their husbands. (Ephesians 5:22–24)

Judaism has also traditionally supported patriarchy. Male Orthodox Jews say the following words in daily prayer:

Blessed art thou, O Lord our God, King of the
   Universe, that I was not born a gentile.
Blessed art thou, O Lord our God, King of the
   Universe, that I was not born a slave.
Blessed art thou, O Lord our God, King of the
   Universe, that I was not born a woman.

Today, Islam and the Roman Catholic Church ban women from the priesthood, as do about half of Protestant denominations. But a growing number of Protestant religious organizations do ordain

Patriarchy is a characteristic of all the world's major religions, including Christianity, Judaism, and Islam. Male dominance can be seen in restrictions that limit religious leadership to men and also in regulations that prohibit women from worshiping alongside men.

Religion			
	Structural-Functional Theory	**Symbolic-Interaction Theory**	**Social-Conflict and Feminist Theories**
What is the level of analysis?	Macro-level	Micro-level	Macro-level
What is the importance of religion for society?	Religion performs vital tasks, including uniting people and controlling behavior. Religion gives life meaning and purpose.	Religion strengthens marriage by giving it (and family life) sacred meaning. People often turn to sacred symbols for comfort when facing danger and uncertainty.	Religion supports social inequality by claiming that the social order is just. Organized religion supports the domination of women by men. Religion turns attention from problems in this world to a "better world to come."

women, who now represent about 18 percent of U.S. clergy. Orthodox Judaism upholds the traditional prohibition against women serving as rabbis, but the Reform, Conservative, and Reconstructionist branches of Judaism look to both men and women as spiritual leaders. Across the United States, the proportion of women in seminaries has never been higher (now roughly one-third), which is more evidence of a trend toward greater equality (Association of Theological Schools, 2012; Hartford Institute for Religious Research, 2012; U.S. Department of Labor, 2012).

EVALUATE Social-conflict and feminist theories emphasize the power of religion to support social inequality. Yet religion also promotes change toward equality. For example, nineteenth-century religious groups in the United States played an important part in the movement to abolish slavery. In the 1950s and 1960s, religious organizations and their leaders formed the core of the civil rights movement. In the 1960s and 1970s, many clergy opposed the Vietnam War, and today many support any number of progressive causes such as feminism and gay rights.

CHECK YOUR LEARNING How does religion help maintain class inequality and gender stratification?

The Applying Theory table summarizes the major theoretical approaches to understanding religion.

Religion and Social Change

19.2 Analyze how religion encourages social change.

Religion can be the conservative force portrayed by Karl Marx. But at some points in history, as Max Weber (1958, orig. 1904–05) explained, religion has promoted dramatic social change.

Max Weber: Protestantism and Capitalism

Weber argued that particular religious ideas set into motion a wave of change that brought about the Industrial Revolution in Western Europe. The rise of industrial capitalism was encouraged by Calvinism, a movement within the Protestant Reformation.

As Chapter 4 ("Society") explains in detail, John Calvin (1509–1564) was a leader in the Reformation who preached the doctrine of *predestination*. According to Calvin, an all-powerful and all-knowing God had selected some people for salvation but condemned most to eternal damnation. Each individual's fate, sealed before birth and known only to God, was either eternal glory or endless hellfire.

Driven by anxiety over their fate, Calvinists understandably looked for signs of God's favor in this world and came to see prosperity as a sign of divine blessing. Religious conviction and a rigid devotion to duty led Calvinists to work hard, and many amassed great wealth. But money was not for selfish spending or even for sharing with the poor, whose plight they saw as a mark of God's rejection. As agents of God's work on Earth, Calvinists believed that they best fulfilled their "calling" by reinvesting profits and achieving ever-greater success in the process.

All the while, Calvinists practiced self-denial by living thrifty lives. In addition, they eagerly adopted technological advances that promised to increase their workplace effectiveness. Together, these traits laid the groundwork for the rise of industrial capitalism. In time, the religious fervor that motivated early Calvinists weakened, leaving a profane "Protestant work ethic." To Max Weber, industrial capitalism itself amounted to a "disenchanted" religion, further showing the power of religion to alter the shape of society (Berger, 2009).

Liberation Theology

Historically, Christianity has reached out to oppressed people, urging all to a stronger faith in a better life to come. In recent decades, however, some church leaders and theologians have taken a decidedly political approach and endorsed **liberation theology**, *the combining of Christian principles with political activism, often Marxist in character.*

This social movement started in the 1960s in Latin America's Roman Catholic Church. Today, Christian activists continue to help people in poor nations liberate themselves from abysmal poverty. Their message is simple: Social oppression runs counter to Christian morality, so as a matter of faith and justice, Christians must promote greater social equality.

Pope Francis has expressed support for the world's poor and also criticized the global economic system for not doing enough to assist people in need. Perhaps the current pope will steer a different course than Pope Benedict XVI and Pope John Paul II, who condemned liberation theology for distorting traditional church doctrine with left-wing politics. In any case, the liberation theology movement has gained strength in the poorest countries of Latin America, where many people's Christian faith drives them to improve conditions for the poor and oppressed (Neuhouser, 1989; J. E. Williams, 2002).

liberation theology the combining of Christian principles with political activism, often Marxist in character

Types of Religious Organizations

19.3 Distinguish among church, sect, and cult.

Sociologists categorize the hundreds of different religious organizations found in the United States along a continuum, with *churches* at one end and *sects* at the other, as shown in Figure 19–1. We can describe any actual religious organization in relation to these two ideal types by locating it on the church–sect continuum.

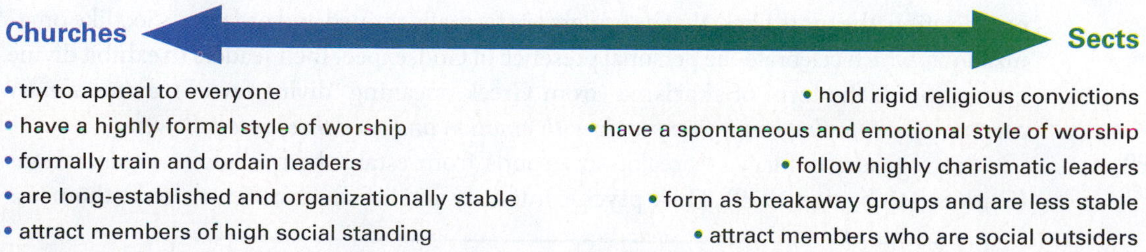

Churches ⟵⟶ **Sects**

- try to appeal to everyone
- have a highly formal style of worship
- formally train and ordain leaders
- are long-established and organizationally stable
- attract members of high social standing

- hold rigid religious convictions
- have a spontaneous and emotional style of worship
- follow highly charismatic leaders
- form as breakaway groups and are less stable
- attract members who are social outsiders

FIGURE 19–1 Church—Sect Continuum

Churches and sects are two opposing ideal types of religious organization. Any real-life religious organization will fall somewhere on the continuum between these two concepts.

Church

Drawing on the ideas of his teacher Max Weber, Ernst Troeltsch (1931) defined a **church** as *a type of religious organization that is well integrated into the larger society.* Churchlike organizations usually persist for centuries and include generations of the same families. Churches have well-established rules and regulations and expect leaders to be formally trained and ordained.

Though concerned with the sacred, a church accepts the ways of the profane world. Church members think of God in intellectual terms (say, as a force for good) and favor abstract moral standards ("Do unto others as you would have them do unto you") over specific rules for day-to-day living. By teaching morality in safely abstract terms, church leaders avoid social controversy. For example, many congregations celebrate the unity of all peoples but say little about their own lack of racial diversity. By downplaying this type of conflict, a church makes peace with the status quo (Troeltsch, 1931).

A church may operate with or apart from the state. As its name implies, a **state church** is *a church formally allied with the state.* State churches have existed throughout human history. For centuries, Roman Catholicism was the official religion of the Roman Empire, and Confucianism was the official religion of China until early in the twentieth century. Today, the Anglican Church is the official church of England, and Islam is the official religion of Pakistan and Iran. State churches count everyone in the society as a member, which sharply limits tolerance of religious differences.

A **denomination**, by contrast, is *a church, independent of the state, that recognizes religious pluralism.* Denominations exist in nations, including the United States, that formally separate church and state. This country has dozens of Christian denominations—including Catholics, Baptists, Episcopalians, Presbyterians, and Lutherans—as well as various categories of Judaism, Islam, and other traditions. Although members of any denomination hold to their own doctrine, they recognize the right of others to have different beliefs.

Sect

The second general religious form is the **sect**, *a type of religious organization that stands apart from the larger society.* Sect members have rigid religious convictions and deny the beliefs of others. Compared to churches, which try to appeal to everyone (the term *catholic* also means "universal"), a sect forms an exclusive group. To members of a sect, religion is not so much one aspect of life as it is a firm plan for living. In extreme cases, members of a sect withdraw completely from society in order to practice their religion without interference. The Amish community is one example of a North American sect that isolates itself. Because our culture generally considers religious tolerance a virtue, members of sects are sometimes accused of being narrow-minded in insisting that they alone follow the true religion (Kraybill, 1994; P. W. Williams, 2002).

In organizational terms, sects are less formal than churches. Sect members may be highly spontaneous and emotional in worship, compared to members of churches, who tend to listen passively to their leaders. Sects also reject the intellectualized religion of churches, stressing instead the personal experience of divine power. Rodney Stark (1985:314) contrasts a church's vision of a distant God ("Our Father, who art in Heaven") with a sect's more immediate God ("Lord, bless this poor sinner kneeling before you now").

Churches and sects also have different patterns of leadership—the more churchlike an organization, the more likely that its leaders are formally trained and ordained. Sectlike organizations, which celebrate the personal presence of God, expect their leaders to exhibit divine inspiration in the form of **charisma** (from Greek, meaning "divine favor"), *extraordinary personal qualities that can infuse people with emotion and turn them into followers.*

Sects generally form as breakaway groups from established religious organizations (Stark & Bainbridge, 1979). Their psychic intensity and informal structure make them less

state church a church formally allied with the state

denomination a church, independent of the state, that recognizes religious pluralism

charisma extraordinary personal qualities that can infuse people with emotion and turn them into followers

church a religious organization that is well integrated into the larger society

sect a religious organization that stands apart from the larger society

cult a religious organization that is largely outside a society's cultural traditions

In global perspective, the range of religious activity is truly astonishing. This woman in Ghana, celebrating the Kokuzahn voodoo festival, throws sand into her open eyes and is not harmed. What religious practices common in the United States might seem astonishing to people living in other countries?

stable than churches, and many sects blossom only to disappear soon after. The sects that do endure typically become more like churches, with declining emphasis on charismatic leadership as they become more bureaucratic.

To sustain their membership, many sects actively recruit, or *proselytize*, new members. Sects highly value the experience of *conversion*, a personal transformation or religious rebirth. For example, members of Jehovah's Witnesses go door-to-door to share their faith with others with the goal of attracting new members.

Finally, churches and sects differ in their social composition. Because they are more closely tied to the world, well-established churches tend to include people of high social standing. Sects attract more disadvantaged people. A sect's openness to new members and its promise of salvation and personal fulfillment appeal to people who feel they are social outsiders.

Cult

A **cult** is *a religious organization that is largely outside a society's cultural traditions.* Most sects spin off from conventional religious organizations. However, a cult typically forms around a highly charismatic leader who offers a compelling message about a new and very different way of life. As many as 5,000 cults exist in the United States (Lottick, 2005).

Because some cult principles or practices are unconventional, the popular view is that they are deviant or even evil. The suicides of thirty-nine members of California's Heaven's Gate cult in 1997—people who claimed that dying was a doorway to a higher existence, perhaps in the company of aliens from outer space—confirmed the negative image the public holds of most cults. In short, calling any religious community a "cult" amounts to dismissing its members as crazy (Shupe, 1995; Gleick, 1997).

This charge is unfair because there is nothing basically wrong with this kind of religious organization. Many longstanding religions—Christianity, Islam, and Judaism included—began as cults. Of course, few cults exist for very long. One reason is that they are even more at odds with the larger society than sects. Many cults demand that members not only accept their doctrine but also adopt a radically new lifestyle. This is why people sometimes accuse cults of brainwashing their members, although research suggests that most people who join cults experience no psychological harm (Kilbourne, 1983; P. W. Williams, 2002).

Religion in History

19.4 Contrast religious patterns in preindustrial and industrial societies.

animism the belief that elements of the natural world are conscious life forms that affect humanity

Like other social institutions, religion shows marked variation according to time and place. Let us look at several ways in which religion has changed over the course of history.

Religion in Preindustrial Societies

Early hunters and gatherers practiced **animism** (from a Latin word meaning "breath of life"), *the belief that elements of the natural world are conscious life forms that affect humanity.* Animists view forests, oceans, mountains, and even the wind as spiritual forces. Many Native American societies are animistic, which explains their reverence for the natural environment.

Belief in a single divine power responsible for creating the world began with pastoral and horticultural societies, which first appeared 10,000 to 12,000 years ago. The conception of God as a "shepherd" arose because Christianity, Judaism, and Islam all began among pastoral peoples.

Religion becomes more important in agrarian societies, which develop a specialized priesthood in charge of religious rituals and organizations. The huge cathedrals that dominated the towns of medieval Europe—many of which remain standing today—are evidence of the central role of religion in the social life of medieval agrarian society.

Religion in Industrial Societies

The Industrial Revolution introduced a growing emphasis on science. More and more, people looked to doctors and scientists for the knowledge and comfort they used to get from priests. But as Durkheim (1965, orig. 1915) predicted almost a century ago, religion persists in industrial societies because science is powerless to address issues of ultimate meaning in human life. In other words, learning *how* the world works is a matter for scientists, but *why* we and the rest of the universe exist at all is a question of faith. In addition, as already noted, the United States stands out as a modern society in which religion has remained especially strong (McClay, 2007; Greeley, 2008).

Animism is widespread in traditional societies, whose members live respectfully within the natural world on which they depend for their survival. Animists see a divine presence not just in themselves but also in everything around them. Their example has inspired "New Age" spirituality, described on pages 561–62.

World Religions

19.5 Contrast six major world religions.

The diversity of religions in the world is almost as wide-ranging as the diversity of culture itself. Many of the thousands of different religions are found in just one place and have few followers. But there are a number of *world religions,* with millions of adherents. We shall briefly examine six world religions, which together claim almost 5 billion believers—just about three-fourths of humanity.

Christianity

Christianity is the most widespread religion with 2.3 billion followers, one-third of the world's people. Most Christians live in Europe or the Americas; more than 80 percent of the people in the United States and Canada identify with Christianity. As shown in Global Map 19–1 on page 549, people who think of themselves as Christian represent a large share of the population in many

Window on the World

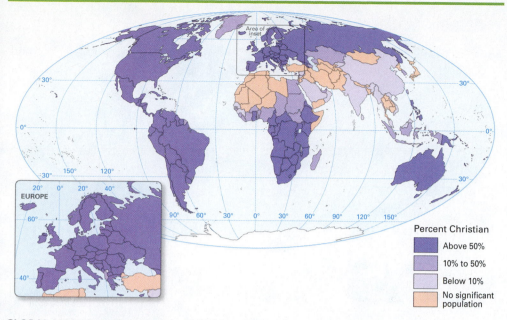

GLOBAL MAP 19–1 Christianity in Global Perspective

Christianity is the dominant religion of Western Europe and became the dominant religion of the Americas and much of southern Africa and Oceania. Can you explain this pattern?

Source: Association of Religion Data Archives (2012).

Percent Christian

- Above 50%
- 10% to 50%
- Below 10%
- No significant population

world regions, with the notable exceptions of northern Africa and Asia. European colonization spread Christianity throughout much of the world over the past 500 years. Its dominance in the West is shown by the fact that our calendar numbers years from the birth of Jesus Christ.

As noted earlier, Christianity began as a cult, drawing elements from Judaism, a much older religion. Like many cults, Christianity was built on the personal charisma of a leader, Jesus of Nazareth, who preached a message of personal salvation. Jesus did not directly challenge the political power of his day, the Roman Empire, telling his followers to "render therefore to Caesar the things that are Caesar's" (Matthew 22:21). But his message was a revolutionary one all the same, promising that faith and love would triumph over sin and death.

Christianity is one example of **monotheism**, *belief in a single divine power*. This new religion was quite different from the Roman Empire's traditional **polytheism**, *belief in many gods*. Yet Christianity views the Supreme Being as a sacred Trinity: God the Creator; Jesus Christ, Son of God and Redeemer; and the Holy Spirit, a Christian's personal experience of God's presence.

monotheism belief in a single divine power

polytheism belief in many gods

The claim that Jesus was divine rests on accounts of his final days on Earth. Brought to trial as a threat to established political leaders, Jesus was tried in Jerusalem and sentenced to death by crucifixion, a common means of execution at the time. This explains why the cross became a sacred Christian symbol. According to Christian belief, three days after his execution, Jesus rose from the dead, revealing that he was the Son of God.

Jesus' followers, especially his twelve closest associates, known as the apostles, spread Christianity throughout the Mediterranean region. At first, the Roman Empire persecuted Christians. But by the fourth century, the empire had adopted Christianity as a state church, the official religion of what became known as the Holy Roman Empire.

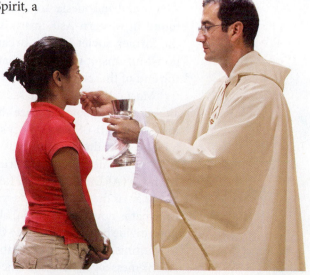

Although it began as a cult, Christianity's 2.3 billion followers make it now the most widespread of the world's religions.

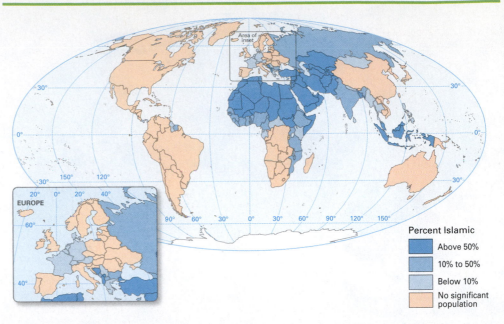

GLOBAL MAP 19–2 Islam in Global Perspective

Islam is the dominant religion of the Middle East, but most of the world's Muslims live in North Africa and Southeast Asia.

Source: Pew Research Center (2011) and Association of Religion Data Archives (2012).

Christianity took various forms, including the Roman Catholic Church and the Eastern Orthodox Church, based in Constantinople (now Istanbul, Turkey). Toward the end of the Middle Ages, the Protestant Reformation in Europe gave rise to hundreds of new denominations. In the United States, dozens of these denominations—the Baptists and Methodists are the two largest—command sizable followings (Kaufman, 1976; Jacquet & Jones, 1991; Hartford Institute for Religious Research, 2012).

Islam

Islam has about 1.6 billion followers, which is almost one-fourth of humanity. Followers of Islam are called Muslims. A majority of people in the Middle East are Muslims, so we tend to associate Islam with Arabs in that region of the world. But most of the world's Muslims live elsewhere: Global Map 19–2 shows that most people in northern Africa and Indonesia are Muslims. In addition, large concentrations of Muslims are found in western Asia in Pakistan, India, Bangladesh, and the southern republics of the former Soviet Union. Because Muslims have a birthrate that is twice the rate for non-Muslims, it is possible that Islam could become the world's dominant religion by the end of this century.

Most estimates put the Muslim population of the United States at about 2.7 million, although a few sources place the number a bit higher. In any case, Islam is clearly an important part of our country's religious life. The Muslim population is not only large but also quite diverse. It includes Arab Americans and others with Middle Eastern ancestry, Asian Americans, and African Americans (Eck, 2001; Association of Religion Data Archives (ARDA), 2012; Pew Research Center, 2012).

Islam is the word of God as revealed to Muhammad, who was born in the city of Mecca (in what is now Saudi Arabia) about the year 570. To Muslims, Muhammad is a prophet, not a divine being as Jesus is to Christians. The text of the Qur'an (Koran), which is sacred to Muslims, is the word of Allah (Arabic for "God") as transmitted through Muhammad, Allah's messenger. In Arabic, the word *islam* means both "submission" and "peace," and the Qur'an urges submission to Allah as the path to inner peace. Muslims express this personal devotion in a ritual of prayers five times each day.

After the death of Muhammad, Islam spread rapidly. Although divisions arose among Muslims, all accept the Five Pillars of Islam: (1) recognizing Allah as the one, true God and Muhammad as God's messenger; (2) ritual prayer; (3) giving alms to the poor; (4) fasting during the month of Ramadan; and (5) making a pilgrimage at least once in one's life to the Sacred House of Allah in Mecca (Weeks, 1988; El-Attar, 1991). Like Christianity, Islam holds people accountable to God for their deeds on Earth. Those who live obediently will be rewarded in heaven, and evildoers will suffer unending punishment.

Muslims are also required to defend their faith, which has led to calls for holy wars against unbelievers (in roughly the same way that medieval Christians fought in the Crusades). Recent decades have witnessed a rise in militancy and anti-Western feeling in much of the Muslim world, where many people see the United States as both militarily threatening and representing a way of life that they view as materialistic and immoral. Many Westerners—who typically know little about Islam and often stereotype all Muslims on the basis of the terrorist actions of a few—respond with confusion and sometimes hostility (Eck, 2001; Ryan, 2001).

Many people in the United States also view Muslim women as socially oppressed. There are differences among Muslim nations in terms of rights given to women: Tunisia allows women far more opportunities than, say, Saudi Arabia, which does not allow women to vote or even drive a car. It is true that many Muslim women lack some of the personal freedoms enjoyed by Muslim men. Yet many—perhaps even most—accept the mandates of their religion and find security in a system that guides the behavior of both women and men (Peterson, 1996). Defenders of Islam also point out that patriarchy was well established in the Middle East long before the birth of Muhammad and that Islam actually improved the social position of women by requiring husbands to deal justly with their wives. For example, Islam permits a man to have up to four wives, but it requires men to have only one wife if having more would cause him to treat any woman unjustly (Qur'an, "The Women," v. 3).

Many religions promote literacy because they demand that followers study sacred texts. As part of their upbringing, most Muslim parents teach their children lessons from the Qur'an; later, the children will do the same for a new generation of believers.

Judaism

In terms of numbers, Judaism's 15 million followers worldwide make it something less than a world religion. Jews make up a majority of the population in only one country—Israel. But Judaism has special importance to the United States because the largest concentration of Jews (5.2 million) is found in this country (with another 500,000 in Canada).

Jews look to the past as a source of guidance in the present and for the future. Judaism has deep historical roots that extend 4,000 years before the birth of Christ to the ancient societies of Mesopotamia. At this time, Jews were animistic, but this belief changed after Jacob—grandson of Abraham, the earliest great ancestor—led his people to Egypt.

Jews survived centuries of slavery in Egypt. In the thirteenth century B.C.E., Moses, the adopted son of an Egyptian princess, was called by God to lead the Jews from bondage. This exodus (a word with Latin and Greek roots mean "marching out") from Egypt is remembered by Jews today in the annual ritual of Passover. After their liberation, the Jews became monotheistic, recognizing a single, all-powerful God.

A distinctive concept of Judaism is the *covenant*, a special relationship with God by which the Jews became God's "chosen people." The covenant implies a duty to observe God's law, especially the Ten Commandments as revealed to Moses on Mount Sinai. Jews regard the Old Testament of the Bible as both a record of their history and a statement of the obligations of Jewish life. Of special importance are the Bible's first five books (Genesis, Exodus, Leviticus, Numbers, and Deuteronomy), called the *Torah* (a word meaning "teaching" and "law"). In contrast to Christianity's central concern with personal salvation, Judaism emphasizes moral behavior in this world.

The Jewish people share a cultural history of oppression as a result of prejudice and discrimination. A collective memory of centuries of slavery in Egypt, conquest by Rome, and persecution in Europe has shaped the Jewish identity. It was Jews in Italy who first lived in an urban ghetto (this word comes from the Italian *borghetto*, meaning "settlement outside the city walls"), and this residential segregation soon spread to other parts of Europe.

Jewish immigration to the United States began in the mid-1600s. The early immigrants who prospered were assimilated into largely Christian communities. But as great numbers entered the country at the end of the nineteenth century, prejudice and discrimination against Jews—commonly termed *anti-Semitism*—increased. Before and during World War II, anti-Semitism reached a vicious peak as the Nazi regime in Germany systematically annihilated 6 million Jews.

Today, in the United States, Judaism has four main denominations: Orthodox, Reform, Conservative, and Reconstructionist. In estimating the size of each denomination, keep in mind that not all people who were born to Jewish parents identify with a specific Jewish denomination, and some do not self-identify as being Jewish at all. Orthodox Jews, who number at least 500,000 people in the United States, strictly observe traditional beliefs and practices, wear traditional dress, physically separate men and women at religious services, and eat only kosher foods (that is, food prepared precisely as prescribed in the Torah). Such traditional practices set off Orthodox Jews in the United States from the larger society, making them the most sectlike denomination.

In the mid-nineteenth century, many Jews wanted to feel a greater part of the larger society, which led to the formation of more churchlike Reform Judaism, which now includes between 1.5 and 2 million people in this country. A third segment, Conservative Judaism, with between 1.5 and 2 million U.S. adherents, has established a middle ground between the other two denominations. Finally, Reconstructionist Judaism, with several hundred thousand followers, is the most recent and most liberal denomination, with a humanistic focus on the importance of secular Jewish culture (Smith, 2005; Grim & Masci, 2008; Kosmin, 2009; Association of Religion Data Archives, 2012; Pew Research Center, Forum on Religion & Public Life, 2012).

The social standing of Jews in the United States is well above average, with high levels of education and income that is well above average. Still, many Jews in this country are concerned about the future of their religion because only half the children growing up in Jewish households are learning Jewish culture and ritual and perhaps half a million adults of Jewish ancestry now prefer to describe themselves as having "no religion." In addition, more than half of young people of Jewish background marry non-Jews. Others are more optimistic, pointing out that many secular Jews who claim no belief in God continue to attend synagogue, suggesting that a rising number of "mixed marriages" may attract new people to Judaism (Keister, 2003; Goldscheider, 2004; Kosmin, 2009; Winston, 2011).

Hinduism

Hinduism is the oldest of all the world religions, originating in the Indus River valley about 4,500 years ago. Today, there are about 950 million Hindus, which is almost 14 percent of the world's people. Global Map 19–3 on page 553 shows that Hinduism remains an Eastern religion, mostly practiced in India and Pakistan but with a significant presence in southern Africa and Indonesia.

Over the centuries, Hinduism and the culture of India have blended so that now one is not easily described apart from the other (although India also has a sizable Muslim population). This connection also explains why Hinduism, unlike Christianity, Islam, and Judaism, has not diffused widely to other nations. But with 1.5 million followers in the United States, Hinduism is an important part of our country's cultural diversity.

Hinduism differs from most other religions in that it is not linked to the life of any single person. In addition, Hinduism envisions God as a universal moral force rather

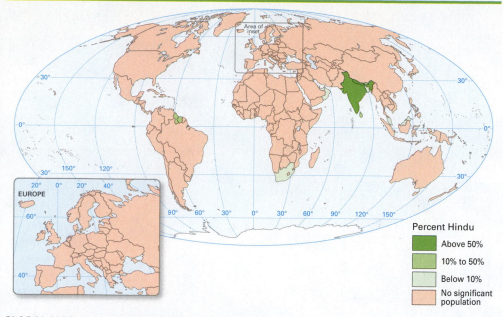

GLOBAL MAP 19–3 Hinduism in Global Perspective

Hinduism is closely linked to the culture of India.

Source: Association of Religion Data Archives (2012).

Percent Hindu

- Above 50%
- 10% to 50%
- Below 10%
- No significant population

than a specific entity. For this reason, Hinduism—like other Eastern religions, as you will see shortly—is sometimes described as an "ethical religion." Hindu beliefs and practices vary widely, but all Hindus believe that they have moral responsibilities, called *dharma.* Dharma, for example, calls people to observe the traditional caste system, described in Chapter 10 ("Social Stratification").

Another Hindu principle, *karma,* involves a belief in the spiritual progress of the human soul. To a Hindu, each action has spiritual consequences, and proper living results in moral development. Karma works through *reincarnation,* a cycle of death and rebirth by which a person is born into a spiritual state corresponding to the moral quality of a previous life. Unlike Christianity and Islam, Hinduism recognizes no ultimate judgment at the hands of a supreme god. But in the ongoing cycle of rebirth, it may be said that people get what they deserve. For those who reach *moksha,* the state of spiritual perfection, the soul has no further need to be reborn.

The case of Hinduism shows that not all religions can be neatly labeled as monotheistic or polytheistic. Hinduism is monotheistic insofar as it views the universe as a single moral system; yet Hindus see this moral force at work in every element of nature. Hindus connect to this moral force through their private meditation and rituals, which vary from village to village across the vast nation of India. Many also participate in public events, such as the *Kumbh Mela,* which every twelve years brings some 20 million pilgrims to bathe in the purifying waters of the sacred Ganges River.

Hinduism is not well understood by most people in the United States, although elements of Hindu thought have entered the New Age movement, discussed later in this chapter. But 2.9 million people in this country claim Asian Indian ancestry, and the number of immigrants from India is rising, which is making Hinduism more and more important in the United States (Larson, 2000; Eck, 2001; U.S. Census Bureau, 2012).

Buddhism

Twenty-five hundred years ago, the rich culture of India gave rise to Buddhism. Today, some 463 million people, or 7 percent of humanity, are Buddhists, and almost all live in Asia. As shown in Global Map 19–4 on page 554, Buddhists are a majority of the population in

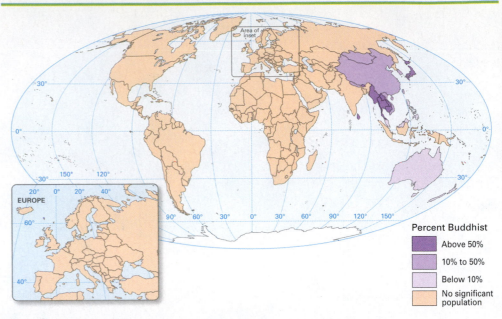

GLOBAL MAP 19–4 Buddhism in Global Perspective

Buddhists represent a large part of the populations of most Asian nations.

Source: Association of Religion Data Archives (2012).

Sri Lanka, Bhutan, Myanmar (Burma), Thailand, Cambodia, Laos, and Japan. Buddhism is also widespread in Vietnam, South Korea, and the People's Republic of China. Buddhism has much in common with Hinduism: It recognizes no god of judgment, sees each daily action as having spiritual consequences, and believes in reincarnation. But like Christianity, Buddhism has origins in the life of one person.

Siddhartha Gautama was born to a high-caste family in Nepal in 563 B.C.E. Even as a young man, he was deeply spiritual. At the age of twenty-nine, he experienced a personal transformation, which led him to years of travel and meditation. By the end of this journey, he achieved what Buddhists describe as *bodhi,* or enlightenment. By gaining an understanding of the essence of life, Gautama became the Buddha.

Drawn by his personal charisma, followers spread the Buddha's teachings—the *dhamma*—across India. In the third century B.C.E., India's ruler became a Buddhist and sent missionaries throughout Asia, transforming Buddhism into a world religion.

Buddhists believe that much of life in this world involves suffering. This idea is rooted in the Buddha's own travels in a very poor society. But, the Buddha claimed, the solution to suffering is not seeking worldly wealth and power. On the contrary, a concern with worldly things is actually the problem, because it holds back spiritual development. Instead, the Buddha taught that we must use meditation to transcend the world—that is, to move beyond selfish concerns and material desires. Only by quieting the mind can people connect with the power of the larger universe—the goal described as *nirvana,* a state of spiritual enlightenment and peace (Thomas, 1975; Van Biema, 1997; Eck, 2001).

Confucianism

From about 200 B.C.E. until the beginning of the twentieth century, Confucianism was a state church—the official religion of China. After the 1949 revolution, the Communist government of the new People's Republic of China repressed all religious expression. But even today, hundreds of millions of Chinese are still influenced by Confucianism. China is still home to Confucian thought, although Chinese immigration has spread this religion to other nations in Southeast Asia. Only a small number of people who follow Confucius live in North America.

Confucius, whose Chinese name was K'ung Fu-tzu, lived between 551 and 479 B.C.E. Like the Buddha, Confucius was deeply moved by people's suffering. The Buddha's response was sectlike—a spiritual withdrawal from the world. Confucius took a more churchlike approach, instructing his followers to engage the world according to a code of moral conduct. In the same way that Hinduism became part of the Indian way of life, Confucianism became linked to the traditional culture of China.

A central idea of Confucianism is *jen*, meaning "humaneness." In practice, this means that we must always place moral principle above our self-interest, looking to tradition for guidance in how to live. In the family, Confucius taught, each of us must be loyal and considerate. For their part, families must remember their duties toward the larger community. In this model, layers of moral obligation unite society as a whole.

Of all world religions, Confucianism stands out as lacking a clear sense of the sacred. Perhaps Durkheim would have said that Confucianism is the celebration of the sacred character of society itself. Others might call Confucianism less a religion than a model of disciplined living. However you look at it, Confucianism shares with religion a body of beliefs and practices through which its followers seek moral goodness and social harmony (Schmidt, 1980; McGuire, 1987; Ellwood, 2000).

Religion: East and West

You may already have noticed two general differences between the belief systems of Eastern and Western societies. First, religions that arose in the West (Christianity, Islam, Judaism) have a clear focus on God as a distinct entity. Eastern religions (Hinduism, Buddhism, Confucianism), however, see divine power in everything, so that these belief systems make little distinction between the sacred and the profane and seem more like ethical codes for living.

Second, followers of Western religions form congregations, worshiping together in a special place at a regular time. Followers of Eastern religions, by contrast, express their religion anywhere and everywhere in their daily lives. Religious temples do exist, but they are used by individuals as part of their daily routines rather than by groups according to a rigid schedule. This is why visitors to a country like Japan are as likely to find temples there filled with tourists as with worshipers.

Despite these two differences, however, all religions have a common element: a call to move beyond selfish, everyday concerns in pursuit of a higher moral purpose. Religions may take different paths to this goal, but they all encourage a spiritual sense that there is more to life than what we see around us.

Religion in the United States

(19.6) Analyze patterns of religiosity in the United States.

Compared to almost every other high-income nation in the world, the United States is a religious country (World Values Survey, 2010). As Figure 19–2 shows, more than 70 percent of U.S. adults claim that religion is important in their life, and this share is higher than in most other high-income countries.

That said, scholars debate exactly how religious we are. Some claim that religion remains central to our way of life, but others conclude that a decline of the traditional family and the growing importance of science are weakening religious faith (Greeley, 2008; Smith, 2012).

Global Snapshot

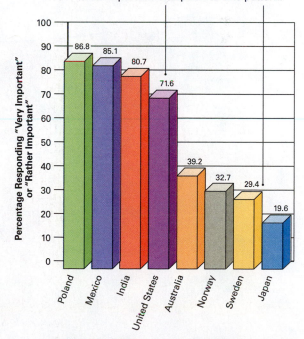

• In general, people in higher-income countries are less religious than those in lower-income nations. The U.S. population is an important exception to this pattern.

Survey Question: "How important is religion in your life?"

FIGURE 19–2 Religiosity in Global Perspective

Religion is stronger in the United States than in many other nations.

Source: World Values Survey (2010).

TABLE 19–1 Religious Identification in the United States, 2012

Religion	Share of Respondents Indicating a Preference
Protestant denominations	**50.7%**
Baptist	17.5
Methodist	6.4
Lutheran	4.5
Presbyterian	1.8
Episcopalian	1.8
All others or no denomination	18.6
Catholic	**24.6**
Jewish	**1.5**
Other or no answer	**1.8**
No religious preference	**21.4**

Source: *General Social Surveys, 1972–2012: Cumulative Codebook* (Chicago: National Opinion Research Center, March 2013).

Religious Affiliation

National surveys show that about 80 percent of U.S. adults identify with a religion (NORC, 2013:261; Gallup, 2013; Pew Research Center, Forum on Religion & Public Life, 2013). Table 19–1 presents the results of the most recent survey of denominational affiliation showing that about half of U.S. adults say they are Protestants, one-fourth Catholics, and 1.5 percent Jews. Large numbers of people follow dozens of other religions, from animism to Zen Buddhism, making our society the most religiously diverse on Earth (Eck, 2001). This remarkable religious diversity results from a constitutional ban on government-sponsored religion and from our historically high numbers of immigrants from all over the world.

About 90 percent of U.S. adults report that they had at least some formal religious instruction when growing up, and 60 percent say they now belong to a religious organization (NORC, 2013:601, 2477). National Map 19–1 shows the share of people who claim to belong to any church across the United States.

National Map 19–2 on page 557 goes a step further, showing that the religion most people identify with varies by region. New England and the Southwest are mostly Catholic, the South is mostly Baptist, and Lutherans predominate in the northern Plains states. In and around Utah, most people belong to the Church of Jesus Christ of Latter-Day Saints, whose followers are more commonly known as Mormons.

Seeing Ourselves

Explore patterns of religious membership in your local community and in counties across the United States in **MySocLab**

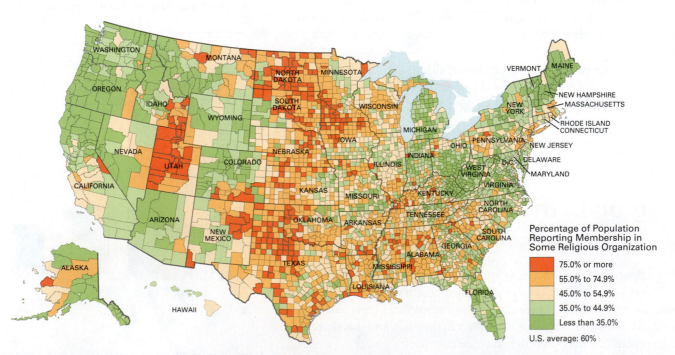

Percentage of Population Reporting Membership in Some Religious Organization

- 75.0% or more
- 55.0% to 74.9%
- 45.0% to 54.9%
- 35.0% to 44.9%
- Less than 35.0%

U.S. average: 60%

NATIONAL MAP 19–1 Religious Membership across the United States

In general, people in the United States are more religious than people in other high-income nations. Yet membership in a religious organization is more common in some parts of the country than in others. What pattern do you see in the map? Can you explain the pattern?

Source: Association of Statisticians of American Religious Bodies (2012).

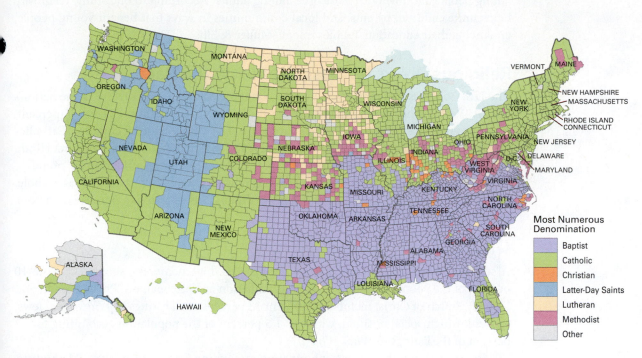

NATIONAL MAP 19–2 Religious Diversity across the United States

In most counties, a large share of people who report having an affiliation are members of the same religious organization. So although the United States is religiously diverse at the national level, most people live in communities where one denomination predominates. What historical facts might account for this pattern?

Source: Association of Statisticians of American Religious Bodies (2012).

Religiosity

Religiosity is *the importance of religion in a person's life.* However, exactly how religious we are depends on how we operationalize this concept. For example, 90 percent of U.S. adults claim to believe in a divine power, although just 59 percent claim that they "know that God exists and have no doubts about it" (NORC, 2013:605). Fifty-nine percent of adults say they pray at least once a day, but just 31 percent report attending religious services on a weekly or almost weekly basis (NORC, 2013:275, 265).

Clearly, the question "How religious are we?" has no easy answer, and it is likely that many people in the United States claim to be more religious than they really are. Although most people in the United States say they are at least somewhat religious, probably no more than about one-third actually are.

Religiosity varies by age. In general, older people are more religious, as suggested by the fact that 90 percent of U.S. adults over the age of sixty-five claim to have a religious affiliation. By contrast, just 67 percent of people between the ages of eighteen and twenty-nine say the same. Researchers conclude that today's young people are less religious than their elders and that they are also less religious than young people were a generation ago (Pew Research Center, 2012; Glenn, 2013).

Religiosity also varies among denominations. Members of sects are the most religious of all, followed by Catholics and then "mainstream" Protestant denominations such as Episcopalians, Methodists, and Presbyterians.

Finally, women are more religious than men. In surveys, 63 percent of women and 49 percent of men say religion is very important in their lives. From another angle, 23 percent of men and 17 percent of women claim to have no religious affiliation (Sherkat & Ellison, 1999; Miller & Stark, 2002; Pew Research Center, Forum on Religion and Public Life, 2009; Pew Research Center, 2013).

religiosity the importance of religion in a person's life

What difference does being more religious make? Researchers have linked a number of social patterns to strong religious beliefs, including low rates of delinquency among young people and low rates of divorce among adults. According to one study, religiosity helps unite children, parents, and local communities in ways that benefit young people, enhancing their educational achievement (Muller & Ellison, 2001).

Religious Diversity: Class, Ethnicity, and Race

The U.S. Congress that took office in 2013 was the most religiously diverse in the nation's history. People who identify themselves as Protestants are a slight majority (56 percent, down from almost 75 percent fifty years ago). The new Congress contains Catholics (31 percent), Jews (6 percent), Mormons (3 percent), the first Buddhist and the first Hindu to serve, and the first person in Congress to describe her religious affiliation as "none."

The changes in Congress reflect increasing religious diversity in the nation as a whole. The following sections explain how religious affiliation is related to a number of factors, including social class, ethnicity, and race.

Social Class

A study of *Who's Who in America,* a listing of U.S. high achievers, showed that the 10 percent of the people who have a religious affiliation as Episcopalians, Presbyterians, and United Church of Christ members represent 33 percent of all listings in *Who's Who.* Jews, too, enjoy high social position, with this 1.5 percent of the population accounting for 12 percent of the listings in *Who's Who.*

Research shows that other denominations, including Congregationalists, Methodists, and Catholics, have moderate social standing. Lower social standing is typical of Southern Baptists, Lutherans, and especially Jehovah's Witnesses and other members of sects. Of course, there is considerable variation within all denominations (Keister, 2003; Smith & Faris, 2005; Pyle, 2006).

Ethnicity

Throughout the world, religion is tied to ethnicity, mostly because one religion stands out in a single nation or geographic region. Islam predominates in the Arab societies of the Middle East, Hinduism is fused with the culture of India, and Confucianism runs deep in Chinese society. Christianity and Judaism do not follow this pattern; although these religions are mostly Western, Christians and Jews are found all over the world.

Religion and national identity are joined in the United States as well. For example, we have Anglo-Saxon Protestants, Irish Catholics, Russian Jews, and people of Greek Orthodox heritage. This linking of nation and creed results from the influx of immigrants from nations with a single major religion. Still, nearly every ethnic category displays some religious diversity. For example, people of English ancestry may be Protestants, Roman Catholics, Jews, Hindus, Muslims, or followers of other religions.

Race

Scholars claim that the church is both the oldest and the most important social institution in the African American community. Transported to the Western Hemisphere in slave ships, most Africans became Christians, the dominant religion in the Americas, but they blended Christian belief with elements of African religions. Guided by this religious mix, African American Christians have developed rituals that seem, by European standards, far more spontaneous and emotional (Frazier, 1965; Paris, 2000; McRoberts, 2003).

When African Americans started moving from the rural South to the industrial cities of the North around 1940, the church played a major role in addressing the problems of dislocation, poverty, and prejudice (Pattillo, 1998). Black churches have also provided an important avenue of achievement for talented men and women. Ralph Abernathy, Martin Luther King Jr., and Jesse Jackson have all achieved world recognition for their work as religious leaders.

Today, with 87 percent of African Americans claiming a religious affiliation, this category of our population is somewhat more religious than the population as a whole. In addition, the trend toward less religious affiliation is almost entirely among white people and does not appear to apply to African Americans (Pew Research Center, 2013).

The vast majority of African Americans favor a Protestant denomination. However, there is an increasing number of non-Christian African Americans, especially in large U.S. cities. Among them, the most common non-Christian religion is Islam, with about 400,000 African American followers. Put otherwise, about 40 percent of native-born Muslims in the United States identify themselves as African American (Paris, 2000; Pew Research Center, Forum on Religion and Public Life, 2009; Pew Research Center, 2013).

Religion in a Changing Society

(19.7) Discuss recent trends in religious life.

Like family life, religion is also changing in the United States. In the following sections, we look at two major aspects of change: changing affiliations over time and the process of secularization.

Changing Affiliation

A lot of change is going on within the world of religion. Within the United States, membership in established, mainstream Protestant churches such as the Episcopalian and Presbyterian denominations has fallen by almost 50 percent since 1960. Within a year or so—if it has not happened already—our nation will no longer have a majority of the population identifying with a Protestant denomination (Pew Research Center, 2012). At the same time, as we shall see shortly, other religious organizations (including Mormons, Catholics, and both liberal "New Age" spiritual movements and conservative fundamentalist organizations) have increased in popularity.

Another dynamic aspect of religion is that many people are moving from one religious organization to another. A survey by the Pew Research Center, Forum on Religion and Public Life (2008) shows that 44 percent of adults in the United States report that they have

Read in **MySocLab**
Document: *Abiding Faith*
by Mark Chaves

Watch in **MySocLab**
Video: *The Big Picture: Religion*

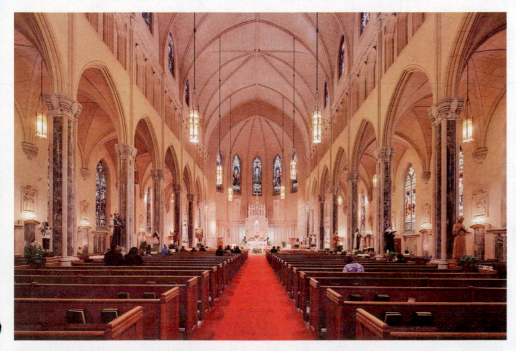

In the last fifty years, traditional "mainstream" religious organizations have lost about half their membership. But during this same period, fundamentalist and new spiritual movements have increased their membership. From another angle, almost half of our people change their religious affiliation over their lifetimes.

switched religious affiliation at some point in their lives. When we add in those who have moved away from religion altogether, the pattern by which people are born and raised with a religious affiliation they keep throughout their lives is no longer the case for at least half of the U.S. population.

Such personal changes mean that religious organizations experience a pattern of people coming and going. Catholics, for example, have represented almost one-fourth of the U.S. adult population for some time. But this fairly stable statistic hides the fact that about one-third of all people raised Catholic have left the church. At the same time, an ever larger number of people—including many immigrants—have joined this church. A more extreme example is the Jehovah's Witnesses: Two-thirds of the people raised in this church have left, but their numbers have been more than replaced by converts recruited by members who travel door-to-door spreading their message.

This pattern of religious "churn" means that there is an active and competitive marketplace of religious organizations in the United States. Perhaps one result of this active competition for members is that U.S. society remains among the most religious in the world. But it also reflects a loosening of ties to the religious organizations people are born into, so men and women now have more choice about their religious beliefs and affiliation.

Secularization

Secularization is *the historical decline in the importance of the supernatural and the sacred.* Secularization (from a Latin word for "worldly," meaning literally "of the present age") is commonly associated with modern, technologically advanced societies in which science is the major way of understanding.

Today, we are more likely to experience the transitions of birth, illness, and death in the presence of physicians (people who claim to have scientific knowledge) than in the company of religious leaders (who share knowledge that is based on faith). This shift alone suggests that religion's relevance to our everyday lives has declined. Harvey Cox (1971:3) explains:

> The world looks less and less to religious rules and rituals for its morality or its meanings. For some [people], religion provides a hobby, for others a mark of national or ethnic identification, for still others an aesthetic delight. For fewer and fewer does it provide an inclusive and commanding system of personal and cosmic values and explanations.

If Cox is right, should we expect religion to disappear someday? Some analysts point to survey data that show that the share of our adult population claiming no religious affiliation has increased from about 2 percent in 1950 to about 20 percent today. Cross-national surveys carried out in thirty nations show a similar pattern, documenting an increasing share of people who identify as atheists (those who claim no divine power exists) in twenty-three of the thirty nations (Pew Research Center, 2011; Smith, 2012).

As Figure 19–3 shows, the share of first-year college students saying they have no religious preference has gone up, doubling between 1990 and 2012. This trend is mirrored in the larger adult population. Other analysts have pointed to the fact that large numbers of unaffiliated adults are now found not only in the Pacific Northwest (a long-time secular region) but also in the Northeast (where Christianity in this country first took hold) and the South (a generally more religious region) (Meacham, 2009).

But other sociologists are not so sure that religion is going away. They point out that the vast majority of people in the United States still say they believe in God, and as many people claim to pray each day as say that they vote in national elections. In fact,

Student Snapshot

- Although the share has been increasing, only about one-quarter of women and men on U.S. campuses claim no religious affiliation.

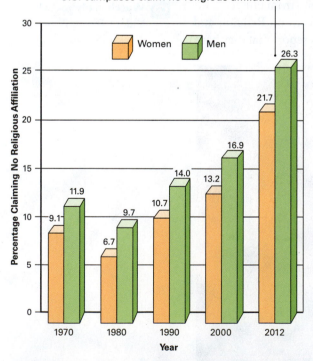

FIGURE 19–3 Religious Nonaffiliation among First-Year College Students, 1970–2012

In recent decades, the share of students claiming no religious affiliation has increased.

Sources: Astin et al. (2002) and Pryor et al. (2013).

researchers remind us, the share of people with a religious affiliation is actually higher today than it was back in 1850. Finally, more people may be switching their religious affiliation from one organization to another, and some may be leaving organized religion entirely, but their spiritual life may continue all the same (McClay, 2007; Greeley, 2008; MacDonald, 2012; Pryor et al., 2013).

Everyone sees religious change; what people disagree about is whether this change is good or bad. Conservatives tend to see any weakening of religion as a mark of moral decline. Progressives view secularization in more positive terms, as liberation from the dictatorial beliefs of the past, giving people greater choice about what to believe. Secularization has also helped bring traditional religious practices—such as ordaining only men—into line with widespread public support for greater gender equality.

According to the secularization thesis, religion weakens in high-income nations as people enjoy higher living standards and greater economic security. A global perspective shows that this thesis holds for the rich countries of Western Europe, where most measures of religiosity have declined and are now low. But the United States—the richest country of all—is an exception, a nation in which, for now at least, religion remains quite strong.

Perhaps the most important event in the history of the secularization debate took place in 1963, when the U.S. Supreme Court banned prayer in public schools, claiming that school prayer violates the principle of separation between church and state.

Court decisions continue to play a part in the secularization debate. In 1950, Congress acted to strengthen religion by establishing a "National Day of Prayer" on the first Thursday in May as an opportunity for people "to turn to God in prayer and meditation." In 2010, however, a federal district court in Wisconsin struck down this law as violating the principle of separation of church and state. In 2011, the federal government made a successful appeal to change this decision so that the "National Day of Prayer" continues (Perez, 2010).

For a closer look at the debate over the place of religion in public schools, **Read More** in **MySocLab**, *Should Students Pray in School?*

Civil Religion

One expression of secularization in the world is the rise of what sociologist Robert Bellah (1975) calls **civil religion**, *a quasi-religious loyalty linking individuals in a basically secular society.* In other words, formal religion may lose power, but citizenship takes on religious qualities. Most people in the United States consider our way of life a force for moral good in the world. Many people also find religious qualities in political movements, whether liberal or conservative (Williams & Demerath, 1991).

Civil religion also involves a wide range of rituals, from singing the national anthem at major sporting events to waving the flag in public parades. At all such events, the U.S. flag serves as a sacred symbol of our national identity, and most members of our society expect people to treat it with respect.

civil religion a quasi-religious loyalty linking individuals in a basically secular society

"New Age" Seekers: Spirituality without Formal Religion

December 29, Machu Picchu, Peru. We are ending the first day exploring this magnificent city built high in the Andes Mountains by the Inca people. Lucas, a local shaman, or religious leader, is leading a group of twelve travelers in a ceremony of thanks. Leading us into a small stone building, he kneels and places offerings—corn and beans, sugar, plants of all colors, and even bits of gold and silver—on the dirt floor in front of him. These he offers as gifts to Pachamama, or Mother Earth. With the gifts, he adds a prayer for harmony, joy, and the hope that all people will do good for others. His heartfelt words amidst such a magnificent setting make the ceremony a magical experience.

In recent decades, more and more people have been seeking spiritual development outside of established religious organizations. This trend has led some analysts to suggest that the United States is becoming a *postdenominational society*. In simple terms, a small but increasing share of people seem to be spiritual seekers, believing in a vital spiritual dimension to human existence that they pursue more or less separately from membership in any formal denomination.

What exactly is the difference between this so-called New Age focus on spirituality and a traditional concern with religion? As one analysis (Cimino & Lattin, 1999:62) puts it, spirituality is

> the search for… a religion of the heart, not the head. It … downplays doctrine and dogma, and revels in direct experience of the divine—whether it's called the "holy spirit" or "divine consciousness" or "true self." It's practical and personal, more about stress reduction than salvation, more therapeutic than theological. It's about feeling good rather than being good. It's as much about the body as the soul.

Millions of people in the United States take part in New Age spirituality. The following six core values define the New Age religious movement (Wesselman, 2001:39–42; Walsh, 2012):

1. **Seekers believe in a higher power.** There exists a higher power, a vital force that is within all things and all people. Each of us, then, is partly divine, and the divine spirit exists everywhere in the world around us.

2. **Seekers believe everything is connected.** Because "spirit" is everywhere in the universe, everything and everyone are interconnected. As New Agers like to say, "We are all one."

3. **Seekers believe in a spirit world.** The physical world we perceive with our five senses is not all there is; more important is the existence of a world beyond the senses, a spiritual reality or "spirit world."

4. **Seekers want to experience the spirit world.** Spiritual development means gaining the ability to experience the spirit world. Many seekers are able to "feel" the presence of spirit within them and they come to understand that helpers and teachers (traditionally called "angels") dwell in the spirit world and can touch their lives.

5. **Seekers pursue transcendence.** Through various techniques (such as yoga, meditation, and prayer) people can gain an increasing ability to rise above the immediate physical world (the experience of "transcendence"), which seekers believe is the larger purpose of life.

6. **Some seekers pursue political change.** While for some seekers spirituality means a turning from the ways of this world, for others spirituality demands seeking both political change to end the destruction of the natural environment and an economic system that is based on competition rather than cooperation.

From a traditional point of view, this New Age concern with spirituality may seem as much psychology or liberal politics as it is religion. Perhaps it would be fair to say that New Age spirituality combines elements of rationality (an emphasis on individualism as well as tolerance and pluralism) with a spiritual focus (searching for meaning beyond everyday concerns). It is this combination that makes New Age seeking particularly popular in the modern world (Tucker, 2002; Besecke, 2003, 2005).

Religious Revival: "Good Old-Time Religion"

At the same time as New Age spirituality is becoming more popular, a great deal of change has been going on in the world of organized religion. Membership in established, mainstream churches has fallen in recent decades, and affiliation with other formal religious organizations, including the Mormons, the Seventh-Day Adventists, and especially Christian sects, has risen dramatically.

These opposing trends suggest that secularization may be self-limiting: As many churchlike organizations become more worldly, many people leave them in favor of more sectlike communities offering a more intense religious experience (Stark & Bainbridge, 1981; Jacquet & Jones, 1991; Iannaccone, 1994; Hout, Greeley, & Wilde, 2001).

Religious Fundamentalism

Fundamentalism is *a conservative religious doctrine that opposes intellectualism and worldly accommodation in favor of restoring traditional, otherworldly religion.* In the United States, fundamentalism has made the greatest gains among Protestants. Southern Baptists, for example, are the largest Protestant religious community in the country. But fundamentalist groups have also grown among Roman Catholics, Jews, and Muslims.

In response to what they see as the growing influence of science and the weakening of the conventional family, religious fundamentalists defend what they call "traditional values." As they see it, liberal churches have been too open to compromise and change. Religious fundamentalism is distinctive in five ways (Hunter, 1983, 1985, 1987):

1. **Fundamentalists take the words of sacred texts literally.** Fundamentalists insist on a literal reading of sacred texts such as the Bible to counter what they see as excessive intellectualism among more liberal religious organizations. For example, fundamentalist Christians believe that God created the world in seven days precisely as described in the biblical book of Genesis.

2. **Fundamentalists reject religious pluralism.** Fundamentalists believe that tolerance and relativism water down personal faith. Therefore, they maintain that their religious beliefs are true and other beliefs are not.

3. **Fundamentalists pursue the personal experience of God's presence.** In contrast to the worldliness and intellectualism of other religious organizations, fundamentalism seeks a return to "good old-time religion" and spiritual revival. To fundamentalist Christians, being "born again" and having a personal relationship with Jesus Christ should be evident in a person's everyday life.

4. **Fundamentalists oppose "secular humanism."** Fundamentalists think that accommodation to the changing world weakens religious faith. They reject "secular humanism," our society's tendency to look to scientific experts rather than to God for guidance about how we should live. There is nothing new in this tension between science and religion; it has existed for centuries, as the Controversy & Debate box on page 564 explains.

fundamentalism
a conservative religious doctrine that opposes intellectualism and worldly accommodation in favor of restoring traditional, otherworldly religion

In this outstanding example of U.S. folk art, Anna Bell Lee Washington's *Baptism 3* (1924) depicts the life-changing experience by which many people enter the Christian faith.

Controversy & Debate

Does Science Threaten Religion?

Cihan: I think someday science will prove religion to be false.
Sophie: You better hope God doesn't prove *you* to be false.
Rasheed: Cool it, both of you. I don't think science and religion are talking about the same thing at all.

About 400 years ago, the Italian physicist and astronomer Galileo (1564–1642) helped launch the Scientific Revolution with a series of startling discoveries. Dropping objects from the Leaning Tower of Pisa, he discovered some of the laws of gravity; making his own telescope, he observed the stars and found that Earth orbited the sun, not the other way around.

For his trouble, Galileo was challenged by the Roman Catholic Church, which had preached for centuries that Earth stood motionless at the center of the universe. Galileo only made matters worse by responding that religious leaders had no business talking about matters of science. Before long, he found his work banned and himself under house arrest.

As Galileo's treatment shows, right from the start, science has had an uneasy relationship with religion. In the twentieth century, the two clashed again over the issue of creation. Charles Darwin's masterwork, *On the Origin of Species,* states that humanity evolved from lower forms of life over the course of a billion years. Yet this theory seems to fly in the face of the biblical account of creation found in Genesis, which states that "God created the heavens and the earth," introducing life on the third day and, on the fifth and sixth days, animal life, including human beings fashioned in God's own image.

Galileo would certainly have been an eager observer of the famous "Scopes monkey trial." In 1925, the state of Tennessee put a small-town science teacher named John Thomas Scopes on trial for teaching Darwinian evolution in the local high school. State law forbade teaching "any theory that denies the story of the Divine Creation of man as taught in the Bible" and especially the idea that "man descended from a lower order of animals." Scopes was found guilty and fined $100. His conviction was reversed on appeal, so the case never reached the U.S. Supreme Court, and the Tennessee law stayed on the books until 1967. A year later, the Supreme Court, in *Epperson* v. *Arkansas,* struck down all such laws as unconstitutional government support of religion.

Today, almost four centuries after Galileo was silenced, many people still debate the apparently conflicting claims of science

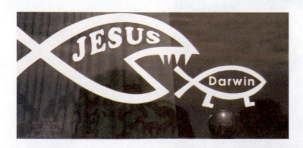

and religion. A third of U.S. adults believe that the Bible is the literal word of God, and many of them reject any scientific findings that run counter to it (NORC, 2013:303). In 2005, all eight members of the school board in Dover, Pennsylvania, were voted out of office after they took a stand that many townspeople saw as weakening the teaching of evolution; at the same time, the Kansas state school board ordered the teaching of evolution to include its weaknesses and limitations from a religious point of view ("Much Ado about Evolution," 2005). And in 2010, an Ohio middle school science teacher was dismissed from his job based on charges that he was teaching Christianity to his students (Boston, 2011).

But a middle ground is emerging: 44 percent of U.S. adults (and also many church leaders) say that the Bible is a book of truths inspired by God without being accurate in a literal, scientific sense. In addition, a recent survey of U.S. scientists found that half of them claimed to believe in God or some form of higher power. So it seems that many people are able to embrace science and religion at the same time. The reason this is possible is that science and religion are two different ways of understanding, and they answer different questions. Both Galileo and Darwin devoted their lives to investigating *how* the natural world works. Yet only religion can address *why* we and the natural world exist in the first place.

This basic difference between science and religion helps explain why our nation is both the most scientific and among the most religious in the world. As one scientist noted, the mathematical odds that a cosmic "big bang" 12 billion years ago created the universe and led to the formation of life as we know it are even smaller than the chance of winning a state lottery twenty weeks in a row. Doesn't such a scientific fact suggest an intelligent and purposeful power in our creation? Can't a person be a religious believer and at the same time a scientific investigator?

In 1992, a Vatican commission concluded that the church's silencing of Galileo was wrong. Today, most scientific and religious leaders agree that science and religion each represent important, but very different, truths. Many also believe that in today's rush to scientific discovery, our world has never been more in need of the moral guidance provided by religion.

What Do You Think?

1. Researchers tell us that a majority of scientists in the United States claim no religious affiliation. Why do you think most scientific people appear to reject religious accounts of human creation?

2. Why do some religious people reject scientific accounts?

3. Do you think religion and science can coexist? Explain.

Sources: Gould (1981), Huchingson (1994), Applebome (1996), Greeley (2008), and Pew Research Center, Forum on Religion and Public Life (2009).

5. **Many fundamentalists endorse conservative political goals.** Although fundamentalism tends to back away from worldly concerns, some fundamentalist leaders (including Christian fundamentalists Pat Robertson and Gary Bauer) have entered politics to oppose what they call the "liberal agenda," which includes feminism and gay rights. Fundamentalists oppose abortion and gay marriage; they support the traditional two-parent family, seek a return of prayer in schools, oppose high levels of immigration, and criticize the mass media for coloring stories with a liberal bias. The Power of Society figure found at the beginning of this chapter shows that evangelical or fundamentalist Protestants are far more likely to support "old-fashioned" values about family and marriage than members of more "mainline" religious organizations or those who have no religious affiliation (Manza & Brooks, 1997; Thomma, 1997; Rozell, Wilcox, & Green, 1998; Pew Research Center, 2012).

Opponents regard fundamentalism as rigid, judgmental, and self-righteous. But many find in fundamentalism, with its greater religious certainty and emphasis on the emotional experience of God's presence, an appealing alternative to the more intellectual, tolerant, and worldly "mainstream" denominations (Marquand, 1997).

Which religions are fundamentalist? In recent years, the world has become familiar with an extreme form of fundamentalist Islam that supports violence directed against Western culture. In the United States, the term is most correctly applied to conservative Christian organizations in the evangelical tradition, including Pentecostals, Southern Baptists, Seventh-Day Adventists, and Assemblies of God. Several national religious movements, including Promise Keepers (a men's organization) and Chosen Women, have a fundamentalist orientation. In national surveys, 25 percent of U.S. adults describe their religious upbringing as "fundamentalist," 40 percent claim a "moderate" upbringing, and 31 percent a "liberal" background (NORC, 2013:265).

The Electronic Church

In contrast to local congregations of years past, some religious organizations, especially fundamentalist ones, have become electronic churches featuring "prime-time preachers" (Hadden & Swain, 1981). Electronic religion has not spread around the world but is found only in the United States. It has made James Dobson, Joel Osteen, Franklin Graham, Robert Schuller, and others more famous than all but a few clergy of the past. About 5 percent of the national television audience (or some 10 million people) regularly view religious television, and 20 percent (about 40 million) watch or listen to some religious programming every week (NORC, 2013:603).

Religion: Looking Ahead

The popularity of media ministries, the growth of fundamentalism, new forms of spirituality, and the connection of millions of people to mainstream churches show that religion will remain a major part of modern society for decades to come. While the evidence suggests that there has been some decline in the importance of religion in the United States, religiosity in this country remains high. Even as some people move away from organized religion, immigration from many religious countries (in Latin America and elsewhere) and the increasing popularity of fundamentalist organizations should increase as well as diversify the religious character of U.S. society in the twenty-first century (Yang & Ebaugh, 2001; T.W. Smith, 2009, 2012).

The world is becoming more complex, and change seems to move more rapidly than our ability to make sense of it all. But rather than weakening religion, this process fires the religious imagination. As new technology gives us the power to change, extend, and even create life, we are faced with increasingly difficult moral questions. Against this backdrop of uncertainty, it is little wonder that many people look to their faith for guidance and hope.

Seeing Sociology in Everyday Life

CHAPTER 19   Religion

How religious is our society?

Compared to most other high-income nations, the United States has a relatively high level of religious belief and activity. We consider ourselves to be a modern, secular society, yet as this chapter explains, most people claim to be religious and at least one-third of the population actually is. Civil religion is also evident in many aspects of our everyday lives. Look at the photos below and on page 567. Can you point to elements of civil religion in each of these familiar situations?

On Thanksgiving Day, most families across the United States gather to share a special dinner and give thanks for their good fortune. What religious or quasi-religious elements are part of a typical Thanksgiving celebration?

What about the Fourth of July? How is this special day an example of civil religion?

In recent decades, football's Super Bowl has emerged as an important annual event. What elements of civil religion can you find in Super Bowl Sunday?

HINT As this chapter explains, civil religion is a quasi-religious loyalty linking members of a mostly secular society. Important events that qualify as civil religion are not formally religious but are typically defined as holidays (a word derived from "holy days"); involve gatherings of family, neighbors, and friends; and include ritual activities and the sharing of specific foods and beverages.

Seeing Sociology in *Your* Everyday Life

1. Make a list of other events, activities, and pastimes that might be considered examples of civil religion. (Start off with Election Day; what about baseball?) Do you know of any college events or local rituals that might be included? In each case, explain the religious element that you see and the way the event or activity affects members of a community.

2. Go to MySocLab and click on the Student Resources link to access the Sociology in Focus blog, where you can read the latest posts by a team of young sociologists who apply the sociological perspective to topics of popular culture.

3. Can you explain the difference between studying religion sociologically and holding personal religious beliefs? To learn more about this difference, go to the "Seeing Sociology in *Your* Everyday Life" feature in MySocLab and read the additional material found there.

Making the Grade

Religion: Concepts and Theories

19.1 Apply sociology's major theories to religion. (pages 540–44)

👁 **Watch** the **Video** in **MySocLab**   👁 **Watch** the **Video** in **MySocLab**

Religion is a major social institution based on setting the *sacred* apart from the *profane*. Religion is grounded in *faith* rather than scientific evidence, and people express their religious beliefs through various rituals.

Theories of Religion

- **Structural functional theory** describes how people celebrate the power of society through religion. Emile Durkheim identified three major functions of religion: Religion unites people, promoting social cohesion; it encourages people to obey cultural norms, promoting conformity; it gives meaning and purpose to life.

- **Symbolic-interaction theory** explains that people use religion to give everyday life sacred meaning; people create rituals that separate the sacred from the profane; Peter Berger claimed that people are especially likely to seek religious meaning when faced with life's uncertainties and disruptions.

- **Social-conflict theory** highlights religion's support of social inequality. Karl Marx claimed that religion justifies the status quo and diverts people's attention from social injustice; in this way, religion discourages change toward a more just and equal society.

- **Feminist theory** highlights the fact that major religions have traditionally been patriarchal, supporting the domination of women by men. A number of major religious organizations bar women from serving as religious leaders.

profane included as an ordinary element of everyday life

sacred set apart as extraordinary, inspiring awe and reverence

religion a social institution involving beliefs and practices based on recognizing the sacred

ritual formal, ceremonial behavior

faith belief based on conviction rather than on scientific evidence

totem an object in the natural world collectively defined as sacred

Religion and Social Change

19.2 Analyze how religion encourages social change. (pages 544–45)

- Max Weber argued, in opposition to Marx, that religion can encourage social change. He showed how Calvinism became "disenchanted," leading to a profane "Protestant work ethic" that contributed to the rise of industrial capitalism.
- **Liberation theology**, a fusion of Christian principles and political activism, tries to encourage social change.

liberation theology the combining of Christian principles with political activism, often Marxist in character

Types of Religious Organizations

19.3 Distinguish among church, sect, and cult. (pages 545–47)

- **Churches** are religious organizations well integrated into their society. They formally train and ordain leaders and have a highly formal style of worship. Churches fall into two categories: *state churches* (e.g., the Anglican Church in England and Islam in Morocco), and *denominations* (e.g., Christian denominations such as Baptists and Lutherans, and various categories of Judaism and Islam).

- **Sects** are the result of religious division. They hold rigid religious beliefs and are marked by charismatic leadership, a spontaneous and emotional style of worship, and members' suspicion of the larger society.

- **Cults** are religious organizations based on new and unconventional beliefs and practices.

church a type of religious organization that is well integrated into the larger society

state church a church formally allied with the state

denomination a church, independent of the state, that recognizes religious pluralism

sect a type of religious organization that stands apart from the larger society

charisma extraordinary personal qualities that can infuse people with emotion and turn them into followers

cult a religious organization that is largely outside a society's cultural traditions

Religion in History

19.4 Contrast religious patterns in preindustrial and industrial societies. (pages 547–48)

- Hunting and gathering societies practiced **animism**, viewing elements of the natural world as spiritual forces.
- Belief in a single divine power began in pastoral and horticultural societies.
- Organized religion gained importance in agrarian societies.
- In industrial societies, scientific knowledge explains *how* the world works, but people look to religion to answer questions about *why* the world exists.

animism the belief that elements of the natural world are conscious life forms that affect humanity

---

World Religions

19.5 Contrast six major world religions. (pages 548–55)

monotheism belief in a single divine power
polytheism belief in many gods

- **Christianity** is the most widespread religion, with 2.3 billion followers—almost one-third of the world's people; Christianity began as a cult built on the personal charisma of Jesus of Nazareth; Christians believe Jesus is the Son of God and follow his teachings.

- **Islam** has about 1.6 billion followers, who are known as Muslims—more than one-fifth of the world's people; Muslims follow the word of God as revealed to the prophet Muhammad and written in the Qur'an, the sacred text of Islam.

- **Judaism's** 15 million followers are mainly in Israel and the United States; Jewish belief rests on the covenant between God and his chosen people, embodied in the Ten Commandments and the Old Testament of the Bible.

- **Hinduism** is the oldest world religion and today has about 950 million adherents; Hindus see God as a universal moral force rather than a specific being and believe in the principles of *dharma* (moral responsibilities) and *karma* (the spiritual progress of the human soul).

- **Buddhists** number about 463 million people; Buddhist teachings are similar to Hindu beliefs, but Buddhism is based on the life of one person, Siddhartha Gautama, who taught the use of meditation as a way to move beyond selfish desires to achieve *nirvana*, a state of enlightenment and peace.

- **Confucianism** was the state church of China until the 1949 Communist revolution oppressed religious expression; it is still strongly linked to Chinese culture; Confucianism teaches *jen*, or "humaneness," meaning that people must place moral principles above self-interest; layers of moral obligations unite society as a whole.

Religion in the United States

19.6 Analyze patterns of religiosity in the United States (pages 555–58)

religiosity the importance of religion in a person's life

 **Explore** the **Map** in **MySocLab**

The United States is one of the most religious and religiously diverse nations.

- 63% of women and 49% of men claim religion is important in their lives
- 59% profess a firm belief in God
- 59% of adults say they pray at least once a day
- 31% say they attend religious services weekly or almost weekly
- 23% of men and 17% of women claim no religious affiliation

Religious affiliation is tied to *social class*, *ethnicity*, and *race*:

- On average, Episcopalians, Presbyterians, and Jews enjoy high standing; lower social standing is typical of Baptists, Lutherans, and members of sects.
- Religion is often linked to the ethnic background of immigrants who came from countries with a major religion.
- Brought here as slaves, most Africans became Christians, but they blended Christian beliefs with elements of African religions.

Religion in a Changing Society

19.7 Discuss recent trends in religious life. (pages 559–65)

 Read the **Document** in **MySocLab**   **Watch** the **Video** in **MySocLab**

- **Secularization** is a decline in the importance of the supernatural and sacred.
- In the United States, while some indicators of religiosity (like membership in mainstream churches) have declined, others (such as membership in sects) have increased.
- **Civil religion** takes the form of a quasi-religious patriotism that ties people to their society.
- *Spiritual seekers* are part of the New Age movement, which pursues spiritual development outside conventional religious organizations.
- **Fundamentalism** opposes religious accommodation to the world, interprets religious texts literally, and rejects religious diversity.

secularization the historical decline in the importance of the supernatural and the sacred
civil religion a quasi-religious loyalty linking individuals in a basically secular society
fundamentalism a conservative religious doctrine that opposes intellectualism and worldly accommodation in favor of restoring traditional, otherworldly religion

20 Education

Listen to Chapter 20 in MySocLab

LEARNING OBJECTIVES

20.1 Compare schooling in high-, middle-, and low-income societies.

20.2 Apply structural-functional theory to schooling.

20.3 Apply social-interaction theory to schooling.

20.4 Apply social-conflict theory to schooling.

20.5 Discuss dropping out, violence, and other problems facing today's schools.

20.6 Summarize the debate over the performance of U.S. schools.

the Power of Society
to open the door to college

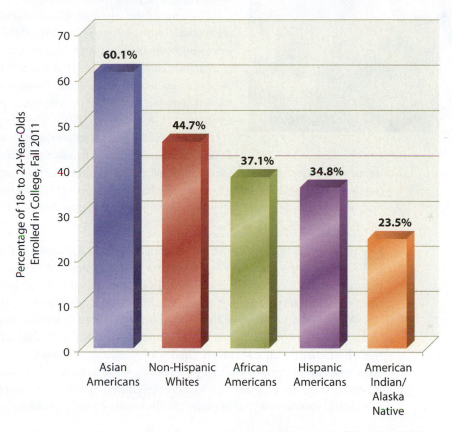

Source: U.S. Department of Education (2013)

Do the odds of going to college simply reflect a personal desire for more schooling? Researchers claim that almost all parents say they would like their children to go to college. But while about 45 percent of white people between the ages of eighteen and twenty-four in the United States were enrolled in college in the fall of 2011, just half that share (23.5 percent) of comparable American Indians and Alaskan Native people were on campus. Asian Americans (who benefit from both higher family income and cultural capital that encourages schooling) are especially likely to attend college. In short, our society is organized in a way that opens the door to higher education far wider for some categories of people than for others.

Chapter Overview

This chapter explains the operation of education, a major social institution. The chapter begins with a global survey of schooling and then focuses on education in the United States.

When Lisa Addison was growing up in Baltimore, her teachers always told her that she was smart and should go to college. "I liked hearing that," she recalls. "But I didn't know what to do about it. No one in my family had ever gone to college. I didn't know what courses to take in high school. I had no idea of how to apply to a college. How would I pay for it? What would it be like if I got there?"

Discouraged and uncertain, Addison found herself "kind of goofing off in school." After finishing high school, she spent the next fifteen years working as a waitress in a restaurant and then as a kitchen helper in a catering company. Now, at the age of thirty-eight, Addison has decided to go back to school. "I don't want to do this kind of work for the rest of my life. I *am* smart. I can do better. At this point, I *am* ready for college."

Addison took a giant step through the door of the Community College of Baltimore County, speaking to counselors and setting her sights on an associate's degree in business. When she finishes the two-year program, she plans to transfer to a four-year university to complete a bachelor's degree. Then she hopes to go back into the food service industry—but this time as a manager at higher pay (Toppo & DeBarros, 2005).

Higher education is part of the American dream for almost all young people in the United States. But many face the types of challenges that delayed Lisa Addison in her journey toward a college degree. Especially for people growing up in low-income families, often with parents who are not college graduates, the odds of getting to college can be small.

Who goes to college in the United States? What difference does higher education make in the type of job you get or the money you make? This chapter answers these questions by focusing on **education**, *the social institution through which society provides its members with important knowledge, including basic facts, job skills, and cultural norms and values.* In high-income nations such as the United States, education is largely a matter of **schooling**, *formal instruction under the direction of specially trained teachers.*

Education: A Global Survey

20.1 Compare schooling in high-, middle-, and low-income societies.

In the United States, young people expect to spend most of their first eighteen years in school. This was not the case a century ago, when just a small elite had the privilege of attending school. Even today, most young people in poor countries receive only a few years of formal schooling.

Schooling and Economic Development

The extent of schooling in any society is tied to its level of economic development. In low- and middle-income countries, which are home to most of the world's people, families and communities teach young people important knowledge and skills. Formal schooling, especially learning that is not directly connected to survival, is available mainly to wealthy people who may not need to work and who can pursue personal enrichment. The word *school* is from a Greek root that means "leisure." In ancient Greece, famous teachers such as Socrates, Plato, and Aristotle taught aristocratic, upper-class men who had plenty of spare time. The same was true in ancient China, where the famous philosopher K'ung Fu-tzu (Confucius) shared his wisdom with a privileged few.

December 30, the Cuzco region, Peru. High in the Andes Mountains of Peru, families send their children to the local school. But "local" can mean 3 miles away or more, and there are no buses, so these children, almost all from poor families, walk at least an hour each way. Schooling is required by law, but in the rural highlands, some parents prefer to keep their children at home where they can help with the farming and livestock.

Today, the limited schooling that takes place in lower-income countries reflects the national culture. In Iran, for example, schooling is closely tied to Islam. Similarly, schooling in Bangladesh (Asia), Zimbabwe (Africa), and Nicaragua (Latin America) has been shaped by the distinctive cultural traditions of these nations.

All lower-income countries have one trait in common when it comes to schooling: There is not much of it. In the world's poorest nations (including several in Central Africa), about one-fourth of all children never get to school (World Bank, 2013). Worldwide, almost one-third of all children never reach the secondary grades (what we call *high school*). As a result, about one-sixth of the world's people cannot read or write. Global Map 20–1 on page 574 shows the extent of illiteracy around the world, and the following national comparisons illustrate the link between the extent of schooling and economic development.

education the social institution through which society provides its members with important knowledge, including basic facts, job skills, and cultural norms and values

schooling formal instruction under the direction of specially trained teachers

Schooling in India

India has recently become a middle-income country, but people there still earn only about 7 percent of U.S. average income, and most poor families depend on the earnings of children. Even though India has outlawed child labor, many children continue to work in factories—weaving rugs or making handicrafts—up to sixty hours per week, which greatly limits their opportunities for schooling.

Today, 92 percent of children in India complete primary school, most often in crowded schoolrooms where one teacher typically faces forty or more children. In comparison, U.S. public schoolteachers have on average about thirty students in a class. Sixty-three percent of students in India go on to secondary school, but just 18 percent enter college. Currently about one-third of India's people are not able to read and write (UNESCO, 2012; World Bank, 2013).

Patriarchy also shapes Indian education. Indian parents are joyful at the birth of a boy because he and his future wife will both contribute income to the family. But there are economic costs to raising a girl: Parents must provide a dowry (a gift of wealth to the groom's family), and after her marriage, a daughter's work benefits her husband's family. Therefore, many Indians see less reason to invest in the schooling of girls, so only 60 percent of girls (compared to 66 percent of boys) reach the secondary grades. What do the girls do while the boys are in school? Most of the children working in Indian factories are girls—a family's way of benefiting from their daughters while they can (World Bank, 2013).

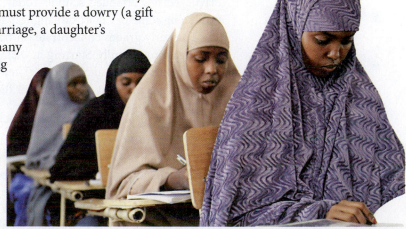

In many low-income nations, children are as likely to work as to attend school, and girls receive less schooling than boys. But the doors to schooling are now opening to more girls and women. These young women are studying nursing at Somalia University in downtown Mogadishu.

Schooling in Japan

Schooling has not always been part of the Japanese way of life. Before industrialization brought mandatory education in 1872, only a

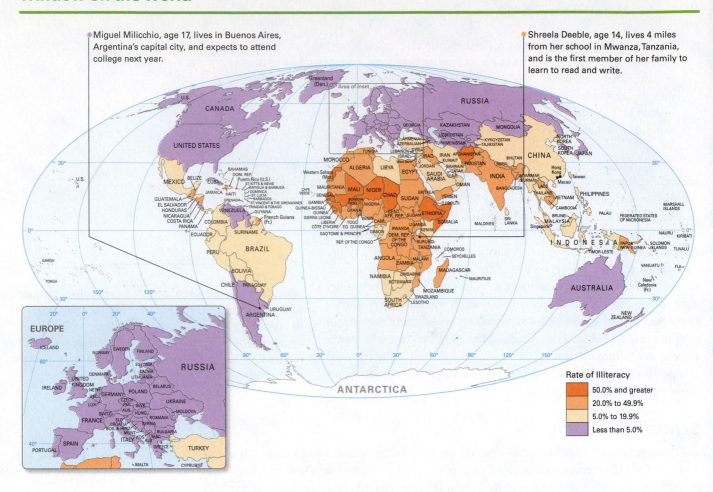

Miguel Milicchio, age 17, lives in Buenos Aires, Argentina's capital city, and expects to attend college next year.

Shreela Deeble, age 14, lives 4 miles from her school in Mwanza, Tanzania, and is the first member of her family to learn to read and write.

Rate of Illiteracy

- 50.0% and greater
- 20.0% to 49.9%
- 5.0% to 19.9%
- Less than 5.0%

GLOBAL MAP 20–1 Illiteracy in Global Perspective

Reading and writing skills are widespread in high-income countries, where illiteracy rates generally are below 5 percent. In much of Latin America, however, illiteracy is more common, one consequence of limited economic development. In eleven nations—almost all of them in Africa—illiteracy is the rule rather than the exception; there people rely on the oral tradition of face-to-face communication rather than the written word.

Sources: UNESCO (2012) and United Nations Development Programme (2012)

privileged few attended school. Today, Japan's educational system is widely praised for producing some of the world's highest achievers.

The early grades concentrate on transmitting Japanese traditions, especially a sense of obligation to family. Starting in their early teens, students take a series of difficult and highly competitive examinations. Their scores on these written tests, which are like the Scholastic Assessment Test (SAT) in the United States, decide the future of all Japanese students.

More men and women graduate from high school in Japan (96 percent) than in the United States (88 percent). But competitive examinations allow just 51 percent of high school graduates—compared to 68 percent in the United States—to enter college. Understandably, Japanese students (and their parents) take entrance examinations very seriously. About half attend "cram schools" to prepare for the exams, which means very late nights completing homework. Such hard work is one reason that Japanese students often nap in class—seen by teachers as the mark of a serious student (Steger, 2006; OECD, 2012).

Japanese schooling produces impressive results. In a number of fields, notably mathematics and science, Japanese students (who rank fourth in the world in science and reading and seventh in mathematics) outperform students in almost every other high-income nation, including the United States (ranked twenty-third in science and thirty-first in mathematics) (World Bank, 2013).

Schooling in Great Britain

During the Middle Ages, schooling was a privilege of the British nobility, who studied classical subjects, having little concern for the practical skills needed to earn a living. But as the Industrial Revolution created a need for an educated labor force, and as working-class people demanded access to schools, a rising share of the population entered the classroom. British law now requires every child to attend school until age sixteen.

Traditional class differences still affect British schooling. Most wealthy families send their children to what the British call *public schools,* which we would refer to as private boarding schools. These elite schools enroll about 7 percent of British students and teach not only academic subjects but also the special patterns of speech, mannerisms, and social graces of the British upper class. Because these academies are very expensive, most British students attend state-supported day schools (Department for Children, Schools, and Families, 2012).

The British have tried to reduce the importance of social background in schooling by expanding their university system and linking admission to competitive entrance examinations. For the students who score the highest, the government pays most of the college costs. But many well-to-do children who do not score very well still manage to get into Oxford or Cambridge, the most prestigious British universities, on a par with our own Yale, Harvard, and Princeton. Many "Oxbridge" graduates go on to positions at the top of the British power elite: Most of the highest-ranking members of the British government—including Prime Minister David Cameron—have "Oxbridge" degrees.

These brief sketches of schooling in India, Japan, and Great Britain show the crucial importance of economic development. In poor countries, many children—especially girls—work rather than go to school. Rich nations enact mandatory education laws to prepare an industrial workforce as well as to satisfy demands for greater equality. But a nation's history and culture still matter, as we see in the intense competition of Japanese schools, the traditional social stratification that shapes schools in Great Britain, and, in the next section, the practical emphasis found in the schools of the United States.

Schooling in the United States

The United States was among the first countries to set a goal of mass education. By 1850, about half the young people between the ages of five and nineteen were enrolled in school. By 1918, all states had passed a *mandatory education law* requiring children to attend school until the age of sixteen or completion of the eighth grade. Table 20–1 shows that a milestone was reached in the mid-1960s when for the first time a majority of U.S. adults had earned high school diplomas. Today, 87.6 percent of U.S. adults twenty-five years of age or older have completed high school, and 30.9 percent have a four-year college degree (U.S. Census Bureau, 2012).

The U.S. educational system is shaped by both our high standard of living (which means that young people typically do not have to work) and our democratic principles (the idea that schooling should be provided to everyone). Thomas Jefferson thought the new nation could become democratic only if people learned to read. Today, the United States has an outstanding record of higher education for its people: The United States is ranked behind only Norway in terms of the share of adults aged twenty-five and older who have earned a university degree (OECD, 2012).

Schooling in the United States also tries to promote *equal opportunity.* National surveys show that most people

TABLE 20–1 Educational Achievement in the United States, 1910–2012

Year	High School Graduates	College Graduates	Median Years of Schooling
1910	13.5%	2.7%	8.1
1920	16.4	3.3	8.2
1930	19.1	3.9	8.4
1940	24.1	4.6	8.6
1950	33.4	6.0	9.3
1960	41.1	7.7	10.5
1970	55.2	11.0	12.2
1980	68.7	17.0	12.5
1990	77.6	21.3	12.4
2000	84.1	25.6	12.7
2010	87.1	29.9	13.0
2012	87.6	30.9	13.1

Notes: Figures are for people 25 years of age and over. Percentage of high school graduates includes those who go on to college. Percentage of high school dropouts can be calculated by subtracting the percentage of high school graduates from 100 percent.

Source: U.S. Census Bureau (2013); World Bank (2013)

think schooling is crucial to personal success, and more people than not also believe that everyone has the chance to get an education consistent with personal ability and talent (NORC, 2013:242, 2199). However, this opinion expresses our cultural ideals rather than reality. A century ago, for example, few women had the chance to go to college, and even today, most men and women who attend college come from families with above-average incomes.

In the United States, the educational system stresses the value of *practical* learning, knowledge that prepares people for future jobs. This emphasis is in line with what the educational philosopher John Dewey (1859–1952) called *progressive education,* having the schools make learning relevant to people's lives. Similarly, students seek out subjects of study that they feel will give them an advantage when they are ready to compete in the job market. For example, as concerns about international terrorism have risen in recent years, so have the numbers of students choosing to study geography, international conflict, and Middle Eastern history and culture (Lord, 2001).

The Functions of Schooling

20.2 Apply structural-functional theory to schooling.

Structural-functional theory looks at ways in which formal education supports the smooth operation and stability of society. We look briefly at five ways in which this happens.

Socialization

Technologically simple societies look to families to teach skills and values and thus to transmit a way of life from one generation to the next. As societies gain more complex technology, they turn to trained teachers to develop and pass on the more specialized knowledge that adults will need to take their place in the workforce.

Watch in **MySocLab**
Video: *Sociology on the Job: Education*

In primary school, children learn language and basic mathematical skills. Secondary school builds on this foundation, and for many students, college allows further specialization. In addition, all schooling teaches cultural values and norms. For example, civics classes instruct students in our political way of life, and rituals such as saluting the flag foster patriotism. Likewise, activities such as spelling bees develop competitive individualism and a sense of fair play.

Cultural Innovation

Faculty at colleges and universities create culture as well as pass it on to students. Research in the sciences, the social sciences, the humanities, and the fine arts leads to discovery and changes in our way of life. For example, medical research at major universities has helped increase life expectancy, just as research by sociologists and psychologists helps us learn how to enjoy life more so that we can take advantage of our longevity.

Social Integration

Schooling molds a diverse population into one society sharing norms and values. This is one reason that states enacted mandatory education laws a century ago at a time

Graduation from college is an important event in the lives of an ever-increasing number of people in the United States. Look over the discussion of the functions of schooling. How many of these functions do you think people in college are aware of? Can you think of other social consequences of going to college?

when immigration was very high. In light of the ethnic diversity of many urban areas today, schooling continues to serve this purpose.

Social Placement

Schools identify talent and match instruction to ability. Schooling increases meritocracy by rewarding talent and hard work regardless of social background and provides a path to upward social mobility.

Latent Functions of Schooling

Schooling also serves several less widely recognized functions. It provides child care for the growing number of one-parent and two-career families. In addition, schooling occupies thousands of young people in their teens and twenties who would otherwise be competing for limited opportunities in the job market. High schools, colleges, and universities also bring together people of marriageable age. Finally, schools establish networks that serve as a valuable career resource throughout life.

EVALUATE Structural-functional theory stresses ways in which formal education supports the operation of a modern society. However, this approach overlooks how the classroom behavior of teachers and students can vary from one setting to another, a focus of symbolic-interaction theory, discussed next. In addition, structural-functional theory says little about many problems of our educational system and how schooling helps reproduce the class structure in each generation, which is the focus of social-conflict theory.

CHECK YOUR LEARNING Identify the five functions of schooling for the operation of society.

Schooling and Social Interaction

20.3 Apply social-interaction theory to schooling.

The basic idea of symbolic-interaction theory is that people create the reality they experience in their day-to-day interaction. We use this approach to explain how stereotypes can shape what goes on in the classroom.

The Self-Fulfilling Prophecy

Chapter 6 ("Social Interaction in Everyday Life") presented the Thomas theorem, which states that situations that people define as real become real in their consequences. Put another way, people who expect others to act in certain ways often encourage that very behavior. Doing so, people set up a *self-fulfilling prophecy.*

Jane Elliott, an elementary school teacher in the all-white community of Riceville, Iowa, carried out a simple experiment that showed how a self-fulfilling prophecy can take place in the classroom. In 1968, Elliot was teaching a fourth-grade class when Dr. Martin Luther King Jr. was assassinated. Her students were puzzled and asked why a national hero had been brutally shot. Elliott responded by asking her white students what they thought about people of color, and she was stunned to find out that they held many powerful negative stereotypes.

To show the class the harmful effects of such stereotypes, Elliott performed a classroom experiment. She found that almost all of the children in her class had either blue eyes or brown eyes. She told the class that children with brown eyes were smarter and worked harder than children with blue eyes. To be sure everyone could easily tell which category a child fell into, pieces of brown or blue colored cloth were pinned to every student's collar.

Elliott recalls the effect of this "lesson" on the way students behaved: "It was just horrifying how quickly they became what I told them they were." Within half an hour,

How good are you as a student? The answer is that you are as good as you and your teachers think you are. The television show *Glee* demonstrates how the help of an inspiring teacher encourages students toward greater self-confidence and higher achievement.

Elliot continued, a blue-eyed girl named Carol had changed from a "brilliant, carefree, excited little girl to a frightened, timid, uncertain, almost-person." Not surprisingly, in the hours that followed, the brown-eyed students came to life, speaking up more and performing better than they had done before. The prophecy had been fulfilled: Because the brown-eyed children thought they were superior, they became superior in their classroom performance—as well as "arrogant, ugly, and domineering" toward the blue-eyed children. For their part, the blue-eyed children began underperforming, becoming the inferior people they believed themselves to be.

At the end of the day, Elliott took time to explain to everyone what they had experienced. She applied the lesson to race, pointing out that if white children thought they were superior to black children, they would expect to do better in school, just as many children of color who live in the shadow of the same stereotypes would underperform in school. The children also realized that the society that teaches these stereotypes, as well as the hate that often accompanies them, encourages the kind of violence that ended the life of Dr. King (Kral, 2000).

EVALUATE Symbolic-interaction theory explains how we all build reality in our everyday interactions with others. When school officials define some students as "gifted," for example, we can expect teachers to treat them differently and the students themselves to behave differently as a result of having been labeled in this way. If students and teachers come to believe that one race is academically superior to another, the behavior that follows may be a self-fulfilling prophecy.

One limitation of this approach is that people do not just make up such beliefs about superiority and inferiority. Rather, these beliefs are built into a society's system of social inequality, which brings us to social-conflict theory.

CHECK YOUR LEARNING How can the labels that schools place on some students affect the students' actual performance and the reactions of others?

Schooling and Social Inequality

(20.4) Apply social-conflict theory to schooling.

Social-conflict theory explains how schooling both causes and perpetuates social inequality. In this way, it can explain how stereotypes of "good" and "bad" students described in the symbolic-interaction discussion arise in the first place. In addition, a social-conflict approach challenges the structural-functional idea that schooling develops everybody's talents and abilities by claiming that schooling plays a part in social stratification.

Social Control

Schooling is a way of controlling people, reinforcing acceptance of the status quo. Samuel Bowles and Herbert Gintis (1976) claim that the rise of public education in the late nineteenth century came at exactly the same time that factory owners needed an obedient and disciplined workforce. Once in school, immigrants learned not only the English language but also the importance of following orders.

Standardized Testing

Here is a question of the kind historically used to measure the academic ability of school-age children in the United States:

> *Painter* is to *painting* as _____ is to *sonnet*.
> (a) driver (b) poet (c) priest (d) carpenter

The correct answer is "(b) poet": A painter creates a painting just as a poet creates a sonnet. This question supposedly measures logical reasoning, but getting the right answer also depends on knowing what each term means. Students who are unfamiliar with the sonnet as a Western European form of written verse are not likely to answer the question correctly.

The organizations that create standardized tests claim that this type of bias has been all but eliminated because they carefully study response patterns and drop any question that favors one racial or ethnic category. But critics insist that some bias based on class, race, or ethnicity will always exist in formal testing. Because test questions will always reflect our society's dominant culture, minority students are placed at a disadvantage (Crouse & Trusheim, 1988; Putka, 1990).

School Tracking

Despite controversy over standardized tests, most schools in the United States use them for **tracking**, *assigning students to different types of educational programs*, such as college preparatory classes, general education, and vocational and technical training.

Tracking supposedly helps teachers meet each student's individual needs and abilities. However, one education critic, Jonathan Kozol (1992), considers tracking an example of "savage inequalities" in our school system. Most students from privileged backgrounds do well on standardized tests and get into higher tracks, where they receive the best the school can offer. Students from disadvantaged backgrounds typically do less well on these tests and end up in lower tracks, where teachers stress memorization and put little focus on creativity.

Based on these concerns, schools across the United States are cautious about making tracking assignments and give students the chance to move from one track to another. Some schools have even dropped tracking entirely. Tracking can help match instruction with students' abilities, but rigid tracking can have a powerful impact on students' learning and self-concept. Young people who spend years in higher tracks tend to see themselves as bright and able; students in lower tracks end up with less ambition and low self-esteem (Bowles & Gintis, 1976; Kilgore, 1991; Gamoran, 1992; Kozol, 1992).

Inequality among Schools

Just as students are treated differently within schools, schools themselves differ in important ways. The biggest difference is between public and private schools.

Public and Private Schools

Across the United States, about 90 percent of the 55.1 million primary and secondary school children attend state-funded public schools. The rest go to private schools.

About 40 percent of private school students attend one of the 6,800 *parochial schools* (*parochial* is from Latin, meaning "of the parish") operated by the Roman Catholic Church. The Catholic school system grew rapidly a century ago as cities swelled with immigrants. Enrolling their children in Catholic schools helped the new arrivals hold onto their religious heritage in a new and mostly Protestant society. Today, after decades of flight from the inner city by white people, many parochial schools enroll non-Catholics, including a growing number of African Americans whose families seek an alternative to the neighborhood public school.

Watch in **MySocLab**
Video: *Sociology in Focus: Education*

tracking assigning students to different types of educational programs

Sociological research has documented the fact that young children living in low-income communities typically learn in classrooms like the one on the left, with large class sizes and low budgets that do not provide for high technology and other instructional materials. Children from high-income communities typically enjoy classroom experiences such as the one shown on the right, with small classes and the latest learning technology.

Another 38 percent of private school students attend one of more than 15,000 schools with some non-Catholic religious affiliation. Many private schools linked to Protestant denominations are known as Christian academies. These schools are favored by parents who want religious instruction for their children as well as higher academic and disciplinary standards.

There are also about 10,600 nonreligious private schools in the United States that enroll the remaining 22 percent of private school students. Many of these students are young people from well-to-do families. These institutions are typically prestigious and expensive preparatory ("prep") schools, modeled on British boarding schools, and they not only provide strong academic programs but also convey the values and teach the way of life of the upper class. Many "preppies" maintain lifelong school-based social networks that provide numerous social advantages.

Are private schools qualitatively better than public schools? Research shows that holding family social background constant, students in private schools do outperform those in public schools on standard measures of academic success. The advantages of private schools include smaller classes, more demanding coursework, and greater discipline (Coleman & Hoffer, 1987; Peterson & Llaudet, 2006).

Inequality in Public Schooling

But even public schools are not all the same. Differences in funding result in unequal resources; consequently, children in more affluent areas receive a better education than children living in poor communities. National Map 20–1 on page 581 shows one key way in which resources differ: Average yearly teacher salaries vary by as much as $35,000 in state-by-state comparisons.

At the local level, differences in school funding can be dramatic. Arlington County, Virginia, one of the richest suburbs in the United States, spends more than $18,500 a year on each of its students, compared to about $5,000 in poor areas like Alpine, Utah, and in recent years, these differences have grown (U.S. Department of Education, 2011). The Thinking About Diversity box on page 582 shows the effects of funding differences in the everyday lives of students.

Because schools are typically funded through local property taxes, schools in more affluent areas will offer a better education than schools in poor communities. This difference also benefits whites over minorities, which is why some districts enacted a policy of *busing*, transporting students to achieve racial balance and equal opportunity in schools. Although only 5 percent of U.S. schoolchildren are bused to schools outside their neighborhoods, this

Seeing Ourselves

 Explore the percentage of people without a high school education in your local community and in counties across the United States in **MySocLab**

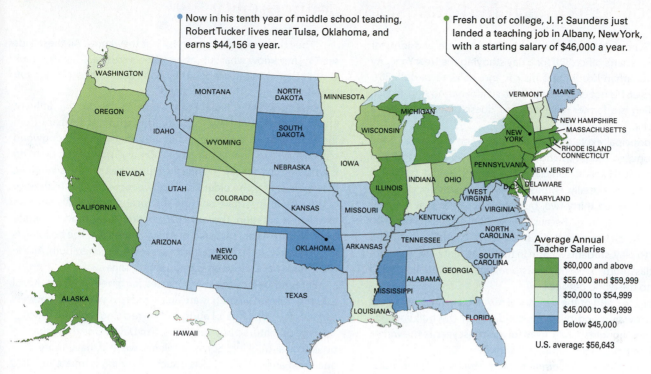

• Now in his tenth year of middle school teaching, Robert Tucker lives near Tulsa, Oklahoma, and earns $44,156 a year.

• Fresh out of college, J. P. Saunders just landed a teaching job in Albany, New York, with a starting salary of $46,000 a year.

Average Annual Teacher Salaries

- $60,000 and above
- $55,000 and $59,999
- $50,000 to $54,999
- $45,000 to $49,999
- Below $45,000

U.S. average: $56,643

NATIONAL MAP 20–1 Teachers' Salaries across the United States

In 2012, the average public school teacher in the United States earned $56,643. The map shows the average teacher salary for all the states ranging from a low of $39,850 in South Dakota to a high of $74,449 in New York. Looking at the map, what pattern do you see? What do high-salary (and low-salary) states have in common?

Source: U.S. Department of Education (2013).

policy is controversial. Supporters claim that given the reality of racial segregation, the only way government will adequately fund schools in poor, minority neighborhoods is if white children from richer areas attend. Critics respond that busing is expensive and undermines the concept of neighborhood schools. But almost everyone agreed on one thing: Given the racial imbalance of most urban areas, an effective busing scheme would have to join inner cities and suburbs, a plan that has never been politically possible. Since the 1990s, busing students to achieve racial balance in schools has sharply declined. Although there was some modest decline in racial segregation in U.S. public schools between 1970 and 1990, there has been little change since then (Logan, Oakley, & Stowell, 2008).

But other policies to address unequal schools have emerged. One plan is to provide money equally across a state. This is the approach taken by Vermont, which passed a law that distributes per-student tax money equally to all communities.

But not everyone thinks that money is the key to good schooling. Consider, for example, that Youngstown, Ohio, spends $14,500 each year on each public school student (40 percent above the national average) but barely manages to graduate half of them. Newark, New Jersey, spends double the national average per student and still does not graduate half of all students (Will, 2011). What other than money is involved? A classic report by a research team headed by James Coleman (1966) confirmed that students in mostly minority schools suffer from larger class size, insufficient libraries, and fewer science labs. But the Coleman report cautioned that more money by itself would not magically improve schooling. More important are the cooperative efforts and enthusiasm of teachers, parents, and the students themselves. In other words, even if school funding were exactly the same everywhere (as in Vermont), students who benefit from more *cultural capital*— that is, those whose parents value schooling, read to their children, and encourage the

Thinking About Diversity: Race, Class, and Gender

Schooling in the United States: Savage Inequality

"Public School 261? Head down Jerome Avenue and look for the mortician's office." Off for a day studying the New York City schools, Jonathan Kozol parks his car and walks toward PS 261. Finding PS 261 is not easy because the school has no sign. In fact, the building is a former roller rink and doesn't look much like a school at all.

The principal explains that this is in a minority area of the North Bronx, so the population of PS 261 is 90 percent African American and Hispanic. Officially, the school should serve 900 students, but it actually enrolls 1,300. The rules say class size should not exceed thirty-two, but Kozol observes that it sometimes approaches forty. Because the school has just one small cafeteria, the children must eat in three shifts. After lunch, with no place to play, students squirm in their seats until told to return to their classrooms. Only one classroom in the entire school has a window to the world outside.

Toward the end of the day, Kozol remarks to a teacher about the overcrowding and the poor condition of the building. She sums up her thoughts: "I had an awful room last year. In the winter, it was 56 degrees. In the summer, it was up to 90."

"Do the children ever comment on the building?" Kozol asks.

"They don't say," she responds, "but they know. All these kids see TV. They know what suburban schools are like. Then they look around them at their school. They don't comment on it, but you see it in their eyes. They understand."

Several months later, Kozol visits PS 24, in the affluent Riverdale section of New York City. This school is set back from the road, beyond a lawn planted with magnolia and dogwood trees, which are now in full bloom. On one side of the building is a playground for the youngest children; behind the school are playing fields for the older kids. Many people pay the high price of a house in Riverdale because the local schools have such an excellent reputation. There are 825 children here; most are white and a few are Asian, Hispanic, or African American. The building is in good repair. It has a large library and even a planetarium. All the classrooms have windows with bright curtains.

Entering one of the many classes for gifted students, Kozol asks the children what they are doing today. A young girl answers confidently, "My name is Laurie, and we're doing problem solving." A tall, good-natured boy continues, "I'm David. One thing that we do is logical thinking. Some problems, we find, have more than one good answer." Kozol asks if such reasoning is innate or if it is something a child learns. Susan, whose smile reveals her braces, responds, "You know some things to start with when you enter school. But we learn some things that other children don't. We learn certain things that other children don't know because we're *taught* them."

What Do You Think?

1. Are there differences between schools in your city or town? Explain.

2. Why do you think there is little public concern about schooling inequality?

3. What changes would our society have to make to eliminate schooling inequality?

Source: Adapted from Kozol (1992:85–88, 92–96).

development of imagination—would still perform better. In short, we should not expect schools alone to overcome marked social inequality in the United States (Schneider et al., 1998; Israel, Beaulieu, & Hartless, 2001; Ornstein, 2010).

Further research confirms the difference that home environment makes in a student's school performance. A research team studied the rate at which school-age children gain skills in reading and mathematics (Downey, von Hippel, & Broh, 2004). Because U.S. children go to school six to seven hours a day, five days a week, and do not attend school during summer months, the researchers calculate that children spend only about 13 percent of their waking hours in school. During the school year, high-income children learn somewhat more quickly than low-income children, but the learning gap is far greater during the summer season when children are not in school. The researchers conclude that when it comes to student performance, schools matter, but the home and local neighborhood matter more. Put another way, schools close some of the learning gap that is created by differences in family resources, but they do not "level the playing field" between rich and poor children the way we like to think they do.

Access to Higher Education

Schooling is the main path to good jobs. But only 68 percent of U.S. high school graduates enroll in college immediately after graduation. Among young people eighteen to twenty-four years old, about 42 percent are enrolled in college (U.S. Department of Education, National Center for Education Statistics, 2013).

A crucial factor affecting access to U.S. higher education is family income. College is expensive: Even at state-supported institutions, annual tuition averages about $8,660, and admission to the most exclusive private colleges and universities exceeds $50,000 a year. This means that college attendance is more common among families with higher incomes. In the United States, some 6.6 million families have at least one child enrolled in college. Of these families, 44 percent have incomes of at least $75,000 annually (roughly the richest 30 percent, who fall within the upper-middle class and upper class), 46 percent have incomes of at least $20,000 but less than $75,000 (the middle class and working class), and only 10 percent have incomes of less than $20,000 a year (the lower class including families classified as poor) (U.S. Census Bureau, 2012).

These economic differences are one reason that the education gap between whites and minorities widens at the college level. As Figure 20–1 shows, African Americans are not quite as likely as non-Hispanic whites to graduate from high school and are much less likely to complete four or more years of college. Hispanics, many of whom speak Spanish as their first language, have a lower rate of high school graduation, and again, the gap is much greater when it comes to college degrees. Schooling is an important path to social mobility in our society, but the promise of schooling has not overcome the racial inequality that exists in the United States.

Completing college brings many rewards, including higher earnings. In the past forty years, as our economy has shifted to work that requires processing information, the gap in average income between people who complete only high school and those who earn a four-year college degree has more than doubled. In fact, today, a college degree adds as much as $1 million to a person's lifetime income. In simple terms, higher education is a good investment.

Table 20–2 on page 584 gives details. In 2011, men who were high school graduates averaged $40,447, and college graduates averaged $66,196. The ratios in parentheses show that a man with a bachelor's degree earns 2.6 times as much in annual income as a man with eight or fewer years of schooling. Across the board, women earn less than men, although as with men, adding years of schooling boosts their income, although not quite as much. Keep in mind that for both men and women, some of the greater earnings have to do with social background, because those with the most schooling are likely to come from relatively well-off families.

Greater Opportunity: Expanding Higher Education

With some 21 million people enrolled in colleges and universities, the United States is a world leader in providing a college education to its people. This country also enrolls more students from abroad than any other, with almost 700,000 nonresident students in 2010.

One reason for this achievement is that there are 4,706 colleges and universities in the United States. This number includes 2,968 four-year institutions (which award bachelor's degrees) as well as 1,738 two-year colleges (which award associate's degrees). Some two-year colleges are private, but most are publicly funded community colleges that serve a

Diversity Snapshot

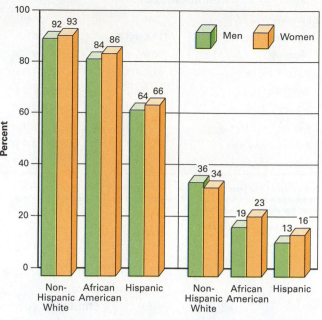

FIGURE 20–1 Educational Achievement for Various Categories of People, Aged 25 Years and Over, 2012

U.S. society still provides less education to minorities.

Source: U.S. Census Bureau (2012).

TABLE 20–2 Median Income by Sex and Educational Attainment, 2011

Education	Men	Women
Professional degree	$119,474 (4.7)	$80,718 (4.0)
Doctorate	100,766 (4.0)	77,458 (3.9)
Master's degree	83,027 (3.3)	60,304 (3.0)
Bachelor's degree	66,196 (2.6)	49,108 (2.4)
1–3 years of college	47,072 (1.9)	34,592 (1.7)
4 years of high school	40,447 (1.6)	30,011 (1.5)
9–11 years of school	30,423 (1.2)	21,113 (1.1)
0–8 years of school	25,223 (1.0)	20,102 (1.0)

Notes: Figures are for persons aged 25 years and over working full time. The earnings ratio, in parentheses, indicates what multiple of the lowest income level a person with the indicated amount of additional schooling earns.

Source: U.S. Census Bureau (2012).

local area (usually a city or a county) and charge a low tuition (U.S. Department of Education, National Center for Education Statistics, 2013).

Because higher education is a key path to better jobs and higher income, the government makes money available to help certain categories of people pay the costs of college. After World War II, the GI Bill provided college funds to veterans, with the result that tens of thousands of men and women were able to attend college. Some branches of the military continue to offer college money to enlistees; in addition, veterans continue to benefit from a number of government grants and scholarships.

Community Colleges

Since the 1960s, the expansion of state-funded community colleges has further increased access to higher education. According to the National Center for Education Statistics (2013), the 1,738 two-year colleges across the United States now enroll 40.8 percent of all college undergraduates.

Community colleges provide a number of specific benefits. First, their relatively low tuition cost places college courses and degrees within the reach of millions of families that could not otherwise afford them. Many students at community colleges today are the first in their families to pursue a college degree. The lower cost of community colleges is especially important during periods of economic recession. When the economy slumps and people lose their jobs, college enrollments soar, especially at community colleges.

Second, community colleges have special importance for minorities. Currently, 39 percent of all African American and 51 percent of Hispanic undergraduates in the United States attend community colleges.

Third, although it is true that community colleges serve local populations, they also attract students from around the world. Many community colleges recruit students from abroad, and about 14 percent of all foreign students enrolled on a U.S. campus are studying at community colleges (U.S. Department of Education, National Center for Education Statistics, 2012).

Fourth, the top priority of faculty who work at large universities is typically research, but the most important job for community college faculty is teaching. Thus, although teaching loads are high (typically four or five classes each semester), community colleges appeal to faculty who find their greatest pleasure in the classroom. Community college students often get more attention from faculty than do students at large universities (Jacobson, 2003). Finally, community colleges teach the knowledge and career skills that countless people depend on to find the jobs they want.

Privilege and Personal Merit

If attending college is a rite of passage for rich men and women, as social-conflict analysis suggests, then *schooling transforms social privilege into personal merit*. Given our cultural emphasis on individualism, we tend to see credentials as badges of ability rather than as symbols of family affluence (Sennett & Cobb, 1973).

When we congratulate the new graduate, we rarely recognize the resources—in terms of both money and cultural capital—that made this achievement possible. Yet young people from families with incomes exceeding $200,000 a year average almost 400 points higher on the SAT college entrance examination than young people from families with less than $20,000 in annual income (College Board, 2013). The richer students are more likely to get into college; once there, they are also more likely to complete their studies and get a degree. In a *credential society*—one that evaluates people on the basis of their schooling—companies hire job applicants with the best education. This process ends up helping people who have advantages to begin with and harming those who are already disadvantaged (Collins, 1979).

Education			
	Structural-Functional Theory	**Symbolic-Interaction Theory**	**Social-Conflict Theory**
What is the level of analysis?	Macro-level	Micro-level	Macro-level
What is the importance of education for society?	Schooling performs many vital tasks for the operation of society, including socializing the young and encouraging discovery and invention to improve our lives. Schooling helps unite a diverse society by teaching shared norms and values.	How teachers define their students—as well as how students think of themselves—can become real to everyone and affect students' educational performance.	Schooling maintains social inequality through unequal schooling for rich and poor. Within individual schools, tracking provides privileged children with a better education than poor children.

EVALUATE Social-conflict theory links formal education to social inequality to show how schooling transforms privilege into personal worthiness and social disadvantage into personal deficiency. However, the social-conflict approach overlooks the extent to which finishing a degree reflects plenty of hard work and the extent to which schooling provides upward social mobility for talented women and men from all backgrounds. In addition, despite the claims that schooling supports the status quo, today's college curricula challenge social inequality on many fronts.

CHECK YOUR LEARNING Explain several ways in which education is linked to social inequality.

The Applying Theory table sums up what each of the theoretical approaches shows us about education.

Problems in the Schools

(**20.5**) Discuss dropping out, violence, and other problems facing today's schools.

An intense debate revolves around the quality of schooling in the United States. Perhaps because we expect our schools to do so much—teach, equalize opportunity, instill discipline, and fire our children's imagination—people are divided on whether public schools are doing their job. Although about half of adults give schools in their local community a performance grade of A or B, the same share gives a grade of C or below (Bushaw & Lopez, 2012).

Discipline and Violence

When many of today's older teachers think back to their own student days, school "problems" consisted of talking out of turn, chewing gum, breaking the dress code, or cutting class. Today schools are grappling with serious issues such as drug and alcohol abuse, teenage pregnancy, and outright violence. Although almost everyone agrees that schools should teach personal discipline, many think the job is no longer being done.

Schools do not create violence; in most cases, violence spills into the schools from the surrounding society. In the wake of a number of school shootings in recent years, many school districts have adopted zero-tolerance policies that require suspension or expulsion for serious misbehavior or bringing weapons on campus.

Deadly school shootings—including the deaths of thirty-three students at Virginia Tech University in 2007, the 2010 death of a student who entered the library at the University of Texas at Austin and shot himself with an AK-47 assault rifle, and the 2012 deaths of six students and one employee at Oikos University in California—have shocked the nation. Such tragic incidents also raise serious questions about balancing students' right to privacy (typically laws forbid colleges from informing parents of a student's grades or mental health issues) and the need to ensure the safety of the campus population. In the Virginia Tech case, had the university been able to bring the young man's mental health problems to the attention of the police or his family, the tragedy might have been prevented (Gibbs, 2007; Shedden, 2008).

Student Passivity

If some schools are plagued by violence, many more are filled with students who are bored. Some of the blame for passivity can be placed on the fact that electronic devices, from television to iPods, now consume more of young people's time than school, parents, and community activities. But schools must share the blame because the educational system itself encourages student passivity (Coleman, Hoffer, & Kilgore, 1981).

Bureaucracy

The small, personal schools that served countless local communities a century ago have evolved into huge educational factories. In a study of high schools across the United States, Theodore Sizer (1984:207–9) identified five ways in which large, bureaucratic schools undermine education:

1. **Rigid uniformity.** Bureaucratic schools run by outside specialists (such as state education officials) generally ignore the cultural character of local communities and the personal needs of their children.

2. **Numerical ratings.** School officials define success in terms of numerical attendance records and dropout rates and "teach to the tests," hoping to raise achievement test scores. In the process, they overlook dimensions of schooling that are difficult to quantify, such as creativity and enthusiasm.

3. **Rigid expectations.** Officials expect fifteen-year-olds to be in the tenth grade and eleventh-graders to score at a certain level on a standardized verbal achievement test. Rarely are exceptionally bright and motivated students permitted to advance more quickly or graduate early. Similarly, poor performers are pushed from grade to grade, doomed to fail year after year.

4. **Specialization.** Students in middle school and high school learn Spanish from one teacher, receive guidance from another, and are coached in sports by still others. Students shuffle between fifty-minute periods throughout the school day. As a result, no school official comes to know the child well.

5. **Little individual responsibility.** Highly bureaucratic schools do not empower students to learn on their own. Similarly, teachers have little say in what they teach in their classes and how they do it; any change in the pace of learning risks disrupting the system.

Of course, with 55 million schoolchildren in the United States, schools must be bureaucratic to get the job done. But Sizer recommends that we "humanize" schools by reducing rigid scheduling, cutting class size, and training teachers more broadly so that they become more involved in the lives of their students. Overall, as James Coleman (1993) has suggested, schools need to be less "administratively driven" and more "output-driven." Perhaps this transformation could begin by ensuring that graduation from high school depends on what students have learned rather than simply on the number of years they have spent in the building.

College: The Silent Classroom

Passivity is also common among college and university students. Sociologists rarely study the college classroom—a curious fact, considering how much time they spend there. One exception was a study at a coeducational university where David Karp and William Yoels (1976) found that, even in small classes, only a few students spoke up. Passivity seems to be a classroom norm, and students may even become irritated if one of their number is especially talkative.

According to Karp and Yoels, most students think classroom passivity is their own fault. Yet as anyone who observes young people outside the classroom knows, they are usually active and vocal. It is clearly the schools that teach students to be passive and to view instructors as experts who serve up "knowledge" and "truth." Most college students find little value in classroom discussion and see their proper role as listening quietly and taking notes. As a result, the researchers estimate, just 10 percent of college class time is used for discussion.

Faculty can bring students to life in their classrooms by making use of four teaching strategies: (1) calling on students by name when they volunteer, (2) positively reinforcing student participation, (3) asking analytical rather than factual questions and giving students time to answer, and (4) asking for student opinions even when no one volunteers a response (Auster & MacRone, 1994).

Dropping Out

If many students are passive in class, others are not there at all. The problem of *dropping out*—quitting school before earning a high school diploma—leaves young people (many of whom are disadvantaged to begin with) unprepared for the world of work and at high risk of poverty. For example, school dropouts account for more than 50 percent of all people receiving welfare assistance and more than 80 percent of the prison population (Christle, Jolivette, & Nelson, 2007).

For all categories of people in the United States, dropping out of school greatly reduces the chances of getting a good job and earning a secure income. Why is the dropout rate particularly high among Hispanic students?

Although the dropout rate has declined slightly in recent decades, a sad fact is that today's children are actually less likely to complete high school than their parents were (Ripley, 2008). Currently, 7.1 percent of people between the ages of sixteen and twenty-four have dropped out of school, a total of some 2.8 million young women and men. Dropping out is least pronounced among non-Hispanic whites (5.0 percent), higher among non-Hispanic African Americans (7.3 percent), and highest of all among Hispanics (13.6 percent) (U.S. Department of Education, National Center for Education Statistics, 2013). These are the official statistics, which include young people who are known to have left school. But a number of researchers estimate that the actual dropout rates are probably at least twice the government's numbers (Thornburgh, 2006).

Some students drop out because of problems with the English language, others because of pregnancy, and some because they must work to help support their family. For children growing up in families with income in the lowest 25 percent, the dropout rate is more than five times higher than for children living in high-income families (U.S. Department of Education, National Center for Education Statistics, 2013). These data suggest that many dropouts are young people whose parents also have little schooling, revealing a multigenerational cycle of disadvantage.

Academic Standards

Perhaps the most serious educational issue confronting our society is the quality of schooling. In 1983, a comprehensive report on the quality of U.S. schools, titled *A Nation at Risk,* was issued by the National Commission on Excellence in Education (NCEE). It begins with this alarming statement:

> If an unfriendly foreign power had attempted to impose on America the mediocre educational performance that exists today, we might well have viewed it as an act of war. As it stands, we have allowed this to happen to ourselves. (1983:5)

Supporting this claim, the report notes that "nearly 40 percent of seventeen-year-olds cannot draw inferences from written material; only one-fifth can write a persuasive essay; and only one-third can solve mathematical problems requiring several steps" (NCEE, 1983:9). Furthermore, scores on the SAT have shown little improvement over time. In 1967, mean scores for students were 516 on the mathematical test and 543 on the verbal test; by 2012, the average in mathematics was about the same, and the verbal average had plunged to just 496. Nationwide, 26 percent of twelfth-graders are below the basic skills in reading, 36 percent are below the basic level in math, and 40 percent are below the basic level in science (Barnes, 2002a; National Assessment of Education Progress, 2010, 2011; College Board, 2013).

functional illiteracy a lack of the reading and writing skills needed for everyday living

For many people, even basic literacy is at issue. **Functional illiteracy**, *a lack of the reading and writing skills needed for everyday living,* is a problem for one in three U.S. children. For older people, about 30 million U.S. adults (about 14 percent of the total) lack basic skills in reading and writing.

A Nation at Risk recommended drastic reform. First, it called for schools to require *all* students to complete several years of English, mathematics, social studies, general science, and computer science. Second, schools should not promote students until they meet achievement standards. Third, teacher training must improve, and teachers' salaries must be raised to draw talent into the profession. The report concluded that schools must meet public expectations and that citizens must be prepared to pay for a job well done.

Read in **MySocLab Document:** *English Learners Still Far Behind Under English-Only Law* by Sarah Garland

What has happened in the years since this report was issued? In some respects, schools have improved. A new report by the National Center for Education Statistics (2012) looked back over the last two decades and noted more students taking courses in science and mathematics, a modest decline in the dropout rate, a trend toward schools offering more challenging courses, fewer high school students working for income, and a larger share of high school graduates going to college. At the same time, the evidence suggests that a majority of elementary school students are falling below standards in reading; in many cases, they can't read at all. In short, although some improvement is evident, much remains to be done.

The United States spends more on schooling its children than almost any other nation—half again more than in Japan and nearly double the average in Europe. Even so, a recent government report comparing the academic performance of fifteen-year-olds in sixty-five countries found that the United States placed twenty-third in science and thirty-first in mathematics. Such statistics fuel fears that our country is losing its leadership in science to other nations, including China, India, and South Korea (European Union, 2013; OECD, 2013).

Cultural values also play a part in how hard students work at their schooling. For example, U.S. students are generally less motivated and do less homework than students in Japan. Japanese young people also spend twenty-one more days in school each year than U.S students. Perhaps one approach to improving academic performance is simply to have students spend more time in school (TIMMS and PIRLS International Study Center, 2013).

Student Snapshot

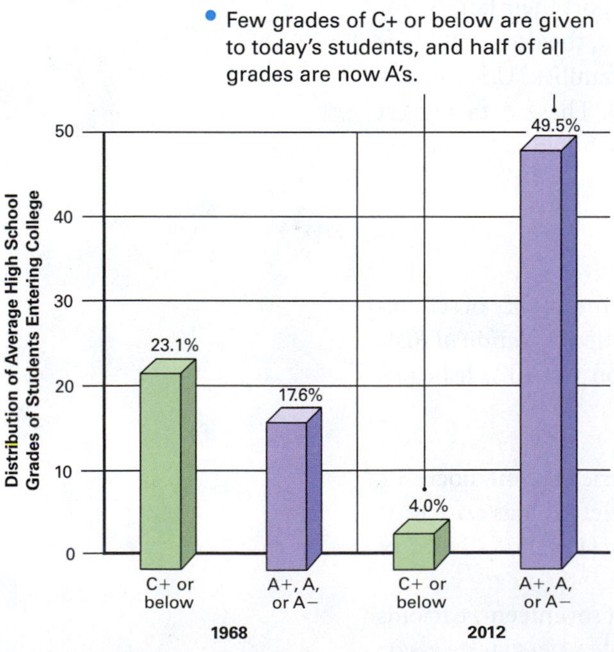

- Few grades of C+ or below are given to today's students, and half of all grades are now A's.

FIGURE 20–2 Grade Inflation in U.S. High Schools

In recent decades, teachers have given higher and higher grades to students.

Sources: Astin et al. (2002) and Pryor et al. (2013).

Grade Inflation

Academic standards depend on using grades that have clear meaning and are awarded for work of appropriate quality. Yet recent decades have seen substantial *grade inflation,* the awarding of ever-higher grades for average work. Though not necessarily found in every school, the trend toward grade inflation is evident across the country in both high schools and colleges.

One study of high school grades revealed a dramatic change in grades between 1968 and 2012. In 1968, as shown in Figure 20–2, the high school records of students who had just entered college included more grades of C+ and below than grades of A–, A, and A+. By 2012, however, these A grades outnumbered grades of C+ and below by more than twelve to one (Pryor et al., 2013).

A few colleges and universities have enacted policies that limit the share of A's (generally to one-third of all grades). But there is little evidence that grade inflation will slow down anytime soon. As a result, the C grade (which used to mean "average") may all but disappear, making just about every student "above average."

What accounts for grade inflation? In part, today's teachers are concerned about the morale and self-esteem of their students and perhaps their own popularity. In any case, teachers clearly are not as "tough" as they used to be. At the same time, the ever more competitive process of getting into college and graduate school puts increasing pressure on high schools and colleges to award high grades (Astin et al., 2002).

Current Issues in U.S. Education

20.6 Summarize the debate over the performance of U.S. schools.

Our society's schools continuously confront new challenges. This section explores several recent and important educational issues, including school choice, home schooling, schooling people with disabilities, adult education, and the teacher shortage.

School Choice

Some analysts claim that our public schools teach poorly because they have no competition. Giving parents options for schooling their children might force all schools to do a better job. This is the essence of a policy called *school choice*.

Watch in MySocLab
Video: *The Big Picture: Education*

The goal of school choice is to create a market for schooling so that parents and students can shop for the best value. According to one proposal, the government would give vouchers to families with school-age children and allow them to spend that money at public, private, or parochial schools. In recent years, major cities, including Indianapolis, Minneapolis, Milwaukee, Cleveland, Chicago, and Washington, D.C., as well as the states of Florida and Illinois, have experimented with choice plans aimed at making public schools perform better to win the confidence of families.

Supporters claim that giving parents a choice about where to enroll their children is the only sure way to improve all schools. But critics (including teachers' unions) charge that school choice amounts to giving up on our nation's commitment to public education and that it will do little to improve schools in central cities, where the need is greatest (Cohen, 1999; Morse, 2002).

In 2002, President George W. Bush signed a new education bill that downplayed vouchers in favor of another approach to greater choice. Starting in the 2005–06 school year, all public schools began testing every child in reading, mathematics, and science in grades three through eight. Although the federal government will provide more aid to schools where students do not perform well, if those schools do not show improvements in test scores over a period of time, their students will have the choice of either special tutoring or transportation to another school. This program, called "No Child Left Behind," has succeeded in showing which schools are not doing a good job educating children and has raised some measures of student performance. At the same time, however, there has been little change in many of the worst-performing schools. By 2012, 48 percent of this nation's public schools had been labeled as failing because they missed their student performance targets. Critics now point to poll numbers that show a majority of U.S. adults supporting major revisions to the No Child Left Behind Act because it has not improved public education. In addition, critics claim that this policy—much of which has been carried forward by the Obama administration under the banner of "Race to the Top"—has directed attention away from the arts, foreign languages, and literature in favor of "teaching to the tests" (Wallis & Steptoe, 2007; Dillon, 2011; Ravitch, 2011; Gallup, 2012; Rich, 2013).

A more modest type of school choice involves *magnet schools,* more than 2,700 of which now exist across the country. Magnet schools offer special facilities and programs that promote educational excellence in a particular field, such as computer science, foreign languages, science and mathematics, or the arts. In school districts with magnet schools, parents can choose the school best suited to their child's particular talents and interests.

Another school choice strategy involves *charter schools*, public schools that are given more freedom to try out new policies and programs. There are more than 5,200 such schools in forty states, Washington, D.C., and Puerto Rico; they enroll 1.8 million students, 63 percent of whom are minorities. In many of these schools, students have demonstrated high academic achievement—a requirement for renewal of the charter—and students who graduate from charter schools are more likely than students in normal public schools to gain admission to a college (U.S. Department of Education, 2012, 2013).

A final development in the school choice movement is *schooling for profit*. Advocates of this plan say that school systems can be operated by private profit-making companies more efficiently than by local governments. Private schooling is nothing new, of course; more than 33,000 schools in the United States are currently run by private organizations and religious groups. What is new is that hundreds of public schools, enrolling hundreds of thousands of students, are now run by private businesses for profit.

Research confirms that many public school systems suffer from bureaucratic bloat, spending too much and teaching too little. And our society has long looked to competition to improve quality. Evidence suggests that for-profit schools have greatly reduced administrative costs, but the educational results appear mixed. Although several companies claim to have improved student learning, some cities have cut back on business-run schools. In recent years, school boards in Baltimore, Miami, Hartford, and Boston have canceled the contracts of for-profit schooling corporations. But other cities are deciding to give for-profit schooling a try. For example, after Philadelphia's public school system failed to graduate one-third of its students, the state of Pennsylvania took over that city's schools and turned over most of them to for-profit companies. Although there was some improvement in student performance, school officials were still dissatisfied and so, in 2010, they turned for assistance to independent companies that operate as nonprofit organizations. In light of conflicting evidence about the performance of for-profit schools, emotions among both supporters and critics of this policy continue to run high, with each side claiming to speak for the well-being of the schoolchildren caught in the middle (Sizer, 2003; Garland, 2007; Richburg, 2008; Mezzacappa, 2010).

Finally, a recent development in the school choice debate is the so-called Parent Empowerment law. First enacted in California in 2010, such laws have been debated in more than twenty states and have been enacted in seven. These laws mandate that, if a school is failing its students, and a significant share of parents formally requests a change, the school must close down (sending students to a better-performing school), replace teachers, or enact some other school choice policy, such as becoming a charter school or being operated by a for-profit company. All "parent trigger" laws, as they are commonly called, have the goal of giving parents more say in the operation of their children's school (Richards, 2011; Russell, 2011; National Conference of State Legislatures, 2013).

All states in the United States permit home schooling. In Europe, however, many nations outlaw this practice. This German family requested and received political asylum in the United States so that they could teach their children at home. Why do you think home schooling has been controversial?

Home Schooling

Home schooling is gaining popularity across the United States. About 1.5 million children (almost 3 percent of all school-age children) receive their formal schooling at home.

Why do parents—especially mothers—undertake the enormous challenge of schooling their own children? Some twenty years ago, most of the parents who pioneered home schooling (which is now legal in every state) wanted to give their children a strongly religious upbringing. Today, however, many home-schooling families simply do not believe that public schools are doing a good job and think they can do better. To benefit their children, they are willing to alter work schedules and relearn algebra or other necessary subjects. Many belong to groups in which parents pool their efforts, specializing in what each knows best (Lois, 2013).

Advocates of home schooling point out that given the poor performance of many public schools, no one should be surprised that a growing number of parents are stepping up to teach their own children. In addition, this system works—on average, students who learn at home outperform those who learn in school. Critics argue that home schooling reduces the amount of funding going to local public schools, which ends up hurting the majority of students. In addition, as one critic points out, home schooling "takes some of the most affluent and articulate parents out of the system. These are the parents who know how to get things done with administrators" (Chris Lubienski, quoted in Cloud & Morse, 2001:48).

Schooling People with Disabilities

Many of the 6.4 million children with disabilities in the United States face special challenges getting to and from school; once there, many with crutches or wheelchairs cannot negotiate stairs and other obstacles inside school buildings. Other children with developmental disabilities such as mental retardation require extensive personal attention from specially trained teachers. Because of these challenges, many children with mental and physical disabilities have received a public education only after persistent efforts by parents and other concerned citizens (Horn & Tynan, 2001; U.S. Department of Education, 2013).

About 60 percent of children with disabilities attend public schools and spend about 80 percent of their time in general classes. This pattern reflects the principle of **mainstreaming**, *integrating students with disabilities or special needs into the overall educational program*. Mainstreaming is a form of *inclusive education* that works best for physically impaired students who have no difficulty keeping up academically with the rest of the class. A benefit of putting children with and without disabilities in the same classroom is allowing everyone to learn to interact with people who differ from one another.

mainstreaming integrating students with disabilities or special needs into the overall educational program

Adult Education

Almost 100 million U.S. adults over the age of twenty-five are enrolled in some type of schooling. These older students range in age from the mid-twenties to the seventies and beyond and make up about 40 percent of students in degree-granting programs. Adults in school are more likely to be women (57 percent) than men (43 percent), and most have above-average incomes.

Why do adults return to the classroom? The most obvious reasons given are to advance a career or train for a new job, but many are in class simply for personal enrichment (U.S. Department of Education, 2013).

The Teacher Shortage

A final challenge for U.S. schools is hiring enough teachers to fill the classrooms. A number of factors—including low salaries and frustration over extensive bureaucracy, as well as increases in class size due to rising enrollments—have combined to

Educators have long debated the best way to teach children with disabilities. On one hand, such children may benefit from separate facilities staffed by specially trained teachers. On the other hand, children are less likely to be stigmatized as "different" if they are included in regular classrooms.

discourage many people from seeking careers in teaching. As a result, there is a shortage of high-quality teachers, especially in mathematics and the sciences.

How will these slots be filled? About the same number of people graduate with education degrees annually. Most of them do not have a degree in a specific field, such as mathematics, biology, or English, and many have trouble passing state certification tests in the subject they want to teach. As a result, many schools, especially in low-income neighborhoods, are staffed by teachers who may be just one chapter ahead of their students. From another angle, almost half of this country's public school teachers have SAT scores that put them in the bottom one-third of all students who took the tests (Quaid, 2008; Kristof, 2011).

What all this adds up to is a need for higher-quality teachers. For our nation's public schools to improve, two things must happen: First, teachers who do not teach well must receive additional training or lose their jobs, and second, well-qualified people need to be attracted into the classroom by higher pay and greater public respect (Ripley, 2008; Kristof, 2011).

Getting rid of bad teachers (and perhaps bad principals, too) means changing rules that make it difficult or impossible to fire someone after a few years on the job. Gaining well-qualified teachers depends on adopting various recruitment strategies. Some schools offer incentives such as higher salaries (the average salary for a thirty-year-old teacher in public schools is only about $40,000 a year) to draw into teaching people who already have had successful careers. Some schools provide signing bonuses (especially for hard-to-fill positions in disciplines such as chemistry) or give housing allowances (in cities such as New York, where housing is often out of the reach of teachers). The pay gap between teachers and other professionals has increased in recent decades. President Obama (2007) has written that he believes that school districts should pay highly qualified and effective teachers as much as $100,000 a year—but, he adds, they also should be able to dismiss unqualified and ineffective teachers.

Other policy ideas include having community colleges play a larger role in teacher education and having government and school boards make it easier for well-trained people to get the certification they need to enter the classroom. Finally, many school districts are going global, actively recruiting in countries such as Spain, India, and the Philippines to bring talented women and men from around the world to teach in U.S. classrooms (Evelyn, 2002; Ripley, 2008; Wallis, 2008; U.S. Census Bureau, 2011).

Debate about education in the United States extends beyond the issues noted here. The Controversy & Debate box on page 593 highlights the declining share of college students who are men.

Schooling: Looking Ahead

Although the United States remains among the world leaders in sending people to college, the public school system continues to struggle with serious problems. In terms of quality of schooling, this country has fallen behind many other high-income nations, a fact that calls into question the future strength of the United States on the world stage.

Many of the problems of schooling discussed in this chapter have their roots in the larger society. We cannot expect schools *by themselves* to provide high-quality education. Schools will improve only to the extent that students, teachers, parents, and local communities commit themselves to educational excellence. In short, educational problems are *social* problems for which there is no quick fix.

For much of the twentieth century, there were just two models for education in the United States: public schools run by the government and private schools operated by nongovernmental organizations. In recent decades, however, many new ideas about schooling have emerged, including schooling for profit and a wide range of school choice programs. In the decades ahead, we are likely to see some significant changes in mass education, guided in part by social science research into the outcomes of different strategies.

Another factor that will continue to reshape schools is new information technology. Today all but the poorest primary and secondary schools use computers for instruction.

Controversy & Debate

The Twenty-First-Century Campus: Where Are the Men?

Meg: I mean, what's with this campus not having enough men?
Tricia: It's no big deal. I'd rather focus on my work.
Mark: I think it's, like, really cool for us guys.

A century ago, the campuses of colleges and universities across the United States might as well have hung out a sign that read "Men Only." Almost all of the students and faculty were male. There were a small number of women's colleges, but many more schools—including some of the best-known U.S. universities such as Yale, Harvard, and Princeton—barred women outright.

Since then, women have won greater social equality. By 1980, the number of women enrolled at U.S. colleges finally matched the number of men.

In a surprising trend, however, the share of women on campus has continued to increase. As a result, in 2011, men accounted for only 43 percent of all U.S. undergraduates. Meg DeLong noticed the gender imbalance right away when she moved into her dorm at the University of Georgia at Athens; she soon learned that just 39 percent of her first-year classmates were men. In some classes, there were few men, and women usually dominated discussions. Out of class, DeLong and many other women soon complained that having so few men on

campus hurt their social life. Not surprisingly, most of the men felt otherwise (Fonda, 2000).

What accounts for the shifting gender balance on U.S. campuses? One theory is that young men are drawn away from college by the lure of jobs, especially in high technology. This pattern is sometimes termed the "Bill Gates syndrome" or the "Mark Zuckerberg syndrome," after the men who dropped out of college to become rich and famous by founding large computer companies. In addition, analysts point to an anti-intellectual male culture. Young women are drawn to learning and seek to do well in school, but young men attach less importance to studying. Rightly or wrongly, more men seem to think they can get a good job without investing years of their lives and a considerable amount of money in getting a college degree.

The gender gap is evident in all racial and ethnic categories and at all class levels. Among African Americans on campus, only 37 percent are men. The lower the income level, the greater the gender gap in college attendance.

Many college officials are concerned about the lack of men on campus. In an effort to attract more balanced enrollments, some colleges are adopting what amounts to affirmative action programs for males. But courts in several states have already ruled such policies illegal. Many colleges, therefore, are turning to more active recruitment; admissions officers are paying special attention to male applicants and stressing a college's strength in mathematics and science—areas traditionally popular with men. In the same way that colleges across the country are striving to increase their share of minority students, the hope is that they can also succeed in attracting a larger share of men.

What Do You Think?

1. Why do you think women outnumber men on the college campus?
2. Is there a gender imbalance on your campus? Does it create problems? What problems? For whom?
3. Should colleges try to balance enrollments by sex? Is affirmative action for men a good or bad way to do this?

Computers encourage students to be more active and allow them to progress at their own pace. Even so, computers will never bring to the educational process the personal insights and imagination of a motivated human teacher.

At the college level, online learning is now available at about three-fourths of all institutions, and about one-fourth of today's college students take one or more courses online. An increasing share of textbooks is now electronic, and this digital format allows readers to become more active in their own learning (Parker, Lenhart, & Moore, 2011).

Technology will never solve all the problems that plague our schools, including violence and rigid bureaucracy. What we need is a broad plan for social change that renews this country's early ambition to provide universal schooling of high quality—a goal that we have yet to achieve.

Seeing Sociology in Everyday Life

How big is our society's inequality in schooling?

All schools, of course, differ in many ways. But there are several tiers of schooling in the United States, and these reflect the social class standing of the students they enroll. The images below and on page 595 provide a closer look at this educational hierarchy.

At the top of the schooling hierarchy are private day and boarding schools. The best of these schools, such as the Hopkins School in New Haven, Connecticut, have large endowments, small classes with extremely well-trained and very dedicated teachers, and magnificent campuses with facilities that rival those of the nation's top colleges. What do you estimate is the annual cost to attend such a school?

In the middle of the educational hierarchy are the best public high schools, most of which are found in suburban communities. This classroom in Briarcliff High School in Briarcliff Manor, New York, has small classes with good teachers and offers many extracurricular activities. What level of income do you think is typical of the families that are able to send their children to schools such as this?

When Barack and Michelle Obama moved to the White House in 2009, they faced the choice of where to enroll their two young daughters. They chose Sidwell Friends, a private school. What factors might they have considered before making this choice?

At the lower end of the hierarchy are the public schools found in our nation's large cities. Thomas Jefferson High School in Los Angeles is better than most, yet compared to suburban and private boarding schools, its classes are larger, its teachers are not as well trained, and the risk of violence within its walls is higher. What can you say about the students who attend inner-city schools?

HINT Private day and boarding schools provide an outstanding education, and the independent living experience of boarding schools also helps students prepare for success in a good college or university. Although schools like Hopkins provide financial aid to many students, the cost of a single year at such a school for most students is at least $35,000, and the typical cost at a boarding school is at least $50,000, which is just about as much as the average family earns in a year. Suburban high schools are supported through tax money; yet the cost of homes in these affluent communities is typically hundreds of thousands of dollars, putting this level of schooling out of reach for a large share of U.S. families. Public schools in the inner city enroll students from families with below-average incomes, which means these schools have the highest percentage of minority students. Liberal Democrats such as the Obamas strongly support public education, but they, like most other residents of the White House (Amy Carter went to public school), have chosen private schooling for their children, whether for educational or security reasons.

Seeing Sociology in *Your* Everyday Life

1. Make a visit to a public or private secondary school near your college or home. What is the typical social background of students enrolled there? Does the school have a tracking policy? If so, find out how it works. How much importance does a student's social background have in the school's process of making a tracking assignment?

2. Go to MySocLab and click on the Student Resources link to access the Sociology in Focus blog, where you can read the latest posts by a team of young sociologists who apply the sociological perspective to topics of popular culture.

3. Why are you in college? What benefits do you expect to receive from continuing your education? Go to the "Seeing Sociology in *Your* Everyday Life" feature in MySocLab to learn more about the benefits of a college education and also for some suggestions about how to get the most out of college.

Making the Grade

Education: A Global Survey

20.1 Compare schooling in high-, middle-, and low-income societies. (pages 572–76)

Education is the social institution for transmitting knowledge and skills, as well as teaching cultural norms and values.

- In preindustrial societies, education occurs informally within the family.
- Industrial societies develop formal systems of schooling to educate their children.
- Differences in schooling in societies around the world today reflect both cultural values and each country's level of economic development.

Schooling in India

- Despite the fact that India is now a middle-income country, patriarchy continues to shape education in India. Many more boys attend school than girls, who are often expected to work in factories at young ages.
- Today, 92% of children in India complete primary school, and 63% go on to secondary school.

Schooling in Japan

- The earliest years of schooling in Japan concentrate on transmitting Japanese cultural traditions.
- More men and women graduate from high school in Japan (96%) than in the United States (88%), but only half of high school graduates gain college admission, which is determined by highly competitive examinations.

Schooling in Great Britain

- During the Middle Ages, schooling was a privilege of the British nobility. The Industrial Revolution created a need for a literate workforce.
- Traditional class differences still affect British schooling; elite schools, which enroll 7% of British students, provide a path for admission to the most prestigious universities.

Schooling in the United States

- The United States was among the first countries to undertake compulsory mass education, reflecting both democratic political ideals and the needs of the industrial-capitalist economy.
- Schooling in the United States claims to promote equal opportunity, but the opportunity to go to college is closely tied to family income.
- The U.S. educational system stresses the value of practical learning that prepares young people for their place in the workforce.

education the social institution through which society provides its members with important knowledge, including basic facts, job skills, and cultural norms and values

schooling formal instruction under the direction of specially trained teachers

The Functions of Schooling

20.2 Apply structural-functional theory to schooling. (pages 576–77) 👁 **Watch** the **Video** in **MySocLab**

Structural-functional theory focuses on the ways in which schooling contributes to the orderly operation of society. Key functions of schooling include

- *Socialization*—teaching the skills that young people need to succeed in life, as well as cultural values and norms
- *Cultural innovation*—providing the opportunity for academic research that leads to important discoveries
- *Social integration*—molding a diverse population into one society by teaching cultural norms and values
- *Social placement*—reinforcing meritocracy and providing a path for upward social mobility
- *Latent functions*—providing child care and the opportunity for building social networks

Schooling and Social Interaction

20.3 Apply social-interaction theory to schooling. (pages 577–78)

Symbolic-interaction theory looks at how we build reality in our day-to-day interactions.

- The "self-fulfilling prophecy" describes how self-image can affect how students perform in school. Students who think they are academically superior are likely to perform better; those who think they are inferior are likely to perform less well.

Schooling and Social Inequality

 20.4 Apply social-conflict theory to schooling. (pages 578–85)

tracking assigning students to different types of educational programs

 Watch the **Video** in **MySocLab**　　 **Explore** the **Map** in **MySocLab**

Social-conflict theory links schooling to inequality involving class, race, and gender.

- Formal education serves as a means of generating conformity to produce obedient adult workers.
- Standardized tests have been criticized as culturally biased tools that may lead to labeling less privileged students as personally deficient.
- **Tracking** has been challenged by critics as a program that gives a better education to privileged youngsters.
- The majority of young people in the United States attend state-funded public schools. A small proportion of students— usually the most well-to-do—attend elite private college preparatory schools.
- Differences in school funding affect the quality of education: Public schools in more affluent areas offer a better education than schools in poorer areas.
- Largely due to the high cost of college, only 68% of U.S. students enroll in college directly after high school graduation; the higher a family's income, the more likely it is that children will attend college.
- Earning a college degree today adds as much as $1 million to a person's lifetime income.

Problems in the Schools

 20.5 Discuss dropping out, violence, and other problems facing today's schools. (pages 585–89)

functional illiteracy a lack of the reading and writing skills needed for everyday living

 Read the **Document** in **MySocLab**

Violence permeates many schools, especially in poor neighborhoods.

- Critics charge that schools today fall short in their attempts to teach personal discipline.

The bureaucratic character of schools fosters **student passivity**. Schools have evolved into huge educational factories that

- demand rigid uniformity
- define success in terms of numerical ratings
- hold rigid expectations of students
- require too much specialization
- instill little individual responsibility in students

The high school **dropout rate**—currently 7.1%—leaves many young people unprepared for the world of work and at high risk of poverty. The dropout rate for children in families with income in the bottom 25% is more than five times higher than for children living in high-income families.

Declining academic standards are reflected in today's lower average scores on achievement tests, the **functional illiteracy** of a significant proportion of high school graduates, and grade inflation.

Current Issues in U.S. Education

20.6 Summarize the debate over the performance of U.S. schools. (pages 589–92)

mainstreaming integrating students with disabilities or special needs into the overall educational program

Watch the **Video** in **MySocLab**

The **school choice movement** seeks to make schools more accountable to the public. Innovative school choice options include magnet schools, schooling for profit, and charter schools.

Home Schooling

- The original pioneers of home schooling did not believe in public education because they wanted to give their children a strongly religious upbringing.
- Home schooling advocates today point to the poor performance of public schools.

Schooling People with Disabilities

- In the past, children with mental or physical disabilities were schooled in special classes.
- **Mainstreaming** affords them broader opportunities and exposes all children to a more diverse student population.

Adult Education

- Adults represent a growing proportion of students in the United States.
- Most older learners are women who are engaged in job-related study.

The Teacher Shortage

- A number of factors—including low salaries and frustration over extensive bureaucracy, as well as increases in class size due to rising enrollments—have combined to discourage many people from seeking careers in teaching, resulting in a shortage of high-quality teachers.
- To address this shortage, many school districts are recruiting teachers from abroad.

21 Health and Medicine

((· **Listen** to **Chapter 21** in **MySocLab**

LEARNING OBJECTIVES

21.1 Explain how patterns of health are shaped by society.

21.2 Contrast patterns of health in low- and high-income countries.

21.3 Analyze how race, class, gender, and age are linked to health.

21.4 Compare the medical systems in nations around the world.

21.5 Apply sociology's major theories to health and medicine.

the Power of Society

to shape patterns of health

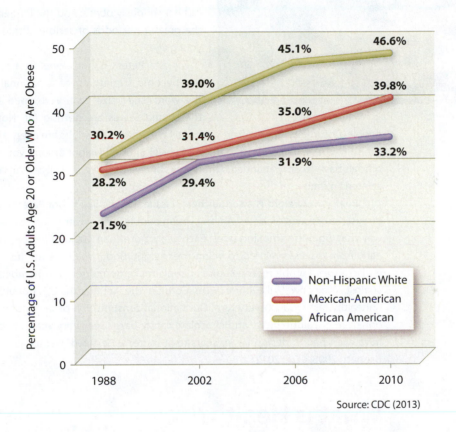

Percentage of U.S. Adults Age 20 or Older Who Are Obese

- Non-Hispanic White
- Mexican-American
- African American

30.2%   39.0%   45.1%   46.6%

28.2%   31.4%   35.0%   39.8%

21.5%   29.4%   31.9%   33.2%

50

40

30

20

10

0

1988   2002   2006   2010

Source: CDC (2013)

What is one of the most disturbing trends in the United States involving health? The answer is the rising rate of obesity. Government studies show that most U.S. adults over the age of twenty are at least somewhat overweight and that rates of obesity (being considerably overweight) are rapidly increasing for all categories of the U.S. population. Since 1988, the share of white people who are obese has risen from about 22 percent to 33 percent. The share of African Americans and Mexican Americans who are obese is even higher and also has been on the rise. While we might think health is a matter of personal choices or sometimes the result of sheer luck, the rise in average body weight in the United States reflects changes in our way of life, including diet and patterns of exercise.

Chapter Overview

This chapter explores health care, including medicine, a social institution of major importance. The chapter begins by explaining why health is a social issue and why sociologists have much to say about human health.

Krista Peters cannot remember a time in her life when she was not on a diet. The sixteen-year-old, who lives in a small Pennsylvania town, shakes her head. "It's, like, I can't do anything about it. I know I don't look good. My mom says I shouldn't eat so much; the nurse at school says the same thing. But if it's up to me, then why can't I ever lose any weight?"

Peters does have a weight problem. Although she stands just 5 feet 2 inches tall, she weighs 240 pounds. Doctors would call her seriously obese, and the longer she remains so heavy, the greater her odds of serious disease and even death at a young age.

Krista Peters is not alone. In a society where fast food has become something of a national dish and people use the word "supersize" as a verb, men and women all across the United States are getting fat. Not some people—*most* people. According to the experts, about 64 percent of U.S. adults are overweight and 36 percent are clinically obese. In response to the rising level of body weight among young people, government officials have recently mandated more fruits and vegetables, as well as limits on junk food, on school cafeteria menus.

Being overweight is a serious health issue. People like Krista Peters are at high risk for heart disease, stroke, and diabetes. Among young people, being overweight carries health risks the same way that cigarette smoking does. Each year, more than 100,000 people in the United States die early from diseases related to being overweight. Body weight is not just a personal problem; it is also a *social* problem. The choices people make do matter, but members of our society are up against some powerful cultural forces. Consider the fact that the U.S. population is confronted with unhealthy fast food at every turn. Our national consumption of salty potato chips, sugar-rich soft drinks, high-calorie pizza, and chocolate candy bars rises every year. Car companies and airlines have even had to design larger seats to fit more "supersized" people (Bellandi, 2003; Witt, 2004; Bennett, 2006; CDC, 2012).

What Is Health?

(21.1) Explain how patterns of health are shaped by society.

 **Watch** in **MySocLab** **Video:** *The Big Picture: Health and Medicine*

health a state of complete physical, mental, and social well-being

In ideal terms, according to the World Health Organization (1946:3), **health** is *a state of complete physical, mental, and social well-being*. This definition underscores the major theme of this chapter: Health is not just a matter of personal choice, nor is it only a biological issue; patterns of well-being and illness are rooted in the organization of society.

Health and Society

Society shapes people's health in four major ways:

1. **Cultural patterns define health.** Standards of health vary from place to place. A century ago, yaws, a contagious skin disease, was so common in sub-Saharan Africa that people there considered it normal (Dubos, 1980). In the United States, a rich diet is so common that most adults and about one-sixth of children are overweight. "Health," therefore, is sometimes a matter of having the same disease as your neighbors (Pinhey, Rubinstein, & Colfax, 1997; CDC, 2012).

What people see as healthful also reflects what they think is morally good. Members of our society (especially men) think a competitive way of life is "healthy" because it fits our cultural mores, but stress contributes to heart disease and many other illnesses. People who object to homosexuality on moral grounds call this sexual orientation "sick," even though it is natural from a biological point of view. Thus ideas about health act as a form of social control, encouraging conformity to cultural norms.

2. **Cultural standards of health change over time.** In the early twentieth century, some doctors warned women not to go to college because higher education would strain the female brain. Others claimed that masturbation was a threat to health. We know now that both of these ideas are false. Fifty years ago, on the other hand, few doctors understood the dangers of cigarette smoking or too much sun exposure, practices that we now recognize as serious health risks. Even patterns of basic hygiene change over time. Today, most people in the United States bathe every day; this is three times as often as fifty years ago (Gillespie, 2000).

3. **A society's technology affects people's health.** In poor nations, infectious diseases are widespread because of malnutrition and poor sanitation. As industrialization raises living standards, people become healthier. But industrial technology also creates new threats to health. As Chapter 22 ("Population, Urbanization, and Environment") explains, high-income ways of life threaten human health by overtaxing the world's resources and creating pollution.

4. **Social inequality affects people's health.** All societies distribute resources unequally. In general, the rich have far better physical and mental health than the poor.

Health: A Global Survey

(21.2) Contrast patterns of health in low- and high-income countries.

We see the close link between health and social life in the fact that human well-being improved over the long course of history as societies developed more advanced technology. Differences in societal development are also the cause of striking differences in health around the world today.

Health in Low-Income Countries

December 25, Yucay, Peru. We're attending the Christmas Day street festival in this small village in the Andes Mountains. There is much excitement and happiness everywhere. I notice something unusual—at least by North American standards— not one of the hundreds of people who have passed by along the main street is wearing glasses. One Peruvian friend says that in this poor community, there are no optometrists or eye doctors, and no one has any extra money to afford glasses.

In the United States and much of the world, severe poverty cuts decades off the long life expectancy that is typical of rich countries. A look back at Global Map 15–1 on page 432 shows that people in most parts of Africa have a life expectancy of barely fifty years, and in the poorest countries, nearly one in ten newborns dies within a year and almost one in four people dies before reaching the age of thirty (Population Reference Bureau, 2012; United Nations, 2011; World Bank, 2013).

The World Health Organization reports that 1 billion people around the world—about one person in six—suffer from serious illness due to poverty. Most poverty-linked disease occurs in low-income countries, where poverty accounts for 70 percent of all illness. In rich countries, by contrast, poverty is the cause of just 7 percent of all illness (Bloom et al., 2011; Murray et al., 2012).

How does poverty threaten health? In simple terms, poor sanitation and malnutrition kill people of all ages. A lack of safe drinking water is also common, and bad water carries

Watch in **MySocLab**
Video: *Sociology on the Job: Health and Medicine*

TABLE 21–1 Leading Causes of Death in the United States, 1900 and 2011

1900	2011
1. Influenza and pneumonia	1. Heart disease
2. Tuberculosis	2. Cancer
3. Stomach and intestinal disease	3. Lung disease (noncancerous)
4. Heart disease	4. Stroke
5. Cerebral hemorrhage	5. Accidents
6. Kidney disease	6. Alzheimer's disease
7. Accidents	7. Diabetes
8. Cancer	8. Influenza and pneumonia
9. Disease in early infancy	9. Kidney disease
10. Diphtheria	10. Suicide

Sources: Information for 1900 is from Cockerham (1986); information for 2011 is from Hoyert and Xu (2012).

a number of infectious diseases, including influenza, pneumonia, and tuberculosis, which are widespread killers in poor societies today. To make matters worse, medical personnel are few and far between; as a result, the world's poorest people—many of whom live in Central Africa—never see a physician.

In a classic vicious circle, poverty breeds disease, which in turn undermines the ability to work. When medical technology controls infectious disease, the populations of poor nations soar. Without resources to provide for the current population, poor societies can ill afford population increases. Therefore, programs that lower death rates in poor countries will succeed only if they are coupled with programs that reduce birth rates.

Health in High-Income Countries

By 1800, as the Industrial Revolution took hold, factory jobs in the cities attracted people from all over the countryside. Cities quickly became overcrowded, causing serious sanitation problems. Factories fouled the air with smoke, which few people recognized as a health threat until well into the twentieth century. Workplace accidents were common.

Gradually, industrialization improved health in Western Europe and North America by providing better nutrition and safer housing for most people, so that by about 1850, health began to improve. Around this time, medical advances began to control infectious diseases. In 1854, for example, a physician named John Snow mapped the street addresses of London's cholera victims and found that they had all drunk contaminated water from the same well. Not long afterward, scientists linked cholera to a specific bacterium and developed a vaccine against the deadly disease. Armed with scientific knowledge, early environmentalists campaigned against common practices such as discharging raw sewage into the same rivers used for drinking water. By the early twentieth century, death rates from infectious diseases had fallen sharply.

A glance at Table 21–1 shows that the leading killers in 1900 were infectious diseases, such as influenza, pneumonia, and tuberculosis. Today, in all but the poorest nations of the world, such diseases account for just a small percentage of deaths. It is now chronic illnesses, such as heart disease, cancer, and stroke, that cause most deaths, usually in old age (Murray et al., 2012).

Health in the United States

21.3 Analyze how race, class, gender, and age are linked to health.

Because the United States is a rich nation, health is generally good by world standards, and it is certainly better than what is typical of poor countries. At the same time, although the United States spends more on health care per person than any other high-income nation, this nation's people have higher rates of disease, are the least likely to live to age fifty, and end up dying sooner than people in other high-income countries (World Health Organization, 2011; Tavernise, 2012). In addition, some categories of people have better health than others.

Who Is Healthy? Age, Gender, Class, and Race

social epidemiology the study of how health and disease are distributed throughout a society's population

Social epidemiology is *the study of how health and disease are distributed throughout a society's population.* Just as early social epidemiologists traced the spread of diseases, researchers today examine the connection between health and our physical and social environments. National Map 21–1 on page 603 surveys life expectancy—a key measure of human health—for counties across the United States where there is more than a ten-year

Seeing Ourselves

 Explore patterns of health in your local community and in counties across the United States in **MySocLab**

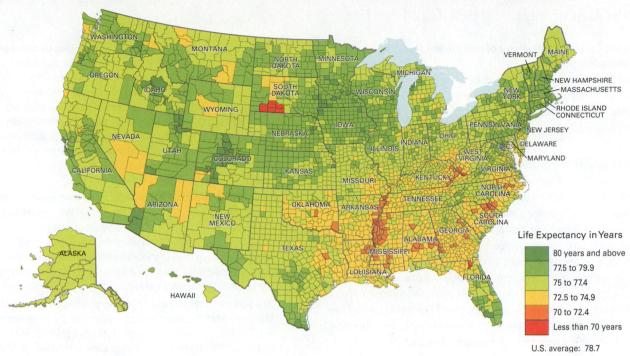

Life Expectancy in Years

- 80 years and above
- 77.5 to 79.9
- 75 to 77.4
- 72.5 to 74.9
- 70 to 72.4
- Less than 70 years

U.S. average: 78.7

NATIONAL MAP 21–1 Life Expectancy across the United States

How long people typically live is a good measure of the overall health of a population. Life expectancy varies from county to county across the United States and reflects factors such as nutrition and diet and smoking habits. Looking at the map, what pattern do you see? Can you explain it?

Source: U.S. Department of Health and Human Services (2009)

difference in average life expectancy between the richest and poorest communities. Patterns of health can be viewed in terms of age, gender, social class, and race.

Age and Gender

In the United States, the death of a young person is a rare event that is typically viewed as unexpected and tragic. Still, young people do fall victim to accidents and, more recently, to acquired immune deficiency syndrome (AIDS).

Across the life course, women have better health than men. First, girls are less likely than boys to die before or immediately after birth. Then, as socialization begins, males become more aggressive and individualistic, which contributes to young males having four times the risk of suicide, and five times the risk of dying from a homicide (CDC, 2012). Later in life, men are also more likely to die from heart disease. As the Thinking About Diversity box on page 604 explains, the combination of chronic impatience, uncontrolled ambition, and frequent outbursts of hostility that doctors call "coronary-prone behavior" is a fairly close match with our culture's definition of masculinity. This is one important way in which gender affects the "bottom line" of longevity, with women, on average, outliving men by about five years.

Social Class and Race

Government researchers tell us that 77 percent of adults in families with incomes over $100,000 think their health is excellent or very good, but only 46 percent of adults in families earning less than $35,000 say the same. Conversely, just 6 percent of higher-income people describe their health as either fair or poor compared with 23 percent of low-income people. Having a higher income and greater wealth boosts people's health by improving their nutrition, enabling them to receive better health care, and allowing them to live in safer and less stressful surroundings (CDC, 2012).

Thinking About Diversity: Race, Class, & Gender

Masculinity: A Threat to Health?

Jeff: Cindy! If you don't get out of there in ten seconds, I'm gonna beat you up!

Cindy: Chill out! I have as much right to be in the bathroom as you do. I'll come out when I am ready.

Jeff: Are you going to take *all day?*

Cindy: Why are you guys always in such a hurry?

Doctors call it "coronary-prone behavior." Psychologists call it the "Type A personality." Sociologists recognize it as our culture's concept of masculinity. This combination of attitudes and behavior, common among men in our society, includes not just impatience ("C'mon! Get outta my bathroom!") but also uncontrolled ambition ("I've gotta have it—I *need* that!") and free-floating hostility ("Why are people *such idiots?*").

This pattern, although normal from a cultural point of view, is one major reason that men who are driven to succeed are at high risk of heart disease. By acting out the Type A personality, we may get the job done, but we set in motion complex biochemical processes that are very hard on the human heart.

Here are a few questions to help you assess your own degree of risk (or that of someone important to you):

1. **Do you believe you have to be aggressive to succeed?** Do "nice guys finish last"? If your answer to this question is yes, for your heart's sake, try to remove hostility from your life. Here's a place to start: Eliminate profanity from your speech. Whenever someone in everyday life starts getting to you, try replacing aggression with compassion, which can be surprisingly effective in dealing with other people. Medically speaking, compassion and humor—rather than irritation and aggravation—will improve your health.

2. **How well do you handle uncertainty and opposition?** Do you have moments when you fume "Why won't the waiter take my order?" or "This customer just doesn't get it!"? We all like to know what's going on, and we like others to agree with us. But the world often doesn't work that way. Accepting uncertainty and opposition makes us more mature and certainly healthier.

3. **Are you uncomfortable showing positive emotions?** Many men think giving and accepting love—from women, from children, and from other men—is a sign of weakness. But the medical truth is that love supports health and anger damages it.

As human beings, we have a great deal of choice about how to live. Think about the choices you make, and reflect on how our society's idea of masculinity often makes us hard on others (including those we love) and, just as important, hard on ourselves.

What Do You Think?

1. Do you think masculinity is harmful to health? Why or why not?

2. Have you had any experiencesthat cause you to link masculinity or femininity to health?

3. How might we try to modify our behavior in the interest of better health?

Sources: Friedman and Rosenman (1974) and M. P. Levine (1990).

Research suggests that African Americans are no different from whites in terms of their desire for good health and willingness to seek medical help. But poverty among African Americans—at almost three times the rate for whites—shapes people's everyday options and helps explain why black people are more likely to die in infancy and, as adults, are more likely to suffer the effects of high blood pressure and heart disease as well as violence and drug abuse (Schnittker, Pescosolido, & Croghan, 2005; McNeil, 2011; CDC, 2012; U.S. Census Bureau, 2012).

The life expectancy of white children born in 2011 is nearly four years greater than that of African Americans (79.0 years versus 75.3). From another angle, 81 percent of white men but just 70 percent of African American men will live to age sixty-five. The comparable figures for women are 88 percent for whites and 81 percent for African Americans (Arias, 2012; CDC, 2012).

Infant mortality—the death rate among children under one year of age—is twice as high for severely disadvantaged children as for children born into privileged families. Although the health of the richest children in our nation is the best in the world, our poorest children are as vulnerable to disease as those in low-income nations such as Nigeria and Cambodia.

Cigarette Smoking

Cigarette smoking tops the list of preventable health hazards in the United States. Only after World War I did smoking become popular in this country. Despite growing evidence of its dangers, smoking remained fashionable until around a generation ago. Today, however, an increasing number of people consider smoking a mild form of social deviance, and an increasing number of states have banned smoking in public buildings (Niesse, 2007).

The popularity of cigarettes peaked in 1960, when 45 percent of U.S. adults smoked. By 2011, according to the Centers for Disease Control and Prevention (2012), only 19 percent were still lighting up. Although smoking is not as common as it was, not everyone who stops using cigarettes stops using tobacco. Government studies show that smoking bans and higher taxes on cigarettes have lowered the consumption of cigarettes, although most of the decline in recent years has been among people who have taken up pipe smoking or the use of smokeless tobacco (CDC, 2012).

Quitting smoking is difficult because cigarette smoke contains nicotine, a physically addictive drug. Many people smoke to cope with stress: Divorced and separated people, the unemployed, and people serving in the armed forces are likely to smoke. Smoking is much more common among working-class people than among those with more income and education. A larger share of men (22 percent) than women (17 percent) smokes. But cigarettes, the only form of tobacco popular with women, have taken a toll on women's health. By 1987, lung cancer surpassed breast cancer as a cause of death among U.S. women, who now account for 39 percent of all smoking-related deaths (Pampel, 2006; CDC, 2010, 2012).

More than 440,000 men and women in the United States die prematurely each year as a direct result of cigarette smoking, a figure that exceeds the death toll from alcohol, cocaine, heroin, homicide, suicide, automobile accidents, and AIDS combined. Smokers also suffer more frequent minor illnesses such as the flu, and pregnant women who smoke increase the likelihood of spontaneous abortion and low-birthweight babies. Even nonsmokers exposed to cigarette smoke have a higher risk of smoking-related diseases; health officials estimate that secondhand smoke causes heart disease or lung cancer that kills about 50,000 people each year (CDC, 2008, 2010).

Tobacco is a $90 billion industry in the United States. With revenues like that, the tobacco industry is able to spend more than $15 million a year employing lobbyists in Washington to influence tobacco policy. It is also able to finance efforts aimed at presenting the controversy over smoking in terms of the "anti-smoking lobby" versus people who choose to smoke and at playing down the ways that tobacco companies threaten public health (Eriksen, Makay, & Ross, 2012).

In 1997, the tobacco industry admitted that cigarette smoking is harmful to health and agreed to stop marketing cigarettes to young people. Despite the antismoking trend in the United States, research shows that 4 percent of middle school students, 16 percent of high school students and 31 percent of college students smoke at least occasionally (American College Health Association, 2012; CDC, 2012). In addition, the use of chewing tobacco— known to cause cancers of the mouth and throat—is increasing among the young.

The tobacco industry has increased its sales abroad, especially in low- and middle-income countries where there is less regulation of tobacco products and where 80 percent of the world's smokers now live. In many countries, especially in Asia, a large majority of men smoke. Worldwide, more than 1 billion adults (about 25 percent of the total) smoke, consuming some 6 trillion cigarettes annually, and there is not yet any sign of the decline in smoking that has occurred in high-income countries. If the current global trends continue, tobacco-related deaths will increase to more than 8 million a year by 2030, which amounts to one person in the world dying every four seconds (Horton, 2012; World Health Organization, 2013).

The harm that can come from cigarette smoking is real. But the good news is that about ten years after quitting, an ex-smoker's health is about as good as that of someone who never smoked at all.

Eating Disorders

eating disorder a physical and mental disorder that involves an intense form of dieting or other unhealthy method of weight control driven by the desire to be very thin

An **eating disorder** is *a physical and mental disorder that involves intense dieting or other unhealthy method of weight control driven by the desire to be very thin.* One eating disorder, *anorexia nervosa,* is characterized by dieting to the point of starvation; another is *bulimia,* which involves binge eating followed by induced vomiting to avoid weight gain.

Gender plays a part in eating disorders: among teenagers, girls are about three times more likely than boys to be affected by these diseases. Among adults, women are three times more likely to suffer from anorexia nervosa and five times more likely to suffer from bulimia than are men. People with eating disorders come from all social backgrounds although risk levels are highest among whites living in affluent families.

For women, U.S. culture equates slimness with being successful and attractive to men. Conversely, we tend to stereotype overweight women (and to a lesser extent men) as lazy, sloppy, and even stupid (U.S. Department of Health and Human Services, National Institute of Mental Health, 2012; Neporent, 2013).

Research shows that most college-age women believe that "guys like thin girls," that being thin is critical to physical attractiveness, and that they are not as thin as men would like. In fact, most college women want to be even thinner than most college men want them to be. Men typically express greater satisfaction with their own body shape (Fallon & Rozin, 1985).

For a close-up look at how the introduction of U.S. culture to the island of Fiji resulted in a sharp increase in eating disorders among women there, **Read More** in **MySocLab**, *Gender and Eating Disorders: A Report from Fiji*

Because few women are able to meet our culture's unrealistic standards of beauty, many women develop a low self-image. This feeling may encourage the sales of makeup, clothes, and various beauty aids, as does the mass media's focus on people's appearance. But it also leads many young women to diet to the point of risking their health and even their lives.

People with eating disorders contend with more than their illness. Research indicates that they are also viewed by others not as people with a mental disorder but as weak individuals who are seeking attention. In fact, the stigma attached to eating disorders was found to be more severe than the stigma attached to depression (Roehrig & McLean, 2010).

Obesity

Eating disorders such as anorexia nervosa and bulimia are serious, but they are not the biggest eating-related problem in the United States. Obesity in the population as a whole is rapidly reaching crisis proportions. For the world as a whole, the average person weighs 137 pounds; for the United States, the average is about 180 pounds (196 pounds for men and 166 pounds for women) (BioMed Central, 2012; CDC, 2013).

As noted in the opening to this chapter, the government reports that 64 percent of U.S. adults are overweight, which is defined in terms of a *body mass index* (BMI) of 25.0 to 29.9, or roughly 10 to 30 pounds over a healthy weight. Of all U.S. adults, 36 percent are clinically obese, with a BMI over 30, which means that they are at least 30 pounds over their healthy weight. National Map 21–2 on page 607 shows the dramatic increase in obesity across the United States between 1996 and 2011.

Being overweight can limit physical activity and raises the risk of a number of serious diseases, including heart disease, stroke, and diabetes. According to the U.S. government, the cost of treating diseases caused by obesity due to such illnesses is about $147 billion every year. Most seriously, some 112,000 people die each year in the United States from diseases related to being overweight (Ferraro & Kelley-Moore, 2003; CDC, 2010).

A cause for national concern is the fact that the obesity rate for the United States is among the highest in the

The obesity rate for the U.S. population is among the highest in the world and it is increasing. As a nation, we are "big gainers" in terms of body mass. This trend has sparked popular television shows such as *Extreme Makeover: Weight Loss Edition,* which celebrates individuals who dramatically drop their weight through a program of fitness training and lifestyle changes. But is the solution to the national trend toward obesity simply a matter of personal effort? What changes to our culture would help move the entire population toward a healthier lifestyle?

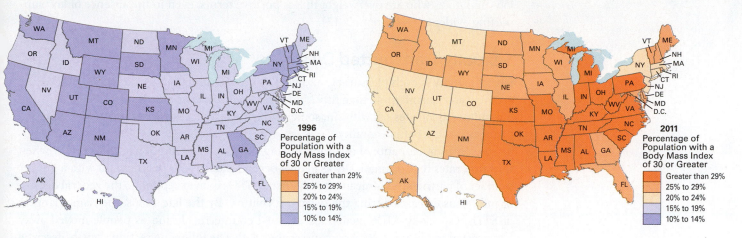

NATIONAL MAP 21–2 Obesity across the United States, 1996 and 2011

The map on the left shows the percentage of each state's population that was medically obese in 1996; the one on the right shows the figures for 2011. What factors do you think are responsible for the trend toward more and more obesity in our country?

Source: Centers for Disease Control and Prevention (2013).

world—well above the rates for Canada, European nations, and Japan—and it is rising. In this country, obesity is evident even in infants. A recent study found that almost one-third of nine-month-old infants were overweight enough to be classified as either obese or at risk for obesity. The trend toward higher rates of obesity among infants and children—the rate is now three times what it was just thirty years ago—suggests that the medical problems of this new generation will be even greater as they reach middle age and may ultimately reverse the historical trend toward greater life expectancy (Moss & Yeaton, 2010; Stockdale, McIntyre, & Sauter, 2011; CDC, 2012; OECD, 2012).

What are the social causes of obesity? One factor is that we live in a society in which more and more people have jobs that keep them sitting in front of computer screens rather than engaging in the type of physical labor that was common a century ago. Even when we are not on the job, most of the work around the house is done by machines (or other people). Children spend more of their time sitting as well—watching television or playing video games.

Then, of course, there is diet. The typical person in the United States is eating more salty and fatty food than ever before (Wells & Buzby, 2008). And as companies try to sell food for less money to gain efficiencies of scale, all meals are getting bigger. The Department of Agriculture reported that in 2000, the typical U.S. adult consumed 140 more pounds of food in a year than was true a decade earlier. Comparing old and new editions of cookbooks, recipes that used to say they would feed six now say they will feed four. As shown in the Power of Society figure at the beginning of this chapter, the obesity problem is greater among minorities than among white people. In large part, this difference reflects income. The odds of being overweight go up among people with lower incomes partly because they may lack the education to make healthy choices and partly because stores in low-income communities offer a greater selection of low-cost, high-fat snack foods and fewer healthful fruits and vegetables (Hellmich, 2002).

Just as researchers have tracked a rising tide of obesity in the United States, they are also finding increasing prejudice directed against people who are overweight. Simply put, many people see being thin as embodying important cultural values such as personal discipline, trying hard, and ambition to succeed. Being overweight, by contrast, seems to imply the absence of these same traits.

Such attitudes are not only widespread but also can be quite harmful. Evidence suggests that physicians are likely to doubt the ability of overweight patients to follow "doctor's

Read in **MySocLab Document:** *Let Them Eat Fat: The Heavy Truths about American Obesity* by Greg Crister orders"; similarly, juries may be less likely to feel sympathy for an overweight person accused of a crime. Perhaps most important of all, employers tend to assess workers and job candidates who are overweight in less positive terms, even in the absence of any supporting evidence (Neporent, 2013).

Sexually Transmitted Diseases

Sexual activity is both pleasurable and vital to the continuation of our species. But sexual activity can transmit more than fifty kinds of *sexually transmitted diseases* (STDs). Because our culture associates sex with sin, some people regard these diseases not only as illnesses but also as marks of immorality.

STDs grabbed national attention during the "sexual revolution" of the 1960s, when infection rates rose dramatically as people began sexual activity earlier and with a greater number of partners. This means that the rise in STDs is an exception to the general decline of infectious diseases during the twentieth century. By the late 1980s, the rising dangers of STDs, especially AIDS, generated a sexual counterrevolution as people moved away from casual sex (Kain, 1987; Laumann et al., 1994). The following sections briefly describe several common STDs.

Gonorrhea and Syphilis

Gonorrhea and syphilis, among the oldest known diseases, are caused by microscopic organisms that are almost always transmitted by sexual contact. Untreated, gonorrhea causes sterility; syphilis damages major organs and can result in blindness, mental disorders, and death.

In 2011, some 251,000 cases of gonorrhea and 13,350 cases of syphilis were officially recorded in the United States, although the actual numbers may be several times higher. Most cases are contracted by non-Hispanic African Americans (66 percent), with lower numbers recorded among non-Hispanic whites (21 percent), Latinos (11 percent), and Asian Americans and Native Americans (1 percent each) (CDC, 2012).

Both gonorrhea and syphilis can easily be cured with antibiotics such as penicillin. Thus neither is a major health problem in the United States.

Genital Herpes

Genital herpes is a virus that is fairly common, infecting at least 25 million adolescents and adults in the United States (one in six). Though far less dangerous than gonorrhea and syphilis, herpes is incurable. People with genital herpes may not have any symptoms, or they may experience periodic, painful blisters on the genitals accompanied by fever and headache. Although not fatal to adults, pregnant women with genital herpes can transmit the disease during a vaginal delivery, and it can be deadly to a newborn. Therefore, women with active infections usually give birth by cesarean section (Sobel, 2001; CDC, 2012).

AIDS

The most serious of all sexually transmitted diseases is *acquired immune deficiency syndrome* (AIDS). Identified in 1981, it is incurable and almost always fatal. AIDS is caused by the *human immunodeficiency virus* (HIV), which attacks white blood cells, weakening the immune system. AIDS thus makes a person vulnerable to a wide range of diseases that eventually cause death.

AIDS deaths in the United States numbered 15,529 in 2010. In addition, officials recorded 32,052 new cases in the United States in 2011, raising the total number of cases on the official record to 1,155,792. Of these people, 636,048 have died (CDC, 2013).

Globally, the number of HIV infections is no longer rapidly increasing. In 2011, about 2.5 million adults and children became infected, which represents a 20 percent drop from a decade earlier. At the same time, the number of infected people is huge, at about 34 million people. The global AIDS death toll now exceeds 25 million, with about 1 percent of the 2011 total of 1.7 million deaths occurring here in the United States (UNAIDS, 2012). Global Map 21–1 on page 609 shows that Africa (especially south of the Sahara) has the

Window on the World

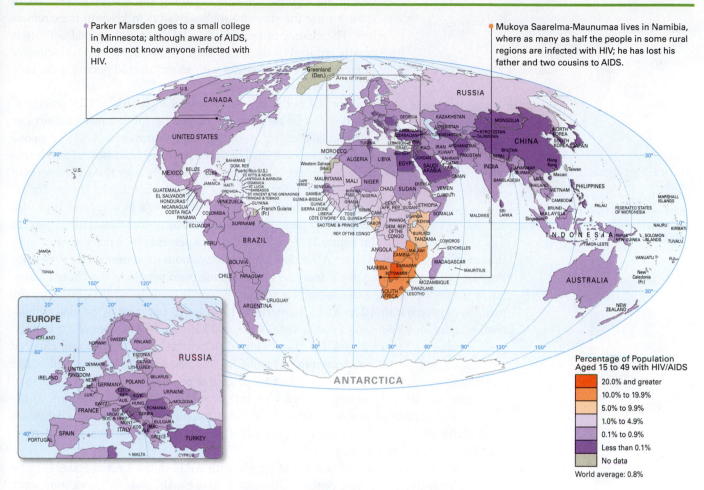

Parker Marsden goes to a small college in Minnesota; although aware of AIDS, he does not know anyone infected with HIV.

Mukoya Saarelma-Maunumaa lives in Namibia, where as many as half the people in some rural regions are infected with HIV; he has lost his father and two cousins to AIDS.

Percentage of Population Aged 15 to 49 with HIV/AIDS

- 20.0% and greater
- 10.0% to 19.9%
- 5.0% to 9.9%
- 1.0% to 4.9%
- 0.1% to 0.9%
- Less than 0.1%
- No data

World average: 0.8%

GLOBAL MAP 21–1 HIV/AIDS Infection of Adults in Global Perspective

Sixty-nine percent of all global HIV infections are in sub-Saharan Africa. In Swaziland, one-fourth of people between the ages of fifteen and forty-nine are infected with HIV/AIDS. This very high infection rate reflects the prevalence of other sexually transmitted diseases and infrequent use of condoms, two factors that promote transmission of HIV. South and Southeast Asia account for about 15 percent of global HIV infections; by contrast, North America and South America taken together account for 8 percent of global HIV infections. From another angle, in Thailand, 1.2 percent of people aged fifteen to forty-nine are now infected compared to 0.6 percent of comparable people in the United States. The incidence of infection in Muslim nations is extremely low by world standards.

Sources: Population Reference Bureau (2012) and UNAIDS (2012).

highest HIV infection rate and accounts for 69 percent of all world cases. The good news is that many of the countries in this region of the world are making dramatic strides toward reducing the rate of infection, especially among children. The risk of infection remains higher for females than for males, not only because HIV is transmitted more easily from men to women but also because many African cultures encourage women to be submissive to men. According to some analysts, the AIDS crisis threatens the political and economic security of Africa, which in turn affects the entire world (Ashford, 2002; UNAIDS, 2012).

Upon infection, people with HIV display no symptoms at all, so most are unaware of their condition. Symptoms of AIDS may not appear for a year or longer, but during this time an infected person may infect others. Within five years, one-third of infected people in the United States develop full-blown AIDS; half develop AIDS within ten years; and almost all become sick within twenty years. In low-income countries, the progression of this illness is much more rapid, with many people dying within a few years of becoming infected.

HIV is infectious but not contagious. That means that HIV is transmitted from person to person through direct contact with blood, semen, or breast milk but not through casual

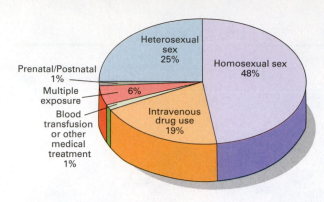

FIGURE 21–1 Types of Transmission for Reported U.S. AIDS Cases as of 2011

There are several ways that people can be infected with HIV.

Source: Centers for Disease Control and Prevention (2013).

contact such as shaking hands, hugging, sharing towels or dishes, swimming together, or even coughing and sneezing. The risk of transmitting the virus through saliva (as in kissing) is extremely low. The chance of transmitting HIV through sexual activity is greatly reduced by the use of latex condoms. However, abstinence or an exclusive relationship with an uninfected person is the only sure way to avoid infection.

Specific behaviors put people at high risk of HIV infection. The first is *anal sex* with an infected person because anal sex can cause rectal bleeding, allowing easy transmission of HIV from one individual to another. The fact that many homosexual and bisexual men engage in anal sex helps explain why these categories of people account for 48 percent of AIDS cases in the United States.

Sharing needles used to inject drugs is a second high-risk behavior. At present, intravenous drug users account for 25 percent (in Figure 21–1, represented as 19 percent plus 6 percent with "multiple exposure") of persons with AIDS. Sex with an intravenous drug user is also very risky. Because intravenous drug use is more common among poor people in the United States, AIDS is now becoming a disease of the socially disadvantaged. Minorities make up the majority of people with AIDS: African Americans (who are 13.1 percent of the total population) account for 43 percent of people with AIDS, and Latinos (16.7 percent of the population) represent 20 percent of AIDS cases. Almost 80 percent of all women and children with the disease are African American or Latino. By contrast, Asian Americans and Native Americans together account for only about 1.4 percent of people with AIDS (CDC, 2013).

Use of any drug, including alcohol, also increases the risk of HIV infection to the extent that it impairs judgment. In other words, even people who understand what places them at risk of infection may act less responsibly if they are under the influence of alcohol, marijuana, or some other drug.

As Figure 21–1 shows, 48 percent of people with AIDS in the United States became infected through homosexual contact, although heterosexuals, infected in various ways, account for about 46 percent of AIDS cases. But heterosexual activity can transmit HIV, and the danger rises with the number of sexual partners one has, especially if they fall into high-risk categories. Worldwide, heterosexual relations are the primary means of HIV transmission, accounting for two-thirds of all infections.

In the United States, treating just one person with AIDS can cost hundreds of thousands of dollars, which is well beyond the reach of many people. Government health programs, private insurance, and personal savings rarely cover more than a fraction of the cost of treatment. In addition, there is the mounting cost of caring for at least 75,000 children orphaned by AIDS (worldwide, the number is around 16.6 million). The good news is that the cost of new drugs and treatment therapies has gone down, and as a result millions of lives have been saved worldwide. Even so, AIDS continues to represent both a medical and a social problem of monumental proportions.

In the early 1980s, the U.S. government responded slowly to the AIDS crisis, largely because the earliest people to be infected, gay men and intravenous drug users, were widely viewed as deviant. But funds allocated for AIDS research and education have increased rapidly (the 2013 federal budget provides $28 billion), and researchers have identified some drugs, including protease inhibitors, that suppress the symptoms of the

In the African nation of Kenya, about 170 people die from AIDS every day. In recent years, the spread of AIDS in sub-Saharan Africa has been greatly reduced. Even so, some 220,000 children under age fourteen in Kenya are now living with HIV. This Nairobi infant, who already has AIDS, is fighting for his life.

disease enough to greatly extend the lives of people infected with HIV. But educational programs remain the most effective weapon against AIDS, since prevention is the only way to stop the spread of a disease that so far has no cure.

Ethical Issues Surrounding Death

Now that technological advances are giving human beings the power to draw the line separating life and death, we must decide how and when to do so. In other words, questions about the use of medical technology have added an ethical dimension to health and illness.

When Does Death Occur?

Common sense suggests that life ceases when breathing and heartbeat stop. But the ability to replace a heart and artificially sustain respiration makes that definition of death obsolete. Medical and legal experts in the United States now define death as an *irreversible* state involving no response to stimulation, no movement or breathing, no reflexes, and no indication of brain activity (Wall, 1980; Jones, 1998).

Do People Have a Right to Die?

Today, medical personnel, family members, and patients themselves face the burden of deciding when a terminally ill person should die. Among the most difficult cases are the roughly 15,000 people in the United States in a permanent vegetative state who cannot express their desires about life and death.

Generally speaking, the first duty of physicians and hospitals is to protect a patient's life. Even so, a mentally competent person in the process of dying may refuse medical treatment and even nutrition, either at the time or, in advance, through a document called a *living will* that states the extent of medical care a person would or would not want in the event of an illness or injury that leaves the person unable to make decisions.

What about Mercy Killing?

Mercy killing is the common term for **euthanasia**, *assisting in the death of a person suffering from an incurable disease*. Euthanasia (from the Greek, meaning "a good death") poses an ethical dilemma, being at once an act of kindness and a form of killing.

Whether there is a "right to die" is one of today's most difficult issues. All people with incurable diseases have a right to refuse treatment that might prolong their lives. But whether a doctor should be allowed to help bring about death is at the heart of the debate. In 1994, three states—Washington, California, and Oregon—asked voters whether doctors should be able to help people who wanted to die. Only Oregon's proposition passed, and the law was quickly challenged and remained tied up in state court until 1997, when Oregon voters again endorsed it. As of 2013, Oregon doctors have legally assisted in the death of about 600 terminally ill patients. In 1997, however, the U.S. Supreme Court decided that under the U.S. Constitution, there is no "right to die," a decision that has slowed the spread of such laws. Only in 2008 did Washington become the second state to allow physician-assisted suicide, and Montana and Vermont have since done the same (Leff, 2008).

Supporters of *active* euthanasia—allowing a dying person to enlist the services of a physician to bring on a quick death—argue that there are circumstances (as when a dying person suffers great pain) that make death preferable to life. Critics counter that permitting active euthanasia invites abuse (see Chapter 15, "Aging and the Elderly"). They fear that patients will feel pressure to end their lives in order to spare family members the burden of caring for them and the high costs of hospitalization. Research in the Netherlands, where physician-assisted suicide is legal, indicates that about one-fifth of all such deaths have occurred without a patient explicitly requesting to die (Gillon, 1999).

In the United States, a majority of adults express support for giving terminally ill people the right to choose to die with a doctor's help (NORC, 2013:427). Therefore, the right-to-die debate is sure to continue.

euthanasia assisting in the death of a person suffering from an incurable disease; also known as *mercy killing*

The Medical Establishment

21.4 Compare the medical systems in nations around the world.

Medicine is *the social institution that focuses on fighting disease and improving health.* Through most of human history, health care was the responsibility of individuals and their families. Medicine emerges as a social institution only as societies become more productive and people take on specialized work.

Members of agrarian societies today still turn to various traditional health practitioners, including acupuncturists and herbalists, who play a central part in improving health. In industrial societies, medical care falls to specially trained and licensed professionals, from anesthesiologists to X-ray technicians. Today's medical establishment in the United States took form over the past 200 years.

medicine the social institution that focuses on fighting disease and improving health

holistic medicine an approach to health care that emphasizes the prevention of illness and takes into account a person's entire physical and social environment

The Rise of Scientific Medicine

In colonial times, physicians, herbalists, druggists, barbers, midwives, and ministers practiced the healing arts. But not all were effective: Unsanitary instruments, lack of anesthesia, and simple ignorance made surgery a terrible ordeal, and physicians probably killed as many people as they saved.

Physicians made medicine into a science by studying the human body and how it works and emphasizing surgery to repair the body and the use of drugs to fight disease. Pointing to their specialized knowledge, these doctors gradually established themselves as professionals who earned medical degrees. The American Medical Association (AMA) was founded in 1847 and symbolized the growing acceptance of a scientific model of medicine.

Still, traditional approaches to health care had their supporters. The AMA opposed them by seeking control of the certification process. In the early 1900s, state licensing boards agreed to certify only doctors trained in scientific programs approved by the AMA. As a result, schools teaching other healing skills began to close, which soon limited the practice of medicine to individuals holding an M.D. degree. In the process, both the prestige and the income of physicians rose dramatically. Today, men and women with M.D. degrees earn high incomes, ranging from an average of about $200,000 annually for doctors practicing family medicine or pediatrics to more than $500,000 for those practicing cardiac surgery (American Medical Group Association, 2012).

Practitioners who did things differently, such as osteopathic physicians, concluded that they had no choice but to fall in line with AMA standards. Thus osteopaths (with D.O. degrees), originally trained to treat illness by manipulating the skeleton and muscles, today treat illness with drugs in much the same way as medical doctors (with M.D. degrees). Chiropractors, herbal healers, and midwives still practice using traditional methods, but they have lower standing within the medical profession. The tension and conflict between scientific medicine and traditional healing continue today, both in the United States and in many other countries.

Scientific medicine, taught in expensive, urban medical schools, also changed the social profile of doctors such that most came from privileged backgrounds and practiced in cities. Women, who had played a large part in many fields of healing, were pushed aside by the AMA. Some early medical schools did focus on the training of women and African Americans, but gradually most of these schools ran out of money and closed. Only in recent decades has the social diversity of medical doctors increased, with women and African Americans representing 34 percent and 5 percent, respectively, of all physicians (U.S. Department of Labor, 2012).

Holistic Medicine

In recent decades, the scientific model of medicine has been combined with the more traditional model of **holistic medicine**, *an approach to health care that emphasizes the prevention of illness and takes into account a person's entire physical and social environment.* Holistic practitioners agree on the need for drugs, surgery, artificial organs, and high technology, but they emphasize treatment of the whole person rather than symptoms and focus on health rather than disease. There are three foundations of holistic health care (Gordon, 1980; Patterson, 1998):

1. **Treat patients as people.** Holistic practitioners concern themselves not only with symptoms but also with how environment and lifestyle affect their patients. Holistic practitioners extend the bounds of conventional medicine, taking an active role in fighting poverty, environmental pollution, and other dangers to public health.

2. **Encourage responsibility, not dependency.** In the scientific model, patients are dependent on physicians. Holistic medicine tries to shift some responsibility for health from physicians to people themselves by encouraging health-promoting behavior. Holistic medicine thus favors an *active* approach to *health* rather than a *reactive* approach to *illness*.

3. **Provide personal treatment.** Scientific medicine locates medical care in impersonal offices and hospitals, both disease-centered settings. By contrast, holistic practitioners favor, as much as possible, a personal and relaxed environment such as the home.

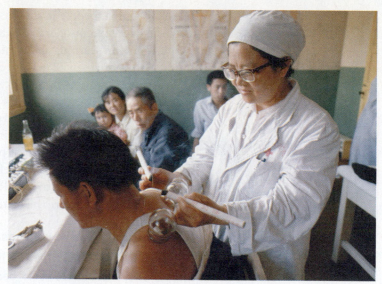

Traditional healers work to improve people's health throughout the world. This patient is receiving a traditional needle therapy in Suining, a city in China's Sichuan province. Do you think people in the United States are accepting of traditional healing practices? Why or why not?

In sum, holistic care does not oppose scientific medicine but shifts the emphasis from treating disease toward achieving the greatest well-being for everyone. Because the AMA currently recognizes more than fifty medical specialties, it is clear that there is a need for practitioners who are concerned with the whole patient.

Paying for Medical Care: A Global Survey

As medicine has come to rely on high technology, the costs of providing medical care have skyrocketed. Countries throughout the world use various strategies to meet these costs.

Medicine in Socialist Nations

In nations with mostly socialist economies, government provides medical care directly to the people. These countries hold that all citizens have the right to basic medical care. The state owns and operates medical facilities and uses public funds to pay salaries to doctors and other medical care workers, who are government employees.

People's Republic of China

This economically growing but mostly agrarian nation faces the immense task of providing for the health of more than 1.3 billion people. China has experimented with private medicine, but the government controls most medical care.

China's "barefoot doctors," roughly comparable to U.S. paramedics, bring some modern methods of medical care to millions of peasants in rural villages. Otherwise, traditional healing arts, including acupuncture and the use of medicinal herbs, are still widely practiced in China. The Chinese approach to health is based on a holistic concern for the interplay of mind and body (Kaptchuk, 1985).

Russian Federation

The Russian Federation has transformed what was a state-dominated economy into more of a market system, so medical care, like so much else, is in transition. But the state remains in charge of health care, and the government claims that everyone has a right to basic medical care.

As in China, people in the Russian Federation do not choose a physician but report to a local government-operated health facility. Russian doctors have much lower incomes than U.S. doctors, earning about the same salary as skilled industrial workers in the United States. Also, more than 72 percent of Russian doctors are women, compared to 34 percent in the United States. As in our society, occupations dominated by women in the Russian Federation offer lower pay.

In recent years, the Russian Federation has suffered setbacks in health care, partly because of a falling standard of living. A rising demand for medical attention has strained a bureaucratic system that at best provides highly standardized and impersonal care. The optimistic view is that as market reforms proceed, both living standards and the quality of medical services will improve. In Russia's uncertain times, what does seem certain is that inequalities in medical care will increase (Landsberg, 1998; Mason, 2003; Zuckerman, 2006).

Medicine in Capitalist Nations

People living in nations with mostly capitalist economies usually pay for medical care out of their own pockets. However, because high cost puts medical care beyond the reach of many people, government programs underwrite much of the expense.

Sweden In 1891, Sweden began a mandatory, comprehensive system of government medical care. Citizens pay for this program with their taxes, which are among the highest in the world. Typically, physicians are government employees, and most hospitals are government-managed. Because this medical system resembles that found in socialist societies, Sweden's system is called **socialized medicine**, *a medical care system in which the government owns and operates most medical facilities and employs most physicians.*

Great Britain In 1948, Great Britain established a dual system of medical service. All British citizens are entitled to medical care provided by the National Health Service, but those who can afford to do so may go to doctors and hospitals that operate privately.

Canada Since 1972, Canada has had a "single-payer" model of medical care that provides health services to all Canadians. Like a giant insurance company, the Canadian government pays doctors and hospitals according to a set schedule of fees. Like Great Britain, Canada also has some physicians working outside the government-funded system and setting their own fees, although costs are regulated by the government.

Canada boasts of providing care for everyone at a lower cost than the (nonuniversal) medical system in the United States. However, the Canadian system uses less state-of-the-art technology and responds more slowly, meaning that people may wait months for major surgery. But the Canadian system provides care for all citizens, regardless of income, unlike the United States, where lower-income people are often denied medical care (Rosenthal, 1991; Macionis & Gerber, 2008).

Japan Physicians in Japan operate privately, but a combination of government programs and private insurance pays their patients' medical costs. As shown in Figure 21–2, the Japanese approach medical care much as the Europeans do, with most medical expenses paid through the government.

Paying for Medical Care: The United States

The United States stands alone among industrialized nations in having no universal, government-sponsored program of medical care. Ours is a **direct-fee system**, *a medical care system in which*

For a close-up look at health in the Russian Federation, **Read More** in **MySocLab**, *When Health Fails: A Report from Russia*

socialized medicine
a medical care system in which the government owns and operates most medical facilities and employs most physicians

direct-fee system
a medical care system in which patients pay directly for the services of physicians and hospitals

Global Snapshot

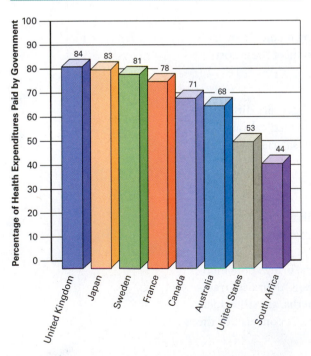

FIGURE 21–2 Extent of Socialized Medicine in Selected Countries

The governments of most high-income countries pay a greater share of their people's medical costs than the U.S. government does.

Source: World Bank (2013).

patients pay directly for the services of physicians and hospitals. Europeans look to government to fund from 70 to nearly 90 percent of their medical costs (paid for through taxation), but the U.S. government pays just 53 percent of this country's medical costs (World Bank, 2013).

In the United States, rich people can purchase the best medical care in the world. Yet the poor are worse off than their counterparts in Europe. This difference explains the relatively high death rates among infants and adults in the United States compared to those in most other high-income nations. In fact, in terms of infant mortality (the odds that an infant will die during the first year of life), the United States is ranked only forty-ninth among global nations and below many European countries. From another angle, researchers report that, despite spending more money per person than other high-income countries, the United States provides its people with higher rates of disease and injury and also a shorter life span (Population Reference Bureau, 2012; *The Lancet*, 2013).

Several states, including Maine, Vermont, and Massachusetts, have enacted programs that provide health care to everyone. Why does the United States have no national program that provides universal care? First, during World War II, the government took control of the economy and froze worker earnings. As a way to increase pay within the wage freeze, more employers began providing health care benefits. Second, labor unions tried to expand health care benefits from employers rather than go after government programs. Third, the public generally favors a private, worker-and-employer system rather than a government-based system because our culture stresses individual self-reliance. Fourth and finally, the AMA and the health insurance industry have strongly and consistently opposed national medical care. There is no question that health care in this country is very expensive. The cost of medical care increased dramatically from $12 billion in 1950 to $2.7 trillion in 2011. This sum amounts to $8,700 per person, more than any other nation in the world spends for medical care (U.S. Department of Health and Human Services, 2012). Who pays the medical bills?

Private Insurance Programs

In 2011, about 170 million people (55 percent) received some medical care benefits from a family member's employer or labor union. Another 30 million people (10 percent) purchased private coverage on their own. Combining these figures, 65 percent of the U.S. population has private insurance, although few such programs pay all medical costs (U.S. Census Bureau, 2012).

Public Insurance Programs

In 1965, Congress created Medicare and Medicaid. Medicare pays a portion of the medical costs of men and women over age sixty-five; in 2011, it covered 47 million women and men, 15 percent of the population. In the same year, Medicaid, a medical insurance program for the poor, provided benefits to 51 million people, about 17 percent of the population. An additional 14 million veterans, 4 percent of the population, can obtain free care in government-operated hospitals. In all, one-third of this country's people get medical benefits from the government, but most also have private insurance (U.S. Census Bureau, 2012).

Health Maintenance Organizations

About 68 million people (22 percent) in the United States belong to a **health maintenance organization (HMO)**, *an organization that provides comprehensive medical care to subscribers for a fixed fee.* HMOs vary in their costs and benefits, and none provides full coverage. Fixed fees make these organizations profitable to the extent that their subscribers stay healthy; therefore, many take a preventive approach to health. At the same time, HMOs have been criticized for refusing to pay for medical procedures that they consider unnecessary. Congress is currently debating the extent to which patients can sue HMOs to obtain better care.

In all, 84 percent of the U.S. population has some medical care coverage, either private or public. Yet most plans do not provide full coverage, so a serious illness threatens

health maintenance organization (HMO) an organization that provides comprehensive medical care to subscribers for a fixed fee

The United States has a culture of individualism, which leads many to think that people should be responsible for their own health and medical care. The 2010 health care reform is a step toward the idea the government should ensure that everyone has at least basic health care. Not surprisingly, even after the 2010 reforms have been found by the U.S. Supreme Court to be constitutional, they remain controversial. Where do you stand on this issue?

even middle-class people with financial hardship. Most programs also exclude certain medical services, such as dental care and treatment for mental health and substance abuse problems. Worse, 49 million people (about 16 percent of the population) have no medical insurance at all, even though 68 percent of these people are working. Almost as many people lose their medical coverage temporarily each year due to layoffs or job changes. Caught in the medical care bind are mostly low- to moderate-income people who do not qualify for Medicaid yet cannot afford the cost of the preventive medical care they need to stay healthy (Brink, 2002; U.S. Census Bureau, 2012; MCOL, 2013).

The 2010 Health Care Law

In 2010, Congress passed a new law (Affordable Care Act of 2010) that made significant changes to the way this country pays for health care. The law extends medical insurance to more people; at the same time, the law has a huge cost—estimated at almost $1 trillion over the first ten years—so that the change will take effect in stages.

Here are some of the most important features of the new health care law:

1. Starting right away, all families will pay an insurance tax. Lower-income families, however, will receive subsidies to help pay the cost of the insurance; high-income families will pay higher taxes on their income to help fund the program.

2. Six months after enactment of the new law, insurance companies could no longer legally drop customers because they get sick or legally refuse coverage to children because of preexisting conditions.

3. Insurance companies cannot set caps on the amount of money they will pay to any individual for medical expenses over a lifetime.

4. Parents can use their health care plans to include children up to the age of twenty-six.

5. By 2014, insurance companies will no longer be able to refuse coverage to anyone of any age due to preexisting health conditions.

6. By 2014, all families will be required to purchase insurance coverage. Government will regulate both the benefits available and the costs.

7. Starting in 2014, the bill provides penalties for people who do not buy insurance; these penalties will increase over time.

In all, the 2010 health care law, reviewed in 2012 and declared to be constitutional by the Supreme Court, will provide health care insurance to some 32 million people (of 49 million total) in the United States who currently do not have this protection. The Obama administration claims that this bill, although providing something short of universal health care coverage, is nonetheless a major step toward that goal.

The Nursing Shortage

Another important issue in medical care is the shortage of nurses across the United States. In 2010, there were nearly 3 million registered nurses (who hold the R.N. degree), an increase of 5 percent since 2004. At the same time, more than 100,000 positions for nurses remain unfilled. Looking ahead, our aging population will require many more nurses in the decades to come so that the number of job openings available to nurses by 2020 will total more than 1 million (American Association of Colleges of Nursing, 2012; U.S. Department of Health and Human Services, 2012).

Our society is experiencing an increasing need for nurses. This increasing demand is due to several factors. First, technological advances in medicine allow more illnesses to be treated. Second, there has been a rapid expansion in hospital out-patient services, such as same-day surgery, rehabilitation, and chemotherapy. Third, an increasing focus on preventive care, rather than simply treating disease or accidents, means more people than ever are receiving care. Fourth, and most important of all, is the aging population of the United States. Compared to young people, the oldest members of our society consume much more medical services.

The challenges of nursing in the emergency room of a large New York City hospital are played out weekly on the television show *Nurse Jackie*. In light of the increasing demand for nurses in the United States, would you consider a career in nursing?

The field of nursing continues to attract young people. More than 500,000 people have entered the field of nursing since 2004. Even so, because the demand for nurses is increasing so quickly, the supply of new nurses continues to fall short of the demand. One reason for this undersupply is a shortage of nursing schools. In 2011, because of this lack of faculty and facilities, nursing programs turned away more than 75,000 qualified applicants (American Association of Colleges of Nursing, 2012).

A broader reason is that today's young women have a wide range of job choices, and fewer are drawn to the traditionally female occupation of nursing. This fact is evident in the rising median age of working nurses, which is now forty-five. Another is that some of today's nurses are unhappy with their working conditions, citing heavy patient loads, too much required overtime, a stressful working environment, and a lack of recognition and respect from supervisors, physicians, and hospital managers.

The nursing shortage is harming health care. One study estimates that more than 6,000 hospital patients die each year for lack of immediate treatment due to the shortage of nurses. Such facts are bringing change to the profession. Salaries, which range from about $45,000 to $65,000 for general-duty nurses to $135,000 and more for certified nurse-anesthetists, are rising, and the typical nurse has enjoyed a steady rise in pay over the last five years. Some hospitals and physicians are also offering signing bonuses in efforts to attract new nurses. In addition, nursing programs are trying harder to recruit a more diverse population, seeking more minorities (which currently represent 23 percent of all nurses) and more men (now only 9 percent of R.N.'s) (Yin, 2002; Marquez, 2006; U.S. Department of Health and Human Services, 2010; American Association of Colleges of Nursing, 2011; U.S. Department of Labor, 2012).

Theories of Health and Medicine

(21.5) Apply sociology's major theories to health and medicine.

Each of sociology's major theoretical approaches—structural-functional theory, symbolic-interaction theory, and social-conflict and feminist theories—helps us organize and interpret facts and issues concerning human health.

Structural-Functional Theory: Role Analysis

 **Watch** in **MySocLab**
Video: *The Basics: Health and Medicine*

Talcott Parsons (1951) viewed medicine as society's strategy to keep its members healthy. According to this model, illness is dysfunctional because it undermines people's abilities to perform their roles.

The Sick Role

sick role patterns of behavior defined as appropriate for people who are ill

Society responds to sickness not only by providing medical care but also by affording people a **sick role**, *patterns of behavior defined as appropriate for people who are ill*. According to Parsons, the sick role releases people from normal obligations such as going to work or attending classes. To prevent abuse of this privilege, however, people cannot simply claim to be ill; they must "look the part" and, in serious cases, get the help of a medical expert. After assuming the sick role, the patient must want to get better and must do whatever is needed to regain good health, including cooperating with health professionals.

The Physician's Role

Physicians evaluate people's claims of sickness and help restore the sick to normal routines. To do this, physicians use their specialized knowledge and expect patients to cooperate with them, providing necessary information and following "doctor's orders" to complete the treatment.

EVALUATE Parsons's analysis links illness and medicine to the broader organization of society. Others have extended the concept of the sick role to some nonillness situations such as pregnancy (Myers & Grasmick, 1989).

One limitation of the sick-role concept is that it applies to acute conditions (like the flu or a broken leg) better than to chronic illnesses (like heart disease), which may not be reversible. In addition, a sick person's ability to assume the sick role (to take time off from work to regain health) depends on the patient's resources; many working poor, for example, cannot afford to assume a sick role. Finally, illness is not entirely dysfunctional; it can have some positive consequences: Many people who experience serious illness find that it provides the opportunity to reevaluate their lives and gain a better sense of what is truly important (D. G. Myers, 2000; Ehrenreich, 2001).

Finally, critics point out that Parsons's analysis gives doctors, rather than patients, the primary responsibility for health. A more prevention-oriented approach gives each of us as individuals the responsibility to pursue health.

CHECK YOUR LEARNING Define the sick role. How does turning illness into a role in this way help society operate?

Symbolic-Interaction Theory: The Meaning of Health

According to the symbolic-interaction approach, society is less a grand system than a complex and changing reality. In this model, health and medical care are socially constructed by people in everyday interaction.

The Social Construction of Illness

If both health and illness are socially constructed, people in a poor society may view hunger and malnutrition as normal. Similarly, many members of our own society give little thought to the harmful effects of a rich diet.

Our response to illness is also based on social definitions that may or may not square with medical facts. People with AIDS may be forced to deal with fear and prejudice that have no medical basis. Likewise, students may pay no attention to signs of real illness on the eve of a vacation but head for the infirmary hours before a midterm examination with a case of the sniffles. In short, health is less an objective fact than a negotiated outcome.

How people define a medical situation may actually affect how they feel. Medical experts marvel at *psychosomatic* disorders (a fusion of Greek words for "mind" and "body"), when state of mind guides physical sensations (Hamrick, Anspaugh, & Ezell, 1986). Applying the sociologist W. I. Thomas's theorem (presented in Chapter 6, "Social Interaction in Everyday Life"), we can say that once health or illness is defined as real, it can become real in its consequences.

The Social Construction of Treatment

Also in Chapter 6, we used Erving Goffman's dramaturgical approach to explain how physicians tailor their physical surroundings (their office) and their behavior (the "presentation of self") so that others see them as competent and in charge.

The sociologist Joan Emerson (1970) further illustrates this process of reality construction in her analysis of the gynecological examination carried out by a male doctor. This situation is vulnerable to serious misinterpretation, since a man's touching of a woman's genitals is conventionally viewed as a sexual act and possibly an assault.

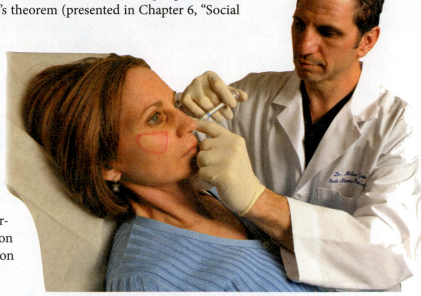

Definitions of health are based on cultural standards, including ideas about beauty. Every year, millions of people undergo cosmetic surgery to bring their appearance into line with societal definitions of how people ought to look.

To ensure that people define the situation as impersonal and professional, the medical staff wear uniforms and furnish the examination room with nothing but medical equipment. The doctor's manner and overall performance are designed to make the patient feel that to him, examining the genital area is no different from treating any other part of the body. A female nurse is usually present during the examination, not only to assist the physician but also to avoid any impression that a man and a woman are "alone together."

Managing situational definitions in this way is only rarely taught in medical schools. The oversight is unfortunate, because as Emerson's analysis shows, understanding how people construct reality in the examining room is as important as mastering the medical skills required for treatment.

The Social Construction of Personal Identity

A final insight provided by the symbolic-interaction approach is how surgery can affect people's social identity. The reason that medical procedures can have a major effect on how we think of ourselves is that our culture places great symbolic importance on some organs and other parts of our bodies. People who lose a limb (say, in military combat) typically experience serious doubts about being "as much of a person" as before. The effects of surgery can be important even when there is no obvious change in physical appearance. For example, Jean Elson (2004) points out that one out of three women in the United States eventually has her uterus surgically removed in a procedure known as a *hysterectomy*. In interviews with women who had undergone the procedure, Elson found that the typical woman faced serious self-doubt about gender identity, asking, in effect, "Am I still a woman?" Only 10 percent of hysterectomies are for cancer; most are for pain, bleeding, or cysts—serious conditions but not so dangerous as to rule out other types of treatment. Perhaps, Elson points out, doctors might be more willing to consider alternative treatment if they were aware of how symbolically important the loss of the uterus is to many women.

Many women who undergo breast surgery have much the same reaction, doubting their own feminine identity and worrying that men will no longer find them attractive. For men to understand the significance of such medical procedures, it is only necessary to imagine how a male might react to the surgical loss of any or all of his genitals.

EVALUATE Symbolic-interaction theory reveals that what people view as healthful or harmful depends on numerous factors that are not, strictly speaking, medical. This approach also shows that in any medical procedure, both patient and medical staff engage in a subtle process of reality construction. Finally, this approach has helped us understand the symbolic importance of limbs and other bodily organs; the loss of any part of the body—through accident or elective surgery—can have important consequences for personal identity.

By directing attention to the meanings people attach to health and illness, symbolic-interaction theory draws criticism for implying that there are no objective standards of well-being. Certain physical conditions do indeed cause definite changes in people, regardless of how we view those conditions. People who lack sufficient nutrition and safe water, for example, suffer from their unhealthy environment, whether they define their surroundings as normal or not.

Self-reported measures of student health show a downward trend. Students' self-assessments of their "emotional health" are now as low as ever recorded (Pryor et al., 2013). And, as Figure 21–3 shows, the share of first-year college students in the United States who describe their physical health as "above average" is lower today than it was in 1985. Do you think such research findings reflect changing perceptions or a real decline in health (due, say, to eating more unhealthy food)?

CHECK YOUR LEARNING Explain what it means to say that health, the treatment of illness, and personal identity are all socially constructed.

Social-Conflict and Feminist Theories: Inequality and Health

Social-conflict analysis points out the connection between health and social inequality and, taking a cue from Karl Marx, ties medicine to the operation of capitalism. Researchers have focused on three main issues: access to medical care, the effects of the profit motive, and the politics of medicine.

Student Snapshot

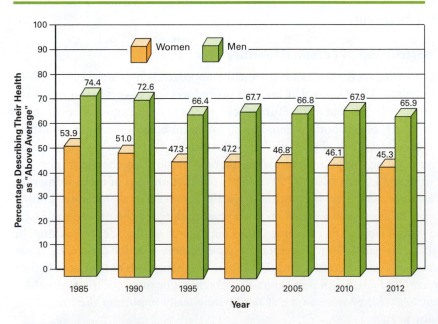

FIGURE 21–3 Self-Assessment of Physical Health by First-Year College Students, 1985–2012

Since 1985, a smaller number of students have described their health as "above average."

Sources: Astin et al. (2002) and Pryor et al. (2013).

Access to Care

Health is important to everyone. Yet by requiring individuals to pay for medical care, capitalist societies allow the richest people to have the best health. The access problem is more serious in the United States than in other high-income nations because we do not have a universal medical care system.

Conflict theorists argue that the capitalist system provides excellent medical care for the rich but not for the rest of the population. Most of the 49 million people who lack medical care coverage at present have low to moderate incomes. When a serious illness strikes, the experience is starkly different for rich and poor people in our society.

The Profit Motive

Some conflict analysts go further, arguing that the real problem is not access to medical care but the nature of capitalist medicine itself. The profit motive turns physicians, hospitals, and the pharmaceutical industry into money-hungry corporations. The drive for higher profits encourages physicians to recommend unnecessary tests and surgery and to rely too much on expensive drugs and treatments rather than focusing on helping people improve their living conditions and lifestyles.

Of about 25 million surgical operations performed in the United States each year, three-fourths are elective, which means that they are intended to promote long-term health and are not prompted by a medical emergency. Of course, any medical procedure or use of drugs is risky, and between 5 and 10 percent of patients are harmed each year as a result. Therefore, the decision to perform surgery, social-conflict theorists argue, reflects not just the medical needs of patients but also the financial interests of surgeons and hospitals (Cowley, 1995; Nuland, 1999).

Finally, say conflict theorists, our society is too tolerant of physicians having a direct financial interest in the tests and procedures they order for their patients (Pear & Eckholm, 1991). Medical care should be motivated by a concern for people, not profits.

Medicine as Politics

Although science claims to be politically neutral, feminists claim that scientific medicine often takes sides on significant social issues. For example, the medical establishment has always strongly opposed government medical care programs and only recently allowed a significant number of women to join the ranks of physicians. The history of medicine itself shows that racial and sexual discrimination has kept women and other minorities out of medicine, but discrimination has been supported by "scientific" opinions about, say, the inferiority of certain categories of people (Leavitt, 1984). Consider the diagnosis of "hysteria," a term that has its origins in the Greek word *hyster*, meaning "uterus." In choosing this word to describe a wild, emotional state, the medical profession suggested that being a woman is somehow the same as being irrational.

Even today, according to conflict theory, scientific medicine explains illness exclusively in terms of bacteria and viruses, ignoring the damaging effects of poverty. In effect, scientific medicine hides the bias in our medical system by transforming this social issue into simple biology.

EVALUATE Social-conflict analysis provides still another view of how health, medicine, and society are related. According to this approach, social inequality is the reason some people have better health than others.

The most common objection to the conflict approach is that it minimizes the gains in U.S. health brought about by scientific medicine and higher living standards. Although there is plenty of room for improvement, health indicators for our population as a whole rose steadily over the course of the twentieth century and compare well with those of other industrial nations.

CHECK YOUR LEARNING Explain how health and medical care are related to social classes, to capitalism, and to gender stratification.

Applying Theory

Health			
	Structural-Functional Theory	**Symbolic-Interaction Theory**	**Social-Conflict and Feminist Theories**
What is the level of analysis?	Macro-level	Micro-level	Macro-level
How is health related to society?	Illness is dysfunctional for society because it prevents people from carrying out their daily roles.	Societies define "health" and "illness" differently according to their living standards.	Health is linked to social inequality with rich people having more access to care than poor people.
	The sick role releases people who are ill from responsibilities while they try to get well.	How people define their own health affects how they actually feel (psychosomatic conditions).	Capitalist medical care places the drive for profits over the needs of people.
			Scientific medicine downplays the social causes of illness, including poverty, racism, and sexism.

In sum, sociology's major theoretical approaches explain why health and medicine are social issues. The Applying Theory table sums up what they teach us. Advancing technology will not solve every health problem. On the contrary, as the Controversy & Debate box on page 623 explains, today's advancing technology is raising new questions and concerns.

The renowned French scientist Louis Pasteur (1822–1895), who spent much of his life studying how bacteria cause disease, said just before he died that health depends less on bacteria than on the social environment in which the bacteria are found (Gordon, 1980:7). Explaining Pasteur's insight is sociology's contribution to human health.

Health and Medicine: Looking Ahead

In the early 1900s, deaths from infectious diseases like diphtheria and measles were widespread. Because scientists had yet to develop penicillin and other antibiotics, even a simple infection from a minor wound might become life-threatening. Today, a century later, most members of our society take for granted good health and long life.

More people in the United States are taking personal responsibility for their health. Even so there are some grounds for concern. The increasing obesity epidemic is one major problem. If this trend continues, the younger generation may become the first in some time to have lower rather than higher life expectancy. Every one of us can live better and longer if we eat sensibly and in moderation, exercise regularly, and avoid tobacco.

Another health problem that our society faces, discussed throughout this chapter, is the double standard that provides good health to the rich but causes higher rates of disease for the poor. International comparisons show that the United States lags in some measures of human health because of the large share of our population that lives at the margins of our society. An important question, even after the recent health care reforms, is what our society should do about the millions of people who live with low income and without the security of medical care.

Finally, we know that health problems are far greater in low-income nations than they are in the United States. The good news is that life expectancy for the world as a whole has been rising—from forty-eight years in 1950 to seventy years today—and the biggest gains have occurred in poor countries (Population Reference Bureau, 2012). But in much of Latin America, Asia, and especially Africa, hundreds of millions of adults and children lack not only medical attention but adequate food and safe drinking water as well. Improving the health of the world's poorest people is a critical challenge in the years to come.

Controversy & Debate

The Genetic Crystal Ball: Do We Really Want to Look?

Felisha: Before I get married, I want my partner to have a genetic screening. It's like buying a house or a car—you should check it out before you sign on the line.

Eva: Do you expect to get a warranty, too?

The liquid in the laboratory test tube seems ordinary enough, like a syrupy form of water. But this liquid is one of the greatest medical breakthroughs of all time; it may even hold the key to life itself. The liquid is deoxyribonucleic acid, or DNA, the spiraling molecule found in cells of the human body that contains the blueprint for making each one of us human as well as different from every other person.

The human body is composed of some 100 trillion cells, most of which contain a nucleus of twenty-three pairs of chromosomes (one of each pair comes from each parent). Each chromosome is packed with DNA in segments called genes. Genes guide the production of protein, the building block of the human body.

If genetics sounds complicated (and it is), the social implications of genetic knowledge are even more complex. Scientists discovered the structure of the DNA molecule in 1952, and in recent years they have made great gains in "mapping" the human genome. Charting the genetic landscape may lead to understanding how each bit of DNA shapes our being.

Scientists are learning more and more about the genetic factors that prompt the eventual development of serious diseases. If offered the opportunity, would you want to undergo a genetic screening that would predict the long-term future of your own health?

But do we really want to turn the key to unlock the secrets of life itself? And what do we do with this knowledge once we have it? Research has already identified genetic abnormalities that cause sickle-cell anemia, muscular dystrophy, Huntington's disease, cystic fibrosis, some forms of cancer, and other crippling and deadly afflictions. Genetic screening—gazing into a person's genetic "crystal ball"—could let people know their medical destiny and allow doctors to manipulate segments of DNA to prevent diseases before they appear.

But many people urge caution in such research, warning that genetic information can easily be abused. At its worst, genetic mapping opens the door to Nazi-like efforts to breed a "superrace." In 1994, the People's Republic of China began to use genetic information to regulate marriage and childbirth with the purpose of avoiding "new births of inferior quality."

It seems inevitable that some parents will want to use genetic testing to evaluate the health (or even the eye color) of their future children. What if they want to abort a fetus because it falls short of their standards? Should parents be allowed to use genetic manipulation to create "designer children"?

Then there is the issue of "genetic privacy." Can a prospective spouse request a genetic evaluation of her fiancé before agreeing to marry? Can a life insurance company demand genetic testing before issuing a policy? Can an employer screen job applicants to weed out those whose future illnesses might drain the company's health care funds? Clearly, what is scientifically possible is not always morally desirable. Society is already struggling with questions about the proper use of our expanding knowledge of human genetics. Such ethical dilemmas will multiply as genetic research moves forward in the years to come.

What Do You Think?

1. Traditional wedding vows join couples "in sickness and in health." Do you think individuals have a right to know the future health of their potential partner before tying the knot? Why or why not?

2. Do you think parents should be able to genetically "design" their children? Why or why not?

3. Is it right that private companies doing genetic research are able to patent their discoveries so that they can profit from the results, or should this information be made available to everyone? Explain your answer.

Sources: D. Thompson (1999) and Golden and Lemonick (2000).

How does society affect patterns of health?

Certain occupations put people at higher-than-average risk of accident or death. One example is coal mining, which has long been one of the deadliest jobs. Although the death toll from mining accidents in the United States has gone down over time, even miners who manage to avoid mine collapses or explosions typically suffer harm from years of breathing coal dust. Look at the photos below and on page 625: How do they link health to a way of life?

Crews on fishing boats such as this one spend months at a time battling high seas and often frigid temperatures. As documented on the television show *The Deadliest Catch*, it is a rare and fortunate fishing season that brings no death or serious injury. What other jobs threaten the health and well-being of U.S. workers?

Are high death tolls in coal mining a thing of the past? In 2007, China reported 3,786 deaths in coal mines in that country. Here, rescuers remove a body from a mine after a gas explosion killed more than 80 miners.

In U.S. history, the deadliest year for coal miners was 1907, when 3,242 miners lost their lives. This photo was taken after a mine explosion near Monongah, West Virginia, that killed 358 people. In 2012, there were 36 mining deaths. What social patterns (think about class, gender, and other factors) can you see in the history of mining and health?

Nº. 10.
Monongah Explosion At The Morgue
Dec. 12-1907

HINT Among the most dangerous jobs in the United States are farming (dangers come from using power equipment), mining, timber cutting, truck driving, and constructing tall buildings. Many members of the military also face danger on a daily basis. In general, people in the working class are at greater risk than middle-class people, who typically work in offices; men also predominate in the most dangerous jobs. Overall, about 4,600 U.S. (nonmilitary) workers lose their lives every year in workplace accidents.

Seeing Sociology in *Your* Everyday Life

1. Take a trip to the local courthouse or city hall to find public records showing people's cause of death and age at death. Compare the records for a century ago and today. What patterns do you find in life expectancy and causes of death?

2. Go to MySocLab and click on the Student Resources link to access the Sociology in Focus blog, where you can read the latest posts by a team of young sociologists who apply the sociological perspective to topics of popular culture.

3. What facts have you learned from this chapter that you can use to improve your own health? For more about sociological study of health, go to the "Seeing Sociology in *Your* Everyday Life" feature in MySocLab, where you can also find suggestions about how the material in this chapter can benefit you.

Making the Grade

What Is Health?

21.1 Explain how patterns of health are shaped by society. (pages 600–601)

health a state of complete physical, mental, and social well-being

 Watch the **Video** in **MySocLab**

Health is a social issue because personal well-being depends on a society's level of technology and its distribution of resources.

- A society's culture shapes definitions of health, which change over time.
- A society's technology affects people's health.
- Social inequality affects people's health.

Health: A Global Survey

21.2 Contrast patterns of health in low- and high-income countries. (pages 601–2)

 Watch the **Video** in **MySocLab**

Health in Low-Income Countries

- Poor nations suffer from inadequate sanitation, hunger, and other problems linked to poverty.
- Life expectancy in low-income nations is about twenty years less than in the United States; in the poorest nations, 10% of children die within a year of birth, and almost 25% die before the age of thirty.

Health in High-Income Countries

- In the nineteenth century, industrialization improved health dramatically in Western Europe and North America.
- A century ago, infectious diseases were leading killers; today, most people in the United States die in old age of chronic illnesses such as heart disease, cancer, or stroke.

Health in the United States

21.3 Analyze how race, class, gender, and age are linked to health. (pages 602–11)

social epidemiology the study of how health and disease are distributed throughout a society's population

eating disorder a physical and mental disorder that involves an intense form of dieting or other unhealthy method of weight control driven by the desire to be very thin

euthanasia assisting in the death of a person suffering from an incurable disease; also known as *mercy killing*

 Explore the **Map** in **MySocLab**   **Read** the **Document** in **MySocLab**

Who Is Healthy? Age, Gender, Class, and Race

- White males (81 years) typically outlive African American men (70 years) and white women (88 years) typically live longer than African American women (81 years).
- Throughout the life course, women have better health than men. Our culture's definition of masculinity promotes aggressive and individualistic behavior that contributes to men's higher rate of coronary disease as well as accidents and violence.
- People of high social position enjoy better health than the poor, a result of better nutrition, wider access to health care, and safer and less stressful living conditions.
- Poverty among African Americans, which is almost three times the rate for whites, helps explain why black people are more likely to die in infancy and to suffer the effects of violence, drug abuse, and poor health.

Cigarette Smoking

- Cigarette smoking is the greatest preventable cause of death; more than 440,000 people in the United States die prematurely each year as a result of smoking cigarettes.
- Many people smoke as a way to relieve stress. Smoking is more common among men, working-class people, divorced people, the unemployed, and those serving in the armed forces.
- Tobacco is a $90 billion industry in the United States; the tobacco industry has increased its sales abroad, especially in low-income countries.

Eating Disorders and Obesity

- Eating disorders—anorexia nervosa and bulimia—are tied to cultural expectations of thinness. Among teens, females are three times more likely than males to suffer from anorexia nervosa and five times more likely to suffer from bulimia.
- In the United States, 64% of adults are overweight; being overweight raises the risk of heart disease, stroke, and diabetes.
- Social causes of obesity include an inactive lifestyle and a diet heavy in salt and fatty foods.

Sexually Transmitted Diseases

- STDs became a matter of national concern during the "sexual revolution" beginning in the 1960s; by the late 1980s, the dangers of STDs, especially AIDS, caused a sexual counterrevolution as people turned away from casual sex.
- Specific behaviors that put people at risk of AIDS include anal sex, sharing needles, and use of any drug.

Ethical Issues Surrounding Death

- Questions about the use of medical technology have added an ethical dimension to health and illness.
- Supporters of a "right to die" argue that individuals should be able to decide for themselves when to use or refuse medical treatment to prolong their lives.

The Medical Establishment

21.4 Compare the medical systems in nations around the world. (pages 612–17)

The Rise of Scientific Medicine

- Health care was historically a family concern but with industrialization became the responsibility of trained specialists.
- The model of scientific medicine is the foundation of the U.S. medical establishment.

Holistic Medicine

- Holistic medicine, focusing on prevention of illness, takes a broader and more traditional approach than scientific medicine.
- Holistic practitioners focus on health rather than disease; they emphasize treating patients as people, encourage people to take responsibility for their own health, and provide treatment in personal, relaxed surroundings.

Paying for Medical Care: A Global Survey

- Socialist societies define medical care as a right; they offer basic care equally to everyone.
- Capitalist societies view medical care as a commodity to be purchased, although most help pay for medical care through socialized medicine or national health insurance.

Paying for Medical Care: The United States

- The 2010 health care reforms are a recent effort to move the United States closer to the goal of having everyone covered by health insurance.
- Most people have private or government health insurance, but about 49 million people in the United States do not have medical insurance.

The Nursing Shortage

- The aging of U.S. society is a major factor raising the demand for nursing.
- More than 100,000 jobs for registered nurses in the United States are currently unfilled, as fewer young women are choosing this traditionally female job. Salary levels are rising and efforts to recruit more men to the profession are under way.

medicine the social institution that focuses on fighting disease and improving health

holistic medicine an approach to health care that emphasizes prevention of illness and takes into account a person's entire physical and social environment

socialized medicine a medical care system in which the government owns and operates most medical facilities and employs most physicians

direct-fee system a medical care system in which patients pay directly for the services of physicians and hospitals

health maintenance organization (HMO) an organization that provides comprehensive medical care to subscribers for a fixed fee

---

Theories of Health and Medicine

21.5 Apply sociology's major theories to health and medicine. (pages 617–22)

 Watch the **Video** in **MySocLab**

sick role patterns of behavior defined as appropriate for people who are ill

Structural-functional theory considers illness to be dysfunctional because it reduces people's abilities to perform their roles. According to Talcott Parsons, society responds to illness by defining roles:

- The *sick role* excuses the ill person from routine social responsibilities.
- The *physician's role* is to use specialized knowledge to take charge of the patient's recovery.

Symbolic-interaction theory investigates how health and medical care are socially constructed by people in everyday interaction:

- Our response to illness is not always based on medical facts.
- How people define a medical situation may affect how they feel.

Social-conflict theory focuses on the unequal distribution of health and medical care. Marxist theory criticizes the U.S. medical establishment for

- its overreliance on drugs and surgery
- the dominance of the profit motive
- overemphasis on the biological rather than the social causes of illness

Feminist theory criticizes the medical establishment for "scientific" statements and policies that effectively allow men to dominate women.

---

22 Population, Urbanization, and Environment

((•)) Listen to Chapter 22 in MySocLab

LEARNING OBJECTIVES

22.1 Explain the concepts of fertility, mortality, and migration, and how they affect population size.

22.2 Analyze population trends using Malthusian theory and demographic transition theory.

22.3 Summarize patterns of urbanization in the United States and around the world.

22.4 Identify the contributions of Tönnies, Durkheim, Simmel, Park, Wirth, and Marx to our understanding of urban life.

22.5 Describe the third urban revolution now under way in poor societies.

22.6 Analyze current environmental problems such as pollution and global warming.

22.7 Evaluate progress toward creating an ecologically sustainable culture.

the Power of Society

to shape our view of global warming

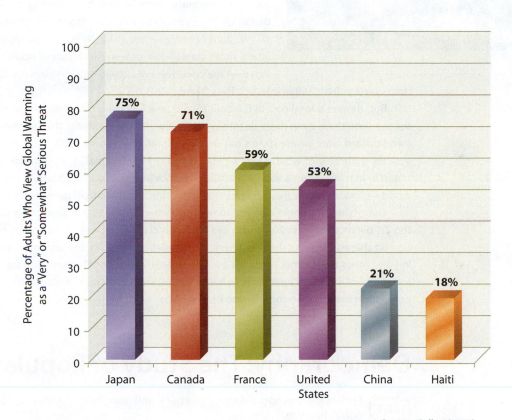

Source: Gallup (2011)

Are attitudes about global warming just our personal opinions? One way to answer this question is to look around the world. The population of the United States has been divided on the issue of global warming, with a slight majority seeing global warming as a "somewhat serious" or "very serious" threat. In most other high-income nations, however, a larger share of adults make this claim. The level of concern about global warming is far lower in low-income nations, where people are more concerned with their basic needs such as food and shelter. Clearly, society has the power to shape our view on environmental issues just as it shapes so many other aspects of our lives.

Chapter Overview

This chapter explores three dimensions of social change: population dynamics, urbanization, and increasing threats to the natural environment. Not only are all three important, but they are closely linked as well.

In the final week of October 2012, most people were making their predictions about the outcome of the presidential election. But weather forecasters were focused on predicting the track of a hurricane that seemed likely to hit the New York region. Officially named Sandy, it was being described as a "superstorm," an especially large hurricane likely to produce exceptional destruction.

On October 30, Hurricane Sandy collided with the coastline of New Jersey, its enormous size spreading punishing winds up and down one thousand miles of the East Coast. Low-lying areas of New York City and nearby communities were flooded by a thirteen-foot-high storm surge that made this event the area's worst storm in memory.

Millions of homes—not just in New York and New Jersey but also in fifteen other states—lost power. Thousands of houses and other buildings near the coast were destroyed or badly damaged. Worst of all, more than one hundred people lost their lives (Webley, 2012).

But, despite a total cost to the country of some $25 billion, analysts wondered if Sandy represented something even more disturbing. With the oceans warming, the weather is changing. The trend toward more severe storms has prompted many to wonder if this "once in a lifetime" storm is actually a preview of what might well become the "new normal." With population highly concentrated in massive urban areas—a pattern found not just in the United States but also in much of the world—climate change may well be putting hundreds of millions of people at risk.

Our planet is a single vast environmental system—one that is shaped for better or worse by the 7.1 billion people (in 2013) who live here. This chapter explores how human society both relies on and shapes the natural environment. Our planet is changing, not only in terms of global warming and other environmental trends but also in terms of a steadily increasing population. Similarly, a majority of the world's people now live in the dense concentrations we call cities and the share of population that is urban continues to rise.

Demography: The Study of Population

(22.1) Explain the concepts of fertility, mortality, and migration, and how they affect population size.

When humans first began to cultivate plants some 12,000 years ago, Earth's entire *Homo sapiens* population was around 5 million, about the number living in just the state of Colorado today. Very slow growth pushed the global total in 1 C.E. to perhaps 300 million, or about the current population of the United States.

Starting around 1750, world population began to spike upward. We now add more than 84 million people to the planet each year; today, the world holds 7.1 billion people (Population Reference Bureau, 2012).

The causes and consequences of this drama are the basis of **demography**, *the study of human population.* Demography (from Greek, meaning "description of people") is a cousin of sociology that analyzes the size and composition of a population and studies how and why people move from place to place. Demographers not only collect statistics but also raise important questions about the effects of population growth and suggest how it might be controlled. The following sections present basic demographic concepts.

Watch in **MySocLab**
Video *The Basics: Population, Urbanization, and Environment*

Fertility

The study of human population begins with how many people are born. **Fertility** is *the incidence of childbearing in a country's population*. During her childbearing years, from the onset of menstruation (typically in the early teens) to menopause (usually in the late forties), a woman is capable of bearing more than twenty children. But *fecundity*, or maximum possible childbearing, is sharply reduced by cultural norms, finances, and personal choice.

Demographers describe fertility using the **crude birth rate**, *the number of live births in a given year for every 1,000 people in a population*. To calculate a crude birth rate, divide the number of live births in a year by the society's total population, and multiply the result by 1,000. In the United States in 2011, there were 3.95 million live births in a population of 311.6 million, yielding a crude birth rate of 12.7 (Hamilton, Martin, & Ventura, 2012).

> **January 18, Coshocton County, Ohio.** Having just finished the mountains of meat and potatoes that make up a typical Amish meal, we have gathered in the living room of Jacob Raber, a member of this rural Amish community. Mrs. Raber, a mother of four, is telling us about Amish life. "Most of the women I know have five or six children," she says with a smile, "but certainly not everybody—some have eleven or twelve!"

A country's birth rate is described as "crude" because it is based on the entire population, not just women in their childbearing years. In addition, this measure ignores differences between various categories of the population: Fertility among the Amish, for example, is quite high, and fertility among Asian Americans is low. But the crude measure is easy to calculate and allows rough comparisons of the fertility of one country or region in relation to others. Part (a) of Figure 22–1 shows that on a global scale the crude birth rate of North America is low.

Global Snapshot

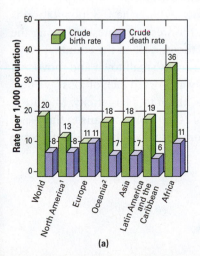
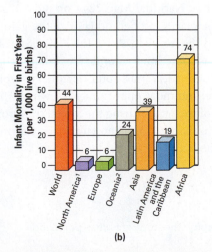
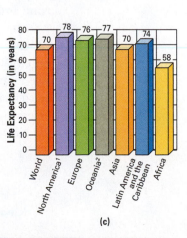

FIGURE 22–1 (a) Crude Birth Rates and Crude Death Rates, (b) Infant Mortality Rates, and (c) Life Expectancy around the World, 2012

By world standards, North America has a low birth rate, an average death rate, a very low infant mortality rate, and high life expectancy.

[1] United States and Canada. [2] Australia, New Zealand, and South Pacific Islands.

Source: Population Reference Bureau (2012).

Mortality

Population size also reflects **mortality**, *the incidence of death in a country's population.* To measure mortality, demographers use the **crude death rate**, *the number of deaths in a given year for every 1,000 people in a population.* This time, we take the number of deaths in a year, divide by the total population, and multiply the result by 1,000. In 2011, there were 2.5 million deaths in the U.S. population of 311.6 million, yielding a crude death rate of 8.1 (Hoyert & Xu, 2012). Part (a) of Figure 22–1 shows that this rate is about average.

A third useful demographic measure is the **infant mortality rate**, *the number of deaths among infants under one year of age for each 1,000 live births in a given year.* To compute infant mortality, divide the number of deaths of children under one year of age by the number of live births during the same year, and multiply the result by 1,000. In 2011, there were 23,910 infant deaths and 3.95 million live births in the United States. Dividing the first number by the second and multiplying the result by 1,000 yields an infant mortality rate of 6.05. Part (b) of Figure 22–1 indicates that by world standards, North American infant mortality is very low.

But remember that differences exist among various categories of people. For example, African Americans, with nearly three times the burden of poverty as whites, have an infant mortality rate of 11.4—more than twice the white rate of 5.1.

Low infant mortality greatly raises **life expectancy**, *the average life span of a country's population.* U.S. males born in 2011 can expect to live 76.3 years, and females can look forward to 81.1 years. As part (c) of Figure 22–1 shows, life expectancy in North America is twenty years greater than is typical of low-income countries in Africa.

Migration

Population size is also affected by **migration**, *the movement of people into and out of a specified territory.* Movement into a territory, or *immigration,* is measured as an *in-migration rate,* calculated as the number of people entering an area for every 1,000 people in the population. Movement out of a territory, or *emigration,* is measured in terms of an *out-migration rate,* the number leaving for every 1,000 people. Both types of migration usually occur at the same time; the difference between them is the *net migration rate.*

All nations experience internal migration, movement within their borders from one region to another. National Map 22–1 on page 633 shows where the U.S. population is moving and the places left behind (notice the gains in the western states and along the East Coast, and the heavy losses in the Plains States in the middle of the country).

Migration is sometimes voluntary, as when people leave a small town and move to a larger city. In such cases, "push-pull" factors are typically at work; a lack of jobs "pushes" people to move, and more opportunity elsewhere "pulls" them to a larger city. Migration can also be involuntary, as during the forced transport of 10 million Africans to the Western Hemisphere as slaves or when Hurricane Katrina forced tens of thousands of people to flee New Orleans.

life expectancy the average life span of a country's population

demography the study of human population

fertility the incidence of childbearing in a country's population

crude birth rate the number of live births in a given year for every 1,000 people in a population

mortality the incidence of death in a country's population

crude death rate the number of deaths in a given year for every 1,000 people in a population

infant mortality rate the number of deaths among infants under one year of age for each 1,000 live births in a given year

migration the movement of people into and out of a specified territory

Seeing Ourselves

✳ **Explore** population density in your local community and in counties across the United States in **MySocLab**

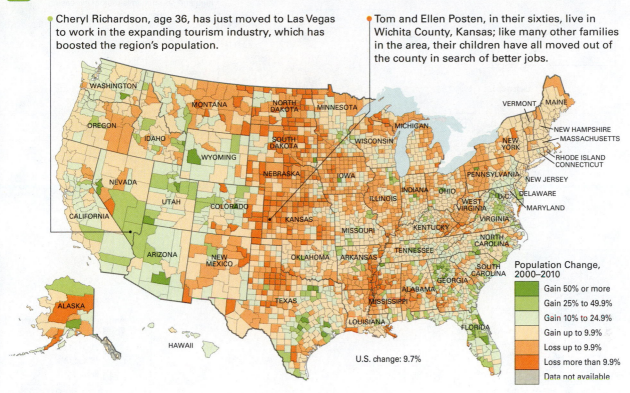

• Cheryl Richardson, age 36, has just moved to Las Vegas to work in the expanding tourism industry, which has boosted the region's population.

• Tom and Ellen Posten, in their sixties, live in Wichita County, Kansas; like many other families in the area, their children have all moved out of the county in search of better jobs.

Population Change, 2000–2010

- Gain 50% or more
- Gain 25% to 49.9%
- Gain 10% to 24.9%
- Gain up to 9.9%
- Loss up to 9.9%
- Loss more than 9.9%
- Data not available

U.S. change: 9.7%

NATIONAL MAP 22–1 Population Change across the United States

This map shows that between 2000 and 2010, population moved from the heartland of the United States toward the coasts. What do you think is causing this internal migration? What categories of people do you think remain in counties that are losing population?

Source: U.S. Census Bureau (2011).

Population Growth

Fertility, mortality, and migration all affect the size of a society's population. In general, rich nations (such as the United States) grow as much from immigration as from natural increase; poorer nations (such as Pakistan) grow almost entirely from natural increase.

To calculate a population's natural growth rate, demographers subtract the crude death rate from the crude birth rate. The natural growth rate of the U.S. population in 2011 was 4.6 per 1,000 (the crude birth rate of 12.7 minus the crude death rate of 8.1), or about 0.5 percent annual growth.

Global Map 22–1 on page 634 shows that population growth in the United States and other high-income nations is well below the world average of 1.2 percent. Earth's low-growth continents are Europe (currently showing no growth) and North America (0.5 percent). Close to the global average are Oceania (1.2 percent), Asia (1.1 percent), and Latin America (1.2 percent). The highest-growth region in the world is Africa (2.4 percent).

A handy rule of thumb for estimating a nation or region's growth is to divide the number 70 by the population growth rate; this yields the *doubling time* in years. Thus an annual growth rate of 2 percent (found in the Latin American nations of Bolivia, Honduras, and Belize) doubles a population in thirty-five years, and a 3 percent growth rate (found in the African nations of Niger, Mali, and Gambia) drops the doubling time to just twenty-three years. The rapid population growth of the poorest countries is deeply troubling because these countries can barely support the populations they have now.

Window on the World

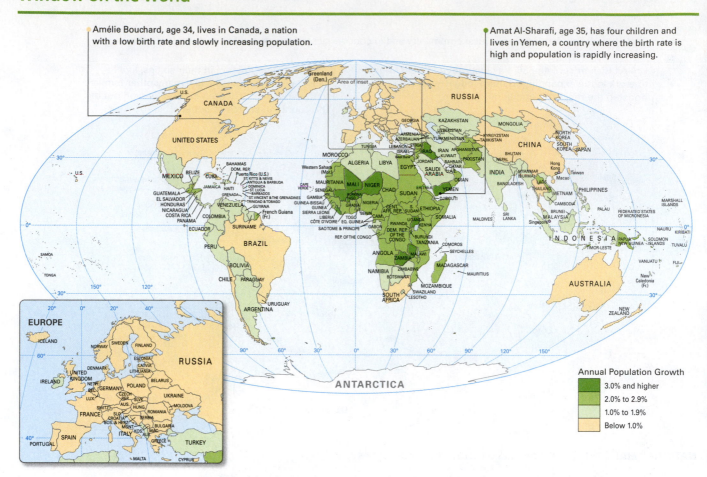

Amélie Bouchard, age 34, lives in Canada, a nation with a low birth rate and slowly increasing population.

Amat Al-Sharafi, age 35, has four children and lives in Yemen, a country where the birth rate is high and population is rapidly increasing.

Annual Population Growth
- 3.0% and higher
- 2.0% to 2.9%
- 1.0% to 1.9%
- Below 1.0%

GLOBAL MAP 22–1 Population Growth in Global Perspective

The richest countries of the world—including the United States, Canada, and the nations of Europe—have growth rates below 1 percent. The nations of Latin America and Asia typically have growth rates around 1.5 percent, a rate that doubles a population in forty-seven years. Africa has an overall growth rate of 2.4 percent (despite only small increases in countries with a high rate of AIDS), which cuts the doubling time to twenty-nine years. In global perspective, we see that a society's standard of living is closely related to its rate of population growth: Population is rising fastest in the world regions that can least afford to support more people.

Source: Population Reference Bureau (2012).

Population Composition

Demographers also study the makeup of a society's population at a given point in time. One variable is the **sex ratio**, *the number of males for every 100 females in a nation's population*. In 2011, the sex ratio in the United States was 97 (96.8 males for every 100 females). Sex ratios are usually below 100 because, on average, women outlive men. In places such as Plainville, Kansas, which has an aging population, the sex ratio is only 89, or 89 males for every 100 females. In India, however, the sex ratio is 108 because, not only is the population much younger, but also many parents value sons more than daughters and may either abort a female fetus or, after birth, give more care to their male children, raising the odds that a female child will die.

A more complex measure is the **age-sex pyramid**, *a graphic representation of the age and sex of a population*. Figure 22–2 on page 635 presents the age-sex pyramids for the populations of the United States and Mexico. Higher mortality with advancing age gives these figures a rough pyramid shape. In the U.S. pyramid, the bulge in the middle reflects high birth rates during the *baby boom* from the mid-1940s to the mid-1960s. The contraction for people in their twenties and thirties reflects the subsequent *baby bust.* The birth rate of 12.7 in 2011 is half what it was (25.3) at the height of the baby boom in 1957.

sex ratio the number of males for every 100 females in a nation's population

age-sex pyramid a graphic representation of the age and sex of a population

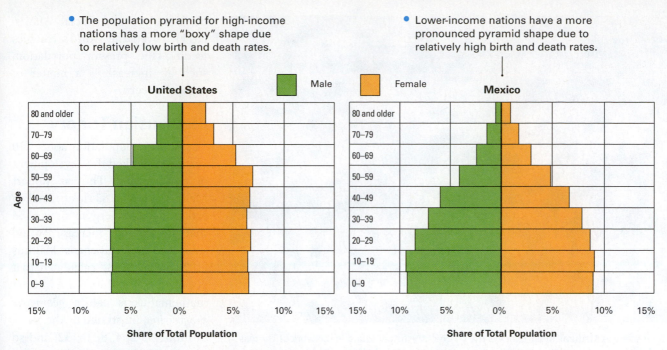

United States

Male   Female

Mexico

Age: 80 and older, 70–79, 60–69, 50–59, 40–49, 30–39, 20–29, 10–19, 0–9

15% 10% 5% 0% 5% 10% 15%

Share of Total Population

Share of Total Population

FIGURE 22–2 Population Age-Sex Pyramids for the United States and Mexico, 2013

By looking at the shape of a country's population pyramid, you can tell its level of economic development and predict future levels of population increase.

Source: U.S. Census Bureau (2013).

Comparing the U.S. and Mexican age-sex pyramids reveals different demographic trends. The pyramid for Mexico, like that of other lower-income nations, is wide at the bottom (reflecting higher birth rates) and narrows quickly by what we would call middle age (due to higher mortality). In short, Mexico is a much younger society, with a median age of twenty-eight compared to thirty-seven in the United States. With a larger share of females still in their childbearing years, Mexico's crude birth rate (19) is considerably higher than our own (12.7), and its annual rate of population growth (1.1 percent) is more than twice the U.S. rate (0.5 percent).

History and Theory of Population Growth

22.2 Analyze population trends using Malthusian theory and demographic transition theory.

In the past, people wanted large families because human labor was the key to productivity. In addition, until rubber condoms were invented in the mid-1800s, prevention of pregnancy was uncertain at best. But high death rates from infectious diseases put a constant brake on population growth.

A major demographic shift began about 1750 as the world's population turned upward, reaching the 1 billion mark by 1800. This milestone (which took all of human history to reach) was repeated barely a century later in 1930, when a second billion people were added to the planet. In other words, not only was population increasing, but the *rate* of growth was accelerating as well. Global population reached 3 billion by 1962 (just thirty-two years later) and 4 billion by 1974 (only twelve years after that). The rate of world population increase has slowed recently, but our planet passed the 5 billion mark in 1987, the 6 billion mark in 1999, and the 7 billion mark early in 2012. In no previous century did the world's population even double; in the twentieth century, it *quadrupled*.

Currently, the world is gaining 84 million people each year; 98 percent of this increase is in poor countries. Experts predict that Earth's population will reach 8 billion by 2025 and will climb more slowly to about 9.3 billion by 2050 (United Nations, Department

This street scene in Madurai, India, conveys the vision of the future found in the work of Thomas Robert Malthus, who feared that population increase would overwhelm the world's resources. Can you explain why Malthus had such a serious concern about population? How is demographic transition theory a more hopeful analysis?

of Economic and Social Affairs, 2011). Given the world's troubles feeding the present population, such an increase is a matter of urgent concern.

Malthusian Theory

The sudden population spurt 250 years ago sparked the development of demography. Thomas Robert Malthus (1766–1834), an English economist and clergyman, warned that population increase would soon lead to social chaos. Malthus (1926, orig. 1798) calculated that population would increase in what mathematicians call a *geometric progression*, illustrated by the series of numbers 2, 4, 8, 16, 32, and so on. At such a rate, Malthus concluded, world population would soon soar out of control.

Food production would also increase, Malthus explained, but only in *arithmetic progression* (as in the series 2, 3, 4, 5, 6, and so on) because even with new agricultural technology, farmland is limited. Thus Malthus presented a distressing vision of the future: people reproducing beyond what the planet could feed, leading ultimately to widespread starvation and war over what resources were left.

Malthus recognized that artificial birth control or abstinence might change his prediction. But he considered one morally wrong and the other impractical. Famine and war therefore stalked humanity in Malthus's mind, and he was justly known as "the dismal parson."

EVALUATE Fortunately, Malthus's prediction was flawed. First, by 1850, the European birth rate began to drop, partly because children were becoming an economic liability rather than an asset and partly because people began using artificial birth control. Second, Malthus underestimated human ingenuity: Modern drip-irrigation techniques, advanced fertilizers, and effective pesticides increased farm production and saved vital resources far more than he could have imagined (Yemma, 2011).

Some people criticized Malthus for ignoring the role of social inequality in world abundance and famine. For example, Karl Marx (1967, orig. 1867) objected to viewing suffering as a "law of nature" rather than the curse of capitalism. More recently, "critical demographers" have claimed that saying poverty is caused by high birth rates in low-income countries amounts to blaming the victims. On the contrary, they see global inequality as the real issue (Horton, 1999; Kuumba, 1999).

Still, Malthus offers an important lesson. Habitable land, clean water, and fresh air are limited resources, and greater economic productivity has taken a heavy toll on the natural environment. In addition, medical advances have lowered death rates, pushing up world population. Common sense tells us that no level of population growth can go on forever. People everywhere must become aware of the dangers of population increase.

CHECK YOUR LEARNING What did Malthus predict about human population increase? About food production? What was his overall conclusion?

Demographic Transition Theory

A more complex analysis of population change is **demographic transition theory**, *a thesis that links population patterns to a society's level of technological development*. Figure 22–3 shows the demographic consequences at four levels of technological development.

Preindustrial, agrarian societies (Stage 1) have high birth rates because of the economic value of children and the absence of birth control. Death rates are also high because of low living standards and limited medical technology. Deaths from outbreaks of disease cancel out births, so population rises and falls only slightly over time. This was the case for thousands of years in Europe before the Industrial Revolution.

Stage 2, the onset of industrialization, brings a demographic transition as death rates fall due to greater food supplies and scientific medicine. But birth rates remain high, resulting in rapid population growth. It was during Europe's Stage 2 that Malthus formulated his ideas, which accounts for his pessimistic view of the future. The world's poorest countries today are in this high-growth stage.

In Stage 3, a mature industrial economy, the birth rate drops, curbing population growth once again. Fertility falls because most children survive to adulthood and because high living standards make raising children expensive. In short, affluence transforms children from economic assets into economic liabilities. Smaller families, made possible by effective birth control, are also favored by women working outside the home. As birth rates follow death rates downward, population growth slows further.

Stage 4 corresponds to a postindustrial economy in which the demographic transition is complete. The birth rate keeps falling, partly because dual-income couples gradually become the norm and partly because the cost of raising children continues to increase. This trend, linked to steady death rates, means that population grows only very slowly or even decreases. This is the case today in Japan, Europe, and the United States.

- The United States is in this historical stage, with both a low birth rate and a low death rate.

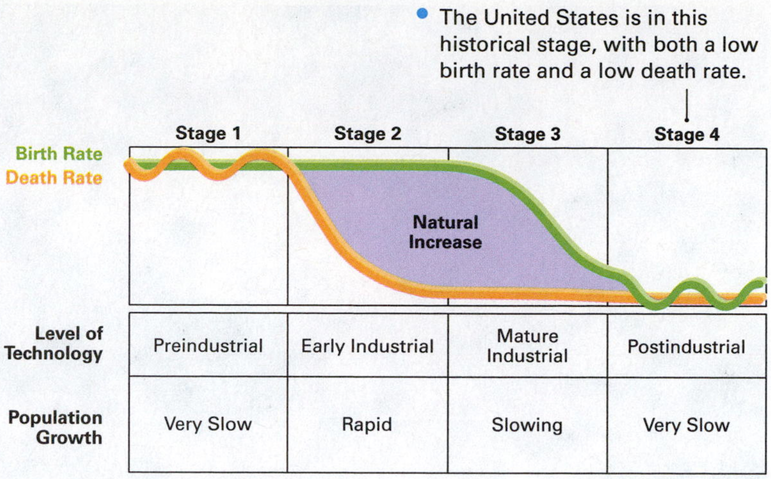

FIGURE 22–3 Demographic Transition Theory

Demographic transition theory links population change to a society's level of technological development.

demographic transition theory a thesis that links population patterns to a society's level of technological development

EVALUATE Demographic transition theory suggests that the key to population control lies in technology. Instead of the runaway population increase feared by Malthus, this theory sees technology slowing growth and spreading material plenty.

Demographic transition theory is linked to modernization theory, one approach to global development discussed in Chapter 12 ("Global Stratification"). Modernization theorists are optimistic that poor countries will solve their population problems as they industrialize. But critics, notably dependency theorists, strongly disagree. Unless there is a redistribution of global resources, they maintain, our planet will become increasingly divided into industrialized "haves," enjoying low population growth, and nonindustrialized "have-nots," struggling in vain to feed more and more people.

CHECK YOUR LEARNING Explain the four stages of demographic transition theory.

Global Population Today: A Brief Survey

What can we say about population in today's world? Drawing on the discussion so far, we can identify important patterns and reach several conclusions.

Fertility in the United States has fallen during the past century and is now quite low. But some categories of the U.S. population have much higher fertility rates. One example is the Amish, a religious society living in rural areas of Ohio, Pennsylvania, and other states. It is common for Amish couples to have five, six, or more children. Why do you think the Amish favor large families?

zero population growth the rate of reproduction that maintains population at a steady level

The Low-Growth North

When the Industrial Revolution began in the Northern Hemisphere, the population increase in Western Europe and North America was a high 3 percent annually. But in the centuries since, the growth rate has steadily declined, and in 1970, it fell below 1 percent. As our postindustrial society settles into Stage 4, the U.S. birth rate is below the replacement level of 2.1 children per woman, a point demographers term **zero population growth**, *the rate of reproduction that maintains population at a steady level.* In 2012, eighty-one nations, almost all of them high-income countries, were at or below the point of zero population growth.

Among the factors that serve to hold down population in these postindustrial societies are a high proportion of men and women in the labor force, rising costs of raising children, trends toward later marriage and singlehood, and widespread use of contraceptives and abortion.

In high-income nations, then, population increase is not the pressing problem that it is in poor countries. On the contrary, many governments in high-income countries, including Italy and Japan, are concerned about a future problem of *underpopulation* because declining population size may be difficult to reverse and because the swelling ranks of the elderly can look to fewer and fewer young people for support (El Nasser & Overberg, 2011; Hamilton, Martin, and Ventura, 2012; Population Reference Bureau, 2012; United Nations Development Programme, 2012).

The High-Growth South

Population is a critical problem in poor nations of the Southern Hemisphere. No nation of the world lacks industrial technology entirely; demographic transition theory's Stage 1 applies today to remote rural areas of low-income nations. But much of Latin America, Africa, and Asia is at Stage 2, with a mix of agrarian and industrial economies. Advanced medical technology, supplied by rich countries, has sharply reduced death rates, but birth rates remain high. This is why lower-income countries now account for about 82 percent of Earth's people and 98 percent of annual global population increase.

In some of the world's poorest countries, such as the Democratic Republic of the Congo in Africa, women still have, on average, more than six children during their lifetimes. But in most poor countries, birth rates have fallen from about six children per woman (typical in 1950) to about three. But this level of fertility is still high enough to make global poverty much worse. This is why leaders in the battle against global poverty point to the importance of reducing fertility rates in low-income nations.

Notice, too, that a key element in controlling world population growth is improving the status of women. Why? Because of this simple truth: Give women more life choices and they will have fewer children. History has shown that women who are free to decide when and where to marry, bear children as a matter of choice, and have access to education and to good jobs will limit their own fertility (Axinn & Barber, 2001; Roudi-Fahimi & Kent, 2007; Population Reference Bureau, 2012).

The Demographic Divide

High- and low-income nations display very different population dynamics, a gap that is sometimes called the *demographic divide*. In Italy, a high-income nation with very low growth, women average just 1.4 children in their lifetimes. Such a low birth rate means that the number of annual births is less than the number of deaths. This means that at the moment, Italy is actually *losing* population. Looking ahead to 2050, and even assuming some gains from immigration, Italy's population is projected to be about the same as it is today. But the share of elderly people in Italy—now 21 percent—will only increase as time goes on.

How different the patterns are in a low-income nation such as the Democratic Republic of the Congo. There, women still average six to seven children, so even with a high mortality rate, this nation's population will more than double by 2050. The share of elderly people is extremely low—about 3 percent—and almost half that country's people are below the age of sixteen. With such a high growth rate, it is no surprise that the problem of poverty is bad and getting worse: About three-fourths of the people are undernourished (Population Reference Bureau, 2012).

In sum, a demographic divide now separates rich countries with low birth rates and aging populations from poor countries with high birth rates and very young populations. Just as humanity has devised ways to reduce deaths around the world, it must now bring down population growth, especially in poor countries where projections suggest a future as bleak as that imagined by Thomas Malthus centuries ago.

Today, China stands out as a nation that has taken a strong stand on reducing population increase. That country's controversial one-child policy, enacted back in the 1970s, has reduced China's population by about 250 million.

> For a closer look at population control in China, **Read More** in **MySocLab**, *Where Are the Girls? China's One-Child Policy*

Urbanization: The Growth of Cities

(22.3) Summarize patterns of urbanization in the United States and around the world.

October 8, Hong Kong. The cable train grinds to the top of Victoria Peak, where we behold one of the world's most spectacular vistas: the city of Hong Kong at night! A million bright, colorful lights ring the harbor as ships, ferries, and traditional Chinese junks slowly slip by. Day or night, few places match Hong Kong for sheer energy: This small city is as economically productive as the state of Wisconsin or the nation of Finland. We could sit here for hours entranced by the spectacle of Hong Kong.

Throughout most of human history, the sights and sounds of great cities such as Hong Kong, Paris, and New York were simply unimaginable. Our distant ancestors lived in small, nomadic groups, moving as they depleted vegetation or hunted migratory game. The tiny settlements that marked the emergence of civilization in the Middle East some 12,000 years ago held only a small fraction of Earth's people. Today, the largest three or four cities of the world hold as many people as the entire planet did back then.

Urbanization is *the concentration of population into cities*. Urbanization redistributes population within a society and transforms many patterns of social life. We will trace these changes in terms of three urban revolutions: the emergence of cities 10,000 years ago, the development of industrial cities after 1750, and the explosive growth of cities in poor countries today.

urbanization the concentration of population into cities

The Evolution of Cities

Cities are a relatively new development in human history. Only about 12,000 years ago did our ancestors begin living in permanent settlements, which set the stage for the *first urban revolution*.

The First Cities

As explained in Chapter 4 ("Society"), hunting and gathering forced people to move all the time; however, once our ancestors discovered how to domesticate animals and cultivate crops, they were able to stay in one place. Raising their own food also created a material surplus, which freed some people from food production and allowed them to build shelters, make tools, weave cloth, and take part in religious rituals. The emergence of cities led to both higher living standards and job specialization.

The first city that we know of was Jericho, which lies to the north of the Dead Sea in what is now the West Bank. When first settled some 10,000 years ago, it was home to only 600 people. But as the centuries passed, cities grew to tens of thousands of people and became the centers of vast empires. By 3000 B.C.E., Egyptian cities flourished, as did cities in China about 2000 B.C.E. and in Central and South America about 1500 B.C.E. In North America, however, only a few Native American societies formed settlements; widespread urbanization had to await the arrival of European settlers in the seventeenth century.

Preindustrial European Cities

European cities date back some 5,000 years to the Greeks and later the Romans, both of whom created great empires and founded cities across Europe, including Vienna, Paris, and London. With the fall of the Roman Empire, the so-called Dark Ages began as people withdrew into defensive walled settlements and warlords battled for territory. Only in the eleventh century did Europe become more peaceful; trade flourished once again, allowing cities to grow.

Medieval cities were quite different from those familiar to us today. Beneath towering cathedrals, the narrow and winding streets of London, Brussels, and Florence teemed with merchants, artisans, priests, peddlers, jugglers, nobles, and servants. Occupational groups such as bakers, carpenters, and metalworkers clustered together in distinct sections or "quarters." Ethnicity also defined communities as residents tried to keep out people who differed from themselves. The term "ghetto" (from the Italian *borghetto,* meaning "outside the city walls") was first used to describe the neighborhood in which the Jews of Venice were segregated.

Industrial European Cities

As the Middle Ages came to a close, steadily increasing commerce enriched a new urban middle class, or *bourgeoisie* (French, meaning "townspeople"). With more and more money, the bourgeoisie soon rivaled the hereditary aristocracy.

By about 1750, the Industrial Revolution triggered a *second urban revolution,* first in Europe and then in North America. Factories unleashed tremendous productive power, causing cities to grow bigger than ever before. London, the largest European city, reached 550,000 people by 1700 and exploded to 6.5 million by 1900 (A. F. Weber, 1963, orig. 1899; Chandler & Fox, 1974).

Cities not only grew but changed shape as well. Older winding streets gave way to broad, straight boulevards to handle the increasing flow of commercial traffic. Steam and electric trolleys soon crisscrossed the expanding cities. Because land was now a commodity to be bought and sold, developers divided cities into regular-sized lots (Mumford, 1961). The center of the city was no longer the cathedral but a bustling central business district filled with banks, retail stores, and tall office buildings.

With a new focus on business, cities became more crowded and impersonal. Crime rates rose. Especially at the outset, a few industrialists lived in grand style, but most men, women, and children barely survived by working in factories.

Organized efforts by workers to improve their lives eventually brought changes to the workplace, better housing, and the right to vote. Public services such as water, sewer systems, and electricity further improved urban living. Today, some urbanites still live in poverty, but a rising standard of living has partly fulfilled the city's historical promise of a better life.

The Growth of U.S. Cities

Most of the Native Americans who inhabited North America for thousands of years before the arrival of Europeans were migratory people who formed few permanent settlements. The spread of villages and towns came after European colonization.

Colonial Settlement, 1565–1800

In 1565, the Spanish built a settlement at Saint Augustine, Florida, and in 1607, the English founded Jamestown, Virginia. The first lasting settlement came in 1624, when the Dutch established New Amsterdam, later renamed New York.

New York and Boston (founded by the English in 1630) started out as tiny villages in a vast wilderness. They resembled medieval towns in Europe, with narrow, winding streets that still curve through lower Manhattan and downtown Boston. When the first census was completed in 1790, as Table 22–1 shows, just 5 percent of the nation's people lived in cities.

Urban Expansion, 1800–1860

Early in the nineteenth century, as cities along the East Coast grew bigger, towns sprang up along the transportation routes that opened the American West. By 1860, Buffalo, Cleveland, Detroit, and Chicago were changing the face of the Midwest, and about one-fifth of the U.S. population lived in cities.

Urban expansion was greatest in the northern states; New York City, for example, had ten times the population of Charleston, South Carolina. The division of the United States into the industrial-urban North and the agrarian-rural South was one major cause of the Civil War (Schlesinger, 1969).

The Metropolitan Era, 1860–1950

The Civil War (1861–65) gave an enormous boost to urbanization as factories strained to produce weapons. Waves of people deserted the countryside for cities in hopes of finding better jobs. Joining them were tens of millions of immigrants, mostly from Europe, forming a culturally diverse urban mix.

In 1900, New York's population soared past the 4 million mark, and Chicago, a city of only 100,000 people in 1860, was closing in on 2 million. Such growth marked the era of the **metropolis** (from the Greek, meaning "mother city"), *a large city that socially and economically dominates an urban area*. Metropolises became the economic centers of the United States. By 1920, urban areas were home to a majority of the U.S. population.

Industrial technology pushed the urban skyline ever higher. In the 1880s, steel girders and mechanical elevators allowed buildings to rise more than ten stories high. In 1930, New York's Empire State Building was hailed as an urban wonder, reaching 102 stories into the clouds.

Urban Decentralization, 1950–Present

The industrial metropolis reached its peak about 1950. Since then, something of a turnaround—termed *urban decentralization*—has occurred as people have left downtown areas for outlying **suburbs**, *urban areas beyond the political boundaries of a city*. The old industrial cities of the Northeast and Midwest stopped growing, and some lost considerable population in the decades after 1950. At the same time, suburban populations increased rapidly. The urban landscape of densely packed central cities evolved into sprawling suburban regions.

Suburbs and Urban Decline

Imitating the European aristocracy, some of the rich had town houses in the city as well as large country homes beyond the city limits. But not until after World War II did ordinary people find a suburban home within their reach. With more and more cars in circulation, new four-lane highways, government-backed mortgages, and inexpensive tract homes, the suburbs grew rapidly. By 1999, most of the U.S. population lived in the suburbs and

TABLE 22–1 Urban Population of the United States, 1790–2050

Year	Population (in millions)	Percentage Living in Cities
1790	3.9	5.1%
1800	5.3	6.1
1820	9.6	7.3
1840	17.1	10.5
1860	31.4	19.7
1880	50.2	28.1
1900	76.0	39.7
1920	105.7	51.3
1940	131.7	56.5
1960	179.3	69.9
1980	226.5	73.7
2000	281.4	79.0
2020 (projected)	337.1	84.4
2040 (projected)	383.5	87.5
2050 (projected)	403.1	88.9

Sources: U.S. Census Bureau (2010) and United Nations (2012).

shopped at nearby malls rather than in the older and more distant downtown shopping districts (Pederson, Smith, & Adler, 1999; Macionis & Parrillo, 2010).

As many older cities of the Snowbelt—the Northeast and Midwest—lost higher-income taxpayers to the suburbs, they struggled to pay for expensive social programs for the poor who remained. Many cities fell into financial crisis, and urban decay became severe. Soon the inner city came to be synonymous with slums, crime, drugs, unemployment, poverty, and minorities.

The urban critic Paul Goldberger (2002) points out that the decline of central cities has also led to a decline in the importance of public space. Historically, the heart of city life was played out on the streets. The French word for a sophisticated person is *boulevardier,* which literally means "street person"—a term that has a negative meaning in the United States today. The active life that once took place on public streets and in public squares now takes place in shopping malls, the lobbies of cineplex theaters, and gated residential communities—all privately owned spaces. Further reducing the vitality of today's urban places is the spread of television, the Internet, and other media that people use without leaving home.

Postindustrial Sunbelt Cities

As older Snowbelt cities fell into decline, Sunbelt cities in the South and the West began to grow rapidly. The soaring populations of cities such as Los Angeles and Houston reflect a population shift to the Sunbelt, where 61 percent of U.S. people now live. In addition, most of today's immigrants enter the country in the Sunbelt region. In 1950, nine of the ten biggest U.S. cities were in the Snowbelt; today, seven of the top ten are in the Sunbelt (U.S. Census Bureau, 2012).

Unlike their colder counterparts, Sunbelt cities came of age after urban decentralization began. So although cities like Chicago have long been enclosed by a ring of politically independent suburbs, cities like Houston have pushed their boundaries outward to include suburban communities. Chicago covers 227 square miles; Houston is more than twice that size, and the greater Houston urban area covers almost 9,000 square miles—an area the size of the state of New Hampshire.

The great sprawl of Sunbelt cities has drawbacks. Many people in cities such as Atlanta, Dallas, Phoenix, and Los Angeles complain that unplanned growth results in traffic-clogged roads, poorly planned housing developments, and schools that cannot keep up with the inflow of children. Not surprisingly, voters in many communities across the United States have passed ballot initiatives seeking to limit urban sprawl (Romero & Liserio, 2002; Sullivan, 2007).

Megalopolis: The Regional City

Another result of urban decentralization is urban regions or regional cities. The U.S. Census Bureau (2010) recognizes 366 *metropolitan statistical areas* (MSAs). Each includes at least one city with 50,000 or more people. The bureau also recognizes 576 *micropolitan statistical areas,* urban areas with at least one city of 10,000 to 50,000 people. *Core-based statistical areas* (CBSAs) include both metropolitan and micropolitan statistical areas.

The biggest CBSAs contain millions of people and cover large areas that extend into several states. In 2011, the

These recent college graduates have migrated to San Francisco in pursuit of economic opportunity. While many smaller cities struggle to keep the young people who are born there, large cities on the West Coast and the East Coast are magnets for young women and men beginning their careers.

metropolis a large city that socially and economically dominates an urban area

suburbs urban areas beyond the political boundaries of a city

megalopolis a vast urban region containing a number of cities and their surrounding suburbs

largest CBSA was New York and its adjacent urban areas in Long Island, western Connecticut, northern New Jersey, and eastern Pennsylvania, with a total population of more than 22 million. Next in size is the CBSA in southern California that includes Los Angeles, Riverside, and Long Beach, with a population of more than 18 million.

As regional cities grow, they begin to overlap. In the early 1960s, the French geographer Jean Gottmann (1961) coined the term **megalopolis** to designate *a vast urban region containing a number of cities and their surrounding suburbs*. Along the East Coast, a 400-mile megalopolis stretches all the way from New England to Virginia. Other supercities cover the eastern coast of Florida and stretch from Cleveland west to Chicago.

Edge Cities

Urban decentralization has also created *edge cities*, business centers some distance from the old downtowns. Edge cities—a mix of corporate office buildings, shopping malls, hotels, and entertainment complexes—differ from suburbs, which contain mostly homes. The population of suburbs peaks at night, but the population of edge cities peaks during the workday.

As part of expanding urban regions, most edge cities have no clear physical boundaries. Some do have names, including Las Colinas (near the Dallas–Fort Worth airport), Tyson's Corner (in Virginia, near Washington, D.C.), and King of Prussia (northwest of Philadelphia). Other edge cities are known only by the major highways that flow through them, including Route 1 in Princeton, New Jersey, and Route 128 near Boston (Garreau, 1991; Macionis & Parrillo, 2013).

Changes to Rural Areas

Most of the United States—75 percent of the land area—is rural. At the same time, most of the nation's people are urban: The 2010 census showed that 83.7 percent of the country's 309 million people were living in urban places.

As shown in Table 22–1, the trend toward becoming an urban society has been under way over the course of U.S. history. Immigration has played a part in the process of urbanization because most newcomers settle in cities. In addition, there has been net migration from rural areas to urban places, typically by people seeking greater social, educational, and economic opportunity.

During the 1990s, however, there developed a new trend, which analysts called the *rural rebound*. What this meant was that, instead of losing population to the urban areas, two-thirds of rural counties actually gained population. These gains were due mostly to migration as more people moved to rural places than left them for cities. The biggest gains in this process were seen in rural counties with special beauty such as lakes or ski areas. People were drawn to such rural communities not only by their natural beauty and clean air but also by their slower pace of life with less traffic and less crime.

Between 2000 and 2010, however, the rural rebound pattern faded, so that once again, most rural counties lost more people to migration than they gained. But the pattern was uneven. Rural counties that were highly scenic continued to

The rural rebound has been most pronounced in towns that offer spectacular natural beauty. There are times when people living in the scenic town of Park City, Utah, cannot even find a parking space.

increase in population due to migration, as did rural areas within commuting distance to large cities. By contrast, remote rural areas and those where the economy was largely based on farming saw little or no population gains or experienced declines.

If rural areas lose more people to migration than they attract, the only way they can maintain their populations is through natural increase—that is, if births outnumber deaths. But while natural increase did occur in some rural counties between 2000 and 2010, it did not occur in most. With typically older populations, most rural counties recorded more deaths than births, which meant that—unless migration made up the difference—populations declined.

Finally, rural places in the United States are becoming more socially diverse. The common view of rural areas as lacking racial and ethnic diversity has some basis in fact, as just 21 percent of this country's rural people fall into minority categories. Even so, keep in mind that some regions of the country have always had large minority populations, including African Americans in the South, Hispanic Americans in the Southwest, and Native Americans in Alaska. But rural areas in general have become more diverse, a trend that is seen in the fact that minorities (that is, people other than non-Hispanic whites) accounted for 83 percent of the rural population increase between 2000 and 2010 (K. M. Johnson, 1999; Johnson & Fuguitt, 2000; K. M. Johnson, 2012).

Urbanism as a Way of Life

(22.4) Identify the contributions of Tönnies, Durkheim, Simmel, Park, Wirth, and Marx to our understanding of urban life.

Early sociologists in Europe and the United States focused their attention on the rise of cities and how urban life differed from rural life. We briefly examine their accounts of urbanism as a way of life.

Ferdinand Tönnies: *Gemeinschaft* and *Gesellschaft*

In the late nineteenth century, the German sociologist Ferdinand Tönnies (1855–1937) studied how life in the new industrial metropolis differed from life in rural villages. From this contrast, he developed two concepts that have become a lasting part of sociology's terminology.

Tönnies (1963, orig. 1887) used the German word ***Gemeinschaft*** ("community") to refer to *a type of social organization in which people are closely tied by kinship and tradition*. The *Gemeinschaft* of the rural village joins people in what amounts to a single primary group.

By and large, argued Tönnies, *Gemeinschaft* is absent in the modern city. On the contrary, urbanization creates ***Gesellschaft*** ("association"), *a type of social organization in which people come together only on the basis of individual self-interest*. In the *Gesellschaft* way of life, individuals are motivated by their own needs rather than by a desire to help improve the well-being of everyone. By and large, city dwellers have little sense of community or common identity and look to others mainly when they need something. Tönnies saw in urbanization a weakening of close, long-lasting social relations in favor of the brief and impersonal ties or secondary relationships typical of business.

Gemeinschaft a type of social organization in which people are closely tied by kinship and tradition

Gesellschaft a type of social organization in which people come together only on the basis of individual self-interest

Emile Durkheim: Mechanical and Organic Solidarity

The French sociologist Emile Durkheim (see Chapter 4, "Society") agreed with much of Tönnies's thinking about cities. However, Durkheim countered that urbanites do not lack social bonds; they simply organize social life differently than rural people.

Durkheim described traditional, rural life as *mechanical solidarity*, social bonds based on common sentiments and shared moral values. With its emphasis on tradition, Durkheim's concept of mechanical solidarity bears a striking similarity to Tönnies's *Gemeinschaft*. Urbanization erodes mechanical solidarity, Durkheim explained, but it also

Peasant Dance (left, c. 1565), by Pieter Breughel the Elder, conveys the essential unity of rural life forged by generations of kinship and neighborhood. By contrast, Lily Furedi's *Subway (right)* communicates the impersonality common to urban areas. Taken together, these paintings capture Tönnies's distinction between *Gemeinschaft* and *Gesellschaft.*

Pieter Breughel the Elder (c. 1525/30–1569), *Peasant Dance,* c. 1565, Kunsthistorisches Museum, Vienna/Superstock. Lily Furedi, American. *Subway.* Oil on canvas, 99 × 123 cm. National Collection of Fine Arts, Washington, D.C./Smithsonian Institute.

generates a new type of bonding, which he called *organic solidarity,* social bonds based on specialization and interdependence. This concept, which parallels Tönnies's *Gesellschaft,* reveals an important difference between the two thinkers. Both thought the growth of industrial cities weakened tradition, but Durkheim optimistically pointed to a new kind of solidarity. Where societies had been built on *likeness* (mechanical solidarity), Durkheim now saw social life based on *difference* (organic solidarity).

For Durkheim, urban society offered more individual choice, moral tolerance, and personal privacy than people find in rural villages. In sum, Durkheim thought that something is lost in the process of urbanization, but much is gained.

Georg Simmel: The Blasé Urbanite

The German sociologist Georg Simmel (1858–1918) offered a microanalysis of cities, studying how urban life shapes individual experience. According to Simmel, individuals perceive the city as a crush of people, objects, and events. To prevent being overwhelmed by all this stimulation, urbanites develop a *blasé attitude,* tuning out much of what goes on around them. Such detachment does not mean that city dwellers lack compassion for others; they simply keep their distance as a survival strategy so that they can focus their time and energy on the people and things that really matter to them.

The Chicago School: Robert Park and Louis Wirth

Sociologists in the United States soon joined the study of rapidly growing cities. Robert Park, a leader of the first U.S. sociology program at the University of Chicago, sought to add a street-level perspective by getting out on the streets and studying real cities. As he said of himself, "I suspect that I have actually covered more ground, tramping about in cities in different parts of the world, than any other living man" (1950:viii). Walking the streets, Park found the city to be an organized mosaic of distinctive ethnic communities, commercial centers, and industrial districts. Over time, he observed, these "natural areas" develop and change in relation to one another. To Park, the city was a living organism—a human kaleidoscope.

Another major figure in the Chicago School of urban sociology was Louis Wirth (1897–1952). Wirth (1938) is best known for blending the ideas of Tönnies, Durkheim, Simmel, and Park into a comprehensive theory of urban life.

Wirth began by defining the city as a setting with a large, dense, and socially diverse population. These traits result in an impersonal, superficial, and transitory way of life. Living among millions of others, urbanites come into contact with many more people than residents of rural areas. So when city people notice others at all, they usually know them not in terms of *who they are* but *what they do*—as, for instance, the bus driver, the florist, or the grocery store clerk. These specialized urban relationships are pleasant for all concerned, but we should remember that self-interest rather than friendship is usually the main reason behind the interaction.

The impersonal nature of urban relationships, together with the great social diversity found in cities today, makes city dwellers more tolerant than rural villagers. Rural communities often jealously enforce their narrow traditions, but the heterogeneous population of a city rarely shares any single code of moral conduct (T. C. Wilson, 1985, 1995).

EVALUATE In both Europe and the United States, early sociologists presented a mixed view of urban living. Rapid urbanization troubled Tönnies, and Wirth saw personal ties and traditional morality lost in the anonymous rush of the city. Durkheim and Park emphasized urbanism's positive face, pointing to more personal freedom and greater personal choice.

One problem with all these views is that they paint urbanism in broad strokes that overlook the effects of class, race, and gender. There are many kinds of urbanites—rich and poor, black and white, Anglo and Latino, women and men—all leading distinctive lives (Gans, 1968). As the Thinking About Diversity box on page 647 explains, the share of minorities in the largest U.S. cities increased sharply since 1990. We see social diversity most clearly in cities where various categories of people are large enough to form distinct, visible communities (Macionis & Parrillo, 2013).

CHECK YOUR LEARNING Which of the urban sociologists—Tönnies, Durkheim, Park, and Wirth—were more positive about urban life? Which were more negative? In each case, explain why.

Urban Ecology

urban ecology the study of the link between the physical and social dimensions of cities

Sociologists (especially members of the Chicago School) developed **urban ecology**, *the study of the link between the physical and social dimensions of cities*. One issue of interest to urban ecologists is why cities are located where they are. Broadly speaking, the first cities emerged in fertile regions where the ecology favored raising crops. Preindustrial people, concerned with defense, built their cities on mountains (ancient Athens was perched on an outcropping of rock) or surrounded by water (Paris and Mexico City were founded on islands). With the coming of the Industrial Revolution, economic considerations gained importance, which explains why all the major U.S. cities were situated near rivers or natural harbors that facilitated trade.

Urban ecologists also study the physical design of cities. In 1925, Ernest W. Burgess, a student and colleague of Robert Park, described land use in Chicago in terms of *concentric zones*. City centers, Burgess observed, are business districts bordered by a ring of factories, followed by residential rings with housing that becomes more expensive the farther it is from the noise and pollution of the city's center.

Homer Hoyt (1939) refined Burgess's observations, noting that distinctive districts sometimes form *wedge-shaped sectors.* For example, one fashionable area may develop next to another, or an industrial district may extend outward from a city's center along a train or trolley line.

Chauncy Harris and Edward Ullman (1945) added yet another insight: As cities decentralize, they lose their single-center form in favor of a *multicentered model.* As cities grow, residential areas, industrial parks, and shopping districts typically push away from one another. Few people wish to live close to industrial areas, for example, so the city becomes a mosaic of distinct districts.

Social area analysis investigates what people in particular neighborhoods have in common. Three factors seem to explain most of the variation: family patterns, social class, and race and ethnicity (Shevky & Bell, 1955; Johnston, 1976). Families with children look for areas with single-family homes or large apartments and good schools. The rich seek

Read in **MySocLab**
Document: *Life and Death in the City: Neighborhoods in Context* by John Logan

Thinking About Diversity: Race, Class, and Gender

Minorities Have Become a Majority in the Largest U.S. Cities

In the nation's largest cities, the "minority-majority" is already here. According to the latest data from the U.S. Census Bureau, minorities—Hispanics, African Americans, and Asians—are now a majority of the population in sixty-five of the one hundred largest U.S. cities. This number is up from forty-eight in 2000 and thirty in 1990.

What accounts for the change? One reason is that large cities have been losing their non-Hispanic white population. For example, between 1990 and 2000, half of Detroit's non-Hispanic white population left that city; between 2000 and 2010, Detroit lost half of the white population that remained. As a result, by 2011, 92 percent of that Snowbelt city's current population included people within various racial and ethnic minority categories.

The same trend toward a larger minority population in cities holds in the Sunbelt. Between 2000 and 2011, the minority population of Garland, Texas, rose from 47 percent to 69 percent. In Phoenix, Arizona, minorities represented 44 percent of the population in 2000, a share that climbed to 53 percent by 2011.

Overall, the minority share of the population of the 100 largest cities in the United States stood at 48 percent in 1990. This share increased to 56 percent by 2000, and it swelled to 60 percent by 2011.

But perhaps the biggest reason for the minority-majority trend in urban population is the increase in immigration. People arriving from other nations, together with higher birth rates among these new immigrants, resulted in a 28 percent gain in the Hispanic population (about 3.7 million people) of the largest 100 cities between 2000 and 2011. The Asian population also surged by 30 percent (more than 1.2 million people). With a far lower level of immigration, African Americans represented a 6 percent smaller share of the people in these large cities in 2011 compared to 2000.

Political officials and other policymakers examine these figures closely. Clearly, the future vitality of the largest U.S. cities depends on meeting the needs and taking advantage of the contributions of the swelling minority—and especially immigrant—populations.

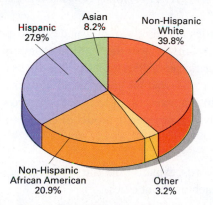

Population Profile for the 100 Largest U.S. Cities, 2011
Racial and ethnic minorities make up a majority of the population of this country's 100 largest cities.
Source: U.S. Census Bureau (2012).

What Do You Think?

1. Why is the minority share of the populations of large U.S. cities increasing?

2. What positive changes and what challenges does a "minority-majority" bring to a city?

3. Before Hurricane Katrina (2005), African Americans represented 67 percent of the population of New Orleans; afterward, the share was about 40 percent. What difference might this change make in the city's immediate future?

Sources: Schmitt (2001) and U.S. Census Bureau (2012).

---

high-prestige neighborhoods, often in the central city near cultural attractions. People with a common race or ethnic heritage tend to cluster in distinctive communities.

Brian Berry and Philip Rees (1969) tied together many of these insights. They explained that distinct family types tend to settle in the concentric zones described by Burgess. Specifically, households with many children tend to live in the outer areas of a city, while "young singles" cluster toward the city's center. Social class differences are primarily responsible for the sector-shaped districts described by Hoyt—for instance, the rich occupy one "side of the tracks" and the poor the other. And racial and ethnic neighborhoods are found at various points throughout the city, consistent with Harris and Ullman's multicentered model.

Urban Political Economy

In the late 1960s, many large U.S. cities were rocked by riots. In the wake of this unrest, some analysts turned away from the ecological approach to a social-conflict understanding of city life. The *urban political economy* model applies Karl Marx's analysis of conflict in the workplace to conflict in the city (Lindstrom, 1995).

The Industrial Revolution created great cities across the United States. In recent decades, however, the movement of industry abroad has brought decline to Detroit and other older cities in the "Rustbelt." Yet today's high levels of immigration are bringing new life to many cities as a new generation of young people joins the urban mix. In the Detroit metropolitan area, much of a recent gain in population is due to surging Arab immigration.

Political economists reject the ecological approach's view of the city as a natural organism with particular districts and neighborhoods developing according to an internal logic. They claim that city life is defined by larger institutional structures, especially the economy. Capitalism is the key to understanding urban life because this economic system transforms the city into real estate traded for profit and concentrates wealth and power in the hands of the few. From this point of view, for example, the decline in industrial Snowbelt cities after 1950 was the result of deliberate decisions by the corporate elite to move their production facilities to the Sunbelt (where labor is cheaper and less likely to be unionized) or to move production out of the country entirely to low-income nations (Molotch, 1976; Castells, 1977, 1983; Lefebvre, 1991; Jones & Wilson, 1999).

EVALUATE The fact that many U.S. cities are in crisis, with widespread poverty, high crime, and barely functioning schools, seems to favor the political economy model over the urban ecology approach. But one criticism applies to both: They focus on U.S. cities during a limited period of history. Much of what we know about industrial cities does not apply to preindustrial U.S. towns in our own past or to the rapidly growing cities in many poor nations today. It is unlikely that any single model of cities can account for the full range of urban diversity.

CHECK YOUR LEARNING In your own words, explain what the urban ecology theory and the urban political economy theory teach us about cities.

Urbanization in Poor Nations

22.5 Describe the third urban revolution now under way in poor societies.

November 16, Cairo, Egypt. People call the vast Muslim cemetery in Old Cairo the "City of the Dead." In truth, it is very much alive: Tens of thousands of squatters have moved into the mausoleums, making this place an eerie mix of life and death. Children run across the stone floors, clotheslines stretch between the monuments, and an occasional television antenna protrudes from a tomb roof. With Cairo's population increasing at the rate of 1,000 people a day, families live where they can.

As noted earlier, twice in its history, the world has experienced a revolutionary expansion of cities. The first urban revolution began about 8000 B.C.E. with the first urban settlements and continued until permanent settlements were in place on several continents. About 1750, the second urban revolution took off; it lasted for two centuries as the Industrial Revolution spurred rapid growth of cities in Europe and North America.

A third urban revolution is now under way. Today, approximately 78 percent of people in industrial societies are already city dwellers. But extreme urban growth is occurring in low-income nations. In 1950, about 25 percent of the people in poor countries lived in cities. In 2008, for the first time in history, the world as a whole became mostly urban, with more than half of humanity living in cities (Population Reference Bureau, 2012).

As the population of our planet continues to climb, the share of humanity living in urban places is also increasing. As noted earlier, global population is projected to reach 9.3 billion by 2050. Almost all of this increase will take place in cities, as the urban share of the world's population climbs to about 68 percent (United Nations, 2012).

Not only are more of the world's people living in cities, but also more of these cities are passing the 10 million mark. In 1975, only three cities in the world, Tokyo, New York, and Mexico City, had populations exceeding 10 million, and all these cities were in high-income nations. In 2011, twenty-three cities had passed this mark, and only five of them were in high-income nations. By 2025, fourteen more "megacities" will be added to the list and only two of these fourteen will be in a high-income nation (nine in Asia, two in Latin America, and one in Africa) (Brockerhoff, 2000; United Nations, 2012).

This third urban revolution is taking place in the developing world because many poor nations have entered the high-growth Stage 2 of the demographic transition. Falling death rates have fueled population increases in Latin America, Asia, and especially Africa. For urban areas, the rate of increase is *twice* as high because in addition to natural increase, millions of people leave the countryside each year in search of jobs, health care, education, and conveniences such as running water and electricity.

Cities do offer more opportunities than rural areas, but they provide no quick fix for the massive problems of escalating population and grinding poverty. Many cities in less economically developed nations—including Mexico City, Egypt's Cairo, India's Kolkata (formerly Calcutta), and Manila in the Philippines—are simply unable to meet the basic needs of much of their populations. All these cities are surrounded by wretched shantytowns—settlements of makeshift homes built from discarded materials. As noted in Chapter 12 ("Global Stratification"), even city dumps are home to thousands of poor people, who pick through the piles of waste hoping to find enough to eat or sell to make it through another day.

Environment and Society

(22.6) Analyze current environmental problems such as pollution and global warming.

The human species has prospered, rapidly expanding over the entire planet. An increasing share of the global population now lives in cities, complex settlements that offer the promise of a better life than that found in rural villages.

But these advances have come at a high price. Never before in history have human beings placed such demands on the planet. This disturbing development brings us to the final section of this chapter: the interplay between the natural environment and society. Like demography, **ecology** is another cousin of sociology, formally defined as *the study of the interaction of living organisms and the natural environment*. Ecology rests on the research of natural scientists as well as social scientists. This text focuses on the aspects of ecology that involve familiar sociological concepts and issues.

The **natural environment** is *Earth's surface and atmosphere, including living organisms, air, water, soil, and other resources necessary to sustain life*. Like every other species, humans depend on the natural environment to survive. Yet with our capacity for culture, humans stand apart from other species; we alone take deliberate action to remake the world according to our own interests and desires, for better and for worse.

Why is the environment of interest to sociologists? Environmental problems, from pollution to acid rain to global warming, do not arise from the natural world operating on its own. Such problems result from the specific actions of human beings, which means they are *social* problems.

The Global Dimension

The study of the natural environment requires a global perspective. The reason is simple: Regardless of political divisions among nations, the planet is a single **ecosystem**, *a system composed of the interaction of all living organisms and their natural environment*.

 **Watch** in **MySocLab**
Video: *Sociology in Focus: Population, Urbanization, and Environment*

ecology the study of the interaction of living organisms and the natural environment

natural environment Earth's surface and atmosphere, including living organisms, air, water, soil, and other resources necessary to sustain life

ecosystem a system composed of the interaction of all living organisms and their natural environment

The Greek meaning of *eco* is "house," reminding us that this planet is our home and that all living things and their natural environment are interrelated. A change in any part of the natural environment ripples throughout the entire global ecosystem.

Consider, from an ecological point of view, our national love of hamburgers. People in North America (and, increasingly, around the world) have created a huge demand for beef, which has greatly expanded the ranching industry in Brazil, Costa Rica, and other Latin American nations. To produce the lean meat sought by fast-food corporations, cattle in Latin America feed on grass, which uses a great deal of land. Latin American ranchers get the land for grazing by clearing thousands of square miles of forests each year. These tropical forests are vital to maintaining Earth's atmosphere. Deforestation ends up threatening everyone, including people in the United States enjoying their hamburgers (N. Myers, 1984a).

Technology and the Environmental Deficit

Sociologists point to a simple formula: $I = PAT$, where environmental impact (I) reflects a society's population (P), its level of affluence (A), and its level of technology (T). Members of societies with simple technology—the hunters and gatherers described in Chapter 4 ("Society")—hardly affect the environment because they are few in number, are poor, and have only simple technology. On the contrary, nature affects their lives as they follow the migration of game, watch the rhythm of the seasons, and suffer from natural catastrophes such as fires, floods, droughts, and storms.

Societies at intermediate stages of technological development, being both larger and richer, have a somewhat greater capacity to affect the environment. But the environmental impact of horticulture (small-scale farming), pastoralism (the herding of animals), and even agriculture (the use of animal-drawn plows) is limited because people still rely on muscle power for producing food and other goods.

Humans' ability to control the natural environment increased dramatically with the Industrial Revolution. Muscle power gave way to engines that burn fossil fuels: coal at first and then oil. Such machinery affects the environment in two ways: We consume more natural resources, and we release more pollutants into the atmosphere. Even more important, armed with industrial technology, we are able to bend nature to our will, tunneling through mountains, damming rivers, irrigating deserts, and drilling for oil in the arctic wilderness and on the ocean floor. This explains why people in rich nations, who represent just 23 percent of humanity, account for nearly half of the world's energy use (World Bank, 2012).

environmental deficit profound long-term harm to the natural environment caused by humanity's focus on short-term material affluence

Not only do high-income societies use more energy, but also they produce 100 times more goods than people in agrarian societies do. Higher living standards in turn increase the problem of solid waste (because people ultimately throw away most of what they produce) and pollution (industrial production generates smoke and other toxic substances).

From the start, people recognized the material benefits of industrial technology. But only a century later did they begin to see the long-term effects on the natural environment. Today, we realize that the technological power to make our lives better can also put the lives of future generations at risk.

Evidence is mounting that we are running up an **environmental deficit**, *profound long-term harm to the natural environment caused by humanity's focus on short-term material affluence* (Bormann, 1990). The

The 2012 film *Promised Land* helped bring hydraulic fracturing, commonly known as "fracking," to the attention of people across the country. What are the arguments in favor of this process of extracting natural gas from the earth? What are the arguments against fracking? Where do you stand?

concept of environmental deficit is important for three reasons. First, it reminds us that environmental concerns are *sociological,* reflecting societies' priorities about how people should live. Second, it suggests that much environmental damage—to the air, land, and water—is unintended, at least in the sense that most people do not realize all the consequences of cutting down forests, strip mining, or using throwaway packaging. Again, sociological analysis is helpful in making such consequences clearer. Third, in some respects, the environmental deficit is *reversible.* Inasmuch as societies have created environmental problems, societies can also undo many of them.

Culture: Growth and Limits

Whether we recognize environmental dangers and decide to do something about them is a cultural matter. Thus along with technology, culture has powerful environmental consequences.

The Logic of Growth

When you turn on the television news, you might hear a story like this: "The government reported bad economic news today, with the economy growing by only half a percent during the first quarter of the year." If you stop to think about it, our culture defines an economy that isn't growing as "stagnant" (which is bad) and an economy that is getting smaller as a "recession" or a "depression" (which is *very* bad). What is "good" is *growth*—lots of it—which makes the economy get bigger and bigger. More cars, bigger homes, more income, more spending—the idea of *more* is at the heart of our cultural definition of living well (McKibben, 2007).

One of the reasons we define growth in positive terms is that we value *material comfort,* believing that money and the things it buys improve our lives. We also believe in the idea of *progress,* thinking the future will be better than the present. In addition, we look to *science* to make our lives easier and more rewarding. In simple terms, "having things is good," "life gets better," and "people are clever." Taken together, such cultural values form the *logic of growth.*

An optimistic view of the world, the logic of growth holds that powerful technology has improved our lives and new discoveries will continue to do so in the future. Throughout the history of the United States and other high-income nations, the logic of growth has been the driving force behind settling the wilderness, building towns and roads, and pursuing material affluence.

However, "progress" can lead to unexpected problems, including strain on the environment. The logic of growth responds by arguing that people (especially scientists and other technology experts) will find a way out of any problem that growth places in our path. For example, before the world runs short of oil, scientists will come up with new hybrid and electric cars, and eventually hydrogen, solar, or nuclear engines (or some yet unknown technology) will develop to meet the world's energy needs.

Environmentalists counter that the logic of growth is flawed because it assumes that natural resources such as oil, clean air, fresh water, and topsoil will always be plentiful. We can and will exhaust these *finite* resources if we continue to pursue growth at any cost. Echoing Malthus, environmentalists warn that if we call on Earth to support increasing numbers of people, we will surely deplete finite resources, destroying the environment—and ourselves—in the process.

The most important insight sociology offers about our physical world is that environmental problems do not simply "happen." Rather, the state of the natural environment reflects the ways in which social life is organized—how people live and what they think is important. The greater the technological power of a society, the greater that society's ability to threaten the natural environment.

The Limits to Growth

If we cannot invent our way out of the problems created by the logic of growth, perhaps we need another way of thinking about the world. Environmentalists therefore counter that growth must have limits. Stated simply, the *limits-to-growth thesis* is that humanity must put in place policies to control the growth of population, production, and use of resources in order to avoid environmental collapse.

In *The Limits to Growth,* a controversial book that was influential in launching the environmental movement, Donella Meadows and her colleagues (1972) used a computer model to calculate the planet's available resources, rates of population growth, amount of land available for cultivation, levels of industrial and food production, and amount of pollutants released into the atmosphere. The authors concede that any long-range predictions are speculative, and some critics think they are plain wrong (Simon, 1981). But right or wrong, the conclusions of the study call for serious consideration. First, the authors claim that we are quickly consuming Earth's finite resources. Supplies of oil, natural gas, and other energy sources are declining and will continue to drop, a little faster or slower depending on the conservation policies of rich nations and the speed with which other nations such as India and China continue to industrialize. Within the next 100 years, resources will run out, crippling industrial output and causing a decline in food production.

This limits-to-growth theory shares Malthus's pessimism about the future. People who accept it doubt that current patterns of life are sustainable for even another century. Perhaps we all can learn to live with less. This may not be as hard as you might think: Research shows, for example, that an increase in material consumption in recent decades has not brought an increase in levels of personal happiness (D. G. Myers, 2000). In the end, environmentalists warn, either we make fundamental changes in how we live, placing less strain on the natural environment, or widespread hunger and conflict will force change on us.

Solid Waste: The Disposable Society

Across the United States, people generate a massive amount of solid waste—about 1.4 billion pounds *every day.* Figure 22–4 shows the average composition of a typical community's trash.

As a rich nation of people who value convenience, the United States has become a *disposable society.* We consume more products than virtually any other nation, and many of these products have throwaway packaging. For example, fast food is served with cardboard, plastic, and Styrofoam containers that we throw away within minutes. Countless other products, from film to fishhooks, are elaborately packaged to make the products more attractive to the customer and to discourage tampering and theft.

Manufacturers market soft drinks, beer, and fruit juices in aluminum cans, glass jars, and plastic containers, which not only consume finite resources but also generate mountains of solid waste. Then there are countless items intentionally designed to be disposable: pens, razors, flashlights, batteries, even cameras. Other products, from light bulbs to automobiles, are designed to have a limited useful life and then become unwanted junk. As Paul Connett (1991) points out, even the words we use to describe what we throw away—*waste, litter, trash, refuse, garbage, rubbish*—show how little we value what we cannot immediately use. But this was not always the case, as the Seeing Sociology in Everyday Life box on page 653 explains.

Living in a rich society, the average person in the United States consumes about 50 times more energy, plastics, lumber, water, and other resources than someone living in a low-income country such as Bangladesh or Tanzania and nearly twice as much as people in some other high-income countries such as Sweden and Japan. This high level of consumption means not only that we in the United States use a disproportionate share of the planet's natural resources but also that we generate most of the world's refuse.

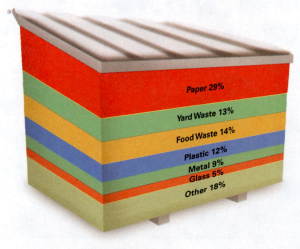

FIGURE 22–4 Composition of Community Trash

We throw away a wide range of material, with paper the single largest part of our trash.

Source: U.S. Environmental Protection Agency (2011).

Paper 29%
Yard Waste 13%
Food Waste 14%
Plastic 12%
Metal 9%
Glass 5%
Other 18%

Seeing Sociology in Everyday Life

Why Grandma Macionis Had No Trash

Grandma Macionis, we always used to say, never threw anything away. Not food, not bottles or cans, not paper. Not even coffee grounds. Nothing.

Grandma was born and raised in Lithuania—the "old country"—where life in a poor village shaped her in ways that never changed, even after she came to the United States as a young woman and settled in Philadelphia.

In her later years, when I knew her, I can remember the family traveling together to her house to celebrate her birthday. We never knew what to get Grandma, because she never seemed to need anything. She lived a simple life and had simple clothes and showed little interest in "fancy things." She had no electric appliances. She used her simple tools until they wore out. Her kitchen knives, for example, were worn narrow from decades of sharpening. The food that was left over from meals was saved. What could not be saved was recycled as compost for her vegetable garden.

Grandma Macionis, in the 1970s, with the author.

After opening a birthday present, she would carefully save the box, refold the wrapping paper, and roll up the ribbon—all of these things meant as much to her as whatever gift they contained. We all knew her routines and we smiled together as we watched her put everything away, knowing she would find a way to use each item again and again.

As strange as Grandma sometimes seemed to her grandchildren, she was a product of her culture. A century ago, in fact, there was little "trash." If socks wore thin, people mended them, probably more than once. When they were beyond repair, they were used as rags for cleaning or sewn with bits of other old clothing into a quilt. Everything had value—if not in one way, then in another.

During the twentieth century, as women joined men in working outside the home, income went up. Families began buying more appliances and other "timesaving" products. Before long, few people cared about the kind of recycling that Grandma practiced. Soon cities sent crews from block to block to pick up truckloads of discarded material. The era of "trash" had begun.

What Do You Think?

1. Just as Grandma Macionis was a product of her culture, so are we. Do you know people who have plenty but never seem to think they have enough?

2. What cultural values make people today demand timesaving products and "convenience" packaging?

3. Do you think recent decades have brought a turnaround so that people are now more aware of a need to recycle? How does today's recycling differ from that practiced by Grandma Macionis?

We like to say that we throw things "away." But most of the 136 million tons of solid waste our society produced in 2010 never went away. Rather, it ended up in landfills, which are, literally, filling up. Material in landfills can pollute underground water supplies. Although in most places, laws now regulate what can be discarded in a landfill, the U.S. Environmental Protection Agency (2011) has identified 1,316 dump sites across the United States containing hazardous materials that are polluting water both above and below the ground. In addition, what goes into landfills all too often stays there, sometimes for centuries. Tens of millions of tires, diapers, and other items we bury in landfills each year do not decompose but will remain as an unwelcome legacy for future generations.

Environmentalists argue that we should address the problem of solid waste by doing what many of our grandparents did: Use less and turn "waste" into a resource. Part of the solution is *recycling*, reusing resources we would otherwise discard. Recycling is an accepted practice in Japan and many other nations, and it is becoming more common in the United States, where we now reuse about one-third of waste materials (U.S. Environmental Protection Agency, 2011). The share is increasing as laws require the recovery and reuse of certain materials such as glass bottles and aluminum cans and as the business of recycling becomes more profitable.

Water and Air

Oceans, lakes, and streams are the lifeblood of the global ecosystem. Humans depend on water for drinking, bathing, cooking, cleaning, recreation, and a host of other activities.

According to what scientists call the *hydrologic cycle,* Earth naturally recycles water and refreshes the land. The process begins as heat from the sun causes Earth's water, 97 percent of which is in the oceans, to evaporate and form clouds. Because water evaporates at lower temperatures than most pollutants, the water vapor that rises from the seas is relatively pure, leaving various contaminants behind. Water then falls to the Earth as rain, which drains into streams and rivers and finally returns to the sea. Two major concerns about water, then, are supply and pollution.

Water Supply

Less than one-tenth of 1 percent of Earth's water is suitable for drinking. It is not surprising, then, that for thousands of years, water rights have figured prominently in laws around the world. Today, some regions of the world, especially the tropics, enjoy plentiful fresh water, using a small share of the available supply. However, high demand, coupled with modest reserves, makes water supply a matter of concern in much of North America and Asia, where people look to rivers rather than rainfall for their water. In China, aquifers are dropping rapidly. In the Middle East, water supply is reaching a critical level. Iran is rationing water in its capital city. In Egypt, the Nile River provides just one-sixth as much water per person as it did in 1900. Across northern Africa and the Middle East, as many as 1 billion people may lack the water they need for irrigation and drinking by 2030. From another angle, by this time the world will be able to provide 40 percent less water than the planet requires (United Nations Environment Programme, 2008; Walsh, 2009).

Rising population and the development of more complex technology have greatly increased the world's appetite for water. The global consumption of freshwater (now estimated at about 3,800 cubic kilometers, or 133 trillion cubic feet per year) has doubled since 1950 and is rising steadily. As a result, even in parts of the world that receive plenty of rainfall, people are using groundwater faster than it can be replenished naturally. In the Tamil Nadu region of southern India, for example, so much groundwater is being used that the water table has fallen 100 feet over the last several decades. Mexico City—which has sprawled to some 1,400 square miles—has pumped so much water from its underground aquifer that the city has sunk 30 feet during the past century and continues to drop about 2 inches per year. Farther north in the United States, the Ogallala aquifer, which lies below seven states from South Dakota to Texas, is now being pumped so rapidly that some experts fear it could run dry in just a few decades.

In light of such developments, we must face the reality that water is a valuable and finite resource. Greater conservation of water by individuals—the average person in the United States consumes about 100 gallons of water a day, which amounts to about 3 million gallons over a lifetime—is part of the answer. However, households around the world account for just 11 percent of water use. It is even more crucial that we curb water consumption by industry, which uses 19 percent of the global total, and farming, which consumes 70 percent of the total for irrigation.

Perhaps new irrigation technology will reduce the future demand for water. But here again, we see how population increase, as well as economic growth, strains our ecosystem (Solomon, 2010; U.S. Department of the Interior, U.S. Geological Survey, 2010; UNESCO World Water Assessment Programme, 2012).

Environmental problems are more serious in low-income communities. This family, living in East Orosi, California, must buy bottled water because water from the ground is no longer safe to drink. More seriously, many families are not aware that they are consuming unsafe water.

Water is vital to life, and it is also in short supply. The state of Gujarat, in western India, has experienced a long drought. In the village of Natwarghad, people crowd together, lowering pots into the local well, taking what little water is left.

Water Pollution

In large cities from Mexico City to Cairo to Shanghai, many people have no choice but to drink contaminated water. Infectious diseases such as typhoid, cholera, and dysentery, all caused by waterborne microorganisms, spread rapidly through these populations. Besides ensuring ample *supplies* of water, then, we must also protect the *quality* of water.

Water quality in the United States is generally good by global standards. However, even here the problem of water pollution is steadily growing. Across the United States, rivers, streams, and underground aquifers absorb hundreds of millions of pounds of pesticides, nitrogen fertilizers, and toxic waste each year. This pollution results not only from intentional dumping but also from the application of agricultural fertilizers and lawn chemicals (Bair, 2011; Galbraith, 2012).

Not all water pollution results from chemicals that people apply to the ground. A special problem is *acid rain*—falling precipitation made acidic by air pollution—which destroys plant and animal life. Acid rain begins with power plants burning fossil fuels (oil and coal) to generate electricity; this burning releases sulfuric and nitrous oxides into the air. As the wind sweeps these gases into the atmosphere, they react with the air to form sulfuric and nitric acids, which turns atmospheric moisture acidic.

This is a clear case of one type of pollution causing another: Air pollution (from smokestacks) ends up contaminating water (in lakes and streams that collect acid rain). Acid rain is truly a global phenomenon because the regions that suffer the harmful effects may be thousands of miles from the source of the original pollution. For instance, British power plants have caused acid rain that has devastated forests and fish in Norway and Sweden, up to 1,000 miles to the northeast. In the United States, we see a similar pattern as smokestacks in the Midwest have harmed the natural environment of upstate New York and New England.

Air Pollution

Because we are surrounded by air, most people in the United States are more aware of air pollution than contaminated water. One of the unexpected consequences of industrial technology, especially the factory and the motor vehicle, has been a decline in air quality. In London in the mid-twentieth century, factory smokestacks, automobiles, and coal fires used to heat homes all added up to probably the worst urban air quality the world has ever known. The fog that some British jokingly called "pea soup" was in reality a deadly mix of pollutants: In 1952, an especially thick haze that hung over London for five days killed 4,000 people.

Air quality improved in the final decades of the twentieth century. Rich nations passed laws that banned high-pollution heating, including the coal fires that choked

London. In addition, scientists devised ways to make factories and motor vehicles operate much more cleanly. In fact, today's vehicles produce only a fraction of the pollution that spewed from models of the 1950s and 1960s. And cleaner air has improved human health: Experts estimate that improvement in U.S. air quality over the past several decades has added almost half a year to the average life span (Chang, 2009).

If high-income countries can breathe a bit more easily than they once did, the problem of air pollution in poor societies is becoming more serious. One reason is that people in low-income countries still rely on wood, coal, peat, and other "dirty" fuels to cook their food and heat their homes. In addition, nations eager to encourage short-term industrial development may pay little attention to the longer-term dangers of air pollution. As a result, many cities in Latin America, Eastern Europe, and Asia are plagued by air pollution as bad as London's "pea soup" back in the 1950s.

The Rain Forests

rain forests regions of dense forestation, most of which circle the globe close to the equator

Rain forests are *regions of dense forestation, most of which circle the globe close to the equator.* The largest tropical rain forests are in South America (notably Brazil), west-central Africa, and Southeast Asia. In all, the world's rain forests cover some 1.5 billion acres, or about 5 percent of Earth's total land surface.

Like other global resources, rain forests are falling victim to the needs and appetites of the surging world population. As noted earlier, to meet the demand for beef, ranchers in Latin America burn forested areas to increase their supply of grazing land. We are also losing rain forests to the hardwood trade. People in rich nations pay high prices for mahogany and other woods because, as the environmentalist Norman Myers (1984b:88) puts it, they have "a penchant for parquet floors, fine furniture, fancy paneling, weekend yachts, and high-grade coffins." Under such economic pressure, the world's rain forests are now just half their original size, and they continue to shrink by about 1 percent (15 million acres) annually, which amounts to about 30 acres a minute. Unless we stop this loss, the rain forests will vanish before the end of this century and with them will go protection for Earth's biodiversity and climate (United Nations, 2011).

Global Warming

Why are rain forests so important? One reason is that they cleanse the atmosphere of carbon dioxide (CO_2). Since the beginning of the Industrial Revolution, the amount of carbon dioxide produced by humans, mostly from factories and automobiles, has risen sharply. Much of this carbon dioxide is absorbed by the oceans. But plants also take in carbon dioxide and expel oxygen. This is why rain forests are vital to maintaining the chemical balance of the atmosphere.

The problem is that production of carbon dioxide is rising while the amount of plant life on Earth is shrinking. To make matters worse, rain forests are being destroyed mostly by burning, which releases even more carbon dioxide into the atmosphere. Experts estimate that the atmospheric concentration of carbon dioxide is now 41 percent higher than it was 150 years ago and rising rapidly (Gore, 2006; Adam, 2008; U.S. Department of Commerce, National Oceanic & Atmospheric Administration, 2013).

global warming a rise in Earth's average temperature due to an increasing concentration of carbon dioxide in the atmosphere

High above Earth, carbon dioxide acts like the glass roof of a greenhouse, letting heat from the sun pass through to the surface while preventing much of it from radiating away from the planet. The result of this *greenhouse effect,* say ecologists, is **global warming**, *a rise in Earth's average temperature due to an increasing concentration of carbon dioxide in the atmosphere.* Over the past century, the global temperature has risen about 1.3° Fahrenheit (to an average of 58° F). Scientists continue to debate the numbers, but they warn that the planet's temperature could rise by 3° F to as much as 5° F during this century. Already, the polar ice caps are melting, and over the last century, the average level of the oceans has risen about six inches. Scientists predict that increasing average temperatures could melt so much ice that the sea level would rise enough to cover low-lying land all around the world: Water would cover all of the Maldive Islands in the Indian Ocean, most of Bangladesh, and much of the coastal United States, including Washington, D.C., right up to the steps of the White House. Such a change would create perhaps 100 million "climate change refugees." On the other hand, this same process of rising temperatures will affect other regions of the world very differently. The U.S. Midwest, currently one of the most productive agricultural regions in the world, would likely become more arid. No wonder that, for more than a decade, government agencies in the United States and elsewhere in the world have been working to "climate-proof" our nation—and especially coastal cities—against the ravages of extreme weather (Gillis, 2011; McMahon, 2011; Reed, 2011; Klinenberg, 2013).

Some scientists point out that we cannot be sure of the consequences of global warming. Others point to the fact that global temperature changes have been taking place throughout history, apparently having little or nothing to do with rain forests or human activity. A few are optimistic, suggesting that higher concentrations of carbon dioxide in the atmosphere might speed up plant growth (since plants thrive on this gas), and this increase would correct the imbalance and push Earth's temperature downward once again. But the consensus among scientists is now clear: Global warming is a serious problem that threatens the future of all of us (Kerr, 2005; Gore, 2006; International Panel on Climate Change, 2007; Singer, 2007; Ridley, 2012).

Declining Biodiversity

Our planet is home to as many as 30 million species of animals, plants, and microorganisms. As rain forests are cleared and humans extend their control over nature, several dozen unique species of plants and animals cease to exist each day, reducing the planet's *biodiversity*.

But given the vast number of living species, why should we be concerned by the loss of a few? Environmentalists give four reasons. First, our planet's biodiversity provides a varied source of human food. Using agricultural high technology, scientists can "splice" familiar crops with more exotic plant life, making food more bountiful as well as more resistant to insects and disease. Certain species of life are even considered vital to the production of human food. Bees, for example, perform the work of pollination, a necessary stage in the growth of plants. The fact that the bee population has declined by one-third in the United States and by two-thirds in the Middle East is cause for serious concern. Thus sustaining biodiversity helps feed our planet's rapidly increasing population.

Second, Earth's biodiversity is a vital genetic resource used by medical and pharmaceutical researchers to produce hundreds of new compounds each year that cure disease and improve our lives. For example, children in the United States now have a good chance of surviving leukemia, a disease that was almost a sure killer two generations ago, because of a compound derived from a tropical flower called the rosy periwinkle. The oral birth control pill, used by tens of millions of women in this country, is another product of plant research involving the Mexican forest yam. Because biodiversity itself allows our ecosystem to control many types of diseases, it is likely that if biodiversity declines, the transmission of disease will increase.

Third, with the loss of any species of life—whether it is the magnificent California condor, the famed Chinese panda, the spotted owl, or even a single species of ant—the beauty and complexity of our natural environment are diminished. There are clear warning signs of such loss: Three-fourths of the world's 10,000 species of birds are declining in number.

Finally, unlike pollution, the extinction of any species is irreversible and final. An important ethical question, then, is whether we who live today have the right to impoverish the world for those who live tomorrow (E. O. Wilson, 1991; Keesing et al., 2010; Capella, 2011).

Environmental Racism

Conflict theory has given rise to the concept of **environmental racism**, *patterns of development that expose poor people, especially minorities, to environmental hazards.* Historically, factories that spew pollution have stood near neighborhoods of the poor and people of color. Why? In part, the poor themselves were drawn to factories in search of work, and their low incomes often meant they could afford housing only in undesirable neighborhoods. Sometimes the only housing that fit their budgets stood in the very shadow of the plants and mills where they worked.

Nobody wants a factory or dump nearby, but the poor have little power to resist. Through the years, the most serious environmental hazards have been located near Newark, New Jersey

Members of small, simple societies, such as the Mentawi in Indonesia, live in harmony with nature; they do not have the technological means to greatly affect the natural world. Although we in complex societies like to think of ourselves as superior to such people, the truth is that there is much we can—indeed, we must—learn from them.

environmental racism
patterns of development that expose poor people, especially minorities, to environmental hazards

(not in upscale Bergen County), in southside Chicago (not wealthy Lake Forest), or on Native American reservations in the West (not in affluent suburbs of Denver or Phoenix) (Commission for Racial Justice, 1994; Bohon & Humphrey, 2000).

Toward a Sustainable Society and World

22.7 Evaluate progress toward creating an ecologically sustainable culture.

The demographic analysis presented in this chapter reveals some disturbing trends. We see, first, that Earth's population has reached record levels because birth rates remain high in poor nations and death rates have fallen just about everywhere. Reducing fertility will remain a pressing need throughout this century. Even with some recent decline in the rate of population increase, the nightmare Thomas Malthus described is still a real possibility, as the Controversy & Debate box on page 658 explains.

Further, population growth remains greatest in the poorest countries of the world, which cannot meet the needs of their present populations, much less future ones. Supporting 84 million additional people on our planet each year, 83 million of them in economically less developed countries, will require a global commitment to provide not just food but housing, schools, and employment as well. The well-being of the entire world may ultimately depend on resolving the economic and social problems of poor, overly populated countries and bridging the widening gulf between "have" and "have-not" nations.

Urbanization is continuing, especially in poor countries. For thousands of years, people have sought out cities in the hope of finding a better life. But the sheer numbers of people who live in today's megacities—including Mexico City, São Paulo (Brazil), Lagos (Nigeria), Mumbai (India), and Manila (Philippines)—have created urban problems on a massive scale.

Around the world, humanity is facing a serious environmental challenge. Part of this problem is population increase, which is greatest in poor countries. But part of the problem is the high levels of consumption in rich nations such as our own. By increasing the planet's environmental deficit, our present way of life is borrowing against the well-being of our children and their children. Globally, members of rich societies, who currently consume so much of Earth's resources, are mortgaging the future security of the poor countries of the world.

The answer, in principle, is to create an **ecologically sustainable culture**, *a way of life that meets the needs of the present generation without threatening the environmental legacy of future generations.* Sustainable living depends on three strategies.

First, the world needs to *bring population growth under control.* The current population of 7.1 billion is already straining the natural environment. Clearly, the higher the world's population climbs, the more difficult environmental problems will become. Even if the recent slowing of population growth continues, the world will have about 9.3 billion people by 2050. Few analysts think that the planet can support this many people; most argue that we must hold the line at about 7 billion, and some argue that we must *decrease* population in the coming decades (Smail, 2007).

A second strategy is to *conserve finite resources.* This means meeting our needs with a responsible eye toward the future by using resources efficiently, seeking alternative sources of energy, and in some cases, learning to live with less.

A third strategy is to *reduce waste.* Whenever possible, simply using less is the best solution. Learning to live with less is not likely to come easily, but keep in mind the research that suggests that as our society has consumed more

Watch in **MySocLab**
Video: *Sociology on the Job: Population, Urbanization, and Environment*

ecologically sustainable culture a way of life that meets the needs of the present generation without threatening the environmental legacy of future generations

If human ingenuity created the threats to our environment that we now face, can humans also solve these problems? In recent years, a number of designs for small, environmentally friendly cars show the promise of new technology. But do such innovations go far enough? Will we have to make more basic changes to our way of life to ensure human survival in the centuries to come?

Controversy & Debate

Apocalypse: Will People Overwhelm the Planet?

Nushawn: I'm telling you, there are too many people already! Where is everyone going to live?

Tabitha: Have you ever been to Kansas? Or Wyoming? There's plenty of empty space out there.

Marco: Maybe now. But I'm not so sure about our children—or their children....

Are you worried about the world's increasing population? Think about this: By the time you finish reading this feature, more than 1,000 people will have been added to our planet. By this time tomorrow, global population will have risen by more than 230,000. Currently, as the table shows, there are more than four births for every two deaths on the planet, pushing the world's population upward by 84 million annually. Put another way, global population growth amounts to adding another Germany to the world each year.

It is no wonder that many demographers and environmentalists are deeply concerned about the future. Earth has an unprecedented population of 7.1 billion; the 3 billion people we have added since 1974 alone roughly equals the planet's total in 1960. Might Thomas Robert Malthus, who predicted that overpopulation would push the world into war and suffering, be right after all? If we do not change our ways, predict Lester Brown and other *neo-Malthusians*, we face a coming apocalypse. Brown admits that Malthus failed to imagine how much technology (especially the use of fertilizers and the ability to genetically modify plants) could boost the planet's agricultural output. But he maintains that Earth's rising population is rapidly outstripping its finite resources. Families in many poor countries can find little firewood, members of rich countries are depleting the oil reserves, and everyone is draining our supply of clean water and poisoning the planet with waste. Some analysts argue that we have already passed Earth's "carrying capacity" for population and we need to hold the line or even reduce global population to ensure humanity's long-term survival.

But other analysts, the *anti-Malthusians,* sharply disagree. Julian Simon points out that two centuries after Malthus predicted catastrophe, Earth supports almost six times as many people who, on average, live longer, healthier lives than ever before. With more advanced technology, people have devised ways to increase productivity and limit population increase. As Simon sees it, this is cause for celebration. Human ingenuity has consistently proved the doomsayers wrong, and Simon is betting it will continue to do so.

Global Population Increase, 2012

	Births	Deaths	Net Increase
Per year	140,541,944	56,238,002	84,303,942
Per month	11,711,829	4,686,500	7,025,329
Per day	385,046	154,077	230,969
Per hour	16,020	6,420	9,600
Per minute	267	107	160
Per second	4.5	1.8	2.7

What Do You Think?

1. Where do you place your bet? Do you think Earth can support 8 or 10 billion people?

2. What, if anything, do you think should be done about global population increase?

3. Were Malthus alive today, would he feel relieved or would he say "I told you so!"? Explain.

Sources: Brown (1995), Simon (1995), Scanlon (2001), Smail (2007), Population Reference Bureau (2012), and U.S. Census Bureau (2013).

and more, people have not become any happier (D. G. Myers, 2000). Recycling programs, too, are part of the answer, and recycling can make everyone part of the solution to our environmental problems.

In the end, making all these strategies work depends on a basic change in the way we think about ourselves and our world. Our *egocentric* outlook sets our own interests as standards for how to live, but a sustainable environment demands an *ecocentric* outlook that helps us see how the present is tied to the future and why everyone must work together. Most nations in the southern half of the world are *underdeveloped,* unable to meet the basic needs of their people. At the same time, most countries in the northern half of the world are *overdeveloped,* using more resources than the planet can sustain over time. The changes needed to create a sustainable ecosystem will not come easily, and they will be costly. But the price of not responding to the growing environmental deficit will certainly be greater (Kellert & Bormann, 1991; Brown et al., 1993; Population Action International, 2000; Gore, 2006).

Finally, consider that the great dinosaurs dominated this planet for some 160 million years and then perished forever. Humanity is far younger, having existed for a mere 250,000 years. Compared to the rather dimwitted dinosaurs, our species has the gift of great intelligence. But how will we use this ability? What are the chances that our species will continue to flourish 160 million years—or even 160 years—from now? The answer depends on the choices that will be made by one of the 30 million species living on Earth: human beings.

Seeing Sociology in Everyday Life

Why is the environment a social issue?

As this chapter explains, the state of the natural environment depends on how society is organized, especially the importance a culture attaches to consumption and economic growth.

We learn to see economic expansion as natural and good. When the economy stays the same for a number of months, we say we are experiencing "stagnation." How do we define a period when the economy gets smaller, as happened during the fall of 2008?

What would it take to convince members of our society that smaller (rather than bigger) might be better? Why do we seem to prefer not just bigger cars but also bigger homes and more and more material possessions?

HINT If expansion is "good times," then contraction is a "recession" or perhaps even a "depression." Such a worldview means that it is normal—or even desirable—to live in a way that increases stress on the natural environment. Sustainability, an idea that is especially important as world population increases, depends on learning to live with what we have or maybe even learning to live with less. Although many people seem to think so, it really doesn't require a 6,000-pound SUV to move around urban areas. Actually, it might not require a car at all. This new way of thinking requires that we do not define social standing and personal success in terms of what we own and what we consume. Can you imagine a society like that? What would it be like?

Seeing Sociology in *Your* Everyday Life

1. Here is an illustration of the problem of runaway growth (Milbrath, 1989:10): "A pond has a single water lily growing on it. The lily doubles in size each day. In thirty days, it covers the entire pond. On which day does it cover half the pond?" When you realize the answer, discuss the implications of this example for population increase.

2. Go to MySocLab and click on the Student Resources link to access the Sociology in Focus blog, where you can read the latest posts by a team of young sociologists who apply the sociological perspective to topics of popular culture.

3. Do you think that the world's increasing population is a problem or not? What about the state of our planet's natural environment? Go to the "Seeing Sociology in *Your* Everyday Life" feature in MySocLab for additional discussion of these issues and suggestions for ways you can become more engaged in promoting a more secure world.

Making the Grade

Demography: The Study of Population

 22.1 Explain the concepts of fertility, mortality, and migration, and how they affect population size. (pages 630–35)

👁 **Watch** the **Video** in **MySocLab**　　🌼 **Explore** the **Map** in **MySocLab**

Demography analyzes the size and composition of a population and how and why people move from place to place.

- **Fertility** is the incidence of childbearing in a country's population. Demographers describe fertility using the **crude birth rate**.
- **Mortality** is the incidence of death in a country's population. Demographers measure mortality using both the **crude death rate** and the **infant mortality rate**.
- The **net migration rate** is the difference between the in-migration rate and the out-migration rate.
- In general, rich nations grow almost as much from immigration as from natural increase; poorer nations grow almost entirely from natural increase.
- Demographers use **age-sex pyramids** to show the composition of a population graphically and to project population trends.

demography the study of human population
fertility the incidence of childbearing in a country's population
crude birth rate the number of live births in a given year for every 1,000 people in a population
mortality the incidence of death in a country's population
crude death rate the number of deaths in a given year for every 1,000 people in a population
infant mortality rate the number of deaths among infants under one year of age for each 1,000 live births in a given year
life expectancy the average life span of a country's population
migration the movement of people into and out of a specified territory
sex ratio the number of males for every 100 females in a nation's population
age-sex pyramid a graphic representation of the age and sex of a population

History and Theory of Population Growth

22.2 Analyze population trends using Malthusian theory and demographic transition theory. (pages 635–39)

- Historically, world population grew slowly, as high birth rates were offset by high death rates.
- About 1750, world population rose sharply, mostly due to falling death rates.
- In the late 1700s, Thomas Robert Malthus warned that population growth would outpace food production, resulting in social calamity.
- **Demographic transition theory** claims that technological advances slow population increase.
- Currently, the world is gaining 84 million people each year, with 98% of this increase taking place in poor countries. World population is expected to reach about 9.3 billion by 2050.

demographic transition theory a thesis that links population patterns to a society's level of technological development
zero population growth the rate of reproduction that maintains population at a steady level

Urbanization: The Growth of Cities

22.3 Summarize patterns of urbanization in the United States and around the world. (pages 639–44)

The **first urban revolution** began with the appearance of cities about 10,000 years ago.

- By about 2,000 years ago, cities emerged in most regions of the world except North America.
- Preindustrial cities have low-rise buildings; narrow, winding streets; and personal social ties.

A **second urban revolution** began about 1750 as the Industrial Revolution propelled rapid urban growth in Europe.

- Cities' physical form changed as planners created wide, regular streets to facilitate commerce.
- The emphasis on business, and the increasing size of cities, made urban life more impersonal.

A **third urban revolution** is now occurring in poor countries.

In the United States, urbanization has been going on for more than 400 years.

- Urbanization came to North America with European colonists.
- By 1850, hundreds of new cities had been founded from coast to coast.
- By 1920, a majority of the U.S. population lived in urban areas.
- Since 1950, the decentralization of cities has resulted in the growth of suburbs and edge cities.
- Rural areas represent 75 percent of the nation's land area; although rural places that are near large cities, as well as those that are especially scenic, are attracting migrants, rural areas currently lose net population through migration to cities.
- Sunbelt cities—but not the older Snowbelt cities—are increasing in size and population.

urbanization the concentration of population into cities
metropolis a large city that socially and economically dominates an urban area
suburbs urban areas beyond the political boundaries of a city
megalopolis a vast urban region containing a number of cities and their surrounding suburbs

Urbanism as a Way of Life

 **Read** the **Document** in **MySocLab**

22.4 Identify the contributions of Tönnies, Durkheim, Simmel, Park, Wirth, and Marx to our understanding of urban life. (pages 644–48)

Rapid urbanization during the nineteenth century led early sociologists to study the differences between rural and urban life.

Ferdinand Tönnies built his analysis on the concepts of *Gemeinschaft* and *Gesellschaft*.

- *Gemeinschaft*, typical of the rural village, joins people in what amounts to a primary group.
- *Gesellschaft*, typical of the modern city, describes individuals motivated by their own needs rather than by a desire to help improve the well-being of the community.

Emile Durkheim agreed with much of Tönnies's thinking but claimed that urbanites do not lack social bonds; the basis of social solidarity simply differs in the two settings. He described

- **mechanical solidarity**—social bonds based on common sentiments and shared moral values. This type of social solidarity is typical of traditional, rural life.
- **organic solidarity**—social bonds based on specialization and interdependence. This type of social solidarity is typical of modern, urban life.

Georg Simmel claimed that the overstimulation of city life produced a blasé attitude in urbanites.

Robert Park, at the University of Chicago, claimed that cities permit greater social freedom.

Louis Wirth saw large, dense, heterogeneous populations creating an impersonal and self-interested, though tolerant, way of life.

Karl Marx's analysis of conflict in the city is echoed in the urban political economy model.

Gemeinschaft a type of social organization in which people are closely tied by kinship and tradition

Gesellschaft a type of social organization in which people come together only on the basis of individual self-interest

urban ecology the study of the link between the physical and social dimensions of cities

Urbanization in Poor Nations

22.5 Describe the third urban revolution now under way in poor societies. (pages 648–49)

- The third urban revolution is taking place now in low-income nations.
- Almost all global population increase is taking place in cities. Of the twenty-three cities with population greater than 10 million, 18 are in poor nations.

Environment and Society

22.6 Analyze current environmental problems such as pollution and global warming. (pages 649–57)

 Watch the **Video** in **MySocLab**

The state of the **environment** is a social issue because it reflects how human beings organize social life.

- Societies increase the **environmental deficit** by focusing on short-term benefits and ignoring the long-term consequences brought on by their way of life.
- The more complex a society's technology, the greater its capacity to alter the natural environment.
- The *logic-of-growth thesis* supports economic development, claiming that people can solve environmental problems as they arise.
- The *limits-to-growth thesis* states that societies must curb development to prevent eventual environmental collapse.
- 54% of the solid waste we throw away ends up in landfills, which are filling up and can pollute groundwater.
- The supply of clean water is already low in some parts of the world. Industrial technology has caused a decline in air quality.
- Rain forests help remove carbon dioxide from the atmosphere and are home to a large share of this planet's living species. Under pressure from development, the world's rain forests are now half their original size and are shrinking by about 1% annually.
- Conflict theory has drawn attention to **environmental racism**.

ecology the study of the interaction of living organisms and the natural environment

natural environment Earth's surface and atmosphere, including living organisms, air, water, soil, and other resources necessary to sustain life

ecosystem a system composed of the interaction of all living organisms and their natural environment

environmental deficit profound long-term harm to the natural environment caused by humanity's focus on short-term material affluence

rain forests regions of dense forestation, most of which circle the globe close to the equator

global warming a rise in Earth's average temperature due to an increasing concentration of carbon dioxide in the atmosphere

environmental racism patterns of development that expose poor people, especially minorities, to environmental hazards

Toward a Sustainable Society and World

22.7 Evaluate progress toward creating an ecologically sustainable culture. (pages 658–59)

 Watch the **Video** in **MySocLab**

- Our planet's population has reached record levels due to high fertility in low-income nations, coupled with declining mortality almost everywhere.
- As population increases, humanity faces environmental challenges that involve both greater consumption of resources and higher levels of pollution.

ecologically sustainable culture a way of life that meets the needs of the present generation without threatening the environmental legacy of future generations

23 Collective Behavior and Social Movements

((• **Listen** to **Chapter 23** in **MySocLab**

LEARNING OBJECTIVES

23.1 Distinguish various types of collective behavior.

23.2 Identify five types of crowds and three explanations of crowd behavior.

23.3 Describe rumor, disasters, and other types of mass behavior.

23.4 Analyze the causes and consequences of social movements.

the Power of Society

to encourage or discourage participation in social movements

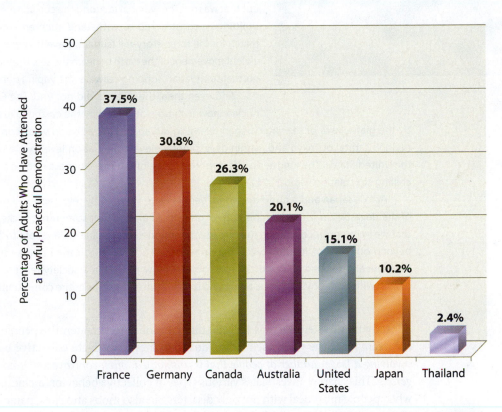

Percentage of Adults Who Have Attended a Lawful, Peaceful Demonstration

- France: 37.5%
- Germany: 30.8%
- Canada: 26.3%
- Australia: 20.1%
- United States: 15.1%
- Japan: 10.2%
- Thailand: 2.4%

Source: Inglehart et al. (2013)

Is being active in a social movement just a matter of personal choice? When asked if they had ever attended a lawful, peaceful demonstration in support of some social movement, about 15 percent of U.S. adults said "yes." In some nations, that share is lower: Just 10 percent of the Japanese say they have engaged in a demonstration and only 2 percent of adults in Thailand say the same. But 20 percent of Australians have engaged in demonstration, as have 26 percent of Canadians, 31 percent of Germans, and 38 percent of the French. Whether people "take to the streets" to show their support for a cause depends on more than decisions made by individuals; it also reflects the culture of the larger society.

Chapter Overview

This chapter explores the wide-ranging patterns of behavior that sociologists describe as "collective behavior," including crowd behavior, rumor and gossip, panics, disasters, and social movements.

Many remember it as the day the earth moved. On March 11, 2011, a 9.0-magnitude earthquake shook the nation of Japan. It pushed the entire country about fifteen feet closer to the United States and even caused a slight change in the way Earth spins on its axis. But these were the observations of scientists. To the people on the ground in northeastern Japan, it was a day they will never forget. For perhaps 20,000 of them, it was the last day of their lives.

The monster earthquake caused countless buildings to collapse. But that was not the worst of it. Along the coastline, even the strongest buildings—constructed to withstand such emergencies—were no match for the three-story-tall tsunami wave that was unleashed by the violent movement of the earth beneath the sea. The wave washed across northeastern Japan, topping seawalls and wiping out entire towns.

And even then, the disaster did not end. The Fukushima Daiichi nuclear power station, damaged by the earthquake and then flooded by the giant wave of seawater, began releasing radiation. The radiation was soon measured in the nation's capital of Tokyo and, within days, slightly elevated radiation levels were even measured in the United States. The long-term effects of this radiation on the Japanese people are still a matter of chilling speculation (Gibbs, 2011).

Across Japan and around the world, people were stunned by television and newspaper images of the devastation caused by this natural disaster. In an age that sometimes tricks us into believing that we have control of nature, the public was reminded how vulnerable we are to forces completely beyond our control. In addition, as happened in 2005 when Hurricane Katrina tore into the city of New Orleans, we had an opportunity to observe how people in a society react to a major disaster, coping with both physical devastation and social disintegration as entire communities are torn apart.

Studying disasters such as the one that continues to threaten the people of Japan is one example of the work sociologists do when they investigate **collective behavior**, *activity involving a large number of people that is unplanned, often controversial, and sometimes dangerous.* This chapter investigates various types of collective behavior, including what happens when people must deal with not only disasters but also mobs and riots, panic and mass hysteria, rumor and gossip, and fashions and fads. In addition, it will examine social movements, a type of collective behavior aimed at changing people's lives in some important way.

Studying Collective Behavior

(**23.1**) Distinguish various types of collective behavior.

Collective behavior is complex and difficult to study for three reasons:

1. **Collective behavior is diverse.** Collective behavior involves a wide range of human action. At first glance, it is difficult to see what disasters have in common with fads, rumors, and mob behavior.

2. **Collective behavior is variable.** Sometimes a rumor about some issue, such as how closely the U.S. government is tracking personal telephone calls and emails, spreads

across the United States and around the world. But other rumors quickly die out. Why does one rumor catch on but others do not?

3. **Much collective behavior is transitory.** Sociologists have long studied social institutions such as the family because they are continuing parts of society. Disasters, rumors, and fads, however, come and go quickly.

Some researchers are quick to point out that these problems apply not just to collective behavior but to most forms of human behavior as well (Aguirre & Quarantelli, 1983). In addition, collective behavior is not always so surprising; anyone can predict that crowds will form at sporting events and music festivals, and sociologists can study these gatherings firsthand or record them on videotape to study later. Researchers can even anticipate some natural disasters such as tornadoes, which are common in some parts of the United States, and be ready to study how people respond to such events (D. L. Miller, 1985).

As a result of their efforts, sociologists now know a great deal about collective behavior. The first lesson to learn is that all collective behavior involves the action of some **collectivity**, *a large number of people whose minimal interaction occurs in the absence of well-defined and conventional norms*. Collectivities are of two types. A *localized collectivity* refers to people physically close to one another, as in the case of crowds and riots. A *dispersed collectivity* or *mass behavior* involves people who influence one another despite being spread over a large area. Examples of this type of collective behavior include rumors, public opinion, and fashion.

Be sure to keep in mind how collectivities differ from the already familiar concept of social groups (see Chapter 7, "Groups and Organizations"). Here are three key differences:

1. **People in collectivities have little or no social interaction.** People in groups interact frequently and directly; by contrast, people in mobs or other localized collectivities interact very little. Most people taking part in dispersed collectivities, such as a fad, do not interact at all.

2. **Collectivities have no clear social boundaries.** Group members share a sense of identity, but people engaged in collective behavior usually do not. People in a local crowd may have the same object of their attention, such as someone on a ledge threatening to jump, but they feel little sense of unity with those around them. Individuals involved in dispersed collectivities, such as students worried about the possibility of a military draft, have almost no awareness of shared membership. To give another example, people may share concerns over many issues, but usually it is difficult to know exactly who falls within the ranks of, say, the environmental or feminist movement.

3. **Collectivities generate weak and unconventional norms.** Conventional cultural norms usually regulate the behavior of people in groups. Some collectivities, such as people traveling together on an airplane, do observe conventional norms, but their interaction is usually limited to polite small talk with respect for the privacy of others sitting nearby. Other collectivities—such as excited fans after a game who take to the streets drinking and overturning cars—behave according to no clear guidelines (Weller & Quarantelli, 1973; Turner & Killian, 1987).

collective behavior activity involving a large number of people that is unplanned, often controversial, and sometimes dangerous

collectivity a large number of people whose minimal interaction occurs in the absence of well-defined and conventional norms

Localized Collectivities: Crowds

23.2 Identify five types of crowds and three explanations of crowd behavior.

One major form of collective behavior is the **crowd**, *a temporary gathering of people who share a common focus of attention and who influence one another*. Crowds are a fairly new development: Most of our ancestors never saw a large crowd. In medieval Europe, for example, about the only time large numbers of people gathered in one

The 2013 Boston Marathon ended with a terrorist blast that killed three people. The two suspects (visible at the back of the crowd) were identified from images taken by many people using their smartphones. In what ways has computer-based technology changed the character of crowds?

place was when armies faced off on the battlefield (Laslett, 1984). Today, however, crowds of 25,000 or more are common at rock concerts and sporting events and even in the registration halls of large universities. Some political events and demonstrations, including the recent rallies in cities of the Middle East, reached 100,000 people or more. Estimates placed the size of the crowd at President Obama's first inauguration ceremony in Washington, D.C., at about 1.5 million (Tucker, 2009; Bialik, 2011).

All crowds include a lot of people, but they differ in their social dynamics. Herbert Blumer (1969) identified four categories of crowds:

A *casual crowd* is a loose collection of people who interact little, if at all. People lying on a beach or people who rush to the scene of an automobile accident have only a passing awareness of one another.

A *conventional crowd* results from deliberate planning, as illustrated by a country auction, a college lecture, or a presidential inauguration. In each case, the behavior of people involved follows a clear set of norms.

An *expressive crowd* forms around an event with emotional appeal, such as a religious revival, an AC/DC concert, or the New Year's Eve celebration in New York City's Times Square. Excitement is the main reason people join expressive crowds, which makes this spontaneous experience exhilarating for those involved.

An *acting crowd* is a collectivity motivated by an intense, single-minded purpose, such as an audience rushing the doors of a concert hall or fleeing from a mall after hearing gunshots. Acting crowds are set in motion by powerful emotions, which can sometimes trigger mob violence.

Any crowd can change from one type to another. In 2001, a conventional crowd of more than 10,000 fans filed into a soccer stadium in Johannesburg, South Africa, to watch a match between two rival teams. After a goal was scored, the crowd erupted, and people began to push toward the field. Within seconds, an acting crowd had formed, and a stampede began, crushing forty-seven people to death (Nessman, 2001). In 2009, when a USAir jet crash-landed in the Hudson River minutes after taking off from a New York airport, some passengers briefly panicked, creating an acting crowd. But by the time the plane came to rest, people followed directions and evacuated the plane in a surprisingly quiet and conventional manner (Ripley, 2009).

Deliberate action by a crowd is not simply the product of rising emotions. Participants in *protest crowds*—a fifth category we can add to Blumer's list—may stage marches, boycotts, sit-ins, and strikes for political purposes (McPhail & Wohlstein, 1983). The anti-government demonstrations that took place in cities across the Middle East during 2010 and 2011 are examples of protest crowds. In some cases, protest crowds have the low-level energy characteristic of a conventional crowd; at other times (especially when government forces go on the offensive), people become emotional enough to form an acting crowd.

Mobs and Riots

When an acting crowd turns violent, the result may be the birth of a **mob,** *a highly emotional crowd that pursues a violent or destructive goal.* Despite, or perhaps because of, their intense emotions, mobs tend to dissipate quickly. How long a mob continues to exist depends on its precise goals and whether its leadership tries to inflame or calm the crowd.

Lynching is the most notorious example of mob behavior in the United States. The term comes from a man named William Lynch, who lived in Virginia during the colonial period. At a time before there were formal police and courts of law, Lynch took it upon himself to enforce law and order in his community. His name soon came to be associated with violence and murder committed outside of the law.

In the United States, lynching has always been colored by race. After the Civil War, so-called lynch mobs terrorized newly freed African Americans. Any person of color who challenged white superiority risked being hanged or burned alive by hate-filled whites.

Lynch mobs—typically composed of poor whites who felt threatened by competition from freed slaves—reached their peak between 1880 and 1930. Police recorded some 5,000 lynchings in that period, though many more undoubtedly occurred. Often lynchings were popular events, attracting hundreds of spectators; sometimes victims were killed quickly, but others were tortured before being put to death. Most of these terrorist killings took place in the Deep South, where the farming economy depended on a cheap and obedient labor force. On the western frontier, lynch mobs targeted people of Mexican and Asian descent. In about 25 percent of reported lynchings, whites killed other whites. Lynching women was rare; only about 100 such cases are known, almost all involving women of color (White, 1969, orig. 1929; Grant, 1975; Lacayo, 2000).

A highly energized crowd with no particular purpose is a **riot**, *a social eruption that is highly emotional, violent, and undirected*. Unlike the action of a mob, a riot usually has no clear goal, except perhaps to express dissatisfaction. The cause of most riots is some long-standing anger or grievance. As a "violent situation waiting to happen," a riot typically is ignited by some minor incident that causes people to start destroying property and harming other persons. A mob action usually ends when some specific violent goal is accomplished (such as a lynching); a riot tends to go on until the rioters run out of steam or police and community leaders gradually bring them under control.

Throughout our nation's history, riots have been sparked by social injustice. Industrial workers, for example, have rioted to vent rage over unfair working conditions. In 1886, a bitter struggle by Chicago factory workers for an eight-hour workday led to the explosive Haymarket Riot, which left eleven dead and scores injured. Prison inmates sometimes express anger and despair through riots.

In addition, race riots have occurred in this country with striking regularity. Early in the twentieth century, crowds of whites attacked African Americans in Chicago, Detroit, and other cities. In the 1960s, seemingly trivial events sparked rage at continuing prejudice and discrimination, causing violent riots in numerous inner-city ghettos. In Los Angeles in 1992, the acquittal of white police officers involved in the beating of black motorist Rodney King set off an explosive riot. Violence and fires killed more than fifty people, injured thousands, and destroyed property worth hundreds of millions of dollars.

Not all riots are fueled by hate. They can also begin with very positive feelings. In 2000, for example, young men celebrating New York City's National Puerto Rican Day began spraying water on young women in the crowd. During the next few hours, sexual violence erupted as dozens of women were groped, stripped, and assaulted—apparently resulting, as one report put it, from a mixture of "marijuana, alcohol, hot weather, testosterone idiocy, and lapses in police [protection]" (Barstow & Chivers, 2000:1). On a number of state university campuses, a win by the home sports team was all it took to send hundreds of students into the streets, drinking alcohol and soon lighting fires and battling with police. As one analyst put it, in an "anything goes" culture, some people think they can get away with whatever they feel like doing (Pitts, 2000; Madensen & Eck, 2006).

Crowds, Mobs, and Social Change

What does a riot accomplish? One answer is "power." As the recent Occupy Wall Street movement illustrates, ordinary people can gain power when they act collectively. The power of the crowd to challenge the status quo and sometimes to force social change

crowd a temporary gathering of people who share a common focus of attention and who influence one another

mob a highly emotional crowd that pursues a violent or destructive goal

riot a social eruption that is highly emotional, violent, and undirected

is the reason crowds are controversial. Throughout history, defenders of the status quo have feared "the mob" as a threat. By contrast, those seeking change have supported collective action.

Theories of Crowd Behavior

What accounts for the behavior of crowds? Social scientists have developed several explanations.

Contagion Theory

An early explanation of collective behavior was offered by the French sociologist Gustave Le Bon (1841–1931). According to Le Bon's *contagion theory* (1960, orig. 1895), crowds have a hypnotic influence on their members. Shielded by the anonymity found in large numbers, people forget about personal responsibility and give in to the contagious emotions of the crowd. A crowd thus assumes a life of its own, stirring up emotions and driving people toward irrational, even violent, action.

EVALUATE Le Bon's idea that crowds provide anonymity and can generate strong emotions is surely true. Yet as Clark McPhail (1991) claims, a considerable body of research shows that "the madding crowd" does not take on a life of its own. Rather, the actions of people in a crowd usually result from some obvious causes. In 2013, for example, 233 people were killed when fire swept through a nightclub in Santa Maria, Brazil. Echoing conventional thinking about crowd behavior, the police described the situation in the club as "very chaotic." There certainly was panic. Later investigation, however, revealed that the panic did not occur because the crowd suddenly and mysteriously "went crazy" but because the band set off some fireworks that set the building ablaze. As smoke quickly filled the large room, people rushed for a single exit, a situation made more difficult by security personnel who blocked the door trying to be sure that anyone who left the room had paid their drink tabs (Barbassa, 2013).

Although collective behavior may involve strong emotions, such feelings may not be irrational, as contagion theory suggests. Emotions—as well as action—can reflect real fear (as panic at a nightclub fire) or result from a sense of injustice (as in political protests) (Jasper, 1998).

CHECK YOUR LEARNING State the contagion theory of crowd behavior. What are several criticisms of this theory?

Convergence Theory

Convergence theory holds that crowd behavior comes not from the crowd itself but also from the particular people who join in. From this point of view, a crowd is a convergence of like-minded individuals. Contagion theory states that crowds cause people to act in a certain way; convergence theory says the opposite, claiming that people who wish to act in a certain way come together to form crowds.

In recent years, the crowds that formed at political demonstrations opposing repressive governments in the Middle East did not cause participants to oppose their government leaders. On the contrary, participants came together because of already existing political attitudes.

People came together in 2012 in response to the devastation caused by Hurricane Sandy along the East Coast of the United States. Which of the theories of crowd behavior discussed in this section of the chapter best explains this event?

EVALUATE By linking crowds to broader social forces, convergence theory rejects Le Bon's claim that crowd behavior is irrational in favor of the view that people in crowds express existing beliefs and values. But in fairness to Le Bon, people some-times do things in a crowd that they would not have the courage to do alone, because crowds can spread responsibility among many people. In addition, crowds can intensify an emotion simply by creating a critical mass of like-minded people.

CHECK YOUR LEARNING State the convergence theory of crowd behavior. What are two criticisms of this theory?

Emergent-Norm Theory

Ralph Turner and Lewis Killian (1987) developed the *emergent-norm theory* of crowd dynamics. These researchers admit that social behavior is never entirely predictable, but if similar interests draw people into a crowd, distinctive patterns of behavior may emerge.

According to Turner and Killian, crowds begin as collectivities containing people with mixed interests and motives. Especially in the case of expressive, acting, and protest crowds, norms may be vague and changing. In the minutes and hours after the earthquake and tsunami devastated Japan, for example, many people fled in terror. But, quickly, people began to come to each other's aid, and the Japanese resolved to undertake a collective effort to rebuild their way of life. In short, the behavior of people in crowds may change over time as people draw on their traditions or make new rules as they go along.

EVALUATE Emergent-norm theory represents a middle-ground approach to crowd dynamics. Turner and Killian (1993) explain that crowd behavior is neither as irrational as contagion theory suggests nor as deliberate as convergence theory implies. Certainly, crowd behavior reflects the desires of participants, but it is also guided by norms that emerge as the situation unfolds.

Decision making does play a role in crowd behavior, although people watching from the sidelines may not realize it. For example, frightened people racing for higher ground may appear to be victims of irrational panic, but from their point of view, fleeing an oncoming tsunami makes a lot of sense.

Emergent-norm theory points out that people in a crowd take on different roles. Some step forward as leaders; others become lieutenants, rank-and-file followers, inactive bystanders, and even opponents (Weller & Quarantelli, 1973; Zurcher & Snow, 1981).

CRITICAL REVIEW State the emergent-norm theory of crowd behavior. What are several criticisms of this theory?

Dispersed Collectivities: Mass Behavior

23.3 Describe rumor, disasters, and other types of mass behavior.

It is not just people clustered together in crowds who take part in collective behavior. **Mass behavior** refers to *collective behavior among people spread over a wide geographic area*.

mass behavior collective behavior among people spread over a wide geographic area

rumor unconfined information that people spread informally, often by word of mouth	**public opinion** widespread attitudes about controversial issues	**fashion** a social pattern favored by a large number of people	**panic** a form of collective behavior in which people in one place react to a threat or other stimulus with irrational, frantic, and often self-destructive behavior	**mass hysteria** or **moral panic** a form of dispersed collective behavior in which people react to a real or imagined event with irrational and even frantic fear
gossip rumor about people's personal affairs	**propaganda** information presented with the intention of shaping public opinion	**fad** an unconventional social pattern that people embrace briefly but enthusiastically		

Rumor and Gossip

A common type of mass behavior is **rumor**, *unconfirmed information that people spread informally, often by word of mouth or by using electronic devices.* People pass along rumors through face-to-face communication, of course, but today's modern technology—including telephones, the mass media, e-mail, text messaging, and the Internet—spreads rumors faster and farther than ever before.

Rumor has three main characteristics:

1. **Rumor thrives in a climate of uncertainty.** Rumors arise when people lack clear and certain information about an issue. In a number of cities, for example, rumors about potential police action spread quickly among members of the "Occupy Wall Street" movement.

2. **Rumor is unstable.** People change a rumor as they pass it along, usually giving it a "spin" that serves their own interests. Conservative people reinforced one point of view as to whether police should clear Occupy encampments; liberal activists encouraged another.

3. **Rumor is difficult to stop.** The number of people aware of a rumor increases very quickly because each person spreads information to many others. The mass media and the Internet can quickly spread local issues and events across the country and around the world. E-mail has particular importance in the process of spreading a rumor because most of us tend to believe something we hear from friends (Garrett, 2011). Eventually, of course, rumors go away. But, in general, the only way to control rumors is for a believable source to issue a clear and convincing statement of the facts.

Rumor can trigger the formation of crowds or other collective behavior. For this reason, officials establish rumor control centers during a crisis in order to manage information. Yet some rumors persist, perhaps just because people enjoy them; the rumor that the Beatles' Paul McCartney had mysteriously died in 1966 is classic example.

Gossip is *rumor about people's personal affairs.* Charles Horton Cooley (1962, orig. 1909) explained that rumor involves some issue many people care about, but gossip interests only a small circle of people who know a particular person. This is why rumors spread widely but gossip tends to be localized.

Communities use gossip as a means of social control, using praise and blame to encourage people to conform to local norms. Also, people gossip about others to put them down and to raise their own standing as social "insiders" (Baumgartner, 1998; Nicholson, 2001). At the same time, no community wants gossip to get out of control to the point that no one knows what to believe, which is why people who gossip too much are criticized as "busybodies."

Public Opinion and Propaganda

Another type of dispersed collective behavior is **public opinion**, *widespread attitudes about controversial issues.* Exactly who is, or is not, included in any "public" depends on the issue involved. Over the years in the United States, publics have formed over numerous controversial issues, from global warming and air pollution to handguns and health care. More recently, the public has debated affirmative action, campaign finance reform, border security, and gun control.

Whatever the issue, a small share of people will have no opinion at all. The absence of an opinion may be due to either ignorance or indifference. Even on many important issues, surveys show that between 5 and 20 percent of people will have no clear opinion. In unusual cases, the undecided share of the public can be a majority of people. One 2011 survey that asked people what they thought of the Tea Party movement, for example, found that 55 percent of U.S. adults claimed that they were either not informed enough to have an opinion (36 percent) or they were undecided (19 percent). Others simply refused to say (2 percent) (Polling Report, 2013).

For a closer look at the rumor that rocked a generation, **Read More** in **MySocLab**, *The Rumor Mill: Paul Is Dead!*

Also, not everyone's opinion carries the same weight. Some categories of people are more likely to be asked for their opinion, and what they say will have more clout because they are better educated, wealthier, or better connected. By forming an organization, various categories of people can increase their voice. Through the American Medical Association, for example, physicians have a lot to say about medical care in the United States, just as members of the National Education Association have a great deal of influence on public education.

Special-interest groups and political leaders all try to shape public tastes and attitudes by using **propaganda,** *information presented with the intention of shaping public opinion.* Although we tend to think of propaganda in negative terms, it is not necessarily false. A thin line separates information from propaganda; the difference depends mostly on the presenter's intention. We offer *information* to enlighten others; we use *propaganda* to sway people toward our own point of view. Political speeches, commercial advertising, and even some college lectures may include propaganda in an effort to steer people toward thinking or acting in some specific way.

Sometimes, of course, propaganda is a matter of saying something that simply is not true. One organization that followed campaign advertising during the 2012 presidential election reported that roughly one-fifth of third-party political ads contained information that was not true (Annenberg Public Policy Center, 2013). Often, however, propaganda is a matter of deciding *which* facts to present—a practice that we often refer to as *spin*. For example, in a recent debate over rising oil prices, President Barack Obama claimed that the United States now imports less than half of the oil the nation consumes. Senator Mitch McConnell countered that the United States imports more than 60 percent of the oil we consume. Is someone lying? No. The two claims were simply based on different ways of calculating the answer. Each person was dealing with facts but *spinning* the facts to support a particular political position (Morse, 2011).

Fashions and Fads

Fashions and fads also involve people spread over a large area. A **fashion** is *a social pattern favored by a large number of people.* People's tastes in clothing, music, and automobiles, as well as ideas about politics, change often, going in and out of fashion.

In preindustrial societies, clothing and personal appearance change very little, reflecting traditional *style*. Women and men, the rich and the poor, lawyers and carpenters wear distinctive clothes and hairstyles that reflect their occupations and social standing (Lofland, 1973; Crane, 2000).

In industrial societies, however, established style gives way to changing fashion. For one thing, modern people care less about tradition and are often eager to try out new "lifestyles." Higher rates of social mobility also cause people to use their appearance to make a statement about themselves. The German sociologist Georg Simmel (1971, orig. 1904) explained that rich people usually stand out as the trendsetters; with plenty of money to spend on luxuries, they attract lots of attention. As the U.S. sociologist Thorstein Veblen (1953, orig. 1899) put it, fashion involves *conspicuous consumption* as people buy expensive products (from designer handbags to Hummers) not because they need them but simply to show off their wealth.

Ordinary people who want to look wealthy are eager to buy less expensive copies of what the rich make fashionable. In this way, a fashion moves downward through the class structure. But eventually, the fashion loses its prestige when too many average people now share "the look," so the rich move on to something new. In short, fashions are born along the Fifth Avenues and Rodeo Drives of the rich, gain popularity in Targets and Walmarts across the country, and are eventually pushed aside in favor of something new.

Fashion refers to social patterns that are popular within a society's population. In modern societies, the mass media play an important part in guiding people's tastes. For example, the popular television show *Project Runway* sets standards for attractive clothing. Fads are patterns that change more quickly. *Project Runway* is one example of the recent fad that had brought so many "reality shows" to television.

Since the 1960s, however, there has been a reversal of this pattern in the United States, and many fashions favored by rich people are drawn from people of lower social position. This pattern began with blue jeans, which have long been worn by people doing manual labor. During the civil rights and antiwar movements of the 1960s, denim jeans became popular among college students who wanted to identify with "ordinary people." Today, emblems of the hip-hop culture allow even the most affluent entertainers and celebrities to mimic styles that began among the inner-city poor. Even rich and famous people often identify with their ordinary roots: In one of her songs, Jennifer Lopez asks her friends not to be fooled by all her new jewelry because she is still the same Jenny who lived with them in the old neighborhood.

A **fad** is *an unconventional social pattern that people embrace briefly but enthusiastically.* Fads, sometimes called *crazes,* are common in high-income societies, where many people have the money to spend on amusing, if often frivolous, things. During the 1950s, two young Californians produced a brightly colored plastic hoop, a version of a toy popular in Australia, that you can swing around your waist by gyrating your hips. The "hula hoop" became a national craze. In less than a year, hula hoops had all but vanished, only to reappear from time to time. Pokémon cards are another example of the rise and fall of a fad. Justin Bieber probably hopes that he does not turn out to be a fad.

How do fads differ from fashions? Fads capture the public imagination but quickly burn out. Because fashions reflect basic cultural values like individuality and sexual attractiveness, they tend to stay around for a while. Therefore, a fashion—but rarely a fad—becomes a more lasting part of popular culture. Streaking, for instance, was a fad that came out of nowhere and soon vanished; denim clothing, however, is an example of fashion that originated in the rough mining camps of Gold Rush California in the 1870s and is still popular today.

Panic and Mass Hysteria

A **panic** is *a form of collective behavior in which people in one place react to a threat or other stimulus with irrational, frantic, and often self-destructive behavior.* The classic illustration of a panic is people streaming toward the exits of a crowded theater after someone yells, "Fire!" As they flee, they trample one another, blocking the exits so that few actually escape.

Closely related to panic is **mass hysteria** or **moral panic**, *a form of dispersed collective behavior in which people react to a real or imagined event with irrational and even frantic fear.* Whether the cause of the hysteria is real or not, a large number of people take it very seriously.

One example of a moral panic occurred during the 1950s as some political leaders encouraged widespread fear of "communists" who had become officials in U.S. government. In the 1960s, another wave of controversy was set off by flag burnings in opposition to the Vietnam War. In the 1980s, fear of AIDS or of people with AIDS caused a moral panic among some people. In early 2013, another moral panic arose as people feared that Congress's failure to resolve budget disagreements might push the United States over a "fiscal cliff."

Sometimes moral panics arise over situations that pose little real danger to anyone. Take, for example, the case of fear arising from AIDS; there is almost no chance of becoming infected with HIV by simply interacting with someone who has this disease. At another level, however, the fear itself can become a danger, as for example, if the fear of AIDS were to give rise to a hate crime targeting a person with AIDS.

One factor that makes moral panics common in our society is the influence of the mass media. Diseases, disasters, and deadly crime all get intense coverage by television and other media, which hope to gain an audience. As sociologist Erich Goode (2000:549) points out, "The mass media *thrive* on scares; contributing to moral panics is the media's stock in trade." It was the mass media, after all, that popularized the term "fiscal cliff" to imply that the country was on a path toward imminent catastrophe.

Mass hysteria is sometimes triggered by an event that, at the extreme, sends people into chaotic flight. Of course, people who see others overcome by fear may become more afraid themselves, and the hysteria feeds on itself. When a presidential 747 chased by an Air Force jet flew low over New York City in a 2009 "photo op," it sent thousands of people who remembered the 9/11 attacks running into the streets, although everyone eventually realized that there was no real danger.

Disasters

A **disaster** is *an event, generally unexpected, that causes extensive harm to people and damage to property*. Disasters are of three types. Earthquakes, floods, hurricanes, and forest fires are all examples of *natural disasters* (K. T. Erikson, 2005a). A second type is the *technological disaster,* which is widely regarded as an accident but is more accurately a failure to control technology (K. T. Erikson, 2005a). The 2011 radiation leak from the Fukushima Daiichi nuclear plant is one recent example of a technological disaster. A second is the 2010 oil spill resulting from the explosion on an oil platform in the Gulf of Mexico, which released as much as 200 million gallons of oil into the water. A third type of disaster is the *intentional disaster,* in which one or more organized groups deliberately harm others. War, terrorist attacks, and genocide in places including Syria (2012–2013), Libya (2011), the Darfur region of Sudan (2003–2010), Yugoslavia (1992–1995), and Rwanda (1994) are all examples of intentional disasters.

The full scope of the harm caused by disasters may become evident only many years after the event takes place. The Thinking Globally box on page 676 provides an example of a technological disaster that is still affecting people and their descendants more than fifty years after it occurred.

Kai Erikson (1976, 1994, 2005a) has investigated dozens of disasters of all types. From the study of floods, nuclear contamination, oil spills, and genocide, Erikson reached three major conclusions about the consequences of disasters.

First, disasters are *social disruptions*. We all know that disasters harm people and destroy property, but only recently have analysts begun to discuss disasters as threats to *human security* (Futamora, Hobson, & Turner, 2011). This concept points to the fact that disasters also damage human community. In 1972, when a dam burst and sent a mountain of water down West Virginia's Buffalo Creek, it killed 125 people, destroyed 1,000 homes, and left 4,000 people homeless. After the waters had returned to normal and help was streaming into the area, the people were paralyzed not only by the loss of family members and friends but also by the loss of their entire way of life. Despite more than forty years

disaster an event, generally unexpected, that causes extensive harm to people and damage to property

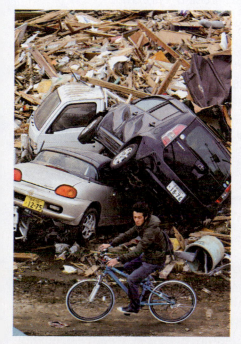

Sociologists classify natural disasters using three types. The 2011 tsunami that brought massive flooding to Japan is an example of a natural disaster. The 2010 Gulf of Mexico oil spill was a technological disaster. The slaughter of hundreds of thousands of people and the displacement of millions more from their homes since 2003 in the Darfur region of Sudan is an example of an intentional disaster.

Thinking Globally

A Never-Ending Atomic Disaster

It was just after dawn on March 1, 1954, and the air was already warm on Utrik Island, a small bit of coral and volcanic rock in the South Pacific that is one of the Marshall Islands. The island was home to 159 people, who lived by fishing much as their ancestors had done for centuries. The population knew only a little about the outside world—a missionary from the United States taught the local children, and two dozen military personnel lived at a small U.S. weather station with an airstrip that received one plane each week.

At 6:45 A.M., the western sky suddenly lit up brighter than anyone had ever seen, and seconds later, a rumble like a massive earthquake rolled across the island. Some of the Utrik people thought the world was coming to an end. And truly, the world they had always known was gone forever.

About 160 miles to the west, on Bikini Island, the United States military had just detonated an atomic bomb, a huge device with 1,000 times the power of the bomb used at the end of World War II to destroy the Japanese city of Hiroshima. The enormous blast vaporized the entire island and sent a massive cloud of dust and radiation into the atmosphere. The military expected the winds to take the cloud north into an open area of the ocean, but the cloud blew east instead. By noon, the radiation cloud had engulfed a Japanese fishing boat ironically called the *Lucky Dragon,* exposing the twenty-three people on board to a dose of radiation that would eventually sicken or kill them all. By the end of the afternoon, the deadly cloud reached Utrik Island.

The cloud was made up of coral and rock dust—all that was left of Bikini Island. The dust fell softly on Utrik Island, and the children, who remembered pictures of snow shown to them by their missionary teacher, ran out to play in the white powder that was piling up everywhere. No one realized that it was contaminated with deadly radiation.

Three-and-one-half days later, the U.S. military landed planes on Utrik Island and informed all the people that they would have to leave immediately, bringing nothing with them. For three months, the island people were housed at another military base, and then they were returned home.

Many of the people who were on the island that fateful morning died young, typically from cancer or some other disease associated with radiation exposure. But even today, those who survived consider themselves and their island poisoned by the radiation, and they believe that the poison will never go away. The radiation may or may not still be in their bodies and in the soil and sand on the island, but it has certainly worked its way deep into their culture. More than fifty years after the bomb exploded, people still talk about the morning that "everything changed." The damage from this disaster turned out to be much more than medical—it was a social transformation that left the people with a deep belief that they are all sick, that life will never be the same, and that powerful people who live on the other side of the world could have prevented the disaster but did not.

What Do You Think?

1. In what sense is a disaster like this one or the 2011 radiation leak in Japan never really over?

2. In what ways did the atomic bomb test change the culture of the Utrik people?

3. The U.S. government never formally took responsibility for what happened. What elements of global stratification do you see in what happened to the people of Utrik Island?

Source: Based on K. T. Erikson (2005a).

---

of effort, they have not been able to rebuild the community life they once knew. We can pinpoint when disasters start, but as Erikson points out, we cannot predict when their effects will end. The full consequences of the radiation leak in Japan following the 2011 earthquake discussed in the opening to this chapter are still far from clear.

Second, Erikson discovered that the social damage is more serious when an event involves some toxic substance, as is usually the case with technological disasters. As the case of radiation falling on Utrik Island shows us, people feel "poisoned" when they have been exposed to a dangerous substance that they fear and over which they have no control.

Third, the social damage is most serious when the disaster is caused by the actions of other people. This can happen through negligence or carelessness (in the case of technological disasters) or through willful action (in the case of intentional disasters). Our belief that "other people will do us no harm" is a basic foundation of social life, Erikson claims. But when others act carelessly (as in the case of the 2010 Gulf oil spill) or intentionally in ways that harm us (as when some Middle Eastern government leaders used deadly force to put down protests in 2011 and 2012), many who survive lose their trust in others to such a degree that it may never be restored.

Social Movements

23.4 Analyze the causes and consequences of social movements.

A **social movement** is *an organized activity that encourages or discourages social change*. Social movements are among the most important types of collective behavior because they often have lasting effects on our society.

Social movements, such as the political movements that swept across the Middle East beginning in 2011, are common in the modern world. But this was not always the case. Preindustrial societies are tightly bound by tradition, making social movements extremely rare. However, the many subcultures and countercultures found in industrial and postindustrial societies encourage social movements dealing with a wide range of public issues. In the United States, for example, the gay rights movement has won legal changes in numerous cities and several states, forbidding discrimination based on sexual orientation and allowing formal domestic partnership and in some places even legal gay marriage. Like any social movement that seeks change, the gay rights movement has prompted a countermovement made up of traditionalists who want to limit the social acceptance of homosexuality. In today's society, almost every important public issue gives rise to a social movement favoring change and an opposing countermovement resisting it.

social movement an organized activity that encourages or discourages social change

claims making the process of trying to convince the public and public officials of the importance of joining a social movement to address a particular issue

Types of Social Movements

Sociologists classify social movements according to several variables (Aberle, 1966; Cameron, 1966; Blumer, 1969). One variable asks, *Who is changed?* Some movements target selected people, and others try to change everyone. A second variable asks, *How much change?* Some movements seek only limited change in our lives, and others pursue radical transformation of society. Combining these variables results in four types of social movements, shown in Figure 23–1.

Alterative social movements are the least threatening to the status quo because they seek limited change in only a part of the population. Their aim is to help certain people *alter* their lives. Promise Keepers, one example of an alterative social movement, encourages men to live more spiritual lives and be more supportive of their families.

Redemptive social movements also target specific people, but they seek radical change. Their aim is to help certain people *redeem* their lives. For example, Alcoholics Anonymous is an organization that helps people with an alcohol addiction to achieve a sober life.

Reformative social movements aim for only limited social change but target everyone. Multiculturalism, described in Chapter 3 ("Culture"), is an educational and political movement that advocates social equality for people of all races and ethnicities. Reformative social movements generally work inside the existing political system. Some are *progressive,* promoting a new social pattern, and others are *reactionary,* opposing those who seek change by trying to preserve the

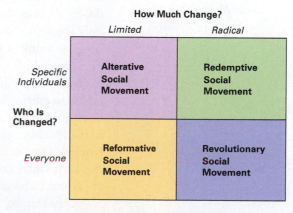

FIGURE 23–1 Four Types of Social Movements

There are four types of social movements, reflecting who is changed and how great the change is.

Source: Based on Aberle (1966).

Claims making is the process of trying to convince others of the importance of some problem and the need for specific change. What claims were made by the Occupy Wall Street movement? In your opinion, how successful has this movement been in reshaping public opinion? Has it brought about change?

status quo or to revive past social patterns. Thus just as multiculturalists push for greater racial equality, white supremacist organizations try to maintain the historical dominance of white people.

Revolutionary social movements are the most extreme of all, seeking the transformation of an entire society. Sometimes pursuing specific goals, sometimes spinning utopian dreams, these social movements reject existing social institutions as flawed in favor of a radically new alternative. Both the left-wing Communist party (pushing for government control of the entire economy) and the right-wing militia groups (advocating the destruction of "big government") seek to radically change our way of life (van Dyke & Soule, 2002).

Claims Making

Watch in **MySocLab**
Video: *Sociology in Focus:*
Collective Behavior and
Social Movements

In 1981, the Centers for Disease Control and Prevention began to track a strange disease that was rapidly killing people, most of them homosexual men. The disease came to be known as AIDS (acquired immune deficiency syndrome). Although AIDS was clearly a deadly disease, there was little public attention and few stories in the mass media. It was only about five years later that the public became aware of the rising number of deaths and began to think of AIDS as a serious social threat.

The change in public thinking was the result of **claims making**, *the process of trying to convince the public and public officials of the importance of joining a social movement to address a particular issue.* In other words, for a social movement to form, some issue has to be defined as a problem that demands public attention. Usually, claims making begins with a small number of people. In the case of AIDS, the gay community in large cities (notably San Francisco and New York) mobilized to convince people of the dangers posed by this deadly disease. Over time, if the mass media give the issue attention and public officials speak out on behalf of the problem, it is likely that the social movement will gain strength.

Considerable public attention has now been given to AIDS, and there is ongoing research aimed at finding a cure for this deadly disease. The process of claims making goes on all the time for dozens of issues. Today, for example, a movement to ban the use of cellular telephones in automobiles has pointed to the thousands of automobile accidents each year related to the use of phones while driving; so far, ten states have passed laws banning the use of handheld phones, thirty-three others ban cell phones for new drivers, and thirty-nine ban text messaging for all drivers; debate continues elsewhere (McVeigh, Welch, & Bjarnason, 2003; Governors' Highway Safety Association, 2013; Macionis, 2013).

Explaining Social Movements

Because social movements are intentional and long-lasting, sociologists find this type of collective behavior easier to explain than brief episodes of mob behavior or mass hysteria described earlier in the chapter. Several theories have gained importance.

Deprivation Theory

Deprivation theory holds that social movements seeking change arise among people who feel deprived. People who feel they lack enough income, safe working conditions, basic political rights, or plain human dignity may organize a social movement to bring about a more just state of affairs (Morrison, 1978; J. D. Rose, 1982).

The rise of the Ku Klux Klan and the passage of Jim Crow laws by whites intent on enforcing segregation in the South after the Civil War illustrate deprivation theory. With the end of slavery, white landowners lost a source of free labor, and poorer whites lost the claim that they were socially superior to African Americans. This change produced a sense of deprivation, prompting whites to try to keep all people of color "in their place" (Dollard et al., 1939). African Americans' deprivation was far greater, of course, but as minorities in a racist society, they had little opportunity to organize. During the twentieth century, however, African Americans did organize successfully in pursuit of racial equality.

As Chapter 7 ("Groups and Organizations") explains, deprivation is a relative concept. Regardless of anyone's absolute amount of money and power, people feel either good or bad about their situation only by comparing themselves to some other category of people. **Relative deprivation,** then, is *a perceived disadvantage arising from some specific comparison* (Stouffer et al., 1949; Merton, 1968).

Alexis de Tocqueville's study of the French Revolution offers a classic illustration of relative deprivation (1955, orig. 1856). Why did rebellion occur in progressive France, where feudalism was breaking down, rather than in more traditional Germany, where

Watch in **MySocLab**
Video: *The Basics: Collective Behavior and Social Movements*

relative deprivation
a perceived disadvantage arising from some specific comparison

A curious fact is that rioting by African Americans in U.S. cities during the 1960s was more common in the North (here, in Detroit), where good factory jobs were available and living standards were higher, than in the South, where a larger share of people lived in rural areas with lower incomes. Relative deprivation theory explains this apparent contradiction by pointing out that it was in the North, where life had improved, that people came to expect equality. Relative to that goal, the reality of second-class citizenship became intolerable.

peasants were much worse off? Tocqueville's answer was that as bad as their condition was, German peasants had known nothing but feudal servitude, and so they could imagine little else and had no basis for feeling deprived. French peasants, by contrast, had seen improvements in their lives that made them eager for more change. Consequently, the French—but not the Germans—felt relative deprivation. As Tocqueville saw it, increasing freedom and prosperity did not satisfy people as much as it sparked their desire for an even better life.

Closer to home, Tocqueville's insight helps explain patterns of rioting during the 1960s. Protest riots involving African Americans took place not in the South, where many black people lived in miserable poverty, but in Detroit at a time when the city's auto industry was booming, black unemployment was low, and black home ownership was the highest in the country (Thernstrom & Thernstrom, 1998).

EVALUATE Deprivation theory challenges our commonsense assumption that the worst-off people are the most likely to organize for change. People do not organize simply because they suffer in an absolute sense; rather, social movements arise out of a sense of *relative* deprivation. Both Tocqueville and Marx—as different as they were in many ways—agreed on the importance of relative deprivation in the formation of social movements.

But most people experience some discontent all the time, so deprivation theory leaves us wondering why social movements arise among some categories of people and not others. A second problem is that deprivation theory suffers from circular reasoning: We assume that deprivation causes social movements, but often the only evidence of deprivation is the social movement itself (Jenkins & Perrow, 1977). A third limitation is that this approach focuses on the cause of a social movement and tells us little about what happens after movements take form (McAdam, McCarthy, & Zald, 1988).

CHECK YOUR LEARNING State the basic idea of the deprivation theory of social movements. What are several criticisms of this theory?

Mass-Society Theory

William Kornhauser's *mass-society theory* (1959) argues that socially isolated people seek out social movements as a way to gain a sense of belonging and importance. From this point of view, social movements are most likely to arise in impersonal, *mass* societies. This theory points out the *personal* as well as the *political* consequences of social movements that offer a sense of community to people otherwise adrift in society (Melucci, 1989).

It follows, says Kornhauser, that categories of people with weak social ties are those most eager to join a social movement. People who are well integrated socially, by contrast, are unlikely to seek membership in a social movement.

Kornhauser concludes that activists tend to be psychologically vulnerable people who eagerly join groups and can be manipulated by group leaders. For this reason, Kornhauser claims, social movements are rarely very democratic.

EVALUATE To Kornhauser's credit, his theory focuses on both the kind of society that produces social movements and the kinds of people who join them. But one criticism is that there is no clear standard for measuring the extent to which we live in a "mass society," so his thesis is difficult to test.

A second criticism is that explaining social movements in terms of people hungry to belong ignores the social-justice issues that movements address. Put otherwise, mass-society theory suggests that flawed people, rather than a flawed society, are responsible for social movements.

What does research show about mass-society theory? The record is mixed. Research by Frances Piven and Richard Cloward (1977) supports Kornhauser's approach. Piven and Cloward found that a breakdown of routine social patterns has encouraged poor people to form social movements. Also, a study of the New Mexico State Penitentiary found that when prison programs that promoted social ties among inmates were suspended, inmates were more likely to protest their conditions (Useem & Goldstone, 2002).

But other studies cast doubt on this approach. Some researchers conclude that the Nazi movement in Germany did not draw heavily from socially isolated people (Lipset, 1963; Oberschall, 1973). Similarly, many of the people who took part in urban riots during the 1960s had strong ties to their communities (Sears & McConahay, 1973). Evidence also suggests that most young people who join religious movements have fairly normal family ties (Wright & Piper, 1986). Finally, researchers who have examined the biographies of 1960s' political activists find evidence of deep and continuing commitment to political goals rather than isolation from society (McAdam, 1988, 1989; Whalen & Flacks, 1989).

CHECK YOUR LEARNING State the basic idea of the mass-society theory of social movements. What are several criticisms of this theory?

Culture Theory

In recent years, sociologists have developed *culture theory*, the recognition that social movements depend not only on material resources and the structure of political power but also on cultural symbols. That is, people in any particular situation are likely to mobilize to form a social movement only to the extent that they develop "shared understandings of the world that legitimate and motivate collective action" (McAdam, McCarthy, & Zald, 1996:6; see also Williams, 2002).

In part, mobilization depends on a sense of injustice, as suggested by deprivation theory. In addition, people must come to believe that they are not able to respond to their situation effectively by acting alone.

Finally, social movements gain strength as they develop symbols and a sense of community that both build strong feelings and direct energy into organized action. Media images of the burning World Trade Center towers after the terrorist attacks on September 11, 2001, helped mobilize people to support the U.S. military campaigns in Afghanistan and Iraq. Likewise, photos of gay couples celebrating their weddings have helped fuel both the gay rights movement and the countermovement trying to prevent the spread of gay marriage. Colorful, rubber bracelets are now used by at least a dozen social movements to encourage people to show support for various causes.

EVALUATE A strength of culture theory is reminding us that social movements depend not just on material resources but also on cultural symbols. At the same time, powerful symbols (such as the flag and ideas about patriotism and respecting our leaders) help

Social movements are often given great energy by powerful visual images, which is one key idea of culture theory. During World War II, this photo of six soldiers raising the U.S. flag on the tiny Pacific island of Iwo Jima increased morale at home and was the inspiration for a memorial sculpture. Some twenty-five years later, newspapers published the photo on the right, showing children running from a napalm strike by U.S. planes in South Vietnam. The girl in the middle of the picture had ripped the flaming clothes from her body. This photo increased the strength of the social movement against the war in Vietnam.

support the status quo. How and when symbols turn people from supporting the system toward protest against it are questions in need of further research.

CHECK YOUR LEARNING State the basic idea of the culture theory of social movements. What is the main criticism of this theory?

Resource-Mobilization Theory

Resource-mobilization theory points out that no social movement is likely to succeed—or even get off the ground—without substantial resources, including money, human labor, office and communications equipment, access to the mass media, and a positive public image. In short, any social movement rises or falls on how well it attracts resources, mobilizes people, and forges alliances.

Outsiders can be just as important as insiders in affecting the outcome of a social movement. Because socially disadvantaged people, by definition, lack the money, contacts, leadership skills, and organizational know-how that a successful movement requires, sympathetic outsiders fill the resource gap. In U.S. history, well-to-do white people, including college students, performed a vital service to the black civil rights movement in the 1960s, and affluent men have joined women as leaders of the women's movement.

Resources connecting people are also vital. The 1989 prodemocracy movement in China was fueled by students whose location on campuses clustered together in Beijing allowed them to build networks and recruit new members (Zhao, 1998). More recently, the Internet, including Facebook and Twitter, was an important resource that helped organizations to mobilize hundreds of thousands of people who took part in the political movements in many nations in the Middle East (Earl & Kimport, 2011; Preston, 2011).

Closer to home, in the 2008 presidential campaign, YouTube videos of Barack Obama were viewed almost 2 billion times, surely contributing to his success in that election. In the months leading up to the 2012 presidential election, 47 percent of all voters identified the Internet as a major source of their political information, which is almost twice the share who said they relied on newspapers and almost as large as the share who claimed to rely on television. Put another way, 41 percent of U.S. voters now claim that they get *most* of their political news from the Internet (Pew Research Center, 2011, 2012).

Of course, Internet-based activism on any particular issue is not equally likely everywhere in the United States. In 2007, the liberal activist organization MoveOn.org used the Internet to create a "virtual march" in which people across the country telephoned their representatives in Congress to oppose the troop "surge" in Iraq. National Map 23-1 on page 683 shows where that organization had more or less success in mobilizing opposition to the war in Iraq.

The availability of organizing ideas online has helped people on campuses and elsewhere increase support for various social movements. For example, Take Back the Night is an annual occasion for rallies at which people speak out in opposition to violence against women, children, and families. Using resources available online, even a small number of people can plan and carry out an effective political event (Passy & Giugni, 2001; Packer, 2003).

EVALUATE Resource-mobilization theory recognizes that both resources and discontent are necessary to the success of a social movement. Research confirms the importance of forging alliances to gaining resources and notes that movements with few resources may, in desperation, turn to violence to call attention to their cause (Grant & Wallace, 1991; Jenkins, Jacobs, & Agone, 2003).

Critics of this theory counter that "outside" people and resources are not always needed to ensure a movement's success. They argue that even relatively powerless segments of a population can promote change if they are able to organize effectively and have strongly committed members (Donnelly & Majka, 1998). Aldon Morris (1981) adds that the success of the civil rights movement of the 1950s and 1960s was due to people of color who drew mostly on their own skills and resources. A second problem with this theory is that it overstates the extent to which powerful people are willing to challenge the status quo. Some rich white people did provide valuable resources to the

Read in **MySocLab**
Document: *The Rise and Fall of Aryan Nations: A Resource Mobilization Perspective* by Robert W. Balch

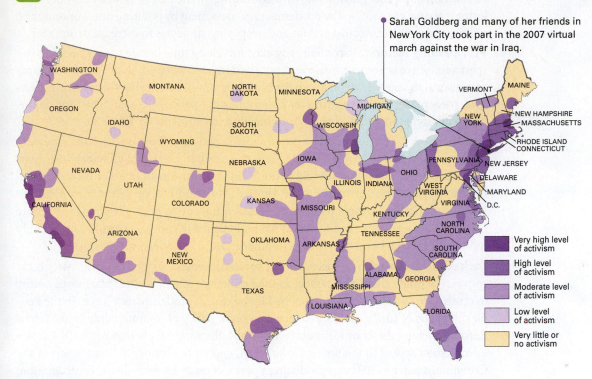

● Sarah Goldberg and many of her friends in New York City took part in the 2007 virtual march against the war in Iraq.

Very high level of activism

High level of activism

Moderate level of activism

Low level of activism

Very little or no activism

NATIONAL MAP 23–1 Virtual March: Political Mobilization across the United States

In early 2007, the political action group MoveOn.org organized a "virtual march on Washington," urging people across the country to call their representatives in Congress to express opposition to the U.S. buildup of troops in Iraq. The map shows the areas in which the most telephone calls were made. What can you say about the places where the mobilization was most and least effective?

Source: MoveOn.org (2007).

black civil rights movement, but probably more often, elites were indifferent or opposed to significant change (McAdam, 1982, 1983; Pichardo, 1995).

CHECK YOUR LEARNING State the basic idea of resource-mobilization theory. What are two criticisms of this theory?

Structural-Strain Theory

One of the most influential theories about social movements was developed by Neil Smelser (1962). *Structural-strain theory* identifies six factors that encourage the development of social movements. Smelser's theory also suggests which factors encourage unorganized mobs or riots and which encourage highly organized social movements. The prodemocracy movement that transformed Eastern Europe during the late 1980s illustrates Smelser's theory.

1. **Structural conduciveness.** Social movements begin to emerge when people come to think their society has some serious problems. In Eastern Europe, these problems included low living standards and political repression by national governments.

2. **Structural strain.** People begin to experience relative deprivation when society fails to meet their expectations. Eastern Europeans joined the prodemocracy movement because they compared their living standards to the higher ones in Western Europe; they also knew that their standard of living was lower than what years of socialist propaganda had led them to expect.

Collective Behavior and Social Movements   **CHAPTER 23   683**

3. **Growth and spread of an explanation.** Forming a well-organized social movement requires a clear statement of not just the problem but also its causes and its solutions. If people are confused about why they are suffering, they will probably express their dissatisfaction in an unorganized way through rioting. In the case of Eastern Europe, intellectuals played a key role in the prodemocracy movement by pointing out economic and political flaws in the socialist system and proposing strategies to increase democracy.

4. **Precipitating factors.** Discontent may exist for a long time before some specific event sparks collective action. Such an event occurred in 1985 when Mikhail Gorbachev came to power in the Soviet Union and began his program of *perestroika* (restructuring). As Moscow relaxed its rigid control over Eastern Europe, people there saw a historic opportunity to reorganize political and economic life and claim greater freedom.

5. **Mobilization for action.** Once people share a concern about some issue, they are ready to take action—to distribute leaflets, stage rallies, and build alliances with sympathetic groups. The initial success of the Solidarity movement in Poland—supported by the Reagan administration in the United States and by Pope John Paul II in the Vatican—mobilized people throughout Eastern Europe to press for change. The rate of change became faster and faster: What had taken a decade in Poland required only months in Hungary and only weeks in other Eastern European nations.

6. **Lack of social control.** The success of any social movement depends in large part on the response of political officials, police, and the military. Sometimes the state moves swiftly to crush a social movement, as happened in the case of prodemocracy forces in the People's Republic of China. But Gorbachev adopted a policy of nonintervention in Eastern Europe, opening the door for change. Ironically, the movements that began in Eastern Europe soon spread to the Soviet Union itself, ending the historical domination of the Communist party in 1991 and producing a new and much looser political confederation.

EVALUATE Smelser's analysis explains how various factors help or hurt the development of social movements. Structural-strain theory also explains why people may respond to their problems either by forming organized social movements or through spontaneous mob action.

Yet Smelser's theory contains some of the same circularity of argument found in Kornhauser's analysis. A social movement is caused by strain, says Smelser, but the only evidence of underlying strain is often the social movement itself. What's more, structural-strain theory is incomplete, overlooking the important role that resources like the mass media or international alliances play in the success or failure of a social movement (Jenkins & Perrow, 1977; McCarthy & Zald, 1977; Olzak & West, 1991).

CHECK YOUR LEARNING According to structural-strain theory, what six factors encourage the formation of social movements? What are two criticisms of this theory?

Political-Economy Theory

Marxist *political-economy theory* also has something to say about social movements. From this point of view, social movements arise in capitalist societies because the capitalist economic system fails to meet the needs of the majority of people. Despite record corporate profits, U.S. society is in crisis with tens of millions of people unable to find good jobs, living below the poverty line, and living without health insurance.

Social movements arise as a response to such conditions. Workers organize to demand higher wages, citizens rally for a health policy that will protect everyone, and people march in opposition to spending billions to fund wars at the expense of social welfare programs (Buechler, 2000).

EVALUATE A strength of political-economy theory is its macro-level approach. Other theories explain the rise of social movements in terms of traits of individuals (such as weak social ties or a sense of relative deprivation) or traits of movements (such as their available resources), but this approach focuses on the institutional structures (the economy and political system) of society itself.

This approach explains social movements concerned with economic issues. But it is less helpful in accounting for the recent rise of social movements concerned with noneconomic issues such as obesity, animal rights, and the state of the natural environment.

CHECK YOUR LEARNING State the basic idea of the political-economy theory of social movements. What is the main criticism of this theory?

New Social Movements Theory

A final theoretical approach addresses what are often called "new social movements." *New social movements theory* suggests that recent social movements in the postindustrial societies of North America and Western Europe have a new focus (McAdam, McCarthy, & Zald, 1988; Pakulski, 1993; Jenkins & Wallace, 1996).

First, older social movements, such as those led by labor organizations, are concerned mostly with economic issues, but new social movements tend to focus on improving our social and physical surroundings. The environmental movement, for example, is trying to stop global warming and address other environmental dangers such as nuclear safety and conservation of natural resources.

Second, most of today's social movements are international, focusing on global ecology, the social standing of women and gay people, animal rights, and opposition to war. In other words, as the process of globalization links the world's nations, social movements are becoming global.

Third, most social movements of the past drew strong support from working-class people, but new social movements that focus on noneconomic issues usually draw support from the middle and upper-middle classes. As discussed in Chapter 17 ("Politics and Government"), more affluent people tend to be more conservative on economic issues (because they have wealth to protect) but more liberal on social issues (partly as a result of extensive education). In the United States and other rich nations, the number of highly educated professionals—the people most likely to support "new social movements"—is increasing, a fact suggesting that these movements will grow (Jenkins & Wallace, 1996; F. Rose, 1997).

EVALUATE One strength of new social movements theory is recognizing that social movements have become international along with the global economy. This theory also highlights the power of the mass media and new information technology to unite people around the world in pursuit of political goals.

However, critics claim that this approach exaggerates the differences between past and present social movements. The women's movement, for example, focuses on many of the same issues—workplace conditions and pay—that have concerned labor organizations for decades. Similarly, many people protesting the use of U.S. military power consider economic equality around the world their primary goal.

CHECK YOUR LEARNING How do "new" social movements differ from "old" social movements? Each of the seven theories presented here offers some explanation of the emergence of social movements. The Summing Up table on page 686 reviews them all.

Gender and Social Movements

Gender figures prominently in the operation of social movements. In keeping with traditional ideas about gender in the United States, more men than women tend to take part in public life, including spearheading social movements.

Concern for the state of the natural environment is one example of a "new social movement," one concerned with improving our social and physical surroundings. Actor Leonardo DiCaprio recently spoke at one of the Live Earth concerts held simultaneously on seven continents to call attention to global warming and other environmental issues.

Theories of Social Movements	
Deprivation Theory	People experiencing relative deprivation begin social movements. The social movement is a means of seeking change that brings participants greater benefits. Social movements are especially likely when rising expectations are frustrated.
Mass-Society Theory	People who lack established social ties are mobilized into social movements. Periods of social breakdown are likely to spawn social movements. The social movement gives members a sense of belonging and social participation.
Culture Theory	People are drawn to a social movement by cultural symbols that define some cause as just. The movement itself tries to become a symbol of power and justice.
Resource-Mobilization Theory	People may join for all the reasons noted for the first three theories and also because of social ties to existing members. But the success or failure of a social movement depends largely on the resources available to it. Also important is the extent of opposition within the larger society.
Structural-Strain Theory	People come together because of their shared concern about the inability of society to operate as they believe it should. The growth of a social movement reflects many factors, including a belief in its legitimacy and some precipitating event that provokes action.
Political-Economy Theory	People unite to address the societal ills caused by capitalism, including unemployment, poverty, and lack of health care. Social movements are necessary because a capitalist economy inevitably fails to meet people's basic needs.
New Social Movements Theory	People who join social movements are motivated by quality-of-life issues, not necessarily economic concerns. Mobilization is national or international in scope. New social movements arise in response to the expansion of the mass media and new information technology.

Investigating Freedom Summer, a 1964 voter registration project in Mississippi, Doug McAdam (1992) found that movement members considered the job of registering African American voters in a hostile white community dangerous and therefore defined it as "men's work." Many of the women in the movement, despite more years of activist experience, ended up working in clerical or teaching assignments behind the scenes. Only the most exceptionally talented and committed women, McAdam found, were able to overcome the movement's gender barriers.

In short, women have played leading roles in many social movements (including the abolitionist and feminist movements in the United States), but male dominance has been the norm even in social movements that otherwise oppose the status quo. At the same time, the recent political movement that brought change to Egypt included women as well as men in the leadership, suggesting a trend toward greater gender equality (Herda-Rapp, 1998; MacFarquhar, 2011).

Stages in Social Movements

Despite the many differences that set one social movement apart from another, all unfold in roughly the same way, as shown in Figure 23–2. Researchers have identified four stages in the life of the typical social movement (Blumer, 1969; Mauss, 1975; Tilly, 1978):

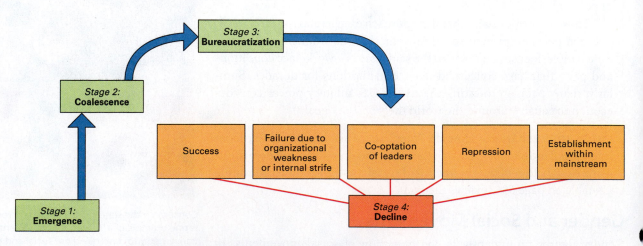

FIGURE 23–2 Stages in the Life of Social Movements

Social movements typically go through four stages. The last is decline, which may occur for any of five reasons.

Stage 1: Emergence

Social movements are driven by the perception that all is not well. Some, such as the civil rights and women's movements, are born of widespread dissatisfaction. Others emerge only as a small vanguard group increases public awareness of some issue. Gay activists, for example, helped raise public concern about the threat posed by AIDS.

Stage 2: Coalescence

After emerging, a social movement must define itself and develop a strategy for "going public." Leaders must determine policies, decide on tactics to be used, build morale, and recruit new members. At this stage, the movement may engage in collective action, such as rallies or demonstrations, to attract the attention of the media and increase public awareness. The movement may also form alliances with other organizations to acquire necessary resources.

Stage 3: Bureaucratization

To become a political force, a social movement must become an established, bureaucratic organization, as described in Chapter 7 ("Groups and Organizations"). As this happens, the movement relies less on the charisma and talents of a few leaders and more on a capable staff. When social movements do not become established in this way, they risk dissolving if the leader steps down, as is the case with many organizations of college activists. By contrast, the National Organization for Women (NOW) is well established and can be counted on to speak for feminists despite its changing leadership.

But becoming more bureaucratic can also hurt a social movement. Surveying the fate of various social movements in U.S. history, Piven and Cloward (1977) found that leaders sometimes become so engrossed in building an organization that they neglect the need to keep people "fired up" for change. In such cases, the radical edge of protest is lost.

Stage 4: Decline

Eventually, most social movements begin to decline. Frederick Miller (1983) suggests four reasons this can occur.

First, if members have met their goals, decline may simply signal success. For example, the women's suffrage movement disbanded after it won the right for women to vote. But as is the case with the modern women's movement, winning one victory leads to the setting of new goals.

Second, a social movement may fold because of organizational failures, such as poor leadership, loss of interest among members, insufficient funds, or repression by authorities. Some people lose interest when the excitement of early efforts is replaced by day-to-day routine. Fragmentation due to internal conflicts over goals and strategies is another common problem. Students for a Democratic Society (SDS), a student movement opposing the Vietnam War, splintered into several small factions by the end of the 1960s as members disagreed over goals and strategies for change.

Third, a social movement can fall apart if leaders are attracted by offers of money, prestige, or power from within the "system." This type of "selling out" is one example of the iron law of oligarchy, discussed in Chapter 7 ("Groups and Organizations"): Organizational leaders can use their position to serve their own interests. For example, Vernon Jordan, once head of the activist National Urban League, became a close adviser to President Clinton and a rich and powerful Washington insider. But this process can also work the other way: Some people give up high-paying careers to become activists. Cat Stevens, a rock star of the 1970s, became a Muslim, changed his name to Yusuf Islam, and since then has devoted his life to the spread of his religion.

Fourth and finally, a social movement can be crushed by repression. Officials may destroy a social movement by frightening away participants, discouraging new recruits, and even imprisoning leaders. In general, the more revolutionary the social movement is, the more officials try to repress it. Until 1990, the government of South Africa banned the African National Congress (ANC), a political organization seeking to overthrow the state-supported system of apartheid. Even suspected members of the ANC were subject to arrest. Only after 1990, when the government lifted the decades-old ban and released from prison ANC leader Nelson Mandela (who was elected the country's president in 1994) did South Africa begin the journey away from apartheid.

Beyond the reasons noted by Miller, a fifth cause of decline is that a social movement may "go mainstream." Some movements become an accepted part of the system—typically, after realizing some of their goals—so that they continue to flourish but no longer challenge the status quo. The U.S. labor movement, for example, is now well established; its leaders control vast sums of money and, according to some critics, now have more in common with the business tycoons they opposed in the past than with rank-and-file workers.

Social Movements and Social Change

Watch in **MySocLab** Video: *The Big Picture: Collective Behavior and Social Movements*

Social movements exist to encourage or to resist social change. The political life of our society is based largely on the claims and counterclaims of social movements about what the problems are and which are the right solutions.

But there is little doubt that social movements have changed our way of life. Sometimes we overlook the success of past social movements and take for granted the changes that other people struggled so hard to win. Beginning a century ago, workers' movements in the United States fought to end child labor in factories, limit working hours, make the workplace safer, and establish workers' right to bargain collectively with employers. Today's laws protecting the environment are another product of successful social movements. In addition, women now enjoy greater legal rights and economic opportunities because of the battles won by earlier generations of women.

As the Controversy & Debate box on page 689 explains, some college students become part of movements seeking social and political goals. What about you? Keeping in mind the importance of social movements to the future direction of society, are you willing to take a stand?

Social Movements: Looking Ahead

Especially since the turbulent 1960s—a decade marked by widespread social protests—U.S. society has been pushed and pulled by many social movements and counter-movements calling attention to issues from abortion to financing political campaigns to medical care to war. Of course, different people define the problems in different ways, just as they are likely to settle on different policies as solutions. In short, social movements and the problems they address are always *political* (Macionis, 2013).

For three reasons, the scope of social movements is likely to increase. First, protest should increase as women, African Americans, gay people, and other historically marginalized categories of our population gain a greater political voice. Second, at a global level, the technology made available by the Information Revolution means that anyone with a television, a personal computer, or a cell phone can be well informed about political events, often as soon as they happen. Third, because of new technology and the emerging global economy, social movements are now uniting people throughout the entire world. Because many problems are global in scope, we can expect the formation of international social movements seeking to solve them.

Controversy & Debate

Are You Willing to Take a Stand?

Myisha: Why don't more students on this campus get involved?
Deanna: I have more to do now than I can handle. Who's got time to save the world?
Justin: Somebody had better care. The world needs a lot of help!

Are you satisfied with our society as it is? Surely, everyone would change some things about our way of life. Indeed, surveys show that if they could, a lot of people would change plenty! There is considerable pessimism about the state of U.S. society, as shown in the responses to this question: "All in all, are you satisfied with the way things are going in this country?" (Pew Research Center, 2013). Just 30 percent of a representative sample of U.S. adults said "yes" and 66 percent said they were dissatisfied (the remaining 4 percent were unsure).

In light of such widespread dissatisfaction, you might think that most people would be willing to do something about it. You'd be wrong. Survey results show that just 23 percent report giving money to some organization seeking social change, and just 6 percent of U.S. adults say they joined a rally or a march in the last five years (NORC, 2013:1527–28).

Many college students probably suspect that age has something to do with such apathy. That is, young people have the interest and idealism to challenge the status quo, but older adults worry only about their families and their jobs. That sentiment was certainly expressed back in one of the popular sayings of the activist 1960s: "You can't trust anyone over thirty."

But the evidence suggests that it is the times that have changed: Students entering college in 2012 expressed less interest in political issues than their counterparts in the 1960s and 1970s.

As the figure shows, when asked about their activities during the past year, just 34.5 percent of first-year students included "keeping up to date with political affairs." In addition, just 26.1 percent of students reported participating in a boycott, rally, or protest in support of a cause, 30.7 percent of students claimed that they had discussed politics frequently during the past year, and just 9.0 percent reported working on a local, state, or national political campaign. The only item that was endorsed by anything approaching half of all students (44.1 percent) was publicly stating their opinion by using e-mail, signing a petition, or joining a blog (Pryor et al., 2013).

Certainly, people cite some good reasons to avoid political controversy. Anytime we challenge the system—whether on campus or in the national political arena—we risk being criticized and perhaps even making enemies.

But the most important reason that people in the United States avoid joining in social movements may have to do with cultural norms about how change should occur. In our individualistic culture, people favor taking personal responsibility over collective action as a means of addressing social problems. For example, when asked about the best way to deal with problems of inequality linked to race, class, and gender, most U.S. adults say that individuals should rely on hard work and their own efforts, and only a few point to social movements and political activism as the best way to bring about change. This individualistic orientation may be the reason that adults in this country are only half as likely as their European counterparts to join in lawful demonstrations (Inglehart et al., 2013).

Sociology, of course, poses a counterpoint to our cultural individualism. As C. Wright Mills (1959) explained decades ago, many of the problems we encounter as individuals are caused by the structure of society. As a result, said Mills, solutions to many of life's problems depend on collective effort—that is, on people willing to take a stand for what they believe.

Student Snapshot

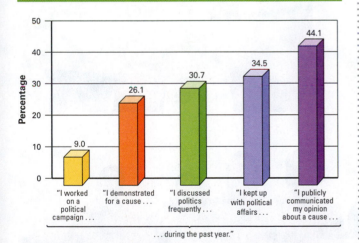

Political Involvement of Students Entering College in 2012: A Survey

First-year college students are mostly younger people who express limited interest in politics.

Source: Pryor et al. (2013).

What Do You Think?

1. Have you ever participated in a political demonstration? What were its goals? What did it accomplish?

2. What about the fact that most eighteen- to twenty-four-year-olds in the United States do not bother to vote? How do you explain such political apathy?

3. What are the most visible political organizations on your campus? Have you considered finding out more about their goals and activities?

Seeing Sociology in Everyday Life

CHAPTER 23 Collective Behavior and Social Movements

What is the scope of today's social movements?

Social movements are about trying to create or resist change. Some movements have a local focus, others are national in scope, and still others tackle international or global issues.

This group of high school students in Austin, Texas, recently took to the streets as part of an "Up in Smoke" movement seeking higher cigarette taxes and other government action to reduce the use of tobacco products by Texans. Can you imagine a countermovement on this issue? What might its goal be?

These students at Philadelphia's Temple University are taking part in a national social movement aimed at promoting the social diversity of college and university campuses. Has a similar social movement been evident on your campus?

The AIDS epidemic is threatening people all around the world. These students at George Washington University recently wrapped themselves in red tape as a way of saying that the federal government needs to do more to combat global AIDS. How might this global issue affect us here in the United States?

HINT Every social movement makes a claim about how the world should be. In just about every case, some people disagree, perhaps giving rise to a countermovement. Certainly, many people might agree that tobacco products are harmful, but they also might argue that the best way to reduce tobacco use is not by government action (reducing people's freedom) but by educating people to make better choices or by instituting programs to help people who try to quit. Likewise, "diversity" movements may attract opposition from people opposed to affirmative action or other programs that they see as favoring some racial category. Finally, almost all global issues are also local issues in that they affect life here at home. After all, a disease spreading around the world is a threat to everyone. Countries ravaged by AIDS or hunger can become unstable, threatening global peace.

Seeing Sociology in *Your* Everyday Life

1. What social movements are represented by organizations on your campus? Invite several leaders to describe their group's goals and strategies to your class.

2. Go to MySocLab and click on the Student Resources link to access the Sociology in Focus blog, where you can read the latest posts by a team of young sociologists who apply the sociological perspective to topics of popular culture.

3. Are you engaged with social movements on your campus or in your local community? Go to the "Seeing Sociology in *Your* Everyday Life" feature in MySocLab to learn more about the importance of social movements and also for suggestions about how you can make a greater difference in the world around you.

Making the Grade

Studying Collective Behavior

23.1 Distinguish various types of collective behavior. (pp. 666–67)

Collective behavior differs from group behavior:
- Collectivities contain people who have little or no social interaction.
- Collectivities have no clear social boundaries.
- Collectivities generate weak and unconventional norms.

collective behavior activity involving a large number of people that is unplanned, often controversial, and sometimes dangerous

collectivity a large number of people whose minimal interaction occurs in the absence of well-defined and conventional norms

Localized Collectivities: Crowds

23.2 Identify five types of crowds and three explanations of crowd behavior. (pp. 667–71)

Crowds, an important type of collective behavior, take various forms:
- casual crowds
- conventional crowds
- expressive crowds
- acting crowds
- protest crowds

crowd a temporary gathering of people who share a common focus of attention and who influence one another

mob a highly emotional crowd that pursues a violent or destructive goal

riot a social eruption that is highly emotional, violent, and undirected

Mobs and Riots

Crowds that become emotionally intense can create violent mobs and riots.
- **Mobs** pursue a specific goal; **rioting** involves unfocused destruction.
- Crowd behavior can threaten the status quo, which is why crowds have figured heavily in social change throughout history.

Theories of Crowd Behavior

Social scientists have developed several explanations of crowd behavior:
- **Contagion theory** views crowds as anonymous, suggestible, and swayed by rising emotions.
- **Convergence theory** states that crowd behavior reflects the desires people bring to them.
- **Emergent-norm theory** suggests that crowds develop their own behavior as events unfold.

Dispersed Collectivities: Mass Behavior

23.3 Describe rumor, disasters, and other types of mass behavior. (pp. 671–77)

Rumor and Gossip

Rumor—unconfirmed information that people spread informally—thrives in a climate of uncertainty and is difficult to stop.
- Rumor, which involves public issues, can trigger the formation of crowds or other collective behavior.
- **Gossip** is rumor about people's personal affairs.

Public Opinion and Propaganda

Public opinion consists of people's positions on important, controversial issues.
- Public attitudes change over time, and at any time on any given issue, a small share of people will hold no opinion at all.
- Special-interest groups and political leaders try to shape public attitudes by using **propaganda.**

Fashions and Fads

People living in industrial societies use **fashion** as a source of social prestige.

mass behavior collective behavior among people spread over a wide geographic area

rumor unconfirmed information that people spread informally, often by word of mouth or by using electronic devices

gossip rumor about people's personal affairs

public opinion widespread attitudes about controversial issues

propaganda information presented with the intention of shaping public opinion

fashion a social pattern favored by a large number of people

fad an unconventional social pattern that people embrace briefly but enthusiastically

panic a form of collective behavior in which people in one place react to a threat or other stimulus with irrational, frantic, and often self-destructive behavior

- **Fads** are more unconventional than fashions; although people may follow a fad with enthusiasm, it usually goes away in a short time.
- Fashions reflect basic cultural values, which make them more enduring.

Panic and Mass Hysteria

A **panic** (in a local area) and **mass hysteria** (across an entire society) are types of collective behavior in which people respond to a significant event, real or imagined, with irrational, frantic, and often self-destructive behavior.

Disasters

Disasters are generally unexpected events that cause great harm to many people. Disasters are of three types:

- *natural disasters* (Example: the 2011 earthquake in Japan)
- *technological disasters* (Example: the 2010 oil spill in the Gulf of Mexico)
- *intentional disasters* (Examples: Syria's recent conflict; Darfur genocide)

mass hysteria (moral panic) a form of dispersed collective behavior in which people react to a real or imagined event with irrational and even frantic fear

disaster an event, generally unexpected, that causes extensive harm to people and damage to property

---

Social Movements

23.4 Analyze the causes and consequences of social movements. (pp. 677–78)

 Watch the **Video** in **MySocLab**   **Watch** the **Video** in **MySocLab**

 Read the **Document** in **MySocLab**   ✳ **Explore** the **Map** in **MySocLab**

 Watch the **Video** in **MySocLab**

Social movements are an important type of collective behavior.

- Social movements try to promote or discourage change, and they often have a lasting effect on society.

Types of Social Movements

Sociologists classify social movements according to the range of people they try to involve and the extent of change they try to accomplish:

- *Alterative social movements* seek limited change in specific individuals. (Example: Promise Keepers)
- *Redemptive social movements* seek radical change in specific individuals. (Example: Alcoholics Anonymous)
- *Reformative social movements* seek limited change in the whole society. (Example: the environmental movement)
- *Revolutionary social movements* seek radical change in the whole society. (Example: the Communist party)

Explaining Social Movements

- **Deprivation theory:** Social movements arise among people who feel deprived of something, such as income, safe working conditions, or political rights.
- **Mass-society theory:** Social movements attract socially isolated people who join a movement in order to gain a sense of identity and purpose.
- **Culture theory:** Social movements depend not only on money and resources but also on cultural symbols that motivate people.
- **Resource-mobilization theory:** Success of a social movement is linked to available resources, including money, labor, and the mass media.
- **Structural-strain theory:** A social movement develops as the result of six factors. Clearly stated grievances encourage the formation of social movements; undirected anger, by contrast, promotes rioting.
- **Political-economy theory:** Social movements arise within capitalist societies that fail to meet the needs of a majority of people.
- **New social movements theory:** Social movements in postindustrial societies are typically international in scope and focus on quality-of-life issues.

social movement an organized activity that encourages or discourages social change

claims making the process of trying to convince the public and public officials of the importance of joining a social movement to address a particular issue

relative deprivation a perceived disadvantage arising from some specific comparison

Stages in Social Movements

A typical social movement proceeds through consecutive stages:

- *emergence* (defining the public issue)
- *coalescence* (entering the public arena)
- *bureaucratization* (becoming formally organized)
- *decline* (due to failure or, sometimes, success)

24 Social Change: Traditional, Modern, and Postmodern Societies

Listen to Chapter 24 in MySocLab

LEARNING OBJECTIVES

24.1 State four defining characteristics of social change.

24.2 Explain how culture, conflict, ideas, and population patterns direct social change.

24.3 Apply the ideas of Tönnies, Durkheim, Weber, and Marx to our understanding of modernity.

24.4 Contrast analysis of modernity as mass society and as class society.

24.5 Discuss postmodernism as one type of social criticism.

24.6 Evaluate possible directions of future social change.

the Power of Society

to shape our view of science

Survey Question: "In the long run, do you think the scientific advances we are making will help or harm humanity?"

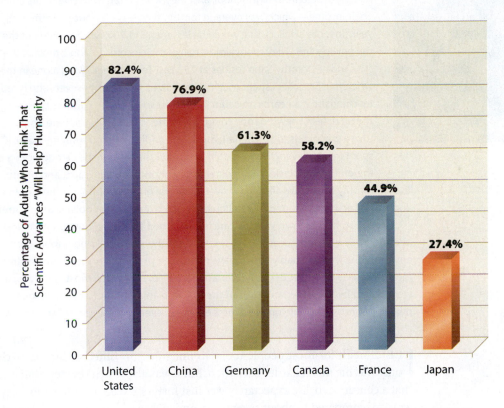

Source: Inglehart et al. (2013)

Doesn't everyone agree that science is useful to humanity? People in the United States overwhelmingly favor science. In fact, the share of our adult population claiming that scientific advances will benefit humanity is 82 percent—the highest of any nation in the world. Most European societies are more divided over whether science is helpful or harmful. Among high-income people, the Japanese (the only population to experience the horrors of the atomic bomb in war) are the least positive about the consequences of science. Clearly, attitudes about scientific advances and other dimensions of change are not simply personal; they also reflect the society in which people live.

Chapter Overview

This chapter explores social change, explaining how modern societies differ from earlier traditional societies. It begins by describing the process of social change and identifying many of its causes.

The five-story, red brick apartment building at 253 East Tenth Street in New York City has been standing for more than a century. In 1900, one of the twenty small apartments in the building was occupied by thirty-nine-year-old Julius Streicher; Christine Streicher, age thirty-three; and their four young children. The Streichers were immigrants, having come in 1885 from their native Germany to New York, where they met and married.

The Streichers probably considered themselves successful. Julius operated a small clothing shop a few blocks from his apartment; Christine stayed at home, raised the children, and did the housework. Like most people in the country at that time, neither Julius nor Christine had graduated from high school, and they worked ten to twelve hours a day, six days a week. Their income—which was average for that time—was about $35 a month, or roughly $425 a year. (In today's dollars, that would be less than $11,700, which would put the family well below the poverty line.) They spent almost half of their income for food; most of the rest went for rent.

Today, Dorothy Sabo resides at 253 East Tenth Street, living alone in the same apartment where the Streichers spent much of their lives. Now eighty-seven, she is retired from a career teaching art at a nearby museum. In many respects, Sabo's life has been far easier than the life the Streichers knew. For one thing, when the Streichers lived there, the building had no electricity (people used kerosene lamps and candles) and no running water (Christine Streicher spent most of every Monday doing laundry using water she carried from a public fountain at the end of the block). There were no telephones, no television, and of course no computers. Today, Dorothy Sabo takes all these conveniences for granted. Although she is hardly rich, her pension and Social Security amount to several times as much (in constant dollars) as the Streichers earned.

But Sabo has her own worries. She is concerned about the environment and often speaks out about global warming. A century ago, if the Streichers and their neighbors complained about "the environment," they probably would have meant the smell coming up from the street. At a time when motor vehicles were just beginning to appear in New York City, most carriages, trucks, and trolleys were pulled by horses—thousands of them. These animals dumped 60,000 gallons of urine and 2.5 million pounds of manure on the streets each and every day (Simon & Cannon, 2001).

It is difficult for most people today to imagine how different life was a century ago. Not only was life much harder back then, but it was also much shorter. Statistical records show that a century ago, life expectancy was just forty-six years for men and forty-eight years for women, compared to about seventy-six and eighty-one years today (Hoyert & Xu, 2012).

Over the past 100 years, much has changed for the better. Yet as this chapter explains, social change is not all positive. Even changes for the better can have negative consequences, creating unexpected new problems. Early sociologists were mixed in their assessment of *modernity,* changes brought about by the Industrial Revolution. Likewise, today's sociologists point to both good and bad aspects of *postmodernity,* the recent transformations of society caused by the Information Revolution and the postindustrial economy. One thing is clear: For better and worse, the rate of change has never been faster than it is now.

What Is Social Change?

24.1 State four defining characteristics of social change.

In earlier chapters, we examined relatively fixed or *static* social patterns, including status and role, social stratification, and social institutions. We also looked at the *dynamic* forces that have shaped our way of life, ranging from innovations in technology to the growth of bureaucracy and the expansion of cities. These are all dimensions of

social change, *the transformation of culture and social institutions over time.* The process of social change has four major characteristics:

social change the transformation of culture and social institutions over time

1. **Social change happens all the time.** "Nothing is constant except death and taxes" goes the old saying. Yet our thoughts about death have changed dramatically as life expectancy in the United States has doubled over the past 100 or so years. And back in the Streichers' day, people in the United States paid no taxes on their earnings; taxation increased dramatically over the course of the twentieth century, along with the size and scope of government. In short, even the things that seem constant are subject to the twists and turns of change.

   Still, some societies change faster than others. As Chapter 4 ("Society") explained, hunting and gathering societies change quite slowly; members of today's high-income societies, by contrast, experience significant change within a single lifetime.

   It is also true that in a given society, some cultural elements change faster than others. William Ogburn's theory of *cultural lag* (1964; see Chapter 3, "Culture") states that material culture (that is, things) usually changes faster than nonmaterial culture (ideas and attitudes). For example, the genetic technology that allows scientists to alter and perhaps even create life has developed more rapidly than our ethical standards for deciding when and how to use the technology.

2. **Social change is sometimes intentional but often it is unplanned.** Industrial societies actively promote many kinds of change. For example, scientists seek more efficient forms of energy, and advertisers try to convince us that life is incomplete without a 4G cell phone or the latest electronic gadget. Yet rarely can anyone envision all the consequences of the changes that are set in motion.

   Back in 1900, when the country still relied on horses for transportation, many people looked ahead to motorized vehicles that would carry them in a single day distances that used to take weeks or months. But no one could see how much the mobility provided by automobiles would alter everyday life in the United States, scattering family members, threatening the environment, and reshaping cities and suburbs. Nor could automotive pioneers have predicted the almost 33,000 deaths that occur in car accidents each year in the United States alone (National Highway Traffic Safety Administration, 2012).

3. **Social change is controversial.** The history of the automobile shows that social change brings both good and bad consequences. Capitalists welcomed the Industrial Revolution because new technology increased productivity and swelled profits. However, workers feared that machines would make their skills obsolete and resisted the push toward "progress."

   Today, as in the past, people disagree about how we ought to live and what we should welcome as "progress." We see this disagreement every day in the changing patterns of social interaction between black people and white people, women and men, and gays and heterosexuals that are welcomed by some people and opposed by others.

4. **Some changes matter more than others.** Some changes (such as clothing fads) have only passing significance; others (like the invention of computers) may change the world. Will the Information Revolution turn out to be as important as the Industrial Revolution? Like the automobile and television, the computer has both positive and negative effects, providing new kinds of jobs while eliminating old ones, linking people in global electronic networks while isolating people in offices, offering vast amounts of information while threatening personal privacy.

In response to the accelerating pace of change in the nineteenth century, Paul Gauguin left his native France for the South Pacific, where he was captivated by a simpler and seemingly timeless way of life. He romanticized this environment in many paintings, including *Nave Nave Moe (Sacred Spring)*.

Paul Gauguin, French (1848–1903), *Nave Nave Moe (Sacred Spring)*, 1894. Hermitage, Saint Petersburg, Russia. Oil on canvas, 73 × 98 cm. © The Bridgeman Art Library International Ltd.

Causes of Social Change

24.2 Explain how culture, conflict, ideas, and population patterns direct social change.

Social change has many causes. In a world linked by sophisticated communication and transportation technology, change in one place often sets off change elsewhere.

Culture and Change

Chapter 3 ("Culture") identified three important sources of cultural change. First, *invention* produces new objects, ideas, and social patterns. Rocket propulsion research, which began in the 1940s, has produced spacecraft that reach toward the stars. Today we take such technology for granted; during this century, a significant number of people may well have an opportunity to travel in space.

Second, *discovery* occurs when people take note of existing elements of the world. For example, medical advances enhance understanding of the human body. Beyond the direct effects on human health, medical discoveries have stretched life expectancy, setting in motion the "graying" of U.S. society (see Chapter 15, "Aging and the Elderly").

Third, *diffusion* creates change as products, people, and information spread from one society to another. Ralph Linton (1937a) recognized that many familiar elements of our culture came from other lands. For example, the cloth used to make our clothing was developed in Asia, the clocks we see all around us were invented in Europe, and the coins we carry in our pockets were devised in what is now Turkey.

In general, material things change more quickly than cultural ideas. That is, breakthroughs such as the science of altering and perhaps even creating life are taking place faster than our understanding of when—and even whether—they are morally desirable.

Conflict and Change

Inequality and conflict in a society also produce change. Karl Marx saw class conflict as the engine that drives societies from one historical era to another (see Chapter 4, "Society," and Chapter 10, "Social Stratification"). In industrial-capitalist societies, he maintained, the struggle between capitalists and workers pushes society toward a socialist system of production.

In the 130 years since Marx's death, this model has proved simplistic. Yet Marx correctly foresaw that social conflict arising from inequality (involving not just class but also race and gender) would force changes in every society, including our own, to improve the lives of working people.

Ideas and Change

Max Weber also contributed to our understanding of social change. Although Weber agreed that conflict could bring about change, he traced the roots of most social change to ideas. For example, people with charisma (Martin Luther King Jr. is one example) can carry a message that changes the world.

Weber also highlighted the importance of ideas by showing how the religious beliefs of early Protestants set the stage for the spread of industrial capitalism (see Chapter 4, "Society"). The fact that industrial capitalism developed primarily in areas of Western Europe where the Protestant work ethic was strong proved to Weber (1958, orig. 1904–05) the power of ideas to bring about change.

These young men are performing in a hip-hop dance marathon in Hong Kong. Hip-hop music, dress style, and dancing have become popular in Asia, a clear case of cultural diffusion. Social change occurs as cultural patterns move from place to place, but people in different societies don't always have the same understanding of what these patterns mean. How might Chinese youth understand hip-hop differently from the young African Americans in the United States who originated it?

Ideas also direct social movements. Chapter 23 ("Collective Behavior and Social Movements") explained how change occurs when people join together in the pursuit of a common goal, such as cleaning up the environment or improving the lives of oppressed people.

Demographic Change

Population patterns also play a part in social change. A century ago, as the chapter opening suggested, the typical household (4.8 people) was almost twice as large as it is today (2.6 people). Women are having fewer children, and more people are living alone. In addition, change is taking place as our population grows older. As Chapter 15 ("Aging and the Elderly") explained, 13 percent of the U.S. population was over age sixty-five in 2011, three times the proportion in 1900. By the year 2035, seniors will account for 20 percent of the U.S. population and their numbers will exceed the nation's entire population in 1900 (U.S. Census Bureau, 2012). Medical research and health care services already focus extensively on the elderly, and life will change in countless additional ways as homes and household products are redesigned to meet the needs of older consumers.

Migration within and among societies is another demographic factor that promotes change. Between 1870 and 1930, tens of millions of immigrants entered the industrial cities in the United States. Millions more from rural areas joined the rush. As a result, farm communities declined, cities expanded, and by 1920, the United States had for the first time become a mostly urban nation. Similar changes are taking place today as people move from the Snowbelt to the Sunbelt and mix with new immigrants from Latin America and Asia.

Where in the United States have demographic changes been greatest, and which areas have been least affected? National Map 24-1 provides one answer, showing counties where the largest numbers of people have lived in their present homes since 1979.

Seeing Ourselves

 **Explore** residential stability in your local community and in counties across the United States in **MySocLab**

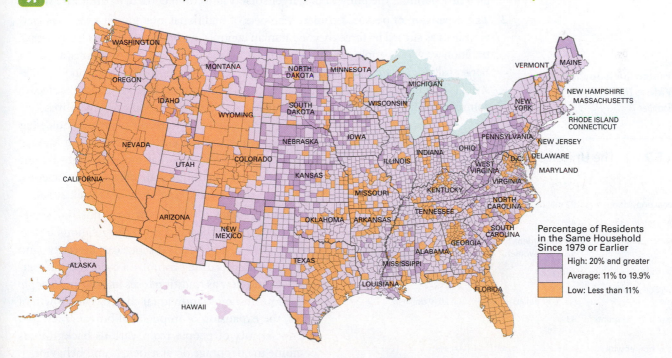

NATIONAL MAP 24-1 Who Stays Put? Residential Stability across the United States

As of 2011, only about 11 percent of housing units in the United States contain people who have lived there since 1979. Counties with a higher proportion of "long-term neighbors" typically have experienced less change over recent decades: Many neighborhoods have been in place since before World War II, and many of the same families live in them. As you look at the map, what can you say about these stable areas? What accounts for the fact that most of these counties are rural and at some distance from the coasts?

Source: U.S. Census Bureau (2012).

Modernity

24.3 Apply the ideas of Tönnies, Durkheim, Weber, and Marx to our understanding of modernity.

modernity changes brought about by the Industrial Revolution

modernization the process of social change begun by industrialization

A central concept in the study of social change is **modernity,** *changes brought about by the Industrial Revolution.* In everyday usage, *modernity* (its Latin root means "lately") refers to the present in relation to the past. Sociologists include in this catchall concept all of the social patterns that were set in motion by the Industrial Revolution, which began in Western Europe in the 1750s. **Modernization,** then, is *the process of social change begun by industrialization.* The timeline in MySocLab highlights important events that mark the emergence of modernity. Table 24-1 provides a snapshot of some of the changes that took place during the twentieth century.

Four Dimensions of Modernization

Peter Berger (1977) identified four major characteristics of modernization, described on the following pages.

1. **The decline of small, traditional communities.** Modernity involves "the progressive weakening, if not destruction, of the … relatively cohesive communities in which human beings have found solidarity and meaning throughout most of history" (1977:72). For thousands of years, in the camps of hunters and gatherers and in the rural villages of Europe and North America, people lived in small communities where social life revolved around family and neighborhood. Such traditional worlds gave each person a well-defined place that, although limiting the range of choice, offered a strong sense of identity, belonging, and purpose.

   Small, isolated communities still exist in remote corners of the United States, of course, but they are home to only a small percentage of our nation's people. These days, their isolation is only geographic: Except among those who are extremely poor or who reject modernity on religious grounds, cars, telephones, television, and the Internet give rural families the pulse of the larger society and connect them to the entire world.

2. **The expansion of personal choice.** Members of traditional, preindustrial societies view their lives as shaped by forces beyond human control—gods, spirits, fate. As the power of tradition weakens, people come to see their lives as an unending series of options, a process Berger calls *individualization.* Many people in the United States, for example, choose a "lifestyle" (sometimes adopting one after another), showing an openness to change. Indeed, a common belief in our modern culture is that people *should* take control of their lives.

   Widespread support for greater personal choice has political consequences. A cultural orientation toward greater individualism means that modern, high-income societies (compared to traditional, low-income societies) are likely to be democratic (Inglehart & Welzel, 2010).

3. **Increasing social diversity.** In preindustrial societies, strong family ties and powerful religious beliefs enforce conformity and discourage diversity and change. Modernization promotes a more rational, scientific worldview as tradition loses its hold and people gain more and more individual choice. The growth of cities, the expansion of impersonal bureaucracy, and the social mix of people from various backgrounds combine to encourage diverse beliefs and behavior.

4. **Orientation toward the future and a growing awareness of time.** Premodern people model their lives on the past, but people in modern societies think more about the future. Modern people are not only forward-looking but also optimistic that new inventions and discoveries will improve their lives.

Watch in **MySocLab**
Video: *The Big Picture: Families*

TABLE 24-1 The United States: A Century of Change

	1910	2010
National population	92 million	309 million
Share living in cities	46%	84%
Life expectancy	48 years (men), 52 years (women)	76 years (men), 81 years (women)
Median age	24.1 years	37.2 years
Average household income	$8,000 (in 2010 dollars)	$60,395 (in 2010 dollars)
Share of income spent on food	43%	13%
Share of homes with flush toilets	10%	99.4%
Average number of cars	1 car for every 64 households	2.2 cars for every household
Divorce rate	about 1 in 20 marriages	about 6 in 20 marriages
Average gallons of petroleum products consumed	34 per person per year	1,100 per person per year

Traditional people organize their lives around sunlight and seasons. With the introduction of clocks in the late Middle Ages, Europeans began to organize their lives in terms of hours and minutes. Focused on personal gain, modern people demand precise measurement of time and are likely to agree that "time is money." Berger (inspired by Weber) points out that one good indicator of a society's degree of modernization is the share of people who keep track of time by continually glancing at their wristwatches (or nowadays, their cell phones).

Recall that modernization touched off the development of sociology itself. As Chapter 1 ("The Sociological Perspective") explained, the discipline originated in the wake of the Industrial Revolution in Western Europe, where social change was proceeding most rapidly. Early European and U.S. sociologists tried to analyze the rise of modern society and its consequences, both good and bad, for human beings.

Finally, in the process of comparing industrial societies with those that came before, we find it easy to assume that *everything* in our world is new. This is not the case, of course, as the Seeing Sociology in Everyday Life box on page 702 explains with a historical look at a favorite form of modern clothing—jeans.

Ferdinand Tönnies: The Loss of Community

The German sociologist Ferdinand Tönnies (1855–1937) produced a lasting account of modernization in his theory of *Gemeinschaft* and *Gesellschaft* (see Chapter 22, "Population, Urbanization, and Environment"). Like Peter Berger, whose work he influenced, Tönnies (1963, orig. 1887) viewed modernization as the progressive loss of *Gemeinschaft,* or human community. As Tönnies saw it, the Industrial Revolution weakened the social fabric of family and tradition by introducing a businesslike emphasis on facts, efficiency, and money. European and North American societies gradually became rootless and impersonal as people came to associate mostly on the basis of self-interest—the state Tönnies termed *Gesellschaft*.

Early in the twentieth century, at least some parts of the United States could be described using Tönnies's concept of *Gemeinschaft*. Families that had lived for generations in small villages and towns were bound together in a hardworking, slow-moving way of life. Telephones (invented in 1876) were rare; not until 1915 could a person place a coast-to-coast call. Living without television (introduced commercially in 1933 and not widespread until after 1950), families entertained themselves, often gathering with friends in the evening to share stories, sorrows, or song. Lacking rapid transportation (Henry Ford's assembly line began in 1908, but cars became common only after World War II), many people knew little of the world beyond their hometown.

Inevitable tensions and conflicts divided these communities of the past. But according to Tönnies, because of the traditional spirit of *Gemeinschaft,* people were "essentially united in spite of all separating factors" (1963:65, orig. 1887).

Modernity turns societies inside out so that, as Tönnies put it, people are "essentially separated in spite of uniting factors" (1963:65, orig. 1887). This is the world of *Gesellschaft,* where, especially in large cities, most people live among strangers and ignore the people they pass on the street. Trust is hard to come by in a mobile and anonymous society where people tend to put their personal needs ahead of group loyalty and an

George Tooker's 1950 painting *The Subway* depicts a common problem of modern life: Weakening social ties and eroding traditions create a generic humanity in which everyone is alike yet each person is an anxious stranger in the midst of others.

Source: George Tooker, *The Subway*, 1950, egg tempera on gesso panel, 18^1/8 × 36^1/8 inches, Whitney Museum of American Art, New York. Purchased with funds from the Juliana Force Purchase Award, 50.23. Photograph © Whitney Museum of American Art

Seeing Sociology in Everyday Life

Tradition and Modernity: The History of Jeans

Sociologists like to contrast "tradition" and "modernity." Tönnies, Durkheim, Weber, and even Marx developed theories that contrasted social patterns that existed "then" with those that exist "now." Such theories are enlightening. But thinking in terms of "tradition versus modernity" encourages us to think that the past and the present have little in common.

All the thinkers discussed in this chapter saw past and present as strikingly different. But it is also true that countless elements of today's society—ranging from religion to warfare—have been part of human society for a very long time. It is also the case that many cultural elements that we think of as "modern" turn out to have been around much longer than many of us realize.

One element of culture that we think of as distinctly modern is jeans. This piece of clothing, common enough to be considered almost a "uniform" among young people, moved to the center of popular culture when it swept college campuses in the late 1960s.

But many people would be surprised to learn that jeans have been worn for centuries. The term *dungarees*, a common name for jeans before the 1960s, is derived from the Hindi word *dungri*, a district of the Indian city Mumbai (formerly Bombay) where the coarse cloth is thought to have originated. From there, the fabric spread westward into Europe. The term *jeans* can be traced back to the name of the Italian city of Genoa, where the cotton fabric was widely worn in the 1650s. Another word for the fabric, *denim*, refers to the French city of Nîmes, reflecting the fact that, somewhat later, people described the cloth as being "de Nîmes."

Art historians have identified paintings from the sixteenth century that show people—typically the poor—wearing jeans. In the 1700s, British sailors used this fabric not only for making sails but also for constructing hammocks to sleep in and for fashioning shipboard clothing.

More than a century later, in 1853, U.S. clothing manufacturer Levi Strauss sold dungarees to miners who were digging for gold in the California gold rush. Strong and durable, jeans became the clothing of choice among people who had limited budgets and who did demanding physical labor.

Cowboys across the West quickly adopted the practical new style, and by the beginning of the twentieth century, jeans were worn by almost all working people. By the 1930s, most prisoners were also wearing denim.

This pattern made jeans a symbol of lower social standing, and many middle-class people looked down on them. As a result, especially in higher-income communities, public school officials banned the wearing of dungarees.

By the 1960s, however, a youth-based counterculture was emerging, that rejected the older pattern of "looking upward" and copying the styles of the rich and famous. Instead, fashion began "looking downward," adopting the look of working people and even the down and out. By the end of the 1960s, rock stars, Hollywood celebrities, and college students favored jeans as a way to make a statement that they identified with working people—part of the era's more left-leaning political attitudes.

Of course, there was money to be made in this new trend. By the 1980s, the fashion industry was cashing in on the popularity of jeans by promoting "designer jeans" among more well-off people who probably had never entered a factory in their lives. A teenage Brooke Shields helped launch Calvin Klein jeans (1980) that became all the rage among people who were able to spend three and four times as much as the jeans worn by ordinary people.

By the beginning of this century, jeans had become an accepted form of dress not only in schools but also in the corporate world. Many CEOs of U.S. corporations—especially in the high-tech fields—now routinely wear jeans to work and even to public events.

As you can see, jeans turn out to have a very long history. The fact that jeans existed both "then" and "now," all the while taking on new and different meanings, reveals the limitation of characterizing cultural elements as either "traditional" or "modern" in a world in which societies invent and reinvent their way of life all the time.

What Do You Think?

1. Is your attitude toward jeans different from that of your parents? If so, how and why?

2. Do you think the changing trend in the popularity of jeans suggests broader changes in our society before and after the 1960s? Explain.

3. How popular is wearing jeans on your campus? What about among your professors? Can you explain these patterns?

  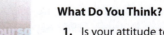

In art from the 1500s, we see poor people wearing denim. In the 1800s, jeans became the uniform for the western cowboy, and by the 1960s, they were the clothing of choice on campus. More recently, corporate executives (especially in tech companies) have made jeans acceptable in the workplace.

Source: Based, in part, on Brazilian (2011).

increasing majority of adults believe "you can't be too careful" in dealing with people (NORC, 2013:2386). No wonder researchers conclude that even as we become more affluent, the social health of modern societies has declined (Myers, 2000).

EVALUATE Tönnies's theory of *Gemeinschaft* and *Gesellschaft* is the most widely cited model of modernization. The theory's strength lies in combining various dimensions of change: growing population, the rise of cities, and increasing impersonality in social interaction. But modern life, though often impersonal, still has some degree of *Gemeinschaft*. Even in a world of strangers, modern friendships can be strong and lasting. Some analysts also think that Tönnies favored—perhaps even romanticized—traditional societies while overlooking bonds of family, neighborhood, and friendship that continue to flourish in modern societies.

CHECK YOUR LEARNING As types of social organization, how do *Gemeinschaft* and *Gesellschaft* differ?

Emile Durkheim: The Division of Labor

The French sociologist Emile Durkheim, whose work is discussed in Chapter 4 ("Society"), shared Tönnies's interest in the profound social changes that resulted from the Industrial Revolution. For Durkheim (1964a, orig. 1893), modernization is defined by an increasing **division of labor**, or *specialized economic activity*. Every member of a traditional society performs more or less the same daily round of activities; modern societies function by having people perform highly specific jobs.

division of labor specialized economic activity

Durkheim explained that preindustrial societies are held together by *mechanical solidarity*, or shared moral sentiments. In other words, members of preindustrial societies view everyone as basically alike, doing the same kind of work and belonging together. Durkheim's concept of mechanical solidarity is virtually the same as Tönnies's *Gemeinschaft*.

With modernization, the division of labor becomes more and more pronounced. To Durkheim, this change means less mechanical solidarity but more of another kind of tie: *organic solidarity*, or mutual dependency between people engaged in specialized work. Put simply, modern societies are held together not by likeness but by difference: All of us must depend on others to meet most of our needs. Organic solidarity corresponds to Tönnies's concept of *Gesellschaft*.

Despite obvious similarities in their thinking, Durkheim and Tönnies viewed modernity somewhat differently. To Tönnies, modern *Gesellschaft* amounts to the loss of social solidarity, because modern people lose the "natural" and "organic" bonds of the rural village, leaving only the "artificial" and "mechanical" ties of the big, industrial city. Durkheim had a different view of modernity, even reversing Tönnies's language to bring home the point. Durkheim labeled modern society "organic," arguing that modern society is no less natural than any other, and he described traditional societies as "mechanical" because they are so regimented. Durkheim viewed modernization not as the loss of community but as a change from community based on bonds of likeness (kinship and neighborhood) to community based on economic interdependence (the division of labor). Durkheim's view of modernity is thus both more complex and more positive than Tönnies's view.

EVALUATE Durkheim's work, which resembles that of Tönnies, is a highly influential analysis of modernity. Of the two, Durkheim was more optimistic; still, he feared that modern societies might become so diverse that they would collapse into **anomie**, *a condition in which society provides little moral guidance to individuals*. Living with weak moral norms and values, modern people can become egocentric, placing their own needs above those of others and, in their social isolation, find little purpose in life.

anomie Durkheim's term for a condition in which society provides little moral guidance to individuals`

The suicide rate—which Durkheim considered a good index of anomie—did in fact increase in the United States over the course of the twentieth century, and the vast majority of U.S. adults report that they see moral questions not in clear terms of right and wrong but in confusing "shades of gray" (NORC, 2013:607). Yet shared norms and values still seem strong enough to give most individuals some sense of meaning and

Max Weber maintained that the distinctive character of modern society was its rational worldview. Virtually all of Weber's work on modernity centered on types of people he considered typical of their age: the scientist, the capitalist, and the bureaucrat. Each is rational to the core: The scientist is committed to the orderly discovery of truth, the capitalist to the orderly pursuit of profit, and the bureaucrat to the orderly conformity to a system of rules.

purpose. Whatever the hazards of anomie, most people seem to value the personal freedom modern society gives them.

CHECK YOUR LEARNING Define mechanical solidarity and organic solidarity. In his view of the modern world, what makes Durkheim more optimistic than Tönnies?

Max Weber: Rationalization

For Max Weber (also discussed in Chapter 4, "Society"), modernity meant replacing a traditional worldview with a rational way of thinking. In preindustrial societies, tradition acts as a constant brake on change. To traditional people, "truth" is roughly the same as "what has always been" (1978:36, orig. 1921). To modern people, however, "truth" is the result of rational calculation. Because they value efficiency and have little reverence for the past, modern people readily adopt new social patterns that allow them to achieve their goals.

Echoing Tönnies and Durkheim, who held that industrialization weakens tradition, Weber declared modern society to be "disenchanted." The unquestioned truths of an earlier time are challenged by rational thinking. In short, said Weber, modern society turns away from the gods just as it turns away from the past. Throughout his life, Weber studied various modern "types"—the capitalist, the scientist, the bureaucrat—all of whom share the forward-looking, rational, and detached worldview that Weber believed was coming to dominate humanity.

EVALUATE Compared with Tönnies and especially Durkheim, Weber was very critical of modern society. He knew that science could produce technological and organizational wonders but worried that science was turning us away from more basic questions about the meaning and purpose of human existence. Weber feared that rationalization, especially in bureaucracies, would erode the human spirit with endless rules and regulations.

CHECK YOUR LEARNING How did Weber understand modernity? What does it mean to say that modern society (think of the scientists, capitalists, and bureaucrats) is "disenchanted"?

Some of Weber's critics think that the alienation he attributed to bureaucracy actually stemmed from social inequality. That criticism leads us to the ideas of Karl Marx.

Karl Marx: Capitalism

For Karl Marx, modern society was synonymous with capitalism; he saw the Industrial Revolution as primarily a *capitalist revolution*. Marx traced the emergence of the bourgeoisie in medieval Europe to the expansion of commerce. The bourgeoisie gradually displaced the feudal aristocracy as the Industrial Revolution gave it a powerful new productive system.

Marx agreed that modernity weakened small communities (as described by Tönnies), increased the division of labor (as noted by Durkheim), and encouraged a rational worldview (as Weber claimed). But he saw these simply as conditions necessary for capitalism to flourish. Capitalism, according to Marx, draws population from farms and small towns into an ever-expanding market system centered in cities; specialization is needed for efficient factories; and rationality is exemplified by the capitalists' endless pursuit of profit.

Earlier chapters have painted Marx as a spirited critic of capitalist society, but his vision of modernity also includes a good bit of optimism. Unlike Weber, who viewed modern society as an "iron cage" of bureaucracy, Marx believed that social conflict in capitalist societies would sow seeds of revolutionary change, leading to an egalitarian socialism. Such a society, as he saw it, would harness the wonders of industrial technology to enrich people's lives and also rid the world of social classes, the source of social conflict and suffering. Although Marx's evaluation of modern, capitalist society was highly negative, he imagined a future of human freedom, creativity, and community.

EVALUATE Marx's theory of modernization is a complex theory of capitalism. But he underestimated the dominance of bureaucracy in modern societies. In socialist societies in particular, the stifling effects of bureaucracy turned out to be as bad as, or even worse than, the dehumanizing aspects of capitalism. The upheavals in Eastern Europe and the former Soviet Union in the late 1980s and early 1990s reveal the depth of popular opposition to oppressive state bureaucracies.

CHECK YOUR LEARNING How did Marx understand modern society? Of the four theorists just discussed—Tönnies, Durkheim, Weber, and Marx—who comes across as the most optimistic about modern society? Who was the most pessimistic? Explain your choices.

Theories of Modernity

24.4 Contrast analysis of modernity as mass society and as class society.

The rise of modernity is a complex process involving many dimensions of change, as described in earlier chapters and summarized in the Summing Up table on page 706. How can we make sense of so many changes going on all at once? Sociologists have developed two broad explanations of modern society, one guided by the structural-functional approach and the other based on social-conflict theory.

Structural-Functional Theory: Modernity as Mass Society

One broad approach—drawing on the ideas of Ferdinand Tönnies, Emile Durkheim, and Max Weber—understands modernization as the emergence of *mass society* (Kornhauser, 1959; Nisbet, 1966; Berger, Berger, & Kellner, 1974; Pearson, 1993). A **mass society** is *a society in which prosperity and bureaucracy have weakened traditional social ties.* A mass society is highly productive; on average, people have more income than ever. At the same time, it is marked by weak kinship and impersonal neighborhoods, leaving individuals feeling socially isolated. Although many people have material plenty, they are spiritually weak and often experience moral uncertainty about how to live.

Summing Up

Traditional and Modern Societies: The Big Picture		
Elements of Society	**Traditional Societies**	**Modern Societies**
Cultural Patterns		
Values	Homogeneous; sacred character; few subcultures and countercultures	Heterogeneous; secular character; many subcultures and countercultures
Norms	Great moral significance; little tolerance of diversity	Variable moral significance; high tolerance of diversity
Time orientation	Present linked to past	Present linked to future
Technology	Preindustrial; human and animal energy	Industrial; advanced energy sources
Social Structure		
Status and role	Few statuses, most ascribed; few specialized roles	Many statuses, some ascribed and some achieved; many specialized roles
Relationships	Typically primary; little anonymity or privacy	Typically secondary; much anonymity and privacy
Communication	Face to face	Face-to-face communication supplemented by mass media
Social control	Informal gossip	Formal police and legal system
Social stratification	Rigid patterns of social inequality; little mobility	Fluid patterns of social inequality; high mobility
Gender patterns	Pronounced patriarchy; women's lives centered on the home	Declining patriarchy; increasing number of women in the paid labor force
Settlement patterns	Small-scale; population typically small and widely dispersed in rural villages and small towns	Large-scale; population typically large and concentrated in cities
Social Institutions		
Economy	Based on agriculture; much manufacturing in the home; little white-collar work	Based on industrial mass production; factories become centers of production; increasing white-collar work
State	Small-scale government; little state intervention in society	Large-scale government; much state intervention in society
Family	Extended family as the primary means of socialization and economic production	Nuclear family retains some socialization functions but is more a unit of consumption than of production
Religion	Religion guides worldview; little religious pluralism	Religion weakens with the rise of science; extensive religious pluralism
Education	Formal schooling limited to elites	Basic schooling becomes universal, with growing proportion receiving advanced education
Health	High birth and death rates; short life expectancy because of low standard of living and simple medical technology	Low birth and death rates; longer life expectancy because of higher standard of living and sophisticated medical technology
Social Change	Slow; change evident over many generations	Rapid; change evident within a single generation

The Mass Scale of Modern Life

November 11, on Interstate 275. From the car window, we see BP and Sunoco gas stations, a Kmart and a Walmart, an AmeriSuites hotel, a Bob Evans, a Chi-Chi's Mexican restaurant, and a McDonald's—all big organizations. And it's the same everywhere. This road happens to circle Cincinnati, Ohio. But it could be in Boston, Saint Louis, Denver, San Diego, or almost anywhere else in the United States.

Mass-society theory argues, first, that the scale of modern life has greatly increased. Before the Industrial Revolution, Europe and North America formed a mosaic of rural villages and small towns. In these local communities, which inspired Tönnies's concept of *Gemeinschaft,* people lived out their lives surrounded by kin and guided by a shared heritage. Gossip was an informal yet highly effective way of ensuring conformity to community standards. These small communities, with their strong moral values and their low tolerance of social diversity, exemplified the state of mechanical solidarity described by Durkheim.

For example, before 1690, English law demanded that everyone participate regularly in the Christian ritual of Holy Communion (Laslett, 1984). On the North American continent, only Rhode Island among the New England colonies tolerated religious dissent. Because social differences were repressed in favor of conformity to established norms, subcultures and countercultures were few, and change proceeded slowly.

Increasing population, the growth of cities, and specialized economic activity driven by the Industrial Revolution gradually altered this pattern. People came to know one another by their jobs (for example, as "the doctor" or "the bank clerk") rather than by their kinship group or hometown. People looked on most others as strangers. The face-to-face communication of the village was eventually replaced by the impersonal mass media: newspapers, radio, television, and the computer-based social media that link people throughout the world. Large organizations steadily assumed more and more responsibility for seeing to the daily tasks that had once been carried out by family, friends, and neighbors; public education drew more and more people to schools; police, lawyers, and courts supervised a formal criminal justice system. Even charity became the work of faceless bureaucrats working for various social welfare organizations.

Geographic mobility, mass communication, and exposure to diverse ways of life all weaken traditional values. People become more tolerant of social diversity, defending individual rights and freedom of choice. Treating people differently because of their race, sex, or religion comes to be defined as backward and unjust. In the process, minorities at the margins of society gain greater power and broader participation in public life. The election of Barack Obama—an African American—to the highest office in the United States is surely one indicator that ours is now a modern society (West, 2008).

The mass media give rise to a national culture that washes over traditional differences that used to set off one region from another. As one analyst put it, "Even in Baton Rouge, La., the local kids don't say 'y'all' anymore; they say 'you guys' just like on TV" (Gibbs, 2000:42). In this way, mass-society theorists fear, transforming people of various backgrounds into a generic mass provides greater moral freedom but it may also end up dehumanizing everyone.

The Ever-Expanding State

In the small-scale preindustrial societies of Europe, government amounted to little more than a local noble. A royal family formally reigned over an entire nation, but without efficient transportation and efficient communication, even absolute monarchs had far less power than today's political leaders.

As technological innovation allowed government to expand, the centralized state grew in size and importance. At the time the United States gained independence from Great Britain, the federal government was a tiny organization with the main purpose of providing national defense. Since then, government has assumed responsibility for more and more areas of social life: schooling the population, regulating wages and working conditions, establishing standards for products of all sorts, providing financial assistance to the elderly, the ill, and the unemployed, providing loans to students, and recently, bailing out corporations facing economic ruin. To pay for such programs, taxes have soared: Today's average worker labors about four months each year to pay for the broad array of services that government provides.

In a mass society, power resides in large bureaucracies, leaving people in local communities with little control over their lives. For example, state officials mandate that local schools must have a standardized educational program, local products must be government-certified, and every citizen must maintain extensive tax records. Although such regulations may protect people and advance social equality, they also force us to deal more and more with nameless officials in distant and often unresponsive bureaucracies, and they undermine the autonomy of families and local communities.

EVALUATE The growing scale of modern life certainly has positive aspects, but only at the price of losing some of our cultural heritage. Modern societies increase individual rights, have greater tolerance of social differences, and raise standards of living (Inglehart & Baker, 2000). But they are prone to what Weber feared most—excessive bureaucracy—as well as to Tönnies's self-centeredness and Durkheim's anomie. Modern society's size, complexity, and tolerance of diversity all but doom traditional values and family patterns, leaving individuals isolated, powerless, and materialistic. As Chapter 17 ("Politics and Government") notes, voter apathy is a serious problem in the United States. But should we be surprised that individuals in vast, impersonal societies think no one person can make much of a difference?

Social-conflict theory sees modernity not as an impersonal mass society but as an unequal class society in which some categories of people are second-class citizens. This Native American family lives on the Pine Ridge Indian Reservation in South Dakota, where poverty is widespread and many trailer homes do not have electricity or running water.

Critics sometimes say that mass-society theory romanticizes the past. They remind us that many people in the small towns of our past were actually eager to set out for a better standard of living in cities. This approach also ignores problems of social inequality. Critics say this theory attracts conservatives who defend conventional morality and overlook the historical inequality of women and other minorities.

CHECK YOUR LEARNING In your own words, state the mass-society theory of modernity. What are two criticisms of it?

Social-Conflict Theory: Modernity as Class Society

The second interpretation of modernity derives largely from the ideas of Karl Marx. From a social-conflict perspective, modernity takes the form of a **class society**, *a capitalist society with pronounced social stratification.* While agreeing that modern societies have expanded to a mass scale, this approach views the heart of modernization as an expanding capitalist economy, marked by inequality (Habermas, 1970; Harrington, 1984; Buechler, 2000).

Capitalism

Class-society theory follows Marx in claiming that the increasing scale of social life in modern society results from the growth and greed unleashed by capitalism. Because a capitalist economy pursues ever-greater profits, both production and consumption steadily increase.

According to Marx, capitalism rests on "naked self-interest" (Marx & Engels, 1972:337, orig. 1848). This self-centeredness weakens the social ties that once united small communities. Under capitalism, people are transformed into commodities: a source of labor and a market for capitalist products.

Capitalism supports science, not just as the key to greater productivity but also as an ideology that justifies the status quo. Modern societies encourage people to view human well-being as a technical puzzle to be solved by engineers and other experts rather than through the pursuit of social justice. For example, a capitalist culture seeks to improve health through advances in scientific medicine rather than by eliminating poverty, despite the fact that poverty is a core cause of poor health.

Business also raises the banner of scientific logic, trying to increase profits through greater efficiency. As Chapter 16 ("The Economy and Work") explains, today's capitalist corporations have reached enormous size and control unimaginable wealth as a result of global expansion. From the class-society point of view, the expanding scale of life is less a function of *Gesellschaft* than the inevitable and destructive consequence of capitalism.

Persistent Inequality

Modernity has gradually worn away the rigid categories that set nobles apart from commoners in preindustrial societies. But class-society theory points out elites are still with us, not as the nobles of an earlier era but in the form of capitalist millionaires. In short, a few people are still born to wealth and power. The United States may have no hereditary monarchy, but the richest 1 percent of the population controls about 35 percent of all privately held property (Wolff, 2012).

Watch in **MySocLab**
Video: *Social Inequalities: Economy and Work*

mass society a society in which prosperity and bureaucracy have weakened traditional social ties

class society a capitalist society with pronounced social stratification

What of the state? Mass-society theorists argue that the state works to increase equality and fight social problems. Marx disagreed; he doubted that the state could accomplish more than minor reforms because as he saw it, real power lies in the hands of capitalists, who control the economy. Other class-society theorists add that to the extent that working people and minorities do enjoy greater political rights and a higher standard of living today, these changes were the result of political struggle, not government goodwill. Despite our pretensions of democracy, they conclude, our political economy leaves most people powerless in the face of wealthy elites.

EVALUATE Class-society theory dismisses Durkheim's argument that people in modern societies suffer from anomie, claiming instead that they suffer from alienation and powerlessness. Not surprisingly, the class-society interpretation of modernity enjoys widespread support among liberals and radicals who favor greater equality and call for extensive regulation (or abolition) of the capitalist marketplace.

A basic criticism of class-society theory is that it overlooks the long-term increasing prosperity of modern societies and the fact that discrimination based on race, ethnicity, religion, and gender is now illegal and is widely regarded as a social problem. In addition, most people in the United States do not want an egalitarian society; they prefer a system of unequal rewards that reflects personal differences in talent and effort.

Based on socialism's failure to generate a high standard of living, few observers think that a centralized economy would cure the ills of modernity. The United States may face a number of social problems—from unemployment to hunger and industrial pollution to war—but these problems are also found in socialist nations.

CHECK YOUR LEARNING In your own words, state the class-society theory of modernity. What are several criticisms of it?

The Summing Up table contrasts the two interpretations of modernity. Mass-society theory focuses on the increasing impersonality of social life and the growth of government; class-society theory stresses the expansion of capitalism and the persistence of inequality.

Modernity and the Individual

Both mass- and class-society theories look at the broad patterns of change since the Industrial Revolution. But from these macro-level approaches we can also draw micro-level insights into how modernity shapes individual lives.

Mass Society: Problems of Identity

Modernity freed individuals from the small, tightly knit communities of the past. Most people in modern societies have the privacy and freedom to express their individuality. However, mass-society theory suggests that so much social diversity, widespread isolation, and rapid social change make it difficult for many people to establish any coherent identity at all (Wheelis, 1958; Berger, Berger, & Kellner, 1974).

As Chapter 5 ("Socialization") explains, people's personalities are largely a product of their social experiences. The small, homogeneous, and slowly changing societies of the past provided a firm, if narrow, foundation for building a personal identity. Even today, the Amish communities that flourish in the United States and Canada teach young men and women "correct" ways to think and behave. Not everyone born into an Amish community

Summing Up

Two Interpretations of Modernity		
	Mass Society	**Class Society**
Process of modernization	Industrialization; growth of bureaucracy	Rise of capitalism
Effects of modernization	Increasing scale of life; rise of the state and other formal organizations	Expansion of the capitalist economy; persistence of social inequality

Mass-society theory relates feelings of anxiety and lack of meaning in the modern world to rapid social change that washes away tradition. This notion of modern emptiness and isolation is captured in the photo at the left. Class-society theory, by contrast, ties such feelings to social inequality, by which some categories of people are made into second-class citizens (or not made citizens at all), an idea expressed in the photo at the right.

can tolerate such rigid demands for conformity, but most members establish a well-integrated and satisfying personal identity (Kraybill & Olshan, 1994; Kraybill & Hurd, 2006).

Mass societies are quite another story. Socially diverse and rapidly changing, they offer only shifting sands on which to build a personal identity. Left to make many life decisions on their own, many people—especially those with greater wealth—face a bewildering array of options. The freedom to choose has little value without standards to help us make good choices, and in a tolerant mass society, people may find little reason to choose one path over another. As a result, many people shuttle from one identity to another, changing their lifestyles, relationships, and even religions in search of an elusive "true self." Given the widespread "relativism" of modern societies, people without a moral compass lack the security and certainty once provided by tradition.

To David Riesman (1970, orig. 1950), modernization brings changes in **social character,** *personality patterns common to members of a particular society.* Preindustrial societies promote what Riesman calls **tradition-directedness,** *rigid conformity to time-honored ways of living.* Members of traditional societies model their lives on those of their ancestors, so that "living a good life" amounts to "doing what our people have always done."

Tradition-directedness corresponds to Tönnies's *Gemeinschaft* and Durkheim's mechanical solidarity. Culturally conservative, tradition-directed people think and act alike. Unlike the conformity sometimes found in modern societies, the uniformity of tradition-directedness is not an effort to imitate a popular celebrity or follow the latest fashions. Instead, people are alike because they all draw on the same solid cultural foundation. Amish women and men exemplify tradition-directedness; in Amish culture, tradition ties everyone to ancestors and descendants in an unbroken chain of righteous living.

Today, members of diverse and rapidly changing societies are likely to view a tradition-directed personality deviant because it seems so rigid. Modern people prize personal flexibility, the capacity to adapt, and sensitivity to others. Riesman calls this type of social character **other-directedness,** *openness to the latest trends and fashions, often expressed by imitating others.* Because their socialization occurs in societies that are continuously in flux, other-directed people develop fluid identities marked by superficiality, inconsistency, and change. They try on different "selves" almost like new clothing, seek out role models, and engage in varied performances as they move from setting to setting

social character personality patterns common to members of a particular society

tradition-directedness rigid conformity to time-honored ways of living

other-directedness openness to the latest trends and fashions, often expressed by imitating others

(Goffman, 1959). In a traditional society, such "shiftiness" marks a person as untrustworthy, but in a changing, modern society, the ability to fit in virtually anywhere—like a chameleon changing its colors to match its environment—is very useful.

In societies that value the up-to-date rather than the traditional, people look to others for approval, using members of their own generation rather than elders as role models. Peer pressure can be irresistible to people without strong standards to guide them. Our society urges individuals to be true to themselves, but when social surroundings change so rapidly, how can people develop the self to which they should be true? This problem lies at the root of the identity crisis so widespread in industrial societies today. "Who am I?" is a nagging question that many of us struggle to answer. In truth, this problem is not so much us as the inherently unstable mass society in which we live.

Class Society: Problems of Powerlessness

Class-society theory paints a different picture of modernity's effects on individuals. This approach maintains that persistent social inequality undermines modern society's promise of individual freedom. For some people, modernity serves up great privilege, but for many, everyday life means coping with economic uncertainty and a growing sense of powerlessness (Newman, 1993; Ehrenreich, 2001).

For racial and ethnic minorities, the problem of relative disadvantage looms even larger. Similarly, although women participate more broadly in modern societies, they continue to run up against traditional barriers of sexism. This approach rejects mass-society theory's claim that people suffer from too much freedom. According to class-society theory, our society still denies a majority of people full participation in social life.

As Chapter 12 ("Global Stratification") explains, the expanding scope of world capitalism has placed more of Earth's population under the influence of multinational corporations. As a result, three-fourths of the world's income is concentrated in the high-income nations, where just 23 percent of its people live. Is it any wonder, class-society theorists ask, that people in poor nations seek greater power to shape their own lives?

The problem of widespread powerlessness led Herbert Marcuse (1964) to challenge Max Weber's statement that modern society is rational. Marcuse condemned modern society as irrational for failing to meet the needs of so many people. Although modern capitalist societies produce unparalleled wealth, poverty remains the daily plight of more than 1 billion people. Marcuse adds that technological advances further reduce people's control over their own lives. High technology gives a great deal of power to a small core of specialists—not the majority of people—who now dominate the discussion of when to go to war, what our energy policy should be, and how people should pay for health care. Countering the common view that technology *solves* the world's problems, Marcuse believed that science *causes* them. In sum, class-society theory asserts that people suffer because modern societies concentrate knowledge, wealth, and power in the hands of a privileged few.

Modernity and Progress

In modern societies, most people expect, and applaud, social change. We link modernity to the idea of *progress* (from the Latin, meaning "moving forward"), a state of continual improvement. We see stability as stagnation.

Given our bias in favor of change, our society tends to regard traditional cultures as backward. But change, particularly toward material affluence, is a mixed blessing. As the Thinking Globally box on page 712 shows, social change is too complex simply to equate with progress.

Even getting rich has both advantages and disadvantages, as the cases of the Kaiapo and the Gullah show. Historically, in the United States, a rising standard of living has made lives longer and more comfortable. At the same time, many people wonder whether today's routines are too stressful, with families often having little time to relax or simply be together. Perhaps this is why, in the United States, measures of happiness over the last twenty-five years have actually gone down (Myers, 2000; Inglehart, Welzel, & Foa, 2009).

Thinking Globally

Does "Modernity" Mean "Progress"? The Kaiapo of the Amazon and the Gullah of Georgia

The firelight flickers in the gathering darkness. Chief Kanhonk sits cross-legged, as he has done at the end of the day for decades, and gathers his thoughts for an evening of animated storytelling (Simons, 2007). This is the hour when the Kaiapo, a small society in Brazil's lush Amazon region, celebrate their heritage. Because the Kaiapo are a traditional people with no written language, the elders rely on evenings by the fire to pass on their culture to their children and grandchildren. In the past, evenings like this have been filled with tales of brave Kaiapo warriors fighting off Portuguese traders who were in pursuit of slaves and gold.

But as the minutes pass, only a few older villagers assemble for the evening ritual. "It is the Big Ghost," one man grumbles, explaining the poor turnout. The "Big Ghost" has indeed descended on them; its bluish glow spills through the windows throughout the village. The Kaiapo children—and many adults as well—are watching reality shows on television. The installation of a satellite dish in the village several years ago has had consequences far greater than anyone imagined. In the end, what their enemies failed to do with guns, the Kaiapo may well do to themselves with prime-time programming.

The Kaiapo are among the 230,000 native peoples who inhabit Brazil. They stand out because of their striking body paint and ornate ceremonial dress. During the 1980s, they became rich from gold mining and harvesting mahogany trees. Now they must decide whether their newfound fortune is a blessing or a curse.

To some, material wealth means the opportunity to learn about the outside world through travel and television. Others, like Chief Kanhonk, are not so sure. Bathed in the firelight, he thinks aloud: "I have been saying that people must buy useful things like knives and fishing hooks. Television does not fill the stomach. It only shows our children and grandchildren white people's things." Bebtopup, the oldest priest, nods in agreement: "The night is the time the old people teach the young people. Television has stolen the night" (Simons, 2007:522).

Far to the north, in the United States, half an hour by ferry from the coast of Georgia, lies the community of Hog Hammock on swampy Sapelo Island. The seventy African American residents of the island today trace their ancestry back to the first slaves who settled there in 1802.

Walking past the colorful houses nestled among pine trees draped with Spanish moss, visitors feel transported back in time. The local people, known as Gullahs (or in some places, Geechees), speak *creole*, a mixture of English and West African languages. They fish, living much as they have for hundreds of years in a region that is an important environmental ecosystem (Dewan, 2010).

But the future of this way of life is now in doubt. The young people who grow up in Hog Hammock can find no work other than fishing and making traditional crafts. "We have been here nine generations and we are still here," says one local. Then, referring to the island's nineteen children, she adds, "It's not that they don't want to be here, it's that there's nothing here for them—they need to have jobs" (Curry, 2001:41).

Just as important, with people on the mainland looking for waterside homes for vacations or year-round living, the island has become prime real estate. Not long ago, one of the larger houses went up for sale, and the community was shocked to learn that its asking price was more than $1 million. The locals know only too well that their property taxes have gone sky high. Edna Holmes, whose family has lived on Hog Hammock for four generations, had long paid about $200 a year in taxes on her house; in recent years, the bill shot up to $2,000. Says Holmes, "The county is trying to tax us out" (Brown, 2013). If this pattern continues, the natural beauty of Hog Hammock is likely to be paved over so that the area becomes another Hilton Head, once a Gullah community on the South Carolina coast that is now home to well-to-do people from the mainland.

It is probably only a matter of time until the people of Hog Hammock sell their homes and move inland. But Edna Holmes and most other residents are unhappy at the thought of selling out, even for a good price. After all, moving away will mean the end of their cultural heritage.

The stories of both the Kaiapo and the people of Hog Hammock show us that change is not a simple path toward "progress." These people may be moving toward modernity, but this process will have both positive and negative consequences. In the end, both groups of people may enjoy a higher standard of living with better homes, more schooling, and new technology. But their newfound affluence will come at the price of their traditions. The drama of these people is now being played out around the world as more and more traditional cultures are being lured away from their heritage by the affluence and materialism of rich societies.

What Do You Think?

1. Why is social change both a winning and a losing proposition for traditional peoples?

2. Do the changes described here improve the lives of the Kaiapo? What about the Gullah community?

3. Do traditional people have any choice about becoming modern? Explain your answer.

Science, too, has its pluses and minuses. As the Power of Society figure at the beginning of this chapter points out, people in the United States are more confident than people in other nations that science improves our lives (Inglehart et al., 2012). But surveys also show that many adults in the United States also see a downside to scientific advances—particularly, that science "makes our way of life change too fast" (NORC, 2013:1727).

New technology has always sparked controversy. A century ago, the introduction of automobiles and telephones allowed more rapid transportation and more efficient communication. But at the same time, such technology weakened traditional attachments to local neighborhoods and even to families. Today, people might well wonder whether smart phones and tablet computers will do the same thing, giving us access to people around the world but shielding us from the community right outside our doors; providing more information than ever before but in the process threatening personal privacy. In short, we all realize that social change comes faster all the time, but we may disagree about whether a particular change is good or bad for society.

Based on everything you have read in this chapter, do you think that, on balance, our society is changing for better or worse? Why?

👁 **Watch** in **MySocLab**
Video: *Sociology in Focus: Health and Medicine*

Modernity: Global Variation

October 1, Kobe, Japan. Riding the computer-controlled monorail high above the streets of Kobe or the 200-mile-per-hour bullet train to Tokyo, we see Japan as the society of the future; its people are in love with high technology. But in other ways, the Japanese remain strikingly traditional: Few corporate executives and almost no senior politicians are women, young people still show seniors great respect, and public orderliness contrasts with the relative chaos of many U.S. cities.

Japan is a nation at once traditional and modern. This contradiction reminds us that although it is useful to contrast traditional and modern societies, the old and the new often coexist in unexpected ways. In the People's Republic of China, ancient Confucian principles are mixed with contemporary socialist thinking. In Saudi Arabia and Qatar, the embrace of modern technology is mixed with respect for the ancient principles of Islam. Likewise, in Mexico and much of Latin America, people observe centuries-old Christian rituals even as they struggle to move ahead economically. In short, although we may think of tradition and modernity as opposites, combinations of traditional and modern are far from unusual; rather, they are found throughout the world.

Postmodernity

24.5 Discuss postmodernism as one type of social criticism.

I f modernity was the product of the Industrial Revolution, is the Information Revolution creating a postmodern era? A number of scholars think so, and they use the term **postmodernity** to refer to *the transformations caused by the Information Revolution and the postindustrial economy.*

Precisely what postmodernism is remains a matter of debate. The term *postmodernism* has been used for decades in literary, philosophical, and even architectural circles. It moved into sociology on a wave of social criticism that has been building since the spread of left-leaning politics in the 1960s. Although there are many variants of postmodern thinking, all share the following five themes (Hall & Neitz, 1993; Inglehart, 1997; Rudel & Gerson, 1999):

postmodernity the transformations caused by the Information Revolution and the postindustrial economy

1. **In important respects, modernity has failed.** The promise of modernity was a life free from want. As postmodernist critics see it, however, the twentieth century was unsuccessful in solving social problems like poverty. This fact is evident in today's high poverty rates, increasing economic inequality, and the widespread sense of financial insecurity.

2. **The bright light of "progress" is fading.** Modern people look to the future, expecting that their lives will improve in significant ways. Members (and even leaders) of postmodern societies, however, are less confident about what the future holds. The strong optimism that carried society into the modern era more than a century ago has given way to widespread pessimism; almost half of U.S. adults do not expect their children's lives to be better than their own (NORC, 2013:402).

3. **Science no longer holds the answers.** The defining trait of the modern era was a scientific outlook and a confident belief that technology would make life better. But postmodern critics argue that science has failed to solve many old problems (such as poor health) and has even created new problems (such as environmental pollution and global warming).

   Postmodernist thinkers discredit science, claiming that it implies a singular truth. On the contrary, they maintain, different people see different "realities," and there are many ways to socially construct the world.

4. **Cultural debates are intensifying.** Now that the world is capable of producing material abundance, ideas are taking on more importance. In this sense, postmodernity is also a postmaterialist era, in which more careers involve working with symbols and in which issues such as social justice, the state of the natural environment, and animal rights command more and more public attention.

5. **Social institutions are changing.** Just as industrialization brought a sweeping transformation to social institutions, the rise of a postindustrial society is remaking society again. For example, the postmodern family no longer conforms to any single pattern; on the contrary, individuals are choosing among many new family forms.

For a closer look at changes in the quality of life in our society, **Read More** in **MySocLab**, *Tracking Change: Is Life in the United States Getting Better or Worse?*

EVALUATE Analysts who claim that the United States and other high-income societies are entering a postmodern era criticize modernity for failing to meet human needs. In defense of modernity, there have been marked increases in longevity and living standards over the course of the past century. If we take the postmodernist view and reject science as bankrupt and progress as a sham, what are the alternatives?

CHECK YOUR LEARNING In your own words, state the characteristics of a postmodern society.

Modernization and Our Global Future

24.6 Evaluate possible directions of future social change.

Imagine the entire world reduced to a village of 1,000 people. About 90 residents of this "global village" come from high-income countries and they earn half of all income. Another 125 people are so poor that their lives are at risk.

The tragic plight of the world's poor shows that the planet is in desperate need of change. Chapter 12 ("Global Stratification") presented two competing views of why more than 1 billion people around the world are so poor. *Modernization theory* claims that in the past, the entire world was poor and that technological change, especially the Industrial Revolution, enhanced human productivity and raised living standards in many nations. From this point of view, the solution to global poverty is to promote technological development and market economies around the world.

For reasons suggested earlier, however, global modernization may be difficult. Recall that David Riesman portrayed preindustrial people as *tradition-directed* and likely to resist change. So modernization theorists claim that the world's rich societies help poor countries grow economically. Industrial nations can speed development by exporting technology to poor regions, welcoming students from these countries, and providing foreign aid to stimulate economic growth.

A review of modernization theory in Chapter 12 points to some success with policies in Latin America and more dramatic results in the small Asian countries of Taiwan, South Korea, Singapore, and Hong Kong (since 1997 part of the People's Republic of China). But jump-starting development in the poorest countries of the world poses greater challenges. And even where dramatic change has occurred, modernization involves a trade-off. Traditional people, such as Brazil's Kaiapo, may gain wealth through economic development, but they lose their cultural identity and values as they are drawn into a global "McCulture" based on Western materialism, pop music, trendy clothes, and fast food. One Brazilian anthropologist expressed hope about the future of the Kaiapo: "At least they quickly understood the consequences of watching television.... Now [they] can make a choice" (Simons, 2007:523).

But not everyone thinks that modernization is really an option. According to a second approach to global stratification, *dependency theory*, today's poor societies have little ability to modernize, even if they want to. From this point of view, the major barrier to economic development is not traditionalism but domination of the global economy by rich capitalist societies.

Dependency theory asserts that rich nations achieved modernization at the expense of poor ones, by taking poor nations' natural resources and exploiting their human labor. Even today, the world's poorest countries remain locked in a disadvantageous economic relationship with rich nations, dependent on wealthy countries to buy their raw materials and in return provide them with whatever manufactured products they can afford. According to this view, continuing ties with rich societies only perpetuates current patterns of global inequality.

Whichever of these two approaches you find more convincing, keep in mind that change in the United States is no longer separate from change in the rest of the world. At the beginning of the twentieth century, most people in today's high-income countries lived in relatively small settlements with limited awareness of the larger world. Today, the world has become one huge village because the lives of all people are increasingly interconnected.

The twentieth century witnessed unprecedented human achievement. Yet solutions to many problems of human existence—including finding meaning in life, resolving conflicts between nations, and eliminating poverty—have eluded us. To this list of pressing matters have been added new concerns, such as controlling population growth and establishing an environmentally sustainable society. In the coming years, we must be prepared to tackle such problems with imagination, compassion, and determination. Our growing understanding of human society gives us reason to be hopeful that we can get the job done.

For a closer look at one dilemma society faces in the twenty-first century, **Read More** in **MySocLab**, *Personal Freedom and Social Responsibility: Can We Have It Both Ways?*

Seeing Sociology in Everyday Life

CHAPTER 24 Social Change: Traditional, Modern, and Postmodern Societies

Is tradition the opposite of modernity?

Conceptually, this may be true. But as this chapter explains, traditional and modern social patterns combine in all sorts of interesting ways in our everyday lives. Look at the photographs below and on page 717, and identify elements of tradition and modernity operating together. Do they seem to go together, or are they in conflict? Why?

These young girls live in the city of Istanbul in Turkey, a country that has long debated the merits of traditional and modern life. What sets off traditional and modern ways of dressing? Do you think such differences are likely to affect patterns of friendship? Would the same be true in the United States?

When the first McDonald's restaurant opened in the city of Kiev in Ukraine, many people stopped by to taste a hamburger and see what "fast food" was all about. As large corporations expand their operations around the world, do they tip the balance away from tradition in favor of modernity? If so, how?

In Riyadh, Saudi Arabia, these young men are shopping for the latest in cell phones. Does such modern technology threaten a society's traditions?

HINT Although sociologists analyze tradition and modernity as conceptual opposites, every society combines these elements in various ways. People may debate the virtues of traditional and modern life, but the two patterns are found almost everywhere. Technological change always has social consequences—for example, the use of cell phones changes people's social networks and economic opportunities; similarly, the spread of McDonald's changes not only what people eat but also where and with whom they share meals.

Seeing Sociology in *Your* Everyday Life

1. How do tradition and modernity combine in your life? Point to several ways in which you are traditional and several ways in which you are thoroughly modern.

2. Go to MySocLab and click on the Student Resources link to access the Sociology in Focus blog, where you can read the latest posts by a team of young sociologists who apply the sociological perspective to topics of popular culture.

3. What do you see as the advantages of living in a modern society? What are the drawbacks?

Go to the "Seeing Sociology in *Your* Everyday Life" feature in MySocLab to learn more about the benefits and challenges of modern living—information you can use to enhance your own life.

Making the Grade

What Is Social Change?

24.1 State four defining characteristics of social change. (pp. 696–97)

Social change is the transformation of culture and social institutions over time. Every society changes all the time, sometimes faster, sometimes more slowly. Social change often generates controversy.

> **social change** the transformation of culture and social institutions over time

Causes of Social Change

24.2 Explain how culture, conflict, ideas, and population patterns direct social change. (pp. 698–99)

 **Explore** the **Map** in **MySocLab**

Culture and Change

- *Invention* produces new objects, ideas, and social patterns.
- *Discovery* occurs when people take notice of existing elements of the world.
- *Diffusion* creates change as products, people, and information spread from one society to another.

Conflict and Change

- Karl Marx claimed that class conflict between capitalists and workers pushes society toward a socialist system of production.
- Social conflict arising from class, race, and gender inequality has resulted in social changes that have improved the lives of working people.

Ideas and Change

Max Weber traced the roots of most social changes to ideas:

- The fact that industrial capitalism developed first in areas of Western Europe where the Protestant work ethic was strong demonstrates the power of ideas to bring about change.

Demographic Change

Population patterns play a part in social change:

- The aging of U.S. society has resulted in changes to family life and the development of consumer products to meet the needs of the elderly.
- Migration within and between societies promotes change.

Modernity

24.3 Apply the ideas of Tönnies, Durkheim, Weber, and Marx to our understanding of modernity. (pp. 700–705)

 **Watch** the **Video** in **MySocLab**   **Read** the **Document** in **MySocLab**

Modernity refers to the social consequences of industrialization, which include

- the decline of traditional communities
- the expansion of personal choice
- increasing social diversity
- focus on the future

Ferdinand Tönnies described modernization as the transition from *Gemeinschaft* to *Gesellschaft*, a process characterized by the loss of traditional community and the rise of individualism.

Emile Durkheim saw modernization as a society's expanding division of labor. *Mechanical solidarity*, based on shared activities and beliefs, is gradually replaced by *organic solidarity*, in which specialization makes people interdependent.

Max Weber saw modernity as the decline of a traditional worldview and the rise of rationality. Weber feared the dehumanizing effects of modern rational organization.

> **modernity** changes brought about by the Industrial Revolution
>
> **modernization** the process of social change begun by industrialization
>
> **division of labor** specialized economic activity
>
> **anomie** Durkheim's term for a condition in which society provides little moral guidance to individuals

Karl Marx saw modernity as the triumph of capitalism over feudalism. Capitalism creates social conflict, which Marx claimed would bring about revolutionary change leading to an egalitarian socialist society.

Theories of Modernity

24.4 Contrast analysis of modernity as mass society and as class society. (pp. 705–13)

 Watch the **Video** in **MySocLab**   **Watch** the **Video** in **MySocLab**

Structural-Functional Theory: Modernity as Mass Society

- According to **mass-society theory**, modernity increases the scale of life, enlarging the role of government and other formal organizations in carrying out tasks previously performed by families in local communities.
- Cultural diversity and rapid social change make it difficult for people in modern societies to develop stable identities and to find meaning in their lives.

Social-Conflict Theory: Modernity as Class Society

- According to **class-society theory**, modernity involves the rise of capitalism into a global economic system resulting in persistent social inequality.
- By concentrating wealth in the hands of a few, modern capitalist societies generate widespread feelings of alienation and powerlessness.

Modernity and the Individual

Both mass-society theory and class-society theory are macro-level approaches; from them, however, we can also draw micro-level insights into how modernity shapes individual lives.

Mass Society: Problems of Identity

- Mass-society theory suggests that the great social diversity, widespread isolation, and rapid social change of modern societies make it difficult for individuals to establish a stable social identity.

David Riesman described the changes in social character that modernity causes:

- Preindustrial societies exhibit **tradition-directedness:** Everyone in society draws on the same solid cultural foundation, and people model their lives on those of their ancestors.
- Modern societies exhibit **other-directedness:** Because their socialization occurs in societies that are continuously in flux, other-directed people develop fluid identities marked by superficiality, inconsistency, and change.

Class Society: Problems of Powerlessness

- Class-society theory claims that the problem facing most people today is economic uncertainty and powerlessness.
- Herbert Marcuse claimed that modern society is irrational because it fails to meet the needs of so many people.
- Marcuse also believed that technological advances further reduce people's control over their own lives.
- People suffer because modern societies have concentrated both wealth and power in the hands of a privileged few.

Modernity and Progress

Social change is too complex and controversial simply to be equated with progress:

- A rising standard of living has made lives longer and materially more comfortable; at the same time, many people are stressed and have little time to relax with their families; there have been no increases in measures of personal happiness over recent decades.
- Science and technology have brought many conveniences to our everyday lives, yet many people are concerned that life is changing too fast; the introduction of automobiles and advanced communications technology has weakened traditional attachments to hometowns and even to families.

mass society a society in which prosperity and bureaucracy have weakened traditional social ties

class society a capitalist society with pronounced social stratification

social character personality patterns common to members of a particular society

tradition-directedness rigid conformity to time-honored ways of living

other-directedness openness to the latest trends and fashions, often expressed by imitating others

---

Postmodernity

24.5 Discuss postmodernism as one type of social criticism. (pp. 713–14)

Postmodernity refers to the cultural traits of postindustrial societies. Postmodern criticism of society centers on the failure of modernity, and specifically science, to fulfill its promise of prosperity and well-being.

postmodernity the transformations caused by the Information Revolution and the postindustrial economy

---

Modernization and Our Global Future

24.6 Evaluate possible directions of future social change. (pp. 714–15)

- *Modernization theory* links global poverty to the power of tradition. Rich nations can help poor countries develop their economies.
- *Dependency theory* explains global poverty as the product of the world economic system. The operation of multinational corporations makes poor nations economically dependent on rich nations.

Sample Test Questions

These questions are similar to those found in the test bank that accompanies this textbook.

Chapter 1   The Sociological Perspective

Multiple-Choice Questions

1. **What does the sociological perspective tell us about whom any individual chooses to marry?**
   a. There is no explaining personal feelings like love.
   b. People's actions reflect human free will.
   c. The operation of society guides many of our personal choices.
   d. In the case of love, opposites attract.

2. **Which early sociologist studied patterns of suicide?**
   a. Peter Berger
   b. Emile Durkheim
   c. Auguste Comte
   d. Karl Marx

3. **The personal value of studying sociology includes**
   a. seeing the opportunities and constraints in our lives.
   b. the fact that it is good preparation for a number of jobs.
   c. being more active participants in society.
   d. All of the above are correct.

4. **The discipline of sociology first developed in**
   a. countries experiencing rapid social change.
   b. countries with little social change.
   c. countries with a history of warfare.
   d. the world's poorest countries.

5. **Which early sociologist coined the term *sociology* in 1838?**
   a. Karl Marx
   b. Herbert Spencer
   c. Adam Smith
   d. Auguste Comte

6. **Which theoretical approach is closest to that taken by early sociologists Auguste Comte and Emile Durkheim?**
   a. the symbolic-interaction approach
   b. the structural-functional approach
   c. the social-conflict approach
   d. None of the above is correct.

7. **Which term refers to the recognized and intended consequences of a social pattern?**
   a. manifest functions
   b. latent functions
   c. eufunctions
   d. dysfunctions

8. **Sociology's social-conflict approach draws attention to**
   a. how structure contributes to the overall operation of society.
   b. how people construct meaning through interaction.
   c. patterns of social inequality.
   d. the stable aspects of society.

9. **Which woman, among the first sociologists, studied the evils of slavery and also translated the writings of Auguste Comte?**
   a. Elizabeth Cady Stanton
   b. Jane Addams
   c. Harriet Martineau
   d. Margaret Mead

10. **Which of the following illustrates a micro-level focus?**
    a. analyzing the operation of the U.S. political system
    b. studying patterns of global terrorism
    c. describing class inequality in the armed forces
    d. observing two new dormitory roommates getting to know one another

ANSWERS: 1 (c); 2 (b); 3 (d); 4 (a); 5 (d); 6 (b); 7 (a); 8 (c); 9 (c);10 (d).

Essay Questions

1. Explain why applying the sociological perspective can make us seem less in control of our lives. In what ways does it actually give us greater power over our lives?

2. Guided by the discipline's three major theoretical approaches, come up with sociological questions about (a) television, (b) war, and (c) colleges and universities.

Chapter 2   Sociological Investigation

Multiple-Choice Questions

1. *Science* **is defined as**
   a. a logical system that bases knowledge on direct, systematic observation.
   b. belief based on faith in some ultimate truth.
   c. knowledge based on a society's traditions.
   d. information that comes from recognized "experts."

2. *Empirical evidence* **refers to**
   a. quantitative rather than qualitative data.
   b. what people consider "common sense."
   c. information people can verify with their senses.
   d. patterns found in every known society.

3. **When trying to measure people's "social class," you would have to keep in mind that**
   a. your measurement can never be both reliable and valid.
   b. there are many ways to operationalize this variable.
   c. there is no way to measure "social class."
   d. in the United States, everyone agrees on what "social class" means.

4. **What is the term for the value that occurs most often in a series of numbers?**
   a. the mode
   b. the median
   c. the mean
   d. All of the above are correct.

5. **When measuring any variable, *reliability* refers to**
   a. whether you are really measuring what you want to measure.
   b. how dependable the researcher is.
   c. results that everyone would agree with.
   d. whether repeating the measurement yields consistent results.

6. **We can correctly say that two variables are *correlated* if**
   a. change in one causes no change in the other.
   b. one occurs before the other.
   c. their values vary together.
   d. both measure the same thing.

7. **Which of the following is *not* a defining trait of a cause-and-effect relationship?**
   a. The independent variable must happen before the dependent variable.
   b. Each variable must be shown to be independent of the other.
   c. The two variables must display correlation.
   d. There must be no evidence that the correlation is spurious.

8. **Interpretive sociology is a research orientation that**
   a. focuses on action.
   b. sees an objective reality "out there."
   c. focuses on the meanings people attach to behavior.
   d. seeks to increase social justice.

9. **To study the effects on test performance of playing soft music during an exam, a researcher conducts an experiment in which one test-taking class hears music and another does not. According to the chapter discussion of the experiment, the class hearing the music is called**
   a. the placebo.
   b. the control group.
   c. the dependent variable.
   d. the experimental group.

10. **In participant observation, the problem of "breaking in" to a setting is often solved with the help of a**
    a. key informant.
    b. research assistant.
    c. bigger budget.
    d. All of the above are correct.

ANSWERS: 1 (a); **2** (c); **3** (b); **4** (a); **5** (d); **6** (c); **7** (b); **8** (c); **9** (d); **10** (a).

Essay Questions

1. Explain the idea that there are various types of truth. What are the advantages and limitations of science as a way of discovering truth?

2. Compare and contrast scientific sociology, interpretive sociology, and critical sociology. Which of these approaches best describes the work of Durkheim, Weber, and Marx?

Chapter 3   Culture

Multiple-Choice Questions

1. **Of all the world's countries, the United States is the most**
   a. multicultural.
   b. culturally uniform.
   c. slowly changing.
   d. resistant to cultural diversity.

2. **Ideas created by members of a society are part of**
   a. high culture.
   b. material culture.
   c. norms.
   d. nonmaterial culture.

3. **Sociologists define a symbol as**
   a. any gesture that insults others.
   b. any element of material culture.
   c. anything that has meaning to people who share a culture.
   d. any pattern that causes culture shock.

4. **U.S. culture holds a strong belief in**
   a. the traditions of the past.
   b. individuality.
   c. equality of condition for all.
   d. All of the above are correct.

5. **Cheating on a final examination is an example of violating campus**
   a. folkways.
   b. symbols.
   c. mores.
   d. high culture.

6. ***Subculture* refers to**
   a. a part of the population lacking culture.
   b. elements of popular culture.
   c. people who embrace high culture.
   d. cultural patterns that set apart a segment of a society's population.

7. **Which region of the United States has the largest share of people who speak a language other than English at home?**
   a. the Southwest
   b. the Northeast
   c. the Northwest
   d. the South

8. **Sociologists use the term "cultural lag" to refer to**
   a. the slowing of cultural change in the United States.
   b. the fact that some societies change faster than others do.
   c. that fact that some elements of culture change faster than others.
   d. people who are less cultured than others.

9. **Which of the following is a description of ethnocentrism?**
   a. taking pride in your ethnicity
   b. judging another culture using the standards of your own culture
   c. seeing another culture as better than your own
   d. judging another culture by its own standards

10. **Which theoretical approach focuses on the link between culture and social inequality?**
    a. the structural-functional approach
    b. the social-conflict approach
    c. the symbolic-interaction approach
    d. the sociobiology approach

Essay Questions

1. In the United States, hot dogs, hamburgers, French fries, and ice cream have long been considered national favorites. What cultural patterns help explain the love of these kinds of foods?

2. From what you have learned in this chapter, do you think that a global culture is emerging? Do you regard the prospect of a global culture as positive or negative? Why?

Chapter 4   Society

Multiple-Choice Questions

1. **Which of the following would Lenski highlight as a cause of change in society?**
   a. new religious movements
   b. conflict between workers and factory owners
   c. the steam engine
   d. the extent to which people share moral values

2. **Horticultural societies are those in which**
   a. people hunt animals and gather vegetation.
   b. people are nomadic.
   c. people have learned to raise animals.
   d. people use simple hand tools to raise crops.

3. **Lenski claims that the development of more complex technology**
   a. has both positive and negative effects.
   b. is entirely positive.
   c. is mostly negative.
   d. has little or no effect on society.

4. **Marx believed that the industrial-capitalist economic system**
   a. was very productive.
   b. concentrated wealth in the hands of a few.
   c. created conflict between two great classes: capitalists and proletarians.
   d. All of the above are correct.

5. **Marx considered which of the following to be the "foundation" of society?**
   a. technology
   b. the economy
   c. dominant ideas
   d. type of solidarity

6. **Unlike Marx, Weber thought alienation was caused by**
   a. social change that is too rapid.
   b. extensive social inequality.
   c. the high level of rationality in modern society.
   d. All of the above are correct.

7. **What Lenski called the "industrial" society and Marx called the "capitalist" society, Weber called**
   a. the "rational" society.
   b. the "ideal" society.
   c. the "traditional" society.
   d. the "technological" society.

8. **Marx's "materialist" analysis contrasts with Weber's**
   a. "optimistic" analysis.
   b. "idealist" analysis.
   c. "traditional" analysis.
   d. "technological" analysis.

9. **Durkheim thought of society as**
   a. existing only in people's minds.
   b. constantly changing.
   c. an objective reality.
   d. having no clear existence at all.

10. **Which of the following questions might Durkheim ask about the ongoing war on terror?**
    a. Would the war on terror unite people across the United States?
    b. Which class benefits most from the war on terror?
    c. How does war lead to new kinds of technology?
    d. How does war increase the scope of bureaucracy?

Essay Questions

1. How would Marx, Weber, and Durkheim imagine U.S. society a century from now? What kinds of questions or concerns would each thinker have?

2. Link Marx, Weber, and Durkheim to one of sociology's theoretical approaches, and explain your choices.

Chapter 5   Socialization

Multiple-Choice Questions

1. **Kingsley Davis's study of Anna, the girl isolated for five years, shows that**
   a. humans have all the same instincts found in other animal species.
   b. without social experience, a child never develops personality.
   c. personality is present in all humans at birth.
   d. many human instincts disappear in the first few years of life.

2. **Most sociologists take the position that**
   a. humans have instincts that direct behavior.
   b. biological instincts develop in humans at puberty.
   c. it is human nature to nurture.
   d. All of the above are correct.

3. **Lawrence Kohlberg explored socialization by studying**
   a. cognition.
   b. the importance of gender in socialization.
   c. the development of biological instincts.
   d. moral reasoning.

4. Carol Gilligan added to Kohlberg's findings by showing that
   a. girls and boys typically use different standards in deciding what is right and wrong.
   b. girls are more interested in right and wrong than boys are.
   c. boys are more interested in right and wrong than girls are.
   d. today's children are far less interested in right and wrong than their parents are.

5. The "self," said George Herbert Mead, is
   a. the part of the human personality made up of self-awareness and self-image.
   b. the presence of culture within the individual.
   c. basic drives that are self-centered.
   d. present in infants from birth.

6. Why is the family so important to the socialization process?
   a. Family members provide vital caregiving to infants and children.
   b. Families give children social identity in terms of class, ethnicity, and religion.
   c. Parents' behavior can greatly affect a child's self-concept.
   d. All of the above are correct.

7. Social class position affects socialization: Lower-class parents tend to stress _____, and well-to-do parents stress _____.
   a. independence; protecting children
   b. independence; dependence
   c. obedience; creativity
   d. creativity; obedience

8. In global perspective, which statement about childhood is correct?
   a. In every society, the first ten years of life are a time of play and learning.
   b. Rich societies extend childhood much longer than poor societies do.
   c. Poor societies extend childhood much longer than rich societies do.
   d. Childhood is defined by being biologically immature.

9. Modern, high-income societies typically define people in old age as
   a. the wisest of all.
   b. the most up-to-date on current fashion and trends.
   c. less socially important than younger adults.
   d. All of the above are correct.

10. According to Erving Goffman, the purpose of a total institution is
    a. to reward someone for achievement in the outside world.
    b. to give a person more choices about how to live.
    c. to encourage lifelong learning in a supervised context.
    d. to change a person's personality or behavior.

ANSWERS: 1 (b); 2 (c); 3 (d); 4 (a); 5 (a); 6 (d); 7 (c); 8 (b); 9 (c);10 (d).

Essay Questions

1. State the two sides of the "nature-nurture" debate. In what important way are nature and nurture not opposed to each other?

2. What are common themes in the ideas of Freud, Piaget, Kohlberg, Gilligan, Mead, and Erikson? In what ways do their theories differ?

Chapter 6   Social Interaction in Everyday Life

Multiple-Choice Questions

1. Which term defines who and what we are in relation to others?
   a. role
   b. status
   c. role set
   d. master status

2. In U.S. society, which of the following is often a master status?
   a. occupation
   b. physical or mental disability
   c. race or color
   d. All of the above are correct.

3. "Role set" refers to
   a. a number of roles found in any one society.
   b. a number of roles attached to a single status.
   c. a number of roles that are more or less the same.
   d. a number of roles within any one organization.

4. Frank excels at football at his college, but he doesn't have enough time to study as much as he wants to. This problem is an example of
   a. role set.
   b. role strain.
   c. role conflict.
   d. role exit.

5. The Thomas theorem states that
   a. our statuses and roles are the keys to our personality.
   b. most people rise to their level of incompetence.
   c. people know the world only through their language.
   d. situations defined as real are real in their consequences.

6. Which of the following is the correct meaning of "presentation of self"?
   a. efforts to create impressions in the minds of others
   b. acting out a master status
   c. thinking back over the process of role exit
   d. trying to take attention away from others

7. Paul Ekman points to what as an important clue to deception by another person?
   a. smiling
   b. using tact
   c. inconsistencies in a presentation
   d. All of the above are correct.

8. In terms of dramaturgical analysis, tact is understood as
   a. helping someone take on a new role.
   b. helping another person "save face."
   c. making it hard for someone to perform a role.
   d. negotiating a situation to get your own way.

9. In her study of human emotion, Arlie Hochschild explains that companies typically
   a. try to regulate the emotions of workers.
   b. want workers to be unemotional.
   c. encourage people to express their true emotions.
   d. profit from making customers more emotional.

10. People are likely to "get" a joke when they
    a. know something about more than one culture.
    b. have a different social background than the joke teller.
    c. understand the two different realities being presented.
    d. know why someone wants to tell the joke.

ANSWERS: 1 (b); 2 (d); 3 (b); 4 (c); 5 (d); 6 (a); 7 (c); 8 (b); 9 (a);10 (c).

Essay Questions

1. Explain Erving Goffman's idea that we engage in a "presentation of self." What are the elements of this presentation? Apply this approach to an analysis of a professor teaching a class.

2. In what ways are human emotions rooted in biology? In what ways are emotions guided by culture?

Chapter 7   Groups and Organizations

Multiple-Choice Questions

1. What term did Charles Cooley give to a small social group whose members share personal and lasting relationships?
   a. expressive group
   b. in-group
   c. primary group
   d. secondary group

2. Which type of group leadership is concerned with getting the job done?
   a. laissez-faire leadership
   b. secondary group leadership
   c. expressive leadership
   d. instrumental leadership

3. The research done by Solomon Asch, in which subjects were asked to pick lines of the same length, showed that
   a. groups encourage their members to conform.
   b. most people are stubborn and refuse to change their minds.
   c. groups often generate conflict.
   d. group members rarely agree on everything.

4. What term refers to a social group that someone uses as a point of reference in making an evaluation or decision?
   a. out-group
   b. reference group
   c. in-group
   d. primary group

5. A network is correctly thought of as
   a. the most close-knit social group.
   b. a category of people with something in common.

c. a social group in which most people know one another.
d. a web of weak social ties.

6. From the point of view of a nurse, a hospital is a
   a. normative organization.
   b. coercive organization.
   c. utilitarian organization.
   d. All of the above are correct.

7. Bureaucracy is a type of social organization characterized by
   a. specialized jobs.
   b. offices arranged in a hierarchy.
   c. lots of rules and regulations.
   d. All of the above are correct.

8. According to Robert Michels, bureaucracy always means
   a. inefficiency.
   b. oligarchy.
   c. alienation.
   d. specialization.

9. Rosabeth Moss Kanter claims that large business organizations
   a. need to "open up" opportunity to encourage workers to perform well.
   b. must have clear and stable rules to survive in a changing world.
   c. do well or badly depending on how talented the leader is.
   d. suffer if they do not adopt the latest technology.

10. The "McDonaldization of society" implies that
    a. organizations can provide food for people more efficiently than families can.
    b. impersonal organizations concerned with efficiency, uniformity, and control are becoming more and more common.
    c. it is possible for organizations to both do their job and meet human needs.
    d. society today is one vast social network.

ANSWERS: 1 (c); 2 (d); 3 (a); 4 (b); 5 (d); 6 (c); 7 (d); 8 (b); 9 (a);10 (b).

Essay Questions

1. How do primary groups differ from secondary groups? Give examples of each in your own life.

2. According to Max Weber, what are the six traits that define bureaucracy? What is the advantage of this organizational form? What are several problems that often go along with it?

Chapter 8   Sexuality and Society

Multiple-Choice Questions

1. What is the term for humans who have some combination of female and male genitalia?
   a. asexual people
   b. bisexual people
   c. transsexual people
   d. intersexual people

2. **A global perspective on human sexuality shows us that**
   a. although sex involves our biology, it is also a cultural trait that varies from place to place.
   b. people everywhere in the world have the same sexual practices.
   c. people in all societies are uncomfortable talking about sex.
   d. All of the above are correct.

3. **Why is the incest taboo found in every society?**
   a. It limits sexual competition between members of families.
   b. It helps define people's rights and obligations toward one another.
   c. It integrates members of a family within the larger society.
   d. All of the above are correct.

4. **The sexual revolution reached its peak during the**
   a. 1890s.
   b. 1920s.
   c. 1960s.
   d. 1980s.

5. **Survey data show that the largest share of U.S. adults reject which of the following?**
   a. extramarital sex
   b. homosexuality
   c. premarital sex
   d. sex simply for pleasure

6. **According to the Laumann study of sexuality in the United States,**
   a. only one-third of the adult population is sexually active.
   b. there is great diversity in levels of sexual activity, so no one stereotype is correct.
   c. single people have more sex than married people.
   d. most married men admit to cheating on their wives at some point in their marriage.

7. **What is the term meaning "sexual attraction to people of both sexes"?**
   a. heterosexuality
   b. homosexuality
   c. bisexuality
   d. asexuality

8. **Compared to 1950, the U.S. rate of teenage pregnancy today is**
   a. higher.
   b. the same, but more teens become pregnant by choice.
   c. the same, but more pregnant teens are married.
   d. lower.

9. **By what point in their lives do most young people in the United States today become sexually active?**
   a. when they marry
   b. by the middle of college
   c. by the end of high school
   d. by age thirteen

10. **If we look back in history, we see that once a society develops birth control technology,**
    a. social control of sexuality becomes more strict.
    b. the birth rate actually goes up.
    c. attitudes about sexuality become more permissive.
    d. people no longer care about incest.

ANSWERS: 1 (d); 2 (a); 3 (d); 4 (c); 5 (a); 6 (b); 7 (c); 8 (d); 9 (c); 10 (c).

Essay Questions

1. What was the "sexual revolution"? What changed? Can you point to reasons for the change?

2. Of the issues discussed in this chapter (prostitution, teen pregnancy, pornography, sexual violence, and abortion), which do you think is the most important for U.S. society today? Why?

Chapter 9 Deviance

Multiple-Choice Questions

1. **Crime is a special type of deviance that**
   a. refers to violations of law.
   b. involves punishment.
   c. refers to any violation of a society's norms.
   d. always involves a particular person as the offender.

2. **Emile Durkheim explains that deviance is**
   a. defined by the rich and used against the poor.
   b. harmful not just to victims but to society as a whole.
   c. often at odds with public morality.
   d. found in every society.

3. **Applying Robert Merton's strain theory, a person selling illegal drugs for a living would be an example of which of the following categories?**
   a. conformist
   b. innovator
   c. retreatist
   d. ritualist

4. **Labeling theory states that deviance**
   a. is a normal part of social life.
   b. always changes people's social identity.
   c. arises not from what people do as much as how others respond.
   d. All of the above are correct.

5. **When Jake's friends began calling him a "dope-head," he left the group and spent more time smoking marijuana. He also began hanging out with others who used drugs, and by the end of the term, he had dropped out of college. Edwin Lemert would call this situation an example of**
   a. primary deviance.
   b. the development of secondary deviance.
   c. the formation of a deviant subculture.
   d. the beginning of retreatism.

6. **A social-conflict approach claims that who a society calls deviant depends on**
   a. who has and does not have power.
   b. a society's moral values.
   c. how often the behavior occurs.
   d. how harmful the behavior is.

7. **Stealing a laptop computer from the study lounge in a college dorm is an example of which criminal offense?**
   a. burglary
   b. motor vehicle theft
   c. robbery
   d. larceny-theft

8. The FBI's criminal statistics used in this chapter to create a profile of the street criminal reflect
   a. all crimes that occur.
   b. offenses known to the police.
   c. offenses that involve violence.
   d. offenses resulting in a criminal conviction.

9. Most people arrested for a violent crime in the United States are
   a. white.
   b. African American.
   c. Hispanic.
   d. Asian.

10. Which of the following is the oldest justification for punishing an offender?
    a. deterrence
    b. retribution
    c. societal protection
    d. rehabilitation

ANSWERS: 1 (a); 2 (d); 3 (b); 4 (c); 5 (b); 6 (a); 7 (d); 8 (b); 9 (a); 10 (b).

Essay Questions

1. How does a sociological view of deviance differ from the commonsense idea that bad people do bad things?

2. Research (Mauer, 1999) shows that one in three black men between the ages of twenty and twenty-nine is in jail, on probation, or on parole. What factors, noted in this chapter, help explain this pattern?

Chapter 10   Social Stratification

Multiple-Choice Questions

1. **Social stratification** refers to
   a. job specialization.
   b. ranking categories of people in a hierarchy.
   c. the fact that some people work harder than others.
   d. inequality of personal talent and individual effort.

2. **Looking back in history and around the world today, we see that social stratification may involve differences in**
   a. how unequal people are.
   b. what resources are unequally distributed.
   c. why a society claims people should be unequal.
   d. All of the above are correct.

3. A caste system is social stratification
   a. based on individual achievement.
   b. based on meritocracy.
   c. based on birth.
   d. in which a person's social position is likely to change over time.

4. **Sally has two advanced degrees, earns an average salary, and is working at a low-prestige job. Which concept best describes her situation?**
   a. low status consistency
   b. horizontal social mobility
   c. upward social mobility
   d. high status consistency

5. According to the Davis-Moore thesis,
   a. equality is functional for society.
   b. the more inequality a society has, the more productive it is.
   c. more important jobs must offer enough rewards to draw talent from less important work.
   d. societies with more meritocracy are less productive than those with caste systems.

6. Karl Marx claimed that society "reproduces the class structure." By this, he meant that
   a. society benefits from inequality.
   b. class differences are passed on from one generation to the next.
   c. class differences are the same everywhere.
   d. a society without classes is impossible.

7. Max Weber claimed that social stratification is based on
   a. economic class.
   b. social status or prestige.
   c. power.
   d. All of the above are correct.

8. A society with which type of productive technology has the least amount of social stratification?
   a. hunting and gathering
   b. horticultural/pastoral
   c. industrial
   d. postindustrial

9. Keeping the Kuznets curve in mind, which type of society has the most social stratification?
   a. hunting and gathering
   b. horticultural/pastoral
   c. agrarian
   d. industrial

10. In our postindustrial society, the degree of economic inequality has been
    a. staying about the same.
    b. increasing.
    c. decreasing.
    d. decreasing, but only among men.

ANSWERS: 1 (b); 2 (d); 3 (c); 4 (a); 5 (c); 6 (b); 7 (d); 8 (a); 9 (c); 10 (b).

Essay Questions

1. Explain why social stratification is a creation of society, not just a reflection of individual differences.

2. How do caste and class systems differ? How are they the same? Why does industrialization introduce a measure of meritocracy into social stratification?

Chapter 11   Social Class in the United States

Multiple-Choice Questions

1. **Which of the following terms refers to earnings from work or investments?**
   a. income
   b. assets
   c. wealth
   d. power

2. The wealthiest 20 percent of people in the United States own about how much of the country's privately owned wealth?
   a. 39 percent
   b. 59 percent
   c. 89 percent
   d. 99 percent

3. About what share of U.S. adults over the age of twenty-five are college graduates?
   a. 10 percent
   b. 30 percent
   c. 50 percent
   d. 70 percent

4. In the United States, average income for African American families is what share of average income for non-Hispanic white families?
   a. 88 percent
   b. 78 percent
   c. 68 percent
   d. 58 percent

5. Which of the following is another term for the "working class"?
   a. upper-middle class
   b. average-middle class
   c. lower-middle class
   d. lower class

6. In terms of health, people living in high-income families
   a. live in safer and less stressful environments.
   b. are more likely to describe their own health as "excellent."
   c. live longer lives.
   d. All of the above are correct.

7. Which quintile (20 percent) of the U.S. population has seen the greatest change in income over the last generation?
   a. the top quintile
   b. the middle quintile
   c. the lowest quintile
   d. All quintiles have seen the same change.

8. Change in social position during a person's own lifetime is called
   a. intergenerational social mobility.
   b. intragenerational social mobility.
   c. structural social mobility.
   d. horizontal social mobility.

9. What share of the U.S. population is officially counted as poor?
   a. 45 percent
   b. 25 percent
   c. 15 percent
   d. 5 percent

10. Which age category of the U.S. population has the highest percentage of people in poverty?
    a. seniors over age sixty-five
    b. middle-aged people
    c. children
    d. people in their thirties

Essay Questions

1. We often hear people say that the United States is a "middle-class society." Where does this idea come from? Based on what you have read in this chapter, how true do you think this claim is? Why?

2. What is the extent of poverty in the United States? Who are the poor in terms of age, race and ethnicity, and gender?

Chapter 12   Global Stratification

Multiple-Choice Questions

1. In global perspective, the richest 20 percent of all people earn about what share of the entire world's income?
   a. 17 percent
   b. 37 percent
   c. 57 percent
   d. 77 percent

2. The United States, Canada, and Japan are all
   a. high-income countries.
   b. middle-income countries.
   c. low-income countries.
   d. in different income categories.

3. Low-income nations
   a. are evenly spread in all world regions.
   b. are found mostly in Africa and Asia.
   c. are all in Latin America.
   d. contain a majority of the world's people.

4. China and India are now
   a. the world's poorest countries.
   b. counted among the world's low-income nations.
   c. counted among the world's middle-income nations.
   d. counted among the world's high-income nations.

5. Which of the following is the range of annual personal income for people living in middle-income nations?
   a. $250 to $1,000
   b. $1,000 to $2,500
   c. $2,500 to $12,500
   d. $12,500 to $25,000

6. How does poverty in poor nations compare to poverty in the United States?
   a. In poor nations, poverty is more likely to involve men.
   b. In most poor nations, the problem of poverty has been all but solved.
   c. In poor nations, most people do not consider poverty a problem.
   d. In poor nations, there is far more absolute poverty.

7. *Neocolonialism* refers to the process by which
   a. rich countries gain new colonies to replace older ones.
   b. multinational corporations dominate the economy of a poor country.
   c. rich countries grant independence to their former colonies.
   d. more and more large corporations do business in many countries at once.

ANSWERS: 1 (a); 2 (c); 3 (b); 4 (d); 5 (c); 6 (d); 7 (a); 8 (b); 9 (c);10 (c).

8. Which of the following statements is the basis of modernization theory?
   a. The main cause of poverty in the world is low productivity due to simple technology and traditional culture.
   b. Poor nations can never become rich if they remain part of the global capitalist economy.
   c. The main cause of poverty in the world is the operation of multinational corporations.
   d. Most poor nations were richer in the past than they are today.

9. According to Walt Rostow, which is the final stage of economic development?
   a. drive to technological maturity
   b. traditional
   c. high mass consumption
   d. take-off

10. Dependency theory differs from modernization theory by saying that
    a. poor nations are responsible for their own poverty.
    b. capitalism is the best way to produce economic development.
    c. economic development is not a good idea for poor countries.
    d. global stratification results from the exploitation of poor countries by rich countries.

ANSWERS: 1 (d); 2 (a); 3 (b); 4 (c); 5 (c); 6 (d); 7 (b); 8 (a); 9 (c);10 (d).

Essay Questions

1. What are the differences between relative poverty and absolute poverty? Describe global social stratification using both concepts.

2. Why do many analysts believe that economic development in low-income countries depends on raising the social standing of women?

Chapter 13 Gender Stratification

Multiple-Choice Questions

1. Gender is not just a matter of difference but also a matter of
   a. power.
   b. wealth.
   c. prestige.
   d. All of the above are correct.

2. The anthropologist Margaret Mead studied gender in three societies in New Guinea and found that
   a. all societies define femininity in much the same way.
   b. all societies define masculinity in much the same way.
   c. what is feminine in one society may be masculine in another.
   d. the meaning of gender is changing everywhere toward greater equality.

3. For all of us raised in U.S. society, gender shapes our
   a. feelings.
   b. thoughts.
   c. actions.
   d. All of the above are correct.

4. There is a "beauty myth" in U.S. society that encourages
   a. women to believe that their personal importance depends on their looks.
   b. beautiful women to think that they do not need men.
   c. men to improve their physical appearance to get the attention of women.
   d. women to think they are as physically attractive as today's men are.

5. In the United States, what share of women work for income?
   a. 80 percent   c. 50 percent
   b. 60 percent   d. 30 percent

6. In the U.S. labor force,
   a. men and women have the same types of jobs.
   b. men and women have the same pay.
   c. women are still concentrated in several types of jobs.
   d. almost all working women hold "pink-collar jobs."

7. For which of the following categories of people in the United States is it true that women do more housework than men?
   a. people who work for income
   b. people who are married
   c. people who have children
   d. All of the above are correct.

8. In the United States, women in the labor force working full time earn how much for every dollar earned by men working full time?
   a. 77 cents   c. 90 cents
   b. 86 cents   d. 98 cents

9. After the 2012 elections, women held about what percentage of seats in Congress?
   a. 9 percent   c. 39 percent
   b. 19 percent   d. 59 percent

10. Which type of feminism accepts U.S. society as it is but wants to give women the same rights and opportunities as men?
    a. socialist feminism   c. radical feminism
    b. liberal feminism   d. All of the above are correct.

ANSWERS: 1 (d); 2 (c); 3 (d); 4 (a); 5 (b); 6 (c); 7 (d); 8 (a); 9 (b);10 (b).

Essay Questions

1. How do the concepts "sex" and "gender" differ? In what ways are they related?

2. Why is gender considered a dimension of social stratification? How does gender intersect with other dimensions of inequality such as class, race, and ethnicity?

Chapter 14 Race and Ethnicity

Multiple-Choice Questions

1. *Race* refers to _____ considered important by a society, and *ethnicity* refers to _____.
   a. biological traits; cultural traits
   b. cultural traits; biological traits
   c. differences; what we have in common
   d. what we have in common; differences

2. What share of the U.S. population consists of people of Hispanic ancestry?
   a. 46.7 percent
   b. 36.7 percent
   c. 26.7 percent
   d. 16.7 percent

3. A minority is defined as a category of people who
   a. have physical traits that make them different.
   b. are less than half the society's population.
   c. are defined as both different and disadvantaged.
   d. are below average in terms of income.

4. In this country, four states now have a "minority majority." Which of the following is not one of them?
   a. California
   b. Florida
   c. Hawaii
   d. New Mexico

5. Research using the Bogardus social distance scale shows that U.S. college students
   a. are less prejudiced than students fifty years ago.
   b. believe that Arabs and Muslims should be kept out of the country.
   c. have the strongest prejudice against African Americans.
   d. All of the above are correct.

6. *Prejudice* is a matter of _____, and *discrimination* is a matter of _____.
   a. biology; culture
   b. attitudes; behavior
   c. choice; social structure
   d. what rich people think; what rich people do

7. The United States is not truly pluralistic because
   a. part of our population lives in "ethnic enclaves."
   b. this country has a history of slavery.
   c. different racial and ethnic categories are unequal in social standing.
   d. All of the above are correct.

8. Which term is illustrated by immigrants from Ecuador learning to speak the English language?
   a. genocide
   b. segregation
   c. assimilation
   d. pluralism

9. During the late 1400s, the first Europeans came to the Americas; Native Americans
   a. followed shortly thereafter.
   b. had just migrated from Asia.
   c. came with them from Europe.
   d. had inhabited this land for 30,000 years.

10. Which of the following is the largest category of Asian Americans in the United States?
    a. Chinese Americans
    b. Japanese Americans
    c. Korean Americans
    d. Vietnamese Americans

ANSWERS: 1 (a); 2 (d); 3 (c); 4 (b); 5 (a); 6 (b); 7 (c); 8 (c); 9 (d);10 (a).

Essay Questions

1. What is the difference between race and ethnicity? What does it mean to say that race and ethnicity are socially constructed?

2. What is a minority? Support the claim that African Americans and Arab Americans are both minorities in the United States, using specific facts from the chapter.

Multiple-Choice Questions

1. Where in the world is the share of the elderly population increasing most quickly?
   a. low-income nations
   b. all the world's nations
   c. high-income nations
   d. Africa

2. What is the average (median) age of the U.S. population?
   a. sixty-seven years
   b. fifty-seven years
   c. forty-seven years
   d. thirty-seven years

3. As we look at older people in the United States, we find a larger share of
   a. men.
   b. women.
   c. well-off people.
   d. married people.

4. What effect does industrialization have on the social standing of the oldest members of a society?
   a. Social standing goes down.
   b. There is little or no effect.
   c. Social standing goes up.
   d. Social standing goes up for men and down for women.

5. The term *gerontocracy* refers to a society where
   a. there is a lot of social inequality.
   b. men dominate women.
   c. religious leaders are in charge.
   d. the oldest people have the most wealth, power, and prestige.

6. The idea of retirement first appears in which type of society?
   a. hunting and gathering
   b. pastoral
   c. industrial
   d. postindustrial

7. In the United States, the poverty rate for people over the age of sixty-five is
   a. higher than the national average.
   b. the same as the national average.
   c. lower than the national average.
   d. higher than among any other age category.

8. Which category of people in the United States provides most of the caregiving to elderly people?
   a. professionals working in the home
   b. nurses
   c. other elderly people
   d. women

9. The structural-functional approach to aging involves
   a. disengagement theory.
   b. activity theory.
   c. social inequality.
   d. All of the above are correct.

10. A document in which a person states which medical procedures he or she wishes to be used or avoided under specific conditions is known as a
    a. death wish.
    b. living will.
    c. legal trust.
    d. power of attorney.

ANSWERS: 1 (c); 2 (d); 3 (b); 4 (a); 5 (d); 6 (c); 7 (c); 8 (d); 9 (a);10 (b).

1. What is the "graying of the United States"? What two factors are causing this trend? What are some of the likely consequences of this trend for our way of life?

2. How is ageism like sexism and racism? How is it different? If older people are disadvantaged, should they be considered a minority? Why or why not?

Chapter 16   The Economy and Work

Multiple-Choice Questions

1. The economy is the social institution that guides
   a. the production of goods and services.
   b. the distribution of goods and services.
   c. the consumption of goods and services.
   d. All of the above are correct.

2. As nations develop economically, which sector represents a steadily decreasing share of all economic production?
   a. primary sector
   b. secondary sector
   c. tertiary sector
   d. All of the three sectors remain the same.

3. Building houses and making cars are examples of production in which economic sector?
   a. the primary sector
   b. the secondary sector
   c. the tertiary sector
   d. the service sector

4. Which of the following marks the rise of a postindustrial economy?
   a. the spread of factories
   b. declining rates of consumption
   c. the development of computer technology
   d. larger machinery

5. Today, about what share of the U.S. labor force has blue-collar work?
   a. about 20 percent
   b. about 50 percent
   c. about 75 percent
   d. about 90 percent

6. What is a result of the globalization of the economy?
   a. Certain areas of the world are specializing in one sector of economic activity.
   b. Industrial jobs in the United States are being lost.
   c. More and more products pass through several nations on their way to consumers.
   d. All of the above are correct.

7. A capitalist society's approach to economic "justice" amounts to
   a. doing what is best for society's poorest members.
   b. freedom of the marketplace.
   c. making everyone more or less socially equal.
   d. All of the above are correct.

8. Socialist economies differ from capitalist economies in that they
   a. are more productive.
   b. create less economic equality.

c. create more economic equality.
d. make greater use of commercial advertising.

9. In the United States, what percentage of nonfarm workers are members of a labor union?
   a. 12 percent
   b. 32 percent
   c. 52 percent
   d. 72 percent

10. The largest 2604 corporations, each with assets exceeding $2.5 billion, represent about what share of all corporate assets in the United States?
    a. 11 percent
    b. 31 percent
    c. 51 percent
    d. 81 percent

ANSWERS: 1 (d); 2 (a); 3 (b); 4 (c); 5 (a); 6 (d); 7 (b); 8 (c); 9 (a);10 (d).

Essay Questions

1. In what specific ways did the Industrial Revolution change the U.S. economy? How is the Information Revolution changing the economy once again?

2. What key characteristics distinguish capitalism from socialism? Compare these two systems in terms of productivity, economic inequality, and extent of personal freedoms.

Chapter 17   Politics and Government

Multiple-Choice Questions

1. According to Max Weber, power is defined as
   a. "the shadow of wealth."
   b. the ability to achieve desired ends despite resistance from others.
   c. a society's form of government.
   d. the creation of bureaucracy.

2. Max Weber claimed that the main difference between power and authority is that
   a. power is a better way to hold a society together.
   b. authority is based on brute force.
   c. power involves a special claim to justice.
   d. people typically view authority as legitimate rather than coercive.

3. Modern societies, including the United States, rely mostly on which type of authority?
   a. charismatic authority
   b. traditional authority
   c. rational-legal authority
   d. no authority

4. In which type of political system does power reside in the hands of the people as a whole?
   a. democracy
   b. aristocracy
   c. totalitarianism
   d. monarchy

5. When sociologists use the term "political economy," they are referring to
   a. the fact that people "vote with their pocketbook."
   b. the fact that the political and economic systems are linked.
   c. any democratic political system.
   d. the most efficient form of government.

6. The claim that socialist societies are democratic is typically based on the fact that
   a. their members have considerable personal liberty.
   b. these societies have no elite.
   c. these societies meet the basic economic needs of everyone.
   d. these societies have a high standard of living.

7. Which type of government concentrates all power in one place and rigidly regulates people's lives?
   a. an aristocratic government
   b. a democratic government
   c. an authoritarian government
   d. a totalitarian government

8. In the 2012 U.S. presidential election, about what share of registered voters actually cast a vote?
   a. close to 100 percent
   b. about 81 percent
   c. about 58 percent
   d. about 27 percent

9. The Marxist political-economy model suggests that
   a. power is concentrated in the hands of a small "power elite."
   b. an antidemocratic bias is built into the capitalist system.
   c. power is spread widely throughout society.
   d. many people do not vote because they are basically satisfied with their lives.

10. Which war resulted in the greatest loss of American lives?
    a. the Civil War
    b. World War II
    c. the Korean War
    d. the Vietnam War

ANSWERS: 1 (b); 2 (d); 3 (c); 4 (a); 5 (b); 6 (c); 7 (d); 8 (c); 9 (b);10 (a).

Essay Questions

1. What is the difference between authority and power? How do preindustrial and industrial societies create authority in different ways?

2. Compare and contrast the pluralist, power-elite, and Marxist political-economy models of political power. Which of these models do you think makes the most sense? Why?

Chapter 18   Families

Multiple-Choice Questions

1. The family is a social institution that is found in
   a. most but not all societies.
   b. low-income nations but typically not in high-income nations.
   c. high-income nations but typically not in low-income nations.
   d. every society.

2. What is the term sociologists use for a family containing parents, children, and other kin?
   a. a nuclear family
   b. an extended family
   c. a family of affinity
   d. a conjugal family

3. A system of marriage that unites one woman with two or more men is called
   a. polygamy.
   b. polygyny.
   c. polyandry.
   d. bilateral marriage.

4. Sociologists claim that marriage in the United States follows the principle of homogamy, which means that partners are
   a. people of the same sex.
   b. people who are socially alike in terms of class, age, and race.
   c. people who marry due to social pressure.
   d. selected based on love rather than by parents.

5. Which of the following are included among the functions of the family?
   a. socialization of children
   b. regulation of sexual activity
   c. social placement of children
   d. All of the above are correct.

6. Which theoretical approach states that people select partners who have about the same to offer as they do?
   a. the structural-functional approach
   b. the social-exchange approach
   c. the social-conflict approach
   d. the feminist approach

7. Which of the following transitions in married life is usually the hardest for people?
   a. birth of the second child
   b. last child leaving home
   c. death of a spouse
   d. retiring from the labor force

8. In the United States, many Latino families are characterized by
   a. strong extended kinship.
   b. parents exerting a great deal of control over their children's courtship.
   c. traditional gender roles.
   d. All of the above are correct.

9. For which category of the U.S. population is the highest proportion of children born to single women?
   a. African Americans
   b. Asian Americans
   c. Hispanic Americans
   d. non-Hispanic white Americans

10. Which category of people in the United States is at the highest risk of divorce?
    a. gay and lesbian couples
    b. young people who marry after a short courtship
    c. a couple whose parents never experienced divorce
    d. a couple facing a wanted and expected pregnancy

ANSWERS: 1 (d); 2 (b); 3 (c); 4 (b); 5 (d); 6 (b); 7 (c); 8 (d); 9 (a);10 (b).

Essay Questions

1. Sociologists point to ways in which family life reflects not just individual choices but the structure of society as well. Provide three examples of how society shapes family life.

2. Overall, do you think families in the United States are becoming weaker or simply more diverse? Support your position.

Chapter 19   Religion

Multiple-Choice Questions

1. What term did Emile Durkheim use to refer to the everyday elements of our lives?
   a. religion
   b. profane
   c. sacred
   d. ritual

2. Faith, or belief in religious matters, is best described as
   a. what we learn from science.
   b. what our senses tell us.
   c. our cultural traditions.
   d. conviction in things unseen.

3. The reason sociologists study religion is to learn
   a. the meaning of life.
   b. whether a particular religion is true or not.
   c. how patterns of religious activity affect society.
   d. which religious organization they wish to join.

4. Which of the following is *not* one of the important functions of religion, according to Durkheim?
   a. generating social conflict
   b. generating social cohesion
   c. providing social control
   d. providing meaning and purpose

5. Peter Berger claims that we are most likely to turn to religion when we experience
   a. social conflict.
   b. the best of times.
   c. familiar, everyday routines.
   d. important events that are out of our control.

6. Which sociologist explained how religion helps support social inequality?
   a. Emile Durkheim
   b. Karl Marx
   c. Max Weber
   d. Ernst Troeltsch

7. Which type of religious organization is most integrated into the larger society?
   a. cult
   b. church
   c. sect
   d. New Age spirituality

8. A sect is a type of religious organization that
   a. has formally trained leaders.
   b. is well integrated into the larger society.
   c. rejects the importance of charisma.
   d. stands apart from the larger society.

9. Which of the following religions is found in the United States?
   a. Islam
   b. Judaism
   c. Christianity
   d. All of the above are correct.

10. The term "secularization" refers to which of the following?
    a. religion becoming more important in people's lives
    b. increasing popularity of fundamentalism
    c. the decline in the importance of religion and the sacred
    d. churches resisting social change

ANSWERS: 1 (b); 2 (d); 3 (c); 4 (a); 5 (d); 6 (b); 7 (b); 8 (d); 9 (d); 10 (c).

Essay Questions

1. What is the basic distinction between the sacred and the profane that underlies all religious belief?

2. In what ways do churches, sects, and cults differ?

Chapter 20   Education

Multiple-Choice Questions

1. In the United States and other countries, laws requiring all children to attend school were enacted following
   a. national independence.
   b. the Industrial Revolution.
   c. World War II.
   d. the computer age.

2. Japan differs from the United States in that getting into college depends more on
   a. athletic ability.
   b. race and ethnicity.
   c. family money.
   d. scores on achievement tests.

3. What share of the U.S. adult population has completed high school?
   a. 45.3 percent
   b. 65.5 percent
   c. 87.6 percent
   d. 99.9 percent

4. Using a structural-functional approach, schooling carries out the task of
   a. tying together a diverse population.
   b. creating new culture.
   c. socializing young people.
   d. All of the above are correct.

5. A social-conflict approach highlights how education
   a. reflects and reinforces social inequality.
   b. helps prepare students for their future careers.
   c. has both latent and manifest functions.
   d. All of the above are correct.

6. The importance of community colleges to U.S. higher education is reflected in the fact that they
   a. greatly expand the opportunity to attend college.
   b. enroll more than 40 percent of all U.S. college students.
   c. enroll half of all Hispanic college students.
   d. All of the above are correct.

7. What share of people in the United States between the ages of sixteen and twenty-four drop out before completing high school?
   a. 1.1 percent
   b. 7.1 percent
   c. 29.1 percent
   d. 39.1 percent

8. Support for the school choice movement is based on the claim that U.S. public schools perform poorly because
   a. they have no competition.
   b. many schools lack enough funding.
   c. the national poverty rate is high.
   d. too many parents are not involved in the schools.

9. This chapter provides lots of evidence to support the claim that
   a. U.S. schools are better than those in other high-income nations.
   b. most public schools perform well and most private schools do not.
   c. without involving the entire society, schools cannot improve the quality of education.
   d. All of the above are correct.

10. About what share of all U.S. college students today are men?
   a. 63 percent
   c. 43 percent
   b. 53 percent
   d. 33 percent

ANSWERS: 1 (b); 2 (d); 3 (c); 4 (d); 5 (a); 6 (d); 7 (b); 8 (a); 9 (c);10 (c).

Essay Questions

1. Why does industrialization lead societies to expand their systems of schooling? In what ways has schooling in the United States been shaped by our economic, political, and cultural systems?

2. From a structural-functional perspective, why is schooling important to the operation of society? From a social-conflict point of view, how does schooling reproduce social inequality in each generation?

Chapter 21   Health and Medicine

Multiple-Choice Questions

1. **Health is a social issue because**
   a. cultural patterns define what people view as healthy.
   b. social inequality affects people's health.
   c. a society's technology affects people's health.
   d. All of the above are correct.

2. **In the very poorest nations of the world today, a majority of people die before reaching**
   a. their teens.
   c. the age of sixty-five.
   b. the age of fifty.
   d. the age of seventy-five.

3. **The Industrial Revolution reduced deaths caused by _____, which increased the share of deaths caused by _____.**
   a. disease; war
   b. starvation; accidents
   c. infectious diseases such as influenza; chronic conditions such as heart disease
   d. chronic conditions such as heart disease; infectious diseases such as influenza

4. **Social epidemiology is the study of**
   a. which bacteria cause a specific disease.
   b. the distribution of health and illness in a population.
   c. what categories of people become doctors.
   d. the distribution of doctors around the world.

5. **What is the largest cause of death among young people in the United States?**
   a. cancer
   c. accidents
   b. influenza
   d. AIDS

6. **In the United States, which category of people has the highest life expectancy?**
   a. African American men
   c. African American women
   b. white men
   d. white women

7. **In the United States, the greatest preventable cause of death is**
   a. sexually transmitted diseases.
   b. automobile accidents.
   c. cigarette smoking.
   d. AIDS.

8. **About what share of U.S. adults are overweight?**
   a. two-thirds
   b. half
   b. one-third
   d. one-fifth

9. **Which sexually transmitted disease is most common among U.S. adults?**
   a. AIDS
   b. genital herpes
   b. gonorrhea
   d. syphilis

10. **A social-conflict analysis claims that capitalism harms human health because**
   a. it does not encourage people to take control of their own health.
   b. it gives physicians little financial incentive to work.
   c. it reduces average living standards.
   d. it makes quality of care dependent on income.

ANSWERS: 1 (d); 2 (a); 3 (c); 4 (b); 5 (c); 6 (d); 7 (c); 8 (a); 9 (b);10 (d).

Essay Questions

1. Why is health as much a social as a biological issue? How does a social-conflict analysis of health and medicine point to the need to define health as a social issue?

2. Describe Talcott Parsons's structural-functional analysis of health and illness. What is the sick role? When and how is it used?

Chapter 22   Population, Urbanization, and Environment

Multiple-Choice Questions

1. *Demography* is defined as the study of
   a. democratic political systems.
   b. human culture.
   c. human population.
   d. the natural environment.

2. **Which region of the world has *both* the lowest birth rate and the lowest infant mortality rate?**
   a. Latin America
   c. Europe
   b. Africa
   d. Asia

3. **Typically, high-income nations grow mostly from _____, and low-income nations grow from _____.**
   a. immigration; natural increase
   b. emigration; natural increase
   c. natural increase; immigration
   d. internal migration; natural increase

4. In general, the higher the average income of a country,
   a. the faster the population increases.
   b. the slower the population increases.
   c. the lower the level of immigration.
   d. the lower the level of urbanization.

5. In the United States, urban decentralization has caused
   a. the expansion of suburbs.
   b. the development of vast urban regions.
   c. the growth of edge cities.
   d. All of the above are correct.

6. Which term was used by Ferdinand Tönnies to refer to a type of social organization in which people come together on the basis of individual self-interest?
   a. mechanical solidarity
   b. organic solidarity
   c. *Gesellschaft*
   d. *Gemeinschaft*

7. The world's third urban revolution is now taking place in
   a. the United States.
   b. Europe and Japan.
   c. middle-income nations.
   d. low-income nations.

8. The *environmental deficit* refers to
   a. long-term harm to the environment caused by a shortsighted focus on material affluence.
   b. the public's lack of interest in the natural environment.
   c. the fact that natural scientists ignore the social dimensions of environmental problems.
   d. the lack of funding for important environmental programs.

9. Which of the following statements reflects the "limits to growth" thesis?
   a. People are rapidly consuming Earth's finite resources.
   b. Whatever problems technology creates, technology can solve.
   c. The quality of life on Earth is getting better.
   d. Higher living standards today will benefit future generations.

10. *Environmental racism* is the idea that
    a. few minorities are found within the environmental movement.
    b. prejudice is the major cause of pollution and other environmental problems.
    c. environmental dangers are greatest for the poor and minorities.
    d. All of the above are correct.

ANSWERS: 1 (c); 2 (b); 3 (a); 4 (b); 5 (d); 6 (c); 7 (d); 8 (a); 9 (a);10 (c).

Essay Questions

1. According to demographic transition theory, how does economic development affect population patterns?

2. According to Ferdinand Tönnies, Emile Durkheim, Georg Simmel, and Louis Wirth, what characterizes urbanism as a way of life? Note several differences in the ideas of these thinkers.

Chapter 23   Collective Behavior and Social Movements

Multiple-Choice Questions

1. Which of the following is true about collective behavior?
   a. It usually involves a large number of people.
   b. It is often spontaneous.
   c. It is often controversial.
   d. All of the above are correct.

2. Which of the following is a good example of a collectivity?
   a. students quietly working out in the college weight room
   b. excited soccer fans throwing bottles as they leave a stadium
   c. students in line in the cafeteria waiting to be served
   d. All of the above are correct.

3. A mob differs from a riot in that the mob
   a. typically has a clear objective.
   b. is not violent.
   c. does not involve people with intense emotion.
   d. lasts a long time.

4. Which theory says that "crowds can make people go crazy"?
   a. emergent-norm theory
   b. convergence theory
   c. contagion theory
   d. subcultural theory

5. When sociologists speak of "mass behavior," they have in mind
   a. people taking part in a riot or mob.
   b. many people spread over a large area thinking or acting in a particular way.
   c. irrational behavior on the part of people in a crowd.
   d. people imitating what they see others do.

6. Which of the following is an example of a technological disaster?
   a. the collapse of the World Trade Center towers on September 11, 2001
   b. the deaths of millions of civilians during World War II
   c. Hurricane Katrina slamming into the Gulf Coast
   d. the radiation leak from the Chernobyl nuclear power plant

7. Hula hoops, streaking, and collecting Pokémon cards are all examples of
   a. style.
   b. fads.
   c. fashion.
   d. popular social movements.

8. Deprivation theory explains that social movements arise among people who
   a. feel adrift in society.
   b. are poor and feel they have little more to lose.
   c. believe that they lack rights, income, or something else that they think they should have.
   d. are moved to action by particular cultural symbols.

9. The claim that social movements cannot arise without factors such as effort, money, and leadership is made by which theory?
   a. resource-mobilization theory
   b. deprivation theory
   c. mass-society theory
   d. political-economy theory

10. The effect of gender on the operation of social movements in the United States is demonstrated by the fact that
    a. few women are interested in most public issues.
    b. men have usually taken leadership roles.
    c. men tend to avoid participation in social movements.
    d. women typically have taken leadership roles.

ANSWERS: 1 (d); 2 (b); 3 (a); 4 (c); 5 (b); 6 (d); 7 (c); 8 (c); 9 (a);10 (b).

Essay Questions

1. The concept of collective behavior encompasses a broad range of social patterns. List some of these patterns. What traits do they have in common? How do they differ?

2. In what respects do some recent social movements (the environment, animal rights, and gun control) differ from older crusades (the right of workers to form unions or the right of women to vote)?

Chapter 24   Social Change: Traditional, Modern, and Postmodern Societies

Multiple-Choice Questions

1. Sociologists use the term "modernity" to refer to social patterns that emerged
   a. with the first human civilizations.
   b. after the fall of Rome.
   c. after the Industrial Revolution.
   d. along with the Information Revolution.

2. Which of the following are common causes of social change?
   a. invention of new ideas and things
   b. diffusion from one cultural system to another
   c. discovery of existing things
   d. All of the above are correct.

3. Karl Marx highlighted the importance of which of the following in the process of social change?
   a. immigration and demographic factors
   b. ideas
   c. social conflict
   d. cultural diffusion

4. Max Weber's analysis of how Calvinism helped create the spirit of capitalism highlighted the importance of which of the following in the process of social change?
   a. invention   b. social conflict
   b. ideas   d. cultural diffusion

5. Which term was used by Ferdinand Tönnies to describe a traditional society?
   a. *Gemeinschaft*
   b. *Gesellschaft*
   c. mechanical solidarity
   d. organic solidarity

6. According to Emile Durkheim, modern societies have
   a. respect for established tradition.
   b. widespread alienation.
   c. common values and beliefs.
   d. an increasing division of labor.

7. For Max Weber, modernity meant the rise of _____; for Karl Marx, modernity meant _____.
   a. capitalism, anomie
   b. rationality, capitalism
   c. tradition, self-interest
   d. specialization, Gesellschaft

8. Which of the following statements about modernity as a mass society is *not* correct?
   a. There is more poverty today than in past centuries.
   b. Kinship ties have become weaker.
   c. Bureaucracy, including government, has increased in size.
   d. People experience moral uncertainty about how to live.

9. Sociologists who describe modernity in terms of class society focus on which of the following?
   a. rationality as a way of thinking about the world
   b. mutual dependency
   c. the rise of capitalism
   d. the high risk of anomie

10. David Riesman described the other-directed social character typical of modern people as
    a. rigid conformity to tradition.
    b. eagerness to follow the latest fashions and fads.
    c. strong individualism.
    d. All of the above are correct.

ANSWERS: 1 (c); 2 (d); 3 (c); 4 (b); 5 (a); 6 (d); 7 (b); 8 (a); 9 (c);10 (b).

Essay Questions

1. Discuss how Tönnies, Durkheim, Weber, and Marx described modern society. What are the similarities and differences in their understandings of modernity?

2. What traits lead some analysts to call the United States a "mass society"? Why do other analysts describe the United States as a "class society"?

Glossary

abortion   the deliberate termination of a pregnancy

absolute poverty   a lack of resources that is life-threatening

achieved status   a social position a person takes on voluntarily that reflects personal ability and effort

activity theory   the idea that a high level of activity increases personal satisfaction in old age

Afrocentrism   emphasizing and promoting African cultural patterns

ageism   prejudice and discrimination against older people

age stratification   the unequal distribution of wealth, power, and privilege among people at different stages of the life course

age-sex pyramid   a graphic representation of the age and sex of a population

agriculture   large-scale cultivation using plows harnessed to animals or more powerful energy sources

alienation   the experience of isolation and misery resulting from powerlessness

animism   the belief that elements of the natural world are conscious life forms that affect humanity

anomie   Durkheim's term for a condition in which society provides little moral guidance to individuals

anticipatory socialization   learning that helps a person achieve a desired position

ascribed status   a social position a person receives at birth or takes on involuntarily later in life

asexuality   a lack of sexual attraction to people of either sex

assimilation   the process by which minorities gradually adopt patterns of the dominant culture

authoritarianism   a political system that denies the people participation in government

authority   power that people perceive as legitimate rather than coercive

beliefs   specific ideas that people hold to be true

bilateral descent   a system tracing kinship through both men and women

bisexuality   sexual attraction to people of both sexes

blue-collar occupations   lower-prestige jobs that involve mostly manual labor

bureaucracy   an organizational model rationally designed to perform tasks efficiently

bureaucratic inertia   the tendency of bureaucratic organizations to perpetuate themselves

bureaucratic ritualism   a focus on rules and regulations to the point of undermining an organization's goals but cooperate closely with the government

capitalism   an economic system in which natural resources and the means of producing goods and services are privately owned

capitalists   people who own and operate factories and other businesses in pursuit of profits

caregiving   informal and unpaid care provided to a dependent person by family members, other relatives, or friends

caste system   social stratification based on ascription, or birth

cause and effect   a relationship in which change in one variable (the independent variable) causes change in another (the dependent variable)

charisma   extraordinary personal qualities that can infuse people with emotion and turn them into followers

charismatic authority   power legitimized by extraordinary personal abilities that inspire devotion and obedience

church   a type of religious organization that is well integrated into the larger society

civil religion   a quasi-religious loyalty linking individuals in a basically secular society

claims making   the process of trying to convince the public and public officials of the importance of joining a social movement to address a particular issue

class conflict   conflict between entire classes over the distribution of a society's wealth and power

class consciousness   Marx's term for workers' recognition of themselves as a class unified in opposition to capitalists and ultimately to capitalism itself

class society   a capitalist society with pronounced social stratification

class system   social stratification based on both birth and individual achievement

cohabitation   the sharing of a household by an unmarried couple

cohort   a category of people with something in common, usually their age

collective behavior   activity involving a large number of people that is unplanned, often controversial, and sometimes dangerous

collectivity   a large number of people whose minimal interaction occurs in the absence of well-defined and conventional norms

colonialism   the process by which some nations enrich themselves through political and economic control of other nations

communism   a hypothetical economic and political system in which all members of a society are socially equal

community-based corrections   correctional programs operating within society at large rather than behind prison walls

concept   a mental construct that represents some aspect of the world in a simplified form

concrete operational stage   Piaget's term for the level of human development at which individuals first see causal connections in their surroundings

conglomerate   a giant corporation composed of many smaller corporations

conspicuous consumption   buying and using products because of the "statement" they make about social position

control   holding constant all variables except one in order to see clearly the effect of that variable

corporate crime   the illegal actions of a corporation or people acting on its behalf

corporation   an organization with a legal existence, including rights and liabilities, separate from that of its members

correlation   a relationship in which two (or more) variables change together

counterculture   cultural patterns that strongly oppose those widely accepted within a society

crime   the violation of a society's formally enacted criminal law

crimes against property   crimes that involve theft of property belonging to others; also known as *property crimes*

crimes against the person   crimes that direct violence or the threat of violence against others; also known as *violent crimes*

criminal justice system   the organizations—police, courts, and prison officials—that respond to alleged violations of the law

criminal recidivism   later offenses by people previously convicted of crimes

critical sociology   the study of society that focuses on the need for social change

crowd   a temporary gathering of people who share a common focus of attention and who influence one another

crude birth rate   the number of live births in a given year for every 1,000 people in a population

crude death rate   the number of deaths in a given year for every 1,000 people in a population

cult   a religious organization that is largely outside a society's cultural traditions

cultural integration   the close relationships among various elements of a cultural system

cultural lag   the fact that some cultural elements change more quickly than others, disrupting a cultural system

cultural relativism   the practice of judging a culture by its own standards

cultural transmission   the process by which one generation passes culture to the next

cultural universals   traits that are part of every known culture

culture   the ways of thinking, the ways of acting, and the material objects that together form a people's way of life

culture shock   personal disorientation when experiencing an unfamiliar way of life

Davis-Moore thesis   the functional analysis claiming that social stratification has beneficial consequences for the operation of society

deductive logical thought   reasoning that transforms general theory into specific hypotheses suitable for testing

democracy   political system that gives power to the people as a whole

demographic transition theory a thesis that links population patterns to a society's level of technological development

demography the study of human population

denomination a church, independent of the state, that recognizes religious pluralism

dependency theory a model of economic and social development that explains global inequality in terms of the historical exploitation of poor nations by rich ones

dependent variable the variable that changes

descent the system by which members of a society trace kinship over generations

deterrence the attempt to discourage criminality through the use of punishment

deviance the recognized violation of cultural norms

direct-fee system a medical care system in which patients pay directly for the services of physicians and hospitals

disaster an event, generally unexpected, that causes extensive harm to people and damage to property

discrimination unequal treatment of various categories of people

disengagement theory the idea that society functions in an orderly way by removing people from positions of responsibility as they reach old age

division of labor specialized economic activity

dramaturgical analysis Erving Goffman's term for the study of social interaction in terms of theatrical performance

dyad a social group with two members

eating disorder a physical and mental disorder that involves an intense form of dieting or other unhealthy method of weight control driven by the desire to be very thin

ecologically sustainable culture a way of life that meets the needs of the present generation without threatening the environmental legacy of future generations

ecology the study of the interaction of living organisms and the natural environment

economy the social institution that organizes a society's production, distribution, and consumption of goods and services

ecosystem a system composed of the interaction of all living organisms and their natural environment

education the social institution through which society provides its members with important knowledge, including basic facts, job skills, and cultural norms and values

ego Freud's term for a person's conscious efforts to balance innate pleasure-seeking drives with the demands of society

empirical evidence information we can verify with our senses

endogamy marriage between people of the same social category

environmental deficit profound long-term harm to the natural environment caused by humanity's focus on short-term material affluence

environmental racism patterns of development that expose poor people, especially minorities, to environmental hazards

ethnicity a shared cultural heritage

ethnocentrism the practice of judging another culture by the standards of one's own culture

ethnomethodology Harold Garfinkel's term for the study of the way people make sense of their everyday surroundings

Eurocentrism the dominance of European (especially English) cultural patterns

euthanasia assisting in the death of a person suffering from an incurable disease; also known as *mercy killing*

exogamy marriage between people of different social categories

experiment a research method for investigating cause and effect under highly controlled conditions

expressive leadership group leadership that focuses on the group's well-being

extended family a family consisting of parents and children as well as other kin; also known as a *consanguine family*

fad an unconventional social pattern that people embrace briefly but enthusiastically

faith belief based on conviction rather than on scientific evidence

false consciousness Marx's term for explanations of social problems as the short-comings of individuals rather than as the flaws of society

family a social institution found in all societies that unites people in cooperative groups to care for one another, including any children

family violence emotional, physical, or sexual abuse of one family member by another

fashion a social pattern favored by a large number of people

feminism support of social equality for women and men, in opposition to patriarchy and sexism

feminization of poverty the trend of women making up an increasing proportion of the poor

fertility the incidence of childbearing in a country's population

folkways norms for routine or casual interaction

formal operational stage Piaget's term for the level of human development at which individuals think abstractly and critically

formal organization a large secondary group organized to achieve its goals efficiently

functional illiteracy a lack of the reading and writing skills needed for everyday living

fundamentalism a conservative religious doctrine that opposes intellectualism and worldly accommodation in favor of restoring traditional, other-worldly religion

Gemeinschaft a type of social organization in which people are closely tied by kinship and tradition

gender the personal traits and social positions that members of a society attach to being female or male

gender roles (also known as sex roles) attitudes and activities that a society links to each sex

gender stratification the unequal distribution of wealth, power, and privilege between men and women

gender-conflict theory (feminist theory) the study of society that focuses on inequality and conflict between women and men

generalized other George Herbert Mead's term for widespread cultural norms and values we use as references in evaluating ourselves

genocide the systematic killing of one category of people by another

gerontocracy a form of social organization in which the elderly have the most wealth, power, and prestige

gerontology the study of aging and the elderly

Gesellschaft a type of social organization in which people come together only on the basis of individual self-interest

global economy economic activity that crosses national borders

global stratification patterns of social inequality in the world as a whole

global warming a rise in Earth's average temperature due to an increasing concentration of carbon dioxide in the atmosphere

gossip rumor about people's personal affairs

government a formal organization that directs the political life of a society

groupthink the tendency of group members to conform, resulting in a narrow view of some issue

hate crime a criminal act against a person or a person's property by an offender motivated by racial or their bias

Hawthorne effect a change in a subject's behavior caused simply by the awareness of being studied

health a state of complete physical, mental, and social well-being

health maintenance organization (HMO) an organization that provides comprehensive medical care to subscribers for a fixed fee

heterosexism a view that labels anyone who is not heterosexual as "queer"

heterosexuality sexual attraction to someone of the other sex

high culture cultural patterns that distinguish a society's elite

high-income countries the nations with the highest overall standards of living

holistic medicine an approach to health care that emphasizes prevention of illness and takes into account a person's entire physical and social environment

homogamy marriage between people with the same social characteristics

homophobia discomfort over close personal interaction with people thought to be gay, lesbian, or bisexual

homosexuality sexual attraction to someone of the same sex

horticulture the use of hand tools to raise crops

hunting and gathering making use of simple tools to hunt animals and gather vegetation for food

hypothesis a statement of a possible relationship between two (or more) variables

id Freud's term for the human being's basic drives

ideal type an abstract statement of the essential characteristics of any social phenomenon

ideology cultural beliefs that justify particular social arrangements, including patterns of inequality

incest taboo a norm forbidding sexual relations or marriage between certain relatives

income   earnings from work or investments

independent variable   the variable that causes the change

inductive logical thought   reasoning that transforms specific observations into general theory

industrialism   the production of goods using advanced sources of energy to drive large machinery

infant mortality rate   the number of deaths among infants under one year of age for each 1,000 live births in a given year

infidelity   sexual activity outside one's marriage

in-group   a social group toward which a member feels respect and loyalty

institutional prejudice and discrimination   bias built into the operation of society's institutions

instrumental leadership   group leadership that focuses on the completion of tasks

intergenerational social mobility   upward or downward social mobility of children in relation to their parents

interpretive sociology   the study of society that focuses on discovering the meanings people attach to their social world

intersection theory   analysis of the interplay of race, class, and gender, which often results in multiple dimensions of disadvantage

intersexual people   people whose bodies (including genitals) have both female and male characteristics

interview   a series of questions a researcher asks respondents in person

intragenerational social mobility   a change in social position occurring during a person's lifetime

kinship   a social bond based on common ancestry, marriage, or adoption

labeling theory   the idea that deviance and conformity result not so much from what people do as from how others

labor unions   organizations of workers that seek to improve wages and working conditions through various strategies, including negotiations and strikes

language   a system of symbols that allows people to communicate with one another

latent functions   the unrecognized and unintended consequences of any social pattern

liberation theology   the combining of Christian principles with political activism, often Marxist in character

life expectancy   the average life span of a country's population

looking-glass self   Cooley's term for a self-image based on how we think others see us

low-income countries   nations with a low standard of living in which most people are poor

macro-level orientation   a broad focus on social structures that shape society as a whole

mainstreaming   integrating students with disabilities or special needs into the overall educational program

manifest functions   the recognized and intended consequences of any social pattern

marriage   a legal relationship, usually involving economic cooperation, sexual activity, and childbearing

Marxist political-economy model   an analysis that explains politics in terms of the operation of a society's economic system

mass behavior   collective behavior among people spread over a wide geographic area

mass hysteria (moral panic)   a form of dispersed collective behavior in which people react to a real or imagined event with irrational and even frantic fear

mass media   the means for delivering impersonal communications to a vast audience

mass society   a society in which prosperity and bureaucracy have weakened traditional social ties

master status   a status that has special importance for social identity, often shaping a person's entire life

material culture   the physical things created by members of a society

matriarchy   a form of social organization in which females dominate males

matrilineal descent   a system tracing kinship through women

matrilocality   a residential pattern in which a married couple lives with or near the wife's family

measurement   a procedure for determining the value of a variable in a specific case

mechanical solidarity   Durkheim's term for social bonds, based on common sentiments and shared moral values, that are strong among members of preindustrial societies

medicalization of deviance   the transformation of moral and legal deviance into a medical condition

medicine   the social institution that focuses on fighting disease and improving health

megalopolis   a vast urban region containing a number of cities and their surrounding suburbs

meritocracy   social stratification based on personal merit

Metaphysical Stage   (the Enlightenment and the ideas of Hobbes, Locke, and Rousseau)

metropolis   a large city that socially and economically dominates an urban area

micro-level orientation   a close-up focus on social interaction in specific situations

middle-income countries   nations with a standard of living about average for the world as a whole

migration   the movement of people into and out of a specified territory

military-industrial complex   the close association of the federal government, the military, and defense industries

minority   any category of people distinguished by physical or cultural difference that a society sets apart and subordinates

miscegenation   biological reproduction by partners of different racial categories

mob   a highly emotional crowd that pursues a violent or destructive goal

modernity   changes brought about by the Industrial Revolution

modernization   the process of social change begun by industrialization

modernization theory   a model of economic and social development that explains global inequality in terms of technological and cultural differences between nations

monarchy   a political system in which a single family rules from generation to generation

monogamy   marriage that unites two partners

monopoly   the domination of a market by a single producer

monotheism   belief in a single divine power

mores   norms that are widely observed and have great moral significance

mortality   the incidence of death in a country's population

multiculturalism   a perspective recognizing the cultural diversity of the United States and promoting equal standing for all cultural traditions

multinational corporation   a large business that operates in many countries

natural environment   Earth's surface and atmosphere, including living organisms, air, water, soil, and other resources necessary to sustain life

neocolonialism   a new form of global power relationships that involves not direct political control but economic exploitation by multinational corporations

neolocality   a residential pattern in which a married couple lives apart from both sets of parents

network   a web of weak social ties

nonmaterial culture   the ideas created by members of a society

nonverbal communication   communication using body movements, gestures, and facial expressions rather than speech

norms   rules and expectations by which a society guides the behavior of its members

nuclear family   a family composed of one or two parents and their children; also known as a *conjugal family*

nuclear proliferation   the acquisition of nuclear weapons technology by more and more nations

objectivity   personal neutrality in conducting research

oligarchy   the rule of the many by the few

oligopoly   the domination of a market by a few producers

operationalize a variable   specifying exactly what is to be measured before assigning a value to a variable

organic solidarity   Durkheim's term for social bonds, based on specialization and interdependence, that are strong among members of industrial societies

organizational environment   factors outside an organization hat affect its operation

organized crime   a business supplying illegal goods or services

other-directedness   openness to the latest trends and fashions, often expressed by imitating others

out-group   a social group toward which a person feels a sense of competition or opposition

panic   a form of collective behavior in which people in one place react to a threat or other stimulus with irrational, frantic, and often self-destructive behavior

participant observation   a research method in which investigators systematically observe people while joining them in their routine activities

pastoralism   the domestication of animals

patriarchy   a form of social organization in which males dominate females

patrilineal descent   a system tracing kinship through men

patrilocality   a residential pattern in which a married couple lives with or near the husband's family

peer group   a social group whose members have interests, social position, and age in common

personal space   the surrounding area over which a person makes some claim to privacy

personality   a person's fairly consistent patterns of acting, thinking, and feeling

plea bargaining   a legal negotiation in which a prosecutor reduces a charge in exchange for a defendant's guilty plea

pluralism   a state in which people of all races and ethnicities are distinct but have equal social standing

pluralist model   an analysis of politics that sees power as spread among many competing interest groups

political action committee (PAC)   an organization formed by a special-interest group, independent of political parties, to raise and spend money in support of political goals

political revolution   the overthrow of one political system in order to establish another

politics   the social institution that distributes power, sets a society's goals, and makes decisions

polyandry   marriage that unites one woman and two or more men

polygamy   marriage that unites a person with two or more spouses

polytheism   belief in many gods

popular culture   cultural patterns that are widespread among a society's population

population   the people who are the focus of research

pornography   sexually explicit material intended to cause sexual arousal

positivism   a scientific approach to knowledge based on "positive" facts as opposed to mere speculation

positivist sociology   the study of society based on systematic observation of social behavior

postindustrial economy   a productive system based on service work and high technology

postindustrialism   the production of information using computer technology

postmodernity   the transformations caused by the Information Revolution and the postindustrial economy

power   the ability to achieve desired ends despite resistance from others

power-elite model   an analysis of politics that sees power as concentrated among the rich

prejudice   a rigid and unfair generalization about an entire category of people

preoperational stage   Piaget's term for the level of human development at which individuals first use language and other symbols

presentation of self   Erving Goffman's term for a person's efforts to create specific impressions in the minds of others

primary group   a small social group whose members share personal and lasting relationships

primary labor market   jobs that provide extensive benefits to workers

primary sector   the part of the economy that draws raw materials from the natural environment

primary sex characteristics   the genitals, organs used for reproduction

profane   included as an ordinary element of everyday life

profession   a prestigious white-collar occupation that requires extensive formal education

proletarians   people who sell their labor for wages

propaganda   information presented with the intention of shaping public opinion

prostitution   the selling of sexual services

public opinion   widespread attitudes about controversial issues

queer theory   a body of research findings that challenges the heterosexual bias in U.S. society

questionnaire   a series of written questions a researcher presents to subjects

race   a socially constructed category of people who share biologically transmitted traits that members of a society consider important

race-conflict theory   the study of society that focuses on inequality and conflict between people of different racial and ethnic categories

racism   the belief that one racial category is innately superior or inferior to another

rain forests   regions of dense forestation, most of which circle the globe close to the equator

rationality   a way of thinking that emphasizes deliberate, matter-of-fact calculation of the most efficient way to accomplish a particular task

rationalization of society   Weber's term for the historical change from tradition to rationality as the main type of human thought

rational-legal authority   power legitimized by legally enacted rules and regulations; also known as *bureaucratic authority*

reference group   a social group that serves as a point of reference in making evaluations and decisions

rehabilitation   a program for reforming the offender to prevent later offenses

relative deprivation   a perceived disadvantage arising from some specific comparison

relative poverty   the lack of resources of some people in relation to those who have more

reliability   consistency in measurement

religion   a social institution involving beliefs and practices based on recognizing the sacred

religiosity   the importance of religion in a person's life

replication   repetition of research by other investigators

resocialization   radically changing an inmate's personality by carefully controlling the environment respond to those actions

retribution   an act of moral vengeance by which society makes the offender suffer as much as the suffering caused by the crime

riot   a social eruption that is highly emotional, violent, and undirected

ritual   formal, ceremonial behavior

role   behavior expected of someone who holds a particular status

role conflict   conflict among the roles connected to two or more statuses

role set   a number of roles attached to a single status

role strain   tension among the roles connected to a single status

routinization of charisma   the transformation of charismatic authority into some combination of traditional and bureaucratic authority

rumor   unconfirmed information that people spread informally, often by word of mouth or by using electronic devices

sacred   set apart as extraordinary, inspiring awe and reverence

sample   a part of a population that represents the whole

Sapir-Whorf thesis   the idea that people see and understand the world through the cultural lens of language

scapegoat   a person or category of people, typically with little power, whom people unfairly blame for their own troubles

schooling   formal instruction under the direction of specially trained teachers

science   a logical system that bases knowledge on direct, systematic observation

scientific management   Frederick Taylor's term for the application of scientific principles to the operation of a business or other large organization

Scientific Stage   (modern physics, chemistry, sociology)

secondary group   a large and impersonal social group whose members pursue a specific goal or activity

secondary labor market   jobs that provide minimal benefits to workers

secondary sector   the part of the economy that transforms raw materials into manufactured goods

secondary sex characteristics   bodily development, apart from the genitals, that distinguishes biologically mature females and males

sect   a type of religious organization that stands apart from the larger society

secularization   the historical decline in the importance of the supernatural and the sacred

segregation   the physical and social separation of categories of people

self   George Herbert Mead's term for the part of an individual's personality composed of self-awareness and self-image

sensorimotor stage   Piaget's term for the level of human development at which individuals experience the world only through their senses

sex   the biological distinction between females and males

sex ratio   the number of males for every 100 females in a nation's population

sexism   the belief that one sex is innately superior to the other

sexual harassment   comments, gestures, or physical contacts of a sexual nature that are deliberate, repeated, and unwelcome

sexual orientation   a person's romantic and emotional attraction to another person

sick role patterns of behavior defined as appropriate for people who are ill

significant others people, such as parents, who have special importance for socialization

social change the transformation of culture and social institutions over time

social character personality patterns common to members of a particular society

social conflict the struggle between segments of society over valued resources

social construction of reality the process by which people creatively shape reality through social interaction

social control attempts by society to regulate people's thoughts and behavior

social dysfunction any social pattern that may disrupt the operation of society

social epidemiology the study of how health and disease are distributed throughout a society's population

social functions the consequences of a social pattern for the operation of society as a whole

social group two or more people who identify with and interact with one another

social institutions the major spheres of social life, or societal subsystems, organized to meet human needs

social interaction the process by which people act and react in relation to others

social media technology that links people in social activity

social mobility a change in position within the social hierarchy

social movement an organized activity that encourages or discourages social change

social stratification a system by which a society ranks categories of people in a hierarchy

social structure any relatively stable pattern of social behavior

social-conflict approach a framework for building theory that sees society as an arena of inequality that generates conflict and change

socialism an economic system in which natural resources and the means of producing goods and services are collectively owned

socialization the lifelong social experience by which people develop their human potential and learn culture

socialized medicine a medical care system in which the government owns and operates most medical facilities and employs most physicians

societal protection rendering an offender incapable of further offenses temporarily through imprisonment or permanently by execution

society people who interact in a defined territory and share a culture

sociobiology a theoretical approach that explores ways in which human biology affects how we create culture

sociocultural evolution Lenski's term for the changes that occur as a society gains new technology

socioeconomic status (SES) a composite ranking based on various dimensions of social inequality

sociological perspective sociology's special point of view that sees general patterns of society in the lives of particular people

sociology the systematic study of human society

special-interest group people organized to address some economic or social issue

spurious correlation an apparent but false relationship between two (or more) variables that is caused by some other variable

state capitalism an economic and political system in which companies are privately owned

state church a church formally allied with the state

status a social position that a person holds

status consistency the degree of uniformity in a person's social standing across various dimensions of social inequality

status set all the statuses a person holds at a given time

stereotype a simplified description applied to every person in some category

stigma a powerfully negative label that greatly changes a person's self-concept and social identity

structural-functional approach a framework for building theory that sees society as a complex system whose parts work together to promote solidarity and stability

structural social mobility a shift in the social position of large numbers of people due more to changes in society itself than to individual efforts

subculture cultural patterns that set apart some segment of a society's population

suburbs urban areas beyond the political boundaries of a city

superego Freud's term for the cultural values and norms internalized by an individual

survey a research method in which subjects respond to a series of statements or questions on a questionnaire or in an interview

symbol anything that carries a particular meaning recognized by people who share a culture

symbolic-interaction approach a framework for building theory that sees society as the product of the everyday interactions of individuals

technology knowledge that people use to make a way of life in their surroundings

terrorism acts of violence or the threat of violence used as a political strategy by an individual or a group

tertiary sector the part of the economy that involves services rather than goods

Theological Stage (the Church in the Middle Ages)

theoretical approach a basic image of society that guides thinking and research

theory a statement of how and why specific facts are related

Thomas theorem W. I. Thomas's claim that situations defined as real are real in their consequences

total institution a setting in which people are isolated from the rest of society and manipulated by an administrative staff

totalitarianism a highly centralized political system that extensively regulates people's lives

totem an object in the natural world collectively defined as sacred

tracking assigning students to different types of educational programs

tradition behavior, values, and beliefs passed from generation to generation

tradition-directedness rigid conformity to time-honored ways of living

traditional authority power legitimized by respect for long-established cultural patterns

transgender appearing or behaving in ways that challenge conventional cultural norms concerning how females and males should look and act

transsexuals people who feel they are one sex even though biologically they are the other

triad a social group with three members

underground economy economic activity involving income not reported to the government as required by law

urban ecology the study of the link between the physical and social dimensions of cities

urbanization the concentration of population into cities

validity actually measuring exactly what you intend to measure

values culturally defined standards that people use to decide what is desirable, good, and beautiful and that serve as broad guidelines for social living

variable a concept whose value changes from case to case

victimless crimes violations of law in which there are no obvious victims

war organized, armed conflict among the people of two or more nations, directed by their governments

wealth the total value of money and other assets, minus outstanding debts

welfare capitalism an economic and political system that combines a mostly market- based economy with extensive social welfare programs

welfare state a system of government agencies and programs that provides benefits to the population

white-collar crime crime committed by people of high social position in the course of their occupations

white-collar occupations higher-prestige jobs that involve mostly mental activity

zero population growth the rate of reproduction that maintains population at a steady level

References

*Blue type denotes reference citations new to this fifteeth edition.

Chapter 1

AMERICAN SOCIOLOGICAL ASSOCIATION. *Careers in Sociology.* 6th ed. Washington, D.C.: American Sociological Association, 2002.

———. "What Can I Do with a Master's Degree?" Washington, D.C. 2011a. [Online] Available at http://www.asanet.org/research/masters.cfm

———. "Research on Jobs and Careers in Sociology." Department of Research and Development. 2011b. [Online] Available at http://www.asanet.org/employment/factsoncareers.cfm

BALTZELL, E. DIGBY. "Introduction to the 1967 Edition." In W. E. B. Du Bois (ed.), *The Philadelphia Negro: A Social Study.* New York: Schocken Books, 1967::ix–xxxvi; orig. 1899.

BARRO, ROBERT, AND JONG-WHA LEE. "Educational Attainment in the World, 1950–2010." National Bureau of Economic Research. 2010. [Online] Available at http://www.nber.org/papers/w15902

BERGER, PETER L. *Invitation to Sociology.* New York: Anchor Books, 1963.

BOWLES, SAMUEL, AND HERBERT GINTIS. *Schooling in Capitalist America: Educational Reform and the Contradictions of Economic Life.* New York: Basic Books, 1976.

CENTERS FOR DISEASE CONTROL AND PREVENTION. "Deaths: Final Data for 2010 (tables only)." 2012. Available at http://www.cdc.gov/nchs/data/dvs/deaths_2010_release.pdf

COMTE, AUGUSTE. *Auguste Comte and Positivism: The Essential Writings.* GERTRUD LENZER, ed. New York: Harper Torchbooks, 1975; orig. 1851–54.

DEUTSCHER, IRWIN. *Making a Difference: The Practice of Sociology.* New Brunswick, N.J.: Transaction, 1999.

DU BOIS, W. E. B. *The Philadelphia Negro: A Social Study.* New York: Schocken Books, 1967; orig. 1899.

EDWARDS, TAMALA M. "Flying Solo." *Time* (August 28, 2000):47–55.

EHRENREICH, BARBARA. *Nickel and Dimed: On (Not) Getting By in America.* New York: Holt, 2001.

FENG HOU, AND JOHN MYLES. "The Changing Role of Education in the Marriage Market: Assortative Marriage in Canada and the United States since the 1970s." *Canadian Journal of Sociology.* Vol. 33, No. 2 (2008):335–64.

FORBES. "Highest-Paid Athletes, 2012—The World's Richest People." June 29, 2012. Available at http://www.therichest.org/sports/forbes-highest-paid-athletes/

HAMILTON, BRADY E., JOYCE A. MARTIN, AND STEPHANIE J. VENTURA. "Births: Preliminary Data for 2011." 2012. Available at http://www.cdc.gov/nchs/data/nvsr/nvsr61/nvsr61_05.pdf

HARRISON, C. KEITH. "Black Athletes at the Millennium." *Society.* Vol. 37, No. 3 (March/April 2000):35–39.

HOEFER, MICHAEL, NANCY RYTINA, AND BRYAN BAKER. "Estimates of the Unauthorized Immigrant Population Residing in the United States: January 2011." 2012. Available at http://www.dhs.gov/xlibrary/assets/statistics/publications/ois_ill_pe_2011.pdf

LAPCHICK, RICHARD, WITH ANTOINETTE LECKY AND AARON TRIGG. "The 2012 Racial and Gender Report Card: National Basketball Association." Orlando: The Institute for Diversity and Ethics in Sport (TIDES), University of Central Florida. June 26, 2012. Available at http://web.bus.ucf.edu/documents/sport/2012-NBA-RGRC.pdf

LAPCHICK, RICHARD, WITH PHILIP COSTA, BRENTON NICKERSON, AND BEN RODRIGUEZ. "The 2012 Racial and Gender Report Card: Major League Baseball." Orlando: The Institute for Diversity and Ethics in Sport (TIDES), University of Central Florida. April 25, 2012. Available at http://web.bus.ucf.edu/documents/sport/2012-MLB-RGRC.pdf

LAPCHICK, RICHARD, WITH PHILIP COSTA, TAMARA SHERROD, AND RAHMAN ANJORIN. "The 2012 Racial and Gender Report Card: National Football League." Orlando: The Institute for Diversity and Ethics in Sport (TIDES), University of Central Florida. September 13, 2012. Available at http://dl.dropbox.com/u/11322904/2012%20NFL%20RGRC.pdf

LENGERMANN, PATRICIA MADOO, AND JILL NIEBRUGGE-BRANTLEY. *The Women Founders: Sociology and Social Theory, 1830–1930.* New York: McGraw-Hill, 1998.

MILLS, C. WRIGHT. *The Sociological Imagination.* New York: Oxford University Press, 1959.

OAKES, JEANNIE. "Classroom Social Relationships: Exploring the Bowles and Gintis Hypothesis." *Sociology of Education.* Vol. 55, No. 4 (October 1982):197–212.

———. *Keeping Track: How High Schools Structure Inequality.* New Haven, Conn.: Yale University Press, 1985.

OECD (THE ORGANISATION FOR ECONOMIC CO-OPERATION AND DEVELOPMENT). "Education at a Glance 2012: OECD Indicators." 2012. Available at http://www.oecd.org/edu/eag2012.htm

POPULATION REFERENCE BUREAU. "Datafinder." 2012. Available at http://www.prb.org/DataFinder.aspx

RUBIN, LILLIAN BRESLOW. *Worlds of Pain: Life in the Working-Class Family.* New York: Basic Books, 1976.

SCHOEN, ROBERT, AND YEN-HSIN ALICE CHENG. "Partner Choice and the Differential Retreat from Marriage." *Journal of Marriage and the Family.* Vol. 68 (2006):1–10.

SCHWARTZ, CHRISTINE R., AND ROBERT D. MARE. "Trends in Educational Assortative Marriage from 1940 to 2003." July 2005. [Online] Available April 22, 2009, at http://www.ccpr.ucla.edu/ccprwpseries/ccpr_017_05.pdf

SHAFER, KEVIN, AND QIAN ZHENCHAO. "Marriage Timing and Educational Assortative Mating." *Journal of Comparative Family Studies* [serial online]. Vol. 45, No. 5 (September 2005):661–91.

SHAULIS, DAHN. "Pedestriennes: Newsworthy but Controversial Women in Sporting Entertainment." *Journal of Sports History.* Vol. 26, No. 1 (Spring 1999):29–46.

STEELE, SHELBY. *The Content of Our Character: A New Vision of Race in America.* New York: St. Martin's Press, 1990.

TOCQUEVILLE, ALEXIS DE. *The Old Regime and the French Revolution.* Stuart Gilbert, trans. Garden City, N.Y.: Anchor/Doubleday, 1955; orig. 1856.

UNESCO (UNITED NATIONS EDUCATIONAL, SCIENTIFIC, AND CULTURAL ORGANIZATION). "Data Centre, Literacy and Educational Attainment." 2012. Available at http://www.uis.unesco.org/Pages/default.aspx

UNITED NATIONS DEVELOPMENT PROGRAMME. "International Human Development Indicators." 2012. Available at http://hdrstats.undp.org/en/indicators/default.html

UPTHEGROVE, TAYNA R., VINCENT J. ROSCIGNO, AND CAMILLE ZUBRINSKY CHARLES. "Big Money Collegiate Sports: Racial Concentration, Contradictory Pressures, and Academic Performance." *Social Science Quarterly.* Vol. 80, No. 4 (December 1999):718–37.

U.S. CENSUS BUREAU. "American Community Survey." 2012. Available at http://www.census.gov/acs/www/

———. "Current Population Survey." 2012. Available at http://www.census.gov/cps/

U.S. DEPARTMENT OF HOMELAND SECURITY, OFFICE OF IMMIGRATION STATISTICS. "Yearbook of Immigration Statistics (Annual)." 2012. Available at http://www.dhs.gov/yearbook-immigration-statistics

WEITZMAN, LENORE J. *The Divorce Revolution: The Unexpected Social and Economic Consequences for Women and Children in America.* New York: Free Press, 1985.

———. "The Economic Consequences of Divorce Are Still Unequal: Comment on Peterson." *American Sociological Review.* Vol. 61, No. 3 (June 1996):537–38.

WELCH, SUSAN, AND LEE SIGELMAN. "Who's Calling the Shots? Women's Coaches in Division I Women's Sports." *Social Science Quarterly.* Vol. 88 (2007, special issue):1415–34.

WORLD BANK. "World DataBank: Education Statistics." 2012. Available at http://databank.worldbank.org/data/views/variableselection/selectvariables.aspx?source=education-statistics

———. "World DataBank: World Development Indicators." 2012. Available at http://databank.worldbank.org/data/views/variableSelection/selectvariables.aspx?source=world-development-indicators

WRIGHT, EARL, II. "The Atlanta Sociological Laboratory, 1896–1924: A Historical Account of the First American School of Sociology." *Western Journal of Black Studies.* Vol. 26, No. 3 (2002a):165–74.

———. "Why Black People Tend to Shout! An Earnest Attempt to Explain the Sociological Negation of the Atlanta Sociological Laboratory Despite Its Possible Unpleasantness." *Sociological Spectrum.* Vol. 22, No. 3 (2002b):325–61.

Chapter 2

AMERICAN SOCIOLOGICAL ASSOCIATION. *Code of Ethics.* Washington, D.C.: American Sociological Association, 1997.

BALTZELL, E. DIGBY. *Puritan Boston and Quaker Philadelphia.* New York: Free Press, 1979.

BENJAMIN, LOIS. *The Black Elite: Facing the Color Line in the Twilight of the Twentieth Century.* Chicago: Nelson-Hall, 1991.

BLACK, CASSANDRA. "Survey Reports More Women Are Having Extramarital Affairs." *Associated Content* (May 4, 2007). [Online] Available April 19, 2009, at http://www.associatedcontent.com/article/231316/survey_reports_more_women_are_having.html

CARDIFF, CHRISTOPHER F., AND DANIEL B. KLEIN. *Critical Review.* Vol. 17, Nos. 3–4 (2005):237–55.

EWOODZIE, JOSEPH. *Break Beats in the Bronx: Symbolic Boundaries and the Making of Hip Hop.* (forthcoming)

FEAGIN, JOE R., AND HERNÁN, VERA. *Liberation Sociology.* Boulder, Colo.: Westview Press, 2001.

FISCHER, CLAUDE W. *The Urban Experience.* 2nd ed. New York: Harcourt Brace Jovanovich, 1984.

GIOVANNINI, MAUREEN. "Female Anthropologist and Male Informant: Gender Conflict in a Sicilian Town." In John J. Macionis and Nijole V. Benokraitis, eds., *Seeing Ourselves: Classic, Contemporary, and Cross-Cultural Readings in Sociology.* 2nd ed. Englewood Cliffs, N.J.: Prentice Hall, 1992:27–32.

HANEY, CRAIG, W. CURTIS BANKS, AND PHILIP G. ZIMBARDO. "Interpersonal Dynamics in a Simulated Prison." *International Journal of Criminology and Penology.* Vol. 1 (1973):69–97.

HESS, BETH B. "Breaking and Entering the Establishment: Committing Social Change and Confronting the Backlash." *Social Problems.* Vol. 46, No. 1 (February 1999):1–12.

KLEIN, DANIEL B., AND CHARLOTTA STERN. "How Politically Diverse Are the Social Sciences and Humanities? Survey Evidence from Six Fields." National Association of Scholars. 2004. [Online] Available January 13, 2005, at http://www.nas.org/aa/klein_launch.htm

LAVIN, DANIELLE, AND DOUGLAS W. MAYNARD. "Standardization vs. Rapport: Respondent Laughter and Interviewer Reaction during Telephone Surveys." *American Sociological Review.* Vol. 66, No. 3 (June 2001):453–79.

LEAVITT, STEVEN D., AND JOHN A. LIST. "Was There Really a Hawthorne Effect at the Hawthorne Plant? An Analysis of the Original Illumination Experiments." Working Paper 15016. Cambridge, Mass.: National Bureau of Economic Research, 2009.

LORENZ, FREDERICK O., AND BRENT T. BRUTON. "Experiments in Surveys: Linking Mass Class Questionnaires to Introductory Research Methods." *Teaching Sociology.* Vol. 24, No. 3 (July 1996):264–71.

MARÍN, GERARDO, AND BARBARA VAN OSS MARÍN. *Research with Hispanic Populations.* Newbury Park, Calif.: Sage, 1991.

NORC. "General Social Surveys, 1972–2010." Chicago: National Opinion Research Center. March 2011. Available at http://www.norc.org/GSS+Website/

PARKER-POPE, TARA. "Love, Sex, and the Changing Landscape of Infidelity." *New York Times* (October 27, 2008). [Online] Available April 22, 2009, at http://www.nytimes.com/2008/10/28/health/28well.html?_r=1

PERRUCCI, ROBERT. "Inventing Social Justice: SSSP and the Twenty-First Century." *Social Problems.* Vol. 48, No. 2 (May 2001):159–67.

ROETHLISBERGER, F. J., AND WILLIAM J. DICKSON. *Management and the Worker.* Cambridge, Mass.: Harvard University Press, 1939.

SMITH, TOM W. "American Sexual Risk Behavior: Trends, Socio-Demographic Differences, and Behavior." March 2006. [Online] Available January 29, 2009, at http://www.norc.org/NR/rdonlyres/2663F09F-2E74-436E-AC81-6FFBF288E183/0/AmericanSexualBehavior2006.pdf

U.S. CENSUS BUREAU. "Census 2010." 2011. Available at http://factfinder2.census.gov/faces/nav/jsf/pages/index.xhtml

———. "American Community Survey." 2012. Available at http://www.census.gov/acs/www/

———. "Current Population Survey." 2012. Available at http://www.census.gov/cps/

U.S. DEPARTMENT OF EDUCATION. "The Condition of Education." 2012. Available at http://nces.ed.gov/programs/coe/tables/table-eda-1.asp

U.S. DEPARTMENT OF JUSTICE. "Correctional Populations in the United States, 2010." 2012. Available at http://bjs.ojp.usdoj.gov/index.cfm?ty=pt&tid=11

WEBER, MAX. *The Protestant Ethic and the Spirit of Capitalism.* New York: Scribner, 1958; orig. 1904–05.

WILSON, WILLIAM JULIUS. *The Declining Significance of Race.* Chicago: University of Chicago Press, 1978.

WOLFF, EDWARD N. "The Asset Price Meltdown and the Wealth of the Middle Class." 2012. Available at http://www.nber.org/authors_papers/edward_wolff

ZIMBARDO, PHILIP G. "Pathology of Imprisonment." *Society.* Vol. 9, No. 1 (April 1972):4–8.

Chapter 3

ASANTE, MOLEFI KETE. *Afrocentricity.* Trenton, N.J.: Africa World Press, 1988.

ASTIN, ALEXANDER W., LETICIA OSEGUERA, LINDA J. SAX, AND WILLIAM S. KORN. *The American Freshman: Thirty-Five Year Trends.* Los Angeles: UCLA Higher Education Research Institute, 2002.

BARASH, DAVID P. *The Whisperings Within.* New York: Penguin Books, 1981.

BARONE, MICHAEL. "Cultures Aren't Equal." *U.S. News & World Report.* Vol. 139, No. 6 (August 22, 2005):26.

BAROVICK, HARRIET. "Tongues That Go out of Style." *Time* (June 10, 2002):22.

BERTEAU, CELESTE. "Disconnected Intimacy: AOL Instant Messenger Use among Kenyon College Students." Senior thesis. Kenyon College, 2005.

CARLE, ROBERT. "Islamists in the 'Rainbow' Coalition." *Society.* Vol. 45, No. 2 (March/April 2008):181–90.

CHAGNON, NAPOLEON A. *Yanomamö: The Fierce People.* 4th ed. Austin, Tex.: Holt, Rinehart and Winston, 1992.

CRYSTAL, DAVID. *The Cambridge Encyclopedia of the English Language.* 3rd ed. Cambridge: Cambridge University Press, 2010.

DARWIN, CHARLES. *On the Origin of Species by Means of Natural Selection, or the Preservation of Favoured Races in the Struggle for Life.* London: Murray, 1859.

DEUTSCHER, GUY. "Does Your Language Shape How You Think?" *New York Times Magazine.* [Online] Available August 26, 2010, at http://www.nytimes.com/2010/08/29/magazine/29language-t.html?_r=1

EUROPEAN UNION. "Europeans and Their Languages." 2012. Available at http://ec.europa.eu/languages/languages-of-europe/eurobarometer-survey_en.htm

FATTAH, HASSAN. "A More Diverse Community." *American Demographics.* Vol. 24, No. 7 (July/August 2002):39–43.

HARRIS, MARVIN. *Cultural Anthropology.* 2nd ed. New York: Harper & Row, 1987.

HAYDEN, THOMAS. "Losing Our Voices." *U.S. News & World Report* (May 26, 2003):42.

HELIN, DAVID W. "When Slogans Go Wrong." *American Demographics.* Vol. 14, No. 2 (February 1992):14.

HOSTETLER, JOHN A. *Amish Society.* 3rd ed. Baltimore: Johns Hopkins University Press, 1980.

IBM. "Web Site by Country/Region and Language." 2012. Available at http://www.ibm.com/planetwide/select/selector.html

INGLEHART, RONALD ET AL. "World Values Survey." 2012. Available at http://www.worldvaluessurvey.com/

INGLEHART, RONALD, AND CHRISTIAN WELZEL. "The WVS Cultural Map of the World." 2010. Available at http://www.worldvaluessurvey.org/wvs/articles/folder_published/article_base_54

KARRFALT, WAYNE. "A Multicultural Mecca." *American Demographics.* Vol. 25, No. 4 (May 2003):54–55.

KAY, PAUL, AND WILLETT KEMPTON. "What Is the Sapir-Whorf Hypothesis?" *American Anthropologist.* Vol. 86, No. 1 (March 1984):65–79.

KELLER, HELEN. *The Story of My Life.* New York: Doubleday Page, 1903.

KRAYBILL, DONALD B. *The Riddle of Amish Culture.* Baltimore: Johns Hopkins University Press, 1989.

KRAYBILL, DONALD B., AND MARC A. OLSHAN, EDS. *The Amish Struggle with Modernity.* Hanover, N.H.: University Press of New England, 1994.

LENHART, AMANDA. "Adults, Cell Phones, and Texting." Pew Research Center Publications. [Online] Available September 2, 2010, at http://pewresearch.org/pubs/1716/adults-cell-phones-text-messages

LEWIS, M. PAUL, ED. *Ethnologue: Languages of the World.* 16th ed. Dallas, Tex.: SIL International, 2009.

LINTON, RALPH. "One Hundred Percent American." *American Mercury.* Vol. 40, No. 160 (April 1937):427–29.

LIPSET, SEYMOUR MARTIN. "Canada and the United States." Charles F. Donan and John H. Sigler, eds. Englewood Cliffs, N.J.: Prentice Hall, 1985.

MARX, KARL, AND FRIEDRICH ENGELS. *The Marx-Engels Reader.* 2nd ed. Robert C. Tucker, ed. New York: Norton, 1978; orig. 1859.

MORELL, VIRGINIA. "Minds of Their Own: Animals Are Smarter Than You Think." *National Geographic.* Vol. 213, No. 3 (March 2008):36–61.

MURDOCK, GEORGE PETER. "The Common Denominator of Cultures." In Ralph Linton, ed., *The Science of Man in World Crisis.* New York: Columbia University Press, 1945:123–42.

NORC. *General Social Surveys, 1972–2010: Cumulative Codebook.* Chicago: National Opinion Research Center, 2011. [Online] Available at http://www.norc.org/GSS+Website

OGBURN, WILLIAM F. *On Culture and Social Change.* Chicago: University of Chicago Press, 1964.

PARSONS, TALCOTT. *Societies: Evolutionary and Comparative Perspectives.* Englewood Cliffs, N.J.: Prentice Hall, 1966.

PEW RESEARCH CENTER, INTERNET AND AMERICAN LIFE PROJECT. "Americans and Text Messaging." 2011. Available at http://www.pewinternet.org/Reports/2011/Cell-Phone-Texting-2011/Summary-of-Findings/Summary-of-Findings.aspx

PINKER, STEVEN. *The Language Instinct.* New York: Morrow, 1994.

PRYOR, JOHN H., KEVIN EGAN, LAURA PALUCKI BLAKE, SYLVIA HURTADO, JENNIFER BERDAN, AND MATTHEW CASE. "The American Freshman: National Norms Fall 2012 (Expanded Edition)." Cooperative Institutional Research Program at the Higher Education Research Institute at UCLA. 2013. Available at http://www.heri.ucla.edu/monographs/TheAmericanFreshman2012-Expanded.pdf

RUBIN, JOEL. "E-Mail Too Formal? Try a Text Message." Columbia News Service. March 7, 2003. [Online] Available April 25, 2005, at http://www.jrn.columbia.edu/studentwork/cns/2003-03-07/85.asp

SAPIR, EDWARD. "The Status of Linguistics as a Science." *Language.* Vol. 5, No. 4 (1929):207–14.

———. *Selected Writings of Edward Sapir in Language, Culture, and Personality.* David G. Mandelbaum, ed. Berkeley: University of California Press, 1949.

SIMONITE, TOM. "AT&T Trials Text-Message Translation." MIT Technology Review. September 26, 2012. Available at http://www.technologyreview.com/news/429375/att-trials-text-message-translation/

Statistics Canada. "Canada Year Book." 2011. Available at http://www.statcan.gc.ca/pub/11-402-x/index-eng.htm

STEYN, MARK. "Is Canada's Economy a Model for America?" *Imprimis.* Vol. 37, No. 1 (January 2008):1–7.

STUESSY, JOE, AND SCOTT LIPSCOMB. *Rock and Roll: Its History and Stylistic Development.* 6th ed. Upper Saddle River, N.J.: Pearson Prentice Hall, 2008.

SUMNER, WILLIAM GRAHAM. *Folkways.* New York: Dover, 1959; orig. 1906.

UNESCO. DATA REPORTED IN "Tower of Babel Is Tumbling Down—Slowly." *U.S. News & World Report* (July 2, 2001):9.

U.S. CENSUS BUREAU. "American Community Survey." 2012. Available at http://www.census.gov/acs/www/

———. "Current Population Survey." 2012. Available at http://www.census.gov/cps/

———. "International Data Base." 2012. Available at http://www.census.gov/population/international/

U.S. DEPARTMENT OF EDUCATION, NATIONAL CENTER FOR EDUCATION STATISTICS. "2003 National Assessment of Adult Literacy." 2008. Available at http://nces.ed.gov/naal/index.asp

U.S. DEPARTMENT OF HOMELAND SECURITY, OFFICE OF IMMIGRATION STATISTICS. "Yearbook of Immigration Statistics (Annual)." 2012. Available at http://www.dhs.gov/yearbook-immigration-statistics

U.S. DEPARTMENT OF LABOR, BUREAU OF LABOR STATISTICS. "Consumer Expenditure Survey." September 25, 2012. Available at http://www.bls.gov/cex/

———. "Labor Force Statistics from the Current Population Survey." 2012. Available at http://www.bls.gov/cps/

WHORF, BENJAMIN LEE. "The Relation of Habitual Thought and Behavior to Language." In *Language, Thought, and Reality.* Cambridge, Mass.: Technology Press of MIT; New York: Wiley, 1956:134–59; orig. 1941.

WILLIAMS, ROBIN M., JR. *American Society: A Sociological Interpretation.* 3rd ed. New York: Knopf, 1970.

WORLD BANK. "World DataBank: Education Statistics." 2012. Available at http://databank.worldbank.org/data/views/variableselection/selectvariables.aspx?source=education-statistics

Chapter 4

BELL, DANIEL. *The Coming of Postindustrial Society: A Venture in Social Forecasting.* New York: Basic Books, 1973.

BERGER, PETER. "Faith and Development." *Society.* Vol. 46, No. 1 (January/February 2009):69–75.

BOULDING, ELISE. *The Underside of History.* Boulder, Colo.: Westview Press, 1976.

BUCKLEY, STEPHEN. "A Spare and Separate Way of Life." *Washington Post* (December 18, 1996):A1, A32–A33.

CHEN, SHAOHUA, AND MARTIN RAVALLION. "An Update to the World Bank's Estimates of Consumption Poverty in the Developing World." World Bank.

February 29, 2012. Available at http://siteresources.worldbank.org/INTPOV-CALNET/Resources/Global_Poverty_Update_2012_02-29-12.pdf

DURKHEIM, EMILE. *The Division of Labor in Society*. New York: Free Press, 1964a; orig. 1893.

———. *The Rules of Sociological Method*. New York: Free Press, 1964b; orig. 1895.

———. *Suicide*. New York: Free Press, 1966; orig. 1897.

———. *Sociology and Philosophy*. New York: Free Press, 1974; orig. 1924.

FISHER, ELIZABETH. *Woman's Creation: Sexual Evolution and the Shaping of Society*. Garden City, N.Y.: Anchor/Doubleday, 1979.

GERTH, H. H., AND C. WRIGHT MILLS, EDS. "Marx and Weber." In *From Max Weber: Essays in Sociology*. New York: Oxford University Press, 1946:46–50.

INTERNATIONAL TELECOMMUNICATIONS UNION (ITU). "ICT Indicators Database." 2012. Available at http://www.itu.int/ITU-D/ict/publications/

LEACOCK, ELEANOR. "Women's Status in Egalitarian Societies: Implications for Social Evolution." *Current Anthropology*. Vol. 19, No. 2 (June 1978):247–75.

LOVGREN, STEFEN. "Will All the Blue Men End Up in Timbuktu?" *U.S. News & World Report* (December 7, 1998):40.

MARX, KARL. EXCERPT FROM "A Contribution to the Critique of Political Economy" (1859). In Lewis S. Feurer, ed. *Karl Marx and Friedrich Engels, Marx and Engels: Basic Writings on Politics and Philosophy*. Garden City, N.Y.: Anchor Books, 1959:42–46.

———. *Karl Marx: Early Writings*. T. B. BOTTOMORE, ed. New York: McGraw-Hill, 1964; orig. 1848.

MARX, KARL, AND FRIEDRICH ENGELS. "Manifesto of the Communist Party." In Robert C. Tucker, ed., *The Marx-Engels Reader*. New York: Norton, 1972:331–62; orig. 1848.

MATLOFF, JUDITH. "Nomadic 'Blue Men' of the Desert Try to Go Roam Again." *Christian Science Monitor* (September 9, 1997):7.

MCCONNELL, TRISTAN. "Tuareg Nomads Set to Intensify Rebellion in Niger." *Christian Science Monitor* (October 11, 2007). [Online] Available October 13, 2008, at http://www.csmonitor.com/2007/1011/p12s01-woaf.html

NOLAN, PATRICK, AND GERHARD E. LENSKI. *Human Societies: An Introduction to Macrosociology*. 11th ed. Boulder, Colo.: Paradigm, 2010.

PEW RESEARCH CENTER. "Demographics of Internet Users." 2012. Available at http://www.pewinternet.org/Static-Pages/Trend-Data-%28Adults%29/Whos-Online.aspx

TURKLE, SHERRY. *Alone Together*. New York: Basic Books, 2011.

UNITED NATIONS. "The Millennium Development Goals Report 2010." New York: United Nations. 2010. [Online] Available at http://mdgs.un.org/unsd/mdg/Resources/Static/Products/Progress2010/MDG_Report_2010_En_low%20res.Pdf

U.S. CENSUS BUREAU. "Current Population Survey." 2012. Available at http://www.census.gov/cps/

WEBER, MAX. *The Protestant Ethic and the Spirit of Capitalism*. New York: Scribner, 1958; orig. 1904–05.

———. *Economy and Society: An Outline of Interpretive Sociology*. Guenther Roth and Claus Wittich, eds. Berkeley: University of California Press, 1978; orig. 1921.

Chapter 5

AMERICAN PSYCHOLOGICAL ASSOCIATION. *Violence and Youth: Psychology's Response*. Washington, D.C.: American Psychological Association, 1993.

ARIÈS, PHILIPPE. *Centuries of Childhood: A Social History of Family Life*. New York: Vintage, 1962.

BEGLEY, SHARON. "Gray Matters." *Newsweek* (March 7, 1995):48–54.

BERGER, PETER L. *Invitation to Sociology*. New York: Anchor Books, 1963.

BEST, RAPHAELA. *We've All Got Scars: What Boys and Girls Learn in Elementary School*. Bloomington: Indiana University Press, 1983.

CENTERS FOR DISEASE CONTROL AND PREVENTION. "National Center for Health Statistics." 2012. Available at http://www.cdc.gov/nchs/fastats/mental.htm

CHODOROW, NANCY. *Femininities, Masculinities, Sexualities: Freud and Beyond*. Lexington: University of Kentucky Press, 1994.

COOLEY, CHARLES HORTON. *Human Nature and the Social Order*. New York: Schocken Books, 1964; orig. 1902.

CURTISS, SUSAN. *Genie: A Psycholinguistic Study of a Modern-Day "Wild Child."* New York: Academic Press, 1977.

DAVIES, MARK, AND DENISE B. KANDEL. "Parental and Peer Influences on Adolescents' Educational Plans: Some Further Evidence." *American Journal of Sociology*. Vol. 87, No. 2 (September 1981):363–87.

DAVIS, KINGSLEY. "Extreme Social Isolation of a Child." *American Journal of Sociology*. Vol. 45, No. 4 (January 1940):554–65.

———. "Final Note on a Case of Extreme Isolation." *American Journal of Sociology*. Vol. 52, No. 5 (March 1947):432–37.

DONOVAN, VIRGINIA K., AND RONNIE LITTENBERG. "Psychology of Women: Feminist Therapy." In Barbara Haber, ed., *The Women's Annual, 1981: The Year in Review*. Boston: Hall, 1982:211–35.

ELLISON, CHRISTOPHER G., JOHN P. BARTKOWSKI, AND MICHELLE L. SEGAL. "Do Conservative Protestant Parents Spank More Often? Further Evidence from the National Survey of Families and Households." *Social Science Quarterly*. Vol. 77, No. 3 (September 1996):663–73.

ERIKSON, ERIK H. *Childhood and Society*. New York: Norton, 1963; orig. 1950.

FELLMAN, BRUCE. "Taking the Measure of Children's TV." *Yale Alumni Magazine* (April 1995):46–51.

FETTO, JOHN. "Me Gusta TV." *American Demographics*. Vol. 24, No. 11 (January 2003b):14–15.

GIBBS, NANCY. "What Kids (Really) Need." *Time* (April 30, 2001):48–49.

GILLIGAN, CAROL. *In a Different Voice: Psychological Theory and Women's Development*. Cambridge, Mass.: Harvard University Press, 1982.

———. *Making Connections: The Relational Worlds of Adolescent Girls at Emma Willard School*. CAMBRIDGE, MASS.: HARVARD UNIVERSITY PRESS, 1990.

GOFFMAN, ERVING. *Asylums: Essays on the Social Situation of Mental Patients and Other Inmates*. Garden City, N.Y.: Anchor Books, 1961.

GOLDBERG, BERNARD. *Bias: A CBS Insider Exposes How the Media Distort the News*. Washington, D.C.: Regnery, 2002.

GOLDSMITH, H. H. "Genetic Influences on Personality from Infancy." *Child Development*. Vol. 54, No. 2 (April 1983):331–35.

GORMAN, CHRISTINE. "Stressed-Out Kids." *Time* (December 25, 2000):168.

HARLOW, HARRY F., AND MARGARET KUENNE HARLOW. "Social Deprivation in Monkeys." *Scientific American* (November 1962):137–46.

HOFFMAN, JAN. "Masculinity in a Spray Can." *New York Times*. January 29, 2010. [Online] Available at http://www.nytimes.com/2010/01/31/fashion/31smell.html

HOYERT, DONNA, AND JIAQUAN XU. "Deaths: Preliminary Data for 2011." National Vital Statistics Reports. Vol. 61, No. 6. Hyattsville, Md.: National Center for Health Statistics. October 10, 2012. Available at http://www.cdc.gov/nchs/data/nvsr/nvsr61/nvsr61_06.pdf

HUESMANN, L. ROWELL, AND LARAMIE D. TAYLOR. "The Role of Media Violence in Violent Behavior." *Annual Review of Public Health*. Vol. 27 (2006):393–415.

HUMAN RIGHTS WATCH. "Children's Rights: Child Labor." 2006. [Online] Available April 9, 2006, at http://www.hrw.org/children/labor.htm

HYMOWITZ, KAY S. "Kids Today Are Growing Up Way Too Fast." *Wall Street Journal* (October 28, 1998):A22.

INTERNATIONAL LABOUR ORGANIZATION, INTERNATIONAL PROGRAMME ON THE ELIMINATION OF CHILD LABOUR (ILO-IPEC). "Global Child Labour Developments: Measuring Trends from 2004 to 2008." 2010. [Online] Available at http://www.ilo.org/ipec/Informationresources/lang--en/index.htm

INTERNATIONAL TELECOMMUNICATIONS UNION. "ICT Indicators Database." 2012. Available at http://www.itu.int/ITU-D/ict/publications/

JORDAN, ELLEN, AND ANGELA COWAN. "Warrior Narratives in the Kindergarten Classroom: Renegotiating the Social Contract?" *Gender and Society*. Vol. 9, No. 6 (December 1995):727–43.

KAO, GRACE. "Group Images and Possible Selves among Adolescents: Linking Stereotypes to Expectations by Race and Ethnicity." *Sociological Forum*. Vol. 15, No. 3 (September 2000):407–30.

KOHLBERG, LAWRENCE. *The Psychology of Moral Development: The Nature and Validity of Moral Stages*. New York: Harper & Row, 1981.

KOHLBERG, LAWRENCE, AND CAROL GILLIGAN. "The Adolescent as Philosopher: The Discovery of Self in a Postconventional World." *Daedalus*. Vol. 100, No. 4 (Fall 1971):1051–86.

KOHN, MELVIN L. *Class and Conformity: A Study in Values*. 2nd ed. Homewood, Ill.: Dorsey Press, 1977.

KONIGSBERG, RUTH DAVIS. "New Ways to Think About Grief." *Time* [Online] Available January 29, 2011, at http://www.time.com/time/magazine/article/0,9171,2042372-2,00.html

KÜBLER-ROSS, ELISABETH. *On Death and Dying*. New York: Macmillan, 1969.

LAREAU, ANNETTE. "Invisible Inequality: Social Class and Childrearing in Black Families and White Families." *American Sociological Review*. Vol. 67, No. 5 (October 2002): 747–76.

LAROSSA, RALPH, AND DONALD C. REITZES. "Two? Two and One-Half? Thirty Months? Chronometrical Childhood in Early Twentieth-Century America." *Sociological Forum*. Vol. 166, No. 3 (September 2001):385–407.

LICHTER, S. ROBERT, AND DANIEL R. AMUNDSON. "Distorted Reality: Hispanic Characters in TV Entertainment." In Clara E. Rodriguez, ed., *Latin Looks: Images of Latinas and Latinos in the U.S. Media*. Boulder, Colo.: Westview Press, 1997:57–79.

MEAD, GEORGE HERBERT. *Mind, Self, and Society*. Charles W. Morris, ed. Chicago: University of Chicago Press, 1962; orig. 1934.

MELTZER, BERNARD N. "Mead's Social Psychology." In Jerome G. Manis and Bernard N. Meltzer, eds., *Symbolic Interaction: A Reader in Social Psychology*. 3rd ed. Needham Heights, Mass.: Allyn & Bacon, 1978.

NIELSEN MEDIA RESEARCH. "State of the Media 2011." 2012. Available at http://blog.nielsen.com/nielsenwire/mediauniverse/

NORC. *General Social Surveys, 1972–2010: Cumulative Codebook*. Chicago: National Opinion Research Center. 2011. Available at http://www.norc.org/GSS+Website

"Ongoing Tally of Newspaper Endorsements." [Online] Available October 27, 2008, at http://www.editorandpublisher.com/eandp/news/article_display.jsp?vnu_content_id=1003875230

PETERS, GERHARD AND JOHN T. WOOLLEY. "2012 General Election Editorial Endorsements by Major Newspapers." The American Presidency Project, University of California, Santa Barbara. 2012. Available at http://www.presidency.ucsb.edu/data/2012_newspaper_endorsements.php

PEW RESEARCH CENTER FOR THE PEOPLE AND THE PRESS. "In Changing News Landscape, Even Television Is Vulnerable: Trends in News Consumption: 1991–2012." 2012. Available at http://www.people-press.org/2012/09/27/in-changing-news-landscape-even-television-is-vulnerable/

———. "Trends in News Consumption: 1991–2012." 2012. Available at http://www.people-press.org/2012/09/27/section-3-news-attitudes-and-habits-2/

RIDEOUT, VICTORIA. "Entertainment Media." June 2007. [Online] Available October 27, 2008, at http://www.kff.org/entmedia/entmedia061907nr.cfm

RIDEOUT, VICTORIA, ULLA G. FOEHR, AND DONALD F. ROBERTS. "Generation M2: Media in the Lives of 8- to 18-Year-Olds." Kaiser Family Foundation. January 2010. [Online] Available at http://www.kff.org/entmedia/8010.cfm

ROBINSON, THOMAS N., ET AL. "Effects of Reducing Children's Television and Video Game Use on Aggressive Behavior." *Archives of Pediatrics and Adolescent Medicine*. Vol. 155, No. 1 (January 2001):17–23.

Rothman, Stanley, Stephen Powers, and David Rothman. "Feminism in Films." *Society.* Vol. 30, No. 3 (March/April 1993):66–72.

Rymer, Russ. *Genie.* New York: HarperPerennial, 1994.

Shute, Nancy. "TV Watching Is Bad for Babies' Brains." *U.S. News & World Report Online.* December 9, 2010. [Online] Available at http://health.yahoo.net/articles/parenting/tv-watching-bad-babies-brains

Smith, Tom W. "Are We Grown Up Yet? U.S. Study Says Not 'til 26." [Online] Available May 23, 2003, at http://news.yahoo.com

Thrupkaew, Noy. "No Minor Issue." *National Geographic.* Vol. 218, No. 5 (November 2010):18.

TVB. "TV Basics." August 2012. Available at http://www.tvb.org/trends/95487

UNICEF. "State of the World's Children." 2012. Available at http://www.unicef.org/sowc/index_sowc.html.

U.S. Census Bureau. "American Community Survey." 2012. Available at http://www.census.gov/acs/www/

———. "Population Estimates." 2012. Available at http://www.census.gov/popest/data/index.html

———. "2012 National Population Projections: Tables and Charts." 2012. Available at http://www.census.gov/population/projections/data/national/2012/summarytables.html

U.S. Department of Justice, Bureau of Justice Statistics. "Corrections Statistics." 2012. Available at http://www.bjs.gov/index.cfm

U.S. Department of Labor, Bureau of International Labor Affairs, Office of Child Labor, Forced Labor and Human Trafficking. "2011 Findings on the Worst Forms of Child Labor." 2012. Available at http://www.dol.gov/ilab/programs/ocft/2011TDA.pdf

U.S. Department of Labor, Bureau of Labor Statistics. "American Time Use Survey." 2012. Available at http://www.bls.gov/tus/

Weitzman, Lenore J. *The Divorce Revolution: The Unexpected Social and Economic Consequences for Women and Children in America.* New York: Free Press, 1985.

———. "The Economic Consequences of Divorce Are Still Unequal: Comment on Peterson." *American Sociological Review.* Vol. 61, No. 3 (June 1996):537–38.

Wilson, Barbara J. "National Television Violence Study." Reported in Julia Duin, "Study Finds Cartoon Heroes Initiate Too Much Violence." *Washington Times* (April 17, 1998):A4.

Chapter 6

Bakalar, Nicholas. "Reactions: Go On, Laugh Your Heart Out." *New York Times* (March 8, 2005). [Online] Available March 11, 2005, at http://www.nytimes.com/2005/03/08/health/08reac.html

Baker, Patricia S., William C. Yoels, Jeffrey M. Clair, and Richard M. Allman. "Laughter in the Triadic Geriatric Encounters: A Transcript-Based Analysis." In Rebecca J. Erikson and Beverly Cuthbertson-Johnson, eds., *Social Perspectives on Emotion.* Vol. 4. Greenwich, Conn.: JAI Press, 1997:179–207.

Benokraitis, Nijole, and Joe R. Feagin. *Modern Sexism: Blatant, Subtle, and Overt Discrimination.* 2nd ed. Englewood Cliffs, N.J.: Prentice Hall, 1995.

Davies, Christie. *Ethnic Humor around the World: A Comparative Analysis.* Bloomington: Indiana University Press, 1990.

Ebaugh, Helen Rose Fuchs. *Becoming an Ex: The Process of Role Exit.* Chicago: University of Chicago Press, 1988.

Ekman, Paul. "Biological and Cultural Contributions to Body and Facial Movements in the Expression of Emotions." In A. Rorty, ed., *Explaining Emotions.* Berkeley: University of California Press, 1980a:73–101.

———. *Face of Man: Universal Expression in a New Guinea Village.* New York: Garland Press, 1980b.

———. *The Expression of Emotions in Man and Animals.* New York: Oxford University Press, 1998.

———. *Emotions Revealed: Recognizing Faces and Feelings to Improve Communication and Emotional Life.* New York: Tribune Books, 2003.

Farrell, Michael B. "Cambridge Becoming Social Media Research Hub." *Boston Globe* (July 28, 2012). Available at http://www.bostonglobe.com/business/2012/07/27/cambridge-becoming-hub-for-social-media-research-from-mit-Microsoft/eG9s355T8Tg5YIJWuulqXN/story.html

Farris, Coreen, Teresa A. Treat, Richard J. Viken, and Richard M. McFall. "Perceptual Mechanisms That Characterize Gender Differences in Decoding Women's Sexual Intent." *Psychological Science.* Vol. 19, No. 4 (2008):348–54.

Flaherty, Michael G. *A Formal Approach to the Study of Amusement in Social Interaction. Studies in Symbolic Interaction.* Vol. 5. New York: JAI Press, 1984:71–82.

———. "Two Conceptions of the Social Situation: Some Implications of Humor." *Sociological Quarterly.* Vol. 31, No. 1 (Spring 1990).

Garfinkel, Harold. *Studies in Ethnomethodology.* Cambridge, Mass.: Polity Press, 1967.

Goffman, Erving. *The Presentation of Self in Everyday Life.* Garden City, N.Y.: Anchor Books, 1959.

———. *Interactional Ritual: Essays on Face to Face Behavior.* Garden City, N.Y.: Anchor Books, 1967.

Gooding, Gretchen E., and Rose M. Kreider. "Women's Marital Naming Choices in a Nationally Representative Sample." *Journal of Family Issues.* Vol. 31, No. 5 (May 2010):681–701. [Online] Available at http://0-journals.ohiolink.edu.dewey2.library.denison.edu/ejc/issue.cgi?issn=0192513x&issue=v31i0005

Henley, Nancy, Mykol Hamilton, and Barrie Thorne. "Womanspeak and Manspeak: Sex Differences in Communication, Verbal and Nonverbal." In John J. Macionis and Nijole V. Benokraitis, eds., *Seeing Ourselves: Classic, Contemporary, and Cross-Cultural Readings in Sociology.* 2nd ed. Englewood Cliffs, N.J.: Prentice Hall, 1992:10–15.

Hochschild, Arlie Russell. "Emotion Work, Feeling Rules, and Social Structure." *American Journal of Sociology.* Vol. 85, No. 3 (November 1979):551–75.

———. *The Managed Heart.* Berkeley: University of California Press, 1983.

Johnson, Cathryn. "Gender, Legitimate Authority, and Leader-Subordinate Conversations." *American Sociological Review.* Vol. 59, No. 1 (February 1994):122–35.

Linton, Ralph. *The Study of Man.* New York: Appleton-Century, 1937.

Macionis, John J. "A Sociological Analysis of Humor." Presentation to the Texas Junior College Teachers Association, Houston, 1987.

Merton, Robert K. *Social Theory and Social Structure.* New York: Free Press, 1968.

Orlansky, Michael D., and William L. Heward. *Voices: Interviews with Handicapped People.* Columbus, Ohio: Merrill, 1981

Pew Research Center. "Pew Internet and American Life Project." 2012. Available at http://www.pewinternet.org/Static-Pages/Trend-Data-(Adults)/Usage-Over-Time.aspx

Pirandello, Luigi. "The Pleasure of Honesty" (1917). In *To Clothe the Naked and Two Other Plays.* New York: Dutton, 1962:143–98.

Powell, Chris, and George E. C. Paton, eds. *Humor in Society: Resistance and Control.* New York: St. Martin's Press, 1988.

Primeggia, Salvatore, and Joseph A. Varacalli. "Southern Italian Comedy: Old to New World." In Joseph V. Scelsa, Salvatore J. La Gumina, and Lydio Tomasi, eds., *Italian Americans in Transition.* New York: American Italian Historical Association, 1990:241–52.

Sansom, William. *A Contest of Ladies.* London: Hogarth, 1956.

Shively, JoEllen. "Cowboys and Indians: Perceptions of Western Films among American Indians and Anglos." *American Sociological Review.* Vol. 57, No. 6 (December 1992):725–34.

Simmel, Georg. *The Sociology of Georg Simmel.* Kurt Wolff, ed. New York: Free Press, 1950; orig. 1902.

Smith-Lovin, Lynn, and Charles Brody. "Interruptions in Group Discussions: The Effects of Gender and Group Composition." *American Journal of Sociology.* Vol. 54, No. 3 (June 1989):424–35.

Speier, Hans. "Wit and Politics: An Essay on Laughter and Power." Robert Jackall, ed. and trans. *American Journal of Sociology.* Vol. 103, No. 5 (March 1998):1352–1401.

Stepanikova, Irena, Qian Zhang, Darryl Wieland, G. Paul Eleazer, and Thomas Stewart. "Non-Verbal Communication between Primary Care Physicians and Older Patients: How Does Race Matter?" *Journal of General Internal Medicine* (December 6, 2011). Available at http://www.springerlink.com/content/d84k724x813755g1/fulltext.html

Svebak, Sven. Cited in Marilyn Elias, "Study Links Sense of Humor, Survival." [Online] Available March 14, 2007, at http://www.usatoday.com

Tannen, Deborah. *You Just Don't Understand: Women and Men in Conversation.* New York: Morrow, 1990.

Thomas, Piri. *Down These Mean Streets.* New York: Signet, 1967.

Thomas, W. I., and Dorothy Swaine Thomas. *The Child in America: Behavior Problems and Programs.* New York: Knopf, 1928.

Thorne, Barrie, Cheris Kramarae, and Nancy Henley, eds. *Language, Gender, and Society.* Rowley, Mass.: Newbury House, 1983.

Turner, Jonathan. *On the Origins of Human Emotions: A Sociological Inquiry into the Evolution of Human Emotions.* Stanford, Calif.: Stanford University Press, 2000.

Turkle, Sherry. *Alone Together: Why We Expect More from Technology and Less from Each Other.* New York: Basic Books, 2012.

United Nations. "The World's Women 2010: Trends and Statistics." 2010. Available at http://unstats.un.org/unsd/demographic/products/Worldswomen/wwwork2010.htm

U.S. Department of Labor, Bureau of Labor Statistics. "Highlights of Women's Earnings." 2012. Available at http://www.bls.gov/cps/cpswom2011.pdf

———. "Labor Force Statistics from the Current Population Survey." 2012. Available at http://www.bls.gov/cps/

Yoels, William C., and Jeffrey Michael Clair. "Laughter in the Clinic: Humor in Social Organization." *Symbolic Interaction.* Vol. 18, No. 1 (1995):39–58.

Chapter 7

Allen, Thomas B., and Charles O. Hyman. *We Americans: Celebrating a Nation, Its People, and Its Past.* Washington, D.C.: National Geographic Society, 1999.

"Army Apologizes over Salutation." *USA Today* (January 8, 2009):6A.

Asch, Solomon. *Social Psychology.* Englewood Cliffs, N.J.: Prentice Hall, 1952.

Baron, James N., Michael T. Hannan, and M. Diane Burton. "Building the Iron Cage: Determinants of Managerial Intensity in the Early Years of Organizations." *American Sociological Review.* Vol. 64, No. 4 (August 1999):527–47.

Bedard, Paul. "Washington Whispers." *U.S. News & World Report* (March 25, 2002):2.

Blau, Peter M. *Inequality and Heterogeneity: A Primitive Theory of Social Structure.* New York: Free Press, 1977.

Blau, Peter M., Terry C. Blum, and Joseph E. Schwartz. "Heterogeneity and Intermarriage." *American Sociological Review.* Vol. 47, No. 1 (February 1982):45–62.

Bobo, Lawrence, and Vincent L. Hutchings. "Perceptions of Racial Group Competition: Extending Blumer's Theory of Group Position to a Multiracial Social Context." *American Sociological Review.* Vol. 61, No. 6 (December 1996):951–72.

Brooks, David. *Bobos in Paradise: The New Upper Class and How They Got There.* New York: Simon & Schuster, 2000.

Castilla, Emilio J. "Gender, Race, and Meritocracy in Organizational Careers." *American Journal of Sociology.* Vol. 113, No. 6 (May 2008):1479–1526.

CTIA (The Wireless Association). "Quick Facts." 2012. Available at http://www.ctia.org/media/industry_info/index.cfm/AID/10323

Etzioni, Amitai. *A Comparative Analysis of Complex Organization: On Power, Involvement, and Their Correlates.* Revised and enlarged ed. New York: Free Press, 1975.

FCC (Federal Communications Commission). "Trends in Telephone Service: Industry Analysis and Technology Division Wireline Competition Bureau." September 2010. Available at http://hraunfoss.fcc.gov/edocs_public/attachmatch/DOC-284932A1.pdf

Fernandez, Roberto M., and Nancy Weinberg. "Sifting and Sorting: Personal Contacts and Hiring in a Retail Bank." *American Sociological Review.* Vol. 62, No. 6 (December 1997):883–902.

Green, Gary Paul, Leann M. Tigges, and Daniel Diaz. "Racial and Ethnic Differences in Job-Search Strategies in Atlanta, Boston, and Los Angeles." *Social Science Quarterly.* Vol. 80, No. 2 (June 1999):263–90.

Gwynne, S. C., and John F. Dickerson. "Lost in the E-Mail." *Time* (April 21, 1997):88–90.

Hagan, Jacqueline Maria. "Social Networks, Gender, and Immigrant Incorporation: Resources and Restraints." *American Sociological Review.* Vol. 63, No. 1 (February 1998):55–67.

Halberstam, David. *The Reckoning.* New York: Avon Books, 1986.

Helgesen, Sally. *The Female Advantage: Women's Ways of Leadership.* New York: Doubleday, 1990.

Heymann, Philip B. "Civil Liberties and Human Rights in the Aftermath of September 11." *Harvard Journal of Law and Public Policy.* Vol. 25, No. 2 (Spring 2002):441–57.

Hui, Sylvia. "Bloomberg Takes Cues from London's Security-Obsessed Security." *The Huffington Post.* [Online] Available May 11, 2010, at http://www.huffingtonpost.com/2010/05/11/bloomberg-taking-cues-fro_n_571359.html

Ide, Thomas R., and Arthur J. Cordell. "Automating Work." *Society.* Vol. 31, No. 6 (September/October 1994):65–71.

Inglehart, Ronald et al. "World Values Survey." 2012. Available at http://www.wvsevsdb.com/wvs/WVSAnalizeQuestion.jsp

International Telecommunications Union. "ICT Indicators Database." 2012. Available at http://www.itu.int/ITU-D/ICTEYE/Indicators/Indicators.aspx

Janis, Irving L. *Victims of Groupthink.* Boston: Houghton Mifflin, 1972.

———. *Crucial Decisions: Leadership in Policymaking and Crisis Management.* New York: Free Press, 1989.

Kaminer, Wendy. "Volunteers: Who Knows What's in It for Them?" *Ms.* (December 1984):93–96, 126–28.

Kanter, Rosabeth Moss. *Men and Women of the Corporation.* New York: Basic Books, 1977.

Kanter, Rosabeth Moss, and Barry A. Stein. "The Gender Pioneers: Women in an Industrial Sales Force." In Rosabeth Moss Kanter and Barry A. Stein, eds., *Life in Organizations.* New York: Basic Books, 1979:134–60.

Klein, Daniel B. "Embarrassed as a Non-Left Professor." *Society.* Vol. 47, No. 5 (September/October 2010):377–78.

Lewis, Lionel S. "Madoff's Victims and Their Day in Court." *Society.* Vol. 45, No. 5 (September/October 2010):439–50.

Lin, Nan, Karen Cook, and Ronald S. Burt, eds. *Social Capital: Theory and Research.* Hawthorne, N.Y.: Aldine de Gruyter, 2001.

Maddox, Setma. "Organizational Culture and Leadership Style: Factors Affecting Self-Managed Work Team Performance." Paper presented at the annual meeting of the Southwest Social Science Association, Dallas, February 1994.

Markoff, John. "Remember Big Brother? Now He's a Company Man." *New York Times* (March 31, 1991):7.

McDonald's Corporation. "Company Profile." 2012. Available at http://www.aboutmcdonalds.com/mcd/investors/company_profile.html

———. "Financial Highlights." 2012. Available at http://www.aboutmcdonalds.com/mcd/investors/financial_highlights.html

Meier, Fred. "Toyota All but Locks Sales Crown for 2012, Dumping GM." *USA Today* (July 25, 2012). Available at http://content.usatoday.com/communities/driveon/post/2012/07/toyota-all-but-locks-sales-crown-for-2012-dumping-gm/1#.UX_AwLXCaSp

Merton, Robert K. *Social Theory and Social Structure.* New York: Free Press, 1968.

Michels, Robert. *Political Parties.* Glencoe, Ill.: Free Press, 1949; orig. 1911.

Milgram, Stanley. "Behavioral Study of Obedience." *Journal of Abnormal and Social Psychology.* Vol. 67, No. 4 (1963):371–78.

———. "Group Pressure and Action Against a Person." *Journal of Abnormal and Social Psychology.* Vol. 69, No. 2 (August 1964):137–43.

———. "Some Conditions of Obedience and Disobedience to Authority." *Human Relations.* Vol. 18, No. 1 (February 1965):57–76.

———. "The Small World Problem." *Psychology Today* (May 1967):60–67.

Miller, Arthur G. *The Obedience Experiments: A Case of Controversy in Social Science.* New York: Praeger, 1986.

Mollenhorst, Gerald. "Networks in Contexts: How Meeting Opportunities Affect Personal Relationships." Ph.D. Dissertation. University of Utrecht, 2009.

O'Harrow, Robert, Jr. "ID Theft Scam Hits D.C. Area Residents." [Online] Available February 21, 2005, at http://news.yahoo.com

"Online Privacy: It's Time for Rules in Wonderland." *Business Week* (March 20, 2000):82–96.

Ouchi, William. *Theory Z: How American Business Can Meet the Japanese Challenge.* Reading, Mass.: Addison-Wesley, 1981.

Petersen, Trond, Ishak Saporta, and Marc-David L. Seidel. "Offering a Job: Meritocracy and Social Networks." *American Journal of Sociology.* Vol. 106, No. 3 (November 2000):763–816.

Philadelphia, Desa. "Tastier, Plusher—and Fast." *Time* (September 30, 2002):57.

Pinchot, Gifford, and Elizabeth Pinchot. *The End of Bureaucracy and the Rise of the Intelligent Organization.* San Francisco: Berrett-Koehler, 1993.

"Places Where the System Broke Down." *Time* (September 19, 2005):34–41.

Podolny, Joel M., and James N. Baron. "Resources and Relationships: Social Networks and Mobility in the Workplace." *American Sociological Review.* Vol. 62, No. 5 (October 1997):673–93.

Pryor, John H., Kevin Egan, Laura Palucki Blake, Sylvia Hurtado, Jennifer Berdan, and Matthew Case. "The American Freshman: National Norms Fall 2012 (Expanded Edition)." Cooperative Institutional Research Program at the Higher Education Research Institute at UCLA. 2013. Available at http://www.heri.ucla.edu/monographs/TheAmericanFreshman2012-Expanded.pdf

Reskin, Barbara F., and Debra Branch McBrier. "Why Not Ascription? Organizations' Employment of Male and Female Managers." *American Sociological Review.* Vol. 65, No. 2 (April 2000):210–33.

Ridgeway, Cecilia L. *The Dynamics of Small Groups.* New York: St. Martin's Press, 1983.

Ritzer, George. *The McDonaldization of Society: An Investigation into the Changing Character of Contemporary Social Life.* Thousand Oaks, Calif.: Pine Forge Press, 1993

Saporito, Bill. "Spotlight: Toyota's Recall." *Time* (February 15, 2010):17.

Schlosser, Eric. *Fast-Food Nation: The Dark Side of the All-American Meal.* New York: Perennial, 2002.

Shipley, Joseph T. *Dictionary of Word Origins.* Totowa, N.J.: Rowman & Allanheld, 1985.

Simmel, Georg. *The Sociology of Georg Simmel.* Kurt Wolff, ed. New York: Free Press, 1950; orig. 1902.

South, Scott J., and Steven F. Messner. "Structural Determinants of Intergroup Association: Interracial Marriage and Crime." *American Journal of Sociology.* Vol. 91, No. 6 (May 1986):1409–30.

Stein, Joel. "Your Data, Yourself." *Time.* Vol. 177, No. 11 (March 21, 2011):40–46.

Stouffer, Samuel A., et al. *The American Soldier: Adjustment during Army Life.* Princeton, N.J.: Princeton University Press, 1949.

Sullivan, Barbara. "McDonald's Sees India as Golden Opportunity." *Chicago Tribune* (April 5, 1995):B1.

Tajfel, Henri. "Social Psychology of Intergroup Relations." *Annual Review of Psychology.* Palo Alto, Calif.: Annual Reviews, 1982:1–39.

Tannen, Deborah. *Talking from 9 to 5: How Women's and Men's Conversational Styles Affect Who Gets Heard, Who Gets Credit, and What Gets Done at Work.* New York: Morrow, 1994.

Taylor, Frederick Winslow. *The Principles of Scientific Management.* New York. Harper Bros., 1911.

Tingwall, Eric. "Auto Insurance Gets Cheaper but Potentially More Invasive." *Automobile* (December 2008):74.

Torres, Lisa, and Matt L. Huffman. "Social Networks and Job Search Outcomes among Male and Female Professional, Technical, and Managerial Workers." *Sociological Focus.* Vol. 35, No. 1 (February 2002):25–42.

U.S. Census Bureau. "Population Estimates." 2012. Available at http://www.census.gov/popest/data/index.html

U.S. Equal Employment Opportunity Commission. "Job Patterns for Minorities and Women in Private Industry (EEO-1)." 2012. Available at http://www1.eeoc.gov/eeoc/statistics/employment/jobpat-eeo1/2011/index.cfm

Watts, Duncan J. "Networks, Dynamics, and the Small-World Phenomenon." *American Journal of Sociology.* Vol. 105, No. 2 (September 1999):493–527.

Weber, Max. *Economy and Society: An Outline of Interpretive Sociology.* Guenther Roth and Claus Wittich, eds. Berkeley: University of California Press, 1978; orig. 1921.

Werth, Christopher. "To Watch the Watchers." *Newsweek* (October 20, 2008):E4.

White, Ralph, and Ronald Lippitt. "Leader Behavior and Member Reaction in Three 'Social Climates.'" In Dorwin Cartwright and Alvin Zander, eds., *Group Dynamics.* Evanston, Ill.: Row & Peterson, 1953:586–611.

Wildavsky, Ben. "Small World, Isn't It?" *U.S. News & World Report* (April 1, 2002):68.

Yeatts, Dale E. "Creating the High-Performance Self-Managed Work Team: A Review of Theoretical Perspectives." Paper presented at the annual meeting of the Southwest Social Science Association, Dallas, February 1994.

Chapter 8

Alan Guttmacher Institute. "Facts on Induced Abortion in the United States." August 2011. Available at http://www.guttmacher.org/pubs/fb_induced_abortion.html#6

———. "U.S. Teenage Pregnancies, Births and Abortions: National and State Trends and Trends by Race and Ethnicity." January 2010. Available at http://www.guttmacher.org/pubs/USTPtrends.pdf

———. "U.S. Teenage Pregnancies, Births, and Abortions, 2008: National Trends by Race and Ethnicity." February 2012. Available at http://www.guttmacher.org/pubs/USTPtrends08.pdf

Astin, Alexander W., Leticia Oseguera, Linda J. Sax, and William S. Korn. *The American Freshman: Thirty-Five Year Trends.* Los Angeles: UCLA Higher Education Research Institute, 2002.

Barton, Bernadette. *Stripped: Inside the Lives of Exotic Dancers.* New York: New York University Press, 2006.

Bearman, Peter S., James Moody, and Katherine Stovel. "Chains of Affection." *American Journal of Sociology.* Vol. 110, No. 1 (July 2004):44–91.

Benedict, Ruth. "Continuities and Discontinuities in Cultural Conditioning." *Psychiatry.* Vol. 1, No. 2 (May 1938):161–67.

Blackwood, Evelyn, and Saskia Wieringa, eds. *Female Desires: Same-Sex Relations and Transgender Practices across Cultures.* New York: Columbia University Press, 1999.

Boyer, Debra. "Male Prostitution and Homosexual Identity." *Journal of Homosexuality.* Vol. 17, Nos. 1–2 (1989):151–84.

Centers for Disease Control and Prevention. "Understanding Teen Dating Violence." 2012. Available at http://www.cdc.gov/ViolencePrevention/pdf/TeenDatingViolence2012-a.pdf

———. "Youth Risk Behavior Survey—Youth Online." 2012. Available at http://apps.nccd.cdc.gov/youthonline/App/Default.aspx

CENTERS FOR DISEASE CONTROL AND PREVENTION, NATIONAL CENTER FOR HEALTH STATISTICS. "National Survey of Family Growth (NSFG)." 2012. Available at http://www.cdc.gov/nchs/nsfg.htm

CHANDRA, ANJANI, WILLIAM D. MOSHER, CASEY COPEN, AND CATLAINN SIONEAN. "Sexual Behavior, Sexual Attraction, and Sexual Identity in the United States: Data from the 2006–2008 National Survey of Family Growth." National Health Statistics Reports. No 36. Hyattsville, Md.: National Center for Health Statistics. 2011. Available at http://www.cdc.gov/nchs/data/nhsr/nhsr036.pdf

COLTON, HELEN. The Gift of Touch: How Physical Contact Improves Communication, Pleasure, and Health. New York: Seaview/Putnam, 1983.

CRACY, DAVID. "Psychologists Repudiate Gay-to-Straight Therapy." Yahoo News. [Online] Available August 5, 2009, at http://news.yahoo.com/s/ap/20090805/ap_on_re_us/us_psychologists_gays

CROSSETTE, BARBARA. "Female Genital Mutilation by Immigrants Is Becoming Cause for Concern in the U.S." New York Times International (December 10, 1995):11.

DAVIDSON, JULIA O'CONNELL. Prostitution, Power, and Freedom. Ann Arbor: University of Michigan Press, 1998.

DAVIS, KINGSLEY. "Sexual Behavior." In Robert K. Merton and Robert Nisbet, eds., Contemporary Social Problems. 3rd ed. New York: Harcourt Brace Jovanovich, 1971:313–60.

DEANGELLIS, TORI. "Is Technology Ruining Our Kids?" Monitor on Psychology APA. Vol. 42, No. 9 (October 2011):62. Available at http://www.apa.org/monitor/2011/10/technology.aspx

DICKINSON, AMY. "When Dating Is Dangerous." Time (August 27, 2001):76.

DWORKIN, ANDREA. Intercourse. New York: Free Press, 1987.

ESTES, RICHARD J. "The Commercial Sexual Exploitation of Children in the U.S., Canada, and Mexico." Reported in "Study Explores Sexual Exploitation." [Online] Available September 10, 2001, at http://dailynews.yahoo.com

FORD, CLELLAN S., AND FRANK A. BEACH. Patterns of Sexual Behavior. New York: Harper Bros., 1951.

FOUCAULT, MICHEL. The History of Sexuality: An Introduction. Vol. 1. Robert Hurley, trans. New York: Vintage, 1990; orig. 1978.

GAGNÉ, PATRICIA, RICHARD TEWKSBURY, AND DEANNA MCGAUGHEY. "Coming Out and Crossing Over: Identity Formation and Proclamation in a Transgender Community." Gender and Society. Vol. 11, No. 4 (August 1997):478–508.

GATES, GARY. "How Many People Are Lesbian, Gay, Bisexual, and Transgender?" The Williams Institute. April 2011. Available at http://williamsinstitute.law.ucla.edu/wp-content/uploads/Gates-How-Many-People-LGBT-Apr-2011.pdf

GAVE, ELENI N. "In the Indigenous Muxe Culture of Mexico's Oaxaca State, Alternative Notions of Sexuality Are Not Only Accepted, They're Celebrated." Travel and Leisure (November 2005). [Online] Available June 15, 2009, at http://travelandleisure.com/articles/stepping-out/page/2/print

GEERTZ, CLIFFORD. "Common Sense as a Cultural System." Antioch Review. Vol. 33, No. 1 (Spring 1975):5–26.

GIDDENS, ANTHONY. The Transformation of Intimacy. Cambridge: Polity Press, 1992.

GREENBERG, DAVID F. The Construction of Homosexuality. Chicago: University of Chicago Press, 1988.

HAMER, DEAN, AND PETER COPELAND. The Science of Desire: The Search for the Gay Gene and the Biology of Behavior. New York: Simon & Schuster, 1994.

HUFFMAN, KAREN. Psychology in Action. New York: Wiley, 2000.

KAPSTEIN, ETHAN B. "The New Global Slave Trade." Foreign Affairs (November/December 2006). [Online] Available April 21, 2009, at http://www.foreignaffairs.com/articles/62094/ethan-b-kapstein/the-new-globalslave-trade

KINSEY, ALFRED, WARDELL BAXTER POMEROY, AND CLYDE E.MARTIN. Sexual Behavior in the Human Male. Philadelphia: Saunders, 1948.

KINSEY, ALFRED, WARDELL BAXTER POMEROY, CLYDE E. MARTIN, AND PAUL H. GEBHARD. Sexual Behavior in the Human Female. Philadelphia: Saunders, 1953.

KLUCKHOHN, CLYDE. "As an Anthropologist Views It." In Albert Deuth, ed., Sex Habits of American Men. New York: Prentice Hall, 1948.

KRUKS, GABRIEL N. "Gay and Lesbian Homeless/Street Youth: Special Issues and Concerns." Journal of Adolescent Health. No. 12 (1991, Special Issue):515–18.

KUNKEL, DALE, ET AL. Sex on TV, 2005. Menlo Park, Calif.: Henry J. Kaiser Family Foundation, 2005. [Online] Available September 13, 2006, at http://www.kff.org/entmedia/upload/Sex-on-TV-4-Full-Report.pdf

LACEY, MARC. "A Distinct Lifestyle: The Muxe of Mexico." New York Times (December 7, 2008):4.

LAUMANN, EDWARD O., JOHN H. GAGNON, ROBERT T. MICHAEL, AND STUART MICHAELS. The Social Organization of Sexuality: Sexual Practices in the United States. Chicago: University of Chicago Press, 1994.

LELAND, JOHN. "Bisexuality." Newsweek (July 17, 1995):44–49.

LEVAY, SIMON. The Sexual Brain. Cambridge, Mass.: MIT Press, 1993.

MARQUARDT, ELIZABETH, AND NORVAL GLENN. Hooking Up, Hanging Out, and Hoping for Mr. Right. New York: Institute for American Values, 2001.

MARTINEZ, GLADYS, CASEY COPEN, AND JOYCE ABMA. "Teenagers in the United States: Sexual Activity, Contraceptive Use, and Childbearing, 2006–2010 National Survey of Family Growth." National Center for Health Statistics. Vital Health Stat. Vol. 23. No. 31. 2011. Available at http://www.cdc.gov/nchs/data/series/sr_23/sr23_031.pdf

MIRACLE, TINA S., ANDREW W. MIRACLE, AND ROY F. BAUMEISTER. Human Sexuality: Meeting Your Basic Needs. Upper Saddle River, N.J.: Prentice Hall, 2003.

MURDOCK, GEORGE PETER. Social Structure. New York: Free Press, 1965; orig. 1949.

MURRAY, STEPHEN O., AND WILL ROSCOE, EDS. Boy-Wives and Female-Husbands: Studies of African Homosexualities. New York: St. Martin's Press, 1998.

NATIONAL CONFERENCE OF STATE LEGISLATURES. "Marriages." 2012. Available at http://www.ncsl.org/programs/cyf/cousins.htm

———. "Same Sex Marriage, Civil Unions and Domestic Partnerships." 2012. Available at http://www.ncsl.org/issues-research/human-services/same-sex-marriage.aspx

NORC. General Social Surveys, 1972–2010: Cumulative Codebook. Chicago: National Opinion Research Center, 2011. [Online] Available at http://www.norc.org/GSS+Website

OLYSLAGER, FEMKE, AND LYNN CONWAY. "On the Calculation of the Prevalence of Transsexualism." 2007. [Online] Available at http://ai.eecs.umich.edu/people/conway/TS/Prevalence/Reports/Prevalence%20of%20Transsexualism.pdf

PEW RESEARCH CENTER. "American Values Survey Question Database." 2012. Available at http://www.people-press.org/values-questions/

———. "With Voters Focused on Economy, Obama Lead Narrows." April 7, 2012. Available at http://www.people-press.org/2012/04/17/with-voters-focused-on-economy-obama-lead-narrows/

PICKERT, KATE. "What Choice?" Time. Vol. 181, No. 1 (January 14, 2013):38–46.

POPULATION REFERENCE BUREAU. "DataFinder: Reproductive Health Variables." 2012. Available at http://www.prb.org/DataFinder.aspx

PRYOR, JOHN H., KEVIN EGAN, LAURA PALUCKI BLAKE, SYLVIA HURTADO, JENNIFER BERDAN, AND MATTHEW CASE. "The American Freshman: National Norms Fall 2012 (Expanded Edition)." Cooperative Institutional Research Program at the Higher Education Research Institute at UCLA. 2013. Available at http://www.heri.ucla.edu/monographs/TheAmericanFreshman2012-Expanded.pdf

REECE, MICHAEL, DEBBY HERBENICK, J. DENNIS FORTENBERRY, STEPHANIE SANDERS, VANESSA SCHICK, BRIAN DODGE, AND SUSAN MIDDLESTADT. "National Survey of Sexual Health and Behavior (NSSHB)." 2010. [Online] Available at http://www.nationalsexstudy.indiana.edu

ROSENBERG, MICA. "Mexican Transvestite Fiesta Rocks Indigenous Town." Reuters. November 23, 2008. [Online] Available June 15, 2009, at http://www.reuters.com/article/lifestyleMolt/idUSTRE4AM1PB20081123

ROSS, LORETTA ROSS. "What Is Reproductive Justice?" The Pro-Choice Public Education Project. 2013. Available at http://www.protectchoice.org/section.php?id=28

SAINT JAMES, MARGO, AND PRISCILLA ALEXANDER. "What Is COYOTE?" 2004. [Online] Available May 28, 2008, at http://www.coyotela.org/what-is.html

SEDGH, GILDA., SINGH, S., HENSHAW, S. K., BANKOLE, A., SHAH, I. H., AHMAN, E. "Induced Abortion: Incidence and Trends Worldwide from 1995 to 2008." The Lancet. Vol. 379, No. 9816 (February 18, 2012):625–32.

SILVERMAN, JAY G. "Adolescent Female Sex Workers: Invisibility, Violence and HIV." Archives of Disease in Childhood. Vol. 96, No. 5 (2011):478–81.

SMITH, TOM W. "American Sexual Risk Behavior: Trends, Socio-Demographic Differences, and Behavior." March 2006. [Online] Available January 29, 2009, at http://www.norc.org/NR/rdonlyres/2663F09F-2E74-436E-AC81-6FFBF288E183/0/AmericanSexualBehavior2006.pdf

SNYDER, HOWARD N. "Sexual Assault of Young Children as Reported to Law Enforcement: Victim, Incident, and Offender Characteristics." 2000. [Online] Available November 9, 2008, at http://www.ojp.usdoj.gov/bjs/pub/pdf/saycrle.pdf

STEINHAUER, JENNIFER. "Sex Sells, So Legislator Urges State to Tax It." New York Times. May 26, 2008. Available at http://www.nytimes.com/2008/05/26/us/26porn.html

STORMS, MICHAEL D. "Theories of Sexual Orientation." Journal of Personality and Social Psychology. Vol. 38, No. 5 (May 1980):783–92.

UNAIDS 2010 PROGRESS REPORTS BY COUNTRY, "UNGASS Country Progress Report: Thailand (Reporting Period January 2008–December 2009)." 2010. [Online] Available at http://www.unaids.org/en/dataanalysis/monitoringcountryprogress/2010progressreportssubmittedbycountries

UNITED NATIONS. "UN World Contraceptive Use 2007." 2008. [Online] Available at http://www.un.org/esa/population/publications/contraceptive2007/contraceptive2007.htm

U.S. DEPARTMENT OF JUSTICE, DEPARTMENT OF JUSTICE STATISTICS. "Criminal Victimization in the United States—NCVS Victimization Analysis Tool." October 17, 2012. Available at http://bjs.ojp.usdoj.gov/index.cfm?ty=nvat

U.S. DEPARTMENT OF JUSTICE, FEDERAL BUREAU OF INVESTIGATION. "Crime in the United States 2011." 2012. Available at http://www.fbi.gov/about-us/cjis/ucr/crime-in-the-u.s/2011/crime-in-the-u.s.-2011

VENTURA, STEPHANIE J., SALLY C. CURTIN, JOYCE C. ABMA, AND STANLEY K. HENSHAW. "Estimated Pregnancy Rates and Rate of Pregnancy Outcomes for the United States, 1990–2008." National Vital Statistics Reports. Vol. 60, No. 7. Hyattsville, Md.: National Center for Health Statistics. June 20, 2012. Available at http://www.cdc.gov/nchs/data/nvsr/nvsr60/nvsr60_07.pdf

WEINBERG, GEORGE. Society and the Healthy Homosexual. Garden City, N.Y.: Anchor Books, 1973.

WEISBERG, D. KELLY. Children of the Night: A Study of Adolescent Prostitution. Lexington, Mass.: Heath, 1985.

WONDERS, NANCY A., AND RAYMOND MICHALOWSKI. "Bodies, Borders, and Sex Tourism in a Globalized World: A Tale of Two Cities—Amsterdam and Havana." Social Problems. Vol. 48, No. 4 (November 2001):545–71.

Chapter 9

AKERS, RONALD L., MARVIN D. KROHN, LONN LANZA-KADUCE, AND MARCIA RADOSEVICH. "Social Learning and Deviant Behavior." American Sociological Review. Vol. 44, No. 4 (August 1979):636–55.

ALLAN, EMILIE ANDERSEN, AND DARRELL J. STEFFENSMEIER. "Youth, Underemployment, and Property Crime: Differential Effects of Job Availability and Job Quality on Juvenile and Young Adult Arrest Rates." American Sociological Review. Vol. 54, No. 1 (February 1989):107–23.

AMERICAN GAMING ASSOCIATION. "Fact Sheet: Types of Gaming by State." 2012. Available at http://www.americangaming.org/industry-resources/research/fact-sheets/states-gaming

Amnesty International. "Death Penalty in 2012." 2012. Available at http://www.amnesty.org/en/death-penalty

Anderson, Elijah. "The Code of the Streets." *Atlantic Monthly* (May 1994):81–94.

———. "The Ideologically Driven Critique." *American Journal of Sociology*. Vol. 197, No. 6 (May 2002):1533–50.

Anti-Defamation League. "State Hate Crimes Statutory Provisions." 2012. Available at http://www.adl.org/99hatecrime/state_hate_crime_laws.pdf

Antlfinger, Carrie. "Homicides Down in Some Large U.S. Cities." *Yahoo News* (January 3, 2009). [Online] Available January 3, 2009, at http://news.yahoo.com/s/ap/20090103/ap_on_re_us/urban_homicides

BBC. "Sudan 'Trousers Woman' Released." *BBC Mobile News*. [Online] Available September 8, 2009, at http://news.bbc.co.uk/2/hi/8244339.stm

Becker, Howard S. *Outside: Studies in the Sociology of Deviance.* New York: Free Press, 1966.

Belofsky, Nathan. *The Book of Strange and Curious Legal Oddities.* New York: Penguin, 2010.

Blau, Judith R., and Peter M. Blau. "The Cost of Inequality: Metropolitan Structure and Violent Crime." *American Sociological Review*. Vol. 47, No. 1 (February 1982):114–29.

Bono, Agostino. "John Jay Study Reveals the Extent of Abuse Problem." [Online] Available September 13, 2006, at http://www.americancatholic.org/news/clergysexabuse/johnjaycns.asp

Brady Campaign to Prevent Gun Violence. 2012. Available at http://www.bradycampaign.org/

CAP Index. 2009. Available at www.capindex.com

Carlson, Norman A. "Corrections in the United States Today: A Balance Has Been Struck." *American Criminal Law Review*. Vol. 13, No. 4 (Spring 1976): 615–47.

Chiricos, Ted, RaneeMcEntire, and Marc Gertz. "Perceived Racial and Ethnic Composition of Neighborhood and Perceived Risk of Crime." *Social Problems*. Vol. 48, No. 3 (August 2001):322–40.

Chopra, Anuj. "Iranian Rap Music Bedevils the Authorities." *U.S. News & World Report* (March 24, 2008):33.

Cloud, John. "A Mind Unhinged." *Time*. Vol. 177, No. 3 (January 24, 2011):32–35.

Cloward, Richard A., and Lloyd E. Ohlin. *Delinquency and Opportunity: A Theory of Delinquent Gangs.* New York: Free Press, 1966.

Cohen, Albert K. *Delinquent Boys: The Culture of the Gang.* New York: Free Press, 1971; orig. 1955.

Cohen, Patricia. "Genetic Basis for Crime: A New Look." *The New York Times* (June 19, 2011).

Cole, George F., and Christopher E. Smith. *Criminal Justice in America.* 3rd ed. Belmont, Calif.: Wadsworth, 2002.

Currie, Elliott. *Confronting Crime: An American Challenge.* New York: Pantheon Books, 1985.

Death Penalty Information Center. "Innocence and the Death Penalty." 2012. Available at http://www.deathpenaltyinfo.org/innocence-and-death-penalty#inn-yr-rc

DeFina, Robert H., and Thomas M. Arvanites. "The Weak Effect of Imprisonment on Crime, 1971–1998." *Social Science Quarterly*. Vol. 83, No. 3 (September 2002):635–53.

Demuth, Stephen, and Darrell Steffensmeier. "The Impact of Gender and Race-Ethnicity in the Pretrial Release Process." *Social Problems*. Vol. 51, No. 2 (May 2004):222–42.

Derber, Charles. *The Wilding of America: Money, Mayhem, and the New American Dream.* 3rd ed. New York: Worth, 2004.

Donahue, John J., III, and Steven D. Leavitt. Research cited in "New Study Claims Abortion Is Behind Decrease in Crime." *Population Today*. Vol. 28, No. 1 (January 2000):1, 4.

Durkheim, Emile. *The Division of Labor in Society.* New York: Free Press, 1964a; orig. 1893.

———. *The Rules of Sociological Method.* New York: Free Press, 1964b; orig. 1895.

Dwyer, Jim. "Dizzying Price for Seeking the Death Penalty." *The New York Times* (June 2, 2011).

Eboh, Camillus. "Nigerian Woman Loses Appeal against Stoning Death." 2002. [Online] Available August 19, 2002, at http://dailynews.yahoo.com

Elias, Robert. *The Politics of Victimization: Victims, Victimology, and Human Rights.* New York: Oxford University Press, 1986.

Elliot, Delbert S., and Suzanne S. Ageton. "Reconciling Race and Class Differences in Self-Reported and Official Estimates of Delinquency." *American Sociological Review*. Vol. 45, No. 1 (February 1980):95–110.

Erikson, Kai T. *Wayward Puritans: A Study in the Sociology of Deviance.* New York: Wiley, 2005b; orig. 1966.

Frank, Thomas. "Coal Mine Deaths Spike Upward." *USA Today* (January 1, 2007). [Online] Available March 4, 2007 at http://www.usatoday.com

Gallup. "U.S. Schools: Whole Lotta Cheatin' Going On." May 11, 2004. [Online] Available November 12, 2008, at http://www.gallup.com/poll/171644/US-Schools-Whole-Lotta-Cheating-Going.aspx

Garfinkel, Harold. "Conditions of Successful Degradation Ceremonies." *American Journal of Sociology*. Vol. 61, No. 2 (March 1956):420–24.

Goffman, Erving. *Stigma: Notes on the Management of Spoiled Identity.* Englewood Cliffs, N.J.: Prentice Hall, 1963.

Goodwin, Liz. "Gun Deaths Set to Outstrip Car Fatalities for First Time in 2015." *The Lookout*. December 19, 2012. Available at http://news.yahoo.com/blogs/lookout/gun-deaths-set-outstrip-car-fatalities-first-time-152632492.html

Gottfredson, Michael R., and Travis Hirschi. "National Crime Control Policies." *Society*. Vol. 32, No. 2 (January/February 1995):30–36.

Greenhouse, Linda. "Supreme Court Allows Lethal Injection for Execution." *New York Times* (April 17, 2008). [Online] Available June 15, 2009, at http://www/nytimes.com/2008/04/17/us/16cnd-scotus.html

Hamilton, Brady E., Joyce A. Martin, and Stephanie J. Ventura. "Births: Preliminary Data for 2011." National Vital Statistics Reports. Vol. 61, No. 5. 2012. Available at http://www.cdc.gov/nchs/data/nvsr/nvsr61/nvsr61_05.pdf

Harries, Keith D. *Serious Violence: Patterns of Homicide and Assault in America.* Springfield, Ill.: Thomas, 1990.

Hartocollis, Anemona. "Man Is Convicted of Attempted Murder as Hate Crime in Village Rampage." *New York Times* (March 2, 2007):B6.

Herpertz, Sabine C., and Henning Sass. "Emotional Deficiency and Psychopathy." *Behavioral Sciences and the Law*. Vol. 18, No. 5 (September/October 2000):567–80.

Hirschi, Travis. *Causes of Delinquency.* Berkeley: University of California Press, 1969.

Hope, Trina L., Harold G. Grasmick, and Laura J. Pointon. "The Family in Gottfredson and Hirschi's General Theory of Crime: Structure, Parenting, and Self-Control." *Sociological Focus*. Vol. 36, No. 4 (November 2003):291–311.

Inciardi, James A. *Elements of Criminal Justice.* 2nd ed. New York: Oxford University Press, 2000.

International Centre for Prison Studies, University of Essex. "World Prison Brief." 2012. Available at http://www.prisonstudies.org/info/worldbrief/

Jefferson, Cord. "Driving Concerns." *National Geographic* (January 2009):33.

Jones, Charisse. "Upon Release from Prison, Some Can Feel Lost." *USA Today* (December 14, 2007):5A.

King, Kathleen Piker, and Dennis E. Clayson. "The Differential Perceptions of Male and Female Deviants." *Sociological Focus*. Vol. 21, No. 2 (April 1988):153–64.

Kittrie, Nicholas N. *The Right to Be Different: Deviance and Enforced Therapy.* Baltimore: Johns Hopkins University Press, 1971.

Kochanek, Kenneth D., Jiaquan Xu, Sherry L. Murphy, Arialdi M. Miniño, and Hsiang-Ching Kung. "Deaths: Final Data for 2009." National Vital Statistics Reports. Vol. 60, No. 3. 2011. Available at http://www.cdc.gov/nchs/data/nvsr/nvsr60/nvsr60_03.pdf

Kubrin, Charles E. "Gangstas, Thugs, and Hustlas: Identity and the Code of the Street in Rap Music." *Social Problems*. Vol. 52, No. 3 (August 2005):360–78.

Langbein, Laura I., and Roseana Bess. "Sports in School: Source of Amity or Antipathy?" *Social Science Quarterly*. Vol. 83, No. 2 (June 2002):436–54.

Lemert, Edwin M. *Social Pathology.* New York: McGraw-Hill, 1951.

———. *Human Deviance, Social Problems, and Social Control.* 2nd ed. Englewood Cliffs, N.J.: Prentice Hall, 1972.

Lemonick, Michael D. "The Search for a Murder Gene." *Time* (January 20, 2003):100.

Leonard, Eileen B. *Women, Crime, and Society: A Critique of Theoretical Criminology.* White Plains, N.Y.: Longman, 1982.

Liazos, Alexander. "The Poverty of the Sociology of Deviance: Nuts, Sluts, and Perverts." *Social Problems*. Vol. 20, No. 1 (Summer 1972):103–20.

Liptak, Adam. "More than 1 in 100 Adults Are Now in Prison in U.S." *New York Times* (February 29, 2008):A14.

Liska, Allen E., and Barbara D. Warner. "Functions of Crime: A Paradoxical Process." *American Journal of Sociology*. Vol. 96, No. 6 (May 1991):1441–63.

Little, Craig, and Andrea Rankin. "Why Do They Start It? Explaining Reported Early-Teen Sexual Activity." *Sociological Forum*. Vol. 16, No. 4 (December 2001):703–29.

Lohr, Steve. "In Bailout Furor, Wall Street Salaries Become a Target." *International Herald Tribune* (September 24, 2008). [Online] Available November 6, 2008, at http://www.iht.com/articles/2008/09/24/business/24pay.php

Martin, John M., and Anne T. Romano. *Multinational Crime: Terrorism, Espionage, Drug and Arms Trafficking.* Newbury Park, Calif.: Sage, 1992.

Martinez, Ramiro, Jr. "Latinos and Lethal Violence: The Impact of Poverty and Inequality." *Social Problems*. Vol. 43, No. 2 (May 1996):131–46.

Merton, Robert K. "Social Structure and Anomie." *American Sociological Review*. Vol. 3, No. 6 (October 1938):672–82.

———. *Social Theory and Social Structure.* New York: Free Press, 1968.

Miller, Walter B. "Lower-Class Culture as a Generating Milieu of Gang Delinquency" (1958). In Marvin E. Wolfgang, Leonard Savitz, and Norman Johnston, eds., *The Sociology of Crime and Delinquency.* 2nd ed. New York: Wiley, 1970:351–63.

Miller, William J., and Rick A. Matthews. "Youth Employment, Differential Association, and Juvenile Delinquency." *Sociological Focus*. Vol. 34, No. 3 (August 2001):251–68.

Mitchell, Chris. "The Killing of Murder." *New York Magazine* (January 8, 2008). [Online] Available February 9, 2008, at http://nymag.com/news/features/crime/2008/42603

Moffitt, Terrie E., et al. "A Gradient of Childhood Self-Control Predicts Health, Wealth, and Public Safety." *Proceedings of the National Academy of Sciences of the United States of America.* [Online] Available January 30, 2011, at http://www.pnas.org/content/early/2011/01/20/1010076108

Morin, Richard. "Getting a Grad Degree in Cheating." Pew Research Center. [Online] Available September 27, 2006, at http://pewresearch.org/pubs/68/getting-a-grad-degree-in-cheating

Munroe, Susan. "Abolition of Capital Punishment in Canada." About.com: Canada Online. July 2007. [Online] Available April 16, 2008, at http://canadaonline.about.com/od/crime/a/abolitioncappun.htm

National Coalition of Anti-Violence Programs. "Hate Violence against Lesbian, Gay, Bisexual, Transgender, Queer and HIV-Affected Communities in the United States in 2011." New York: National Coalition of Anti-Violence Programs. 2012. Available at http://www.avp.org/resources/avp-resources/107

National Conference of State Legislatures. "Same Sex Marriage, Civil Unions and Domestic Partnerships." 2012. Available at http://www.ncsl.org/issues-research/human-services/same-sex-marriage.aspx

National Conference of State Legislatures. "State Medical Marijuana Laws." 2012. Available at http://www.ncsl.org/issues-research/health/state-medical-marijuana-laws.aspx

National Conference of State Legislatures. "State Traffic Safety Legislation." 2012. Available at http://www.ncsl.org/programs/transportation/trafsafdb.cfm?action=billresults

Newcomb, Alyssa. "Texting While Walking Banned in New Jersey Town." abcNews (May 13, 2012). Available at http://gma.yahoo.com/blogs/abc-blogs/texting-while-walking-banned-jersey-town-152720795-abc-news-topstories.html

NORC. General Social Surveys, 1972–2010: Cumulative Codebook. Chicago: National Opinion Research Center. 2011. Available at http://www.norc.org/GSS+Website

"Our Cheating Hearts." Editorial. U.S. News & World Report (May 6, 2002):4.

Ozersky, Josh. "Got Raw?" Time. Vol. 176, No. 12 (September 20, 2010):69–70.

Pew Center on the States. "Prison Count 2010." April 2010. [Online] Available at http://www.pewcenteronthestates.org/uploadedFiles/Prison_Count_2010.pdf?n=880

Pew Research Center for the People and the Press. 2012. Available at http://www.people-press.org/question-search/?qid=1814733&pid=51&ccid=50#top

Pinker, Steven. "Are Your Genes to Blame?" Time (January 20, 2003):98–100.

Pryor, John H., Kevin Egan, Laura Palucki Blake, Sylvia Hurtado, Jennifer Berdan, and Matthew Case. "The American Freshman: National Norms Fall 2012 (Expanded Edition)." Cooperative Institutional Research Program at the Higher Education Research Institute at UCLA. 2013. Available at http://www.heri.ucla.edu/monographs/TheAmericanFreshman2012-Expanded.pdf

Quillian, Lincoln, and Devah Pager. "Black Neighbors, Higher Crime? The Role of Racial Stereotypes in Evaluations of Neighborhood Crime." American Journal of Sociology. Vol. 107, No. 3 (November 2001):717–67.

Quinney, Richard. Class, State and Crime: On the Theory and Practice of Criminal Justice. New York: McKay, 1977.

Reckless, Walter C., and Simon Dinitz. "Pioneering with Self-Concept as a Vulnerability Factor in Delinquency." Journal of Criminal Law, Criminology, and Police Science. Vol. 58, No. 4 (December 1967):515–23.

Rogers, Richard G., Rebecca Rosenblatt, Robert A. Hummer, and Patrick M. Krueger. "Black-White Differentials in Adult Homicide Mortality in the United States." Social Science Quarterly. Vol. 82, No. 3 (September 2001): 435–52.

Rosenfeld, Richard. "Crime Decline in Context." Contexts. Vol. 1, No. 1 (Spring 2002):20–34.

Scheff, Thomas J. Being Mentally Ill: A Sociological Theory. 2nd ed. New York: Aldine, 1984.

Shanks, Pete. "Promoting a Genetic Basic for Crime." Psychology Today and the Center for Genetics and Society (June 27, 2011). Available at http://www.psychogytoday.com/blog/genetic-crossroads/201106/promoting-genetic-basis-crime

Sheldon, William H., Emil M. Hartl, and Eugene McDermott. Varieties of Delinquent Youth. New York: Harper Bros., 1949.

Sherman, Lawrence W., and Douglas A. Smith. "Crime, Punishment, and Stake in Conformity: Legal and Informal Control of Domestic Violence." American Sociological Review. Vol. 57, No. 5 (October 1992):680–90.

Shover, Neal, and Andrew Hochstetler. Choosing White-Collar Crime. New York: Cambridge University Press, 2006.

Smith, Douglas A. "Police Response to Interpersonal Violence: Defining the Parameters of Legal Control." Social Forces. Vol. 65, No. 3 (March 1987): 767–82.

Smith, Douglas A., and Patrick R. Gartin. "Specifying Specific Deterrence: The Influence of Arrest on Future Criminal Activity." American Sociological Review. Vol. 54, No. 1 (February 1989):94–105.

Smith, Douglas A., and Christy A. Visher. "Street-Level Justice: Situational Determinants of Police Arrest Decisions." Social Problems. Vol. 29, No. 2 (December 1981): 167–77.

Spitzer, Steven. "Toward a Marxian Theory of Deviance." In Delos H. Kelly, ed., Criminal Behavior: Readings in Criminology. New York: St. Martin's Press, 1980:175–91.

Stack, Steven, Ira Wasserman, and Roger Kern. "Adult Social Bonds and the Use of Internet Pornography." Social Science Quarterly. Vol. 85, No. 1 (March 2004):75–88.

State of Oregon. "Governor Kitzhaber Issues Reprieve—Calls for Action on Capital Punishment." November 22, 2011. Available at http://www.oregon.gov/gov/media_room/pages/press_releasesp2011/press_112211.aspx

Statistics Canada. "Canada Year Book: Homicide in Canada, 2010." 2011. Available at http://www.statcan.gc.ca/pub/85-002-x/2011001/article/11561-eng.htm

Steele, Randy. "Awful but Lawful." Boating (June 2000):36.

Sutherland, Edwin H. "White Collar Criminality." American Sociological Review. Vol. 5, No. 1 (February 1940):1–12.

Swartz, Steve. "Why Michael Milken Stands to Qualify for Guinness Book." Wall Street Journal (March 31, 1989):1, 4.

Szasz, Thomas S. The Myth of Mental Illness: Foundations of a Theory of Personal Conduct. New York: Dell, 1961.
———. The Manufacturer of Madness: A Comparative Study of the Inquisition and the Mental Health Movement. New York: Harper & Row, 1970.
———. "Cleansing the Modern Heart." Society. Vol. 40, No. 4 (May/June 2003):52–59.
———. "Protecting Patients against Psychiatric Intervention." Society. Vol. 41, No. 3 (March/April 2004):7–10.

Sullivan, Andrew. Lecture delivered at Kenyon College, Gambier, Ohio, April 4, 2002.

Terry, Don. "In Crackdown on Bias, a New Tool." New York Times (June 12, 1993):8.

Thornberry, Terrance, and Margaret Farnsworth. "Social Correlates of Criminal Involvement: Further Evidence on the Relationship between Social Status and Criminal Behavior." American Sociological Review. Vol. 47, No. 4 (August 1982):505–18.

Tierney, John. "Prison and the Poverty Trap." New York Times. February 18, 2013. Available at http://www.nytimes.com/2013/02/19/science/long-prison-terms-eyed-as-contributing-to-poverty.html?emc=tnt&tntemail1=y&_r=0

Tittle, Charles R., Wayne J. Villemez, and Douglas A. Smith. "The Myth of Social Class and Criminality: An Empirical Assessment of the Empirical Evidence." American Sociological Review. Vol. 43, No. 5 (October 1978): 643–56.

Uggen, Christopher. "Ex-Offenders and the Conformist Alternative: A Job-Quality Model of Work and Crime." Social Problems. Vol. 46, No. 1 (February 1999):127–51.

U.S. Census Bureau. "Current Population Survey." 2012. Available at http://www.census.gov/cps/
———. "Population Estimates." 2012. Available at http://www.census.gov/popest/data/index.html

U.S. Department of Health and Human Services, SAMHSA. "Results from the 2011 National Survey on Drug Use and Health." 2012. Available at http://www.samhsa.gov/data/NSDUH/2011SummNatFindDetTables/

U.S. Department of Justice, Bureau of Justice Statistics. "Capital Punishment." 2011, 2012. Available at http://bjs.ojp.usdoj.gov/index.cfm?ty=tp&tid=18
———. "Prisoners in 2010." 2011. Available at http://bjs.ojp.usdoj.gov/content/pub/pdf/p10.pdf
———. "Criminal Victimization 2011." 2012. Available at http://bjs.gov/content/pub/pdf/cv11.pdf
———. "Criminal Victimization in the United States—NCVS Victimization Analysis Tool." 2012. Available at http://bjs.ojp.usdoj.gov/index.cfm?ty=nvat
———. "Federal Justice Statistics Resource Center." 2012. Available at http://bjs.ojp.usdoj.gov/fjsrc/index.cfm

U.S. Department of Justice, Federal Bureau of Investigation. "Crime in the United States 2011." 2012. Available at http://www.fbi.gov/about-us/cjis/ucr/crime-in-the-u.s/2011/crime-in-the-u.s.-2011

U.S. Department of Justice, Federal Bureau of Investigation. "Hate Crime Statistics." 2012. Available at http://www.fbi.gov/about-us/cjis/ucr/hate-crime/2011

U.S. Department of Labor, Bureau of Labor Statistics. "Injuries, Illnesses, and Fatalities." 2012. Available at http://www.bls.gov/iif/#tables

U.S. Department of Labor, Mine Safety and Health Administration. "Mine Safety and Health at a Glance." 2012. Available at http://www.msha.gov/MSHAINFO/FactSheets/MSHAFCT10.HTM

Valdez, A. "In the Hood: Street Gangs Discover White-Collar Crime." Police. Vol. 21, No. 5 (May 1997):49–50, 56.

Vera Institute of Justice. "The Price of Prisons: What Incarceration Costs Taxpayers." 2012. Available at http://www.vera.org/project/price-prisons

Vold, George B., and Thomas J. Bernard. Theoretical Criminology. 3rd ed. New York: Oxford University Press, 1986.

Von Drehle, David. "One Madman and a Gun." Time. Vol. 177, No. 3 (January 24, 2011):26–31.

Warr, Mark, and Christopher G. Ellison. "Rethinking Social Reactions to Crime: Personal and Altruistic Fear in Family Households." American Journal of Sociology. Vol. 106, No. 3 (November 2000):551–78.

Winship, Christopher, and Jenny Berrien. "Boston Cops and Black Churches." Public Interest (Summer 1999):52–68.

Witkin, Gordon. "The Crime Bust." U.S. News & World Report (May 25, 1998):28–40.

Wittenauer, Cheryl. "Saggy Pants May Not Be Lawful." 2007. [Online] Available at http://www.yahoonews.com

Wolfgang, Marvin E., Robert M. Figlio, and Thorsten Sellin. Delinquency in a Birth Cohort. Chicago: University of Chicago Press, 1972.

Wolfgang, Marvin E., Terrence P. Thornberry, and Robert M. Figlio. From Boy to Man, from Delinquency to Crime. Chicago: University of Chicago Press, 1987.

Wright, Richard A. In Defense of Prisons. Westport, Conn.: Greenwood Press, 1994.

Zakaria, Fareed. "Incarceration Nation." Time. Vol. 179, No. 13 (April 2, 2012):18.

Chapter 10

Arrow, Kenneth, Samuel Bowles, and Steven Durlauf. Meritocracy and Economic Inequality. Princeton, N.J.: Princeton University Press, 2000.

Badenhausen, Kurt. "Mayweather Tops List of the World's Highest-Paid Athletes." Forbes (June 19, 2012). Available at http://sports.yahoo.com/news/mayweather-tops-list-worlds-100-highest-paid-athletes-164158726-spt.html

Baltzell, E. Digby. The Protestant Establishment: Aristocracy and Caste in America. New York: Vintage Books, 1964.

Beck, Rachel, and Ellen Simon. "CEOs Who Got Out before Crisis Left with Millions." Yahoo News (September 25, 2008). [Online] Available September 25, 2008, at http://news.yahoo.com/s/ap/20080925/ap_on_bi_ge/bailout_ceo_pay&printer=1;_ylt=Ak3oDhhSUwYZqhuaJh10BZ9v24cA

Beech, Hannah. "Murder, Lies, Abuse of Power and Other Crimes of the Chinese Century." Time (May 14, 2012). Available at http://www.time.com/time/magazine/article/0,9171,2113802-3,00.html

Beeghley, Leonard. The Structure of Social Stratification in the United States. Needham Heights, Mass.: Allyn & Bacon, 1989.

Bian, Yanjie. "Chinese Social Stratification and Social Mobility." Annual Review of Sociology. Vol. 28 (2002):91–116.

Brinton, Mary C. "The Social-Institutional Bases of Gender Stratification: Japan as an Illustrative Case." American Journal of Sociology. Vol. 94, No. 2 (September 1988):300–34.

Central Intelligence Agency. "CIA World Factbook." 2012. Available at https://www.cia.gov/library/publications/the-world-factbook/index.html

Chang, Leslie T. *Factory Girls: From Village to City in a Changing China*. New York: Spiegel & Grau, 2008.

Clark, Margaret S., ed. *Prosocial Behavior*. Newbury Park, Calif.: Sage, 1991.

Dahrendorf, Ralf. *Class and Class Conflict in Industrial Society*. Stanford, Calif.: Stanford University Press, 1959.

Davis, Kingsley, and Wilbert Moore. "Some Principles of Stratification." *American Sociological Review*. Vol. 10, No. 2 (April 1945):242–49.

Defense Finance and Accounting Service. "Military Pay Tables." 2012. Available at http://www.dfas.mil/militarypay/militarypaytables.html

Domhoff, G. William. *Who Rules America Now? A View of the '80s*. Englewood Cliffs, N.J.: Prentice Hall, 1983.

Federal Reserve Board. "2010 Survey of Consumer Finances." 2012. Available at http://www.federalreserve.gov/econresdata/scf/files/2010_SCF_Chartbook.pdf

Fletcher, Michael A. "Research Ties Economic Inequality to Gap in Life Expectancy." *Washington Post* (March 10, 2013). Available at http://articles.washingtonpost.com/2013-03-10/business/37605505_1_life-expectancy-eligibility-age-retirement-age

Foroohar, Rana. "Your Incredible Shrinking Paycheck." *Time*. Vol. 177, No. 8 (February 28, 2011):24.

French, Howard W. "Teaching Japan's Salarymen to Be Their Own Men." *New York Times* (November 27, 2002):A4.

Gerber, Theodore P., and Michael Hout. "More Shock than Therapy: Market Transition, Employment, and Income in Russia, 1991–1995." *American Journal of Sociology*. Vol. 104, No. 1 (July 1998):1–50.

Grossman, Lev. "2010 Person of the Year: Mark Zuckerberg." *Time*. Vol. 176, No. 26 (December 27, 2010–January 3, 2011):44–75.

Herrnstein, Richard J., and Charles Murray. *The Bell Curve: Intelligence and Class Structure in American Life*. New York: Free Press, 1994.

Hout, Michael, Clem Brooks, and Jeff Manza. "The Persistence of Classes in Post-Industrial Societies." *International Sociology*. Vol. 8, No. 3 (September 1993):259–77.

Jacoby, Russell, and Naomi Glauberman, eds. *The Bell Curve Debate*. New York: Random House, 1995.

Johnson, Ian. "China's Aristocratic Class Wields Its Influence to Shape Politice." *New York Times* (November 13, 2012).

Kohn, Melvin L. "*The Bell Curve* from the Perspective of Research on Social Structure and Personality." *Sociological Forum*. Vol. 11, No. 2 (June 1996): 395.

Kuznets, Simon. "Economic Growth and Income Inequality." *American Economic Review*. Vol. 14, No. 1 (March 1955):1–28.

———. *Modern Economic Growth: Rate, Structure, and Spread*. New Haven, Conn.: Yale University Press, 1966.

Lenski, Gerhard E. *Power and Privilege: A Theory of Social Stratification*. New York: McGraw-Hill, 1966.

Liu, Melinda, and Duncan Hewitt. "The Rise of the Sea Turtles." *Newsweek* (August 18, 2008):29–31.

Long, Jason, and Joseph Ferrie. "The Path to Convergence: Intergenerational Occupational Mobility in Britain and the U.S. in Three Eras." *Economic Journal*. Vol. 117, No. 519 (2007):C61–C71.

Lord, Walter. *A Night to Remember*. Rev. ed. New York: Holt, Rinehart and Winston, 1976.

Mabry, Marcus, and Tom Masland. "The Man after Mandela." *Newsweek* (June 7, 1999):54–55.

Marx, Karl, and Friedrich Engels. "Manifesto of the Communist Party." In Robert C. Tucker, ed., *The Marx-Engels Reader*. New York: Norton, 1972:331–62; orig. 1848.

Mason, David S. "Fairness Matters: Equity and the Transition to Democracy." *World Policy Journal*. Vol. 20, No. 4 (Winter 2003–04). 2004. [Online] Available at http://www.worldpolicy.org/journal/articles/wpj03-4/mason.htm

McGroarty, Patrick, and Devon Maylie. "Zuma Renews Push for Power." *Wall Street Journal* (June 27, 2012):A13.

McKee, Victoria. "Blue Blood and the Color of Money." *New York Times* (June 9, 1996):49–50.

Moore, Michael J. "Wall Street Bonuses Cut." *Bloomberg Businessweek* (November 15, 2012). Available at http://www.businessweek.com/articles/2012-11-15/wall-street-bonuses-cut

Murphy, John. "Some Rise but Most Sink in Soweto's Sea of Slums." *Baltimore Sun* (October 6, 2002). [Online] Available November 15, 2008, at http://www.baltimoresun.com/news/health/balte.soweto06oct06,0,1833961.story

New York Times. "The Pay at the Top." April 9, 2011. Available at http://projects.nytimes.com/executive_compensation

Norbeck, Edward. "Class Structure." In *Kodansha Encyclopedia of Japan*. Tokyo: Kodansha, 1983:322–25.

OECD. "Stat. Extracts." 2009. Available at http://stats.oecd.org/index.aspx?

Packard, Mark. Personal communication, 2002.

Perry, Alex. "South Africa Looks for a Leader." *Time* (April 27, 2009):38–41.

Pomerantz, Dorothy, and Lacey Rose. "Forbes: The Celebrity 100." *Forbes*. June 28, 2010. Available at http://www.forbes.com/2010/06/22/oprah-winfrey-ladygaga-twilight-business-entertainment-celeb-100-10-intro_2.html

Powell, Bill. "Postcard: Dongguan." *Time* (December 15, 2008):4.

Richburg, Keith B. "China's Communist Rulers Find Newly Rich a Headache." *The Richmond Times-Dispatch* (September 14, 2011):A2.

Roth, Zachary. "Labor: Lavish CEO Pay Still Rising." *The Lookout*. April 20, 2011. Available at http://news.yahoo.com/s/yblog_thelookout/20110420/ts_yblog_thelookout/labor-lavish-ceo-pay-still-rising

Roth, Zachary. "Wall Street Pay Hits New Record." *The Lookout*. [Online] Available February 2, 2011, at http://news.yahoo.com/s/yblog_thelookout/20110202/ts_yblog_thelookout/wall-street-pay-hits-new-record

Scherer, Ron. "Could Bailout's Pay Caps Launch Wall Street Trend?" *Yahoo News* (September 30, 2008). [Online] Available September 29, 2008, at http://news.yahoo.com/s/csm/20080930/ts_csm/apaycut&printer=1;_ylt=Al3doZ_4Ps07Lcen.QIvU92Oe8UF

Tumin, Melvin M. "Some Principles of Stratification: A Critical Analysis." *American Sociological Review*. Vol. 18, No. 4 (August 1953):387–94.

United Nations. "Human Development Stat. Extracts." 2011. Available at http://stats.oecd.org/index.aspx?

U.S. Census Bureau. "American Community Survey." 2012. Available at http://www.census.gov/acs/www/

———. "Current Population Survey." 2012. Available at http://www.census.gov/cps/

———. "Families and Living Arrangements." 2012. Available at http://www.census.gov/population/www/socdemo/hh-fam.html

———. "Housing Vacancies and Homeownership." 2012. Available at http://www.census.gov/housing/hvs/

U.S. House of Representatives. *1991 Green Book*. Washington, D.C.: U.S. Government Printing Office, 1991.

Vonnegut, Kurt, Jr. "Harrison Bergeron." In *Welcome to the Monkey House*. New York: Delacorte Press, 1968:7–13.

Wendle, John. "Russia's Millionaires Keep Their Heads Up." *Time* (January 12, 2009):4.

Williamson, Jeffrey G., and Peter H. Lindert. *American Inequality: A Macroeconomic History*. New York: Academic Press, 1980.

Williamson, Samuel H. "Six Ways to Compute the Relative Value of a U.S. Dollar Amount, 1790 to Present." *Measuring Worth*. 2012. Available at http://www.measuringworth.com/index.html

Wolff, Edward N. "The Asset Price Meltdown and the Wealth of the Middle Class." 2012. Available at http://www.nber.org/authors_papers/edward_wolff

World Bank. "Russian Economic Report #26." September 25, 2011. [Online] Available at http://documents.worldbank.org/curated/en/2011/09/15115904/growing-risks

———. "Russian Federation Partnership, Country Program Snapshot." September 2011. [Online] Available at http://siteresources.worldbank.org/INTRUSSIANFEDEpiRATION/Resources/Russia_Snapshot.pdf

———. "World Development Indicators." 2010, 2011. [Online] Available at http://data.worldbank.org/data-catalog/world-development-indicators

———. "World DataBank: World Development Indicators." 2012. Available at http://data.worldbank.org/data-catalog/world-development-indicators

Wu, Xiaogang, and Donald J. Treiman. "Inequality and Equality under Chinese Socialism: The Hukou System and Intergenerational Occupational Mobility." *American Journal of Sociology*. Vol. 113, No. 2 (September 2007): 415–45.

Zuckerman, Mortimer B. "The Russian Conundrum." *U.S. News & World Report* (March 13, 2006):64.

Chapter 11

Adams, Patricia F., Whitney K. Kirzinger, and Michael E. Martinez. "Summary Health Statistics for the U.S. Population: National Health Interview Survey, 2011." National Center for Health Statistics. Vital Health Stat. Vol. 10, No. 255. 2012. Available at http://www.cdc.gov/nchs/data/series/sr_10/sr10_255.pdf

Applebaum, Binyamin. "Family Net Worth Drops to Level of Early 90s, Fed Says." *New York Times* (June 11, 2012). Available at http://finance.yahoo.com/news/family-net-worth-drops-level-185603451.html

Bainbridge, Jay, Marcia k.Meyers, and Jane Waldfogel. "Childcare Reform and the Employment of Single Mothers." *Social Science Quarterly*. Vol. 84, No. 4 (December 2003):771–91.

Baltzell, E. Digby. *Sporting Gentlemen: From the Age of Honor to the Cult of the Superstar*. New York: Free Press, 1995.

Beller, Emily, and Michael Hout. "Intergenerational Social Mobility: The United States in Comparative Perspective." *The Future of Children*. Vol. 16, No. 2 (Fall 2006). [Online] Available April 30, 2008, at http://www.futureofchildren.org/information2826/information_show.htm?doc_id=389282

Bohannan, Cecil. "The Economic Correlates of Homelessness in Sixty Cities." *Social Science Quarterly*. Vol. 72, No. 4 (December 1991):817–25.

Bott, Elizabeth. *Family and Social Network*. New York: Free Press, 1971; orig. 1957.

CNBC. "What's It Take to Be Middle Class? A Job." [Online] Available September 6, 2012, at http://finance.yahoo.com/news/whats-middle-class-job-193336311.html

Coleman, Richard P., and Bernice L. Neugarten. *Social Status in the City*. San Francisco: Jossey-Bass, 1971.

Corporate Library, The. "Executive Compensation." 2012. Available at http://www.thecorporatelibrary.com/info.php?id=60#ec

Creswell, Julie, and Azam Ahmed. "Large Hedge Funds Fared Well in 2011." *New York Times* (March 29, 2012). Available at http://dealbook.nytimes.com/2012/03/29/large-hedge-funds-fared-well-in-2011/

Eisenstadt, Jill. "The Maid's Tale." *New York Times* (July 25, 2004). [Online] Available March 22, 2005, at http://www.researchnavigator.com

Forbes. "The Forbes 400." 2012. Available at http://www.forbes.com/wealth/forbes-400

Fox, Justin. "Pay Them Less? Hell, Yes." *Time* (March 2, 2009):30.

Harford, Tim. "The American Dream: Getting to the Starting Line." [Online] Available October 9, 2007, at http://www.forbes.com/entrepreneurs/2007/10/09/income-mobility-opportunity-ent-dream1007-cx_th_1009harford.html

Helman, Christopher. *America's 25 Highest-Paid CEOs*. *Forbes*. October 12, 2011. Available at http://www.forbes.com/sites/christopherhelman/2011/10/12/americas-25-highest-paid-ceos/

Hout, Michael. "More Universalism, Less Structural Mobility: The American Occupational Structure in the 1980s." *American Journal of Sociology*. Vol. 95, No. 6 (May 1998):1358–1400.

IBOPE Inteligência. "Poll: Faith in American Dream Sinking as U.S. Adults Become Split Over Whether or Not They Can Achieve It." 2011. Available at http://zogbyworldwide.com/news/

Internal Revenue Service. "SOI Tax Stats—Individual Statistical Tables by Tax Rate and Income Percentile." 2012. Available at http://www.irs.gov/uac/SOI-Tax-Stats-Individual-Statistical-Tables-by-Tax-Rate-and-Income-Percentile

Kaufman, Leslie. "Surge in Homeless Families Sets Off Debate on Cause." *New York Times* (July 29, 2004). [Online] Available May 4, 2009, at http://www.nytimes.com/2004/06/29/us/surge-in-homeless-families-sets-off-debate-oncause.html?fta=y

Keister, Lisa A. *Getting Rich: America's New Rich and How They Got That Way*. New York: Cambridge University Press, 2005.

Keister, Lisa A., and Darby E. Southgate. *Inequality: A Contemporary Approach to Race, Class, and Gender*. Cambridge: Cambridge University Press, 2011.

Kohn, Melvin L. *Class and Conformity: A Study in Values*. 2nd ed. Homewood, Ill.: Dorsey Press, 1977.

Kohut, Andy. "Public and Occupy Wall Street Movement Agree on Key Issues." Pew Research Center. October 19, 2011. Available at http://www.people-press.org/2011/10/19/haves-and-have-nots/

Kozol, Jonathan. *Rachel and Her Children: Homeless Families in America*. New York: Crown, 1988.

Krugman, Paul. "For Richer: How the Permissive Capitalism of the Boom Destroyed American Equality." *New York Times Magazine* (September 20, 2002):62–67, 76–77, 141–42.

Lareau, Annette. "Invisible Inequality: Social Class and Childrearing in Black Families and White Families." *American Sociological Review*. Vol. 67, No. 5 (October 2002):747–76.

Lewis, Oscar. *The Children of Sanchez*. New York: Random House, 1961.

Lichter, Daniel T., and Martha L. Crowley. "Poverty in America: Beyond Welfare Reform." *Population Bulletin*. Vol. 57, No. 2 (June 2002):3–34.

Lichter, Daniel T., and Rukmalie Jayakody. "Welfare Reform: How Do We Measure Success?" *Annual Review of Sociology*. Vol. 28 (August 2002):117–41.

Lin, Nan, and Wen Xie. "Occupational Prestige in Urban China." *American Journal of Sociology*. Vol. 93, No. 4 (January 1988):793–832.

Lino, Mark. "Expenditures on Children by Families, 2011." Miscellaneous Publication Number 1528–2011. U.S. Department of Agriculture Center for Nutrition Policy and Promotion. 2012. Available at http://www.cnpp.usda.gov/Publications/CRC/crc2011.pdf

McLeod, Jay. *Ain't No Makin' It: Aspirations and Attainment in a Low-Income Neighborhood*. Boulder, Colo.: Westview Press, 1995.

Miller, Matthew, and Peter Newcomb, eds. "The Forbes 400." *Forbes* (October 10, 2005, Special issue).

Mouw, Ted. "Job Relocation and the Racial Gap in Unemployment in Detroit and Chicago, 1980 to 1990." *American Sociological Review*. Vol. 65, No. 5 (October 2000):730–53.

NORC. *General Social Surveys, 1972–2010: Cumulative Codebook*. Chicago: National Opinion Research Center, 2011. [Online] Available at http://www.norc.org/GSS+Website

Ostrander, Susan A. "Upper-Class Women: The Feminine Side of Privilege." *Qualitative Sociology*. Vol. 3, No. 1 (Spring 1980):23–44.

———. *Women of the Upper Class*. Philadelphia: Temple University Press, 1984.

Pew Research Center. "Growing Share of Americans Live in Income-Segregated Neighborhoods." August 1, 2012. Available at http://pewresearch.org/pubs/2316/census-segregation-lower-income-middle-upper-neighborhood-rise-major-metropolitan-tract-household-data-analysis-1980-majority-inequality-class-mixed

———. "The Lost Decade of the Middle Class." August 22, 2012. Available at http://www.pewsocialtrends.org/2012/08/22/the-lost-decade-of-the-middle-class/

———. "A Third of Americans Now Say They Are in the Lower Classes." 2012. Available at Available at http://pewresearch.org/pubs/2349/more-americans-lower-class-demographics-change-republicans-youth

Pyle, Ralph E., and Jerome R. Koch. "The Religious Affiliation of American Elites, 1930s to 1990s: A Note on the Pace of Disestablishment." *Sociological Focus*. Vol. 34, No. 2 (May 2001):125–37.

Roth, Zachary. "Labor: Lavish CEO Pay Still Rising." *The Lookout*. April 20, 2011. Available at http://news.yahoo.com/s/yblog_thelookout/20110420/ts_yblog_thelookout/labor-lavish-ceo-pay-still-rising

Roth, Zachary. "Wall Street Pay Hits New Record." *The Lookout*. [Online] Available February 2, 2011, at http://news.yahoo.com/s/yblog_thelookout/20110202/ts_yblog_thelookout/wall-street-pay-hits-new-record

Russell, Cheryl. "Are We in the Dumps?" *American Demographics*. Vol. 17, No. 1 (January 1995):6.

Saez, Emmanuel, and Thomas Piketty. "Income Inequality in the United States, 1913–1998." *Quarterly Journal of Economics*. Vol. 118, No. 1 (2003): 1–39. Tables and figures updated to 2010 in Excel format, March 2012. Available at http://www.econ.berkeley.edu/~saez/

Singh, Gopal K. "Child Mortality in the United States, 1935–2007: Large Racial and Socioeconomic Disparities Have Persisted Over Time." Rockville, Md.: U.S. Department of Health and Human Services. 2010. [Online] Available at http://www.hrsa.gov/healthit/images/mchb_child_mortality_pub.pdf

Taylor, Paul. "Ask the Expert: The Rise in Residential Segregation by Income." Pew Research Center Publications. August 2, 2012. Available at http://pewresearch.org/pubs/2318/residential-segregation-income

U.S. Bureau of Economic Analysis. "National Income and Product Account Tables." 2012. Available at http://www.bea.gov/iTable/iTable.cfm?ReqID=9&step=1

U.S. Census Bureau. "American Community Survey." 2010. [Online] Available at http://www.census.gov/acs/www

———. "Current Population Survey." September 2010. [Online] Available at http://www.census.gov/cps

———. "Voting and Registration." 2011. Available at http://www.census.gov/hhes/www/socdemo/voting/index.html

———. "American Community Survey." 2012. Available at http://www.census.gov/acs/www/

———. "Current Population Survey." 2012. Available at http://www.census.gov/cps/

———. "Families and Living Arrangements." 2012. Available at http://www.census.gov/population/www/socdemo/hh-fam.html

———. "Housing Vacancies and Homeownership." 2012. Available at http://www.census.gov/housing/hvs/

———. "Population Estimates." 2012. Available at http://www.census.gov/popest/data/index.html

———. "Small Area Income and Poverty Estimates (SAIPE)." 2012. Available at http://www.census.gov/did/www/saipe/data/statecounty/maps/index.html

U.S. Conference of Mayors. "A Status Annual Report on Hunger and Homelessness in America's Cities." December 2011. Available at http://usmayors.org/pressreleases/uploads/2011-hhreport.pdf

U.S. Department of Agriculture, Economic Research Service. "Food Security in the United States: Key Statistics and Graphics." 2012. Available at http://www.ers.usda.gov/Briefing/FoodSecurity/stats_graphs.htm

U.S. Department of Commerce, Bureau of Economic Analysis. "National Income and Product Account Tables." 2012. Available at http://www.bea.gov/iTable/iTable.cfm?ReqID=9&step=1

U.S. Department of Health and Human Services, Administration for Children and Families, Office of Family Assistance. "Characteristics and Financial Circumstances of TANF Recipients." 2012. Available at http://www.acf.hhs.gov/programs/ofa/character/index.html

U.S. Department of Housing and Urban Development, Office of Community Planning and Development. "The Fifth Annual Homeless Assessment Report to Congress." June 2011. Available at http://www.hudhre.info/index.cfm?do=viewResource&ResourceId=4450

U.S. Department of Labor, Bureau of Labor Statistics. "Current Employment Statistics." 2012. Available at http://www.bls.gov/ces/home.htm

U.S. Department of Labor, Wage and Hour Division. 2012. Available at http://www.dol.gov/whd/flsa/index.htm

Von Drehle, David. "The Financial Crisis: Who Can Lead Us Out of This Mess?" *Time* (October 6, 2008):32–36.

Wahl, Jenny B. "From Riches to Riches: Intergenerational Transfers and the Evidence from Estate Tax Returns." *Social Science Quarterly*. Vol. 84, No. 2 (June 2003):278–96.

Walker, Karen. "'Always There for Me': Friendship Patterns and Expectations among Middle- and Working-Class Men and Women." *Sociological Forum*. Vol. 10, No. 2 (June 1995):273–96.

Weitzman, Lenore J. "The Economic Consequences of Divorce Are Still Unequal: Comment on Peterson." *American Sociological Review*. Vol. 61, No. 3 (June 1996):537–38.

Wilson, William Julius. *When Work Disappears: The World of the New Urban Poor*. New York: Knopf, 1996a.

———. "Work." *New York Times Magazine* (August 18, 1996b):26ff.

Wolff, Edward N. "The Asset Price Meltdown and the Wealth of the Middle Class." 2012. Available at http://www.nber.org/authors_papers/edward_wolff

Zagorsky, Jay. "Divorce Drops a Person's Wealth by 77 Percent." Press release (January 18, 2006). [Online] Available January 19, 2006, at http://www.eurekalert.org/pub_releases/2006-01/osu-dda011806.php

Chapter 12

Anti-Slavery International. 2012. Available at http://www.antislavery.org/english/default.aspx

Bangladesh Garment Manufacturers & Exporters Association. 2012. Available at http://www.bgmea.com.bd/home/pages/aboutus

Bauer, P. T. *Equality, the Third World, and Economic Delusion*. Cambridge, Mass.: Harvard University Press, 1981.

Bearak, Barry. "Lives Held Cheap in Bangladesh Sweatshops." *New York Times* (April 15, 2001):A1, A12.

Berger, Peter L. *The Capitalist Revolution: Fifty Propositions about Prosperity, Equality, and Liberty*. New York: Basic Books, 1986.

Bergesen, Albert, ed. *Crises in the World-System*. Beverly Hills, Calif.: Sage, 1983.

Bonanno, Alessandro, Douglas H. Constance, and Heather Lorenz. "Powers and Limits of Transnational Corporations: The Case of ADM." *Rural Sociology*. Vol. 65, No. 3 (September 2000):440–60.

Bricker, Jesse, Arthur Kennickell, Kevin Moore, and John Sabelhaus. "Changes in U.S. Family Finances from 2007 to 2010: Evidence from the Survey of Consumer Finances." *Federal Reserve Bulletin*, Vol. 98, No. 2 (2012). Available at http://www.federalreserve.gov/Pubs/Bulletin/2012/PDF/scf12.pdf

Burkett, Elinor. "God Created Me to Be a Slave." *New York Times Magazine* (October 12, 1997):56–60.

Chen, Shaohua, and Martin Ravallion. "An Update to the World Bank's Estimates of Consumption Poverty in the Developing World." World Bank. 2012. Available at http://siteresources.worldbank.org/INTPOVCALNET/Resources/Global_Poverty_Update_2012_02-29-12.pdf

Consortium for Street Children. "Street Children Statistics." 2011. Available at http://www.streetchildren.org.uk/_uploads/resources/Street_Children_Stats_FINAL.pdf

Davies, James, Rodrigo Lluberas, and Anthony Shorrocks. "Credit Suisse Global World Databook, 2012." 2012. Available at https://infocus.credit-suisse.com/data/_product_documents/_shop/369553/2012_global_wealth_databook.pdf

Davies, James B., Susanna Sandström, Anthony Shorrocks, and Edward N. Wolff. *The World Distribution of Household Wealth.* Helsinki: United Nations University/World Institute for Development Economics Research, March 2008.

Delacroix, Jacques, and Charles C. Ragin. "Structural Blockage: A Cross-National Study of Economic Dependency, State Efficacy, and Underdevelopment." *American Journal of Sociology.* Vol. 86, No. 6 (May 1981):1311–47.

Dixon, William J., and Terry Boswell. "Dependency, Disarticulation, and Denominator Effects: Another Look at Foreign Capital Penetration." *American Journal of Sociology.* Vol. 102, No. 2 (September 1996):543–62.

Economist, The. "Paving the Way." [Online] Available January 27, 2011, at http://www.economist.com/node/18013822?story_id=18013822&fsrc=rss

Firebaugh, Glenn. "Growth Effects of Foreign and Domestic Investment." *American Journal of Sociology.* Vol. 98, No. 1 (July 1992):105–30.

——. "Does Foreign Capital Harm Poor Nations? New Estimates Based on Dixon and Boswell's Measures of Capital Penetration." *American Journal of Sociology.* Vol. 102, No. 2 (September 1996):563–75.

——. "Empirics of World Income Inequality." *American Journal of Sociology.* Vol. 104, No. 6 (May 1999):1597–1630.

Firebaugh, Glenn, and Dumitru Sandu. "Who Supports Marketization and Democratization in Post-Communist Romania?" *Sociological Forum.* Vol. 13, No. 3 (September 1998):521–41.

Firebaugh, Glenn, and Frank D. Beck. "Does Economic Growth Benefit the Masses? Growth, Dependence, and Welfare in the Third World." *American Sociological Review.* Vol. 59, No. 5 (October 1994):631–53.

Fisher, Max. "The Country Where Slavery Is Still Normal." *The Atlantic* (June 28, 2011). Available at http://www.theatlantic.com/international/archive/2011/06/the-country-where-slavery-is-still-normal/241148/

Forbes. "World's Billionaires." 2012. Available at http://www.forbes.com/wealth/billionaires

Frank, André Gunder. *On Capitalist Underdevelopment.* Bombay: Oxford University Press, 1975.

——. *Crisis: In the World Economy.* New York: Holmes & Meier, 1980.

——. *Reflections on the World Economic Crisis.* New York: Monthly Review Press, 1981.

Frayssinet, Fabiana. "Agribusiness Driving Land Concentration." Inter Press Service News Agency. [Online] Available October 5, 2009, at http://ipsnews.net/news.asp?idnews=48734

Galano, Ana Maria. "Land Hungry in Brazil." August 1998. [Online] Available December 4, 2008, at http://www.unesco.org/courier/1998_08/uk/somm/intro.htm

Goesling, Brian. "Changing Income Inequalities within and between Nations: New Evidence." *American Sociological Review.* Vol. 66, No. 5 (October 2001):745–61.

Hossain, Naomi. "Exports, Equity, and Empowerment: The Effects of Ready-made Garments Manufacturing Employment on Gender Equality in Bangladesh." World Bank. 2011. Available at http://siteresources.worldbank.org/INTWDR2012/Resources/7778105-1299699968583/7786210-1322671773271/Hossain-Export-Equity-employment.pdf

IBGE (Instituto Brasileiro de Geografia e Estatística). Census of Agriculture, 2006. [Online] Available at http://www.ibge.gov.br/english/presidencia/noticias/noticia_visualiza.php?id_noticia=1464&id_pagina=1

International Labour Organization. "Forced Labour." 2012. Available at http://www.ilo.org/global/topics/forced-labour/lang-en/index.htm

Kentor, Jeffrey. "The Long-Term Effects of Foreign Investment Dependence on Economic Growth, 1940–1990." *American Journal of Sociology.* Vol. 103, No. 4 (January 1998):1024–46.

——. "The Long-Term Effects of Globalization on Income Inequality, Population Growth, and Economic Development." *Social Problems.* Vol. 48, No. 4 (November 2001):435–55.

Landsea Center for Women's Land Rights. 2011. Available at http://www.landesa.org/women-and-land

Lappé, Frances Moore, and Joseph Collins. *World Hunger: Twelve Myths.* New York: Grove Press/Food First Books, 1986.

Lappé, Frances Moore, Joseph Collins, and Peter Rosset. *World Hunger: Twelve Myths.* 2nd ed. New York: Grove Press, 1998.

Leopold, Evelyn. "Sudan's Young Endure 'Unspeakable' Abuse: Report." [Online] Available April 19, 2007, at http://www.news.yahoo.com

Levinson, F. James, and Lucy Bassett. "Malnutrition Is Still a Major Contributor to Child Deaths." Population Reference Bureau. 2007. [Online] Available December 4, 2008, at http://www.prb.org/pdf07/Nutrition2007.pdf

Lindauer, David L., and Akila Weerapana. "Relief for Poor Nations." *Society.* Vol. 39, No. 3 (March/April 2002):54–58.

Milanovic, Branko. "Global Income Inequality: New Results and Implications for 21st Century Policy." World Bank. 2011. Available at http://siteresources.worldbank.org/EXTABCDE/Resources/7455676-1292528456380/7626791-1303141641402/7878676-1306699356046/Parallel-Sesssion-6-Branko-Milanovic.pdf

Moore, Wilbert E. "Modernization as Rationalization: Processes and Restraints." In Manning Nash, ed., *Essays on Economic Development and Cultural Change in Honor of Bert F. Hoselitz.* Chicago: University of Chicago Press, 1977:29–42.

——. *World Modernization: The Limits of Convergence.* New York: Elsevier, 1979.

Orhant, Melanie. "Human Trafficking Exposed." *Population Today.* Vol. 30, No. 1 (January 2002):1, 4.

Parsons, Talcott. *Societies: Evolutionary and Comparative Perspectives.* Englewood Cliffs, N.J.: Prentice Hall, 1966.

Perry, Alex. "Africa Rising." *Time.* Vol. 180, No. 23 (December 3, 2012):48–52.

Population Reference Bureau. "Datafinder." 2012. Available at http://www.prb.org/DataFinder.aspx

——. "World Population Data Sheet." 2012. Available at http://www.prb.org/pdf12/2012-population-data-sheet_eng.pdf

Rostow, Walt W. *The Stages of Economic Growth: A Non-Communist Manifesto.* Cambridge: Cambridge University Press, 1960.

——. *The World Economy: History and Prospect.* Austin: University of Texas Press, 1978.

Sala-i-Martin, Xavier. "The World Distribution of Income." Working Paper No. 8933. Cambridge, Mass.: National Bureau of Economic Research, 2002.

Schaffer, Michael. "American Dreamers." *U.S. News & World Report* (August 26, 2002):12–16.

UNICEF. "ChildInfo Statistics by Area: Child Survival and Health." 2012. Available at http://www.childinfo.org

United Nations. "Millennium Development Goals." 2011. [Online] Available at http://www.un.org/millenniumgoals

United Nations, Department of Economic and Social Affairs. "World Population Prospects: The 2010 Revision." 2011. Available at http://esa.un.org/unpd/wpp/index.htm

United Nations, Department of Economic and Social Affairs. "World Urbanization Prospects: The 2011 Revision." 2012. Available at http://esa.un.org/unpd/wup/pdf/WUP2011_Highlights.pdf

United Nations Development Programme. "Human Development Report 2007–08." 2008. [Online] Available at http://hdr.undp.org/en/reports/global/hdr2007-8/

United Nations Development Programme. "International Human Development Indicators." 2012. Available at http://hdrstats.undp.org/en/indicators/default.html

United Nations, Food and Agriculture Organization (FAO). "Women in Agriculture: Closing the Gender Gap for Development." 2011. Available at http://www.fao.org/docrep/013/i2050e/i2050e.pdf

——. "The State of Food Insecurity in the World 2012." 2012. Available at http://www.fao.org/fileadmin/user_upload/newsroom/docs/sofi-faqs.pdf

United Nations, Food and Agriculture Organization, Statistics Division. "Prevalence of Undernourishment in Total Population." Food Security Statistics. 2012. Available at http://www.fao.org/economic/ess/ess-fs/fs-data/en/

United Nations, Inter-agency Group for Child Mortality Estimation. "Levels and Trends in Child Mortality, 2012." 2012. Available at http://www.childinfo.org/files/Child_Mortality_Report_2012.pdf

United Nations Statistics Division. "The World's Women 2010: Trends and Statistics." Chapter 8: Poverty. 2010. Available at http://unstats.un.org/unsd/demographic/products/Worldswomen/WW2010pub.htm

United Nations World Food Programme. "Undernutrition: Women and Children Paying the Price." 2008. Available at http://www.wfp.org/english/?n=37

U.S. Agency for International Development (USAID). "U.S. Overseas Loans and Grants." 2012. Available at http://gbk.eads.usaidallnet.org/

U.S. Census Bureau, Foreign Trade Division. "Foreign Trade Statistics." 2012. Available at http://www.census.gov/foreign-trade/index.html

U.S. Department of Labor. "List of Goods Produced by Child Labor or Forced Labor, 2012." 2012. Available at http://www.dol.gov/ilab/programs/ocft/2012TVPRA.pdf

Vogel, Ezra F. *The Four Little Dragons: The Spread of Industrialization in East Asia.* Cambridge, Mass.: Harvard University Press, 1991.

Wallerstein, Immanuel. *The Modern World-System: Capitalist Agriculture and the Origins of the European World-Economy in the Sixteenth Century.* New York: Academic Press, 1974.

——. *The Capitalist World-Economy.* New York: Cambridge University Press, 1979.

——. "Crises: The World Economy, the Movements, and the Ideologies." In Albert Bergesen, ed., *Crises in the World-System.* Beverly Hills, Calif.: Sage, 1983:21–36.

——. *The Politics of the World Economy: The States, the Movements, and the Civilizations.* Cambridge: Cambridge University Press, 1984

Weber, Max. *The Protestant Ethic and the Spirit of Capitalism.* New York: Scribner, 1958; orig. 1904–05.

World Bank. "World DataBank: Health, Nutrition, and Population Statistics." 2012. Available at http://data.worldbank.org/data-catalog/health-nutrition-and-population-statistics

——. "World DataBank: World Development Indicators." 2012. Available at http://data.worldbank.org/data-catalog/world-development-indicators

Worsley, Peter. "Models of the World System." In Mike Featherstone, ed., *Global Culture: Nationalism, Globalization, and Modernity.* Newbury Park, Calif.: Sage, 1990:83–95.

Chapter 13

American Bar Association. "Legal Education, Statistics." 2012. Available at http://www.americanbar.org/content/dam/aba/administrative/legal_education_and_admissions_to_the_bar/council_reports_and_resolutions/1947_2010_enrollment_by_gender.authcheckdam.pdf

American Sociological Association. "Number of Doctoral Degrees Awarded in Sociology Since 1966 by Gender." Available at http://www.asanet.org/research/stats/gender/number_doctorate.cfm

Armstrong, Elisabeth. *The Retreat from Organization: U.S. Feminism Reconceptualized.* Albany: State University of New York Press, 2002.

"The Barrier That Didn't Fall." *The Daily Beast.* [Online] Available November 18, 2008, at http://www.thedailybeast.com/blogs-and-stories/2008-11-18/thebarrier-that-didnrsquot-fall

Baydar, Nazli, and Jeanne Brooks-Gunn. "Effect of Maternal Employment and Child-Care Arrangements on Preschoolers' Cognitive and Behavioral Outcomes: Evidence from Children from the National Longitudinal Survey of Youth." *Developmental Psychology.* Vol. 27, No. 6 (November 1991):932–35.

Bem, Sandra Lipsitz. *The Lenses of Gender: Transforming the Debate on Sexual Inequality.* New Haven, Conn.: Yale University Press, 1993.

Bernard, Jessie. *The Female World.* New York: Free Press, 1981.

Bonner, Jane. Research presented in the Public Broadcast System telecast *The Brain #6: The Two Brains.* Videocassette VHS 339. Newark, N.J.: WNET-13 Films, 1984.

Boyle, Elizabeth Heger, Fortunata Songora, and Gail Foss. "International Discourse and Local Politics: Anti-Female-Genital-Cutting Laws in Egypt, Tanzania, and the United States." *Social Problems.* Vol. 48, No. 4 (November 2001):524–44.

Catalyst. "*Fortune* 500 Board Seats Held by Women." 2012. Available at http://www.catalyst.org/knowledge/fortune-500-board-seats-held-women

——. "Women CEOs of the *Fortune* 1000." 2012. Available at http://www.catalyst.org/publication/271/women-ceos-of-the-fortune-1000

CBS News Polls. "Poll: Women's Movement Worthwhile." [Online] Available October 23, 2005, at http://www.cbsnews.com/stories/2005/10/22/opinion/polls/main965224.shtml

Ceci, Stephen J., and Wendy M. Williams. "Understanding Current Causes of Women's Underrepresentation in Science." *The Proceedings of the National Academy of Sciences.* 2011. [Online] Available at http://www.human.cornell.edu/hd/loader.cfm?csModule=security/getfile&PageID=60893

Center for American Women and Politics. "Women in Elective Office." 2012. Available at http://www.cawp.rutgers.edu/fast_facts/index.php

Centers for Disease Control and Prevention. "Deaths: Final Data for 2010, Tables." 2012. Available at http://www.cdc.gov/nchs/data/dvs/deaths_2010_release.pdf

Chronicle of Higher Education. "Survey Finds a Drop in Minority Presidents Leading Colleges." March 12, 2012. Available at http://chronicle.com/article/Who-Are-College-Presidents-/131138/

Cohen, Philip N., and Matt L. Huffman. "Individuals, Jobs, and Labor Markets: The Devaluation of Women's Work." *American Sociological Review.* Vol. 68, No. 3 (June 2003):443–63.

College Board, The. "2012 College-Bound Seniors: Total Group Profile Report." [Online] 2012. Available at http://research.collegeboard.org/programs/sat/data/cb-seniors-2012

Collins, Patricia Hill. *Black Feminist Thought: Knowledge, Consciousness, and the Politics of Empowerment.* 2nd ed. New York: Routledge, 2000.

Coltrane, Scott, and Melinda Messineo. "Mass Mediated Inequality: Images of Race and Gender in 1990s' Television Advertising." *Sex Roles.* Vol. 42, No. 5/6 (2000):363–89.

Correll, Shelley J. "Gender and the Career Choice Process: The Role of Biased Self-Assessment." *American Journal of Sociology.* Vol. 106, No. 6 (May 2001):1691–1730.

Cortese, Anthony J. *Provocateur: Images of Women and Minorities in Advertising.* Lanham, Md.: Rowman & Littlefield, 1999.

Crossette, Barbara. "Female Genital Mutilation by Immigrants Is Becoming Cause for Concern in the U.S." *New York Times International* (December 10, 1995):11.

Davis, Donald M., cited in "TV Is a Blonde, Blonde World." *American Demographics, special issue: Women Change Places,* 1993.

Domi, Tanya L. "Women in Combat: Policy Catches Up with Reality." *New York Times.* February 8, 2013. Available at http://www.nytimes.com/2013/02/09/opinion/women-in-combat-policy-catches-up-with-reality.html?_r=0

Doyle, James A. *The Male Experience.* Dubuque, Iowa: Brown, 1983.

Dworkin, Andrea. *Intercourse.* New York: Free Press, 1987.

Ehrenreich, Barbara. *The Hearts of Men: American Dreams and the Flight from Commitment.* Garden City, N.Y.: Anchor Books, 1983.

——. "The Real Truth about the Female Body." *Time* (March 15, 1999):56–65.

Engels, Friedrich. *The Origin of the Family.* Chicago: Kerr, 1902; orig. 1884.

England, Paula, Joan M. Hermsen, and David A. Cotter. "The Devaluation of Women's Work: A Comment on Tam." *American Journal of Sociology.* Vol. 105, No. 6 (May 2000):1741–60.

Ferree, Myra Marx, and Beth B. Hess. *Controversy and Coalition: The New Feminist Movement across Four Decades of Change.* 3rd ed. New York: Routledge, 1995.

Forbes. "*Forbes* 400." 2012. Available at http://www.forbes.com/forbes-400/

Foroohar, Rana. "The 100% Solution." *Time.* Vol. 177, No. 21 (May 23, 2011):22.

Freedman, Estelle B. *No Turning Back: The History of Feminism and the Future of Women.* New York: Ballantine Books, 2002.

French, Marilyn. *Beyond Power: On Women, Men, and Morals.* New York: Summit Books, 1985.

Frias, Sonia M., and Ronald J. Angel. "Stability and Change in the Experience of Partner Violence among Low-Income Women." *Social Science Quarterly.* Vol. 88, No. 5 (2007):1281–1306.

Fry, Richard, and D'Vera Cohn. "Women, Men and the New Economics of Marriage." Pew Research Center. 2010. [Online] Available at http://pewsocialtrends.org/files/2010/10/new-economics-of-marriage.pdf

Fryar, Cheryl D., Qiuping Gu, and Cynthia Ogden. "Anthropometric Reference Data for Children and Adults: United States, 2007–2010." National Center for Health Statistics. Vital Health Stat. Vol. 11, No. 252. 2012. Available at http://www.cdc.gov/nchs/data/series/sr_11/sr11_252.pdf

Fuller, Rex, and Richard Schoenberger. "The Gender Salary Gap: Do Academic Achievement, Intern Experience, and College Major Make a Difference?" *Social Science Quarterly.* Vol. 72, No. 4 (December 1991):715–26.

Gallup. "In U.S., Half of Women Prefer a Job Outside the Home; Most Men, Regardless of Education, Marital Status, or Party, Want an Outside Job." September 7, 2012. Available at http://www.gallup.com/poll/157313/half-women-prefer-job-outside-home.aspx

Gewertz, Deborah. "A Historical Reconsideration of Female Dominance among the Chambri of Papua New Guinea." *American Ethnologist.* Vol. 8, No. 1 (1981):94–106.

Gibbs, Nancy. "What Kids (Really) Need." *Time* (April 30, 2001):48–49.

Gilligan, Carol. *In a Different Voice: Psychological Theory and Women's Development.* Cambridge, Mass.: Harvard University Press, 1982.

Goffman, Erving. *Gender Advertisements.* New York: Harper Colophon, 1979.

Goldberg, Steven. *The Inevitability of Patriarchy.* New York: Morrow, 1974.

Goudreau, Jenna. "Best-Paying Jobs for Women in 2012." *Forbes.* July 27, 2012. Available at Available at http://finance.yahoo.com/news/top-20-best-paying-jobs-for-women-in-2012.html

Grandoni, Dino. "Women Who Took the Pill Had an 8 Percent Higher Income by Age 50." *The Atlantic Wire.* March 6, 2012. Available at http://news.yahoo.com/women-took-pill-had-8-percent-higher-income-195424592.html

Graybow, Martha. "Women Directors Help Boost Corporate's Financial Performance: Study." *International Business Times.* October 2, 2007. [Online] Available December 2, 2008, at http://in.ibtimes.com/articles/20071002/women-directors-help-boost-corporate-financial-performance.htm

Gurnett, Kate. "On the Forefront of Feminism." *Albany Times Union* (July 5, 1998):G-1, G-6.

Haney, Lynne. "After the Fall: East European Women since the Collapse of State Socialism." *Contexts.* Vol. 1, No. 3 (Fall 2002):27–36.

Harpster, Paula, and Elizabeth Monk-Turner. "Why Men Do Housework: A Test of Gender Production and the Relative Resources Model." *Sociological Focus.* Vol. 31, No. 1 (February 1998):45–59.

Heath, Julia A., and W. David Bourne. "Husbands and Housework: Parity or Parody?" *Social Science Quarterly.* Vol. 76, No. 1 (March 1995):195–202.

Henley, Nancy, Mykol Hamilton, and Barrie Thorne. "Womanspeak and Manspeak: Sex Differences in Communication, Verbal and Nonverbal." In John J. Macionis and Nijole V. Benokraitis, eds., *Seeing Ourselves: Classic, Contemporary, and Cross-Cultural Readings in Sociology.* 2nd ed. Englewood Cliffs, N.J.: Prentice Hall, 1992:10–15.

Herman, Dianne. "The Rape Culture." In John J. Macionis and Nijole V. Benokraitis, eds., *Seeing Ourselves: Classic, Contemporary, and Cross-Cultural Readings in Sociology.* 5th ed. Upper Saddle River, N.J.: Prentice Hall, 2001.

Hewlett, Sylvia Ann. "As Careers Paths Change, Make On-Ramping Easy." [Online] Available July 8, 2010, at http://blogs.hbr.org/hbr/hewlett/2010/07/as_careers_paths_change_make_o.html

Hewlett, Sylvia Ann, and Carolyn Buck Luce. "Off-Ramps and On-Ramps: Keeping Talented Women on the Road to Success." March 2005. [Online] Available December 8, 2008, at http://0-search.ebscohost.dewey2.library.denison.edu:80/login.aspx?direct=true&db=buh&AN=16235203&site=ehostlive

hooks, bell. *Feminist Theory: From Margin to Center.* 2nd ed. London: Pluto Press, 2000.

Hoyert, Donna, and Jiaquan Xu. "Deaths: Preliminary Data for 2011." National Vital Statistics Reports. Vol. 61, No 6. Hyattsville, Md.: National Center for Health Statistics. 2012. Available at http://www.cdc.gov/nchs/data/nvsr/nvsr61/nvsr61_06.pdf

Internal Revenue Service. "SOI Tax Stats—Personal Wealth Statistics." 2012. Available at http://www.irs.gov/uac/SOI-Tax-Stats---Personal-Wealth-Statistics

Inter-Parliamentary Union. "Women in National Parliaments." 2012. Available at http://www.ipu.org/wmn-e/classif.htm

Johnson, Barry W., and Brian G. Raub. "Personal Wealth, 2001." *Statistics of Income Bulletin* (Winter 2005–06). 2006. [Online] Available September 20, 2006, at http://www.irs.gov/pub/irs-soi/01pwart.pdf

Kaminer, Wendy. "Demasculinizing the Army." *New York Times Review of Books* (June 15, 1997):7.

Kane, Emily W. "Racial and Ethnic Variations in Gender-Related Attitudes." *Annual Review of Sociology.* Vol. 26 (August 2000):419–39.

Kochlar, Rakesh. "Two Years of Economic Recovery: Women Lose Jobs, Men Find Them." Pew Research Center. July 6, 2011. Available at http://www.pewsocialtrends.org/2011/07/06/two-years-of-economic-recovery-women-lose-jobs-men-find-them/

Kristof, Nicholas, and Sheryl Wu Dunn. *Half the Sky: Turning Oppression into Opportunity for Women Worldwide.* New York: Vintage Books, 2010.

Lamm, Dottie. "Our Boys Are Falling Behind in Education." Denverpost.com [Online]. Available April 18, 2010, at http://www.denverpost.com/opinion/ci_14893585

Lengermann, Patricia Madoo, and Ruth A. Wallace. *Gender in America: Social Control and Social Change.* Englewood Cliffs, N.J.: Prentice Hall, 1985.

Lever, Janet. "Sex Differences in the Complexity of Children's Play and Games." *American Sociological Review.* Vol. 43, No. 4 (August 1978):471–83.

Lewin, Tamar. "Girls' Gains Have Not Cost Boys, Report Says." *New York Times* (May 20, 2008). [Online] Available December 7, 2008, at http://www.nytimes.com/2008/05/20/education/20girls.html?partner=permalink&exprod=permalink

LITVAN, LAURA. "Women Winning Senate Races Will Set Record in January." *Bloomberg News*. November 7, 2012. Available at http://www.businessweek.com/news/2012-11-07/women-winning-senate-races-will-set-record-in-january

MARATHONGUIDE.COM. "Marathon Records." 2012. Available at http://www.marathonguide.com/history/records/index.cfm

MARSHALL, SUSAN E. "Ladies against Women: Mobilization Dilemmas of Antifeminist Movements." *Social Problems*. Vol. 32, No. 4 (April 1985):348–62.

MARTIN, CAROL LYNN, AND RICHARD A. FABES. "The Stability and Consequences of Young Children's Same-Sex Peer Interactions." *Developmental Psychology*. Vol. 37, No. 3 (May 2001):431–46.

McGIRK, TIM. "Crossing the Lines." *Time* (February 27, 2006):36–43.

MEAD, MARGARET. *Sex and Temperament in Three Primitive Societies*. New York: Morrow, 1963; orig. 1935.

MESSINEO, MELINDA. "Does Advertising on Black Entertainment Television Portray More Positive Gender Representations Compared to Broadcast Networks?" *Sex Roles*. Vol. 59, No. 9/10 (2008):752–64.

MURDOCK, GEORGE PETER. "Comparative Data on the Division of Labor by Sex." *Social Forces*. Vol. 15, No. 4 (May 1937):551–53.

NOLAN, PATRICK, AND GERHARD E. LENSKI. *Human Societies: An Introduction to Macrosociology*. 11th ed. Boulder, Colo.: Paradigm, 2010.

NORC. *General Social Surveys, 1972–2010*. Chicago: National Opinion Research Center. March 2011. [Online] Available at http://www.norc.org/GSS+Website

OVADIA, SETH. "Race, Class, and Gender Differences in High School Seniors' Values: Applying Intersection Theory in Empirical Analysis." *Social Science Quarterly*. Vol. 82, No. 2 (June 2001):341–56.

PAPPAS, STEPHANIE. "Americans Like Baby Boys Best." *Live Science*. June 24, 2011. Available at http://news.yahoo.com/s/livescience/20110624/sc_livescience/americanslikebabyboysbest

PARSONS, TALCOTT. "Age and Sex in the Social Structure of the United States." *American Sociological Review*. Vol. 7, No. 4 (August 1942):604–16.

———. *The Social System*. New York: Free Press, 1951.

———. *Essays in Sociological Theory*. New York: Free Press, 1954.

PATON, GRAEME. "Boys Falling Behind Girls at the Age of Five." *The Telegraph*. [Online]. Available March 25, 2010, at http://www.telegraph.co.uk/education/educationnews/7521315/Boys-falling-behind-girls-at-the-age-offive.html

PAXTON, PAMELA, MELANIE M. HUGHES, AND JENNIFER L. GREEN. "The International Women's Movement and Women's Political Participation, 1893–2003." *American Sociological Review*. Vol. 71, No. 6 (December 2006):898–920.

PEW RESEARCH CENTER FOR THE PEOPLE AND THE PRESS. "Values Survey 2012." April 2012. Available at http://www.people-press.org/2012/04/17/section-2-issues-of-the-2012-campaign/

POPENOE, DAVID. "Parental Androgyny." *Society*. Vol. 30, No. 6 (September/October 1993b):5–11.

POPULATION REFERENCE BUREAU. "Datafinder." 2012. Available at http://www.prb.org/DataFinder.aspx

———. "Female Genital Mutilation/Cutting: Data and Trends: Update 2010." 2010. Available at http://www.prb.org/pdf10/fgm-wallchart2010.pdf

RAPHAEL, RAY. *The Men from the Boys: Rites of Passage in Male America*. Lincoln: University of Nebraska Press, 1988.

RIDGEWAY, CECILIA L., AND LYNN SMITH-LOVIN. "The Gender System and Interaction." *Annual Review of Sociology*. Vol. 25 (August 1999):191–216.

ROESCH, ROBERTA. "Violent Families." *Parents*. Vol. 59, No. 9 (September 1984): 74–76, 150–52.

ROSENDAHL, MONA. *Inside the Revolution: Everyday Life in Socialist Cuba*. Ithaca, N.Y.: Cornell University Press, 1997.

ROSSI, ALICE S. "Gender and Parenthood." In Alice S. Rossi, ed., *Gender and the Life Course*. New York: Aldine, 1985:161–91.

SABATINI, JOSHUA. "San Francisco Circumcision Ban Headed for November Ballot." *The Examiner*. [Online] Available February, 18, 2011, at http://www.sfexaminer.com/local/2011/02/san-francisco-circumcision-ban-headednovember-ballot

SAINT JEAN, YANICK, AND JOE R. FEAGIN. *Double Burden: Black Women and Everyday Racism*. Armonk, N.Y.: Sharpe, 1998.

SEGAL, MADY WECHSLER, AND AMANDA FAITH HANSEN. "Value Rationales in Policy Debates on Women in the Military: A Content Analysis of Congressional Testimony, 1941–1985." *Social Science Quarterly*. Vol. 73, No. 2 (June 1992):296–309.

SHEA, RACHEL HARTIGAN. "The New Insecurity." *U.S. News & World Report* (March 25, 2002):40.

SHELLENBARGER, SUE. "The Name Change Dilemma." *The Wall Street Journal* (May 13, 2011). Available at http://finance.yahoo.com/family-home/article/112736/name-change-dilemma-women-marriage-wsj?mod=family-love_money

SMOLOWE, JILL. "When Violence Hits Home." *Time* (July 4, 1994):18–25.

SOMMERS, CHRISTINE HOFF. *The War against Boys: How Misguided Feminism Is Harming Our Young Men*. New York: Simon & Schuster, 2000.

STACEY, JUDITH. *Patriarchy and Socialist Revolution in China*. Berkeley: University of California Press, 1983.

STIER, HAYA. "Continuity and Change in Women's Occupations following First Childbirth." *Social Science Quarterly*. Vol. 77, No. 1 (March 1996):60–75.

STRATTON, LESLIE S. "Why Does More Housework Lower Women's Wages? Testing Hypotheses Involving Job Effort and Hours Flexibility." *Social Sciences Quarterly*. Vol. 82, No. 1 (March 2001):67–76.

TALLICHET, SUZANNE E. "Barriers to Women's Advancement in Underground Coal Mining." *Rural Sociology*. Vol. 65, No. 2 (June 2000):234–52.

TANNEN, DEBORAH. *You Just Don't Understand: Women and Men in Conversation*. New York: Morrow, 1990.

———. *Talking from 9 to 5: How Women's and Men's Conversational Styles Affect Who Gets Heard, Who Gets Credit, and What Gets Done at Work*. New York: Morrow, 1994.

TAVRIS, CAROL, AND CAROL WADE. *Psychology in Perspective*. 3rd ed. Upper Saddle River, N.J.: Prentice Hall, 2001.

TONG, ROSEMARIE. *Feminist Thought: A More Comprehensive Introduction*. 3rd ed. Boulder, Colo.: Westview, 2009.

UDRY, J. RICHARD. "Biological Limitations of Gender Construction." *American Sociological Review*. Vol. 65, No. 3 (June 2000):443–57.

UNITED NATIONS DEVELOPMENT PROGRAMME. "Human Development Report 2011." Statistical Tables. [Online] Available at http://hdr.undp.org/en/statistics/data/

U.S. CENSUS BUREAU. "Economic Survey: Survey of Business Owners." 2010. Available at http://www.census.gov/newsroom/releases/archives/business_ownership/cb10-184.html

———. "Current Population Survey." 2012. Available at http://www.census.gov/cps/

———. "Families and Living Arrangements." 2012. Available at http://www.census.gov/hhes/families/data/cps2012.html

———. "Income, Poverty and Health Insurance Coverage in the United States: 2011." 2012. Available at http://www.census.gov/newsroom/releases/archives/income_wealth/cb12-172.html

U.S. DEPARTMENT OF DEFENSE. "Military Personnel Statistics." 2012. Available at http://siadapp.dmdc.osd.mil/personnel/MILITARY/Miltop.htm

U.S. DEPARTMENT OF EDUCATION, NATIONAL CENTER FOR EDUCATION STATISTICS. "U.S. Digest of Education Statistics 2012." 2012. Available at http://nces.ed.gov/programs/digest/2012menu_tables.asp

U.S. DEPARTMENT OF JUSTICE, DEPARTMENT OF JUSTICE STATISTICS. "Criminal Victimization 2011." October 17, 2012. Available at http://bjs.gov/content/pub/pdf/cv11.pdf

U.S. DEPARTMENT OF JUSTICE, FEDERAL BUREAU OF INVESTIGATION. "Crime in the United States 2011." 2012. Available at http://www.fbi.gov/about-us/cjis/ucr/crime-in-the-u.s/2011/crime-in-the-u.s.-2011

U.S. DEPARTMENT OF LABOR. "Women's Employment During the Recovery." 2011. Available at http://www.dol.gov/_sec/media/reports/FemaleLaborForce/FemaleLaborForce.pdf

U.S. DEPARTMENT OF LABOR, BUREAU OF LABOR STATISTICS. "American Time Use Survey 2012." 2012. Available at http://www.bls.gov/TUS/CHARTS/HOUSEHOLD.HTM

———. "Highlights of Women's Earnings." 2012. Available at http://www.bls.gov/cps/cpswom2011.pdf

———. "Labor Force Statistics from the Current Population Survey." 2012. Available at http://www.bls.gov/cps/

———. "Women in the Labor Force: A Databook." 2011. Available at http://www.bls.gov/cps/wlf-databook2011.htm

U.S. DEPARTMENT OF LABOR, OCCUPATIONAL EMPLOYMENT STATISTICS (OES). "National Occupational Employment and Wage Estimates." 2012. Available at http://www.bls.gov/oes/current/oes_nat.htm

VOGEL, LISE. *Marxism and the Oppression of Women: Toward a Unitary Theory*. New Brunswick, N.J.: Rutgers University Press, 1983.

VON DREHLE, DAVID. "The Myth About Boys." *Time*. [Online]. Available July 26, 2007, at http://www.time.com/time/magazine/article/0,9171,1647452,00.html

WALDFOGEL, JANE. "The Effect of Children on Women's Wages." *American Sociological Review*. Vol. 62, No. 2 (April 1997):209–17.

WANG, WENDY, AND KIM PARKER. "Women See Value and Benefits of College; Men Lag on Both Fronts Study Finds." Pew Research Center. August 17, 2011. Available at http://www.pewsocialtrends.org/2011/08/17/women-see-value-and-benefits-of-college-men-lag-on-both-fronts-survey-finds/

WOLF, NAOMI. *The Beauty Myth: How Images of Beauty Are Used against Women*. New York: Morrow, 1990.

WORLD HEALTH ORGANIZATION, DEPARTMENT OF REPRODUCTIVE HEALTH AND RESEARCH. "Prevalence of Female Genital Mutilation." 2012. Available at http://www.who.int/reproductivehealth/topics/fgm/prevalence/en/index.html

Chapter 14

ADORNO, THEODORE W., ELSE FRENKEL-BRUNSWIK, DANIEL J. LEVINSON, AND R. NEVITT SANFORD. *The Authoritarian Personality*. New York: HARPER & BROTHERS, 1950.

ALBON, JOAN. "Retention of Cultural Values and Differential Urban Adaptation: Samoans and American Indians in a West Coast City." *Social Forces*. Vol. 49, No. 3 (March 1971):385–93.

ALI, LORRAINE, AND VANESSA JUAREZ. "We Love This Country." *Newsweek*. April 7, 2003.

ALI, LORRAINE, TAMARA LIPPER, AND MOHAMMED MACK. "Voters: A Demographic Shift." *Newsweek*. October 25, 2004.

AMERICAN SOCIOLOGICAL ASSOCIATION. *The Importance of Collecting Data and Doing Social Scientific Research on Race*. Washington, D.C.: American Sociological Association, 2003.

BALTZELL, E. DIGBY. *The Protestant Establishment: Aristocracy and Caste in America*. New York: Vintage Books, 1964.

BARBASSA, JULIANA. "Asian-American Political Profile Rising in U.S." *Yahoo News* (January 18, 2009). [Online] Available January 18, 2009, at http://news.yahoo.com/s/ap/20090118/ap_on_re_us/asian_american_politics

BARTLETT, DONALD L., AND JAMES B. STEELE. "Wheel of Misfortune." *Time* (December 16, 2002):44–58.

BLANTON, KIMBERLY. "Borrowers Sue Subprime Lender, Allege Race Bias." *Boston Globe* (July 13, 2007). [Online] Available March 9, 2008, at http://www.boston.com/business/personalfinance/articles/2007/07/13/borrowers_sue_subprime_lender_allege_race_bias/

BLAUSTEIN, ALBERT P., AND ROBERT L. ZANGRANDO. *Civil Rights and the Black American*. New York: Washington Square Press, 1968.

BOGARDUS, EMORY S. "Social Distance and Its Origins." *Sociology and Social Research.* Vol. 9 (July/August 1925):216–25.

———. *A Forty-Year Racial Distance Study.* Los Angeles: University of Southern California Press, 1967.

BOOTH, WILLIAM. "By the Sweat of Their Brows: A New Economy." *Washington Post* (July 13, 1998):A1, A10–A11.

BOSWELL, TERRY E. "A Split Labor Market Analysis of Discrimination against Chinese Immigrants, 1850–1882." *American Sociological Review.* Vol. 51, No. 3 (June 1986):352–71.

BOWEN, WILLIAM G., AND DEREK K. BOK. *The Shape of the River: Long-Term Consequences of Considering Race in College and University Admissions.* Princeton, N.J.: Princeton University Press, 1999.

BRODKIN, KAREN B. "How Did Jews Become White Folks?" In John J. Macionis and Nijole V. Benokraitis, eds. *Seeing Ourselves: Classic, Contemporary, and Cross-Cultural Readings in Sociology.* 7th ed. Upper Saddle River, N.J.: Prentice Hall, 2007.

CALIFORNIA NEWSREEL. "Race: The Power of an Illusion: Genetic Diversity Quiz." 2003. [Online] Available February 9, 2006, at http://www.pbs.org/race/000_About/002_04_a-godeeper.htm

CAMARA, EVANDRO. PERSONAL COMMUNICATION, 2000.

CARMICHAEL, STOKELY, AND CHARLES V. HAMILTON. *Black Power: The Politics of Liberation in America.* New York: Vintage Books, 1967.

CENTER FOR AMERICAN WOMEN AND POLITICS. "Women's Votes Decisive in 2012 Presidential Race." 2012. Available at http://www.cawp.rutgers.edu/press_room/news/documents/PressRelease_11-07-12-gendergap.pdf

CENTER FOR COMMUNITY AND ETHNIC MEDIA, CUNY. 2013. Available at http://ccem.journalism.cuny.edu/research/

CHUA-EOAN, HOWARD. "Profiles in Outrage." *Time* (September 25, 2000):38–39.

CUMMINGS, SCOTT, AND THOMAS LAMBERT. "Anti-Hispanic and Anti-Asian Sentiments among African Americans." *Social Science Quarterly.* Vol. 78, No. 2 (June 1997):338–53.

DOBYNS, HENRY F. "An Appraisal of Techniques with a New Hemispheric Estimate." *Current Anthropology.* Vol. 7, No. 4 (October 1966):395–446.

DOLLARD, JOHN, ET AL. *Frustration and Aggression.* New Haven, Conn.: Yale University Press, 1939.

EMERSON, MICHAEL O., GEORGE YANCEY, AND KAREN J. CHAI. "Does Race Matter in Residential Segregation? Exploring the Preferences of White Americans." *American Sociological Review.* Vol. 66, No. 6 (December 2001):922–35.

EWERS, JUSTIN. "Saving Symbols of Shame." *U.S. News & World Report.* Vol. 144, No. 7 (March 10, 2008):31.

FIREBAUGH, GLENN, AND KENNETH E. DAVIS. "Trends in Antiblack Prejudice, 1972–1984: Region and Cohort Effects." *American Journal of Sociology.* Vol. 94, No. 2 (September 1988):251–72.

FLYNN, KEVIN. "Colorado Voters Preserve Affirmative Action." *Rocky Mountain News* (November 7, 2008). [Online] Available December 7, 2008, at http://www.rockymountainnews.com/news/2008/nov/06/colorado-voters-preserveaffirmative-action

FRANKLIN, JOHN HOPE. *From Slavery to Freedom: A History of Negro Americans.* 3rd ed. New York: Vintage Books, 1967.

GALLAGHER, CHARLES A. "Miscounting Race: Explaining Whites' Misperceptions of Racial Group Size." *Sociological Perspectives.* Vol. 46, No. 3 (2003):381–96.

GESCHWENDER, JAMES A. *Racial Stratification in America.* Dubuque, Iowa: Brown, 1978.

GILBERTSON, GRETA A., AND DOUGLAS T. GURAK. "Broadening the Enclave Debate: The Dual Labor Market Experiences of Dominican and Colombian Men in New York City." *Sociological Forum.* Vol. 8, No. 2 (June 1993):205–20.

GOTHAM, KEVIN FOX. "Race, Mortgage Lending, and Loan Rejections in a U.S. City." *Sociological Focus.* Vol. 31, No. 4 (October 1998):391–405.

HAGOPIAN, ELAINE C. *Civil Rights in Peril: The Targeting of Arabs and Muslims.* London: Photo Press, 2004.

HANDLIN, OSCAR. *Boston's Immigrants, 1790–1865: A Study in Acculturation.* Cambridge, Mass.: Harvard University Press, 1941.

HARRIS, DAVID R., AND JEREMIAH JOSEPH SIM. "Who Is Multiracial? Assessing the Complexity of Lived Race." *American Sociological Review.* Vol. 67, No. 4 (August 2002):614–27.

HERRNSTEIN, RICHARD J., AND CHARLES MURRAY. *The Bell Curve: Intelligence and Class Structure in American Life.* New York: Free Press, 1994.

HILL, MARK E. "Race of the Interviewer and Perception of Skin Color: Evidence from the Multi-City Study of Urban Inequality." *American Sociological Review.* Vol. 67, No. 1 (February 2002):99–108.

HSU, FRANCIS L. K. *The Challenge of the American Dream: The Chinese in the United States.* Belmont, Calif.: Wadsworth, 1971.

ICELAND, JOHN, ET AL. "Racial and Ethnic Residential Segregation and Household Structure: A Research Note." *Social Science Research.* Vol. 39, No. 1 (2010):39–47.

INCIARDI, JAMES A., HILARY L. SURRATT, AND PAULO R. TELLES. *Sex, Drugs, and HIV/AIDS in Brazil.* Boulder, Colo.: Westview Press, 2000.

JIMÉNEZ, TOMÁS R. "Weighing the Costs and Benefits of Mexican Immigration: The Mexican American Perspective." *Social Science Quarterly.* Vol. 88, No. 3 (2007):599–618.

JONES, KATHARINE W. *Accent on Privilege: English Identities and Anglophilia in the U.S.* Philadelphia: Temple University Press, 2001.

JOSEPHY, ALVIN M., JR. *Now That the Buffalo's Gone: A Study of Today's American Indians.* New York: Knopf, 1982.

KANTROWITZ, BARBARA, AND PAT WINGERT. "What's at Stake." *Newsweek* (January 27, 2003):30–37.

KAUFMAN, ROBERT L. "Assessing Alternative Perspectives on Race and Sex Employment Segregation." *American Sociological Review.* Vol. 67, No. 4 (August 2002):547–72.

KEWALRAMANI, ANGELINA, LAUREN GILBERTSON, MARY ANN FOX, AND STEPHEN PROVASNIK. *Status and Trends in the Education of Racial and Ethnic Minorities, 2005.* National Center for Education Statistics. September 2007. [Online] Available May 19, 2008, at http://nces.ed.gov/pubs2007/minoritytrends

KINKEAD, GWEN. *Chinatown: A Portrait of a Closed Society.* New York: HarperCollins, 1992.

KRYSAN, MARIA. "Community Undesirability in Black and White: Examining Racial Residential Preferences through Community Perceptions." *Social Problems.* Vol. 49, No. 4 (November 2002):521–43.

LAI, H. M. "Chinese." In *Harvard Encyclopedia of American Ethnic Groups.* Cambridge, Mass.: Harvard University Press, 1980:217–33.

LEACH, COLIN WAYNE. "Democracy's Dilemma: Explaining Racial Inequality in Egalitarian Societies." *Sociological Forum.* Vol. 17, No. 4 (December 2002):681–96.

LEE, BARRET A., AND MATHEW MARLAY. "The Right Side of the Tracks: Affluent Neighborhoods in the Metropolitan United States." *Social Science Quarterly.* Vol. 88, No. 3 (2007):766–89.

LING, PYAU. "Causes of Chinese Emigration." In Amy Tachiki et al., eds., *Roots: An Asian American Reader.* Los Angeles: UCLA Asian American Studies Center, 1971:134–38.

LOGAN, JOHN R., RICHARD D. ALBA, AND WENQUAN ZHANG. "Immigrant Enclaves and Ethnic Communities in New York and Los Angeles." *American Sociological Review.* Vol. 67, No. 2 (April 2002):299–322.

LOVEMAN, MARA. "Is 'Race' Essential?" *American Sociological Review.* Vol. 64, No. 6 (December 1999):890–98.

MARÍN, GERARDO, AND BARBARA VAN OSS MARÍN. *Research with Hispanic Populations.* Newbury Park, Calif.: Sage, 1991.

MARZÁN, GILBERT, ANDRÉS TORRES, AND ANDREW LUECKE. "Puerto Rican Outmigration from New York City: 1995–2000." Centro de Estudios Puertorriqueños, Hunter College (CUNY), *Policy Report.* Vol. 2, No. 2 (2008). [Online] Available at http://www.centropr.org/documents/working_papers/Outmigration091108.pdf

MASSEY, DOUGLAS S., AND NANCY A. DENTON. "Hypersegregation in U.S. Metropolitan Areas: Black and Hispanic Segregation along Five Dimensions." *Demography.* Vol. 26, No. 3 (August 1989):373–91.

MATTHIESSEN, PETER. *Indian Country.* New York: Viking Press, 1984.

METZGER, KURT. "Cities and Race." *Society.* Vol. 39, No. 1 (December 2001):2.

MYRDAL, GUNNAR. *An American Dilemma: The Negro Problem and Modern Democracy.* New York: Harper Bros., 1944.

NATIONAL GOVERNOR'S ASSOCIATION. 2012. Available at http://www.nga.org

NAVARRO, MIREYA. "Puerto Rican Presence Wanes in New York." *New York Times* (February 28, 2000):A1, A20.

NEWMAN, WILLIAM M. *American Pluralism: A Study of Minority Groups and Social Theory.* New York: Harper & Row, 1973.

NORC. *General Social Surveys, 1972–2010: Cumulative Codebook.* Chicago: National Opinion Research Center. 2011. Available at http://www.norc.org/GSS+Website

O'HARE, WILLIAM P., WILLIAM H. FREY, AND DAN FOST. "Asians in the Suburbs." *American Demographics.* Vol. 16, No. 9 (May 1994):32–38.

OLZAK, SUSAN. "Labor Unrest, Immigration, and Ethnic Conflict in Urban America, 1880–1914." *American Journal of Sociology.* Vol. 94, No. 6 (May 1989):1303–33.

OWEN, CAROLYN A., HOWARD C. ELSNER, AND THOMAS R. MCFAUL. "A Half-Century of Social Distance Research: National Replication of the Bogardus Studies." *Sociology and Social Research.* Vol. 66, No. 1 (1977):80–98.

PARRILLO, VINCENT. "Diversity in America: A Sociohistorical Analysis." *Sociological Forum.* Vol. 9, No. 4 (December 1994):42–45.

PARRILLO, VINCENT, AND CHRISTOPHER DONOGHUE. "Updating the Bogardus Social Distance Studies: A New National Survey." *Social Science Journal.* Vol. 42, No. 2 (April 2005): 257–71.

PATTERSON, DAVID ROYSTON. "Will Puerto Rico Be America's 51st State?" *New York Times.* November 24, 2012. Available at https://docs.google.com/viewer?a=-v&pid=sites&srcid=ZGVmYXVsdGRvbWFpbnxzb2Npb2xvZ3kxNWV8Z3g6Njc5ODE0Y2NhNGJkYTliZQ

PATTILLO, MARY. *Black on the Block: The Politics of Race and Class in the City.* Chicago: University of Chicago Press, 2007.

PERLMUTTER, PHILIP. "Minority Group Prejudice." *Society.* Vol. 39, No. 3 (March/April 2002):59–65.

PEW RESEARCH CENTER. "Muslim Americans: No Signs of Growth in Alienation or Support for Extremism." 2011. Available at http://www.people-press.org/2011/08/30/section-1-a-demographic-portrait-of-muslim-americans/

———. "The Rise of Asian Americans." 2012. Available at http://www.pewsocialtrends.org/2012/06/19/the-rise-of-asian-americans/

PEW RESEARCH CENTER, FORUM ON RELIGIOUS AND PUBLIC LIFE. "The Future of the Global Muslim Population: Projections for 2010–2030." 2011. Available at http://pewforum.org/The-Future-of-the-Global-Muslim-Population.aspx

———. "The Global Religious Landscape: A Report on the Size and Distribution of the World's Major Religious Groups as of 2010." 2012. Available at http://www.pewforum.org/global-religious-landscape.aspx

PORTES, ALEJANDRO, AND LEIF JENSEN. "The Enclave and the Entrants: Patterns of Ethnic Enterprise in Miami before and after Mariel." *American Sociological Review.* Vol. 54, No. 6 (December 1989):929–49.

ROTHENBERG, PAULA. *White Privilege.* 3rd ed. New York: Worth, 2008.

SALE, KIRKPATRICK. *The Conquest of Paradise: Christopher Columbus and the Columbian Legacy.* New York: Knopf, 1990.

SANDER, RICHARD, AND STUART TAYLOR, JR. "The Unraveling of Affirmative Action." *Wall Street Journal.* (October 13–14, 2012):C1–2.

SHESKIN, IRA M., AND ARNOLD DASHEFSKY. "Jewish Population in the United States." 2011. Available at http://www.jewishdatabank.org/

SMITH, RYAN A. "Race, Gender, and Authority in the Workplace: Theory and Research." *Annual Review of Sociology.* Vol. 28 (2002):509–42.

SMITH, TOM W. "Anti-Semitism Decreases but Persists." *Society.* Vol. 33, No. 3 (March/April 1996):2.

SOWELL, THOMAS. *Ethnic America.* New York: Basic Books, 1981.

———. *Race and Culture.* New York: Basic Books, 1994.

———. "Ethnicity and IQ." In Steven Fraser, ed., *The Bell Curve Wars: Race, Intelligence, and the Future of America.* New York: Basic Books, 1995:70–79.

STEELE, SHELBY. *The Content of Our Character: A New Vision of Race in America.* New York: St. Martin's Press, 1990.

STOUT, DAVID. "Supreme Court Splits on Diversity Efforts at University of Michigan." [Online] Available June 23, 2003, at http://news.yahoo.com

SUN, LENA H. "WWII's Forgotten Internees Await Apology." *Washington Post* (March 9, 1998):A1, A5, A6.

TAKAKI, RONALD. *Strangers from a Different Shore.* Boston: Back Bay Books, 1998.

TAYLOR, PAUL, ANA GONZOLEZ-BARRERA, JEFFREY PASSEL, AND HARK HUGO LOPEZ. "An Awakening Giant: The Hispanic Electorate Is Likely to Double by 2030." Pew Research Center. November 14, 2012. Available at http://www.pewhispanic.org/2012/11/14/an-awakened-giant-the-hispanic-electorate-is-likely-to-double-by-2030/

TAYLOR, PAUL, MARK HUGO LOPEZ, JESSICA HAMAR MARTÍNEZ, AND GABRIEL VELASCO. "When Labels Don't Fit: Hispanics and Their Views of Identity." Pew Research Center. April 4, 2012. Available at http://www.pewhispanic.org/2012/04/04/when-labels-dont-fit-hispanics-and-their-views-of-identity/

THOMAS, W. I. "The Relation of Research to the Social Process." In Morris Janowitz, ed., *W. I. Thomas on Social Organization and Social Personality.* Chicago: University of Chicago Press, 1966:289–305; orig. 1931.

THOMAS, W. I., AND DOROTHY SWAINE THOMAS. *The Child in America: Behavior Problems and Programs.* New York: Knopf, 1928.

TUMULTY, KAREN. "Should They Stay or Should They Go?" *Time* (April 10, 2006):30–41.

TYLER, S. LYMAN. *A History of Indian Policy.* Washington, D.C.: U.S. Department of the Interior, Bureau of Indian Affairs, 1973.

U.S. CENSUS BUREAU. "2012 Boundary and Annexation Survey." 2012. Available at http://www.census.gov/geo/www/bas/bas12/bas12_codes.html

———. "American Community Survey." 2012. Available at http://www.census.gov/acs/www/

———. "Census 2010." 2011. Available at http://factfinder2.census.gov/faces/nav/jsf/pages/index.xhtml

———. "Current Population Survey." 2012. Available at http://www.census.gov/cps/

———. "Families and Living Arrangements." 2012. Available at http://www.census.gov/hhes/families/data/cps2012.html

———. "Most Children Younger Than Age 1 Are Minorities, Census Bureau Reports." May 17, 2012. Available at http://www.census.gov/newsroom/releases/archives/population/cb12-90.html

———. "2012 National Population Projections: Tables and Charts." 2012. Available at http://www.census.gov/population/projections/data/national/2012/summarytables.html

———. "Population Estimates." 2012. Available at http://www.census.gov/popest/data/index.html

———. "Statistical Abstract of the United States: 2010 (129th Edition)." 2010. Available at http://www.census.gov/compendia/statab/

———. "World Vital Events per Time Unit, 2011." 2011. [Online] Available at http://www.census.gov/population/popclockworld.html

U.S. DEPARTMENT OF HOMELAND SECURITY, OFFICE OF IMMIGRATION STATISTICS. "Yearbook of Immigration Statistics." 2012. Available at http://www.dhs.gov/yearbook-immigration-statistics

U.S. DEPARTMENT OF LABOR, BUREAU OF LABOR STATISTICS. "Labor Force Statistics from the Current Population Survey." 2012. Available at http://www.bls.gov/cps/

WALDMAN, CARL. *Atlas of the North American Indian.* New York: Facts on File, 2000.

WEST, CORNEL. "The Obama Moment." *U.S. News & World Report* (November 17, 2008):29.

WILKES, RIMA, AND JOHN ICELAND. "Hypersegregation in the Twenty-First Century." *Demography.* Vol. 41, No. 1 (February 9, 2004):23–36.

WILSON, JAMES Q. "Crime, Race, and Values." *Society.* Vol. 30, No. 1 (November/December 1992):90–93.

WONG, BUCK. "Need for Awareness: An Essay on Chinatown, San Francisco." In Amy Tachiki et al., eds., *Roots: An Asian American Reader.* Los Angeles: UCLA Asian American Studies Center, 1971:265–73.

Chapter 15

AARP PUBLIC POLICY INSTITUTE. "Caregiving in the U.S.: A Focused Look at Caring for Someone Age 50 or Older." 2009. Available at http://assets.aarp.org/rgcenter/il/caregiving_09.pdf

———. "Valuing the Invaluable: 2011 Update. The Growing Contributions and Costs of Family Caregiving." 2012. Available at http://assets.aarp.org/rgcenter/ppi/ltc/i51-caregiving.pdf

ARIAS, ELIZABETH. "United States Life Tables, 2008." Revised using intercensal populations. 2012. Available at http://www.cdc.gov/nchs/data/dvs/Revised_Tables_2008.pdf

ARIÈS, PHILIPPE. *Western Attitudes toward Death: From the Middle Ages to the Present.* Baltimore: Johns Hopkins University Press, 1974.

ASSOCIATED PRESS. "Japan Population Shrinks by Record in 2010." [Online] Available January 1, 2011, at http://news.yahoo.com/s/ap/20110101/ap_on_re_as/as_japan_population

ATCHLEY, ROBERT C. *Aging: Continuity and Change.* Belmont, Calif.: Wadsworth, 1983.

BALTES, PAUL B., AND K. WARNER SCHAIE. "The Myth of the Twilight Years." *Psychology Today.* Vol. 7, No. 10 (March 1974):35–39.

BARR, BOB. "Euthanasia … or a 'Dutch Treat'?" *Washington Times* (December 26, 2004). [Online] Available July 29, 2007, at http://www.bobbarr.org/default.asp?pt=newsdescr&RI=585

BRANDON, EMILY. "Why the Retirement Age Is Increasing." [Online] Available November 15, 2010, at http://finance.yahoo.com/news/Why-the-Retirement-Age-Is-usnews-3042824221.html?x=0&sec=topStories&pos=5&asset=&ccode=

BROOKS, DAVID, AND GAIL COLLINS. "Raise the Retirement Age or Find New Jobs for Youths?" *New York Times* (March 9, 2011). Available at http://opinionator.blogs.nytimes.com/2011/03/09/raise-the-retirement-age-or-find-jobs-for-youths/

BUTLER, ROBERT N. *Why Survive? Being Old in America.* New York: Harper & Row, 1975.

CALLAHAN, DANIEL. *Setting Limits: Medical Goals in an Aging Society.* New York: Simon & Schuster, 1987.

———. "Life Extension: Rolling the Technological Dice." *Society.* Vol. 46, No. 3 (May/June, 2009):214–20.

CARRNS, ANN. "Pushing 80, and Still Punching the Clock." *New York Times* (November 13, 2012). Available at http://www.nytimes.com/2012/11/14/your-money/for-some-retirement-age-may-be-well-past-75.html

CENTERS FOR DISEASE CONTROL AND PREVENTION, NATIONAL CENTER FOR HEALTH STATISTICS. "Health Data Interactive." 2012. Available at http://www.cdc.gov/nchs/hdi.htm

CENTERS FOR MEDICARE AND MEDICAID SERVICES. "Medicare Data for Calendar Year 2011." 2012. Available at http://www.cms.gov/Research-Statistics-Data-and-Systems/Statistics-Trends-and-Reports/ReportsTrustFunds/index.html

COHEN, ELIAS. "The Complex Nature of Ageism: What Is It? Who Does It? Who Perceives It?" *Gerontologist.* Vol. 41, No. 5 (October 2001):576–78.

CORNWELL, ERIN YORK, AND LINDA J. WAITE. "Social Disconnectedness, Perceived Isolation, and Health among Older Adults." *Journal of Health and Social Behavior.* Vol. 50, No. 1 (March 2009):31–48.

CORTEZ, MICHELLE FAY. "Memory Loss Grows Less Common among Older Americans, Study Says." Bloomberg.com. February 20, 2008. [Online] Available January 8, 2009, at http://www.bloomberg.com/apps/news?pid=20601103&sid=a667F2gzkXoE&refer=us

CUMMING, ELAINE, AND WILLIAM E. HENRY. *Growing Old: The Process of Disengagement.* New York: Basic Books, 1961.

CUTCLIFFE, JOHN R. "Hope, Counseling, and Complicated Bereavement Reactions." *Journal of Advanced Nursing.* Vol. 28, No. 4 (October 1998): 754–62.

DANFORTH, MARION M., AND J. CONRAD GLASS, JR. "Listen to My Words, Give Meaning to My Sorrow: A Study in Cognitive Constructs in Middle-Aged Bereaved Widows." *Death Studies.* Vol. 25, No. 6 (September 2001):413–30.

DELLA CAVA, MARCO R. "For Dutch, It's as Easy as Asking a Doctor." *USA Today* (January 7, 1997):4A.

ERIKSON, ERIK H. *Childhood and Society.* New York: Norton, 1963; orig. 1950.

FEDERAL INTERAGENCY FORUM ON AGING-RELATED STATISTICS. "Older Americans 2012: Key Indicators of Well-Being." 2012. Available at http://www.agingstats.gov/agingstatsdotnet/Main_Site/Data/2012_Documents/Docs/EntireChartbook.pdf

FETTO, JOHN. "Drug Money." *American Demographics.* Vol. 25, No. 2 (March 2003a):48.

FOLIART, DONNE E., AND MARGARET CLAUSEN. "Bereavement Practices among California Hospices: Results of a Statewide Survey." *Death Studies.* Vol. 25, No. 5 (July 2001): 461–68.

FRIEDAN, BETTY. *The Fountain of Age.* New York: Simon & Schuster, 1993.

GARDYN, REBECCA. "Retirement Redefined." *American Demographics.* Vol. 22, No. 11 (November 2000):52–57.

GILLON, RAANAN. "Euthanasia in the Netherlands: Down the Slippery Slope?" *Journal of Medical Ethics.* Vol. 25, No. 1 (February 1999):3–4.

GOKHALE, JAGADEESH. "Mandatory Retirement Age Rules: Is It Time to Reevaluate?" Statement before the United States Senate. September 9, 2004. [Online] Available January 1, 2009, at http://www.cato.org/testimony/ct-jg040909.html

GOLDMAN, RUSSELL. "Deaf Twins Going Blind Euthanized." ABC News. January 14, 2013. Available at http://news.yahoo.com/deaf-twins-going-blind-euthanized-165500992--abc-news-topstories.html

HAUB, CARL. "Tracking Trends in Low Fertility Countries: An Uptick in Europe?" Population Reference Bureau. September 2008. [Online] Available January 8, 2009, at http://www.prb.org/Articles/2008/tfrtrendsept08.aspx

HOLMSTROM, DAVID. "Abuse of Elderly, Even by Adult Children, Gets More Attention and Official Concern." *Christian Science Monitor* (July 28, 1994):1.

HOLWERDA, TJALLING JAN, ET AL. "Feelings of Loneliness, but Not Social Isolation, Predict Dementia Onset: Results from the Amsterdam Study of the Elderly." *Journal of Neurology, Neurosurgery and Psychiatry.* December 2012. Available at http://jnnp.bmj.com/content/early/2012/11/06/jnnp-2012-302755

HOYERT, DONNA, AND JIAQUAN XU. "Deaths: Preliminary Data for 2011." National Vital Statistics Reports. Vol. 61, No. 6 (2012). Available at http://www.cdc.gov/nchs/data/nvsr/nvsr61/nvsr61_06.pdf

INSTITUTE FOR WOMEN'S POLICY RESEARCH. "The Economic Security of Older Women and Men in the United States." November 2007. [Online] Available January 3, 2009, at http://www.iwpr.org/pdf/BPD480.pdf

INTERNATIONAL LABOUR ORGANIZATION, BUREAU OF STATISTICS. "LABORSTA." 2012. Available at http://laborsta.ilo.org/data_topic_E.html

JONES, D. GARETH. "Brain Death." *Journal of Medical Ethics.* Vol. 24, No. 4 (August 1998):237–43.

KADLEC, DANIEL. "Everyone, Back in the (Labor) Pool." *Time* (July 29, 2002): 22–31.

Konigsberg, Ruth Davis. "New Ways to Think About Grief." *Time* [Online] Available January 29, 2011, at http://www.time.com/time/magazine/article/0,9171,2042372-2,00.html

Koskela, Roger. "Life after Work: 'Stage' Your Retirement to Max Your Transition." *Kitsap* (Wash.) *Sun.* August 17, 2008. [Online] Available January 1, 2009, at http://www.kitsapsun.com/news/2008/aug/17/life-after-work-145stage-yourretirement-to-max

Kübler-Ross, Elisabeth. *On Death and Dying.* New York: Macmillan, 1969.

Lah, Kyung. "Report: More Elderly Japanese Turn to Petty Crime." CNN.com/Asia. December 24, 2008. [Online] Available April 20, 2009, at http://www.cnn.com/2008/WORLD/asiapcf/12/24/elderly.shoplifters

Lee, Felicia R. "Long Buried, Death Goes Public Again." *New York Times* (November 2, 2002). [Online] Available November 2, 2002, at http://www.nytimes.com/2002/11/02/arts/long-buried-death-goes-public-again.html

Leff, Lisa. "California Gay Marriage Vote Still Undecided." November 5, 2008. [Online] Available November 5, 2008, at http://news.yahoo.com/s/ap/20081105/ap_on_el_ge/ballot_measures

Leland, John. "Skills to Learn, to Restart Earnings." *New York Times* (April 1, 2009). Available at http://www.nytimes.com/2009/04/02/business/retirementspecial/02reskill.html

Lin, Ge, and Peter Rogerson. Research reported in Diane Crispell, "Sons and Daughters Who Keep in Touch." *American Demographics.* Vol. 16, No. 8 (August 1994):15–16.

Longino, Charles F., Jr. "Myths of an Aging America." *American Demographics.* Vol. 16, No. 8 (August 1994):36–42.

Lund, Dale A. "Conclusions about Bereavement in Later Life and Implications for Interventions and Future Research." In Dale A. Lund, ed., *Older Bereaved Spouses: Research with Practical Applications.* London: Taylor-Francis-Hemisphere, 1989:217–31.

———. "Caregiving." In *Encyclopedia of Adult Development.* Phoenix, Ariz.: Oryx Press, 1993: 57–63.

Lund, Dale A., Michael S. Caserta, and Margaret F. Dimond. "Gender Differences through Two Years of Bereavement among the Elderly." *Gerontologist.* Vol. 26, No. 3 (1986):314–20.

Mauro, Tony. "Ruling Likely Will Add Fuel to Already Divisive Debate." *USA Today* (January 7, 1997):1A, 2A.

McCartney, Scott. "U.S. Mulls Raising Pilot Retirement Age." *Baltimore Sun* (February 28, 2005). [Online] Available April 16, 2005, at http://www.Baltimoresun.com

Metz, Michael E., and Michael H. Miner. "Psychosexual and Psychosocial Aspects of Male Aging and Sexual Health." *Canadian Journal of Human Sexuality.* Vol. 7, No. 3 (Summer 1998):245–60.

Moen, Phyllis, Donna Dempster-McClain, and Robin M. Williams. "Successful Aging: A Life-Course Perspective on Women's Multiple Roles and Health." *American Journal of Sociology.* Vol. 97, No. 6 (May 1992):1612–38.

Morin, Rich, and Richard Fry. "More Americans Worry about Financing Retirement." Pew Research Center. October 22, 2012. Available at http://www.pewsocialtrends.org/2012/10/22/more-americans-worry-about-financing-retirement/

National Center on Elder Abuse. "Elder Abuse Prevalence and Incidence." March 31, 2005. Available at http://www.ncea.aoa.gov/ncearoot/Main_Site/pdf/publication/FinalStatistics050331.pdf

———. "Elder Abuse 2010 Fact Sheet." 2010. Available at http://www.ncea.aoa.gov/ncearoot/Main_Site/pdf/publication/NCEA_WhatIsAbuse-2010.pdf

Neugarten, Bernice L. "Grow Old with Me. The Best Is Yet to Be." *Psychology Today* (December 1971):45–48, 79, 81.

———. "Personality and Aging." In James E. Birren and K. Warner Schaie, eds., *Handbook of the Psychology of Aging.* New York: Van Nostrand Reinhold, 1977:626–49.

NORC. *General Social Surveys, 1972–2010: Cumulative Codebook.* Chicago: National Opinion Research Center. 2011. Available at http://www.norc.org/GSS+Website

Ogawa, Naohiro, and Robert D. Retherford. "Shifting Costs of Caring for the Elderly Back to Families in Japan: Will It Work?" *Population and Development Review.* Vol. 23, No. 1 (March 1997):59–95.

Ogden, Russel D. "Nonphysician-Assisted Suicide: The Technological Imperative of the Deathing Counterculture." *Death Studies.* Vol. 25, No. 5 (July 2001): 387–402.

Olson, Elizabeth. "Community Colleges Want You." *New York Times* (October 24, 2006):E2.

Onishi, Norimitsu. "In a Graying Japan, Lower Shelves and Wider Aisles." *New York Times* (September 4, 2006):A4.

Oregon Public Health Division. "Death with Dignity Act Annual Report." 2012. Available at http://www.oregon.gov/DHS/ph/pas/index.shtml

Palmore, Erdman. "Predictors of Successful Aging." *Gerontologist.* Vol. 19, No. 5 (October 1979):427–31.

Parini, Jay. "The Meaning of Emeritus." *Dartmouth Alumni Magazine* (July/August 2001):40–43.

Population Reference Bureau. "DataFinder." 2012. Available at http://www.prb.org/DataFinder.aspx

Porter, Eduardo. "Old, in the Way, and Hard at Work." *New York Times* (August 29, 2004). [Online] Available May 5, 2009, at http://www.nytimes.com/2004/08/29/weekinreview/the-world-economic-strains-old-in-the-way-and-hard-at-work.html?sec=health&&n=Top%2FReference%2FTimes%20Topics%2FSubjects%2FL%2FLabor

Rimer, Sara. "Blacks Carry Load of Care for Their Elderly." *New York Times* (March 15, 1998):1, 22.

Rubenstein, Eli A. "The Not So Golden Years." *Newsweek* (October 7, 1991):13.

Savishinsky, Joel S. *Breaking the Watch: The Meanings of Retirement in America.* Ithaca, N.Y.: Cornell University Press, 2000.

Schiller, Jeannine, Jacqueline Lucas, Brian Ward, and Jennifer Peregoy. "Summary Health Statistics for U.S. Adults: National Health Interview Survey, 2010." National Center for Health Statistics. Vital Health Stat. Vol. 10, No. 252. 2012. Available at http://www.cdc.gov/nchs/data/series/sr_10/sr10_252.pdf

Schultz, R., and J. Heckhausen. "A Lifespan Model of Successful Aging." *American Psychologist.* Vol. 7, No. 7 (July 1996):702–14.

Shapiro, Joseph P. "Back to Work, on Mission." *U.S. News & World Report* (June 4, 2001).

Sheehan, Tom. "Senior Esteem as a Factor in Socioeconomic Complexity." *Gerontologist.* Vol. 16, No. 5 (October 1976):433–40.

Smart, Tim. "Not Acting Their Age." *U.S. News & World Report* (June 4, 2001):54–60.

Spitzer, Steven. "Toward a Marxian Theory of Deviance." In Delos H. Kelly, ed., *Criminal Behavior: Readings in Criminology.* New York: St. Martin's Press, 1980:175–91.

Streib, Gordon F. "Are the Aged a Minority Group?" In Bernice L. Neugarten, ed., *Middle Age and Aging: A Reader in Social Psychology.* Chicago: University of Chicago Press, 1968:35–46.

Thompson, Mark. "Fatal Neglect." *Time* (October 27, 1997):34–38.

———. "Shining a Light on Abuse." *Time* (August 3, 1998):42–43.

Toossi, Mitra. "Labor Force Projections to 2018: Older Workers Staying More Active." *Monthly Labor Review.* (November 2009):30–51. [Online] Available at http://www.bls.gov/opub/mlr/2009/11/art3full.pdf

Treas, Judith. "Older Americans in the 1990s and Beyond." *Population Bulletin.* Vol. 50, No. 2 (May 1995).

Trumbull, Mark. "How Retirement Is Being Reinvented Worldwide." *The Christian Science Monitor.* [Online] Available January 16, 2011, at http://www.csmonitor.com/World/Global-Issues/2011/0116/How-retirement-is-beingreinvented-worldwide

U.S. Administration on Aging. "National Survey of OAA Participants: Caregiver." AGID (Aging Integrated Database). 2012. Available at http://www.agid-net.org/CustomTables/NPS

U.S. Census Bureau. "Current Population Survey." 2010. [Online] Available at http://www.census.gov/cps

———. "Population Estimates." 2010. [Online] Available at http://www.census.gov/popest/estimates.html

———. "American Community Survey." 2012. Available at http://www.census.gov/acs/www/

———. "Current Population Survey." 2012. Available at http://www.census.gov/cps/

———. "International Data Base." 2012. Available at http://www.census.gov/population/international/

———. "2012 National Population Projections: Tables and Charts." 2012. Available at http://www.census.gov/population/projections/data/national/2012/summarytables.html

———. "Population Estimates." 2012. Available at http://www.census.gov/popest/data/index.html

———. "Statistical Abstract of the United States: 2012 (131st Edition)." Washington, D.C. 2011. Available at http://www.census.gov/compendia/statab/

U.S. Department of Agriculture. "2007 Census of Agriculture." 2009. Available at http://www.agcensus.usda.gov/Publications/2007/Online_Highlights/index.asp

U.S. Department of Labor, Bureau of Labor Statistics. "Labor Force Statistics from the Current Population Survey." 2012. Available at http://www.bls.gov/cps/

U.S. Social Security Administration. "The 2012 Annual Report of the Board of Trustees of the Federal Old-Age and Survivors Insurance and Federal Disability Insurance Trust Funds." 2012. Available at http://www.ssa.gov/OACT/TRSUM/index.html

Wall, Thomas F. *Medical Ethics: Basic Moral Issues.* Washington, D.C.: University Press of America, 1980.

Walsh, Mary Williams. "No Time to Put Your Feet Up as Retirement Comes in Stages." *New York Times* (April 15, 2001):1, 18.

Wangsness, Lisa. "A Coalition of Forces Beat Back Question 2." *Boston Globe* (November 7, 2012). Available at http://www.bostonglobe.com/2012/11/07/dying/22ppArgemoWeHEF6GnsE5H/story.html

Wolfe, David B. "Targeting the Mature Mind." *American Demographics.* Vol. 16, No. 3 (March 1994):32–36.

Yudelman, Montague, and Laura J. M. Kealy. "The Graying of Farmers." *Population Today.* Vol. 28, No. 4 (May/June 2000):6.

Chapter 16

Allen, Mike. "Card Check Battle Starts Tomorrow." *Politico* (March 9, 2009). [Online] Available May 8, 2009, at http://www.politico.com/news/stories/0309/19786.html

Alliance for Board Diversity. "Alliance for Board Diversity Data Sheet, 2011 Update." 2011. Available at http://theabd.org/

Berger, Peter L. *The Capitalist Revolution: Fifty Propositions about Prosperity, Equality, and Liberty.* New York: Basic Books, 1986.

Carlson, Allan. "Agrarianism Reborn: The Curious Return of the Small Family Farm." *Intercollegiate Review.* Vol. 43, No. 1 (Spring 2008):13–23.

Central Intelligence Agency. "CIA World Factbook." 2012. Available at https://www.cia.gov/library/publications/the-world-factbook/index.html

Clark, Kim. "Bankrupt Lives." *U.S. News & World Report* (September 16, 2002):52–54.

Clawson, Dan, and Mary Ann Clawson. "What Has Happened to the U.S. Labor Movement? Union Decline and Renewal." *Annual Review of Sociology.* Vol. 25 (1999):95–119.

DALMIA, SHIKHA. "Obama and Big Labor." *Forbes* (October 29, 2008). [Online] Available May 8, 2009, at http://www.forbes.com/2008/10/28/obama-card-check-oped-cx_sd_1029dalmia.html

DECARLO, SCOTT, ED. "*Forbes*: The Global 2000." 2012. Available at http://www.forbes.com/global2000/list/

DIXON, WILLIAM J., AND TERRY BOSWELL. "Dependency, Disarticulation, and Denominator Effects: Another Look at Foreign Capital Penetration." *American Journal of Sociology.* Vol. 102, No. 2 (September 1996):543–62.

DUDLEY, KATHRYN MARIE. *Debt and Dispossession: Farm Loss in America's Heartland.* Chicago: University of Chicago Press, 2000.

EISLER, BENITA. *The Lowell Offering: Writings by New England Mill Women, 1840–1845.* Philadelphia: Lippincott, 1977.

FIREBAUGH, GLENN, AND DUMITRU SANDU. "Who Supports Marketization and Democratization in Post-Communist Romania?" *Sociological Forum.* Vol. 13, No. 3 (September 1998):521–41.

FIREBAUGH, GLENN, AND FRANK D. BECK. "Does Economic Growth Benefit the Masses? Growth, Dependence, and Welfare in the Third World." *American Sociological Review.* Vol. 59, No. 5 (October 1994):631–53.

FOROOHAR, RANA. "Don't Hold Your Breath." *Time.* Vol. 177, No. 25 (June 20, 2011):22–26.

FOX, JUSTIN. "Why Denmark Loves Globalization." *Time* (November 15, 2007). [Online] Available March 15, 2008, at http://www.time.com/time/magazine/article/0,9171,1684528,00.html

FRIEDMAN, MILTON, AND ROSE FRIEDMAN. *Free to Choose: A Personal Statement.* New York: Harcourt Brace Jovanovich, 1980.

GENERAL MOTORS. "Corporate Strategy." 2012. Available at http://www.gm.com/company/investors/corporate-strategy.html

GERLACH, MICHAEL L. *The Social Organization of Japanese Business.* Berkeley: University of California Press, 1992.

GOODE, WILLIAM J. "Encroachment, Charlatanism, and the Emerging Profession: Psychology, Sociology, and Medicine." *American Sociological Review.* Vol. 25, No. 6 (December 1960):902–14.

GRAY, STEPHEN. "In Ohio, An Era Nears Its End." *Time.* Vol. 177, No. 11 (March 21, 2011):15.

GRAYBOW, MARTHA. "Women Directors Help Boost Corporate's Financial Performance: Study." *International Business Times.* October 2, 2007. [Online] Available December 2, 2008, at http://in.ibtimes.com/articles/20071002/women-directors-help-boost-corporate-financial-performance.htm

GREENHOUSE, LINDA. "Many Entry-Level Workers Find Pinch of Rough Market." *New York Times* (September 4, 2006).

GUTIERREZ, CARL. "Bear Stearns Announces More Job Cuts." *Forbes* (October 3, 2007). [Online] Available May 28, 2008, at http://www.forbes.com/markets/2007/10/03/bear-stearns-layoffs-markets-equity-cx_cg_1003markets23.html

HARFORD, TIM. "The Beauty of Everyday Economics." *U.S. News & World Report* (January 28, 2008):14.

HOWDEN, DANIEL. "Latin America's New Socialist Revolution." *The New Zealand Herald.* December 20, 2005. [Online] Available at http://www.nzherald.co.nz/world/news/article.cfm?c_id=2&objectid=10360679

IGNATIUS, ADI. "A Tsar Is Born." *Time* (December 31, 2007):46–62.

INTERNAL REVENUE SERVICE. "SOI Tax Stats—Business Tax Statistics." 2012. Available at http://www.irs.gov/uac/SOI-Tax-Stats---Business-Tax-Statistics

———. "Tax Gap Estimates." 2012. Available at http://www.irs.gov/uac/The-Tax-Gap

INTERNATIONAL LABOUR ORGANIZATION. "Key Indicators of the Labour Market." 2012. Available at http://www.ilo.org/empelm/what/WCMS_114240/lang--en/index.htm

KALLEBERG, ARNE L., BARBARA F. RESKIN, AND KEN HUDSON. "Bad Jobs in America: Standard and Nonstandard Employment Relations and Job Quality in the United States." *American Sociological Review.* Vol. 65, No. 2 (April 2000):256–78.

KELLEHER, JAMES B. "Wisconsin a Big Setback to Unions in Benefits Battles." Reuters. June 6, 2012. Available at http://www.reuters.com/article/2012/06/06/us-usa-wisconsin-recall-idUSBRE85313220120606

KENTOR, JEFFREY. "The Long-Term Effects of Foreign Investment Dependence on Economic Growth, 1940–1990." *American Journal of Sociology.* Vol. 103, No. 4 (January 1998):1024–46.

KIVANT, BARBARA. "Reassessing Risk." *Time* (November 17, 2008):Global 1–4.

KONO, CLIFFORD, DONALD PALMER, ROGER FRIEDLAND, AND MATTHEW ZAFONTE. "Lost in Space: The Geography of Corporate Interlocking Directorates." *American Journal of Sociology.* Vol. 103, No. 4 (January 1998):863–911.

MCGEEHAN, PATRICK. "Adding to Recession's Pain, Thousands to Lose Job Benefits." *New York Times* (January 11, 2009). [Online] Available January 12, 2009, at http://www.nytimes.com/2009/01/12/nyregion/12benefits.html.

MILLER, TERRY, KIM HOLMES, AND EDWIN FEULNER. "2012 Index of Economic Freedom." 2012. Available at http://www.heritage.org/index/Default.aspx

MONTAIGNE, FEN. "Russia Rising." *National Geographic.* Vol. 200, No. 5 (September 2001): 2–31.

MURPHY, MIKE. "The Real Stakes in Wisconsin." *Time.* Vol. 177, No. 10 (March 14, 2011):24.

NATIONAL CONFERENCE OF STATE LEGISLATURES. "State 'Right to Work' Laws." 2012. Available at http://www.ncsl.org/issues-research/labor/laborandemploymentlegislation.aspx

NELSON, JOEL I. "Work and Benefits: The Multiple Problems of Service Sector Employment." *Social Problems.* Vol. 42, No. 2 (May 1994):240–55.

OECD. "Social Issues: Key Tables from OECD." 2012. Available at http://dx.doi.org/10.1787/socxp-gov-table-2012-1-en

———. "Stat. Extracts: Labour." 2012. Available at http://www.oecd.org/statistics/

———. "Country Statistical Profile: Denmark." 2012. Available at http://www.oecd-ilibrary.org/economics/country-statistical-profile-denmark_20752288-table-dnk

PEW RESEARCH CENTER. "Confidence in Democracy and Capitalism Wanes in Former Soviet Union." December 5, 2011. Available at: http://pewresearch.org/pubs/2139/russia-lithuania-ukraine-former-soviet-union-democracy-capitalism-individualismeconomic-conditions?src=prc-newsletter

———. "The Future of the Global Muslim Population: Muslim Population by Country." 2011. [Online] Available at http://features.pewforum.org/muslim-population

POPULATION REFERENCE BUREAU. "DataFinder." 2012. Available at http://www.prb.org/DataFinder.aspx

PRYOR, JOHN H., SYLVIA HURTADO, LINDA DEANGELO, LAURA PALUCKI BLAKE, AND SERGE TRAN. *The American Freshman: National Norms Fall 2010.* Los Angeles: Cooperative Institutional Research Program at the Higher Education Research Institute at UCLA, 2011.

RASMUSSEN POLL. Reported in the *Dayton Daily News.* [Online] Available February 23, 2011, at http://www.daytondailynews.com/news/dayton-news/americanssplit-on-union-issues-1089409.html?cxtype=ynews_rss

RILEY, NAOMI SCHAEFER. "Why Unions Hurt Higher Education." *USA Today* (March 3, 2011):9A.

RIPLEY, AMANDA. "Meet Your Government Workers." *Time.* Vol. 177, No. 9 (March 7, 2011):40–44.

RITZER, GEORGE, AND DAVID WALCZAK. *Working: Conflict and Change.* 4th ed. Englewood Cliffs, N.J.: Prentice Hall, 1990.

ROUSSEAU, CARYN. "Unions Rally at Wal-Mart Stores." [Online] Available November 22, 2002, at http://dailynews.yahoo.com

RULE, JAMES, AND PETER BRANTLEY. "Computerized Surveillance in the Workplace: Forms and Delusions." *Sociological Forum.* Vol. 7, No. 3 (September 1992): 405–23.

SACHS, JEFFREY D. "The Case for Bigger Government." *Time* (January 19, 2009):34–36.

SAPORITO, BILL. "Can Wal-Mart Get Any Bigger?" *Time* (January 13, 2003):38–43.

SMITH, ADAM. *An Inquiry into the Nature and Causes of the Wealth of Nations.* New York: Modern Library, 1937; orig. 1776.

SULZBERGER, A. G. "Union Bill Is Law, but Debate Is Far from Over." *New York Times.* March 11, 2011. Available at http://www.nytimes.com/2011/03/12/us/12wisconsin.html

UNITED NATIONS DEVELOPMENT PROGRAMME. *Human Development Report 1990.* New York: Oxford University Press, 1990.

U.S. CENSUS BUREAU. "Federal, State, and Local Governments State Government Tax Collections." 2012. Available at http://www.census.gov/govs/statetax/

———. "Population Estimates." 2012. Available at http://www.census.gov/popest/data/index.html

U.S. DEPARTMENT OF LABOR, BUREAU OF LABOR STATISTICS. "Current Employment Statistics - CES (National)." 2012. Available at http://www.bls.gov/ces/home.htm

———. "Employment Situation." 2012. Available at http://www.bls.gov/news.release/empsit.toc.htm

———. "Employment Projections; Labor Force (Demographic) Data." 2012. Available at http://www.bls.gov/emp/emplab1.htm

———. "International Labor Comparisons." 2012. Available at http://www.bls.gov/fls/

———. "Labor Force Statistics from the Current Population Survey." 2012, 2013. Available at http://www.bls.gov/cps/

———. "Union Members Survey—2012." January 23, 2013. Available at http://www.bls.gov/news.release/union2.nr0.htm

U.S. EQUAL EMPLOYMENT OPPORTUNITY COMMISSION. "Job Patterns for Minorities and Women in Private Industry." 2012. Available at http://www1.eeoc.gov/eeoc/statistics/employment/jobpat-eeo1/2011/index.cfm

VALLAS, STEPHEN P., AND JOHN P. BECK. "The Transformation of Work Revisited: The Limits of Flexibility in American Manufacturing." *Social Problems.* Vol. 43, No. 3 (August 1996): 339–61.

WALLERSTEIN, IMMANUEL. *The Capitalist World-Economy.* New York: Cambridge University Press, 1979.

WALMART. "Corporate and Financial Facts." 2012. Available at http://news.walmart.com/walmart-facts/corporate-financial-fact-sheet

WALSH, BRYAN. "How Business Saw the Light." *Time* (January 15, 2007):56–57.

WEIDENBAUM, MURRAY. "The Evolving Corporate Board." *Society.* Vol. 32, No. 3 (March/April 1995):9–20.

WERTHEIMER, BARBARA MAYER. "The Factory Bell." In Linda K. Kerber and Jane DeHart Mathews, eds., *Women's America: Refocusing the Past.* New York: Oxford University Press, 1982:130–40.

WESSEL, DAVID. "What's Wrong with America's Job Engine?" *The Wall Street Journal.* July 27, 2011. Available at http://finance.yahoo.com/banking-budgeting/article/113206/americas-job-engine-wsj?mod=bb-budgeting%20&sec=topStories&pos=4&asset=&ccode=

WILES, P. J. D. *Economic Institutions Compared.* New York: Halsted Press, 1977.

WORLD BANK. "Countries and Regions." 2012. Available at http://go.worldbank.org/9FV1KFE8P0

———. "World DataBank: World Development Indicators." 2012. Available at http://data.worldbank.org/data-catalog/world-development-indicators

ZAKARIA, ZAKARIA. "Why It's Different This Time." *Time.* Vol. 177, No. 8 (February 28, 2011):30–31.

Chapter 17

"ABRAMOFF EFFECT: LEAPING OUT OF BED WITH THE LOBBYISTS." *New York Times* (January 16, 2006). [Online] Available May 2, 2009, at http://query.nytimes.com/gst/fullpage.html?res=9D04EEDC143FF935A25752C0A9609C8B63&sec=&spon=

AL ARABIYA. "Syria Video Shows Assad Militia Stabbing and Stoning Victims." Al Arabiya News. January 2, 2013. Available at Available at http://english.alarabiya.net/articles/2013/01/02/258348.html

ARENDT, HANNAH. *Between Past and Future: Six Exercises in Political Thought.* Cleveland, Ohio: Meridian Books, 1963.

ASTIN, ALEXANDER W., LETICIA OSEGUERA, LINDA J. SAX, AND WILLIAM S. KORN. *The American Freshman: Thirty-Five Year Trends.* Los Angeles: UCLA Higher Education Research Institute, 2002.

BALTZELL, E. DIGBY. *The Protestant Establishment: Aristocracy and Caste in America.* New York: Vintage Books, 1964.

BARNES, JULIAN E. "War Profiteering." *U.S. News & World Report* (May 13, 2002b):20–24.

BARTLETT, DONALD L., AND JAMES B. STEELE. "How the Little Guy Gets Crunched." *Time* (February 7, 2000):38–41.

BELL, JIM. "Will Enthusiasm for Democracy Endure in Egypt and Elsewhere?" Pew Research Center. [Online] Available March 8, 2011, at http://pewresearch.org/pubs/1918/enthusiasm-for-democracy-in-egypt-tunisiafragile-eastern-europe-experience-shows?src=prc-latest&proj=peoplepress

BIPARTISAN POLICY CENTER. "2012 Election Turnout Dips Below 2008 and 2004 Levels: Number of Eligible Voters Increases by Eight Million, Five Million Fewer Votes Cast." November 8, 2012. Available at http://bipartisanpolicy.org/sites/default/files/2012%20Voter%20Turnout%20Report.pdf

BRIANS, CRAIG LEONARD, AND BERNARD GROFMAN. "Election Day Registration's Effect on U.S. Voter Turnout." *Social Science Quarterly.* Vol. 82, No. 1 (March 2001):170–83.

CENTER FOR RESPONSIVE POLITICS. "Lobbying Database." 2012. Available at http://www.opensecrets.org/lobbyists/index.

———. "Campaign Spending." 2012. Available at http://www.opensecrets.org/outsidespending/summ.php

CHANCE, DAVID, AND JACK KIM. "North Korea Mourns Dead Leader, Son Is 'Great Successor'." Reuters. December 19, 2011. Available at http://news.yahoo.com/north-koreastate-tv-says-kim-jong-il-031257363.html

DAHL, ROBERT A. *Who Governs?* New Haven, Conn.: Yale University Press, 1961.

———. *Dilemmas of Pluralist Democracy: Autonomy vs. Control.* New Haven, Conn.: Yale University Press, 1982.

DEDRICK, DENNIS K., AND RICHARD E. YINGER. "MAD, SDI, and the Nuclear Arms Race." Unpublished manuscript. Georgetown, Ky.: Georgetown College, 1990.

FEDERAL ELECTION COMMISSION. "PAC Count—1974 to Present." 2012. Available at http://www.fec.gov/press/cf_summaries.shtml

FISHER, ROGER, AND WILLIAM URY. "Getting to Yes." In William M. Evan and Stephen Hilgartner, eds., *The Arms Race and Nuclear War.* Englewood Cliffs, N.J.: Prentice Hall, 1988:261–68.

FREEDOM HOUSE. "Freedom in the World Comparative and Historical Data." 2012. [Online] Available at http://www.freedomhouse.org/report-types/freedom-world

———. "Freedom in the World Comparative and Historical Data." 2013. Available at http://www.freedomhouse.org/report-types/freedom-world

GELLMAN, BARTON. "Julian Assange." *Time.* Vol. 176, No. 26 (December 27, 2010–January 3, 2011):90–94.

GHOSH, BOBBY. "Rage, Rap, and Revolution." *Time.* Vol. 177, No. 8 (February 28, 2011):32–37.

GIBBS, NANCY. "Terrified ... or Terrorist?" *Time.* Vol. 174, No. 20 (November 23, 2009):28–31.

GORENSTRIN, PETER. "Don't Call It a Stimulus: 2012 Election Spending Likely to Top $8 Billion." *The Daily Ticker.* April 14, 2011. Available at http://finance.yahoo.com/blogs/daily-ticker/don-t-call-stimulus-2012-election-spending-likely-2011-414-084921-208.html

GRIER, PETER. "How to Slow the Spread of the Bomb." *Christian Science Monitor* (June 5, 2006). [Online] Available July 29, 2006, at http://news.yahoo.com/s/csm/20060605

Guardian (The). "Elections 2012." November 2012. Available at http://www.guardian.co.uk/news/datablog/2012/nov/07/us-2012-election-county-results-download#data

HALBFINGER, DAVID M., AND STEVEN A. HOLMES. "Military Mirrors Working-Class America." *New York Times* (March 20, 2003). [Online] Available May 4, 2009, at http://www.cwalocal4250.org/news/binarydata/Military%20Mirrors%20Working-Class%20America.pdf

HORWITZ, JULIANA. "Winds of Political Change Haven't Shifted Public's Ideological Balance." November 25, 2008. [Online] Available January 23, 2009, at http://pewresearch.org/pubs/1042/winds-of-political-change-haventshifted-publics-ideology-balance

JENKINS, J. CRAIG. *Images of Terror: What We Can and Can't Know about Terrorism.* Hawthorne, N.Y.: Aldine de Gruyter, 2003.

JOHNSON, PAUL. "The Seven Deadly Sins of Terrorism." In Benjamin Netanyahu, ed., *International Terrorism.* New Brunswick, N.J.: Transaction Books, 1981:12–22.

KAPLAN, DAVID E., AND MICHAEL SCHAFFER. "Losing the Psywar." *U.S. News & World Report* (October 8, 2001):46.

KARATNYCKY, ADRIAN. "The 2001–2002 Freedom House Survey of Freedom: The Democracy Gap." In *Freedom in the World: The Annual Survey of Political Rights and Civil Liberties, 2001–2002.* New York: Freedom House, 2002:7–18.

KOHUT, ANDREW. "Misreading Election 2012." *Wall Street Journal* (November 13, 2012). Available at http://online.wsj.com/article/SB10001424127887323894704578113231375465160.html

LIAZOS, ALEXANDER. *People First: An Introduction to Social Problems.* Needham Heights, Mass.: Allyn & Bacon, 1982.

LIPTAK, ADAM. "Justices, 5–4, Reject Corporate Spending Limit." *New York Times.* [Online] Available January 21, 2010, at http://www.nytimes.com/2010/01/22/us/politics/22scotus.html

LYND, ROBERT S., AND HELEN MERRELL LYND. *Middletown in Transition.* New York: Harcourt, Brace & World, 1937.

MARULLO, SAM. "The Functions and Dysfunctions of Preparations for Fighting Nuclear War." *Sociological Focus.* Vol. 20, No. 2 (April 1987):135–53.

MILITARY DIVERSITY LEADERSHIP COMMISSION. "From Representation to Inclusion: Diversity Leadership in the 21st Century Military." March 7, 2011. Available at http://mldc.whs.mil/index.php/final-report

MILLS, C. WRIGHT. *The Power Elite.* New York: Oxford University Press, 1956.

MOORE, GWEN, ET AL. "Elite Interlocks in Three U.S. Sectors: Nonprofit, Corpgrate, and Government." *Social Science Quarterly.* Vol. 83, No. 3 (September 2002):726–44.

New York Times. "Election Results 2012." 2012. Available at http://elections.nytimes.com/2012/results/president/exit-polls

NOLAN, PATRICK, AND GERHARD E. LENSKI. *Human Societies: An Introduction to Macrosociology.* 11th ed. Boulder, Colo.: Paradigm, 2010.

NORC. *General Social Surveys, 1972–2010: Cumulative Codebook.* Chicago: National Opinion Research Center. 2011. [Online] Available at http://www.norc.org/GSS+Website

OECD. "Economic Outlook No. 90 Annex Tables." 2013. Available at http://www.oecd.org/eco/outlook/economicoutlook.htm

OHLEMACHER, STEPHEN. "Obama's Victory May Show the Way to Win in Future." *USA Today* (November 9, 2008). [Online] Available January 13, 2009, at http://www.usatoday.com/news/politics/2008-11-08-1164297038_x.htm

PEW RESEARCH CENTER FOR THE PEOPLE AND THE PRESS. "Changing Face of America Helps Assure Obama Victory." November 7, 2012. Available at http://www.people-press.org/2012/11/07/changing-face-of-america-helps-assure-obama-victory/

———. "After Newtown, Modest Change in Opinion about Gun Control: Most Say Assault Weapons Make Nation More Dangerous." December 20, 2012. Available at http://www.people-press.org/2012/12/20/after-newtown-modest-change-in-opinion-about-gun-control/

———. "Young Voters Supported Obama Less, but May Have Mattered More." November 26, 2012. Available at http://www.people-press.org/2012/11/26/young-voters-supported-obama-less-but-may-have-mattered-more/

PEW RESEARCH CENTER, FORUM ON RELIGION AND PUBLIC LIFE. "The Global Religious Landscape: A Report on the Size and Distribution of the World's Major Religious Groups as of 2010." December 2012. Available at http://www.pewforum.org/global-religious-landscape.aspx

PEW RESEARCH CENTER, SOCIAL AND DEMOGRAPHIC TRENDS. "The Growing Electoral Clout of Blacks Is Driven by Turnout, Not Demographics." December 26, 2012. Available at http://www.pewsocialtrends.org/2012/12/26/the-growing-electoral-clout-of-blacks-is-driven-by-turnout-not-demographics/3/

POLSBY, NELSON W. "Three Problems in the Analysis of Community Power." *American Sociological Review.* Vol. 24, No. 6 (December 1959):796–803.

PRYOR, JOHN H., KEVIN EGAN, LAURA PALUCKI BLAKE, SYLVIA HURTADO, JENNIFER BERDAN, AND MATTHEW CASE. "The American Freshman: National Norms Fall 2012 (Expanded Edition)." Cooperative Institutional Research Program at the Higher Education Research Institute at UCLA. 2013. Available at http://www.heri.ucla.edu/monographs/TheAmericanFreshman2012-Expanded.pdf

PRYOR, JOHN H., SYLVIA HURTADO, LINDA DEANGELO, LAURA PALUCKI BLAKE, AND SERGE TRAN. *The American Freshman: National Norms for Fall 2007.* Los Angeles: UCLA Higher Education Research Institute, 2007.

ROGERS, MARTIN. "In Memory of Kim Jong-Il: Dear Leader, G.O.A.T." *The Daily Take.* December 21, 2011. Available at http://www.thepostgame.com/blog/daily-take/201112/memory-kim-jong-il-dear-leader-and-goat

ROTHMAN, STANLEY, AND AMY E. BLACK. "Who Rules Now? American Elites in the 1990s." *Society.* Vol. 35, No. 6 (September/October 1998):17–20.

SAX, LINDA J., ET AL. *The American Freshman: National Norms for Fall 2003.* Los Angeles: UCLA Higher Education Research Institute, 2003.

SCHOUTEN, FREDREKA. "GOP Keeps Control of House." *USA Today.* November 7, 2012. Available at http://www.usatoday.com/story/news/politics/2012/11/06/house-congress-election/1683163/

SCHUR, LISA A., AND DOUGLAS L. KRUSE. "What Determines Voter Turnout? Lessons from Citizens with Disabilities." *Social Science Quarterly.* Vol. 81, No. 2 (June 2000):571–87.

SENTENCING PROJECT. "Felony Disenfranchisement Laws in the United States." 2012. Available at http://www.sentencingproject.org/Admin%5CDocuments%5Cpublications%5Cfd_bs_fdlawsinus.pdf

SIVARD, RUTH LEGER. *World Military and Social Expenditures, 1987–88.* 12th ed. Washington, D.C.: World Priorities, 1988.

SKOCPOL, THEDA. *States and Social Revolutions: A Comparative Analysis of France, Russia, and China.* Cambridge: Cambridge University Press, 1979.

STOCKHOLM INTERNATIONAL PEACE RESEARCH INSTITUTE. "SIPRI Military Expenditure Database." 2012. Available at http://milexdata.sipri.org/

———. "SIPRI Yearbook." 2012. Available at http://www.sipri.org/yearbook

THOMPSON, MARK. "The Other 1%." *Time.* Vol. 178, No. 20 (November 1, 2011):33–39.

THOMPSON, MARK, AND DOUGLAS WALLER. "Shield of Dreams." *Time* (May 8, 2001):45–47.

TILLY, CHARLES. "Does Modernization Breed Revolution?" In Jack A. Goldstone, ed., *Revolutions: Theoretical, Comparative, and Historical Studies.* New York: Harcourt Brace Jovanovich, 1986:47–57.

TOCQUEVILLE, ALEXIS DE. *The Old Regime and the French Revolution.* Stuart Gilbert, trans. Garden City, N.Y.: Anchor/Doubleday, 1955; orig. 1856.

UGGEN, CHRISTOPHER, AND JEFF MANZA. "Democratic Contraction? Political Consequences of Felon Disenfranchisement in the United States." *American Sociological Review.* Vol. 67, No. 6 (December 2002):777–803.

U.S. CENSUS BUREAU, GOVERNMENTS DIVISION. "Federal, State, and Local Governments." 2012. Available at http://www.census.gov/govs/www/index.html

———. "Population Estimates." 2012. Available at http://www.census.gov/popest/data/index.html

———. "Voting and Registration." 2009. Available at http://www.census.gov/hhes/www/socdemo/voting/index.html

U.S. Department of Defense. "Population Representation in the Military Services." 2012. Available at http://prhome.defense.gov/RFM/MPP/ACCESSIONPOLICY/poprep.aspx

———. "Military Casualty Information." 2012. Available at http://siadapp.dmdc.osd.mil/personnel/CASUALTY/castop.htm

———. "Military Personnel Statistics." 2012. Available at http://siadapp.dmdc.osd.mil/personnel/MILITARY/Miltop.htm

U.S. Department of Labor, Bureau of Labor Statistics. "Employment Situation." 2013. Available at http://www.bls.gov/news.release/empsit.toc.htm

U.S. Department of State, Bureau of Intelligence and Research. "Independent States in the World." 2012. Available at http://www.state.gov/s/inr/rls/4250.htm

U.S. Department of State, National Counterterrorism Center. "Annual Report on Terrorism." 2012. Available at http://www.nctc.gov/docs/2011_NCTC_Annual_Report_Final.pdf

U.S. House of Representatives. "Committee on Veterans Affairs." Veterans in Congress, 2013. Available at http://veterans.house.gov/veterans-congress-112th-congress

U.S. Office of Management and Budget. "The Budget for Fiscal Year 2013." 2012. Available at http://www.gpo.gov/fdsys/browse/collectionGPO.action?collectionCode=BUDGET

Vinovskis, Maris A. "Have Social Historians Lost the Civil War? Some Preliminary Demographic Speculations." *Journal of American History.* Vol. 76, No. 1 (June 1989):34–58.

Weber, Max. *Economy and Society: An Outline of Interpretive Sociology.* Guenther Roth and Claus Wittich, eds. Berkeley: University of California Press, 1978; orig. 1921.

Whitaker, Mark. "Ten Ways to Fight Terrorism." *Newsweek* (July 1, 1985):26–29.

Wright, Quincy. "Causes of War in the Atomic Age." In William M. Evan and Stephen Hilgartner, eds., *The Arms Race and Nuclear War.* Englewood Cliffs, N.J.: Prentice Hall, 1987:7–10.

Yom, Sean L., and F. Gregory Gause III. "Resilient Royals: How Arab Monarchies Hang on." *Journal of Democracy.* Vol. 23, No. 4 (October 2012):74–88.

Xia, Renee. "In China, Activists Watch and Cheer." *Wall Street Journal.* [Online] Available March 12, 2011, at http://online.wsj.com/article/SB10001424052748704823004576192642010298086.html

Zakaria, Zakaria. "Why It's Different This Time." *Time.* Vol. 177, No. 8 (February 28, 2011):30–31.

Chapter 18

AARP Foundation. "GrandFacts." October 2007. [Online] Available July 3, 2008, at http://www.grandfactsheets.org/doc/National%20Resources%20Fact%20Sheet.pdf

Allen, Walter R. "African American Family Life in Social Context: Crisis and Hope." *Sociological Forum.* Vol. 10, No. 4 (December 1995):569–92.

Amato, Paul R. "What Children Learn from Divorce." *Population Today.* Vol. 29, No. 1 (January 2001):1, 4.

Amato, Paul R., and Juliana M. Sobolewski. "The Effects of Divorce and Marital Discord on Adult Children's Psychological Well-Being." *American Sociological Review.* Vol. 66, No. 6 (December 2001):900–21.

Anderson, John Ward. "Early to Wed: The Child Brides of India." *Washington Post* (May 24, 1995):A27, A30.

Bernard, Jessie. *The Future of Marriage,* 2nd ed. New Haven, Conn.: Yale University Press, 1982.

Besharov, Douglas J., and Lisa A. Laumann. "Child Abuse Reporting." *Society.* Vol. 34, No. 4 (May/June 1996):40–46.

Bianchi, Suzanne M., and Daphne Spain. "Women, Work, and Family in America." *Population Bulletin.* Vol. 51, No. 3 (December 1996).

Blankenhorn, David. *Fatherless America: Confronting Our Most Urgent Social Problem.* New York: HarperCollins, 1995.

Blau, Peter M. *Exchange and Power in Social Life.* New York: Wiley, 1964.

Booth, Alan, and Ann C. Crouter, eds. *Just Living Together: Implications of Cohabitation on Families, Children, and Policy.* Mahwah, N.J.: Erlbaum, 2002.

Brines, Julie, and Kara Joyner. "The Ties That Bind: Principles of Cohesion in Cohabitation and Marriage." *American Sociological Review.* Vol. 64, No. 3 (June 1999):333–55.

Centers for Disease Control and Prevention. "Marriage and Divorce Data." National Marriage and Divorce Rate Trends. 2012. Available at http://www.cdc.gov/nchs/nvss/marriage_divorce_tables.htm

———. "Cohabitation, Marriage, Divorce, and Remarriage in the United States." Vital Health Stat. Vol. 23, No. 22. 2002. Available at http://www.cdc.gov/nchs/data/series/sr_23/sr23_022.pdf

Centers for Disease Control and Prevention, National Center for Health Statistics. "National Survey of Family Growth (NSFG)." 2012. Available at http://www.cdc.gov/nchs/nsfg.htm

Cherlin, Andrew J., Linda M. Burton, Tera R. Hart, and Diane M. Purvin. "The Influence of Physical and Sexual Abuse on Marriage and Cohabitation." *American Sociological Review.* Vol. 69, No. 6 (December 2004):768–89.

Cohn, D'Vera. "Do Parents Spend Enough Time with Their Children?" Population Reference Bureau. January 2007. [Online] Available July 3, 2008, at http://www.prb.org/Articles/2007/DoParentsSpendEnoughTimeWithTheirChildren.aspx

Copen, Casey E., Kimberly Daniels, Jonathan Vespa, and William D. Mosher. "First Marriages in the United States: Data From the 2006–2010 National Survey of Family Growth." National Health Statistics Reports. No. 49. 2012. Available at http://www.cdc.gov/nchs/data/nhsr/nhsr049.pdf

Cornwell, Erin York, and Linda J. Waite. "Social Disconnectedness, Perceived Isolation, and Health among Older Adults." *Journal of Health and Social Behavior.* Vol. 50, No. 1 (March 2009):31–48.

Duncan, Greg J., W. Jean Yeung, Jeanne Brooks-Gunn, and Judith R. Smith. "How Much Does Childhood Poverty Affect the Life Chances of Children?" *American Sociological Review.* Vol. 63, No. 3 (June 1998):406–23.

Ember, Melvin, and Carol R. Ember. "The Conditions Favoring Matrilocal versus Patrilocal Residence." *American Anthropologist.* Vol. 73, No. 3 (June 1971):571–94.

———. *Anthropology.* 6th ed. Englewood Cliffs, N.J.: Prentice Hall, 1991.

Engels, Friedrich. *The Origin of the Family.* Chicago: Kerr, 1902; orig. 1884.

England, Paula. "Three Reviews on Marriage." *Contemporary Sociology.* Vol. 30, No. 6 (November 2001):564–65.

Etzioni, Amitai. "How to Make Marriage Matter." *Time* (September 6, 1993):76

European Union, European Communities Statistical Office. "Eurostat." 2012. Available at http://epp.eurostat.ec.europa.eu/portal/page/portal/population/data/database

Furstenberg, Frank F., Jr., and Andrew J. Cherlin. *Divided Families: What Happens to Children When Parents Part.* Cambridge, Mass.: Harvard University Press, 1991.

———. "Children's Adjustment to Divorce." In Bonnie J. Fox, ed. *Family Patterns, Gender Relations.* 2nd ed. New York: Oxford University Press, 2001.

Fustos, Kata. "Marriage and Partnership Turnover for American Families." Population Reference Bureau. June 2010. [Online] Available at http://www.prb.org/Articles/2010/usmarriagepolicyseminar.aspx

———. "Marriage Benefits Men's Health." Population Reference Bureau. September 2010. Available at http://www.prb.org/Articles/2010/usmarriage-menshealth.aspx

Gilbert, Neil. "Family Life: Sold on Work." *Society.* Vol. 42, No. 3 (2005):12–17.

Glenn, Norval D., and BethAnn Shelton. "Regional Differences in Divorce in the United States." *Journal of Marriage and the Family.* Vol. 47, No. 3 (August 1985):641–52.

Goldstein, Joshua R., and Catherine T. Kenney. "Marriage Delayed or Marriage Forgone? New Cohort Forecasts of First Marriage for U.S. Women." *American Sociological Review.* Vol. 66, No. 4 (August 2001):506–19.

Goode, William J. "The Theoretical Importance of Love." *American Sociological Review.* Vol. 24, No. 1 (February 1959):38–47.

Green, Penelope. "Under One Roof, Building for Extended Families." *New York Times* (November 29, 2012). Available at http://www.nytimes.com/2012/11/30/us/building-homes-for-modern-multigenerational-families.html?emc=eta1&_r=0

Greenspan, Stanley I. *The Four-Thirds Solution: Solving the Child-Care Crisis in America.* Cambridge, Mass.: Perseus, 2001.

Holwerda, Tjalling Jan, et al. "Feelings of Loneliness, but Not Social Isolation, Predict Dementia Onset: Results from the Amsterdam Study of the Elderly." *Journal of Neurology, Neurosurgery and Psychiatry.* December 2012. Available at http://jnnp.bmj.com/content/early/2012/11/06/jnnp-2012-302755

Kantrowitz, Barbara, and Pat Wingert. "Unmarried with Children." *Newsweek* (May 28, 2001):46–52.

Kent, Mary Mederios. "Most Americans Marry Within Their Race." Population Reference Bureau. August 2010. [Online] Available at http://www.prb.org/Articles/2010/usintermarriage.aspx

———. "U.S. Women Delay Marriage and Children for College." Population Reference Bureau. January 2011. [Online] Available at http://www.prb.org/Articles/2011/usmarriageandchildbirth.aspx

Kreider, Rose M., and Renee Ellis. "Number, Timing, and Duration of Marriages and Divorces: 2009." *Current Population Reports,* P70–125. U.S. Census Bureau. 2011. [Online] Available at http://www.census.gov/prod/2011pubs/p70–125.pdf

Laumann, Edward O., John H. Gagnon, Robert T. Michael, and Stuart Michaels. *The Social Organization of Sexuality: Sexual Practices in the United States.* Chicago: University of Chicago Press, 1994.

Levine, Samantha. "The Price of Child Abuse." *U.S. News & World Report* (April 9, 2001):58.

Lino, Mark. "Expenditures on Children by Families, 2011." Miscellaneous Publication Number 1528-2011. U.S. Department of Agriculture, Center for Nutrition Policy and Promotion. 2012. Available at http://www.cnpp.usda.gov/Publications/CRC/crc2011.pdf

Lobo, Susan. "Census-Taking and the Invisibility of Urban American Indians." *Population Today.* Vol. 30, No. 4 (May/June 2002):3–4.

Lund, Dale A. "Caregiving." *Encyclopedia of Adult Development.* Phoenix, Ariz.: Oryx Press, 1993:57–63.

Luo, Ye, Tracey A. LaPierre, Mary Elizabeth Highes, and Linda J. White. "Grandparents Providing Care to Grandchildren: A Population-Based Study of Continuity and Change." *Journal of Family Issues.* Vol. 33, No. 9 (2012):1143–1167.

Mace, David, and Vera Mace. *Marriage East and West.* Garden City, N.Y.: Doubleday/Dolphin, 1960.

Macionis, John J. "Intimacy: Structure and Process in Interpersonal Relationships." *Alternative Lifestyles.* Vol. 1, No. 1 (February 1978):113–30.

Martin, Joyce A., Brady E. Hamilton, Stephanie J. Ventura, Michelle J. K. Osterman, Elizabeth Wilson, and T. J. Mathews. "Births: Final Data for 2010." National Vital Statistics Reports. Vol. 61, No 1. 2012. Available at http://www.cdc.gov/nchs/data/nvsr/nvsr61/nvsr61_01.pdf

Mayo, Katherine. *Mother India.* New York: Harcourt, Brace, 1927.

McLanahan, Sara. "Life without Father: What Happens to the Children?" *Contexts.* Vol. 1, No. 1 (Spring 2002):35–44.

McLeod, Jane D., and Michael J. Shanahan. "Poverty, Parenting, and Children's Mental Health." *American Sociological Review.* Vol. 58, No. 3 (June 1993):351–66.

MOELLER, PHILIP. "Financial Safeguards Needed as Senior Divorces Soar." *U.S. News & World Report*. July 6, 2012. Available at http://finance.yahoo.com/news/financial-safeguards-needed-senior-divorces-151329123.html

MURDOCK, GEORGE PETER. *Social Structure*. New York: Free Press, 1965; orig. 1949.

NATIONAL CONFERENCE OF STATE LEGISLATURES. "Same Sex Marriage, Civil Unions and Domestic Partnerships." 2013. Available at http://www.ncsl.org/issues-research/human-services/same-sex-marriage.aspx

NAVARRO, MIREYA. "For Younger Latinas, a Shift to Smaller Families." *New York Times* (December 5, 2004). [Online] Available April 30, 2005, at http://www.researchnavigator.com

NEWPORT, FRANK. "Americans Turn More Negative toward Same-Sex Marriage." Gallup News Service, April 2005. [Online] Available July 3, 2008, at http://www.gallup.com/poll/15889/Americans-Turn-More-Negative-Toward-SameSex-Marriage.aspx

New York Times. "Times Topics: Same-Sex Marriage, Civil Unions, and Domestic Partnerships." 2013. Available at http://topics.nytimes.com/top/reference/timestopics/subjects/s/same_sex_marriage/index.html

NORC. *General Social Surveys, 1972–2010*. Chicago: National Opinion Research Center. March 2011. [Online] Available at http://www.norc.org/GSS+Website

OECD. "Stat. Extracts." 2012. Available at http://stats.oecd.org/index.aspx

———. "Employment Policies and Data." 2012. Available at http://www.oecd.org/els/emp/howdoecdlabourmarketsperform.htm

———. "Society at a Glance 2011." 2012. Available at http://www.oecd-ilibrary.org/social-issues-migration-health/society-at-a-glance-2011_soc_glance-2011-en

PARKER, KIM. "The Boomerang Generation." Pew Research: Social and Demographic Trends. March 15, 2012. Available at http://www.pewsocialtrends.org/2012/03/15/the-boomerang-generation/3/

PASSEL, JEFFREY, WENDY WANG, AND PAUL TAYLOR. "One-in-Seven New U.S. Marriages Is Interracial or Interethnic." Pew Research Center Social and Demographic Trends. [Online] Available June 4, 2010, at http://pewsocialtrends.org/2010/06/04/marrying-out *Peters Atlas of the World*. New York: Harper & Row, 1990.

PEW RESEARCH CENTER. "American Values Survey Question Database." 2012. Available at http://www.people-press.org/values-questions/

PEW RESEARCH CENTER FORUM ON RELIGION AND PUBLIC LIFE. "U.S. Religious Landscape Survey." 2008. [Online] Available at http://religions.pewforum.org/reports

———. "Gay Marriage Around the World." July 9, 2009. Available at http://www.pewforum.org/Gay-Marriage-and-Homosexuality/Gay-Marriage-Around-the-World.aspx

———. "Same-Sex Marriage: Redefining Marriage Around the World." 2009. [Online] Available at http://pewforum.org/docs/?DocID=235

PEW RESEARCH CENTER ON THE PEOPLE AND THE PRESS. "Political Survey Report, March 3, 2011." 2011. [Online] Available at http://people-press.org/2011/03/03/section-3-attitudes-toward-social-issues

PEW RESEARCH CENTER, SOCIAL AND DEMOGRAPHIC TRENDS. "As Marriage and Parenthood Drift Apart, Public Is Concerned about Social Impact." July 1, 2007. Available at http://pewsocialtrends.org/pubs/526/marriage-parenthood

———. "Modern Marriage." July 18, 2007. Available at http://www.pewsocialtrends.org/2007/07/18/modern-marriage/

———. "The Decline of Marriage and Rise of New Families." November 18, 2010. Available at http://www.pewsocialtrends.org/2010/11/18/the-decline-of-marriage-and-rise-of-new-families/

———. "Fighting Poverty in a Tough Economy, Americans Move in With Relatives." October 3, 2011. Available at http://www.pewsocialtrends.org/files/2011/10/Multigenerational-Households-Final1.pdf#

PHILLIPS, MELANIE. "What about the Overclass?" *Public Interest* (Fall 2001):38–43.

POPENOE, DAVID. "Can the Nuclear Family Be Revived?" *Society*. Vol. 36, No. 5 (July/August 1999):28–30.

———. "Family Decline in the Swedish Welfare State." *Public Interest*. No. 102 (Winter 1991):65–77.

POPENOE, DAVID, AND BARBARA DAFOE WHITEHEAD. *Should We Live Together? What Young Adults Need to Know about Cohabitation before Marriage*. New Brunswick, N.J.: National Marriage Project, 1999.

POPULATION REFERENCE BUREAU. "Who Speaks for Me? Ending Child Marriage Fact Sheet." May 2011. [Online] Available at: http://www.prb.org/pdf11/child-marriagefact-sheet.pdf

RALEY, R. KELLY, T. ELIZABETH DURDEN, AND ELIZABETH WILDSMITH. "Understanding Mexican-American Marriage Patterns Using a Life Course Approach." *Social Science Quarterly*. Vol. 85, No. 4 (December 2004):872–90.

ROESCH, ROBERTA. "Violent Families." *Parents*. Vol. 59, No. 9 (September 1984):74–76, 150–52.

ROSENFELD, MICHAEL J., AND BYONG-SOO KIM. "The Independence of Young Adults and the Rise of Interracial and Same-Sex Unions." *American Sociological Review*. Vol. 70, No. 4 (August 2005):541–62.

ROUDI-FAHIMI, FARAZZEH. "Child Marriage in the Middle East and North Africa." Population Reference Bureau. (April 2010). [Online] Available at http://www.prb.org/Articles/2010/menachildmarriage.aspx

RUBIN, LILLIAN BRESLOW. *Worlds of Pain: Life in the Working-Class Family*. New York: Basic Books, 1976.

SHUPE, ANSON, WILLIAM A. STACEY, AND LONNIE R. HAZLEWOOD. *Violent Men, Violent Couples: The Dynamics of Domestic Violence*. Lexington, Mass.: Lexington Books, 1987.

SMITH, TOM W. "American Sexual Risk Behavior: Trends, Socio-Demographic Differences, and Behavior." March 2006. [Online] Available January 29, 2009, at http://www.norc.org/NR/rdonlyres/2663F09F-2E74-436E-AC81-6FFBF288E183/0/AmericanSexualBehavior2006.pdf

SNELL, MARILYN BERLIN. "The Purge of Nurture." *New Perspectives Quarterly*. Vol. 7, No. 2 (Winter 1990):1–2.

STACEY, JUDITH. *Brave New Families: Stories of Domestic Upheaval in Late Twentieth-Century America*. New York: Basic Books, 1990.

———. "Good Riddance to 'the Family': A Response to David Popenoe." *Journal of Marriage and the Family*. Vol. 55, No. 3 (August 1993):545–47.

STONE, LAWRENCE. *The Family, Sex, and Marriage in England, 1500–1800*. New York: Harper & Row, 1977.

TAVERNISE, SABRINA, AND ROBERT GEBELOFF. "Once Rare in Rural America, Divorce Is Changing the Face of Its Families." *The New York Times*. [Online] Available March 23, 2011, at http://www.nytimes.com/2011/03/24/us/24divorce.html?_r=1&ref=sabrinatavernise

UNITED NATIONS ECONOMIC COMMISSION FOR EUROPE. "UNECE Statistical Database: Fertility, Families and Households." Available March 14, 2011, at http://w3.unece.org/pxweb/

UNITED NATIONS STATISTICS DIVISION. "Demographic Yearbook." December 2012. Available at http://unstats.un.org/unsd/demographic/products/dyb/dyb2.htm

U.S. CENSUS BUREAU (KREIDER, ROSE M. AND RENEE ELLIS). "Number, Timing, and Duration of Marriages and Divorces: 2009." *Current Population Reports*, P70-125. 2011. Available at http://www.census.gov/prod/2011pubs/p70-125.pdf

U.S. CENSUS BUREAU. "Survey of Income and Program Participation: Childcare." 2011. Available at http://www.census.gov/population/www/socdemo/childcare.html

———. "Census 2010." 2011, 2012. Available at http://factfinder2.census.gov/faces/nav/jsf/pages/wc_dec.xhtml

———. "American Community Survey." 2012. Available at http://www.census.gov/acs/www/#

———. "Current Population Survey." 2012. Available at http://www.census.gov/cps/

———. "Families and Living Arrangements." 2012. Available at http://www.census.gov/hhes/families/data/cps2012.html

———. "Fertility." 2012. Available at http://www.census.gov/hhes/fertility/data/cps/supplemental.html

———. "Population Estimates." 2012. Available at http://www.census.gov/popest/data/index.html

U.S. DEPARTMENT OF HEALTH AND HUMAN SERVICES, ADMINISTRATION ON CHILDREN, YOUTH AND FAMILIES. "Child Maltreatment." 2012. Available at http://www.acf.hhs.gov/programs/cb/research-data-technology/statistics-research/child-maltreatment

U.S. DEPARTMENT OF JUSTICE, DEPARTMENT OF JUSTICE STATISTICS. "Criminal Victimization 2011." October 17, 2012. Available at http://bjs.gov/content/pub/pdf/cv11.pdf

U.S. DEPARTMENT OF JUSTICE, FEDERAL BUREAU OF INVESTIGATION. "Crime in the United States 2011." 2012. Available at http://www.fbi.gov/about-us/cjis/ucr/crime-in-the-u.s/2011/crime-in-the-u.s.-2011

U.S. DEPARTMENT OF LABOR, BUREAU OF LABOR STATISTICS. "American Time Use Survey." 2012. Available at http://www.bls.gov/tus/

WALLERSTEIN, JUDITH S., AND SANDRA BLAKESLEE. *Second Chances: Men, Women, and Children a Decade after Divorce*. New York: Ticknor & Fields, 1989.

WANG, WENDY. "The Rise of Intermarriage." Pew Research Center, Social and Demographic Trends. 2012. Available at http://www.pewsocialtrends.org/2012/02/16/the-rise-of-intermarriage/

WANG, WENDY, AND PAUL TAYLOR. "For Millennials, Parenthood Trumps Marriage." Pew Research Center. 2011. [Online] Available at http://pewsocialtrends.org/2011/03/09/for-millennials-parenthood-trumps-marriage

Chapter 19

APPLEBOME, PETER. "70 Years after Scopes Trial, Creation Debate Lives." *New York Times* (March 10, 1996):1, 10.

APRILL, ELLEN P. "Churches, Politics, and the Charitable Contribution Deduction." *Boston College Law Review*. Vol. 42, No. 4 (2004):843–874. [Online] Available April 19, 2009, at http://www.bc.edu/bc_org/avp/law/lwsch/journals/bclawr/42_4/04_FMS.htm

ASSOCIATION OF RELIGION DATA ARCHIVES (ARDA). 2012. Available at http://www.thearda.com/

ASSOCIATION OF STATISTICIANS OF AMERICAN RELIGIOUS BODIES. 2010 Religious Congregations and Membership Survey. 2012. Available at http://www.rcms2010.org/

ASSOCIATION OF THEOLOGICAL SCHOOLS. "Annual Data Tables/FactBooks." 2012. Available at http://www.ats.edu/Resources/PublicationsPresentations/Documents/AnnualDataTables/2011-12AnnualDataTables.pdf

ASTIN, ALEXANDER W., LETICIA OSEGUERA, LINDA J. SAX, AND WILLIAM S. KORN. *The American Freshman: Thirty-Five Year Trends*. Los Angeles: UCLA Higher Education Research Institute, 2002.

BELLAH, ROBERT N. *The Broken Covenant*. New York: Seabury Press, 1975.

BERGER, PETER L. *The Sacred Canopy: Elements of a Sociological Theory of Religion*. Garden City, N.Y.: Doubleday, 1967.

———. "Faith and Development." *Society*. Vol. 46, No. 1 (January/February 2009):69–75.

BESECKE, KELLY. "Speaking of Meaning in Modernity: Reflexive Spirituality as a Cultural Resource." *Sociology of Religion*. Vol. 62, No. 3 (2003):365–81.

———. "Seeing Invisible Religion: Religion as a Societal Conversation about Transcendent Meaning." *Sociological Theory*. Vol. 23, No. 2 (June 2005):179–96.

BOSTON, ROB. "Ohio Creationism Teacher John Freshwater Fired." *Opposing Views*. [Online] Available January 12, 2011, at http://www.opposingviews.com/i/ohio-creationism-teacher-john-freshwater-fired

CIMINO, RICHARD, AND DON LATTIN. *Shopping for Faith: American Religion in the New Millenium*. New York: Jossey-Bass, 1999.

COX, HARVEY. *The Secular City*. Rev. ed. New York: Macmillan, 1971.

Durkheim, Emile. *The Elementary Forms of Religious Life.* New York: Free Press, 1965; orig. 1915.

Eck, Diana L. *A New Religious America: How a "Christian Country" Has Become the World's Most Religiously Diverse Nation.* San Francisco: HarperSanFrancisco, 2001.

El-Attar, Mohamed. Personal communication, 1991.

Ellwood, Robert S. "East Asian Religions in Today's America." In Jacob Neusner, ed. *World Religions in America: An Introduction.* Louisville, Ky.: Westminster John Knox Press, 2000:154–71.

Frazier, E. Franklin. *Black Bourgeoisie: The Rise of a New Middle Class.* New York: Free Press, 1965.

Gallup. "In U.S., Rise in Religious 'Nones' Slows in 2012." January 10, 2013. Available at http://www.gallup.com/poll/159785/rise-religious-nones-slows-2012.aspx

Gleick, Elizabeth. "The Marker We've Been Waiting For." *Time* (April 7, 1997):28–42.

Glenn, Heidi. "Losing Our Religion: The Growth of the 'Nones.'" The Two-Way. National Public Radio. January 13, 2013. Available at http://www.npr.org/blogs/thetwo-way/2013/01/14/169164840/losing-our-religion-the-growth-of-the-nones

Goldscheider, Calvin. *Studying the Jewish Future.* Seattle: University of Washington Press, 2004.

Gould, Stephen J. "Evolution as Fact and Theory." *Discover* (May 1981):35–37.

Greeley, Andrew M. "Symposium: Neo-Darwinism and Its Discontents." *Society.* Vol. 45, No. 2 (2008):162–63.

Grim, Brian J., and David Masci. "The Demographics of Faith." August 19, 2008. [Online] Available February 23, 2009, at http://www.america.gov/st/diversity-english/2008/August/20080819121858cmretrop0.5310633.html

Hadden, Jeffrey K., and Charles E. Swain. *Prime-Time Preachers: The Rising Power of Televangelism.* Reading, Mass.: Addison-Wesley, 1981.

Hartford Institute for Religious Research. 2012, 2013. Available at http://hirr.hartsem.edu/index.html

Hout, Michael, Andrew M. Greeley, and Melissa J. Wilde. "The Demographic Imperative in Religious Change in the United States." *American Journal of Sociology.* Vol. 107, No. 2 (September 2001):468–500.

Huchingson, James E. "Science and Religion." *Miami Herald* (December 25, 1994):1M, 6M.

Hunter, James Davison. *American Evangelicalism: Conservative Religion and the Quandary of Modernity.* New Brunswick, N.J.: Rutgers University Press, 1983.

———. "Conservative Protestantism." In Philip E. Hammond, ed., *The Sacred in a Secular Age.* Berkeley: University of California Press, 1985:50–66.

———. *Evangelicalism: The Coming Generation.* Chicago: University of Chicago Press, 1987.

Iannaccone, Laurence R. "Why Strict Churches Are Strong." *American Journal of Sociology.* Vol. 99, No. 5 (March 1994):1180–1211.

Jacquet, Constant H., and Alice M. Jones. *Yearbook of American and Canadian Churches, 1991.* Nashville, Tenn.: Abingdon Press, 1991.

Kaufman, Walter. *Religions in Four Dimensions: Existential, Aesthetic, Historical, and Comparative.* New York: Reader's Digest Press, 1976.

Keister, Lisa A. "Religion and Wealth: The Role of Religious Affiliation and Participation in Early Adult Asset Accumulation." *Social Forces.* Vol. 82, No. 1 (September 2003):175–207.

Kilbourne, Brock K. "The Conway and Siegelman Claims against Religious Cults: An Assessment of Their Data." *Journal for the Scientific Study of Religion.* Vol. 22, No. 4 (December 1983):380–85.

Kosmin, Barry. "The Changing Population Profile of American Jews, 2000–2008." Paper presented at the Fifteenth World Congress of Jewish Studies, Jerusalem, Israel. 2009. Available at http://commons.trincoll.edu/aris/files/2011/08/AJIS08.pdf

Kraybill, Donald B. "The Amish Encounter with Modernity." In Donald B. Kraybill and Marc A. Olshan, eds., *The Amish Struggle with Modernity.* Hanover, N.H.: University Press of New England, 1994:21–33.

Larson, Gerald James. "Hinduism in India and in America." In Jacob Neusner, ed., *World Religions in America: An Introduction.* Louisville, Ky.: Westminster/John Knox, 2000:124–41.

Lottick, Edward A. "Prevalence of Cults: A Review of Empirical Research in the U. S. A." International Cultic Studies Association, Universidad Autonoma de Madrid. 2005. Available at http://www.pressbox.co.uk/detailed/Health/Prevalence_of_Cults_in_the_USA_32794.html

MacDonald, G. Jeffrey. "Who's Filling America's Church Pews." *Christian Science Monitor.* December 23, 2012. Available at http://www.csmonitor.com/USA/Society/2012/1223/Who-s-filling-America-s-church-pews

Manza, Jeff, and Clem Brooks. "The Religious Factor in U.S. Presidential Elections, 1960–1992." *American Journal of Sociology.* Vol. 103, No. 1 (July 1997):38–81.

Marquand, Robert. "Worship Shift: Americans Seek Feeling of 'Awe.'" *Christian Science Monitor* (May 28, 1997):1, 8

Marx, Karl. *Karl Marx: Early Writings.* T. B. Bottomore, ed. New York: McGraw-Hill, 1964; orig. 1848.

McClay, William M. "Secularism, American Style." *Society.* Vol. 44, No. 6 (2007):160–63.

McGuire, Meredith B. *Religion: The Social Context.* 2nd ed. Belmont, Calif.: Wadsworth, 1987.

McRoberts, Omar M. *Streets of Glory: Church and Community in a Black Urban Neighborhood.* Chicago: University of Chicago Press, 2003.

Meacham, Jon. "The End of Christian America." *Newsweek.* [Online] Available April 4, 2009, at http://www.newsweek.com/2009/04/03/the-end-of-christian-america.html

Miller, Alan S., and Rodney Stark. "Gender and Religiousness: Can Socialization Explanations Be Saved?" *American Journal of Sociology.* Vol. 107, No. 6 (May 2002):1399–1423.

Muller, Chandra, and Christopher G. Ellison. "Religious Involvement, Social Capital, and Adolescents' Academic Progress: Evidence from the National Education Longitudinal Study of 1988." *Sociological Focus.* Vol. 34, No. 2 (May 2001):155–83.

Neuhouser, Kevin. "The Radicalization of the Brazilian Catholic Church in Comparative Perspective." *American Sociological Review.* Vol. 54, No. 2 (April 1989):233–44.

NORC. *General Social Surveys, 1972–2010.* Chicago: National Opinion Research Center. March 2011. Available at http://www.norc.org/GSS+Website

———. *General Social Surveys, 1972–2012.* Chicago: National Opinion Research Center. March 2013. Available at http://www.norc.org/GSS+Website

Paris, Peter J. "The Religious World of African Americans." In Jacob Neusner, ed. *World Religions in America: An Introduction.* Revised and expanded ed. Louisville, Ky.: Westminster/John Knox, 2000:48–65.

Pattillo, Mary. "Church Culture as a Strategy of Action in the Black Community." *American Sociological Review.* Vol. 63, No. 6 (December 1998):767–84.

Perez, Evan. "Justice Department Files Appeal to Preserve National Prayer Day." *The Wall Street Journal.* [Online] Available April 22, 2010, at http://online.wsj.com/article/SB10001424052748703876404575200441140766602.html

Peterson, Scott. "Women Live on Own Terms behind the Veil." *Christian Science Monitor* (July 31, 1996):1, 10.

Pew Research Center for the People and the Press. "American Values Survey Database." 2012. Available at http://www.people-press.org/values-questions/

———. "Muslim Americans: No Signs of Growth in Alienation or Support for Extremism." August 30, 2011. Available at http://www.people-press.org/2011/08/30/section-1-a-demographic-portrait-of-muslim-americans/

Pew Research Center, Forum on Religion and Public Life. "A Religious Portrait of African Americans." 2009. [Online] Available at http://www.pewforum.org/A-Religious-Portrait-of-African-Americans.aspx

———. "Scientists and Belief." 2009. [Online] Available at http://www.pewforum.org/Science-and-Bioethics/Scientists-and-Belief.aspx

———. "The Future of the Global Muslim Population: Projections for 2010–2030." 2011. Available at http://www.pewforum.org/The-Future-of-the-Global-Muslim-Population.aspx

———. "The Global Religious Landscape: A Report on the Size and Distribution of the World's Major Religious Groups as of 2010." 2012. Available at http://www.pewforum.org/global-religious-landscape.aspx

———. "'Nones' on the Rise: One-in-Five Adults Have No Religious Affiliation." 2013. Available at http://www.pewforum.org/Unaffiliated/nones-on-the-rise.aspx

———. "U.S. Religious Landscape Survey." 2008. Available at http://www.pewforum.org/The-Stronger-Sex----Spiritually-Speaking.aspx

———. "Faith on the Hill: The Religious Composition of the 113th Congress." November 16, 2012. Available at http://www.pewforum.org/Government/Faith-on-the-Hill--The-Religious-Composition-of-the-113th-Congress.aspx

Pryor, John H., Kevin Egan, Laura Palucki Blake, Sylvia Hurtado, Jennifer Berdan, and Matthew Case. "The American Freshman: National Norms Fall 2012 (Expanded Edition)." Cooperative Institutional Research Program at the Higher Education Research Institute at UCLA. 2013. Available at http://www.heri.ucla.edu/monographs/TheAmericanFreshman2012-Expanded.pdf

Pyle, Ralph E. "Trends in Religious Stratification: Have Religious Group Socioeconomic Distinctions Declined in Recent Decades?" *Sociology of Religion.* Vol. 67, No. 1 (Spring 2006):61–79.

Rozell, Mark J., Clyde Wilcox, and John C. Green. "Religious Constituencies and Support for the Christian Right in the 1990s." *Social Science Quarterly.* Vol. 79, No. 4 (December 1998):815–27.

Ryan, Patrick J. "The Roots of Muslim Anger." *America* (November 26, 2001):8–16.

Schmidt, Roger. *Exploring Religion.* Belmont, Calif.: Wadsworth, 1980.

Sheler, Jeffrey L. "Faith in America." *U.S. News & World Report* (May 6, 2002):40–44.

Sherkat, Darren E., and Christopher G. Ellison. "Recent Developments and Current Controversies in the Sociology of Religion." *Annual Review of Sociology.* Vol. 25 (1999):363–94.

Shupe, Anson. *In the Name of All That's Holy: A Theory of Clergy Malfeasance.* Westport, Conn.: Praeger, 1995.

Smith, Tom W. *Jewish Distinctiveness in America: A Statistical Portrait.* American Jewish Committee New York: 2005.

———. "Religious Change around the World." Chicago: NORC/University of Chicago. August 2009. Available at http://publicdata.norc.org:41000/gss/documents/CNRT/CNR%2030%20Religious%20Change%20Around%20the%20World.pdf

———. "Beliefs about God across Time and Countries." Chicago: NORC/University of Chicago. April 18, 2012.

Smith, Christian, and Robert Faris. "Socioeconomic Inequality in the American Religious System: An Update and Assessment." *Journal for the Scientific Study of Religion.* Vol. 44, No. 1 (March 2005):95–104.

Stark, Rodney. *Sociology.* Belmont, Calif.: Wadsworth, 1985.

Stark, Rodney, and William Sims Bainbridge. "Secularization and Cult Formation in the Jazz Age." *Journal for the Scientific Study of Religion.* Vol. 20, No. 4 (December 1981):360–73.

Thomas, Edward J. *The Life of Buddha as Legend and History.* London: Routledge & Kegan Paul, 1975.

Thomma, Steven. "Christian Coalition Demands Action from GOP." *Philadelphia Inquirer* (September 14, 1997):A2.

TROELTSCH, ERNST. *The Social Teaching of the Christian Churches.* New York: Macmillan, 1931.

TUCKER, JAMES. "New Age Religion and the Cult of the Self." *Society.* Vol. 39, No. 2 (February 2002):46–51.

U.S. CENSUS BUREAU. "American Community Survey." 2012. Available at http://www.census.gov/acs/www/

U.S. DEPARTMENT OF LABOR, BUREAU OF LABOR STATISTICS. "Labor Force Statistics from the Current Population Survey." 2012. Available at http://www.bls.gov/cps/

VAN BIEMA, DAVID. "Buddhism in America." *Time* (October 13, 1997):71–81.

———. "A Surge of Teen Spirit." *Time.* Vol. 153, No. 20 (May 31, 1999):58–59.

WALSH, NEALE DONALD. "The Overhaul of Humanity." *Light of Consciousness: Journal of Spiritual Awareness.* Vol. 24, No. 4 (Winter 2012):23–25.

WEBER, MAX. *The Protestant Ethic and the Spirit of Capitalism.* New York: Scribner, 1958; orig. 1904–05.

WEEKS, JOHN R. "The Demography of Islamic Nations." *Population Bulletin.* Vol. 43, No. 4 (December 1988):5–54.

WESSELMAN, HANK. *Visionseeker: Shared Wisdom from the Place of Refuge.* Carlsbad, Calif.: Hay House, 2001.

WILLIAMS, JOHNNY E. "Linking Beliefs to Collective Action: Politicized Religious Beliefs and the Civil Rights Movement." *Sociological Forum.* Vol. 17, No. 2 (June 2002): 203–22.

WILLIAMS, PETER W. *America's Religions: From Their Origins to the Twenty-First Century.* Urbana: University of Illinois Press, 2002.

WILLIAMS, RHYS H., and N. J. DEMERATH III. "Religion and Political Process in an American City." *American Sociological Review.* Vol. 56, No. 4 (August 1991):417–31.

WINSTON, KIMBERLY. "Atheist Jews: Judaism Without God." *Huffington Post.* September 23, 2011. Available at http://www.huffingtonpost.com/2011/09/23/atheist-jews-judaism-without-god_n_978418.html

WORLD VALUES SURVEY. 2010. Available at http://www.wvsevsdb.com/wvs/WVSAnalizeQuestion.jsp

YANG, FENGGANG, and HELEN ROSE FUCHS EBAUGH. "Transformations in New Immigrant Religions and Their Global Implications." *American Sociological Review.* Vol. 66, No. 2 (April 2001):269–88.

Chapter 20

ASTIN, ALEXANDER W., LETICIA OSEGUERA, LINDA J. SAX, and WILLIAM S. KORN. *The American Freshman: Thirty-Five Year Trends.* Los Angeles: UCLA Higher Education Research Institute, 2002.

AUSTER, CAROL J., and MINDY MACRONE. "The Classroom as a Negotiated Social Setting: An Empirical Study of the Effects of Faculty Members' Behavior on Students' Participation." *Teaching Sociology.* Vol. 22, No. 4 (October 1994):289–300.

BARNES, JULIAN E. "Wanted: Readers." *U.S. News & World Report* (September 9, 2002a):44–45.

BOWLES, SAMUEL, and HERBERT GINTIS. *Schooling in Capitalist America: Educational Reform and the Contradictions of Economic Life.* New York: Basic Books, 1976.

BUSHAW, WILLIAM J., and SHANE J. LOPEZ. "Public Education in the United States A Nation Divided." *Phi Delta Kappan.* Vol. 94, No. 1 (September 2012).

CHRISTLE, CHRISTINE A., KRISTINE JOLIVETTE, and C. MICHAEL NELSON. "School Characteristics Related to High School Dropout Rates." *Remedial and Special Education.* Vol. 28, No. 6 (2007):325–39.

CLOUD, JOHN, and JODIE MORSE. "Home Sweet School." *Time* (August 27, 2001):46–54.

COHEN, ADAM. "A First Report Card on Vouchers." *Time* (April 26, 1999):36–38.

COLEMAN, JAMES S. "The Design of Organizations and the Right to Act." *Sociological Forum.* Vol. 8, No. 4 (December 1993):527–46.

COLEMAN, JAMES S., ET AL. *Equality of Educational Opportunity.* Washington, D.C.: U.S. Government Printing Office, 1966.

COLEMAN, JAMES S., and THOMAS HOFFER. *Public and Private High Schools: The Impact of Communities.* New York: Basic Books, 1987.

COLEMAN, JAMES S., THOMAS HOFFER, and SALLY KILGORE. *Public and Private Schools: An Analysis of Public Schools and Beyond.* Washington, D.C.: National Center for Education Statistics, 1981.

COLLEGE BOARD, THE. "Trends in Higher Education: Average Published Undergraduate Charges by Sector, 2012–13." 2013. Available at http://trends.collegeboard.org/college-pricing/figures-tables/average-published-undergraduate-charges-sector-2012-13

COLLINS, RANDALL. *The Credential Society: A Historical Sociology of Education and Stratification.* New York: Academic Press, 1979.

CROUSE, JAMES, and DALE TRUSHEIM. *The Case against the SAT.* Chicago: University of Chicago Press, 1988.

DEPARTMENT FOR CHILDREN, SCHOOLS, AND FAMILIES (UK). "DCSF: Pupil Characteristics and Class Sizes in Maintained Schools in England: January 2012." 2012. Available at http://www.education.gov.uk/rsgateway/DB/SFR/s000925/index.shtml

DILLON, SAM. "Most Public Schools May Miss Targets, Education Secretary Says." *New York Times.* [Online] Available March 9, 2011, at http://www.nytimes.com/2011/03/10/education/10education.html?_r=1

———. "Failure Rate of Schools Overstated, Study Says." *New York Times.* December 15, 2011. [Online] Available at http://www.nytimes.com/2011/12/15/education/education-secretary-overstated-failing-schools-under-no-child-leftbehind-study-says.html

DOWNEY, DOUGLAS B., PAUL T. VON HIPPEL, and BECKETT A. BROH. "Are Schools the Great Equalizer? Cognitive Inequality during the Summer Months and School Year." *American Sociological Review.* Vol. 59, No. 5 (October 2004):613–35.

EUROPEAN UNION, EUROPEAN COMMUNITIES STATISTICAL OFFICE. "Eurostat: Education and Training." 2013. Available at http://epp.eurostat.ec.europa.eu/portal/page/portal/education/introduction

EVELYN, JAMILAH. "Community Colleges Play Too Small a Role in Teacher Education, Report Concludes." *Chronicle of Higher Education Online* (October 24, 2002). [Online] Available October 24, 2002, at http://chronicle.com/daily/2002/10/2002102403n.htm

FONDA, DAREN. "The Male Minority." *Time* (December 11, 2000):58–60.

GALLUP. "No Child Left Behind Rated More Negatively Than Positively." August 20, 2012. Available at http://www.gallup.com/poll/156800/no-child-left-behind-rated-negatively-positively.aspx

GAMORAN, ADAM. "The Variable Effects of High-School Tracking." *American Sociological Review.* Vol. 57, No. 6 (December 1992):812–28.

GARLAND, SARAH. "Study Backs Results of For-Profit Schools." *New York Sun Online.* April 11, 2007. [Online] Available March 31, 2008, at http://www2.nysun.com/article/52198

GIBBS, NANCY. "Darkness Falls." *Time* (April 30, 2007):36–52.

HORN, WADE F., and DOUGLAS TYNAN. "Revamping Special Education." *Public Interest.* No. 144 (Summer 2001):36–53.

ISRAEL, GLENN D., LIONEL J. BEAULIEU, and GLEN HARTLESS. "The Influence of Family and Community Social Capital on Educational Achievement." *Rural Sociology.* Vol. 66, No. 1 (March 2001):43–68.

JACOBSON, JENNIFER. "Professors Are Finding Better Pay and More Freedom at Community Colleges." *Chronicle of Higher Education Online* (2003). [Online] Available March 7, 2003, at http://www.chronicle.com

KARP, DAVID A., and WILLIAM C. YOELS. "The College Classroom: Some Observations on the Meaning of Student Participation." *Sociology and Social Research.* Vol. 60, No. 4 (July 1976):421–39.

KILGORE, SALLY B. "The Organizational Context of Tracking in Schools." *American Sociological Review.* Vol. 56, No. 2 (April 1991):189–203.

KOZOL, JONATHAN. *Savage Inequalities: Children in America's Schools.* New York: Harper Perennial, 1992.

KRAL, BRIGITTA. "The Eyes of Jane Elliott." *Horizon Magazine* (2000). [Online] Available June 8, 2005, at http://www.horizonmag.com/4/jane-elliott.asp

KRISTOFF, NICHOLAS. "Pay Teachers More." *New York Times* (March 13, 2011). [Online] Available at http://www.nytimes.com/2011/03/13/opinion/13kristof.html?ref=education

LOGAN, JOHN R., DEIDRE OAKLEY, and JACOB STOWELL. "School Segregation in Metropolitan Regions, 1970–2000: The Impacts of Policy Choices on Public Education." *American Journal of Sociology.* Vol. 113, No. 6 (May 2008):1611–44.

LOIS, JENNIFER. *Home Is Where the School Is: The Logic of Homeschooling and the Emotional Labor of Mothering.* New York: New York University Press, 2013.

LORD, MARY. "Good Teachers the Newest Imports." *U.S. News & World Report* (April 9, 2001):54.

MEZZACAPPA, DALE. "Only Six Providers Approved for 'Turnaround.'" *Philadephia Public Schools Notebook.* 2010. [Online] Available at http://www.thenotebook.org/blog/102296/six-providers-approved-turnaround

MORSE, JODIE. "A Victory for Vouchers." *Time* (July 8, 2002):32–34.

NATIONAL COMMISSION ON EXCELLENCE IN EDUCATION. *A Nation at Risk.* Washington, D.C.: U.S. Government Printing Office, 1983.

NATIONAL CONFERENCE OF STATE LEGISLATURES. "Parent Trigger Laws in the States." 2013. Available at http://www.ncsl.org/issues-research/educ/state-parent-trigger-laws.aspx

NORC. *General Social Surveys, 1972–2010.* Chicago: National Opinion Research Center. March 2011. [Online] Available at http://www.norc.org/GSS+Website

OBAMA, BARACK. *The Audacity of Hope: Thoughts on Reclaiming the American Dream.* New York: Random House, 2007.

OECD. "Education at a Glance 2012: OECD Indicators." 2012. Available at http://www.oecd.org/edu/eag2012.htm

———. "Stat. Extracts." 2012. Available at http://stats.oecd.org/index.aspx

ORNSTEIN, ALLAN C. "Achievement Gaps in Education." *Society.* Vol. 47, No. 5 (September/October 2010):424–29.

PARKER, KIM, AMANDA LENHART, and KATHLEEN MOORE. "The Digital Revolution and Higher Education." *Pew Research: Social and Demographic Trends* (August 28, 2011). Available at http://www.pewsocialtrends.org/2011/08/28/the-digital-revolution-and-higher-education/

PETERSON, PAUL E., and ELENA LLAUDET. "On the Public-Private School Achievement Debate." Paper prepared for the annual meetings of the American Political Science Association, August 2006. [Online] Available July 15, 2008, at http://www.hks.harvard.edu/pepg/PDF/Papers/PEPG06-02-PetersonLlaudet.pdf

PHILADELPHIA, DESA. "Rookie Teacher, Age 50." *Time* (April 9, 2001):66.

PRYOR, JOHN H., KEVIN EGAN, LAURA PALUCKI BLAKE, SYLVIA HURTADO, JENNIFER BERDAN, and MATTHEW CASE. "The American Freshman: National Norms Fall 2012 (Expanded Edition)." Cooperative Institutional Research Program at the Higher Education Research Institute at UCLA. 2013. Available at http://www.heri.ucla.edu/monographs/TheAmericanFreshman2012-Expanded.pdf

PUTKA, GARY. "SAT to Become a Better Gauge." *Wall Street Journal* (November 1, 1990):B1.

QUAID, LIBBY. "Study: Math Teachers One Chapter ahead of Students." *Yahoo News* (November 25, 2008). [Online] Available November 25, 2008, at http://news.yahoo.com/s/ap/20081125/ap_on_re_us/qualified_teachers

RAVITCH, DIANE. "Obama's War on Schools." *Newsweek.* [Online] Available March 20, 2011, at http://www.newsweek.com/2011/03/20/obama-s-waron-schools.html

RICH, MOTOKO. "Holding States and Schools Accountable." *New York Times* (February 9, 2013). Available at http://www.nytimes.com/2013/02/10/education/debate-over-federal-role-in-public-school-policy.html

RICHARDS, JENNIFER SMITH. "Parents Could Get Club to Fix Bad Schools." *The Columbus Dispatch* (April 4, 2011):A1, A4.

RICHBURG, KEITH B. "School Privatization Plan Sputters." *Washington Post* (June 29, 2008). [Online] Available February 3, 2009, at http://www.boston.com/news/education/k_12/articles/2008/06/29/school_privatization_plan_sputters

RIPLEY, AMANDA. "Can She Save Our Schools?" *Time* (December 8, 2008):36–44.

RUSSELL, DEBORAH. "'Parent Trigger' Laws Give Parents More Power." *The Notebook*. [Online] Available April 1, 2011, at http://www.thenotebook.org/blog/113429/trigger-happy

SCHNEIDER, MARK, MELISSA MARSCHALL, PAUL TESKE, AND CHRISTINE ROCH. "School Choice and Culture Wars in the Classroom: What Different Parents Seek from Education." *Social Science Quarterly*. Vol. 79, No. 3 (September 1998):489–501.

SENNETT, RICHARD, AND JONATHAN COBB. *The Hidden Injuries of Class*. New York: Vintage Books, 1973.

SHEDDEN, DAVID. "School Shootings (1997–2008)." Poynteronline. April 16, 2008. [Online] Available July 15, 2008, at http://www.poynter.org/column.asp?id=49&aid=1025

SIZER, THEODORE R. *Horace's Compromise: The Dilemma of the American High School*. Boston: Houghton Mifflin, 1984.

———. "Private Profit, Public Good?" *Frontline* interview. July 3, 2003. [Online] Available May 20, 2006, at http://www.pbs.org/wgbh/pages/frontline/shows/edison/etc/private.html

STEGER, BRIGITTE. "Sleeping through Class to Success." *Time and Society*. Vol. 15, No. 2–3 (2006):197–214. [Online] Available January 17, 2009, at http://tas.sagepub.com/cgi/content/abstract/15/2-3/197

THORNBURGH, NATHAN. "Dropout Nation." *Time* (April 17, 2006):30–40.

TIMMS AND PIRLS INTERNATIONAL STUDY CENTER. "Trends in International Mathematics and Science Study." 2013. Available at http://timss.bc.edu/timss2011/international-database.html

TOPPO, GREG, AND ANTHONY DEBARROS. "Reality Weighs Down Dreams of College." *USA Today* (February 2, 2005):A1.

UNESCO INSTITUTE OF STATISTICS. "Data Centre." 2010. Available at http://stats.uis.unesco.org/unesco/tableviewer/document.aspx?ReportId=143

———. "Data Centre." 2012. Available at http://stats.uis.unesco.org/unesco/tableviewer/document.aspx?ReportId=143

U.S. CENSUS BUREAU. "Current Population Survey." 2010. [Online] Available at http://www.census.gov/cps

———. "Educational Attainment." 2010. [Online] Available at http://www.census.gov/population/www/socdemo/educ-attn.html

———. "Population Estimates." 2010. [Online] Available at http://www.census.gov/popest/estimates.html

———. *Statistical Abstract of the United States: 2010*. 129th ed. Washington, D.C., 2010. [Online] Available at http://www.census.gov/compendia/statab

———. *Statistical Abstract of the United States: 2011*. 130th ed. Washington, D.C., 2010. [Online] Available at http://www.census.gov/statab/www

———. "Current Population Survey." 2012. Available at http://www.census.gov/cps

———. "Educational Attainment." 2012. Available at http://www.census.gov/hhes/socdemo/education/data/cps/2012/tables.html

———. "Population Estimates." 2012. Available at http://www.census.gov/popest/data/index.html

U.S. DEPARTMENT OF EDUCATION, NATIONAL CENTER FOR EDUCATIONAL STATISTICS. "National Assessment of Educational Progress (Nation's Report Card)." 2010, 2011. Available at http://nces.ed.gov/nationsreportcard/naepdata/

———. "Private School Universe Survey (PSS)." 2011. Available at http://nces.ed.gov/surveys/pss/

———. "The Condition of Education." May 2012. Available at http://nces.ed.gov/programs/coe/

———. "U.S. Digest of Education Statistics 2012." 2012. Available at http://nces.ed.gov/programs/digest/2012menu_tables.asp

———. "Common Core of Data (CCD)." February 2013. Available at http://nces.ed.gov/ccd/

———. "National Household Education Surveys (NHES)." February 2013. Available at http://nces.ed.gov/nhes/

———. "Projections of Education Statistics to 2021." 2013. Available at http://nces.ed.gov/programs/projections/projections2021/index.asp

U.S. DEPARTMENT OF LABOR, OCCUPATIONAL EMPLOYMENT STATISTICS (OES). "Occupational Employment and Wages." May 2012. Available at http://www.bls.gov/oes/current/oes252021.htm

WALLIS, CLAUDIA. "How to Make Great Teachers." *Time* (February 14, 2008). [Online] Available March 1, 2008, at http://www.time.com/time/nation/article/0,8599,1713174,00.html

WALLIS, CLAUDIA, AND SONJA STEPTOE. "How to Fix No Child Left Behind." *Time*. Vol. 169, No. 23 (June 4, 2007):34–41.

WILL, GEORGE F. "Spoiling for a Fight in Ohio." *The Berkshire Eagle* (February 6, 2011):A6.

WORLD BANK. "World DataBank: Education Statistics." 2013. Available at http://data.worldbank.org/data-catalog/ed-stats

———. "World DataBank: World Development Indicators." 2013. Available at http://data.worldbank.org/data-catalog/world-development-indicators

Chapter 21

AMERICAN ASSOCIATION OF COLLEGES OF NURSING (AACN). "Fact Sheet: Nursing Shortage." 2012. Available at http://www.aacn.nche.edu/media-relations/fact-sheets/nursing-shortage

AMERICAN COLLEGE HEALTH ASSOCIATION. "National College Health Assessment Reference Group Data Report." Baltimore: American College Health Association. 2012. Available at http://www.acha-ncha.org/pubs_rpts.html

AMERICAN MEDICAL GROUP ASSOCIATION. "Total Compensation." 2012. Available at http://www.amga.org/Research/2011ExecSummary.pdf

ARIAS, ELIZABETH. "United States Life Tables, 2008." Revised using intercensal populations, 2012. Available at http://www.cdc.gov/nchs/data/dvs/Revised_Tables_2008.pdf

ASHFORD, LORI S. "Young Women in Sub-Saharan Africa Face a High Risk of HIV Infection." *Population Today*. Vol. 30, No. 2 (February/March 2002):3, 6.

ASTIN, ALEXANDER W., LETICIA OSEGUERA, LINDA J. SAX, AND WILLIAM S. KORN. *The American Freshman: Thirty-Five Year Trends*. Los Angeles: UCLA Higher Education Research Institute, 2002.

BECKER, ANNE E. "The Association of Television Exposure with Disordered Eating Among Ethnic Fijian Adolescent Girls." Paper presented at the annual meeting of the American Psychiatric Association, Washington, D.C., May 19, 1999.

———. "New Global Perspectives on Eating Disorders." *Culture, Medicine, and Psychiatry*. Vol. 28, No. 4 (December 2004):434–37.

BELLANDI, DEANNA. "Study Finds Meal Portion Sizes Growing." [Online] Available January 3, 2003, at http://www.yahoo.com

BENNETT, JESSICA. "No More Junk." *Newsweek* (April 18, 2006). [Online] Available April 25, 2007, at http://www.msnbc.msn.com/id/12359367/site/newsweek

BIOMED CENTRAL. Data cited in *Time*. (July 9, 2012):11.

BLOOM, D. E., ET AL. *The Global Economic Burden of Non-Communicable Diseases*. Geneva: World Economic Forum, September 2011.

BRINK, SUSAN. "Living on the Edge." *U.S. News & World Report* (October 14, 2002):58–64.

———. "Economic Facts about U.S. Tobacco Use and Tobacco Production." 2008. Available at http://www.cdc.gov/tobacco/data_statistics/fact_sheets/economics/econ_facts/index.htm

———. "Smoking-Attributable Mortality, Years of Potential Life Lost, and Productivity Losses—United States, 2000–2004." *Morbidity and Mortality Weekly Report (MMWR)*. Vol. 57, No. 45 (November 14, 2008). Available at http://www.cdc.gov/tobacco/data_statistics/mmwrs/byyear/2008/mm5745a3/highlights.htm

———. "Smoking and Tobacco Use." 2010. Available at http://www.cdc.gov/tobacco/index.htm

———. "CDC Health Disparities and Inequalities Report—United States, 2011." *Morbidity and Mortality Weekly Report (MMWR)*. Vol. 60, Suppl. (2011). Available at http://www.cdc.gov/mmwr/pdf/other/su6001.pdf

CENTERS FOR DISEASE CONTROL AND PREVENTION. "Behavioral Risk Factor Surveillance System: Mapping." 2012. Available at http://www.cdc.gov/brfss/index.htm

———. "Behavioral Risk Factor Surveillance System: Prevalence and Trends Data." 2012. Available at http://apps.nccd.cdc.gov/BRFSS/

———. "Current Cigarette Smoking Among Adults—United States, 2011." *Morbidity and Mortality Weekly Report (MMWR)*. Vol. 61, No. 44 (November 9, 2012):889–94. Available at http://www.cdc.gov/mmwr/preview/mmwrhtml/mm6144a2.htm?s_cid=%20mm6144a2.htm_w

———. "Current Tobacco Use Among Middle and High School Students—United States, 2011." *Morbidity and Mortality Weekly Report (MMWR)*. Vol. 61, No. 31 (August 10, 2012):581–85. Available at http://www.cdc.gov/mmwr/preview/mmwrhtml/mm6131a1.htm?s_cid=mm6131a1_w

———. "Health, United States, 2011 with Chartbook." 2012. Available at http://www.cdc.gov/nchs/hus.htm

———. "Sexually Transmitted Diseases." 2012. Available at http://www.cdc.gov/std/stats11/toc.htm

———. "Diagnoses of HIV Infection in the United States and Dependent Areas, 2011." 2013. Available at http://www.cdc.gov/hiv/library/reports/surveillance/2011/surveillance_Report_vol_23.html

———. "FastStats." 2013. Available at http://www.cdc.gov/nchs/fastats/bodymeas.htm

———. "HIV/AIDS Surveillance Report." 2013. Available at http://www.cdc.gov/hiv/topics/surveillance/

———. "Overweight and Obesity." 2013. Available at http://www.cdc.gov/obesity/index.html

———. "State Tobacco Activities Tracking and Evaluation (STATE) System." 2012. Available at http://apps.nccd.cdc.gov/StateSystem/Default/Default.aspx

CENTERS FOR DISEASE CONTROL AND PREVENTION, NATIONAL CENTER FOR HEALTH STATISTICS. "Summary Health Statistics for the U.S. Population: National Health Interview Survey, 2011." *Vital and Health Statistics*, Series 10, No. 256. 2012. Available at http://www.cdc.gov/nchs/nhis.htm

———. "Health Data Interactive." 2013. Available at www.cdc.gov/nchs/hdi.htm

COCKERHAM, WILLIAM C. *Medical Sociology*, 2nd ed. Englewood Cliffs, N.J.: Prentice Hall, 1986:24.

COWLEY, GEOFFREY. "The Prescription That Kills." *Newsweek* (July 17, 1995):54.

DUBOS, RENÉ. *Man Adapting*. Enlarged ed. New Haven, Conn.: Yale University Press, 1980.

EHRENREICH, BARBARA. *Nickel and Dimed: On (Not) Getting By in America*. New York: Holt, 2001.

ELSON, JEAN. *Am I Still a Woman? Hysterectomy and Gender Identity*. Philadelphia: Temple University Press, 2004.

EMERSON, JOAN P. "Behavior in Private Places: Sustaining Definitions of Reality in Gynecological Examinations." In H. P. Dreitzel, ed., *Recent Sociology*. Vol. 2. New York: Collier, 1970:74–97.

ERIKSEN, MICHAEL, JUDITH MACKAY, AND HANA ROSS. *The Tobacco Atlas*, 4th ed. Atlanta, Ga.: American Cancer Society; New York: World Lung Foundation. 2012. Available at http://www.TobaccoAtlas.org

FALLON, A. E., AND P. ROZIN. "Sex Differences in Perception of Desirable Body Shape." *Journal of Abnormal Psychology*. Vol. 94, No. 1 (1985):100–105.

FERRARO, KENNETH F., AND JESSICA A. KELLEY-MOORE. "Cumulative Disadvantage and Health: Long-Term Consequences of Obesity?" *American Sociological Review*. Vol. 68, No. 5 (October 2003):707–29.

Friedman, Meyer, and Ray H. Rosenman. *Type A Behavior and Your Heart.* New York: Fawcett Crest, 1974.

Gillepsie, Mark. "Trends Show Bathing and Exercise Up, TV Watching Down." January 2000. [Online] Available April 9, 2006, at http://www.gallup.com

Gillon, Raanan. "Euthanasia in the Netherlands: Down the Slippery Slope?" *Journal of Medical Ethics.* Vol. 25, No. 1 (February 1999):3–4.

Golden, Frederic, and Michael D. Lemonick. "The Race Is Over." *Time* (July 3, 2000):18–23.

Gordon, James S. "The Paradigm of Holistic Medicine." In Arthur C. Hastings et al., eds., *Health for the Whole Person: The Complete Guide to Holistic Medicine.* Boulder, Colo.: Westview Press, 1980:3–27.

Hamrick, Michael H., David J. Anspaugh, and Gene Ezell. *Health.* Columbus, Ohio: Merrill, 1986.

Hellmich, Nanci. "Environment, Economics Partly to Blame." *USA Today* (October 9, 2002):9D.

Horton, Richard. "GBD 2010: Understanding Disease, Injury, and Risk." *The Lancet,* Vol. 380, No. 9859 (December 15, 2012):2053–54. Available at http://www.thelancet.com/journals/lancet/article/PIIS0140-6736(12)62133-3/fulltext

Hoyert, Donna, and Jiaquan Xu. "Deaths: Preliminary Data for 2011." National Vital Statistics Reports. Vol. 61, No. 6. Hyattsville, Md.: National Center for Health Statistics. October 10, 2012. Available at http://www.cdc.gov/nchs/data/nvsr/nvsr61/nvsr61_06.pdf

Jones, D. Gareth. "Brain Death." *Journal of Medical Ethics.* Vol. 24, No. 4 (August 1998):237–43.

Kain, Edward L. "A Note on the Integration of AIDS into the Sociology of Human Sexuality." *Teaching Sociology.* Vol. 15, No. 4 (July 1987):320–23.

Kaptchuk, Ted. "The Holistic Logic of Chinese Medicine." In Shepard Bliss et al., eds. Berkeley Holistic Health Center, *The New Holistic Health Handbook: Living Well in a New Age.* Lexington, Mass.: Greene Press, 1985:41.

The Lancet. "Wealth But Not Health in the USA." Vol. 381, No. 9862 (January 19, 2013). Available at http://www.thelancet.com/journals/lancet/article/PIIS0140-6736(13)60069-0/fulltext

Landsberg, Mitchell. "Health Disaster Brings Early Death in Russia." *Washington Times* (March 15, 1998):A8.

Laumann, Edward O., John H. Gagnon, Robert T. Michael, and Stuart Michaels. *The Social Organization of Sexuality: Sexual Practices in the United States.* Chicago: University of Chicago Press, 1994.

Leavitt, Judith Walzer. "Women and Health in America: An Overview." In Judith Walzer Leavitt, ed., *Women and Health in America.* Madison: University of Wisconsin Press, 1984:3–7.

Leff, Lisa. "California Gay Marriage Vote Still Undecided." November 5, 2008. [Online] Available November 5, 2008, at http://news.yahoo.com/s/ap/20081105/ap_on_el_ge/ballot_measures

Levine, Michael P. "Reducing Hostility Can Prevent Heart Disease." *Mount Vernon* (Ohio) *News* (August 7, 1990):4A.

Macionis, John J., and Linda Gerber. *Sociology.* 6th Canadian ed. Scarborough, Ontario: Prentice Hall Allyn & Bacon Canada, 2008.

Marquez, Laura. "Nursing Shortage: How It May Affect You." *ABC News.* January 21, 2006. [Online] Available April 1, 2008, at http://abcnews.go.com/WNT/Health/story?id=1529546

Mason, David S. "Fairness Matters: Equity and the Transition to Democracy." *World Policy Journal.* Vol. 20, No. 4 (Winter 2003). [Online] Available February 21, 2008, at http://www.worldpolicy.org/journal/articles/wpj03-4/mason.html

McNeil, Donald G., Jr. "Broad Racial Disparities Seen in Americans' Ills." *New York Times.* [Online] Available January 13, 2011, at http://www.nytimes.com/2011/01/14/health/14cdc.html?_r=2

MCOL. "Current National Managed Care Enrollment." 2013. Available at http://www.mcol.com/current_enrollment

Moss, Brian G., and William H. Yeaton. "Young Children's Weight Trajectories and Associated Risk Factors: Results from the Early Childhood Longitudinal Study—Birth Cohort." *American Journal of Health Promotion.* Vol. 25, No. 3 (January–February 2010):190–98.

Murray, Christopher, et al. "Disability-Adjusted Life Years (DALYs) for 291 Diseases and Injuries in 21 Regions, 1990–2010: A Systematic Analysis for the Global Burden of Disease Study 2010." *The Lancet.* Vol. 380, No. 9859 (December 15, 2012):2197–223. Available at http://www.thelancet.com/journals/lancet/article/PIIS0140-6736(12)61689-4/fulltext

Myers, David G. *The American Paradox: Spiritual Hunger in an Age of Plenty.* New Haven, Conn.: Yale University Press, 2000.

Myers, Sheila, and Harold G. Grasmick. "The Social Rights and Responsibilities of Pregnant Women: An Application of Parsons' Sick Role Model." Paper presented at the Southwestern Sociological Association, Little Rock, Ark., March 1989.

Neporent, Liz. "Stigma against Fat People, the Last Acceptable Prejudice, Studies Find." *ABC News.* January 22, 2013. Available at http://abcnews.go.com/Health/stigma-obese-acceptable-prejudice/story?id=18276788

Niesse, Mark. "Some Bars Pan Hawaii's Tough Smoking Ban." [Online] Available February 19, 2007, at http://news.yahoo.com

NORC. *General Social Surveys, 1972–2010.* Chicago: National Opinion Research Center. March 2011. [Online] Available at http://www.norc.org/GSS+Website

Nuland, Sherwin B. "The Hazards of Hospitalization." *Wall Street Journal* (December 2, 1999):A22.

OECD. "Obesity Update 2012." 2012. Available at http://www.oecd.org/health/49716427.pdf

Pampel, Fred C. "Socioeconomic Distinction, Cultural Tastes, and Cigarette Smoking." *Social Science Quarterly.* Vol. 87, No. 1 (March 2006):19–35.

Parsons, Talcott. *The Social System.* New York: Free Press, 1951.

Patterson, Elissa F. "The Philosophy and Physics of Holistic Health Care: Spiritual Healing as a Workable Interpretation." *Journal of Advanced Nursing.* Vol. 27, No. 2 (February 1998):287–93.

Pear, Robert, and Erik Eckholm. "When Healers Are Entrepreneurs: A Debate over Costs and Ethics." *New York Times* (June 2, 1991):1, 17.

Pinhey, Thomas K., Donald H. Rubinstein, and Richard S. Colfax. "Overweight and Happiness: The Reflected Self-Appraisal Hypothesis Reconsidered." *Social Science Quarterly.* Vol. 78, No. 3 (September 1997):747–55.

Population Reference Bureau. "Datafinder." 2012. Available at http://www.prb.org/DataFinder.aspx

Pryor, John H., Kevin Egan, Laura Palucki Blake, Sylvia Hurtado, Jennifer Berdan, and Matthew Case. "The American Freshman: National Norms Fall 2012 (Expanded Edition)." Cooperative Institutional Research Program at the Higher Education Research Institute at UCLA. 2013. Available at http://www.heri.ucla.edu/monographs/TheAmericanFreshman2012-Expanded.pdf

Roehrig, James P., and Carmen P. McLean. "A Comparison of Stigma Toward Eating Disorders Versus Depression." *International Journal of Eating Disorders.* Vol. 43, No. 7 (November 2010):671–74.

Rosenthal, Elizabeth. "Canada's National Health Plan Gives Care to All, with Limits." *New York Times* (April 30, 1991):A1, A16.

Schnittker, Jason, Bernice A. Pescosolido, and Thomas W. Croghan. "Are African Americans Really Less Willing to Use Health Care?" *Social Problems.* Vol. 52, No. 2 (May 2005):255–71.

Sobel, Rachel K. "Herpes Tests Give Answers You Might Need to Know." *U.S. News & World Report* (June 18, 2001):53.

Stockdale, Charles B., Douglas A. McIntyre, and Michael B. Sauter. "10 States with the Deadliest Eating Habits." *24/7 Wall Street.* [Online] Available February 9, 2011, at http://finance.yahoo.com/family-home/article/112083/10-states-with-the-deadliest-eating-habits

Tavernise, Sabrina. "Life Expectancy Rises Around the World, Study Finds." *New York Times* (December 13, 2012). Available at http://www.nytimes.com/2012/12/14/health/worlds-population-living-longer-new-report-suggests.html?ref=childrenshealth&_r=1&

Thompson, Dick. "Gene Maverick." *Time* (January 11, 1999):54–55.

UNAIDS. "2012 Report on the Global AIDS Epidemic." 2012. Available at http://www.unaids.org/en/media/unaids/contentassets/documents/epidemiology/2012/gr2012/20121120_UNAIDS_Global_Report_2012_with_annexes_en.pdf

U.S. Census Bureau. "Current Population Survey." 2012. Available at http://www.census.gov/cps/

U.S. Department of Health and Human Services. "National Health Expenditure Data." 2012. Available at http://www.cms.gov/Research-Statistics-Data-and-Systems/Statistics-Trends-and-Reports/NationalHealthExpendData/NHE-Fact-Sheet.html

U.S. Department of Health and Human Services, Community Health. "Community Health Status Indicators." 2009. Available at http://wwwn.cdc.gov/CommunityHealth/HomePage.aspx

U.S. Department of Health and Human Services, Health Resources and Services Administration. "The Registered Nurse Population 2008 Survey." 2010. Available at http://bhpr.hrsa.gov/healthworkforce/rnsurvey/initialfindings2008.pdf

U.S. Department of Health and Human Services, National Institute of Mental Health. "Eating Disorders." 2012. Available at http://www.nimh.nih.gov/health/publications/eating-disorders/complete-publication.shtml

———. "Statistics." 2012. Available at http://www.nimh.nih.gov/statistics/index.shtml

U.S. Department of Health and Human Services, Substance Abuse and Mental Health Services Administration (SAMHSA). "Results from the 2011 National Survey on Drug Use and Health: National Findings." 2012. Available at http://www.samhsa.gov/data/NSDUH/2011SummNatFindDetTables/

U.S. Department of Labor, Bureau of Labor Statistics. "Census of Fatal Occupational Injuries (CFOI)." 2012. Available at http://stats.bls.gov/iif/oshcfoi1.htm

———. "Labor Force Statistics from the Current Population Survey." 2012. Available at http://www.bls.gov/cps/

U.S. Department of Labor, Mine Safety and Health Administration. "Mine Safety and Health at a Glance." 2012. Available at http://www.msha.gov/MSHAINFO/FactSheets/MSHAFCT10.HTM

U.S. Department of Labor, Occupational Employment Statistics (OES). "May 2012 National Occupational Employment and Wage Estimates, United States." 2012. Available at http://www.bls.gov/oes/current/oes_nat.htm#29-0000

Wall, Thomas F. *Medical Ethics: Basic Moral Issues.* Washington, D.C.: University Press of America, 1980.

Wells, Hodan Farah, and Jean C. Buzby. *Dietary Assessment of Major Trends in U.S. Food Consumption, 1970–2005.* Economic Information Bulletin No. (EIB 33).Washington, D.C.: U.S. Department of Agriculture, March 2008.

Witt, Louise. "Why We're Losing the War against Obesity." *American Demographics.* Vol. 25, No. 10 (January 2004):27–31.

World Bank. "World DataBank: Health, Nutrition, and Population Statistics." 2013. Available at http://data.worldbank.org/data-catalog/health-nutrition-and-population-statistics

World Health Organization. *Constitution of the World Health Organization.* New York: World Health Organization Interim Commission, 1946.

———. "Russian Federation." 2007. [Online] Available July 9, 2007, at http://www.who.int/countries/rus/en

———. "Highlights on Health in the Russian Federation." 2011. Available at http://www.euro.who.int/en/where-we-work/member-states/russian-federation/publications/highlights-on-health-in-the-russian-federation

——. "Progress Report 2011: Global HIV/AIDS Response." November 2011. Available at http://www.who.int/hiv/pub/progress_report2011/en/index.html

——. "Tobacco." 2013. Available at http://www.who.int/mediacentre/factsheets/fs339/en/index.html

——. "WHO Report on the Global Tobacco Epidemic, 2011." 2011. Available at http://www.who.int/tobacco/global_report/2011/en/index.html

YIN, SANDRA. "Wanted: One Million Nurses." *American Demographics*. Vol. 24, No. 8 (September 2002):63–65.

ZUCKERMAN, MORTIMER B. "The Russian Conundrum." *U.S. News & World Report* (March 13, 2006):64.

Chapter 22

ADAM, DAVID. "World CO₂ Levels at Record High, Scientists Warn." *Guardian* (May 12, 2008). [Online] Available July 16, 2008, at http://www.guardian.co.uk/environment/2008/may/12/climatechange.carbonemissions

AXINN, WILLIAM G., AND JENNIFER S. BARBER. "Mass Education and Fertility Transition." *American Sociological Review*. Vol. 66, No. 4 (August 2001):481–505.

BAIR, JULENE. "Running Dry on the Great Plains." *New York Times*. November 30, 2011. Available at http://www.nytimes.com/2011/12/01/opinion/polluting-the-ogallala-aquifer.html?_r=0

BAOCHANG, GU, WANG FENG, GUO ZHIGANG, AND ERLI ZHANG. "China's Local and National Fertility Policies at the End of the Twentieth Century." *Population and Development Review*. Vol. 33, No. 1 (2007):129–48.

BERRY, BRIAN L., AND PHILIP H. REES. "The Factorial Ecology of Calcutta." *American Journal of Sociology*. Vol. 74, No. 5 (March 1969):445–49.

BOHON, STEPHANIE A., AND CRAIG R. HUMPHREY. "Courting LULUs: Characteristic of Suitor and Objector Communities." *Rural Sociology*. Vol. 65, No. 3 (September 2000):376–95.

BORMANN, F. HERBERT. "The Global Environmental Deficit." *BioScience*. Vol. 40, No. 2 (1990):74.

BROCKERHOFF, MARTIN P. "An Urbanizing World." *Population Bulletin*. Vol. 55, No. 3 (September 2000):1–44.

BROWN, LESTER R. "Reassessing the Earth's Population." *Society*. Vol. 32, No. 4 (May/June 1995):7–10.

BROWN, LESTER R., ET AL., EDS. *State of the World 1993: A Worldwatch Institute Report on Progress toward a Sustainable Society*. New York: Norton, 1993.

CAPELLA, PETER. "UN Alarmed at Huge Decline in Bee Numbers." Yahoo.com [Online] Available March 10, 2011, at http://news.yahoo.com/s/afp/20110310/sc_afp/unenvironmentspeciesanimalfarmbee_20110310124832

CASTELLS, MANUEL. *The Urban Question*. Cambridge, Mass.: MIT Press, 1977.

——. *The City and the Grass Roots*. Berkeley: University of California Press, 1983.

CHANDLER, TERTIUS, AND GERALD FOX. *3000 Years of Urban History*. New York: Academic Press, 1974.

CHANG, ALICIA. "Study: Cleaner Air Adds 5 Months to U.S. Life Span." *Yahoo News* (January 21, 2009). [Online] Available April 10, 2009, at http://www.newsvine.com/_news/2009/01/21/2339450-study-cleaner-air-adds-5-months-to-us-life-span

COMMISSION FOR RACIAL JUSTICE. *CRJ Reporter*. New York: United Church of Christ, 1994.

CONNETT, PAUL H. "The Disposable Society." In F. Herbert Bormann and Stephen R. Kellert, eds., *Ecology, Economics, and Ethics: The Broken Circle*. New Haven, Conn.: Yale University Press, 1991:99–122.

EL NASSER, HAYA, AND PAUL OVERBERG. "U.S. Growth Slows, Still Envied." *USA Today* (January 7–9, 2011):1A.

GALBRAITH, KATE. "Push Comes to Shove Over Water Restrictions." *New York Times* (March 17, 2012). Available at http://www.nytimes.com/2012/03/18/us/in-west-texas-push-comes-to-shove-over-water-restrictions.html?pagewanted=all

GALLUP. "Fewer Americans, Europeans View Global Warming as a Threat." April 20, 2011. Available at http://www.gallup.com/poll/147203/Fewer-Americans-Europeans-View-Global-Warming-Threat.aspx#2

GANS, HERBERT J. *People and Plans: Essays on Urban Problems and Solutions*. New York: Basic Books, 1968.

GARREAU, JOEL. *Edge City*. New York: Doubleday, 1991.

GILLIS, JUSTIN. "Sea-Level Science." *Conservation*. Vol. 12, No. 1 (Spring 2011):44–45.

GOLDBERGER, PAUL. Lecture delivered at Kenyon College, Gambier, Ohio, September 22, 2002.

GORE, AL. *An Inconvenient Truth: The Crisis of Global Warming*. Emmaus, Pa.: Rodale Books, 2006.

GOTTMANN, JEAN. *Megalopolis*. New York: Twentieth Century Fund, 1961.

HAMILTON, BRADY E., JOYCE A. MARTIN, AND STEPHANIE J. VENTURA. "Births: Preliminary Data for 2011." National Vital Statistics Reports. Vol. 61, No. 5 (2012). Available at http://www.cdc.gov/nchs/data/nvsr/nvsr61/nvsr61_05.pdf

HARRIS, CHAUNCY D., AND EDWARD L. ULLMAN. "The Nature of Cities." *Annals of the American Academy of Political and Social Sciences*. Vol. 242, No. 1 (November 1945):7–17.

HESKETH, THERESE, LI LU, AND ZHUWEI XING. "The Effects of China's One-Child Family Policy after 25 Years." *New England Journal of Medicine*. Vol. 353, No. 11 (November 2005):1171–76.

HORTON, HAYWARD DERRICK. "Critical Demography: The Paradigm of the Future?" *Sociological Forum*. Vol. 14, No. 3 (September 1999):363–67.

HOYERT, DONNA, AND JIAQUAN XU. "Deaths: Preliminary Data for 2011." National Vital Statistics Reports. Vol. 61, No. 6. Hyattsville, Md.: National Center for Health Statistics. October 10, 2012. Available at http://www.cdc.gov/nchs/data/nvsr/nvsr61/nvsr61_06.pdf

HOYT, HOMER. *The Structure and Growth of Residential Neighborhoods in American Cities*. Washington, D.C.: Federal Housing Administration, 1939.

INTERNATIONAL PANEL ON CLIMATE CHANGE. *Climate Change, 2007*. New York: United Nations, 2007.

——. "The Rural Rebound." *Population Reference Bureau Reports on America*. Vol. 1, No. 3 (September 1999). [Online] Available October 9, 2004, at http://www.prb.org/Content/NavigationMenu/PRB/AboutPRB/Reports_on_America/ReportonAmericaRuralRebound.pdf

JOHNSON, KENNETH M. "Rural Demographic Change in the New Century: Slower Growth, Increased Diversity." Carsey Institute, University of New Hampshire. Winter 2012. Available at http://www.carseyinstitute.unh.edu/publications/IB-Johnson-Rural-Demographic-Trends.pdf

JOHNSON, KENNETH M., AND GLENN V. FUGUITT. "Continuity and Change in Rural Migration Patterns, 1950–1995." *Rural Sociology*. Vol. 65, No. 1 (March 2000):27–49.

JOHNSTON, R. J. "Residential Area Characteristics." In D. T. Herbert and R. J. Johnston, eds., *Social Areas in Cities. Vol. 1: Spatial Processes and Form*. New York: Wiley, 1976:193–235.

JONES, ANDREW E. G., AND DAVID WILSON. *The Urban Growth Machine: Critical Perspectives*. Albany: State University of New York Press, 1999.

KEESING, FELICIA, ET AL. "Impacts of Biodiversity on the Emergence and Transmission of Infectious Disease." *Nature: International Weekly Journal of Science*. Vol. 468, No. 7324. [Online] Available December 2, 2010, at http://www.nature.com/nature/journal/v468/n7324/full/nature09575.html

KELLERT, STEPHEN R., AND F. HERBERT BORMANN. "Closing the Circle: Weaving Strands among Ecology, Economics, and Ethics." In F. Herbert Bormann and Stephen R. Kellert, eds., *Ecology, Economics, and Ethics: The Broken Circle*. New Haven, Conn.: Yale University Press, 1991:205–10.

KERR, RICHARD A. "Climate Models Heat Up." *Science Now* (January 26, 2005):1–3.

KLINENBERG, ERIC. "Adaptation." *The New Yorker* (January 7, 2013):32–37.

KUUMBA, M. BAHATI. "A Cross-Cultural Race/Class/Gender Critique of Contemporary Population Policy: The Impact of Globalization." *Sociological Forum*. Vol. 14, No. 3 (March 1999):447–63.

LEFEBVRE, HENRI. *The Production of Space*. Oxford: Blackwell, 1991.

LINDSTROM, BONNIE. "Chicago's Post-Industrial Suburbs." *Sociological Focus*. Vol. 28, No. 4 (October 1995):399–412.

MACIONIS, JOHN J., AND VINCENT N. PARRILLO. *Cities and Urban Life*. 5th ed. Upper Saddle River, N.J.: Pearson Prentice Hall, 2010.

——. *Cities and Urban Life*. 6th ed. Upper Saddle River, N.J.: Pearson, 2013.

MALTHUS, THOMAS ROBERT. *First Essay on Population, 1798*. London: Macmillan, 1926; orig. 1798.

MARX, KARL. *Capital*. Friedrich Engels, ed. New York: International Publishers, 1967; orig. 1867.

McGURN, WILLIAM. "The Not So Dismal Science: Humanitarians v. Economists." *Imprimis*. Vol. 40, No. 5 (March 2011):1–7.

McKIBBEN, BILL. *Deep Economy: The Wealth of Communities and the Durable Future*. New York: Times Books, 2007.

McMAHON, BUCKY. "Vanishing Point." *Conservation*. Vol. 12, No. 1 (Spring 2011):40–48.

MEADOWS, DONELLA H., DENNIS L. MEADOWS, JORGAN RANDERS, AND WILLIAM W. BEHRENS III. *The Limits to Growth: A Report on the Club of Rome's Project on the Predicament of Mankind*. New York: Universe, 1972.

MILBRATH, LESTER W. *Envisioning a Sustainable Society: Learning Our Way Out*. Albany: State University of New York Press, 1989.

MOLOTCH, HARVEY. "The City as a Growth Machine." *American Journal of Sociology*. Vol. 82, No. 2 (September 1976):309–33.

MUMFORD, LEWIS. *The City in History: Its Origins, Its Transformations, and Its Prospects*. New York: Harcourt, Brace & World, 1961.

MYERS, DAVID G. *The American Paradox: Spiritual Hunger in an Age of Plenty*. New Haven, Conn.: Yale University Press, 2000.

MYERS, NORMAN. "Humanity's Growth." In Sir Edmund Hillary, ed., *Ecology 2000: The Changing Face of the Earth*. New York: Beaufort Books, 1984a:16–35.

——. "The Mega-Extinction of Animals and Plants." In Sir edmund hillary, ed., *Ecology 2000: The Changing Face of the Earth*. New York: Beaufort Books, 1984b:82–107.

PARK, ROBERT E. *Race and Culture*. Glencoe, Ill.: Free Press, 1950.

PEDERSON, DANIEL, VERN E. SMITH, AND JERRY ADLER. "Sprawling, Sprawling …" *Newsweek* (July 19, 1999):23–27.

POPULATION ACTION INTERNATIONAL. *People in the Balance: Population and Resources at the Turn of the Millennium*. Washington, D.C.: Population Action International, 2000.

POPULATION REFERENCE BUREAU. "Datafinder." 2011, 2012. Available at http://www.prb.org/DataFinder.aspx

——. "World Population Data Sheet." 2012. Available at http://www.prb.org/pdf12/2012-population-data-sheet_eng.pdf

REED, BRIAN. "Could People from Kiribati Be 'Climate Change Refugees'?" *The Two-Way*. National Public Radio news blog. [Online] Available February 17, 2011, at http://www.npr.org/templates/archives/archive.php?thingId=131216964

RIDLEY, MATT. "Cooling Down the Fears of Climate Change." *Wall Street Journal*. (December 19, 2012):A19.

ROMERO, FRANCINE SANDERS, AND ADRIAN LISERIO. "Saving Open Spaces: Determinants of 1998 and 1999 'Antisprawl' Ballot Measures." *Social Science Quarterly*. Vol. 83, No. 1 (March 2002):341–52.

ROUDI-FAHIMI, FARZANEH, AND MARYMEDERIOS KENT. "Challenges and Opportunities: The Population of the Middle East and North Africa." *Population Bulletin*. Vol. 65, No. 2 (June 2007). Washington, D.C.: Population Reference Bureau, 2007.

SCANLON, STEPHAN J. "Food Availability and Access in Less Industrialized Societies: A Test and Interpretation of Neo-Malthusian and Technoecological Theories." *Sociological Forum*. Vol. 16, No. 2 (June 2001):231–62.

Schlesinger, Arthur M., Jr. "The City in American Civilization." In A. B. Callow Jr., ed., *American Urban History*. New York: Oxford University Press, 1969:25–41.

Schmitt, Eric. "Whites in Minority in Largest Cities, the Census Shows." *New York Times* (April 30, 2001):A1, A12.

Shevky, Eshref, and Wendell Bell. *Social Area Analysis*. Stanford, Calif.: Stanford University Press, 1955.

Simon, Julian. *The Ultimate Resource*. Princeton, N.J.: Princeton University Press, 1981.

———. "More People, Greater Wealth, More Resources, Healthier Environment." In Theodore D. Goldfarb, ed., *Taking Sides: Clashing Views on Controversial Environmental Issues*. 6th ed. Guilford, Conn.: Dushkin, 1995.

Singer, S. Fred. "Global Warming: Man-Made or Natural?" *Imprimis*. Vol. 36, No. 8 (2007):1–5.

Smail, J. Kenneth. "Let's *Reduce* Global Population!" In John J. Macionis and Nijole V. Benokraitis, eds., *Seeing Ourselves: Classic, Contemporary, and Cross-Cultural Readings in Sociology*. 7th ed. Upper Saddle River, N.J.: Prentice Hall, 2007.

Solomon, Steven. *Water: The Epic Struggle for Wealth, Power, and Civilization*. New York: Harper Collins, 2010.

Sullivan, Will. "Road Warriors." *U.S. News & World Report* (May 7, 2007):42–49.

Tönnies, Ferdinand. *Community and Society (Gemeinschaft und Gesellschaft)*. New York: Harper & Row, 1963; orig. 1887.

United Nations Development Programme. "International Human Development Indicators." 2012. Available at http://hdrstats.undp.org/en/indicators/default.html

United Nations Environment Programme (UNEP). *Vital Water Graphics—An Overview of the State of the World's Fresh and Marine Waters*. 2nd ed. Nairobi, Kenya, 2008. [Online] Available at http://www.unep.org/dewa/vitalwater/index.html

———. "Vital Forest Graphics: Stopping the Downswing?" 2009. [Online] Available at http://www.fao.org/forestry/home/en

UNESCO World Water Assessment Programme. "World Water Development Report 4: Managing Water Under Uncertainty and Risk." March 2012. Available at http://www.unesco.org/new/en/natural-sciences/environment/water/wwap/wwdr/wwdr4-2012/

United Nations, Department of Economic and Social Affairs. "World Population Prospects: The 2010 Revision." May 2011. Available at http://esa.un.org/unpd/wpp/index.htm

———. "World Urbanization Prospects: The 2011 Revision." March 2012. Available at http://esa.un.org/unpd/wup/pdf/WUP2011_Highlights.pdf

United Nations, Food and Agriculture Organization (FAO). "Global Forest Resources Assessment." 2010. Available at http://www.fao.org/forestry/fra/fra2010/en/

———. "The State of Forests in the Amazon Basin, Congo Basin and Southeast Asia." June 2011. Available at http://www.fao.org/forestry/fra/70893/en/

———. "Water Development and Management Unit." AQUASTAT database. April 2012. Available at http://www.fao.org/nr/water/aquastat/main/index.stm

———. "Water at a Glance: The Relationship between Water, Agriculture, Food Security and Poverty." 2012. Available at http://www.fao.org/nr/water/docs/waterataglance.pdf

United Nations Statistics Division. "Environmental Indicators." 2011. Available at http://unstats.un.org/unsd/ENVIRONMENT/qindicators.htm

United Nations, UN Water. "Statistics: Graphs and Maps." January 2013. Available at http://www.unwater.org/statistics.html

U.S. Census Bureau. "State and County Quick Facts." 2010. [Online] Available at http://www.fedstats.gov/qf

U.S. Census Bureau. "Census 2010." 2011, 2012. Available at http://factfinder2.census.gov/faces/nav/jsf/pages/wc_dec.xhtml

———. "2010 Census Brief: Population Distribution and Change: 2000 to 2010." March 2011. Available at http://www.census.gov/prod/cen2010/briefs/c2010br-01.pdf

———. "American Community Survey." 2012. Available at http://www.census.gov/acs/www/

———. "Population Estimates." 2012. Available at http://www.census.gov/popest/data/index.html

———. "State and County QuickFacts." 2012. Available at http://www.fedstats.gov/qf/

———. "International Data Base." 2013. Available at http://www.census.gov/population/international/

U.S. Department of Commerce, National Oceanic and Atmospheric Administration. "National Climatic Data Center." State of the Climate Annual Global Analysis. 2011. Available at http://www.ncdc.noaa.gov/sotc/

———. "Trends in Atmospheric Carbon Dioxide, Mauna Loa." January 2013. Available at http://www.esrl.noaa.gov/gmd/ccgg/trends/

U.S. Department of the Interior, U.S. Geological Survey. "Estimated Use of Water in the United States." 2010. Available at http://water.usgs.gov/watuse/

U.S. Environmental Protection Agency. "Municipal Solid Waste (MSW) in the United States: Facts and Figures." 2011. Available at http://www.epa.gov/epawaste/nonhaz/municipal/msw99.htm

———. "National Priorities List (NPL)." Superfund Sites. March 2013. Available at http://www.epa.gov/superfund/sites/query/queryhtm/nplfin1.htm

U.S. Environmental Protection Agency, Office of Water. "Estimated Per Capita Water Ingestion and Body Weight in the United States—An Update." 2004. Available at http://www.epa.gov/waterscience/criteria/drinking/percapita/2004.pdf

Walsh, Bryan. "A River Ran Through It." *Time*. Vol. 174, No. 23 (December 14, 2009):56–63.

Weber, Adna Ferrin. *The Growth of Cities*. New York: Columbia University Press, 1963; orig. 1899.

Webley, Kayla. "Hurricane Sandy by the Numbers: A Superstorm's Statistics, One Month Later." *Time*. National online edition. November 26, 2012. Available at http://nation.time.com/2012/11/26/hurricane-sandy-one-month-later/

Wilson, Edward O. "Biodiversity, Prosperity, and Value." In F. Herbert Bormann and Stephen R. Kellert, eds., *Ecology, Economics, and Ethics: The Broken Circle*. New Haven, Conn.: Yale University Press, 1991:3–10.

Wilson, Thomas C. "Urbanism and Tolerance: A Test of Some Hypotheses Drawn from Wirth and Stouffer." *American Sociological Review*. Vol. 50, No. 1 (February 1985):117–23.

———. "Urbanism and Unconventionality: The Case of Sexual Behavior." *Social Science Quarterly*. Vol. 76, No. 2 (June 1995):346–63.

Wirth, Louis. "Urbanism as a Way of Life." *American Journal of Sociology*. Vol. 44, No. 1 (July 1938):1–24.

Yardley, Jim. "China Sticking with One-Child Policy." *New York Times* (March 11, 2008). [Online] Available December 23, 2008, at http://www.nytimes.com/2008/03/11/world/asia/11china.html?_r=1

Yemma, John. "As the World's Population Heads Toward a Peak, Malthusian Worries Reemerge." *The Christian Science Monitor*. [Online] Available February 7, 2011, at http://www.csmonitor.com/Commentary/editors-blog/2011/0207/Asworld-population-heads-toward-a-peak-Malthusian-worries-reemerge

Chapter 23

Aberle, David F. *The Peyote Religion among the Navaho*. Chicago: Aldine, 1966.

Aguirre, Benigno E., and E. L. Quarantelli. "Methodological, Ideological, and Conceptual-Theoretical Criticisms of Collective Behavior: A Critical Evaluation and Implications for Future Study." *Sociological Focus*. Vol. 16, No. 3 (August 1983):195–216.

Aguirre, Benigno E., E. L. Quarantelli, and Jorge L. Mendoza. "The Collective Behavior of Fads: Characteristics, Effects, and Career of Streaking." *American Sociological Review*. Vol. 53, No. 4 (August 1988):569–84.

Annenberg Public Policy Center. 2013. Available at http://factcheck.org/

Barbassa, Juliana. "Funerals Begin for 233 Killed in Brazil Blaze." *Associated Press*. January 28, 2013. Available at http://news.yahoo.com/funerals-begin-233-killed-brazil-133908722.html

Barstow, David, and C. J. Chivers. "A Volatile Mixture Exploded into Rampage in Central Park." *New York Times* (June 17, 2000):A1, B7.

Baumgartner, M. P. "Introduction: The Moral Voice of the Community." *Sociological Focus*. Vol. 31, No. 2 (May 1998):105–17.

Bialik, Carl. "Counting Crowds in Cairo." *Wall Street Journal*. [Online] Available February 4, 2011, at http://blogs.wsj.com/numbersguy/countingthe-crowds-in-cairo-1035

Blumer, Herbert G. "Collective Behavior." In Alfred McClung Lee, ed., *Principles of Sociology*. 3rd ed. New York: Barnes & Noble Books, 1969:65–121.

Buechler, Steven M. *Social Movements in Advanced Capitalism: The Political Economy and Cultural Construction of Social Activism*. New York: Oxford University Press, 2000.

Cameron, William Bruce. *Modern Social Movements: A Sociological Outline*. New York: Random House, 1966.

Cooley, Charles Horton. *Social Organization*. New York: Schocken Books, 1962; orig. 1909.

Crane, Diana. *Fashion and Its Social Agenda: Class, Gender, and Identity in Clothing*. Chicago: University of Chicago Press, 2000.

Dollard, John, et al. *Frustration and Aggression*. New Haven, Conn.: Yale University Press, 1939.

Donnelly, Patrick G., and Theo J. Majka. "Residents' Efforts at Neighborhood Stabilization: Facing the Challenges of Inner-City Neighborhoods." *Sociological Forum*. Vol. 13, No. 2 (June 1998):189–213.

Earl, Jennifer, and Earl Kimport. *Digitally Enabled Social Change: Activism in the Internet Age*. Massachusetts Institute of Technology, 2011.

Erikson, Kai T. *Everything in Its Path: Destruction of Community in the Buffalo Creek Flood*. New York: Simon & Schuster, 1976.

———. *A New Species of Trouble: Explorations in Disaster, Trauma, and Community*. New York: Norton, 1994.

———. Lecture at Kenyon College, February 7, 2005.

Futamora, Madoka, Christopher Hobson, and Nicholas Turner. "Natural Disasters and Human Security." United Nations University. (April 29, 2011). Available at http://unu.edu/publications/articles/natural-disasters-and-human-security.html

Garrett, R. Kelly. "Web Use Doesn't Encourage Belief in Political Rumors, but E-mail Does." 2011. Available at http://researchnews.osu.edu/archive/polirumor.htm

Gibbs, Nancy. "The Day the Earth Moved." *Time*. (March 28, 2011):26.

Governors Highway Safety Association. "State Cell Phone Driving Laws." 2013. Available at http://www.ghsa.org/html/stateinfo/laws/cellphone_laws.html

Grant, Donald L. *The Anti-Lynching Movement*. San Francisco: R&E Research Associates, 1975.

Grant, Don Sherman, II, and Michael Wallace. "Why Do Strikes Turn Violent?" *American Journal of Sociology*. Vol. 96, No. 5 (March 1991):1117–50.

Herda-Rapp, Ann. "The Power of Informal Leadership: Women Leaders in the Civil Rights Movement." *Sociological Focus*. Vol. 31, No. 4 (October 1998):341–55.

Inglehart, Ronald, et al. "World Values Survey: Online Data Analysis." Available February 2013, at http://www.wvsevsdb.com/wvs/WVSAnalizeQuestion.jsp

Inglehart, Ronald, and Christian Welzel. *World Values Survey*. 2011. [Online] Available at http://www.worldvaluessurvey.org

Jasper, James M. "The Emotions of Protest: Affective and Reactive Emotions in and around Social Movements." *Sociological Forum*. Vol. 13, No. 3 (September 1998):397–424.

JENKINS, J. CRAIG, AND CHARLES PERROW. "Insurgency of the Powerless: Farm Worker Movements, 1946–1972." *American Sociological Review.* Vol. 42, No. 2 (April 1977):249–68.

JENKINS, J. CRAIG, AND MICHAEL WALLACE. "The Generalized Action Potential of Protest Movements: The New Class, Social Trends, and Political Exclusion Explanations." *Sociological Forum.* Vol. 11, No. 2 (June 1996):183–207.

JENKINS, J. CRAIG, DAVID JACOBS, AND JON AGONE. "Political Opportunities and African-American Protest, 1948–1997." *American Journal of Sociology.* Vol. 109, No. 2 (September 2003):277–303.

KAPFERER, JEAN-NOEL. "How Rumors Are Born." *Society.* Vol. 29, No. 5 (July/August 1992):53–60.

KORNHAUSER, WILLIAM. *The Politics of Mass Society.* New York: Free Press, 1959.

LACAYO, RICHARD. "Blood at the Root." *Time* (April 10, 2000):122–23.

LASLETT, PETER. *The World We Have Lost: England before the Industrial Age.* 3rd ed. New York: Scribner, 1984.

LE BON, GUSTAVE. *The Crowd: A Study of the Popular Mind.* New York: Viking Press, 1960; orig. 1895.

LIPSET, SEYMOUR MARTIN. *Political Man: The Social Bases of Politics.* Garden City, N.Y.: Anchor/Doubleday, 1963.

LOFLAND, LYN. *A World of Strangers.* New York: Basic Books, 1973.

MACFARQUHAR, NEIL. "After Revolt, Egyptians Try to Shape New Politics." *New York Times.* [Online] Available March 18, 2011, at http://www.nytimes.com/2011/03/19/world/middleeast/19egypt.html?scp=5&sq=Women%20and%20Cairo&st=cse

MACIONIS, JOHN J. *Social Problems.* 5th ed. Upper Saddle River, N.J.: Pearson Prentice Hall, 2013.

MADENSEN, TAMARA D., AND JOHN E. ECK. "The Problem of Student Party Riots." Center for Problem-Oriented Policing. 2006. [Online] Available January 25, 2009, at http://www.popcenter.org/problems/student_riots

MAUSS, ARMAND L. *Social Problems of Social Movements.* Philadelphia: Lippincott, 1975.

MCADAM, DOUG. *Political Process and the Development of Black Insurgency, 1930–1970.* Chicago: University of Chicago Press, 1982.

———. "Tactical Innovation and the Pace of Insurgency." *American Sociological Review.* Vol. 48, No. 6 (December 1983):735–54.

———. *Freedom Summer.* New York: Oxford University Press, 1988.

———. "The Biographical Consequences of Activism." *American Sociological Review.* Vol. 54, No. 5 (October 1989):744–60.

———. "Gender as a Mediator of the Activist Experience: The Case of Freedom Summer." *American Journal of Sociology.* Vol. 97, No. 5 (March 1992):1211–40.

MCADAM, DOUG, JOHN D. MCCARTHY, AND MAYER N. ZALD. "Social Movements." In Neil J. Smelser, ed., *Handbook of Sociology.* Newbury Park, Calif.: Sage, 1996.

MCCARTHY, JOHN D., AND MAYER N. ZALD. "Resource Mobilization and Social Movements: A Partial Theory." *American Journal of Sociology.* Vol. 82, No. 6 (May 1977):1212–41.

MCPHAIL, CLARK. *The Myth of the Maddening Crowd.* New York: Aldine, 1991.

MCPHAIL, CLARK, AND RONALD T. WOHLSTEIN. "Individual and Collective Behaviors within Gatherings, Demonstrations, and Riots." *Annual Review of Sociology.* Vol. 9. Palo Alto, Calif.: Annual Reviews, 1983:579–600.

MCVEIGH, RORY, MICHAEL WELCH, AND THORODDUR BJARNASON. "Hate Crime Reporting as a Successful Social Movement Outcome." *American Sociological Review.* Vol. 68 (2003):843–67.

MELUCCI, ALBERTO. *Nomads of the Present: Social Movements and Individual Needs in Contemporary Society.* Philadelphia: Temple University Press, 1989.

MERTON, ROBERT K. *Social Theory and Social Structure.* New York: Free Press, 1968.

MILLER, DAVID L. *Introduction to Collective Behavior.* Belmont, Calif.: Wadsworth, 1985.

MILLER, FREDERICK D. "The End of SDS and the Emergence of Weatherman: Demise through Success." In Jo Freeman, ed., *Social Movements of the Sixties and Seventies.* White Plains, N.Y.: Longman, 1983:279–97.

MILLS, C. WRIGHT. *The Sociological Imagination.* New York: Oxford University Press, 1959.

MORRIS, ALDON. "Black Southern Sit-In Movement: An Analysis of Internal Organization." *American Sociological Review.* Vol. 46, No. 6 (December 1981):744–67.

MORRISON, DENTON E. "Some Notes toward Theory on Relative Deprivation, Social Movements, and Social Change." In Louis E. Genevie, ed., *Collective Behavior and Social Movements.* Itasca, Ill.: Peacock, 1978:202–209.

MORSE, MICHAEL. "Obama, McConnell Take Oil Import Data for Spin." Annenberg Public Policy Center. [Online] Available March 14, 2011, at http://factcheck.org/2011/03/obama-mcconnell-take-oil-import-data-for-spin/

MOVEON.ORG. 2007. Available at http://pol.moveon.org/virtualmarch/

NESSMAN, RAVI. "Stampede at Soccer Match Kills 47." [Online] Available April 11, 2001, at http://www.news.yahoo.com

NICHOLSON, NIGEL. "Evolved to Chat: The New Word on Gossip." *Psychology Today* (May/June 2001):41–45.

NORC. "General Social Surveys, 1972–2010." Chicago: National Opinion Research Center. March 2011. Available at http://www.norc.org/GSS+Website/

OBERSCHALL, ANTHONY. *Social Conflict and Social Movements.* Englewood Cliffs, N.J.: Prentice Hall, 1973.

OLZAK, SUSAN, AND ELIZABETH WEST. "Ethnic Conflict and the Rise and Fall of Ethnic Newspapers." *American Sociological Review.* Vol. 56, No. 4 (August 1991):458–74.

PACKER, GEORGE. "Smart-Mobbing the War." *New York Times Magazine* (March 9, 2003):46–49.

PAKULSKI, JAN. "Mass Social Movements and Social Class." *International Sociology.* Vol. 8, No. 2 (June 1993):131–58.

PASSY, FLORENCE, AND MARCO GIUGNI. "Social Networks and Individual Perceptions: Explaining Differential Participation in Social Movements." *Sociological Forum.* Vol. 16, No. 1 (March 2001):123–53.

PEW RESEARCH CENTER ON THE PEOPLE AND THE PRESS. "Republicans Are Losing Ground on the Deficit, But Obama's Not Gaining." March 2011. [Online] Available at http://people-press.org/report/717

———. "Low Marks for the 2012 Election: Voters Pessimistic About Partisan Cooperation." November 15, 2012. Available at http://www.people-press.org/2012/11/15/low-marks-for-the-2012-election/#

———. "Obama in Strong Position at Start of Second Term: Support for Compromise Rises, Except Among Republicans." January 17, 2013. Available at http://www.people-press.org/2013/01/17/obama-in-strong-position-at-start-of-second-term/

PEW RESEARCH CENTER PROJECT FOR EXCELLENCE IN JOURNALISM. "The State of the News Media 2011." March 2011. [Online] Available at http://stateofthemedia.org/2011/overview-2/key-findings

———. "The State of the News Media 2012." 2012. Available at http://stateofthemedia.org/

PICHARDO, NELSON A. "The Power Elite and Elite-Driven Countermovements: The Associated Farmers of California during the 1930s." *Sociological Forum.* Vol. 10, No. 1 (March 1995):21–49.

PITTS, LEONARD, JR. "When a Win Sparks a Riot." *Philadelphia Inquirer* (June 26, 2000):A11.

PIVEN, FRANCES FOX, AND RICHARD A. CLOWARD. *Poor People's Movements: Why They Succeed, How They Fail.* New York: Pantheon Books, 1977.

POLLING REPORT, THE. CBS News. 2013. Available at http://www.pollingreport.com/index.html

PRESTON, JENNIFER. "Movement Began with Outrage and a Facebook Page That Gave It an Outlet." *New York Times.* [Online] Available February 5, 2011, at http://www.nytimes.com/2011/02/06/world/middleeast/06face.html?_r=1

PRYOR, JOHN H., KEVIN EGAN, LAURA PALUCKI BLAKE, SYLVIA HURTADO, JENNIFER BERDAN, AND MATTHEW CASE. "The American Freshman: National Norms Fall 2012 (Expanded Edition)." Cooperative Institutional Research Program at the Higher Education Research Institute at UCLA. 2013. Available at http://www.heri.ucla.edu/monographs/TheAmericanFreshman2012-Expanded.pdf

RIPLEY, AMANDA. "The Moment." *Time* (February 2, 2009):17.

ROSE, FRED. "Toward a Class-Cultural Theory of Social Movements: Reinterpreting New Social Movements." *Sociological Forum.* Vol. 12, No. 3 (September 1997):461–94.

ROSE, JERRY D. *Outbreaks.* New York: Free Press, 1982.

ROSNOW, RALPH L., AND GARY ALAN FINE. *Rumor and Gossip: The Social Psychology of Hearsay.* New York: Elsevier, 1976.

SEARS, DAVID O., AND JOHN B. MCCONAHAY. *The Politics of Violence: The New Urban Blacks and the Watts Riot.* Boston: Houghton Mifflin, 1973.

SIMMEL, GEORG. "Fashion." In Donald N. Levine, ed., *Georg Simmel: On Individuality and Social Forms.* Chicago: University of Chicago Press, 1971; orig. 1904.

SMELSER, NEIL J. *Theory of Collective Behavior.* New York: Free Press, 1962.

STOUFFER, SAMUEL A., ET AL. *The American Soldier: Adjustment during Army Life.* Princeton, N.J.: Princeton University Press, 1949.

THERNSTROM, ABIGAIL, AND STEPHAN THERNSTROM. "American Apartheid? Don't Believe It." *Wall Street Journal* (March 2, 1998):A18.

TILLY, CHARLES. *From Mobilization to Revolution.* Reading, Mass.: Addison-Wesley, 1978.

TOCQUEVILLE, ALEXIS DE. *The Old Regime and the French Revolution.* Stuart Gilbert, trans. Garden City, N.Y.: Anchor/Doubleday, 1955; orig. 1856.

TUCKER, MARIA. "How Big Was the Inaugural Crowd? Good Question." *News & Observer* (January 21, 2009). [Online] Available April 28, 2009, at http://www.sacbee.com/inauguration/story/1563105.html

TURNER, RALPH H., AND LEWIS M. KILLIAN. *Collective Behavior.* 3rd ed. Englewood Cliffs, N.J.: Prentice Hall, 1987.

———. *Collective Behavior.* 5th ed. Upper Saddle River, N.J.: Prentice Hall, 1993.

VAN DYKE, NELLA, AND SARAH A. SOULE. "Structural Social Change and the Mobilizing Effect of Threat: Explaining Levels of Patriot and Militia Organizing in the United States." *Social Problems.* Vol. 49, No. 4 (November 2002):497–520.

VEBLEN, THORSTEIN. *The Theory of the Leisure Class.* New York: New American Library, 1953; orig. 1899.

WELLER, JACK M., AND E. L. QUARANTELLI. "Neglected Characteristics of Collective Behavior." *American Journal of Sociology.* Vol. 79, No. 3 (November 1973):665–85.

WHALEN, JACK, AND RICHARD FLACKS. *Beyond the Barricades: The Sixties Generation Grows Up.* Philadelphia: Temple University Press, 1989.

WHITE, WALTER. *Rope and Faggot.* New York: Arno Press/New York Times, 1969; orig. 1929.

WILLIAMS, JOHNNY E. "Linking Beliefs to Collective Action: Politicized Religious Beliefs and the Civil Rights Movement." *Sociological Forum.* Vol. 17, No. 2 (June 2002):203–22.

WRIGHT, STUART A., AND ELIZABETH S. PIPER. "Families and Cults: Familial Factors Related to Youth Leaving or Remaining in Deviant Religious Groups." *Journal of Marriage and the Family.* Vol. 48, No. 1 (February 1986):15–25.

ZHAO, DINGXIN. "Ecologies of Social Movements: Student Mobilization during the 1989 Prodemocracy Movement in Beijing." *American Journal of Sociology.* Vol. 103, No. 6 (May 1998):1493–1529.

ZURCHER, LOUIS A., AND DAVID A. SNOW. "Collective Behavior and Social Movements." In Morris Rosenberg and Ralph H. Turner, eds., *Social Psychology: Sociological Perspectives.* New York: Basic Books, 1981:447–82.

Chapter 24

BERGER, PETER L. *Facing Up to Modernity: Excursions in Society, Politics, and Religion.* New York: Basic Books, 1977.

BERGER, PETER L., BRIGITTE BERGER, AND HANSFRIED KELLNER. *The Homeless Mind: Modernization and Consciousness.* New York: Vintage Books, 1974.

BRAZILIAN, ALEXA. "Forever in Blue Jeans." *Wall Street Journal* (January 8, 2011. Available at http://online.wsj.com/article/SB100014240527487041115045760 60150008236490.html

BROWN, ROBBIE. "History-Rich Georgia Island Wins Second Look at Taxes." *New York Times.* Available January 29, 2013, at http://www.nytimes.com/2013/01/30/us/history-rich-georgia-island-wins-second-look-on-taxes.html

BUECHLER, STEVEN M. *Social Movements in Advanced Capitalism: The Political Economy and Cultural Construction of Social Activism.* New York: Oxford University Press, 2000.

CURRY, ANDREW. "The Gullahs' Last Stand?" *U.S. News & World Report* (June 18, 2001):40–41.

DEWAN, SHAILA. "Ecosystem vs. an Endangered Culture." *New York Times.* [Online] Available July 1, 2010, at http://green.blogs.nytimes.com/2010/07/01/ecosystem-vs-an-endangered-culture/?scp=1&sq=Gullah&st=cse

DURKHEIM, EMILE. *The Division of Labor in Society.* New York: Free Press, 1964a; orig. 1893.

EHRENREICH, BARBARA. *Nickel and Dimed: On (Not) Getting By in America.* New York: Holt, 2001.

ETZIONI, AMITAI. "How to Make Marriage Matter." *Time* (September 6, 1993):76.

———. "The Responsive Community: A Communitarian Perspective." *American Sociological Review.* Vol. 61, No. 1 (February 1996):1–11.

———. *My Brother's Keeper: A Memoir and a Message.* Lanham, Md.: Rowman & Littlefield, 2003.

GIBBS, NANCY. "The Pulse of America along the River." *Time* (July 10, 2000):42–46.

———. "THE HAPPINESS PARADOX." *Time.* Vol. 174, No. 20 (November 23, 2009):116.

GOFFMAN, ERVING. *The Presentation of Self in Everyday Life.* Garden City, N.Y.: Anchor Books, 1959.

HABERMAS, JÜRGEN. *Toward a Rational Society: Student Protest, Science, and Politics.* Jeremy J. Shapiro, trans. Boston: Beacon Press, 1970.

HALL, JOHN R., AND MARY JO NEITZ. *Culture: Sociological Perspectives.* Englewood Cliffs, N.J.: Prentice Hall, 1993.

HARRINGTON, MICHAEL. *The New American Poverty.* New York: Penguin Books, 1984.

HOYERT, DONNA, AND JIAQUAN XU. "Deaths: Preliminary Data for 2011." National Vital Statistics Reports. Vol. 61, No. 6 (October 10, 2012). Available at http://www.cdc.gov/nchs/data/nvsr/nvsr61/nvsr61_06.pdf#

INGLEHART, RONALD. *Modernization and Postmodernization: Cultural, Economic, and Political Change in 43 Societies.* Princeton, N.J.: Princeton University Press, 1997.

———, et al. "World Values Survey: Online Data Analysis." Available February 2013. Available at http://www.wvsevsdb.com/wvs/WVSAnalizeQuestion.jsp

INGLEHART, RONALD, AND CHRISTIAN WELZEL. "World Values Survey." Inglehart-Welzel Cultural Map of the World. 2010. Available at http://www.worldvaluessurvey.com/

INGLEHART, RONALD, AND WAYNE E. BAKER. "Modernization, Cultural Change, and the Persistence of Traditional Values." *American Sociological Review.* Vol. 65, No. 1 (February 2000):19–51.

INGLEHART, RONALD, CHRISTIAN WELZEL, AND ROBERTO FOA. "Happiness Trends in 24 Countries, 1946–2006." 2009. [Online] Available February 15, 2009, at http://margaux.grandvinum.se/SebTest/wvs/articles/folder_published/article_base_106

KORNHAUSER, WILLIAM. *The Politics of Mass Society.* New York: Free Press, 1959.

KRAYBILL, DONALD B., AND JAMES P. HURD. *Horse-and-Buggy Mennonites: Hoofbeats of Humility in a Postmodern World.* University Park: Pennsylvania State University Press, 2006.

KRAYBILL, DONALD B., AND MARC A. OLSHAN, EDS. *The Amish Struggle with Modernity.* Hanover, N.H.: University Press of New England, 1994.

LASLETT, PETER. *The World We Have Lost: England before the Industrial Age.* 3rd ed. New York: Scribner, 1984.

LINTON, RALPH. "One Hundred Percent American." *American Mercury.* Vol. 40, No. 160 (April 1937a):427–29.

MARCUSE, HERBERT. *One-Dimensional Man.* Boston: Beacon Press, 1964.

MARX, KARL, AND FRIEDRICH ENGELS. "Manifesto of the Communist Party." In Robert C. Tucker, ed., *The Marx-Engels Reader.* New York: Norton, 1972:331–62; orig. 1848.

MIRINGOFF, MARC, AND MARQUE-LUISA MIRINGOFF. "The Social Health of the Nation." *Economist.* Vol. 352, No. 8128 (July 17, 1999):suppl. 6–7.

MYERS, DAVID G. *The American Paradox: Spiritual Hunger in an Age of Plenty.* New Haven, Conn.: Yale University Press, 2000.

NATIONAL HIGHWAY TRAFFIC SAFETY ADMINISTRATION, NHTSA's NATIONAL CENTER FOR STATISTICS AND ANALYSIS. "Fatality Analysis Reporting System (FARS)." 2012. Available at http://www-fars.nhtsa.dot.gov/Main/index.aspx

———. "2011 Traffic Safety Annual Assessment—Alcohol-Impaired Driving Fatalities." 2013. Available at http://www-nrd.nhtsa.dot.gov/Pubs/811700.pdf

NEWMAN, KATHERINE S. *Declining Fortunes: The Withering of the American Dream.* New York: Basic Books, 1993.

NISBET, ROBERT A. *The Sociological Tradition.* New York: Basic Books, 1966.

NORC. *General Social Surveys, 1972–2010.* Chicago: National Opinion Research Center. March 2011. [Online] Available at http://www.norc.org/GSS+Website

OGBURN, WILLIAM F. *On Culture and Social Change.* Chicago: University of Chicago Press, 1964.

PEARSON, DAVID E. "Post-Mass Culture." *Society.* Vol. 30, No. 5 (July/August 1993):17–22.

———. "Community and Sociology." *Society.* Vol. 32, No. 5 (July/August 1995):44–50.

RIESMAN, DAVID. *The Lonely Crowd: A Study of the Changing American Character.* New Haven, Conn.: Yale University Press, 1970; orig. 1950.

RUDEL, THOMAS K., AND JUDITH M. GERSON. "Postmodernism, Institutional Change, and Academic Workers: A Sociology of Knowledge." *Social Science Quarterly.* Vol. 80, No. 2 (June 1999):213–28.

SIMON, ROGER, AND ANGIE CANNON. "An Amazing Journey." *U.S. News & World Report* (August 6, 2001):10–19.

SIMONS, MARLISE. "The Price of Modernization: The Case of Brazil's Kaiapo Indians." In John J. Macionis and Nijole V. Benokraitis, eds., *Seeing Ourselves: Classic, Contemporary, and Cross-Cultural Readings in Sociology.* 7th ed. Upper Saddle River, N.J.: Prentice Hall, 2007.

TÖNNIES, FERDINAND. *Community and Society (Gemeinschaft und Gesellschaft).* New York: Harper & Row, 1963; orig. 1887.

U.S. CENSUS BUREAU. "American Community Survey." 2012. Available at http://www.census.gov/acs/www/

———. "Current Population Survey." 2012. Available at http://www.census.gov/cps/

———. "Educational Attainment." 2012. Available at http://www.census.gov/hhes/socdemo/education/

———. "2012 National Population Projections: Tables and Charts." 2012. Available at http://www.census.gov/population/projections/data/national/2012/summarytables.html

———. "Population Estimates." 2012. Available at http://www.census.gov/popest/data/index.html

———. "Statistical Abstract of the United States: Historical Statistics." January 2013. Available at http://www.census.gov/compendia/statab/hist_stats.html

U.S. DEPARTMENT OF HEALTH AND HUMAN SERVICES, ADMINISTRATION ON CHILDREN, YOUTH AND FAMILIES. "Child Maltreatment." 2012. Available at http://www.acf.hhs.gov/programs/cb/research-data-technology/statistics-research/child-maltreatment

U.S. DEPARTMENT OF HEALTH AND HUMAN SERVICES, SUBSTANCE ABUSE AND MENTAL HEALTH SERVICES ADMINISTRATION (SAMHSA). "Results from the 2011 National Survey on Drug Use and Health: National Findings." 2012. Available at http://www.samhsa.gov/data/NSDUH/2011SummNatFindDetTables/

U.S. DEPARTMENT OF JUSTICE, FEDERAL BUREAU OF INVESTIGATION. "Crime in the United States 2011." 2012. Available at http://www.fbi.gov/about-us/cjis/ucr/crime-in-the-u.s-2011

U.S. DEPARTMENT OF LABOR, BUREAU OF LABOR STATISTICS. "Employment Situation." 2013. Available at http://www.bls.gov/news.release/empsit.toc.htm

WEBER, MAX. *The Protestant Ethic and the Spirit of Capitalism.* New York: Scribner, 1958; orig. 1904–05.

———. *Economy and Society: An Outline of Interpretive Sociology.* Guenther Roth and Claus Wittich, eds. Berkeley: University of California Press, 1978; orig. 1921.

WEST, CORNEL. "The Obama Moment." *U.S. News & World Report* (November 17, 2008):29.

WHEELIS, ALLEN. *The Quest for Identity.* New York: Norton, 1958.

WOLFF, EDWARD N. "The Asset Price Meltdown and the Wealth of the Middle Class." 2012. Available at http://www.nber.org/authors_papers/edward_wolff

Credits

Text Credits

CHAPTER 1: 4: Berger, 1963; **6:** Data from Hamilton et al. (2012), Population Reference Bureau (2012); **7: (f):** Centers for Disease Control and Prevention (2012); **8:** C. Wright Mills (1959). Excerpted text from Mills (1959:3–5). *The Sociological Imagination* by C. Wright Mills Oxford Univ. Press, 1959); **9:** Excerpted text from Mills (1959:3–5). *The Sociological Imagination* by C. Wright Mills Oxford Univ. Press, 1959); **10:** Calculations by the author based on international data from the Population Reference Bureau (2012), UNESCO (2012), United Nations Development Programme (2012), U.S. Census Bureau (2012), World Bank (2012); **14:** Anglican hymn," All Things Bright and Beautiful"; **15:** Tocqueville, Alexis De. *The Old Regime and the French Revolution.* Stuart Gilbert, trans. Garden City, N.Y.: Anchor/Doubleday, 1955; orig. 1856; **15:** Tocqueville, Alexis De. *The Old Regime and the French Revolution.* Stuart Gilbert, trans. Garden City, N.Y.: Anchor/Doubleday, 1955; orig. 1856; **17:** Centers for Disease Control and Prevention (2012); **19:** Karl Marx; **21:** Based in part on Baltzell (1967), Du Bois (1967, orig. 1899), Wright (2002a, 2002b), and personal communication with Earl Wright II.; **24: (f):** Lapchick (2012); **24:** Lapchick, 2012.

CHAPTER 2: 31: Source: U.S. Department of Education (2012) and U.S. Department of Justice (2012); **34:** T. W. Smith (2006), Black (2007), Parker-Pope (2008), and NORC (2011); **41:** Feagin, Joe R., and Hernán, Vera. Liberation Sociology. Boulder, Colo:Westview Press, 2001; **47:** Haney, Craig, W. Curtis Banks, and Philip G. Zimbardo. "Interpersonal Dynamics in a Simulated Prison." *International Journal of Criminology and Penology. Vol. 1* (1973):69–97; **47:** Zimbardo 1972:4 "Pathology of Imprisonment" Society, Vol. 9, #1, April 1972; **50:** Adapted from Lois Benjamin, *The Black Elite: Facing the Color Line in the Twilight of the Twentieth Century* (Chicago: Nelson-Hall, 1991); **55:** U.S. Census Bureau, 2010.

CHAPTER 3: 71: J. Rubin (2003), Berteau (2005), Bacher (2009), Lenhart (2010), Pew Research Center (2011); **72:** Keller, Helen. *The Story of My Life.* New York: Doubleday Page, 1903; **73:** Lewis (2009), and European Union (2012); **77: (f):** Inglehart, Ronald, and Christian Welzel. *Modernization, Culture Change, and Democracy.* New York: Cambridge University Press, 2005. "Inglehart-Welzel Cultural Map of the World." 2010. [Online] Available at http://www.worldvalues survey.com; **78:** Mark Twain; **79:** Hostetler 1980; Kraybill 1994; **82:** Asante, Molefi Kete. Afrocentricity. Trenton, N.J.: Africa World Press, 1988; Tony Blair; **83:** U.S. Census Bureau (2012); **84:** Astin, Alexander W., Leticia Oseguera, Linda J. Sax, and William S. Korn. The American Freshman: Thirty-Five Year Trends. Los Angeles: UCLA Higher Education Research Institute, 2002.; Pryor, John H., Sylvia Hurtado, Linda Deangelo, Laura Palucki Blake, and Serge Tran. The American Freshman: National Norms for Fall 2010. Cooperative Institutional Research Program at the Higher Education Research Institute. Los Angeles: UCLA Higher Education Research Institute, 2013; **86:** Stuessy, Joe, and Scott Lipscomb. *Rock and Roll: Its History and Stylistic Development.* 6th ed. Upper Saddle River, N.J.: Pearson Prentice Hall, 2008; **87:** (Confucius, Whose Chinese name was K'ung Fu-tzu, lived between551 and 479 B.C.E. Like the Buddha); Helin, David W. "When Slogans Go Wrong." American Demographics. Vol. 14, No. 2 (February 1992):14; **90:** Marx, Karl, and Friedrich Engels. The Marx-Engels Reader. 2nd ed. Robert C. Tucker, ed. New York: Norton, 1978; orig. 1859; **91–92:** Barash, David P. *The Whisperings Within.* New York: Penguin Books, 1981.

CHAPTER 4: 99: http://www.pewinternet.org/Static-Pages/Trend-Data-(Adults)/Whos-Online.aspx (CH 4 Pew Research Center (2012); **100:** Buckley, Stephen. "A Spare and Separate Way of Life."Washington Post (December 18, 1996):A1, A32–A33.; Matloff, Judith. "Nomadic 'Blue Men' of the Desert Try to Go Roam Again."Christian Science Monitor (September 9, 1997):7.; Lovgren, Stefan. "Will All the Blue Men End Up in Timbuktu?" U.S. News & World Report (December 7, 1998):40.; & McConnell, Tristan. "Tuareg Nomads Set to Intensify Rebellion in Niger." Christian Science Monitor (October 11, 2007). [Online] Available October 13, 2008, at http://www.csmonitor.com/2007/1011/p12s01-woaf.html"; **103:** Psalm 23; **108:** Marx, Karl, and Friedrich Engels. "Manifesto of the Communist Party." in Robert C. Tucker, ed., The Marx-Engels Reader. New York: Norton, 1972:331–62; orig. 1848; **110:** Karl Marx: Early Writings. T. B. Bottomore, ed. New York: McGraw-Hill, 1964; orig. 1848; Marx, Karl, and Friedrich Engels. "Manifesto of the Communist Party." in Robert C. Tucker, ed., The Marx-Engels Reader. New York: Norton, 1972:362; orig. 1848; **112:** United Nations (2010) and International Telecommunication Union (2012); **114:** Max Weber 1978:974, orig. 1921 from *Economy and Society*

ed. Roth & Wittich (U of CA Press, 1978); **115:** Max Weber, 1978:988, orig. 1921; Durkheim, Emile. Sociology and Philosophy. New York: Free Press, 1974; orig. 1924; **116:** Durkheim, Emile. Suicide. New York: Free Press, 1966; orig. 1897.

CHAPTER 5: 134: George Herbert Mead; **136:** NORC, 2011; **137:** U.S. Census Bureau (2012); **140: (f):** International Telecommunication Union (2012); TVB (2012); **143:** UNICEF (2012).

CHAPTER 6: 153: http://pewinternet.org/Commentary/2012/March/Pew-Internet-Social-Networking-full-detail.aspx; **156:** Orlansky, Michael D., and William L. Heward. Voices: Interviews with Handicapped People. Columbus, Ohio: Merrill, 1981; **158:** United Nations (2010); **159:** From The Pleasure of Honesty by Luigi Pirandello Source: 1962:157–158, 54 words from Source: *To Clothe the Naked and Two Other Plays* tr. Wiliam Murray (Dutton 1962); **160:** Thomas, W. I., and Dorothy Swaine Thomas. *The Child in America: Behavior Problems and Programs.* New York: Knopf, 1928."; Garfinkel, Harold. *Studies in Ethnomethodology.* Cambridge, Mass.: Polity Press, 1967."; **163:** William Sansom, 1956:230–31: words from story in *A Contest of Ladies* (Hogarth 1956); **167:** Abraham Lincoln; William Shakespeare, (As You Like It, act 2, scene 7); **171:** Macionis, John J. "A Sociological Analysis of Humor." Presentation to the Texas Junior College Teachers Association, Houston, 1987; **173:** Bakalar, Nicholas. "Reactions: Go On, Laugh Your Heart Out."New York Times (March 8, 2005). [Online] Available March 11, 2005, at http://www.nytimes.com/2005/03/08/health/08reac.html; SVEBAK, SVEN. Cited in Marilyn Elias, "Study Links Sense of Humor, Survival."[Online] Available March 14, 2007, at http://www.usatoday.com 2007.

CHAPTER 7: 179: WVS 2010-2012 Questionnaire on http://www.worldvaluessurvey.org/index_surveys; **183:** Asch, Solomon. Social Psychology. Englewood Cliffs, N.J.: Prentice Hall, 1952; **184:** Janis, Irving L. Victims of Groupthink. Boston: Houghton Mifflin, 1972; **185: (f)** Created by the author; **187:** International Telecommunications Union (2012); **187:** Kaminer, Wendy. "Volunteers: Who Knows What's in It for Them?" Ms. (December 1984):93–96, 126–28; **192:** Weber, Max. *Economy and Society: An Outline of Interpretive Sociology.* Guenther Roth and Claus Wittich, eds. Berkeley: University of California Press, 1978; orig. 1921; **193:** "Places Where the System Broke Down." *Time* (September 19, 2005):34–4; **193:** Weber, Max. *Economy and Society: An Outline of Interpretive Sociology.* Guenther Roth and Claus Wittich, eds. Berkeley: University of California Press, 1978; orig. 1921; Michels, Robert. Political Parties. Glencoe, Ill.: Free Press, 1949; orig. 1911; **194:** Allen, Thomas B., and Charles O. Hyman. *We Americans: Celebrating a Nation, Its People, and Its Past.* Washington, D.C.: National Geographic Society, 1999; **195: (f)** U.S. Census Bureau (2012) and U.S. Equal Employment Opportunity Commission (2012); **197: (f)** Created by the author; **197:** Brooks, David. *Bobos in Paradise: The New Upper Class and How They Got There.* New York: Simon & Schuster, 2000; **198:** Brooks, David. *Bobos in Paradise: The New Upper Class and How They Got There.* New York: Simon & Schuster, 2000; **200:** Online Privacy: It's Time for Rules in Wonderland." Business Week (March 20, 2000):82–96.; Heymann, Philip B. "Civil Liberties and Human Rights in the Aftermath of September 11." Harvard Journal of Law and Public Policy. Vol. 25, No. 2 (Spring 2002):441–57.; O'harrow, Robert, Jr. "ID Theft Scam Hits D.C. Area Residents." [Online] Available February 21, 2005, at http://news.yahoo.com; Tingwall, Eric. "Auto Insurance Gets Cheaper but Potentially More Invasive." Automobile (December 2008):74.; Werth, Christopher. "To Watch the Watchers." Newsweek (October 20, 2008):E4.; Hui, Sylvia."Bloomberg Takes Cues from London's Security-Obsessed Security." The Huffington Post. [Online] Available May 11, 2010, at http://www.huffingtonpost.com/2010/05/11/bloomberg-taking-cues-fro_n_571359.html; & Stein, Joel. "Your Data, Yourself." Time. Vol. 177, No. 11 (March 21, 2011): 40–46."; **201:** Ritzer, George. *The McDonaldization of Society: An Investigation into the Changing Character of Contemporary Social Life.* Thousand Oaks, Calif.: Pine Forge Press, 1993."

CHAPTER 8: 207: NORC: http://www.norc.org/PDFs/sexmoralfinal_06-21_FINAL.PDF; **212:** National Conference of State Legislatures (2012); **214: (f):** Laumann, Edward O., John H. Gagnon, Robert T. Michael, and Stuart Michaels. *The Social Organization of Sexuality: Sexual Practices in the United States.* Chicago: University of Chicago Press, 1994; **215:** Data from United Nations (2008) and Population Reference Bureau (2012); **215:** NORC. General Social Surveys, 1972–2010: Cumulative Codebook. Chicago: National Opinion Research Center, 2011. [Online] Available at http://www.norc.org/GSS+Website; **216:** General Social Surveys, 1972–2010: Codebook (Chicago: National Opinion Research Center, 2011); **217: (f):** Adapted from

Storms, Michael D. "Theories of Sexual Orientation." Journal of Personality and Social Psychology. Vol. 38, No. 5 (May 1980):783–92; **219:** (f): Mosher, William D., Anjani Chandra, and Jo Jones. "Sexual Behavior and Selected Health Measures: Men and Women, 15–44 Years of Age, United States, 2002." September 15, 2005. [Online] Available November 8, 2008, at http://www.cdc.gov/nchs/data/ad/ad362.pdf; **219:** Gave, Eleni N. "In the Indigenous Muxe Culture of Mexico's Oaxaca State, AlternativeNotions of Sexuality Are Not Only Accepted, They're Celebrated." Travel and Leisure (November 2005). [Online] Available June 15, 2009, at http://travelandleisure.com/articles/stepping-out/page/2/print; Lacey, Marc. "A Distinct Lifestyle: The Muxe of Mexico." New York Times(December 7, 2008):4.; & Rosenberg, Mica. "Mexican Transvestite Fiesta Rocks Indigenous Town." Reuters, November 23, 2008. [Online] Available June 15, 2009, at http://www.reuters.com/article/lifestyleMolt/idUSTRE4AM1PB20081123"; **220:** (f): Astin, Alexander W., Leticia Oseguera, Linda J. Sax, and William S. Korn. The American Freshman: Thirty-Five Year Trends. Los Angeles: UCLA Higher Education Research Institute, 2002.; Pryor, John H., Sylvia Hurtado, Linda Deangelo, Laura Palucki Blake, and Serge Tran. The American Freshman: National Norms for Fall 2008. Los Angeles: UCLA Higher Education Research Institute, 2008.; **222:** Alan Guttmacher Institute. "U.S. Teenage Pregnancies, Births and Abortions: National and State Trends and Trends by Race and Ethnicity." January 2010. [Online] Available at http://www.guttmacher.org/pubs/USTPtrends.pdf; **222:** NORC. General Social Surveys, 1972–2010: Cumulative Codebook. Chicago: National Opinion Research Center, 2011. [Online] Available at http://www.norc.org/GSS+Website; **225:** Marquardt, Elizabeth, and Norval Glenn. Hooking Up, Hanging Out, and Hoping for Mr. Right. New York: Institute for American Values, 2001; **226:** Miracle, Tina S., Andrew W. Miracle, and Roy F. Baumeister. Human Sexuality: Meeting Your Basic Needs. Upper Saddle River, N.J.: Prentice Hall, 2003; **230:** Women's Access to Abortion in Global Perspective; **231:** NORC. General Social Surveys, 1972–2010: Cumulative Codebook. Chicago:National Opinion Research Center, 2011. [Online] Available at http://www.norc.org/GSS+Website": **410–11.**

CHAPTER 9: 237: Source: U.S. Department of Justice (2011) and U.S. Department of Health and Human Services (2012); **243:** Durkheim, Emile. The Rules of Sociological Method. New York: Free Press, 1964b; orig. 1895; **243:** Merton, Robert K. Social Theory and Social Structure. New York: Free Press, 1968; **245:** Our Cheating Hearts." Editorial. U.S. News & World Report (May 6, 2002):4.; Bono, Agostino. "John Jay Study Reveals the Extent of Abuse Problem." [Online] Available September 13, 2006, at http://www.americancatholic.org/news/clergysexabuse/johnjaycns.asp; & Lohr, Steve. "In Bailout Furor, Wall Street Salaries Become a Target." International Herald Tribune (September 24, 2008). [Online] Available November 6, 2008, at http://www.iht.com/articles/2008/09/24/business/24pay.php"; **249:** Quinney, Richard. Class, State and Crime: On the Theory and Practice of Criminal Justice. New York: McKay, 1977; **253:** Terry, Don. "In Crackdown on Bias, a New Tool." New York Times (June 12, 1993):8.; Sullivan, Andrew. Lecture delivered at Kenyon College, Gambier, Ohio, April 4, 2002. & Hartocollis, Anemona. "Man Is Convicted of Attempted Murder as Hate Crime in Village Rampage." New York Times (March 2, 2007):B6."; **255:**CAP Index (2009). [Online] Available www.capindex.com; **256:** (f)Federal Bureau of Investigation (2012); **260:** Amnesty International (2012); **265:** State of Oregon, 2011; **267:** Winship & Berrien (1999), Donahue & Leavitt (2000), Rosenfeld (2002), Liptak (2008), C. Mitchell (2008), Antlfinger (2009), and Federal Bureau of Investigation (2012).

CHAPTER 10: 273: U.S. Department of Justice (2011) and U.S. Department of Health and Human Services (2012); **277:** Mabry & Masland (1999), Murphy (2002), Perry (2009), and (McGroarty & Maylie, 2012); **284:** (f): U.S. Census Bureau (2012) and World Bank (2012); **287:** Michael J. Moore, "Wall Street Bonuses Cut", Bloomberg Businessweek, Markets & Finance, November 15, 2012. http://www.businessweek.com/articles/2012–11–15/wall-street-bonuses-cut; **288:** Marx, Karl, and Friedrich Engels. "Manifesto of the Communist Party." In Robert C. Tucker, ed., The Marx-Engels Reader. New York: Norton, 1972:331–62; orig. 1848; **293:** (f): Kuznets, Simon. "Economic Growth and Income Inequality." American Economic Review. Vol. 14, No. 1 (March 1955): 1–28.; & Lenski, Gerhard E. Power and Privilege: A Theory of Social Stratification. New York: McGraw-Hill, 1966; **294:** Based on Gini coefficients obtained from Central Intelligence Agency (2012) and World Bank (2012); **295:** Harrison Bergeron" from Welcome to the Monkey House by Kurt Vonnegut, Jr, 14-page story from collection Welcome to the Monkey House (Doubleday 1968); **295:** Herrnstein & Murray (1994), Jacoby & Glauberman (1995), Kohn (1996), and Arrow, Bowles, & Durlauf (2000).

CHAPTER 11: 302: Eisenstadt, Jill. "The Maid's Tale." New York Times (July 25, 2004). [Online] Available March 22, 2005, at http://www.research navigator.com; **303:** (f): Income data from U.S. Census Bureau (2012); wealth data based on Wolff (2012) and author estimates; **304:** Adapted from General Social Surveys, 1972–2010: Cumulative Codebook (Chicago: National Opinion Research Center, 2011); **309:** U.S. Census Bureau (2010); **314:** (f): U.S. Census

Bureau (2012); **315:** (f): U.S. Census Bureau (2012); **317:** (f): U.S. Census Bureau (2012); **319:** U.S. Census Bureau (2010); **321:** Wilson, William Julius. When Work Disappears: The World of the New Urban Poor. New York: Knopf, 1996a; **323:** Lichter & Crowley (2002), Lichter & Jayakody (2002), Von Drehle (2008), U.S. Census Bureau (2012); U.S. Department of Health and Human Services (2012); **324:** (f): Internal Revenue Service (2012) and Saez and Piketty (2012); **324:** Kohut, 2011; **324:** NORC, 2011:2270.

CHAPTER 12: 331: UNICEF (2012) http://www.unicef.org/sowc2012/pdfs/UNDER-FIVE-MORTALITY-RANKINGS.pdf; **333:** (f): Based on Milanovic (2009, 2011) and Davies, Lluberas, & Shorrocks (2012); **335:** Data from United Nations Development Programme (2012) and the World Bank (2012); **337:** Based on Schaffer, Michael. "American Dreamers." U.S. News & World Report (August 26, 2002):12–16 and The Economist (2011); **339:** (f): Based on Population Reference Bureau (2012) and World Bank (2012); **340:** United Nations Development Programme (2012), World Bank (2012); **341:** United Nations. "Millennium Development Goals." 2011. [Online] Available at http://www.un.org/millenniumgoals; **342:** World Bank (2012); **343:** Based on Burkett (1997), Fisher (2011); Anti-Slavery International (2012); **344:** Universal Declaration of Human Rights, 1948; **353:** World Bank (2012).

CHAPTER 13: 359: Gallup (2012) http://www.gallup.com/poll/157313/half-women-prefer-job-outside-home.aspx; **361:** "Marathonguide.com. 2012. [Online] Available at http://www.marathonguide.com/history/records/index.cfm"; **363:** Data from United Nations Development Programme (2011); **368:** U.S. Bureau of Labor Statistics (2012); **370:** U.S. Bureau of Labor Statistics (2012); **371:** Sommers (2000), von Drehle (2007), Lamm (2010), and Paton (2010); **372:** Center for American Women and Politics (2012); **374:** Population Reference Bureau (2010), World Health Organization (2006, 2011), and United Nations (2012); **375:** Crossette (1995), Boyle, Songora, & Foss (2001), and Sabatini (2011); **382:** Equal Rights Amendment (ERA) to the U.S. Constitution; **383:** Population Reference Bureau (2012); **384:** Pew Research Center, 2012; **385:** NORC, 2011: 438.

CHAPTER 14: 391: Center for American Women and Politics (2012); **394:** U.S. Census Bureau (2012); **395:** U.S. Census Bureau, 2013; **396:** U.S. Census Bureau (2012); **397:** Booth (1998), Tumulty (2006), U.S. Department of Homeland Security (2012), and U.S. Department of Labor (2012); **399:** Parrillo, Vincent, and Christopher Donoghue. "Updating the Bogardus Social Distance Studies: A New National Survey." Social Science Journal.Vol. 42, No. 2 (April 2005): 257–71; **400:** Martin Luther King Jr.; **403:** Metzger, Kurt. "Cities and Race." Society. Vol. 39, No. 1 (December 2001):2; **404:** Emma Lazarus,; **405:** Waldman (2000) and U.S. Census Bureau (2011); **406:** U.S. Census Bureau (2012); **408:** Blaustein, Albert P., and Robert L. Zangrando. Civil Rights and the Black American. New York:Washington Square Press, 1968; **408:** Declaration of Independence; **409:** U.S. Census Bureau (2012); **411:** U.S. Census Bureau (2011, 2012); **412:** U.S. Census Bureau (2012); **414:** U.S. Census Bureau (2012); **416:** U.S. Census Bureau (2012); **417:** Handlin, Oscar. Boston's Immigrants, 1790–1865: A Study in Acculturation. Cambridge, Mass.: Harvard University Press, 1941; **418:** Bowen & Bok (1999), Kantrowitz & Wingert (2003), Flynn (2008), Leff (2008), NORC (2011), and (Sander & Taylor), Jr., 2012.

CHAPTER 15: 425: U.S. Department of Health and Human Services (2012); **426:** Carrns, 2012; **427:** U.S. Census Bureau (2012); **428:** Porter (2004), Haub (2008), Associated Press (2011), and U.S. Census Bureau (2012); **429:** U.S. Census Bureau (2012); **432:** Population Reference Bureau (2012); **433:** RUBENSTEIN, ELI A. "The Not So Golden Years." Newsweek (October 7, 1991):13; **434:** U.S. Census Bureau (2012), Federal Interagency Forum on Aging-Related Statistics (2012); **436:** Kadlec (2002), Koskela (2008),Trumbull (2011), and U.S. Bureau of Labor Statistics (2012); **436:** U.S. Census Bureau (2012); **442:** Ariès, Philippe. Western Attitudes toward Death: From the Middle Ages to the Present. Baltimore: Johns Hopkins University Press, 1974"; **442:** Biblical book of Ecclesiastes; **445:** Della Cava (1997), Mauro (1997), and B. Barr (2004); **447:** Callahan (1987, 2009) and Centers for Medicare & Medicaid Research (2012).

CHAPTER 16: 456: Estimates based on World Bank (2012); **457:** Data from International Labour Organization (2012); **458:** Data from International Labour Organization (2012); **462:** Fox (2007), Population Reference Bureau (2012), World Bank (2012), and OECD (2012); **463:** Pryor et al Figure: The Changing Pattern of Work in the United States, 1900–2011. Pearson Education Source: Estimates based on U.S. Department of Labor (2012); **465:** National Conference of State Legislatures (2012); **466:** Gray (2011), Murphy (2011), Rasmussen (2011), Ripley (2011), Sulzberger (2011), and Kelleher (2012); **467:** Pryor et al. (2011); **468:** U.S. Department of Labor (2013); **470:** U.S. Department of Labor (2012).

CHAPTER 17: 479: Pew Research Center (2012) http://www.people-press.org/2011/11/03/the-generation-gap-and-the-2012-election-3/11-3-11-1/; **484:**Freedom House (2013); **487:** Liazos, Alexander. People First: An Introduction to Social Problems. Needham Heights,Mass.: Allyn & Bacon, 1982;

487: Xia, Renee. "In China, Activists Watch and Cheer." Wall Street Journal. [Online] Available March 12, 2011, at http://online.wsj.com/article/SB1000 1424052748704823004576192642010298086.html; Zakaria, Zakaria. "Why It's Different This Time." Time. Vol. 177, No. 8 (February 28, 2011):30–31; **488:** OECD (2013); **490:** Astin et al. (2002), Sax et al. (2003), and Pryor et al. (2007); **491:** Copyright Guardian News & Media Ltd 2012; **497:** Compiled from various SOURCE by Maris A. Vinovskis (1989) and the author; **497:** quoted in Whitaker, Mark. "Ten Ways to Fight Terrorism." Newsweek (July 1, 1985):26–29; **498:** Halbfinger, David M., and Steven A. Holmes. "Military Mirrors Working-Class America."New York Times (March 20, 2003). [Online] Available May 4, 2009, at http://www.cwalocal4250.org/news/binarydata/ Military%20Mirrors%20Working-Class%20America.pdf; **499:** Thompson (2011), U.S. Department of Defense (2012), New York Times (2013), U.S. House Committee on Veterans Affairs (2013); **501:** Albert Einstein; **503:** Karatnycky (2002), Pew Forum on Religious & Public Life (2012), and Freedom House (2013).

CHAPTER 18: 509: Copen et al. (2012) http://www.cdc.gov/nchs/data/nhsr /nhsr049.pdf; **512:** Martin et al. (2012), U.S. Census Bureau (2012); European Union Statistical Division (2012); OECD (2012); United Nations Economic Commission for Europe (2012), and U.S. Bureau of Labor Statistics (2012); **513:** Peters Atlas of the World (1990) with updates by the author; **518:** Anderson, John Ward. "Early to Wed: The Child Brides of India." Washington Post (May 24, 1995):A27, A30. Roudi-Fahimi, Farazzeh. "Child Marriage in the Middle East and North Africa." Population Reference Bureau. (April 2010). [Online] Available at http://www.prb.org/Articles/2010/menachildmarriage.aspx; **522:** U.S. Census Bureau (2012); **524:** Based on Kent (2010), Taylor (2010), Pew Research Center (2012); U.S. Census Bureau (2012); and Wang (2012) U.S. Constitution, First Amendment; **525:** National Center for Health Statistics (2011) and U.S. Census Bureau (2012); **526:** National Center for Health Statistics (2012); **527:** U.S. Census Bureau (2011); **528:** Roesch, Roberta. "Violent Families." Parents. Vol. 59, No. 9 (September 1984):74–76, 150–52; **529:** Phillips, Melanie. "What about the Overclass?" Public Interest (Fall 2001): 38–43.

CHAPTER 19: 540: Durkheim, Emile. The Elementary Forms of Religious Life. New York: Free Press, 1965; orig. 1915; **540:** Shelter, Jeffrey L. "Faith in America." U.S. News & World Report (May 6, 2002):40–44; April, 2004; **541:** 2 Corinthians 5:7; **541:** Hebrews 11:1; **543:** 1 Corinthians 11:7–9; **543:** 1 Corinthians 14:33–35; **543:** Ephesians 5:22–24; **543:** Marx, Karl. Karl Marx: Early Writings. T. B. Bottomore, ed. New York: McGraw-Hill, 1964; orig. 1848; **543:** Qur'an 4:34, quoted in Kaufman,Walter. Religions in Four Dimensions: Existential, Aesthetic, Historical, and Comparative. New York: Reader's Digest Press, 1976: 163"; **549:** Association of Religion Data Archives (2012); **549:** Matthew 22:21; **550:** Pew Research Center (2011) and Association of Religion Data Archives (2012); **553:** Association of Religion Data Archives (2012); **554:** Association of Religion Data Archives (2012); **555:** Inglehart, Ronald, and Christian Welzel. "World Values Survey." 2010. [Online] Available at http://www.worldvaluessurvey .com; **556:** Association of Statisticians of American Religious Bodies; **556:** General Social Surveys, 1972–2010: Cumulative Codebook (Chicago: National Opinion Research Center, March 2011); **557:** Association of Statisticians of American Religious Bodies; **557:** NORC. General Social Surveys, 1972–2010. Chicago: National Opinion Research Center. March 2011. [Online] Available at http://www.norc.org/GSS+Website; **560:** Astin, Alexander W., Leticia Oseguera, Linda J. Sax, and William S. Korn. The American Freshman: Thirty-Five Year Trends. Los Angeles: UCLA Higher Education Research Institute, 2002 and Pryor, John H., Sylvia Hurtado, Linda Deangelo, Laura Palucki Blake, and Serge Tran. The American Freshman: National Norms Fall 2010. Los Angeles: Cooperative Institutional Research Program at the Higher Education Research Institute at UCLA, 2012; **560:** Cox, Harvey. The Secular City. Rev. ed. New York: Macmillan, 1971; **562:** Cimino & Lattin, 1999:62; **564:** Gould, Stephen J. "Evolution as Fact and Theory." Discover (May 1981):35–37. Greeley, Andrew M. "Symposium: Neo-Darwinism and Its Discontents." Society. Vol. 45, No. 2 (2008):162–63. Huchingson, James E. "Science and Religion." Miami Herald (December 25, 1994):1M, 6M. Applebome, Peter. "70 Years after Scopes Trial, Creation Debate Lives." New York Times (March 10, 1996):1, 10. Pew Research Center, Forum on Religion and Public Life. "A Religious Portraitof African-Americans." 2009. [Online] Available at http:// pewforum.org/A-Religious-Portrait-of-African-Americans.aspx#a.

CHAPTER 20: 574: UNESCO (2012) and World Bank (2012); **575:** U.S. Census Bureau (2012); **575:** U.S. Census Bureau (2013); World Bank (2013); **581:** U.S. Department of Education (2013); **582:** Kozol, Jonathan. Savage Inequalities: Children in America's Schools. New York: Harper Perennial, 1992; **584:** U.S. Census Bureau (2012); **587:** NCEE, 1983:9. Reference: A Nation at Risk, was issued by the National Commission on Excellence in Education (NCEE). (1983:5) Published by the Government Printing Office; **588:** Astin, Alexander W., Leticia Oseguera, Linda J. Sax, and William S. Korn. The American Freshman: Thirty-Five Year Trends. Los Angeles: UCLA Higher Education Research Institute, 2002.Pryor, John H., Sylvia Hurtado, Linda Deangelo, Laura Palucki

Blake, and Serge Tran. The American Freshman: National Norms Fall 2010. Los Angeles: Cooperative Institutional Research Program at the Higher Education Research Institute at UCLA, 2013; **591:** Chris Lubienski, quoted in Cloud, John, and Jodie Morse. "Home Sweet School." Time (August 27, 2001):46–54.

CHAPTER 21: 599: CDC (2013) http://www.cdc.gov/diabetes/atlas /countydata/Obesity_Prevalence.pdf; **602:** Information for 1900 is from William C. Cockerham, Medical Sociology, 2nd ed. (Englewood Cliffs, N.J.: Prentice Hall, 1986); **603:** Copyright © by Pearson Education, Upper Saddle River, NJ; **604:** Friedman, Meyer, and Ray H. Rosenman. Type A Behavior and Your Heart. New York: Fawcett Crest, 1974. Levine, Michael P. Student Eating Disorders: Anorexia Nervosa and Bulimia. Washington, D.C.: National Educational Association, 1987; **607:** Centers for Disease Control and Prevention (2013); **609:** Population Reference Bureau (2012) and UNAIDS (2012); **610:** Centers for Disease Control and Prevention (2012); **614:** World Bank (2013); **620:** Astin, Alexander W., Leticia Oseguera, Linda J. Sax, and William S. Korn. The American Freshman: Thirty-Five Year Trends. Los Angeles: UCLA Higher Education Research Institute, 2002.Pryor, John H., Sylvia Hurtado, Linda Deangelo, Laura Palucki Blake, and Serge Tran. The American Freshman: National Norms Fall 2010. Los Angeles: Cooperative Institutional Research Program at the Higher Education Research Institute at UCLA, 2012; **623:** Thompson, Dick. "Gene Maverick." Time (January 11, 1999):54–55.Golden, Frederic, and Michael D. Lemonick. "The Race Is Over." Time (July 3, 2000):18–23; **624:** information for 2011 is from Hoyert & Xu (2012).

CHAPTER 22: 629: Gallup (2011) http://www.gallup.com/poll/153653/ Americans-Worries-Global-Warming-Slightly.aspx; **629:** Park, Robert E. Race and Culture. Glencoe, Ill.: Free Press, 1950; **631:** Population Reference Bureau (2012); **633:** U.S. Census Bureau (2011); **634:** Population Reference Bureau (2012); **635:** U.S. Census Bureau (2013); **639:** Hesketh, Therese, Li Lu, and Zhuwei Xing. "The Effects of China's One-ChildFamily Policy after 25 Years."New England Journal ofMedicine.Vol. 353, No. 11(November 2005):1171– 76. Baochang, Gu, Wang Feng, Guo Zhigang, and Erli Zhang. "China's Local and National Fertility Policies at the End of the Twentieth Century." Population and Development Review. Vol. 33, No. 1 (2007):129–48.McGurn,William. "The Not So Dismal Science: Humanitarians v. Economists."Imprimis. Vol. 40, No. 5 (March 2011):1–7. EL NASSER, HAYA, and PAUL OVERBERG. "U.S. Growth Slows, Still Envied." USA Today (January 7–9, 2011):1A; Population Reference Bureau (2013)" **641:** U.S. Census Bureau (2010) and United Nations (2012); **647:** Schmitt, Eric. "Whites in Minority in Largest Cities, the Census Shows." New York Times (April 30, 2001):A1, A12; U.S. Census Bureau (2012); **650:** Bormann, F. Herbert. "The Global Environmental Deficit." BioScience. Vol. 40, No. 2 (1990):74; **652:** U.S. Environmental Protection Agency (2011); **656:** Myers, Norman. "The Mega-Extinction of Animals and Plants." In Sir Edmund Hillary, ed., Ecology 2000: The Changing Face of the Earth. New York: Beaufort Books, 1984b:82–107; **659:** Brown, Lester R. "Reassessing the Earth's Population." Society. Vol. 32, No. 4 (May/June 1995):7–10; Simon (1995); Scanlon, Stephan J. "Food Availability and Access in Less Industrialized Societies: A Test and Interpretation of Neo-Malthusian and Technoecological Theories." Sociological Forum. Vol. 16, No. 2 (June 2001):231–62; Smail, J. Kenneth. "Let's Reduce Global Population!" In john J. Macionis and Nijole V. Benokraitis, eds., Seeing Ourselves: Classic, Contemporary, and Cross-Cultural Readings in Sociology. 7th ed. Upper Saddle River, N.J.: Prentice Hall, 2007; Population Reference Bureau (2012), and U.S. Census Bureau (2013)".

CHAPTER 23: 669: Barstow, David, and C. J. Chivers. "A Volatile Mixture Exploded into Rampage in Central Park." New York Times (June 17, 2000):A1, B7; **672:** Goode, Erich. "No Need to Panic? A Bumper Crop of Books on Moral Panics." Sociological Forum. Vol. 15, No. 3 (September 2000):543–52; **674:** Jennifer Lopez; **676:** Based on K. T. Erikson (2005a); **677:** Aberle, David F. The Peyote Religion among the Navaho. Chicago: Aldine, 1966; **681:** McAdam, McCarthy & Zald, 1996:6; see also J. E. Williams, 2002; **683:** MoveOn.org (2007); **685:** Jenkins, J. Craig, and Michael Wallace. "The Generalized Action Potential of Protest Movements: The New Class, Social Trends, and Political Exclusion Explanations." Sociological Forum. Vol. 11, No. 2 (June 1996):183–207. Rose, Fred. "Toward a Class-Cultural Theory of Social Movements: Reinterpreting New Social Movements." Sociological Forum. Vol. 12, No. 3 (September 1997): 461–94."; **689:** Pryor et al. (2013).

CHAPTER 24: 695: Questionnaire on http://www.worldvaluessurvey.org /index_surveys; **699:** U.S. Census Bureau (2012); **700:** Berger, Peter L. Facing Up to Modernity: Excursions in Society, Politics, and Religion. New York: Basic Books, 1977; **701:** Tönnies, Ferdinand. Community and Society (Gemeinschaft und Gesellschaft).New York: Harper & Row, 1963; orig. 1887; **702:** Based, in part, on Brazillian (2011); **703:** NORC. General Social Surveys, 1972–2010. Chicago: National Opinion ResearchCenter.March 2011. [Online] Available at http://www .norc.org/GSS+Website; **704:** Weber, Max. Economy and Society: An Outline of Interpretive Sociology. Guenther Roth and Clauswittich, eds. Berkeley: University of California Press, 1978; orig. 1921; **707:** Gibbs, Nancy. "The Pulse of America along the River." Time (July 10, 2000):42–46; **713:** NORC, 2011:1762;

714: NORC (2011): U.S. Census Bureau (2012); U.S. Department of Health and Human Services (2012); U.S. Department of Justice (2012); U.S. Department of Labor (2012); 715: Simons, Marlise. "The Price of Modernization: The Case of Brazil's Kaiapo Indians." In John J.Macionis and Nijole v. Benokraitis, eds., Seeing Ourselves: Classic, Contemporary, and Cross-Cultural Readings in Sociology. 7th ed. Upper Saddle River, N.J.: Prentice Hall, 2007.

Photo Credits

CHAPTER 1: Gallo Images/Alamy, 2; Jupiterimages/Thinkstock, 4; Allen Brown/dbimages/Alamy, 5(tl); Outdoor-Archiv/Alamy, 5(tc); Paul W. Liebhart, 5(tr); Jamie Marshall/DK Images, 5(bl); UpperCut Images/SuperStock, 5(bc); Paul W. Liebhart, 5(br); AP Images/Gary He, 8; Jeff Greenberg/PhotoEdit, 12; s70/Zuma Press/Newscom, 13; Frank Zullo/Science Source, 15; Splash News/Corbis, 18; Library of Congress Prints and Photographs Division, 19; Schomburg Center/Art Resource, NY, 21; Warner Bros. Pictures/Everett Collection, 23; Pearson Education, 25; Photo by Rex USA/Everett Collection, 26; Mark Savage/Corbis, 27(l); RW3 WENN Photos/Newscom, 27(r); Jupiterimages/Thinkstock, 28.

CHAPTER 2: The Star-Ledger/Jennifer Brown/The Image Works, 30; Photo by Reuben Burrell/Courtesy of Lois Benjamin, 32; Rick Rycroft/AP Images, 33; Travel Ink/Gallo Images/Getty Images, 35; Steve McCurry/Magnum Photos, 40(l); Jeffry W. Myers/CORBIS, 40(r); Bill Bachman/Alamy, 43; Ted Foxx/Alamy, 44; Philip G. Zimbardo, Inc., 46(r); Philip G. Zimbardo, Inc., 46(l); Alamy Limited, 49; John Macionis, 53; Courtesy George J. Mitchell Department of Special Collections & Archives, Bowdoin College Library, 56; Tom Grill/Corbis, 60(l); Sean Justice/Corbis, 60(r); Olivier Cadeaux/Corbis, 60(b); Stephen Derr/Getty Images, 61(l); Photo by Reuben Burrell/Courtesy of Lois Benjamin, 62.

CHAPTER 3: AP Photo/Manuel Balce Ceneta, 64; TongRo Images/Thinkstock, 66; Paul W. Liebhart, 67(tl); Boaz Rottem/Alamy, 67(tc); szefei/Shutterstock, 67(tr); Paul W. Liebhardt, 67(cl); Jon Arnold Images Ltd/Alamy, 67(c); Hubertus Kanus/Science Source, 67(cr); Photononstop/SuperStock, 67(bl); Susanna Bennett/Alamy, 67(bc); George Doyle/Stockbyte/Getty Images, 67(br); Herve Collart/Sygma/Corbis, 68; Hazel Thompson/The New York Times/Redux Pictures, 69; Tomas Rodriguez/Corbis, 71; Keren Su/China Span/Alamy, 72; FOX/Contributor/Getty Images, 75; jochem wijnands/Horizons WWP/Alamy, 78; Thibault Monnier/PacificCoastNe/Newscom, 80; Janine Wiedel Photolibrary/Alamy, 81; Carlos Rene Perez/AP Images, 86(l); Bettmann/Corbis, 86(c); Michael Ochs Archives/Stringer/Getty Images, 86(r); Thomas L. Kelly/Aurora Photos/Alamy, 87; Ignacio Palacios/age fotostock/SuperStock, 89; GoGo Images Corporation/Alamy, 92; Hulton Archive/Getty Images, 94(l); HBO / JOHNSON, JOHN P./Album/Newscom, 94(r); Melissa Moseley/Sony Pictures/Bureau L.A. Collection/Corbis, 95; jochem wijnands/Horizons WWP/Alamy, 96;

CHAPTER 4: Exactostock/SuperStock, 98; Blickwinkel/Alamy, 100; Penny Tweedie/Corbis, 101; Monty Brinton/CBS via Getty Images, 102; Everett Collection, 106(l); Pictorial Press Ltd/Alamy, 106(r); Moviestore Collection Ltd/Alamy, 109; Tim Boyle/Getty Images, 111; George Tooker "Landscape with Figures" 1966, Egg tempera on gesso panel, 26 x 30 inches., Private Collection, Courtesy DC Moore Gallery, NY, 114; Elliott Landy/Magnum Photos, 116(l); Elliott Landy/Magnum Photos, 116; James Crump/WireImage/Getty Images, 116(c); Alain Fulconis/AFP/Getty Images/Newscom, 116(cr); Geoffrey Robinson/Alamy, 116(r); Mike Booth/Alamy, 117(l); Getty Images/Jupiter Images, 117(r); Stacy Walsh Rosenstock/Alamy, 118; Jeff Greenberg/PhotoEdit, 119; i love images/Fotolia, 120; Gijsbert Hanekroot/Alamy, 120(r); London Ent/Splash News/Newscom, 121(l); Moviestore Collection Ltd/Alamy, 122.

CHAPTER 5: Radius Images/Alamy, 124; Blend Images/Alamy, 126(tl); yeo2205/Shutterstock, 127(tl); Picture Partners/Science Source, 127(tc); Dorling Kindersley, 127(tr); Bradley Secker/The Washington Post/Getty Images, 128(bl); Exactostock/SuperStock, 133(tr); Uppercut RF/Glowimages, 134; Levranii/Shutterstock, 136(bl); Jack Hollingsworth/Photodisc/Thinkstock, 138(c); Splash News/Newscom, 141(br); Splash News/Corbis, 142(bl); Steven Tackeff/Zuma Press/Newscom, 145(br); Jim West/Alamy, 146(b); James Porto/Taxi/Getty Images, 147(bl); Remi Benali/Terra /Corbis, 148(b); Anders Ryman/Encyclopedia/Corbis, 148(tl); Chung Sung-Jun/Getty Images Entertainment/Getty Images, 149(cl); Blend Images/Alamy, 150(tl).

CHAPTER 6: David J. Green - lifestyle themes/Alamy, 152; Ingram Publishing/SuperStock, 154; Jason Merritt/Getty Images, 155; Michael Hanson/Aurora/Getty Images, 156; Goodshoot/Thinkstock, 160; Staton R. Winter/The New York Times/Redux Pictures, 161; PHILIPPE LOPEZ/AFP/GettyImages, 162; David Sipress/Cartoon Bank, 163; Paul W. Liebhardt, 164(l); Paul W. Liebhardt, 164(c); Paul W. Liebhardt, 164(r); Barbara Penoyar/Photodisc/Getty Images, 167(l); allOver photography/Alamy, 167; George Hunter / SuperStock, 167; Lucian Coman/Shutterstock, 167(cr); iStockphoto/Thinkstock, 167(cr); Thinkstock, 167(r); ImageSelect/Alamy, 168(l); Esther Lim/Actionplus/Newscom, 168(c); Jim West / Alamy, 168(r); Furgolle/BSIP/Corbis, 169; David J. Green - lifestyle themes/Alamy, 170; AW3 WENN Photos/Newscom, 172; Blend Images/Alamy, 174; George Doyle/Getty Images, 175; Goodshoot/Thinkstock, 176.

CHAPTER 7: Paul Bradbury/OJO Images/Getty Images, 178; Everett Collection Historical/Alamy, 180(tl); George Robinson/Alamy, 181(br); Cultura Creative/Alamy, 186(tl); Merrick Morton/Columbia Pictures/Courtesy Everett Collection, 188(tl); Jordin Althaus/©Fox/Everett Collection, 190(bl); George Tooker, Government Bureau, 1956. Egg tempera on gesso panel, 19 Ã— 29 inches. The Metropolitan Museum of Art, George A. Hearn Fund, 1956 (56.78). Photograph Â© 1984 The Metropolitan Museum of Art/Image source Art Resource, NY, 193(tr); Catherine Karnow/Encyclopedia/Corbis, 199(tl); David Levenson/Alamy, 199(tr); AP Photo/Rick Bowmer, 201(br); Lisa F. Young/Shutterstock, 202(b); B Christopher/Alamy, 203(tl); Robert Harbison, 203(tr), George Robinson/Alamy, 204.

CHAPTER 8: Rob Melnychuk/Photodisc/Getty Images, 206; Ariel Skelley/Blend Images/Alamy, 208(tl); David Keith Jones/Images of Africa Photobank/Alamy, 209(tl); John Cancalosi/Alamy, 209(tc); Leah-Anne Thompson/Shutterstock, 209(tr); Jon Arnold Images Ltd/Alamy, 209(bl); Jon Arnold Images Ltd/Alamy, 209(bc); Photo Researchers, Inc., 209(br); SLP/G Features Grosby Group Latin America/Newscom SpecialHispanic US & Canada Central and South America Rights, 210(bl); Alamy, 213(bl); Thomas Schweizer/Comet/Corbis, 213(br); Jose Perez/Splash News/Corbis, 218(tl); Cortesa/Notimex/Corbis, 221(br); AP Photo/Victor R. Caivano, 224(tl); Whitney Macionis, 225(cl); akg-images, 226(bl); Richard Lord/The Image Works, 228(bl); Bill Aron/PhotoEdit, Inc., 232(br); Studio 101/Alamy, 233(tl); Richard Lord/The Image Works, 234.

CHAPTER 9: AP Photo/The Kentucky Enquirer, Patrick Reddy, 236; Hechtenberg/Caro/Alamy, 238(tl); Melissa Moore/The Image Works, 239(br); Pearson Education, 241(bl); Christian Abraham/AP Images, 242(bl); A. Ramey/PhotoEdit, 244(bl); Pool/Getty image, 246(bl); Joe Koshellek/MCT/Newscom, 248(tl); Adam Taylor/© Netflix/Everett Collection, 250(tl); Abbot Genser/HBO/Everett Collection, 251(br); c99/ZUMA Press/Newscom, 253(cl); Peter Turnley/CORBIS, 257(tr); David Sipress/Cartoon Bank, 258(tl); Richard Ellis/Alamy, 259(br); Angel Zayas/Demotix/Corbis, 261(tr); Christos Kalohoridis/© USA Network/Everett Collection, 262(tl); US Information Agency, 265(tr); Reuters/Lucy Nicholson, 267(bl); AP Photo/The Star-Democrat, Charlie Campbell, 268(b); AP Photo/Miguel Angel Morenatti, 269(tl); Bill Greenblatt/UPI/Landov, 269(tr); Joe Koshellek/MCT/Newscom, 270.

CHAPTER 10: Ferdinando Scianna/Magnum Photos, Inc., 272; AF archive/Alamy, 274(tl); Viviane Moos/Corbis News/Corbis, 275(tr); William Albert Allard/National Geographic Stock, 276(bl); AP Photo/Gurinder Osan, 276(br); Per-Anders Pettersson/Getty Images, 277(bl); WUF/Splash News/WUF/Splash News/Newscom, 279(br); De Agostini Picture Library/Getty Images, 281(br); AP Photo/Imaginechina, 283(tr); Ben Rose/WireImage/Getty Images, 286(tl); AP Photo/Rich Pedroncelli, 288(tl); Aleksandar Todorovic/Shutterstock, 290(tl); Getty Images, 292(cl); Dex Images, Inc./Corbis, 296(b); Visions of America, LLC/Alamy, 296; Tobias Hase/dpa/Corbis, 297(tl); White House/Handout/CNP/Corbis, 297(tr); Viviane Moos/Corbis News/Corbis, 298.

CHAPTER 11: Robert Nickelsberg/Getty Images, 300; David Bacon/The Image Works, 302(tl); ZUMA Press, Inc/Alamy, 306(bl); Jupiterimages/Goodshoot/Thinkstock, 307(bl) ; H. Mark Weidman Photography/Alamy, 307(br); AP Photo/History, 308(bl); Russell Lee/Historical/Corbis, 310(bl); Penny Tweedie/Stone /Getty Images, 311(bl); Art Resource, NY, 318(bl); Carl Wagner/KRT/Newscom, 321(bl); David Urbina/PhotoEdit, 322(br); Jim West/Alamy, 325; Everett Collection, 326(bl); ABC/Everett Collection, 326(br); Lauren Browdy/Alamy, 327(tl); Jupiterimages/Goodshoot/Thinkstock, 328.

CHAPTER 12: John Miles /The Image Bank/Getty images, 330; x99/ZUMA Press/Newscom, 332(tl); Songquan Deng/Alamy, 334(tl); Norbert Michalke/imagebroker/Alamy, 334(tr); Asia Alan King/Alamy, 334(bl); Alison Wright/Encyclopedia/Corbis, 337(cl); Leonard Zhukovsky/Fotolia, 338(tl); AP Photo/CHESNOT/SIPA, 338(tr); AP Photo/Aijaz Rahi, 341(br); Malcolm Linton/Liaison, 343(cl); Joe McDonald/Corbis, 346(bl); Robert van der Hilst/Corbis, 346(bc); Justin Eckersall/Alamy, 346(br); Andrea Comas/Reuters/Corbis, 348(bl); Jan Sochor/Alamy, 351(tr); RabihMoghrabi/AFP/Getty Images/Newscom, 354(cl); Kamran Jebreili/AP Images, 354(cl); Matt Shonfeld/Redux, 355(tl); AP Photo/Aijaz Rahi, 356.

CHAPTER 13: Cultura Creative/Alamy, 358; Corbis, 360(tl); Carol Beckwith/Robert Estall Photo Agency/Alamy, 362(tl); Biddiboo/Getty Images, 365(tr); AP Images, 366(cl); Murray Close/Lionsgate/Everett Collection, 367(tr); Kuenzig/Laif/Aurora Photos, 375(cl); AMC/Everett Collection, 376(bl); FPG/Archive Photos/Getty Images, 378(tl); Jeff Greenberg/Alamy, 381(tr); Peter Foley/Bloomberg/Getty Images, 382(tl); AE Pictures Inc./Photodisc/Getty Images, 385(br); Image Courtesy of The Advertising Archives, 386(c); PHCP Incorporated-www.phcpinc.com, 387(tl); Image Courtesy of The Advertising Archives, 387(c); Carol Beckwith/Robert Estall Photo Agency/Alamy, 388.

CHAPTER 14: Joseph Sohm Visions of America/Newscom, 390; CREATISTA/Shutterstock, 392(tl); Paul Matthew Photography/Shutterstock, 393(tl); Sanjay Deva/Shutterstock, 393(tc); Owen Franken/Corbis, 393(tr); Charles O'Rear/Corbis, 393(bl); Paul W. Liebhardt, 393(bc); Buddy Mays/Alamy, 393(br);

Joe Raedle/Getty Images, **397(cl)**; PETER FOLEY/EPA /LANDOV, **401(br)**; Cheryl Diaz Meyer/Dallas Morning News/Corbis, **403(tr)**; Library of Congress Prints and Photographs Division [LC-USZ62-98729], **406(tr)**; Bettmann/Corbis, **408(tl)**; Library of Congress Prints and Photographs Division [LC-USZ62-7816], **408(tl)**; Everett Collection Inc/Alamy, **408(tc)**; Bettmann/Corbis, **408(tr)**; Benjamin J. Myers/Corbis, **409(b)**; Phil Schermeister/Corbis, **410(bl)**; Hill Street Studios/Crystal Cartier/Blend Images/Getty Images, **415(tr)**; Peter Yates/Corbis, **416(tl)**; Jeff Greenberg/Alamy, **417(t)**; Carl D. Walsh/Aurora Photos, **418(bl)**; David De Lossy/Getty Images, **420(b)**; Ronnie Kaufman/Corbis, **421(tr)**; Cheryl Diaz Meyer/Dallas Morning News/Corbis, **422**.

CHAPTER 15: Dennis MacDonald/PhotoEdit, Inc., **424**; Europics/Newscom, **426(tl)**; DK Images, **431(tl)**; TAO Images Limited/Getty Images, **431(tr)**; TV Land/Everett Collection, **434(tl)**; Pearson Education/PH College, **437(tr)**; © robert lerich/Fotolia.com, **440(cr)**; Dominic Lipinski/AP Images, **445(cl)**; AP Images/Beth A. Keiser, **446(t)**; Marty Katz/The Image Works, **447(cl)**; Ryan Remiorz, CP/AP Images, **448(bl)**; James Devaney/WireImage/Getty Images, **448(br)**; Henny Ray Abrams/AP Images, **449(tl)**; Evan Agostini/AP Images, **449(tr)**; AP Images/Beth A. Keiser, **450**.

CHAPTER 16: Rafael Maldonado-Pool/Getty Images, **452**; Carlos Barria/Reuters, **454(tl)**; Chris Thomaidis/Stone/Getty Images, **455(tr)**; Allen Brown/dbimages/Alamy, **460(tl)**; T.Lehne/Lotuseaters/Alamy, **460(tr)**; National Geophysical Data Center, **462(tl)**; Trent Dietsche/Alamy, **466(bl)**; Zelig Shaul/ACE Pictures/Newscom, **469(tr)**; Norbert Michalke/Imagebroker/Alamy, **471(tr)**; Feng Yu/Alamy, **474(cl)**; Joerg Boethling/Alamy, **474(br)**; Dwight Cendrowski/Alamy, **475(tr)**; Chris Thomaidis/Stone/Getty Images, **476**.

CHAPTER 17: Chris Fitzgerald/Candidate Photos/Newscom, **478**; Hasan Jamali/AP Images, **480(c)**; Fahad Shadeed/Reuters, **483(tr)**; KCNA/Xinhua/Landov, **486(tl)**; Jeff Greenberg/Alamy, **489(bl)**; David Hancock/Alamy, **489(br)**; p72/Zuma Press/Newscom, **493(tr)**; epa european pressphoto agency b.v. /Alamy, **495(br)**; Kent Smith/Everett Collection, **496(bl)**; KARIM SAHIB/AFP/Getty Images/Newscom, **498(bl)**; Zhang Jun/Xinhua/Photoshot/Newscom, **499(bl)**; Time & Life Pictures/Getty Images, **500(bl)**; Dr. Billy Ingram/WireImage/Getty Images, **504(b)**; William Thomas Cain/Getty Images, **505(tr)**; Lawidjaja Rudy/SIPA/Newscom, **505(cl)**; Dr. Billy Ingram/WireImage/Getty Images, **506**.

CHAPTER 18: Steve Skjold/Alamy, **508**; © Blend Images/Alamy, **510(tl)**; Jordan Strauss/Invision/AP Images, **511(br)**; John Terence Turner/Taxi/Getty Images, **512(bl)**; Westend61/Newscom, **515(br)**; AKM-GSI/ /Splash News/Corbis, **517(tr)**; Robert Weber/The Cartoon Bank, **519(tr)**; Andi Berger/Shutterstock, **520(b)**; Adrian Burke/Corbis, **523(tr)**; MarkBarrett/MIRA.com, **527(tr)**; Steven Greaves/Corbis, **530(tl)**; AP Photo/NBC, Trae Patton, **531(bl)**; Juice Images/Alamy, **533(bl)**; Ursula Coyote/AMC/Everett Collection, **534(c)**; Cliff Lipson/©Showtime/Everett Collection, **535(tl)**; Patrick McElhenney/©Fox/Everett Collection, **535(tr)**; Westend61/Newscom, **536**.

CHAPTER 19: Wunder Images/Alamy, **538**; Shaul Schwarz/Getty images, **540(tl)**; SCPhotos/Alamy, **541(tr)**; Reuters/Corbis, **542(b)**; © SHIGEMITSU TAKAHASHI/Alamy, **543(br)**; Robert Estall photo agency/Alamy, **547(t)**; ITAR-TASS/Newscom, **548(tl)**; P Deliss/Godong/Photononstop, **549(br)**; Annie Griffith/National Geographic, **551(tr)**; Nikreates/Alamy, **559(bl)**; Anna Belle Lee Washington/SuperStock, **563(bl)**; Gary Braasch/CORBIS, **564(bl)**; Larry Williams/Corbis, **566(b)**; Hero Images/Corbis, **567(tl)**; Denver Post, Glen Martin/AP Images, **567(tr)**; Annie Griffith/National Geographic, **568**.

CHAPTER 20: Glow Asia RF/Alamy, **570**; © Cultura Creative (RF)/Alamy, **572(tl)**; Antony Njuguna/Reuters/Landov, **573(br)**; Visions of America, LLC/Alamy, **576(bl)**; Michael Yarish/Fox/Everett Collection, **578(tr)**; Cleve Bryant/PhotoEdit, **580(tl)**; Jim Cummins/Corbis, **580(tr)**; Peter Byron/Photo Edit, **582(cl)**; Spencer Grant/PhotoEdit, **587(tr)**; ZUMA/Alamy, **590(bl)**; Jeff Greenberg/PhotoEdit, **591(br)**; Corbis/SuperStock, **593(cl)**; Michael J. Doolittle/The Image Works, **594(cr)**; Suzanne DeChillo/The New York Times/Redux, **594(b)**; David McNew/Getty Images News /Getty Images, **595(tl)**; Obama Transition Office, Callie Shell/AP Images, **595(tr)**; Visions of America, LLC/Alamy, **596**.

CHAPTER 21: Guy Somerset/Alamy, **598**; Martin Parr/Magnum Photos, **600(tl)**; Corbis, **604(bl)**; infusny-146/RogerWong/INFphoto.com/Newscom, **606(bl)**; Antony Njuguna/Reuters, **610(bl)**; Tom Nebbia/Encyclopedia/Corbis, **613(tr)**; The Des Moines Register, Rodney White/AP Images, **616(tl)**; Phil Caruso/Showtime Network/Everett Collection, **617(tr)**; Robin Nelso /PhotoEdit, **619(tr)**; Steve Murez/Black Star, **623(bl)**; Dan Rafla/Aurora Photos, **624(c)**;

Xinhua, Wang Song/AP Images, **625(tl)**; US Department of Labor, **625(c)**; Antony Njuguna/Reuters, **626**.

CHAPTER 22: jeremy sutton-hibbert / Alamy, **628**; Leonard Zhukovsky/Fotolia, **630(tl)**; dbimages/Alamy, **636(tl)**; David Turnley/Corbis, **638(tl)**; Jack Hollingsworth/Corbis, **642(bl)**; Michael Smith/Getty Images News/Getty Images, **643(br)**; SuperStock, **645(tl)**; Smithsonian American Art Museum, Washington, DC/Art Resource, NY, **645(tr)**; Clark Brennan/Alamy, **648(tl)**; Scott Green/Focus Features/Everett Collection, **650(bl)**; Wilfried Krecichwost/Bridge/Corbis, **651(br)**; John Macionis, **653(cl)**; ZUMA /ZUMA Press, Inc./Alamy, **654(bl)**; Amit Dave/Reuters/Landov, **655(tl)**; Remi Benali/Terra/Corbis, **657(tr)**; REUTERS/Mark Blinch, **658(bl)**; Henny Ray Abrams/AP Images, **660(c)**; David Cooper/TorontoStar/ZUMAPRESS.com/Newscom, **661(t)**; Amit Dave/Reuters/Landov, **662**.

CHAPTER 23: PHOTOPQR/OUEST FRANCE/EDU/Newscom, **664**; Aflo Foto Agency/Alamy, **666(tl)**; AP Photo/Bob Leonard, File, **668(tl)**; Scott Houston/Alamy, **670(bl)**; Barbara Nitke/Lifetime/Everett Collection, **673(br)**; Mike Clarke/AFP/Getty Images/Newscom, **675(bl)**; Barry Lewis/Alamy, **675(bc)**; Salah Omar/AFP/Getty Images, **675(br)**; Historical/Corbis, **676(bl)**; Norma Jean Gargasz/Alamy, **678(tr)**; Alvan Quinn/AP Images, **679(bl)**; MPVHistory/Alamy, **681(bl)**; Nick Ut/AP Images, **681(br)**; Mike Segar/Reuters, **685(br)**; Bob Daemmrich/PhotoEdit, **690(c)**; Chris Gardner/AP Images, **690(b)**; Jacquelyn Martin/AP Images, **691(t)**; Scott Houston/Alamy, **692**.

CHAPTER 24: Guillaume Plisson/Bloomberg via Getty Images, **694**; Nelson Hancock/Rough Guides/DK Images, **696(tl)**; Nave Nave Moe (Sacred Spring), 1894 (oil on canvas), Gauguin, Paul (1848-1903) / Hermitage, St. Petersburg, Russia/The Bridgeman Art Library, **697(br)**; Mike Clarke/AFP/Getty Images, **698(bl)**; Source: George Tooker, The Subway, 1950, egg tempera on gesso panel, 18 1/8 Ã— 36 1/8 inches, Whitney Museum of American Art, New York. Purchased with funds from the Juliana Force Purchase Award, 50.23. Photograph Â© Whitney Museum of American Art, **701(br)**; By Courtesy Galerie Canesso, **702(bl)**; Michael Gallacher/The Missoulian/AP Images, **702(bc)**; Mantel/SIPA/Newscom, **702(br)**; Pearson Education/PH College, **704(t)**; Allen Russell/Alamy, **708(tl)**; Ed Pritchard/Stone/Getty images, **710(tl)**; Timothy A. Clary/AFP/Getty Images, **710(tr)**; Mauri Rautkari/Ecophoto Ltd., **712(bl)**; Brad Rickerby/Stone/Getty Images, **713(tr)**; paul prescott/Alamy, **716(b)**; SHAWN BALDWIN /The New York Times/Redux, **717(cr)**; AP Images/Efrem Lukatsky, **717(tl)**; Mike Clarke/AFP/Getty Images, **718**.

MySocLab Photo Credits

Chapter 2: Photoedit; **Chapter 3:** 1: Bettmann/Corbis; 2: Oldrich Karasek/isifa Image Service s.r.o./Alamy; **Chapter 5:** iStockphoto/Thinkstock; **Chapter 6:** Ryan McVay/Photodisc/Getty Images; **Chapter 8:** Shaul Schwarz/Getty Images; **Chapter 9:** stester/Shutterstock.com; **Chapter 10:** Daniel Gluskoter/UPI/Newscom; **Chapter 11:** AP Photo/Indianapolis Star, Charlie Nye; **Chapter 12:** Maciej Dakowicz/Alamy; **Chapter 15:** 1: Paul S. Howell; 2: Ji Chunpeng/Xinhua/Newscom; **Chapter 16:** 1: Library of Congress Photographs and Prints Division; 2: Stephanie Maze/Corbis; 3: Rob Colvin/Photodisc/Getty Images; **Chapter 17:** 1: Christoph Papsch/vario images GmbH & Co.KG/Alamy; 2: Dinodia/The Image Works; **Chapter 19:** Don Hammond/Design Pics/Corbis; **Chapter 21:** 1: Michael DeFreitas Pacific/Alamy; 2: Sergei Karpukhin/AP Images; **Chapter 22:** Bohemian Nomad Picturemakers/Documentary Value/Corbis; **Chapter 23:** Pictorial Press Ltd/Alamy; **Chapter 24:** 1: Buccina Studios/Photodisc/Getty Images; 2: Jim West/Alamy.

Timeline: 1807: MPI/Stringer/Hulton Archive/Getty Images; **1829:** Vintage Images/Alamy; **1848:** Bettmann/CORBIS; **1869:** Alexey Klementiev/Fotolia; **1876:** Courtesy of AT&T Archives and History Center; **1886:** Irene Springer/Pearson Education; **1893:** Bettmann/CORBIS; **1903:** Library of Congress Prints and Photographs Division, [LC-DIG-ppmsca-19075]; Schomburg Center/Art Resource, NY; **1910:** DK Images; **1912:** Chris Alan Wilton/The Image Bank/Getty Images; **1913:** Library of Congress Prints and Photographs Division, [LC-USZ62-19261]; **1921:** Hulton Archive/Getty Images; **1927:** Bettmann/Corbis; **1933:** Bettmann/Corbis; **1945:** Photo Courtesy of U.S. Air Force; **1946:** AP Photos/University of Pennsylvania; **1947:** Bettmann/Corbis; **1953:** Bettmann/Corbis; **1952:** DK Images; **1955:** AP Images; **1964:** Photo by CBS Photo Archive/Getty Images; **1969:** AP Photos; NASA; **1980:** Laima Druskis/Pearson Education; **1981:** Jan Butchofsky/Corbis; **1987:** puckillustrations/Fotolia; **1990:** DK Images; **2000:** Brady/Pearson Education; Horst Schmidt/Fotolia; **2007:** taniho/Fotolia; **2011:** Jim West/Alamy; **2012:** Leonard Zhukovsky/Fotolia; **2013:** Steven Greaves/Corbis.

Author Index

Subject Index

workplace issues for, 194–96, 281,
315, 342, 359, 367–69, 376, 385,
455–56, 467, 470
Women's movement
basic feminist ideas in, 382
feminism as element of (*see*
Feminism)
origins of, 360, 381–82
public support for, 384–85
resources for, 682
sexual and reproductive freedom in,
382, 383
social change through, 90
types of feminism in, 382–84
voting rights in, 360–61, 371, 382
Woodhull, Victoria, 371
Woodward, Charlotte, 360
Work and workplace
See also Corporations and businesses;
Economy
blue-collar, 289, 304, 308–9, 463–64
changing nature of work, 196–98
child labor in, 85, 87, 142, 143,
342–43, 346, 455, 573
cultural diversity addressed in, 66, 87
division of labor in, 105, 107, 109,
116–17, 118, 190, 455, 703–4
dual labor market, 464
education impacting, 306, 465–67,
468, 469, 576, 583, 584
elderly adults in, 145, 426, 432–33,
435–36, 439–40
emotional expression in, 168, 170

families impacted by, 511, 519
farming/agricultural (*see* Farming and
agriculture)
forced labor, 342
formal organizations in, 180, 184,
189–201
gay rights in, 219
gender issues in, 194–96, 281, 315,
342, 359, 367–70, 376, 385, 455–56,
467, 470
globalization impacting, 317, 352–53,
457–58
global stratification impacting, 332,
354–55
government-based, 483–84, 487
health care benefits in, 615
immigrant issues in, 397, 410–13,
417, 455
income from (*see* Income)
industrial era changes in, 14, 104–5,
107–10, 116–17, 455–56, 703–4
information technology in,
469–71, 475
Japanese work organization, 196
labor unions in, 289, 464–65, 466
low-wage employment in, 12, 109,
309, 332, 397
minimum wage for, 321–22
modern challenges for, 474–75
occupational prestige of, 304–5,
453, 612
postindustrial changes in, 456,
463–71

poverty and poor people's desire for,
34, 320–22
professions in, 465–67
racial and ethnic issues in, 194–95,
321, 397, 408–9, 410–13, 417, 453,
468, 469, 470
regulation of, 289, 459, 464–65, 466
retirement from, 145, 426,
435–36, 440
right-to-work laws, 464–65
safety issues in, 332, 624–25
scientific management in, 194,
196–97
self-employment, 466, 467
service-sector, 456–57, 458, 463
sexual harassment in, 229–30,
254, 376
social class relationship to, 35, 36,
179, 276–83, 286–89, 304–5, 307–9,
313–14, 316, 321
social movements in, 688
social stratification relationship to,
276–83, 286–89
sociology applied in, 13–14
teachers in, 591–92
technology impacting, 14, 104–5,
196–98, 346, 455, 469–71, 475
underemployment, 468
unemployment in (*see*
Unemployment)
urban, 321, 640, 641
white-collar, 289, 304, 308, 463–64,
465–67

women's issues in, 194–96, 281, 315,
342, 359, 367–70, 376, 385, 455–56,
467, 470
working poor, 309, 320–22
Working class
definition and description of, 308
group and organization involvement
of, 179
World War II, 412

Xi Jinping, 283

Yanomamö people, 68, 78, 498
Yemen
childbearing statistics in, 7
culture in, 67
deviance and crime in, 259
gender stratification in, 363
politics and government in, 480
Yniguez, Rosa, 510
Youth. *See* Children and
adolescents
Yugoslavia, disasters in, 675

Zimbabwe
economy of, 351
education in, 573
life expectancy in, 432
television watching in, 140
Zimbardo, Philip, 46–47, 58
Zuckerberg, Mark, 188, 285
Zuma, Jacob, 277